Maine

Christina Tree

EXP

Maine

FOURTEENTH EDITION

Christina Tree & Nancy English

The Countryman Press ✷ Woodstock, Vermont

We welcome your comments and suggestions. Please contact Explorer's Guide Editor, The Countryman Press, P.O. Box 748, Woodstock, Vermont 05091, or e-mail countrymanpress@wwnorton.com.

Fourteenth Edition

ISBN 978-0-88150-793-5
ISSN 1533-6883

Maps by Mapping Specialists, © 2008 The Countryman Press
Book design by Bodenweber Design
Text composition by PerfecType, Nashville, TN
Cover photograph © Carol Latta
Interior photographs as noted

Published by The Countryman Press, P.O. Box 748, Woodstock, Vermont 05091

Distributed by W. W. Norton & Company, Inc., 500 Fifth Avenue, New York, NY 10110

Printed in Canada

10 9 8 7 6 5 4 3 2 1

DEDICATION

To Timothy and Yuko, married in Maine, and for our grandchildren, Aki and Taiga.
—C. T.

To Emma.
—N. E.

EXPLORE WITH US!

We have been fine-tuning *Maine: An Explorer's Guide* for the past 27 years, a period in which lodging, dining, and shopping opportunities have more than quadrupled in the state. As we have expanded our guide, we have also been increasingly selective, making recommendations based on years of conscientious research and personal experience. We describe the state by locally defined regions, giving you Maine's communities, not simply her most popular destinations. With this guide you'll feel confident to venture beyond the tourist towns, along roads less traveled, to places of special hospitality and charm.

WHAT'S WHERE

In the beginning of the book you'll find an alphabetical listing of special highlights and important information that you may want to reference quickly. You'll find advice on everything from where to buy the best local lobster to where to write or call for camping reservations and park information.

LODGING

We've selected lodging places for mention in this book based on their merit alone; we do not charge innkeepers to be listed. The authors always check every bed & breakfast, farm, sporting lodge, and inn in Maine personally.

Prices. Please don't hold us or the respective innkeepers responsible for the rates listed as of press time in 2008. Some changes are inevitable. **The 7 percent state rooms and meals tax should be added to all prices unless we specifically state that it's included in a price.** We've tried to note when a gratuity is added, but it's always wise to check before booking.

Smoking. Maine B&Bs, inns, and restaurants are now generally smoke-free, but many lodging places still reserve some rooms for smokers and, depending on their license, some restaurants still offer a smoking area. If this is important to you, be sure to ask when making reservations.

RESTAURANTS

In most sections please note a distinction between *Dining Out* and *Eating Out*. By their nature, restaurants included in the *Eating Out* group are generally inexpensive.

KEY TO SYMBOLS

ⵔⵔ **Weddings**. The wedding-ring symbol appears next to lodging venues that specialize in weddings.

Special value. The blue-ribbon symbol appears next to selected lodging and restaurants that combine quality and moderate prices.

Pets. The dog-paw symbol appears next to venues that accept pets.

Child-friendly. The crayon symbol appears next to lodging, restaurants, activities, and shops of special interest or appeal to youngsters.

♿ **Handicapped access**. The wheelchair symbol appears next to lodging, restaurants, and attractions that are partially or completely handicapped accessible.

((ɪ)) **Wireless Internet**. The wireless symbol appears next to lodging, restaurants, and attractions that offer wireless Internet access.

We would appreciate any comments or corrections. Please write to:

Explorer's Guide Editor
The Countryman Press
P.O. Box 748
Woodstock, VT 05091

You can also e-mail
countrymanpress@wwnorton.com, or ctree@traveltree.net

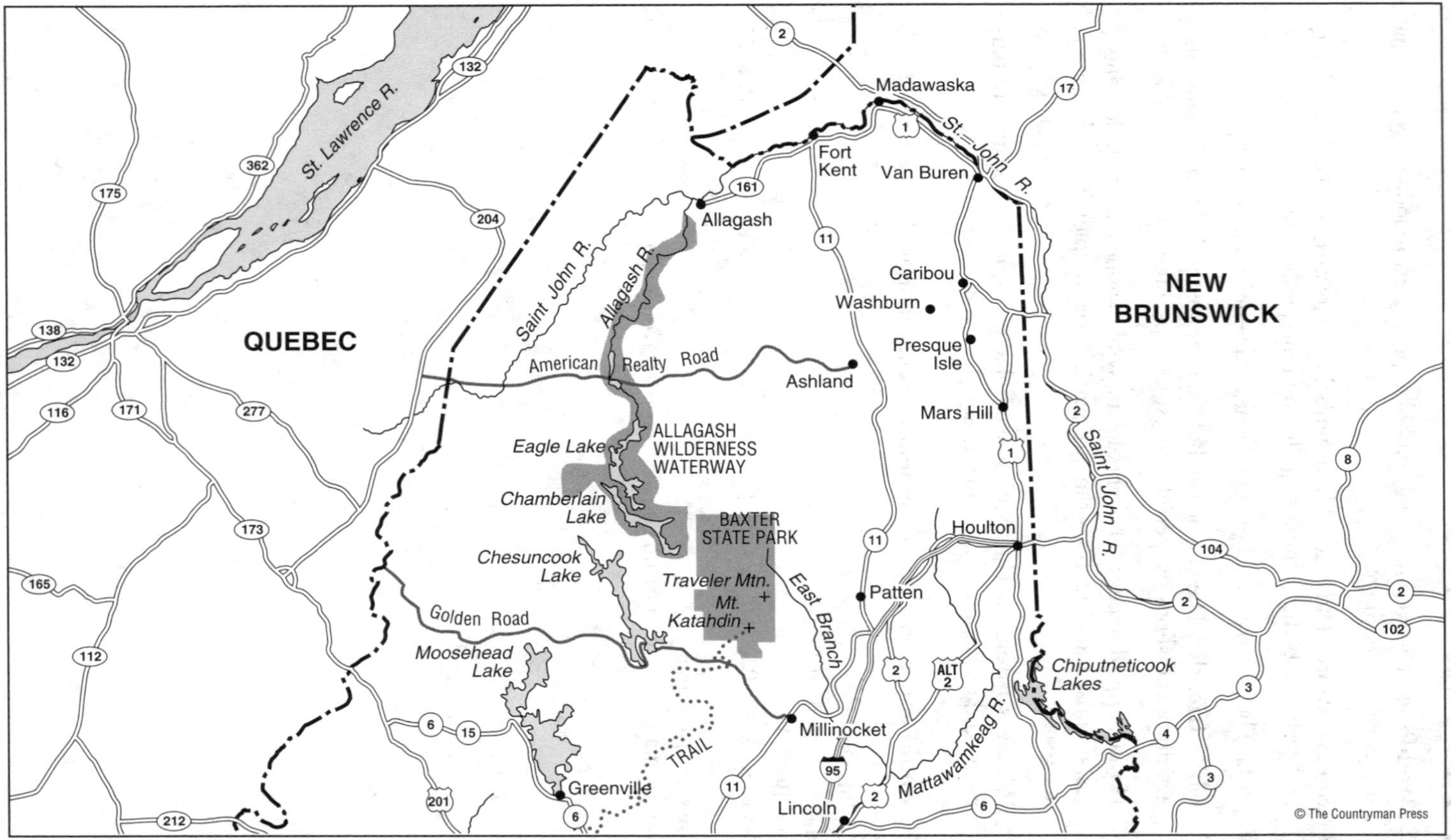
QUEBEC
NEW BRUNSWICK
St. Lawrence R.
Madawaska
St. John R.
Fort Kent
Van Buren
Allagash
Saint John R.
Allagash R.
Caribou
Washburn
Presque Isle
American Realty Road
Ashland
Mars Hill
ALLAGASH WILDERNESS WATERWAY
Eagle Lake
Chamberlain Lake
BAXTER STATE PARK
Houlton
Saint John R.
Chesuncook Lake
Traveler Mtn.
Mt. Katahdin
East Branch
Patten
Golden Road
Moosehead Lake
Chiputneticook Lakes
Millinocket
Mattawamkeag R.
TRAIL
Greenville
Lincoln
© The Countryman Press

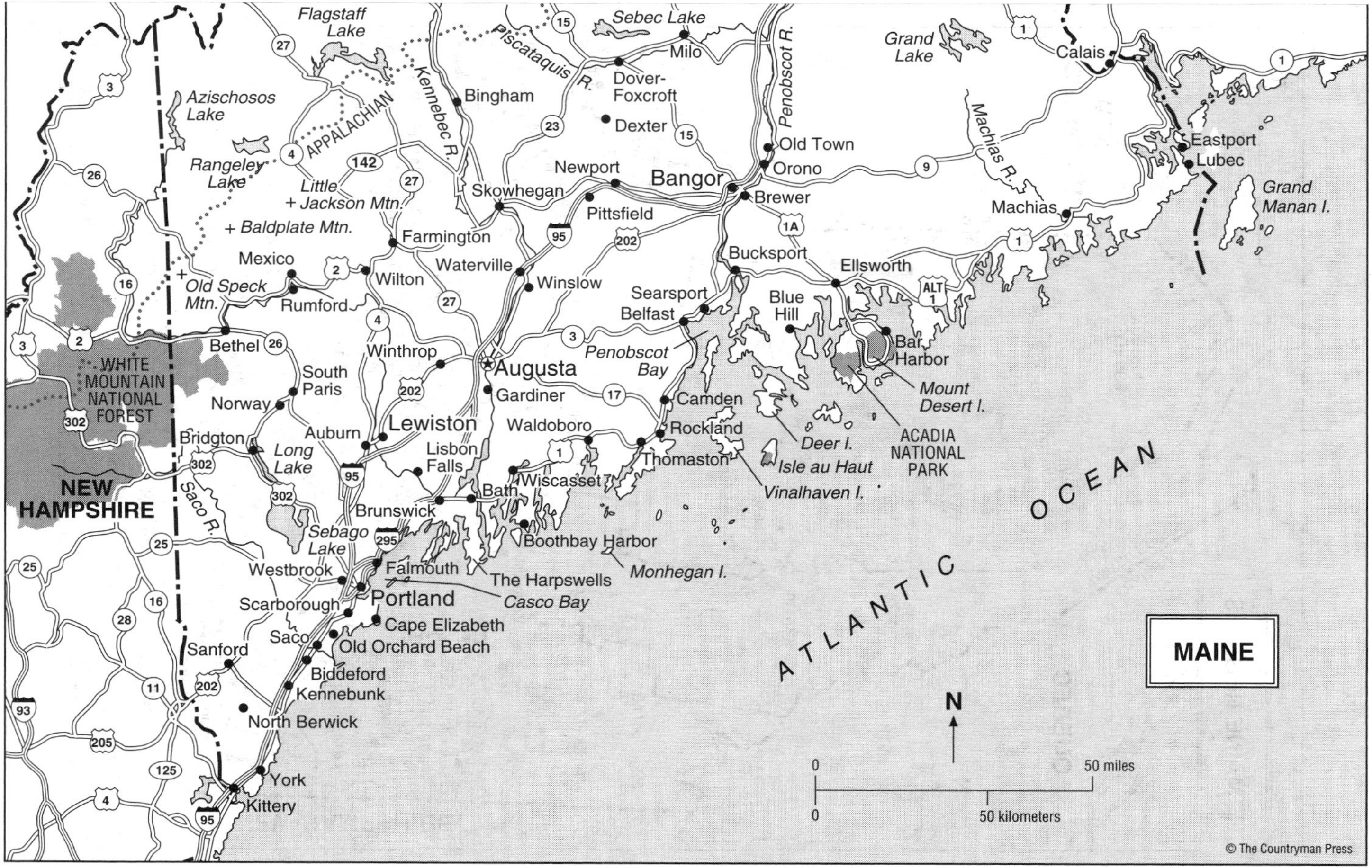
MAINE
NEW HAMPSHIRE
WHITE MOUNTAIN NATIONAL FOREST
ATLANTIC OCEAN
APPALACHIAN
Flagstaff Lake
Sebec Lake
Grand Lake
Calais
Milo
Dover-Foxcroft
Piscataquis R.
Kennebec R.
Penobscot R.
Machias R.
Bingham
Aziscoshos Lake
Rangeley Lake
Dexter
Old Town
Orono
Bangor
Brewer
Newport
Skowhegan
Pittsfield
Little Jackson Mtn.
Baldplate Mtn.
Old Speck Mtn.
Farmington
Mexico
Rumford
Wilton
Waterville
Winslow
Bucksport
Ellsworth
Searsport
Belfast
Blue Hill
Bar Harbor
Mount Desert I.
ACADIA NATIONAL PARK
Eastport
Lubec
Grand Manan I.
Machias
Bethel
Winthrop
Augusta
Gardiner
South Paris
Norway
Penobscot Bay
Camden
Rockland
Thomaston
Deer I.
Isle au Haut
Vinalhaven I.
Lewiston
Auburn
Waldoboro
Lisbon Falls
Bridgton
Long Lake
Saco R.
Wiscasset
Bath
Brunswick
Sebago Lake
Boothbay Harbor
Monhegan I.
Westbrook
Falmouth
The Harpswells
Portland
Casco Bay
Scarborough
Cape Elizabeth
Saco
Old Orchard Beach
Sanford
Biddeford
Kennebunk
North Berwick
York
Kittery
N
0
50 miles
0
50 kilometers
© The Countryman Press

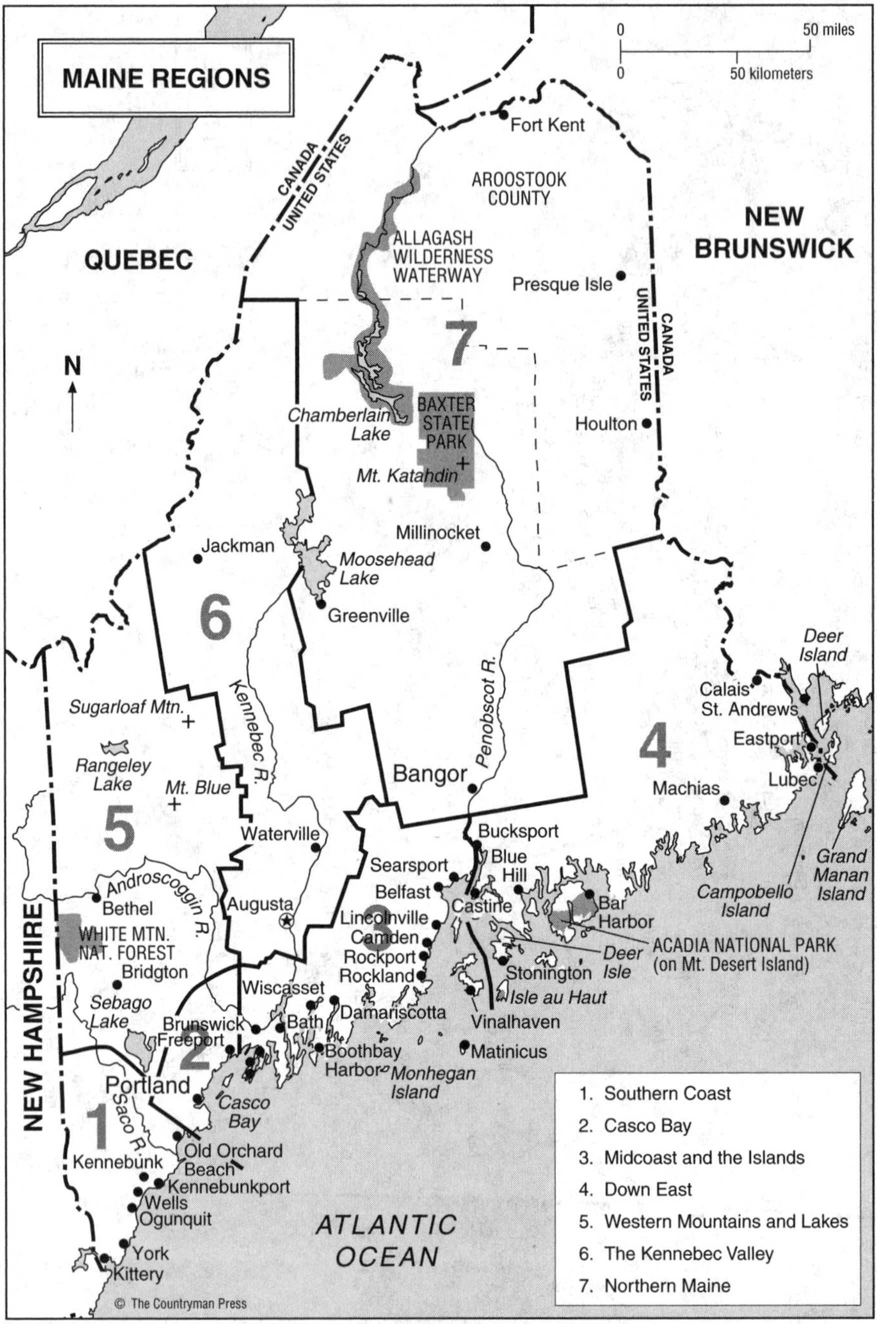

MAINE REGIONS
0
50 miles
0
50 kilometers
QUEBEC
CANADA
UNITED STATES
NEW BRUNSWICK
NEW HAMPSHIRE
N
Fort Kent
AROOSTOOK COUNTY
ALLAGASH WILDERNESS WATERWAY
Presque Isle
7
Chamberlain Lake
BAXTER STATE PARK
Mt. Katahdin
Houlton
Millinocket
Jackman
Moosehead Lake
Greenville
6
Kennebec R.
Penobscot R.
Sugarloaf Mtn.
Rangeley Lake
Mt. Blue
5
Waterville
Augusta
Bangor
Bucksport
4
Machias
Deer Island
Calais
St. Andrews
Eastport
Lubec
Grand Manan Island
Campobello Island
Androscoggin R.
Bethel
WHITE MTN. NAT. FOREST
Bridgton
Sebago Lake
Searsport
Belfast
Lincolnville
Camden
Rockport
Rockland
3
Castine
Blue Hill
Bar Harbor
ACADIA NATIONAL PARK (on Mt. Desert Island)
Deer Isle
Stonington
Isle au Haut
Vinalhaven
Matinicus
Wiscasset
Brunswick
Freeport
Bath
Damariscotta
Boothbay Harbor
Monhegan Island
2
Portland
Casco Bay
1
Saco R.
Old Orchard Beach
Kennebunk
Kennebunkport
Wells
Ogunquit
York
Kittery
ATLANTIC OCEAN
1. Southern Coast
2. Casco Bay
3. Midcoast and the Islands
4. Down East
5. Western Mountains and Lakes
6. The Kennebec Valley
7. Northern Maine
© The Countryman Press

CONTENTS

INTRODUCTION

He who rides and keeps the beaten track studies the fences chiefly.
—Henry David Thoreau, The Maine Woods, *1853*

Over the past 27 years *Maine: An Explorer's Guide* has introduced hundreds of thousands of people to many Maines.

When this book first appeared in 1982, it was the first 20th-century guidebook to describe New England's largest state region by region, rather than to focus only on the most touristed communities, listed alphabetically. From the start, we critiqued places to stay and to eat as well as everything to see and to do—based on merit rather than money.

The big news, however, isn't that *Maine: An Explorer's Guide* was first but that readers constantly tell us that it remains the best Maine guidebook—that despite current competition, this "Maine Bible" gets better with each edition.

This 2008 edition includes more Web sites than ever as a way of amplifying our own descriptions. We like to think of this book as the ultimate Maine search engine. With this edition we also introduce our own Web site: www.maineguidebook.com. We haven't put our entire book online, but we have adapted our format to the Web.

With each new edition we build on what we know, spending months on the road, checking every lodging we include, making sure it's a place we would personally like to stay.

Back in 1981, this didn't seem like a tall order. Chris's three sons—ages 3, 6, and 8—helped her research reasonably priced rental cottages, ice cream stands, and beaches. The guide, however, quickly grew as inns, B&Bs, and other lodging options proliferated, as did things to do and see, dining venues, and shopping options. The book also soon included all the parts of Maine in which a visitor can find commercial lodging, from Kittery to Caribou and from the White Mountains to the island of Monhegan, not to mention all of Rt. 1 from Kittery to Fort Kent. After the first couple of editions it became obvious that no one person could explore this immense and richly textured state during one season.

We now describe more than 500 places to stay, ranging from campgrounds to grand old resorts and including farms as well as B&Bs, inns, and sporting camps—in all corners of the state and in all price ranges. We have also checked out a similar number of places to dine and to eat (we make a distinction between dining and eating), and, since shopping is an important part of everyone's travels, we include special stores we've encountered. We have opinions about everything we've found, and we don't hesitate to share them. In every category we record exactly what we see.

While the number of Maine guidebooks has multiplied, we remain proud of the depth and scope of this one. We strive not only to update details but also to simplify the format and to sharpen the word pictures that describe each area.

This book's introductory section, "What's Where in Maine," is a quick-reference

TOURISM IN MAINE

We are fascinated by Maine's history in general and her tourism history in particular. It seems ironic that back in the 1920s "motor touring" was hailed as a big improvement over train and steamer travel because it meant you no longer had to go where everyone else did—over routes prescribed by railroad tracks and steamboat schedules. In Maine cars seem, however, to have had precisely the opposite effect. Now 90 percent of the state's visitors follow the coastal tourist route faithfully, as though their wheels were grooved to Rt. 1.

Worse still, it's as though many tourists are on a train making only express stops—at rush hour. At least half of those who follow Rt. 1 stop, stay, and eat in all the same places—Kennebunkport, Boothbay or Camden, and Bar Harbor, for example—in August.

Tourism has always been driven by images. In the 1840s Thomas Cole, Frederic Church (both of whom sketched and painted scenes of Mount Desert), and lesser-known artists began projecting Maine as a romantic, remote destination in the many papers, magazines, and children's books of the decade. While Henry David Thoreau's *The Maine Woods* was not published until 1864, many of its chapters appeared as magazine articles years earlier (Thoreau first climbed Katahdin in 1846), and in 1853 *Atlantic Monthly* editor James Russell Lowell visited and wrote about Moosehead Lake.

After the Civil War, Maine tourism boomed. Via railroad and steamboat, residents of cities throughout the East and Midwest streamed into the Pine Tree State, most toting guidebooks, many published by rail and steamboat lines to boost business. "Sports" in search of big game and big fish patronized "sporting camps" throughout the North Woods. Thanks to the rise in popularity of fly-fishing and easily maneuverable canoes, women were able to share in North Woods soft adventure. Splendid lakeside hotels were built on the Rangeleys and Moosehead, and farms took in boarders throughout the Western Lakes region. Along the coast and on dozens of islands, hotels

directory to a vast array of information about the state. The remainder of the book describes Maine region by region.

Note that "off-season" prices are often substantially lower than those in July and August. September is dependably sparkling and frequently warm. Early October in Maine is just as spectacular as it is in New Hampshire and Vermont, with magnificent mountains rising from inland lakes as well as the golds and reds set against coastal blue. Be aware that the inland ski resorts of Sunday River near Bethel and the Sugarloaf area are "off-season" all summer as well as fall.

Maine is almost as big as the other five New England states combined, but

of every size were built, most by Maine natives. Blue-collar workers came by trolley to religious camp meetings, and the wealthy built themselves elaborate summer "cottages" on islands and around Bar Harbor, Camden, and Boothbay Harbor. Developments and sophisticated landscaping transformed much of the previously ignored sandy Southern Coast.

Although it's difficult to document, it's safe to say that Maine attracted the same number of visitors in the summer of 1900 that it did in 2000. This picture altered little for another decade. Then came World War I, coinciding with the proliferation of the Model A.

The 1922 founding of the Maine Publicity Bureau (the present Maine Tourism Association), we suspect, reflects the panic of hoteliers (founder Hiram Ricker himself owned three of the state's grandest hotels: the Mount Kineo House, the Poland Spring House, and the Samoset). Over the next few years these hotels went the way of passenger service, and "motorists" stuck to motor courts and motels along Rt. 1 and a limited number of inland roads.

By the late 1960s, when Chris began writing about Maine, much of the state had all but dropped off the tourist map; in the decades since, she has chronicled the reawakening of most of the old resort areas. Whale-watching and whitewater rafting, skiing and snowmobiling, windjamming and kayaking, outlet shopping, and the renewed popularity of country inns and B&Bs have all contributed to this reawakening. Maine is, after all, magnificent. It was just a matter of time.

Recently the extent of waterside (both coastal and inland) walks open to the public has dramatically increased. It's interesting to note that this phenomenon of preserving and maintaining outstanding landscapes—from Ogunquit's Marginal Way to the core of what's now Acadia National Park—was also an offshoot of Maine's first tourism boom. In this 14th edition we note the dramatic growth of coastal trails way Down East in Washington County and the ever-increasing ways of exploring the North Woods.

A proliferation of fabulous restaurants, too, can be found in the Portland chapter and beyond, with an ever-increasing use of things locally grown.

her residents add up to less than half the population of greater Boston. That means there is plenty of room for all who look to her for renewal—both residents and out-of-staters.

It's our hope that, although this book should help visitors and Maine residents alike enjoy the state's resort towns, it will be particularly useful for those who explore off the beaten track.

THE AUTHORS

Chris was born in Hawaii and bred in Manhattan, came to New England to attend Mount Holyoke College, and has been living in Massachusetts since she began to work for the *Boston Globe* in 1968. She is addicted to many Maines. As a toddler she learned to swim in the Ogunquit River and later watched her sons do the same in Monhegan's icy waters—and then learn to sail at summer camp in Raymond and paddle canoes on the Saco River and down the St. John. Her number two son was married on Little Cranberry Island off Mount Desert. For the *Globe* and *Yankee* magazine she continues to write about a variety of things to do in Maine. She has skied Sugarloaf and Sunday River and dogsledded and cross-country skied between North Woods sporting camps, llama trekked and camped in Evans Notch, and sea kayaked off points from Portland to Pembroke as well as sailed and windjammed whenever possible on Penobscot Bay. She values her Boston vantage point, far enough away to give her the perspective on what it means to be a visitor, yet near enough to comfortably and continually explore Maine.

Born in New York City and raised in northeastern Vermont, Nancy has spent most of her adult life in Portland, Maine. She has heard the cry of a bobcat at night in Vermont and the calls of loons on lakes in Maine, along with the honks of geese migrating over Congress Street in the middle of Portland's downtown. Nature and wildlife have been an enduring interest throughout her writing career, spent most recently as the restaurant reviewer for the *Maine Sunday Telegram.* Her travel writing started in the 1970s while still an undergraduate at Vassar College, with articles in *Vermont Life* magazine; it includes work on a new edition of the *Coast of Maine Book* in 2000. She has written a first and the recent second edition of *Chow Maine*, a guide to the best restaurants, cafés, lobster shacks, and markets on the Maine coast. Working on this *Explorer's Guide* took her inland, to great restaurants far from the summer crowds, although some of them are the favorites of year-round tourists, like The Oxford House Inn in Fryeburg. Traveling in Maine is a pastime she shares with many other Mainers, who have their own seasonal traditions, from eating a lobster roll at Harraseeket Lunch every summer to fly-fishing in the North Maine Woods every fall.

We would like to thank Jennifer Thompson for her production help and Kristin Sperber for her careful copyediting of this edition. We would both also like to thank Nancy Marshall, Charlene Williams, and Rose Whitehouse for unfailing response to all cries for help with gathering information whenever called for, and to Elizabeth Roundy Richards and K. W. Oxnard for their contributions to previous editions.

Chris owes thanks to many more people than those listed here. As always, thanks to Virginia Fieldman in Jonesboro, also to Linda and Robert Godfry and

Gregg Noyes of Eastport, Linda Corey and Jim Thompson of Calais, Joyce Owen and Janice Meiners of Campobello, and Valery Kidney and Melissa Bochar of New Brunswick Tourism. Moving down the coast, thanks to Barbara Maurer of Downeast Acadia, to Richard Malaby in Hancock, and Shari Closter and Captains Ken and Ellen Barnes in Rockland, and Phil Crossman on Vinalhaven. In the Damariscotta area, thank you to Karen and Dave Bragg and to Bobby and Sherry Weare; Lucy Finny in Bath, thank you Elizabeth Knowlton and in Georgetown Carolyn and Tom Church. In the Brunswick area, thank you Mercie Norman, Phyllis Truesddell, Richard Mosley and Heather Collins and her chamber staff, and in York, Sue Antal and Carrie Eisner.

Turning inland, first and foremost I owe thanks to East Vassalboro's Elizabeth Davidson, also Kimberly Lindloff of the Waterville Chamber. For help with the Upper Kennebec Valley, thanks to Wende Gray. In Rockwood thank you to John Willard and, in Greenville to Ruth McLaughlin, in Millinocket to Jean Hoekwater of Baxter State Park, and to Matt Polstein for continuous help. Finally, thanks are due the world's most helpful, talented, and long-suffering husband, former *Boston Globe* travel editor William A. Davis, who drove thousands of miles through Maine with me, doubling our efforts and contributing copy in every pinch.

Nancy wishes to thank Kate McCartney and Terry Ouellette in Aroostook County, and Connie Boivin and Sarah Faragher in Bangor, along with Amy Kenney of Hollywood Slots, which is undergoing huge growth and a move into a massive new building. For help in Rangeley, Nancy Birkett Vincent, the staff of Ecopelagicon, and the volunteers at the Rangeley Historical Society deserve many thanks—as well as the volunteers everywhere, who answer so many questions. In western regions, Nancy thanks Julie Whelchel and John and Phyllis Morris, all area innkeepers with a fine talent for hospitality. In Bethel, thanks go to Wende Gray; and, at Sugarloaf, to Greg Sweetser. Along the coast the help has been generous. Thanks go to Helene Harton and Roy Kasindorf of Bar Harbor, Jennie Cline of the quiet side of Mount Desert, Caroline Sulzer and David Walker of Surry, Linda Chilton of the Camden chamber, and all the friendly people in Down East Maine who took time from their busy schedule to answer questions. Farther south Carolyn Shubert at Boothbay Region Land Trust, Kate Fletcher at Maine Media Workshops, and many more business people and hospitality professionals helped make sure the updated information I had was correct. The chambers of commerce of Maine are staffed with courteous and generous people who have contributed many details to this book.

Thanks also are due to my daughter, who has provided details of meals and perceptions about inns that make descriptions come alive, while clocking many miles alongside me as we travel through Maine.

Both authors would like to thank all the people who have taken the time to write about their experiences in Maine. We can't tell you how much your input—or simply your reactions to how we describe things—means to us. We welcome your comments and appreciate all your thoughtful suggestions for the next edition of *Maine: An Explorer's Guide*. You can contact us directly by e-mail: ctree@traveltree.net.

WHAT'S WHERE IN MAINE

AREA CODE The area code throughout Maine is **207**.

ABENAKI See *Wabanaki*.

ACADIANS Acadians trace their lineage to French settlers who came to Nova Scotia in the early 1600s and who, in 1755, were forcibly deported by an English governor. This "Great Disturbance" dispersed a population of some 10,000 Acadians and brutally divided families. In a meadow overlooking the St. John River at Madawaska's **Tante Blanche Museum**, a large marble cross marks the spot on which several hundred displaced Acadians landed in 1787. **Village Acadien**, a dozen buildings forming a mini museum village just west of Van Buren, only begins to tell the story. While the sizable Franco-American communities in Biddeford, Lewiston, and Brunswick have a different history (their forebears were recruited from Quebec to work in 19th-century mills), they, too, have experienced a long repression of their culture and recent resurgence of pride in a shared French heritage. **La Kermesse**, held in late June in Biddeford, is a major Franco-American festival, as is the **Festival de Joie** in Lewiston. Contact the **Maine Acadian Heritage Council** (207-728-6826) for more information.

AGRICULTURAL FAIRS The season opens in late June and runs through the first week of October, culminating with the large, colorful, immensely popular (traffic backs up for miles) **Fryeburg Fair**. Among the best traditional fairs are the **Union Fair** (late August) and the **Blue Hill Fair** (Labor Day weekend). **The Common Ground Country Fair** (third weekend in September, at the fairgrounds in Unity), sponsored by the Maine Organic Farmers and Gardeners Association (www.mofga.org), features wholesome food, folk dancing, and music and draws back-to-the-earth and organic gardeners from all corners of the state. For details about fairs see the **Maine Department of Agriculture** site: www.getrealmaine.com.

AIRPORTS AND AIRLINES **Portland International Jetport** (207-774-7301), with connections to most large American and Canadian cities, is served by several carriers: Delta Air Lines (1-800-221-1212; www.delta.com), Continental Airlines (1-800-

523-3272; www.continental.com), United Express (1-800-864-8331; www.ual.com), U.S. Airways (1-800-428-4322; www.usair.com), JetBlue (1-800-538-2583; www.jetblue.com), AirTran (1-800-247-8726; www.air tran.com), and Northwest (1-800-225-2525; www.nwa.com). **Bangor International Airport** (207-947-0384; www.flybangor.com), serving northern and Down East Maine, also offers connections to all parts of the United States via U.S. Airways Express (1-800-428-4322), Delta Connection (1-800-221-1212), Northwest (1-800-225-2525), Continental Airlines (1-800-523-3272), and Allegiant Air (702-505-8888). Colgan Air operates U.S. Airways flights (1-800-428-4322) to **Hancock County Regional Airport** (Trenton/Bar Harbor), **Augusta State Airport**, **Knox County Regional Airport** (Rockland/Owls Head), and **Northern Maine Regional Airport** (Presque Isle). **Manchester, N.H.,** and Boston's **Logan International Airport** are both popular gateways for Maine travelers; both are served by Mermaid Transportation (www.gomermaid .com) to Portland. Concord Trailways (see *Bus*) offers express service from Logan to Portland.

AIR SERVICES Also called flying services, these are useful links to wilderness camps and coastal islands. Greenville, prime jumping-off point for the North Maine Woods, claims to be New England's largest seaplane base. In this book flying services are also listed under *Getting There* or *Getting Around* in "Rangeley Lakes Region," "Moosehead Lake Area," "Katahdin Region," and "Washington County." Check *Getting There* in "Rockland/Thomaston Area" for air taxis to several islands, including Vinalhaven, North Haven, and Matinicus.

AMTRAK Maine passenger service is not just back but moving more and more passengers every year! Amtrak's **Downeaster** (www.thedowneaster .com) offers five round-trips per day between Boston's North Station and the Portland rail–bus station just off I-95 (shuttles connect with the Old Port). It's two-and-a-half hours each way, the way train rides should be, with comfortable seats, friendly service, and a sense of the shoreline you otherwise never see. Northbound from Boston you cross the wide Merrimac River into Haverhill (Mass.) and stop in the middle of the University of New Hampshire campus in Durham. In Maine the first stop is Wells at a regional transportation center, served by taxis and a seasonal trolley to the beach. In Saco the station is just beyond the mighty falls (taxi service and shuttlebus). In Old Orchard the stop is on the beach itself, beside the chamber of commerce. The Portland station doubles as a stop for Concord Trailways. The 9:05 AM from Boston arrives in Portland at 11:30 and there's a southbound 8:10 PM train with a same-day round-trip fare of s $39.

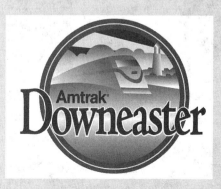

AMUSEMENT PARKS **Funtown/Splashtown USA** in Saco is Maine's biggest, with rides, waterslides, and pools. **Aquaboggan** (pools and slides) is also on Rt. 1 in Saco. **Palace Playland** in Old Orchard Beach is a classic, with a carousel, Ferris wheel, rides, and a 60-foot water slide. **York's Wild Kingdom** at York Beach has a zoo and amusement area.

ANTIQUARIAN BOOKS Maine is well known among book buffs as a browsing mecca. **Maine Antiquarian Booksellers** publishes a printed directory of more than 80 members. Download it at www.mainebooksellers.org.

ANTIQUES A member directory listing more than 260 dealers is produced by the **Maine Antiques Dealers' Association, Inc.** The association's active Web site lists a greater number of members as well as auctions (www.maineantiques.org). The *Antique Dealer Directory* is another good resource, and you can order it online or download it instantly. For a "Maine Antiquing Trail" with three loop tours, see www.visitmaine.com.

Christina Tree

APPALACHIAN TRAIL (www.appalachiantrail.org). The 267-mile Maine section of this 2,175-mile Georgia-to-Maine footpath enters the state in the Mahoosuc Range—accessible there from Grafton Notch State Park (the Mahoosuc Notch section is extremely difficult)—and continues north into the Rangeley and Sugarloaf areas, on up through the Upper Kennebec Valley to Monson. West of Moosehead Lake it runs through Gulf Hagas and on around Nahmakanta Lake, through Abol Bridge to Baxter State Park, ending at the summit of 5,267-foot Mount Katahdin. Hikes along the trail are noted within specific chapters; lodging places catering to AT through-hikers include **Northern Outdoors** in The Forks, and **Little Lyford Pond Camps** near Gulf Hagas. July, August, and September are the best months to hike this stretch. The **Maine Appalachian Trail Club** (www.matc.org) helps with maintenance and in other ways. For a list of publications, write to Appalachian Trail Conference, P.O. Box 807, Harpers Ferry, WV 25425-0807.

APPALACHIAN MOUNTAIN CLUB (www.outdoors.org). In recent years the Boston-based AMC, the country's oldest nonprofit outdoor recreation/conservation group, has acquired 37,000 acres in the North Woods (see "Moosehead Lake Area"), along with three historic sporting camps, and is working to maintain an extensive trail system geared to nonmotorized recreational use. The **AMC** has long offered seasonal "family camp" programs for adults and families seeking an organized outdoor-geared vacation at **Echo Lake** (www.amcecholakecamp.org) on Mount Desert, at **Cold**

River Camp (www.amccoldriver camp.org) in Evans Notch (within the White Mountain National Forest) and most recently at Medawisla near Greenville. Also see *Hiking* and *Cross-Country Skiing*.

APPLES Fall brings plenty of pick-your-own opportunities across the state, and many orchards also sell apples and cider. For a map/guide to PYO orchards, see www.maineapples .org or the Department of Agriculture's Web site: www.getrealmaine .com. And check out the Cornish Apple Festival and Apple Acres Bluegrass Festival, both held in Cornish in late September.

AQUARIUMS The **Marine Resources Aquarium** in Boothbay Harbor displays regional fish and sea creatures, many of them surprisingly colorful. The stars of the show are the sharks and skates in a large touch tank. The **Mount Desert Oceanarium** is a commercial attraction with several locations in the Bar Harbor area.

ARTISTS, ART PROGRAMS, AND ART GALLERIES Maine's landscape has drawn major artists since the mid–19th century. The **Maine Arts Commission** (www.mainearts.com) offers a searchable database of artists, arts organizations, and events. Within each chapter we describe commercial galleries, which seemed to have clustered in Portland, Rockland, Northeast Harbor, Stonington, Blue Hill, and Eastport. A number of books profile the work of current Maine artists; a standout is *Art of the Maine Islands* by Carl Little and Arnold Skolnick (Down East Books). Artist-owned galleries, which have become destinations in their own right, are found in Sullivan and Stonington and on the islands of Monhegan, North Haven, Vinalhaven, and Little Cranberry. Summer arts workshops are offered in Stonington and at **Rock Gardens Inn** (www.rockgardensinn.com), and the Maine College of Art (www.meca.org) in Portland. The most prestigious summer arts workshop in Maine is the **Skowhegan School of Painting and Sculpture** (207-474-9345 or 212-529-0505; www.skowheganart.org).

ART MUSEUMS Seven of the state's museums have formed a partnership and created the **Maine Art Museum Trail** (www.maineartmuseums.org). The **Portland Museum of Art** (www .portlandmuseum.org) is known for its strong collection of works by impressionist and postimpressionist masters as well as Winslow Homer. **The Farnsworth Art Museum** with its **Center for the Wyeth Family in Maine** in Rockland(www.farnsworth museum.org) has a stellar collection of Maine art, as well as frequent special exhibits. The seasonal **Ogunquit Museum of American Art** (www .ogunquitmuseum.org), the **Colby College Museum of Art** (www .colby.edu/museum) in Waterville, and the newly expanded Bowdoin College Museum of Art (www.bow doin.edu/artmuseum) are also outstanding and described within their respective chapters. The **University of Maine Museum of Art** in Bangor (www.umma.umaine.edu) is another worth exploring.

ATVS **Alliance Trail Vehicles of Maine** (www.atvmaine.com) offers information about the state's all-terrain vehicle clubs and riding opportunities.

BALLOONING Hot-air balloon rides are available across the state from **Balloons Over New England** (1-800-788-5562) in Kennebunkport, **Hot Fun** (www.hotfunballoons.com) in South Portland, and **Sails Aloft** (207-623-1136) in Augusta.

BEACHES Given the summer temperature of the Atlantic Ocean (from 59 degrees in Ogunquit to 54 degrees at Bar Harbor), swimming isn't the primary reason you come to the Maine coast. But Maine beaches (for instance at York, Wells, the Kennebunks, Portland, Popham, and Pemaquid) can be splendid walking, sunning, and kite-flying places. At **Ogunquit** and in **Reid State Park** in Georgetown, there are also warmer backwater areas in which small children can paddle. Other outstanding beaches include 7-mile-long **Old Orchard Beach** and, nearby, state-maintained **Crescent Beach** on Cape Elizabeth, **Scarborough Beach** in Scarborough, **Ferry Beach** in Saco, and **Sand Beach** in Acadia National Park. The state-maintained freshwater beaches are on **Lakes Damariscotta**, **St. George**, **Sebec**, **Rangeley**, **Sebago**, and **Moosehead**; also on **Pleasant Pond** in Richmond. All state beaches include changing facilities, restrooms, and showers; many have snack bars. The town of **Bridgton** has several fine little lakeside beaches and **Lake George Regional Park** (between Skowhegan and Canaan) offers sandy beaches and facilities on two shores.

Christina Tree

BED & BREAKFASTS We have visited just about every B&B in Maine. They range from elegant town houses and country mansions to farms and fishermen's homes. Prices vary from $65 to more than $600 (on the coast in August) for a double and average $110–150 in high season on the coast. With few exceptions, they offer a friendly entrée to their communities.

BICYCLING **Mountain biking** is particularly popular on the carriage roads in **Acadia National Park**. Biking is also popular on Swan's Island off Acadia and on islands in Casco Bay. Rt. 1 is heavily traveled, and should be avoided. Dedicated recreation paths are beginning to appear, notably in Portland and Brunswick/Bath, along the Kennebec between Augusta and Gardiner, and farther north between Solon and Bingham. Bicycling also makes sense in heavily touristed resort areas in which a car can be a nuisance; rentals are available in Ogunquit, Kennebunkport, Camden, Southwest Harbor, and Bar Harbor.

Check out the excellent Maine DOT site, **www.exploremaine.org/bike**, for tours ranging from 20 to 100 miles. The **Bicycle Coalition of Maine** (207-623-4511; www.bikemaine.org) serves as a conduit for information about both off- and on-road bicycling throughout the state and maintains a calendar of bicycling

Northern Outdoors

events. Guided multiday tours are offered by **Summer Feet Cycling** (www.summerfeet.net) and by **Bike Vermont** (www.bikevermont.com); two-day camping tours are offered by L. L. Bean (www.llbean.com).

BIRDING **Maine Audubon** (207-781-2330; www.maineaudubon.org), based at Gilsland Farm Audubon Center in Falmouth, maintains a number of birding sites and sponsors nature programs and field trips, which include cruises to Matinicus Rock and to Eagle Island. Note the special programming at Maine Audubon's Adirondack-style lodges on their 1,600-acre preserve at Borestone Mountain. **Laudholm Farm** in Wells, **Biddeford Pool**, **Scarborough Marsh**, **Merrymeeting Bay**, and **Mount Desert** are also popular birding sites. **Monhegan** is the island to visit in May and September. The **Moosehorn National Wildlife Refuge** (207-454-3521) in Washington County represents the northeastern terminus of the East Coast chain of wildlife refuges and is particularly rich in bird life. We recommend *Birder's Guide to Maine* by Elizabeth Cary Pierson, Jan Erik Pierson, and Peter D. Vickery (Down East Books). The annual **Downeast Birding Festival**, featuring guided hikes, cruises, and lectures, is held in the Cobscook Bay area Memorial Day weekend (www.downeastbirdfest.org). Also see *Puffin-Watching* and *Nature Preserves, Coastal* and *Inland*. The site **www.mainebirding.net** has checklists, events, and detailed descriptions.

BLUEBERRYING Maine grows 98 percent of America's lowbush blueberries. More than 65.5 million pounds are harvested annually from an estimated 25,000 acres. There are absolutely no human-planted wild blueberry fields. Few growers allow U-pick, at least not until the commercial harvest is over. (One exception is **Staples Homestead Blueberries** in Stockton Springs.) Then the public is invited to go "stumping" for leftovers. On the other hand, berrying along roads and hiking paths is a rite of summer. The **blueberry barrens**—thousands of blueberry-covered acres—spread across Cherryfield, Columbia, and Machias (site of the state's most colorful blueberry festival in August) in Washington County. For more about Maine's famous fruit, click on **www.wildblueberries.com**.

BOATBUILDING **WoodenBoat School** (207-359-4651; www.thewoodenboatschool.com) in Brooklin (see "Blue Hill Area") offers a plethora of courses, including more than 100 on various aspects of boatbuilding. The **Maine Maritime Museum** (www.mainemaritimemuseum.org) in Bath offers some classes in boatbuilding; Atlantic Challenge's program, the

Apprenticeshop (207-594-1800), in Rockland offers two-year apprentice programs and six-week (or longer) internships; and the **Washington County Community College Marine Trades Center** at Eastport attracts many out-of-staters.

BOAT EXCURSIONS You really won't know what Maine is about until you stand off at sea to appreciate the beauty of the cliffs and island-dotted bays. For the greatest concentrations of boat excursions, see "Boothbay Harbor Region," "Rockland/Thomaston Area," and "Bar Harbor and Ellsworth"; there are also excursions from Ogunquit, Kennebunkport, Portland, Belfast, Camden, Castine, Stonington, Jonesport, Machias, Lubec, and Eastport. (Also see *Coastal Cruises*; *Ferries, in Maine* and *to Canada*; *Sailing*; and *Windjammers*. See "Sebago and Long Lakes Region" and "Moosehead Lake Area" for lake excursions.)

BOOKS Anyone who seriously sets out to explore Maine should read the following mix of Maine classics and guidebooks: *The Maine Woods* by **Henry David Thoreau**, first published posthumously in 1864, remains very readable and gives an excellent description of Maine's mountains (we recommend the Penguin edition). Our favorite relatively recent Maine author is **Ruth Moore**, who writes about Maine islands in *The Weir*, *Spoonhandle*, and *Speak to the Wind* (originally published in the 1940s and reissued by Blackberry Books, Nobleboro). Happily, the 1940s books by **Louise Dickinson Rich**, among which our favorites are *The Coast of Maine: An Informal History* and *We Took to the Woods*, are now published by Down East Books in Camden, along with **Henry Beston**'s 1940s classic *Northern Farm: A Chronicle of Maine*. **Sarah Orne Jewett**'s classic *The Country of the Pointed Firs and Other Stories* (W. W. Norton), first published in 1896, is set on the coast around Tenants Harbor and still an excellent read. For historical fiction, try any one of Pulitzer Prize–winner **Kenneth Roberts**'s novels about Maine during the Revolutionary War. **John Gould**, an essayist who wrote a regular column for the *Christian Science Monitor* for more than 50 years, has published several books, including *Dispatches from Maine*, a collection of those columns, and *Maine Lingo* (with **Lillian Ross**), a humorous look at Maine phrases and expressions.

Maine has been home to the authors of many of our most beloved children's classics. **Robert McCloskey**, author of *Blueberries for Sal, Time of Wonder*, and *One Morning in Maine* resided on an island off the Blue Hill peninsula, also summer home to **E. B. White**, known for wonderful essay collections, and his ever-popular children's novels, *Charlotte's Web* and *Stuart Little*. Damariscotta-based **Barbara Cooney** wrote and illustrated some 200 books, among them *Miss Rumphius, Island Boy*, and *Hattie and the Wild Waves*,

Recent classics set in Maine include **Carolyn Chute**'s *The Beans of Egypt, Maine* (1985), *Letourneau's Used Auto Parts* (1988), and *Merry Men* (1994); and **Cathie Pelletier**'s *The Funeral Makers* (1987) and *The Weight of Winter* (1991). *Maine Speaks*, an anthology of Maine literature published by the **Maine Writers and Publishers Alliance** (www.mainewriters.org), contains all the obvious poems and essays and many pleasant surprises. **Linda Greenlaw**'s *The Lobster Chronicles* (2002) describes the island of Isle au Haut. It's a good read with insights into life on all Maine's surviving island communities.

Guides to exploring Maine include the indispensable *Maine Atlas and Gazetteer* (DeLorme) and, from Down East Books, *Birder's Guide to Maine* by Elizabeth Cary Pierson, Jan Erik Pierson, and Peter D. Vickery; *Walking the Maine Coast* by John Gibson; and *Islands in Time: A Natural and Cultural History of the Islands of the Gulf of Maine* by Philip W. Conkling. Serious hikers should secure the *AMC Maine Mountain Guide* (AMC Books); also *50 Hikes in the Maine Mountains* by Cloe Chunn and *50 Hikes in Coastal and Southern Maine* by John Gibson (both Countryman Press).

Also worth noting: *Maine*, by Charles C. Calhoun (Compass American Guides), complements this guide with its superb illustrations and well-written background text.

BUS SERVICE **Concord Trailways** (1-800-639-3317; www.concord trailways.com) serves Portland, Brunswick, Bath, Wiscasset, Damariscotta, Waldoboro, Rockland, Camden, Belfast, Searsport, Bangor, and the University of Maine at Orono (when school is in session). Its Boston/Portland/Bangor Express is the fastest service to eastern Maine. **Greyhound Bus Lines/Vermont Transit** (1-800-231-2222 or 1-800-451-3292; www .vermonttransit.com) serves Augusta, Lewiston, Waterville, Portland, Bangor, and (seasonally but crucially) Bar Harbor. See www.exploremaine.org for details about public transit buses. **West's Coastal Connection** (www .westbusservice.com), offers daily service year-round between Bangor Airport (stopping at both bus terminals) to Calais, with stops in Machias and Perry, with many flag-down stops (call ahead) in between.

CAMPING See "North Maine Woods" for details about camping within these vast fiefdoms, and also for camping in **Baxter State Park** (see "Katahdin Region") and along the **Allagash Wilderness Waterway** (see *To Do—Canoeing* in "Aroostook County"). For camping within **Acadia National Park**, see "Acadia National Park." For the same within the **White Mountain National Forest**, see "Bethel Area." For private campgrounds, the booklet ***Maine Camping Guide***, published by the Maine Campground Owners Association (207-782-5874; www.campmaine.com), lists most privately operated camping and tenting areas. Reservations are advised for the state's 13 parks that offer camping (www.campwithme.com; also see *Parks, State*). We have attempted to describe the state parks in detail wherever they appear in this book (see Damariscotta, Camden, Cobscook Bay, Sebago, Rangeley, and Greenville). Note that state campsites can accommodate average-sized campers and trailers, but only Sebago and Rangeley offer trailer hook-ups. **Warren Island** (just off Islesboro) and **Swan Island** (just off Richmond) offer organized camping, and primitive camping is permitted on a number of islands through the **Maine Island Trail Association** (MITA; see *Islands*). Within this book we occasionally describe outstanding private campgrounds.

CAMPS AND LEARNING PROGRAMS FOR ADULTS **Outward Bound** (1-866-846-7745; www.outwardbound wilderness.org) offers a variety of adult-geared outdoor adventures in Maine as well as throughout the country. **L. L. Bean** (www.llbean .com) offers introductions to a variety of sports with programs lasting from a couple hours to multiday family adventures and Outdoor Discovery Schools. The **Hog Island Audubon Camp** on Hog Island off Bremen offers a series of weeklong courses (see "Damariscotta/Newcastle"). The **AMC** (See *Appalachian Mountain Club*) also offers week-long "Family Camps" programs at several Maine venues. Photographers should check out the **Maine Media Workshops** (www.theworkshops.com) in Rockport. Also see *Boatbuilding* (**WoodenBoat** offers much more than boatbuilding); check **Elderhostel** (1-800-454-5768; www.elderhostel.org), which offers a variety of programs throughout Maine for everyone over age 60; and the **Haystack Mountain School** under *Crafts* and arts workshops under *Artists and Art Galleries*. Entries under *Music School, Art Programs, and Sailing* also have workshop information. Potters should also check out the **Watershed Center for Ceramic Arts** (www.watershed centerceramicarts.org) in Newcastle. **The National Theatre Workshop of the Handicapped** (www.ntwh .org) is a residential program in Belfast.

CAMPS, FOR CHILDREN More than 200 summer camps are listed in the exceptional booklet published annually by the Maine Youth Camping Association (1-800-536-7712; www.maine camps.org).

CANOEING, GUIDED TRIPS Developed by the Wabanaki and still proudly manufactured in Old Town (see "Bangor Area"), the canoe remains the craft of choice on Maine rivers. Novices might begin with the slow-moving, shallow **Saco River**, which offers a number of well-maintained camping sites. Several outfitters in the Fryeburg area (see *To Do* in "Sebago and Long Lakes Region") offer rentals and shuttle service, and **Saco Bound**, just over the New Hampshire line, offers guided tours. The **Moose River** near Jackman (see *To Do* in "Upper Kennebec Valley") offers a similar camping/canoeing trip, and **Sunrise International**, based in Bangor (see *To Do* in "Bangor" and "Washington County and the Quoddy Loop"), offers staging for trips down the Grand Lake chain of lakes and the St. Croix River. Also see **www .northernforestcanoetrail.org** for the 348-mile portion of the Maine stretch. Within each chapter canoe rentals and guided trips are described under *To Do*.

CANOEING THE ALLAGASH The ultimate canoe trip in Maine (and on the entire East Coast) is the seven- to 10-day expedition up the **Allagash Wilderness Waterway**, a 92-mile ribbon of lakes, ponds, rivers, and streams in the heart of northern Maine's vast commercial forests. We advise using a shuttle service. The general information number for the Allagash Wilderness Waterway is 207-941-4014; ask for the free map that pinpoints the 65 authorized campsites within the zone (and details other crucial information). A detailed topographical map, backed with historical and a variety of other handy information, is DeLorme's *Map and Guide to* *the Allagash and St. John*. The **North Maine Woods** offers its own information about campsites and a publication with a map (www.northmainewoods.org). Be aware of blackflies in June and no-see-ums when warm weather finally comes. For further information, see *Camping* and *Guide Services*, and check out www.maineoutdoors.com. Also see *To Do—Canoeing* in "Aroostook County." A map tracing **Henry David Thoreau's three canoe/hiking journeys** described in *The Maine Woods* has been produced by Maine Woods Forever (www.thoreauwabanakitrail.org).

CHEESE Maine's more than 20 cheese-makers claim to create more than 150 artisan cheeses, but with the exception of Seal Cove Farm in Lamoine (producing goat cheese since 1980), most are available only locally. Check out **www.mainecheeseguild.org** for more information and about **Open Creamery Day** in early October.

CHILDREN, ESPECIALLY FOR Throughout this book, restaurants, lodgings, and attractions that are of special interest to families with children are indicated by the crayon symbol .

CHRISTMAS TREES AND WREATHS Maine is a prime source of Christmas trees for the Northeast. The **Maine Christmas Tree Association** (www.mainechristmastree.com) maintains a list of farms that sell wreaths and garlands and those that welcome visitors to cut their own trees in November. The Maine Department of Agriculture maintains a more detailed "Choose and Cut" list at www.getrealmaine.com.

CLAMMING Maine state law permits shellfish harvesting for personal use only, unless you have a commercial license. But rules vary with each town, so check with the town clerk (source of licenses) before you dig, and make sure there's no red tide. Some towns do prohibit clamming, and in certain places there is a temporary stay on harvesting while the beds are being seeded.

COASTAL CRUISES *Cruise* is a much-used (and -abused) term along the Maine coast, chiefly intended to mean a boat ride. Within each chapter we describe what's currently available, from ferries to multiday sails. (Also see *Windjammers*).

COTTAGE RENTALS Cottage rentals are a reasonably priced way for families to stay in one Maine spot for a week or more. Request the booklet *Maine Guide to Inns and Bed & Breakfasts and Camps & Cottages* from the Maine Tourism Association (www.mainetourism.com). Many local chambers of commerce also keep a list of available rentals, and we list cottage rental Web sites in most chapters.

COVERED BRIDGES Of the 120 covered bridges that once spanned Maine rivers, just nine survive. The most famous, and certainly picturesque, is the **Artists' Covered Bridge** (1872) over the Sunday River in Newry, northwest of Bethel. The others are **Porter Bridge** (1876), over the Ossipee River, 0.5 mile south of Porter; **Babb's Bridge**, rebuilt after burning in 1973, over the Presumpscot River between Gorham and Windham; **Hemlock Bridge** (1857), 3 miles northwest of East Fryeburg;

Lovejoy Bridge (1883), over the Ellis River in South Andover; **Bennett Bridge** (1901), over the Magalloway River, 1.5 miles south of the Wilson's Mills post office; **Robyville Bridge** (1876), Maine's only completely shingled covered bridge, in the town of Corinth; the **Watson Settlement Bridge** (1911), between Woodstock and Littleton; and **Low's Bridge**, carefully reconstructed in 1990 after a flood took the 1857 structure, across the Piscataquis River between Guilford and Sangerville.

CRAFTS *Maine Guide to Crafts and Culture*, available free from the **Maine Crafts Association** (www.mainecrafts.org), is a geographic listing of studios, galleries, and museums throughout Maine. **United Maine Craftsmen, Inc.** (207-621-2818; www.unitedmainecraftsmen.com) also sponsors six large shows each year. **Haystack Mountain School of Crafts** (www.haystack-mtn.org; see "Deer Isle, Stonington") is a summer school nationally respected in a variety of crafts with three-week courses mid-June through mid-September. The surrounding area (Blue Hill to Stonington) contains the largest concentration of Maine craftspeople, many with open studios. More than 130 fiber studios plus fiber farms and galleries are listed at www.mainefiberarts.org; a hard copy of the map/guide is also available.

Christina Tree

DOGSLEDDING Although racing is a long-established winter spectator sport, riding on a dogsled is an activity growing in popularity. **Telemark Inn** (www.telemarkinn.com) in West Bethel offers dogsledding. In the Moosehead Lake region, Stephen Medera's **Song in the Woods** (www.songinthewoods.com) and Ed Mathieu's **Moose Country Safaris and Dogsled Trips** (www.maineguide.com/sportsmen/dogsled) offer a choice of trips. Don and Angel Hibbs have traveled more than 40,000 miles by dog team. Their **Nahmakanta Lake Camps** (www.nahmakanta.com) in Rainbow Township serve as a base for driving teams (guests can ride or drive) on trails in a 27,000-acre preserve that's Maine's largest roadless preserve outside Katahdin—which is clearly visible from the trail system. Guests ski in 10 miles from the Golden Road. The New England Dogsled Championships are held in Jackman in March.

EVENTS We have listed outstanding annual events within each chapter of this book; also see event listings on www.visitmaine.com and www.mainetourism.com. A community calendar is posted at www.mainepublicradio.org.

FACTORY OUTLETS We note individual outlet stores in their respective chapters throughout; we also describe the state's two major outlet clusters: in **Freeport** (www.freeportusa.com) and **Kittery** (www.thekitteryoutlets .com). L. L. Bean (www.llbean.com), Freeport's anchor store, is open 24 hours and is the single most spectacular store in northern New England. New Balance also makes sneakers and maintains major sports clothing outlets in Fryeburg, Norway, and Skowhegan.

FALL FOLIAGE Autumn days tend to be clear, and the changing leaves against the blue sea and lakes can be spectacular. Off-season prices sometimes prevail, in contrast with the rest of New England at this time of year. Check the Maine Office of Tourism Web site, www.mainefoliage.com, for a map reporting leaf colors and places to visit.

FARM B&BS **The Maine Farm Vacation B&B Association** describes its 18 members in its brochure and at www.mainefarmvacation.com. This is a promotional association, not an official approval and inspection group. Properties vary widely. Some offer plenty of space, animals, big breakfasts, and friendly informal atmosphere, but others are not working farms.

FARM STANDS, FARMS, AND FARMER'S MARKETS The **Maine Department of Agriculture** (207-287-3491; www.getrealmaine.com), 28 State House Station, Augusta 04333, publishes a handy 151-page guide listing more than 65 markets.

FERRIES The Maine Department of Transporation mantians a brilliant Web site (www.exploremaine.org) with schedules for **Maine State Ferry**

Christina Tree

Service (1-800-491-4883) from Rockland to Vinalhaven, North Haven, and Matinicus, from Lincolnville to Islesboro, and from Bass Harbor to Swans Island and Frenchboro. They also list services to Monhegan Island, Isle au Haut and the Cranberry Islands, and Casco Bay islands; from Portland and Bar Harbor to Canada on "The Cat" (www.catferry.com), as well as the Quoddy Loop ferries from Eastport and Campobello Island to the New Brunswick mainland via Deer Island and from Black Harbor to Grand Manan.

FILM **Northeast Historic Film** (1-800-639-1636; www.oldfilm.org) is based at "The Alamo," a vintage-1916 movie house in Bucksport. This admirable group has created a regional moving-image archive of films based on or made in New England that were shown in every small town during the first part of the 20th century. Request the catalog *Videos of Life in New England*. The **International Film & Television Workshops** in Rockport offers a variety of weeklong courses in various aspects of film. The **Maine International Film Festival** is a ten-day event, with more than 60 films shown in Waterville

(www.miff.org). Portland hosts the **Maine Jewish Film Festival** in mid-March. There are still four functioning **drive-ins** in Maine, in Saco, Bridgton, Skowhegan, and Westbrook.

FIRE PERMITS Maine law dictates that no person shall kindle or use outdoor fires without a permit, except at authorized campsites or picnic grounds. Fire permits in the organized townships are obtained from the local town warden; in the unorganized townships, from the nearest forest ranger. Portable stoves fueled by propane gas, gasoline, or Sterno are exempt from the rule.

FISHING **Maine sporting camps** (www.mainesportingcamps.com) catering to fishermen can be found in "Western Mountains and Lakes Region," "North Maine Woods," and "Upper Kennebec Valley." The Maine Department of Marine Resources (207-633-9500) furnishes species information and launch sites at www.maine.gov/dmr/index.htm (look for "recreational fishing" on the left). **The Maine Department of Inland Fisheries and Wildlife** (207-287-8000) publishes a weekly fishing report at www.mefishwildlife.com. **Registered Maine Guides (www.maineguides.org)** know where and how to fish, and offer frequent courses. One-day fishing licenses are available at general stores and from outfitters throughout the state and come with a regulations book. Also check out FISHING at **www.visitmaine.com**.

FORTS Maine's 20 forts are actually a fascinating lot, monuments to the state's largely forgotten history. **Fort Knox** (see "Bucksport") is the state's grandest fort and offers a lively seasonal schedule of events. **Fort William Henry** at Pemaquid (see "Damariscotta/Newcastle") is genuinely fascinating, while **Fort Edgecomb** off Rt. 1 in Edgecomb, just east of Wiscasset, is an easy hit. Also check out **Fort George** in Castine, **Fort McClary** in Kittery, **Fort Popham** near Bath, **Fort Pownall** at Stockton Springs, **Fort O'Brien** in Machiasport, and, at the northern end of Rt. 1, **Fort Kent** in Fort Kent.

GOLDEN ROAD This legendary 96-mile road is the privately owned high road of the North Maine Woods, linking Millinocket's paper mills on the east with commercial woodlands that

Christina Tree

extend to the Quebec border. Its name derives from its multimillion-dollar cost in 1975, but its value has proven great to visitors heading up from Moosehead Lake, as well as from Millinocket to Baxter State Park. It's also used by the whitewater rafting companies on the Penobscot River and the Allagash Wilderness Waterway, and for remote lakes like Chesuncook. Expect to pull to the side to permit lumber trucks to pass. Much of the road is now paved and well maintained, even (especially) in winter. Be sure to bring along your Maine atlas or another detailed map. At this writing the Greenville Road—until recently a toll road linking Kokadjo and the Golden Road—is free but not well maintained.

GOLF The **Golf Maine Association Web site** (www.golfme.org) offers information and links to its member courses. Also check out the **Maine Golf Trail** at www.visitmaine.com and the Maine State Golf Association (www.mesga.org). Within the book we list golf courses within each chapter. The major resorts catering to golfers are the **Samoset** in Rockport, the **Bethel Inn** in Bethel, **Sebasco Harbor Resort** near Bath, the **Country Club Inn** in Rangeley, and **Sugarloaf/USA** in the Carrabassett Valley (where you should also inquire about **Moose Meadows**). Check out **Sunday River**'s course in Newry.

GORGES Maine has the lion's share of the Northeast's gorges. There are four biggies. The widest is the **Upper Sebois River Gorge** north of Patten, and the most dramatic, "Maine's Miniature Grand Canyon," is **Gulf Hagas** near the Katahdin Iron Works (see "Katahdin Region"). Both **Kennebec Gorge** and **Ripogenus Gorge** are now popular whitewater rafting routes.

GUIDE SERVICES In 1897 the Maine legislature passed a bill requiring hunting guides to register with the state; the first to do so was Cornelia Thurza Crosby (better known as "Fly Rod" Crosby), whose syndicated column appeared in New York, Boston, and Chicago newspapers at the turn of the 20th century. Becoming a Registered Maine Guide entails passing one of several specialized tests—in hunting, fishing, or one of a growing number of recreational categories, including whitewater rafting, canoeing, or kayaking—administered by the Maine Department of Inland Fisheries and Wildlife. There are currently some 6,000 **Registered Maine Guides**, but just a few hundred are full-time professional guides. The Web site of the 500-member Maine Professional Guides Association is www.maineguides.org.

HANDICAPPED ACCESS Within this book, handicapped-accessible lodging, restaurants, and attractions are marked with a wheelchair symbol ♿. Maine, by the way, offers an outstanding handicapped snow sports program, including cross-country and alpine skiing, shoeshoeing, and snowboarding (1-800-639-7770; www.skimhs.org). Summer programs offer paddling, golf, and cycling.

HIKING For organized trips, see ***Appalachian Mountain Club***. Also see the exciting new ***Maine Huts and Trails System***. While we list hikes we like within most chapters, we strongly suggest acquiring detailed trail guides. In addition to the *AMC*

Maine Mountain Guide and the AMC map/guide to trails on Mount Desert, we recommend investing in *50 Hikes in Coastal and Southern Maine* by John Gibson and *50 Hikes in the Maine Mountains* by Cloe Chunn (both from Backcountry Publications), which offer clear, inviting treks up hills of every size throughout the state. *The Maine Atlas and Gazetteer* (DeLorme) also outlines a number of rewarding hikes. While hiking is generally associated with inland Maine and with Acadia, in recent years tens of thousands of acres of dramatic shore property have been preserved, much of it traversed by coastal trails detailed in *Cobscook Trails*, available from the Quoddy Regional Land Trust (www.qrlt.org). Also see *Appalachian Trail*; Baxter State Park in "Katahdin Region"; and "Acadia National Park."

HISTORY We tell Maine's rich history through the places that still recall or dramatize it. See *Wabanaki* for sites that tell of the long precolonial history. For traces of early 17th-century settlement, see our descriptions of **Phippsburg**, **Pemaquid**, and **Augusta**. The French and Indian Wars (1675–1760), in which Maine was more involved than most of New England, are recalled in the reconstructed English **Fort William Henry** at Pemaquid and in historical markers scattered around **Castine** (Baron de Saint Castine, a young French nobleman married to a Penobscot Indian princess, controlled the coastal area we now call "Down East"). A striking house built in 1760 on **Kittery Point** (see "Kittery and the Yorks") evokes Sir William Pepperrell, credited with having captured the fortress at Louisburg from the French, and restored buildings in **York Village** (www.oldyork.org) suggest Maine's brief, peaceful colonial period.

In the **Burnham Tavern** at **Machias** you learn that townspeople captured a British man-of-war on June 1, 1775, the first naval engagement of the Revolution. Other reminders of the Revolution are less triumphant: At the Cathedral Pines in **Eustis** and spotted along Rt. 202 in the **Upper Kennebec Valley**, historical markers tell the poignant saga of Colonel Benedict Arnold's ill-fated 1775 attempt to capture Quebec. Worse: Markers at **Fort George** in Castine detail the ways in which a substantial patriot fleet utterly disgraced itself there. Maine's brush with the British didn't end with the Revolution: The Barracks Museum in **Eastport** tells of British occupation again in 1814.

Climb the six steep floors of the **Portland Observatory** (built in 1807) and hear how Portland ranked second among New England ports, its tonnage based on lumber, the resource that fueled fortunes like those evidenced by the amazingly opulent **Colonel Black Mansion** in Ellsworth and the elegant **Ruggles House** way Down East in Columbia Falls. In 1820 Maine finally became a state (the 23rd), but, as we note in our introduction to "The North Maine Woods," not without a price. The mother state (Massachusetts), her coffers at their usual low, stipulated an even division of all previously undeeded wilderness, and some 10.5 million acres were quickly sold off, vast privately owned tracts that survive today as the unorganized townships.

Plagued in 1839 by boundary disputes with Canada that were ignored in Washington, the new, timber-rich state built its own northern forts (the **Fort Kent Blockhouse** survives). This "Aroostook War" was terminated by the Webster-Ashburton Treaty of 1842. In 1844 the state built massive **Fort Knox** at the mouth of the Penobscot River (see "Bucksport"), just in case. Never entirely completed, it makes an interesting state park. This era was, however, one of great prosperity and expansion within the new state.

As we note in the introduction to "Brunswick and the Harpswells," it can be argued that the Civil War began and ended there. Unfortunately the state suffered heavy losses: Some 18,000 young soldiers from Maine died, as Civil War monuments remind us. The end of the war, however, ushered in a boom decade. Outstanding displays in the **Vinalhaven Historical Society Museum** (see "The Fox Islands") and in the **Deer Isle Granite Museum** in Stonington (see "Deer Isle, Stonington") present the ways that Maine granite fed the demand for monumental public buildings throughout the country, and both schooners and Down Easters (graceful square-rigged vessels) were in great demand (see the **Penobscot Marine Museum** in "Belfast, Searsport" and the **Maine Maritime Museum** in "Bath Area").

In the late 19th century many Maine industries boomed, tourism included. We describe Maine's tourism history in our introduction because it is so colorful, little recognized, and so much a part of what you see in Maine today.

Maine, the Pine Tree State from Prehistory to the Present by Richard Judd, Edwin Churchill, and Joel Eastman (University of Maine Press) is a good, recent, readable history (paperback).

HORSEBACK RIDING **Northern Maine Riding Adventures** (see "Katahdin Region") offers entire days and overnights as well as shorter stints in the saddle, and special-needs riders are welcomed. We describe other riding options throughout the book.

HORSE RACING Harness racing can be found at **Scarborough Downs** (207-883-4331), Rt. 1 (exit 6 off the Maine Turnpike), April through November. The **Bangor Raceway** is open late May through late July. Both allow betting on races, but Bangor offers slot machines and more in a new, huge casino called Hollywood Slots (see *Gambling*). Many of the agricultural fairs also feature harness racing. Contact the Maine Harness Racing Commission (207-287-3221) for more information, or check the Web site of the Maine Harness Racing Promotions Board at www.maineharnessracing.com for schedules.

HUNTING Hunters should obtain a summary of Maine hunting and trapping laws from the **Maine Department of Inland Fisheries and Wildlife** (207-287-3371; www.mefishandwildlife.com). Also see *Registered Maine Guides.* Within the book check out "Moosehead Lake Area," "Katahdin Region," "Upper Kennebec" and "Calais." Also see HUNTING at www.visitmaine.com.

ICE CREAM Here's the scoop on our favorite ice cream sources. **John's Homemade Ice Cream**, Rt. 3, Liberty, puts local berries into its homemade fruit purées. The **Scoop Deck**, Rt. 1 in Wells (40 flavors for 20 years); **Round Top** ice cream, Business Rt. 1 in Damariscotta (in business 80 years); **Dorman's Dairy Dream** (closed Sunday; ginger is best), Rt. 1 in Thomaston; **Morton's Ice Cream** in Ellsworth; and **Phil's Not-So-Famous Ice Cream** in Lubec. Inland, check out **Shaner's Family Dining** in South Paris and **Smedberg's Crystal Spring Farm** in Oxford. **Gifford's** (www.giffords icecream.com) is a Skowhegan-based creamery that's been in the same family for a century, with a long list of flavors and the coveted "World's Best Vanilla" award.

Christina Tree

INNS Each edition of this book has become more selective as the number of places to stay increases. For each edition we personally inspect hundreds of inns and B&Bs. Our choices reflect both what we have seen and the feedback we receive from others; they are not paid listings. The **Maine Innkeepers Association** maintains a Web site of their members at www.maineinns.com. Also check listings at www.visitmaine.com and www.maine tourism.com.

ISLANDS Most of Maine's 3,250 offshore islands are uninhabited. We describe those that offer overnight

INFORMATION (OFFICIAL) ABOUT MAINE

The **Maine Office of Tourism** maintains www.visitmaine.com, a Web site almost good enough to compensate for the lack of any staff person to answer specific questions. The 24-hour information line, 1-888-624-6345, connects (if you hold on long enough) with a fulfillment clerk who will send you the thick, helpful, four-season guide *Maine Invites You,* and—if you request them—*Maine Guide to Inns and Bed & Breakfasts and Camps & Cottages.* These are published by the **Maine Tourism Association** (MTA; 207-623-0363), which maintains its own helpful Web site: www.maine tourism.com. The MTA also operates well-stocked and -staffed welcome centers at its southern gateway at **Kittery** (207-439-1319) on I-95 northbound (also accessible from Rt. 1); in **Yarmouth** just off Rt. 1 and I-95 (207-846-0833); in **Hampden** near Bangor on I-95 both northbound and southbound (207-862-6628 or 207-862-6638); at the Downeast Heritage Museum in **Calais** (207-454-2211); and in **Houlton** (207-532-6346). There's also a new information center near the New Hampshire line on Rt. 302 in **Fryeburg** (207-935-3639). In each chapter we describe the local information sources under *Guidance.*

lodging—**Chebeague**, **Long**, and **Peaks Islands** in Casco Bay; **Monhegan**, **Vinalhaven**, **North Haven**, **Islesboro**, and **Matinicus** along the Midcoast; and **Isle au Haut**, **Islesford** (also known as **Little Cranberry**), **Swans Island**, **Campobello,** and **Grand Manan** (New Brunswick) in the Down East section—in varying detail. In Casco Bay the ferry also serves **Cliff Island** (summer rentals are available); **Eagle Island**, former home of Admiral Peary, is served by daily excursion boats from Portland and South Freeport. For information on public and private islands on which low-impact visitors are welcome, contact the **Maine Island Trail Association** (207-596-6456; www.mita.org). MITA maintains 80 islands and charges $45 for membership, which brings with it a detailed guidebook and the right to land on these islands. **The Island Institute** (207-594-9209; www.islandinstitute.org) serves as an umbrella organization for the island communities; with the $50 membership come its publications: *Island Journal* and *Working Waterfront*.

KAYAKING Outfitters who offer guided half-day and full-day trips, also overnight and multiday expeditions with camping on Maine islands, are too numerous to be listed here but are described within each relevant chapter. The leading outfitters are **Maine Island Kayak Company** (www.maineisland kayak.com) on Peaks Island off Portland, **Maine Sport Outfitters** (207-236-7120) in Rockport, **H2Outfitters** (207-833-5257) on Orrs Island, **Old Quarry Ocean Adventures, Inc.** (www.oldquarry.com) in Deer Isle, **Tidal Transit** (207-633-7140) in Boothbay Harbor, and **Castine Kayak Adventures** (www.castinekayak.com) in Machias. **L. L. Bean** offers instruction in kayaking in many different classes of its **Outdoor Discovery Schools** (1-888-552-3261; www.llbean.com), Rt. 1, Freeport, and guides half- and full-day trips all season long. Their mid-June **Paddle Sports Festival** offers lectures, demonstrations, classes, and sea tours, and you can try out all the different boats sold. Also see **www.MaineSeaKayakGuides.com** for a listing of members of the Maine Association of Sea Kayaking Guides & Instructors. *Sea Kayaking Along the New England Coast* by Tamsin Venn (Appalachian Mountain Club) includes detailed kayaking routes from Portland to Cobscook Bay as well as an overall introduction to the sport. Dorcas Miller's comprehensive *Kayaking the Maine Coast: A Paddler's Guide to Day Trips from Kittery to Cobscook* (Countryman Press) is an excellent resource for kayak owners and competent kayakers.

LAKES Maine boasts some 6,000 lakes and ponds, and every natural body of water of more than 10 acres is theoretically available to the public for "fishing and fowling." Access is, however, limited by the property owners.

Christina Tree

Because paper companies and other land management concerns permit public use (see *Camping*), there is ample opportunity to canoe or fish in solitary waters. **Powerboat owners** should note that most states have reciprocal license privileges with Maine; the big exception is New Hampshire. A milfoil sticker is required by law of all motorized boats using Maine rivers, lakes, ponds, and streams (www.maine.gov/ifw). For more about the most popular resort lakes in the state, see the Bridgton, Rangeley, Moosehead, and Belgrade Lakes chapters. State parks on lakes include **Aroostook** (camping, fishing, swimming; Rt. 1 south of Presque Isle), **Damariscotta Lake State Park** (Rt. 32, Jefferson), **Lake St. George State Park** (swimming, picnicking, fishing; Rt. 3 in Liberty), **Lily Bay State Park** (8 miles north of Greenville), **Peacock Beach State Park** (swimming, picnicking; Richmond), **Peaks-Kenny State Park** (Sebec Lake in Dover-Foxcroft), **Rangeley Lake State Park** (swimming, camping; Rangeley), **Range Pond State Park** (Poland), **Sebago Lake State Park** (swimming, picnicking, camping; near Bridgton), **Mount Blue State Park** (Weld), and **Swan Lake State Park** (Swanville). Families with small children should note the coastal area lakes surrounded by rental cottages (see *Cottage Rentals*).

LIGHTHOUSES Maine takes pride in its 65 lighthouses. The most popular to visit is **Portland Head Light** (completed in 1790, automated in 1990, now a delightful museum featuring the history of lighthouses) on Cape Elizabeth. Others that feature museums are the **Marshall Point Light** at Port Clyde, **Pemaquid Point** (the lighthouse itself is now open seasonally and has rocks below that are peerless for scrambling), **Monhegan Light** on Monhegan Island, **Grindle Point** on Islesboro, and **West Quoddy Head Light** in Lubec, now part of a state park with a stunning shore path. At **Burnt Island Light Station** in Boothbay Harbor guides dress as lighthouse keepers from the 1950s and show visitors how life was lived on an isolated island. **Cape Neddick (Nubble) Light** is just off Sohier Park in York. **Fort Point Light** at Stockton Springs and **Bass Harbor Head Light** at Bass Harbor are accessible, as are Rockland's two distinctive lighths—**Owls Head** (1825) and the **Rockland Breakwater Light** (1827, pictured on our book cover). Rockland's **Gateway Visitor Center** is also home to the **Maine Lighthouse Museum** (www.mainelighthousemuseum.com). True lighthouse buffs also make the pilgrimage to **Burnt Harbor Light** on Swan's Island and to **Matinicus Rock**, the setting for several children's books. **East Quoddy Head Lighthouse** on the island of Campobello, accessible at low tide, is the ultimate adventure; it is also a prime

Christina Tree

whale-watching post. In recent years many lighthouses have been restored by volunteers, such as those who rallied around **Little River Light** on an island at the head of Cutler Harbor which in 2008 opens to the public not as a daytrip but as an overnight destination. Desriptions of all these lights are detailed in their respective chapters; also see: **www.LighthouseFoundation.org.**

LITTER Littering in Maine is punishable by a $100 fine; this applies to dumping from boats as well as other vehicles. Most cans and bottles are redeemable.

L. L. BEAN (www.llbean.com). With nine stores in Japan, dozens more scattered throughout the East Coast, and a hugely popular catalog, L. L. Bean remains a distinctly Maine icon and its Freeport campus is a major, ever-expanding destination. Ninety out of the first 100 boots Leon Leonwood Bean sold in 1912 fell apart. Bean refunded the purchasers' money, establishing a company tradition of guaranteed customer satisfaction. The Freeport store's 24/7 hours began as a way to serve outdoorsmen passing through in the wee hours. While outdoor clothing and equipment remain its mainstay, the elaborate anchor store now carries far more, and there is now a separate **Hunting and Fishing Store, a Bike, Boot & Ski Store** and a choice of **Outdoor Discovery Schools** and **Walk-on Adventures**, ranging from kayaking to fly-fishing. See the *Freeport* chapter for details.

LLAMA TREKKING The principle is appealingly simple: The llama carries your gear; you lead the llama. From the **Telemark Inn** (www.telemarkinn.com), surrounded by semiwilderness west of Bethel, Steve Crone offers single- and multiday treks. At **Pleasant Bay Bed & Breakfast** (www.pleasantbay.com) in Addison you can walk the property's waterside trails with the llamas.

LOBSTERS It's no secret that Maine's clean, cold waters produce some of the world's tastiest lobster. This hard-shelled crustacean has a long body and five sets of legs, including two large front claws, one large, flat, and heavy and the other smaller, thinner. They don't like light, hiding by day and emerging at night to eat mussels, sea urchins, and crabs. Most are at least seven years old by the time they are caught, because Maine regulates the minimum (also maximum) size of what can sold. The state also prohibits catching pregnant females, and imposes trap limits and license controls. In the 1880s most lobster was canned. Currently 90 percent of what's caught by Maine's 7,500 lobstermen is shipped live, out of state. For more on the industry see www.lobsterfrommaine.com.

LOBSTERS, EATING While lobster is just another item on the menu elsewhere in the world, in Maine it's an experience. While elsewhere it's appeal may be the fanciful ways it's prepared, in Maine it's the opposite. The shorter the time between a lobster's last crawl—not in a restaurant tank but in its home waters—the better. The preferred cooking method: 10–15 minutes in boiling seawater for an average-size (1 to 1½ lb.) lobster. Selecting the lobster is a bit more complicated. Choices may include a "cull" (a lobster with one claw), a "chicken" (a female, usually 1 pound, and considered to have the most delicate meat), and "hard shell" or "soft shell." Lobsters molt, usually shedding their shells in summer. The soft shell fills with sea water, which is replaced by new meat as the animal grows and the shell hardens. Which is better depends on who you talk to. Many prefer "shedders" because the shells are easy to crack and the meat is sweet. These actually transport less well than the full and firmly meated "hard shells," so chances are you won't have a chance to sample one outside Maine. *How* to eat a lobster is a no-holds-barred experience best embarked upon (and always explained) at lobster pounds (read on).

amazingmaine.com

LOBSTER BOAT RACING

LOBSTER POUNDS Technically this term refers to the saltwater holding areas in which lobsters are literally impounded, but in tourist talk a *lobster pound* is a no-frills seaside restaurant serving lobsters and clams steamed in seawater and consumed outside, with a nearby sink for washing off. Short of a lobster bake or boil on a beach, this is the only way to eat lobster in Maine. We have grouped lobster pounds, describing them in detail within each relevant chapter, but here's a quick overview of our favorites. The **Pemaquid Peninsula** (see "Damariscotta/Newcastle") is especially blessed: Check out **Shaw's** in New Harbor; the nearby **Harbor View Restaurant** at the Pemaquid Fisherman's Co-op; and, in Round Pond, **Muscongus Bay Lobster** and the **Round Pond Lobster Co-Op**. Near Rockland look for **Cod End** in Tenants Harbor. **Miller's Lobster Company** on Spruce Head, and **Waterman's Beach Lobsters** in South Thomaston are both good. In the Harpswells south of Brunswick the two standouts are **Allen's Seafood** (exceptional clams too) and **Morse's at Holbrook Wharf**. Other lobster-eating landmarks include **Robinson's Wharf** at Townsend Gut near Boothbay, the **Lobster Shack** in Cape Elizabeth near Portland, **Young's Lobster Pound** in East Belfast, the **Lobster Pound** in Lincolnville Beach, and **Union River Lobster Pot** in Ellsworth. At the entrance to Mount Desert Island, the **Trenton Bridge Lobster Pound** has been in George Gascon's family a long time and the view is great. On Mount Desert **Beal's** is in Southwest Harbor, and **Thurston's**, which we prefer, is in Bernard. Minutes from Freeport's outlets, the **Harraseeket Lunch & Lobster Company** in South Freeport is a find. On the Southern Coast the **Ogunquit Lobster Pound** on Rt. 1 in Ogunquit is now a full-service restaurant, but waterside **Chauncey Creek** in Kittery is still no frills (BYO everything from salad to wine) and a good value. **Nunan's Lobster Hut** in Cape Porpoise and **Fisherman's Catch** in Wells Harbor are also the real thing. The farthest Down East lobster pound is **Tidal Falls Lobster**

Restaurant in Hancock, sited by tidal reversing falls.

LOBSTER-BOAT RACES The season's races (www.lobsterboatracing.com) represent one of the best spectator events along the Maine coast. Races begin mid-June in Boothbay Harbor, and the "World's Fastest Lobster Boat Races" are always held on Moosabec Reach between Jonesport and Beals Island on July 4. Other venues are Rockland, Stonington, Harpswell, Friendship, Winter Harbor, and Searsport. Participants accumulate points as they go along, and there's an awards ceremony and pig roast in late September.

MAINE GROWN Locally produced items include venison and beeswax as well as blueberries, Christmas wreaths, smoked seafood, teas, beer, wine, maple syrup, and lobster stew, to name just a few. The Maine Department of Agriculture (**www.getrealmaine.com**) publishes several helpful guides. The Web site lists farmer's markets, orchards, farm stores, and much more.

MAINE HUTS AND TRAILS Check **www.mainehuts.org** for updates and details on this ambitious Kingfield-based, 180-mile hut-to-hut trail system that will eventually run from the Mahoosuc Mountains to Moosehead Lake. The first of a planned series of a dozen huts has opened at Poplar Stream Falls, just 2.5 miles from the Carrabassett Valley. It consists of main building, three small bunkhouses (with private and semi-private lodging) and a wood-fired sauna. There's a full-time staff of four who provide dinner, breakfast, and educational programming for guests (reservations: 1-877-ME-HUT2HUT). Two more huts are planned . The first 36 miles of trail—8 feet wide and maintained for nonmotorized use (hiking, mountain biking, and cross-country skiing)—follow the Dead River to The Forks.

MAINE MADE Maine craftspeople and entrepreneurs produce an ever-increasing variety of specialty foods, handcrafted furniture and furnishings, apparel, toys, and much more (www.mainemade.com).

MAINE MAPS Free state maps are available from the Maine Tourism Association welcome center, but we are sad to see the way these have deteriorated in recent years. The AAA map to Northern New England states is a step up and within this book we have done our best to detail obvious destinations. Sooner or later, however, serious Maine explorers have to invest in DeLorme's ***Maine Atlas & Gazetteer*** (www.DeLorme.com). See www.visitmaine.maine for printable maps to specialized trails and http://iceagetrail.unmaine.edu for a glacial geology guide to the Maine Ice Age Trail Down East. The Bureau of Parks and Lands (207-287-3824; www.maine.gov/ifw) publishes a map worth securing in its glossy, hard-copy form. It lists, locates, and describes state parks and public reserved lands and indicates abandoned railroad corridor trails.

MAINE PUBLIC BROADCASTING Public broadcasting (www.mpbc.org) offers statewide television and radio. **Maine Public Television** stations are Channel 10 in Augusta, Channel 12 in Orono, Channel 13 in Calais, Channel 10 in Presque Isle, and Channel 26 in Biddeford. Local programming includes *Home: The Story of Maine*, *Made in Maine*, and *Maine Watch*, highlighting important issues in Maine each week. **Maine's seven public radio stations** can be found on the dial at 89.7 in Calais, 90.1 in Portland, 90.9 in Bangor, 91.3 in Waterville, 106.1 in Presque Isle, 90.5 in Camden, and 106.5 in Fort Kent. Local programming includes *Maine Watch*; *Maine Things Considered*, a news program highlighting state news; *The Humble Farmer*, a quirky jazz and talk show hosted by local celebrity Robert Skoglund; and *Maine Stage*, a classical music series. Check out www.mainepublicradio.org.

MAINE TURNPIKE For travel conditions and construction updates, phone 1-800-675-PIKE, or check **www.maineturnpike.com**. New exit numbers will throw you if your map predates 2004. Tolls are now a flat rate paid when getting on—and sometimes off—the turnpike. Heading north, the first booth is in York. If you remain on the turnpike all the way to Augusta, you will pass through two more booths requiring a toll (New Gloucester and Gardiner). Unless you need to exit at Gray or Lewiston/Auburn, it's cheaper and quicker to follow I-295 rather than the Maine Turnpike (I-95) north to Augusta.

MAPLE SUGARING Maine produces roughly 8,000 gallons of syrup a year, and the Maine Maple Producers Association (www.mainemapleproducers.com) publishes a list of producers who welcome visitors on **Maine Maple Sunday** (also known as Sap Sunday) in late March.

MARITIME MUSEUMS **Maine Maritime Museum** (www.mainemaritimemuseum.org) in Bath stands in a class by itself and should not be missed. The **Penobscot Marine Museum** (www.penobscotmarinemuseum.org) in Searsport is smaller but still substantial, focusing on the merchant captains and their experiences in far corners of the world, featuring yearlong special exhibits. Also see www.maritimemaine.net.

MOOSE The moose, Maine's state animal, has made a comeback from near extinction in the 1930s and now numbers more than 30,000 in the North Maine Woods alone. Moose are the largest animal found in the wilds of New England. They grow to be 10 feet tall and average 1,000 pounds. The largest member of the deer family, they have a large, protruding upper lip and a distinctive "bell" or "dewlap" dangling from their muzzle.

"Bull" (male) moose have long been prized for their antlers, which grow to a span of up to 6 feet. They are shed in January and grow again. Female moose ("cows") do not grow antlers, and their heads are lighter in color than the bull. All moose, however, are darker in spring than summer, grayer in winter.

Front hooves are longer than the

Lori Duff

rear, as are the legs, the better to cope with deep snow and water. In summer they favor wetlands and can usually be found near ponds or watery bogs. They also like salt and so tend to create and frequent "wallows," wet areas handy to road salt (the attraction of paved roads).

Moose are vegetarians, daily consuming more than 50 pounds of leaves, grass, and other greenery when they can find it. In winter their diet consists largely of bark and twigs. Mating season is in mid-September until late October. Calves are born in early spring and weigh in at 30 pounds. They grow quickly but keep close to their mothers for an entire year. At best moose live 12 years.

Your chances of spotting one are greatest in early morning or at dusk on a wooded pond or lake or along logging roads. If you are driving through moose country at night, go slowly, because moose typically freeze rather than retreat from oncoming headlights. For details about commercial moose-watching expeditions, check "Rangeley Lakes Region," "Moosehead Lake Area," and the "Katahdin Region." The Moosehead Lake Region Chamber of Commerce sponsors **Moosemainea** mid-May through mid-June, with special events and a huge moose locator map. Suspicious that this promotion coincided with Moosehead's low tourist season, we queried the state's moose expert, who assures us that moose are indeed most visible in late spring. **Warning:** The state records hundreds of often deadly collisions between moose and cars or trucks. The common road sign and bumper sticker reading BRAKE FOR MOOSE means just that. Be extremely wary at dusk when vision is difficult and moose are active.

MUSEUMS Also see *Art Museums, Museum Villages, Maritime Museums*, and *Wabanaki*. Easily the most undervisited museum in the state, the **Maine State Museum** (www.mainestatemuseum.org) in Augusta has outstanding displays on the varied Maine landscape and offers historical exhibits ranging from traces of the area's earliest people to rifles used by State of Mainers in Korea; it also includes exhibits on fishing, agriculture, lumbering, quarrying, and shipbuilding. The **Seashore Trolley Museum** (www.trolleymuseum.org) in Kennebunkport and the **Owls Head Transportation Museum** (www.owlsehead.org) near Rockland are family finds (inquire about special events at both). Our favorites also include the **Peary-MacMillan Arctic Museum** at Bowdoin College in Brunswick, the **Wilson Museum** (www.wilsonmuseum.org) in Castine, and the **L. C. Bates Museum** (www.gwh.org) in Hinckley, a true "cabinet of curiosities" filled with stuffed animals and Indian artifacts and surpassingly lively. The **Lumbermen's Museum** in Patten (www.lumbermensmuseum.org) and the **Rangeley Lakes Region Logging Museum** are both glimpses of a recently vanished way of life in the North Maine Woods. The museum at the **Colonial**

VINALHAVEN HISTORICAL SOCIETY

Christina Tree

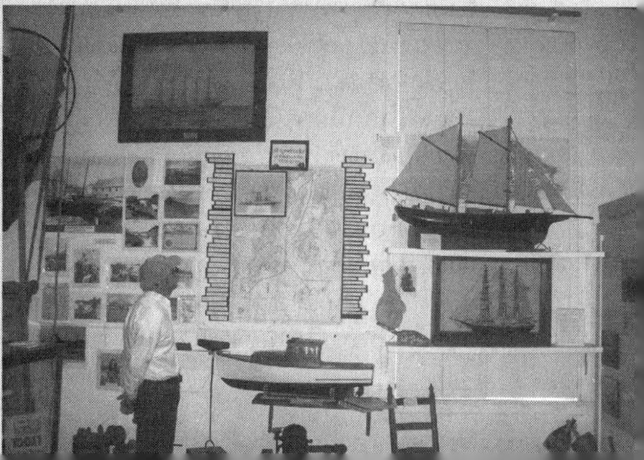

Pemaquid Restoration in Pemaquid, presenting archaeological finds from the adjacent early 17th-century settlement, is also unexpectedly fascinating. The **Downeast Heritage Museum** (www.downeast heritage.org) in Calais dramatizes the 1604 settlement of nearby St. Croix Island and the culture of the local Passamaquoddy Nation. Also see **www.mainemuseums.org** for an overview of museums, historical societies, historic sites, and archives.

MUSIC CONCERT SERIES Click on **www.mainemusic.org** for a daily updated list of musical events in Maine. **Bowdoin International Music Festival** (www.bowdoin festival.org) in Brunswick is the state's most prestigious and varied chamber music series, and the **Kneisel Hall Chamber Music Festival** (www.kneisel.org) in Blue Hill is its oldest chamber music festival, also still outstanding. The **Mount Desert Festival of Chamber Music** (www.mt desertfestical.org), the **Bar Harbor Festival** (www.barharbormusic festival.org), and the **Arcady Music Festival** (www.arcady.org) are all highlights of the season on Mount Desert. The **Sebago/Long Lakes Region Chamber Music Festival** (207-583-6747) at the Deertrees Theatre and Cultural Center in Harrison is noteworthy, and **Bay Chamber Concerts** (www.baychamberconcerts.org), present a summer series in Rockport and Rockland. The **Machias Bay Chamber Concerts** are held in the Machias Congregational church. There is, of course, the **Portland Symphony Orchestra** (www.port landsymphony.org), which has a summertime pops series, and the **Bangor Symphony Orchestra** (www.bangor symphony.com). Music lovers should also take note of the **American Folk Festival** the last weekend in August in Bangor, the **Lincoln Arts Festival** (www.lincolnartsfestival.org) of classical and choral music held throughout the Boothbay Harbor region in summer months, and the **Bluegrass Festival** at Thomas Point Beach in September. **SummerKeys** (www.summerkeys.com) offers a series of summer Wednesday-evening concerts in Lubec, with water taxi service from Eastport.

MUSIC SCHOOLS Notable are the **Bowdoin International Festival** (www.summermusic.org); **Kneisel Hall** in Blue Hill (www.kneisel.org); **Monteux School of Conducting** in Hancock (www.monteuxschool.org); **New England Music Camp** in Oakland (www.nemusiccamp.com); and **Maine Jazz Camp** (www.mainejazz camp.com) at the University of Maine, Farmington. A popular recent addition is **SummerKeys** (www.summer keys.com) in Lubec, specializing in piano but welcoming students of all levels in a variety of instruments.

NATURE PRESERVES, COASTAL Within each chapter we describe these under *Green Space* or *To Do—Hiking*. On the Southern Coast the **Wells National Estuarine Research Reserve at Laudholm Farm** (www.wellsreserve.org) includes two barrier beaches. On Casco Bay the Maine Audubon (www.maineaudubon.org) headquarters at **Gilsland Farm** in Falmouth includes 70 acres of nature trails; Maine Audubon also offers canoe tours and many summer programs at their **Scarborough Marsh Audubon Center** and maintains picnic and tenting sites at **Mast Landing Sanctuary** in Freeport. In Midcoast the **Boothbay Region Land Trust** (www.bbrlt.org) and the **Damariscotta River Association** (www.draclt.org) maintain some exceptional preserves, and **Camden Hills State Park** includes miles of little-used trails with magnificent views. Down East in the Blue Hill area, the 1,350-acre **Holbrook Island Sanctuary** in West Brooksville is a beauty, and in Ellsworth 40-acre **Birdsacre** (www.birdsacre.com) includes nature trails and a museum honoring ornithologist Cordelia Stanwood. **Acadia National Park** (www.nps.gov/acad), the state's busiest preserve, offers 120 miles of hiking paths on Mount Desert, also trails on Isle au Haut and at Schoodic Point. **Schoodic Mountain** north of Sullivan is one of the area's most spectacular hikes. Right across the line in Washington County, Steuben's **Maine Coastal Islands Refuge** (www.fws.gov/northeast/mainecoastal) is a 2,166-acre preserve with 47 offshore islands. Near Jonesport, **Great Wass Island** (accessible by road from Jonesport), maintained by the Maine Chapter of The Nature Conservancy, is a beautiful preserve with a 2-mile shore trail. **Western Head**, near Machias, is now maintained by Maine Coast Heritage Trust; Maine's Bureau of Parks and Lands maintains a 5.5-mile **Bold Coast Trail** along the high bluffs west of Cutler; **West Quoddy Light State Park** includes a splendid 2-mile shore trail. **Roosevelt Campobello International Park** also includes many miles of shore paths, and **Cobscook Bay State Park** (see "Eastport and Cobscook Bay") and **Moosehorn National Wildlife Refuge** (see "Calais and the St. Croix Valley") also offer hiking trails. The Nature Conservancy has protected more than a million acres in Maine; see the Maine chapter's site for details (www/nature.org/maine/). **The Maine Coast Heritage Trust** (www.mcht.org/) also publishes useful brochures about its holdings.

NATURE PRESERVES, INLAND In the Rangeley area the **Rangeley Lakes Heritage Trust** (www.rlht.org) has preserved more than 10,000 acres, including 20 miles of lake and river frontage and ten islands. In the Sugarloaf area the Maine Bureau of Parks and Lands now offers detailed maps to trails within the 35,000-acre **Bigelow Preserve**. Within each chapter we describe nature preserves along with state parks under *Green Space* or *To Do—Hiking*. Among our favorites are trails to the top of **Mount Kineo** overlooking Moosehead Lake, **Gulf Hagas**, a remote part of the Appalachian Trail corridor, jointly owned and managed by the AT Conference and the National Park Service, and **Baxter State Park** (www.baxterstateauthority.com). The Bureau of Parks and Lands Web site (www.parksandlands.com) is helpful in locating public preserves scattered throughout the state, including the North Maine Woods.

PARKS AND FORESTS, NATIONAL **Acadia National Park** (207-288-3338; www.nps.gov/acad), which occupies roughly half of Mount Desert Island, plus scattered areas on Isle au Haut, Little Cranberry Island, Baker Island, Little Moose Island, and Schoodic Point, adds up to more than 40,000 acres offering hiking, ski touring, swimming, horseback riding, canoeing, and a variety of guided nature tours and programs, as well as a scenic 27-mile driving tour. Note that an entry fee is charged to drive the Park Loop Road. Camping is by reservation only at Blackwoods, and first come, first served at Seawall. The **White Mountain National Forest** encompasses 41,943 acres in Maine, including five campgrounds under the jurisdiction of the Evans Notch Ranger District (207-824-2134).

PARKS, STATE The **Bureau of Parks and Lands** (207-287-3821; www.parksandlands.com), can send a packet of information describing each of the 32 parks and the 12 (plus the Allagash Wilderness Waterway) that offer camping facilities. We have described parks as they appear geographically. In 2008 day-use fees are between $2 and $4.50 per adult, $1 for ages 5–11, and free for those under 5 and or over 65. Seasonal park passes are $30 per individual, $60 per vehicle (www.mainestateparkpass.com). Thirteen state parks offer camping (www.campwithme.com); the fee per site is $11–15 for residents, $14–20 for nonresidents. There is an additional fee for trailer hookups in the two parks that now offer them, Camden Hills and Sebago, also a $2-per-night reservation fee for camping. Call the reservations hotline (within Maine, 1-800-332-1501; from out of state, 207-624-9950 at least two days in advance to make a campground reservation, or use the real-time online registration form. (Also see *Lakes*.)

PETS Throughout this book, lodgings and selected other places that accept pets are indicated with the dog-paw symbol 🐾. Most lodgings require a reservation and an additional fee. Always call ahead when traveling with your pet.

PLOYE This traditional Acadian pancake/flat bread, as delicate as a crêpe, is a specialty throughout the St. John Valley. The **Bouchard Family Farm** (1-800-239-3237) produces a line of French Canadian food products.

POPULATION 1,321,574.

PUFFIN-WATCHING Atlantic puffins are smaller than you might expect. They lay just one egg a year and were almost extinct at the turn of the 20th century, when the only surviving birds nested on either Matinicus Rock or Machias Seal Island. Since 1973 Audubon has helped reintroduce nesting on Eastern Egg Rock in Muscongus Bay, 6 miles off Pemaquid Point, and since 1984 there has been a similar puffin-restoration project on Seal Island in outer Penobscot Bay, 6 miles from Matinicus Rock. The best times for viewing puffins are June and July or the first few days of August. The only place you are allowed to view the birds on land is **Machias Seal Island**, where visitors are permitted in limited numbers. Contact **Andrew Patterson** (www.boldcoast.com) in Cutler or **John Norton** (www.machiassealisland.com) in Jonesport. With the help of binoculars (a must), you can also view the birds from the water via tours with **Cap'n Fish** (207-633-3244) from Boothbay Harbor, **Hardy Boat Cruises** (www.hardyboat.com) from New Harbor, and the Monhegan Boat Line (www.monheganboat.com) from Port Clyde. The **Hog Island Audubon Camp** (www.maineaudubon.org) also offers guided boat cruises to Eastern Egg Rock. For those who can't make time to get out on the water the **Project Puffin Visitor Center** (www.projectpuffin.org) in Rockland uses live-streaming minicams and audio to provide a virtual visit with nesting puffins on Machias Seal Island.

RAIL TRAVEL See *Amtrak* for passenger service on the **Downeaster** from Boston to Portland. The seasonal Maine Eastern Railroad runs between Brunswick and Rockland; see *Railroad Excursions*.

Christina Tree

MAINE EASTERN RAILROAD ENGINE

RAILROAD EXCURSIONS AND MUSEUMS **Boothbay Railway Village** (www.railwayvillage.org) delights small children and offers railroad exhibits in its depot. **The Maine Eastern Railroad** (www.maineeastern railroad.com) offers 54-mile seasonal runs between Rockland and Brunswick, stopping in Bath and Wiscasset. It's a beautiful trip along the coast in plush 1940s and '50s coaches and a dining car, pulled by a 1950s diesel electric engine. In 2007 there were round-trip runs Wed.–Sun., but check the Web site for current information. In Portland the **Maine Narrow Gauge Railroad Company & Museum** (www.mngrr.org) combines displays and a 3-mile shoreside excursion. Inland, the **Sandy River & Rangeley Lakes Railroad** (www.srrl-rr.org) in Phillips in the Rangeley region operates short excursions one Sunday per month in summer. In Wiscasset, **Waterville & Farmington Railway Museum** (www.wwfry.org) at Sheepscot Station, Alna, preserves the history of another 2-foot narrow-gauge railroad and displays an 1891 2-footer locomotive, billed as the oldest in the United States. Rail buffs also find their way to **Maine Central Model Railroad** (207-497-2255) in Jonesport.

RATES Please do not regard any prices listed for *Lodging* as set in stone. Call ahead to confirm them. Rates are those in effect as we go to press. *MAP* stands for "Modified American Plan": breakfast and dinner included in rate. *AP* stands for "American Plan": three meals included in rate. *EP* stands for "European Plan": no meals. *B&B* stands for "bed & breakfast": breakfast is included.

RENYS Billed as "A Maine Adventure," and as "a part of the state's culture since 1949," Renys (www.renys .com) is a family-owned chain of 14 discount stores which, like hermit crabs, occupy spaces vacated by previous owners. The Farmington Renys fills a former music hall, the Madison space was an opera house, and in Damariscotta Renys Underground was a bowling alley. Several Renys fill former supermarkets and in Bath, Gardiner, Dexter, and Damariscotta the shops effectively fill the void left by small town clothing and department stores. Listing what Renys stocks is harder than saying what it doesn't. There are linens and shoes, name-brand clothing and toys, electronics, clamming and camping gear, stationery, Maine-made products, and always surprises. Renys has recently become less about odd lots (that niche is now filled by Marden's,

Maine's other discount chain), and more about quality, service, and good value. "When you want socks, we have socks," says John Reny. For big-time discounts hit any Renys on the first Saturday in November at 6 AM. The biggest discounts are during the first hour, diminishing but still substantial savings every hour until 9 AM.

ROCKHOUNDING Maine is a famous source of pink and green tourmaline, especially plentiful in the Bethel area. **Perham's of West Paris** (207-674-2341) at Trap Corner displays Maine minerals and offers access to its four quarries and information on gem hunting throughout the state. Thanks to the high price of gold, prospectors are back—panning Maine streambeds. The **Maine Geological Survey** (207-287-2801) has an online edition of *A Collector's Guide to Maine Mineral Localities.* Also see Maine collecting sites at www.rockhounds.com.

Christina Tree

SAILING Windjammers and yacht charter brokers aside, there are a limited number of places that will rent small sailing craft, fewer that will offer lessons to adults and children alike. The **Mansell Boat Rental Company** (www.mansellboatrentals.com), Southwest Harbor, rents sailboats by the day or longer. **Learn-to-sail programs** are offered by **WoodenBoat School** (www.woodenboatschool.com) in Brooklin, at the **Camden Yacht Club** (www.camdenyachtclub.org), which offers a junior sailing program to nonmembers, and **Bay Island Sailing School** (www.sailme.com) based at Journey's End Marina in Rockland. On Vinalhaven the volunteer-run, nonprofit **Island Sail School** (www.islandsail.org) is open to both children and adults. **Sawyer's Sailing School** (1-866-783-6882), geared to adults, is based at the Dolphin Marina in Harpswell. **Old Quarry Ocean Adventures** (www.oldquarry.com) in Deer Isle rents a variety of sailboats and offers lessons. Other rentals and daysails are listed throughout the book. (Also see *Windjammers.*)

SHAKERS **Sabbathday Lake Shaker Village and Museum** (www.shaker.lib.me.us) in New Gloucester is the country's last functioning Shaker religious community. Visitors are welcome to walk the grounds, take seasonal tours of six of the 18 existing structures, visit the museum reception center and gift shop, and attend seasonal Sunday services in the meetinghouse. Frequent workshops and special events are scheduled Mar.–Dec.

SKIING, CROSS-COUNTRY More than 20 cross-country ski centers are listed at **www.skimaine.com**. The **Sugarloaf/USA Outdoor Center** is the state's largest commercial nordic network. Bethel, with three trail networks (**Sunday River Inn**, **Bethel Inn**, and **Carter's Farm X-C Ski Center**), offers varied terrain. The towns of **Rangeley** and **Millinocket** also maintain extensive trail networks that enjoy dependable snow cover. For the most adventurous touring check the Katahdin/Moosehead area. The **Birches Resort** in Rockwood and the AMC-owned **Little Lyford Pond** and **Medawisla** sporting camps near Greenville offer guided wilderness tours in conjunction with West Branch Pond; reserve through the Appalachian Mountain Club (www.outdoors.org). **Chesuncook Lake House** (www.chesuncooklakehuse.com), **Nahmakanta Lake Camps** (www.nahmakanta.com) and Katahdin Lake Wilderness Camps (www.katahdinlakewildernesscamps.com) all cater to cross-country skiers. Also see *Maine Huts and Trails* for progress on an evolving 186-mile trail maintained year-round exclusively for nonmotorized traffic with full-service, winterized huts, running from Bethel to Sugarloaf, up along the Dead River to The Forks, and on up to Rockwood.

SKIING, DOWNHILL **Ski Maine Association** (207-773-SNOW; www.skimaine.com) provides information about mountains in Maine, snow conditions, and more. **Sugarloaf/USA** in the Carrabassett Valley and **Sunday River** in the Bethel area vie for the title of Maine's number one ski resort. The two are very different and actually complement each other well. Sugarloaf is a high, relatively remote mountain with New England's only lift-serviced snowfields on its summit and a classy, self-contained condo village at its base. Sunday River, just an hour north of Portland, consists of eight adjoining (relatively low-altitude) mountains; snowmaking is a big point of pride, and facilities include a variety of slope-side condo lodgings. **Saddleback Mountain** (in the Rangeley area) is a big mountain undergoing development with an enthusiastic following. **Mount Abram** (also in the Bethel area) is a true family area with a strong ski school and some fine runs. **Shawnee Peak** in Bridgton is a medium-sized, family-geared area that offers night as well as day skiing. The **Camden Snow Bowl** in Camden is small but satisfying.

SNOWMOBILING Maine has reciprocal agreements with nearly all states and provinces; for licensing and rules, contact the Department of Inland Fisheries and Wildlife (www.maine.gov/ifw). You can register online. **The Maine Snowmobile Association** (MSA; www.mesnow.com) represents more than 280 clubs and maintains some 13,000 miles of an ever-expanding cross-state trail network. Aroostook County, given its reliable snow conditions, is an increasingly popular destination. The Upper Kennebec Valley and Jackman as well as the entire Moosehead, Katahdin, and Rangeley Lake areas are snowmobiling meccas.

SPORTING CAMPS The Maine sporting camp—a gathering of log cabins around a log hunting lodge by a remote lake or stream—is a distinctly Maine phenomenon that began appearing in the 1860s. "Sports" (guests) were met by a guide at a train or steamer and paddled up lakes and rivers to a camp. With the advent of floatplanes, many of these camps became more accessible (see *Air Services*), and the proliferation of private logging roads has put most within reach of sturdy vehicles. True sporting camps still cater primarily to anglers in spring and hunters in fall, but since summer is neither a hunting season nor a prime fishing season, they all host families who just want to be in the woods. True sporting camps still include a central lodge in which guests are served all three meals; boats and guide service are available. The **Maine Sporting Camp Association** (www.mainesportingcamps.com) maintains lists and links with than 60 members. Also see *Maine Sporting Camps: A Year-round Guide to Vacationing at Traditional Hunting and Fishing Camps* by Alice Arlen (Countryman Press).

THEATER, SUMMER **The Ogunquit Playhouse** (www.ogunquitplayhouse.org) is among the oldest and most prestigious summer theaters in the country, and the **Arundel Barn Playhouse** (www.arundelbarnplayhouse.com) in Kennebunk is the newest. The **Hackmatack Playhouse** in Berwick (www.hackmatack.org) and **Biddeford City Theater** (www.citytheater.org) are other Southern Coast options. In Portland note the **Portland Stage Company** (www.portlandstage.com), and in Brunswick the **Maine State Music Theater** at Bowdoin College (www.msmt.org). Farther along the coast look for the **Camden Civic Theatre** (www.camdentivictheater.com), based in the refurbished Opera House in Camden, the **Belfast Maskers** in Belfast (www.belfastmaskerstheater.com), the new Northport Music Theater (www.northportmusictheater.com), the **Acadia Repertory Theatre** in Somesville (www.acadiarep.com), and **Downriver Theater Productions** in Machias. Inland look for the **Theater at Monmouth** (www.theateratmonmouth.org), **Lakewood Theater** in Skowhegan (www.lakewoodtheater.org), **Deer-trees Theatre** in Harrison (www.deertreestheatre.com, and **Celebration Barn Theater** in South Paris (www.celebrationbarn.com).

THEATER, YEAR-ROUND **Penobscot Theatre Company** in Bangor offers a variety of winter productions (www.penobscottheatre.org) . Other companies are the **Chocolate Church Arts Center** in Bath (207-442-8455) and the **Camden Civic Theatre** in Camden (www.camdentivictheater.com). **Portland Stage Company** (www.portlandstage.com) presents a series of productions. **The Portland Players** (www.portlandplayers.org) present a winter season of productions, as does the **Public Theatre** (www.thepublictheatre.org) in Auburn. In Brunswick the **Theater Project** (207-729-8584) performs year-round. Most universities and colleges also offer performances throughout the school year.

TRAFFIC AND HIGHWAY TRAVEL TIPS Maine coastal travel has its sticky wickets. By far the worst is the backup at the tolls at the entrance to the Maine Turnpike as well as those not far south in New Hampshire. Get E-ZPass (www.ezpassmaineturnpike.com), or avoid passing through these tolls, if at all possible, at obvious peak travel times. Within their respective chapters we suggest ways around bottlenecks at Brunswick, Wiscasset, and

Camden. Note that it takes no longer to reach a Down East than a Midcoast destination, thanks to the way the highways run. The quickest way to reach Rockland or Camden from points south is up I-295 to Brunswick and then coastal Rt. 1. Belfast and destinations east through the Blue Hill Peninsula, however, can be reached in roughly the same time by taking I-295 to Augusta and then Rt. 3 to coastal Rt. 1. You can reach Ellsworth (gateway to Mount Desert and points east) in equal time by traveling I-95 to the Maine Turnpike to Bangor and then down Rt. 1A. For current information on road conditions and delays dial 511 in Maine, 1-866-282-7578 from out-of-state or check www.511maine.go.

TRAFFIC RULES Seat belts are the law in Maine and turns on a red light are permitted unless otherwise stated, after a stop to check for oncoming traffic. Headlights should be turned on with windshield wipers.

WABANAKI *Wabanaki* means "people of the dawn." Native Americans have lived in Maine and eastern Canada for many thousands of years, judging from shell heaps and artifacts found in areas ranging from the coastal Damariscotta/Boothbay and Blue Hill areas to the Rangeley Lakes in western Maine. Ancient pictographs can be found on the Kennebec River and around Machias Bay. An excellent exhibit, *12,000 Years in Maine*, in the **Maine State Museum** (www.mainestatemuseum.org) in Augusta, depicts the distinct periods in this history and features the Red Paint People, named for the red pigments found sprinkled in their burial sites. They flourished between 5,000 and 3,800 years ago and are said to have fished from large, sturdy boats. The **Abbe Museum** (www.abbemuseum.org) in Bar Harbor is dedicated to showcasing the cultures of Maine's Wabanaki, the less than 7,000 members of the **Penobscot, Passamaquoddy, Micmac**, and **Maliseet** tribes who live in the state. The permanent collection of 50,000 objects ranges from 10,000-year-old artifacts to exquisite basketry and craftswork from several centuries. The time line begins with the present and draws visitors back through 10,000 years and to its core, "the Circle of Four Directions." Two North Maine Woods sites are said to have been sacred: the **Katahdin Iron Works**, in Brownville Junction, source of the pigments found in burial sites; and **Mount Kineo** on Moosehead Lake, source of the flintlike volcanic stone widely used for arrowheads. Early French missions at Mount Desert and Castine proved battlegrounds between the French and English, and by the end of the 17th century thousands of Wabanaki had retreated either to Canada or to the Penobscot community of **Old Town** and to **Norridgewock**, where Father Sebastian Rasle insisted that the Indian lands "were given them of God, to them and their children forever, according to the Christian oracles." The mission was obliterated (it's now a pleasant roadside rest area), and by the end of the French and Indian Wars only four tribes remained. Of these the Micmacs and Maliseets made the unlucky choice of siding with the Crown and were subsequently forced to flee (but communities remain near the Aroostook County–Canadian border in Presque Isle and Littleton, respectively). That left only the Penobscots and the Passamaquoddys.

In 1794 the Penobscots technically deeded most of Maine to Massachusetts in exchange for the 140 small islands in the Penobscot River, and in 1818 Massachusetts agreed to pay them an assortment of trinkets for the land. In 1820, when Maine became a state, a trust fund was set aside but ended up in the general treasury. The state's three reservations (two belonging to the Passamaquoddys and one to the Penobscots) were termed "enclaves of disfranchised citizens bereft of any special status." Indians loomed large in Maine lore and greeted 19th-century tourists as fishing and hunting guides in the woods and as snowshoe and canoe makers and guides, while Native American women sold their distinctive sweetgrass and ash-splint baskets and beadwork at the many coastal and inland summer hotels and boardinghouses.

In 1972 the Penobscots and Passamaquoddys sued to reclaim 1.5 million acres of land allegedly illegally appropriated by the state, and in 1980 they received an $80.6 million settlement, which they have since invested in a variety of enterprises. The Indian Island Reservation in **Old Town** is presently home to 500 of the tribe's 2,000 members, and the **Penobscot Nation Museum** (www.penobscotnation.org/museum) there, while small, is open regularly and well worth checking. The Passamaquoddy tribe today numbers 3,369 members, roughly divided between the reservations at **Indian Township** on Schoodic Lake and at **Pleasant Point** (www.wabanaki.com), near Eastport, site of the **Indian Ceremonial Days**, held annually in mid-August to celebrate Passamaquoddy culture and climaxing in dances in full regalia.

The new **Downeast Heritage Museum** (www.downeastheritage.org) in Calais features displays on Passamaquoddy history, language, and craftsmanship. The 1,000-member Aroostook Band of Micmacs are headquartered in Presque Isle; tribal offices for the 800-member Houlton Band of Maliseet Indians are in Littleton. The **Hudson Museum** at the University of Maine, Orono, has a small display on local tribes. Members of all four tribes form **The Maine Indian Basketmakers Alliance** (wwww.maineindianbaskets.org), which publishes *Wabanaki Cultural Resource Guide*, and makes and markets traditional ash-splint and sweetgrass baskets through the **Wabanaki Arts Center** in Old Town and at special sales events, held in July in Bar Harbor and December at the University of Maine, Orono.The **L. C. Bates Museum** in Hinckley displays ancient artifacts and 19th- and early 20th-century craftsmanship, and **Nowetah's American Indian Museum** in New Portland (see "Sugarloaf and the Carrabassett Valley") displays a large collection of authentic basketry.

WATERFALLS The following are all easily accessible to families with small children: **Snow Falls Gorge** off Rt. 26 in West Paris offers a beautiful cascade (ask for directions at Perham's Gem Store); **Small's Falls** on the Sandy River, off Rt. 4 between Rangeley and Phillips, has a picnic spot with a trail beside the falls; **Jewell Falls** is located in the Fore River Sanctuary in the heart of Portland; **Step Falls** is on Wight Brook in Newry off Rt. 26; and just up the road in Grafton Notch State Park is **Screw Auger Falls**, with its natural gorge.

Another Screw Auger Falls is in Gulf Hagas (see *Gorges*), off the Appalachian Trail near the Katahdin Iron Works Road, north of Brownville Junction. **Kezar Falls**, on the Kezar River, is best reached via Lovell Road from Rt. 35 at North Waterford. An extensive list of "scenic waterfalls" is detailed in the *Maine Atlas and Gazetteer* (DeLorme). Check out 90-foot **Moxie Falls** at The Forks.

WEDDINGS At this writing no one conduit exists for information about the ever-increasing number of services (photographers, musicians, carriage operators, caterers, and florists, as well as inns and venues) geared to helping couples wed near Maine water. Several chambers of commerce, notably York, Kennebunkport, Boothbay, and Camden, are particularly helpful. Within the book we note properties that specialize in weddings with our ring symbol ⚭. A Maine marriage license currently costs just $30.

WHALE-WATCHING Each spring humpback, finback, and minke whales migrate to New England waters, where they remain until fall, cavorting, it sometimes seems, for the pleasure of excursion boats. One prime gathering spot is **Jefferies Ledge**, about 20 miles off Kennebunkport, and another is the **Bay of Fundy**. For listings of whale-watch cruises, see "The Kennebunks," "Portland Area," "Bar Harbor," and "Washington County." The East Quoddy (Campobello) and West Quoddy (Lubec) Lighthouses are also prime viewing spots. Whales are sighted more often than not on the ferry ride from Black Harbor, New Brunwick, to the island of **Grand Manan**, another hub for whale-watch cruises.

WHITEWATER RAFTING In Maine, this phenomenon's beginnings coincided with the last log drive on the Kennebec River. Logs were still hurtling through Kennebec Gorge on that day in the spring of 1976 when fishing guide Wayne Hockmeyer (and eight bear hunters from New Jersey) plunged through it in a rubber raft. At the time Hockmeyer's rafting know-how stemmed solely from having seen *River of No Return*, in which Robert Mitchum steered Marilyn Monroe down the Salmon River.

Hockmeyer founded **Northern Outdoors** and there are now more than a dozen other major outfitters positioned around The Forks, near the confluence of the Kennebec and Dead Rivers, all skilled in negotiating the rapids through nearby 12-mile-long Kennebec Gorge. Numbers on the river are now strictly limited, and rafts line up to take their turns riding the releases—which gush up to 8,000 cubic feet of water per second—from the Harris Hydroelectric Station above the gorge. Several rafting companies—notably **Northern Outdoors** (www.northernoutdoors.com), **Crab Apple** (www.crabappleinc.com), and **Magic Falls Rafting Company**

Raft Maine

(www.magicfalls.com)—have built fairly elaborate base facilities in and around The Forks. **New England Outdoor Center** (www.noec.com), and **Three Rivers White Water** (www.threerivers.com) have established food and lodging facilities for patrons who want to raft the Penobscot near Baxter State Park. For information about a number of outfitters, contact **Raft Maine** (1-800-723-8633; www.raft maine.com). *Note*: Online promotions project images in which all outfitters seem to offer the same experience and to differ only in price. This isn't true. Read about the real differences between outfitters in the "Upper Kennebec" and "Katahdin" chapters.

WINDJAMMERS In 1935 artist Frank Swift outfitted a few former fishing and cargo schooners to carry passengers around the islands of Penobscot Bay. At the time these old vessels were moored in every harbor and cove, casualties of progress. Swift's fleet grew to include more than a dozen vessels. Competitors also prospered throughout the 1950s, but the entire windjammer fleet appeared doomed by rigorous Coast Guard licensing requirements in the 1960s. The 1970s and 1980s saw the rise of a new breed of windjammer captain. Almost every one of those now sailing has built or restored the vessel he or she commands or acquired it from the captain who did. Members of the current Maine windjammer fleet range from the *Stephen Taber* and the *Lewis R. French*, both originally launched in 1871, to the *Heritage*, launched in 1983, to the *Hallie & Matthew*, launched in Eastport in 2005.

Former *Taber* co-captain Ellen Barnes recalls her own discovery of windjammers: "No museums had gobbled up these vessels; no cities had purchased them to sit at piers as public relations gimmicks. These vessels were the real thing, plying their trade as they had in the past with one exception: The present-day cargo was people instead of pulpwood, bricks, coal, limestone, and granite."

Choosing which vessel to sail on is the most difficult part of a windjammer cruise. All have ship-to-shore radios and sophisticated radar; some offer more in the way of creature comforts; some are known for their food. Windjammers accommodate between 12 and 44 passengers. Excessive drinking is discouraged on all the vessels, and guests are invited to bring musical instruments. Children under 14 are permitted only on some. In relevant chapters we have described each vessel in the kind of detail we devote to individual inns. Questions you might like to ask in making your reservation: (1) What's the bunk arrangement? Double bunks and cabins for a family or group do exist. (2) What's the cabin ventilation? Some vessels offer cabins with portholes or windows that open. (3) What's the rule about children? Several schooners schedule special family cruises with activities geared to kids. (4) What's the extent of weatherproof common space? It varies widely. (5) Is smoking allowed? (6) Is there evening entertainment of any kind? **The Maine Windjammers Association** (1-800-807-WIND; www.sailmaine coast.com) represents most windjammers.

Southern Coast

KITTERY, SOUTH BERWICK, AND THE YORKS

OGUNQUIT AND WELLS

THE KENNEBUNKS

OLD ORCHARD BEACH, SACO, AND BIDDEFORD

Christina Tree

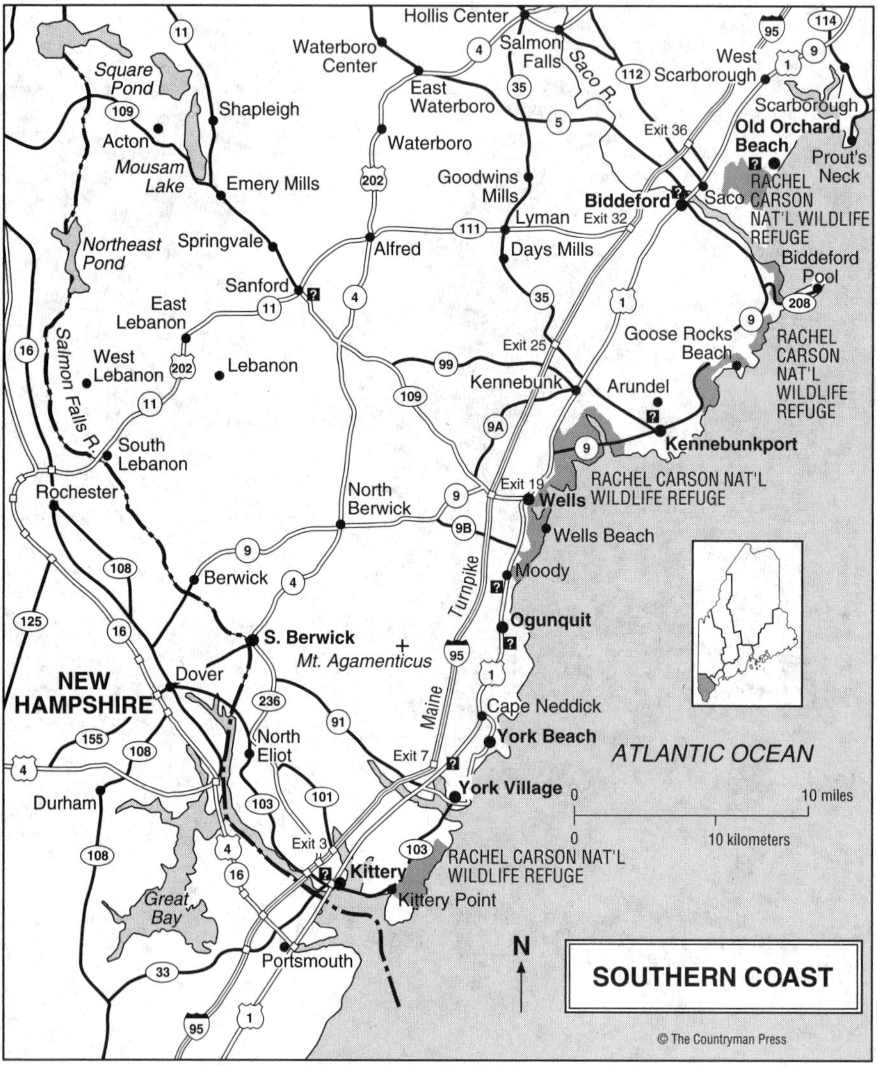
SOUTHERN COAST
Hollis Center
Waterboro Center
Salmon Falls
Saco R.
West Scarborough
Scarborough
Square Pond
Shapleigh
Acton
Mousam Lake
East Waterboro
Waterboro
Emery Mills
Goodwins Mills
Old Orchard Beach
Prout's Neck
Exit 36
Biddeford
Saco
Exit 32
RACHEL CARSON NAT'L WILDLIFE REFUGE
Lyman
Springvale
Alfred
Days Mills
Northeast Pond
Biddeford Pool
Sanford
East Lebanon
Goose Rocks Beach
Exit 25
RACHEL CARSON NAT'L WILDLIFE REFUGE
West Lebanon
Lebanon
Kennebunk
Arundel
Salmon Falls R.
Kennebunkport
South Lebanon
RACHEL CARSON NAT'L WILDLIFE REFUGE
Rochester
North Berwick
Exit 19
Wells
Wells Beach
Berwick
Moody
Maine Turnpike
Ogunquit
S. Berwick
Mt. Agamenticus
NEW HAMPSHIRE
Dover
Cape Neddick
North Eliot
York Beach
ATLANTIC OCEAN
Exit 7
York Village
Durham
0
10 miles
0
10 kilometers
Exit 3
Kittery
RACHEL CARSON NAT'L WILDLIFE REFUGE
Great Bay
Kittery Point
Portsmouth
N
© The Countryman Press

SOUTHERN COAST

The smell of pine needles and salt air, the taste of lobster and saltwater taffy, the shock of cold green waves, and, most of all, the promise of endless beach—this is the Maine that draws upward of half the state's visitors, those who never get beyond its Southern Coast. The southern Maine coast makes up just 35 miles of the state's 3,500 coastal miles but contains 90 percent of its sand.

The early history of these towns differs sharply but all have been shaped since the Civil War by the summer tide of tourists. York Village and Kittery are recognized as the oldest communities in Maine; Wells dates from the 1640s, and Kennebunkport was a shipbuilding center by the 1790s. All were transformed in the second half of the 19th century, an era when most Americans—not just the rich—began to take summer vacations, each in his or her own way.

Maine's Southern Coast was one of the country's first beach resort areas, and it catered then—as it does today—to the full spectrum of vacationers, from blue-collar workers to millionaires. Before the Civil War, Old Orchard Beach rivaled Newport, Rhode Island, as the place to be seen; when the Grand Trunk Railroad to Montreal opened in 1854, it became the first American resort to attract a sizable number of Canadians.

While ocean tides are most extreme way Down East, the ebb and flow of tourist tides wash most dramatically over this stretch of Maine. Nowhere are the 1930s-era motor courts thicker along Rt. 1, now sandwiched between elaborate condo-style complexes with indoor pools and elevators. Most of the big old summer hotels vanished by the 1950s, the era of the motor inns that now occupy their sites. But in the past few decades many former sea captains' homes and summer mansions have been transformed into small inns and bed & breakfasts, rounding out the lodging options. Luckily, the lay of the land—salt marsh, estuarine reserves, and other wetlands—largely limits commercial clutter.

GUIDANCE The **Maine Beaches Association** maintains a toll-free number that connects with the major chambers: 1-800-639-2442; www.mainebeaches association.com.

The Maine Tourism Association's Kittery Information Center (207-439-1319; www.mainetourism.com), Maine's gatehouse in a real sense, is on I-95 northbound in Kittery, with exhibits on Maine regions and products and a staffed information desk good for local as well as statewide advice on lodging, dining, and attractions. You can also check regional Web sites and lodging by computer. Open daily except Christmas and Thanksgiving, 8–6 in summer months, otherwise 9–5:30 (bathrooms open 24 hours daily). The rest area also includes vending machines and picnic tables under the pines.

KITTERY, SOUTH BERWICK, AND THE YORKS

The moment you cross the Piscataqua River you know you are in Maine. Kittery and York both have their share of deep coves and rocky ocean paths.

Both towns claim to be Maine's oldest community. Technically Kittery wins, but York looks older . . . depending, of course, on which Kittery and which York you are talking about.

Kittery Point, an 18th-century settlement overlooking Portsmouth Harbor, boasts Maine's oldest church and some of the state's finest mansions. The village of Kittery itself, however, has been shattered by so many bridges and rotaries that it initially seems to exist only as a gateway, on the one hand for workers at the Portsmouth Naval Shipyard and on the other for patrons of the outlet malls strung along Rt. 1. However, don't overlook the shops and restaurants around downtown Waterman Square, or the strolling and swimming spots along coastal Rt. 103.

In the late 19th century artists and literati gathered at Kittery Point. Novelist and *Atlantic Monthly* editor William Dean Howells, who summered here, became keenly interested in preserving the area's colonial-era buildings. Novelist Sarah Orne Jewett, a contributor to the *Atlantic*, spearheaded restoration of the magnificent 18th-century Hamilton House in her hometown, nearby South Berwick. Her friend Sam Clemens (otherwise known as Mark Twain), who summered in York, was involved in the effort to buy up that town's splendid old school, church, burial ground, and abundance of 1740s homes, recognizing York as Maine's oldest surviving community.

In 1896 Howells suggested turning York Village's "old gaol" into a museum. At the time you could count the country's historic house museums on your fingers. In the Old Gaol of today you learn about the village's bizarre history, including its origins as a Native American settlement called Agamenticus, one of many wiped out by a plague in 1616. In 1630 it was settled by English colonists, and in 1642 it became Gorgeana, America's first chartered city. It was then demoted to the town of York, part of Massachusetts, in 1670. Fierce Native American raids followed, but by the middle of the 18th century the present colonial village was established, a crucial way station between Portsmouth and points east.

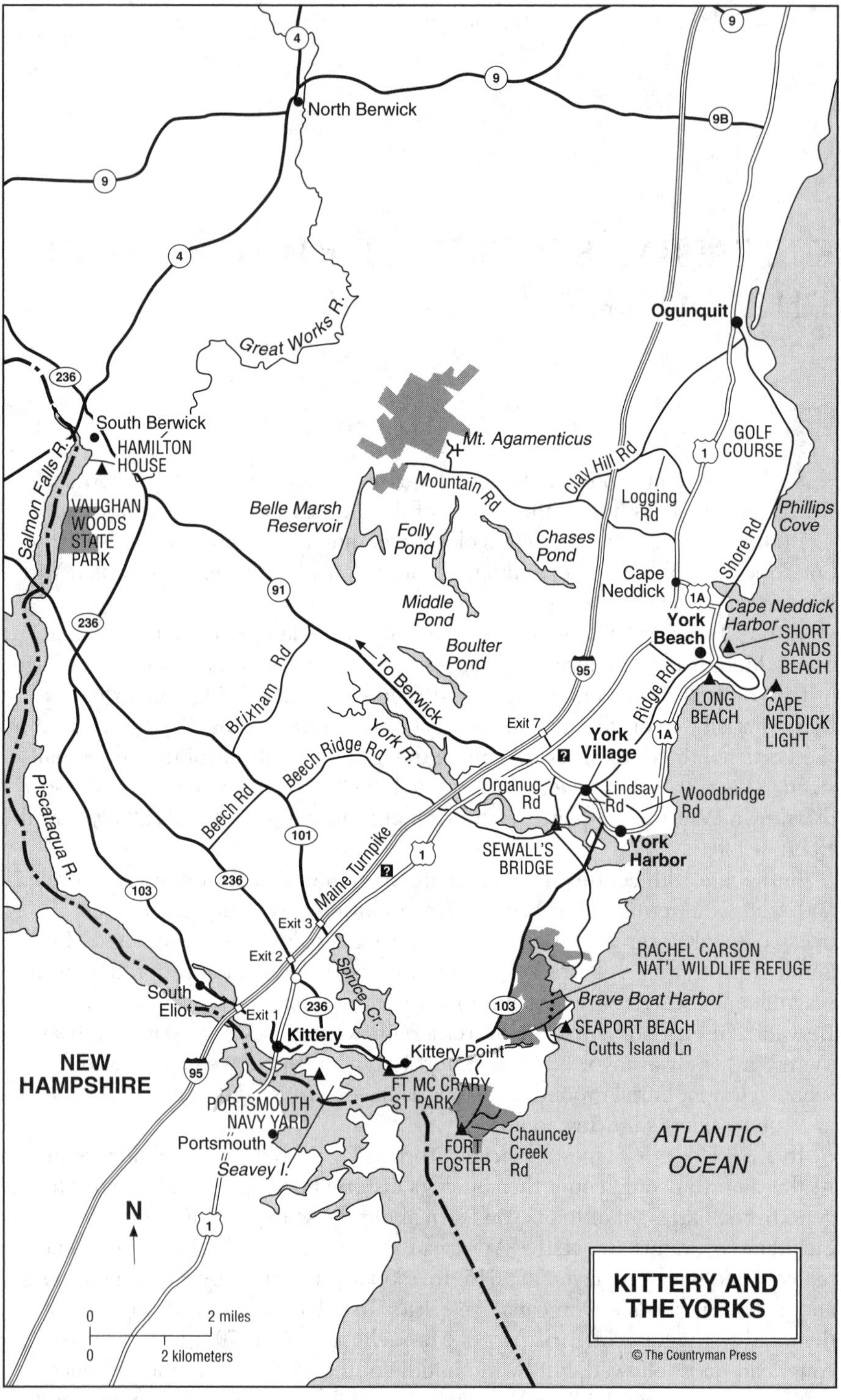

KITTERY AND THE YORKS
© The Countryman Press
North Berwick
Great Works R.
South Berwick
HAMILTON HOUSE
Salmon Falls R.
VAUGHAN WOODS STATE PARK
Mt. Agamenticus
Mountain Rd
Belle Marsh Reservoir
Folly Pond
Chases Pond
Middle Pond
Boulter Pond
Clay Hill Rd
Logging Rd
GOLF COURSE
Ogunquit
Shore Rd
Phillips Cove
Cape Neddick
Cape Neddick Harbor
SHORT SANDS BEACH
York Beach
LONG BEACH
CAPE NEDDICK LIGHT
Ridge Rd
York Village
Lindsay Rd
Woodbridge Rd
York Harbor
Organug Rd
SEWALL'S BRIDGE
To Berwick
York R.
Brixham Rd
Beech Ridge Rd
Beech Rd
Exit 7
Maine Turnpike
Exit 3
Exit 2
Exit 1
Piscataqua R.
South Eliot
Kittery
Spruce Cr.
Kittery Point
FT MC CRARY ST PARK
RACHEL CARSON NAT'L WILDLIFE REFUGE
Brave Boat Harbor
SEAPORT BEACH
Cutts Island Ln
Chauncey Creek Rd
FORT FOSTER
NEW HAMPSHIRE
PORTSMOUTH NAVY YARD
Portsmouth
Seavey I.
ATLANTIC OCEAN
N
0
2 miles
0
2 kilometers
1
1A
4
9
9B
91
95
101
103
236

York is divided into so many distinct villages that Clemens once observed, "It is difficult to throw a brick . . . in any one direction without danger of disabling a postmaster." Not counting Scotland and York Corners, York includes York Village, York Harbor, York Beach, and Cape Neddick—such varied communities that locals can't bring themselves to speak of them as one town; they refer instead to "the Yorks."

The rocky shore beyond York Village was Lower Town until the Marshall House was opened near the small gray-sand beach in 1871 and its address was changed to York Harbor. Soon the hotel had 300 rooms, and other mammoth frame hotels appeared at intervals along the shore. Now all the old hotels are gone. All, that is, except the Cliff House, a resort which, although physically in York, has long since changed its address and phone to Ogunquit, better known these days as a resort town.

Still, York Harbor remains a delightful, low-key retreat. The Marshall House has been replaced by the contemporary Stage Neck Inn, and several dignified old summer "cottages" are now inns and B&Bs. A narrow, mile-or-so path along the shore was first traced by fishermen and later smoothed and graced with small touches such as the Wiggly Bridge, a graceful little suspension bridge across the river and through Steedman Woods.

Landscaping and public spaces were among the consuming interests of the 19th-century summer residents, who around the turn of the century also became interested in zoning. In *Trending into Maine* (1935) Kenneth Roberts noted York Harbor's "determination to be free of billboards, tourist camps, dance halls and other cheapening manifestations of the herd instinct and Vacationland civilization."

A York Harbor corporation was formed to impose its own taxes and keep out unwanted development. The corporation's biggest fight, wrote Roberts, was against the Libby Camps, a tent-and-trailer campground on the eastern edge of York Harbor that "had spread with such funguslike rapidity that York Harbor was in danger of being almost completely swamped by young ladies in shorts, young men in soiled undershirts, and fat ladies in knickerbockers."

Libby's Oceanside Camp still sits on Roaring Rock Point, its trailers neatly angled along the shore. Across from it is matching Camp Eaton, established in 1923. No other village boundary within a New England town remains as clearly defined as this one between York Harbor and York Beach.

Beyond the campgrounds stretches 2-mile Long Sands Beach, lined with a simpler breed of summer cottage than those in York Village or York Harbor. There is a real charm to the strip and to the village of York Beach, with its Victorian-style shops, boardwalk amusements, and the Goldenrod—known for its taffy Goldenrod Kisses. This restaurant is still owned by the same family that opened it in 1896, about the time the electric streetcar put York Beach within reach of the "working class."

During this "trolley era" half a dozen big hotels accommodated 3,000 summer visitors, and 2,000 more patronized boardinghouses in York Beach. Today's lodgings are a mix of motels, cottages, and B&Bs. There are beaches (with metered parking), Fun-O-Rama games and bowling, and York's Wild Kingdom, with exotic animals and carnival rides. York Beach, too, has now gained "historic" status, and the Old York Historical Society, keeper of eight buildings open to the public in York Village, now sponsors York Beach walking tours.

GUIDANCE **Greater York Region Chamber of Commerce** (207-363-4422; via the Southern Maine link, 1-800-639-2442; www.gatewaytomaine.org), 1 Stonewall Lane, York 03909. On Rt. 1 just off I-95 exit 7 northbound (York), this handsome information center (with restrooms) modeled on a Victorian summer "cottage" is open year-round, high season daily 9–5, off-season Mon.–Fri. 9–4, Sat. 10–4.

At **Sohier Park,** overlooking Nubble Light on York Beach, a seasonal information center with restrooms is open May–mid-Oct., 10 AM–sunset.

GETTING THERE York is off I-95 exit 7, the last exit before the Maine Turnpike tolls. The nearest bus service is to Portsmouth, New Hampshire, and the nearest train stop is Wells, Maine. For air service check for flights to Portsmouth (NH) Airport. At this writing the former U.S. air base is served by bargain-priced flights from unlikely places. The I-95 exits for Kittery are 1, 2, and 3.

GETTING AROUND **York Trolley Company** (207-748-3030; www.yorktrolley.com). Late June–Labor Day, trolleys circle all day along the beaches and around the Nubble. Inquire about special narrated tours and service to the Kittery Outlet Malls. $8 all-day pass, $4 for ages 10 and under; free under age 2.

WHEN TO COME With the exception of York Beach, which is highly seasonal, this area can be an appealing seaside getaway June through December. It's packed on July and August weekends. Thanks to the sizable year-round population, most restaurants remain open year-round. The Kittery outlets and Stonewall Kitchen draw holiday shoppers.

✷ To See

In Kittery

♿ **Kittery Historical and Naval Museum** (207-439-3080), Rt. 1, just north of the Rt. 236 rotary. Open June–Columbus Day, Tue.–Sat. 10–4, and by appointment. $3 adults, $1.50 ages 7–15, $6 per family. A fine little museum filled with ships' models and exhibits about the early history of this stretch of the Southern Coast. Displays include archaeological finds, early shipbuilding tools, navigational instruments, and mariner folk art, including samples of work by Kittery master ship's carver John Haley Bellamy (1836–1914). The lens from Boon Island Light is also displayed.

Fort McClary, Rt. 103. A state park open seasonally (grounds accessible year-round). A hexagonal 1846 blockhouse on a granite base, it was the site of fortifications in 1715, 1776, and 1808. Its picnic area is across the road but on a fine day the grounds of the fort itself, with a spectacular view of Portsmouth Harbor, are far more inviting. This site was first fortified to protect Massachusetts's vessels from being taxed by the New Hampshire colony. $2 contribution requested.

In York

First Parish Church, York Village. An outstanding, mid-18th-century meetinghouse with a fine cemetery full of old stones with death's heads and Old English spelling.

Christina Tree

FORT MCCLARY

Civil War Monument, middle of York Village. Contrary to the local legend that this was a Civil War memorial meant for a town in the South (the uniform suggests a Confederate rather than Union soldier), it's intended to honor all the town's "fallen heroes." Admittedly it's confusing: This particular soldier is wearing a Spanish-American War uniform, but the only years chiseled into its base are 1861–65.

In York Harbor and York Beach

Sayward-Wheeler House (207-384-2454; www.historicnewengland.org), 79 Barrell Lane, York Harbor. Open June–Oct 15, first and third Sat. of the month, 11–4; tours on the hour, $5. A fine, early-18th-century house built by Jonathan Sayward—merchant, shipowner, judge, and representative to the Massachusetts General Court—who earned the respect of the community despite his Tory leanings. It remained in the same family for 200 years and retains its Queen Anne and Chippendale furnishings, family portraits, and china brought back as booty from the expedition against the French at Louisburg in 1745.

Note: Historic New England also maintains the **Hamilton House** and the **Sarah Orne Jewett House** in South Berwick, described in *Scenic Drives*.

Nubble Light, York Beach. From Rt. 1A (Long Beach Ave.), take Nubble Rd. out through the Nubble (a cottage-covered peninsula) to Sohier Park at the tip of the peninsula. The 1879 Cape Neddick Lighthouse Station (better known as "Nubble Light") is perched on a small island of its own—but that's all the better for taking pictures from the park, which offers parking and a seasonal information center with restrooms and a small gift shop.

NUBBLE LIGHT

Christina Tree

✎ ♿ **York's Wild Kingdom** (207-363-4911; www.yorkzoo.com), York Beach. In July and Aug. the zoo is open daily 10–6 and the amusement area, noon–9:30; varying hours in shoulder seasons, so call ahead to check. This is an old-fashioned amusement area and zoo with goats, bears, ducks, swans,

OLD YORK HISTORICAL SOCIETY (207-363-4974; www.oldyork.org). This nonprofit group maintains eight historic buildings, open to the public early June–Columbus Day weekend, Mon.–Sat. 10–5. Admission is $5 adult for one building, $10 for all, $1 less for seniors, children's rates. It's best to pay the umbrella price and spend several hours wandering through the 18th-century buildings scattered through the village. Begin with the orientation film screened in the newly reconstructed 1830s Remick Barn **Visitors Center,** attached to the vintage-1754 **Jefferds' Tavern,** corner of Lindsay Rd. and York St. Exhibits change, and food is frequently cooking on the hearth at the tavern kitchen. If you have time to visit only one building, pick the "**Old Gaol**" with its dank and dismal cells and stories of luckless patrons, many of them women. Dating in part from 1719, this was the jail for the entire province of Maine until 1760. In the vintage-1742 **Emerson-Wilcox House** on York Street, period rooms and gallery space trace the development of local decorative arts, and feature a complete set of bed hangings embroidered by Mary Bulman before 1745. The **Elizabeth Perkins House**, South Side Rd. (at Sewall Bridge), is our favorite building, a 1730 house by the York River. It is filled with colonial-era antiques and with the spirit of Elizabeth Perkins, the real powerhouse behind the original Society for the Preservation of Historic Landmarks in York County. Nearby at 140 Lindsay Rd. are the 18th-century **John Hancock Warehouse and Wharf** and **George Marshall Store**, which was built in 1869 as a chandlery for the large schooners that once docked here; it's now a contemporary art gallery. Also on Lindsay Road: **Ramsdell House**, in the 1740s a farm laborer's home, today a work in progress, and **Old School House** (1745) with exhibits on mid-18th-century education. The society also sponsors walking tours and special events and offers a local historical research library (open year-round) and archives in its headquarters, a former bank building at 207 York St. in the middle of York Village.

Old York Historical Society

PORTRAIT IN THE ELIZABETH PERKINS HOUSE, OLD YORK HISTORICAL SOCIETY

and a number of unhappy-looking exotic animals. There is also mini golf, a butterfly kingdom, and both pony and elephant rides. $18.25 adults, $14.25 ages 4–10, and $4 ages 3 and under for zoo/ride admission; less for zoo only. Rides are also priced individually.

SCENIC DRIVES **Kittery Point**, **Pepperrell Cove**, and **Gerrish Island**. From Rt. 1, find your way to Rt. 103 and follow its twists and turns along the harbor until you come to the white **First Congregational Church** and a small green across from a striking, privately owned Georgian-style house. An old graveyard overlooking the harbor completes the scene. Park at the church (built in 1730, Maine's oldest), notice the parsonage (1729), and walk across the road to the old **graveyard**. The neighboring magnificent house was built in 1760 for the widow of Sir William Pepperrell, the French and Indian Wars hero who captured the fortress at Louisburg from the French. Knighted for his feat, Pepperrell went on to become the richest man in New England. For a splendid view of the harbor, continue along Rt. 103 to **Fort McClary** (see *To See*). **Frisbee's Market**, in business since 1828, claims to be America's oldest family-run grocery store (also known for its handmade corned beef). Four large hotels once clustered in this corner of Kittery, but today it's one of the quietest along the Southern Coast. At the back of the parking lot across from Frisbee's, a seemingly forgotten tomb is inscribed with a plaque commemorating Colonel William Pepperrell, born in Devonshire in 1646, died in Kittery in 1734, and Sir William Pepperrell (1696–1759). Just beyond you can still see the foundations of one of the former summer hotels. Turn right beyond Pepperrell Cove and follow Gerrish Island Lane to a T; then take Pocahontas (the name of another vanished hotel) to World War I–era **Fort Foster**, now a park. Also check out **Chauncey Creek Lobster Pound** and **Seapoint Beach**. Rt. 103 winds on by the mouth of the York River and into York Harbor.

South Berwick. A short ride north of the Rt. 1 outlets transports you to a bend in the Salmon Falls River that is anchored by a splendid 1780s Georgian mansion, restored through the efforts of local author Sarah Orne Jewett; a formal garden and riverside trails through the woods add to the unusual appeal of this place. From Kittery, take either Rt. 236 north from the I-95 Eliot exit or more rural Rt. 101 north from Rt. 1 at exit 3 (turn right at its junction with Rt. 236). From York, take Rt. 91 north. Hamilton House and **Vaughan Woods State Park** are the first left after the junction of Rts. 236 and 91 (Brattle St.); follow signs. **Hamilton House** is open June–Oct. 15, Wed.–Sun. 11–4, with tours on the hour ($8 adults); grounds open every day dawn to dusk. Come at 4 PM on Sunday in July for picnic concerts in the restored flower gardens. The foursquare Georgian mansion built in 1785 on a promontory above the Salmon Falls River had fallen into disrepair by the

FRISBEE'S 1828 MARKET

Christina Tree

Christina Tree

HAMILTON HOUSE

time Jewett (1849–1909) was growing up in nearby South Berwick; she used it as the setting for her novel *The Tory Love* and persuaded wealthy Boston friends to restore it in 1898 (during that same period William Dean Howells was involved in restoring nearby York Village). Historic New England (207-384-2454; www.historicnewengland.org) also maintains the **Sarah Orne Jewett House** farther up Rt. 236, at its junction with Rt. 4 (5 Portland St.), in the middle of the pleasant village of South Berwick (open Fri.–Sun. 11–4, with tours on the hour. $5). This is another fine 1774 Georgian house. Jewett, who is best known for her classic novel *The Country of the Pointed Firs*, actually grew up in the clapboard house next door, now the delightful town library. Here you learn that in the mid–19th century this picturesque village was home to extensive mills. The brick **Counting House Museum** (207-384-0000) by the Salmon Falls on Main St. (Rt. 4 at the bridge) is open July 1–Oct. 1, weekends. It houses the Old Berwick Historical Society collection with exhibits on 17th- through 19th-century rural life in southern Maine. Inquire about monthly lectures and events.

✷ To Do

BICYCLING **Mount Agamenticus** (see *Green Space*) is webbed with trails beloved by mountain bikers. **Berger's Bike Shop** (207-363-4070) in York Village rents mountain and hybrid bikes.

BOAT EXCURSIONS **Isles of Shoals Steamship Co.** (603-431-5500 or 1-800-441-4620; www.islesofshoals.com), Portsmouth, New Hampshire. Daily cruises in-season stop at Star Island, site of a vast old white summer hotel that's now a Unitarian conference center. Visitors are welcome to this barren but fascinating place, webbed with walking trails. The ride on the 90-foot replica of an old steamboat takes 1 hour each way.

Captain & Patty's Piscataqua River Tours (207-439-8976), Town Dock, Pepperell Rd., Kittery Point. June–Oct. 15, frequent daily departures for a tour aboard launch *Sir William Pepperrell*.

BOAT RENTALS **York Harbor Marine Service** (207-363-3602; www.yorkharbormarine.com), 20 Harris Island Rd., York. Boston Whalers and other runabouts can be rented to explore the river and nearby coast.

FISHING Check with the Greater York Region Chamber of Commerce about the half-dozen deep-sea-fishing boats operating from York Harbor and Kittery. Surf casting is also popular along Long Sands and Short Sands Beaches and from Sohier Park in York. **Eldredge Bros. Fly Shop** (207-363-9269; www.eldredge

flyshop.com), 1480 Rt. 1, Cape Neddick, is a full-service outfitter offering guided freshwater and saltwater trips.

FRIGHTS **Ghostly Tours** (207-363-0000; www.ghostlytours.com), 250 York St. (Rt. 1A), York Village. Late June–Halloween, Mon.–Sat. Candlelight tours through Old York Village guided by a hooded ghost-tale teller.

GOLF **The Ledges Golf Club** (207-351-3000; www.ledgesgolf.com), 1 Ledges Dr. (off Rt. 91), York. This is a destination course for much of southern Maine. eighteen holes, carts, pro shop, favored by local residents.

Cape Neddick Country Club (207-361-2011; www.capeneddickgolf.com), Shore Rd., Cape Neddick. Designed in the early 1900s by Donald Ross, redesigned by Brian Silva in 1998, the 18 holes feature rolling fairways integrated with ledge outcroppings and wetlands. A pro shop and restaurant, **The Cape Neddick Grille** (207-361-2112).

The Links at Outlook (207-384-4653), Rt. 4, South Berwick. An 18-hole Scottish-style course and driving range.

SEA KAYAKING The tidal York River, stretches of the Piscataqua around and above Eliot, and the Salmon Falls River (accessible from Vaughan Woods State Park in South Berwick) are particularly appealing to kayakers. **Harbor Adventures** (207-363-8466; www.harboradventures.com) in York Harbor and **Coastal Maine Excursions** (207-363-0181; www.excursionsinmaine.com), Rt. 1, Cape Neddick, offer guided tours and rentals; **Eldredge Bros. Fly Shop** (see *Fishing*) also offers rentals.

SPAS The **Cliff House Resort & Spa** (207-361-1000; www.cliffhousemaine.com), Shore Rd., on the York–Ogunquit line. A variety of massage, face care, and body care services are offered and include use of the fully equipped fitness area as well as large indoor and outdoor pools. Exercise classes are also offered.

Portsmouth Harbor Inn & Spa (207-439-7060; www.innatportsmouth.com), 6 Water St., Kittery. A full-service spa housed in the attractive carriage house of this waterside inn, offering facials, body treatments, massage, manicures, and pedicures. Inquire about both day and two-night packages.

SUMMER YOUTH PROGRAMS ✐ **York Parks & Recreation Department** (207-363-1040) offers summer baseball, basketball, mountain biking, and dance programs for younger children and teens.

✻ Green Space

BEACHES

In Kittery

Seapoint Beach, Kittery, is long with silky soft sand. Parking is residents-only right at the sand, but there's limited public parking 0.5 mile back up Curtis Island Lane (off Rt. 103).

✐ **Fort Foster**, Gerrish Island, is shallow a long way out and also has low-tide tidal pools with crabs and snails.

In York

Long Sands is a 2-mile expanse of coarse gray sand stretching from York Harbor to the Nubble, backed by Rt. 1A and summer cottages, great for walking. Metered parking the length of the beach and a bathhouse midway. Lifeguard in high season.

✐ **Short Sands** is a shorter stretch of coarse gray sand with a bathhouse, parking lot (meters), and playground, just in front of the village of York Beach.

York Harbor Beach is small and pebbly, but pleasant. Very limited parking, bathrooms.

PARKS **Fort Foster Park**, Kittery. Beyond Pepperrell Cove, look for Gerrish Island Lane and turn right at the T onto Pocahontas Rd., which leads, eventually, to this 92-acre town park. The World War I fortifications are ugly, but there is a choice of small beaches with different exposures (one very popular with sailboarders), extensive walking trails, and picnic facilities. Fee.

Piscataqua River Boat Basin (207-439-1813), Main St., Eliot. Open May–Oct. Boat launch, picnic area, beach, restrooms.

Mount Agamenticus (207-363-1040), York. Just 580 feet high but billed as the highest hill on the Atlantic seaboard between York and Florida. A defunct ski area now owned by the town of York, it can be reached by an access road from Mountain Rd. off Rt. 1 (turn at Flo's Hot Dogs). The summit is cluttered with satellite dishes and cell towers, but 8 miles of trails are set in pristine woods, with trail maps available at each trailhead. Spring and fall raptor migrations can be viewed from the summit.

Vaughan Woods State Park (207-384-5160), South Berwick. Seasonal. $2 age 12 and above. Take Old Fields Rd. off Brattle St. A 250-acre preserve on the banks of the Salmon Falls River; picnic facilities and 3 miles of nature trails. The first cows in Maine are said to have been landed here at Cow Cove in 1634. See directions under South Berwick in *Scenic Drives*.

Sohier Park, Rt. 1A, York. See Nubble Light under *To See*. A popular picnic spot.

Goodrich Park, York. A good picnic spot on the banks of the York River, accessible from Rt. 1 south; look for the entrance just before the bridge.

Mason Park, Rt. 1A, York Harbor, adjoining Harbor Beach. Created in 1998 when several classic York Harbor cottages were destroyed in accordance with the wills of their former owners.

WALKS **Cliff Path** and **Fisherman's Walk**, York Harbor. For more than a mile, you can pick your way along the town's most pleasant piece of shorefront. Begin at the George Marshall Store and walk east along the river and through the shady Steedman Woods. Go across the Wiggly Bridge (a mini suspension bridge), then continue across Rt. 103, past the Sayward House, along the harbor, down the beach, and along the top of the rocks. Continue east from Mason Park above York Harbor Beach until the path ends at a private property line. This portion is a bit rough, and walkers are advised to keep to the path. Returning the way you've come is no hardship.

✷ Lodging

Note: York Beach offers many **summer cottage rentals**, and rentals can also be found elsewhere in town. Check with the Greater York Chamber of Commerce for individual rentals as well as reliable realtors. Also see www.seasiderentals.com.

Kim Grant

THE WIGGLY BRIDGE IN YORK

INNS AND RESORTS *Note:* For details about the largest local resort, The Cliff House resort and spa, which sits on the Ogunquit–York line, see the "Ogunquit" chapter.

Dockside Guest Quarters (207-363-2868 or 1-800-270-1977; www.docksidegq.com), 22 Harris Island Rd., York 03909. Open April–mid-Dec. Sited on a peninsula in York Harbor, this family-run inn faces the outlet to the harbor. From the porch and front rooms of the gracious, 19th-century Maine House, the view usually includes fishing boats, sailing yachts, and kayakers, always gulls and the Boon Island Light. The inn forms the centerpiece of a 7-acre compound that includes four contemporary, multiunit cottages. In all there are 25 guest rooms—including several with gas fireplace and six apartment/suites with kitchenette—all with private deck and water views. Breakfast is served buffet-style in the Maine House, a morning gathering place for guests who check the blackboard weather forecast and plan their day. Guests have access to fishing equipment, bicycles, a rowing skiff, and Boston whalers. River tours are also offered by innkeeper Eric Lusty. Two-night minimum stay during July and Aug. $216–229 in high season, $104–125 off-season; $197–276 for a suite with living room and kitchenette. Phil Lusty serves lunch and dinner in the neighboring Dockside Restaurant (see *Dining Out*).

Stage Neck Inn (207-363-3850 or 1-800-222-3238; www.stageneck.com), Stage Neck Rd., York Harbor 03911. Open year-round. An attractive 1970s complex of 58 rooms built on the site of the 19th-century Marshall House. Located on its own peninsula, the inn offers some water views, a formal dining room (see Harbor Porches in *Dining Out*), less formal **Sandpiper Grille**, tennis courts, an outdoor pool, a small indoor pool, and Jacuzzi; its grounds adjoin sandy Harbor Beach. $270–385 per room in-season, $145–275 off-season, no meals included.

York Harbor Inn (207-363-5119 or 1-800-343-3869; www.yorkharborinn.com), P.O. Box 573, York St., Rt. 1A, York Harbor 03911. Open year-round. The beamed lobby is said to have been built in 1637 on the Isles of Shoals. An exclusive men's club in the 19th century, this is now a popular dining spot (see *Dining Out*); the Ship's Cellar Pub features an elaborately carved bar. The 54 rooms are outfitted with handsome furnishings, a private bath, and air-conditioning. Several have a working fireplace, some in the **Harbor Hill Inn** have a Jacuzzi, and many have water views. The neighboring **Harbor Cliffs B&B**, a former summer mansion, and 1730 **Harbor Crest** hold elegant common rooms, all the amenities, and several suites. $109–349, continental breakfast included.

"1" **The Union Bluff** (207-363-1333 or 1-800-833-0721; www.unionbluff.com), 8 Beach St., P.O. Box 1860, York Beach 03910. Open year-round. First opened in 1868, this landmark has been recently renovated. There's not much of a lobby, but the elevator accesses comfortable rooms with an ocean and beach view. A neighboring Meeting House with a function hall accommodating up to 250 guests was added in 2007. All three meals are served, and there's a choice between the **Beach Street Grill** and an informal pub. Rooms are divided between the original hotel, a three-story motel-like annex with balconies, and the new Meeting House. $179–279 for ocean-view rooms mid-June–Labor Day, from $129 for street side. From $59 off-season; rates include golf privileges.

BED & BREAKFASTS

In York Harbor 03911

"1" **Inn at Tanglewood Hall** (207-351-1075; www.tanglewoodhall.com), 611 York St., P.O. Box 490. Open year-round. In this shingled 1880s summer mansion, onetime home of bandleader Tommy Dorsey, owners Su and Andy Wetzel offer six nicely decorated and air-conditioned guest rooms, all with queen beds and private bath, three with gas fireplace or porch. The York Harbor Suite holds hand-painted flowers on its floors and porch. Guests mingle on the wrap-around veranda overlooking the wooded garden. A full breakfast is served between 8 and 10 on the veranda or in the dining room, or brought to your room. Although the house has no water views, the most dramatic stretch of the Cliff Path is just down the road. $115–235, depending on season.

"1" **Edwards' Harborside Inn** (207-363-3037; www.edwardsharborside.com), P.O. Box 866. Open year-round. Location! Location! Sited across from York Harbor Beach with a long wharf of its own, this solidly built summer mansion is owned by Jay Edwards, a third-generation innkeeper. Breakfast is served in one of the sunporches with a view of the harbor. Many of the 10 guest rooms (seven with private bath) also have water views, and all are air-conditioned and have TV, and phone; the York Suite is a lulu, with water views on three sides and a Jacuzzi overlooking the water, too. Rooms $220, suites $320 in July, Aug., and holidays; $150–220 in shoulder months; $110–200 in winter. $50 per extra person.

♿ **Chapman Cottage** (207-363-2059 or 1-877-363-2059; www.chapmancottagebandb.com), 370 York St. Open year-round. Donna and Paul Archibald have transformed this three-story 1899 summer home into a luxurious B&B with four exceptional guest rooms and two suites. The spacious suites each have two gas fireplaces, one to enjoy from your Jacuzzi, but our favorite is the third-floor Elizabeth's Room, bright and simple with a deck. All rooms have air-conditioning and a welcoming fruit basket, water, and sherry (no phones or TV). The ground-floor parlors now serve as dining room and wine/martinini bar. Dinner by reservation Wed.–Sun. (see *Dinng Out*). There's also a porch set high above the sloping lawn with distant water views. Paul is known locally as a superb chef; his skill demonstrated at breakfast as well as at dinner. $175–185 per couple for rooms, $200–250 for suites in high season, from $140 in fall and from $130 in spring. Rates include breakfast and, usually, Paul's chocolate truffles.

Inn at Harmon Park (207-363-2031; santal@maine.rr.com), P.O. Box 495. Open for B&B Sep.–May and by the week in summer. Sue Antal's hospitable, big 1899 Victorian is within walking distance of Arbor Beach and the shore paths. She offers a comfortable living room with wood-burning fireplace and four guest rooms, from cozy Celia Thaxter with its water view (nice if you are alone) to the suite with fireplace (nice if you aren't). All have private bath and are furnished in wicker and antiques, with radio, small TV, and VCR. Sue is a justice of the peace and knows all the likely local wedding venues, inside and out. $89–129 includes a great breakfast served on the delightful sun porch.

In York Beach 03910

The Katahdin Inn (207-363-1824; in winter, 617-938-0335), 11 Ocean Ave. Extension, P.O. Box 93. Open mid-May–Columbus Day. "Bed and beach" is the way innkeeper Rae LeBlanc describes her golden-colored 1890s guest house overlooking Short Sands Beach and the ocean. Eight of the nine guest rooms have water views. Number 9 on the third floor is small and white with a window and skylight that seem to suspend it above the water. All rooms have a small fridge. The porch is lined with rockers. From $95 (shared bath) to $125 for a large room (private bath); from $65 off-season. No breakfast, but morning tea and coffee are served.

Sand and Surf (207-363-2554 in-season; sand_and_surf@hotmail.com), 53 Ocean Ave. Extension. Open June–Labor Day, weekends from Memorial Day to Columbus Day. The porch is what it's all about in this classic seaside lodging that's been welcoming guests for more than a century. There's a fireplace in the sitting room but no TV. The 11 rooms include a two-room suite; most have half baths. $60–142.

Candleshop Inn (1-207-363-4087; www.candleshopinn.com), 44 Freeman St., P.O. Box 1216. Open year-round. Barbara and Michael Sheff have transformed an old summer home into a tasteful, restful, and distinctive B&B. The 10 guest rooms offer a range of beds (from twin to king) and come with and without private bath; many have water views. Therapeutic massage and Reiki are offered. Rates ($110–170 in-season) include a full vegetarian breakfast and morning yoga. Children under age 5 stay free then $5 up until age 12, otherwise $15 per extra person. Inquire about off-season yoga and pampering weekends or creating your own group retreat.

In York 03909

Morning Glory Inn (207-363-2062; www.morninggloryinnmaine.com), 129 Seabury Rd. Bonnie and

Bill Alston, formerly of the Inn at Tanglewood Hall, have designed and opened their idea of what a B&B should be. What began more than 200 years ago as a post-and-beam cottage on The Isles of Shoals now has the feel of contemporary house, banked in flowers and squirreled away down a rural road near the water. There are three guest rooms, each with a patio or deck, new bath (one with jets), TV, DVD, and mini fridge. Our favorite is Sandpiper. The spacious living and dining area has plenty of space to relax and a wood-burning fireplace. From $115 midweek in winter to $175–225 for a July-Oct. weekend. Rates include a full breakfast.

The Apple Blossom Bed & Breakfast (207-351-1727; www.appleblossombandb.com), 25 Brixham Rd., lies in a rural corner of York that was, until recently, all farms and orchards. Bob and Mary Lou Erickson's rambling white farmhouse dates in part to 1717 and is set on 11 pristine acres. The six comfortable guest rooms are divided between the second and third floors and offer a choice of queens and twins, all with private bath, cable TV, air-conditioning, and antiques. A hot tub stands in an attractive screened building on the lawn. $120–140, $90 off-season, includes a full breakfast served in the dining room or on the screened porch.

In Kittery and South Berwick

The Portsmouth Harbor Inn and Spa (207-439-4040; www.innatportsmouth.com), 6 Water St., Kittery 03904. Open year-round. Nathaniel and Lynn Bowditch are the innkeepers at this 1890s redbrick garden spot in the village just off the Kittery green, across the road from the Piscataqua River, within walking distance (across the bridge) of downtown Portsmouth, New Hampshire. Common rooms are cheerful and spacious, and the six guest rooms are smallish but carefully, imaginatively furnished; all have private bath (some with claw-foot tub), air-conditioning, ceiling fan, phone, and cable TV/VCR (there's an extensive video library). Minx has a gorgeous bathroom. Nat, for many years one of Maine's top tourism officers, is your enthusiastic breakfast chef, while Lynn, a lawyer in a previous life, supervises staff in the full-service spa, housed in the carriage house. $145–200 in-season includes a full breakfast. From $100 off-season.

The Academy Street Inn (207-384-5633), 15 Academy St., South Berwick 03908. Open year-round. We highly recommend this 1903 mansion, adjacent to the attractive village that's home to Maine's oldest private school and to the several historic houses associated with the author Sarah Orne Jewett (1849–1909). Paul Fopeano displays his antique snowshoe collection and Lee Fopeano, manager of Grissini in Kennebunkport, knows how to organize excellent breakfasts. The twin parlors are richly paneled with carved mantels. Five spacious guest rooms have private baths and solid furnishings. A full breakfast is served at the dining room table under the crystal chandelier. Early coffee is set out upstairs, within steps of the guest rooms. $84–94.

OTHER LODGING **View Point** (207-363-2661; www.viewpointhotel.com), 229 Nubble Rd., York 03909. Office open daily in summer, selected days off-season. A nicely designed, oceanfront, condominium-style com-

Nancy English

ACADEMY STREET INN

plex overlooking the Nubble Lighthouse. All nine suites have a living room, kitchen, porch or patio, gas fireplace, phone, cable TV, CD stereo, VCR, washer-dryer. From $225 in off-season for one-bedroom to $575 in season for three-bedroom units. Weekly rates. Specials.

🖍 ♿ **The Anchorage Inn** (207-363-5112; www.anchorageinn.com), Rt. 1A, Long Beach Ave., York Beach 03910. A total of 179 motel-style rooms, most with water views across from Long Sands Beach, a good choice for families. Facilities include indoor and outdoor pools; some rooms sleep four, some with TV, small fridge. In high season $159–360 (for a four-person spa suite) and in low season $61–282; inquire about packages.

🏵 🐾 "1" **Country View Motel & Guesthouse** (207-363-7160 or 1-800-258-6598; www.countryviewmotel.com), 1521 Rt. 1, Cape Neddick 03902. Open year-round. True to its name, this complex faces one of the few remaining meadows on this stretch of Rt. 1, an anomaly like this big old house. Margaret Bowden offers six rooms with private bath (from $110 in-season with continental breakfast) in the house itself and 16 units in the two-story motel (beyond the swimming pool), varying from standard units (with direct-dial phone, cable TV, and air-conditioning) to a two-story apartment ($94–220 in-season). From $49 off-season. Inquire about the two-bedroom cottage. Pets are $10 each per night with the proviso they not be left alone.

✻ Where to Eat

DINING OUT **Anneke Jans** (207-439-0001; www.annekejans.net), 60 Wallingford Square, Kittery. Open for dinner Tue.–Sat. This dramatically dark dining room creates the illusion of sitting in theater. The drama unfolds in the well-lit kitchen, visible beyond a stainless-steel framed counter. The chefs perform well. The signature Bangs Island mussels with Great Hill blue cheese, applewood smoked bacon, and pommes frits begs for an encore. Entrées $16–31. Fully licensed with a wide selection of wines by the glass. Save room for steamed lemon pudding or chocolate truffle cake.

Chapman Cottage (207-363-2059; www.chapmancottagebandb.com), 370 York St. Open year-round, Wed.–Sun. 5–9. Reservations requested. Innkeeper Paul Archibald is an accomplished chef and his à la carte menu is surprisingly broad, ranging on a given night from house-made raviolis with a Gorgonzola cheese sauce ($18) to fresh lobster, diver scallops, and jumbo shrimp with a creamy risotto ($27). The setting is the parlor of this elegant 19th-century "cottage." Lighter plates and tapas are served in the inn's other former parlor, now an attractive martini/wine bar.

Clay Hill Farm (207-361-2272; www.clayhillfarm.com), 220 Clay Hill Rd., Cape Neddick. Open year-round for dinner but generally closed Mon. and Tue. in winter. Call for off-season hours and reservations. A gracious old farmhouse set in landscaped gardens halfway up Mount Agamenticus, with valet parking and an elegant decor the farm is geared to functions. You might begin with escargot in mushroom caps and dine on seared scallops with napa cabbage, sweet red peppers, bean sprouts, and lemon-pepper sauce. Entrées $22–33. Early-bird specials Sunday to Friday at 5:30 PM.

The York Harbor Inn (207-363-5119; www.yorkharborinn), Rt. 1A, York Harbor. Open year-round for dinner and Sunday brunch. Four pleasant dining rooms, most with water views. The menu is large. The seafood chowder is studded with shrimp, scallops, crabmeat, and haddock ($7.25 a cup); fresh seafood is the specialty. Dinner entrées might include Yorkshire lobster supreme (lobster stuffed with a scallop-and-shrimp filling,) and lobster-stuffed breast of chicken. The less formal downstairs **Ship's Cellar Pub** (open 4–11 PM) offers chowders, burgers, sandwiches, and salads but also New York sirloin and pan-roasted swordfish. Entrées $23–28.

Harbor Porches (207-363-3850; www.stageneck.com), Stage Neck Rd., York Harbor. Open year-round for breakfast, lunch, dinner, and Sunday brunch. The Gilded Era decor evokes the glory days of the Marshall House, a grand hotel that occupied this site for many decades, and the glass walls overlook the open ocean. The menu ranges from a vegetarian selection—maybe potato artichoke gratinée, grilled marinated vegetables, or tomato and fava bean ragout ($20)—to petite filet and lobster tail ($32) and includes several seafood choices. No shorts in the formal dining room, but the casual restaurant alongside uses the same menu as well as its own.

Dockside Restaurant (207-363-2722; www.docksidegq.com), Harris Island Rd. off Rt. 103, York Harbor. Open for lunch and dinner late May–Columbus Day. Reservations suggested for dinner. Docking as well as parking. The view of yacht-filled York Harbor from Phil and Anne Lusty's glass-walled dining room and screened porch is hard to beat. At lunch try the Maine crabcakes or lobster ravioli; at dinner the specialties are seafood and roast stuffed duckling, and we can also recommend the grilled wild salmon and mussels with ginger and basil gnocchi. Dinner entrées $18–29. Children's menu.

Cap'n Simeon's Galley (207-439-3655), Rt. 103, Pepperrell Cove, Kittery Point. Open year-round for lunch and dinner and Sunday brunch; closed Mon.–Wed. off-season. A special place with a water view. You enter through the original Frisbee's Store (the building is said to date back to 1680, the store to 1828). The dining area's picture windows overlook the cove and beyond to Portsmouth Harbor. Seafood is the specialty and the chowder is good, but you can also just have a grilled cheese sandwich. All seafood is fried in 100 percent vegetable oil. The all-day menu ranges from burgers to a quart of fried oysters ($28).

Frankie & Johnny's Natural Foods (207-363-1909), 1594 Rt. 1, Cape Neddick. Open for dinner Wed.–Sun. in July and Aug., Thu.–Sun. in spring and fall. No credit cards. BYOB. This colorful place offers vegan and vegetarian dishes but also plenty of seafood and meat. It can hit the spot if you're in the mood for a blackened fish salad, toasted peppercorn-seared sushi-grade tuna on gingered vegetables, or homemade "harvest" pasta. Daily specials. Entrées $17–27.

Sun 'n' Surf Restaurant (207-363-2961), 165 Long Sands Beach Ave. (Rt. 1A). Open for three meals. Still owned by the family who opened a snack bar on this prime spot on Long Sands Beach in 1963, this is now a popular full-service restaurant. Breakfast specials, lunch salads and sandwiches, seafood and steak and dinner. Entrées $15 (for fish 'n' chips) to $25 (for N.Y. sirloin).

Also see **Arrows**, in "Ogunquit and Wells."

EATING OUT

Along Rt. 1 in Kittery and York (south to north)

Beach Pea Baking Co. (207-439-555), 59 State Rd. (Rt. 1 south), Kittery, south of the exit 2 Kittery traffic circle. Open Tue.–Sat., 7:30–6. The aromas alone are worth a stop. Known for artisan breads—from roasted garlic boules through country French and baguettes to focaccia—and fabulous cakes, also a source of great sandwiches to go or eat on the deck.

Bob's Clam Hut (207-439-4233; www.bobsclamhut.com), Rt. 1 south, next to the Kittery Trading Post, Kittery. Open daily year-round, 11–9. Here since 1956 and definitely the best fried clams on the strip—some say the entire coast. The menu includes all the usual fried (using "cholesterol-free oil") seafood plus burgers and sandwiches. Order at the take out and look for seating either inside or at the picnic tables around back.

Stonewall Kitchen Café (207-351-2719), 2 Stonewall Lane, just off Rt. 1, beside the chamber of commerce, York. Open Mon.–Sat. 8–6, Sun. 9–6. At the Stonewall Kitchen flagship store (see *Selective Shopping*) you order from the espresso bar and the deli (breakfast specials, soup, salad, and sandwiches). Take out or take your plate to a stand-up table or (weather permitting) or an outside café table.

Wild Willy's Burgers (207-363-9924), 765 Rt. 1, York. Daily (except Sun.) 11–7:30. This wildly popular family eatery features 100 percent certified Angus ground chuck hand shaped daily into burgers, topped with more combinations than you thought possible, and served with "country fair" fries.

Flo's Hot Dogs, Rt. 1 north, Cape Neddick. Open only 11–3 and not a minute later. The steamers are bargain priced, but that doesn't explain the long lines, and it's not Flo who draws the crowds because Flo has passed away. Her daughter-in-law Gail carries on. Request the special sauce.

BOB'S CLAM HUT IN KITTERY

Christina Tree

LOBSTER **Cape Neddick Lobster Pound** (207-363-5471; www.capeneddick.com), 60 Shore Rd. (Rt. 1A), Cape Neddick. Open Mar.–Nov. for lunch and dinner but call for hours in shoulder seasons. In August come early or be prepared to wait. Sited by a tidal river, this attractive building with dining inside and on a deck is a local favorite. Besides lobster and clams, the menu offers a variety of choices, from vegetable stir-fry to soups and salads to filet mignon and bouillabaisse. Dinner entrées $14–29, but you can always get a grilled cheese and chips ($4.95). Fully licensed.

Chauncey Creek Lobster Pound (207-439-1030), 16 Chauncey Creek Rd., Kittery Point. Open daily 11–8 in summer, weekends in Oct. Owned by the Spinney family since the 1950s, specializing in reasonably priced lobster dinners with steamers, served on picnic tables right on a pier on a tidal river walled by pine trees. Also available: lobster in rolls and in the rough, mussels, chowders, baked beans, a chicken dinner, pizza, and a raw bar. Coleslaw, corn, baked beans, and even popcorn shrimp and individual pizzas are also available. On summer weekends expect a wait. BYOB.

The Lobster Barn (207-363-4721; www.thelobsterbarn.com), Rt. 1, York. Open year-round for lunch and dinner. A pubby, informal, popular dining room with wooden booths and a full menu. Steak and lobster are what this is about. In summer lobster dinners (in the rough) are served under a tent out back. Salad bar and fresh-made bread. Early-bird and daily specials. Children's menu. Live music on the deck Sun. 3–7. Steak $11–19; lobster, market price.

Warren's Lobster House (207-439-1630; www.lobsterhouse.com), 1 Water St., Kittery. Open year-round for lunch, dinner, and Sunday brunch; docking facilities. The rambling, knotty-pine dining room overlooks the Piscataqua River and Portsmouth, New Hampshire, beyond; a dining landmark with 1940s decor. The salad bar, with more than 50 selections, provides a meal in itself. The specialty is "Lobster, Lobster, and More Lobster." The menu is, however, large and includes several beef dishes and plenty of seafood. Entrées $13–17, more for lobster.

Fox's Lobster House (207-363-2643; www.foxslobster.com), Nubble Point, York Beach. Open daily in-season 11:45–9. A large, tourist-geared place near the Nubble, with a water view and a menu ranging from fried clam rolls to lobster, $21.95 for a 1.5-pounder with drawn butter.

Foster's Downeast Clambake (207-263-3255 or 1-800-552-0242; www.fostersclambake.com), P.O. Box 486, York Harbor 03991. This is all about lobster bakes for groups, at their place or yours, anywhere in the world (including the White House).

In York Village

The Rowan Tree Café (207-363-2035), 241 York St. Open Mon.–Fri. 8–3, Sat. 9–2. This sandwich and salad spot makes its own chewy, exemplary whole-grain ciabatta; taste it with apple chutney chicken salad or the BLT with lemon basil aioli. Salads feature grilled chicken or seared salmon with intriguing additions, like fruit, or walnuts and Asiago cheese.

Rick's All Seasons Restaurant (207-363-5584), 240 R York St. Open daily from 5 AM for breakfast until 2 PM weekdays, closing earlier on weekends; for dinner only Wed. and Thu., until 8 PM. A reasonably priced local hangout; specialties include omelets, quiche, corned beef hash, and hot apple pie with cheese.

In York Harbor

Maud Hutchins Seafood Restaurant (207-363-6192), 1 Axholme Rd. (off Rt. 1A) at Foster's Downeast Clambake. Open 10–8. No view but a serious seafood place, good for steamed clams and mussels, lobster cakes with roasted red pepper sauce and Portuguese seafood stew.

Lobster Cove (207-351-1100), 756 York St. Open for breakfast through dinner. Just west of Long Sands Beach with an upstairs deck and water views. The Talpey family, owners of the Goldenrod, have created this moderately priced eatery. No surprises, but a good dinner bet for broiled haddock or baked stuffed shrimp. Burgers all day plus a children's menu.

In York Beach

York Beach Fish Market (207-363-2763), Railroad St. Billed as and generally agreed to be the best lobster rolls in York Beach. Eat in booths or walk to the beach to enjoy. Crab rolls, chowder, hot dogs, and more.

The Goldenrod (207-363-2621; www.thegoldenrod.com), Rt. 1A. Open Memorial Day–Labor Day for breakfast, lunch, and dinner. Still owned by the Talpey family, who first opened for business here in 1896—just in time to serve the first electric trolleys rolling into York Beach from Portsmouth and Kittery. One of the best family restaurants in New England; same menu all day 8 AM–10:30 PM, but lunch and dinner specials are served up at time-polished, wooden tables in the big dining room with a fieldstone fireplace as well as at the old-style soda fountain. Their famous Goldenrod Kisses are made from saltwater taffy cooked and pulled in the windows. A wide selection of homemade ice creams and yogurts, good sandwiches. (Where else can you still get a cream cheese and olives or nuts sandwich?) The dinner menu features basics like meatloaf, broiled haddock, and chicken teriyaki.

Inn at Long Sands (207-363-5132), York Beach Ave. This 50-seat restaurant, across from Long Sands beach,

THE GOLDENROD, YORK BEACH

is a find. All three meals are prepared by trained chefs who seem to know what they are doing. Reasonable prices, wine and beer. This is also a B&B with rooms overlooking the beach.

Shore Road Restaurant & Deli (207-363-6533), junction of Rt.1A and Shore Road. Open 7–5 most of the year, from 6 in summer. Features the usual but reasonably priced sandwiches and burgers (good grilled reubens). The dining area is at the back of the general store, with easy parking and handy to Cape Neddick beach.

Elsewhere

Crooked Lane Café (207-439-2244), 70 Wallingford Square, Kittery. Open daily (except Sun.), 7–3. A brick-walled, storefront eatery in downtown Kittery. Good for "concoct-your-own" sandwiches, good salads, great coleslaw, wine, and cheese; some outdoor seating.

Fogarty's Restaurant and Bakery (207-384-8361), South Berwick Village. Open daily 11–8, until 9 Sat. and Sun. Closed Mon. in Jan. Big, casual, and friendly, a local institution with sandwiches, salads, and burgers served for dinner along with Yankee pot roast, tenderloin tips, and ham steak, all at amazingly digestible prices. Indian pudding and Aunt Pat's pies for dessert. Children's menu.

Muddy River Marketplace (207-748-3400; www.muddyriver.com), junction Rts. 236 and 101, Eliot. Open daily for lunch and dinner. While there's more on the menu, this is all about barbecue: pulled pork, baby backs, beef brisket, and smoked pulled chicken, lobster bakes. An offshoot of the Portsmouth eatery (which has since closed) so there's more happening here than ever. All you can eat Tuesday buffet for $13.95. A pleasant eat-in space with picnic tables as well. Children's menu.

SNACKS, TREATS, AND TAKE-HOME

Brown's Ice Cream (207-363-4077), Nubble Rd., 0.25 mile beyond the lighthouse, York Beach. Seasonal. Family-owned, all extra-creamy ice creams—55 flavors—are made on the premises. Try the "Maine Survivor." From $2.75 for a kiddy cone. "Small" is enormous. Picnic tables but no view.

Pie in the Sky Bakery (207-363-2656), Rt. 1, Cape Neddick. Open Thu.–Mon. except Jan.; hours vary off-season. The purple house at the corner of River Rd. is filled with delicious smells and irresistible muffins, pies, and scones baked here by John and Nancy Stern.

Cacao Chocolates (207-438-9001), 64 Government St. in downtown Kittery. Open noon–4, Sat. 10–4; closed Sun., Mon., and the month of Aug. Susan Tuveson and Greta Evans make amazing chocolates. Truffles and caramels are made by hand in small batches using fresh dairy cream, butter, and pure, natural flavorings, some of them surprising—like fine teas, chiles, and cheese. We were skeptical about a goat cheese and cognac truffle. Tasting was bliss.

Terra Cotta Pasta Company (207-375-3025), Rt. 1 north, below the Kittery traffic circle. Open Mon.–Sat. 9–6. Freshly made parsley and garlic linguine and wild mushroom lasagna are a sampling of what's offered, along with dozens of full-bodied sauces. It's also a good spot to pick up a sandwich for a picnic at nearby Fort McClary.

Food & Co. (207-363-0900; www.foodnco.com), 1 York St., York. Open

Mon.–Sat. 8–6. A sleek gourmet market and café featuring artisan cheeses, small-producer wines, deli items, take-home dishes, and "handcrafted" sandwiches.

✷ Entertainment

Ogunquit Playhouse (see *To See* in "Ogunquit and Wells") is the nearest and most famous summer theater. Special children's presentations.

Hackmatack Playhouse (207-698-1807; www.hackmatack.org), in Berwick, presents summer-stock performances most evenings; Thursday matinees.

Seacoast Repertory Theatre (603-433-3372; www.seacoastrep.org), 125 Bow St., Portsmouth, New Hampshire. Professional theater productions.

The Kittery Art Association (see *Art Galleries*) offers a summer series of Friday concerts and lectures.

✷ Selective Shopping

ANTIQUES Half a dozen antiques dealers can be found along Rt. 1 between **Bell Farm Antiques** in York and **Columbary Antiques** (a group shop) in Cape Neddick. Stop in one and pick up the leaflet guide to the couple of dozen member shops between York and Arundel.

TJ's (207-363-5673), 1287 Rt. 1, Cape Neddick. In a class of its own. All reproduction antiques, including fine arts and fabrics. Operated by interior designers Jerry Rippletoe and Tony Sienicki.

ART GALLERIES **York Art Association Gallery** (207-363-4049 or 207-363-2918), Rt. 1A, York Harbor. Annual July art show, films, and workshops.

Nancy English

PIE IN THE SKY BAKERY, CAPE NEDDICK

George Marshall Store Gallery, 140 Lindsay Rd., York. Open mid-June–mid-Oct., Thu. 11–4, Sun. 1–4. Housed in an 18th-century store maintained by the Old York Historical Society. Exhibits feature regional contemporary art and fine crafts. Free.

Kittery Art Association (207-451-9384; www.kitteryart.org), 8 Coleman Ave., Kittery Point. Open seasonally Thu. 3–6, Sat. noon–6, Sun. noon–5. Housed in a former firehouse marked (and just off) Rt. 103, changing shows by member artists. The Web site lists Friday night music and other events.

CRAFTS **Village Marketplace** (207-363-7616), 211 York St. (Rt. 1A), York Village. Open mid-Apr.–Dec. 24, daily 9:30–5:30, Fri. until 8. Housed in the vintage 1834 "Olde Church" in the center of York Village: locally crafted toys, needlework, baskets, jellies, and much more.

SPECIAL STORE Kittery Trading Post (207-439-2700; www.kitterytradingpost.com), Rt. 1, Kittery. A local institution since 1926, the sprawling store completed a major expansion in 2004 and is always jammed with shoppers in search of quality sportswear, shoes, children's clothing, firearms, outdoor books, and fishing or camping gear. The summer-end sales are legendary, and many items are routinely discounted, but this is not an outlet store.

In York

Stonewall Kitchen (207-351-2712; www.stonewallkitchen.com), Stonewall Lane, Rt. 1, beside the chamber of commerce, York. Open in high season 8–8 except Sun. 9–6; check for off-season hours. What began as a display of offbeat vinegars at a local farmer's market in 1991 is now a mega specialty food business with a big wholesale and mail-order component. Owners Jonathan King and Jim Stott are quick to claim, however, that all their products—from roasted garlic and onion red pepper jelly or raspberry peach champagne jam through sun-dried tomato mustard to fresh lemon curd and dozens of vinegars, chutneys, and barbecue sauces—still represent homemade care. Sample them in the open-kitchen-style shop, pick up free recipes and find kitchen-supplies, home furnishings, and more. (Also see *Eating Out*).

Old York Historical Society Museum Shop, 196 York St. (Rt. 1A), York Village. Open May–Dec., Mon.–Sat. 10–5. Some great gifts, cards, books.

Gravestone Artwear (1-800-564-4310), 250 York St., York Village. Open weekdays, 10:30–4. This departure point for Ghostly Tours (see *To Do*) is a trove of ghostly and grave-yard-related products, from carvings to cards, T-shirts, and more.

Rocky Mountain Quilts (207-363-6800 or 1-800-762-5940), 130 York St., York Village. Open May–mid-Oct., Mon. to Sat. 10–5, Sun. 12–5; call off-season. Betsey Telford restores quilts and sells antique quilts (more than 450 in stock, "from doll to king"), blocks, and fabrics from the late 1700s to the 1940s.

Knight's (207-361-2500; www.mainequiltshop.com), 1901 Rt. 1, Cape Neddick. Bright fabrics, quilt supplies, and small quilted gifts (but no quilts) are sold here. Inquire about quilting classes.

When Pigs Fly (207-439-3114; www.sendbread.com), 447 Rt. 1. This is the company store for these widely distributed, all-natural breads.

Woods to Goods (207-363-6001; www.woodstogoods.com), 891 Rt. 1, York. Open daily 10–6; 10–5 off-season. Not all but many of the lamps, ships' models, and other decorative items in this roadside shop are made by inmates of Maine prisons. The "Prison Blues" T-shirts and sweatshirts with the catchy line MADE ON THE INSIDE TO BE WORN ON THE OUTSIDE are produced by Oregon inmates.

In Kittery

The antithesis of the mammoth eponymous Trading Post and outlet malls on Rt. 1 north of the I-95 exit 2 traffic circle, half a dozen distinctive owner-operated shops have recently opened south of the circle and in downtown Kittery. See Cacao Chocolates, Beach Pea Baking Co., Terra Cotta, and Crooked Lane Café under *Where to Eat*. **Papers, Ink!** (207-439-1955), 64 Wallingford Square, is part of this renaissance, selling cards, stationery, and fun things.

OUTLET MALLS **Kittery Outlets** (1-888-548-8379; www.thekitteryoutlets.com). Open daily year-round, May–Jan. 1, Mon.–Sat. 9–9, Sun. 10–6; off-season Sun.–Thu. 10–6, Sat. 10–8. Take I-95, exit 3. At this writing more than 120 discount stores within a 1.3-mile strip of Rt. 1 in Kittery represent a mix of clothing, household furnishings, gifts, and basics. All purport to offer savings of at least 20 percent on retail prices.

✱ Special Events

Note: Be sure to pick up the area's unusually lively *Calendar of Events* at the Greater York Region Chamber of Commerce (see *Guidance*).

June: **Strawberry Festival**, South Berwick.

July: **Ellis Park Concerts** almost nightly, and **band concerts** Wednesday evening at Short Sands Pavilion, York Beach. **York Days Celebration** (*last days of the month*)—flower show, church supper, concerts, square dances, parade, and sand-castle contest.

September–Oct. **Zach's Corn Maze** (www.zachscornmaze.com) in York.

October: **Harvestfest** (*the weekend after Columbus Day weekend, usually coinciding with peak foliage here*), York Village—an ox roast, oxcart races, hay- and horse rides, music, and live entertainment.

Sunday of Thanksgiving weekend: **Lighting of the Nubble**, Sohier Park, 5:45–7, with a shuttle bus from Ellis Park (207-363-1040). The famous lighthouse is illuminated in sparkling white lights for the Christmas season.

December: **Christmas Open House Tours**. Kittery Christmas Parade and Tree Lighting and York Festival of Lights Parade (*first weekend of the month*).

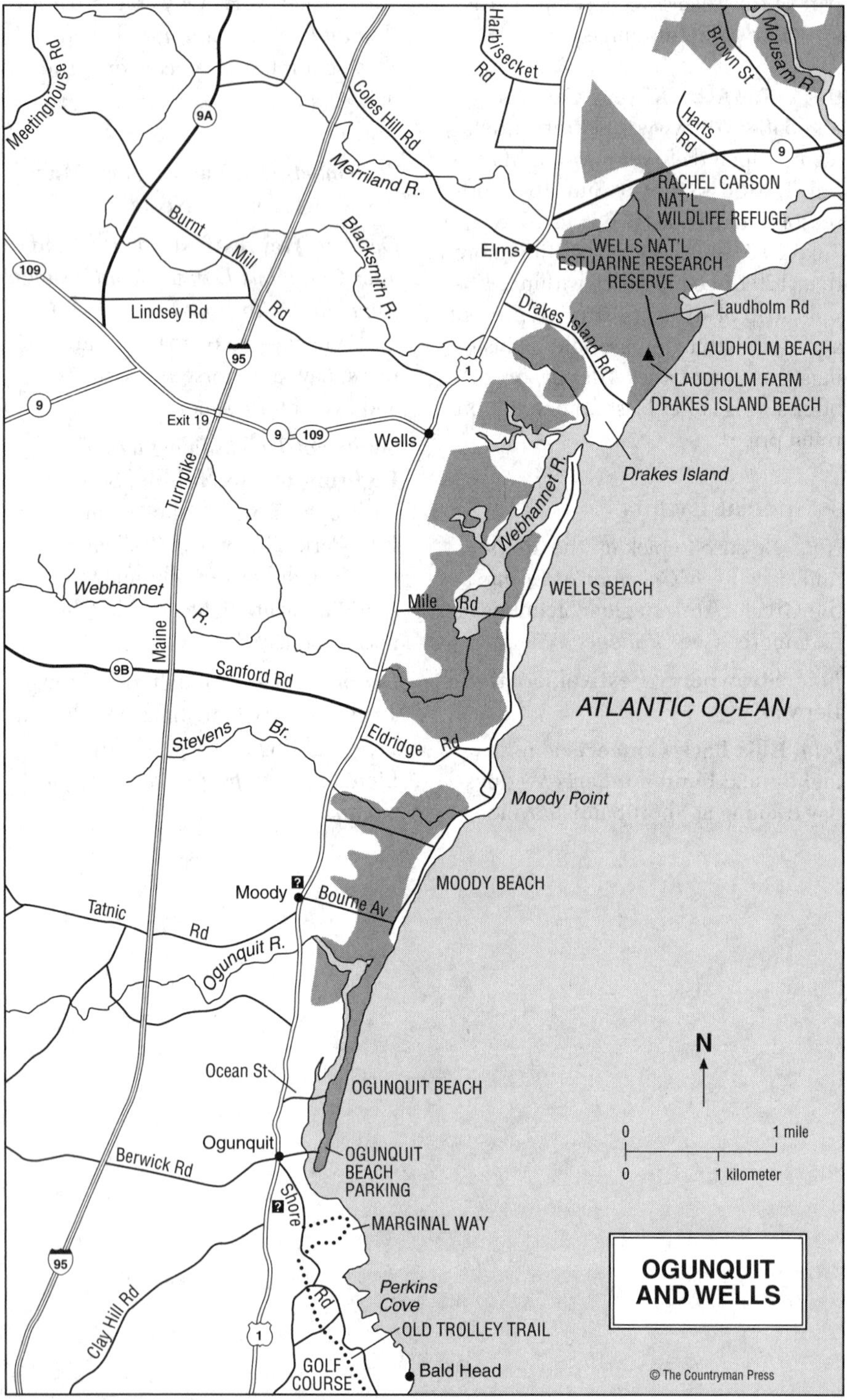

OGUNQUIT AND WELLS
Meetinghouse Rd
9A
Coles Hill Rd
Harbisecket Rd
Brown St
Mousam R.
Harts Rd
9
Merriland R.
RACHEL CARSON NAT'L WILDLIFE REFUGE
Burnt Mill Rd
Blacksmith R.
Elms
WELLS NAT'L ESTUARINE RESEARCH RESERVE
109
Lindsey Rd
Laudholm Rd
Drakes Island Rd
LAUDHOLM BEACH
95
1
LAUDHOLM FARM
DRAKES ISLAND BEACH
Exit 19
Wells
Drakes Island
Maine Turnpike
Webhannet R.
Webhannet R.
WELLS BEACH
Mile Rd
9B
Sanford Rd
ATLANTIC OCEAN
Stevens Br.
Eldridge Rd
Moody Point
MOODY BEACH
Moody
Bourne Av
Tatnic Rd
Ogunquit R.
N
Ocean St
OGUNQUIT BEACH
0
1 mile
0
1 kilometer
Ogunquit
Berwick Rd
OGUNQUIT BEACH PARKING
Shore Rd
MARGINAL WAY
Perkins Cove
Clay Hill Rd
OLD TROLLEY TRAIL
GOLF COURSE
Bald Head
© The Countryman Press

OGUNQUIT AND WELLS

Ogunquit and Wells share many miles of uninterrupted sand, and the line between the two towns also blurs along Rt. 1, a stretch of restaurants, family attractions, and family-geared lodging places. The two beach resorts are, however, very different.

Named for the English cathedral town, Wells was incorporated in 1653 and remains a year-round community of 10,000 with seasonal cottages, condo complexes, and campgrounds strung along the beach and Rt. 1—parallel strips separated by a mile-wide swatch of salt marsh. Wells is a resort for families, the place to find a reasonably priced weekly rental.

Ogunquit was part of Wells until 1980 but seceded in spirit long before that, establishing itself as a summer resort in the 1880s and a magnet for artists in the 1890s through the 1940s. It remains a compact, walk-around resort village clustered between its magnificent beach and picturesque Perkins Cove; these two venues are connected by the mile-long Marginal Way, an exceptional shore path. The village offers a vintage movie house and the Ogunquit Playhouse, one of New England's most famous summer theaters. Most of Ogunquit's big old wooden hotels were razed during the 1960s and replaced by motor inns.

With the 1980s came condos, B&Bs, more restaurants, and boutiques. Luckily, the decade also brought trolleys-on-wheels to ease traffic at Perkins Cove and the beach. With a year-round population of 1,100 and 3,000 rooms for rent, Ogunquit regularly draws 40,000 on a summer weekend, 80,000 on holiday weekends year-round. A reservation on summer weekends, or even on a weekday in August, is wise—but call the Ogunquit Chamber (listed below) for help if you are without one, and they can usually help.

GUIDANCE **Ogunquit Chamber of Commerce** (207-646-2939; www.ogunquit.org), P.O. Box 2289, Rt. 1, Ogunquit 03907 (beside the Ogunquit Playhouse). Open year-round, Mon.–Sat. 9–5; until 8 on Fri. and 6 on Sat. in July and Aug. Staff are helpful, and this large visitors center is well stocked with pamphlets and offers restrooms.

Wells Chamber of Commerce (207-646-2451 or 1-800-639-2442; www.wellschamber.org), 136 Post Rd. (Rt. 1, northbound side) in Moody. Open mid-May–Columbus Day, daily 9–5; weekdays and some Saturdays the rest of the year.

GETTING THERE *By car:* Coming north on I-95, take exit 7 (York) and drive up Rt. 1 to the village of Ogunquit. Coming south on the Maine Turnpike/I-95, take turnpike exit 19 (Wells).

By train: The **Downeaster**, Amtrak's popular Boston–Portland service, makes five round-trips daily, year-round. The Wells Transportation Center stop is at 696 Sanford Rd. (Rt. 109) at the exit 2 tollbooth of the Maine Turnpike (I-95).

Brewster's Taxi (207-646-2141), billed as serving Ogunquit since 1898, offers local and long-distance service.

Coastal Taxi (207-229-0783) is on-call 24 hours, year-round.

GETTING AROUND Mid-May–Columbus Day **open-sided trolleys** circle through the village of Ogunquit, Perkins Cove, and out Rt. 1 in Wells, stopping at the main entrance to Ogunquit Beach and at Footbridge Beach. Fare is nominal. Trolley stops are mapped, and maps are available from the chambers of commerce.

PARKING Park and walk or take the trolley. In summer this is no place to drive. There are at least seven public lots; rates are $12–24 per day, but are constantly changing. There is also free parking (1-hour limit) on Rt. 1 across from the Leavitt Theatre just north of Ogunquit Square or adjacent to Cumberland Farms. Parking at the main entrance to Ogunquit Beach is $4 per hour ($15 weekdays in good weather, maybe less if it's raining, per day). In Wells parking at the five public lots is $15 per day; monthly permits are available from the town office. Perkins Cove parking has a minimum charge of $4 for an hour, with a three-hour maximum.

PUBLIC RESTROOMS *In Ogunquit:* At Footbridge Beach, Main Beach, Perkins Cove, Jacob's Lot, the Dunaway Center, and the information center.

In Wells: At the jetty, Wells Harbor Pier, Wells Beach, and Drakes Island parking areas.

WHEN TO COME Ogunquit shuts down in winter, with most of its restaurants closed and even the best operating on a shortened schedule. Wells, too, slows to a crawl. But since the height of summer is so busy in both places, visiting in September and October or June makes for a more leisurely experience.

* To See

Perkins Cove, Ogunquit. Maine's most painted fishing cove, with some 40 restaurants and shops now housed in weathered fish shacks. It is the departure point for the area's excursion and fishing boats, based beside the famous draw-footbridge. Parking is nearly impossible in summer, but public lots are nearby, and the trolley stops here regularly. The cove can also be reached on foot via the Marginal Way.

Ogunquit Museum of American Art (207-646-4909; www.ogunquitmuseum.org), Shore Rd., Ogunquit (0.4 mile west of Perkins Cove). Open July–Oct. 15, Mon.–Sat. 10:30–5; Sun. 2–5. Closed Labor Day. $7 adults, $5 seniors, $4 students, free under 12. Founded in 1952 and built superbly of local stone and wood, with enough glass to let in the beauty of the cove it faces, the museum displays selected paintings from its permanent collection, which includes the strong, bright oils of Henry Strater and other one-time locals such as Reginald Marsh; also Thomas Hart Benton, Marsden Hartley, Edward Hopper, Rockwell Kent, and William and Marguerite Zorach. Special exhibitions feature nationally recognized artists.

Nancy English

THE DRAWBRIDGE SPANNING PERKINS COVE

Ogunquit Heritage Museum (207-646-0296; www.ogunquitheritagemuseum.org), 86 Obeds Ln., Ogunquit. Open June–Sept., Tues.–Sat. 1–5. Set inside the Captain James Winn House, an 18th-century cape with a unique Federal staircase and original paneling and flooring, this museum exhibits artifacts of Ogunquit's artistic and fishing history and houses the Littlefield Genealogical Library.

Historical Society of Wells & Ogunquit (207-646-4755), 936 Post Rd. (Rt. 1, opposite Wells Plaza). Open mid-May–mid-Oct., Tue.–Thu. 10–4; off-season, Wed.–Thu. 10–4. $2 donation per adult. Housed in a historic meetinghouse still used for weddings, concerts, and numerous special events; also a genealogy library, old photos, memorabilia, ships' models, and a gift shop.

✐ ♿ **Wells Auto Museum** (207-646-9064), Wells. Open Memorial Day–Columbus Day, daily 10–5. Admission fee. More than 80 cars dating from 1900 to 1963, including a 1919 Stutz Bearcat and a 1941 Packard convertible, plus nickelodeons, toys, and bicycles. Rides in antique cars are offered.

✷ To Do

BICYCLING **Wheels & Waves** (207-646-5774), 579 Post Rd. (Rt. 1), Wells. Rents as well as sells bikes; also a source of wetsuits and everything surf related.

BOAT EXCURSIONS

From Perkins Cove

Finestkind Cruises (207-646-5227;

OGUNQUIT MUSEUM OF ART

Christina Tree

www.finestkindcruises.com) offers scenic cruises and "lobstering trips." Both the ***Ugly Anne*** (207-646-7202; www.uglyanne.com) and the ***Bunny Clark*** (207-646-2214; www.bunnyclark.com) offer deep-sea-fishing trips. The excursion boat ***Deborah Ann*** (207-361-9501; www.deborahannwhalewatch.com) offers four-and-a-half-hour whale-watching cruises out to Jefferies Ledge.

FISHING FROM SHORE Tackle can be rented at Wells Harbor, bait is available as well. The obvious fishing spots are the municipal dock and harbor jetties. There is surf casting near the mouth of the Mousam River. Also see "Kittery and the Yorks" and "The Kennebunks."

GOLF The area's major 18-hole golf courses are described in "Kittery and the Yorks."

Merriland Farm (207-646-0508; www.merrilandfarm.com), 545 Coles Hill Rd. (off Rt. 1), Wells. Nine-hole, par-three course on a working farm. Also a café serving Memorial Day weekend to early fall, 8–4.

MINI GOLF ♿ **Wells Beach Mini-Golf** (1-800-640-2267), 1000 Post. Rd. (Rt. 1, next to Big Daddy's Ice Cream, Wells. Open daily mid-May–mid-Oct.

Wonder Mountain (207-646-9655), Rt. 1, Wells. Open Memorial Day–Columbus Day. Two 18-hole courses include mountain mania, complete with waterfalls. Arcade with skee ball and video games.

Sea-Vu Mini Golf (207-646-7732) is another Rt. 1 option in Wells. 18-holes.

SEA KAYAKING **World Within Sea Kayaking** (207-646-0455; www.worldwithin.com), 746 Ocean Ave., Wells. Registered Maine Guide Andrew French offers guided estuary and ocean tours from the Ogunquit River Plantation, on the Ogunquit–Wells line.

TENNIS Three public courts in Ogunquit. Inquire at **Dunaway Center** (207-646-9361). **Wells Recreation Area**, Rt. 9A, Wells, has four courts.

Green Space

BEACHES Three-mile-long **Ogunquit Beach** offers surf, soft sand, and space for kite flying, as well as a sheltered strip along the mouth of the Ogunquit River for toddlers. It can be approached three ways: (1) The most popular way is from the foot of Beach St. There are boardwalk snacks, changing facilities, and toilets, and it is here that the beach forms a tongue between the ocean and the Ogunquit River (parking in the lot here is $4 per hour in-season). (2) The Footbridge Beach access (take Ocean St. off Rt. 1 north of the village) offers restrooms and is less crowded. $15 a day weekdays, $20 weekends for parking. (3) Moody Beach parking lot, Wells. Be sure to park in the lot provided; $20 a day. Walk west onto Ogunquit Beach, not to Moody Beach, now private above the high-water mark.

Wells Beach. Limited free parking right in the middle of the village of Wells Beach; also parking at the east end by the jetty. Wooden casino and boardwalk, clam shacks, clean public toilets, a cluster of motels, concrete benches—a gathering point for older people who sit while enjoying the view of the wide, smooth beach.

Drakes Island, Wells. Take Drakes Island Rd. off Rt. 1. There are three small parking areas on this spit of land lined with private cottages.

NATURE PRESERVES AND PARKS **Wells National Estuarine Research Reserve at Laudholm Farm** (207-646-1555; www.wellsreserve.org), Laudholm Rd. (off Rt. 1, just south of its junction with Rt. 9; look for the blinking yellow light just south of the Maine Diner on Rt. 1), Wells. This 1,600-acre estuary, an area formed where ocean tides meet freshwater currents, is one of 27 in the nation with a research facility. The reserve consists of two parts: the meadows and two barrier beaches at the mouth of the Little River, and Laudholm Farm, a former estate that began as a saltwater farm in the 1620s. Owned by the Lord family from 1881 until 1986 (George C. Lord was president of the Boston & Maine Railroad), it was farmed until the 1950s. Today it's a birder's mecca. A visitor center is open year-round (weekdays 10–4; also May–Oct., Sat. 10–4 and Sun. noon–4), with a slide show, exhibits, restrooms, and parking. Seven miles of trails meander through fields, woods, and wetlands (bring a bathing suit if you want to swim at the beach). The Laudholm Trust grounds are open daily year-round (gates open daily at 8 and remain open until 8 in summer months; otherwise, until 5; entrance fee Memorial Day–Columbus Day is $2 adults, $1 ages 6–16); no dogs allowed. Inquire about guided trail walks, artists' workshops, and programs for kids ages 6–9. The Laudholm Nature Crafts Festival is the weekend after Labor Day. Punkinfiddle (www.punkinfiddle.org), the last Sat. in Sept., is a celebration of National Estuaries Day with fiddle bands, sheep herding, pumpkin rolling, and more.

Rachel Carson National Wildlife Refuge, off Rt. 9 on the Wells–Kennebunk line. See the description in "The Kennebunks."

Dorothea Grant Common. Hidden away between Rt. 1 and the Dunaway Center, this quiet park surrounds the Ogunquit Heritage Museum at Winn House (see *To See*).

WALKS **Marginal Way**. In 1923 Josiah Chase gave Ogunquit this windy path along the ocean. A farmer from the town of York, just south of here, Chase had driven his cattle around rocky Israel's Head each summer to pasture on the marsh grass in Wells, just to the north. Over the years he bought land here and there until, eventually, he owned the whole promontory. He then sold off sea-view lots at a tidy profit and donated the actual ocean frontage to the town, thus preserving his own right-of-way. There is very limited parking at the mini lighthouse on Israel's Head.

🍼 ♿ **Wells Harbor**. Here is a pleasant walk along a granite jetty and a good fishing spot. There is also a playground, and a gazebo where concerts are held.

Old Trolley Trail. An interesting nature walk and cross-country ski trail that begins on Pine Hill Rd. N., Ogunquit.

WHALE WATCH ***Deborah Ann*** **Whale Watch** (207-361-9501; www.deborahannwhalewatch.com). Perkins Cove, Ogunquit. Two trips daily, one in the morning, one in the afternoon, May–Oct. $50 adults, $45 seniors, $35 ages 12 and under. Jefferies Ledge takes and hour and a half to reach; if you don't see any whales (which doesn't happen very often), you'll get a free trip to try again.

✷ Lodging

Note: Ogunquit's 2,500 "rooms" include many family-geared efficiencies, especially along Rt. 1. We do not attempt to critique them here, but all are listed on the Ogunquit Chamber of Commerce Web site (www.ogunquit.org) and in its *Vacation Planner.*

All listings are in Ogunquit 03907, or have an Ogunquit mailing address, and are most convenient to Ogunquit, unless otherwise noted.

RESORT ✐ ♿ 🐾 **The Cliff House** (207-361-1000; www.cliffhousemaine.com), Shore Rd., P.O. Box 2274. Open late Mar.–Dec. Over the last few years, the Cliff House, opened in 1872 with a single building on the top of its spectacular location, has expanded with a monumental spa facility and 32 new, large rooms that feature gas fireplaces and of course ocean views. Guests in any of the 194 rooms in the entire resort can use the "vanishing-edge" pool (set out on the terrace it gives swimmers the illusion of a sea dip without the low temperature of Maine ocean water). The spa, open to the public as well as to guests, gives guests the reality of luxurious massages and facials.

THE CLIFF HOUSE RESORT AND SPA

Nancy English

Innkeeper Kathryn Weare is the great-granddaughter of the woman who opened this hotel, and hospitality remains her focus. Although the decor in the rooms in the main building is undistinguished (a problem also in the new building), every amenity you need is close to hand, from a dining room with that great view and good food (see *Dining Out*) to nearby golf courses, two indoor heated pools, and an exercise room.

This place rose from its own ashes after being run down during the temporary, exclusive use of the U.S. military, which used it as a lookout for Nazi submarines in World War II. Innkeeper Charles Weare tried to sell it for $50,000 in 1946 with an ad in the *Wall Street Journal*, but received no offers.

High-season summer rates range $255–350 with no meals; $155–245 off-season.

RESORT MOTOR INNS Our usual format places inns before motels, but in the 1960s some of Ogunquit's leading resorts replaced their old hotel buildings with luxury "motor inns."

Sparhawk (207-646-5562; www.thesparhawk.com), 85 Shore Rd., P.O. Box 936. Open mid-Apr.–late Oct. Fifty-one-unit Oceanfront overlooks the confluence of the Ogunquit River and the Atlantic Ocean, as well as Ogunquit Beach (waves lap below the balconies). Twenty units in neighboring Ireland House (with balconies canted toward the water) are combination living room/bedroom suites. The Barbara Dean and Jacobs Houses, formerly village homes, add another 11 suites and four apartments, some with gas fireplace and Jacuzzi. The two-bedroom Little White House is overlooks the ocean. Guests register and gather in Sparhawk Hall. Amenities include outdoor pool (heated mid-June–mid-Sep.), shuffleboard, croquet, tennis, and privileges at the local golf course and fitness center. One-week minimum stay July–mid-Aug.; $185–305 per night in high summer, $100–270 in spring and fall.

Aspinquid (207-646-7072; www.aspinquid.com), Beach St., P.O. Box 2408. Open mid-Mar.–Oct. This weathered-shingle complex sits just across the bridge from Ogunquit Beach. Built in 1971 by the owners of the old hotel, the two-story clusters still look modern. Rooms all have two double beds, phone, and TV; most have kitchenette. Some sliding doors on private decks overlook the water, and you can hear the surf pounding on the beach. Facilities include a pool, lighted tennis court, and fishpond with a waterfall ideal for relaxation. $165–380 in-season, $90–215 in spring and fall.

INNS AND HOTELS **The Beachmere Inn** (207-646-2021 or 1-800-336-3983; www.beachmereinn.com), 62 Beachmere Place. Open late Mar.–mid-Dec. Extensive renovations are scheduled for completion in 2008. Beachmere Inn consists of a rambling, updated mansion and a streamlined building that border a huge lawn on Ogunquit Beach. The inn, owned by female members of the same family since 1937, has 39 rooms and 33 suites; number 35 is a blue aerie set over Marginal Way and ocean waves, with handmade furniture and gas fireplace. All rooms have kitchenette and cable TV, and many have a private balcony, deck, or terrace. Four handicapped accessible rooms are new additions, as are a new breakfast area and wedding rooms. Attention to detail throughout and hospitality make a stay here a pleasure. High-season rates, $150–349, drop in the off-season and after Columbus Day to as low as $60–180.

The Grand Hotel (207-646-1231 or 1-800-806-1231; www.thegrandhotel.com), 276 Shore Dr. Open Mar.–Nov. Twenty-eight suites in this hotel, originally a condominium complex, each have two rooms, wet bar, fridge, cable TV, and private deck or balcony; fireplace in top floor rooms. There's an elevator, an interior atrium, an indoor pool, and an outdoor hot tub; in 2007 all queen-sized beds were replaced with kings. $180–240 in high season, $95–210 right after Labor Day, from $70 off-season.

BED & BREAKFASTS **The Trellis House** (207-646-7909 or 1-800-681-7909; www.trellishouse.com), 2 Beachmere Place, P.O. Box 2229. Open year-round. Pat and Jerry

Houlihan's shingled, turn-of-the-20th-century summer cottage offers appealing common areas, including a wraparound screened porch and comfortable seating around the hearth. Upstairs are three guest rooms, all with full private bath, one with a water view; the English Suite has a canopied four-poster. A romantic cottage in the garden is private. This is one of those places where guests feel at ease, because the Houlihans are genuine hosts. $125–250 in-season, from $85 off-season, includes a breakfast (served anytime between 8:30 and 10) that might include apple-cinnamon French toast and sausage. The inn is handy both to the village and to Perkins Cove via the Marginal Way.

Marginal Way House and Motel (207-646-8801; in winter, 207-363-6566; www.marginalwayhouse.com), Wharf Lane, P.O. Box 697. Open late Apr.–Oct. Just a short walk from the beach and really in the middle of the village, this delightful complex is hidden down a waterside lane; its landscaped lawn has a water view. Geoffrey Blake and his family have run this property since 1968. There are old-fashioned guest rooms—number 8 has flowered wallpaper and a beach view—in the Main and Wharf Houses, each with private bath. Dockside houses six standard motel units, and there are seven (high-season weekly rental) apartments. High season $102–246, low $49–159.

Morning Dove (207-646-3891; www.morningdove.com), 13 Bourne Ln., P.O. Box 1940. Open Mar.–Jan. 2. On a quiet side street off Shore Road, within walking distance of everything, this is a handsome, spotless 1860s farmhouse. We like the living room with its white marble fireplace; there are two suites, one with gas fireplace, and four guest rooms. Innkeeper Rob Leary took over in 2007. $150–190 in-season, $95–150 off-season, full breakfast included.

Above Tide Inn (207-646-7454; www.abovetideinn.com), 66 Beach St. Open May 15–Oct. 15. Location! Location! Sited right at the start of the Marginal Way and steps from the bridge leading over to Ogunquit Beach, also steps from village shops and jutting right out into the water. Meghan and John Hubacz host nine rooms, each with an outdoor sitting area, and small fridge, TV, shower or bath. All but one room have water views, and local artists painted the pictures hanging inside. Mid-July–Labor Day rates are $185–250; $100–140 off-season, continental breakfast included.

The Beauport Inn on Clay Hill (207-361-2400 or 1-800-646-8681; www.beauportinn.com), 339 Clay Hill Rd. Open year-round. Who says, "They don't build 'em like that anymore"? This new stone manor, a luxuriously apppointed riverside retreat created by George and Cathy Wilson, has vintage-1835 English oak floor-to-ceiling paneling in its great room. Each room has a gas fireplace, cable TV, and VCR; there's also a two-room suite and a fully equipped apartment. A lap pool, steam room, and Jacuzzi are shared by all guests. $110–185 (depending on the season) includes a very full breakfast. The apartment is $1,100–1,350.

Beach Farm Inn (207-646-8493; www.beachfarminn.com), 97 Eldridge Rd., Wells 04090. Open year-round. This handsome, restored farmhouse has been taking in guests since the 19th century, when it was a working salt-marsh farm. Today loyal repeat customers and many French Canadians appreciate the great hospitality of Nancy Swenson and Craig White. Victorian upholstery by Nancy and furniture by Craig give the interior panache. A full breakfast featuring apple-baked French toast (or homemade pierogi in winter) is served on the bright sunporch. The guest pantry stocks Carpe Diem coffee, and the swimming pool beckons from the lawn. Eight attractive bedrooms, three with private bath—others can be rented with an unattached bath for private use—and two efficiency cottages. $100–150 per couple June–Sep. and holiday weekends, including breakfast, $70–90 off-season.

COTTAGES *Note:* We have noted just a few of the dozens of the area's summer rentals, especially plentiful in Wells. Contact the Wells Chamber of Commerce, which keeps track of rental cottages and condos.

Garnsey Bros. Rentals (207-646-8301) specializes in Wells, and **Seaside Vacation Rentals** (207-646-7671) offers hundreds of rentals throughout the area.

The Dunes (207-646-2612; www.dunesonthewaterfront.com) 518 Main St., P.O. Box 917. Open May–Oct. Owned by the Perkins family for more than 70 years, this is really a historic property, the best of the coast's surviving "cottage colonies," as well as a great family find. The 36 units include 19 old-style white cottages with green trim, many with fireplaces, scattered over well-kept grounds fronting on the Ogunquit River, with direct access to Ogunquit Beach by rowboat at high tide and on foot at low tide. All rooms have refrigerator and color TV. Minimum stay in July and Aug. in the larger cottages. $105–350 in-season, $75–221 off-season.

Cottage in the Lane Motor Lodge (207-646-7903; www.cottageinthelane.com), 84 Drakes Island Rd., Wells 04090. There are 10 housekeeping cottages, all facing landscaped grounds under the pines (an artistic play structure and a pool form the centerpiece); salt marsh beyond. It's a 0.75-mile walk or bike ride to the beach. The quiet setting borders the Rachel Carson Wildlife Refuge and Laudholm Farm (see *Green Space*). $940 per week for a two-bedroom cottage in season, $560–750 per week for a two-bedroom cottage off-season.

The Seagull Inn and Condominiums (207-646-5164; www.seagullvacations.com), 1413 Post Rd. (Rt. 1), Wells 04090. Open May.–Oct. Two three-story townhouses (available year-round), 27 two-bedroom cottages, 1 one-bedroom cottage, all with a screened porch, fill what used to be an open field. Private driveway, gas grills, and new cottages have ocean view. The seven remaining old cottages have been updated with bathrooms and kitchens. Two heated pools, one with hot tub, the other with a wading pool for children. Rentals by the week in summer (three-night minimum off-season), $800–1,500 for the housekeeping cottages; $1,000–2,600 a week for townhouses.

MOTEL **Riverside Motel** (207-646-2741; www.riversidemotel.com), Shore Rd, P.O. Box 2244. Open late Apr.–late Oct. Just across the drawfootbridge and overlooking Perkins

Cove is this trim, friendly place with 42 units; also four rooms in the 1874 house. The property has been in Michael Staples's family for more than 100 years. All rooms have cable TV and full bath, most tiled, and all overlook the cove; continental breakfast is served in the lobby around the fireplace or on the sundeck. $90–190, depending on season and location of room. Three-day minimum July 28–Aug. 17.

✷ Where to Eat

DINING OUT Technically in Cape Neddick but just as handy to Ogunquit, **Clay Hill Farm** is described in "Kittery and the Yorks."

Ⓜ **Arrows** (207-361-1100; www.arrowsrestaurant.com), Berwick Rd., Ogunquit. Open Tue.–Sun. in July and Aug. at 6 PM, fewer days of the week off-season, and closed Jan.–Mar. Voted one of the country's top 50 restaurants by *Gourmet*, this is one of the area's destination restaurants. The food is sometimes extraordinary; lobster cannelloni with ricotta, part of a multi-lobster concoction entrée, rang with flavor. The big wine list is expensive, as are the wines by the glass. A strict dress code is enforced (no one in shorts or jeans will be seated), and 24-hour notice is required for cancellations or a fee is charged on the credit card required to make the reservation. Immaculate gardens surround the old house, and guests often tour the garden before dinner, when some of the produce they have observed will be on their plates. Entrées $42 and up.

THE RIVERSIDE MOTEL, OVERLOOKING PERKINS COVE

Nancy English

98 Provence (207-646-9898; www.98provence.com), 262 Shore Rd., Ogunquit. Open Apr.–Dec. 1, daily except Tue. for dinner (5:30–9:30) in summer, fewer days off-season. This classic French Provençal restaurant gets all the details right. The herb-crusted log of foie gras pâté, with buttered toast, creates happiness. The house cassoulet might hold duck confit, rabbit sausage, and lamb shank. The wine list is dominated by France, and some lovelies are sold by the glass. Reservations advised. Entrées $21–30.

♿ **Joshua's Restaurant** (207-646-3355; www.joshuas.biz), 1637 Post Rd. (Rt. 1), Wells. Open for dinner daily in summer, closed Sunday. The Mather family farm grows a lot of its restaurant's vegetables, and chef Joshua Mather puts them to spectacular use as sides for grilled rack of lamb, haddock with a caramelized onion crust, and lobster pie. An elegant, refurbished farmhouse dining room and bar. Entrées $19–28.

The Cliff House (207-361-1000; www.cliffhousemaine.com), Shore Rd., Ogunquit. Open daily for dinner late Mar.–Dec. Jackets required; no shorts, jeans, or sneakers allowed. Intelligent combinations fill the menu, like crabcakes with Asian slaw and lemon aioli. Fresh gnocchi with walnut butter, grilled sirloin, and cod on wilted Swiss chard with a roasted corn and pancetta chowder are from a fall menu. The view over the water from the high cliff is mesmerizing. Entrées $26–38.

MC Perkins Cove (207-646-6263; www.mcperkinscove.com), Perkins Cove. Lunch and dinner daily in summer, closed some days of the week off-season. Wonderful water view. Owned by the inventive chefs of Arrows (see above), this is a casual place for fresh raw oysters, grilled steak, fried chicken or trout, and other seafood with splendid touches. Choose your own sides and sauces. Entrées $19–34.

Five'O Shore Road (207-646-5001; www.fiveo-shoreroad.com), 50 Shore Rd., Ogunquit Village. Open for dinner in-season nightly, light fare served until 11 PM; Thu.–Sun. in winter. The beef tenderloin brochette we tried remains a high point of dining out, and the skilled preparation of everything else is memorable too. Fried sweetbreads made one menu, as did Peking chicken and scallion crêpes, and rack of lamb. Good wine and cocktails. Entrées $25–33.

Gypsy Sweethearts (207-646-7021; www.gypsysweethearts.com), 30 Shore Rd., Ogunquit. Open Apr.–Oct. for dinner Tue.–Sun. from 5:30; weekends off-season. Meals with a Caribbean twist are served in a charming old house that is the dependable neighborhood dinner spot for demanding locals. Chef-owner Judie Clayton's green pumpkin seed secret sauce is a tangy delight on the rack of lamb. Poblano rellenos, and shelled lobster with spinach tagliatelle. Many wines available by the glass. Entrées $17–28.

Jonathan's Restaurant (207-646-4777; www.jonathansrestaurant.com), 92 Bourne Lane, Ogunquit. Open year-round. There are two entirely distinct parts to this big place. The downstairs restaurant consists of a series of dimly lit, nicely decorated rooms (one with a 600-gallon tropical aquarium). Choices range from grilled steak to caramelized salmon, marinated in a triple sec vinaigrette and served with a lemon *beurre blanc*. Entrées $18–26. For more about what happens upstairs, see *Entertainment*.

LOBSTER *Note:* Maine's southernmost beach resorts are the first place many visitors sample real "Mane Lobstah" the way it should be eaten: messily, with bib, broth, butter, and a water view.

Barnacle Billy's, Etc. (207-646-5575 or 1-800-866-5575; www.barnbilly.com), Perkins Cove. Open May–Oct. for lunch and dinner. What began as a no-frills lobster place (the one that's still next door) has expanded over 40 years to fill a luxurious dining space created for a more upscale waterside restaurant. Lobster and seafood dishes remain the specialty, and it's difficult to beat the view combined with comfort, which frequently includes the glow from two great stone fireplaces. Full bar; dinner entrées from $16.75 for grilled chicken to $35 for a big boiled lobster. You can also order lobster at the counter and wait for your number, dine on the outdoor deck, or order burgers.

Lobster Shack (207-646-2941), end of Perkins Cove. Open mid-Apr.–mid-Oct., 11–9 in-season. A family-owned, old-style, serious lobster-eating place since the 1940s (when it was known as Maxwell and Perkins). The tables are wide slabs of shellacked pine with plenty of room for lobster by the pound, steamer clams, good chowder, house coleslaw; also reasonably priced burgers, apple pie à la mode, wine, beer.

Blue Water Inn (207-646-5559; www.bluewaterinn.com), Beach St., Ogunquit. The view of the Ogunquit River is hard to beat, and the specialty is fish—haddock, halibut, and lobster in a variety of ways. Entrées $16–27.

✐ **Ogunquit Lobster Pound** (207-646-2516), Rt. 1 (north of Ogunquit Village). Open April–Oct. Expanded gradually over the years, this log landmark still retains its 1930s atmosphere and is still all about selecting your lobster and watching it (if you so choose) get steamed in the huge outdoor pots. "Steamers" (steamed clams) are the other specialty. The large menu, however, now ranges from angel-hair pasta to filet mignon with wild mushroom ravioli. Beer and wine are available. Entrées $14–30 and up for lobster.

✐ **Fisherman's Catch** (207-646-8780; www.fishermanscatchwells.com), 134 Harbor Rd., Wells Harbor. Open May–Columbus Day, daily 11:30–9 in summer, closing earlier off-season. Set in a salt marsh, with rustic tables; a traditional seafood place with unbeatable prices. Good chowder and really good lobster stew, homemade crabcakes, lobster dinners, children's menu, beer on tap. Try the bread pudding with whiskey sauce. Entrées $12–18, higher for lobster.

EATING OUT **Amore Breakfast** (207-646-6661; www.amorebreakfast.com), 178 Shore Rd., Ogunquit. Open early spring–mid-Dec., in-season 7 AM–1 PM, closed Wed. and Thu. Relaxed and pleasant, this pine restaurant makes exuberant omelets and a lobster eggs Benedict as pretty as an ocean sunset. Also ingenious French toast, bagels with smoked salmon, and a place to park. Breakfast $5–13.

Lord's Harborside Restaurant (207-646-2651), Harbor Rd., Wells Harbor. Open end of Apr.–Oct. for lunch and dinner; closed Tue. A big, ungarnished dining room with a harbor view serving fried and broiled fish and seafood. Lobster boiled and baked. Entrées $15–26.

The Steakhouse (207-646-4200; www.the-steakhouse.com), Rt. 1, Wells. Lobster and seafood, but the emphasis is on corn-fed prime and choice beef, and all steak dinners include a choice of two: baked beans, fries, baked potato, pasta with meat sauce, vegetable, salad, applesauce, or cottage cheese with pear. Entrées $14–26.

Jake's Seafood (207-646-6771), 127 Post Rd. (Rt. 1),, Moody. Open for all three meals Apr.–Oct., breakfast and lunch Nov.–Mar. Specializes in good American cooking, fresh seafood, ice cream.

Congdon's Donuts Family Restaurant (207-646-4219), 1090 Post Rd. (Rt. 1), Wells. Open from 6 AM year-round. Fresh muffins, breads, pastries, and doughnuts; also ice cream made on the premises and a full menu for lunch and dinner. We've heard the doughnuts are fried in lard—the best way of all, for some of us.

Mike's Clam Shack (207-646-5999; www.mikesclamshack.com), 1150 Post Rd. (Rt. 1), Wells. Open daily in-season 11–9:30. An enormous place with enormous crowds, and a reputation for good fried clams. Sandwiches, burgers, pasta, and fried seafood, $10–22.

 Billy's Chowder House (207-646-7558; www.billyschowderhouse.com), Mile Rd., Wells. Open daily mid-Jan.–early Dec. Overlooking Wells Harbor and a salt marsh, a family favorite with a big menu, a famous chowder, and a selection of fried seafood, steamed shellfish, broiled scallops, and, of course, boiled lobster. There's also plenty of meat on the menu, including a hot dog and fries. Entrées $13–21.

Maine Diner (207-656-4441), 2265 Post Rd. (Rt. 1), Wells, near the junction of Rts. 1 and 9. Open year-round 7 AM–9 PM. This packed place can still boast about its seafood chowder, shrimp, scallops, lobster, and clams in a milky broth. Avoid the chicken pot pie. Hot dog $5; lobster pie $20.

 Village Food Market (207-646-2122), 230 Main St., Ogunquit. This landmark grocery store has gone with the times, adding daily baked goods, soups, salads, and a deli—even an upscale summer takeout called Fancy That, with an outdoor eating area. Call before 11 for a picnic takeout order to avoid the line.

SNACKS **Bread & Roses Bakery** (207-646-4227), 28 Main St., Ogunquit. Over the years Mary Breen's pleasant bakery has expanded into an attractive café serving muffins and coffee, and well known for delectable pastries. Some vegan and kosher items are made here.

Scoop Deck (207-646-5150), Eldridge Road (just off Rt. 1), Wells. Open Memorial Day–Columbus Day. Mocha almond fudge and Dinosaur Crunch (blue vanilla) are among the more than 40 flavors; the ice cream is from Thibodeau Farms in Saco. Also yogurt, cookies, brownies, and hot dogs.

Borealis Breads (207-641-8800; www.borealisbreads.com), Rt. 1, Wells. Open 7:30–6 daily. Great bread and sandwiches—don't overlook the fabulous bread sticks—and the brownies and other treats are excellent. More than 80,000 pounds of whole wheat flour for the breads is milled from wheat grown in Aroostook County.

✷ Entertainment

THEATERS **Hackmatack Playhouse** (207-698-1807), 538 School St. (Rt. 9), Berwick, stages live performances throughout the season.

Arundel Barn Playhouse (207-985-5552; www.arundelbarnplayhouse.com), 53 Old Post Rd., Arundel. Mid-June–Labor Day. Professional musical theater in a restored 1800s barn.

 Booth Theater (207-646-8142; www.boothproductions.com), 13 Beach St., Ogunquit. A black-box theater (based in Worcester, Massachusetts, in winter) with productions Mon.–Sat., June–Aug. The theater seats 74, and the productions vary from musicals to dramas. Inquire about children's matinees and youth camp programs.

Leavitt Fine Arts Theatre (207-646-3123), 259 Main St., Ogunquit Village. An old-time theater with new screen and sound; showing first-run films since 1923.

Ogunquit Playhouse (207-646-5511; www.ogunquitplayhouse.org), Rt. 1 (just south of Ogunquit Village). Open mid-June–Labor Day. Billing itself as "America's Foremost Summer Theater," this grand old summer-stock theater opened for its first season in 1933 and is now owned by the Ogunquit Playhouse Foundation. It continues to feature top stars in productions staged Mon.–Fri. at 8 PM, Sat. at 8:30 PM; matinees are Wed. and Thu. at 2:30 PM, Sat. at noon for kids; Sun. concerts at 8 PM.

OTHERS **Jonathan's Restaurant** (207-646-4777), 92 Bourne Ln., Ogunquit. Memorial Day–Oct. You can check the current schedule on the Web site, www.jonathansrestaurant.com. Folk singer David Wilcox and comedian Paula Poundstone were two performers in 2007.

Ogunquit Performing Arts (207-646-6170) sponsors the Chamber Music Festival in June and the Capriccio annual arts festival at the beginning of September; also film, social dances, and theater year-round.

Hope Hobbs Gazebo at Wells Harbor Park is the site of Saturday-night concerts in summer.

✷ Selective Shopping

ANTIQUARIAN BOOKS Boston book lovers drive to Wells to browse in this cluster of exceptional bookstores along Rt. 1. **Douglas N. Harding Rare Books** (207-646-8785; www.hardingsbooks.com), 2152 Post Rd., open year-round, which is huge and excellent with some 200,000 titles, including rare finds, maps, and prints. **East Coast Books** (207-646-0416), Depot St. at Rt. 109 in Wells, open by appointment only, has a large general collection, autographed copies, and art and historical books. **The Arringtons** (207-646-4124), 1908 Post Rd. (Rt. 1), specialize in military subjects as well as vintage paperbacks and postcards.

OGUNQUIT PLAYHOUSE

Kim Grant

ANTIQUES SHOPS Rt. 1 from York through Wells and the Kennebunks is studded with antiques shops, among them: **MacDougall-Gionet** (207-646-3531; www.macdougall-gionet.com), open Tue.–Sun. 10–5, a particularly rich trove of country furniture in a barn; 60 dealers are represented. **R. Jorgensen Antiques** (207-646-9444; www.rjorgensen.com) has nine rooms filled with antique furniture, including fine formal pieces from a number of countries.

ART GALLERIES In addition to the Ogunquit Museum of Art there is the **Barn Gallery**, home of the **Ogunquit Art Association** (207-646-8400), Shore Rd. and Bourne Ln., Ogunquit. Open late May–early Oct., Mon.–Sat. 11–5 and Sun. 1–5. The Barn Gallery showcases work by members; also stages frequent workshops, lectures, films, and concerts. Ogunquit's galleries (all seasonal) also include, in Perkins Cove, the **George Carpenter Gallery** (207-646-5106). A longtime area resident, Carpenter paints outdoors in the tradition and style of New England's 1920s marine and landscape artists. **Shore Road Gallery** (207-646-5046), 294 Shore

Rd., open Memorial Day–Columbus Day weekend, daily in July–Aug, offers fine arts, jewelry, and fine crafts by nationally known artists.

SPECIAL SHOPS **Perkins Cove**, the cluster of former fish shacks by Ogunquit's famous draw-footbridge, harbors more than a dozen shops and galleries. Our favorite is the **Carpenter Gallery** (see above).

Ogunquit Camera (207-646-2261), at the corner of Shore Rd. and Wharf Lane in Ogunquit Village. Open year-round, and featuring one-hour film developing. A great little shop that's been here since 1952. It's also a trove of toys, towels, windsocks, beach supplies, and sunglasses.

Harbor Candy Shop (207-646-8078; www.harborcandy.com), 26 Main St., Ogunquit. Open since 1956, this family-owned store makes turtles with Belgian chocolate and handmade caramel (made with cream and sugar and no preservatives); they are their most popular item. Small-batch fudge made with cream, brittles, and coconut "snowflakes," coconut shreds in chocolate. Time to get in the car and drive over.

Merriland Farm (207-646-5040; www.merrilandcafe.com), 545 Coles Hill Rd. (off Rt. 1), Wells. This 200-year-old farm offers a view of Wells that was here for centuries before its sandy shore was developed. In addition to operating a café specializing in pies and berry shortcake, and a nine-hole golf course, this is a place to pick cultivated highbush blueberries in July and August and to buy jam, raspberry vinegar, and gift baskets.

Lighthouse Depot (207-646-0608; www.lighthousedepot.com), 2178 Post Rd. (Rt. 1), Wells. Look for the lighthouses outside (just before the turnoff for Laudholm Farm). Open daily in summer, fewer days in winter. Billed as "the largest selection of lighthouse gift items in the world," this is two floors filled with lawn lighthouses, lighthouse books, ornaments, jewelry, paintings, replicas, and much more.

* Special Events

April: Big **Patriot's Day celebration** at Ogunquit Beach.

June: **Ogunquit Chamber Music Festival** (*first week*). **Laudholm Farm Day** (*midmonth*). **Wells Week** (*end of the month*)—a weeklong celebration centering on Harbor Park Day, with boat launchings, a chicken barbecue, a sand-sculpture contest, and a crafts fair.

July: **Fireworks** on July 4 and three-day **Harbor Fest** in Wells.

August: **Sidewalk Art show** in Ogunquit.

September: **Open Homes Day**, sponsored by the Wells Historical Society. **Nature Crafts Festival** (*second weekend*) at Laudholm Farm. **Capriccio**, a celebration of the performing arts, and **Kite Day**, in Ogunquit. **Punkinfiddle** (www.punkinfiddle.org), a celebration of National Estuaries Day

October: **Ogunquit Fest** (*third week*)—ghost tours and costume parade.

December: **Christmas parade** in Wells. **Christmas by the Sea** in Ogunquit.

THE KENNEBUNKS

The Kennebunks began as a fishing stage near Cape Porpoise as early as 1602, but the community was repeatedly destroyed by Native American raids. In 1719 the present "port" was incorporated as Arundel, a name that stuck through its lucrative shipbuilding and seafaring years until 1821, when it became Kennebunkport. Later, when the novel *Arundel,* by Kenneth Roberts (born in Kennebunk), had run through 32 printings, residents gave the old name to North Kennebunkport.

That the Kennebunks prospered as a shipbuilding center is obvious from the quantity and quality of its sea captains' and shipbuilders' mansions, the presence of its brick customhouse (now the library), and the beauty of its churches.

In his 1891 guidebook, *The Pine-Tree Coast*, Samuel Adams Drake noted that "since the beginning of the century more than eight hundred vessels have been sent out from the shipyards of this river." He recalled: "When I first knew this place, both banks of the river were lined with shipyards . . . all alive with the labor of hundreds of workmen." But by the 1890s, Drake noted, shipbuilding was "moribund" and Kennebunkport had become "a well-established watering-place."

In 1872 this entire spectacular 5-mile stretch of coast—from Lords Point at the western end of Kennebunk Beach all the way to Cape Porpoise on the east—was acquired by one developer, the Sea Shore Company. Over the next couple of decades no fewer than 30 grand hotels and dozens of summer mansions evolved to accommodate the summer visitors that train service brought. The Kennebunks then shared the 1940s-to-1960s decline suffered by all Maine coastal resorts, losing all but a scattering of old hotels.

According to the locals, the Kennebunks developed an almost countercultural feel in the 1960s and '70s. Then the tourist tide again turned, and over the past few decades the area has grown increasingly upscale: Surviving hotels have been condoed, inns have been rehabbed, and dozens of B&Bs and inns have opened. Still, if you look beyond the clichés, you'll discover the real Maine here, too. Dock Square's world-class shopping district now rivals those in Palm Beach (where many retail stores have sister shops) and other swanky spots, but a walk through the historic streets of Kennebunkport is free and quite idyllic. And a meal at one of the lobster shacks is as rustic, delicious, and affordable as any on the Maine coast.

You can bed down a few steps from Dock Square's lively shops and restaurants, 2 miles away in the quiet village of Cape Porpoise, or out at Goose Rocks, where the only sound is the lapping of waves on endless sand. Most B&Bs are, however, the former sea captains' homes grouped within a few stately streets of each other, many within walking distance of both Dock Square and the open ocean.

GUIDANCE **Kennebunk/Kennebunkport Chamber of Commerce** (207-967-0857 or 1-800-982-4421; www.visitthekennebunks.com), P.O. Box 740, Kennebunk 04043. Open Mon.–Fri. year-round, plus Sat. and Sun. late May–late Oct. The information center, a yellow building on Rt. 9 just east of its junction with Rt. 35 (at the light in Lower Village), offers plenty of parking in the rear. Staff are unusually helpful, and the chamber publishes an excellent free guide. An office in the **Brick Store Museum** (see *Museums*) in Kennebunk is open Apr.–mid-Dec.

Kennebunkport Information and Hospitality Center (207-967-8600). Open May–mid-Dec. Restrooms and information at Dock Square.

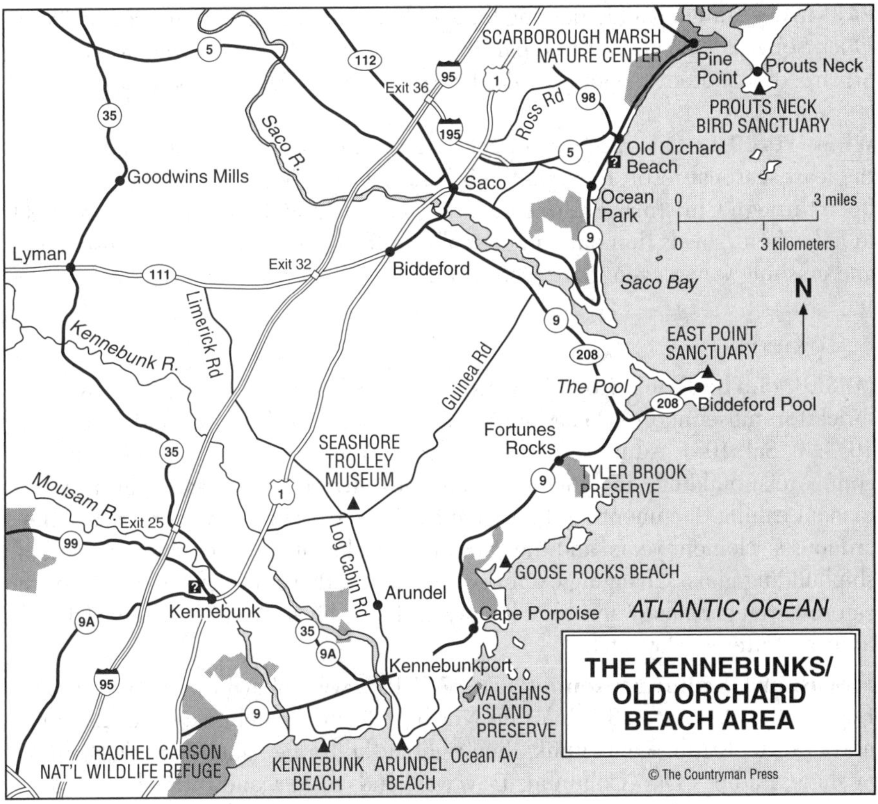

GETTING THERE *By air:* You can fly your own plane into **Sanford Airport**; otherwise, **Portland International Jetport** (see "Portland Area") is served by various airlines and taxi services.

By car: Drive up I-95 to exit 25 and take Rt. 35 into Kennebunk, on to Kennebunkport and Kennebunk Beach. Coming up Rt. 1, take Rt. 9 east from Wells.

By train: See *Amtrak* in "What's Where." The **Downeaster** service from Boston's North Station takes about two hours and stops in Wells.

GETTING AROUND Kennebunk is a busy commercial center straddling the strip of Rt. 1 between the Mousam and Kennebunk Rivers. A 10-minute ride down Summer St. (Rt. 35) brings you to Kennebunkport. Then there are Kennebunk Beach, Cape Porpoise, Goose Rocks Beach, Cape Arundel, and Kennebunk Lower Village. Luckily, free detailed maps are readily available.

Intown Trolley Co. (207-967-3686; www.intowntrolley.com), Kennebunkport, offers narrated sightseeing tours; $13 adults, $6 ages 14 and under, free for those 2 and under. The tickets are good for the day, so you can also use them to shuttle between Dock Square and Kennebunk Beach. Also available for private charter.

Bicycles work well here and are a good way to handle the mile between Dock Square and Kennebunk Beach.

PARKING A municipal fee parking lot is hidden behind the commercial block in Dock Square. You can find free parking at 30 North St., a short walk to Dock Square, and another fee lot near the bridge in Lower Village. Good luck!

WHEN TO COME One nice side effect of the Kennebunk tourist trade: This is the least seasonal resort town on the Southern Coast. Most inns and shops stay open through Christmas Prelude in early December, and many never close. Visit in fall, when crowds thin out and the colorful foliage makes the old mansions and crashing waves even more picturesque.

✷ To See

MUSEUMS The Brick Store Museum and Archives (207-985-4802; www.brickstoremuseum.org), 117 Main St., Kennebunk. Open year-round, Tue.–Fri. 10–4:30, Sat. 10–1. Admission is by donation. This block of early-19th-century commercial buildings, including William Lord's **Brick Store** (1825), hosts a permanent exhibit documenting the region from the days of Native Americans, the arduous settlement years, and the subsequent colonial era through the period of shipbuilding glory. Changing exhibits focus on a wide variety of subjects. Visitors can research genealogy and local history in the archives. Architectural walking tours are offered May–Oct.

✐ **Seashore Trolley Museum** (207-967-2712; www.trolleymuseum.org), 195 Log Cabin Rd., located 3.2 miles up North St. from Kennebunkport or 2.8 miles north on Rt. 1 from Kennebunk, then right at the traffic light. Open daily, rain or shine, Father's Day–Columbus Day, weekends in May and through Oct.; $8 adults, $5.50 ages 6–16, $6 seniors over 60, children under 6 free. This nonprofit museum preserves the history of the trolley era, displaying more than 200 vehicles from all over the world. The impressive collection began in 1939, when the last open-sided Biddeford–Old Orchard Beach trolley was retired to an open field straddling the old Atlantic Shore Line. A 4-mile trolley excursion takes visitors through woods and fields along a stretch once traveled by summer guests en route to Old Orchard Beach. Interesting fact: In recent years the U.S. Marines have used the museum for "urban training operations"—war games with paintball guns. Boy scouts come here on the merit badge programs.

Kennebunkport Historical Society (207-967-2751; www.kporthistory.org) has three facilities. **Pasco Exhibit Center**, 125 North St., $3 adults, is open year-round, Tue.–Fri. 10–4; mid-June–mid-Oct., Sat. 10–1. The **Town House School**, at 135 North St., is used for research, $10, and is open year-round, Tue.–Fri. 10–1. Free on-site parking at both. The society also maintains the **Nott House**, 8 Maine St. (no parking), a Greek Revival mansion with Doric columns, original wallpapers, carpets, and furnishings. Open mid-June–Labor Day, Tue., Wed., and Fri. 1–4, Sat. 10–1, Thu. 10–4; Labor Day–Columbus Day, closed on Tue. Guided walking tours available. $5 adults. Gift shop.

HISTORIC SITES **Wedding Cake House**, Summer St. (Rt. 35), Kennebunk. This privately owned 1826 house is laced up and down with ornate white gingerbread. Legend has it that a local sea captain had to rush off to sea before a proper wedding cake could be baked, but he more than made up for it later.

South Congregational Church, Temple St., Kennebunkport. Just off Dock Square, built in 1824 with a Christopher Wren–style cupola and belfry; Doric columns added in 1912.

Louis T. Graves Memorial Library (207-967-2778), 18 Maine St., Kennebunkport. Built in 1813 as a bank, which went bust, it later served as a customhouse. It was subsequently donated to the library association by artist Abbott Graves, whose pictures alone make it worth a visit. You can still see the bank vault and the sign from the custom collector's office. At the Perkins House next door, the book saleroom is full of bargains.

First Parish Unitarian Church, Main St., Kennebunk. Built between 1772 and 1773 with an Asher Benjamin–style steeple added between 1803 and 1804, along with a Paul Revere bell. In 1838 the interior was divided in two levels, with the church proper elevated to the second floor. Popular legend holds that the pulpit was carved from a single log found floating in the Caribbean Sea and towed back to Maine.

SCENIC DRIVE Ocean Avenue, starting in Kennebunkport, follows the **Kennebunk River** for a mile to Cape Arundel and the open ocean, then winds past many magnificent summer homes. Stop along **Parson's Way,** located off Ocean Ave. on the right just after the Colony Hotel, and enjoy the park benches that take advantage of the magnificent view of the mouth of the Kennebunk River and **Gooch's Beach**. Continue north and east to **Walker's Point**, former president George H. W. Bush's summer estate (it fills a private 11-acre peninsula). Built by his grandfather in 1903, its position is uncannily ideal for use as a president's summer home, moated by water on three sides yet clearly visible from pullouts along the avenue. In July and August gawkers lined up by the dozen in the hope of catching a glimpse of our 43rd president, George W. Continue along the ocean (you don't have to worry about driving too slowly, because everyone else is, too). Follow the road to **Cape Porpoise**, site of the area's original 1600s settlement. The cove is still a base for lobster and commercial fishing boats, and the village is a good place to lunch or dine. Continue along Rt. 9 to **Clock Farm Corner** (you'll know it when you see it) and turn right onto Dyke Rd. to **Goose Rocks Beach**; park and walk. Return to Rt. 9 and cross it, continuing via Goose Rocks Rd. to the Seashore Trolley Museum and then Log Cabin Rd. to Kennebunkport.

✱ To Do

BALLOONING **Balloons Over New England** (207-499-7575 or 1-800-788-5562; www.balloonsovernewengland.com), based in Kennebunk, offers flights year-round.

BICYCLING **Cape-Able Bike Shop** (207-967-4382; www.capeablebikes.com), 83 Arundel Rd. (off Log Cabin Rd.), Kennebunkport. Billed as Maine's biggest bike shop, Cape-Able rents a variety of bikes, including tandems and trail bikes. Any one of the good staff is a good source of advice. Open most of the year; in summer months, Mon.–Sat. 9–6, Sun. 8–3; closed Sun. off-season. The Kennebunks lend themselves well to exploration by bike, a far more satisfying way to go in summer than by car since you can stop and park wherever the view and urge hit you. Inquire about the **Bridle Path** (an old trolley-line route) and **Wonderbrook Park**. Guided on- and off-road tours offered.

BOATBUILDING SCHOOL **The Landing School of Boat Building and Design** (207-985-7976; www.landingschool.edu), 286 River Rd., Arundel, offers a Sept.–June program in building and designing sailing craft. Visitors welcome if you call ahead.

CARRIAGE RIDES **Rockin' Horse Stables** (207-967-4288; www.geocities.com/rockinhorsestables), 245 Arundel Rd., Kennebunkport. Tour Kennebunkport's historic district (25 minutes) in a spiffy white vis-à-vis carriage with burgundy-colored velvet seats and antique lanterns. Sleigh rides in winter.

FISHING Deep-sea fishing is available on the charter boat *Lady J* (207-985-7304; www.ladyjcharters.com).

Stone Coast Anglers, Inc. (207-985-6005; www.stonecoastanglers.com), Kennebunk. They specialize in chartered boat trips along the coast for up to three guests as well as guided wading trips for saltwater and game fish.

GOLF **Cape Arundel Golf Club** (207-967-3494), 19 River Rd., Kennebunkport, 18 holes. The local links former president George H. W. Bush frequents are open to the public Apr.–Nov. except 11–2:30. **Webhannet Golf Club** (207-967-

2061), 26 Golf Club Dr., off Sea Rd., Kennebunk Beach, 18 holes. Open to the public, but semiprivate, with limited tee times especially in July and Aug. **Dutch Elm Golf Course** (207-282-9850), Arundel, 18 holes; cart and club rentals, lessons, pro shop, snack bar, putting greens. ✐ **Hillcrest Golf** (207-967-4661), Kennebunk. Open daily 8 AM–dark; balls and clubs furnished.

KAYAKING **Harbor Adventures** (207-363-8466; www.harboradventures.com), Kennebunkport. Guided sea kayak tours for individuals and groups.

SAILING ***Bellatrix* Sailing Trips** (207-967-8685; www.sailingtrips.com), Kennebunkport. Up to six passengers can experience the rugged southern Maine coastline from the comfortable cockpit of a 37-foot ocean racing yacht. Guests are even allowed to take the helm, and free sailing instruction is available if desired. $50 for a half-day sail.

Schooner *Eleanor* (207-967-8809; www.gwi.net/schoonersails). Two-hour sailing trips aboard a traditional, gaff-rigged, 55-foot schooner set sail from the docks at the Arundel Wharf Restaurant.

WHALE-WATCHING AND OCEAN TOURS This is a popular departure point for whale-watching on Jefferies Ledge, about 20 miles offshore. If you have any tendency toward seasickness, be sure to choose a calm day or take antinausea medication. Chances are you'll see more than a dozen whales. Frequently sighted species include finbacks, minkes, rights, and humpbacks. **First Chance** (207-967-5507 or 1-800-767-2628; www.firstchancewhalewatch.com), 4 Western Ave. in the Lower Village (at the bridge), also offers a scenic lobster cruise.

✷ Winter Pastimes

CROSS-COUNTRY SKIING **Harris Farm** (207-499-2678; www.harrisfarm.com), 252 Buzzell Rd., Dayton. A 500-acre dairy farm with more than 20 miles of trails. Equipment rentals available, including snowshoes and ice skates. Located 1.5 miles from the Rt. 5 and Rt. 35 intersection.

SLEIGH RIDES **Rockin' Horse Stables** (207-967-4288), 245 Arundel Rd., Kennebunkport, offers 30- to 40-minute sleigh rides on a 100-acre farm.

✷ Green Space

BEACHES The Kennebunks discourage day-trippers by requiring a permit to park at major beaches. Day, week, and seasonal passes must be secured from the chamber of commerce, town hall, police department, or local lodging places. You can also park in one of the town lots and walk, bike, or take a trolley to the beach.

Goose Rocks Beach, a few miles north of Kennebunkport Village on Rt. 9, is the area's most beautiful beach: a magnificent wide, smooth stretch of silver-white sand backed by high dunes. Children here seem to mimic their less frenetic 19th-century counterparts, doing wonderfully old-fashioned things like flying kites, playing paddleball, and making sand castles.

Kim Grant

GOOSE ROCKS BEACH

Kennebunk and **Gooch's Beaches** in Kennebunk are both long, wide strips of firm sand backed by Beach Ave., divided by Oak's Neck. Beyond Gooch's Beach, take Great Hill Rd. along the water to **Strawberry Island**, a great place to walk and examine tidal pools. Please don't picnic. Keep going and you come to **Mother's Beach**, small and very sandy.

Arundel Beach, near the Colony Hotel at the mouth of the Kennebunk River, offers nice rocks for climbing and good beachcombing for shell and beach-glass enthusiasts.

NATURE PRESERVES ✐ ♿ **Rachel Carson National Wildlife Refuge** (207-646-9226; TDD/voice 1-800-437-1220). Headquarters for this almost 50-mile, 5,000-acre preserve is just south of the Kennebunkport line at 321 Port Rd. (Rt. 9) in Wells. The refuge is divided among 10 sites along Maine's Southern Coast. Pick up a leaflet guide to the mile-long, wheelchair-accessible nature trail here. Kayakers can enter the refuge traveling up the rivers, but no put-ins or takeouts allowed to avoid disturbing the wildlife. (Also see Laudholm Farm in "Ogunquit and Wells.")

Kennebunkport Conservation Trust (www.thekennebunkportconservationtrust.org), P.O. Box 7028, Cape Porpoise 04014, maintains several properties. These include the **Tyler Brook Preserve** near Goose Rocks, the 148-acre **Emmons Preserve** along the Batson River (access from unpaved Gravelly Rd., off Beachwood Rd.), the 740-acre **Kennebunkport Town Forest**, and the **Vaughns Island Preserve**, which offers nature trails on a wooded island separated from the mainland by two tidal creeks. Cellar holes of historic houses are accessible by foot from three hours after to three hours before high tide. The Trust also maintains 14-acre **Butler Preserve** on the Kennebunk River, including Picnic Rock.

The Nature Conservancy (207-729-5181) owns 135 acres of the **Kennebunk Plains Preserve** and assists in the management of 650 state-owned acres in West Kennebunk (take Rt. 99 toward Sanford) with nearly 4 miles of shoreline on the Mousam River in Kennebunk.

East Point Sanctuary, off Rt. 9 (east of Goose Rocks Beach) in Biddeford Pool. A 30-acre Maine Audubon property, well known to birders, who flock here during migrating seasons. Beautiful any time of year. From Rt. 9 turn right just beyond Goose Rocks Beach onto Fortune Rocks Beach Rd. to Lester B. Orcutt Blvd.; turn right, drive almost to the end, and look for a chain-link fence and AUDUBON sign. The trail continues along the golf course and sea.

WALKS **Henry Parsons Park**, Ocean Ave., is a path along the rocks leading to Spouting Rock and Blowing Cave, both sights to see at midtide. A great way to view the beautiful homes along Ocean Ave.

St. Anthony Monastery and Shrine (207-967-2011), Kennebunkport. Some 20 acres of peaceful riverside fields and forests on Beach Rd., now maintained by Lithuanian Franciscans as a shrine and retreat. Visitors are welcome; gift shop. (See St. Anthony's Franciscan Monastery and Guesthouse in *Other Lodging*.)

✷ Lodging

The Kennebunks represent one of the Maine coast's largest concentrations of inns and B&Bs, with more than 80 lodging places, or 1,400 rooms. We list a number of options in different price ranges, but still just a fraction of what's available. These places tend to stay open at least through the first two weekends in December, when the town celebrates Christmas Prelude, and many are open year-round.

All listings are in Kennebunkport 04046 unless otherwise noted.

TOP-DOLLAR INNS AND B&BS **Captain Lord Mansion** (207-967-3141 or 1-800-522-3141; www.captainlord.com), P.O. Box 800, at the corner of Pleasant and Green Sts. Open year-round. This three-story Federal home, built in 1812, is topped with a widow's walk from which guests can contemplate the town and sea. All 16 rooms have a gas fireplace and private bath; large high beds are equipped with steps to climb into them. The decor here is possibly the most elaborate in the state, and the Merchant Captain's Suite may have the most elaborate bathroom, including its gas fireplace. The Captain's Garden House holds four more ornate rooms. This is home when what you covet is perfection and every amenity. $289–499 per room in high season, $149–399 off-season, breakfast and tea included. Spa services include massage for couples and facials.

White Barn Inn (207-967-2321; www.whitebarninn.com), 37 Beach Ave., P.O. Box 560C, Kennebunk 04043. Open year-round. The "barn" is now an elegant dining room (see *Dining Out*) attached to the inn. Built in the 1860s as a farmhouse, later enlarged as the Forest Hills House, this complex lies midway between Dock Square and Kennebunk Beach. Courteous staff wear black, a sleek hotel version of the brown-robed Franciscan monks nearby (see St. Anthony's Franciscan Monastery and Guesthouse in *Other Lodging*). Choose an antiques-furnished room in the original farmhouse; a suite in the carriage house with four-poster king bed, fireplace, and marble bath with whirlpool tub; a cottage suite with specially crafted furnishings, a double-

RESORT HOTEL

The Colony Hotel (207-967-3331 or 1-800-552-2363; www.thecolonyhotel.com), 140 Ocean Ave. and King's Hwy. Open May–Oct. With 124 rooms (all with private bath) in three buildings, this is among the last of New England's coastal resorts maintained in the grand style. The Colony is also environmentally conscious, placing recycling bins in guest rooms, composting, and earning the accolade "Certified Wildlife Habitat" from the National Wildlife Federation. None of these practices, however, diminishes the luxuriousness of the hotel with historic Waverly wallpaper and handsome old furniture. Set on a rise overlooking the point at which the Kennebunk River meets the Atlantic, it's been owned by the Boughton family since 1948; many guests have been coming for generations. Amenities include a heated saltwater pool, a private beach, an 18-hole putting green, and a social and nature walk program. A three-night minimum is required for weekend reservations for July and Aug. $185–800 single or double per day includes a full breakfast; plus $5-per-person service charge. Pets are $25 per day.

THE COLONY HOTEL COMBINES OLD-FASHIONED VIRTUES WITH SUSTAINABILITY.

Nancy English

sided fireplace, Jacuzzi, and steam shower. Guests breakfast in the inn's original, old-fashioned dining room; some rooms overlook the landscaped pool area. $320–860 per couple for rooms includes breakfast, afternoon tea and aperitifs, and use of touring bikes. Three waterfront cottages are also for rent. A 5.35 percent housekeeping fee is added.

"I" **The Beach House** (207-967-3850; www.beachhseinn.com), 211 Beach Ave., Kennebunk 04043. Open year-round. An elegant inn with 35 rooms across the street from Kennebunk Beach. The sitting room and breakfast room are posh; a smallish corner room with magnificent views has an immaculate tiled bathroom. Breakfast is a bountiful continental spread, and afternoon tea and aperitifs—Taylor Port and E&J Brandy—are served. Bikes included. The 35 rooms are $199–525 Apr.–Nov., $189–399 off-season, plus a 5.35 percent housekeeping fee.

MODERATELY EXPENSIVE INNS AND B&BS

On the water

Cape Arundel Inn (207-967-2125; www.capearundelinn.com), 208 Ocean Ave., P.O. Box 530A. Open Mar.–New Year's Eve. The most dramatic location in town, facing the open ocean with just the estate of former president George H. W. Bush interrupting the water view. Jack Nahil, former owner of the White Barn Inn and On the Marsh Tavern, has transformed this 19th-century mansion "cottage" room by unique room. Seven rooms in the main house and six in an addition are now fully enhanced by his good taste in furnishings; those in the addition all have picture windows and decks facing the water, parking in back, and TVs. A carriage house water-view suite (up a flight of stairs) has a deck and sitting area. The living room is hung with interesting art, some of it Nahil's own. The dining room, which is open for dinner to the public (see *Dining Out*), is deservedly well loved. $295–375 in-season, from $150 off-season, includes a "creative continental" breakfast.

Tides Inn By-the-Sea (207-967-3757; www.tidesinnbythesea.com), 252 Kings Hwy., Goose Rocks Beach. Open June–Oct. Marie Henriksen and her daughter Kristin Blomberg continue to make this very Victorian inn a delightful anachronism. No in-room phones or TVs, loads of charming chintz and lace—even a ghost who shakes one bed upstairs—mean a true Maine coast getaway. A few short miles from Dock Square, the inn overlooks the area's long and silvery Goose Rocks Beach. Built by Maine's foremost shingle-style architect, John Calvin Stevens, in 1899, the Tides Inn has hosted Teddy Roosevelt and Sir Arthur Conan Doyle. The Belvidere Club serves great meals (see *Dining Out*), and rooms in the main building feature new, bigger windows. We

THE CAPE ARUNDEL INN OVERLOOKS THE OCEAN.

Nancy English

were lulled to sleep in a front room listening to the waves. High-season rates range $195–325 for ocean-view (two guests) and family rooms (four guests); less in the off-season. Next door, **Tides Too** offers two-bedroom oceanfront suites.

Seaside Inn & Cottages (207-967-4461; www.kennebunkbeach.com), 80 Beach Ave., Kennebunk 04043. The motor inn is open year-round; cottages are rented May–Oct. An attractive complex formed by a 1720s homestead, a 1756 inn, a modern 22-room motor inn, and 10 housekeeping cottages—all set on 20 landscaped acres on a private beach next to one of Maine's best public strands. This property has been in the Gooch-Severance family for 13 generations. The homestead, which was built as a tavern (the tavern keeper operated the ferry across the mouth of the Kennebunk River here), is now rented as a cottage. The cheery breakfast room is a former boathouse for the 19th-century inn that stood here until the 1950s. Motor inn rooms feature two queen beds, air-conditioning, a discreet cable TV, phone, and balcony or patio. Cottages, which vary in size and view, are per month in July and August, per week the rest of the season. One-week minimum in oceanfront rooms and two-day minimum in terrace-side rooms in high season. Inn rooms are $229–239 per night, including continental breakfast, less off-season; cottage rates range from $995 weekly to $9,500 monthly. Pets accepted in all cottages.

Bufflehead Cove Inn (207-967-3879; www.buffleheadcove.com), Box 499, off Rt. 35. Open May–Nov. This hidden gem, sequestered on six acres at the end of a dirt road and overlooking an 8-foot-deep tidal cove, sits less than a mile from the village of Kennebunkport. Harriet Gott, a native of nearby Cape Porpoise, and her husband, Jim, and their son Erin offer four good-looking guest rooms, a suite, and a separate deluxe cottage. River View cottage lies off by itself, with a deck, kitchen, wood-burning fireplace, and whirlpool tub. The inn living room has a hearth and deep window seats. $155–375 includes a full breakfast on the white porch if the weather is fine, and afternoon wine and cheese.

♿ **Kennebunkport Inn** (207-967-2621 or 1-800-248-2621; www.kennebunkportinn.com), 1 Dock Square, P.O. Box 111. Open year-round. Owners Debbie Lennon and Tom Nill have redecorated most of the 50 rooms; number 303 is now a "mansion room" with canopied four-poster, gas fireplace, and bathtub. The inn has four sections—the main house (originally an 1890s mansion), a 1980s Federal-style addition, a 1930s river house with smaller rooms, and the Wharfside, with 14 rooms including two family suites. In summer a small, enticing pool on the terrace offers respite from the Dock Square hubbub, and guests can dine in the **Port Tavern and Grill** year-round. The cocktail lounge with a huge old bar offers evening piano music. High-season rates $199–329 per room, less off-season.

♿ **The Captain Fairfield Inn** (207-967-4454 or 1-800-322-1928; www.captainfairfield.com), P.O. Box 2690, corner of Pleasant and Green Sts. Open year-round. Owners Rob and Leigh Blood have put the final touches on this elegant inn. The lawn stretches back across the width of the block, where guests make themselves comfortable with cookies and lemonade served in the afternoon. Notable among the nine handsome rooms, the Library features a private porch and double whirlpool; Sweet Liberty has a huge, newly tiled shower. Sunday breakfast always includes blueberry crêpes. $225–340 in high season, $145–285 in low.

♿ **The Breakwater Inn, Hotel and Spa** (207-967-5333; www.thebreakwaterinn.com), 127 Ocean Ave., P.O. Box 560C, across from Mabel's Lobster Claw. A 19th-century riverside complex renovated in 2002 by Laurie Bongiorno. Open year-round, the 37 rooms are split between three buildings. Each room is equipped with CD player, TV, phone, air-conditioning, and a granite-and-tile bath; rooms vary in view and size. The inn, made up of two buildings, has rooms on four floors and no elevator; only the hotel has an elevator. Guests can dine at Stripers Waterside Restaurant (see *Eating Out*). In-season rates as high as $399 at the inn and $475 for a suite in the hotel, and include continental breakfast and afternoon tea; $150–349 off-season and midweek. Waterside Cottage is $650 a night. A 5.35 percent housekeeping fee is added. Request specific details about your room before booking to keep confusion at a minimum.

Old Fort Inn (207-967-5353 or 1-800-828-FORT; www.oldfortinn.com), 8 Old Fort Ave., P.O. Box M. Open mid-Apr.–mid-Dec. Stepping into David and Sheila Aldrich's quiet respite is like falling into a plush wing chair after a long, hard day. The inn, set on 15 acres, feels miles away from humming Dock Square yet it's actually little more than a mile's walk. The 16 guest rooms in the stone-and-brick carriage house are filled with four-poster beds and elegant furnishings, and all include TV, phone, and air-conditioning. The property includes a heated pool, tennis court, horseshoes, and shuffleboard. Two-night minimum during high season. $175–390; less off-season. Rates include a full buffet breakfast.

The Captain Jefferds Inn (207-967-2311 or 1-800-839-6844; www.captainjefferdsinn.com), 5 Pearl St., Box 691. Eric and Sarah Lindblom are your hosts at this handsome Federal-era mansion with two suites and 13 rooms; nine have wood or gas fireplaces and all have air-conditioning, feather beds, and down comforters. Baxter, in the carriage house, is decorated in a "Maine camp" style—except for the two-person whirlpool with a round-stone surround. A screen porch is one feature of the suites. First-floor Chatham has a four-poster and two wingback chairs by the fireplace. The spacious common rooms include a sun porch where tea and coffee are always available. $150–360, depending on the season.

Maine Stay Inn and Cottages (207-967-2117 or 1-800-950-2117; www.mainestayinn.com), 34 Maine St., Box 500A. Open year-round. A terrific place for families with children, the inn offers six guest rooms in the main house and 11 suites in five cottages nestled in nicely landscaped grounds—including a full swing set. The house was built in 1860 by Melville Walker and given to his wife as a Christmas present five years later. A wicker-filled wraparound porch, a spiral staircase, and several ornate fireplace mantels sustain the history.

A full breakfast and afternoon tea are offered by owners Janice and George Yankowski. $219–299 in-season, $109–189 off-season.

♿ **The 1802 House** (207-967-5632 or 1-800-932-5632; www.1802inn.com), 15 Locke St. P.O. Box 646-A. Open year-round. Linda Van Goor and Jay Durepo offer six guest rooms, all with queen four-poster bed, five with fireplace, and four with whirlpool tub. A three-room suite with a fireplace, fridge, double shower, Roman garden room, and double whirlpool tub overlooks a private deck. The house, shaded by large pines and on the 15th fairway of the Cape Arundel Golf Course, has an out-in-the-country feel; golf packages available. $189–369 in high season, $139–299 in low, includes full breakfast.

MODERATELY PRICED INNS AND B&BS ♿ **The Green Heron** (207-967-3315; www.greenheroninn.com), 126 Ocean Ave. P.O. Box 2578. Open year-round except for two weeks in January. A friendly little hotel with a casual atmosphere, owned and run by Tony Kusuma and Dan Oswald, The Green Heron has 10 small but pleasant rooms and a coveside cottage with private bath, air-conditioning, and TV; some also have a refrigerator and a fireplace. "Portland Head," with oak furniture, shares a deck on the inlet on the inn's west side, where herons and other waterbirds find their own breakfast. In-season $165–310 for a double, off-season $130–230, including a full breakfast and afternoon refreshments.

Chetwynd House Inn (207-967-2235; www.chetwyndhouse.com), 4 Chestnut St. P.O. Box 130. Open year-round. In 1972 Susan Chetwynd opened Chetwynd, Kennebunkport's first B&B. Now owned by Robert Knowles, her son, it remains a gracious 1840s home near Dock Square. The four antiques-furnished guest rooms have private bath, TV, refrigerator, and air-conditioning; a top-floor junior suite has skylights and a river view. Generous breakfasts—with eggs cooked to order and a quarter melon with peaches, blueberries, and bananas or other fruit—are served family-style at the dining room table. $170–210 in-season; discounts come with off-season specials.

Harbor Inn (207-967-2074; www.harbor-inn.com), 90 Ocean Ave., P.O. Box 538A. Open year-round. Kathy and Barry Jones, longtime Port residents and owners of Cove House (see below), filled this fine old house with flowers and their warm friendliness. The five rooms and two-room suite (all with private bath) feature a mix of family antiques, paintings, and prints, and the long front porch is lined with wicker. It's a short walk to the ocean, a longer but pleasant walk to Dock Square. $155–180 for rooms in-season, $95–135 off-season. Woodbine Cottage in-season is $225 a night or $1,500 weekly.

Cove House Bed & Breakfast (207-967-3704; www.covehouse.com), 11 S. Maine St. Open year-round. Decorated with period antiques and gorgeous Oriental rugs, this inn features architectural details such as a pretty side porch, original fireplace mantels, and richly burnished, foot-wide plank floors. Barry doubles as a volunteer EMT and fireman, and his relaxed manner and Maine accent lend a refreshing authenticity to the place. Cove House is within walking distance of a beach and easy bicycling distance of Dock Square. Two of the four pleasant guest rooms have a private bath. Inn rooms are $150; $850 per week for Cove Cottage in July and Aug. (three-night minimum; when available, $150 a night), breakfast is included.

The Waldo Emerson Inn (207-985-4250 or 1-877-521-8776; www.waldoemersoninn.com), 108 Summer St. (Rt. 35), Kennebunk 04043. This special house was built in 1784 by a shipbuilder who inherited the land and original 1753 cottage (the present kitchen) from Waldo Emerson, the great-uncle of the famous poet and essayist. The building was later a stop on the Underground Railroad. John and Kathy Daamen offer four cozy guest rooms with private bath and air-conditioning; two include a fireplace. Each is handsomely decorated with antique wallpaper and period details. A quilt store is on the property and the Wedding Cake House is next door. $95–155 per couple includes a full gourmet breakfast and afternoon tea in one of the two handsome 18th-century parlors (one with a large-screen TV).

OTHER LODGING **St. Anthony's Franciscan Monastery and Guest House** (207-967-4865; www.franciscanguesthouse.com), 26 Beach Ave., Kennebunk 04043. Open mid-May–Dec. With private bath, air-conditioning, and television, the 60 rooms here have the feeling of Maine the way it used to be. The rooms at this 1908 estate on the Kennebunk River were converted to a guesthouse in the 1960s; the monks live in the Tudor great house. The 66-acre garden is open to the public year-round during daylight hours (no pets), and walking the trails might take an hour and a half, past formal gardens and the Stations of the Cross, Our Lady of Lourdes, and other shrines and fountains. A modern abstract statue, with colored glass from the Vatican Pavilion at the 1964 World's Fair, stands beside the monastery. Maps of the trees and shrubs planted under Frederick Law Olmsted's design, and of the shrines, are available. $80–135 in-season, $60–80 off-season, with breakfast made by the Lithuanian cook—a cross between a European and an American breakfast that includes homemade farmer's cheese, raisin bread, carrot bread, and potato bread.

🐾 ✎ ♿ **Yachtsman Lodge and Marina** (207-967-2511; www.yachtsmanlodge.com), Ocean Ave., P.O. Box 560C. Open late April and into the fall. This 30-room inn is great for the cruising crowd, who can sail right up the Kennebunk River to the lodge and take advantage of its 59-slip marina. The Yachtsman features rooms decorated to resemble the inside of a yacht, with private riverside patios. $175–379 includes continental breakfast in the marble-tiled breakfast room or under the pergola. Children and pets are okay and wheelchair access is easy. Bicycle and canoe rentals are free for guests.

✿ 🐾 ✎ **Shorelands** (207-985-4460 or 1-800-99-BEACH; www.shorelands.com), Rt. 9, P.O. Box 769. Open May–Oct. A family-owned, family-geared motel and cottage complex of 28 units ranging from cottages to small motel rooms, all within walking distance of the beach. Facilities include outdoor pool, outdoor hot tub, yard games, horseshoes, basketball, lobster cookers, and gas grills.

$75–175 in-season, $49–149 off-season, with $10 additional per night Memorial Day and $20 Columbus Day weekends. Weekly rates, off-season packages. "We're not posh," they say, and their many repeat customers like it that way.

✱ Where to Eat

DINING OUT ♿ **Academe at the Kennebunk Inn** (207-985-3351; www.thekennebunkinn.com), 45 Main St. Kennebunk. Open Wed.–Sat. for dinner; daily for the more informal tavern menu, lunch on weekdays. Chef-owners Brian O'Hea and Shanna Horner O'Hea make high-quality meals at a moderate price. Bacon-wrapped meatloaf, fish 'n' chips, and braised short rib with brie, mushroom, and fig ravioli are on the Academe menu; grilled pizza, sandwiches, burgers on the Sun.–Mon. dinner menu. Entrées $14–23.

Cape Arundel Inn (207-967-2125), Ocean Ave., Kennebunkport. Open daily mid-Apr.–Dec. for dinner, closed Mon. off-season. Jack Nahil, one of the area's most highly respected restaurateurs, has made this a superb dining room, matching its great location facing the ocean with skilled cooking that draws loyal customers from near and far. Chef Rich Lemoine extols his "fabulous staff," many of whom have worked with Nahil for decades. Certainly the service feels seamless, and the care is both genuine and unaffected. Lobster stew is equally perfect, as is rack of lamb, prime sirloin *au poivre,* and halibut, whichever way they are doing it when you dine here. A pianist plays every night in the summer.

White Barn Inn (207-967-2321), 37 Beach Ave., Kennebunkport. Open for dinner year-round Mon.–Sat. (except Jan.), daily in summer. Reservations required with credit card; $25 per-person fee charged if canceled less than 24 hours in advance. This award-winning restaurant is set in two restored 19th-century barns with a three-story glassed rear wall, exposed beams, and extravagant seasonal floral displays. Original art, hotel silver, and fine linens are accessories to extraordinary meals. The four-course prix fixe menu, under Chef Jonathan Cartwright, changes frequently. In 2007 dinner started with quail breast with Quebec foie gras, and went on to chilled pea soup, roast cod with morels and pea and lobster ravioli or blue cheese and bone marrow glazed beef tenderloin; roasted banana soufflé with chocolate ice cream could complete the evening. Jackets required. $91 prix fixe plus tax, beverage, and gratuity.

On the Marsh Tavern (207-967-2299; www.onthemarsh.com), Rt. 9, Kennebunk Lower Village. Open daily for dinner May–Oct.; closed Mon. and Tue. off-season. Continental dining with style overlooking a lovely salt marsh. Executive Chef Jeff Savage takes pride in his high-quality ingredients. Grilled Quebec foie gras is a standard appetizer with truffle demiglace, and Maine crab bake with polenta matsutake features locally foraged mushrooms. Deconstructed beef Wellington is topped with foie gras torchon and duxelles, and seared diver scallops with lobster risotto and baby toymoi, a kind of Asian cabbage. The wines are wonderful; there are 240 to choose from. Entrées $21–35.

The Belvidere Club at the Tides Inn By-the-Sea (207-967-3757), Goose Rocks Beach, 6 miles northeast of Dock Square. Open mid-May–mid-Oct. for dinner. Kristin Blomberg and Marie Henriksen added to their inn a 19th-century mahogany bar, salvaged from the demolished Shawmut Inn in Kennebunkport (word has it the presidential press corps used to swap stories around the antique brass rail), and an Eastlake molding around the back shelves. Robert Rossow made the summer of 2007 "even better than before," and may return. Fried oysters with tuscan kale might be an appetizer, and organic pork loin chops or lobster al Rossow (with ricotta salata, prosciutto, cream, and spinach) might be entrées. Kids' menu. Entrées $20–36.

♿ **Bandaloop** (207-967-4994; www.bandaloop.biz), 2 Dock Square. Open daily for dinner in summer, less often in winter. A mix-and-match list of entrées and sauces appeals to any adventurous diner, but daily specials get the choices right for everyone else. How about a Coleman Ranch all-natural steak with roasted garlic gravy, or seared scallops with pineapple salsa? Entrées $15–25.

Lucas on 9 (207-967-0039; www.lucason9.com), 62 Mills Rd. (Route 9), Cape Porpoise. Open late April to mid-Dec. This cheerful, family-owned place cooks up 10 to 12 specials at both lunch and dinner. Baked stuffed haddock, lobster ravioli, and Mediterranean pasta with feta, red peppers, and olives are made by Jonathan Lane, who uses his own Cajun rub on the swordfish. Locally-picked lobster stuffs the fine lobster rolls; bread pudding with warm whiskey sauce is the signature dessert. Deborah Lane, the chef's mother, and Corey Lane, his sister, run the dining room. Entrées $7–29.

♿ **Pier 77** (207-967-8500; www.pier77restaurant.com), Pier Rd., Cape Porpoise. Open daily for lunch, dinner at 5, June–Columbus Day, Wed.–Sun. St. Patrick's Day–May and Columbus Day–Dec., closed Jan–mid-Mar. This restaurant came under new ownership in 2004 and the well-made dinners upstairs and lunches downstairs deserve the big following they've earned. Seared halibut with crispy mussels, or gumbo with andouille, scallops, prawns, crawdads, okra, and broccoli rabe are two possible dishes in summer; pulled pork sandwiches or chicken taquitos might be for lunch. Entrées $16–30.

Grissini Italian Bistro (207-967-2211; www.restaurantgrissini.com), 27 Western Ave., Kennebunkport. Open year-round, except Jan., for dinner. A northern Italian 120-seat trattoria with seasonal outdoor terrace dining and an à la carte menu. You might start with penne Bolognese, then dine on grilled salmon or portobello mushrooms layered with fresh mozzarella and polenta, or a rack of lamb with smoked bacon cannellini. Large portions. Entrées $19–29.

♿ **Stripers Waterfront Restaurant** (207-967-3625), 131–133 Ocean Ave., Kennebunkport. Open in-season daily for lunch and dinner. This upscale seafood place has a long, thin aquarium harboring little blue fish that match pale blue slip-covered chairs. Dinner entrées, like farmed striped bass with lemon caper beurre blanc ($29.50) and scallops with figs and prosciutto in vanilla balsamic ($26.50), vie with tempura-fried cod, shrimp, and scallops ($24 to $25) on a menu that includes meat dishes.

LOBSTER AND CLAMS **Nunan's Lobster Hut** (207-967-4362), Rt. 9, Cape Porpoise. Open for dinner weekends in May and then daily June to mid-Oct. A long telescope of a building full of old benches, with buoys hanging from the rafters, Nunan's has been feeding lobster lovers since 1953 when Bertha Nunan started working here, and she just retired, and her two sons and their wives are in charge, with decades of experience to guide them. The place can fill up by 5:15; people outside get a number and wait for a table. A 1.5-pound lobster comes with melted butter, potato chips, a roll, and pickles. Grilled cheese and a hamburger supply other tastes, and pie, brownies, and cheesecake are on the dessert list. Beer and wine. No credit cards.

The Clam Shack (207-967-3321 or 207-967-2560), Kennebunkport (at the bridge). Clams, lobsters, and fresh fish. A year-round seafood market and Mother's Day–Columbus Day takeout stand that's worth the wait. Other seafood markets include **Cape Porpoise Lobster Co.** (207-967-4268) in Cape Porpoise, where the locals get their fish and steamed lobster to go, and **Port Lobster** (207-967-2081), 122 Ocean Ave., Kennebunkport, which offers live or cooked lobsters packed to travel or ship, and lobster, shrimp, and crab rolls to go (several obvious waterside picnic spots are within walking distance). Other local businesses get their picked lobster here; it won't be fresher anywhere else.

THE CLAM SHACK, KENNEBUNKPORT

Kim Grant

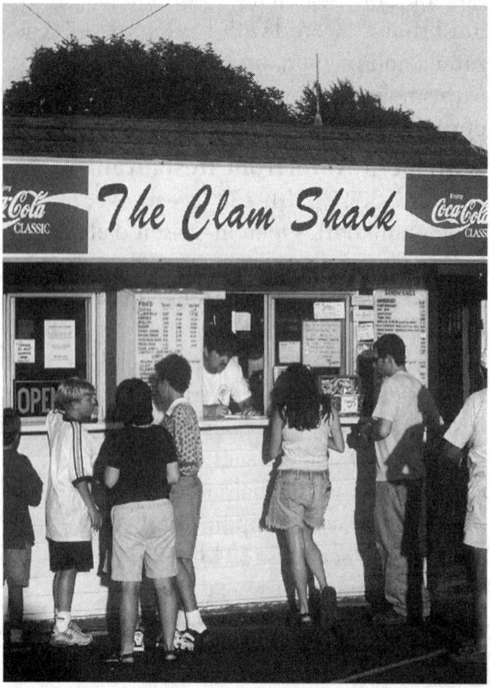

Mabel's Lobster Claw (207-967-2562), Ocean Ave., Kennebunkport. Open Apr.–early Nov. daily for lunch and dinner. An informal favorite with locals, including former president Bush. Reservations recommended for dinner. Specialties include stuffed lobster Savannah, lobster stew, and shore dinner (clam chowder, lobster, and steamed clams). The lunch special is a lobster roll in a buttery, grilled hot-dog roll. Dinner entrées $13–30.

EATING OUT **The Wayfarer** (207-967-8961), 1 Pier Rd., Cape Porpoise. Open Tue.–Sat. for breakfast, lunch, and dinner, Sun. breakfast. Closed Mon. The chowder comes with high praise, and the lobster roll we enjoyed was the best of its kind, on a toasted hot-dog bun with lots of sweet fresh lobster meat and not too much mayonnaise. Pies are homemade. BYOB from the general store across the road. Entrées $11–22.

Seafood Center (207-985-7391), 1181 Portland Rd. (Rt. 1), Arundel. Open Wed.–Sun. 11–8 year-round. The locals say this is the best place for fried seafood, with a high degree of cleanliness and frequently changed oil. You will taste the delicate fish, clams, or shrimp, and the onions in the onion rings, and not the oil.

Alisson's (207-967-4841; www.alissons.com), 5 Dock Square, Kennebunkport. Open at 11 for lunch and 5 for dinner. Casual dining in this busy, family-run spot features standards with occasional outstanding twists, like the Dee Dee Burger with blue cheese. **The Market Pub** is Dock Square's meeting place. Entrées $14–25.

Federal Jack's Restaurant & Brew Pub (207-967-4322), 8 Western Ave., Kennebunk Lower Village. Open from 11:30 for lunch and dinner, offering a variety of handcrafted ales. This is the original Shipyard Ale brewery with parking right in the thick of things. The restaurant is upstairs, spacious, sleek, and sunny, with seasonal terrace dining on the river. There are lobster rolls, burgers, seafood and pasta dishes, and the Blue Fin stout might go with the Captain Jack's Feast—chowder, lobster, and mussels. Live acoustic music on weekends. Stick with the simple stuff to eat well.

Bartley's Dockside (207-967-5050; www.bartleys-dockside.com), by the bridge, Kennebunkport. Lunch and dinner daily. Since 1977 this friendly, family-owned place has been a reliable bet for meals that range from lunchtime chowders and stews to a dinner bouillabaisse. The juicy blueberry pie comes in a bowl.

✷ Entertainment

Arundel Barn Playhouse (207-985-5552; www.arundelbarnplayhouse.com), 53 Old Post Rd. (just off Rt. 1), Arundel. Opened in 1998 in an 1800s revamped barn, this is a thoroughly professional, classic summer theater with performances Tues.–Sat., some Sundays, June–Labor Day., matinees Wed. and some Fridays. Tickets $24–35.

Hackmatack Playhouse (207-698-1807; www.hackmatack.org), 538 Rt. 9, Beaver Dam, Berwick. Local actors, rave reviews.

River Tree Center for the Arts (207-967-9120; www.rivertreearts.org), 35 Western Ave., Kennebunk. Encompassing the Chappell School of Music and the Irvine Gallery and School of Art, this multifaceted organization stages local concerts, productions, and happenings, as well as workshops in the visual and performing arts for all ages.

Also see **Federal Jack's** under *Eating Out*, and *Entertainment* in "Ogunquit and Wells."

✷ Selective Shopping

ANTIQUES SHOPS The Kennebunks are known as an antiques center, with half a dozen shops, most on Rt. 1, representing a number of dealers.

ART GALLERIES You'll find some 50 galleries, most of them seasonal; **Mast Cove Galleries** (207-967-3453) on Maine St., Kennebunkport, is touted as the "largest group gallery in the area." Pick up a free copy of the annual *Guide to Fine Art, Studios, and Galleries*, published by the **Art Guild of the Kennebunks** (207-985-2959) and available at the chamber of commerce and most galleries.

FARMS **Harris Farm** (207-499-2678; www.harrisfarm.com), Buzzell Rd., Dayton. July–Oct. Visitors are welcome to tour the dairy barn; fresh milk, eggs, produce, and maple syrup are sold. Pick-your-own pumpkins on the last Sunday in Sept. and the first two Sundays in Oct., with hayrides offered to the pumpkin patch. A short, pleasant ride up Rt. 35; call for directions.

Blackrock Farm (207-967-5783; www.blackrockfarm.net), 293 Goose Rocks Rd., Kennebunkport. A beautifully planted perennial garden and nursery with unusual plants and trees, and a pick-your-own-raspberry patch. Bring a picnic and feast your eyes on the stone walls, grape arbor, and sculpture.

SPECIAL SHOPS **Kennebunk Book Port** (207-967-3815), 10 Dock Square, Kennebunkport. Open year-round. The oldest commercial building in the Port (1775) is one of the most pleasant bookstores in New England. Climb an outside staircase into this inviting mecca, which is dedicated to reading as well as to buying. Helpful handwritten notes with recommendations from staff make browsing even easier. Books about Maine and the sea are specialties.

Tom's of Maine Natural Living Store (207-985-6331), 106 Lafayette Center, Kennebunk. Open daily year-round. This is the outlet for a variety of Tom's of Maine products made in town.

The Good Earth (207-967-4160), Dock Square, Kennebunkport. Open daily May–Oct., varying hours otherwise; closed Jan.–Mar. Stoneware in unusual designs—mugs, vases, and bowls. Great browsing in the loft showroom.

KBC Coffee & Drygoods (207-967-1261), 8 Western Ave., Kennebunkport. Hidden away down on the river beneath Federal Jack's, this is a source of Kennebunk Brewing Company ales and brew gear as well as souvenir clothing and gifts; also good for cappuccino, cookies, and muffins.

✷ Special Events

Many of the events below are listed with the Kennebunk/Kennebunkport Chamber of Commerce (207-967-0857 or 1-800-982-4421; www.visitthekennebunks.com), P.O. Box 740, Kennebunkport 04043.

February: **Wedding Expo**. **Winter Carnival Weekend** with **hay- and sleigh rides** in Kennebunk. Weekend **"February Is for Lovers"** events (207-967-0857).

June: **Métis of Maine Annual Pow-wow**—dance, rituals and crafts made by people of Native American ancestry.

July: **Bed & Breakfast Inn and Garden Tour**. Old-fashioned July 4 **picnic**, **fireworks**, and **band concert**.

August: **Riverfest** (*first Saturday*).

September: **Old-Time Fiddlers Contest and Country Music Show** (*second Saturday*).

October: **Presidential Road Race** (www.presidentialroadrace.com).

November: **Holiday Auction**. **Holiday Presents Weekend**.

December: **Christmas Prelude** (*first and second weekends*)—Dock Square is decked out for Yuletide, and there are champagne receptions, church suppers, concerts, and carols; holiday fairs and house tours.

OLD ORCHARD BEACH, SACO, AND BIDDEFORD

Old Orchard's name stems from an apple orchard, one of the first in Maine, planted in 1657 by pioneer settler Thomas Rogers. It was also one the first Maine towns to prosper by catering to tourists.

In 1837 a canny local farmer, Ebenezer C. Staples, recognized the region's summer playground potential. Initially taking in boarders on his farm for $1.50 a week, he later opened the first hotel, the still-operating Old Orchard Beach Inn. Staples's instincts proved right: The new railroads soon brought a wave of tourists from both the United States and Canada to frolic on Old Orchard's superb 7-mile-long white sand beach.

Thanks to the Grand Trunk Railroad, Old Orchard became the closest ocean beach resort to Montreal. The area, which has a large Franco-American population, is still a popular destination for French Canadian visitors, and in summer you are likely to hear Quebec-accented French spoken almost anywhere you go.

When the first pier at Old Orchard Beach was built in 1898, it stood 20 feet above and 1,800 feet out over the water and was constructed entirely of steel. The pavilions housed animals, a casino, and a restaurant. In the decades that followed, the original pier was rebuilt many times after being damaged by fire and storms, until a wider and shorter wooden pier was built in 1980.

An amusement area appeared in 1902 and grew after World War I. The 1920s brought big-name bands such as those led by Guy Lombardo and Duke Ellington to the Pier Casino, and thousands danced under a revolving crystal ball.

Fire, hard economic times, and the decline of the railroad and steamboat industries all took their toll on Old Orchard Beach over the years, but then a major revitalization plan widened sidewalks, added benches and streetlights, and passed and enforced ordinances that prevent "cruising" (repeatedly driving the same stretch of road). The result is a cleaner, more appealing, yet still lively and fun vacation spot. For families, it can't be beat, with the beach, amusement park rides, mini golf just down the road, and reasonable lodging rates.

The area is also well known for the camp meetings that began in the mid-1800s, first by Methodists, then by Baptists and the Salvation Army. These meetings continue throughout the summer in the Ocean Park community today.

Biddeford and Saco, separated by the Saco River, are often called "the twin cities." Saco is a classic Yankee town with white-clapboard mansions, a prestigious museum, and a long, dignified main street. However, it also has a rather garish strip of amusement and water parks along Rt. 1 that is a big draw in summer for families with young children.

Although it also includes the stately old seaside resort village of Biddeford Pool, the city of Biddeford is essentially a classic mill town with a strong French Canadian heritage and mammoth 19th-century brick textile mills that have largely stood idle since the 1950s.

Pine Point in Scarborough and its surrounding area is the easternmost tip of Old Orchard Beach and is often a less crowded, quieter spot to visit. A large saltwater marsh in Scarborough is also good for quiet relaxation and exploring by foot, bike, and canoe.

GUIDANCE **Old Orchard Beach Chamber of Commerce** (207-934-2500; to get a free vacation planner by mail, 1-800-365-9386; www.oldorchardbeach maine.com), P.O. Box 600 (1st St.), Old Orchard Beach 04064, maintains a year-round walk-in information center (open 8:30–4:30 weekdays, also Sat. and Sun., June–Aug.) and offers help with reservations.

Biddeford-Saco Chamber of Commerce & Industry (207-282-1567; www .biddefordsacochamber.org), 110 Main St., Saco Island, Suite 1202, Saco 04072. Stocks many local brochures; helpful, friendly staff.

GETTING THERE *By air:* **Portland International Jetport** is 13 miles north, and rental cars are available at the airport. You can also fly your own plane into **Sanford Airport**.

By hired car: **D&P Associated Limousine Services** (207-865-0203, 1-800-750-6757), 96 Oakland Ave., Westbrook 04092, and **Maine Limousine Service** (207-883-0222, 1-800-646-0068; www.mainelimo.com), P.O. Box 1478, Scarborough 04070 can also pick you up and bring you to the region.

By car: Exits 36 and 42 off the Maine Turnpike (I-95) take you easily to Rt. 9 and the center of Old Orchard Beach. You can also find the town from Rt. 1.

By train: The **Downeaster** (1-800-USA-RAIL; www.thedowneaster.com), Amtrak's train service between Boston and Portland, makes five stops a day year-round at Saco and seasonally, May–Oct., at Old Orchard Beach.

GETTING AROUND From many accommodations in Old Orchard Beach, you are close enough to walk to the pier, the town's center of activity. **Shuttle Bus**, the local transportation service, connects the downtowns of Biddeford, Saco, Portland, and Old Orchard Beach. Call 207-282-5408 for schedules.

PARKING There are a number of privately owned lots in the center of Old Orchard Beach and one municipal lot. Most charge $5–15 for any length of time—10 minutes or all day. There are meters on the street if you don't mind circling a few times to catch an available one, but at 15 minutes for a quarter, you're better off in lots if you plan to stay long.

WHEN TO COME Biddeford is especially worth visiting during La Kermesse, the colorful four-day Franco-American festival in late June. This festival—which features a colorful parade (some marching bands wear snowshoes), concerts, dances, fireworks, and public suppers with traditional stick-to-the-ribs French Canadian food—is one of the largest ethnic events in New England. Old Orchard Beach quiets way down after Columbus Day, but there are still many places to stay and four year-round restaurants for off-season visitors. The pier closes after Columbus Day weekend.

✷ Villages

Ocean Park is a historic community founded in 1881 by Free Will Baptists and well known for its outstanding religious, educational, and cultural programs. The Ocean Park Association (207-934-9068; www.oceanpark.org) sponsors lectures, concerts, movies, and other events throughout the summer in the cluster of old buildings known as Temple Square. Within the community there is also a recreation hall, shuffleboard and tennis courts, an old-fashioned ice cream parlor, and a smattering of gift shops. The entire community is a state game preserve, and you can find great walking trails through cathedral pines. A comprehensive guide to programs and recreation is put out by the association.

Pine Point. This quiet and less crowded end of the beach offers a selection of gift shops, restaurants, lobster pounds, and places to stay.

Camp Ellis. At the end of a peninsula where the Saco River blends with the ocean. Residents fight a constant battle with beach erosion, and some of the homes are frighteningly close to the shore. Fishing trips, whale-watching, a long breakwater great for walking, interesting shops, and a couple of restaurants.

Biddeford Pool. A small yachting port with lots of low-key charm where well-to-do families have been summering in the same big old shingled houses for generations. You'll find a few shops, a lobster pound, and a small restaurant, but not much else. Although politically part of blue-collar Biddeford, "the pool" is socially closer to fashionable nearby Kennebunkport.

✷ To See and Do

APPLE PICKING **Snell Farm** (207-929-6166; www.snellfamilyfarm.com), 1000 River Rd. (Rt. 112), Buxton. Pick-your-own-apples in Sept. and Oct., when the farm stand here moves from its summer spot across the street over toward the farmhouse, and the greenhouse is jammed with pumpkins ready for carving. In summer and fall the farm stand is stuffed with the best produce imaginable.

BERRY PICKING **Libby & Sons U-Pick** (207-793-4749; www.libbysonupick.com), Limerick. This popular inland spot for high-bush blueberry picking is growing 7,500 bushes to keep up with the demand. Even so, call in advance to make sure it's open, and not closed for a day to let more berries ripen. In fall, the apple orchard is open for picking, with both berries and apples ripe in Sept. Freshly pressed cider and pumpkins too.

FOR FAMILIES The Rt. 1 strip in Saco and nearby Old Orchard Beach makes up Maine's biggest concentration of "family attractions." Kids go wild. Parents fear they may go broke.

Funtown/Splashtown USA (207-284-5139; www.funtownsplashtownusa.com), Rt. 1, Saco. Open daily (depending on the weather) mid-June–Labor Day, weekends in spring and fall. Water activities and a large amusement park. In addition to the 100-foot wooden roller coaster Excalibur, the park has bumper cars, New England's largest log flume, plenty of carnival rides, a hydrofighter, kiddie rides, antique cars.

Aquaboggan Water Park (207-282-3112; www.aquaboggan.com), Rt. 1, Saco. Open mid-June–Labor Day. Several waterslides, including a high-thrills slide with mats or tubes, Aquasaucer, swimming pool, bumper boats, mini golf, arcade, shuffleboard, toddler area, wave pool.

Pirate's Cove Adventure Golf (207-934-5086), 70 1st St., Old Orchard Beach. Thirty-six up-and-down mini golf holes, waterfalls, ponds. Two separate courses available.

Palace Playland (207-934-2001; www.palaceplayland.com), 1 Old Orchard St., Old Orchard Beach. Open daily June–Labor Day; arcade open through Columbus Day on weekends. For more than 60 years fun seekers have been wheeled, lifted, shaken, spun, and bumped in Palace Playland rides. There's a carousel (though it no longer contains the original 1906 horses), a Ferris wheel, a 60-foot-high (Maine's largest) waterslide, and a roller coaster. You can pay by the ride or buy an all-day pass.

GOLF Dunegrass (207-934-4513), 200 Wild Dunes Way, Old Orchard Beach, 18 holes.

Biddeford-Saco Country Club (207-282-5883), 101 Old Orchard Rd., Saco, 18 holes.

Dutch Elm Golf Course (207-282-9850), 5 Brimstone Rd., Arundel, 18 holes.

Deep Brook Golf Course (207-282-3500), 36 New County Rd. (Rt. 5), Saco, nine holes.

Cascade Golf Center (207-282-3524), 955 Portland Rd., Saco, driving range.

MUSEUMS Saco Museum (207-283-3861; www.sacomuseum.org), 371 Main St., Saco. Open year-round Tue., Wed., Fri., and Sat. noon–4; Thu. noon–8; Sun. noon–4 from June–Dec.15. $4 adults, $3 seniors, $2 students, under 6 free (free to all 4–8 Thu.). Larger than it looks from the outside, and very well maintained and organized. Rotating exhibits, original paintings, furniture, decorative arts, tools, and natural history specimens. Lectures, tours, and special exhibits. The institute's **Dyer Library** next door has an outstanding Maine history collection.

Harmon Historical Museum, (207-934-9319), 4 Portland Ave., Old Orchard Beach, is open June–Labor Day weekend, Tue.–Fri. 1–4, Sat. 9–12; winter hours Tues. 10–2 and by appointment. Home of the Old Orchard Beach Historical Society, the building is full of exhibits from the town's past. Each year, in addition to the regular school, fire, and aviation exhibits, there is a special exhibit. Pick up the time line of the area's history and the walking map of historic sites.

SCENIC DRIVE From Saco there's a loop that heads up Rt. 112, past the Way-Way General Store. On the left a few miles out is the Saco Heath Preserve, worth a stop to explore. From there, continue on Rt. 112 until it intersects with Rt. 202. Turn left and stay on 202 until you see the intersection with Rt. 5. Turn left again and follow Rt. 5 along the river, back to the center of Saco.

TENNIS The **Ocean Park Association** (207-934-9068; www.oceanpark.org) maintains public tennis courts, open to the public for a fee in summer.

* Green Space

BEACHES Obviously, **Old Orchard Beach** is the big draw in this area, with 7 miles of sand and plenty of space for sunbathing, swimming, volleyball, and other recreation.

Ferry Beach State Park is marked from Rt. 9 between Old Orchard Beach and Camp Ellis, in Saco. The 100-plus-acre preserve includes 70 yards of sand, a boardwalk through the dunes, bike paths, nature trails, a picnic area with grills, lifeguards, changing rooms, and pit toilets. Even in the middle of summer it isn't terribly crowded here. $3 per person, $1 ages 5–11, free under 5 or over 65 with identification. Off-season the Iron Ranger (a green pole with a green can beside the booth) collects $1.50 adults, 50¢ for ages 5–11.

Bay View Beach, at the end of Bay View Rd. near Ferry Beach, is 200 yards of mostly sandy beach; lifeguards, free parking.

Camp Ellis Beach, Rt. 9, Saco. Some 2,000 feet of beach backed by cottages; also a long fishing pier. The commercial parking lots fill quickly on sunny days.

Pine Point, Rt. 9 (at the very end), Scarborough, is small and uncrowded, with a lobster pound and restaurant. The larger beach area, just a bit closer to Old Orchard, with snack bar, changing room, and bathrooms, charges $10 a day in summer for parking in the adjacent lot.

HIKING **Saco Trails**, P.O. Box 852, Saco 04072, publishes *Take a Hike in Saco*, a booklet that lists several trails maintained for hiking. Copies available at the Biddeford-Saco Chamber of Commerce.

NATURE PRESERVES **Scarborough Marsh Audubon Center** (207-883-5100), Pine Point Rd. (Rt. 9), Scarborough. Open daily mid-June–Labor Day, 9:30–5:30. The largest salt marsh (3,000 acres) in Maine, this is a great place for quiet canoe exploration. This Maine Audubon center offers canoe rentals, exhibits, a nature store, and guided walking and canoe tours throughout the summer.

Saco Heath Preserve, Rt. 112, Saco. Maybe this small Nature Conservancy preserve isn't crowded because nobody knows it's here, but it shouldn't be overlooked. The sign is hard to spot; look for it on the right a few miles out of Saco. A quiet, peaceful stroll through a peat bog on a wooden boardwalk.

East Point Sanctuary (207-781-2330), Lester B. Orcutt Blvd., Biddeford Pool. Open sunrise–sunset year-round. A 30-acre Maine Audubon Society preserve with trails, a view of Wood Island Light, and terrific birding in spring and fall.

✷ Lodging

INNS AND BED & BREAKFASTS **The Atlantic Birches Inn** (207-934-5295 or 1-888-934-5295; www.atlanticbirches.com), 20 Portland Ave., Old Orchard Beach 04064. A Victorian, shingle-style home, built in the area's heyday. Five guest rooms in the main house are named for former grand hotels; they're cheerful, with a mix of old and new furnishings. The "cottage" next door offers three rooms and two kitchenette suites with separate entrances. The in-ground pool is perfect on a hot day. $116–182 in high season includes an enhanced continental breakfast.

Hobson House Celtic Inn (207-284-4113; www.hobsonhouse.com), 398 Main St., Saco 04072. A big yellow mansion in the heart of Saco's historic district, Hobson House was built in the 1820s by Joseph Hobson, Saco's first mayor. It wears its dignity lightly, however, in the hands of owner Frank Zayac. There are four pleasant and comfortably furnished bedrooms, two with a private bath (the Alice May Hobson Suite also has a canopy bed, fireplace, and sitting area) and two sharing a bath. Common space includes a beautiful back garden with a large, free-form swimming pool. $100–125 with full breakfast.

🍴 ✐ **Old Orchard Beach Inn** (207-934-5834 or 1-877-700-6624; www.oldorchardbeachinn.com), 6 Portland Ave., Old Orchard Beach 04064. Ebenezer Staples's original hostelry, part of this inn dates from the 1730s, and the building is on the National Register of Historic Places as Maine's oldest continually operated inn. Now updated, it retains traditional wide-pine floorboards, antique furnishings, and a lot of period touches; some rooms have ventless fireplace. All 18 rooms, one a two-bedroom suite, have air-conditioning, cable TV, and private bath. $125–450 high season, $89–225 off-season, with a continental breakfast that includes homemade muffins and breads.

OTHER LODGING Old Orchard Beach offers an overwhelming number of motel, cottage, and condominium complexes both along the beach and on main roads. The chamber of commerce publishes a helpful *Old Orchard Beach Vacation Planner*.

Aquarius Motel (207-934-2626; www.aquariusmotel.com), 1 Brown St., Old Orchard Beach 04064. A small, family-owned and -operated 14-unit motel that's exceptionally clean, and right on the beach. The patio is a great place to relax after a day of sightseeing. $159 for a double with kitchenette in-season. Family-sized units also available. Many special rates in early spring and late fall.

Ocean Walk Hotel (207-934-1716 or 1-800-992-3779; www.oceanwalkhotel.com), 197 E. Grand Ave., Old Orchard Beach 04064. Forty-four well-kept rooms, from studios to oceanfront suites. The top-floor rooms in one building have very high ceilings, giving them a light, airy, spacious feel. $160–280 in-season, $75–200 off-season.

♿ **Sea View Motel** (207-934-4180 or 1-800-541-8439; www.seaviewgetaway.com), 65 W. Grand Ave., Old Orchard Beach 04064. Forty-nine rooms, some with ocean views. Pretty landscaping, with an outdoor pool and a beautiful fountain in front. Rooms are modern, bright, and clean. Two-bedroom suites with kitchenettes are also available. $87–310 in-season, $57–125 off-season.

The Gull Motel & Inn (207-934-4321; www.gullmotel.com), 89 W. Grand Ave., Old Orchard Beach 04064. An attractive motel, immaculate and family oriented. The inn is right on the beach, with a great porch. Cottages also available by the week. Inn rates $80–150 per night; motel rates $75–160; cottages $1,250 per week.

♿ **Billowhouse** (207-934-2333 or 1-888-767-7776; www.billowhouse.com), 2 Temple Ave., Ocean Park 04063. This 1881 Victorian seaside guesthouse is Mary Kerrigan's retirement project, completely renovated yet with old-fashioned charm. There are three ground-level efficiency apartments and six kitchenette units in the adjoining motel. The four B&B units include a large three-room suite with private deck, in-room Jacuzzi, and full kitchen; a two-room suite with private deck and outside hot tub; two oceanfront rooms with private bath share a deck overlooking the ocean. The beach is just steps away. $115–210 in-season, less for extended stays, breakfast included for B&B guests only; $80–140 off-season.

The Nautilus by the Sea (207-934-2021 or 1-800-981-7018; www.nautilusbythesea.com), 2 Colby Ave., Ocean Park 04063. This 12-room B&B, built in 1890 as a private home, is smack up against the beach. A couple of rooms share baths, but all have beach or ocean views, with the most dramatic vista from the fourth-floor "penthouse suite," where you can lie in bed at night and watch the beam of Wood Island Light play across the water. Owners Dick and Patte Kessler have kept the decor simple and traditional, much as it would have been when the house was built. $85–170 in-season, $65–125 off-season, with continental breakfast.

CAMPGROUNDS Camping is a budget-minded family's best bet in this area. There are at least a dozen campgrounds here (more than 4,000 sites in the area), many geared to families and offering games, recreational activities, and trolley service to the beach in-season. Following are a few recommendations; check with the chamber for a full listing.

Silver Springs Campground (207-283-3880; www.silverspringscampgroundandcottages.com), 705 Portland Rd. (Route 1), Saco. May–mid-Oct. A total renovation of the 13 cottages and addition of sites to a new total 130 sites with full hook-ups for RV have been keeping Mary Ann and Bryce Ingraham busy. "Most people who come, come back," Mary Ann said. Although the exterior of the 1940s cottages is old, the inside is newly paneled with pine, rewired and -plumbed. Two swimming pools and rec hall. The Ingrahams are eager to start doing weddings with the 40 acres at their disposal. Camping sites $30–45, cottages $99–175.

♿ **Bayley's Camping Resort** (207-883-6043; www.bayleys-camping.com),

52 Ross Rd., Scarborough 04074. Just down the road from Pine Point are paddleboats, swimming pool, Jacuzzi, fishing, game room, special programs for children and adults—and a shuttle to take you to Pine Point Beach and Old Orchard's downtown. More than 400 sites and 50 rental trailers. $43–64 depending on hook-ups; lower rates in spring and fall.

♂ ♿ **Powder Horn** (207-934-4733; www.mainecampgrounds.com), P.O. Box 366, Old Orchard Beach 04064. A 450-site campground with plenty of recreation options—playgrounds, shuffleboard, horseshoes, volleyball, rec hall and game room, activities program, mini golf, trolley service to the beach in-season. $46–51 per night in-season, $37–47 off-season. **Hidden Pines** is a sister campground next door for basic to premium sites.

✱ Where to Eat

DINING OUT ♿ **Joseph's by the Sea** (207-934-5044; www.josephsbythesea.com), 55 W. Grand Ave., Old Orchard Beach. Open Apr.–Oct. Serving breakfast and dinner daily in-season; hours vary the rest of the year, so call ahead. The dining rooms overlook the water, or you can dine on the garden patio. This family-run restaurant is one of the few to keep high standards over years of operation. While not as formal as in years past, the dinners are still as polished and well made. Wonderful grilled steaks, braised pork shanks, and the popular Pasta Maison—Maine shrimp, scallops, salmon, and mussels on angel hair pasta with real cream—for once the cream is light, enhancing and not overwhelming the seafood. Entrées $18–29.

♂ **The Landmark** (207-934-0156; www.landmarkfinedining.com), 28 E. Grand Ave., Old Orchard Beach. Open at 5 for dinner Mar.–Dec.; daily June–Columbus Day; otherwise, closed on Mon. Fine dining in a 1910 Victorian house. Menu specialties include lacquered duck, lobster stew, and barbequed ribs. Entrées $18–27. Early-bird specials.

Bufflehead's (207-284-6000; www.buffleheadsrestaurant.com), 122 Hills Beach Rd., Biddeford. Open year-round, daily for lunch and dinner in summer; call for hours off-season. Offering indoor and outdoor seating with a terrific ocean view, this great family place makes quality food. Try the seafood crêpes with lobster, shrimp, and crab in a spicy cream ($9). Baked manicotti with a side of Italian sausage could do for someone ready to switch from seafood. Entrées $11–25.

EATING OUT **French Quarter** (207-286-8568; www.frenchquarterbiddeford.com), 140 Main St., Biddeford. Open Tues.–Fri. for lunch and dinner, Sat. dinner only. Shrimp etouffée, jambalaya, and seafood gumbo are recommended. Entrées $8–13.

Bebe's Burritos (207-283-4222), 140 Main St., Biddeford. Open Tues.–Sun. for lunch and dinner. Great burritos with all the fixings, including homemade beans and slow-cooked beef and chicken. Live entertainment Thur.–Sat. nights.

Huot's Restaurant (207-282-1642; www.huotsseafoodrestaurant.com), Camp Ellis Beach, Saco. Open mid-Apr.–mid-Sept. Tues.–Sun. 11–9. The third generation of the Huot family is carrying on the tradition of good fresh seafood at this clean, simple spot in Camp Ellis, begun in 1935. Entrées $7–25.

Traditions (207-282-6661), 162 Main St., Saco. A cozy trattoria-style restaurant specializing in pasta and traditional Italian meat and seafood dishes. Open for lunch and dinner. Entrées $8–16.

Wormwoods (207-282-9679), 16 Bay Ave., Camp Ellis Beach, Saco. Open daily year-round for lunch and dinner. An old-fashioned place, with dark green booths, by the breakwater. They go all-out decorating for the seasons—watch out for the screeching skull in October—and can be counted on for fried seafood.

BREAKFAST AND LUNCH **Cole Road Café** (207-283-4103), 1 Cole Rd., Biddeford. Open for breakfast and lunch Wed.–Sat. 7 AM–1:45 PM, breakfast only Sun., same hours. Deservedly popular, this colorful, friendly place makes all the breakfast standards; specials might include blueberry-stuffed French toast with cream cheese or Granny Smith apple pancakes topped with granola, or for lunch, a butternut squash goat cheese tart. Six specials daily for each meal. Joyce Rose has run Cole Road Café for 15 years. Breakfast $2–7.

The Blue Elephant (207-281-3070; www.blueelephantcatering.com), 12 Pepperell Square, Saco. Open Mon.–Fri. 7–5, Sat. 8–4 for breakfast and lunch. A former Philadelphia caterer and restaurant manager serve fine breakfast sandwiches; housemade croissants, scones, and cinnamon rolls; and Carpe Diem coffee. Lunch features chowder, panini, Cuban sandwiches, and lobster mac 'n' cheese. Lunch $3–15.

Hattie's (207-282-3435), 109 Milestretch Rd., Biddeford Pool. The favorite local gathering spot for breakfast and lunch, now with a new owner.

LOBSTER POUND **Lobster Claw** (207-282-0040), 4 Ocean Park Rd. (Rt. 5), Saco. Lobsters cooked outside in giant kettles, stews and chowders, cozy dining room, and takeout available. Twin lobster specials, also steamers, fried seafood. Lobster packed to travel.

TAKEOUT Near Old Orchard Beach's pier and on the main drag are an abundance of takeout stands and informal restaurants serving pizza, burgers, hot dogs, fried seafood, fried dough, pier fries, ice cream, and more. Our favorites are **Bill's** for pizza, **Lisa's** for pier fries.

Rapid Ray's (207-282-1847), 179 Main St., Saco. Open daily until around midnight. A local icon since 1953. Quick and friendly service from people who seem to know everyone who walks through the door. Burgers, hot dogs, lobster rolls, fries, onion rings, and the like at great prices.

✷ Entertainment

City Theater (207-282-0849; www.citytheater.org), Main St., Biddeford. This 500-seat, 1890s theater offers a series of live performances.

Saco Drive-In (207-284-1016), Rt. 1, Saco. Double features in spring, summer, and . . .? "Sunday September 3. My wife says close. So we're closed. Thank you for a good season; see you in the spring," spoke a recorded message heard in fall 2007.

✷ Selective Shopping

Cascade Flea Market, Rt. 1, Saco. One of Maine's largest outdoor flea markets, open daily in summer.

Stone Soup Artisans (207-283-4715; www.stonesoupartisans.com), 228 Main St., Saco. Quality crafts from more than 60 Maine artisans.

✱ Special Events

January: **Annual Lobster Dip**—hundreds of participants dip into the chilly Atlantic to benefit Special Olympics of Maine, in Old Orchard Beach.

Late June: **La Kermesse**, Biddeford—parade, public suppers, dancing, and entertainment highlighting Franco-American culture and traditions.

Early July: **Greek Heritage Festival**, St. Demetrius on Bradley St. in Saco.

Late July: **Saco Art Festival** and **Shriners Football Game** in Biddeford.

June–Labor Day: **Fireworks** at the Old Orchard Beach square Thursday at 9:45 PM.

August: **Ocean Park Festival of Lights** and **Salvation Army camp meetings** under the pavilion in Ocean Park. **Beach Olympics**—three days of competitions, music, displays, and presentations to benefit the Special Olympics of Maine. Annual **5K Race and Kids' Fun Run**, scholarship fund-raiser.

September: Annual **Car Show**—with a car lineup and parade, Old Orchard Beach.

October: **Saco Pumpkin Fest**.

December: **Celebrate the Season by the Sea**—a tree-lighting ceremony with horse-drawn haywagon rides, refreshments, holiday bazaar, caroling, and a bonfire on the beach, in Old Orchard.

Casco Bay

PORTLAND AREA

FREEPORT

Maine Office of Tourism

PORTLAND AREA

Lively, walkable, sophisticated, Maine's largest city is still a working port. Greater Portland accounts for one-quarter of Maine's total population, but Portland's most populated area is a 3.5-mile-long peninsula facing Casco Bay. Visitors head first for the Old Port, more than five square blocks built exuberantly during the city's peak shipping era and now laced with restaurants, cafés, shops, and galleries.

Portland's motto, *Resurgam* ("I shall rise again"), could not be more appropriate. The 17th-century settlement was expunged twice by Native Americans, then torched by the British. Finally it prospered as a lumbering port in the 1820s—as still evidenced by its many Federal-era mansions and commercial buildings, like the granite-and-glass Mariner's Church in the Old Port, built in 1820 to be the largest building in the capital of a brand-new state. Then on Independence Day in 1866 a firecracker flamed up in a Commercial Street boatyard and quickly destroyed most of the downtown. Again the city rose like the legendary phoenix, rebuilding quickly and beautifully, this time in sturdy brick, to create the core of northern New England's shipping, rail, and manufacturing businesses.

These very buildings, a century later, were "going for peanuts," in the words of a real estate agent who began buying them up in the late 1960s, when its handsome Grand Trunk Station was demolished. Down by the harbor artists and craftspeople were renting shop fronts for $50 per month. They formed the Old Port Association, hoping to entice people to stroll through the no-man's-land. That first winter they strung lights through upper floors to convey a sense of security, and they shoveled their own streets, a service the city had ceased to provide to that area. At the end of the winter they celebrated their survival by holding the first Old Port Festival, a street fair that is still held each June.

Lining a ridge above the Old Port, Congress Street was the city's fashionable shopping and financial strip in the first half of the 20th century. The present Maine Bank & Trust Building was the tallest in all New England when it was built in 1909. By the mid-1990s, however, the three department stores here had closed and foot traffic had shifted to the Maine Mall. Now some of it is back.

The Maine College of Art (MECA) has replaced Porteus Department Store in a five-story Beaux Arts building and maintains the street-level Institute of Contemporary Art. With a student body of more than 400 and a far larger con-

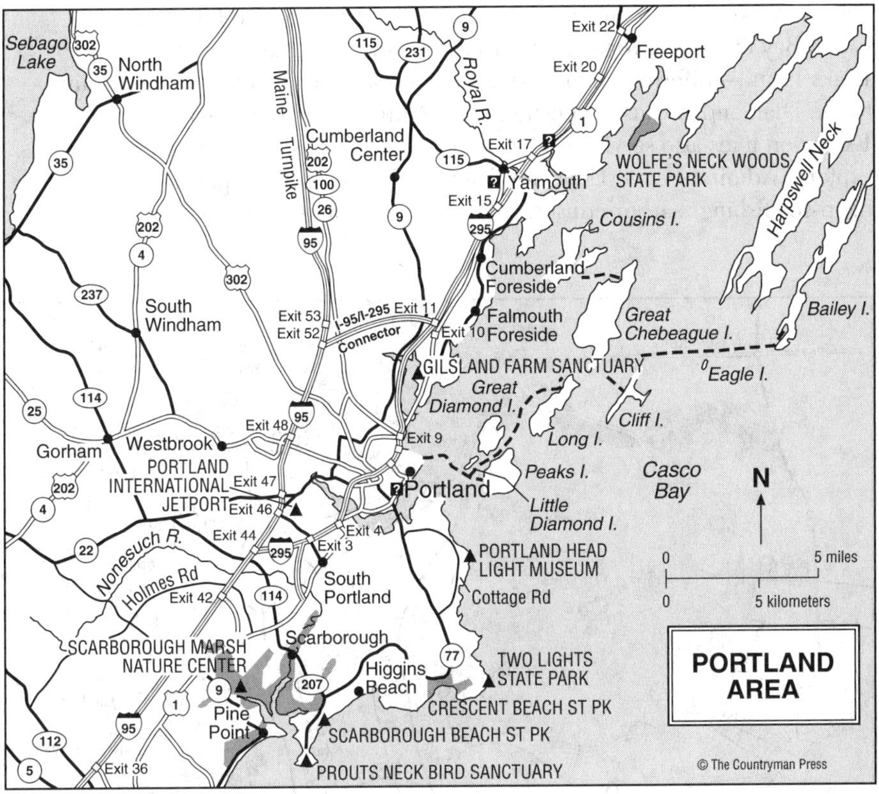

tinuing-education program, MECA has had a visual impact up and down Congress Street, which is now called the Arts District. Contemporary art galleries proliferate around the Portland Museum of Art.

Scattered throughout the city are members of Portland's growing immigrant community, with families from Bosnia, Russia, Somalia, Congo, Vietnam, Puerto Rico, and Mexico, making Portland the state's most diverse city.

Longfellow Square abuts the gracious residential blocks of the West End. Spared by the fire that destroyed the Old Port, its leafy streets are lined with town houses and mansions in a range of graceful architectural styles (several are B&Bs).

The Western Promenade was laid out as an overlook for the West End way back in 1836; the Eastern Promenade was at the opposite end of the peninsula, along the verge of Munjoy Hill, overlooking Casco Bay. In 1879, the city gained Deering Oaks Park and was blessed by the design of city civil engineer William Goodwin. In 1917, with turn-of-the-century plans by Frederick Law Olmsted, a dream of James Phinney Baxter, a mayor of Portland, came true when the Baxter Boulevard along Back Cove was opened to pedestrians.

Commercial Street, with condominiums and fish processing plants, is a departure point for the ferry to Yarmouth, Nova Scotia, and for the fleet of Casco Bay liners that regularly transport people, mail, and supplies to nearby Peaks Island—offering rental bikes, guided sea kayaking, lodging, and dining—to the Diamond islands, Chebeague, and Cliff Island, more than an hour's ride. Excursion lines also service Eagle Island, preserved as a memorial to Arctic explorer Admiral Peary. The waterfront is, moreover, the departure point for deep-sea fishing, harbor cruises, whale-watching, and daysailing.

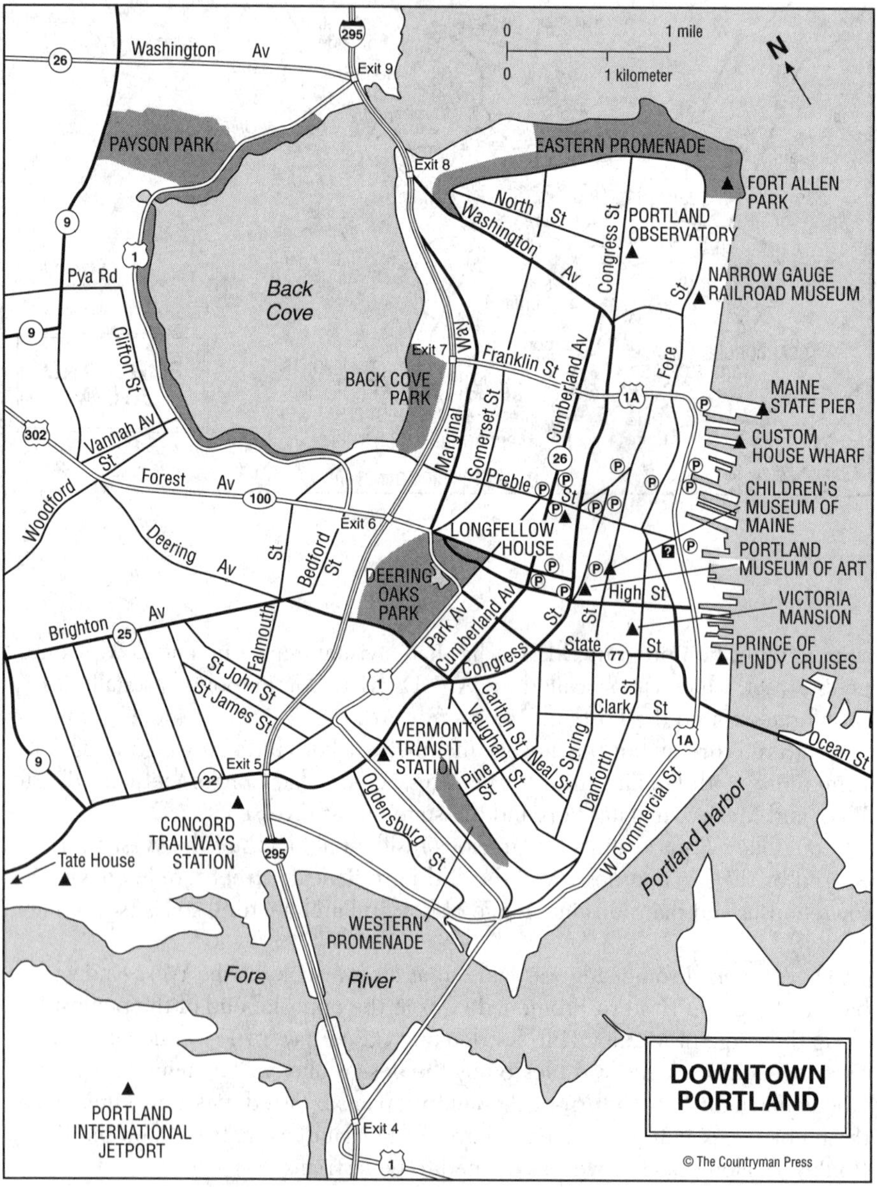

South Portland's waterfront has become far more visitor-friendly in recent years, with the Spring Point Lighthouse, recently restored Bug Light, and Portland Harbor Museum as focal points, along with a burgeoning trail system.

Beyond South Portland lies Cape Elizabeth, home of the vintage-1791 Portland Head Light and its museum. Nearby Scarborough to the south and both Falmouth and Yarmouth, just north of the city, also offer surprisingly secluded seaside reserves for walking, boating, and birding.

GUIDANCE **Convention and Visitors Bureau of Greater Portland** (207-772-5800; www.visitportland.com), 245 Commercial St., Portland 04101, publishes *Greater Portland Visitors Guide*, listing restaurants, sights, museums, and accommodations, including cottages. Last-minute discount rates might be available here, lower than published rates because of cancellations or availability. The walk-in information center is open Mon.–Fri. 8:30–5, Sat. 9:30–4:30 through summer, and Sat. 10–3 Columbus Day–Memorial Day. The CVB has a center (207-775-5809) at the Portland International Jetport. **Deering Oaks Visitor Center** (207-828-0149) is located in Deering Oaks Park just off the State St. extension and Forest Ave. When the cruise ships are in, the Visitors Center opens an office near Casco Bay Lines.

Portland's Downtown District (207-772-6828; www.portlandmaine.com), 549 Congress St., Portland 04101, offers information about performances, festivals, and special events. They publish a guide to services, attractions, dining, and lodging.

For current entertainment, weather, and dining ratings, click onto one of several local newspaper Web sites: **www.pressherald.com**, the *Portland Press Herald* site, or the *Portland Phoenix*'s page, **www.portlandphoenix.com**. *The Portland Forecaster*—a free weekly available in street vending boxes and at coffeehouses and shops—carries listings for galleries, music, and events. A Web site, **www.portlandfoodmap.com**, holds the most complete listing of Portland restaurants.

The Maine Tourism Association (207-846-0833) staffs a major state information center on Rt. 1 in Yarmouth, just off I-295, exit 17.

Also see **Greater Portland Landmarks** under *To See*.

GETTING THERE *By air:* **Portland International Jetport** (207-774-7301; www.portlandjetport.org) is served by Delta Air Lines (1-800-221-1212; www.delta.com), Continental Airlines (1-800-523-3272; www.continental.com), United Express (1-800-864-8331; www.ual.com), U.S. Airways (1-800-428-4322; www.usair.com), JetBlue (1-800-538-2583; www.jetblue.com), AirTran (1-800-247-8726; www.airtran.com), and Northwest (1-800-225-2525; www.nwa.com). Car rentals at the airport include National, Avis, Hertz, Budget, and Alamo.

By bus: **Concord Trailways** (207-828-1151 or 1-800-639-3317; www.concordtrailways.com) stops en route from Boston to Bangor and coastal points at a modern station just off I-295 (it's also the new train station—see *By train*); the buses offer movies, music, and a nonstop express to Boston and its Logan

Airport. It's a $10 taxi ride from the bus station to downtown, or try the new Explorer bus (see *Getting Around*). **Vermont Transit** (207-772-6587 or 1-800-552-8737; www.vermonttransit.com) offers frequent service among Portland, Boston, and Maine's coastal and inland points, using the Greyhound terminal, which unfortunately is dingy and offers little parking.

By ferry: **The Cat** (1-888-249-7245; www.catferry.com), a high-speed car ferry, makes four trips to Nova Scotia from July 14 to Aug. 31 in 2008, departing at 8 AM Thur.–Sun. Three trips a week are scheduled before and after those dates. Schedule changes in the future are inevitable, so call or check the Web site before making plans.

By car: From I-95, take I-295 to exit 44 (Portland Waterfront) and follow signs for the ferry. The **Convention and Visitors Bureau** information center (see *Guidance*) is at 245 Commercial St. between Becky's Diner and DiMillo's Restaurant, on the other side of the street.

By train: Amtrak service (1-800-USA-RAIL; www.thedowneaster.com or www.amtrak.com). The **Downeaster** is so successful more trips have been added. It now runs five times daily between Boston's renovated North Station and Portland's clean new rail–bus station on outer Congress St.; the trip takes about two-and-a-half hours. Paid parking is available, and even when cars overflow the big lots, helpful attendants seem to find a space for you. The trip is tranquil and the view of Scarborough Marsh beautiful. Stops in Old Orchard Beach, Saco/Biddeford, and Wells give another option to Portland visitors who would like to skip driving. The trip to Old Orchard Beach, for instance, takes just 15 minutes, and drops you off next to the amusement park.

GETTING AROUND Portland, like many interesting small cities, holds beautiful 18th- and 19th-century facades, engaging street musicians, and creative window displays. It's a great place for walking.

Portland Explorer Express Bus Service (207-772-4457; www.vipchartercoaches.com) runs a 26-passenger, air-conditioned shuttle among the airport, the bus–rail station, the Maine Mall, and major downtown locations such as the Old Port and the Casco Bay lines ferry terminal 12:15–7 PM daily including most holidays between May and October. $2 one-way. Pay as you get on the bus.

The Metro (207-774-0351; www.gpmetrobus.com) bus transfer system serves Greater Portland. Metro city buses connect airport and city, and offer convenient routes around the city. $1.25 one-way, or $5 for a day pass; less for seniors over 65 and those with disabilities, 60¢. Students need to call about the discount.

PORTLAND WATERFRONT

Kim Grant

PARKING Portland meters are 25¢ per half hour, but, as we have discovered the hard way, you get a $10 ticket after

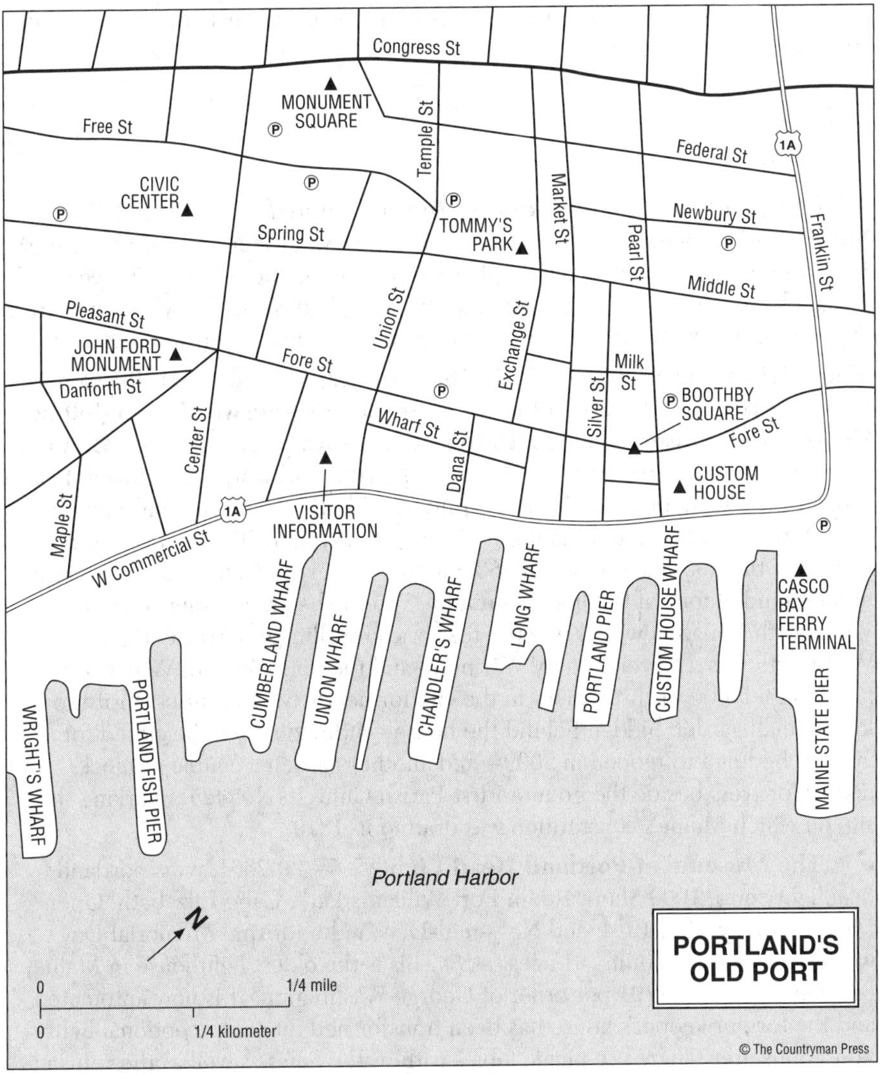

2 hours, which climbs to $15 if you keep feeding the meter. The city urges visitors to use its many parking garages. The **Fore Street Garage** (439 Fore St.) puts you at one end of the Old Port, and the **Custom House Square Garage** (25 Pearl St.) at the other. The **Casco Bay Garage** (Maine State Pier) and **Free Street Parking** (130 Free St., just up from the art museum) are also handy.

WHEN TO COME Portland, with its thriving restaurant and museum scene makes a great destination any time of year. The Victoria Mansion and the Tate House dress up in Christmas finery and offer holiday tours, though a whale-watching trip would have to be scheduled in the months of better weather. And the winter wind can blow bitterly cold on Portland streets—even when some of us are still out skating on Deering Oaks pond.

✱ To See

MUSEUMS

All listings are in Portland unless otherwise noted

Museum of African Culture (207-871-7188; www.museumafricanculture.org), 13 Brown St. With more than 500 pieces representing more than 1,000 years of African history and art, including masks, bronzes, batiks, and wooden sculptures, this museum was closed while moving to its new location when we went to press.

Maine Historical Society (207-774-1822; www.mainehistory.org), 485 Congress St. Maine Historical Society's offices are here, as are **Wadsworth-Longfellow House**, **MHS Museum**, and **MHS Research Library**, as well as the **Maine memory network** (www.mainememory.net). The Wadsworth-Longfellow House is open May–Oct., daily 10–5 (closed July 4 and Labor Day); the museum is open Mon.–Sat. 10–5, and the library is open year-round, Tue.–Sat. 10–4. $8 adults for the house and museum, $3 children under 18. Call for hours for a 45-minute guided tour of the house. Built in 1785 by the grandfather of Henry Wadsworth Longfellow, this was the first brick dwelling in town. Peleg Wadsworth was a Revolutionary War hero, and the entire clan of Wadsworths and Longfellows was prominent in the city for nearly two centuries. Visit the lovely small garden hidden behind the house—although it will be closed for 2008, scheduled to reopen in 2009—and another garden a couple of blocks down Congress beside the granite First Parish Church (No. 425), marking the site on which Maine's constitution was drafted in 1819.

🖍 ♿ **The Museum at Portland Head Light** (207-799-2661; www.portlandheadlight.com), 1000 Shore Rd. in Fort Williams Park, Cape Elizabeth. Open Memorial Day–Oct, 10–4, and Nov.–mid-Dec. and mid-Apr.–Memorial Day weekends 10–4. $2 adults, $1 ages 6–18. This is the oldest lighthouse in Maine, first illuminated in 1791 per order of George Washington. It is now automated, and the former keeper's house has been transformed into an exceptional lighthouse museum. There are picnic tables with water views as well as the ruins of an old fort in the surrounding Fort Williams Park, just 4 miles from downtown Portland. Take State St. (Rt. 77) south across the bridge to South Portland, then turn left onto Broadway and right onto Cottage St., which turns into Shore Rd.

Institute of Contemporary Art/MECA (207-879-5742; www.meca.edu/ica), 522 Congress St. Changing exhibits frequently worth checking; free. The ICA is a street-level gallery at the Maine College of Art (MECA), which enrolls more than 400 full-time students and many times that number in continuing-studies programs.

🖍 **Maine Narrow Gauge Railroad Co. & Museum** (207-828-0814; www.mngrr.org), 58 Fore St. Open mid-May–mid-Oct., daily 11–4, and weekends year-round except Jan. 2–Feb. 12. A 1½ mile round-trip excursion along Casco Bay is offered regularly May–Oct. Valentine's Train on Valentine's Day, Ghost Train around Halloween, and from the day after Thanksgiving to Dec. 23, Santa

Fest, when the train's route is lined with lights in shapes ranging from a deer family to a North Pole castle. Entrance to the museum and gift shop are free if your buy a train ticket; excursion fares are $9 round-trip adults and seniors, $6 ages 3–12. Drive through the complex of brick buildings and park on the waterside. The museum sells the tickets. From the 1870s to the 1940s, five narrow-gauge lines carrying visitors linked rural Maine communities.

Portland Museum of Art (207-775-6148; for a weekly schedule of events and information, 207-773-ARTS; www.portlandmuseum.org), 7 Congress Square. Open Tue., Wed., Thu., Sat., and Sun. 10–5, Fri. 10–9; Memorial Day–Columbus Day open Mon. 10–5; closed New Year's Day, Thanksgiving, and Christmas. $10 adults, $8 students and seniors (with ID), and $4 ages 6–17; under 6 free. Free admission Fri. 5–9 PM. Tours daily—inquire about times. Maine's largest art museum is a striking building designed by I. M. Pei's firm. Featured American artists include Winslow Homer, Edward Hopper, Rockwell Kent, Louise Nevelson, Andrew and N. C. Wyeth, John Singer Sargent, and Marguerite Zorach; the museum also has interesting European works by Renoir, Degas, Prendergast, Matisse, and Picasso. In 2002 the neighboring McLellan House, the lovely Federal-period home of the museum's original collection, was reopened, along with the Sweat Memorial Galleries, an impressive collection of 19th-century American paintings and decorative arts. The museum has bought the Winslow Homer Studio on Prouts Neck, in Scarborough, but it is closed to the public. The museum hopes to complete work in the spring of 2009; check the Web site or call.

WEATHERBEATEN BY WINSLOW HOMER (UNITED STATES, 1836–1910), 1894

🔧 ♿ **Children's Museum of Maine** (207-828-1234; www.kitetails.com), 142 Free St. Open Memorial Day–Labor Day, Mon.–Sat. 10–5, Sun. noon–5; otherwise, closed Mon. $7 per person (under 1 free). Next door to the Portland Museum of Art, this fun museum features three levels of interactive, hands-on exhibits designed to help the young and old learn together. Permanent exhibits include *Our Town* (with car repair shop, farm, supermarket, lobster boat, and fire department), a climbing wall, and a shipyard outside good for a picnic lunch in good weather. There's also a science center, a toddler area, and a black-box room that's a walk-in camera obscura.

🔧 **Portland Observatory** (207-774-5561, ext. 104; www.portlandlandmarks.org), 138 Congress St. Open Memorial Day–Columbus Day, daily 10–5. $6 adults, $4 ages 6–16. Built in 1807, this imposing, octagonal, 86-foot-high shingled landmark atop Munjoy Hill is the last surviving 19th-century maritime signal station in the country. During a recent restoration, interpretive displays were added. Climb the 103 steps to the top and watch for ships entering Casco Bay.

Portland Harbor Museum (207-799-6337; www.portlandharbormuseum.org), on Fort Rd., marked from Rt. 77 in South Portland. Open Memorial Day–Columbus Day, daily 10–4:30; mid-Apr.–May, and Columbus Day–Nov., Fri.–Sun. 10-4:30. $4 adults, free under 18. Sited in a brick repair shop that was part of Fort Preble and is now part of Southern Maine Community College, this museum mounts changing exhibits on local maritime history and features pieces of the *Snow Squall*, an 1850s Portland clipper ship wrecked in the Falkland Islands, and artifacts of the ship's restoration. Spring Point Lighthouse, at the end of a breakwater, is another good vantage point on the harbor.

🔧 ♿ **Portland Fire Museum** (207-772-2040; www.portlandfiremuseum.com), 157 Spring St. (near the corner of State). Open June–Aug., Tues. and Sat. 10–2, Wed. and Fri. 6–8, and by appointment. The only remaining firehouse in Portland with horse stalls, this wonderful old brick structure was built in 1837 and originally housed a girls' grammar school. The artifacts, photos, paintings, and fire equipment (including a 1938 pumper truck) chronicle the city's contentious relationship with fire, from the fire department's humble beginnings in 1768 and the city's destruction by fire at the hands of the British in 1775, to the Great Fire of 1866.

HISTORIC SITES

All listings are in Portland unless otherwise noted

🔧 **Victoria Mansion**, the Morse-Libby House (207-772-4841; www.victoriamansion.org), 109 Danforth St. (at the corner of Park St.). Open for tours May–Oct., Mon.–Sat. 10–4, Sun. 1–5 (closed July 4 and Labor Day); $10 adults, $9 seniors, $3 students 6–17, under 6 free. Christmas hours and rates: day after Thanksgiving–Dec., Tues.–Sun. 11–5; $12 adults (no senior discount), $5 students. Ruggles Sylvester Morse, a Maine native who made his fortune as a New Orleans hotelier, built this elaborately gilded, frescoed, carved, and many-mirrored mansion in 1858 as a summer home after relocating south just before the Civil War. The Italianate brownstone palazzo features a three-story grand hall with stained-glass windows, a stunning skylight, and a flying staircase with 377 balusters hand carved from Santo Domingo mahogany. It was rescued from destruction and opened to the public in 1941. The gift shop sells well-chosen Victoriana. In December the house is dressed to the hilt.

Tate House Museum (207-774-6177; www.tatehouse.org), 2 Waldo St. Follow Congress St. (Rt. 22) west across the Fore River to Westbrook Street (it's just outside the Portland Jetport). Open mid-June 15–mid-Oct., Tue.–Sat. 10–4, first Sun. of the month 1–4. $7 adults, $5 seniors, $2 ages 6–12, under 6 free. George Tate, mast agent for the Royal Navy, built this Georgian house in 1755 to reflect his important position. Both the interior and exterior are unusual, distinguished by clerestory windows, a gambrel roof, wood paneling, and elegant furniture. An 18th-century herb garden is part of the historic landscape.

Neal Dow Memorial (207-773-7773; www.mewctu.org), 714 Congress St. Open year-round, Mon.–Fri. 11–4. Donation requested. Currently the headquarters of the Maine Women's Christian Temperance Union, this handsome Greek Revival mansion was built in 1829 by Neal Dow, the man responsible for an 1851 law that made Maine the first state to prohibit alcohol. He also championed women's rights and abolition.

GUIDED TOURS **Greater Portland Landmarks** (207-774-5561; www.portlandlandmarks.org), 165 State St., Portland 04101. From July through Sept. this nonprofit organization offers downtown walking tours of the Old Port Mon.–Sat. beginning at 10:30 AM; $7 per adult, free under age 16 if accompanied by an adult. Tours depart from the Convention and Visitors Bureau at 245 Commercial St. Also note the organization's many excellent books and its *Discover Historic Portland on Foot* series of walking guides. GPL also runs the Portland Observatory (see above).

Mainely Tours and Gifts, Inc. (207-774-0808; www.mainelytours.com), 3 Moulton St., Portland. Mid-May–Oct. This narrated, 90-minute trolley tour begins on Commercial Street in the Old Port and includes Portland Head Light. $16 adults, $15 seniors, $9 ages 3–12.

Downeast Duck Tours (207-774-3825; www.downeastduck.com), Harbor View Gifts, 177 Commercial St., Portland. The Duck Tour, about an hour long, takes you around Portland and into Casco Bay after the amphibious vehicle rolls into the harbor. Narrated tours run from the end of June to mid-Oct., daily, with five a day before Labor Day and fewer in the fall. $22 adults, $19 seniors, $17 ages 6–12, $5 under 5.

TATE HOUSE

Nancy English

Scenic Drives

Cape Elizabeth and Prouts Neck. From State St. in downtown Portland, head south on Rt. 77 across the Casco Bay Bridge to South Portland, then turn left onto Broadway and right onto Cottage St., which turns into Shore Rd. Enter 94-acre **Fort Williams Park** (4 miles from downtown) to see the **Museum at Portland Head Light**. There are also picnic tables with water views and a beach, as well as the ruins of the old fort. Many people like to come here early in the morning (Stop at **Terra Cotta Pasta Co.**, 501 Cottage Rd., for gelato and cannoli and terrific take-out Italian meals and salads.) Follow Shore Rd. south to Rt. 77 and continue through Pond Cove, the main village in residential Cape Elizabeth, and on to **Two Lights State Park**, with its views of Casco Bay and the open Atlantic, good for fishing and picnicking. **Crescent Beach State Park**, just beyond, is a mile of inviting sand, the area's premier beach.

Rt. 77 continues through **Higgins Beach**, a Victorian-era summer community of reasonable rentals and lodging with plenty of beach but limited parking. At the junction of Rts. 207 and 77 continue on Black Point Rd., past **Scarborough Beach State Park**, and on to exclusive **Prouts Neck**. Unless you are staying or eating at the **Black Point Inn**, parking in-season is all but impossible here. Park back at Scarborough Beach and walk or bike to the **Cliff Walk**, site of **Winslow Homer's studio**. Return by the same route (you are just 15 miles from downtown). A short and rewarding detour: At the junction of Cottage Rd. and Broadway, turn right onto Broadway to Southern Maine Technical College. A granite breakwater leads to the **Spring Point Light**, overlooking Casco Bay. Look for signs for the **Spring Point Shoreway Path**, which follows the bay 3 miles to **Willard Beach**.

Falmouth Foreside. From downtown Portland, take Rt. 1 north across the mouth of the Presumpscot River. Signs for the Governor Baxter School for the Deaf direct you down Andres Ave. and across a causeway to 100-acre **Mackworth Island**. Park and walk (dogs permitted) the 1.5-mile path that circles the island. Views are off across the bay, and a small beach invites strolling. Return to Rt. 1 and continue north, looking for signs for **Gilsland Farm Audubon Center**, headquarters for Maine Audubon. The blue sign comes up in less than 0.5 mile; follow the dirt road to the visitor center.

THE OLD PORT

Kim Grant

Yarmouth. From downtown Portland, take I-295 to exit 17. Commercial and tourist-geared businesses are relegated to Rt. 1, leaving the inner village lined with 18th- and 19th-century homes. The village green retains its round railroad station, and **Royal River Park** offers recreation (the Royal River is popular with sea kayakers) in all seasons. Also check out **Lower Falls Landing**, a former sardine cannery that now houses interesting shops. Don't miss the DeLorme

Map Store on Rt. 1 with "Eartha," the world's largest rotating and revolving globe.

✷ Island Excursions

No one seems quite sure how many islands there are in Casco Bay. Printed descriptions range from 136 to 222. Seventeenth-century explorer John Smith dubbed them the Calendar Islands, saying there was one for every day of the year. Regardless of the actual number, there are plenty of offshore places for poking around. Regular year-round ferry service runs to six of the islands, five of which invite exploration.

For listings of summer cottages and other rentals in the Casco Bay Islands, contact **Port Island Realty** (207-766-5966; www.portisland.com) and **Ashmore Realty** (207-766-5702; www.ashmorerealty.com).

Portland Express Water Taxi (207-415-8493; www.portlandexpresswatertaxi.com) goes to all the islands visited by Casco Bay lines as well as Jewel and Cushing islands.

PEAKS ISLAND Just 3 miles from Portland (a 20-minute ferry ride), Peaks is the most accessible island. Ferry service runs regularly, even off-season, because many of the island's approximately 1,000 year-round residents commute to the mainland for work and school. In summer the population swells to between 5,000 and 6,000, and day-trippers are common. Check out the bulletin boards at the top of Welch St. and at **Hannigan's Market**. The 5-mile shore road around the island is great for walking or bicycling. Rent a pair of wheels at **Brad's ReCycled Bike Shop** (207-766-5631), 115 Island Ave., the most adorable bike rental place in the U.S. of A.; when Brad isn't there, folks fill out a form, place payment in the box, and return the bikes when you're through. The **Fifth Maine Regiment Museum** (207-766-3330; www.fifthmainemuseum.org), Seashore Ave., is a striking building erected in 1888 to house Maine's largest collection of Civil War memorabilia (local history exhibits are on the second floor). Open June–Sept., weekends 12–4; July and Aug., daily 12–4, or by appointment. **Maine Island Kayak Co.** (207-766-2373 or 1-800-796-2373; www.maineislandkayak.com) offers excellent, superbly guided half-day to multiday trips in Casco Bay, along the Maine coast, and elsewhere, along with renowned kayaking instruction. Food sources (some are open in summer only) include sandwiches at **Hannigan's Market** year-round. **The Cockeyed Gull** (207-766-2800; www.cockeyedgull.com), 78 Island Ave., serves the best dinner on the island, and has a deck perched over the bay. The restaurant is open year-round, and makes a good destination off-season for an island day trip. The **Inn on Peaks Island** (207-766-5100; www.innonpeaksisland.com), 33 Island Ave., has big, airy rooms and is open year-round with its own lunch and dinner restaurant, **The Pub**. All rooms include TV/DVD, phone, ceiling fan, fireplace, whirlpool tub, and balcony, $225–300 for a double, and includes vouchers for breakfast across the street, at fabulous **Peaks Café** (207-766-2479), Welch St., which offers a complete range of coffee choices, as well as pastries, bagels, fruit, and juices, and is the locals' favorite place for breakfast.

Peaks Island House (207-766-4400; www.thepeaksislandhouse.com), 20 Island Ave., open May–Sept., serves lunch and dinner and has outside deck seating in nice weather. This place also provides overnight lodging (207-766-4406 for reservations). Four rooms, decorated in floral and sea motifs, with private bath and water views. $125–145 per night.

DownFront (207-766-5500), 50 Island Ave., at the top of the hill from the boat, sells great ice cream, candy, and souvenirs.

CHEBEAGUE ISLAND Chebeague is the largest island in Casco Bay: 4.5 miles long and 2 miles wide. Its population of 350 swells to eight times that in summer. A bike is the best way to explore. Mack Passano (207-846-7829), 168 South Rd., is know as the Bike Man of Chebeague, and was written up in *Down East* magazine. More than 100 second-hand bikes here for free.

Slow Bell Café (207-847-9317), 2 Walker Road. This 40-seat restaurant serves steamed lobsters, take-out available. Jonathan Komlosy is the owner.

The Chebeague Orchard Inn (207-846-9488; www.chebeague-orchard.com), 66 North Rd., open May 15–Oct.15. Enthusiastic kayakers, the hosts offer 15 percent discount if guests arrive here by sea kayak, as well as common room with fireplace, and five antiques-furnished guest rooms, three with private bath, some with water views. Vickie and Neil Taliento are helpful hosts who keep bikes for guests and include a full breakfast with fresh-picked berries in season. $125–165. Workshops in painting, photography, and sea kayaking. **The Sunset House** (207-846-6568), 74 South Rd., is no longer a B&B but is now offered for rent by the week or month.

You can pick up takeout at **Doughty's Island Market** (207-846-9997). To relax and enjoy the scenery, head to **Chandler's Cove**, a white sand beach, or the beach near **Coleman's Cove**. Golfers will want to try the **Chebeague Island Golf Club** (207-846-9478), a beautiful nine-hole course founded in 1920, where nonmembers can play anytime except Monday or Thursday morning. Facilities on the island include a recreation center with an Olympic-sized outdoor heated swimming pool, indoor gym, weight room, and outdoor tennis/basketball courts. The **Chebeague Island Historical Society** has restored the old District No. 9 Schoolhouse, open all day in summer with a visitor center and museum. Call 207-846-5237 for more details.

Casco Bay Lines ferries dock at the southern end of the island, and **Chebeague Transportation Company** (207-846-3700; www.chebeaguetrans.com), runs the ferry that travels between Cousins Island and Chebeague. Call for directions and parking details.

LONG ISLAND Three miles long and approximately a mile wide, Long Island, like the others, has a thriving summer population. The **Chestnut Hill Inn** (207-766-5272; www.chestnuthillinn.com) is a seven-room (four with private bath) establishment open year-round. On weekdays continental breakfast is included, and on weekends a full breakfast is served. $145–200. Dinner is available by reservation, both to guests and to the public.

GREAT DIAMOND ISLAND A pleasant half-hour ferry ride from downtown, this 2-mile-long island is the site of Fort McKinley, built sturdily of brick in the 1890s, now restored as **Diamond Cove** (www.diamondcove.com), a resort-style development featuring 121 town houses. A rental agency, Great Diamond Rentals (207-766-3005; www.greatdiamondrentals.com) can be contacted for summer rentals—but unless you are staying there, or take a guided tour (given by Diamond Cove management company), the resort grounds are not open to the public. ⚭ **Diamond's Edge** (207-766-5850; www.diamondsedge.com) is the big attraction here, a casually elegant restaurant open late May–Sept., dinner only except mid-June–Labor Day, when lunch is also served. A popular place for weddings.

CLIFF ISLAND Cliff Island is a full one-and-a-half-hour ride down the bay. It is the most rustic of the islands, with 8 miles of dirt roads, no overnight accommodations, a peaceful feel, and sandy beaches. There's a seasonal sandwich shop on the wharf, and the general store sells sandwiches year-round. For **cottage rentals** check with the Greater Portland CVB.

✷ To Do

BALLOONING **Hot Fun** (207-799-0193; www.hotfunballoons.com), P.O. Box 2825, South Portland. Hot-air balloon rides for up to six passengers.

BICYCLING **Map Adventures** (1-800-891-1534; www.mapadventures.com) makes very readable small maps of bike routes. **Portland Trails** (207-775-2411; www.trails.org) prints a *Map and Trail Guide*. The Maine Department of Transportation publishes a spiral-bound book with bike routes in Maine; separate tours are published in smaller books. These maps are stocked at **Back Bay Bicycle** (207-773-6906; www.backbaybicycle.com; 333 Forest Ave., Portland), where bikes can be repaired or purchased. Back Bay Bicycle and **Cycle Mania** (207-774-2933; www.cyclemania1.com; 59 Federal St., Portland) sponsor weekly group rides. Cycle Mania is the only city bike shop that rents bicycles. They recommend you make a reservation, and also stock the Map Adventures, DOT Bike trail booklets, and Portland Trails map.

Eastern Trail (207-284-9260; www.easterntrail.org) is an ambitious trail system that will someday connect Casco Bay to Kittery (and Maine to Florida) with a 68.8-mile off-road greenway. Parts of the route now stretch through Scarborough Marsh, with its flocks of birds and summer scenery, up through South Portland, but at the moment it mostly follows heavily trafficked roads.

BOATING **Chebeague Transportation Company** (207-846-3700; www.chebeaguetrans.com), runs the ferry that travels between Cousins Island and Chebeague. Call for directions and parking details.

Casco Bay Lines (207-774-7871; www.cascobaylines.com), Casco Bay Ferry Terminal, 56 Commercial St. at the foot of Franklin Arterial, Portland. Founded in 1845, this business was said to be the oldest continuously operating ferry company in the country when it went bankrupt in 1980. The present, quasi-municipal

Casco Bay Island Transit District now carries 870,000 passengers and 26,000 vehicles out to the bay's beautiful islands every year. The brightly painted ferries are still lifelines to six islands, carrying groceries and lumber as well as mail. The year-round, daily mail-boat run (three hours) puts into all the islands in the morning and again in the afternoon. A variety of seasonal, special excursions includes a five-and-a-half-hour Bailey Island Cruise and a Moonlight Run at 9:15 PM. Also year-round, daily car ferry service to Peaks Island.

Eagle Island Tours (207-774-6498; www.eagleislandtours.com), Long Wharf, Portland. Runs Memorial Day–Columbus Day. Visit the former home of Admiral Peary, now maintained by the state as a historic site and nature preserve; the company also offers Lighthouse Lovers and sunset cruises. Group charters available. Land and Sea Tour includes tickets for the Mainely Tours trolley (see *Guided Tours*) run by the same family. Ask about Capt. William Frappier's book, *Steamboat Yesterdays on Casco Bay*.

Bay View Cruises (207-761-0496; www.bayviewcruises-me.com), Fisherman's Wharf, Portland. Mid-June–Sept. Daily narrated harbor cruises aboard the *Bay View Lady* in summer, weekends May and Oct.

✐ ***Lucky Catch* Lobstering** (207-761-0941; www.luckycatch.com), 170 Commercial St., Portland. Instead of just eating them, why not land one of those tasty crustaceans yourself? Memorial Day–Columbus Day, Captain Tom takes tourists and locals out to haul traps on the *Lucky Catch* five times daily Mon.–Sat., with side trips to Portland Head Light and White Head Passage. Each 80- to 90-minute cruise costs $22 per adult, $20 ages 13–18 and seniors, $14 ages 12 and under.

Olde Port Mariner Fleet (207-775-0727; www.oldportmarinefleet.com), Long Wharf, Portland. Whale-watches daily in summer 10–3, weekends in early June and after Labor Day in *The Odyssey*, a 93-passenger boat. Starts Memorial Day weekend, ends last Sun. in Sept. Harbor cruises by private charter.

Deep-sea fishing and sailing. Several deep-sea-fishing boats and sailing yachts are based in Portland every summer. Check with the Convention and Visitors Bureau (207-772-5800) for current listings.

BREWERY TOURS Like its namesake city in Oregon, Portland is famous for its microbreweries, and many feature restaurants alongside them. Most give tours, either on a regular basis or by appointment. For information, contact individual breweries: **Allagash Brewing** (207-878-5385 or 1-800-330-5385; www.allagash.com), 100 Industrial Way, Portland; **Casco Bay Brewing** (207-797-2020; www.cascobaybrewing.com), 57 Industrial Way, Portland; **D. L. Geary Brewing** (207-878-BEER; www.gearybrewing.com), 38 Evergreen Dr., Portland; **Gritty McDuff's Brew Pub** (207-772-2739; www.grittys.com), 396 Fore St., Portland; **Shipyard Brewing** (207-761-0807; www.shipyard.com), 86 Newbury St., Portland; and **Sebago Brewing Company** (207-775-2337; www.sebagobrewing.com), 15 Philbrook Ave., South Portland.

FOR FAMILIES ✐ **Southworth Planetarium** (207-780-4249; www.usm.maine

.edu/~planet), University of Southern Maine, 96 Falmouth St., Portland. Astronomy shows throughout the year. Special shows for young children in summer and on holidays, including an astronomical exploration of the biblical Star of Bethlehem. Children's matinees on Saturdays.

GOLF There are several popular nine- and 18-hole courses in the area, notably **Sable Oaks Golf Club** (207-775-6257), South Portland, considered among the most challenging and best courses in Maine (18 holes); **Riverside North** (18 holes, 207-797-3524) and **Riverside South** (nine holes, 207-797-5588), in Portland; **Val Halla** (18 holes, 207-829-2225), in Cumberland; and **Twin Falls** (nine holes, 207-854-5397), in Westbrook.

Willowdale Golf Club (207-883-9351), off Rt. 1, Scarborough, has 18 holes.

RACING **Scarborough Downs** (207-883-4331), off I-95, exit 6, in Scarborough. From Apr. to Dec. Scarborough Downs, the largest facility of its kind in New England, has live harness racing with betting windows; year-round thoroughbred and harness racing is available via simulcast with Off-Track Betting. **Downs Club Restaurant** (207-883-3022) is open for dinner Mon., Tues., Sat., and Sun. in-season, and you can place your bets from the top of the multilevel dining room with great views of the track.

Beech Ridge Motor Speedway (207-883-5227), Holmes Rd., Scarborough. Summer stock-car racing every Sat. night.

SAILING ***Bagheera*** (207-766-2500 or 1-87-SCHOONER; www.portland schooner.com), Maine State Pier, Portland. Built in 1924 of long-leaf yellow pine, oak, and mahogany, this vintage Alden sailed all over the world before making Casco Bay her home port in 2002. She can carry as many as 48 passengers. Four cruises daily, Memorial Day–Columbus Day. $30 ($35 for sunset) adults, $15 children 12 and under. ***Wendameen***, a schooner built in 1912, is available for private charters and overnight cruises.

SEA KAYAKING ✐ **Maine Island Kayak Co.** (207-766-2373 or 1-800-796-2373; www.maineislandkayak.com), 70 Luther St., Peaks Island. Late May–Oct. We love this company for many reasons, including its exceptional guides, its state-of-the-art equipment, and its commitment to the leave-no-trace philosophy, crucial in heavily trafficked Casco Bay. MIKCO offers a limited schedule of trips, call for information.

✴ Green Space

BEACHES ✐ ♿ **Crescent Beach State Park** (207-799-5871), 66 Two Lights Road, Cape Elizabeth; 8 miles from Portland on Rt. 77. A mile of sand complete with changing facilities, a playground, picnic tables, and a snack bar. Fee charged for adults and ages 5–11. Good for young children, because it's protected from heavy surf.

✐ ♿ **Wolfe's Neck Woods State Park** (207-865-4465; off-season, 207-865-

6080), 425 Wolfe's Neck Rd. (take Bow St., across from L. L. Bean), Freeport. Open Apr.–Oct. Day-use fee. A 233-acre park with shoreline hiking along Casco Bay, the Harraseeket River, and salt marshes, as well as excellent birding with ospreys as the local stars. Guided nature walks, and scattered picnic tables and grills.

Kettle Cove is just down the road from Crescent Beach—follow the road behind the (excellent) ice cream shop on Rt. 77. There is no admission fee to this rocky end of Crescent Beach, but parking is limited.

Higgins Beach, farther down Rt. 77 in Scarborough, is an extensive strand within walking distance of lodging—but there is no parking on the street. Private lots charge a fee. The swell can kick up quite a bit here, so beware the undertow. Surfers are always here when the waves are high.

Scarborough Beach State Park, Black Point Rd. (Rt. 207), 3 miles south of Rt. 1 on Prouts Neck. Open Memorial Day–Sept. ($4 admission), also for walking year-round. A 243-acre park with a superb beach, but only a 65-foot stretch is technically public. Get there early because parking is minimal. For the scenic route from Portland, see *Scenic Drives*.

PARKS ✐ **Deering Oaks**, Portland's 51-acre city park designed by city civil engineer William Goodwin, has a pond, ducks and swans, fountains, a playground, a fine grove of oak trees, a beautifully cared for rose garden, and a refurbished urban "ravine" complete with a wading pool and spray jets for summertime frolicking. A farmer's market is held here Wed. and Sat. mornings May–Nov. Ice skating on the pond in winter, with the newly renovated stone "Castle" to be open for refreshment and warming up. No admission fee.

Two Lights State Park, 66 Two Lights Rd., Cape Elizabeth, is open year-round. No swimming, but 40 acres of shore with stunning water views for picnicking and fishing.

Also see **Fort Williams Park** in *Scenic Drives* and **Fort Allen Park** under Eastern Promenade in *Walks*.

NATURE PRESERVES ✐ **Gilsland Farm Audubon Center** (207-781-2330; www.maineaudubon.org), 20 Gilsland Farm Rd., Falmouth (3 miles east of Portland). Open Mon.–Sat. 9–5, Sun. noon–5 in warm weather, 2–5 in cold weather. Maine Audubon's headquarters are located at this 65-acre wildlife sanctuary, along with trails, rolling fields, river frontage, and salt marsh. The education center features exhibits throughout the year, a wildlife discovery room for children, and a Maine Audubon Nature Store selling binoculars and great books. The education center hosts day and evening wildlife-related programs year-round and runs camps for children during summer and school breaks. The sanctuary is also open year-round for walking, sunrise to sunset.

Scarborough Marsh Audubon Center (207-883-5100), Pine Point Rd. (also marked as Rt. 9 west), Scarborough (10 miles south of downtown Portland). Visitors can walk the property any day of the year, dawn to dusk; the nature center is open May–June, Sat. and Memorial Day weekend; June–Labor Day, daily

9:30–5:30. The state's largest salt marsh can also be explored by canoe or kayak. The nature center houses an aquarium and mounted birds and mammals and sponsors walks, canoe tours, and rentals.

Fore River Sanctuary, (207-775-2411; www.trails.org). Located near Maine Turnpike exit 8, off Brighton Ave., Portland, and managed by Portland Trails. This 85-acre preserve is hidden behind a suburban neighborhood where explorers may not think to look. The 2.5 miles of hiking trails offer access to Portland's only waterfall, **Jewell Falls**. A set of railroad tracks (be careful—they are active) marks the beginning of a trail that leads you through woods and marshland.

Prouts Neck Cliff Walk and Wildlife Sanctuary. Winslow Homer painted many of his seascapes in a small studio here (now owned by Portland Museum of Art and scheduled to open to the public sometime in 2008). This exclusive community on Prouts Neck is not far from the Black Point Inn. Winslow Homer Road marks the start of the Cliff Path (unmarked), a beautiful stroll along the rocks, around Eastern Point, and back almost to the inn. You can also walk through the sanctuary between Winslow Homer Road (just east of St. James Episcopal Church) and Library Lane, donated by Winslow's brother Charles.

WALKS **Portland Trails** (207-775-2411; www.trails.org), 305 Commercial St., Portland, an organization committed to developing hiking and walking trails in the city, sells a map describing several city parks and more than 30 miles of trails as well as bus routes to take you there. The Portland Trails Map costs $4.95 and can be bought from the Web site or at the visitor information center. A favorite walk is the Presumpscot River trail, one of the prettiest walks full of wildflowers and wildlife.

The Eastern Promenade. Follow Congress St. east to the Portland Observatory atop Munjoy Hill and then continue the extra block to the Eastern Promenade, a park-lined street high on this same bluff with sweeping views of Casco Bay. Follow it around, back toward the harbor, to 68-acre **Fort Allen Park**, which dates to 1814, set on a blustery point above the bay. Down along the bay itself the paved **Eastern Promenade Trail** runs along the base of Munjoy Hill, good for biking and walking. (The railroad museum's excursion train runs alongside it.)

The Western Promenade. It's ironic that Munjoy Hill (see above), the poorer (but vibrant) section of town, has the million-dollar view while the Western Promenade overlooks the airport and gas holding tanks. Still, this is Portland's most architecturally interesting residential neighborhood. Pick up a copy of the Portland Landmarks leaflet *Guide to the Western Promenade* ($1) from the visitors bureau.

Baxter Boulevard. A 3.5-mile path around the tidal flats of Back Cove connects with the Eastern Promenade Trail. It's a popular spot for dog walking, jogging, and biking. Adjacent fields provide good kite flying and soccer venues.

Eastern Cemetery, Congress St. and Washington Ave. (near the Portland Observatory on Munjoy Hill). The oldest cemetery in Portland, it is listed in the National Trust for Historic Places. Its six acres hold more than 4,000 headstones dating from the mid-17th century to the early 19th; some are embellished with angels and death's heads.**Spirits Alive** (207-846-7753; www.spiritsalive.org) runs guided tours ($7 adults, $4 seniors and students, under 12 free) usually on weekends in the summer, a Halloween Walk Among the Shadows tour, and others. The group restores gravestones, and is installing botanical markers. Over 100 trees are being planted, and granite benches are in place for meditation.

Clark's Pond Trail, maintained by the South Portland Land Trust (www.spland trust.org). Home Depot in South Portland is located at the trailhead of this plunge into the woods, a 1.2 mile trail located near the Maine Mall with a secret waterfall and turkeys and deer. South Portland's master plan will someday connect many neighborhoods with walkways and bike trails.

✷ Lodging

HOTELS There are more than 2,000 hotel and motel rooms in and around Portland.

In the Old Port 04101

♿ **Portland Regency** (207-774-4200 or 1-800-727-3436; www.the regency.com), 20 Milk St. We like the Regency for its quiet stateliness in the midst of the Old Port, even though some of the rooms don't have much in the way of windows. Stay in one of 95 rooms (including nine suites) housed in a century-old armory. Rooms come with reproduction beds (a king or two doubles), floral chintz spreads and drapes, cable TV, and air-conditioning; some suites feature a whirlpool tub. **Twenty Milk Street** is a good steak house with a formal dining room, and the **Armory Lounge** offers cocktails and lighter fare in an upscale sports bar. A downstairs gym and day spa with luxurious locker rooms, each with private sauna; also coed sauna and steam room, and 10-person, tiled whirlpool with a waterfall. Complimentary van service and valet parking. From $139–179 Jan.–Apr.; in-season (Memorial Day weekend–Oct.) $249–299.

♿ **Portland Harbor Hotel** (207-775-9090 or 1-888-798-9090; www.theportlandharborhotel.com), 468 Fore St. The choice of granite-look-alike rigid foam garnered some controversy when this hotel was being built, but so far the exterior is holding up. An enviable location in the heart of the Old Port and an in-hotel restaurant and elevators make it a good bet for those who wish for comfort. Amenities include cable TV and radio, marble bath, European-style glass shower, granite counters, and free pickup service from the Jetport or train station. Jacuzzi suites feature an oval spa tub, separate sitting area with sofa bed. **Eve's** serves fine dinners. $159–299, depending on view and season. Pets are allowed with a $25 fee per day.

♿ **Hilton Garden Inn Portland Downtown Waterfront** (207-780-0780; www.hiltongardeninn portland.com), 65 Commercial St. Portland's corporate and leisure hotel rents 120 rooms, all with a bath, refrigerator, and microwave. Two corner suites with views and a sitting area are also available. A small indoor pool and fitness center, and impressive views of the harbor from half of the rooms—the inn is located in the middle of the Old Port—make this a fun place to stay. Rates $259–344 in summer, as low as $159 in winter.

Midtown Portland

🐾 ✐ ♿ **Eastland Park Hotel** (207-775-5411 or 1-888-671-8008; www.eastlandparkhotel.com), 157 High St. This 1927 landmark's $2.5 million face-lift refurbished everything from the gilt-and-marble lobby, ballroom, and 202 guest rooms and suites to the beloved **Top of the East** cocktail lounge, with stunning 360-degree views. All rooms have private bath, cable TV, new windows that open, and air-conditioning. Shuttle service from the Jetport is free, as is use of the in-hotel exercise room or nearby Bay Club Fitness. $169–254 in-season, $99–174 in winter. $25 fee for pets includes a goody bag, perhaps with lobster dog bones.

✐ ♿ **Holiday Inn by the Bay** (207-775-2311 or 1-800-HOLIDAY; www.innbythebay.com), 88 Spring St. Portlanders love to hate this ugly, 11-story, downtown high-rise, especially since it took over a beautiful neighborhood. But perhaps someday we'll regard its utilitarian architecture fondly, and the harbor and skyline views are great from the inside. Amenities include an indoor pool, small fitness center, cable TV with in-room movies and video-game hook-ups, free parking, laundry facility, and a restaurant and lounge. Two suites and 239 rooms range from $180 in high season.

Note: Portland does host the major chains, many located by I-95 at exit 8 in Westbrook or in South Portland.

Beyond Portland

✐ ♿ **Black Point Inn Resort** (207-883-2500 or 1-800-258-0003; www.blackpointinn.com), 510 Blackpoint Rd., Prouts Neck 04074. Open May–Jan. 1. This vintage-1878 summer hotel blessedly remains the same or even more so, after a renovation tore down newer additions. The oldest elevator in the state of Maine is still hand operated by a polite staff member, and there is a wonderful widow's walk has 360-degree views of Scarborough, Old Orchard Beach, and the mighty Atlantic Ocean. Guests use the Prouts Neck Country Club's 18-hole golf course and 14 tennis courts, and can also rent boats at the local yacht club; bikes are available at the inn. Two sandy beaches, outdoor heated pool, a room with exercise equipment, and in-room massages by appointment. There are 25 rooms, afternoon tea, evening cocktails with a pianist, and a casual and formal dining rooms (see *Dining Out*). In high season $440–540 for double MAP per night plus 18 percent gratuity; from $360–460 off-season.

🐾 ✐ ♿ **Inn by the Sea** (207-799-3134; www.innbythesea.com), 40 Bowery Beach Rd., Cape Elizabeth 04107. A 15-minute drive from downtown Portland, this shingled complex maintains a high reputation for great hospitality and beautiful rooms. The 43 one- and two-bedroom condo-style suites hold a living/dining area, full kitchen, and porch or deck with water view. Beach house units are generally larger, with a gas-burning fireplace and full water views. Fourteen rooms are being added in 2008. Amenities include outdoor pool, tennis courts, and shuffleboard, a fitness center and spa with six treatment rooms (new in 2008), and a lobby bar, plus walking and jogging trails, and golf privileges at nearby Purpoodock Club. A boardwalk leads to the tip of Crescent Beach State Park. $419–789 summer, $189–369 winter.

✐ **Higgins Beach Inn** (207-883-6684; www.higginsbeachinn.com), 34

Ocean Ave., Scarborough 04074 (7 miles south of Portland). Open mid-May–mid-Oct. A well-cared-for 1890s three-story wooden summer hotel near sandy, gorgeous Higgins Beach. The dining room, **Garofalo's**, features seafood and pasta dishes from owner Diane's Sicilian family recipes (entrées $17–24). There is also a cocktail lounge and a sunporch. Upstairs, the 22 guest rooms are archetypal summer hotel rooms—simple, clean, and airy—13 with private bath. Full breakfast available but not included in the room rates: $85–150 double, with a minimum two-night stay most weekends.

INNS AND BED & BREAKFASTS ♿ **Pomegranate Inn** (207-772-1006 or 1-800-356-0408; www.pomegranateinn.com), 49 Neal St., Portland 04102. Peter Morneau, general manager, and new owner Kim Swan, plan to preserve the distinctive look of the inn. Among the eight amazing rooms, most have bold, hand-painted walls by Heidi Gerquest, a Portland artist; all have discreet TV and private bath, and five have a gas fireplace. Breakfast might be leek and goat cheese omelet with prosciutto. The fireplace surround and columns in the dining rooms are painted a green faux stone that exactly mimics green onyx. $175–265 per room in-season, $95–155 off-season, including breakfast.

Wild Iris Inn (207-775-0224 or 1-800-600-1557; www.wildirisinn.com), 273 State St., Portland 04101. This small Victorian on the hill into Portland's main street, Congress, is the favorite stop for business travelers and tourists who like a quiet place with all the basic comforts. Seven rooms, all but two with private bath, have been furnished by owner Diane Edwards with attractive quilts and furniture; all are air-conditioned. A Shaker-inspired dining room holds biscotti and tea at all hours, as well as a full breakfast in the morning. Downtown is a close walk, and a computer and printer are available for visitors. $85–175.

Carleton Inn (207-775-1910 or 1-800-639-1779; www.innoncarleton.com), 46 Carleton St., Portland 04102. Phil Cox has lovingly restored this handsome 1869 town house, even the trompe l'oeil artwork in the entryway. Each of the six rooms are furnished with spectacularly heavy, high-Victorian bedroom sets, including one Egyptian Revival headboard found in Colorado. The breakfast table is another big antique. $135–259 in-season. Two Maine coon cats in residence.

West End Inn (207-772-1377 or 1-800-338-1377; www.westendbb.com), 146 Pine St., Portland 04102. This 1871 brick town house combines natural elegance with colorful decor, and is now owned by Dan and Michele Brown. The most popular of the six rooms is Cliff Island, with 12-foot ceilings, private deck, and white and blue accents. All come with private bath, cable TV, ceiling fan, and air-conditioning. $159–199 in-season, including full breakfast and afternoon tea. Children 10 and older welcome.

Morrill Mansion Bed & Breakfast (207-774-6900; www.morrillmansion.com), 249 Vaughan St., Portland 04102. Seven bedrooms are named after local neighborhoods and old families in this new B&B close to Maine Medical Center and on the edge of the West End, an easy walk to midtown. The building was completely done over in 2006 by David Parker. All rooms have private bath and cable TV. $88–219 includes a breakfast buffet, with an egg custard and warm fruit crisp and yogurt, fresh fruit, cereals, and more. Afternoon treats are served in the second floor guest living room.

Inn at Park Spring (207-774-1059 or 1-800-437-8511; www.innatparkspring.com), 135 Spring St., Portland 04101. This inn features one of the most convenient locations in town. Nancy and John Gonsalves offer six guest rooms with private bath and sitting area, and many days fresh flowers. A breakfast is served in the formal dining room with floor-to-ceiling windows; a French toast croissant stuffed with marmalade and cream cheese is a possibility. June–Oct. $149–180, otherwise $99–139.

Inn at St. John (207-773-6481 or 1-800-636-9127; www.innatstjohn.com), 939 Congress St., Portland 04102. A 39-room hotel built in 1897 to accommodate railroad passengers arriving at Union Station (unfortunately long gone), this place has undergone a renovation that brings many of its rooms into the modern age. Convenient for guests arriving by Vermont Transit, it's a hike to downtown, but the moderate rates and quality make up for the distance. Attractive rooms are well managed by innkeeper Paul Hood. $60–250 (depending on season) includes continental breakfast, air-conditioning, and cable TV; $10 fee per pet, but not to exceed a maximum of $20.

* Where to Eat

The quality of the dining is exceptional in Portland. Some of the chefs have national reputations, with an award from *Food and Wine* magazine to Steve Corry of 555, from the James Beard Foundation to Sam Hayward of Fore Street; one local star has won awards from both—Rob Evans of Hugo's.

But many more chefs are distinguished by incredibly consistent, reliably wonderful dinners. Several women have made their marks with their new restaurants, including Abby Harmon of Caiola's, a great neighborhood spot in the West End, and Krista Kern, whose teeny Bresca was all the buzz in 2007.

DINING OUT

In Portland

Back Bay Grill (207-772-8833; www.backbaygrill.com), 65 Portland St. It's always a good night for dinner at Back Bay Grill, a comfortable, elegant restaurant with a fresh, lively menu. A lot of history hasn't made this dining room stiff, perhaps because the mural on the wall always provides such a good example of bon temps. The Maine crabcake is excellent, seared foie gras with pickled cherries divine. Flat iron steak, black truffle fettucini, and monkfish with wilted spinach might be your welcome dinner. Entrées $18–35.

Bresca (207-772-1004), 111 Middle St. A 20-seat mocha dining room is usually stuffed with Krista Kern's happy customers, who might have a fetish for the wilted greens, pancetta, and a six-minute egg. Steak and fish are made with precision and flair, the homemade pasta is tender and seasoned with invention. Desserts by the chef-owner, a former bigwig pastry chef, pull out all the stops. Entrées $16–24.

Caiola's (207-772-1110; www.caiolas.com), 58 Pine St. A short walk into the West End, this bustling restaurant's kitchen is run by Abby Harmon, head of the kitchen at Street and Co. for 16 years. Her sure touch makes scallops perfect and duck crispy and tender; try the braised stuffed cabbage with chicken of the woods mushrooms, or house-made cannoloni stuffed with caramelized onions, spinach, and peppers. The fine wine list and well-run dining room, managed by Lisa Vaccaro, makes the atmosphere welcoming. Entrées $13–23.

Cinque Terre (207-347-6154; www.cinqueterremaine.com), 56 Wharf St. Northern Italian food is served in an open-plan dining room with tile floors and second-floor gallery. Lee Skawinski runs the kitchen, turning out homemade gnocchi, each like a cheesy, buttery little soufflé. Any of the homemade stuffed pasta dishes will be wonderful, and the risottos are perfectly mated with Maine lobster. Try the great Italian wine. Entrées $20–27.

♿ **five fifty-five** (207-761-0555; www.fivefifty-five.com), 555 Congress St. Chef-owner Steve Corry smiled from the July 2007 cover of *Food and Wine* magazine, named one of top 10 best new chefs. His skills make even hamburgers an unusual pleasure. But try the black pepper ice cream, or whatever wild flavor the evening menu offers, for real adventure. Smoked trout risotto with fresh corn and pork tenderloin with apple crisp were featured on a fall menu. Entrées $23–29. Reservations advised.

Fore Street (207-775-2717; www.forestreet.biz), 288 Fore Street. Open for dinner nightly. Reservations a must in summer, but there are a few open tables at 5:30 when the dining room opens. Sam Hayward oversees meals full of his signature integrity. Great roast pork, turned on a spit in the open kitchen, or wood-fired oven-roasted fish, or roast quail, or just a few chicken livers quickly sautéed, and the best steamed mussels with garlic almond butter. The local vegetable side dishes are not to be missed. Desserts like chocolate soufflé cake and peach tarte tatin are favorites on the menu. Entrées $18–35.

Hugo's (207-774-8538; www.hugos.net), 88 Middle St. Rob Evans came to Portland in 2000. A la carte dishes and a four-course, fixed price, $68 menu create an exuberant evening packed with revelations. Combinations of flavors and oddball juxtapositions—an oyster cracker made with oyster, mussels and Maine periwinkles, beet risotto as deep red as garnet—make meals entertaining and delicious. Bring your open mind and dive in, or for less, sample something at the bar. Or try Evans's casual Duckfat, further down on Middle St. (see *Eating Out*). Plates $10–26.

♿ **Local 188** (207-761-7909; www.local188.com), 685 Congress St. Open Tue.–Sat. for dinner, and Sunday brunch. A tapas bar and dinner restaurant with a great lounge and bar. The Spanish bias is evident, as is local produce, and a stray Turkish or elsewhere influence. Spanish wines are a specialty. Try the gazpacho, and the garlic shrimp, grilled chourico, and paella. Entrées $15–19; tapas $6.

♿ **Mims Brasserie** (207-347-7478; www.mimsportland.com), 205 Commercial St. Open daily for breakfast, lunch, and dinner, weekend brunch.

This restaurant opened in 2004 with an à la carte menu for every part of the meal. Meals could be short rib with fava beans and lobster bouillabaisse with crème fraîche, with sides like spinach with garlic or haricot vert. Entrées $15–22.

♿ **Street & Company** (207-775-0887), 33 Wharf St. Open for dinner daily 5:30–9:30, Fri. and Sat. until 10. Reservations recommended. The noisy, packed dining rooms here, and a comfortable bar with upholstered seats, are filled with lovers of the wonderful fish, inventive specials, and comfortable standards like lobster diavolo for two, mussels Provençal, and scallops in Pernod and cream. The raw bar serves up the best oysters in town. Bourbon pecan pie and peach crisp might be on the dessert menu. Entrées $22–29.

On Munjoy Hill

♿ **The Front Room** (207-773-3366; www.thefrontroomrestaurant.com), 73 Congress St. Open daily for all three meals. Bustling and hectic on weekends, this neighborhood mainstay serves a wide range of fine dinners, from meatloaf to roasted pork chops, grilled flat iron steak to corned hake in cream with red potatoes and bacon. Easy to understand why it's full, isn't it? The noise can overwhelm some. Entrées $12–18.

♿ **Bar Lola** (207-775-5652), 100 Congress St. Open Wed.–Sat. for dinner. Little dishes offer customers a chance to tailor dinner to their appetite, with the smallest being really just a taste, and even the largest courses modestly sized. Owners Guy and Stella Hernandez take pride in the changing menu, and its respect for seasonal meat and fish, but spinach salad with warm vinaigrette and a fried egg is a popular classic you can usually find on the menu. Entrées $12-14.

♿ **Blue Spoon** (207-773-1116), 89 Congress St. Open for lunch and dinner Tue.–Sat., brunch on Sun. This small restaurant at the top of Munjoy Hill cooks up straightforward dishes with skill and keeps them reasonably priced. Local stuff in season, and seasonal dishes. The juicy burger and large bowls of mussels with lemon and garlic are popular mainstays on an otherwise changing menu. Entrées $13–18.

Outside of Portland

♿ **The Point Oceanfront Dining at The Black Point Inn Resort** (207-883-2500 or 1-800-258-0003; www.blackpointinn.com), 510 Blackpoint Rd., Prouts Neck 04074. Open May–Jan.1, dinner in the formal room by reservation only. Cheryl Lewis is the chef, Norine Kotts the dining room manager at this inn that has revived its reputation for great dinners and fine casual food (in the Chart Room). The cocktails on the porch are always fine, but with new management the dinners are delightful too. Hanger steak, roast poussin, and braised short ribs are expertly made; desserts are in fine hands. Entrées $19–36.

♿ **SeaGrass Bistro** (207-846-3885; www.seagrassbistro.com), 30 Forest Falls Drive, Yarmouth. Stephanie Brown takes her obsession with fresh and local straight into fall and winter, with mushroom and leek soufflé, molasses-glazed pork loin with Maine cattle greens and wilted kale or Swiss chard. House ice creams and a chocolate molten cake made here. Brown offers cooking classes and enjoys many repeat customers. Entrées $23–28.

🔌 ♿ **Saltwater Grille** (207-799-5400; www.saltwatergrille.com), 231 Front St., South Portland. Open daily for lunch and dinner, with fabulous views across the bay to Portland. The food has steadied and improved here. Entrées include scallops carbonara (scallops sautéed with bacon, mushrooms, and peas in a Parmesan cream sauce on bow-tie pasta) and saffron seafood and gnocchi that adds sweet sausages. Big servings. Entrées $18–26.

EATING OUT *Note:* Most of the restaurants described under *Dining Out* also serve a reasonably priced lunch.

In and around the Old Port

Vignola (207-772-1330; www.vignolamaine.com), 10 Dana St. Open daily until 12 AM for dinner, lunch Thurs.–Sat., Sunday brunch 10–2:30. The casual sister restaurant of Cinque Terre (see Dining Out), Vignola makes some of the best pizza in town, one with boar sausage. An old-fashioned pork and veal terrine, or tartare of beef appetizers, roast Maine rabbit, or grilled quail stuffed with foie gras—it doesn't sound casual at all, just terrific. Sides ordered separately. Entrées $16–20.

♿ **PepperClub** (207-772-0531; www.pepperclubrestaurant.com), 78 Middle St. Open for dinner Sun.–Thu. 5–9, Fri. and Sat. 5–10. A creative menu is written on two large blackboards and smaller table versions. Choose from six vegetarian, three fish, and three meat entrées every night, perhaps the wonderful meatloaf, organic salmon, Indian curry with dal and chutney, or roasted vegetables with orzo. Entrées $12-16.50. Free parking across the street.

Flatbread Pizza (207-772-8777; www.flatbreadcompany.com), 72 Commercial St. One of a small chain of pizza joints (six others include one in Paia Maui, Hawaii). Flatbread bakes its pies in a clay, wood-fired oven shaped like a low igloo—right in the middle of the restaurant. Kids are always sitting on a stone, mesmerized by the fire. Our favorite pizza features house maple-fennel sausage, sun-dried tomatoes, onions, mushrooms, mozzarella, and Parmesan ($16.75), but everything here is good, including the salads and desserts. Outside deck overlooks the ferry terminal.

Duckfat (207-774-8080; www.duckfat.com), 43 Middle St. Open Mon.–Thur. 11–8, Fri.–Sat. 11–9, Sun. 12–6. Sister restaurant to Hugo's (see *Dining Out*), with the soul of an eccentric on a budget. Incredible fries rise from a mix of duckfat and vegetable oil. Panini are crisp cases of vegetable ratatouille or bacon, goat cheese, and tomatoes. Rich milk shakes, tender beignets, sweet dessert sandwiches of brioche and jam. Salads and iced coffee for a light lunch. Panini $7–9.

Ribollita (207-774-2972), 41 Middle St. Open for dinner Tues.–Sat. The classics are the draw at this welcoming place, with pansanella, crispy calamari, handmade pasta in the butternut squash ravioli, good wine, and main dishes of salmon with pesto or seared rib-eye. Bean and bread soup, the ribollita of its name, is always available. Desserts include the creamiest flan in town. Entrées $11.50–19.50.

🔌 **Gilbert's Chowder House** (207-871-5636), 92 Commercial St. Open for lunch and dinner. As the name implies, Gilbert's serves delicious and filling chowders, but they also have a nice range of seafood appetizers and entrées, such as lovely steamed mussels with garlic butter. The decor is Early Dive, but you can sit outside on the wharf in-season.

Federal Spice (207-774-6404), 225 Federal St. (across from the downtown post office). Open Mon.–Sat. from 11 AM. The soups du jour zing with flavor, as does the chili. Homemade falafel, yam fries, and sweet potato jalapeño corn bread round out the creative menu of hot and cold wraps and soft tacos.

Japanese, Indian, and Thai

Miyake (207-871-9170), 129 Spring St. Open for dinner daily, lunch Tues.–Fri. In-season, a variety of wild salmon allows a taste of the Pacific's best; all the sushi is fresh and perfectly cut. Uni and ankimo are exceptional, and even the miso soup is of the highest quality.

Benkay (207-773-5555), 2 India St. A happening sushi bar with Western- and Japanese-style tables (one in the shape of a dory), and Rock 'n' Roll Sushi Friday and Saturday nights.

Restaurant Sapporo (207-772-1233; www.sappororestaurant.com), 230 Commercial St. Open for lunch and inner daily. Portland's oldest sushi place has kept its high standards. You can count on Sapporo for a great dinner.

Yosaku (207-780-0880), 1 Danforth St. Open daily for lunch and dinner. High quality sushi and other good Japanese meals.

Fuji (207-773-2900; www.fujimaine.com), 29 Exchange St. Open daily for lunch and dinner, with fine sushi and Japanese dishes. Japanese steakhouse-style meals are served on hibachis in the lower dining room; a reservation is a good idea for three or more.

Tandoor (207-775-4259), 88 Exchange St. Open daily for lunch and dinner. We've tried them all, and we still think this is the best Indian place in town. Choose from classics like chicken and lamb cooked in the tandoor oven, or vegetarian favorites like dal (yellow lentils sautéed with cream and spices) and *sag paneer* (spinach with homemade cheese).

Viet Bangkok Cuisine (207-347-7279), 249 St. John St. Open Mon.–Sat. for lunch and dinner. Great pho, Vietnamese noodle soup, and authentic Thai curries. Try the cold Thai beef salad for intense lime and spice. Entrées $7.50–17.

Around Portland

♿ **Becky's Diner** (207-773-7070; www.beckys.com), 390 Commercial St. Open daily 4 AM–9 PM, this is a genuine local favorite, known for soups and pies. Breakfast on fruit salad, granola-and-yogurt bowl, and delicious grilled, homemade corn and blueberry muffins. Also reasonably priced lunch and dinner specials, and good chowder. An long-awaited expansion has allowed the morning lines to diminish and find cover.

Norm's Bar & Grill (207-828-9944), 606 Congress St. Open daily for dinner, lunch Mon.–Sat. And for barbeque fans **Norm's East End Grill** (207-253-1700), 47 Middle St. Barbequed ribs, chicken, and more goes well with sweet potato fries at the Middle St. branch, and steak salads and pork chops dinners are wonderful on Congress. Both spots are busy.

Artemisia Café (207-761-0135), 61 Pleasant St. (just behind and to the east of Holiday Inn by the Bay). Lunch Mon.–Fri., brunch Sat. and Sun., dinner Thu.–Sat. Salads, wraps, and sandwiches, from salade Niçoise to the Tuscan grill with portobello mushrooms, pesto, and goat cheese. A friendly spot for a quiet and good brunch or dinner.

Bonobo (207-347-8267), 46 Pine St. Open Mon. 5–11, Tues.-Sun. 11–11. A wood-fired oven bakes pizza with a thin crust made with wet dough; many organic ingredients are used. Sausage and onion is one popular pie. The house pizza, Bonobo, holds mushrooms, prosciutto, spinach, spinach, cream, fontina, and thyme. Pizza $9–16.

The Bayou Kitchen (207-774-4935), 543 Deering Ave. (across the street from Big Sky Bakery and an excellent art supply store). Serving breakfast and lunch Wed.–Sat. 7–2, Sun. 8–2. This hole-in-the-wall off Forest Ave. offers the best grits and eggs in town, plus decent jambalaya, crawfish po'boys, and Cajun burgers.

Beyond Portland

158 Pickett Street Café (207-799-8998), 158 Bejamin Pickett St., South Portland. Breakfast and lunch Tues.–Sun. They make the bagels so exactly right: chewy, slightly sour, utterly delicious, and golden brown. A variety of original soups in winter, local salads in summer, and sandwiches like ham and brie with roasted grapes on baguette, Anestes Fotiades's favorite (and see www.portland foodmap.com, his work of art).

THE LOBSTER SHACK AT TWO LIGHTS

Nancy English

Beale Street Barbeque and Grill (207-767-0130; www.mainebbq.com), 725 Broadway, South Portland. Open daily for lunch and dinner. This place serves authentic, hickory-smoked chicken, beef, sausage, and pork, plus good corn bread, barbecued beans, and coleslaw.

The Lobster Shack (207-799-1677; www.lobstershack-twolights.com), 225 Two Lights Rd., Cape Elizabeth (off Rt. 77 at the tip of the cape, near Two Lights State Park). Open Apr.–late Oct., 11–8. Dine inside or out at this local landmark built in the 1920s, set below the lighthouse and next to the foghorn. Herb and Martha Porch have gotten their line management down to a science. Lobsters, chowders and lobster stew, fried Maine shrimp, scallops, and clams, or the lobster and crabmeat rolls.

The Good Table (207-799-4663), 526 Ocean House Rd. (Rt. 77), Cape Elizabeth. Open Tue.–Sun. for breakfast, lunch, and dinner 8 AM–9 PM in summer, from 11 AM in winter, with 3 PM Sun. closing year-round. Beloved by its loyal regulars, the restaurant serves home-style entrées for lunch and dinner, but the specials board is where some of the best meals can be found. Weekend brunch menu might include eggs Benedict and interesting quiches.

Ken's Place (207-883-6611), 207 Pine Point Road, Scarborough. Open daily for lunch and dinner April to Oct. You can depend on David Wilcox to make sure things are running smoothly here, and that the kitchen is scrupulous about changing the oil, and serving the freshest seafood. Great fried clams, and wonderful seafood.

First and Last Tavern (207-883-8383), 240 Pine Point Rd. (Route 9), Scarborough. Open Tues.–Sun. in summer, fewer days off-season, closed Jan.–Apr. A family branch of the well-known First and Last Tavern in Hartford, Conn., the Italian dishes here deliver flavor; pizza is crisp and wonderful Homemade gelato. Entrées $10–17.

COFFEE BARS At **Java Net** (207-773-2469 or 1-800-528-2638), 39 Exchange St., travelers can sip on a latte, cider, or chai while checking their e-mail or conducting business via the Internet. Bring your laptop or use their computers (hourly rates). **Coffee by Design** (207-772-5533), 620 Congress St., is the first in this friendly local chain (now also at 67 India St.), a cheerful spot with plenty of tables (sidewalk tables in summer), local art on display (and for sale), and all the usual coffee and espresso choices. **Arabica** (207-879-0792), 16 Free St. We like this place's baked goods, Victorian love seat, high ceilings, and cinnamon toast.

ICE CREAM **Maple's Organic Desserts** (207-774-2665; www.maplesorganics.com), 151 Middle St. Open Mon.–Sat. 11–10, Sun. 12–9. Here is dessert, all organic. The maple gelato is a favorite, but the changing flavors always entice—cardomom ginger, toasted coconut, and apple cobbler, are a few that are beloved. Whoopie pies and cakes too.

✷ Entertainment

All listings are in Portland unless otherwise noted

Cumberland County Civic Center (207-775-3458; www.theciviccenter.com), 1 Civic Center Square. An arena with close to 8,000 seats, the center hosts year-round concerts, ice-skating spectaculars, Portland Pirates hockey games, and more.

Top of the East (207-775-5411; www.eastlandparkhotel.com), Eastland Hotel, 157 High St. Open for lunch daily from 11–2, light fare till 4, then appetizers until 1 AM. Portland's only rooftop lounge, with a marble bar, leather banquettes, and floor-to-ceiling windows taking in views of Mount Washington and Casco Bay.

MUSIC **Portland Symphony Orchestra** (207-773-6128; www.portlandsymphony.com), Merrill Auditorium, 20 Myrtle St. (just off Congress St. behind city hall). The winter series runs Sept.–May; in summertime, outdoor pops concerts at different locations along the shores of Casco Bay.

Portland Opera Repertory Theatre (207-879-7678; www.portopera.org), Merrill Auditorium. This critically acclaimed company enters its 14th season in 2008. Past productions include *The Barber of Seville* and *Faust*.

PCA Great Performances (207-773-3150; www.pcagreatperformances.com). A series of orchestra, jazz, and musical theater performances staged in fall and winter at Merrill Auditorium.

Everything from *Momix* to the Ellis Marsalis Trio.

PROFESSIONAL SPORTS The **Portland Pirates** (207-828-4665; www.portlandpirates.com), a professional minor-league hockey team, play their home games at the Cumberland County Civic Center. The **Portland Sea Dogs** (1-800-936-3647; www.portlandseadogs.com), a double-A baseball team and Boston Red Sox affiliate, play in Hadlock Stadium on Park Ave. (next to the Expo).

THEATER **Portland Stage Company** (207-774-0465; www.portlandstage.com) is based in the city's old Odd Fellows Hall (25A Forest Ave.), now an elegant, intimate, 290-seat theater. This Equity group stages a variety of shows Oct.–Apr.

Portland Players (207-799-7338), Thaxter Theater, 420 Cottage Rd., South Portland. An excellent community theater, the Players put on productions Sept.–June.

Lyric Music Theater (207-799-6509), Cedric Thomas Playhouse, 176 Sawyer St., South Portland. Four musicals each winter.

St. Lawrence Arts & Community Center (207-775-5568; www.stlawrencearts.org), 76 Congress St. An umbrella performance space for several local professional theater companies, musicians, filmmakers, dance companies, and other artists. The schedule changes constantly, so call to see what's doing.

* Selective Shopping

All listings are in Portland unless otherwise noted

Angela Adams (207-774-3523; www.angelaadams.com), 273 Congress St. This store sells the swirling, colorful carpets and handbags designed by Angela Adams. Her work has won praise from all kinds of designers, and her pricey rugs are now coveted items. Sales held at the end of the retail seasons.

Ferdinand (207-761-2151; www.ferdinandhomestore.com), 243 Congress St. Just steps from Angela Adams, Ferdinand is stuffed with low chic—T-shirts with charming animals, and cheap pins, earrings, and jewelry, all infused with owner Diane Toepfer's eccentric aesthetic.

ANTIQUES There are a plethora of small shops, especially in the Old Port, along Congress St., and along Rt. 1 from south of town and north into Yarmouth. Here two good ones:

Allen and Walker (207-772-8787), 600 Congress St. A mix of 1960s modern and older antiques, with some Japanese pottery.

Zinnia's (780-6622), 662 Congress St. Chock-full of interesting 19th- and 20th-century antiques, this place specializes in antique lighting and furniture.

ART GALLERIES **Art Walks** are held the first Friday of every month, when galleries citywide hold open house.

Greenhut Galleries (207-772-2693 or 1-888-772-2693; www.greenhutgalleries.com), 146 Middle St. Peggy Golden Greenhut represents many of Maine's top artists and sculptors.

June Fitzpatrick Gallery (207-772-1961; www.fitzpatrickgallery.com), 112 High St. Well established and showcasing contemporary and fine art.

Aucocisco (207-874-2060; www.aucocisco.com), 615A Congress St. Andres Verzosa's expanded gallery is worth checking out, showcasing brilliant area artists.

Salt Gallery (207-761-0660; www.salt.edu), 110 Exchange St. (but may move—call first). The Salt Institute for Documentary Studies brings students from all over the United States and abroad to study photography, nonfiction writing, and documentary radio. You can view the fruits of their photographic work, usually about the state of Maine, in this 19th-century Old Port building.

CRAFTS GALLERIES **Edgecomb Potters Gallery** (207-780-6727; www.edgecombpotters.com), 49 Exchange St. One of four in the state; a fine collection of reasonably priced, interesting pottery.

Abacus (207-772-4880; www.abacusgallery.com), 44 Exchange St. A fascinating array of fine glass, ceramics, jewelry, textiles, and home furnishings.

Maine Potters Market (207-774-1633; www.mainepottersmarket.com), 376 Fore St. Work by 15 Maine potters.

BOOKSTORES **Books Etc.** (207-774-0626; www.mainebooksetc.com), 38 Exchange St., fills two storefronts and features a terrific Maine books section. They also own a second store in Falmouth (207-781-3784), 240 Rt. 1 (the Shops at Falmouth Village). **Longfellow Books** (207-772-4045; www.longfellowbooks.com), 1 Monument Way, stocks a full range of titles and hosts frequent readings by local and national authors. **Borders Books and Music** (207-775-6110) in the Maine Mall parking lot (I-95, exit 7) has a huge selection and its own café.

Antiquarian-book lovers should check out **Carlson-Turner Books** (207-773-4200; www.carlsonturnerbooks.com), 241 Congress St.; **Emerson Maps and Books** (207-874-2665), 18 Exchange St.; **Cunningham Books** (207-775-2246), 188 State St. on Longfellow Square, with a well-arranged selection of some 50,000 titles; and Pat Murphy's famous **Yes Books** (207-775-3233), 589 Congress St., considered by some to be the best used-book store in Maine.

Newest on the list is **Rabelais** (207-774-1044; www.rabelaisbooks.com), 86 Middle St., devoted to books on food, wine, and cooking. Don Lindgren is a rare-book dealer. Samantha Lindgren's pastry-chef past helps her advise on the best food books available. The best gift supply in the world for a friend who cooks, including yourself.

FOOD **Public Market House** (207-228-2056; www.publicmarkethouse.com), 28 Monument Square. Open Mon.–Fri. 8–6, Sat. 9–6, Sun. 10–3. **K. Horton Specialty Foods** with fine cheeses, many from Maine, **Maine Beer and Beverage Company** with beers, many from Maine's great breweries, **Big Sky Bread** with its good bread and terrific granola, and **A Country Bouquet**, with beautiful flowers.

Rosemont Market (207-774-8129), 559 Brighton Ave., Portland. Open daily 8–6, Sun. 9–4. Fabulous bread, foccacia sandwiches, cheeses, and a wide selection of reasonable, terrific wine.

Two Fat Cats (207-347-5144; www.twofatcatsbakery.com), 47 India St.,

Nancy English

THE HEIGHT OF BERRY SEASON AT PORTLAND'S MONUMENT SQUARE FARMERS' MARKET.

Portland. This bakery made the best pie Nancy tasted in 2007, and it was blueberry, and as the *Maine Sunday Telegram* restaurant reviewer, a guide writer, and 2007 Cumberland County Fair apple pie judge, she tasted a lot of pie.

Maine Pantry (207-228-2028; www.mainespantry.com), 111 Commercial St. Many of the best food products made in Maine can be found here, like Stanchfield Farms high quality jams and jellies, and Captain Mowett Blue Flame hot sauce, made with blueberries, and they are all perfect souvenirs.

Len Libby's Candies (207-883-4897; www.lenlibby.com), 419 Route 1, Scarborough. The candies made here are good, but the real draw is the enormous moose named Lenny—made with 1,700 pounds of milk chocolate, the only life-sized chocolate moose in the world. You can watch a video about how he was put together in 1997. The pond he's standing in is blue-tinted white chocolate.

Standard Baking Co. (207-773-2112), 75 Commercial St. (below Fore Street restaurant). Open Mon.–Fri. 7–6, weekends 7–5. Artisanal French and Italian breads are exceptional, and so are the rolls, baguettes, brioches, and pastries. Small gingerbread cakes, brownies, morning buns with or without nuts, croissants, and *pain au chocolat*.

Browne Trading Market (207-775-7560), 260 Commercial St. Open Mon.–Sat. 10–6. Formerly a fish wholesaler serving upscale restaurants throughout the United States, now selling their own smoked salmon, trout, shrimp, scallops, mussels, fresh seafood, and caviar, along with a wide assortment of cheeses and wine.

Portland Farmer's Market. May–Nov., Wed. 7–noon at Monument Square, and Sat. 7–noon in Deering Oaks Park. Produce, flowers, seeds, baked goods, and more, some organic and all grown and made in Maine. Visit the wading pool nearby in the park.

Harbor Fish Market (207-775-0251 or 1-800-370-1790; www.harborfish.com), 9 Custom House Wharf. Open Mon.–Sat. 8:30–5:30. The epicenter of fish, lobster, crabs, oysters, clams, eels, and squid, to name a few, able to ship anywhere you like.

MORE SPECIAL SHOPS **Portmanteau** (207-774-7276; www.portmanteauonline.com), 11 Free St. Nancy Lawrence began by stitching canvas bags but has long since established a reputation for the distinctive tapestry handbags, totes, backpacks, luggage, and cloaks fabricated in her store.

Leroux Kitchen (207-553-7665), 161 Commercial St. Everything you could possibly need to make a gourmet meal, from marble mortar and pestles and Henckels knives to Viking cookware and wines and prepared foods.

🐾 **Fetch** (207-773-5450), 195 Commercial St. Fetch sells all-natural pet foods, supplements, and litter, as well as a smattering of chew toys and shampoos. Owner Kathy and her pug Zip host a Pug Night every Wednesday in summer. Pets welcome.

Beyond Portland proper is the **Maine Mall** (exit 7 off I-95), whose immediate complex of more than 100 stores is supplemented by large shopping centers and chain stores.

Cabela's (www.cabelas.com) Haigis Parkway, Scarborough 04070. Located at I-95's exit 42. Cabela's, a nationwide chain, plans to open this new 130,000-square-foot showroom in spring 2008. A competitor of Freeport's L. L. Bean, Cabela's offers a huge array of sporting equipment and clothing, along with wild game displays, an indoor archery range, an aquarium of native fish, and recreations of habitats with trophy animals.

✻ Special Events

First Sunday in June: **Old Port Festival**—a celebration that began in the 1970s with the revival of the Old Port; includes a parade, various performances, street vendors, and special sales.

Mid-July: **Yarmouth Clam Festival**—arts and crafts, plenty of clams, performances, more.

August: **Cumberland Crafts Fair**, Cumberland Fairgrounds. **Sidewalk Art Festival**, Congress St.

September: **Cumberland County Fair**, Cumberland

October: **Halloween Parade with Shoestring Theater.**

First weekend in November: **Maine Brewer's Festival**. Each year this event grows in size, due to the increasing number of Maine microbreweries.

Post-Thanksgiving—Christmas: **Victorian Holiday Portland**—with tree lighting, the arrival of Father Christmas, costumed carolers, special events through Christmas.

FREEPORT

Think of Freeport, and you'll likely think of shopping. This is one coastal town that welcomes visitors every day of the year, even on Christmas morning, when the famous L. L. Bean store is open for business. A 24-hour, 365-day-a-year superstore, L. L. Bean has been a landmark since the famous boot was developed back in 1912. The store grew in popularity in 1951 when it opened around the clock, and is now recreating itself as an activity center, offering activities and tours with its Outdoor Discovery Schools. But it was with the influx of seconds and factory stores in the early 1980s that the reputation of Freeport as a shopping mecca took hold.

Freeport is definitely a bargain shopper's dream, but it has always featured upscale retailers as well, such as Cole-Haan and Burberry, and famous furniture makers like Thomas Moser.

The retail facades, however, belie a rich and varied history dating back more than 200 years. The first known residents of the area were several tribes of the Wabanaki. Attempts by colonists to settle in the area resulted in a series of wars throughout the 1600s and early 1700s. By 1715 epidemics of European diseases and the settlers' persistence ended the Native American hold on the area, and a peace treaty with the Penobscots was signed in 1725.

Originally a part of North Yarmouth, Freeport was granted a charter, separating it from the town in 1789. A longtime legend (somewhat controversial, because there is no documented evidence of the occurrence) holds that in 1820 the papers separating Maine from Massachusetts were signed in the historical Jameson Tavern.

Early citizens made a living through agriculture and timber. During the War of 1812, shipbuilding became an important industry, with one famous boat inspiring Whittier's poem "The Dead Ship of Harpswell." In the 1880s shoe factories sprouted up in Freeport, adding another industry to its economy.

Transportation advances also had their effect on Freeport's history. When an electric trolley was built to connect Portland and Yarmouth with Brunswick and Lewiston, it passed through Freeport. Many trolley companies built parks to encourage ridership; likewise a developer built the Casco Castle Hotel to draw tourists to South Freeport. The hotel burned down, but a stone tower remains (on private property) and can be best viewed from Winslow Memorial Park or from the harbor.

Despite the proliferation of shops, the village has retained the appearance of older days—even McDonald's has been confined to a gracious old house, with no golden arches in sight. The Freeport Historical Society operates a research library and museum in a historic house, in the midst of the retail sector. You can take a self-directed walking tour of Freeport historic sites.

Some come to the area simply to stroll wooded paths in Wolfe's Neck Woods State Park and the Mast Landing Audubon Sanctuary. Bradbury Mountain is just a short drive, and Pettengill Farm offers a look at 19th-century coastal life. The Desert of Maine is a quirky attraction as well.

GUIDANCE **The Freeport Merchants Association** (207-865-1212 or 1-800-865-1994; www.freeportusa.com), P.O. Box 452, Freeport 04032, operates a visitors center in a replica of a historic hose tower on Depot St. Brochures, information, and restrooms can be found here. Among their materials is an excellent, free visitor walking map with a list of stores, restaurants, accommodations, attractions, and other services.

The Maine Tourism Association's welcome center in Kittery stocks some Freeport brochures, and there is another state information center on Rt. 1 just south of Freeport, in Yarmouth, at exit 17 off I-95.

THE BIG INDIAN IS A RT. 1 LANDMARK, VISIBLE FROM I-95.

Nancy English

GETTING THERE A number of **bus tour companies** also offer shopping trips to Freeport from Boston and beyond. Most people drive, which means there can be a shortage of parking spaces in peak season. One solution to this problem is to stay at one of the dozen or so inns or B&Bs within half a mile of L. L. Bean and leave your car there. The Amtrak **Downeaster** brings you from Boston to Portland, where you can get a bus, or just take one from Boston. Excellent bus service on **Concord Trailways** (see *Getting There* in "Portland Area") runs from Boston to Brunswick.

WHEN TO COME The holiday shopping season is one of Freeport's busiest times, and a special "Sparkle" weekend celebrates it in December. For hiking and swimming, summer months are best.

✷ Villages

South Freeport has been a fishing center from its beginning, when it was known as Strout's Port. Between 1825 and 1830 up to 12,000 barrels of mackerel were packed and shipped from here each year. Later the area specialty became lobster packing. Offering a very different feel from the chaotic shopping frenzy of downtown Freeport, the harbor features great seafood. From here you can take a cruise to explore Eagle and Seguin Islands in summer.

Porter's Landing. Once the center of commercial activity, this now-quiet residential neighborhood nestles amid rolling hills, woods, and streams. The village is part of the Harraseeket Historic District on the National Register of Historic Places.

✷ To See and Do

♿ **Desert of Maine** (207-865-6962; www.desertofmaine.com), 95 Desert Rd., Freeport. Open daily, early May–mid-Oct., 9–5. Admission runs $8.75 adults, $6.25 ages 13–16, $5.25 ages 5–12. Narrated tram tours and self-guided walks through 40 acres of sand that was once the Tuttle Farm. Heavily farmed, then extensively logged to feed the railroad, the topsoil eventually gave way to the glacial sand deposit beneath it, which spread . . . and spread until entire trees sank below the surface. It is an unusual sand, rich in mineral deposits that make it unsuitable for commercial use but interesting to rock-hounds. Children love it, especially the gem hunt (stones have been scattered in a section of the desert for children to find). Overnight camping is available (see *Lodging*).

BOAT EXCURSIONS **Atlantic Seal** (207-865-6112), Town Wharf, South Freeport. Memorial Day–mid-Oct. Captain Thomas Ring (owner of the charming Atlantic Seal B&B) runs daily narrated trips into Casco Bay, including three-hour cruises to Eagle Island, the former summer home of Admiral Robert E. Peary, the first person to reach the North Pole; Thu. six-hour cruises to Seguin Island Lighthouse to see—and climb inside—the fascinating first-order Fresnel lens, and a visit to the museum run by the Friends of the Seguin Lighthouse Caretakers (with 50-foot humpback whale and porpoise sightings on the trip to the island); seal- and osprey-sighting trips; and fall foliage cruises mid-Sept. and Oct. Lobstering demonstrations usually included, except on Sunday, when lobstering is prohibited by Maine law. Fee for state historical site is included.

CANOEING The **Harraseeket River** in Freeport is particularly nice for canoeing. Start at Mast Landing, the northeastern end of the waterway; there are also launching sites at Winslow Memorial Park on Staples Point Rd. and at South Freeport Harbor. Phone **Maine Audubon** headquarters in Falmouth (207-781-2330; www.maineaudubon.org) for details about periodic, scheduled guided trips through the area. Nearby lake canoeing can be found at **Run Around Pond** in North Pownal (the parking lot is off Lawrence Rd., 1 mile north of the intersection with Fickett Rd.).

CROSS-COUNTRY SKIING The areas listed under *Green Space* are good cross-country skiing spots; rent or purchase equipment from L. L. Bean, which also offers classes (see *Special Learning Programs*).

GOLF **Freeport Country Club** (207-865-0711), 2 Old County Rd., Freeport. Nine holes, golf clinics, pro shop, and snack bar.

JEWELRY MAKING ✐ **The Beadin' Path** (207-865-4785; www.beadinpath.com), 15 Main St., Freeport. Choose beads and findings from a wide variety (including vintage and contemporary Swarovski crystal), then sit at the table and create your own jewelry pieces. Prices are based on the beads you choose, so this can be a good, inexpensive rainy-day activity for kids (and adults).

MUSEUM ✐ **Harrington House** (207-865-3170; www.freeporthistoricalsociety.com), 45 Main St., Freeport. Open Tue., Thu., and Fri. 10–2:30, Wed. 10–7. Donations appreciated. Built of local brick and granite, this 1830 house and garden is maintained by the Freeport Historical Society as a museum, research library, and archive.

SPECIAL LEARNING PROGRAMS **L. L. Bean Outdoor Discovery Schools** (1-888-552-3261; www.llbean.com/walkon), Rt. 1, Freeport. You can get your toes wet—literally, if you're kayaking—with L.L. Bean's Walk-On Adventures program. For $15 (in 2007) participants can take a shuttle bus from the downtown store to enjoy one-and-a-half to two-and-a-half hours of fly casting, kayaking, cross-country skiing, archery, showshoeing, and clay shooting, all offered seasonally. All you need to do is sign up at the store on the day of the program; all equipment is provided. Schedules at the Freeport store are listed online.

The Outdoor Discovery School offers half-day or longer tours and classes that cover the basics—the Women's Kayak Touring Essentials II, for instance, covers strokes and boat handling. A Maine bike tour involves a two-day trip on coastal roads with camping at the private L. L. Bean Freeport waterfront campground, and a lobster dinner ($249, min. age 10, all equipment provided). A family camping trip with kayaks to Maine islands is another possibility. The school will customize tours for groups, and works with local inns.

L. L. Bean is well into planning stages to develop a theme park for outdoor activities on 700 acres of its property on Desert Road, 1 mile from its downtown stores. Lodging in the park could keep customers there for an entire vacation—with daytime activities like biking, archery, golf, and cross-country skiing. Kayaking and fishing will be offered on Casco Bay. If L.L.Bean decides to pursue it, the idea might become a reality in 2010.

✱ Green Space

✐ **Winslow Memorial Park** (207-865-4198), Staples Point Rd., South Freeport. Open Memorial Day–Sept. A 90-acre municipal park with a sandy beach and large grassy picnicking area; also boating and 100-site oceanside campground

($18–20 per night). Facilities include restrooms with showers. Admission fee.

Mast Landing Sanctuary (207-781-2330; www.maineaudubon.org), Upper Mast Landing Rd. (take Bow St. south), Freeport. Maintained by Maine Audubon, this 140-acre sanctuary offers trails through apple orchards, woods, meadows, and along a millstream. Several paths radiate from a 1-mile loop trail. You might even get lucky and see mink, deer, or porcupines.

Wolfe's Neck Woods State Park (207-865-4465), 425 Wolfe's Neck Rd. (take Bow St., across from L. L. Bean), Freeport. Open Apr.–Nov. A 233-acre park with shoreline hiking along Casco Bay, the Harraseeket River, and salt marshes, with excellent birding. Ospreys nest here, and an eagle is nearby. Guided nature walks and scattered picnic tables and grills. $1.50 day-use fee ages 12–64.

Bradbury Mountain State Park (207-688-4712), Rt. 9, 528 Hallowell Rd., Pownal (6 miles from Freeport: from I-95, take exit 20 and follow signs). Open year-round. $3 ages 12 and older, $1 ages 5–11, under 5 free. The summit, accessible by an easy (even for young children) 0.5-mile hike, yields a splendid view of Casco Bay and New Hampshire's White Mountains. Facilities in the 1,000-acre park include a small playground, a softball field, hiking trails, toilets, and a 35-site overnight camping area.

Pettengill Farm (207-865-3170; www.freeporthistoricalsociety.com), Pettengill Rd., Freeport. Managed by the Freeport Historical Society (which conducts periodic guided tours), the grounds are open anytime. A saltwater farm with 140 acres of open fields and woodland that overlook the Harraseeket Estuary, with a totally unmodernized vintage-1810 saltbox house. Come the weekend after Labor Day for the annual Pettengill Farm Days celebration.

✷ Lodging

All listings are in Freeport 04032 unless otherwise noted

INN **Harraseeket Inn** (207-865-9377 or 1-800-342-6423; www.stayfreeport.com), 162 Main St. The Gray family—Nancy, her son Chip, and daughter Penelope (all former Maine Guides)—have a passion for Maine expressed through meticulous and warm innkeeping. Two blocks north of L. L. Bean, their luxury hotel is the largest in the area, with 84 rooms (including five suites) plus nine town houses. The inn began as a five-room B&B in the 1800 Federal house next door. Many of the rooms feature antiques and reproductions, canopy bed, and Jacuzzi; 20 have a fireplace. The inn has formal dining rooms (see *Dining Out*), conference spaces (one with outdoor terrace), and the casual and popular Broad Arrow Tavern (see *Eating Out*). Other public spaces include a drawing room, library, gym, ballroom, and a pretty, glassed-in pool overlooking the gardens. Rates in-season are $221–304, full buffet breakfast and afternoon high tea included. Two-night minimum stay required on some holiday weekends. Package plans available.

BED & BREAKFASTS 🐾 ✐ **White Cedar Inn** (207-865-9099 or 1-800-853-1269; www.whitecedarinn.com), 178 Main St. Open year-round. This restored Victorian is former home of Arctic explorer Donald B. MacMillan, who traveled nearly to the North Pole with Admiral Peary—till frostbite set in. Seven bedrooms come with private bath, down comforters, and air-conditioning; some have a fireplace. A spiral staircase leads down to the Bowdoin room, with a private entrance, sitting area, and TV (pets are welcome here). Owners Rock Nadeau and Monica Kissane, who are constantly updating the inn's rooms and common spaces, serve a full breakfast at small tables in the sunroom. Doubles $130-200 in-season, $105-175 off-season.

🐾 **Captain Briggs House** (207-865-1868 or 1-888-217-2477; www.captainbriggs.com), 8 Maple Ave. Simple, pleasant rooms with private bath, all botanically named. Evergreen had a large full bath with beadboard wainscoting. This place is quieter than some because it's set well off Rt. 1. The sitting room has cable TV, games, and books. $95–225 in-season includes full breakfast made with local eggs.

The James Place Inn (207-865-4486 or 1-800-964-9086; www.jamesplaceinn.com), 11 Holbrook St. This well-appointed place run by Victoria and Robert Baron has everything we love in a B&B: charm, luxury, beautiful furnishings, and a relaxed atmosphere. Single women enjoy a stay in Wisteria, with its single whirlpool bath. All seven rooms have air-conditioning and cable TV; one features a kitchenette and three have a whirlpool bath. Enjoy the full breakfast at the café tables on the deck or in the pretty glassed-in breakfast room. $155–185 double in-season.

🐾 **Applewood Inn** (207-865-9705 or 1-877-954-1358; www.applewoodusa.com), 8 Holbrook St. Jay and Jennifer Yilmaz have 11 rooms in two well-kept, modern buildings for nightly rentals, and one has a kitchen. Local artists are the creators of much of the engaging decor, including a giraffe clock. Two blocks north of L. L. Bean, the inn sits far enough off Rt. 1 to be very quiet. Private bath in each room; some have a fireplace, skylights, Jacuzzi, and TV/VCR. Full breakfast included in the $140–250 in-season rates; longer term rentals available. The family also operates six AJ Dogs stands and two ice cream stands on Freeport's busy Main Street.

✐ **Atlantic Seal B&B** (207-865-6112 or 1-877-ATL-SEAL), 25 Main St., Box 146, South Freeport 04078. Open year-round. Captain Tom Ring is the real deal: A fifth-generation Mainer with an authentic Maine accent, he still lives in his family's cozy 1850 Cape and skippers boat cruises to neighboring islands in high season. Each room is named for a ship built in Freeport, and we're crazy about The Dash, with brass queen and double beds, Jacuzzi tub, gas fireplace, and fabulous private deck overlooking the tidal Harraseeket River. Ask Captain Tom about the trunk his grandfather brought on board when he sailed four-masted schooners along the Maine coast. Swim off the private dock; a rowboat and two mountain bikes are available for guest use. There is a resident cat. Summer rates, including a "hearty sailor's breakfast"—like apple pancakes and blueberry muffins—start at $150 and go to $225. Guests receive a discount on morning cruises.

Kendall Tavern (207-865-1338; www.kendalltavern.com), 213 Main St. This 200-year-old farmhouse, owned by Loree and Tim Rudolph, features seven rooms, all with private bath and air-conditioning. Pastel walls, quilts, and antiques, like hand-painted armoires and four-poster beds, make the rooms attractive; two are under the eaves on the top floor. Sit in one of two parlors with fireplaces, or hang out on the lovely front porch in summer; the shops are a 10-minute walk away. Rates range up to $175 in-season, and include a full breakfast. Children over 8 welcome.

🐾 ✐ ♿ **Royalsborough Inn at the Bagley House** (207-865-6566 or 1-800-765-1772; www.royalsboroughinn.com), 1290 Royalsborough Rd., Durham 04222. A 10-minute drive from downtown Freeport in a serene country setting, this is the oldest house in town, built as a public house in 1772. The town's first worship services were held here, and this was the site of the first schoolhouse. Marianne and Jim Roberts have furnished the eight rooms with antiques and hand-sewn quilts. Emma's room, with its red and white coverlet, holds its antiques with panache. $129–179 double in-season includes full breakfast and afternoon refreshments. Alpacas graze in a paddock behind the house; their wool and woven goods are for sale in the store. Massage therapy is available.

MOTELS **The Village Inn** (207-865-3236, reservations only 1-800-998-3649; www.freeportvillageinn.com), 186 Main St., has rates starting at $85 and is within easy walking distance of all the shops. The very basic decor is perfectly clean, and the owners since 1986, Lewis and Jackie Corliss, are downhome Mainers who can tell you the history of their transformed town or help you get your disabled car fixed, as they did for us. A breakfast of pancakes, French toast, or scrambled eggs is included.

On Rt. 1 south of Freeport near the Yarmouth town line are a number of modern motels. Among these is the 🐾 **Best Western Freeport Inn** (207-865-3106 or 1-800-99-VALUE; www.freeportinn.com), 31 Rt. 1. Set on 25 acres of lawns and nature trails, this place offers an upscale motel ambience at reasonable prices. All rooms have pretty designer bedspreads, carpeting, cable TV, air-conditioning, and in-room phone. Swimming pool, playground, and canoes to paddle Cousins River. Pets are allowed in 16 of the 80 rooms. Doubles are $130–150 in-season. The inn's restaurant and bakery, the Freeport Café, serves meals all day.

The Casco Bay Inn (207-865-4925 or 1-800-570-4970; www.cascobayinn.com) is family run, clean, comfortable, and completely refurbished in 2001, with budget rates ($64–125).

CAMPGROUNDS 🐾 ✐ ♿ **Cedar Haven Campground** (207-865-6254; reservations only, 1-800-454-3403; www.campcedarhaven.com), 39 Baker Rd. Fifty-eight mostly wooded sites, each with fireplace and picnic table. Water and electricity hook-ups, 12 with sewer as well. Cable TV at selected sites. Twelve tent sites. Store with wood, ice, and groceries; mini golf, playground, and pond for swimming. Two miles from Rt. 1 and downtown Freeport. $21.50–40 per night.

Desert Dunes of Maine Campground (207-865-6962; www.desertofmaine.com), 95 Desert Rd. Located next to a kitschy attraction with a natural glacial sand deposit (see *To See and Do*), this campground offers 50 wooded and open sites with hook-ups, hot showers, laundry, convenience store, propane, fire rings, picnic tables, horseshoe pits, nature trails, and swimming pool. Campsites are $24–39 per night.

Where to Eat

All listings are in Freeport unless otherwise noted

DINING OUT **Harraseeket Inn Maine Dining Room** (207-865-9377 or 1-800-342-6423), 162 Main St. Open year-round for dinner and Sunday brunch 11:30–2. Continental cuisine and elegant service in three formal dining rooms. The chefs use fresh, in-season, and often organic ingredients from local gardeners and farmers to create mouthwatering entrées like roast quail with figs and mushrooms, and sirloin with ancho bordelaise. Entrées $24–76 (for the rack of lamb for two). The Harraseeket is also known for its outstanding Sunday brunch, which often features such delicacies as caviar, oysters on the half shell, and even venison ($25).

Mediterranean Grill (207-865-1688; www.mediterraneangrill.biz), 10 School St. Open in summer Sun.–Thu. 11–9, till 10 Fri. and Sat., closes one hour earlier off-season. A Turkish dinner awaits you here: falafel and stuffed eggplant to kebabs, moussaka, and lamb shanks. Choose from Turkish wines as well as the usual from California, and baklava or rice pudding to end. Entrées $17–25.

Jameson Tavern (207-865-4196; www.jamesontavern.com), 115 Main St. Lunch 11:30–2:30 and dinner 5–closing. The 1779 building's interior needs a little TLC, but it has an interesting history: Locals claim that the papers separating Maine from Massachusetts were signed here in 1820. Dine on the outside patio in summer, or by one of several indoor fireplaces during cold months, on scallops Florentine or a lazy man lobster. If there's a wait, you can order from the same menu in the neighboring Tap Room (see *Eating Out*). $18–24.

EATING OUT **The Broad Arrow Tavern** (207-865-9377), Harraseeket Inn, 162 Main St. Open 11:30–10:30, with drinks till midnight. A ground-floor dining room overlooking the terrace, this place is constantly packed with locals, tourists, and inn guests, who come for the delicious food, unstuffy pub atmosphere, and interesting collection of stuffed animals on the wall (moose, fisher, deer). The open kitchen has a wood-fired oven and grill, and it serves up everything from brick-oven pizzas, sandwiches, and grilled steak to a Caesar we found a little overweighted by dressing. Rich desserts follow, like a double chocolate chip cookie, dished up hot out of the oven with double vanilla ice cream and chocolate sauce. Lunch entrées $10–35.

Jacqueline's Tea Room (207-865-2123; www.jacquelinestearoom.com), 201 Main St. Open for 11 AM to 1 PM, seatings Tues. to Fri. and every other weekend. No credit cards. Just north of the main business district, this is a stunning celebration of femininity and tea. For $19.50 and a reservation, you can enjoy tea sandwiches of smoked salmon or cucumber, delicate, crumbling scones with clotted cream and lemon curd, and cakes, tarts, and English toffee. The list of over 90 teas (also available to purchase), served in 2-cup teapots, means a visitor won't run out of options during the leisurely two hours the hostess recommends. Every inch of the place is decorated, and many of the decorations are for sale, like the pagoda bird feeder hanging over my table. The gift shop is open without reservation.

Conundrum (207-865-0303), 117 Rt. 1, South Freeport. This bistro, set right under the Big Indian, serves good burgers and other casual meals in an intimate, dark blue room decorated with local artists' work. We like the varieties of pâté and cheese (also sold in the neighboring shop, Old World Gourmet; see *Snacks*), which you can order as entrées, and the wine selection is amazing. More than 500 bottles are available here; 60 wines are offered by the glass. You can get a taste before deciding on a glass, or half glass, to drink. The best place in Maine to taste wine. Entrées $10–27.

Tap Room (207-865-4196; www.jamesontavern.com), Jameson Tavern, 115 Main St. This informal tavern to the rear of the building serves the full Jameson Tavern menu plus pub fare from 11:30 AM until late in the evening.

♿ **Gritty McDuff's** (207-865-4321), 187 Lower Main St. The only brewpub in Freeport, this branch of the popular Portland pub offers outdoor dining, lobster, seafood, pizza, and pub food. Great ales and nachos, and we like the festive murals.

♿ **Muddy Rudder** (207-846-3082; www.muddyrudder.com), Rt. 1, Yarmouth. Operated by the nearby Freeport Inn, this popular restaurant overlooks the water and serves a wide selection of seafood dishes plus steaks, sandwiches, and salads; you can also have a full clambake on the deck. Renovated in 2001, the Rudder is still relaxed.

Harraseeket Lunch & Lobster Co. (207-865-4888), foot of Main St., South Freeport (turn off Rt. 1 at the giant wooden Indian, then turn right at a stop sign a few miles down). Open May–Columbus Day. At this traditional lobster shack in the middle of the Harraseeket boatyard, order lobsters and clams on one side, fried food on the other, and eat at picnic tables (of which there are never enough at peak hours) overlooking a boat-filled harbor. Lobsters are fresh from the pound's boats; homemade desserts. There is also a small inside dining room. Be aware that it is a busy place; you may have to wait to eat.

HARRASEEKET LUNCH & LOBSTER CO.
Nancy English

The Lobster Cooker (207-865-4349; www.lobstercooker.net), 39 Main St. Steamed lobster, excellent fresh-picked lobster and crabmeat rolls, sandwiches, and chowders; cafeteria-style dining on the outdoor patio. Beer and wine.

The Freeport Café (207-865-3106), Rt. 1 (next to the Freeport Inn). Open daily 6 AM–9 PM. A bona fide local hangout, this small café makes up for its unappealing location right on Rt. 1 with good food at great prices. Extremely friendly service, great dinner specials, and a children's menu.

SNACKS **Old World Gourmet** (207-865-4477), Rt. 1 (next to the Big Indian). Foreign cheese, pâté, prepared food, and wine are ready to fill picnic baskets or take over dinner duty. You can eat lunch here at one of the tables nestled next to the shop's shelves. Try one of their grilled panini, vegetarian sandwiches, composed salads, baked goods, Italian sodas, or lattes flavored with Torani syrup.

Royal River Natural Foods (207-865-0046; www.rrnf.com), 443 Rt. 1. A great place to buy vegetarian snacks for the road, such as organic fruits and local vegetables, freshly made soups, pasta and green salads, sandwiches, and muffins, which you can eat in the café too. Also a full line of natural grocery items.

The Village Store (207-865-4230), 97 South Freeport Rd. (across the street from the South Freeport church). With two picnic tables in back and multicolored stools inside, locals gather here for the baked doughnut muffins in the morning and the "ham ultimate," a popular sub. Wine, beer, salads, ice cream, and six newspapers along with Wicked Joe coffee.

Selective Shopping

FREEPORT FACTORY OUTLETS As noted in the chapter's introduction, Freeport's 125-plus factory outlets constitute what has probably become Maine's mightiest tourist magnet. *Boston Globe* writer Nathan Cobb called it, "A shoppers' theme park spread out at the foot of L. L. Bean, the high church of country chic."

A grand scheme is underway to construct a $45 million open-air commercial center on more than three acres of L. L. Bean–owned land in the middle of town. With a plaza surrounded by three large and several smaller buildings, each sized for a boutique, it will be called Freeport Village Station. It will be located on the site of the L. L. Bean Outlet Store (now temporarily open on Main St.). Proposed hours of 10–10 are intended to lure shoppers.

L. L. Bean contends that it attracts at least 3 million customers annually—almost three times the population of Maine. In the early 1980s neighboring property owners began to claim a portion of this traffic. Instead of relegating the outlets to malls, they have deftly draped them in brick and clapboard, actually improving on the town's old looks (although longtime shopkeepers who were forced to move because of skyrocketing real estate prices might well disagree). Ample parking lots are sequestered behind the Main Street facade, and the new construction will add a parking garage for 550 cars.

In summer a festive atmosphere reigns, with hot dog and ice cream vendors on key corners. But it's the quality of the shops that ensures a year-round crowd, with well-known clothing, accessories, or home furnishing line factory stores. The following is a selected list of the more interesting outlets. Many stores claim 20 to 70 percent off suggested retail prices, and even L. L. Bean has a separate outlet, which you should check for bargains before heading to the main store.

L. L. Bean Factory Store, 568 Rt. 1. Seconds, samples, and irregular merchandise of all kinds. You never know what you'll find, but it's always worth a look. Unlike the main store, the outlet is not open 24 hours a day.

Thomas Moser Cabinetmakers (207-865-4519, 1-800-708-9041; www.thosmoser.com), 149 Main St. Open Mon.–Sat. 10–6, Sun. 11–5. Fine furniture inspired by Shaker, Arts and Crafts, Japanese, and art deco designs. This family business has been a Freeport institution for more than 35 years.

Dooney & Bourke (207-865-1366; www.dooney.com), 56 Main St. (in back). Stylish pocketbooks, shoulder bags, belts, wallets, and portfolios.

Burberry (207-865-4400), 42 Main St. Not just the raincoats lined with

L. L. BEAN

Kim Grant

L. L. Bean (1-800-559-0747, ext. 37222; www.llbean.com), 95 Main St. Open 24 hours a day, 365 days a year, as are the two other stores listed below (but not the outlet). With a kid's department, a camping department, a pond stocked with brown or brook trout, and a trail "rock" to test new hiking boots, the building resembles a fancy shopping mall more than it does a single store. Back in 1912 Leon Leonwood Bean developed his boot, or Maine

their famous tan tartan; you'll find chic women's, men's, and children's clothing; sweaters, hats, and accessories, too.

♿ **Cuddledown of Maine Factory Store** (207-865-1713; www.cuddledown.com), 475 Rt. 1. Comforters, pillows, gift items, all filled with goose down.

♿ **Maine Wreath & Flower Factory Outlet** (207-865-3019 or 1-800-973-4987; www.mainewreath.com), 13 Bow St. Quality Maine-dried flowers and wreaths at discount prices.

Cole-Haan Footwear and Accessories (207-865-6321; www.colehaan.com), 66 Main St. Beautiful shoes, handbags, and socks. Pricey, but their quality is famous.

♿ **Lenox Factory Outlet** (207-865-6125; www.dansk.com, www.lenox.com), 100 Main St., Suite 11. Dinnerware, stemware, flatware, in a variety of company lines, including Kate Spade and Dansk.

SPECIAL SHOPS

All listings are in Freeport unless otherwise noted

Brown Goldsmiths (207-865-4126; www.browngoldsmiths.com), 11 Mechanic St. Open Mon.–Sat.

Hunting Shoe, a unique combination of rubber bottom and leather top. "You cannot expect success hunting deer or moose if your feet are not properly dressed," Bean wrote in his very first catalog. Ninety out of the first 100 boots he built literally fell apart at the seams, so Bean refunded the purchasers' money and began a company tradition of guaranteed customer satisfaction, including all-night hours for the outdoorsmen who passed through in the wee hours. Bean himself died in 1967, but his grandson Leon Gorman, chairman of the board, and company president Christopher McCormick now oversee an empire of outdoor equipment.

L. L. Bean Hunting and Fishing Store (1-877-552-3268; www.llbean.com), 95 Main St. All the fishing equipment is here, along with archery gear and hunting rifles. Beans also sells used guns, and will buy guns in good condition. Fish and game mounts are hung around the store, giving the place a hunting lodge atmosphere. With 33,000 square feet, L. L. Bean is showing off more of its equipment in one space than it ever has. Hunting clothing and boots could outfit anyone for the trip of a lifetime.

L. L. Bean Bike, Boot & Ski Store (1-877-552-3268; www.llbean.com), 95 Main St. When the weather warms up, the bike and boat displays bloom; when it's getting colder it's time for all the ski equipment, snowshoes, toboggans, and sleds to take a bigger share of the space. You can bring a bike in for repair, or get bindings mounted to skis. A wide selection of kayaks, paddles, and accessories. Down the road behind corporate headquarters you can also try your hand at fly casting, archery, and clay shooting, or kayak from the company's private beach on a nearby cove (see Outdoor Discovery Schools and Walk-on Adventures in *To See and Do*).

Original designs in rings, earrings, and bracelets.

Bridgham & Cook, Ltd. (207-865-1040 or 1-800-UK-BUYER; www.britishgoods.com), 116 Main St. Packaged British and Irish foods, toiletries, teas, gifts—a must for the Anglophile, who might also like Jacqueline's Tearoom, and the Harraseeket Inn (see *Where to Eat*) for a proper cup of tea.

Cold River Vodka (207-865-4828; www.coldrivervodka.com), 437 Rt. 1, south of Rt. 295 exit 20. Open daily in-season, fewer days off. Using Maine potatoes grown on his farm in Fryeburg, Donnie Thibodeau teamed up with a professional brewer to open Maine's first vodka distillery in 2005. A gallery dramatizes the history of Maine potato farming. Tours are offered 11–5 in-season, 12–5 off-season. Tastings are not offered because Maine law doesn't allow it.

DeLorme's Map Store (207-865-4171), Rt. 1 (south of downtown Freeport). A good place to spend a couple of rainy hours watching the world turn—literally—and sifting through DeLorme's impressive offerings. Check out the publishing company's maps, atlases, pamphlets, and guidebooks of the United States and the world, as well as some interesting educational toys. A large bank of computers invites visitors to try mapping software. Many people come just to see Eartha, the world's largest rotating and revolving globe, which spins quietly in a glassed-in lobby.

Edgecomb Potters/Hand in Hand Gallery (207-865-1705 or 1-800-343-5529; www.edgecombpotters.com), 8 School St. Fine contemporary American crafts, including colorful porcelain made in Maine, jewelry, blown glass, and iron.

♿ **Mangy Moose** (207-865-6414 or 1-800-606-6517; www.themangymoose.com), 112 Main St. Moose, moose, and more moose. A fun store filled with gifts, books, mounts—meaning stuffed moose, mountain lion, bobcat, caribou, and bear heads. "It's moosely fun for everyone."

♿ **Play and Learn** (207-865-6434 or 1-888-865-6434), 200 Lower Main St. A great source for educational toys and teaching resources.

Sherman's Book & Stationery Store (207-869-9000; www.shermans.com), 128 Main St. A branch of the Maine bookseller (also in Bar Harbor, Camden, and Boothbay Harbor), featuring Maine books and gifts, cards, and toys.

Special Events

Mid-June: **L.L. Bean Paddlesports Festival**

Summer: Frequent musical and comedy performances in the **L. L. Bean Discovery Park**.

Labor Day weekend: **Sidewalk Sale**, with sales galore. **Fall in the Village** art exhibition.

Fall: **Pettengill Farm Days**—living history demonstrations, horse-drawn wagon rides, inside/outside house tours, children's days, fresh-pressed cider.

December: **Sparkle Weekend** (*first full weekend*)—caroling, horse-drawn wagons, Santa arriving in a Maine yacht, musical entertainment, holiday readings, storytelling, complimentary refreshment and hot-cocoa stops, **Christmas Open House Tours**.

Midcoast and the Islands

BRUNSWICK AND THE HARPSWELLS

BATH AREA

WISCASSET AREA

BOOTHBAY HARBOR REGION

DAMARISCOTTA/NEWCASTLE AND PEMAQUID AREA

ROCKLAND/THOMASTON AREA

MIDCOAST ISLANDS

CAMDEN/ROCKPORT AREA

ISLEBORO

BELFAST, SEARSPORT, AND STOCKTON SPRINGS

Christina Tree

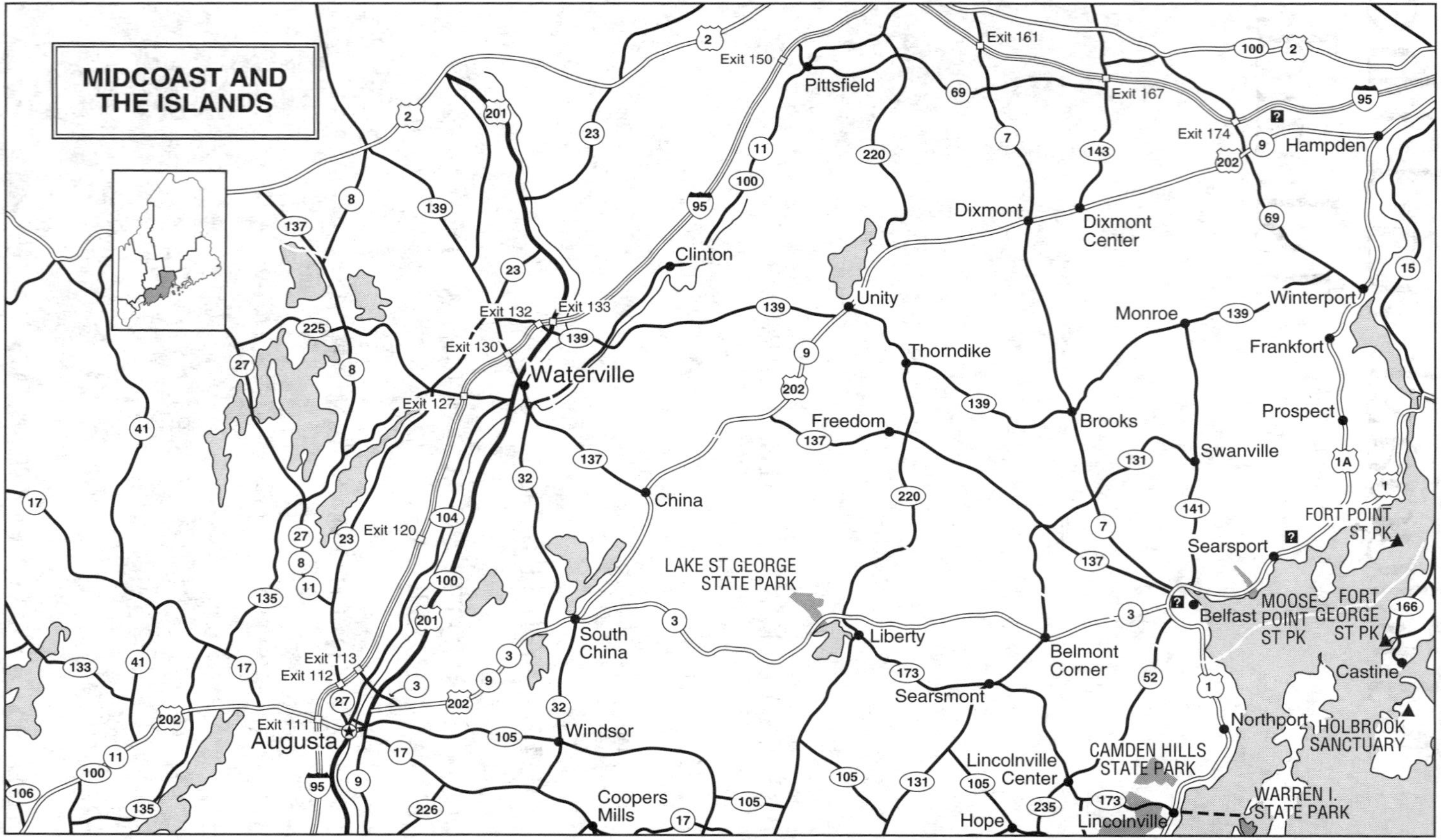

MIDCOAST AND THE ISLANDS
Pittsfield
Clinton
Unity
Waterville
Thorndike
Freedom
Dixmont
Dixmont Center
Hampden
Winterport
Monroe
Frankfort
Prospect
Brooks
Swanville
Searsport
FORT POINT ST PK
Belfast
MOOSE POINT ST PK
FORT GEORGE ST PK
Castine
HOLBROOK SANCTUARY
Northport
CAMDEN HILLS STATE PARK
WARREN I. STATE PARK
Lincolnville
Lincolnville Center
Hope
Belmont Corner
Searsmont
Liberty
LAKE ST GEORGE STATE PARK
China
South China
Windsor
Coopers Mills
Augusta
Exit 111
Exit 112
Exit 113
Exit 120
Exit 127
Exit 130
Exit 132
Exit 133
Exit 150
Exit 161
Exit 167
Exit 174

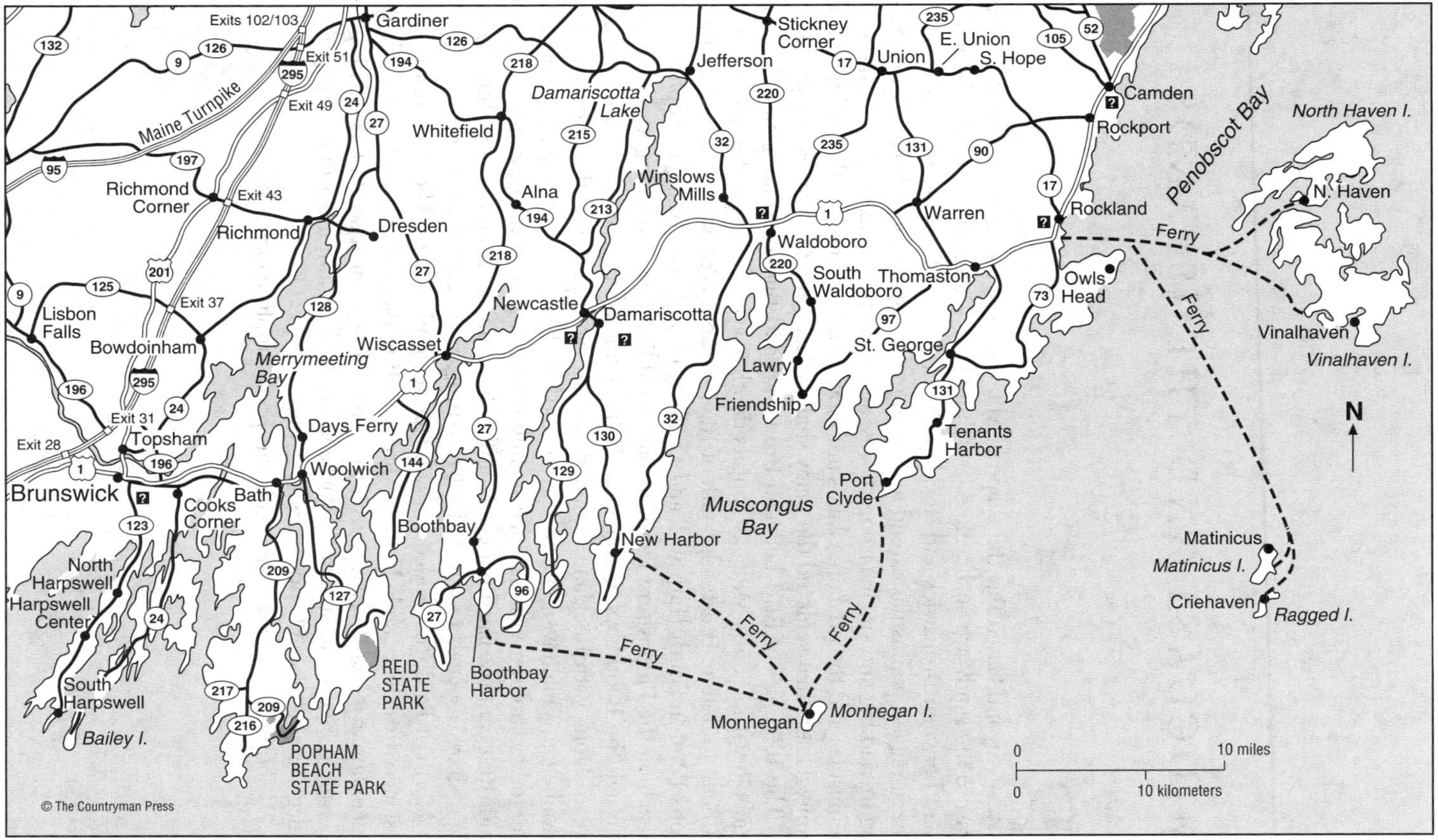
Gardiner
Exits 102/103
Exit 51
Exit 49
Exit 43
Exit 37
Exit 31
Exit 28
Maine Turnpike
Stickney Corner
Jefferson
Union
E. Union
S. Hope
Camden
Rockport
Penobscot Bay
North Haven I.
N. Haven
Whitefield
Damariscotta Lake
Winslows Mills
Alna
Richmond Corner
Richmond
Dresden
Warren
Rockland
Waldoboro
South Waldoboro
Thomaston
Owls Head
Vinalhaven
Vinalhaven I.
Lisbon Falls
Bowdoinham
Newcastle
Damariscotta
Wiscasset
Merrymeeting Bay
St. George
Lawry
Friendship
Topsham
Days Ferry
Woolwich
Tenants Harbor
Brunswick
Bath
Cooks Corner
Boothbay
Port Clyde
Muscongus Bay
New Harbor
North Harpswell
Harpswell Center
Matinicus
Matinicus I.
Criehaven
Ragged I.
REID STATE PARK
Boothbay Harbor
Ferry
South Harpswell
Bailey I.
Monhegan
Monhegan I.
POPHAM BEACH STATE PARK
N
0 10 miles
0 10 kilometers
© The Countryman Press

MIDCOAST AND THE ISLANDS

Beyond Casco Bay the shape of Maine's coast changes—it shreds. In contrast to the sandy arc of shoreline stretching from Kittery to Cape Elizabeth, the coast between Brunswick and Rockland is composed of a series of more than a dozen ragged peninsulas extending like so many fingers south from Rt. 1, creating myriad big and small harbors, coves, and bays. Scientists tell us that these peninsulas and the offshore islands are mountains drowned by the melting of the same glaciers that sculpted the many shallow lakes and tidal rivers in this area.

The 100 miles of Rt. 1 between Brunswick and Bucksport are generally equated with Maine's Midcoast, but its depth is actually far greater and more difficult to define. It extends south of Rt. 1 to the tips of every peninsula, from Potts Point in South Harpswell and Land's End on Bailey Island to Popham Beach on the Phippsburg Peninsula and Reid State Park in Georgetown and on through the Boothbays to Pemaquid Point, Friendship, Port Clyde, and Spruce Head. Along with Rockland, Camden, Belfast, Searsport, and the islands of Monhegan, Vinalhaven, North Haven, and Islesboro, these communities have all catered to summer visitors since steamboats began off-loading them in the mid–19th century. Each peninsula differs in character from the next, but all offer their share of places to stay and eat in settings you rarely find along Rt. 1.

North of Rt. 1, this midcoast region also extends inland. Above Bath, for instance, five rivers meld to form Merrymeeting Bay, and north of Newcastle the tidal Damariscotta River widens into 13-mile-long Damariscotta Lake. This gently rolling, river- and lake-laced backcountry harbors a number of picturesque villages and reasonably priced lodging places.

We hope that no one who reads this book simply sticks to Rt. 1.

BRUNSWICK AND THE HARPSWELLS

The Civil War began and ended in Brunswick, or so say local historians. A case can be made. Harriet Beecher Stowe was attending a service in Brunswick's First Parish Church when she is said to have had a vision of the death of Uncle Tom and hurried home to begin penning the book that has been credited with starting the war. Joshua Chamberlain, a longtime parishioner in this same church, was the Union general chosen for the honor of receiving the surrender of General John Gordon, commander of the Confederate infantry, at Appomattox.

Thanks largely to the Ken Burns PBS series *The Civil War*, and to the film *Gettysburg*, Joshua Chamberlain has been rediscovered. Annual admissions to his house have soared, fueling its restoration. This scholar-soldier-governor is, in fact, an appropriate figurehead for a town that's been home to Brunswick Naval Air Station as well as to Bowdoin College, over which Chamberlain presided as president after four terms as governor of Maine.

Brunswick began as an Indian village named Pejepscot, at the base of the Androscoggin River's Great Falls. In 1688 this site became a Massachusetts outpost named Fort Andross, and subsequently it has been occupied by a series of mills. Its current population of 21,170 is a mix of Franco-Americans whose great-grandparents were recruited to work in mills, of military- and Bowdoin-related families, and of an increasing number of professionals who commute a half hour to work in Portland or Augusta (Brunswick is halfway between).

Brunswick's Maine Street is the state's widest, laid out in 1717 with a grassy "mall"—a long strip of greenery that's the scene of concerts and of farmer's markets—at the upper end, near the neo-Gothic First Parish Church and the Bowdoin College campus.

A prestigious college, chartered in 1794, Bowdoin is the July and August venue for the Bowdoin International Music Festival, and for the Maine State Music Theatre. The newly renovated Bowdoin College Museum of Art and its Peary-MacMillan Arctic Museum are also well worth a stop.

Brunswick isn't a tourist town. No kiosk proclaims the schedule of plays and concerts, because patrons know enough to read about them in the Thursday edition of the *Times Record*. Maine Street's shops, galleries, and restaurants cater to residents, and the Eveningstar Cinema and Frontier Café and Cinema screen art

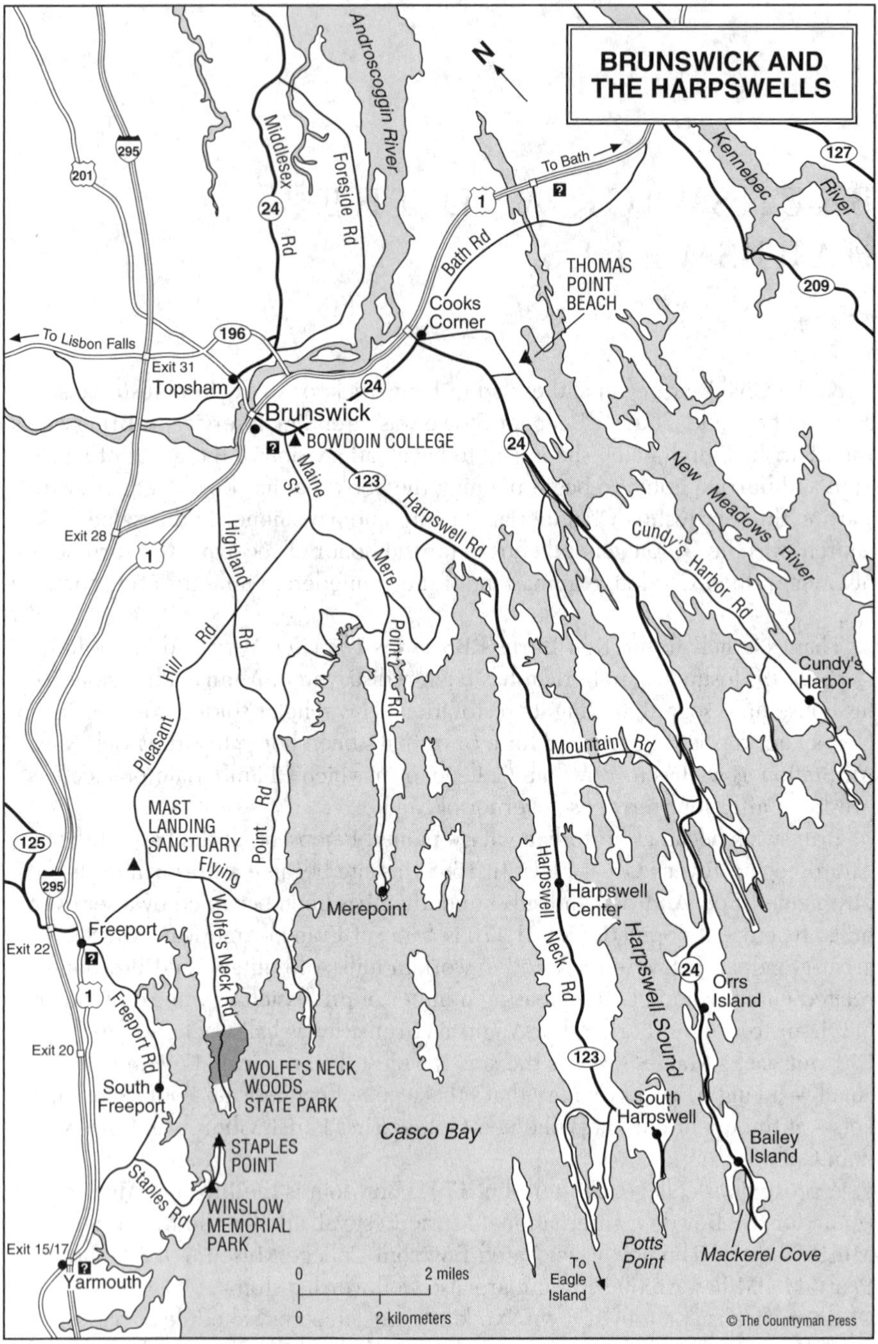

BRUNSWICK AND THE HARPSWELLS
N
Androscoggin River
Middlesex Rd
Foreside Rd
24
295
201
1
To Bath
127
Kennebec River
Bath Rd
THOMAS POINT BEACH
209
Cooks Corner
To Lisbon Falls
196
Exit 31
Topsham
24
Brunswick
BOWDOIN COLLEGE
Maine St
123
Harpswell Rd
New Meadows River
Cundy's Harbor Rd
Exit 28
1
Highland Rd
Mere Point Rd
Pleasant Hill Rd
Cundy's Harbor
Mountain Rd
Point Rd
MAST LANDING SANCTUARY
125
295
Flying Point Rd
Wolfe's Neck Rd
Merepoint
Harpswell Center
Harpswell Neck Rd
Harpswell Sound
Freeport
Exit 22
1
Freeport Rd
Exit 20
24
Orrs Island
WOLFE'S NECK WOODS STATE PARK
South Freeport
123
South Harpswell
Casco Bay
STAPLES POINT
Bailey Island
Staples Rd
WINSLOW MEMORIAL PARK
Exit 15/17
Yarmouth
0
2 miles
0
2 kilometers
To Eagle Island
Potts Point
Mackerel Cove
© The Countryman Press

films for local consumption. Grand City is still a genuine five-and-dime with a lunch counter, a basement stocked with furniture and fabrics, boots and gloves for clammers. Freeport's nearby outlet stores seem light-years away.

South of Brunswick one peninsula and several bridge-linked islands stretch seaward, defining the eastern rim of Casco Bay. Collectively they form the town of Harpswell, better known as "the Harpswells" because it includes so many coves, points, and islands (notably Orrs and Bailey). Widely known for their seafood restaurants, these peninsulas are surprisingly sleepy, salted with crafts, galleries, and some great places to stay. They are Maine's most convenient peninsulas, yet they seem much farther Down East.

GUIDANCE **Southern Midcoast Maine Chamber** (207-725-8797; www.midcoastmaine.com), Border Trust Business Center, 1 Main St., Topsham 04086.

GETTING THERE *By bus:* Bus service to downtown Brunswick from Logan Airport and downtown Boston is unusually good: two-and-a-half hours both via **Concord Trailways**, which stops on Rt. 1, and **Vermont Transit/Greyhound**, which stops in downtown Brunswick.

By car: The I-295 (formerly I-95) exit for Brunswick and coastal points north is exit 28 to Rt. 1. Continue straight ahead up Pleasant St., which forms a T with Maine St. Turn right for the Bowdoin College campus and the Harpswells. For Topsham the new exits are 31 northbound and 31A southbound.

By train: Plans call for Amtrak's **Downeaster** to extend service on to Brunswick from Portland but in the meantime you can come by rail from Rockland and points between. See **The Maine Eastern Railroad** (see *Railroad Excursion* under *To Do*).

By air and limo: **Mid-Coast Limo** (1-800-937-2424; www.midcoastlimo.com) makes runs by reservation from Portland International Jetport.

WHEN TO COME Brunswick is a lively year-round community, but if you want to visit all its museums and take advantage of summer music and theater, come in July or August—but never on Monday.

✷ To See

Bowdoin College (207-725-3100; www.bowdoin.edu), Brunswick. Tours of the 215-acre campus with more than 120 buildings begin at the admissions office. Phone for current hours. Maine was part of Massachusetts when the college was founded in 1794, and the school is named for a Massachusetts governor. Nathaniel Hawthorne and Henry Wadsworth Longfellow were classmates here in 1825; other notable graduates include U.S. president Franklin Pierce and North Pole explorer Robert Edwin Peary. Founded as a men's college, the school has been coed since the early 1970s. Bowdoin ranks among the nation's top both in status and in cost (the college provides substantial financial aid). It isn't necessary to take a tour to see the sights: visitors can park in any parking area on campus unless otherwise noted.

JOSHUA LAWRENCE CHAMBERLAIN

JOSHUA LAWRENCE CHAMBERLIN

Joshua Lawrence Chamberlain (1828–1914) was Maine's greatest Civil War hero, a college professor who became one of the most remarkable soldiers in American history.

An outstanding scholar—he had a graduate degree in theology and was teaching rhetoric and languages (he spoke or could read eight) at his alma mater, Bowdoin College, when the war began—Chamberlain proved to be an even better soldier. He fought in some of the bloodiest battles of the war, had horses shot out from under him five times, and was wounded six times, once so severely that he was given up for dead and his obituary appeared in Maine newspapers.

Of all his military achievements Chamberlain is best remembered for his valor and leadership on the second day of the battle of Gettysburg, July 2, 1863. A lieutenant colonel commanding an inexperienced and understrength regiment, the 20th Maine Volunteer Infantry, he defended Little Round Top, a key position on the extreme left of the Union line. Repeatedly attacked by a much larger Confederate force, he refused to retreat; when defeat seemed imminent—there was no more ammunition and most of his men were dead or wounded—he ordered an unorthodox bayonet charge that routed the Confederates.

Had the southerners taken Little Round Top they could have outflanked the Union army and won the battle—and with it, possibly, the war. Eventually, more than 30 years later, Chamberlain received the nation's highest military award, the Medal of Honor, for his "daring heroism and great tenacity" at Gettysburg.

He ended the war a major general and was chosen by General Ulysses S. Grant to accept the surrender of the Confederate Army of Northern Virginia following General Robert E. Lee's capitulation at Appomattox. As the Confederate regiments marched into the Union camp to lay down their arms, Chamberlain had his troops salute them, a gesture of respect that infuriated some northerners but helped reconcile many southerners to their defeat.

After the war Chamberlain served four one-year terms as governor of Maine. From 1871 to 1883 he was president of Bowdoin College, where he introduced science courses to modernize the curriculum and tried unsuccessfully to make military training compulsory. (Students rioted in protest.) He died in 1914, "of his wounds," it was said. Late in life he wrote *The Passing of the Armies,* an account of the final campaign of the Union's Army of the Potomac from the point of view of its Fifth Corps, which he commanded. Filled with vivid descriptive passages, the book is still in print.

A household name in his day, Chamberlain's memory eventually faded. That began changing in 1975 with the publication of Michael Shaara's best-selling and Pulitzer Prize–winning novel about the battle of Gettysburg, *Killer Angels,* in which Chamberlain was a major protagonist. In 1990 the story of his desperate defense of Little Round Top was a highlight of the acclaimed PBS television series *The Civil War.* A few years later actor Jeff Daniels convincingly portrayed Chamberlain, drooping handlebar mustache and all, in *Gettysburg,* the epic film based on Shaara's novel. Daniels played Chamberlain again in a 2003 Civil Warm movie, *Gods and Generals.*

The Pejepscot Historical Society maintains Chamberlain's old home at 226 Main St., across from the Bowdoin campus. On display are Chamberlain's uniforms, medals, sword, bullet-dented boots, and the ornate chair he used as governor and college president. Note the statue depicting him as a major general, set in the small park beside the house. Seemingly as tenacious and enduring after death as he was in battle, Chamberlain appears to have now finally won from posterity the full recognition he deserves. The Chamberlain House is open late May–late Oct. Tue.–Sat. 10–4. Guided tours are on the hour; the last begins at 4. $5 adults, $2.50 children.

JOSHUA LAWRENCE CHAMBERLIN HOUSE AND MUSEUM

Pejepscot Historical Society

♿ **Bowdoin College Museum of Art** (207-725-3275; www.bowdoin.edu/art museum), Park Row. Open year-round, Tue.–Sat. 10–5, Thurs. til 8:30, Sunday 2–5. Closed Mon. and holidays. Free. Reopened in 2007 after a four-year, $20.8 million renovation that increased its space by 63 percent, this is one of New England's oldest (established 1811) and most significant art collections, housed in a copper-domed 1894 building designed by McKim, Mead, and White, now with an entrance through a discrete glass pavilion facing the street. There are seven galleries and a rotunda with murals by Abbott Thayer, Kenyon Cox, and John LaFarge. Current collections include more than 14,000 objects ranging from Assyrian bas-reliefs and Far Eastern works to American portraits by Gilbert Charles Stuart and Thomas Eakins to Maine-based works by Winslow Homer, Rockwell Kent, John Sloan, and Andrew Wyeth. Check the Web site for current exhibits.

Peary-MacMillan Arctic Museum (207-725-3416), Hubbard Hall, Bowdoin College, Brunswick. Open year-round, Tue.–Sat. 10–5, Sun. 2–5; closed Mon. and holidays. Free. A well-displayed collection of clothing, trophy walruses and seals, polar bears and caribou, and other mementos from expeditions to the North Pole by two Bowdoin alumni. Robert Edwin Peary (class of 1877) was the first person to reach the North Pole (in 1909), and Donald Baxter MacMillan (class of 1898), who was Peary's chief assistant, went on to dedicate his life to exploring Arctic waters and terrain. Displays include an interactive touch screen, photo blowups, and artifacts to tell the story.

Eagle Island State Historic Site (207-624-6080; www.pearyeagleisland.org). Open mid-June–Labor Day, 10–sunset. Accessible six days a week from South Freeport with Capt. Thomas Ring via ***Atlantic Seal*** (207-865-6112), $28 per adult, $20 per child 15 and under (free parking); five days a week from Portland's Long Wharf via Eagle Island Tours (207-774-6498; www.eagleislandtours), $26 per adult, $24 senior, $15 children

Sea Escape Charters (207-833-5531) offers charter runs out from Bailey Island. Private boats welcome; there is a nominal landing and admission charge. Just 17 acres, this is the site of Admiral Robert E. Peary's shingled summer home where, on September 6, 1909, his wife received the news that her husband had become the first person to reach the North Pole. Peary positioned his house to face northeast on a rocky bluff that resembles the prow of a ship. He designed the three-sided living room hearth, made from island stones and Arctic quartz crystals, and stuffed many of the birds on the mantel. Bedrooms appear as though someone has just stepped out for a walk, and the dining room is strewn with photos of men and dogs battling ice and snow. A nature path circles the island, passing the pine trees filled with seagulls (the trails open after bird nesting season).

BOWDOIN COLLEGE

Dan Gair / Blind Dog Photo, Inc.

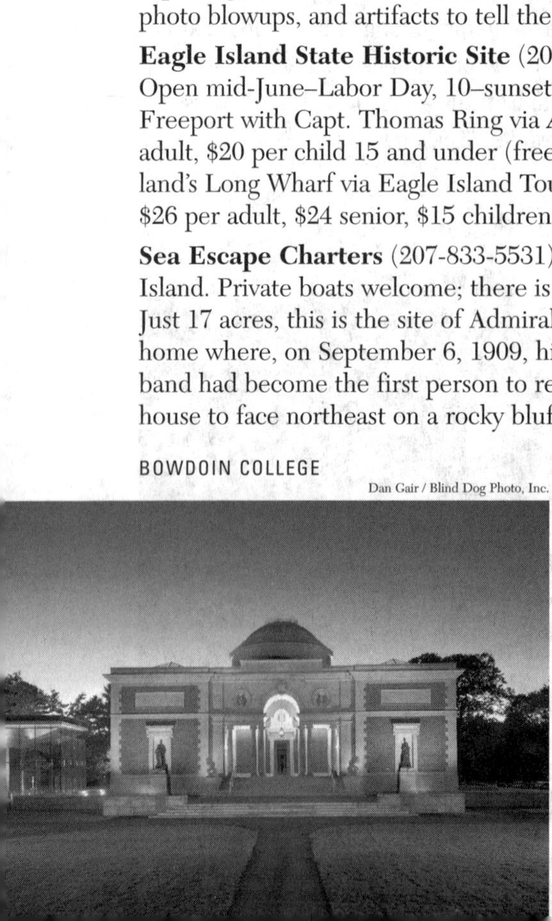

Pejepscot Historical Society Muse-

Christina Tree

CRIBSTONE BRIDGE

ums (207-729-6606). Founded in 1888 and named for an ancient Indian settlement, this is one of Maine's oldest historical societies. It maintains three downtown Brunswick museums. For the first—the Joshua L. Chamberlain Museum—see box on page 178. **The Pejepscot Museum**, 159 Park Row (Tue.–Fri. 10–5; free), is a massive, cupola'd mansion that displays changing exhibits on the history of Brunswick, Topsham, and Harpswell. The **Skolfield-Whittier House**, part of the same mid-19th-century Italianate double house (open May–Oct. Tue., Thurs.–Sat. 10–2:30), is virtually unchanged since the 1925 death of Dr. Frank Whittier. Its high-Victorian drawing room is hung with crystal chandeliers and heavy velvet drapes, furnished in wicker and brocade, and filled with the photos, books, and paintings of three generations. A combination ticket for all three museums is $8 adults, $4 children. Inquire about walking tours.

The First Parish Church (UCC) (207-729-7331), Maine St. at Bath Rd., Brunswick. Open for noon-time summer organ concerts and tours July–mid-Aug., Tue. 12:10–12:50; for Sunday services; and by chance. This graceful neo-Gothic building was designed in the 1840s by Richard Upjohn, architect of New York City's Trinity Church. A dramatic departure from its Puritan predecessors, it's open beamed, is mildly cruciform in shape, and has deeply colored stained-glass windows. The large sanctuary window was donated by Joshua Chamberlain, one of the first people to be married here. The Hutchings-Plastid tracker organ was installed in 1883.

SCENIC DRIVE **A tour of the Harpswells, including Orrs and Bailey Islands**. Allow a day for this rewarding peninsula prowl. From Brunswick, follow Rt. 123 south past Bowdoin College 9 miles to the picturesque village of Harpswell Center. The white-clapboard **Elijah Kellogg Church** faces the matching **Harpswell Town Meeting House**, built in 1757. The church is named for a former minister who was a prominent 19th-century children's-book author. Continue south through West Harpswell to **Potts Point**, where multicolored 19th-century summer cottages cluster on the rocks like a flock of exotic birds that have wandered in among the gulls.

Retrace your way up Rt. 123, and 2 miles north of the church turn right onto Mountain Rd., leading to busier Rt. 24 on Great (also known as Sebascodegan) Island. Drive south along **Orrs Island** across the only remaining **cribstone bridge** in the world, a National Historic Civil Engineering Landmark. (Its granite blocks are laid in honeycomb fashion—without cement—to allow tidal flows.) This bridge brings you to **Bailey Island**, with its restaurants, lodging places, picturesque Mackerel Cove, and rocky **Land's End**, with a statue honoring all Maine fishermen. Return up Rt. 24 and take Cundy's Harbor Rd. 4.3 miles to another picturesque fishing harbor with a couple of good little restaurants.

✷ To Do

BICYCLING **The Androscoggin River Bicycle Path**, a 2.6-mile, 14-foot-wide paved bicycle/pedestrian trail, begins at Lower Water St. in Brunswick and runs along the river to Grover Lane in Cooks Corner. It connects with Topsham along the way via a bicycle lane on the new Merrymeeting Bridge.

BOAT EXCURSIONS From Bailey Island both Capt. Jay McGowen Sportfishing (207-833-6054) and Sea Escape Charters (207-833-5531) offer fishing trips, scenic cruises, and excursions in Casco Bay. Sea Escape specializes in tours to Eagle Island (see *To See*). Casco Bay Lines (207-774-7871) offers a daily seasonal excursion from Cook's Lobster House on Bailey Island. It takes one hour and 45 minutes to circle around Eagle Island and through this northern end of Casco Bay. *Symbion II* (207-725-0969) is Captain Ken Brigham's 38-foot Hunter sailboat, offering three-hour daysails and overnight charters. Nautic Video (207-833-5713; www.nauticvideo.com) is Capt. James Jones outfit; he offers charter tours from Orrs Island aboard his modified 34-foot lobster boat, featuring a live underwater video cam.

RAILROAD EXCURSION

✐ **The Maine Eastern Railroad** (1-866-637-2457; www.maineeasternrailroad.com), runs Fri. and Sat. Memorial Day weekend through late June, then Wed.–Sun. until early November. The best excursion train in New England! The 54-mile run from Brunswick to Rockland—with stops in Bath and Wiscasset—takes just over two hours, traveling along the coast in plush, streamlined 1940s and '50s coaches and dining car, pulled by a 1950s diesel electric engine. Check the Web site for current schedule and fares. At this writing you can depart Brunswick at 10:20 AM and arrive in Rockland at 12:25. That gives one plenty of time of see that community's museums before returning at 6:30. Alternately, one family member can drive and meet the train at any of its stops. Note that it's now once more *almost* possible to travel by train from Washington, D.C., to Brunswick, thanks to Amtrak's *Downeaster* (see *What's Where*), which now comes as far as Portland, 30 miles south of Brunswick. Plans call to close that gap.

GOLF **Brunswick Golf Club** (207-725-8224), River Rd., Brunswick. Incorporated in 1888, an 18-hole course known for its beauty and challenging nature. Snack bar, lounge, and cart rentals.

Mere Creek Golf Club (207-721-9995) is a nine-hole course at the Brunswick Naval Station is open to the public.

SEA KAYAKING **H2Outfitters** (207-833-5257; www.h2outfitters.com). Based just north of the cribstone bridge on Orrs Island, this is one of Maine's oldest kayaking outfitters. No rentals. Lessons for all abilities, from beginners to instructor certification; guided day trips and overnight excursions are also offered.

Seaspray Kayaking (207-443-3646; www.seaspraykayaking.com), with a base on the New Meadows River in Brunswick, offers rentals and a variety of guided trips and rentals.

✱ Green Space

BEACHES AND SWIMMING HOLES ✐ **White's Beach** (207-729-0415), Durham Rd., Brunswick. Open mid-May–mid-Oct. A pond in a former gravel pit (water no deeper than 9 feet). Facilities include a small slide for children. Sandy beach, lifeguards, picnic tables, grills, and a snack bar. Inquire about campsites.

✐ **Thomas Point Beach** (207-725-6009), off Thomas Point Rd., marked from Rt. 24, Cooks Corner. Open Memorial Day–Labor Day, 9 AM–sunset. Admission fee. The beach is part of an 85-acre private preserve on tidal water overlooking the New Meadows River and Thomas Bay. It includes groves for picnicking (more than 500 picnic tables plus a main lodge snack bar, playground, and arcade) and 75 tent and RV sites. It's the scene of a series of August events, including the Maine Highland Games and Bluegrass Festival.

✐ **Coffin Pond** (207-725-6656), River Rd., Brunswick. Open mid-June–Labor Day 10–7. Admission fee. A strip of sandy beach surrounding a circular, spring-fed pond. Facilities include a 55-foot-long waterslide, a playground, and changing rooms maintained by the town.

WALKS **Giant's Staircase**, Bailey Island. Turn off Rt. 24 at Washington Ave., park at the Episcopal church, and walk down to Ocean St.; follow the path along the water and follow the small sign to the well-named "stairs."

Brunswick Topsham Swinging Bridge. This restored footbridge spans the Androscoggin River, and was originally built in 1892 by John A. Roebling Sons Co., the firm that built the Brooklyn Bridge, for workers walking to the Cabot Mill.

Brunswick-Topsham Land Trust (207-729-7694), 108 Maine St., Brunswick. The land trust has preserved more than 700 acres in the area. Pick up a map and guides to the nature loops at **Skolfield Nature Preserve**, Rt. 123, Brunswick (4 miles or so south of town), adjoining an ancient Indian portage between Middle Bay and Harpswell Cove, and to the **Bradley Pond Farm Preserve** in Topsham, a 2.5-mile trail system in a 162-acre preserve. **Crystal Spring Farm**

Trails, a 2.5-mile trail on the 160-acre farm on Pleasant Hill Road in Brunswick.

Town of Harpswell Walking Trails. By far the most famous of these leads to the Giant Stairs (see above) but there are a half dozen more options. Stop by the town offices on Mountain Road (between Rts. 24 and 123) and pick up a trail map to seven local properties with walking trails. Check out the **The Cliff Trail**, that begins around back. This 2.3-mile loop features a shore walk along tidal Strawberry Creek, two "fairy house" zones and a view from 150-foot cliffs over Long Reach.

Swan Island (207-547-5322; www.mefishwildlife.com). Open by reservation only May–Labor Day and on a limited basis until the end of Sept. No pets allowed. Managed by the Maine Department of Inland Fisheries and Wildlife. Day use and overnight camping, but only 60 visitors at a time are allowed; $5 adult day-use, $8 overnight. The landing is in Richmond Village, and transport is provided. Tours are available in an open slat-sided truck, and there is plenty of area for walking. At the head of Merrymeeting Bay, the island is 4 miles long and less than a mile wide, a haven for wood ducks, mergansers, white-tailed deer, bald eagles, wild turkeys, and more. It was the site of an Indian village, and in 1614 Capt. John Smith visited. Several early houses survive; Aaron Burr slept in one.

✷ Lodging

In and around Brunswick

Middle Bay Farm Bed & Breakfast (207-373-1375; www.middlebayfarm.com), 287 Pennellville Rd., Brunswick 04011. Open year-round. Sited on a quiet cove minutes from downtown Brunswick, this handsome clapboard house dates to the 1830s. In the early 1900s it was a summer boardinghouse (Helen Keller is said to have stayed here), but it had stood empty for 10 years when the Truesdells bought and renovated it. Phyllis Truesdell is a warm and skilled hostess who makes guests feel invited. There's a living room with a baby grand, a gracious dining room, and a big country kitchen. The four spacious guest rooms have private full bath, water view, sitting area, and cable TV/VCR hidden in an armoire. There's also a porch from which to survey lawn, sky, and water. The neighboring Sail Loft Cottage houses two rustic suites, each with a living area, cooking facility, and two small bedrooms. The five landscaped acres are on a rise above a tidal cove; kayaks and canoes are available. $150 in-season, $135 off-season in the house, including a full breakfast; $170 in-season $150 off-season in the Sail Loft.

♿ **Brunswick Inn at Park Row** (207-729-4914 or 1-800-299-4914; www.brunswickinnparkrow.com), 165 Park Row, Brunswick 04011. Under new ownership, the former Brunswick Bed & Breakfast is now more boutique hotel than B&B. The Bar Harbor–based owners have redecorated the 15 guest rooms, divided between the original mid-1800s Greek Revival home and a contemporary Carriage House in the rear. Each is equipped with phone, desk, clock radio; TV on request. The elegant old double parlor is filled with brown leather armchairs, and the former common room is now a wine bar. Art on the walls is for sale. The location remains prime. $125–190 includes a full breakfast.

"1" **The Black Lantern** (207-725-4165 or 1-888-306-4165; www.blacklanternbandb.com), 37 Elm St., Topsham 04086. Open most of the year. Longtime local B&B owners Tom and Judy Connelie are now a few blocks from their previous location, giving them—and their guests—a view of the Andsocoggin River and direct access to the bike path (also good for jogging) along its banks. Of the three cheerful rooms (all with private bath) we recommend the back room with its river view. $95–110 ($90 off-season) includes a full breakfast. Quilters are particularly welcome and guests can borrow a bike.

Captain Daniel Stone Inn (207-725-9898 or 1-877-573-5151; www.captaindanielstoneinn.com), 10 Water St., Brunswick 04011. Thirty-four modern rooms and four suites are annexed to a Federal mansion. All have TV, phone, VCR, and alarm clock–cassette player; some feature a whirlpool bath. Continental breakfast. $140–255 per room in-season. Guests have access to bikes for use on the nearby path. Inquire about last-minute deals, long-term rates, and catered events.

In Harpswell

Harpswell Inn (207-833-5509 or 1-800-843-5509; www.harpswellinn.com), 108 Lookout Point Rd., Harpswell 04079. Innkeepers Richard and Anne Mosley have deep ties to Haprswell and a keen interest in its history, in which their gracious three-story white-clapboard B&B has played a significant part. Built as the cookhouse for an adjacent boatyard, it was subsequently the Lookout Point House, one of no less than 52 Harpswell hotels and boardinghouses that accommodated guests during the steamboating era. The 12 guest rooms vary widely and come with and without hearth, deck, water views, whirlpool, and bath (only two share); there are also three suites with kitchens. The large living room has a fireplace and plenty to read, more seating with water views is scattered about the lawns. Allen's, one of the area's best sources for lobster and clams (see *Eating Out*) is next door. In high season $110–159 for rooms, $235–245 for suites, includes a very full breakfast. There is also a 50-seat function room for which Richard, a professional chef, supplies catering. Inquire about four cottages available for weekly rental.

"1" **The Captain's Watch B&B** (207-725-0979), 926 Cundy's Harbor Rd. and Pinkham Point Rd., Harpswell 04079. Open year-round. Donna Dillman and Ken Brigham offer eight guest rooms that, at this writing, are divided between their longtime property, the Civil War–era former Union Hotel in Cundy's Harbor, and their contemporary waterside home on Card Cove. Your choice is between spacious traditional rooms with fireplaces and antiques ($140–175, including a full breakfast) and two rooms in a modern house, directly facing the water ($150 with breakfast). A large upstairs apartment is $1,000 per week. Capt. Ken offers daysails aboard 38-foot *Symbion II* (see *To Do*).

The Log Cabin, An Island Inn (207-833-5546; www.logcabin-maine.com), Rt. 24, Bailey Island 04003. Open Apr.–Oct. Built decades ago as a lavish log summer home with a huge hearth (a moose head, of course, hangs above), this was for many years a popular restaurant, but the owners refitted it to offer nine rooms—four with kitchen, two with hot tub, all with private bath, fridge, coffee machine, and waterside deck—and heated swimming pool. Breakfast is included for $99–299, $329 for the Harspswell Room, really a fully equipped cottage. Dinner is still served, but the restaurant's no longer open to the public (entrées $15–29).

Driftwood Inn and Cottages (207-833-5461; www.thedriftwoodinnmaine.com), 81 Washington Ave., Bailey Island 04003. Open late May to mid-October; the dining room (which is open to the public) is open July–Labor Day. Location, location! Sited on a rocky point within earshot of a foghorn and walking distance of the Giant's Staircase, Driftwood is classically "Maine rustic." This term was once generally understood to mean naturally air-conditioned, heated by fireplaces (there are also gas stoves in the common rooms), and shared baths (some guest rooms are now private), and this 1905 complex is one of the last of its breed along Maine's coast. Breakfast and dinner (BYOB) are served in a pine-walled dining room. The cottages contain a total of 16 doubles and eight singles (nine with half-bath); there are also six housekeeping cottages. We recommend Room 7 in Driftwood, pine walled with a firm queen bed, a half-bath, and windows on the water. There is a small saltwater swimming pool set in the rocks. Innkeeper David Conrad's family has owned Driftwood for more than 60 years. $90–135 per couple, $75 single (no minimum stay). Housekeeping cottages, available by the week, are $645–680; children under 10 years stay for half-price. On a per diem basis, breakfast is $6.50; dinner, $16.50–19. Inquire about weekly rates. No credit cards. Pets are accepted in the cottages ($50 fee).

DRIFTWOOD INN

Christina Tree

MOTELS **Little Island Motel** (207-833-2392; www.littleislandmotel.com), 44 Little Island Rd., Orrs Island 04066. Open mid-May–mid-Oct. An attractive motel with terrific views. Jo Atlass offers eight units, each with a small refrigerator and color TV. The motel is on its own mini island with a private beach, connected to land by a narrow neck. $120–140 per couple includes continental breakfast and use of boats, bicycles, and the outdoor picnic area. $10 extra for each child under 12, $20 for anyone over.

♿ **Bailey Island Motel** (207-833-2886; www.baileyislandmotel.com), Rt. 24, Bailey Island 04003. Open mid-May–mid-Oct. Located just over the cribstone bridge. A pretty, gray-shingled building on the water's edge, offering ocean views and landscaped lawns with rocks and a dock to walk out on. The 11 rooms are clean and comfortable, with cable TV. No smoking. Morning coffee and muffins are included in $95–125. Guests are welcome to tie their boat up to the dock or a mooring.

COTTAGES **The Southern Midcoast Maine Chamber** (see *Guidance*) lists cottage rentals on Orrs and Bailey Islands.

✷ Where to Eat

DINING OUT

In Brunswick

Note: This is a college town, and the quality of the food is higher than prices imply.

Henry & Marty (207-721-9141; www.henryandmarty.com), 61 Maine St. Open for dinner Tue.–Sun. Reservations recommended. Filling two warmly colored and decorated storefronts. Ownership has changed but the staff remains and quality of the food continues to rank among the best along Maine's Midcoast. Patrons share a smug sense of being savvy enough to be here, whether they're dining on thin-crust pizza, a halibut Niçoise salad, or the slow-roasted natural (local) beef brisket. Entrées $11–29.

Sweet Leaves Teahouse (207-725-1376; www.sweetleaves.com), 22 Pleasant St. Open Tues.–Sat., 11:30–9. Bright and airy, this is a relaxing space to savor a wide variety of teas—and herbs (this may be your only chance to sample catnip or black dandelion root), unusual soups (we can vouch for the chilled carrot, ginger with coconut milk, and lemon balm) and panini, which might include a crabmeat salad, or avocado with bacon, spinach, and red pepper mayo. Come for high tea in the afternoon. Dinner entrées, available after 5, might range from local snap peas, oyster mushrooms, and pak chai in a green curry broth with basmati rice coquettes to seared hangar steak with asparagus. As much produce as possible is local. Pastry is a specialty and yogurts, ice creams, and sorbets are made here. "Dinnerly Plates" $15.75–18.75. Beer and wine are served.

Scarlet Begonias (207-721-0403), 212 Maine St. Open Mon.–Thu. 11–8, Fri. 11–9, Sat. noon–9; closed Sun. In their attractive storefront "bistro," Doug and Colleen Lavallee serve some great sandwiches (we recommend the turkey spinach with mozzarella and basil mayo, grilled on sourdough bread) and chunky, fresh-herbed pastas like rose begonia. Entrees $7–13.

Back Street Bistro (207-725-4060), 11 Town Place. Open nightly. Just off Maine Street by the fire station, you can depend on a good meal. A fish and shellfish gumbo varies nightly, but always comes with a deeply flavored broth. Entrées $16–25.

The Great Impasta (207-729-5858), 42 Maine St. Open daily (except Sun.) for lunch and dinner. A great stop even if you're simply traveling up or down Rt. 1, but arrive early to get a booth (plaques honor booth regulars). Specialties include pasta dishes like seafood lasagna; try the eggplant stuffed with smoked mozzarella, mushrooms, onions, and tomatoes and topped with roasted vegetables. Wine and beer served. Dinner entrées $11–19.

El Camino (207-725-8228), 15 Cushing St. Open for dinner Tues.–Sat. An unpromising exterior disguises a hip, funky interior, the setting for highly inventive Mexican food, with a dedication to using chemical-free seafood and meats as well as organic—local wherever possible—produce. Vegans as well as vegetarians have options and everything is spicy and good. The chips are warm, the selection of beers large, and the margaritas famous. Entrées $12–15.

Richard's Restaurant (207-729-9673), 115 Maine St. Open for lunch and dinner Mon.–Sat. Continental fare like veal Oscar and grilled New York sirloin is featured, also satisfying dishes like *Gemischter salat*, Wiener schnitzel, and *Schlachtplatte*. Nightly specials include *Rinds-rouladen* (thinly sliced beef rolled with onions, bacon, mustard, and pickles). The beer list is impressive. Dinner entrées $11–21. Lighter fare and German beer are on tap in the Eidelweiss Lounge, also live piano music on weekends.

EATING OUT

In and near Brunswick

Frontier Café & Cinema Gallery (207-725-5222; www.explorefrontier.com) 14 Maine St. (Fort Andross). Open Mon.–Thurs. 9–9, Fri. 9–11, Sat. 11–11. A theater, gallery, and café is a winning combination that's difficult to pigeonhole. In the café huge windows along two walls overlook the Androscoggin River, its dam, and the picturesque Bowdoin Mill in Topsham. Tables by these windows maximize light and views, which frequently include ospreys, sometimes eagles and peregrine falcons. There are coffees and teas, wine, and beer; a menu of soups and salads, sandwiches and panini changes weekly. There are reasonably priced cheeses and "marketplates" representing different parts of the world. Check the Web site for wine tastings and other special events. Owner Michael "Gil" Gilroy, who traveled the world for his previous work, has used largely salvaged and recycled materials to turn this raw factory space into his vision of a cultural crossroads. Also see *Entertainment*.

HOLBROOK WHARF AND SNACK BAR

Christina Tree

Sea Dog Brewing (207-725-0162; www.seadogbrewing.com), Great Mill Island, 1 Main St., Topsham. Open daily 11:30–1 AM. Music Thu.–Sat. Housed in a picturesque (former) paper mill, vintage 1868. A big, friendly brewpub with seasonal outdoor dining overlooking the churning Androscoggin. This is a good bet for families. Specialties include fried scallops, grilled or teriyaki sirloin, potato-crusted haddock, and cioppino (seafood stew). The wide choice of beers includes more than half a dozen ales brewed here or in Bangor. Dinner entrées $15–19.

111 Maine (207-729-9111; www.111Maine.com), 111 Maine St. Open Tue.–Thu. 11–4, Fri. until 9, Sat. and Sun. 10–2. This welcome addition to Maine Street is a chic storefront café featuring soups, salads, and farm-fresh produce along with "small plates," such as spring rolls with local tomatoes and marinated mozzarella and citrus-grilled shrimp skewers with mango-napa slaw. The brunch menu features fritatta and perhaps Belgian waffles with whipped heavy cream and apple compote.

Joshua's Restaurant & Tavern (207-725-7981), 121 Maine St. Open 11:30 AM–11 PM. Named for General Joshua Chamberlain, reliably good for burgers and basics, including a first-rate crab salad. Don't be put off by the downstairs pub. Head upstairs for the deck or dining room. It's a big menu—plenty of fried and broiled fish, soups, stews, and a wide choice of beers.

Bangkok Garden Restaurant (207-725-9708), 14 Maine St. (Fort Andross). Open daily for lunch and dinner, Sun. 4–9. This attractive restaurant gets good reviews for classic dishes like green curry and pad Thai.

Wild Oats Bakery and Café (207-725-6287), Tontine Mall, 149 Maine St. Open Mon.–Sat. 7:30–5, Sun. 8–3. Set back from Maine St. with tables on the terrace and inside. A town meeting place serving coffees and teas, from-scratch pastries and breads, healthy sandwiches, and salads.

Fat Boy Drive-In (207-729-9431), Old Rt. 1. Open for lunch and dinner, late Mar.–mid-Oct. This is no 1950s reconstruct, just a real drive-in with carhops that's survived because it's so good and incredibly reasonably priced. If you own a pre-1970 car, you can come to the annual "sock hop."

Little Dog Coffee Shop (207-721-9500), 87 Maine St. Open 6 AM-8 PM. An inviting waystop with soothing eggplant-colored walls, widely spaced tables, a couch or two. The daily changing menu includes soup and grilled panini. We recommend the mushroom, avocado, and tomato combo. Also coffees, teas, pastries, and newspapers.

The Barn Door Café (207-721-3229), 4 Bowdoin Mill Island. Open Mon.–Fri. 7–6, Sat. 9–2. A small café, just off Rt. 1 and well known to locals for soups and sandwiches, like "crunchy tuna" (with slivered Granny Smith apples) and crunchy Thai chicken (marinated chicken with veggies and peanut sauce). A cup of soup and half sandwich are $5.50.

The Humble Gourmet (207-721-8100), 103 Pleasant St. (Rt. 1 northbound), open 8–7 daily, except Sun. A road-food find with baked goods, great sandwiches on homemade bread, soups, and salads. A couple of doors up from the Miss Brunswick Diner (see below, easier to spot).

Miss Brunswick Diner (207-729-5948), 101 Pleasant St. (Rt. 1 northbound). Open daily 5 AM–9 PM. A convenient road-food stop, a remake of a diner that originally stood in Norway (Maine) but has now been here several decades; the neon lights, booths, and jukebox are all new, but the food is what it claims to be: "home cooking at a down-home good price."

Tess's Market (207-729-9531), 54 Pleasant St. Strictly takeout, but a great source of sandwiches, pizza, and the area's best selection of wine.

In the Harpswells

Dolphin Chowder House (207-833-6000; www.dolphinchowderhouse.com), South Harpswell (marked from Rt. 123, it's 2.5 miles; also accessible by water). Open seasonally, 11–8 daily. The nicest kind of small Maine restaurant—owned by the Saxton family, overlooking a small but busy harbor. The dining room fills early for lunch and dinner. Chowder, lobster stew, and fried seafood are specialties. Wine and beer are served.

Block & Tackle (207-725-5690), Cundy's Harbor Rd. Open mid-May–mid-Oct., 11–8, breakfast from 7 AM on weekends. A family-run and -geared restaurant. Try shrimpster stew or real homemade clamcakes. The Friday special is corned hake.

In Richmond

Railway Café (207-737-2277), 64 Main St. Open Mon.–Thurs. 6:30 AM–8 PM, Fri. and Sat 6:30 AM–9 PM; Sun. 7–4. Minutes off I-295 exit 43,

LOBSTER **Morse's at Holbrooks** (207-729-9050), Cundy's Harbor. Open Memorial Day–mid June on weekends, then daily until Labor Day, 11–8. Members of the Morse family own this nicely sited lobster landmark with its harbor view. The chowder is great again, and the tartar sauce is homemade. Tables are topped with umbrellas and banked in flowers, and lobster is available right off the boat in all the usual ways. Also first-rate crab rolls. BYOB.

Allen's Seafood (207-833-2828), 119 Lookout Point Rd., Harpswell. Open Apr.–Oct, Tue.–Sun. 11–7. This longtime seafood wholesaler has added a take-out menu and picnic benches to take advantage of the glorious view. The steamed clams are locally picked and processed on the spot, served with broth and butter. The lobster couldn't be fresher. Order from the stand and eat at picnic tables, some with umbrellas. The menu includes fried scallops, shrimp, and haddock, as well as seafood rolls, burgers, dogs, and the usual sides. Also strawberry shortcake and doughboys. BYOB.

Middlebay Lobster (207-798-5868), 45 Ellen Way, Cundy's Harbor. The view is nonexistent, but the quality and price of fish and seafood are good. The menu includes a wide choice of sandwiches and "other stuff" as well as wine and beer. Try Mud Season for dessert.

Estes Lobster House (207-833-6340), Rt. 123, South Harpswell. Open daily May–Oct., 11–9. Since 1947, a classic "shore dinner" place with red-checked oilcloth tables. It's on a causeway with water views and the basics: steamed and fried clams and lobster every which way, broiled seafood baskets. Wine and beer, some waterside tables.

Cook's Lobster House (207-833-2818), Bailey Island. Open year-round, 11:30–10. A landmark barn of a place right on the water (beyond the parking lots) with knotty-pine walls, booths, and a classic Maine seafood menu. Founded in 1955 and little changed since. No surprises. If there's a line and you don't mind settling for light fare, head for the deck where there's open seating. In July and August try to get here before noon, when the Casco Bay liner arrives with its load of day-trippers from Portland.

this pleasant restaurant makes a good road-food stop: a wide choice of morning omelets and lunchtime sandwiches, burgers, salads, and pizzas, and a huge, reasonably priced dinner menu includes "Just for Kids." Allow a few minutes to walk around this historic Kennebec River town.

✐ **The Old Goat** (207-737-4628) 2 Main St. This small, cozy pub specializes in paninis, traditional Italian grilled sandwiches. The wide selection includes kid-friendly grilled cheese and peanut butter versions. All sandwiches $7. Open for lunch, dinner, and beyond.

✷ Entertainment

MUSIC **Bowdoin International Music Festival** (207-373-1400; www.bowdoinfestival.org), Brunswick. Famed in classical music circles since 1964, this late June through early August festival brings together talented young performers and internationally acclaimed musicians for six concert series of both classical and contemporary works. Wednesday and Friday evening concerts, featuring festival faculty and guest artists, are staged in Crooker Theater at Brunswick High School. Daily student concerts and the Gamper Festival of Contemporary Music are held in the new, state-of-the-art Studzinski Recital Hall on the Bowdoin College campus. Additional concerts, staged throughout the local community, are free, as are all student and Gamper Festival concerts.

Music on the Mall (207-729-4439). July–Aug., concerts at 7 PM Wed. on Brunswick's grassy downtown mall. Free.

Also see **First Parish Church** under *To See.*

Nancy English

DOLPHIN CHOWDER HOUSE

THEATER ✐ **Maine State Music Theatre** (207-725-8769; www.msmt.org), Bowdoin College, Brunswick. Summer performances at 8 PM, Tue.–Sat.; matinees Tue., Thu., and Fri. Special children's shows. Air-conditioned Pickard Theater is housed in Memorial Hall, an 1873 memorial to the Bowdoin students who fought and died in the Civil War—ordered built, of course, by Joshua Chamberlain. It's a fit stage for Maine's premier performing-arts group. This highly professional Equity company strives for a mix of classics and new scripts and frequently gets rave reviews.

The Theater Project (207-729-8584), 14 School St., Brunswick. Serious drama presented year-round in a black-box theater, Wed.–Sun. at 8. Inquire about late-night cabarets and dinner theater.

FILM **Eveningstar Cinema** (207-729-6796 or 1-888-304-5486), Tontine Mall, 149 Maine St., Brunswick. The specialty is alternative film: foreign, art, biography, documentary, and educational. Also a monthly venue for folk, jazz, and other music performances.

Frontier Café & Cinema Gallery (207-725-5222; www.explorefrontier.com) 14 Main St. (Fort Andross). Open Mon.–Wed. 9–9, until 11 Thu. and Fri., Sat. 11–11. Check the Web site for frequent films and lectures in the 75-seat cinema (seats are recycled from the Biddeford Theater, converted into swivel/rocking chairs and coffee tables). Visual story telling, workshops, and special events too (also see *Eating Out*).

✷ Selective Shopping

ANTIQUES Cabot Mill Antiques (207-725-2855), 14 Maine St. (at Rt. 1; Fort Andross), Brunswick. Open daily 10–5. A vast, 140-dealer space with quality antiques; flea markets on summer weekends.

Day's Antiques (207-725-6959), 153 Park Row, Brunswick. Open Mon.–Sat. 10–5.

ART AND CRAFTS GALLERIES

In Brunswick
Galleries at the north end of Brunswick's Maine St. include **Bayview Gallery** (207-729-5500), 58 Maine St., showing traditional Maine, and the edgier, innovative **Icon Contemporary Art** (207-725-8157), around the corner at 19 Mason St. Check out **Spindleworks** (207-725-8820), 7 Lincoln St., an artists' cooperative for people with disabilities that produces some striking handwoven fiber clothing and hangings, quilts, accessories, paintings, prints, and more. The **Window Tree Gallery and Frame Shop** (207-729-4366), 44 Maine St., is also worth checking. **Maine Fiber Arts Visitors Center**, 13 Main St., Topsham (207-721-0678; www.fiberarts.org), open weekdays and for special events, exhibits work and serves as a resource center for this active statewide association of farmers, artists, and craftsmen.

Second Friday Art Walks May–Dec. (207-798-6985; www.fiveriverartsalliance.org) are major events, with open houses at a number of studios as well as galleries and other art venues.

In the Harpswells
The Gallery at Widgeon Cove (207-833-6081; www.widgeoncove.com), Open most of the year but call before coming. This waterside gallery features Georgann Kuhl's watercolors and monotypes, mostly landscapes, on her handmade papers, and the gold and silver jewelry and sculptures of Condon Kuhl; it's worth a detour. **Ash Cove Pottery** (207-833-6004), farther down the road, displays a variety of hand-thrown and -glazed functional stoneware by Susan Horowitz and Gail Kass. On Rt. 24 (north of Mountain Rd.) the former Gunpoint Church now serves as a gallery for **Sebascodegan Artists** (named for the island on which it stands), a cooperative with 20 members. It's open July 4–Labor Day, Mon.–Sat. 10–5.

Hawke's Lobster (207-721-0472) in Cundy's Harbor is a seasonal source of not only seafood but also the work of local craftspeople. It may be the world's only gift shop with a tank full of freshly caught lobsters as its centerpiece.

BOOKSTORES Gulf of Maine Books (207-729-5083), 134 Maine St., Brunswick. A laid-back, full-service bookstore with a wide inventory, particularly rich in Maine titles, poetry, and "books that fall through the holes in bigger stores." Owners are photographer Beth Leonard and Gary Lawless, founder of Blackberry Press (note the full line here), which has reissued many out-of-print Maine classics. A true Renaissance man, Lawless is a well-known poet with an international following.

Brunswick Bookland & Cafe (207-725-2313), Cooks Corner Shopping Center. Open Mon.–Sat. 9 AM–10 PM, Sun. 9–6. A major, full-service independent bookstore that includes the **Hardcover Café**, serving light meals, espresso, desserts, and good daily specials.

Borders Books, Music, Movies & Café (207-271-1178), 147 Bath Rd., is a big, recent addition to the lineup around Cooks Corner.

SPECIAL STORES **Island Candy Company** (207-833-6639), Rt. 24, Orrs Island. Open year-round, 11–8. Melinda Harris Richter makes everything from lollipops to truffles. Try the almond cups.

Grand City V&S (207-725-8964), 128 Maine St., Brunswick. Open Mon.–Sat. 9–6, Sun. 10–4. See the chapter introduction. A must-stop for anyone who misses genuine five-and-dimes.

Wyler Crafts & Clothiers (207-729-1321), 150 Maine St., Brunswick, is a great mix of quality pottery, glassware, jewelry, and clothing; an offshoot Wyler Furniture and Home shop is at 100 Maine St.

✷ Special Events

Mid-May–June: **Fishway Viewing Room** (207-795-4290), Brunswick-Topsham Hydro Station, next to Fort Andross. Open during the spawning season, Wed.–Sun. 1–5. Watch salmon, smallmouth bass, and alewives climb the 40-foot-high fish ladder that leads to a holding tank beside the viewing room.

Throughout summer: **Farmer's Market** (Tue. and Fri., May–Nov.) on the downtown Brunswick Mall (the town common), and Saturday mornings at Crystal Spring Farm, Pleasant Hill Rd. Check the Thursday edition of Brunswick's *Times Record* for current happenings.

July: **Annual Lobster Luncheon**, Orrs Island United Methodist Church. **Bailey Island Fishing Tournament** (to register, phone Cook's Lobster House at 207-833-2818).

August: **Topsham Fair** (*first week*)—a traditional agricultural fair complete with ox pulls, crafts and food competitions, a carnival, and livestock; held at Topsham Fairgrounds, Rt. 24, Topsham. **Maine Highland Games**, Thomas Point Beach (*third Sat.*), a daylong celebration of Scottish heritage, with piping, country dancing, sheepdog demonstrations, and Highland fling competitions.

September: **Annual Thomas Point Bluegrass Festival** (*Labor Day weekend*), Thomas Point Beach. **Family Arts Festival** (*midmonth*)—music, dance, and storytelling on the downtown mall, Brunswick.

BRUNSWICK FARMER'S MARKET

Christina Tree

BATH AREA

Over the years some 5,000 vessels have been built in Bath. Think about it: In contrast to most communities—which retain what they build—here an entire city's worth of imposing structures have sailed away. Perhaps that's why, with a population of fewer than 9,300, Bath is a city rather than a town, and why the granite city hall, with its rounded, pillared facade and cupola (with a Paul Revere bell and a three-masted schooner for a weather vane), seems meant for a far larger city.

American shipbuilding began downriver from Bath in 1607 when the 30-ton pinnace *Virginia* was launched by Popham Colony settlers. The tradition continues with naval vessels regularly constructed at the Bath Iron Works (BIW).

With around 5,700 workers, BIW employs fewer people than worked in Bath's shipyards in the 1850s. At its entrance a sign proclaims: THROUGH THESE GATES PASS THE WORLD'S BEST SHIPBUILDERS. This is no idle boast, and many current employees have inherited their skills from a long line of forebears.

Obviously, this is the place for a museum about ships and shipbuilding, and the Maine Maritime Museum has one of the country's foremost collections of ships' models, journals, logs, photographs, and other seafaring memorabilia. It includes a 19th-century working shipyard.

Both BIW and the Maine Maritime Museum are sited on a 4-mile-long reach of the Kennebec River where the banks slope at precisely the right gradient for laying keels. Offshore, the channel is 35 to 150 feet deep; the open Atlantic is 18 miles downriver.

In the 1850s Bath was the fourth largest port in the United States in registered tonnage, and throughout the 19th century it consistently ranked among America's eight largest seaports. Its past prosperity is reflected in the blend of Greek Revival, Italianate, and Georgian Revival styles in the brick storefronts along Front Street and in the imposing wooden churches and mansions in similar styles along Washington, High, and Middle Streets. Front Street more offers a healthy mix of shops, and restaurants.

Today BIW dominates the city's economy as dramatically as its 400-foot-high construction crane—the biggest on the East Coast—does the city's waterfront. One of the largest civilian employers in Maine, the company actually produced more destroyers during World War II than did all of Japan, and it continues to

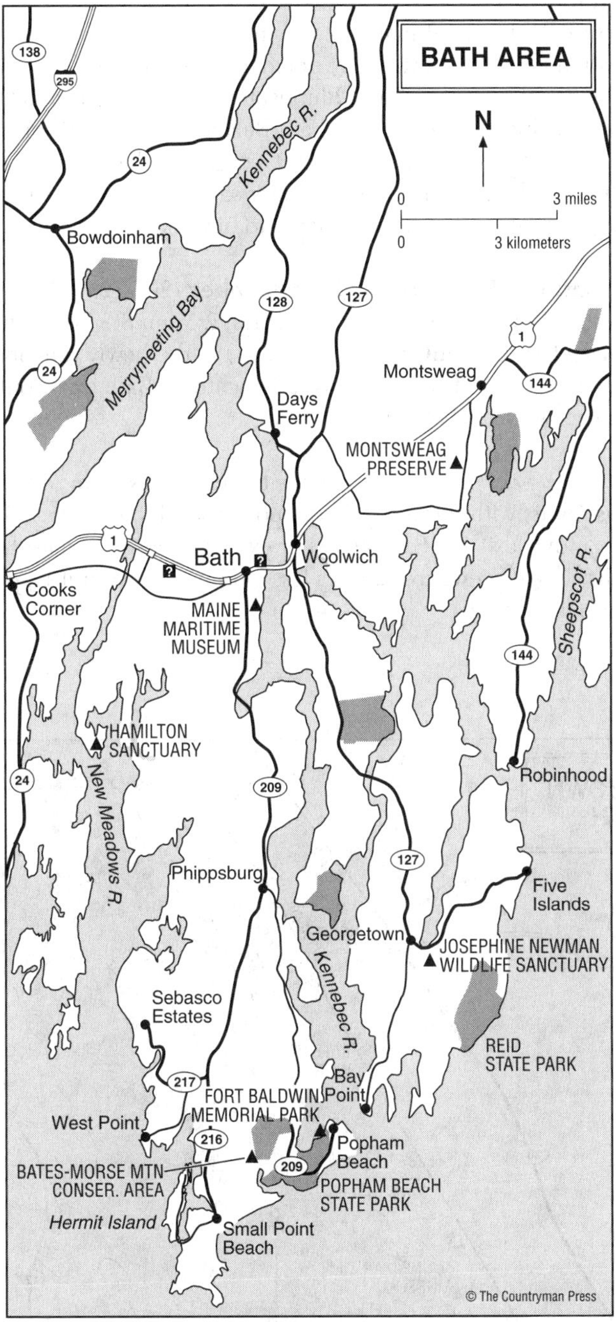

BATH AREA
N
0
3 miles
0
3 kilometers
138
295
24
Kennebec R.
Bowdoinham
Merrymeeting Bay
128
127
1
Montsweag
144
Days Ferry
MONTSWEAG PRESERVE
Bath
Woolwich
Cooks Corner
MAINE MARITIME MUSEUM
Sheepscot R.
HAMILTON SANCTUARY
New Meadows R.
209
Robinhood
Phippsburg
Five Islands
Georgetown
JOSEPHINE NEWMAN WILDLIFE SANCTUARY
Kennebec R.
Sebasco Estates
REID STATE PARK
217
Bay Point
FORT BALDWIN MEMORIAL PARK
West Point
216
Popham Beach
BATES-MORSE MTN CONSER. AREA
POPHAM BEACH STATE PARK
Hermit Island
Small Point Beach
© The Countryman Press

keep to its pledge to deliver naval ships ahead of schedule and under budget. Note the 750-foot floating dry dock (visible from Washington Street) used for launching and retrieval.

The story of BIW is one of many told in the Maine Maritime Museum—for which you should allow the better part of a day. Save another to explore the Phippsburg Peninsula south of Bath. Phippsburg's perimeter is notched with coves filled with fishing boats, and Popham Beach near its southern tip is a grand expanse of sand. Reid State Park on Georgetown Island, just across the Kennebec River, is the Midcoast's other major sandy strand. North of Bath, Merrymeeting Bay is a major flyway well known to birders.

GUIDANCE **Southern Midcoast Maine Chamber** (207-725-8797; www.midcoastmaine.com), Border Trust Business Center, 2 Main St., Topsham 04086 with a seasonal **Visitors Center** (207-442-7371) in the newly rehabbed Bath Railroad Station (take Rt. 1 to the Historic Downtown Bath exits south of the bridge). Also see www.visitbath.com.

GETTING THERE *By car:* Rt. 1 passes above the city; exits from the elevated road access various points within the city. From points south take I-95 to I-295 (formerly I-95) to either exit 28 (Brunswick) or exit 31 (Topsham) and the connector (Rt. 196) to Rt. 1. We prefer exit 28 (it's less confusing), but if it's a peak traffic time try your luck with 31.

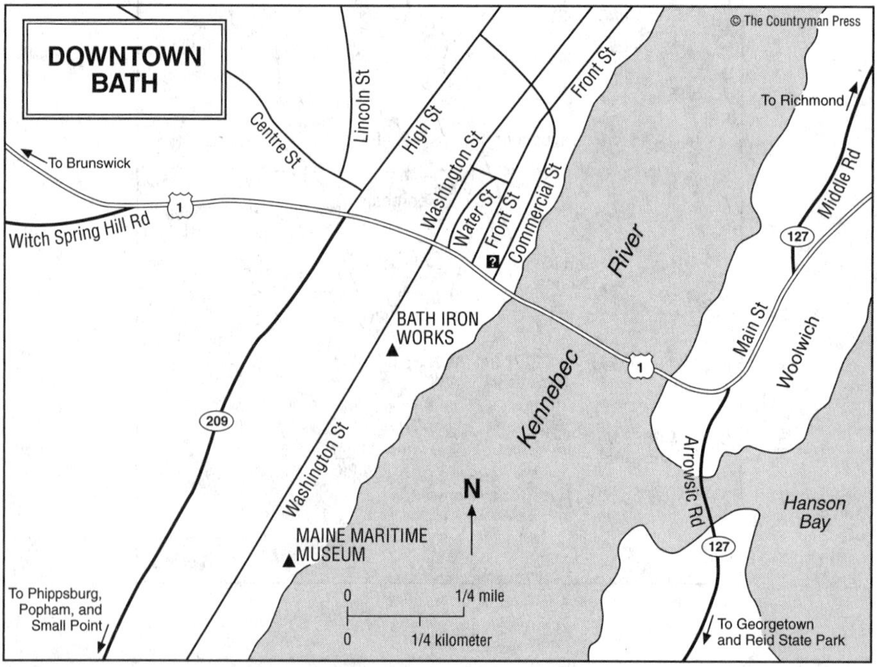

By bus: **Concord Trailways** (1-800-639-3317), en route to and from Boston, stops in Bath at Coastal Plaza just off Rt. 1.

By air and limo: **Mid-Coast Limo** (1-800-937-2424; www.midcoastlimo.com) makes runs by reservation from Portland International Jetport.

By train: **The Maine Eastern Railroad** (1-866-636-2457; www.maineeastern railroad.com) offers 54-mile seasonal runs between Brunswick and Rockland, stopping in Bath and Wiscasset.

GETTING AROUND **Bath Trolley Company** (www.bathtrolley.org) operates a loop throughout the city, daily July through Labor Day, weekends in the shoulder seasons. $1 per ride.

WHEN TO COME Bath itself remains lively year-round, but the Popham and Georgetown areas are June-through-Columbus-Day destinations.

✷ To See

Bath Historic District. In the 18th and 19th centuries Bath's successful families built impressive mansions. **Sagadahoc Preservation, Inc.** (207-443-2174; www.sagadahocpreservation.org), publishes an excellent brochure: *Architectural Tours—Self-Guided Walking and Driving Tours of the City of Bath.*

Woolwich Historical Society Museum (207-443-4833; www.woolwich history.org), Rt. 1 and Nequasset Rd., Woolwich. Open mid-June–mid-Aug., Wed.–Fri. 12–4. Volunteer-run, this 19th-century rural life museum displays antique clothing, quilts, and seafaring memorabilia from local attics. Special events.

SCENIC DRIVES **The Phippsburg Peninsula**. From the Maine Maritime Museum drive south on Rt. 209, down the narrow peninsula that's the town of Phippsburg. Pause at the first causeway you cross. This is **Winnegance Creek**, an ancient shortcut between Casco Bay and the Kennebec River; look closely to your left and you'll see traces of the 10 tide mills that once operated here.

Continue south on Rt. 209 until you come to the **Phippsburg Center Store** on your right. Turn left on Parker Head Rd. into the tiny hamlet of **Phippsburg Center**. This is one of those magical places, far larger in memory than in fact—perhaps because it was once larger in fact, too. Notice the **giant linden tree** planted in 1774 between the white-clapboard Congregational church (1802) and its small cemetery. Another surviving linden was also planted in 1774, the year the striking Georgian mansion next

BATH CITY HALL

Kim Grant

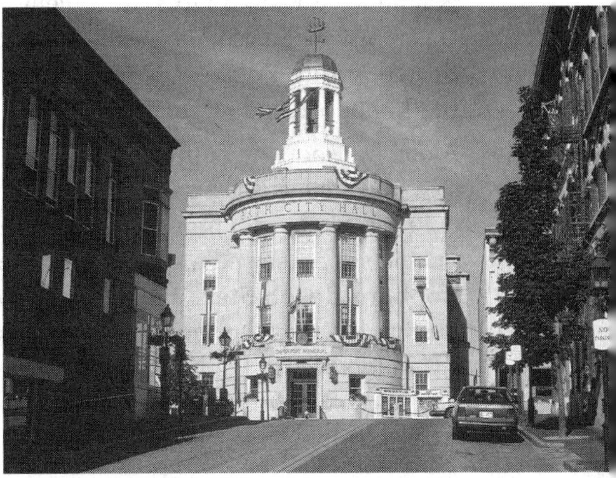

Maine Maritime Museum
MAINE MARITIME MUSEUM

Maine Maritime Museum (207-443-1316; www.mainemaritimemuseum.org), 243 Washington St., Bath (watch for the turnoff from Rt. 1). Open daily year-round 9:30–5 except Thanksgiving, Christmas, and New Year's Day. $10 adults, $9 seniors, and $7 ages 7–16. Sited just south of Bath Iron Works on the banks of the Kennebec River, this extensive complex, 10 riverside acres, includes the brick-and-glass Maritime History Building and the Percy & Small Shipyard, the country's only surviving wooden shipbuilding yard (its turn-of-the-20th-century belts for driving

door was built. Also look for the stumps of piers on the river shore beyond, remnants of a major shipyard.

Continue along the peninsula's east shore on the Parker Head Rd., past a former millpond where ice was once harvested. At the junction with Rt. 209, turn left. The road threads a salt marsh and the area at Hoss Ketch Point, from which all traces of the ill-fated **Popham Colony** have long since disappeared. Rt. 209 winds around Sabino Head and ends at the parking lot for **Fort Popham**, a granite Civil War–era fort (with picnic benches) at the mouth of the Kennebec River. A wooded road, for walking only, leads to World War I and II fortifications that constitute **Fort Baldwin Memorial Park**; a six-story tower yields views up the Kennebec and out to sea.

Along the shore at **Popham Beach**, note the pilings, in this case from vanished steamboat wharves. Around the turn of the 20th century, two big hotels served the passengers who transferred here from Boston to Kennebec River steamers, or who simply stayed a spell to enjoy the town's spectacular beach. Now **Popham Beach State Park**, this immense expanse of sand remains a popular destination for fishermen, beach walkers, sunbathers, and even a few hardy swimmers. From Popham Beach, return to Rt. 209 and follow it west to Rt. 217 and out to **Sebasco Harbor**, then back up to Phippsburg Center.

machinery have been restored). Museum exhibits focus on the era beginning after the Civil War when 80 percent of this country's full-rigged ships were built in Maine, almost half of these in Bath.

The pride of Bath, you learn, were the Down Easters, a compromise between the clipper ship and the old-style freighter that plied the globe from the 1870s through the 1890s, and the big multi-masted schooners designed to ferry coal and local exports like ice, granite, and lime. A fine example, the six-masted *Wyoming* was the largest wooden sailing vessel ever built. A full-scale steel sculpture suggests it mammoth size and height.

The museum's permanent collection of artwork, artifacts, and documents totals more than 20,000 pieces, and there is an extensive research library. Permanent exhibits include "Distant Lands of Palm and Spice," a fascinating, occasionally horrifying glimpse of where and why Maine ships sailed in the 18th and 19th centuries. Another exhibit chronicles the history of Maine's lobstering business, including displays on the19th-century canning boom and a vintage 1954 film, *The Maine Lobsterman,* written and narrated by E. B. White. The late Victorian home of a prominent Bath family is open seasonally.

There are also changing exhibits and a full schedule of tours and boat cruises (see *To Do*) as well as lectures, concerts, and other special events. Trolley tours of Bath Iron Works are offered several times a week.

Arrowsic and Georgetown Islands. Just east of the Sagadahoc Bridge (at the Dairy Queen that's been there forever), turn south on Rt. 127. Cross a shorter bridge and you are on Arrowsic Island. Note **Robinhood Road**, which leads to two of the area's top restaurants (see *Dining Out*). Farther down Rt. 127 in **Georgetown Center** look for **Georgetown Pottery**; the general store has a snack bar and is good for sandwiches. The **Georgetown Historical Society and Cultural Center** (207-371-9200; www.georgetownhistoricalsociety.org), open weekends, is just south at 20 Bay Point Rd.; check the Web site for a schedule of lectures and events. Continue on Rt. 127 to **Reid State Park**, the big draw (see *Swimming*). The road ends at the **Five Islands** lobster pound.

✱ To Do

BOAT EXCURSIONS **Maine Maritime Museum** (www.mainemaritimemuseum.org; see *To See*) offers an extensive choice of regularly scheduled one- to three-hour narrated tours down the Kennebec River, and Merrymeeting Bay, heading along the coast to Boothbay Harbor to view lighthouses (as many as 10 of them). Also special cruises upriver to Swan Island and other destinations.

The M/V *Ruth*, based at Sebasco Estates (207-389-1161); the **M/V *Yankee*** (207-389-1788), based at Hermit Island Campground at Small Point; and

Kennebec Charters (207-389-1883) at Popham Beach all offer coastal excursions.

Maine Island Touring Company (207-371-9930) offers tours to see birds and seals. **Gillies & Fallon Guide Service** (207-389-2300) also offers scenic cruises, lobster hauling, and sportfishing.

Sun Rae Charters (207-371-2813) offers evening excursions in a comfortably outfitted lobster boat.

Rivercruise (207-442-9769) operates from the Kennebec Tavern dock, Bath. Capt. Dick Bloxam offers charter trips upriver to Richmond and Hallowell, or down to Seguin Island, or across to Boothbay.

Seguin Island Light Station (www.seguinisland.org). Guarding the mouth of the Kennebec River, this 186-foot granite lighthouse stands on a bluff on a 64-acre island. Commissioned by George Washington in 1795, it's one of the oldest lighthouses in the country. It's accessed regularly by **Mid-Maine Water Taxi** (207-371-2288), ***Atlantic Seal*** (877-285-7325), and local charter boats.

CANOE AND KAYAK RENTALS This area's many coves and quiet stretches of smaller tidal rivers lend themselves to kayaking, and outfitters have multiplied in recent years. **Seaspray Kayaking** (207-443-3646; www.seaspraykayaking.com), with bases at Sebasco Harbor, Georgetown Center, and on the New Meadows River between Bath and Brunswick, offers rentals and daily tours, also inn-to-inn trips and multilevel instruction. **Up the Creek** (207-442-4845), 39 Main Rd. (Rt. 209), is sited beside a put-in not far south of Bath, renting Old Town canoes and kayaks. **Sea Taylor Rentals** (207-725-7400), 271 Bath Rd., Brunswick, rents canoes to explore Merrymeeting Bay.

FISHING **Kennebec Angler** (207-442-8239), 97 Commercial St., Bath, is fishing central for the area, a referral service for guides and charter boats. The shop is filled with tackle and gear and offers demo rods for full-day trials before purchasing. Surf fishing is popular at Popham Beach. Nearly 20 boats offer fishing on the river, while **Obsession Sportfishing Charters** (207-442-8581) offers deep-sea-fishing charters. Also see *Boat Excursions*.

PERCY & SMALL SHIPYARD

GOLF **Bath Country Club** (207-442-8411), Whiskeag Rd., Bath, has 18 holes and a pro shop; lessons available. **Sebasco Harbor Resort Golf Club** (207-389-9060) is a recently renovated, waterside nine-hole course open to the public. Reservations advised. Also see *Brunswick*.

RAILROAD EXCURSION **The Maine Eastern Railroad** (1-866-636-2457; www.maineeasternrailroad

.com) offers 54-mile seasonal runs between Brunswick and Rockland, stopping in Bath and Wiscasset. Travel along the coast in plush 1940s and '50s coaches and a dining car, pulled by a 1950s diesel electric engine. Check the Web site for current information. The Bath stop is in the renovated RR station at the foot of Main Street.

SWIMMING 🐾 If you're traveling with a dog, it's important to know that they're allowed only in picnic areas, not on the beaches.

Popham Beach State Park (207-389-1335; 207-389-9125 for current parking and tide updates), Rt. 209, Phippsburg; 14 miles south of Bath. One of the best state park swimming and walking beaches in Maine: 3 miles of sand at the mouth of the Kennebec River, only part of the park's 519 acres. Facilities include bathhouses, showers, and picnic areas with grills. Also a sandbar, tidal pools, and smooth rocks. It can be windy; extra layers are recommended. Day-use fees ($4 adults, $1 ages 5–11, under 5 free), are charged mid-Apr.–Oct.

Reid State Park (207-371-2303), Rt. 127, Georgetown (14 miles south of Bath and Rt. 1). Open daily year-round. A 766-acre preserve with rock ledges, woodlands, and salt marshes as well as sand beaches. Good for year-round walking and birding. The bathhouse and snack bar overlook 2 miles of sand in three distinct beaches that seldom become overcrowded, although the limited parking area does fill by noon on summer weekends. You can choose surf or slightly warmer sheltered backwater. Little River, around the corner from Half-Mile Beach, is a tidal estuary that warms on sunny days, especially good for children. Entrance fee ($4.50 under age 65) charged mid-Apr.–mid-Oct.

Charles Pond, Rt. 27, Georgetown (about 0.5 mile past the turnoff for Reid State Park; 15 miles down the peninsula from the Carlton Bridge). Often considered the best all-around swimming hole in the area, this long and narrow pond has clear water and is surrounded by tall pines.

Pleasant Pond (207-582-2813), Peacock Beach State Park, Richmond. Open Memorial Day–Labor Day. $3 adult. A sand-and-gravel beach with lifeguards on duty. Water depth drops off gradually to about 10 feet in a 30-by-50-foot swimming area removed from boating and enclosed by colored buoys. Picnic tables and barbecue grills.

Sewall Pond, Woolwich. Visible from Rt. 1, this popular swimming hole is just behind the Woolwich Historical Society Museum.

SPECIAL LEARNING PROGRAM **Shelter Institute** (207-442-7938; www.shelterinstitute.com), 873 Rt. 1, Woolwich. A year-round resource center for people who want to build or retrofit their own energy-efficient home, offering a wide variety of classes.

✷ Green Space

Fort Baldwin Memorial Park, Phippsburg. Follow the short, narrow road around a one-lane corner to Point Sebago, the site of the Popham Colony. An interpretive panel in the parking lot details the remarkable extent of the 1607–08 settlement here. An undeveloped area with a six-story tower to climb (steep stairs, but the railing is sturdy) for a beautiful view up the Kennebec and, downriver, out to sea. There are also remnants of fortifications from World Wars I and II.

Fort Popham Historic Site (207-389-1335), Hunniwell's Point at Popham Beach. Open Memorial Day–Sept. Picnic sites are scattered around the ruins of this 1861 granite fort, built to guard the Kennebec during the Civil War. Beach and ocean fishing access.

Josephine Newman Wildlife Sanctuary, Georgetown. Bounded on two sides by salt marsh, the 119 acres maintained by Maine Audubon provide good birding along 2.5 miles of walking trails. Look for the sign on Rt. 127, 9.1 miles south of Rt. 1.

Bates–Morse Mountain Conservation Area consists of some 600 acres extending from the Sprague to the Morse River and out to Seawall Beach. Allow two hours for the walk to and from this unspoiled private beach. Pack a picnic and towel, but please, no radios or beach paraphernalia: Seawall Beach is an important nesting area for piping plovers and least terns. There's a great view from the top of Morse Mountain, which is reached by an easy hike, just over a mile along a partially paved road. Parking is very limited.

Hamilton Sanctuary, West Bath. Situated on a peninsula in the New Meadows River, offering a 1.5-mile trail system and great bird-watching. Take the New Meadows exit off Rt. 1 in West Bath; turn left on New Meadows Rd., which turns into Foster Point Rd.; follow it 4 miles to the sanctuary sign.

Montsweag Preserve, Montsweag Rd., Woolwich. A 1.5-mile trail takes visitors through woods, fields, and a salt marsh, and along the water. This 45-acre preserve is owned by The Nature Conservancy (207-729-5181). You will have to watch carefully for the turns (right onto Montsweag Rd. about 6.5 miles from Bath on Rt. 1, then 1.3 miles and a left into the preserve).

Also see **Reid State Park** under *Swimming*.

* Lodging

RESORTS **Sebasco Harbor Resort** (207-389-1161 or 1-800-225-3819; www.sebasco.com), P.O. Box 75, Sebasco Estates 04565. Open May–Oct. This 575-acre, 132-room, family-geared waterside resort dates back to 1930, featuring a nine-hole golf course, tennis courts, a large swimming pool, kayaking, and full children's and adult activities programs. Sailing lessons and excursions, lobster cookouts, and live entertainment are also offered. The newest additions are luxury Harbor Village Suites ($319–459) and the Fair Winds Spa Suites ($319–399), handy to the full-service Fair Winds Spa and Wellness Center. Lodging is otherwise divided between the main lodge ($189–319), a lighthouse-shaped annex ($259–359), and 22 widely scattered and differing cottages, some with fireplace and kitchenette ($375–1,890). Rates drop in shoulder seasons. All rates are based on two people, $15 per extra person. Add $48 per person MAP (breakfast and dinner), another $20 for golf. Weddings and family reunions are a specialty.

Informal dining is at The Ledges, more formal at The Pilot House (entrées $14–23). A spa menu is also available. Children under 10 dine at no charge when accompanied by an adult and ordering from the children's menu. Inquire about golf, spa, and other special packages. Pets are accepted in some cottages ($25 per night).

🖉 **Rock Gardens Inn** (207-389-1339; www.rockgardensinn.com), Sebasco Estates 04565. Open mid-June–late Sept. A hidden gem, sited on its own narrow peninsula between a cove and bay, within but beyond the Sebasco Harbor Resort grounds. Accommodating just 60 guests, it offers a more intimate atmosphere but access to all of Sebasco Harbor Resort's facilities as well as its own pool and dock with kayaks. Rock Gardens dates back more than 90 years, and Ona Barnet has preserved the old-style atmosphere but constantly updates the 10 cottages (accommodating three to eight) and three inn rooms. August is family geared. In June, July, and September a series of Sebasco Art Workshops feature some surprisingly well-known teachers (Ona's father, Will Barnet, is a prominent artist). In high season $130–190 per person MAP (ask about children's rates) includes a four-course dinner (BYOB) as well as breakfast; five-night minimum in July and Aug., but check for cancellations; add 15 percent for service.

BED & BREAKFASTS

In Bath 04530

"1" 🏵 🐾 🖉 ♿ **The Inn at Bath** (207-443-4294 or 1-800-423-0964; www.innatbath.com), 969 Washington St. Open year-round. Elizabeth Knowlton is the keeper of Bath's leading inn. A restored 1830s mansion in the city's historic district, the inn features deeply colored and richly decorated twin living rooms with marble fireplaces, eight luxurious guest rooms with private bath, and a two-bedroom suite. Four rooms have a wood-burning fireplace; two of these also feature a Jacuzzi. Most rooms have a writing desk and small niceties that add up to comfort. We enjoyed a night in the Lavender Room with its soft colors, Hitchcock dressing table, a rocker, and king bed with a spool headboard. All guest rooms have air-conditioning, phone, cable TV, VCR, and clock radio. There's also a guest computer. $140–185, with a breakfast that includes homemade granola and fresh fruit and perhaps quiche. $25 per additional guest. Children (over 5) and dogs are welcome.

Pryor House (207-443-1146; www.pryorhouse.com), 360 Front St. Don and Gwenda Pryor offer three crisp, attractive upstairs guest rooms with air-conditioning and private bath in this late-Federal-style home. The Captain's Room has a rich red wallpaper, white wicker, and tall four-poster king; the Tall Chimney Room features a small deck and big Jacuzzi. Downstairs common space is inviting. Breakfast, which may feature tomato basil quiche, banana crèpes, or blueberry French toast, is included ($105–150). Forest, the brown greyhound, will undoubtedly greet you.

🐾 🖉 **Fairhaven Inn** (207-443-4391 or 1-888-443-4391; www.mainecoast.com/fairhaveninn), 118 North Bath Rd. Open year-round. Hidden away (not a place to find after dark) on the Kennebec River as it meanders down from Merrymeeting Bay, Andrew and

Dawn Omo's 1790s house has eight pleasant, air-conditioned guest rooms, six with private bath. The inn's 13 acres of meadow invite walking in summer and cross-country skiing in winter, and the inn is handy to the Bath Country Club. Two-night minimum stay on holidays and summer weekends. In-season rates $90–145, including a full breakfast, $15 per pet. Inquire about the cottage.

Kismet Inn (207-443-3399; www.kismetinnmaine.com), 44 Summer St., Bath. Open May–Oct. You know the world is shrinking when a former lumber baron's mansion becomes a yoga retreat featuring organic Middle Eastern food and Japanese-style baths. "I like color" is the way innkeeper Shad Towfighi explains the deep reds, lavenders, and yellows on the walls and the brightly patterned fabrics. Born in Iran, Towfighi has decorated with Persian carpets and hangings but also commissioned local craftspeople to reupholster locally found antiques and to create beds of her own design. Guests are welcome to just come for the night and enjoy an organic breakfast, but you might want to take advantage of morning yoga in the specially designed studio or a 40-minute exfoliation treatment in your 3-foot deep tub. $200–$255 for B&B, $315 with yoga plus $200 for an exfoliation scrub. Organic dinner menus are $60–85. No credit cards.

On the Phippsburg Peninsula south of Bath

The 1774 Inn at Phippsburg (207-389-1774; www.1774inn.com), 44 Parker Head Rd., Phippsburg 04562. Open year-round. Ranked among the most beautiful houses in Maine, this is an imposing cupola-topped, foursquare mansion, built in 1774 at the heart of picturesque Phippsburg Center. The home of Maine's first U.S. congressman, this landmark has been restored by Debbie and Joe Braun. Guests can choose from four splendid Federal-style guest rooms and three smaller bedrooms, all decorated in Willamsburg colors and fabrics, furnished with antiques, and all with private bath. $125–195.

Popham Beach Bed & Breakfast (207-389-2409; www.pophambeachbandb.com), 4 Riverview Ave., Popham Beach 04562. Open year-round. Peggy Johannessen has restored this former Coast Guard station, built in 1883 right on Popham Beach, to create a B&B with as much character as the building itself. The four guest rooms all have private bath and some of the most superb water views along the entire coast. The second-floor Bunkroom, despite its name, may just be the most spectacular beachside room in New England. Breakfast is full and served at a common table, and the sitting room is large and beautifully furnished. $185–225 in high season, with a two-night minimum stay; from $150 off-season.

EdgeWater Farm Bed & Breakfast (207-389-1322 or 1-877-389-1322; www.ewfbb.com), 71 Small Point Rd., Phippsburg 04562. Carol and Bill Emerson are passionate gardeners, and their restored circa-1800 farmhouse is set in four acres of gardens and fruit trees. It's well suited to small-group gatherings, with a large Sun Room to gather in. Another wing houses an indoor pool with a large recreation room above, along with several guest rooms and an outdoor hot tub on a back deck. The six guest rooms include two suites (all with private bath). $90–225. Dogs, $25 per stay.

On the Georgetown Peninsula

Coveside Bed and Breakfast (207-371-2807 or 1-800-232-5490; www.covesidebandb.com), Georgetown (Five Islands) 04548. Open Memorial Day–mid-Oct. Twelve miles down Rt. 127 from Rt. 1, beyond the turnoff for Reid State Park. Tucked into a corner of a quiet, lobster-filled cove, Carolyn and Tom Church have created a rare retreat. The seven guestrooms are divided between a century-old farmhouse and a matching, shingled (built from scratch) cottage with its own common space and screened porch. All of the many-windowed rooms face the water and those in the cottage have French doors opening onto decks. There's a wood-burning fireplace and Jacuzzi in one of the original rooms, and gas fireplaces warm the new rooms, but still really any room here is special. All have high, angled, or cathedral ceilings with fans, and there's a sense of uncluttered spaciousness, real comfort. Weather permitting, the multi-course breakfast is served on the brick terrace from which the lawn slopes away down beneath high trees to the shorefront. Amenities include a canoe and rental bikes. $125–190.

The Mooring (207-371-2790; www.themooringb-b.com), 132 Seguinland Rd., Georgetown 04548. Open May–Oct. Paul and Penny Barabe, the great-granddaughter of Walter Reid—donor of the land for his namesake state park—share their home as a B&B. The five guest rooms all have private bath; there are gracious common spaces and a great wicker-furnished porch overlooking the lawns and water. Weddings are a specialty. $150–170 in high season includes a full breakfast.

Tide's End Farm (207-371-9050; www.tidesendfarm.com), 98 Knubble Rd., Georgetown 04548. This 1770s farmhouse and its surrounding 48-acre island (connected to the rest of Georgetown by a causeway) belonged to Liia Becker's grandparents. An accomplished horsewoman who breeds Cleveland Bays (a mount favored and actually saved from probable extinction by Queen Elizabeth). She offers a variety of riding programs but it's not necessary to sign on to enjoy a stay at this saltwater farm, which offers three guest rooms with shared bath. $100–175 includes a full breakfast.

Grey Havens (207-371-2616; www.greyhavens.com), Senguinland Rd., P.O. Box 308, Georgetown 04548. Theoretically open May–Oct., but call. The donor of the land for neighboring Reid State Park also built this turreted, gray-shingled summer hotel, which opened in 1904. The 14 rooms, all with private bath are $160–280.

OTHER LODGING **Hermit Island Campground** (207-443-2101; www.hermitisland.com), 6 Hermit Island Rd., Phippsburg 04562; winter mailing address: 42 Front St., Bath 04530. This 255-acre almost-island at Small Point offers 271 nicely scattered campsites, 51 on the water. Only tents, small to medium pop-ups, and small pickup campers are permitted. Owned since 1953 by the Sewall family, Hermit Island also has a central lodge with a recreation room and snack bar where kids can meet.

Beyond the camping area are acres of private beach and hiking trails through unspoiled woods and meadows. $34–53 per night; less off-season. Repeat customers tend to mail in their reservations Jan. 2, but it's always worth a try. No pets.

Cottage listings are available from the Southern Midcoast Maine Chamber (see *Guidance*). Also see *Cottage Rentals* in "What's Where."

✱ Where to Eat

DINING OUT

Also see "Brunswick and the Harpswells."

Ⓞ **The Robinhood Free Meetinghouse** (207-371-2188; www.robinhoodmeetinghouse.com), 210 Robinhood Rd. (off Rt. 127), Robinhood. Open nightly mid-May–Oct., Thu.–Sat. off-season. Reservations advised. Michael Gagné, known regionally for his fresh, innovative dishes, has turned the vintage-1855 Robinhood Free Meetinghouse into an attractive dining space. The second-floor chapel, with a 16-foot ceiling and 10-foot windows, seems designed for wedding parties. There's also an intimate ground-floor dining room, a totally different feel with contemporary art. The soup of the day might be cream of mushroom hazelnut ($6.50); as an entrée, you might select grilled curry marinated lamb with pear chutney, lemon yogurt, paratha bread, and jasmine rice, or butter-poached lobster with chives, beets, and "pommes Maxim." Entrées $24–30. The irresistible dessert menu runs from home-made ice creams ($7.50) to raspberry vanilla souffe ($12).

Mary Ellenz Italian Café (207-442-0960), 15 Vine St., Bath. Summer hours are Tue.–Sat. for dinner, Tue.–Fri. for lunch. From its original riverside site this delightful restaurant (named for the two Mary Ellens who began it) has moved downtown, beside the bridge. Well worth finding. The atmosphere is soothing, hip, and informal; food is fabulous. We recommend the crabcakes on wilted greens with red onion, fresh lemon, and buerre blanc. Most dishes come with the house crispy polenta and grilled veggies. Wine priced to sell. Entrées $11–24. Tapas and a lighter menu are also offered.

Kennebec Tavern and Marina (207-442-9636), 119 Commercial St., Bath. Open for lunch and dinner daily; Sunday brunch 11–2. A casual, relaxing barn of a place with booths and tables overlooking the Kennebec River, and a seasonal waterside deck. The choice of seafood, chicken, steak, and combos is wide. It can hit the spot for us after a long day of driving. Dinner entrées $12–25.

♂ ♿ **Mae's Cafe** (207-442-8577; www.maescafeandbakery.com), 160 Center St. (corner of High), Bath. Mon.–Wed. 8–3, Thurs.–Sat. 8–8, Sun. 8–2. Andy and Kate Winglass are the owners of this cheerful restaurant/café, expanded to include an attractive upstairs dining room. At lunchtime the place to come for quiche, salads, and such specialty entrées as pan-seared crabcakes. You might dine on oven-roasted duck breast with Maine blueberry honey glaze, or blackened scallops. Dinner entrées $15–19, including salad. The bakery case is filled with delectable cakes and most patrons walk away with at least a cookie. Fully licensed.

Solo Bistro (207-443-3373), 128 Front St., Bath. Open for lunch and dinner. Handy to downtown shops, this cool spot makes popular lobster, crabcakes, and seafood curry, as well as meat and vegetarian dishes. The menu changes monthly, and features local produce when available. Basement wine bar, jazz some Fridays. Dinner entrées $18–28.

The Osprey (207-371-2530), at Robinhood Marina, Robinhood (just off Rt. 127, near Reid State Park). Open daily mid-June–Labor Day for lunch and dinner; Tues.–Sun. mid-May–June (lunch weekends only) and till Columbus Day. Under the same ownership as J. P. Maxwell in Bath, sited in the Robinhood Marine Center, a full-service yacht yard with waterfront views, including an osprey nest on the day marker. Burgers, sandwichs, steamed clams, fried seafood and lobster. Entrées might include sweet-potato-encrusted haddock ($19) and chippino (a seafood medley in a spicy red bouillon, $21).

EATING OUT

In Bath

Beale Street Barbeque and Grill (207-442-9514; www.mainebbq.com), 215 Water St. Open for lunch and dinner. No reservations. Mark, Mike, Rebecca and John Quigg have built their slow-cooking pits and are delivering the real Tennessee (where Mark lived for six years) goods: pulled pork, ribs, sausage, a big Reuben; also nightly specials (frequently fish) to round out the menu.

THE OSPREY

Christina Tree

Starlight Café (207-443-3005), 15 Lambard St. Open weekdays. This bright, funky place is a real find. Large, sandwiches (create your own by picking bread, meat, cheese, and veggies) and daily specials. Crowded at lunchtime, but worth a wait.

J. R. Maxwell &Co. (207-443-2014), 122 Front St., Bath. Open year-round for lunch and dinner daily. In the middle of Bath's shopping street, in a renovated 1840s building, originally a hotel. A bit dark and tired but with dependably good burgers, sandwiches, and prime rib. Children's menu. Dinner entrées $14–23.

The Cabin (207-443-6224), 525 Washington St., across from Bath Iron Works. Open from lunch until 10 until 11 Thur.–Sat. This is the real thing and looks it, a working-man's gathering place claiming "the only real pizza in Maine," rated among the best in the state. Beer by the pitcher, outdoor terrace.

On the Popham Peninsula

Spinney's Restaurant (207-389-1122), at the end of Rt. 209, Popham Beach. Open weekends May; call to check in June, daily July–Oct. for lunch and dinner. Our kind of beach restaurant: a pleasant atmosphere, basic chowder-and-a-sandwich menu, and (if you're lucky) a table on the glassed-in porch with water views. Glen and Diane Theal specialize in fresh fish and seafood, fried, steamed, and broiled; good lobster and crabmeat rolls. Fully licensed.

Anna's Water's Edge (207-389-1803), Black's Landing Rd., Sebasco Estates. Open daily 11–9. Located on a commercial fishing wharf, a great place to eat steamed lobster. Less well known and crowded than Spinney's but with a great view from the attractive dining room (and the outdoor seating). Standout chowder and crabcakes top the full menu with nightly specials. Beer and wine served.

♿ **Lobster House** (207-389-1596), 395 Small Point Rd. (follow Rt. 1 to Rt. 209, then Rt. 209 to Rt. 216). Open weekends in June, Tues.–Sun. in July and Aug. Down near Small Point, surrounded by salt marsh, this is a classic old lobster place specializing in seafood dinners and homemade pastry. Beer and wine are served.

North Creek Farm (207-389-1341; www.northcreekfarm.org), 24 Sebasco Road, Phippsburg. Open year-round 9–6:30. Suzy Verrier's nursery and extensive perennial gardens (see *Selective Shopping*) is also the setting for a great little eatery with limited inside seating and picnic benches. The tables by the woodstove are especially inviting off-season, as are the freshly made soups. Homemade pies are another draw.

COVESIDE RESTAURANT & MARINA

Christina Tree

On the Georgetown Peninsula

Five Islands Lobster and Grill (207-371-2990), Georgetown. Thirteen miles south of Rt. 1 at the end of Rt. 127 on Five Islands wharf. Open seasonally 11:30–8. It's hard to beat the view from this end-of-the-road commercial lobster wharf. It's all outdoors and all about steamed lobsters and clams, lobster rolls, fried clams, and fried seafood. Blackboard specials usually include Jenny's special crabcake and the haddock sandwich.

Sarah's Dockside (207-371-2722), Moore's Turnpike Rd., Five Islands. Now owned by Sarah's, a popular Wiscasset restaurant and off to a shaky start in 2007, but Sarah is a Georgetown native and we figure that this seasonal lobster pound that overlooks Gott's Cove will be well worth finding (don't give up halfway down the dirt access road).

✷ Entertainment

Chocolate Church Arts Center (207-442-8455), 804 Washington St., Bath. Year-round presentations include plays, concerts, and a wide variety of guest artists. Special children's plays and other entertainment are included on the schedule. There is also a very nice gallery in a separate building beside the Chocolate Church.

✷ Selective Shopping

ANTIQUES Along **Front Street** in Bath there are a number of interesting antiques shops. Of special note: **Brick Store Antiques** (207-443-2790), 143 Front St., and **Front Street Antiques and Books** (207-443-8098), 190–192 Front St., a multiple-dealer shop.

ART AND ARTISANS **Five River Arts Alliance** (207-798-6964; www.fiveriverartsalliance.org) is a source of information about Third Friday Art Walks, involving some 20 local galleries and studios.

West Island Gallery (207-371-9090; westislandgallery.com), 37 Bay Point Rd. (just off Rt. 127), Georgetown. Open June–Dec. Susie Westly Wren's outstanding gallery represents more than 40 artists and craftspeople, filling two floors of her house. Changing art exhibits.

Georgetown Pottery (207-371-2801; www.georgetownpottery.com), Rt. 127, Georgetown (some 9 miles south of Rt. 1). Open daily 8:30–5, later in summer. Jeff Peters has been handcrafting his distinctive style of pottery here since 1972 and, while there are branches in Brunswick and Freeport, this is a showroom worth a drive. An extensive selection of dishes, mugs, and other practical pieces in a variety of hand-painted and deeply colored designs, from casseroles to ikebana "Zen pots."

Saltbox Pottery (207-443-5586; www.saltboxpottery.com), 4 Shaw Rd., Woolwich. Open daily year-round, 10–5:30. Traditional-style stoneware.

BOOKSTORE **Bath Book Shop** (207-443-9338), 96 Front St., Bath. Finally, a good independent bookstore located in Bath's downtown district.

Christina Tree

FIVE ISLANDS WHARF

FARMER'S MARKET Waterfront Park, Bath, May–Nov., Thu. and Sat. 8:30–12:30 (207-586-5067).

FLEA MARKET **Montsweag Flea Market** (207-443-2809), Rt. 1, Woolwich. Open Wed., Fri.–Sun., 6:30–3. A field filled with tables weighted down by every imaginable collectible and curiosity. Wednesday is Antique Day; on weekends look for collectibles, crafts, and good junk. Come early.

SPECIAL SHOPS Bath's **Front Street** is lined with mid-19th-century red-brick buildings. Among the clothing and specialty shops, don't overlook **Reny's** (46 Front St.), one in a chain of Maine department stores good for genuine bargains and good value in an amazing range of things. **Springer's Jewelers** (76 Front St.) is a vintage emporium with mosaic floors, chandeliers, and ornate glass sales cases.

Halcyon Yarn (207-442-7909; www.halcyonyarn.com), 12 School St., Bath. Warehouse open Mon.–Sat. 10–4, Wed. until 8. A mecca for knitters, spinners, and rug-hookers with yarns distributed worldwide.

Woodbutcher Tools (207-442-7938), 873 Rt. 1, Woolwich. The Shelter

Institute (see *Special Learning Programs*) maintains this woodworker's discovery, specializing in hard-to-find woodworking tools.

North Creek Farm (207-389-1341; www.northcreekfarm.org), 24 Sebasco Rd. (junction of Rts. 217 and 209). Open year-round 9–6:30. Suzy Verrier, an authority on *Rosa rugosa* and the author of two books on roses, maintains an extensive nursery and perennial gardens through which visitors are invited to wander. The store sells her organically grown produce, eggs, cut flowers, wine and beers, cheese, gardening implements, and gifts (also see *Eating Out*).

Five Islands Farm (207-371-9383; www.fiveislandsfarm.com), Rt. 127, Five Islands. Open mid-May–Dec., Wed.–Mon. 10:30–6. Heidi Klingelhofer's small, shingled emporium overflows with flowers and is a seasonal trove of Maine cheeses, wines, local produce, and specialty foods. Cheese is Heidi's passion, and she carries one of the largest selections of Maine artisan cheeses available anywhere.

Native Arts (207-442-8399), Rt. 1, Woolwich. Open 10–6 daily, year-round. Native American art and craftwork from throughout the country.

NORTH CREEK FARM

Christina Tree

✷ Special Events

Details for most events at www.visitbath.com

June: **Bath House and Garden Tour**, sponsored by Sagadahoc Preservation, Inc. (207-443-2174; www.sagadahocpreservation.org).

Three days surrounding the Fourth of July: **Bath Heritage Days**—a grand celebration with an old-time parade of antique cars, marching bands, clowns, guided tours of the historic district, crafts sales, art shows, musical entertainment in two parks, a triathlon, strawberry shortcake festival, carnival, train, and Fireman's Follies featuring bed races, bucket relays, and demonstrations of equipment and firefighting techniques. **Fireworks** over the Kennebec.

Second Saturday in July: **Popham Circle Fair** at the Popham Chapel features the sale of bird feeders (shaped like the chapel) that residents make all year; profits keep the chapel going.

July–August: Wednesday-evening concerts by the **Bath Municipal Band**, Library Park.

August: **Annual Antique Show and Sale**.

October: **AutumnFest** (*Saturday of Columbus Day weekend*)

December: **Old-Fashioned Christmas** (*all month*), with competitions and special events.

WISCASSET AREA

Sea captains' mansions and mid-19th-century commercial buildings line Rt. 1 in this historic village—and on July and August weekends motorists have plenty of time to study them as they inch along. The wide new bridge across the Sheepscot River here was to have eased the traffic snarl, but Wiscasset is the only village through which cars heading up and down the Midcoast on Rt. 1 must all file, stopping at pedestrian crossings.

It's an obvious stop. The places to eat are varied and good, antiques stores abound, and the historic buildings are worth visiting.

Still the shire town of Lincoln County, Wiscasset is only half as populous as it was in its shipping heyday—which, judging from the town's clapboard mansions, began after the Revolution and ended around the time of the Civil War. Lincoln County Courthouse, built in 1824 on the town common, is the oldest functioning courthouse in New England.

From Wiscasset, Rt. 27 runs northwest to Dresden Mills. From there it's just a few miles to the haunting Pownalborough Court House and on to Dresden, the Kennebec River, and Swan Island at Richmond. Rt. 218 veers northeast, paralleling the Sheepscot River through backcountry to Head Tide Village and Alna, home of the Wiscasset, Waterville, and Farmington Railway. Rt. 144 heads south down the spine of the quiet Westport Island to the Squire Tarbox Inn.

GUIDANCE **Southern Midcoast Maine Chamber** (207-725-8797; www.midcoastmaine.com) and **Damariscotta Region Chamber of Commerce** (207-563-8340; www.damariscottaregion.com) both cover this area.

GETTING THERE *By bus:* **Concord Trailways** (1-800-639-3317; www.concordtrailways.com) stops twice daily.

By car: Note the shortcut around traffic northbound; turn right on Lee St., continue to Fore St. and Water St., and either park or continue north (right) on Rt. 1.

By air and limo: **Mid-Coast Limo** (1-800-937-2424; www.midcoastlimo.com) makes runs by reservation from Portland International Jetport.

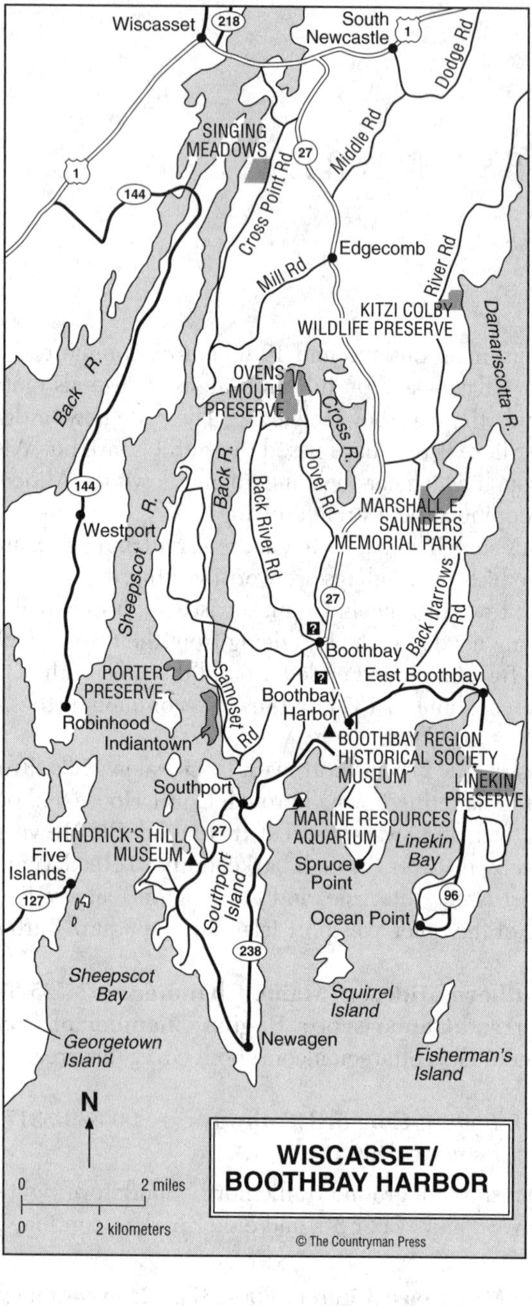

Wiscasset
218
South Newcastle
1
Dodge Rd
SINGING MEADOWS
27
Middle Rd
Cross Point Rd
1
144
Edgecomb
Mill Rd
River Rd
KITZI COLBY WILDLIFE PRESERVE
Damariscotta R.
Back R.
OVENS MOUTH PRESERVE
Cross R.
Back R.
Dover Rd
Back River Rd
144
Westport
Sheepscot R.
MARSHALL E. SAUNDERS MEMORIAL PARK
27
Back Narrows Rd
Boothbay
East Boothbay
PORTER PRESERVE
Samoset Rd
Boothbay Harbor
Robinhood
Indiantown
BOOTHBAY REGION HISTORICAL SOCIETY MUSEUM
Southport
LINEKIN PRESERVE
MARINE RESOURCES AQUARIUM
HENDRICK'S HILL MUSEUM
27
Linekin Bay
Five Islands
Spruce Point
127
Southport Island
96
Ocean Point
238
Sheepscot Bay
Squirrel Island
Georgetown Island
Newagen
Fisherman's Island
N
0
2 miles
0
2 kilometers
WISCASSET/ BOOTHBAY HARBOR
© The Countryman Press

PARKING Parking is surprisingly easy. You can usually find a slot in the parking lot or along Water St.

PUBLIC RESTROOMS Restrooms are in the **Waterfront Park**, corner of Water and Fore Sts. *Note:* This is also a great spot for a picnic.

✷ To See

In Wiscasset Village

Musical Wonder House (207-882-7163 or 1-800-336-3725; www.musicalwonderhouse.com), 18 High St. Open Memorial Day–Halloween, Mon.–Sat. 10–5; Sun. 12–5. $10 per adult, $8 per child for a half-hour tour, $20 per adult, $10 per child for a 75-minute tour; $45 for a three-hour tour of the entire seven-room house. No admission charge for the gift shop or for the Entrance Hall, with its 23 antique coin-operated machines. A truly magnificent collection covering two centuries of musical history. Some 2,000 music boxes, player grand pianos and organs, spring-wound phonographs, musical birds, porcelains, furniture, clocks, steins, whistlers, and a musical painting—all displayed in a fine 1852 sea captain's mansion.

Nickels-Sortwell House (207-882-6218; www.historicnewengland.org), 121 Main St. (Rt. 1). Open June 1–Oct. 15, Fri.–Sun. Tours on the hour, 11–4. Admission: $5. This classic Federal-era mansion in the middle of town was built by a shipowner and trader. After he lost his fortune, the house became a hotel for many years. In 1895 a Cambridge, Massachusetts, mayor purchased the property; some of the furnishings date to that time. It's now maintained by Historic New England.

NICKELS-SORTWELL HOUSE

Kim Grant

Castle Tucker (603-436-3205; www.historicnewengland.org), Lee and High Sts. Same nonprofit owner as the Nickels-Sortwell House, same season, tour hours, and admission price but open Wed.–Sun. Castle Tucker was built in 1807 by Judge Silas Lee, who overextended his resources to present his wife with this romantic house. After his death it fell into the hands of his neighbors, to whom it had been heavily mortgaged, and passed through several owners until it was acquired in 1858 by Captain Richard Holbrook Tucker, whose descendants owned the house until 1997. Highlights include a freestanding elliptical staircase, Victorian furnishings, and original wallpapers.

Old Lincoln County Jail and Museum (207-882-6817; www

.lincolncountyhistory.org), 133 Federal St. (Rt. 218). Open July and Aug., Tue.–Sat. 10–4. In June and Sept., open Sat. 10–4. $4 per adult, $2 per child. The museum consists of a chilling 1811 jail (in use until 1930) with damp, thick granite walls (some bearing interesting 19th-century graffiti), window bars, and heavy metal doors. The jailer's house (in use until 1953) displays tools and changing exhibits.

In Dresden

Pownalborough Court House (207-882-6817; www.lincolncountryhistory.org), Rt. 128. Same hours and admission as the county jail, and worth the drive. Maine's only surviving pre–Revolutionary War courthouse, this striking three-story building, which includes living quarters upstairs for the judge, gives a sense of this countryside along the Kennebec in 1761, when it was built to serve as an outpost tavern as well as a courtroom. The courthouse is on the second floor, and the third floor is a museum of rural life. Bring a picnic (there are tables). Special events include a mustering of the militia and wreath-laying ceremonies on Memorial Day, and a cider pressing in October. From Wiscasset take Rt. 27 north for 8 miles to Dresden Mills, then Rt. 127 south for 3.7 miles to Rt. 197 and on to Rt. 128, where you head north for 1.3 miles.

In Edgecomb

Fort Edgecomb State Memorial (207-882-7777); the turnoff from Rt. 1 is just across the Sheepscot River. The fort is open May 30–Labor Day, daily 9–6. Nominal donation. This 27-foot, two-story octagonal blockhouse (built in 1808) overlooks a narrow passage of the Sheepscot River. For the same reasons that it was an ideal site for a fort, it is today an ideal picnic site, and tables are provided.

FOR FAMILIES **Morris Farm** (207-882-4080; www.morrisfarm.org) 156 Gardiner Road (Rt. 27), Wiscasset. A 60-acre organic working farm, with trails open to the public during daylight hours; phone to check on current programming, which includes day camps and farm tours.

Sheepscot Village, **Head Tide Village**, and the **Wiscasset, Waterville, and Farmington Railway Museum** (207-882-4193; www.wwfry.org), Sheepscot Station, Alna. The museum is open 9–5 on Sat. year-round, also Sun. Memorial Day–Columbus Day. Steam trains run most weekends; inquire about Halloween and Victorian Christmas runs. Volunteers preserve the history of this 2-foot narrow-gauge railroad. The museum's pride is Engine No. 9, an 1891 2-footer locomotive, billed as the oldest in the United States. Volunteers have built replicas of the engine house and shop, original station, and freight

POWNALBOROUGH COURT HOUSE

Christina Tree

shed, which now houses the gift shop and museum. Half a mile of track has been laid. Trains are usually pulled by a diesel locomotive, but on special occasions a vintage-1904 steam engine is used. **Sheepscot Village** itself is a picturesque gathering of early-19th-century buildings. It's a few miles north of Wiscasset, just off Rt. 218. At the Alna Fire Station turn right and drive 1.2 miles to the parking lot for the 32-acre **Bass Falls Preserve**, with a mile-long trail down to the river. It's maintained by the Sheepscot Valley Conservation Association (207-586-5616). Farther north on Rt. 218 signs point to **Head Tide Village**, another quiet cluster of old homes around the Old Head Tide Church (1858). Note the swimming hole beneath the milldam.

✷ Green Space

Sunken Garden, Main St., Wiscasset. Down a few steps, easy to miss, but a wonderful little garden surrounded by a stone wall. Planted by the Sortwell family in the foundation of an old inn, the property was donated to the town in 1959.

Sherman Lake Rest Area, Rt. 1 between Edgecomb and Newcastle. Pick up the fixings in Wiscasset and picnic at this scenic rest area.

✷ Lodging

INN "1" **Squire Tarbox Inn** (207-882-7693 or 1-800-818-0626; www.squiretarboxinn.com), 1181 Main Rd. (Rt. 144; turn off Rt. 1 south of Wiscasset), Westport 04578. Open mid-Apr.–Dec. "A good country inn must be tasted" maintains Swiss chef Mario De Pietro, and food is indeed what draws most patrons to his handsome Federal-style farmhouse, a full 8 miles down a winding country road from Rt. 1. Those who come as guests also savor one of the quietest country locations to be found on the coast. Boards and timbers in the low-ceiling dining room date to 1763, while the parlor and four largest guest rooms, all with working fireplaces, are in the "new" (1825) section of house. The remaining seven, more rustic guest rooms are in the converted 1820s Carriage Barn, off an inviting sitting room with a gas fireplace, books, and games. De Pietro and his wife, Roni, perpetuate the inn's reputation for hospitality as well as food, encouraging guests to follow walking paths on their 13 acres, row on the saltwater pond, or explore Westport Island on a mountain bike. $135–195 per couple; off-season $110–175 per couple. Breakfast is included, and features freshly baked croissants, home-made muesli, and a hot dish prepared by the chef, with fresh-laid eggs from his hens. In a previous life De Pietro was corporate chef of NYC-based Restaurant Associates, overseeing 50 restaurants. Inquire about cooking classes. Also see *Dining Out*.

BED & BREAKFASTS **Marston House** (207-882-6010 or 1-800-852-4137; www.marstonhouse.com), Main St., P.O. Box 517, Wiscasset 04578. Open May–Oct. The front of the house is Sharon Mrozinski's antiques shop, specializing in 18th- and early-19th-century textiles and painted furnishings. In the carriage house behind—well away from the Rt. 1 traffic noise—are two exceptional guest rooms, each with private entrance, each with working fireplace and private bath. Breakfast is served in the flowery gardens or in your room and features fresh fruit, yogurt, home-baked muffins, and fresh orange juice. $100 double.

"1" **Snow Squall Inn** (207-882-6892 or 1-800-775-7245; www.snowsquallinn.com), 5 Bradford Rd., Wiscasset 04578. Open May–Oct. and by special reservation off-season. Melanie (a trained yoga instructor and massage therapist) and Paul Harris (a professional chef) offer comfortably elegant accommodations in this 1850s house named for a clipper ship. The four guest rooms in the main house, each named for a vessel, have a private bath, king or queen bed, phone, and air-conditioning. Each of the three suites in the Carriage House has two bedrooms (one and a half baths) and a private entrance. Plenty of common space here, gardens and lounges with hearths and TV. $100–150 for rooms; $140–220 for suites, depending on the number of guests. Full breakfast included. Less off-season. Inquire about massage and yoga.

✱ Where to Eat

DINING OUT **Squire Tarbox Inn** (207-882-7693; www.squiretarboxinn.com), 1181 Main Rd. (Rt. 144; turn off Rt. 1 south of Wiscasset), Westport (see *Lodging*). Open daily Memorial Day–Oct.; Thurs.–Sat. in Apr., May, Nov., and Dec., when Thurs. is Swiss night. Reserve. Dinner is served 6–8:30 PM in an 18th-century former summer kitchen with a large colonial fireplace and ceiling timbers that were once part of a ship. In warm weather months an attractive screened and canopied deck. Swiss chef-owner Mario De Pietro could start you off with Scandinavian dill-cured salmon, then serve entrées like rosemary-roasted rack of lamb or sautéed sliced veal with Swiss-style roesti potatoes. Several nightly specials feature the freshest available produce. Strawberries (served with double cream) along with salad greens and many vegetables come from the inn's extensive organic farm. Entrees: $25–29. A 15 percent gratuity is added.

SQUIRE TARBOX INN

Christina Tree

Le Garage (207-882-5409; www.legarageme.com), Water St., Wiscasset. Open daily in summer for lunch and dinner. Closed Jan. and Mon. off-season. A 1920s-era garage, now a good restaurant with a glassed-in porch overlooking the Sheepscot River (when you make reservations, request a table on the porch). Frequently less crowded for lunch than restaurants on the main drag. Try a crèpe. The dinner menu features plenty of seafood choices, steaks, and vegetarian meals. Specialties include traditional creamed finnan haddie, charbroiled native lamb, and chicken pie. Entrées are $10–25. "Light suppers" are also available from $9.50, giving you the option of smaller portions of many menu selections.

EATING OUT ✐ **Sarah's** (207-882-7504; www.sarahscafe.com), Main and Water Sts., Wiscasset. Open daily for lunch and dinner, with an outdoor deck for summer dining. Everything in this popular waystop is prepared from scratch, and the extensive menu includes good pizza (try the Greek pizza with extra garlic), salads, sandwiches in pita pockets or baked in dough, vegetarian dishes, Mexican fare, and lobster more than 15 different ways. Well known for their soup and bread bar.

The Sea Basket (207-882-6581 or 1-800-658-1883), Rt. 1, south of Wiscasset. Open 11–8; closed Tue. Call for hours. The Belanger family has owned and operated this cheerful diner for more than 20 years, keeping it shipshape and humming. "Famous" lobster stew is also sold frozen and shipped all over the country. Other seafood choices include lobster rolls and sea scallops. Bring your own beer or wine.

✐ **Red's Eats**, Water St., just before the bridge, Wiscasset. Open Apr.–Sept. until 2 AM on Fri. and Sat., until 11 weeknights, and noon–6 on Sun. Al Gagnon, now assisted by his daughter, has operated this classic hot-dog stand/lobster shack since 1977. Tables on the sidewalk and behind, overlooking the river. Too many write-ups have raised prices, lengthened lines, and reduced portions. No complaints, however, about the lobster, fried clams, and hot dogs.

Sprague's Lobster (207-882-7814), Water St., also just before the bridge but the other side of Rt.1,Wiscasset. Open seasonally. Picnic tables on a pier beside the river are a great place to sample the fresh, bargain-priced lobsters with all the fixings, or crab rolls and road-food staples. No legend, no lines, a great view, and really good clam fritters.

✷ Selective Shopping

ANTIQUES SHOPS Antiques are everywhere in Wiscasset. On and just off Water Street, in or attached to attractive old homes, more than 20 shops by our count. Pick up a map (available in most shops) and browse the day away; many specialize in nautical pieces and country primitives. **Avalon Antiques Market** (207-882-4029), Rt. 1, 2 miles south of Wiscasset Village, open daily 9–7, represents more than 100 dealers.

ART GALLERIES Maine Art Gallery (207-882-7511; www.maineartgallery.org), Warren St. (in a vintage 1807 academy), Wiscasset. A nonprofit gallery since 1954 with changing exhibits June–mid-Nov., featuring prominent Maine artists and photographers.

Wiscasset Bay Gallery (207-882-7682; www.wiscassetbaygallery.com), 67 Main St., Wiscasset. Changing exhibits in attractive, spacious exhibit rooms. Specializes in 19th- and 20th-

SPRAGUE'S LOBSTER

Nancy English

century Maine and New England marine and landscape paintings.

OTHER **Sheepscot River Pottery** (pastel, floral designs), Rt. 1 just north of Wiscasset in Edgecomb, home base for one of Maine's major potteries.

Tandem Glass Gallery & Studio (207-737-4511), 6 Eagle Lodge Lane (on Rt. 127, 8 miles from Wiscasset near the Pownalborough Courthouse), Dresden. Open Tues.–Sun. 10–5. Visitors can observe glass blowing. Courses offered.

FARM **Winters Gone Farm** (207-882-9191 or 1-800-645-0188; www.wintersgone.com), 145 Alna Rd. (Rt. 218), Wiscasset. An alpaca farm with nature trails and picnic areas, a store selling sweaters, scarves, jackets, teddy bears, toys, and more.

BOOTHBAY HARBOR REGION

The water surrounding the village of Boothbay Harbor brings with it more than just a view. You must cross it—via a footbridge—to get from one side of town to the other, and you can explore it on a wide choice of excursion boats and in sea kayaks. It is obvious from the very lay of this old fishing village that its people have always gotten around on foot or in boats. Though parking has increased in recent years, cars don't have room to pass each other, and still feel like an obvious intrusion. In the peninsula's other coastal villages, Southport and East Boothbay, roads are walled by pines, permitting only occasional glimpses of water, and offer little or no shoulder for pedestrians or cyclists.

Boats are what all three of the Boothbays have traditionally been about. Boats are built, repaired, and sold here, and sailing and fishing vessels fill the harbors. Excursions range from an hour-long sail around the outer harbor to a 90-minute crossing (each way) to Monhegan Island. Fishermen can pursue giant tuna, stripers, and blues, and nature lovers can cruise out to see seals, whales, and puffins.

In the middle of summer Boothbay Harbor itself is chockablock full of tourists licking ice cream cones, chewing freshly made taffy and fudge, browsing in shops, looking into art galleries, listening to band concerts on the library lawn, and, of course, eating lobster. You get the feeling it's been like this every summer since the 1870s.

Boothbay Harbor is just a dozen miles south of Rt. 1 as the road (Rt. 27) runs, down the middle of the peninsula. The coastline is, however, a different story, measuring 100 miles as it wanders down the Sheepscot, around Southport Island and up into Boothbay Harbor, out around Spruce Head, around Linekin Bay, out Ocean Point, and back up along the Damariscotta River.

Thanks to the fervor of developers from the 1870s on, this entire coastline is distinguished by the quantity of its summer cottages, many of which can be rented by the week for much less than you might think. Still, thanks to the Boothbay Region Land Trust, there are now also easily accessible waterside preserves with many miles of trail meandering through hundreds of acres of spruce and pine, down to smooth rocks and tidal pools. The area's roads may not allow strolling, but you can find plenty of places to indulge a walking habit in the Linekin Preserve and elsewhere.

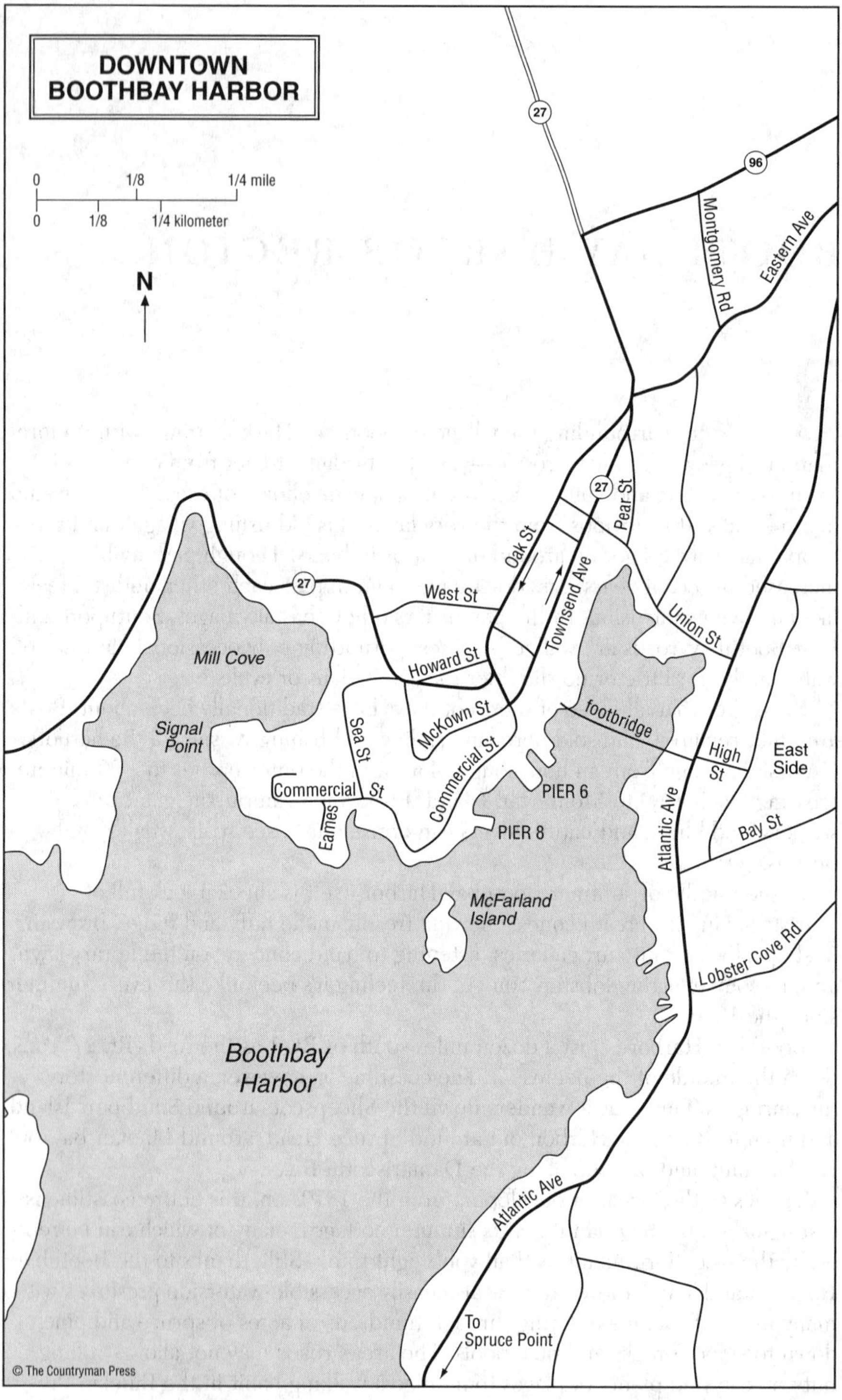

DOWNTOWN
BOOTHBAY HARBOR
0
1/8
1/4 mile
0
1/8
1/4 kilometer
N
27
96
Montgomery Rd
Eastern Ave
27
Pear St
Oak St
Townsend Ave
27
West St
Union St
Mill Cove
Howard St
McKown St
footbridge
Signal
Point
Sea St
Commercial St
High
St
East
Side
Commercial
St
PIER 6
Atlantic Ave
Eames
PIER 8
Bay St
McFarland
Island
Lobster Cove Rd
Boothbay
Harbor
Atlantic Ave
To
Spruce Point
© The Countryman Press

It was precisely this landscape that inspired Rachel Carson, who first summered on the peninsula in 1946 and built a cottage on the Sheepscot River in 1953, to write much of *The Edge of the Sea* (1955) and then *Silent Spring* (1962), the book that changed global thinking about human beings' relation to basic laws of nature.

GUIDANCE **Boothbay Harbor Region Chamber of Commerce** (207-633-2353 or 1-800-266-8422; www.boothbayharbor.com), Rt. 27, P.O. Box 356, Boothbay Harbor 04538. Open year-round. A satellite information booth near the **Cod Cove Inn** (207-882-5539), junction of Rts. 1 and 27, is open mid-May–Oct., weekends in fringe times, daily in high season. This user-friendly chamber publishes an annual guide, maintains a Rt. 27 office stocked with brochures, keeps detailed books of cottage listings and photos, and tracks availability for cottages weekly and for lodgings daily. They also publish the walking map.

The Boothbay Information Center (207-633-4743), Rt. 27, Boothbay. Open daily Memorial Day–Columbus Day. An unusually friendly walk-in center that does its best to help people without reservations find places to stay. It keeps an illustrated scrapbook of options, also a cottage rental list.

GETTING THERE *By air or bus:* Private planes can fly into the Wiscasset Airport. If you fly into the Portland International Jetport, **Platinum Plus Taxi or Harbor Tour and Shuttle** (207-443-9166) can take you to Boothbay or pick you up at the nearest Concord Trailways bus stop (in Wiscasset, 14 miles away). **D&P Associated Limousine Services** (207-865-0203, 1-800-750-6757), 96 Oakland Ave., Westbrook 04092, and **Maine Limousine Service** (207-883-0222, 1-800-646-0068; www.mainelimo.com), P.O. Box 1478, Scarborough 04070 can also pick you up and bring you to the Boothbay Harbor region.

By car: Take I-295 from Portland, getting off at exit 28 (Brunswick) or exit 31 (Topsham). We prefer the Topsham exit, because you miss the commercial stretch of Rt. 1 that leads into Brunswick. Follow signs to Rt. 1 north through Bath and Wiscasset, turning onto Rt. 27 into Boothbay and Boothbay Harbor.

GETTING AROUND A trolley-on-wheels circulates by the Rocktide Inn on the east side of the harbor, the shops on the west, and the Aquarium on Southport Island. Runs every 30 minutes daily, 10–5, mid-June–Labor Day.

PARKING In-town parking has increased substantially in the past few years. We had a little trouble in August, when finding a spot in the center of Boothbay Harbor can mean circling the block a couple of times. Stop on your way into town at one of the information centers and pick up a detailed map to downtown. The biggest public lot is at the municipal building.

WHEN TO COME At least half of Boothbay's B&Bs are staying open year-round now, even in midwinter when the gas fireplaces are on high. Enjoying the area off-season gives you a glimpse of how the locals like it, along with uncrowded restaurants and a calm pace. But if it's bright warm days you're looking for, or a room by the sea in one of the older inns, summer can't be beat.

✱ To See

Boothbay Region Historical Society Museum (207-633-0820; www.boothbayhistorical.org), 72 Oak St., Boothbay Harbor. Open year-round Wed.-Sat. 10–2. Free. Seven rooms are filled with vintage lobster traps, Native American artifacts, ships' bells, Fresnel lens from Ram Island, and genealogical resources. The gift shop stocks books, maps, coins, photos, and more.

Hendricks Hill Museum (207-633-1102; www.hendrickshill.org), 417 Hendricks Hill Rd., Rt. 27, Southport Island. Open July 1–Labor Day, Tue., Thu., and Sat. 11–3. The house looks much as it did in 1810, with a period kitchen, including a beehive oven, and pictures of Southport's grand hotels as well as other village memorabilia, wooden boats, and farm implements. While in Southport, visit the Southport Memorial Library, which has an impressive butterfly collection. Southport lies in the narrow heart of the migratory route of the monarch butterfly.

Burnt Island Lighthouse Program (207-633-9559 for Maine gov.; www.maine.gov/dmr/education; 207-633-2284 for reservations; www.balmydayscruises.com). Twice a day Mon.–Fri. July–Aug. $22 adults, $12 under 12. This three-hour living history tour of Burnt Island Light Station is a must-do on a visit to the Boothbay region. Guides in 1950 wardrobes portray the family that once maintained the light in the lantern room; the family children give tours of the island's five acres and surrounding water. Volunteers from many organizations turned this formerly abandoned site into a well-maintained destination good for walks on trails as well as learning about the past and the hazards of navigation on the coast of Maine.

BOOTHBAY HARBOR

Kim Grant

FOR FAMILIES 🖍 ♿ **Boothbay Railway Village** (207-633-4727; www.railwayvillage.org), Rt. 27 (about 3 miles north of Boothbay Harbor). Open daily 9:30–5, June–Columbus Day; a Ghost Train ($5) runs at the end of Oct. Regular admission $8 adults, $4 ages 3–16. A 2-foot narrow-gauge railway wends its way through a miniature village made up of several restored buildings, including vintage railroad stations, the Boothbay Town Hall (1847), and the Spruce Point chapel (1923). Displays include a general store, a doll museum, and a 1920s-era home with an authentic 1929 GE refrigerator and period furniture. More than 55 antique autos (1907–49) are also on display. Many special events, including a weekend antique auto meet (more than 150 cars) in late July. Thomas and Friends railroad cars here late July and early Aug. of 2008.

🌧 🖍 **Kenneth Stoddard Shell Museum** (207-633-4828), Hardwick Rd., Boothbay Harbor. Features one of the world's largest private collections of seashells, including lobster claws and sand dollars. Open daily May–mid-Sept.; by appointment the rest of the year. Admission free.

🌧 🖍 **Daffy Taffy and Fudge Factory,** the By-Way, Boothbay Harbor (see *Snacks*). If the weather is bad and the kids are restless, take them to watch the sweets being made by huge machines. No charge, unless they work up an appetite.

🌧 🖍 ♿ **Knickerbocker Lake**, Barter's Island Rd., Boothbay (near Knickerkane Island Park). Salt water too cold for the little ones? Head to this lovely freshwater lake for a dip.

🖍 **The By-Way**. Don't miss Boothbay Harbor's old-fashioned harborside boardwalk area. Walk from the By-Way down to the footbridge across the harbor.

✷ To Do

BICYCLING **Tidal Transit Co.** (207-633-7140; www.kayakboothbay.com), by the footbridge, Boothbay Harbor, rents bikes in-season. Our favorite bike route begins at Boothbay Village and follows lightly trafficked Barter's Island Rd. past Knickerbocker Lake and Knickerkane Island Park to Hodgdon Island, and then on to Barter's Island and the Porter Preserve.

BOAT EXCURSIONS 🖍 **Balmy Days Cruises** (207-633-2284 or 1-800-298-2284; www.balmydayscruises.com), Pier 8, Boothbay Harbor. *Balmy Days II* offers sails to Monhegan every morning early June–early Oct. and weekends in shoulder seasons (see Monhegan" in *Midcoast Islands*). The crossing takes 90 minutes each way, and you have close to four hours on the island (a 30-minute boat ride around the island is also possible on the way back). Bring a picnic and hit the trail. Adults $32, children $18. *Novelty* makes one-hour Boothbay Harbor tours all day. Balmy Days also offers mackerel fishing on the *Miss Boothbay* daily in-season, a great idea for families.

🖍 **Boothbay Whale Watch** (207-633-3500 or 1-888-942-5363; www.whaleme.com), Fisherman's Wharf, Pier 6, Boothbay Harbor. This company offers guaranteed whale-watches: If you don't see a whale, your next trip is free. They also run Sunday reggae and Thursday classic oldies evening cruises with full bar and galley. In 2007 whale-watches were $35 adults, $22 ages 6–12; children 5 and under are free; call for changes.

Cap'n Fish Boat Cruises (207-633-3244 or 1-800-636-3244; www.mainewhales.com), Pier 1 (red ticket booth), Boothbay Harbor. Operates mid-May–mid-Oct. daily. A variety of cruises: whale-watch, puffin, Pemaquid Point Lighthouse, seal-watch, Kennebec River–Bath, and a sunset sail. Coffee, snacks, soft drinks, full bar are available on board (don't bring your own). Children under 12 are half price. Dogs allowed on board.

Schooner ***Lazy Jack*** (207-633-3444; www.sailschoonerlazyjack.com), Pier 1, Boothbay Harbor. Captain Joe Tassi operates May–Oct., offering two-hour trips, and can accommodate 13 passengers.

Maine State Aquarium (207-633-9559; www.maine.gov/dmr/rm/aquarium), McKown Point Rd., West Boothbay Harbor. Open Memorial Day weekend–Aug. daily 10–5, Sept. Wed.–Sun. $5 adults, $3 ages 5–18 and over 60; 4 and under free. At this octagonal waterside aquarium, kids and adults alike can view tanks filled with sea creatures found in Maine waters such as striped bass, cod, alewives, and a 17-pound lobster. Dip your hands into the touch tank and feel the surprisingly smooth skin of a dogfish (a gentle species of shark) and skates. Presentations several times a day in summer, but get there early (except Sept.) to ensure a good view.

BOAT RENTALS **Charger Charters** (day, 207-380-4556; night, 207-882-9309), 80 Commercial St., Boothbay Harbor, and **Finest Kind Wooden Boats** (207-633-5082), West Boothbay, offer both power- and sailboat rentals.

BOWLING **Romar Bowling Lanes** (207-633-5721), at the By-Way, Boothbay Harbor. Open summer months only. In business since 1929, under the same ownership since 1946, this log-sided pleasure hall with its sandwich bar, pool tables, and video games is a genuine throwback. A great rainy-day haven.

FISHING Several deep-sea-fishing charters are based in Boothbay Harbor. Check with the chamber of commerce. Also see *Boat Rentals*.

The Tackle Shop at the White Anchor (207-633-3788; www.whiteanchorinnboothbay.com), RR 1, Box 438 (Rt. 27), Boothbay, is one of the largest tackle shops on the Maine coast. Open daily, 9–7, call for hours in winter. Rod and reel rentals, bait, plus a full line of fishing gear.

Charger Charters (207-882-9309; www.geocities.com/chargercharters/index.html), 80 Commercial St., Boothbay Harbor. The *Charger* runs three fishing trips daily for mackerel, stripers, and bluefish. Also half- and full-day private charter options for cod, cusk, pollack, and shark.

Blackjack Sportfishing & Charters (207-633-6445, cell 207-380-5445), Pier 7, next to Whale Park, Boothbay Harbor. Capt. Dan Stevens offers charters on his six-passenger, 28-foot bass boat for sportfishing, sightseeing, and transportation.

Redhook Charters (207-633-3807), P.O. Box 45, Boothbay. Leaves from Tugboat Inn Marina. Capt. Mark Stover provides tackle for charters, sightseeing, and transportation.

Shark Five Charters (207-633-5929; www.saltwatermaine.com); Brown's Wharf Inn & Marina, 121 Atlantic Ave., Boothbay Harbor. Capt. Barry Gibson has spent more than 36 years fishing striped bass fishing; tackle provided when on his 28-foot center console boat.

Sweet Action Charters (207-633-4741; www.sweetactioncharters.com), Kaler's Crab and Lobster House, 48 Commercial St., Boothbay Harbor. Inshore fishing for mackerel, stripers, and bluefish on a 19-foot Seaway T-top, gear included.

GOLF AND MINI GOLF **Boothbay Region Country Club** (207-633-6085), Country Club Dr. (off Rt. 27), Boothbay. Open spring–Dec. Eighteen holes, restaurant and lounge, carts and clubs for rent, and a driving range.

Dolphin Mini-Golf (207-633-4828), off Rt. 27 (turn at the lighthouse), Boothbay. Eighteen holes including lakes stocked with fish and a covered bridge.

RECREATIONAL FACILITY **Boothbay Region YMCA** (207-633-2855; www.brymca.com), Townsend Ave., Rt. 27 (on your left as you come down the stretch that leads to town). An exceptional facility open to nonmembers (user fee charged) with swimming and other programs for children. Worth checking out if you're in the area. Tennis, racquetball, gymnastics, aerobics, soccer, swimming in a heated six-lane indoor pool, saunas, and a fieldhouse with a three-lane track.

SAILING ***Bay Lady*** (207-633-2284 or 1-800-298-2284; www.balmydayscruises.com), Pier 8, Boothbay Harbor. A 13-passenger boat offers 30- and 60-minute excursions; part of Balmy Day cruises (see *Boat Excursions*).

SEA KAYAKING **Tidal Transit Company** (207-633-7140; www.kayakboothbay.com), Boothbay Harbor, in the "Chowder House" building by the footbridge, offers guided tours as well as hourly, half-day, and full-day rentals (basic instruction included). Offerings include a lighthouse tour, wildlife tours, and sunset tours. They also rent bikes.

Additional kayak companies in the Boothbays are at **Gray's Homestead Camping** (207-633-4612; www.graysoceancamping.com) on Southport Island (rentals only); and **East Boothbay Kayak Company** (207-633-7411 or 1-866-633-7411; www.eastboothbaykayaks.com) at Ocean Point Marina in East Boothbay.

TENNIS Public tennis courts are located across Rt. 27 from the YMCA, which also has indoor courts.

WALKING **Ocean Point**, at the tip of the East Boothbay peninsula, offers beautiful views of the ocean and several windswept islands, but parking can be tricky. Leave your car in the lot operated by the Linekin Preserve (part of Boothbay Region Land Trust, see *Green Space*) or in designated parking areas and walk the point by foot, being mindful of NO TRESPASSING signs.

✷ Green Space

BEACHES ✐ Beaches are all private, but visitors are permitted in a number of spots. Here are four: (1) Follow Rt. 27 toward Southport, across the Townsend Gut Bridge to a circle (white church on your left, monument in the center, general store on your right); turn right and follow Beach Rd. to the beach, which offers roadside parking and calm, shallow water. (2) Right across from the Boothbay Harbor Yacht Club (Rt. 27 south), just beyond the post office and at the far end of the parking lot, is a property owned by the yacht club, which puts out a float by July. There are ropes to swing from on the far side of the inlet, a grassy area in which to sun, and a small sandy area beside the water (which is too deep for small children). (3) **Barrett Park**, Lobster Cove (turn at the Catholic church, east side of Boothbay Harbor), is a place to picnic and get wet. (4) **Grimes Cove** has a little beach with rocks to climb at the very tip of Ocean Point, East Boothbay. (Also see **Knickerkane Island Park** under *Nature Preserves*.)

GARDEN **Coastal Maine Botanical Gardens** (207-633-4333; www.mainegardens.org), P.O. Box 234, Boothbay. Open weekdays 9–5, until 8 Wed. July–Aug., 9–6 Sat.–Sun. $10 adults, $8 seniors 65 and over, $5 ages 5–17, under 5 free. Accessible from Barter's Island Rd. This gorgeous, newly expanded public garden emphasizes more than 300 native species on 128 acres. The visitors center, gift shop, and café at the entrance sit near the Kitchen Garden and Rose Garden. A downward sloping path brings you through the Woodland Garden, and connects with the original Shore Walk, now called Shoreland Trail, where you can find the Fern Walk, fairy village, and Hillside and Meditation gardens. At the other end of the property a growing rhododendron collection puts on its finery in spring. The Fern and Heath walks focus on mosses, lichens, heaths, and ferns.

NATURE PRESERVES **Boothbay Region Land Trust** (207-633-4818; www.bbrlt.org), 1 Oak St., P.O. Box 183, Boothbay Harbor. Open Mon.–Fri. 9:30–4:30. Pick up a brochure and map (showing 30 miles of trails) to the easily accessible properties, here or at the chamber of commerce; 1,700 acres of land is under its protection, including three islands. Kiosks at the trailheads also provide maps and information. In the Porter Preserve (23 wooded acres, including a beach) on Barters Island, an osprey peered from its nest atop a marker along a ledge just offshore, and another ledge was so thick with seals that they seemed like some kind of brown growth—until a dog barked and the entire ledge seemed to heave and rise, then flop and splash off in

COASTAL MAINE BOTANICAL GARDENS

Nancy English

different directions. The Ovens Mouth Preserve is a narrow passage between the Sheepscot and Back Rivers and a tidal basin. Separated by the two peninsulas that constitute this preserve is Ice House Cove, and across it are the remnants of the 1880s dam that once turned it into a freshwater pond. Schooners once moored outside the dam, loaded their hulls with ice, and sailed for the Caribbean. The pond has reverted to salt marsh and teems with wildlife. The trust has numerous other properties; for a full listing, go to their Web site. Ten of the 15 preserves have geocaching sites.

Knickerkane Island Park, Barter's Island Rd., Boothbay. Paths lead from the parking lot onto a small island with picnic tables and swimming.

✷ Lodging

The chamber of commerce lists more than 100 lodging places in its regional guide, from resorts to B&Bs to campgrounds and cottages. Families should explore the possibilities of the area's many rental cottages. Because the chamber of commerce is open year-round, it's possible to contact the people there in time to reserve well in advance. See *Guidance* for the numbers you can call to check current vacancies in the area.

RESORTS 🖍 **Spruce Point Inn Resort & Spa** (207-633-4152 or 1-800-553-0289; www.sprucepointinn.com), 88 Grandview Ave., P.O. Box 237, Boothbay Harbor 04538. Open mid-May–mid-Oct. A full-service resort at the end of a 100-acre wooded peninsula jutting into Boothbay Harbor, the inn offers nine guest rooms in the main building; 12 rooms with Maine traditional decor, some with cathedral ceilings and hardwood floors; 56 deluxe rooms featuring unusually large bedrooms and marble baths, TVs, gas fireplace, and balconies with water views; and five cottages, two oceanfront, perfect for families. We loved swimming in the cold saltwater pool and warming back up again in the hot tub beside it, both on the edge of the sea. Large living room, TV room and study, recreation room (geared to kids), heated freshwater pool, clay tennis courts, lawn games, fitness center, full-service spa, and private pier. Organized children's programs in July and Aug. Good food (see *Dining Out*). High season $169–359 for guest rooms; cottages and condos $419–560. Children free under age 18. A service charge, 10 percent on rooms and 15 percent on cottages, is added for use of amenities, including kayaks, 42 acres for hiking, and bicycles.

🖍 ♿ **Newagen Seaside Inn** (207-633-5242 or 1-800-654-5242; www.newagenseasideinn.com), Rt. 27, Southport Island, Cape Newagen 04576. Open mid-May–mid-Oct. This resort reminds us of a Connecticut mansion in a 1940s Kate Hepburn movie, with dark green Adirondack chairs set out on the lawn, a playground set in sight, and the stony coast filling the horizon. The 27 rooms and three suites in the main inn all have private bath; first-floor rooms have private deck. Take a chilly plunge in the bay off the dock, then hightail it to the heated freshwater pool and finish in the hot tub overlooking the little harbor. Also included are tennis courts, bicycles, lawn games, rowboats, and the Pine Room, which houses two funky 1940s-era candlepin bowling lanes, pool table, Ping-Pong. A video library and breakfast are in the main building, and a spa room offers massage therapy. Boxed lunches and dinner available. Rooms $135–285, depending on room and season. The three cottages begin at $1,500 per week.

Ocean Point Inn (207-633-4200 or 1-800-552-5554; www.oceanpointinn.com), 191 Shore Rd., P.O. Box 409, East Boothbay 04544. Open mid-June–Columbus Day. Owner David Dudley has worked at Ocean Point since 1969, and he bought the inn in 1985—he even met his wife here! He has outfitted many of the 61 rooms, suites, cottages, and apartments with pretty wallpaper borders (scenes of ducks, early American houses, and the like), king and queen four-posters, and botanical prints. All rooms and cottages have private bath, air-conditioning, cable TV, mini refrigerator, and phone; some have a fireplace, ocean view, and porch. Guests can relax in the heated pool with a hot tub or the Adirondack chairs overlooking the ocean. The inn also offers an oceanfront dining room (see *Dining Out*). $136–216 in-season, when breakfast is $12.95 per person.

TOPSIDE INN

Nancy English

INNS AND BED & BREAKFASTS

Five Gables Inn (207-633-4551 or 1-800-451-5048; www.fivegablesinn.com), 107 Murray Hill Rd. (off Rt. 96), P.O. Box 335, East Boothbay 04544. Open mid-May–Oct. Five Gables combines luxury with unstuffy relaxation, two desirable qualities that don't always go hand in hand. Fifteen of the 16 rooms offer gorgeous views of Linekin Bay; most have queen-sized beds (many with handmade quilts), and five have a working fireplace. Try one of the smaller third-floor gable rooms, which offer some of the best views of the water. An extensive buffet breakfast, prepared by Mike, a Culinary Institute of America graduate, is included in a $150–225 double. Afternoon tea comes with home-baked goodies and port.

Topside Inn (207-633-5404 or 1-877-486-7466; www.topsideinn.com), 60 McKown St., Boothbay Harbor 04538. Open May 1–Nov. 1. Brian Lamb and Ed McDermott have redone this inn. With a great location at the top of McKown Hill, some of the 21 rooms in the 1876 house and a pair of two-story motel-style annexes have water views of the lighthouses and islands; all have private bath and TV. Room 1 in the Main House has two double beds, handsome decor, and a Victorian love seat in a window alcove. Reasonable rates: $135–185, including a breakfast with great house granola, yogurt, a bowl packed with all kinds of fruit, and a hot entrée as well as fresh muffins. $25 fee for pets.

Hodgdon Island Inn (207-633-7474, 1-800-314-5160; www.hodgdonislandinn.com), Barter's Island Rd., P.O. Box 603, Boothbay 04571. Open year-round. Situated on a quiet road overlooking a cove (and the hand-cranked drawbridge featured in the film *In the Bedroom*). Dan and Joy Moody have added luxurious new bedding and curtains to the nine air-conditioned rooms with water views, all with private bath and ceiling fan; two of the rooms share a porch. The heated swimming pool is set in a landscaped garden; more gardens are a half mile away at the Coastal Maine Botanical Garden (see *Green Space*). Guests can enjoy breakfast on the front porch overlooking a saltwater cove. $140–235 includes breakfast.

🐾 **Welch House** (207-633-3431 or 1-800-279-7313; www.welchhouse.com), 56 McKown St., Boothbay Harbor 04538. Open year-round. Susan Hodder and Michael Feldmann have put their heart and soul into making this place sing. All 14 rooms have private bath, air-conditioning, cable TV and VCR, and phone; some include whirlpool tub, fireplace, and a private deck. The Captain's Lady, with its king bed and gas fireplace, looks out on the harbor. $135–205 in high season, $85–155 in low, which includes a full breakfast, possibly lobster Benedict, served on the breathtaking second-floor deck.

🐾 ✐ **Lawnmere Inn** (207-633-2544 or 1-800-633-7645; www.lawnmere inn.com), P.O. Box 29, Southport 04576 (on Rt. 27 on Southport Island, 2 miles from downtown Boothbay Harbor). Open Memorial Day–mid-Oct. The location is difficult to beat, with broad lawns sloping to the water's edge, lupine and herb gardens, and seal's-eye views of lobster boats and the Sheepscot River. Most of the 11 rooms in the main inn and the 18 rooms (with decks) in the motel wing have water views; there's also a small cottage and the Pine View Guest House. The Lawnmere, built as a summer hotel in the 1890s, has a small, personal feel with lots of attractive common space. There is also a popular dining room (see *Dining Out*). Small pets are accepted in a few of the motel wing rooms ($20 fee). $115–185 in summer; less off-season, includes a fine breakfast. Two-night minimum weekends in July and Aug.

Atlantic Ark Inn (1-800-579-0112; www.atlanticarkinn.com), 62 Atlantic Ave., Boothbay Harbor 04538. Open late May–Oct. Donna Piggot's clean, airy inn is located at a remove from (but accessible by footbridge to) the bustle of the harbor. The six guest rooms are all decorated with white walls, duvet covers, and drapes. All have private bath; some feature harbor views and private balcony. Our favorite: a third-floor room with a cathedral ceiling, Jacuzzi, panoramic view of the harbor, and French doors opening onto a balcony. Full breakfast is served on formal china; a cheese plate with whole-grain breads is served in the afternoon. $105–195 depending on season. Two-night stays on weekends.

Linekin Bay Bed & Breakfast (207-633-9900 or 1-800-596-7420; www.linekinbaybb.com), 531 Ocean Point Rd., East Boothbay 04544. Open year-round. A haven overlooking Linekin Bay, with four charming rooms, all with water views, fireplace, and private bath. Owners Larry Brown, a retired police sergeant, and Marti Booth are friendly hosts. The Holbrook Suite, with its wonderful purple bedding, couch, and gas fireplace, looks like it could make a vacation. $140–190 in season, $105–125 off, includes a full breakfast, perhaps with Downeast egg casserole (eggs, zucchini, onion, and cheese). Brown also makes a great brownie and sweets in the afternoon. Children 12 and over welcome.

"1" **1830 Admiral's Quarters Inn** (207-633-2474; www.admiralsquarters inn.com), 71 Commercial St., Boothbay Harbor 04538. Open year-round. This big sea captain's house is just steps from the busy harbor. Seven tidy, bright rooms, most two-room suites, have a private bath, phone, cable TV, hair dryer, air-conditioning, fireplace, and deck, with a gull's-eye view of the waterfront. The sitting room is a solarium with that same great view. $185–215 in high season includes full breakfast.

"1" **The Greenleaf Inn** (207-633-7346; www.greenleafinn.com), 65 Commercial St., Boothbay Harbor 04538. Open year-round. Jeff Teel, who has spent 10 years rebuilding and refurbishing his inn, runs it with meticulous attention. The library is full of games and good books, and a hot tub, porches, sunroom, and pretty grounds are more amentiities. Seven rooms with fireplace, private bath, air-conditioning, cable TV, and wireless Internet. Great service has brought many return customers. $125–205 depending on season.

Sprucewold Lodge (207-633-3600, 1-800-732-9778; www.sprucewold lodge.com), 4 Nahanada Rd., Boothbay Harbor 04538. Open end of June–mid-Oct. Richard Pizer runs this unique log lodge, built in the 1920s, with three stone fireplaces that fill in during chilly weather. Surrounded by spruce, pine, oak, and birch, in a rare wooded part of Boothbay Harbor, it's tucked away, but just a 20-minute walk to the village. A buffet breakfast is served in the cathedral-ceilinged dining hall, with eggs, peach French toast, bacon, breads, and pastries. twenty-nine rooms, most with private bath. $65–109, depending on room and season.

COTTAGES *Note:* Contact the chambers of commerce for lists of rental cottages. In addition, the locally based **Cottage Connection of Maine** (1-800-823-9501; www.cottageconnec tion.com) represents dozens of properties.

MOTELS **Ship Ahoy Motel** (207-633-5222; www.shipahoymotel .com), Rt. 238, Southport Island (mailing address: P.O. Box 235, Boothbay Harbor 04538). Open Memorial Day weekend–Columbus Day. Great views at a sensational price. A family-owned motel with 54 tidy units, all with TV and air-conditioning, 30 with a private balcony right on the water, others tucked into the granite ledges and pines of the island. Guests who hanker for kitschy 1960s decor are in for a real treat. Amenities include an unheated freshwater pool, coffee shop, and dock on 0.75 mile of waterfront. $49–79 in high season; $39–59 off-season; breakfast extra.

"1" **1828 Vintage House & Cottages** (207-633-3411; www.1828 vinatgehouse.com), 301 Adams Pond Rd., Boothbay 04537. Open year-round. Nine cottages, some with kitchenettes, one suite, and four "condo" units with full kitchens have been renovated since Win and Lori Mitchel bought this charming property in 2006; two large cottages, each with two bedrooms and kitchen, have been built. The swimming pool in front of the smaller, sweet cottages on the front lawn is a draw, and guests can golf at nearby private Boothbay Country Club. $75–169 (depending on season) includes continental breakfast in summer. **1828 Vintage House Specialties,** in the main house, is a wine and cheese shop with more than 100 beers.

"1" ♿ **Flagship Inn** (207-633-5094 or 1-800-660-5094; www.boothbaylodging.com), 200 Townsend Ave. (Rte. 27), Boothbay Harbor 04538. Open year-round. This completely renovated, affordable motel has air-conditioning, a swimming pool, hot tub, and cable TV. $69–139, depending on the season. On-site restaurant.

Boothbay Harbor has a number of inviting motels, many on the water, but we defer to the Mobil and AAA guides.

CAMPING ♿ **Gray Homestead Campground** (207-633-4612; www.graysoceancamping.com), 21 Homestead Rd., Southport Island 04576. Open May 1–Columbus Day. You can't beat the location—30 beautiful acres on the east coast of Southport Island. Forty sites for tents and RVs. Stephen Gray's family has been here since 1800. $32–46 per night for RVs, tents starting at $32 for a family of four.

Little Ponderosa (207-633-2700; www.littleponderosa.com), 159 Wiscasset Road, Boothbay. Open mid-May–Columbus Day. A big, family-oriented place, with 96 shaded sites, 36 on a tidal inlet. Many amenities and diversions. $25 per day for water-only tent sites in-season, $37 for RV sites on the water.

Shore Hills Campground (207-633-4782; www.shorehills.com), 553 Wiscasset Road, Boothbay. Open May 1–Columbus Day, with 150 sites, some on the waterfront. Amenities and recreation opportunities, and the motto "No rig too big." Tent sites $27, full-service RV sites $38 in summer.

✷ Where to Eat

DINING OUT **Lawnmere Inn** (207-633-2544 or 1-800-633-SMILE), Hendricks Hill Rd. (Route 27), Southport Island (just across the bridge). Open for breakfast and dinner daily in-season. Off-season hours vary; call ahead. Reservations appreciated. In a dining room paneled with knotty pine, overlooking a lawn sloping to the sea, we ate savory bruschetta with portobello mushrooms and chèvre. Entrées might include honey-pecan-crusted halibut, lobster strudel, or t-bone lamb chops. And when we hankered for a bowl of berries for dessert, our helpful waitress said she'd make one up for us. Entrées $17–29.

Andrews' Harborside Restaurant (207-633-4074; www.andrewsharborside.com), 12 Bridge St., Boothbay Harbor (downtown, next to the municipal parking lot and footbridge). Open for breakfast, lunch, and dinner, daily May–Oct.; off-season closed Sun. afternoon. The chef-owner specializes in creative seafood and traditional New England dishes. Wonderful cinnamon rolls at breakfast, crab rolls and burgers at lunch, Round Top ice cream and seafood entrées at dinner. Entrées $10–30.

Lobsterman's Wharf (207-633-3443), Rt. 96, East Boothbay (adjacent to a boatyard). Open mid-May–Columbus Day, serving 11:30–9, until 10 on weekends. Just far enough off the beaten track to escape crowds, this place is popular with locals. The large menu includes all the usual seafood, lobster stew, and crabcakes, as well as spinach salad, pastas, and decent house wine. Entrées $7–30.

♂ ♿ **Spruce Point Inn** (207-633-4152), east side of the outer harbor at Spruce Point. Open May–mid-Oct. Reservations advised. Diners can enjoy a lobster roll or a steak in a relaxed setting at Bogie's Hideaway, or dine in the more formal 88 Grandview (open July–Aug.), where they can also contemplate great water views. Dine on clam chowder and "Caveman cut," a 14-ounce Black Angus New York sirloin ($28). The atmosphere is elegant in the big front room, more casual in the inner rooms. Entrées $14–28. Full breakfast available to the public.

♂ ♿ **Newagen Seaside Inn** (207-633-5242 or 1-800-654-5242), Rt. 27, Southport Island, Cape Newagen. Open for breakfast and dinner seasonally; usually closed Sat. nights. A pleasant, old-fashioned dining room with ocean and sunset views, and splendid grounds to walk off the meal. The Cape Harbor Grill, the name of the inn's dining room, serves veal osso bucco, Tao's chicken, and marinated steaks. A pub menu offers casual meals. Entrées $18–32.

♂ ♿ **Ocean Point Inn Restaurant** (207-633-4200 or 1-800-552-5554), East Boothbay. Open mid-June–Columbus Day weekend. Full breakfast buffet $12.95, and dinner nightly. Reservations suggested. More than 100 years of tradition in these three informal dining rooms with ocean views. Choices might include roast beef, fresh Maine salmon, swordfish, and Black Angus steaks. Children's menu and vegetarian options. Entrées $19–35.

Ports of Italy (207-633-1011; www.portsofitaly.com), 47 Commercial St., Boothbay Harbor. Open for dinner daily, Apr.–mid-Nov. Christina Rossi and her husband, David Rossi, from Milan, are cooking real Italian meals with homemade pasta in this bright upstairs dining room. An outside dining area is lovely in summer. Strawberries or blueberries appear in the fabulous zabaglione for dessert. The *risotto alla pescatore* is full of shrimp, scallops, and the best things from the sea ($22). Grilled fish and meat too. Entrées $16–28.

Also, see **Carousel Music Theatre and Supper Club** in *Entertainment*.

EATING OUT **Blue Moon Café** (207-633-2220; www.bluemoonboothbayharbor.com), 54 Commercial St., Boothbay Harbor. Open Mon.–Sat. 7:30 AM–2:30 PM, Sun. 8–1, April–Oct. This little café with a seaside deck makes perfect crabcakes, and the side salad was filled with fresh greens. The chicken quesadilla with big pieces of chicken and melted Boursin and tomato made another great lunch. Order at the counter.

❀ ♂ **Ebb Tide** (207-633-5692), Commercial St., Boothbay Harbor. Open year-round, 7 AM–9 PM; until 9:30 PM Fri. and Sat., closing 7:30 off-season. Nothing fancy about this place, but they offer breakfast all day, plus lobster rolls, club sandwiches, fisherman's platters, and reasonably priced specials. Homemade desserts like peach shortcake and frappes are legendary. Old-fashioned, but with air-conditioning, and knotty-pine booths.

♂ ♿ **Chowder House** (207-633-

5761; www.chowderhouseinc.com), Granary Way, Boothbay Harbor (beside the municipal parking lot and footbridge). Serving a light menu 11:30–9, mid-June–Labor Day. Situated off a waterfront deck, in an outdoor boat bar, a racing sloop under an awning with 30 bar stools and four tables. The menu includes chowders, crab rolls, Buffalo wings, grilled ribs, and crab dip; full bar for daiquiris and other specialty drinks. Desserts will be just two: Tollhouse Squares, a big chocolate chip cookie, and homemade blueberry pie.

89 Baker's Way (207-633-1119), 89 Townsend Ave., Boothbay Harbor. Open 6 AM–9 PM daily. Just the place for fried apple dumpling, you think, and then you smell lemongrass cooking and wonder where you are. There are two worlds here: a full bakery, very popular with locals, and a restaurant that serves traditional Vietnamese foods. Available 11 AM–closing, the Vietnamese menu includes appetizers like steamed buns with ground pork, onion, garlic, peas, eggs, and scallions and fresh spring rolls. Try the fabulous stir-fried squid—or chicken or shrimp—and dine in the back garden by the magnolia. Entrées $9.50.

The Rocktide Inn (207-633-4455 or 1-800-762-8433; www.rocktideinn.com), 35 Atlantic Ave., Boothbay Harbor. Open daily for breakfast 7:30–9:30 AM, dinner 5:30–9 PM, or drinks 4–11 PM; until 8:30 after Labor Day. Closed Columbus Day–mid-June. Come by boat or car for dinner (jackets required in the formal dining room) or a Rocktide martini in the **On the Rocks Bar**.

MacNab's Premium Teas & Tea Room (207-633-7222 or 1-800-884-7222), Back River Rd. (first driveway on your left), Boothbay. Open Tue.–Sat. 10–5 in July and Aug.; closes at 4 the rest of the year. A Scottish-style tearoom serving cock-a-leekie soup, scone sandwiches, salads, and Highland pie as well as tea and scones; afternoon tea and high tea by reservation. Great cookies and sweets, and wonderful tea. More than 100 varieties of teas and tisanes sold wholesale and retail.

Dunton's Doghouse, Sea St., Boothbay Harbor. Open May–Sept., 11–8. Good, reasonably priced takeout food, including a tasty crabmeat roll.

SNACKS ✐ **East Boothbay General Store** (207-633-7800), 255 Ocean Point Rd. (Rt. 96), East Boothbay. Open Tues.–Sun. The former head chef for Jimmy Buffet's yacht, Liz Evans Pochee, is here now, but there isn't any attitude. Try the $3 bottle of wine. She and her husband Dominic Pochee make great sandwiches and pizza, and in the morning donuts are made here.

✐ **Down East Ice Cream Factory** (207-633-3016), the By-Way, Boothbay Harbor. Homemade hard ice cream and frozen yogurt, and a make-your-own sundae bar; all sorts of toppings, including real hot fudge. Open 10:30–10:30 in the height of summer; hours vary off-season.

✐ **Daffy Taffy and Fudge Factory** (207-633-5178), the By-Way, Boothbay Harbor. No credit cards. Watch taffy being pulled, designed, and wrapped—then chew! The fudge is made with fresh cream and butter. Open 10–10 in the height of the season, fewer hours off-season.

Cream teas are served at **MacNab's**; see *Eating Out*.

LOBSTER POUNDS **The Lobster Dock** (207-633-7120; www.thelobsterdock.com), 49 Atlantic Ave., Boothbay Harbor, at the east end of the footbridge. Open 11:29–8:31 Memorial Day weekend–weekend before Columbus Day weekend. Chef–owner Mitch Weiss and his crabcakes starred on a 2007 Bobby Flay "Throwdown" on the Food Network, but this is still the place for a lobster roll, either hot with drawn butter, or cold with a dab of mayo, both fantastic. Also lobster and shore dinners, steamed clams, mussels, steaks, and prime rib. Lobster spring rolls, and seared, exceptional tuna might be specials. Some people love the seafood fra diavolo: shrimp, scallops, mussels, an entire lobster, simmered in a zesty broth with herbs, garlic, bay leaf, tomato, red pepper flakes, and wine ($25).

Robinson's Wharf (207-633-3830; www.robinsonswharf.net), Rt. 27, Southport Island (just across Townsend Gut from West Boothbay Harbor). Open mid-June–Columbus Day for lunch and dinner daily; children's menu. On a sunny day sit on the dock at one of the picnic tables and watch the boats unload their catch. Lobsters and lobster rolls, fried shrimp, clams, scallops, fish chowder, lobster stew, sandwiches, and homemade desserts.

Clambake at Cabbage Island (207-633-7200; www.cabbageislandclambakes.com). The *Argo* departs Pier 6 at Fisherman's Wharf daily in summer, twice on Sat. and Sun., carrying passengers to six-acre Cabbage Island for a traditional clambake with lobsters, clams, corn, and potatoes steamed in seaweed then served on picnic tables. In bad weather a circa-1900 lodge seats up to 100 people by a huge fireplace. About $53 per person including boat ride and tax.

✷ Entertainment

Carousel Music Theatre and Supper Club (207-633-5297; www.carouselmusictheatre.com), Rt. 27, Boothbay Harbor. Performances mid-May–Labor Day. Doors open at 5:30 PM; show begins at 7. Closed Sun. and Mon. A full dinner menu, with entrées like beef tips with mushrooms and onions; cocktails are served by the cast before an evening of Broadway tunes sung cabaret-style begins.

Thursday-evening concerts by the Hallowell Band on the library lawn, Boothbay Harbor. July 4–Labor Day, 8 PM.

Lincoln Arts Festival (207-633-4676). Concerts throughout the summer in varied locations.

✷ Selective Shopping

ART GALLERIES **Gold/Smith Gallery** (207-633-6252), 41 Commercial St., Boothbay Harbor. Shows upstairs have featured Jean Swan Gordon, with watercolors of flowers, and John Wissemann, color pencil drawings.

Gleason Fine Art (207-633-6849; www.gleasonfineart.com), 31 Townsend Ave., Boothbay Harbor. Tue.–Sat. 10–5. Museum-quality paintings by Fairfield Porter and James Fitzgerald, paintings by Scott Kelley of birds, and other best contemporary artists in Maine.

Mathias Fine Art (207-633-7404), on Barter's Island, 10 Mathias Dr. in Trevett. Featuring works by Culver, Bettinson, and others.

Ateliers Villard Studios (207-633-3507), 57 Campbell St., Boothbay Harbor. A studio and gallery featuring interesting woodblock prints, woodcarvings, and oil paintings by artists Kim and Philippe Villard.

Decker's Cove Art Studio (207-633-7992; www.margaretcanepa.com), 48 Plummer Rd., Southport. Open June–Sept. Check out Margaret Canepa's lush, colorful paintings of Genoa, Italy, and the Maine coast.

ARTISANS ***The Lincoln County Cultural Guide***, available at the chamber, is a great starting point for searching out artisans in the area. Categorical listings make it simple to find what you're looking for.

Boothbay Harbor Artisans (207-633-1152; www.mainecraftcoop.org/boothbay.html), 4 Boothbay House Hill Rd., Boothbay Harbor. A cooperative crafts market featuring quilts, soap, stained glass, pottery, maple syrup, jewelry, and more.

Boothbay Region Art Foundation (207-633-2703; www.boothbayartists.org), 1 Townsend Ave., Boothbay Harbor. Open May–late Oct., Mon.–Sat. 10–5, Sun. 12–5. Four juried shows are held in the summer season. "Art in the Square" (Thanksgiving–Dec.) features 12 x 12-inch paintings by area artists; their sale raises money for scholarships.

Andersen Studio (207-633-4397), Rt. 96 at Andersen Rd., East Boothbay. Acclaimed stoneware animal sculptures of museum quality made here for more than 50 years.

The Silver Lining (207-633-4103), 17 Townsend Ave., Boothbay Harbor. Working metalsmiths. Original sculpture and jewelry in brass, sterling, and gold; an exceptional store.

Edgecomb Potters (207-882-9493 or 1-800-343-5529; www.edgecombpotters.com), Rt. 27, Edgecomb. Open year-round. Maine's largest, most famous pottery store (with branches in Portland and Freeport). A two-tiered gallery filled with deeply colored pots, vases, and table settings, lamps, bowls, cookware, and jewelry. There's also a sculpture garden and a small seconds corner.

Abacus Gallery (207-633-2166; www.abacusgallery.com), 12 McKown St., Boothbay Harbor. We love this shop (which has a sister store in Portland) full of artsy silver jewelry, whimsical wooden pepper grinders, hand-painted furniture, and gifts.

Gold/Smith Gallery (207-633-6252), 41 Commercial St., Boothbay Harbor. An unusual selection of 14- and 18-carat gold jewelry.

SPECIAL SHOPS **The Palabra Shop** (207-633-4225; www.palabrashop.com), 53 Commercial St., Boothbay Harbor. Open in summer, Sun.–Thur. 9–6, opened later on weekends. A warren of 10 rooms offering everything from kitschy souvenirs to handcrafts and jewelry to a few antiques. Upstairs (open by appointment) is a Poland Spring Museum with an impressive collection of the Moses bottles this natural springwater used to come in.

Coast and Cottage (207-633-0671), 129 Commercial St. (at Sample's Shipyard), Boothbay Harbor. Home accessories with coastal elegance.

House of Logan (207-633-2293 or 1-800-414-5144), 20 Townsend Ave., Boothbay Harbor. Great men's and women's clothing, with a companion store, **The Village Store and Children's Shop**, selling gifts and furnishings at 34 Townsend Ave.

Sherman's Book & Stationery Store (1-800-371-8128; www.shermans.com), 5 Commercial St., Boothbay Harbor. A two-story emporium filled with souvenirs, kitchenware, and games, as well as a full stock of books; specializing in nautical titles. Art and school supplies.

Rare Books at Vagabonds' House (207-633-7518), 5 Lincoln St., East Boothbay. Pam and Ron Riml stock rare and used books, and specialize in travel, nautical, and maritime books.

Calypso (207-633-3831), 50 Commercial St., Boothbay Harbor. Women's clothing. Open seasonally. The clothes are all good looking.

✷ Special Events

January: **The Penguin Plunge**, East Boothbay.

April: **Fishermen's Festival**—contests for fishermen and lobstermen, cabaret ball, crowning of the Shrimp Princess, tall-tale contest, boat parade, and blessing of the fleet.

May: **Rocky Coast 10-K Road Race and Bunny Run**.

June: **Windjammer Days**—parade of windjammers into the harbor, fireworks, band concert, parade of floats and bands up Main St., visiting U.S. Navy and Coast Guard vessels, live music on the waterfront, food, children's activities, and two crafts shows. The big event of summer.

July: **Antique Auto Days**, Boothbay Railway Village, Rt. 27. Also **Antique Tractor Show and Engine Meet**. **Harbor Jazz Weekend**. **Boothbay in Bloom** celebrates the season with summer merchandise, a fashion show, flower box competitions, special nature tours, pink lady's slipper count, pooches on parade, and more. **Rock-skipping Contest** held at the footbridge parking lot, on the east side of the bridge.

August: **Boat Builders Festival,** East Boothbay. **Boothbay Region Fish and Game Saltwater Fishing Tournament**, Boothbay Harbor (207-633-3788). **YMCA Southport Rowgatta.**

September: Held the weekend after Labor Day, the **Shipyard Cup** (www.shipyardcup.com), organized by East Boothbay's Hodgdon Yachts and the Boothbay Shipyard, brings some America's Cup boats here; all entrants are a minimum of 70 feet long, with many much longer.

October: **Fall Foliage Festival**—boat cruises to view foliage, as well as food booths, crafts sales, live entertainment, antique auto museum, steam train rides.

Early December: **Harbor Lights Festival**—parade, crafts, holiday shopping.

DAMARISCOTTA/NEWCASTLE AND PEMAQUID AREA

Damariscotta is a small region of large, quiet lakes, long tidal rivers, and almost 100 miles of meandering coastline, all within easy striking distance of Rt. 1. It encompasses the Pemaquid Peninsula communities of Bristol, Pemaquid, New Harbor, and Round Pond, as well as communities around Lake Damariscotta, the exceptional twin villages of Damariscotta and Newcastle, and neighboring Waldoboro.

Damariscotta's musical name means "meeting place of the alewives," and in spring spawning alewives can indeed be seen climbing more than 40 feet up a fish ladder from Great Salt Bay to the fresh water in Damariscotta Lake.

The area's first residents also found an abundance of oysters here, judging from the shells they heaped over the course of 2,400 years, on opposite banks of the river just below Salt Bay. Native Americans also had a name for the peninsula jutting 10 miles seaward from this spot: *Pemaquid*, meaning "long finger."

Pemaquid loomed large on 16th- and 17th-century maps because its protected inner harbor was the nearest mainland haven for Monhegan, a busy fishing center for European fishermen. It was from these fishermen that the Pemaquid Native American Samoset learned the English with which he welcomed the Pilgrims at Plymouth in 1621. It was also from these fishermen that Plimoth Plantation, the following winter, secured supplies enough to see it through to spring. Pemaquid, however, lacked a Governor William Bradford. Although it is occasionally referred to as this country's first permanent settlement, its history remains murky.

The site of Maine's "Lost City" is a mini peninsula bordered by the Pemaquid River and Johns Bay (named for Captain John Smith, who explored here in 1614). At one tip stands a round stone tower, a re-creation of part of a fort built here in 1692. In recent years more than 100,000 artifacts have been unearthed in the adjacent meadow, many of them now on display in a small state-run museum. An old cemetery full of crooked slate headstones completes the scene.

Since 19th-century steamboats began bringing guests, this region has supported summer inns and cottages. It is especially appealing to families with young children since it offers warm-water lakes, including 15-mile-long Damariscotta, which has the kind of clarity and largely wooded shore that one expects to find much farther inland.

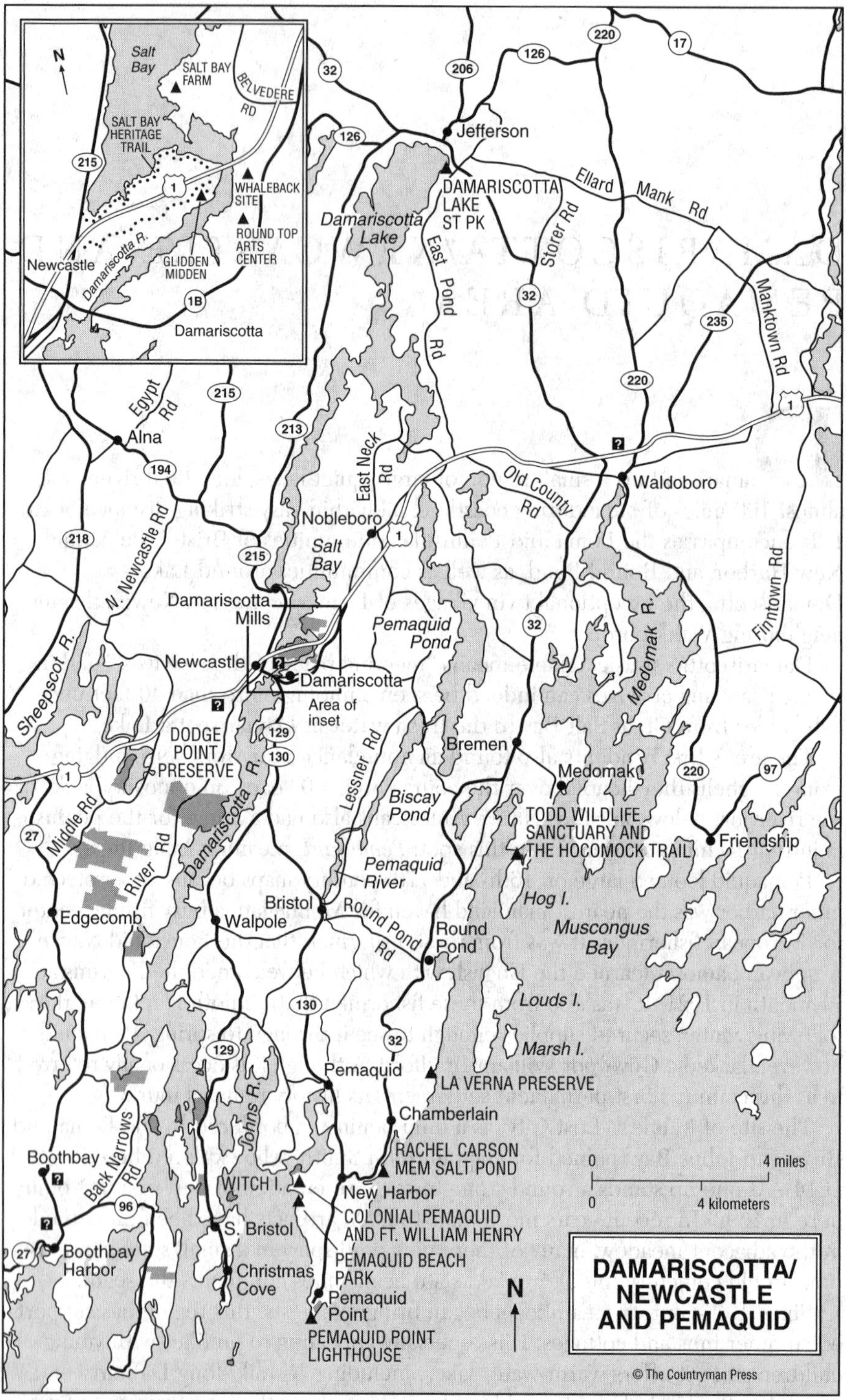
DAMARISCOTTA/
NEWCASTLE
AND PEMAQUID
© The Countryman Press
Salt Bay
SALT BAY FARM
BELVEDERE RD
SALT BAY HERITAGE TRAIL
WHALEBACK SITE
ROUND TOP ARTS CENTER
GLIDDEN MIDDEN
Newcastle
Damariscotta R.
Damariscotta
N
215
1
1B
Jefferson
DAMARISCOTTA LAKE ST PK
Damariscotta Lake
East Pond Rd
Storer Rd
Ellard Mank Rd
Manktown Rd
Egypt Rd
Alna
N. Newcastle Rd
East Neck Rd
Old County Rd
Waldoboro
Nobleboro
Salt Bay
Damariscotta Mills
Pemaquid Pond
Medomak R.
Finntown Rd
Sheepscot R.
Newcastle
Damariscotta
Area of inset
DODGE POINT PRESERVE
Lessner Rd
Bremen
Medomak
Middle Rd
River Rd
Damariscotta R.
Biscay Pond
TODD WILDLIFE SANCTUARY AND THE HOCOMOCK TRAIL
Friendship
Pemaquid River
Edgecomb
Walpole
Bristol
Round Pond Rd
Round Pond
Hog I.
Muscongus Bay
Louds I.
Marsh I.
Pemaquid
LA VERNA PRESERVE
Chamberlain
Johns R.
Back Narrows Rd
Boothbay
RACHEL CARSON MEM SALT POND
WITCH I.
New Harbor
COLONIAL PEMAQUID AND FT. WILLIAM HENRY
S. Bristol
Boothbay Harbor
Christmas Cove
PEMAQUID BEACH PARK
Pemaquid Point
PEMAQUID POINT LIGHTHOUSE
0
4 miles
0
4 kilometers
220
17
126
206
32
126
235
220
1
215
213
194
218
215
129
130
97
220
27
130
129
32
96
27

Pemaquid Light is pictured on Maine's quarter as well as on countless calendars and books because it looks just like a lighthouse should and stands atop dramatic but clamber-friendly rocks. These are composed of varied seams of granite schist and softer volcanic rock, ridged in ways that invite climbing, and pocked with tidal pools that demand stopping.

While there is plenty to see and to do (and to eat), it's all scattered just widely enough to disperse tourist traffic. The villages are small. Damariscotta, with easy off/on access to Rt. 1, is just a few waterside streets built of mellow old local brick; it's the region's compact shopping, dining, and entertainment hub.

GUIDANCE **Damariscotta Region Chamber of Commerce** (207-563-8340; www.damariscottaregion.com). The chamber office is open year-round weekdays 9–5 at 15 Courtyard St., just off Main St. beside the Salt Bay Café. Inquire about cottage rentals.

The Damariscotta Region Information Bureau at the eastern end of Main St., junction of Rt. 1B and Vine St., is a walk-in center. Open seasonally.

GETTING THERE *By bus:* **Concord Trailways** (1-800-639-8080) stops in Damariscotta and Waldoboro en route from Portland to Bangor.

By air: **Mid-Coast Limo** (within Maine, 1-800-834-5500; outside the state, 1-800-937-2424) runs to and from the **Portland International Jetport**. Most inns on the peninsula will pick up guests in Damariscotta, but you do need a car—or a boat—to get around.

By car: The obvious way is up Rt. 1, but in high season many locals avoid traffic by taking I-295 to exit 43 and cutting cross-country through Richmond and Alna/Head Tide to Damariscotta Mills. Not a straight shot but a pretty ride.

PARKING Parking in Damariscotta is much better than it first looks. Large lots are sequestered behind buildings on both sides of Main Street.

✷ Villages

Damariscotta/Newcastle. The twin villages of Newcastle (pop. 1,748, as of the 2000 census) and Damariscotta (2,041 residents) are connected by a bridge and form the commercial center of the region. Damariscotta's Main Street is flanked by fine brick commercial buildings built after the fire of 1845. It's studded with shops and restaurants, and more of the same are tucked down alleyways and around parking lots. Note the towns' two exceptional churches, and check the program of downtown concerts and art openings listed in *The Lincoln County News*. Damariscotta Mills, a short drive up Rt. 215 from Newcastle, on Lake Damariscotta, is worth a visit.

Waldoboro. (pop. 4,920) An inscription in the cemetery of the Old German Church (see *Historic Churches*) relates the deceptive way in which landholder General Samuel Waldo lured the town's first German settlers here. The church and much of the town overlook the tidal Medomak (pronounced with the emphasis on *med*) River. Bypassed by Rt. 1, this village includes some architecturally interesting buildings, one of the country's oldest continuously operating five-and-dimes, and the Waldo Theater (see *Entertainment*). The **Waldoborough Historical Society Museum** (207-832-4713) 1664 Main St. (Rt. 220, just south of Rt. 1) is open regularly in summer months. It includes a vintage school, a barn and hall housing plenty of colorful local memorabilia.

Round Pond. The name was obviously inspired by the village's almost circular harbor, said to have been a pirate base. It was once a major shipbuilding spot and then a quarrying center. It remains a working fishing harbor with competing lobster pounds, a good restaurant, several interesting shops and a famous Independence Day parade.

New Harbor. As picturesque a working harbor as any in Maine. Take South Side Road to Back Cove and walk out on the wooden pedestrian bridge for a great harbor view. Note the Samoset Memorial, honoring the Native American who greeted the Pilgrims at Plymouth and also sold land here, creating the first deed executed in New England. The village itself is far bigger than it looks at first. **Hanna's Garage** looks like a gas station but inside is a serious hardware and marine supply store with an upstairs (past the huge moose head) stocked with clothing and hunting and clamming gear. **C. E. Reilly & Son** (established 1828) offers far more than most supermarkets.

South Bristol. Chances are you will be stopped at "The Gut," the narrow channel spanned by the busiest swing bridge in Maine. This is the place to photograph lobster and fishing boats, always in view. Rt. 129 continues south to Christmas Cove, a long-established summer colony.

Jefferson, the village at the head of Damariscotta Lake, also at the junction of Rts. 126, 32, and 206. Old farmhouses, a general store, and summer homes along the river now form the core of the village, and Damariscotta Lake State Park, with its sandy beach, is on the fringe. Be sure to drive west a couple of miles on Rt. 213 to Bunker Hill, with its old church commanding a superb panorama down the lake.

✱ To See

HISTORIC SITES Shell Middens. The upper Damariscotta River is known for its enormous heaps ("middens") of oyster shells, amassed over a thousand years by Native Americans who camped on the sites now occupied by the villages of Newcastle and Damariscotta. A trail to the **Glidden Midden**, now on the National Register of Historic Places, 30 feet deep and said to date back 2,400 years, begins beside the Newcastle Post Office on Rt. 215. Park next door at Lincoln Co. Publishing. This is part of

THE BRIDGE AT SOUTH BRISTOL GUT
Christina Tree

the **Great Salt Bay Preserve Heritage Trail**, maintained by the **Damariscotta River Association** (207-563-1393). Visit its nearby headquarters (see *Green Space*) for more about this and the **Whaleback Shell Midden State Historic Site**, with access well marked on Business Rt. 1, just north of Round Top Ice Cream. A path leads to the river bank; the surviving midden, mostly covered with vegetation, is directly across the river. This bank was once the site of an even larger shell heap that was substantially removed in the 1880s to supply a factory, built on the spot, to process oyster shells into chicken feed. The factory is gone and, once more, this is a great picnic spot.

Thompson Ice House Rt. 129 in South Bristol. Open July and Aug., Wed., Fri., and Sat. 1–4. A 150-year-old commercial icehouse is preserved, displaying traditional tools for cutting ice from an adjacent pond, and a video presentation on how ice continues to be harvested here. Naturally ice can be found in the outside cooler.

Old Rock Schoolhouse, Bristol (follow signs from Rt. 130 to Rt. 132). Open during summer months, Tue. and Fri. 2–4. Dank and haunting, this 1827 rural stone schoolhouse stands at a crossroads in the woods.

Chapman-Hall House, 270 Main St., Damariscotta. Open July–Labor Day Tues.–Sun., volunteer dependent. Built in 1754, this is the oldest homestead in the region. The house has been restored with its original kitchen, and an herb garden.

HISTORIC CHURCHES This particular part of the Maine coast possesses an unusual number of fine old meetinghouses and churches, all of which are open to the public.

Old German Church (207-832-5100), Rt. 32, Waldoboro. Open daily during July and Aug., 1–4. Built in 1772 with square-benched pews and a wineglass pulpit; note the inscription in the cemetery: "This town was settled in 1748 by Germans who immigrated to this place with the promise and expectation of finding a prosperous city, instead of which they found nothing but wilderness." Bostonian Samuel Waldo—owner of a large tract of land in this area—had not been straight with the 40 German families he brought to settle it. This was the first Lutheran church in Maine and is the setting of one of Andrew Wyeth's most famous Helga paintings.

St. Patrick's Catholic Church (207-563-6038), Academy Rd., Newcastle (Rt. 215 north of Damariscotta Mills). Open year-round daily, to sunset. This is the oldest surviving Catholic church (1808) in New England. It's an unusual building: brick construction, very narrow, and graced with a Paul Revere bell. The pews and stained glass date to 1896, and there's an old graveyard out back. Mass is frequently said in Latin.

NEW HARBOR

Christina Tree

Colonial Pemaquid State Historic Site (207-677-2423; www.friendsofcolonialpemaquid.org). Marked from Rt. 130, this eight-acre complex includes a state-maintained visitors center and museum, Fort William Henry, and the Old Fort House. Open Memorial Day–Labor Day, 9:30–6:30; $2 ages 12–64. This small peninsula at the mouth of the Pemaquid River offers a glimpse into many layerings of history, beginning with a circa-1610 seasonal English fishing station that evolved into a year-round fur trading outpost circa 1630–50. In recent decades archaeologists have uncovered the foundations of homes, a customhouse, and a tavern, all of which are now on view. The 17th-century tools and pottery, Spanish oil jars, and wampum found in these cellar holes are displayed in the museum.

Local farmers had filled in the foundations, but in the late 19th century, when this area became a popular steamship stop and summer colony, the series of forts at the very mouth of the river were excavated. In 1908 the state re-created a portion of 1692 **Fort William Henry**, the second and most substantial of these, built to be "the most expensive and strongest fortification that has ever been built on American soil," and destroyed by the French a year later. The crenellated stone tower contains exhibits on the early explorations of Maine and on the French and Indian Wars, and enshrines the "Rock of Pemaquid," obviously meant as a rival to Plymouth Rock, suggesting that settlers alighted on it long before the Pilgrims ever got to Plymouth. Both the proven and possible history of this place are fascinating.

The distinctive square clapboard **Fort House**, beside the tower, contains a library, restored parlor, changing exhibits, and a gift store that sells, among other things, a DVD about the settlement's long history. Picnic tables on the grounds command water views. For a schedule of frequent summer lectures, tours, and reenactments check the Web site. Even if the museum and fort are closed, this is a beautiful, haunting site. A burial ground, dating to the early 1700s, overlooks the quiet, inner harbor.

Pemaquid Point Lighthouse (www.lighthousefoundation.org), Rt. 130 (at

St. Andrew's Episcopal Church (207-563-3533), Glidden St., Newcastle. A charming half-timbered building on the bank of the Damariscotta River. Set among gardens and trees, it was the first commission in this country for Henry Vaughan, the English architect who went on to design the National Cathedral in Washington, D.C.

Old Walpole Meeting House, Rt. 129, South Bristol. Open Sun. during July and Aug. for 3 PM services. A 1772 meetinghouse with box pews and a pulpit with a sounding board.

Harrington Meeting House, Rt. 130, Pemaquid. Open during July and Aug.,

PEMAQUID LIGHT

the end), Pemaquid Point. The tower is open mid-May–mid-Oct. 9–5, but is closed on rainy days. Pemaquid Point is owned by the town, which charges a $2 per person parking fee during summer. The lighthouse, built in 1824 and automated in 1934, is a beauty. It's just a 39-step climb to the top of the tower, but the light looms high above the rocks below and the real place to appreciate it is gained by climbing down, not up. The rocks offer a wonderfully varied example of geologic upheaval, with tilted strata and igneous intrusions. The tidal pools are exceptional, but take care not to get too close to the dangerous waves. The rocks stretch for half a mile to Kresge Point. The **Fishermen's Museum** (207-677-2494) in the former lighthouse keeper's home (open Memorial Day–Columbus Day, daily 9–5) contains photographs, ships' models, and other artifacts related to the Maine fishing industry and lighthouses. Donations are requested. The complex also includes the Pemaquid Art Gallery, picnic tables, and public toilets. Another fabulous site, even when the museum is closed.

Mon., Wed., Fri., and Sat. 2–4:30. Donations accepted. The 1772 building has been restored and serves as a museum of Old Bristol. A nondenominational service is held here once a year, usually on the third Sunday in August.

OTHER **Skidompha Library** (207-563-5513; www.skidompha.org), 184 Main St., Damariscotta. Open except Tues.–Sat. from 9 AM; until 8 PM Thu. and noon on Sat., otherwise until 5 PM. This stunning library forms the heart of town, the scene of many programs geared to visitors as well as regulars. There are also frequent authors' nights and classic films.

Christina Tree

HARRINGTON MEETING HOUSE

Fawcett's Antique Toy & Art Museum (207-832-7398), 3506 Rt. 1., Waldoboro. Open Memorial Day–Columbus Day, Thu., Fri., and Mon. 10–4, Sat.–Sun. 12–4. $3 admission. Comic-book and antique-toy lovers alert: This is a major collection of original cartoon art, billed as the finest Lone Ranger collection in the world, also antique Disneyana, space toys, and the like. Antique toys bought and sold.

SCENIC DRIVES From Newcastle, Rt. 215 winds along **Damariscotta Lake** to Damariscotta Mills; continue along the lake and through farm country on Rt. 213 (note the scenic pullout across from the Bunker Hill Church, with a view down the lake) to Jefferson for a swim at **Damariscotta Lake State Park**. The turn off Rt. 215 onto 194 above Damariscotta Mills brings you to the picturesque villages of **Alna** and **Head Tide** (see "Wiscasset Area"). Cross the bridge at Head Tide. Turn south on Rt. 218 to Wiscasset or follow it north through North Whitefield and east across Rt. 126 along Clary Lake to Jefferson.

Pemaquid Peninsula. Follow Rt. 129 south from Damariscotta, across the **South Bristol Bridge** to **Christmas Cove**. Backtrack and cross the peninsula via **Harrington Meeting House Road** to **Colonial Pemaquid** and **Pemaquid Beach** (this corner of the world is particularly beautiful at sunset). Turn south on Rt. 130 to **Pemaquid Point** and return via Rt. 32 and **Round Pond**; take Biscay Rd. back to Damariscotta or continue on Rt. 32 into Waldoboro.

✷ To Do

BIRDING ✐ **Audubon Camp**, Hog Island (0.25 mile offshore at the head of Muscongus Bay). June–Aug. One-week programs including family and adult camps and youth and teen sessions focusing on the island's wildlife; also boat trips to see the puffins that were reintroduced to nearby Eastern Egg Rock by the Audubon Puffin Project. There are 5 miles of spruce trails; wildflower and herb gardens, as well as mudflats, surround rustic bungalows. The dining room is in a restored 19th-century farmhouse. For details, contact Maine Audubon (207-781-2339; www.maineaudubon.org). For **puffin-watching** and **birding cruises**, see Hardy Boat Cruises (below). Also see *Green Space*.

BOAT EXCURSIONS ✐ **Hardy Boat Cruises** (Stacie and Capt. Al Crocetti: 207-677-2026 or 1-800-278-3346; www.hardyboat.com), Shaw's Wharf, New Harbor. May–Oct. The 60-foot Maine-built *Hardy III* offers daily (twice daily in high season) hour-long service to Monhegan Island (for a detailed description, see "Midcoast Islands"). Pick a calm day. It doesn't matter if it's foggy, but the passage is more than an hour and no fun if it's rough. Another cruise circles **East-**

ern Egg Rock, one of only five Maine islands on which puffins breed, with narration by an Audubon naturalist. There are also seal-watching and harbor cruises. Parking is free but roughly 0.25 mile back up the road (Gosnold Arms [see *Lodging*] guests are just steps away).

Salt Water Charters (207-677-6229; www.saltwater-charters.com), based in Round Pond Harbor, offers island-hopping and coastal excursions for up to six people on a 38-foot lobster boat.

GUIDED KAYAK TOURS AND RENTALS **Midcoast Kayak** (207-563-5732; www.midcoastkayak.com), 47 Main St., Damariscotta, offers a variety of guided paddles in and around Muscongus Bay, also rentals. **Maine Kayak** (1-866-624-6352;www.mainekayak.com) offers guided trips, rentals, and packages from a variety of bases, including New Harbor.

BOAT RENTALS **Lake Pemaquid Camping** (207-563-5202; www.lakepemaquid.com), Egypt Rd., Damariscotta, rents canoes, kayaks, and paddle- and motorboats.

FISHING **Damariscotta Lake** is a source of bass, landlocked salmon, and trout. See Mill Pond Inn under *Bed & Breakfasts*.

GOLF **Wawenock Country Club** (207-563-3938), Rt. 129 (7 miles south of Damariscotta), Walpole. Open May–Nov. A nine-hole course with 18 tee boxes and a full-service clubhouse.

Sheepscot Links (207-549-7060), 822 Townhouse Rd., Whitefield. A rural, nine-hole golf course set on a former dairy farm. Clubhouse, pull carts.

SWIMMING **Pemaquid Beach Park** (207-677-2754), Rt. 130, Pemaquid. A town-owned area open Memorial Day–Labor Day, 9–5. Nominal admission. Bathhouse, restrooms, refreshment stand, and picnic tables. This is also a great place to walk and watch the sunset in the evening.

Damariscotta Lake State Park, Rt. 32, Jefferson. A fine sandy beach with changing facilities, picnic tables, and grills at the northern end of the lake. No pets allowed. $4 per car.

On Pemaquid Peninsula the big freshwater swimming holes are **Biscay Pond**, (from Rt. 1 take Biscay Rd. 3 miles), and at **Bristol Dam** on Rt. 130, 5 miles south of Damariscotta.

* Green Space

NATURE PRESERVES **Damariscotta River Association** (207-563-1393; www.draclt.org), based at 115-acre **Heritage Center Farm**, 110 Belvedere Rd., a quarter mile north of Rt. 1 in Damariscotta. Open year-round. Sited on 100-acre Salt Pond Farm with hayfields, salt- and freshwater marshes, and woods, laced with walking/skiing paths, this is also the site of seasonal **Friday Farmers Markets**, a summer concert series, special programs, and tours. DRA properties total more than 1,200 acres in more than a dozen easily accessible places, including **Great Salt Bay Preserve Heritage Trail**, which loops around Glidden Point and leads to the Glidden Midden (*To See*). **Dodge Point Preserve** is a 506-acre property on Newcastle's River Rd. (2.6 miles south of Rt. 1), which includes a sand beach as well as a freshwater pond, a beaver bog, and trails.

Rachel Carson Memorial Salt Pond, Rt. 32, north of New Harbor. The pond is on the opposite side of the road from the parking lot. There's a beautiful view of the open ocean from here, and at low tide the tidal pools are filled with tiny sea creatures. Look for blue mussels, hermit crabs, starfish, and green sea urchins. Here Rachel Carson researched part of her book *The Edge of the Sea.* Inland from the pond, the preserve includes fields and forest.

Griggs Preserve, Newcastle, is maintained by the Sheepscot Valley Conservation Association (207-586-5616). A loop trail through 56 acres brings you to a view of the reversing falls at Sheepscot Village. Take Rt. 1 south to Cochran Rd. (turn right at Skip Cahill's Tires). After a mile turn left onto Trails End Rd. to the trailhead (on the left, before the bridge).

Todd Wildlife Sanctuary and the Hocomock Trail, Bremen (take Keene Neck Rd. off Rt. 32). A visitors center (207-529-5148) is open June–Aug., daily 1–4. The nature trail leads down to the beach. This is a great family picnic spot, accessible with short legs.

Witch Island, South Bristol. An 18-acre wooded island lies 0.25 mile offshore at the east end of "the Gut," the narrow channel that serves as South Bristol's harbor. A trail around the island threads through oaks and pines, and there are two sheltered beaches.

✷ Lodging

INNS **The Newcastle Inn** (207-563-5685 or 1-800-832-8669; www.newcastleinn.com), River Rd., Newcastle 04553. Open year-round. Laura and Peter Barclay offer 15 tasteful and comfortable rooms, all with private bath, some with water views, several with canopy bed, nine with gas fireplace, and two with Jacuzzi. An inviting little bar with French doors opens onto a wide, awning-shaded deck with water views—the breakfast venue weather permitting. Dining is important here; a four-course dinner ($46 prix fixe) might begin with Pemaquid oysters and include a mix of locally grown greens, lobster en casserole, and a rich chocolate pot de crème. The setting is Lupines, a dining room decorated with a mural of the village Damariscotta. The Barclays have added many plantings to the grounds, which slope to the river and overlook Damariscotta. $175–255 in

DAMARISCOTTA LAKE

Christina Tree

high season, $125–225 in low, including a three-course breakfast. Inquire about special getaway weekends.

Gosnold Arms (207-677-3727; winter, 561-575-9549; www.gosnold.com), 146 Rt. 32, New Harbor 04554. Open mid-May–mid-Oct. Sited at the entrance to a picturesque working harbor, steps from Shaws Wharf, a good place to eat lobster and departure point for the Hardy Boat cruises to Monhegan Island and around Egg Rock. Originally a saltwater farm, this friendly inn has been owned by the Phinney family for more than three decades. It rambles on along the water with rockers on the porch and ample rainy-day space. There are 10 simple but comfortable guest rooms upstairs (all private bath, eight with water views) and 20 cottage units, six with deck, smack-dab on the harbor. The Hillside units, squirreled away at the top of the property, are good for families. Breakfast on the enclosed porch is served buffet-style, the better to catch the boat. Guests who overnight on Monhegan are permitted to keep their car in an upper lot. $105–285 double B&B in the inn, 15 percent less off-season.

Bradley Inn (207-677-2105 or 1-800-942-5560; www.bradleyinn.com), 3063 Pemaquid Point, New Harbor 04554. Open year-round. Warren and Beth Busteed are energetic innkeepers who have established a culinary reputation for this turn-of-the-20th-century inn (see *Dining Out*). The 13 guest rooms and two suites are divided among the main house, the carriage house, and a cottage, all nicely furnished (each with private bath). Clunker bicycles are free, and the inn is less than a mile from Pemaquid Lighthouse and Kresge Point. When we stopped by in 2007, a spa with sauna and treatment rooms was in the works. From $145 off-season to $325 (for a carriage house suite) in-season; special birding and spa weekends.

The Hotel Pemaquid (207-677-2312; www.hotelpemaquid.com), 3098 Bristol Rd., New Harbor 04554. Open mid-May–mid-Oct. A century-old summer hotel a short walk from Pemaquid Point but without water views. The 25 rooms are divided among the main house and new annexes. Most rooms have private bath (four rooms in the inn itself share two baths). Coffee is set out at 7 and the nearby Sea Gull Shop (see *Eating Out*) serves three meals. From $65 off-season with shared bath to $240 for a suite in Aug.; a four-bedroom housekeeping cottage is $775–825 per week.

BED & BREAKFASTS

In Newcastle/Damariscotta

The Flying Cloud (207-563-2484; www.theflyingcloud.com), River Rd., Newcastle 04553. Open year-round. An 1840s sea captain's home expanding on a 1790s cape with five spacious guest rooms, one a two-bedroom suite, and all with private bath, four with water views. All are named for ports of call of the clipper ship *Flying Cloud.* Our favorites are the second-floor San Francisco room, with floor-to-ceiling six-over-six windows overlooking the river and a high pencil-post king bed, adjoining the well-stocked library; and the smaller, skylit, third-floor Melbourne room, also with a river view. The living room and dining room are both light-filled and comfortably elegant. There's an informal TV room and a screened porch overlooking flower gardens, the venue for bountiful breakfasts that might begin with a chilled melon soup. Karen and Dave Bragg are caring hosts. $90–190 per couple.

Mill Pond Inn (207-563-8014; www.millpondinn.com), Rt. 215, Damariscotta Mills (mailing address: 50 Main St., Nobleboro 04555). Open year-round. Two-person hammocks swing under the willow trees beside a pond. Enter the red door of Sherry and Bobby Whear's 1780 gray-clapboard house and you immediately feel at home. The six rooms—including a two-bedroom suite with its own entrance—all have private bath and are so different from each other that you might want to ask for descriptions, but all cost $130 per couple. Breakfast might be a crabmeat omelet with veggies from the garden. In winter pack a picnic lunch and skate across the lake to an island. In summer take a dip off the dock or ask for a ride in the 16-foot restored antique motorboat. Bobby, a Registered Maine Guide, is happy to arrange fishing trips. No credit cards please.

The Harbor View Inn at Newcastle (207-563-2900; www.theharborview.com), P.O. Box 791, Newcastle 04553. Open year-round. Set above Main St. in Newcastle, this handsome 1840s house has a spacious, beamed, and many-windowed living room and second-floor reading room; there's also a deck overlooking the harbor. Joe McEntee offers just three guest rooms, all unusually large and luxurious. The two upstairs have a fireplace, river views, and private deck. Breakfast is special. $170–210 mid-May–Oct. Less for singles and in the off-season

MILL POND INN

Christina Tree

Oak Gables (207-563-1476; 1-800-335-7748; www.oakgablesbb.com), 36 Pleasant St., Damariscotta 04543. Open year-round. Set on 11 riverside acres, with a heated swimming pool and boathouse. Martha Scudder's gracious house has four second-floor rooms, shared bath ($95–150 with breakfast). Inquire about weekly rentals for the riverside three-bedroom cottage, a two-person studio, an apartment in the guest wing, and a river-view apartment above the garage.

The Tipsy Butler (207-563-3394; www.thetipsybutler.com), 11 High St., P.O. Box 239, Newcastle 04553. Open year-round. The facade of this 1980s mansion is formally pillared and the four guest rooms are variously named for the butler, maid, cook, and groundskeeper. We like the Maid's Room with its pencil-post king-sized bed and bath with bidet. All have TV with HBO, VCR, and DVD. Innkeepers Sarah and Tony pride themselves on their breakfasts. $135–190; two-night minimum in high season.

Pemaquid Peninsula south of Damariscotta

Brannon-Bunker Inn (207-563-5941, 1-800-563-9225; www.brannonbunkerinn.com), 349 Rt. 129, Walpole 04573. Open Mar.–Dec.

We like the feel of this 1820s inn, which at one point became a Prohibition-era dance hall. Your hosts are the Hovance family, and children are welcome. In the main house there are five guest rooms, one on the first floor with private bath, four upstairs (two with shared bath). The neighboring Carriage House includes a suite with two bedrooms and a kitchen/living room, also two more rooms with private bath. There's ample common space, with a big fieldstone fireplace for foggy mornings and a screened porch for sunny afternoons. The upstairs sitting area walls are hung with memorabilia from World War I and all rooms are tastefully furnished in country antiques. $90–110 for rooms; $110–170 for the Carriage House suite. Breakfast features freshly baked muffins and fresh fruit.

The Inn at Round Pond (207-529-2004; www.theinnatroundpond.com), 1442 Rt. 31, Round Pond 04564. Sue and Bill Morton have brought new life to this 1830s Colonial with its mansard-roofed third floor, added around the turn of the last century, when it became the Harbor View Hotel. This remains the only place to stay in this picturesque waterside village. Rooms have been reduced to three suites. Our favorite is the third-floor Monhegan Suite with a king-sized iron bed and a sitting area. An adjoining room with twins is available for an additional charge. $150–190 Memorial Day–Columbus Day, otherwise $100–125 per couple, with breakfast.

Sunset Bed and Breakfast (207-644-8849; www.sunsetbnb.com), 16 Sunset Loop, P.O. Box 91, South Bristol 04568. Open May–Oct. Kay and Dick Miller have turned a vintage summer cottage into a surprisingly comfortable B&B with two second-floor rooms, one with twins and the other with a queen, both with skylights and sharing a bath. $130 with private bath (they don't rent the other room), $90 with shared, $70 single, including a full breakfast.

In Waldoboro 04572

Blue Skye Farm (207-832-0300; www.blueskyefarm.com), 1708 Friendship Rd. (Rt. 220). What a treasure! This is an exquisite house, dating back to 1775 but with an elegant Federal facade. It retains all its original woodwork and working fireplaces (in two of the five guest rooms as well as in common rooms); the stenciling in the front hall is thought to be by Moses Eaton. Brits Peter and Jan Davidson have restored all the original detailing. The two upstairs front rooms and one downstairs (the former North Parlor) are classically proportioned; a smaller downstairs guest room (the Library) overlooks the marshes. A full breakfast is served, but because their hosts live in an adjoining cottage, guests have access to the kitchen as well as outdoor grills for other meals. The 100-acre property includes gardens, hiking trails, and a skating pond. $110–145 in-season, from $95 off-season. This is a great house to rent in its entirety. Candlelit lobster dinners can be arranged when booking.

Also see "Rockland/Thomaston Area" for Harbor Hill and Outsiders' Inn in Friendship, just down the peninsula from Waldoboro.

North of Damariscotta Lake in Jefferson 04348

Jefferson House (207-549-5768; www.jeffersonhousebb

.com), 95 Washington Rd. (Rt. 126), P.O. Box 985. The large, bright kitchen with its big old cookstove is the center of this 1835 farmhouse. You can also breakfast on the deck overlooking the village and millpond. Guests can use the canoe on the river and it's a half-mile to the beach at Damariscotta Lake State Park. Jim and Barbara O'Halloron's make you feel like invited guests. The five rooms are comfortable but four are shared bath. $60 double, $50 single; $75 for a room with a private bath. $10 additional per extra person.

Blueberry Hill Farm (207-549-7448; www.mainefarmvacation.com), 101 Old Madden Rd. This is another find: a secluded 125-acre farm with a 1774 farmhouse, tastefully restored and furnished with antiques and original art. JoAnn Tribby and Ellis Percy offer three guest rooms in their house, one with a fireplace and one a small single (all shared bath). This is an organic farm raising Highland cattle, Shetland ponies, pigs, and chickens, along with a kitchen garden. Clary Lake, within walking distance, is good for swimming, canoeing, and fishing. Damariscotta Lake State Park is also near. $50 for the single room, $65 per couple for the doubles, $15 for additional guests, full breakfast included.

COTTAGES Many rental properties are listed with the Damariscotta area chamber; for cottages and apartments down on the peninsula, also request a copy of the current *Map & Guide* published by the Pemaquid Area Association (Chamberlain 04541). **Newcastle Square Vacation Rentals** (207-563-6500; www.mainecoastcottages.com), 87 Main St., Damariscotta, handles more than 100 area cottages and houses.

The Thompson House and Cottages (207-677-2317; www.thompsoncottages.net), New Harbor 04554. Open May–Nov. Merle and Karen Thompson are the third generation of a family that's been offering hospitality since they began taking guests in an 1874 house in 1920. There are still two sparkling clean rooms in the house, but the big attractions are the 21 equally tidy housekeeping cottages (maximum of five people), many with ocean views and facing New Harbor or Back Cove, all with fireplace (wood supplied). $1,050–1,600 per week, less off-season. Rooms (with private bath) in the house are $70 per night, $400 per week, and there are three apartments ($600 per week) on the property.

Ye Olde Forte Cabins (207-677-2261), 18 Old Fort Rd., Pemaquid Beach 04554. Nostalgia buffs take note: These are classic 1922 cabins (sleeping one to four), stepped roof to roof along a wide central lawn sloping to a private beach on John's Bay. There's a cookhouse equipped with everything you need to make meals, along with immaculate men's and women's shower houses. $439–631 per week, less if you bring your own linen. The neighboring **Seaside Apartments**, under the same ownership, includes four efficiencies and accepts pets, and also offers a dock at which guests can keep canoes and kayaks, $478–690 per week.

CAMPING **Lake Pemaquid Camping** (207-563-5202; www.lakepemaquid.com), Box 967, Damariscotta 04543. Off Biscay Rd. More than 200 tent and RV sites, also cabin and cottage rentals on 7-mile Lake Pemaquid. Facilities include tennis, a pool, 18-hole mini golf, a game room, laundry facilities, a sauna, Jacuzzi, a snack bar, and store, along with a marina with boat rentals.

Christina Tree

YE OLD FORTE CABINS

✷ Where to Eat

DINING OUT

In Damariscotta/Newcastle

Damariscotta River Grill (207-563-2992), 155 Main St. Open for lunch and dinner. A brick-walled, two-floor, middle-of-Main-Street gem under the same ownership as the long and justly popular Anchor Inn in Round Pond. Begin either meal by splitting an order of Pemaquid oysters on the half shell, served with the house horseradish. At dinner feast on pan-seared scallops with roasted tomatoes and wilted spinach, drizzled with balsamic vinegar, or try the lobster cakes with eggplant. Children's menu. Dinner entrées $13–20.

Augustine's Backstreet Restaurant (207-563-5666), Elm St. Plaza. Open daily 11:30–9. This pleasant restaurant is hidden back behind Main St. and overlooks the Damariscotta River. At lunch you might try the house smoked chicken salad or Portuguese seafood and sausage stew. Dinner options might include rum pepper painted salmon and tempura jumbo shrimp skewers with a soba noodle salad. Entrees: $19–27.

74 Maine Bistro (207-563-7444; www.74maine.com). Open for dinner but days change; check. Chef-owner James Metzger specializes in fresh fish with fresh salsa and relishes. It was late, we wanted something light, and so ordered the honey-mustard frilled salmon on mixed greens tossed in Asian vinaigrette. It's the best salmon I've ever tasted and my husband was equally enthusiastic about his wasabi sesame tuna. Both are $15. Entrees are $16–34.

Salt Bay Café (207-563-3302), 88 Main St. Open for breakfast 7:30–10:30, lunch 11–4, dinner 4 until closing. What this chef-owned restaurant lacks in a view, it makes up for in comfort, reliably good food, and service. Lunch features soups, salads, and sandwich combos. The large dinner menu ranges from pasta dishes to roast leg of lamb and includes the widest variety of vegetarian dishes around. Children's menu. Entrées $7–22.

King Eider's Pub (207-563-6008; www.kingeiderspub.com), 2 Elm St. Open year-round 10:30–11. The downstairs pub is a good foggy-evening spot for light grub and a boutique brew. Crabcakes are also the specialty in the pleasant upstairs restaurant, and they're bigger than the norm, the two offered as an appetizer can work as dinner for most appetites, especially if you begin with Damariscotta River oysters and add the house salad. The dinner menu is large, ranging from burgers to chargrilled steaks, Entrées $9–20.

Also see Lupines at the Newcastle Inn under *Lodging*.

On the Pemaquid Peninsula

Anchor Inn (207-529-5584), Round Pond. Open daily for lunch (11–2), dinner (from 5), and Sunday brunch (noon–3), mid-May–Labor Day, then Wed.–Sun. until Columbus Day. Jean and Rick Hirch's tiered dining room overlooking the harbor is a real standout. Reservations are necessary for dinner; ask for a table on the porch, hanging over the harbor. At either meal try the Italian seafood stew, loaded with fish, scallops, and mussels, served with garlic bread ($17.76). Dinner options include shrimp and scallops baked with crabmeat, and chicken sautéed with dried tomatoes and baby spinach, finished with melted Gruyère and fresh basil cream. Children's menu. Dinner entrées $16–26. Shore dinners and lobster priced to market.

Bradley Inn (207-677-2105; www.bradleyinn.com), Pemaquid Point Rd., New Harbor. Open by reservation for dinner year-round; Thu.–Tues. in-season; Thu.–Sun. Nov.–Mar. Fine dining is what these two attractive dining rooms are about. The rooms are decorated in nautical antiques and soothing colors; tables

LOBSTER POUNDS

Note: Muscongus Bay is a particularly prime lobster source, and genuine lobster pounds are plentiful around the harbors of the Pemaquid Peninsula.

Harbor View Restaurant at the **Pemaquid Fisherman's Co-op** (207-677-2801; www.pemaquidlobsterco-op.com), off Pemaquid Harbor Rd., Pemaquid Harbor. Open Memorial Day–Columbus Day, 11–8. Operated by Maine's oldest continuously run fishermen's cooperative. Lobster, steamed clams and mussels, and shrimp, shore dinners and baskets, enjoyed at indoor and outdoor tables with a great view across John's Bay to Colonial Pemaquid. There's a play area for kids while you wait for your lobster.

Shaw's Wharf (207-677-2200), Rt. 32, New Harbor. Open early May–mid-Oct., daily for lunch and supper. You can't get closer to a working harbor than this popular dockside spot. Pick your lobster out of the pool below and feed on it upstairs at picnic tables, either inside or out. Chowders and stews, a wide choice of sandwiches, dinner salads, sides, and fried and seafood dinners are also on the menu. Fully licensed.

On the dock at Round Pond two competing lobster shacks are both open daily for lunch through dinner in season.

Muscongus Bay Lobster Company (207-529-5528) Still pretty basic but expanded in recent years with plenty of picnic tables on the deck. Sample the area's oysters on the half shell, as well as the freshest of crabmeat, lobsters, corn, and fixings.

Round Pond Lobster (207-529-5725). Really no-frills but locals swear by it. Check out the nightly special and BYOB and salad.

are well spaced and candlelit. The à la carte menu changes nightly but might include lavender risotto with black mission figs and roasted corn, or Maine crabcakes with a lobster corn compote, peas, and fava beans. Entrées $23–37. The inviting bar features house cocktails and grilled flatbreads.

EATING OUT

In Damariscotta

Schooner Landing (207-563-7447), Schooner Wharf, Main St. Open May–Sept. daily for lunch and dinner, just weekends in Apr. and Oct.; the pub remains open for live music on weekends through winter. A harborside restaurant on the Damariscotta River; the view is the big draw here, along with the informal feel and draft brews. This is the best location in town, but service tends to be slow.

Mediterranean Kitchen (207-563-2882), 189 Main St. Open for lunch and dinner except Sunday year-round. Greek-style pizzas are the house specialty, but the lamb and beef gyros with the house sauce get rave reviews. Dinner options include moussaka and all the classic Greek salads and side dishes.

Weatherbird Café (207-563-8993), 72 Courtyard St. If you are browsing the shops and want a quick but delicious lunch, this baker/market/clothing and gift store serves up delicious deli sandwiches on their fresh baked breads and panini, all $5.

Andrew's Pine View Restaurant (207-563-2899), Rt. 1 north of the village, Damariscotta. Open daily for lunch and dinner, Sunday brunch 9–2:30. A good, family-geared way stop with dining mainstays like country-style chicken pie and baked stuffed haddock. Beer and wine served.

Larson's Lunch Box (207-563-57550), 430 Upper Main St. (Business Rt. 1), Open daily year-round, 11–3:30, until 7 in July and August. Beloved by locals, this roadside stand is known for its fresh and generous crab and lobster rolls. Billy and Barbara Ganem have installed a serious restaurant kitchen and also pride themselves on from-scratch clam chowder, sweet potato fries, and cookies. Picnic tables and unbeatable prices.

Paco's Tacos (207-563-5355), off Main St. in the alley beside Sheepscot River Pottery. Open weekdays 11–4. Better than average and handy to the public landing (parking and a picnic spot).

On or just off Rt. 1

Moody's Diner (207-832-7785), Rt. 1, Waldoboro. Open Mon.–Fri. 4 AM–11:30 PM, Sat. 5 AM–11:30 PM, Sun. 6 AM–11:30 PM. A clean and warm, classic 1930s diner run by sev-

MOODY'S DINER

Nancy English

eral generations of the Moody family along with other employees who have been there so long they've become part of the family. Renovated and expanded, it retains all the old atmosphere and specialties like cream pies and family-style food—corned beef hash, meat loaf, and stews—at digestible prices. You can buy T-shirts and other Moody's paraphernalia, but you can also still get chicken croquettes at prices that haven't soared with fame.

Bullwinkle's Family Steakhouse (207-832-6272), Rt. 1, Waldoboro. Locally loved and a good bet for road food. Steaks are the specialty, along with baby back ribs, seafood baskets, and subs.

Narrows Tavern (207-832-2210), 15 Friendship St., Waldoboro. Open 11:30 AM–1 AM, dinner until 9. A welcoming village pub with picnic-style tables and a TV screen in back, also local art on old brick walls. Good chowder, salads, and pastas with fresh veggies and fish, also burgers and sweet potato fries. Great pies. Good selection of wine by the glass.

On the Pemaquid Peninsula: Rt. 130

Country Cupboard (207-677-3911), 137 Huddle Rd., New Harbor. Open Tue.–Sat. 8–3, Sun. 8–12; until 7 Tues.–Sat in summer. A family-run log eatery specializing in from-scratch baking (try the cinnamon buns). Given its local fame, we were disappointed in the chowder but agree this is a great new food option within striking distance of Pemaquid Light and the beach. Luncheon options include blackboard specials as well as salads, burgers, and sandwiches. Sunday is breakfast service only, with table service.

Sea Gull Shop (207-677-2374), next to the Pemaquid Lighthouse at Pemaquid Point. Open daily in-season, 8–8, serving all three meals. The Monhegan Room, hidden behind the shop but overlooking the water, is delightfully old fashioned. Standard menu. Entrées $5–20. BYOB.

The Contented Sole (207-677-3000) at Colonial Pemaquid. Open seasonally for lunch and dinner, this barn of a wharf-side restaurant changes names frequently. Full license.

On the Pemaquid Peninsula: Along Rt. 129 to Christmas Cove

Coveside Restaurant & Marina (207-644-8282; www.covesiderestaurant.com), Christmas Cove, South Bristol. Open seasonally, 11–9. Geared to customers arriving by yacht (call for moorings) and to the neighboring old summer colony, this is a good excuse to drive all the way down to Christmas Cove. The big, open-timbered, pine-paneled dining room has picture windows and a deck on the water. Even the lunch menu is sophisticated, with such offerings as bouillabaisse and calamari salad in addition to burgers and baskets. Dinner choices include orange horseradish crusted grouper and scallop and shrimp linguine with spicy ham and mushrooms. Entrées: $17–23.

Harborside Café (207-644-8751), South Bristol. Open year-round for breakfast, lunch, supper. Just north of the drawbridge at "the Gut," this is a general store that we passed many times before noticing all the pickups gathered at noon. Inside we found a six-stool counter and several booths, a standard road-food menu—fresh-dough pizza, omelets all day, sandwiches, fried seafood, daily specials—plus standout chowder and fresh fruit pies.

Elsewhere

Morse's Kraut House (207-832-5569; www.morsessauerkraut.com), 3856 Washington Rd. (8 miles north of Rt. 1, on Rt. 220), Waldoboro. Open year-round, daily except Wed., 9–4. Avoid the Saturday rush. Since 1918 sauerkraut has been made from fresh cabbage and sold on this premises, which now includes a store and a four-booth restaurant. On weekends the line stretches out the door for deep-fried Kraut Balls, beet borscht, sweet and sour braised red cabbage, German potato salad, Morse's fresh, finely chopped coleslaw, grilled "schinken," sauerbraten, beef goulash, a wide variety of sausages, and famous freshly made sauerkraut. Desserts include Black Forest liqueur cakes and apple strudel. The store sells many of the house specialties and more.

Country Farm (207-549-5985), corner of Rts. 126 and 218 in Whitefield. Open daily (except Mon.) for lunch and dinner. Very busy on Saturday night, popular with locals. The menu is large and varied. $20–35 for two.

ICE CREAM **Round Top Ice Cream** (207-563-5307), Business Rt. 1, Damariscotta. Open early Apr.–Columbus Day, 11:30–10, until 8 off-season. You'll find delicious Round Top Ice Cream, made with 15 percent butterfat, offered at restaurants throughout the region, but this is the original shop just up the road from the farm where it all began in 1924. The ice cream comes in 60 flavors, including fresh blueberry.

✱ Entertainment

Lincoln Theater (207-563-3424; www.lcct.org), entrance off Main St., Damariscotta. The biggest hall east of Boston in 1875, later boasting the largest motion-picture screen in the state. A second-floor theater was restored (with elevator access) by the Lincoln County Community Theater, which stages its own productions here. Also first-run films and special programs.

Waldo Theatre (207-832-6060; www.waldotheatre.org), Main St., Waldoboro. Mar.–Dec., a schedule of films, concerts, and live performances.

The DaPonte String Quartet (207-529-4555; www.daponte.org) perform in St. Patrick's and in the Second Congregational Church, Newcastle

Also check the film and lecture schedule at Damriscotta's Skidompha Library (see *To See*).

Colonial Pemaquid State Historic Site (207-677-2423; www.friendsofcolonialpemaquid.org) is a venue for frequent reenactments, lectures and other special events (see *Historic Sites*).

✱ Selective Shopping

ANTIQUES *Antiquing in the Midcoast Pemaquid Region*, a free pamphlet guide, lists more than two dozen dealers in this small area. Check local papers for auctions or call **Robert Foster** (207-563-8110), based at his auction gallery on Rt. 1, Newcastle.

ART, CRAFTS, AND MORE

In Damariscotta unless otherwise noted

The Firehouse Gallery (207-563-7299; www.thefirehousegallery.com), corner of Main St. and Rt. 130. Open Apr.–Dec., representing many of Maine's most prominent artists, also carrying fine crafts including distinctive jewelry.

Gallery 170 (207-563-5098; www.gallery170.com), 170 Main St. The library's former clapboard home is now a serious contemporary gallery.

River Gallery (207-563-6330), Main St. Open in-season Mon.–Sat. 10–3; features 19th- and early-20th-century landscapes.

Tin Fish Etc. (207-563-8204), above the Weatherbird Store, Northey Square. Dana Moses fashions remarkable art pieces in all sizes made from recycled metal, mostly corrugated iron.

Damariscotta Pottery (207-563-8843), around back of the Weatherbird. Open year-round except Sun. Majolica ware, decorated in floral designs. You won't see this advertised. It doesn't have to be. Watch it being shaped and painted.

The Stable Gallery (207-563-1991), 26 Water St. Open daily May–Oct. A cooperative showing work of member artists and a variety of craftspeople.

Watershed Center for Ceramic Arts (207-882-6705; www.watershedceramics.org), 19 Rick Hill Rd., Newcastle. An old brickworks serves as a seasonal studio in which artists use the local clay to create work. Inquire about studio tours, and Salad Days.

Pine Tree Yarns (207-563-8909; www.pinetreeyarns.com), Main St. A knitter's heaven, seemingly thousands of yarns in a riot of colors, many hand-dyed by Elaine Eskesen on the premises. Elaine also designs patterns geared to current as well as classic tastes.

✐ **Weatherbird**, Northey Square. Open Mon.–Sat. 8:30–5:30. A combination café and gift shop with mouth-watering pastries and specialty foods, wines, home accessories, clothing, gifts, toys, and cards.

Sheepscot River Pottery (207-882-9410 or 1-800-659-4794), Main St. The big shop is on Rt. 1 in Edgecomb, but this gift shop features the distinctive hand-painted dinnerware, plates, lamps, and more.

In Round Pond

Natural Expressions (207-529-4411; www.peapodjewelry.com), 1794 Rt. 32, north of Round Pond. Open Mon.–Sat. May–Dec. or by appointment. This jewel-like gallery displays an extensive range of peapod jewelry and local pearl pieces designed and made on the premises.

Round Pond Art Gallery, seemingly transplanted from the rue Sisley, displays an interesting mix of "les beaux arts."

✐ **Granite Hall Store** (207-529-5864), Rt. 32, Round Pond. Open daily in season 10–8:30. Penny candy up front, also Scottish-, Irish-, and Maine-made woolens, books, and cards, among many other things, plus an ice cream takeout window.

In New Harbor and Pemaquid Point

Pemaquid Craft Co-Op (207-677-2077), Rt. 130, New Harbor. Open May–Oct., daily 10–6, then Fri.–Sun. until Dec. 24. Fifteen rooms filled with varied work by 50 Maine crafters.

Saltwater Artists Gallery (207-677-2490; www.saltwaterartists.com), corner of Rt. 30 and Lighthouse Road. Open Memorial Day–Columbus Day, 10–5. A nonprofit cooperative featuring 30 local artists in a wide variety of media.

Pemaquid Art Gallery (207-677-2753), Pemaquid Lighthouse Park, displays the work of local artists.

North Country Wind Bells (207-677-2224; www.mainebuoybells.com), 544 Rt. 32, Chamberlain. Open daily June–Labor Day, weekdays off-season. North of New Harbor on the pretty coastal road to Round Pond. Buoy wind bells, wilderness bells, and lighthouse bells are made and sold, along with garden and home accessories.

BOOKS **Maine Coast Book Shop** (207-563-3207), 158 Main St., Damariscotta. One of Maine's best bookstores, with a large children's section and knowledgeable staff members who delight in making suggestions and helping customers shop. It now fills the entire first floor of the Lincoln Theater building and includes an inviting cyber café with a blackboard menu and freshly made soups as well as espressos, and teas.

Jean Gillespie Books (207-529-5555), Rt. 32 south of Round Pond. Open 1–5 seasonally, or by appointment. An exceptional antiquarian bookstore, since 1961. Some 20,000 titles line shelves in a barnlike annex to the house. Specialties include the Civil War, cookbooks, and Maine.

SPECIAL SHOPS **Borealis Breads Store** (207-832-0655; www.borealisbreads.com), 1860 Rt. 1 (across from Moody's Diner), Waldoboro. Open Mon.–Fri. 8:30– 5:30, Sat. and Sun. 9–4. Maine's most popular bread, made from all-natural ingredients, including local grains, and baked here on a stone hearth; more than a dozen kinds are widely distributed.

S. Fernald's Country Store (207-832-4624), 17 Friendship St., Waldoboro Village. Open daily except Sunday. Billed as the oldest five-and-dime in the country (established 1927), this friendly establishment now offers an eclectic stock. "You never know what you will find here," says owner Sumner Richards, who serves deli-style sandwiches, soups, and specials at the old-style soda fountain (see *Eating Out*).

I'm Puzzled (207-563-5719), Nobleboro, marked from Rt. 1. Jigsaw puzzle buffs should follow the signs to Robert Havenstein's two-car garage, filled to overflowing with jigsaw puzzles, more than 850 different offerings ranging from $2 yard-sale rejects to antique wooden puzzles prized by collectors.

Reny's (207-563-3177; www.renys.com), Main St., Damariscotta. First opened in Damariscotta in 1949, family-owned Reny's has since become a small-town Maine institution with 14 stores from Wells to Ellsworth as well as many inland. Corporate headquarters are south of town. Main Street hosts two stores: the original sells quality clothing, and **Reny's Underground**, which sells everything from tea to TVs, bedding, china, toys; a wide assortment of canned and boxed foodstuffs at amazing savings; also a wide assortment of shoes, sandals, and boots; beach equipment and all manner of staples and things you didn't realize you needed. The antithesis of Walmart, Renys has been the subject of two Maine musicals. The biggest sales of the year here begin at 6 AM on the first Saturday of November.

✱ Special Events

February: **Annual ice-harvest** at the Thompson Ice House, South Bristol.

May–early June: **Return of the alewives** to Damariscotta Lake.

July: **Annual July 4 fireworks** in Damariscotta and Wiscasset and a famously unorthodox parade in Round Pond.

Early August: **Olde Bristol Days**, Old Fort Grounds, Pemaquid Beach—parade, fish fry, chicken barbecue, bands, bagpipers, concerts, pancake breakfast, road race, boat race, firemen's muster, crafts, and the annual Bristol Footlighters Show.

First Saturday in November. Early Bird Sale at Reny's and at stores throughout town. Free coffee, doughnuts and bargains. From 6 AM.

Columbus Day weekend: **Round Pond Roundabout**, sponsored by local crafts studios and art galleries (207-529-4411).

ROCKLAND/THOMASTON AREA

Long billed as the "Lobster Capital of the World," Rockland is now better known as home of the Farnsworth Museum, with its exceptional collection of Maine-based paintings, and for the galleries, shops, attractions, and restaurants lining its mile-long, floridly brick Main Street. Departure point for ferries to the islands of Vinalhaven, North Haven, and Matinicus, it is also home port for the majority of Maine's windjammers, as well as for several daysailers and excursion boats.

This city of nearly 8,000 has never, however, been a "tourist town" like Camden or Boothbay. Until recently odors from its harborside fish-rendering plant were famous. A popular jingle ran: "Camden by Sea, Rockland by Smell." SeaPro has since gone the way of the city's two sardine-packing and other fish-processing plants, and the huge harbor, protected by a nearly mile-long granite—and walkable—breakwater, is now sparkling clean and equipped to accommodate pleasure boats. Along the waterfront old industrial sheds have disappeared, replaced by office space. The harborside walking trail is lengthening. A former newspaper plant is now the chamber of commerce visitors center and Lighthouse Museum.

Still Rockland prides itself on its grit. The city's industrial base still includes FMC Bio-Polymer (processing carrageenan from seaweed) and homegrown Fisher Snowplow, and the harbor, Maine's second largest after Portland, remains home to 700 vessels, including a sizable fishing and lobstering fleet, tugs, and U.S. Coast Guard and commercial vessels.

Rockland has remade itself several times over the centuries. Initially known for its shipbuilding, the city became synonymous in the late 19th century with the limestone it quarried, burned, and shipped off to be made into plaster. When wallboard replaced plaster, Rockland quickly switched to catching and processing fish. Now with fishing on the decline, city entrepreneurs are once more widening their base.

A century ago summer people heading for Bar Harbor, as well as the islands, took the train as far as Rockland, switching here to steamboats. Today a similar summer crowd rides the bus to the ferry terminal or flies into Knox County Regional Airport on Owls Head, just south of town, transferring to rental cars, air taxis, or windjammers, to charter boats as well as ferries. The old train

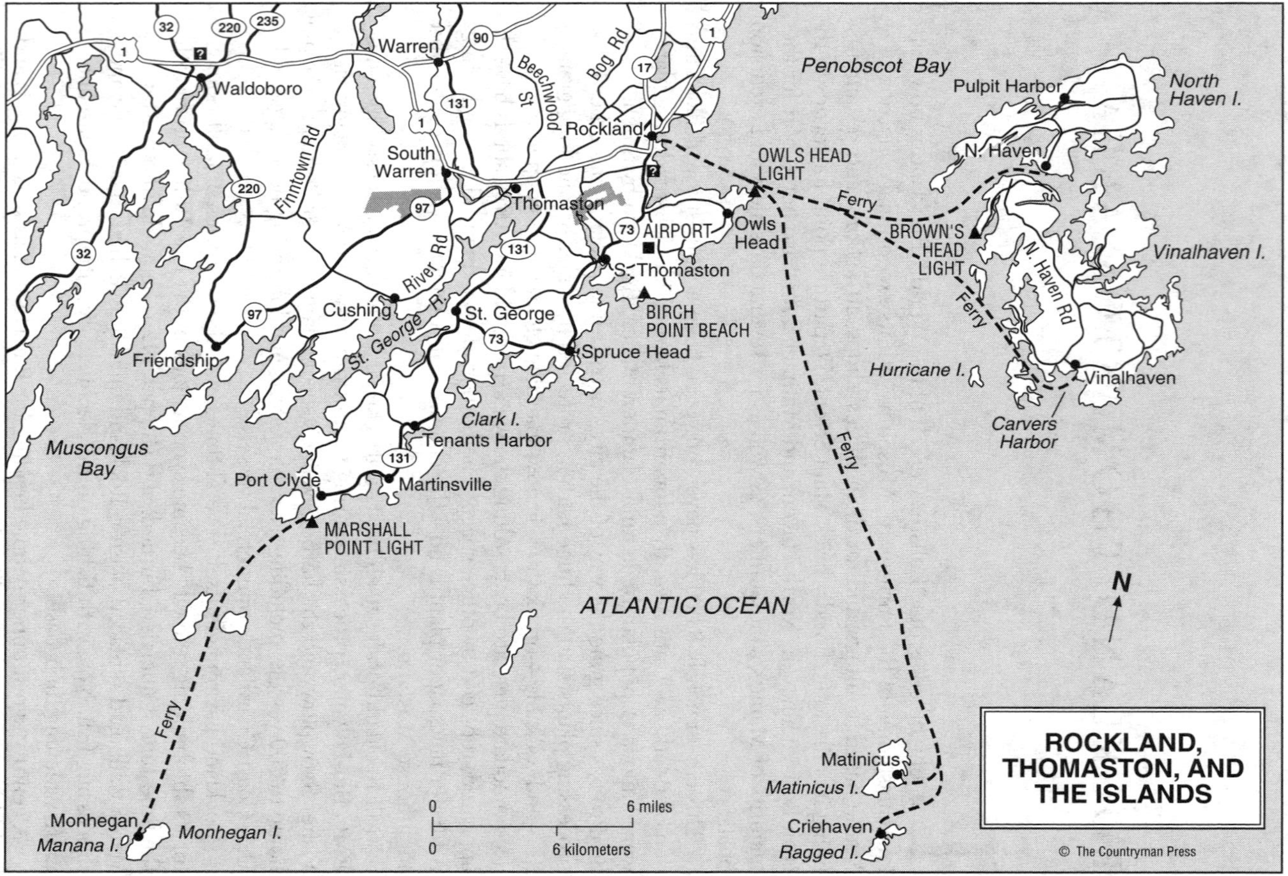
ROCKLAND, THOMASTON, AND THE ISLANDS
© The Countryman Press
Penobscot Bay
Muscongus Bay
ATLANTIC OCEAN
Waldoboro
Warren
South Warren
Thomaston
Rockland
Beechwood St
Bog Rd
Finntown Rd
River Rd
Cushing
St. George R.
St. George
Friendship
AIRPORT
Owls Head
OWLS HEAD LIGHT
S. Thomaston
BIRCH POINT BEACH
Spruce Head
Clark I.
Tenants Harbor
Martinsville
Port Clyde
MARSHALL POINT LIGHT
Monhegan
Manana I.
Monhegan I.
Ferry
Pulpit Harbor
North Haven I.
N. Haven
BROWN'S HEAD LIGHT
N. Haven Rd
Vinalhaven I.
Vinalhaven
Hurricane I.
Carvers Harbor
Matinicus
Matinicus I.
Criehaven
Ragged I.
N
0
6 miles
6 kilometers
1
32
220
235
90
17
131
97
73

terminal on Union St. is now a restaurant and terminus of the popular Eastern Maine excursion train from Brunswick (see *To Do*).

Southwest of Rockland, two peninsulas separate Muscongus Bay from Penobscot Bay. One is the fat arm of land on which the villages of Friendship and Cushing doze. The other is the skinnier St. George Peninsula with Port Clyde at its tip, the departure point for the year-round mail boat to Monhegan Island. The peninsulas are divided by the 10-mile-long St. George River, on which past residents of Thomaston launched their share of wooden ships.

GUIDANCE **Penobscot Bay Regional Chamber of Commerce** (207-596-0376 or 1-800-562-2529; www.therealmaine.com), 1 Park Dr., Rockland. Open daily Memorial Day–Labor Day, Mon.–Fri. 9–5 and Sat. 10–4; then weekdays and 10–2 Sat. through the Columbus Day weekend. The chamber's spacious **Maine Discovery Visitor Center** serves the entire Rockland area, which includes Owls Head, Thomaston, the peninsula villages, and the islands. It also lists cottage and vacation rentals.

GETTING THERE *By air:* **Knox County Regional Airport** (207-594-4131), at Owls Head, just south of Rockland. Daily service via **U.S. Airways Express** (operated by Colgan Air: 1-800-428-4322) to Boston, Bar Harbor, Augusta, and New York. Inquire about charter services to the islands. **Penobscot Island Air** (www.penobscotislandair.net) offers both scheduled and charter service to Vinalhaven, North Haven, and Maticinus. **Maine Atlantic Aviation** (1-800-780-6071; www.maineatlantic.com) offers charter service. Rental cars are available at the airport. Also see *By taxi* under *Getting Around*; all offer service to **Portland International Jetport** (see "Portland Area"). **Mid-Coast Limo** (1-800-937-2424; www.midcoastlimo.com) also serves Boston's Logan Airport.

NORTH HAVEN

Christina Tree

By bus: **Concord Trailways** (1-800-639-3317; www.concordtrailways.com) stops in Rockland at the Maine State Ferry Terminal.

By boat: **For moorings** contact the **harbormaster** (office: 207-594-0312; dock: 207-594-0314).

By train: **The Maine Eastern Railroad** (1-866-637-2457; www.maineeasternrailroad.com) offers seasonal Wed.–Sun. service from Brunswick (ample parking).

GETTING AROUND *By taxi:* **Schooner Bay Limo & Taxi** (207-594-5000), **Hit the Road Driver Service** (207-230-0095; cell, 207-691-0295), and **Joe's Taxi** (207-975-3560) will get you there. **All Aboard Trolley** (207-594-9300; www.aatrolley.com) offers seasonal daily, narrated, 10–3 service on a loop around Rockland.

By ferry: Frequent service from the **Maine State Ferry Service Terminal** (207-596-2022 or 1-800-491-4883) to Vinalhaven, North Haven, and, less frequently, to Matinicus (see "Midcoast Islands"). **Monhegan Boat Line** (207-372-8848) serves Monhegan from Port Clyde.

Note: Rockland can be accessed and thoroughly enjoyed without a car.

WHEN TO COME Rockland stages a series of festivals that draw weekend crowds from mid-July through September. The biggest is the Maine Lobster Festival, first weekend in August. The Farnsworth Museum, major galleries, restaurants, and lodging all remain open year-round.

✷ Villages and Islands

Friendship. Best known as the birthplace of the classic Friendship sloop, first built by local lobstermen to haul their traps (originals and reproductions of this sturdy vessel hold races here every summer), Friendship remains a quiet fishing village. The **Friendship Museum** (207-832-4826), housed in a former brick schoolhouse at the junction of Rt. 220 and Martin's Point Rd., is open Late June–Labor Day, also Sept. weekends, Mon.–Sat. 1–4 and Sun. 2–4. Displays feature Friendship sloops.

DOWNTOWN ROCKLAND

Christina Tree

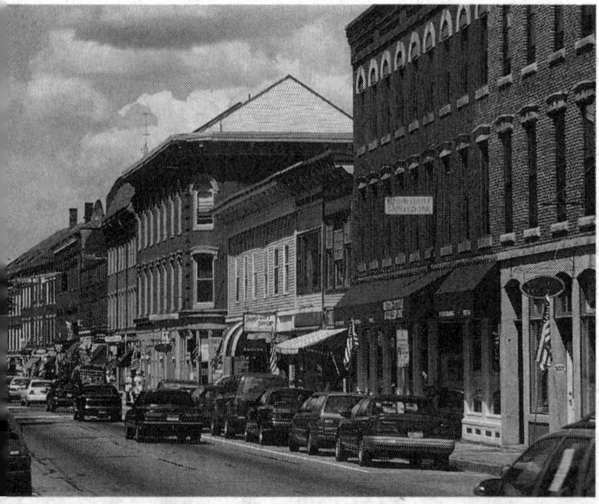

Tenants Harbor has a good little library and, beyond, rock cliffs, tidal pools, old cemeteries, and the kind of countryside described by Sarah Orne Jewett in *The Country of the Pointed Firs.* Jewett lived just a few bends down Rt. 131 in Martinville while she wrote the book.

Port Clyde marks the end of Rt. 131 and the tip of the St. George Peninsula. The departure point for the year-round ferries to Monhegan, it's tranquil and picturesque, with the exception of ferry departures and arrivals, when it's chaotic. Note the two B&Bs, good restaurant, and **The Marshall Point Light** around the bend.

amazingmaine.com

MARSHALL POINT LIGHT

Union is a short ride from the coast but surrounded by gentle hills and farm country (the **Union Fair** and the **State of Maine Wild Blueberry Festival** are big). This place is also a good spot to swim, eat, and explore the **Matthews Museum of Maine Heritage** at the fairgrounds (open daily July and Aug., noon–4).

Islands. An overnight or longer stay on an island is far preferable to a day trip. From Rockland you can take a Maine State (car) Ferry to **Vinalhaven** and **North Haven**. Together these form the Fox Islands, divided by a narrow passage. Vinalhaven is Maine's largest off-shore island with its largest year-round population and lobstering fleet. A number of shops, eating and lodging options cluster in the picturesque fishing village of Carver's Harbor. North Haven offers fewer and more seasonal places to eat, shop, and stay, but a more open landscape. **Matinicus**, also accessible from Rockland, is the most remote Maine island and quietly beautiful. Tiny **Monhegan**, accessible from Port Clyde, offers the most dramatic cliff scenery and the most hospitable welcome to visitors. For details, see the descriptions of each island in the next chapter.

✷ To See

MUSEUMS AND HISTORIC HOMES ✐ **General Henry Knox Museum (Montpelier)** (207-354-8062; www.knoxmuseum.org), High St., Thomaston. Open Memorial Day–Columbus Day, Tue.–Sat. 10–4. Admission $6 adults, $5 seniors, $3 ages 5–14 (family: $15). A 1926 re-creation of the grand mansion built (on another spot) in 1794 by General Henry Knox, the portly 5-foot-6-inch, 300-pound Boston bookseller who became a Revolutionary War hero, then our first secretary of war. He married a granddaughter of Samuel Waldo, the Boston developer who owned all of this area and for whom the county is named. The re-creation was financed by *Saturday Evening Post* publisher and Camden summer resident Cyrus Curtis.

OWL'S HEAD LIGHT

Christina Tree

Farnsworth Art Museum

WHARF SCENE BY GEORGE BELLOWS

Farnsworth Art Museum and Wyeth Center (207-596-6457; www.farnsworth museum.org), 16 Museum St., Rockland. Open year-round, Columbus Day–Memorial Day Tues.–Sun. 10–5; in summer daily 10–5, Wed. until 8. Admission to the museum and Farnsworth Homestead (see below) is $10 adults, $8 senior citizens, $8 students over 18; no charge under 18. This exceptional art museum was established by Lucy Farnsworth, who amazed everyone when, on her death at age 97 in 1935, she left $1.3 million to preserve her house and build a library and art gallery to honor the memory of her father. From the beginning the collection included paintings of Maine by Winslow Homer, George Bellows, and a (then) little-known local summer resident, Andrew Wyeth.

The museum's collection now numbers over 9,000 objects housed in five buildings and remains Maine-focused. A permanent exhibit, *Maine in America: Two Hundred Years of American Art,* traces the evolution of Maine landscape paintings. There are also Hudson River School artists like Thomas Cole, and 19th-century marine artist Fitz Henry Lane; American impressionists Frank Benson, Willard Metcalf, Childe Hassam, and Maurice Prendergast; early-20th-century greats like Rockwell Kent and Charles Woodbury; and such "modernists" as John Marin and Marsden Hartley. Rockland-raised painter and sculptor Louise Nevelson is also well represented. The Farnsworth's original Georgian Revival library houses changing exhibits of reference materials and is the site for regularly scheduled lectures and concerts. **The Jamien Morehouse Wing** has added four galleries of exhibition space on Main Street. Gardens connect the main museum with the **Wyeth Center**, a two-story exhibit space in a former church, displaying works by N. C. Wyeth (1882–1945) and Jamie Wyeth (born 1946). Exhibits vary. Andrew Wyeth's paintings are shown in the main museum.

Farnsworth Homestead (207-596-6457), Elm St., Rockland. Open Memorial Day–Columbus Day and weekends in December, when it's decorated for Christmas. Built in 1850 by Miss Lucy's father, a tycoon with revenues from the lime industry and a fleet of ships, filled with its original Victorian furnishings, it remains—according to a stipulation in Miss Lucy's will—just as it was when she died at the age of 97. Walls are hung with inexpensive copies of oil paintings known as chromolithographs, a fireplace mantel is glass painted to resemble marble, and doors are not made of fine wood grains but, rather, have been painted to imitate them.

The Olson House (207-596-6457), Hawthorn Point Rd., Cushing. Open Memorial Day–Columbus Day, daily 11–4. $4 over age 18; free under. Administered by the Farnsworth Art Museum, this house served as a backdrop for many works by Andrew Wyeth, including *Christina's World.* It's been intentionally left unrestored except for interpretive materials. On Pleasant Point, accessed by quiet back roads, this saltwater farm makes a good bicycle destination. Built in the late 1700s, it was remodeled in 1872 but remained in the same family, ultimately passing to Alvara and Christina (1892–1968) Olson. It has been owned by the Farnsworth since 1991. The house, both inside and out, evokes the familiar painting.

THE OLSON HOUSE

Farnsworth Art Museum

Owls Head Transportation Museum (207-594-4418; www.owlshead.org), adjacent to the Knox County Regional Airport off Rt. 73, Owls Head (2 miles south of Rockland). Open daily year-round except Christmas, Thanksgiving, New Year's Day. Apr.–Nov. 10–5, Dec.–Mar. 10–4. $8 adults, $7 seniors, $5 under 17, under 5 free, $20 for families (a couple dollars more on special-event days such as antique air shows, or antique car and motorcycle auctions). One of the country's outstanding collections of antique planes and automobiles, and everything works. In the exhibition hall you can take a 100-year journey through the evolution of transportation, from horse-drawn carriages to World War I fighter planes; from a 16-cylinder Cadillac to a Rolls-Royce; from the Red Baron's Fokker triplane to a Ford trimotor. Exhibits are constantly changing and evolving. If you haven't been here in a few years, you are in for a pleasant surprise. On weekends there are special demonstrations of such magnificent machines as a 1901 Oldsmobile and visitors can take a ride in Model-T Fords.

Project Puffin Visitor Center (207-596-5566; www.projectpuffin.org), 311 Main St., Rockland. Open daily June 15–Oct. 10–5, until 7:30 Wed. Call for off-season hours. Free. Live-streaming minicams and audio provide a virtual visit with nesting puffins on Machias Seal Island. A joint project of National Audubon and Maine Audubon, this is a must-stop, with exhibits cleverly designed for children, like the "burrow" into which they can crawl and observe puffins feeding their chicks in a similar burrow. Exhibits include a video chronicling the 33-year effort to restore these seabirds to the Maine Coast.

Maine Lighthouse Museum (207-594-3301; www.mainelighthousemuseum.com), Maine Discovery Center, 1 Park Dr., Rockland. Open daily Memorial Day–Labor Day, Mon.–Fri. 9–5; Sat. and Sun. 10–4; then weekdays and 10–2 Sat. through Columbus Day. Nominal entrance fee. Billed as the country's largest exhibit of lighthouse lenses and lifesaving artifacts, the display showcases more than a dozen Fresnel lenses. Working foghorns, flashing lights, search-and-rescue gear, buoys, bells, rescue boats, and half models round out rotating exhibits.

More Lighthouses Maine has 65 lighthouses, and Penobscot Bay boasts the largest concentration. Three in the Rockland area are accessible by land. **Rockland Breakwater Light** (207-785-4609; www.rocklandlighthouse.com), pictured on the cover of this book, is a pleasant walk out along the almost mile-long granite breakwater (turn off Rt. 1 onto Waldo Ave. just north of Rockland, then right onto Samoset Rd., follow to the end). **Owls Head Light**, built in 1825 atop sheer cliffs, nonetheless has safe trails down one side to the rocks below—good for scrambling and picnicking. From Rockland or the Owls Head Transportation Museum, take Rt. 73 to North Shore Dr. After about 2 miles you come to a small post office at an intersection. Turn left onto Main St. and after 0.25 mile make a left onto Lighthouse Dr. Just north of the village of Port Clyde (turn off Rt. 131 onto Marshall Point Rd.) is the **Marshall Point Lighthouse Museum** (207-372-6450; www.marshallpoint.org), open Memorial Day–Columbus Day, Sun.–Fri. 1–5 and Sat. 10–5. Built in 1885, deactivated in 1971, this is a small light on a scenic point; part of the former lighthouse keeper's home is now a lively museum dedicated to the history of the town of St. George in general and the light station (established in 1832) in particular. Even if the lighthouse isn't open, this is a great spot to sit, walk, and picnic.

Island Institute (207-594-9209; www.islandinstitute.org), 386 Main St., Rockland. A nonprofit organization focusing on the human dimension of Maine's 15 surviving year-round island communities (a century ago there were 300). The idea initially was to get residents of different islands talking to each other. The monthly *Working Waterfront* newspaper, as well as the glossy *Island Journal,* focus on shared concerns ranging from fisheries to schools to mapping. Changing exhibits.

✷ To Do

BICYCLING **Bikesenjava** (207-596-1004; www.haybikesenjava.com), 481 Main St., Rockland, now sited conveniently near the ferry terminal, is a source of rental hybrid and mountain bikes, as well as tag-a-longs, and 21-speed kid's mountain bikes, car racks, coffees, and chai.

Georges River Bikeways is the name of a free map and guide that traces routes along the river and in its watershed area from Thomaston north into Liberty. Check with the **Georges River Land Trust** (207-594-5166), 328 Main St., Rockland.

Note: Both Vinalhaven and North Haven are popular biking destinations. Please ride single file. Roads are narrow.

BOAT EXCURSIONS Check with the chamber of commerce for a complete list of current excursions. Also see the Maine State Ferry Service under *Getting Around.* The ferry rides to both North Haven and Vinalhaven are reasonably priced and a good way to get out on the water. Both islands make good day trips, but Monhegan is far more walkable; Monhegan Boat Line (207-372-8848; www.monheganboat.com) in Port Clyde offers a variety of cruises as well as regular service. See the "Midcoast Islands" chapter.

Daysails and longer

***Summertime* Cruises** (1-800-562-8290; www.schoonersummertime.com), 115 South St., Rockland, offers three- and six-day cruises on a 53-foot pinky schooner for up to six passengers throughout the summer. In spring and autumn Capt. Bill Brown offers daysails.

A Morning in Maine (207-691-7245; www.amorninginmaine.com), Rockland City Pier. A classic coastal ketch with an overall length of 55 feet, captained by marine biologist Bob Pratt, offers sails ranging from a few hours to overnights for up to 21 people.

Bugeye Schooner *Jenny Norman* (207-542-3695; www.sailmainebugeye.com). Captains Mike and Julie Rogers have restored this classic 49-foot Chesapeake Bay vessel and offer daysails May–Oct. from Rockland. Inquire about sunset music and massage cruises.

BOAT RENTALS **Midcoast Yacht Sales and Rentals** (207-882-6445), Rockland,

WINDJAMMERS

Note: Most of these vessels are members of the **Maine Windjammer Association** (1-800-807-WIND; www.sailmainecoast.com). Also see Windjammers in "What's Where" and "Camden/Rockport Area." In three days aboard a windjammer you can explore islands and remote mainland harbors that would take hundreds of miles of driving and several ferries to reach. Three- and six-day cruises are offered late May–mid-Oct. and run $400–950. All the vessels are inspected and certified each year by the Coast Guard.

American Eagle (207-594-8007 or 1-800-648-4544; www.schooner americaneagle.com), North End Shipyard, Rockland. One of the last classic Gloucester fishing schooners to be launched (in 1930), this 92-foot vessel continued to fish (minus her original stern and masts, plus a pilothouse) off Gloucester until 1983, when Capt. John Foss brought her to Rockland's North End Shipyard and spent the next two years restoring and refitting her. The *Eagle* was built with an engine (so she still has one) as well as sails, and she offers some comfortable below-decks spaces. The *Eagle* sails farther out to sea (to see whales and seabirds) than other windjammers and also offers an 11-day July cruise to New Brunswick and a Labor Day sail to Gloucester (Massachusetts) to participate in a race. Most cruises are three- to 11-days, accommodating 26 guests in 14 double cabins.

Heritage (207-594-8007 or 1-800-648-4544; www.schoonerheritage.com), North End Shipyard, Rockland. Capt. Doug Lee likes to describe his graceful, 95-foot, 30-passenger vessel as "the next generation of coasting schooner rather than a replica." He notes that schooners were modified over the years to suit whatever cargo they carried. Here headroom in the cabins and the top of the companionways was raised to accommodate upright cargo, and the main cabin is an unusually airy, bright space in which to gather. Lee

SCHOONER *AMERICAN EAGLE*

Greg Cranna

Maine Windjammer Association

WINDJAMMER *NATHANIEL BOWDITCH*

is a marine historian who, with his wife and co-captain, Linda, designed and built the *Heritage* in Rockland's North End Shipyard. Their two daughters, Clara and Rachel, have always summered aboard ship and now sometimes sail as crew. Both captains are unusually warm hosts.

Stephen Taber (207-594-4723 or 1-800-999-7352; www.stephentaber.com) was launched in 1871 and is the oldest documented U.S. sailing vessel in continuous use. She is 68 feet long and accommodates 22 passengers; cabins have windows; two are singles, four have full-sized double beds and six have twins; all have sink with running water. Heads and showers are on deck. Capt. Noah Barnes is the first second-generation windjammer captain, taking over the helm from his parents (both licensed captains), who restored the vessel and sailed it for 25 years. The *Taber* continues to have an enthusiastic following, known for its exceptional food, also for wine-tasting and other special-interest cruises.

Victory Chimes (207-594-0755 or 1-800-745-5651; www.victorychimes.com). "There was nothing special about this boat in 1900 when she was built," Capt. Kip Files is fond of telling his passengers at their first breakfast aboard. "But now she's the only three-masted American-built schooner left. And she's the largest commercial sailing vessel in the United States." The *Chimes* is 132 feet long, accommodating 40 passengers in a variety of cabins (four singles, two quads, one triple, 12 doubles).

Nathaniel Bowditch (207-236-7032 or 1-800-288-4098; www.windjammervacation.com) was built in East Boothbay as a racing yacht in 1922. Eighty-two feet long, she took special honors in the 1923 Bermuda Race and served in the Coast Guard during World War II. She has since been rebuilt. Capt. Owen Dorr's great-grandfather was mate aboard one of the last five-masted schooners to sail the East Coast and in the 1940s Owen's parents worked for Capt. Frank Swift, creator of the Maine windjammer tradition.

Capt. Owen and Cathie Dorr met aboard a Maine schooner (she was a passenger, he, a crew member). The *Bowditch* accommodates 24 passengers in 11 double-bunked cabins and two single "Pullmans"; in-cabin sinks.

Isaac H. Evans (207-594-7956 or 1-877-238-1325; www.isaacevans.com). A trim 22-passenger schooner dating (in part) to 1886, built for oystering in Delaware Bay, now back in service with owner-captain Brenda G. Walker. There are 11 double berths, some side-by-side, some upper–lower bunks. Three- and four-day and weeklong cruises are offered. Specializes in family trips; children 6 and over welcome on all cruises.

J&E Riggin (207-594-1875 or 1-800-869-0604; www.mainewindjammer.com) was built in 1927 for the oyster-dredging trade. A speedy 90-footer, she was extensively rebuilt in the 1970s before joining the windjammer trade. Capts. Jon Finger and Anne Mahle take 24 passengers in nine double and two triple cabins. Mahle is an outstanding chef, author of the cookbook, *At Home, At Sea*. The *J&E Riggin* welcomes families with children ages 6 and up on special family cruises.

rents powerboats. **Bay Island, Inc.** (207-596-7550 or 1-800-421-2492; www.sailme.com), 117A Tilson Ave., Rockland, rents sailboats and motorboats. **Johanson Boatworks** (207-596-7060 or 1-877-456-4267), 11 Farwell Dr., Rockland, offers sailboat charters.

SEA KAYAKING **Breakwater Kayak** (207-596-6895; www.breakwaterkayak.com), behind Landings Restaurant (see *Eating Out*) on Commercial St., Rockland. Two-hour to multiday guided kayaking tours.

Port Clyde Kayaks (207-372-8128; www.portclydekayaks.com), 6 Cold Storage Rd., Port Clyde. Guided tours take you across Port Clyde Harbor to Marshall Point Light and beyond.

FISHING, HUNTING, AND CANOEING **The Penobscot Bay Chamber of Commerce** (see *Guidance*) offers information on fishing (both salt and fresh water) and registered duck-hunting guides.

Maine Outdoors (207-785-4496; www.maineoutdoors.biz), 69 Beote Rd., Union, offers fishing and other paddling adventures.

GOLF **Rockland Golf Club** (207-594-9322; www.rocklandgolf.com), 606 Old County Rd., Rockland. Open Apr.–Oct. This 18-hole public course gets high marks from pros; complete with a modern clubhouse serving meals from 7 AM.

For the local resort that specializes in golf, see **Samoset Golf Course** in "Camden/Rockport Area."

RAILROAD EXCURSION ✐ **The Maine Eastern Railroad** (1-866-636-2457; www.maineeasternrailroad.com) offers 54-mile seasonal runs between Rockland

and Brunswick, stopping in Bath and Wiscasset. It's a beautiful trip along the coast in plush 1940s and '50s coaches and a dining car pulled by a 1950s diesel electric engine.

SPECIAL LEARNING PROGRAM **Hurricane Island Outward Bound School** (207-594-5548, 845-424-4000; www.outwardbound.org). Outward Bound challenges participants to do things they never thought they could—and then push themselves just a little farther. May–Oct. courses are offered in sailing, sea kayaking, and rock climbing in Wheeler Bay and Hurricane Island (near Vinalhaven).

✷ Green Space

BEACHES ✐ **Johnson Memorial Park**, Chickawaukee Lake, Rt. 17, 2 miles north of downtown Rockland. Restrooms, picnic area, a sand beach, and warm water add up to the area's best swimming, good for small children.

✐ **Birch Point Beach State Park**, also known as Lucia Beach, off Ash Point Rd. in Owls Head. Sandy, with smooth boulders for sunning, wooded walking trails, and picnic benches. Marked from Rt. 73.

Drift Inn Beach in Port Clyde, down Drift Inn Rd. by the Harpoon Restaurant, just off Rt. 131; a small beach in a great spot.

WALKING/PICNICKING **Rockland waterfront**. The area's most spectacular stretch of the **Rockland Harbor Trail** begins on the Samoset Hotel property just over the Rockport line and runs 1.7 miles out along the Rockland Breakwater to the lighthouse. There's always plenty of boat traffic. Another rewarding section of the trail runs from Harbor Park at the public landing south along the water past **Sandy Beach Park** (picnic benches) to Mechanic St. and on to **Snow Marine Park**. Along Park Dr. **Gilbert and Adams Central Park** offers benches, flowers, a gazebo, and harbor views.

Owls Head Light State Park. This classic lighthouse is set into a beautiful point with walks and views on both the bay and harbor sides, picnic tables. See *Lighthouses* for directions.

Waldo Tyler Wildlife Sanctuary, Buttermilk Ln. (off Rt. 73), South Thomaston, is a birding spot on the Weskeag River.

✐ A Rt. 1 picnic area overlooks Glen Cove, between Rockland and Rockport.

The Georges River Land Trust (207-594-5166), 328 Main St., Studio 206, Rockland, publishes a map/guide to the Georges Highland Path, a foot trail through the hills of the Georges River watershed. Maps are available at the chamber of commerce.

FOXBORO THOROUGHFAIR

Christina Tree

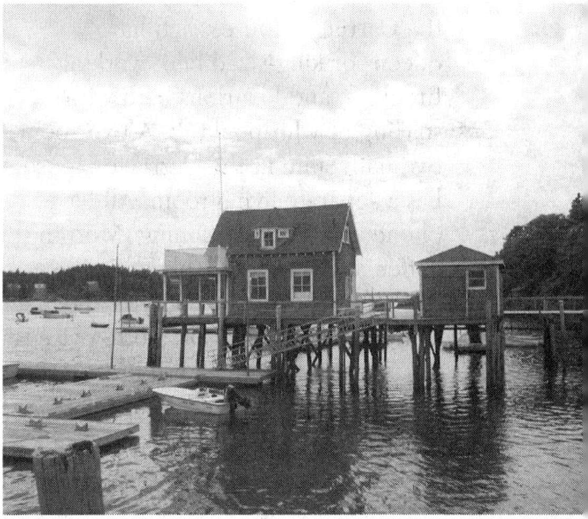

✱ Lodging

INNS AND BED & BREAKFASTS

In Rockland 04841

♿ "ı" **The Captain Lindsey House** (207-596-7950 or 1-800-523-2145; www.lindseyhouse.com), 5 Lindsey St. Built in 1837 as one of Rockland's first inns, the current feel is that of a small, boutique hotel. With richly paneled public rooms and nine spacious guest rooms (one handicapped accessible), it's a gem, and the most convenient lodging to the Farnsworth Museum and Main Street shops. It's the creation of schooner captains Ken and Ellen Barnes, who also restored and operated the windjammer *Stephen Taber* for more than 25 years. Each guest room is different, but all have air-conditioning, phone, TV, and private bath. $156–211, from $99–156 off-season, including a full buffet breakfast, served in the garden, weather permitting.

"ı" **Berry Manor Inn** (207-596-7696 or 1-800-774-5692; www.berrymanor inn.com), 81 Talbot Ave., P.O. Box 1117. This expansive 19th-century shingle-style mansion is a sumptuous retreat. The 12 guest rooms, divided among the second and third floors of the mansion and the second floor of the Carriage House, each have queen- or king-sized bed, working fireplace, and luxurious bath with soaking or whirlpool tub. A two-room, two-bath suite in the Carriage House has a separate living room. All have phone and air-conditioning. Morning coffee and juice available at 7 AM. $155–255 for rooms, $360 for the suite mid-June–mid-Oct., otherwise $115–240, including a full breakfast and Mom's homemade pies.

"ı" **LimeRock Inn** (207-594-2257 or 1-800-LIME-ROC; www.limerock inn.com), 96 Limerock St. P. J. Walter and Frank Isganites are the innkeepers of this 1890s Queen Anne–style mansion on a quiet residential street with a wraparound front porch and two living rooms to relax in. The eight guest rooms, all with private bath, are opulently furnished with antiques. The turret room is over the top. Amenities include a 24-hour guest pantry and computer. $130–225 ($110–255 off-season) includes a full breakfast.

"ı" 🐾 ♿ **Old Granite Inn** (207-594-9036 or 1-800-386-9036; www.old graniteinn.com), 546 Main St. An 1840s mansion built of local granite, attached to a 1790 house, set in a flower a garden, across from the Maine State Ferry Terminal (also the Concord Trailways stop). Ideal if you come without a car and are bound for an island, but innkeepers Edwin and Joan Hantz have added plenty of other reasons to stay here. There's a sparely comfortable feel to the living room, and dining room (or common spaces). Eight guest rooms (seven with private bath) are furnished with a blend of antiques and contemporary furniture. The four ground-floor rooms are all wheelchair accessible. Second-floor rooms include a two-room suite; the two with harbor views are the largest and most expensive. One small back room is reserved for people who miss the ferry. $100–185 per night in high season, less off-season, includes a full breakfast.

✎ "ı" **Ripples Inn at the Harbor** (207-594-2771; www.ripplesinnatthe harbor.com) 16 Pleasant St. Open year-round. Sandi Dillon has restored this pleasant house with imagination and skill. Rooms are not overly fussy but nicely decorated with an eye to comfort. There are four rooms and a family suite (accommodating four) with a whirlpool tub and private entrance. In addition to the usual common spaces an "UN-common room" has a microwave, fridge, and TV. $150–180 with full breakfast.

Lakeshore Inn (207-594-4209 or 1-866-540-8800; www.lakeshorebb com), 184 Lakeview Dr. (Rt. 17). A much-modified 1767 home set above Rt. 17, overlooking Lake Chickawaukee (good swimming), 2 miles north of downtown Rockland. Californians Jim and Susan Rodiger (and their two corgis, Ben and Frisco) offer four air-conditioned rooms with private bath, phone, and data ports. Amenities include an enclosed outdoor hot tub. Two-night minimum. Breakfast is full. $145–155 double in-season. Inquire about spa weekends.

On Spruce Head and on the St. George Peninsula

Craignair Inn (207-594-7644 or 1-800-320-9997; www.craignair.com), Clark Island Rd., Spruce Head 04859. Open Apr.–Dec. Steve and Neva Joseph breathed new life into this old inn. Sited on four shorefront acres, it offers 20 guest rooms, divided between the main house (six with private bath; six share five baths) and those with less of a view but private bath in the Vestry, a former chapel set in gardens in the rear. We like Room 8 with its view of water and Clark Island. The dining room overlooks the water and is open to the public for dinner. Walk across the causeway to the Clark Island shoreline. $60–140 per couple, depending on season, including breakfast. Two-night minimum stay on holiday weekends. $10 extra for a pet.

Ocean House (207-372-6691 or 1-800-269-6691; www.oceanhouse hotel.com), P.O. Box 66, Port Clyde 04855. Open May–Oct. This friendly old village inn is the logical place to spend the night before or after boarding the ferry to Monhegan. Former islander Bud Murdock offers 10 pleasant upstairs guest rooms (eight with private bath; two share), and several have water views This is a good place for a single traveler, thanks to the single rates and the ease of meeting fellow guests. Rooms are $110 (shared bath), $125 double with private bath, and $145 for a room with two double beds, less solo. The adjacent cottage is available weekly.

East Wind Inn (207-372-6366 or 1-800-241-8439; www.eastwindinn .com), Mechanic St., P.O. Box 149, Tenants Harbor 04860. Open Apr.–Nov. Longtime innkeeper Tim Watts offers a total of 22 guest rooms divided between the three-story inn itself and the waterside Meeting House. They vary from singles with shared baths ($109) and standard double with private bath ($179) to suites ($201) and apartments in the Meeting House ($221). All rates include a full breakfast. This rather formal waterside inn has a large parlor with a piano, but the best seats in the house are on the wraparound porch overlooking Tenants Harbor. Dinner is open to the public (see *Dining Out*). A number of guests sail in. **The Chandlery** on the wharf offers light food as well as marine supplies and gifts.

Seaside Inn Bed and Breakfast (207-372-0700 or 1-800-279-5041; www.seasideportclyde.com), 5 Cold Storage Rd., PO Box 215, Port Clyde 04855. Maggie Evans is the new innkeeper here, offering eight rooms (six with private bath), steps from the Monhegan Boat Line. There's a fireplace, TV, and VCR in the library and a cheery breakfast room, scene of bountiful breakfasts unless you are catching the 7 AM ferry, in which you still get continental. $109–149.

Weskeag Inn (207-596-6676 or 1-800-596-5576; www.weskeag.com), Rt. 73, P.O. Box 213, South Thomaston 04858. Open year-round. Handy to the Owls Head Transportation Museum and to Knox County Regional Airport (pickups provided, perhaps in an antique car). A hospitable 1830s home overlooking the Weskeag estuary, near a public boat landing. Six attractive guest rooms have private bath; two share or are rented as a suite. Request a water view. The lawn slopes to the tidal Weskeag River. $120–150 in-season, $85–95 off-season with full breakfast.

Blue Lupin Bed & Breakfast (207-594-2673), 372 Waterman Beach Rd., South Thomaston 04858. In her delightfully old-fashioned home with its many books, Helen Mitchell offers three rooms and one suite, all with private bath, overlooking the Atlantic. Handy to the Waterman's Beach Lobsters (see *Lobster Pounds*) and to the beach at Birch Point State Park. All rooms have TV/VCR, and the library is well stocked with videos. $75–160 includes a full breakfast. Children 12 and older welcome.

In Friendship 04547

Harbor Hill B&B (207-832-6646), P.O. Box 35, 5 Harbor Hill Lane. Open May–Nov. 1, also winter weekends by arrangement. Liga and Len (Chip) Jahnke's 1800s farmhouse is set on a hillside sloping to the sea, with stunning views of the islands in Muscongus Bay. The large downstairs front suite is a beauty, furnished in antiques and overlooking the harbor. All three suites have water views and private bath. Rates of $100–115 include a three-course Scandinavian-style breakfast. A two-bedroom cottage is $625 per week or $145 daily (two-night minimum stay). Children welcome. Pets can stay in the cottage.

Outsiders' Inn (207-832-5197), corner of Rts. 97 and 220, 4 Main St. Open in summer months and by reservation off-season. Bill and Debbie Michaud have created a casually comfortable atmosphere in an 1830 house. Many guests take advantage of Bill's kayaking expertise; sea kayaks are available for rent and for guided expeditions in nearby Muscongus Bay. Pleasant doubles with private bath are $85; $65 with shared bath, $5 less for singles, breakfast included. A small cottage in the garden is $385 per week. Facilities include a sauna.

MOTEL **Navigator Motor Inn** (207-594-2131 or 1-800-545-8025; www.navigatorinn.com), 520 Main St., Rockland 04841. Open all year with 81 rooms and suites. Geared to families bound for the islands. The Maine State Ferry Terminal is across the street, so you can park your car in line for the early-morning ferry and walk back to your room. This is a five-story, 80-room motor inn with cable TV and a restaurant that serves from 6:30 AM. $59–169.

COTTAGES AND EFFICIENCIES A list of cottages, primarily in the Owls Head and Spruce Head areas, is available from the **Penobscot Bay Regional Chamber of Commerce** (see *Guidance*).

✱ Where to Eat

DINING OUT **Primo** (207-596-0770; www.primorestaurant.com), 2 S. Main St. (Rt. 73), Rockland. Open daily in summer, otherwise Wed.–Mon., 5:30–9:30 or less; call first. Reservations are a must at this very special restaurant, one that grows much of what it serves. "Primo" was chef and co-owner Melissa Kelly's grandfather and a butcher. Kelly raises her own pork and makes several kinds of sausages as well as preparing cuts of meats and overseeing the gardens and greenhouses on the property. Some water-view tables, but most patrons have their eyes on their plates, which perhaps hold pan-seared scallops with local turnip, and wild mushrooms tossed with cress, Jerusalem artichokes, and a truffle. Appetizers might include roast Pemaquid oyster with deviled crab and a salad gathered outside the kitchen door. You might also dine on a great flatbread pizza with tomato and house-made sausage. The house cannoli are crisp, rich, and excellent. A big wine list, and good mojitos and other special drinks. The menu is also available in the bar. Entrées $23–32.

Amalfi on the Water (207-596-0012; www.amalfionthewater.com), 12 Water St., Rockland. Open daily year-round (except Mon.) for dinner. Chef David Cooke's downtown restaurant, larger than it looks from the street, deserves rave reviews for specialties drawn from all sides of the Mediterranean. You might want to begin with mussels steamed with garlic, shallots, and white wine, or calamari fritte. Paella is the specialty, in the traditional mix of seafood, chorizo, and chicken, but also in all-seafood and vegetarian versions. Entrées $17–21.

Café Miranda (207-594-2034; www.cafemiranda.com), 15 Oak St., Rockland. Open year-round 5:30–9:30 and Sunday brunch, also lunch daily in summer. Reserve for dinner. In 1993 Kerry Altiero was the first chef in Rockland to offer the hip kind of dining for which the city has since become known. His small restaurant has, however, neither expanded (unless you count seasonal café tables) nor moved from its side street. Single diners sit up at the counter watching an amazing variety of food emerge from the brick oven (fueled by logs from Altiero's farm). The menu lists 89 items, half of them entrées and the other half lighter, eclectic fare to mix and match. On our last visit we began with a delectable kale dish roasted with mushrooms, garlic, and feta, followed by mussels roasted with curry. Entrées $11–22.50.

Rustica (207-594-0015), 315 Main St. Open Mon.–Sat. 11–3 and 5–10, Sun. 11–8; Tues.–Sat. off-season. High quality at reasonable prices, a pleasant atmosphere, and decent wine are a winning combination for this "cucina Italiana." Chef-owner John Stowe serves up a hearty soups and perhaps deep-fried risotto stuffed with proscuitto and fresh mozzarella; pizza too. Dinner might be veal marsala or any number of pastas. Entrées $13–19.

Suzuki's Sushi Bar (207-596-7447; www.suzukisushi.com), 419 Main St. Open Tues.–Sat. for dinner. Where better to sample the full variety this ocean's yield than a sophisticated Japanese restaurant? The large menu includes raw nigiri dishes and spicy sushi rolls, entrées such as shrimp with skitake, wakame, and scallions in a kelp dashi borth, and many delectable salads and vegetarian dishes. Entrées $10–30.

Spruce Head to Tenants Harbor

Sul Mare (207-372-9995), 13 River Rd., Tenants Harbor. Open year-round 5–10 PM daily. Chef-owner Kevin Kieley—"100 percent Irish but I went to school in Italy" presides in a stuccoed and tile-roofed-style trattoria. He's known for grilled steaks and seafood. You might begin with wood-grilled Italian sausage with white beans and roasted pepper ($8) and dine on steamed mussels over linguini ($16) or sautéed sea scallops with fresh basil, tomato, and pignole over linguini ($25). The lobstermen who come here prefer to eat prime rib and drink Budweiser, Kieley says, but he has good Italian wine for the rest of us. Entrées $10–25.

Craignair Inn (207-594-7644), Clark Island Rd., off Rt. 73, Spruce Head. Walk the shore before dining by a water-view window. Begin with the house crabcakes, serve crispy with Dijon remoulade on mixed greens. The entrée specialty is baked haddock stuffed with fresh seafood and served with rice. The house salad ($4.50) is extra. Entrées $18–26.

East Wind Inn (207-372-6366; www.eastwindinn.com), Tenants Harbor. Open for dinner daily Apr.–Nov. Reservations suggested. A formal dining room overlooking the working harbor with a porch on which cocktails are served in summer. Featuring local seafood and produce, dinners might include roast Atlantic salmon pan seared and drizzled with a lemon buerre blanc and fried capers ($19.95) or filet mignon, char-grilled with a blueberry demi-glace on the side ($23.95).

EATING OUT

In Rockland

Atlantic Baking Co. (207-596-0505), 351 Main St. Open Mon.–Sat. 1–6, Sun. 8–4; Tues.–Sat. in winter. Sited near the Farnsworth Museum this busy place seduces passersby with the aroma of fresh-baked bread. There's a blackboard sandwich menu and plenty of help-yourself salads and such in deli cases. The plastic and Styrofoam, however, are seemingly at odds with the from-scratch, PC ethos of the place.

Sunfire Mexican Grill (207-594-6196), 488 Main St. Open for lunch Tues.–Sat. 11–3, for dinner Thurs. and Sat. 5–8. This is exceptional Mexican fare, all the basics but with very fresh veggies (try the mango avocado salad) and just the right taste.

✐ **Rockland Café** (207-596-7556; www.rocklandcafe.com), 441 Main St. Open daily 6 AM–9 PM. This is a reliable family eatery, good for fish-and-chips, soups, salad, clam rolls, and daily specials. Warning: The crabcakes are more like crab pancakes. Look for the green-and-white-striped awning.

The Brown Bag (207-596-6372), 606 Main St. (north of downtown). Open Mon.–Sat. 6:30 AM–4 PM. This expanded storefront restaurant is a local favorite, with an extensive breakfast and sandwich menu, soups, chowders, and daily specials. Make your selection at the counter and carry it to your table when it's ready.

✐ **The Landings Restaurant & Marina** (207-596-6563), 1 Commercial St. Open year-round. On the harbor with outside as well as inside seating; serves 11:30–9 from a menu that ranges from a hot dog to steak, lobster, and a full-scale clambake.

Fried clams, fish-and-chips, and a good selection of sandwiches.

✐ **Union Station Grille** (207-594-7745), 4 Union St. Open daily for lunch and dinner. "A lot of people don't know we're here" observes chef Milli Salo, about the vintage railroad station, rehabbed and decorated with blow-up photos from Rockland's past. It's a big menu and we lunched happily on the salad bar.

The Brass Compass Café (207-596-5960), 305 Main St. Open daily for breakfast and lunch. No surprises, just generous portions, good food at reasonable prices, beer and wine.

✐ **Wasses Wagon,** 2 N. Main St. A local institution for hot dogs.

In Thomaston

Harbor View Restaurant (207-354-8173), Thomas Harbor Point. Basically open year-round. This harborside standby is good for daily soups, sandwiches, and salads at lunch. At dinner, seafood—baked, broiled, and fried—is the specialty. Dinner entrées range $11–26, but burgers are always available. Nightly specials. Full license. In-season there's dining on the deck.

Thomaston Café and Bakery (207-354-8589; www.thomastoncafe.com), 154 Main St., Thomaston. Open year-round Mon.–Sat. 7–2, Sun. brunch 8:30–1:30. Chef-owner Herbert and Eleanor Peters have won many awards and acquired a strong following. Lunch on fresh-made soups, great sandwiches, specials like fish cakes with home fries, salads. The dinner menu ranges from wild mushroom hash to fresh fettuccine with brandied lobster meat. Wine and beer are served. Dinner entrées $13–22.

In the Port Clyde area

The Dip Net Restaurant (207-372-6307), at the end of Rt. 131. Open seasonally 11–9. Seating inside is very limited, but on a pleasant evening this is a great spot for steamed clams and mussels, served at a waterside table right on the dock. The bouillabaisse ($20) gets raves. Soups, salads, sandwiches, a raw bar, mahogany clams

LOBSTER POUNDS

Miller's Lobster Company (207-594-7406; www.millerslobster.com), Wheeler's Bay, off Rt. 73, Spruce Head. Open 11–7, late June–Labor Day. This is our hands-down favorite: on Wheeler's Bay, family owned and operated, with a loyal following. Tables are on the wharf; lobsters and clams are cooked in seawater, served with fixings, topped off with fresh-made pies. BYOB.

✐ **Cod End Cookhouse** (207-372-8981; www.codend.com), on the wharf, Tenants Harbor. Open seasonally, daily 11–8:30. Hidden down a lane, a combination fish shop and informal wharfside eatery (tables inside and out) right on Tenants Harbor with a separate cookhouse: chowders and lobster rolls, lobster dinners, steamed clams and mussels. Also burgers and sandwiches. Children's menu. Beer and wine served.

Waterman's Beach Lobsters (207-594-7819), off Rt. 73, South Thomaston. Open Thu.–Sun. 11–7 in summertime. Oceanfront feasting on the deck: lobster and clam dinners, seafood rolls, pies.

and mussels over linguini, and a veggie platter are also on Scott Yokovenko's menu. Beer, wine, and homemade desserts. The neighboring **Port Clyde General Store** makes good sandwiches and has picnic benches on the same deck.

✐ **Farmer's Restaurant** (207-372-6111), Rt. 131, Tenants Harbor. Open year-round for three meals. Bill and Gayle Stuart are the owners of this dependable family restaurant with breakfast sides like corned beef hash and fish cakes; soups, sandwiches, and fried baskets for lunch; and moderately priced fried or broiled seafood dinners.

The Harpoon (207-372-6304), corner of Drift Inn and Marshall Point Rds., Port Clyde. Open May–mid-Oct. for dinner, Wed.–Sat. in shoulder months. This engaging seafood restaurant in the seaside village of Port Clyde (just off Rt. 131, around the corner from the harbor) specializes in the local catch. Try the blackened seafood, lazy lobster, fried combo plate, or prime rib. The bar is lively.

OTHER **In Good Company** (207-593-9110), 415 Main St., Rockland. Open from 4:30 except Mon. A wine bar in a living-room-like setting, serving salads, cheeses, nibbles, and light meals such as cedar-planked salmon and cold sliced beef tenderloin.

Rock City Books and Coffee (207-594-4123), 328 Main St., Rockland, Mon.–Sat. 7–6, Sun. 8–6. Coffee is a serious deal here, roasted by Rock City Coffee Roasters. Chai and tea too, along with bagels, scones and such. Also a wide selection of new and used books.

Hardcover Café at the Breakwater Bookland (207-593-9272; www.booklandcafe.com), 91 Camden St. Open Mon.–Sat. 9–8:45, Sun. 9–5:45. The café offers espresso, sandwiches, and salads in a a major bookstore, housed in a former waterside factory.

✷ Entertainment

The Farnsworth Museum (207-596-6457; www.farnsworthmuseum.org) in Rockland stages a year-round series of Sunday concerts, free with museum admission; reservations advised.

The Strand Theatre (207-594-0070; www.rocklandstrand.com), 345 Main St., Rockland. Vintage 1923, a beautifully restored classic downtown theater offering films, concerts, and live performances including a summer Wednesday evening series of Bay Chamber Concerts.

✷ Selective Shopping

ART AND CRAFTS GALLERIES Since the opening of the **Farnsworth Museum Store** (corner of Main and Elm Sts.), so many galleries have opened around the Farnsworth area that an *Arts in Rockland* walking map is available at most. **Wednesday Receptions** (6–8) in summer routinely involve two dozen art venues. Galleries include the prestigious, recently expanded **Caldbeck Gallery** (207-594-5935; www.caldbeck.com), at 12 Elm St. since 1982; goldsmith Thomas O'Donovan's **Harbor Square Gallery** (www.harborsquaregallery.com), filling three floors of a former bank building (374 Main St.) with art but also featuring fine jewelry; and the stunning new **Eric Hopkins Gallery** (207-594-1996; www.erichopkins.com), 21 Winter St. A North Haven native, Hopkins is one of Maine's most popular, distinctive, and accessible artists. Others to check: **Kimber's Fine Art** (207-594-

3634); **Mulford Gallery** (207-594-4775), 313 Main St., has frequently changing exhibits worth checking as does **Art Space Gallery** (207-594-8784; www.artspacemaine.com), 342 Main St. **Archipelago Fine Arts** (207-596-0701; www.thearchipelago.net) at the Island Institute (386 Main St.) represents roughly 300 artists and craftspeople on "hinged" as well as real islands. **Playing with Fire! Glassworks and Gallery** (207-594-7805; www.playingwithfire.com) 485 Main St., and **Lucky Dog Gallery** (207-596-0120; www.luckydog.com), 485 Main St.

Deborah Beckwith Winship's bright, primitive-style graphics are familiar to Maine visitors, and her studio at 53 Fulton St (207-594-5321) is an excuse to explore Rockland's South End.

More Selective Shopping along Rockland's mile-long Main Street
Huston Tuttle & Gallery One (No. 365) is a serious art store with a gallery upstairs; **The Store** (No. 435) features a wide selection of cooking supplies; **The Grasshopper Shop** (No. 400), a major link in a small Maine chain; **G. F. MacGregor** (No. 338), a blend of tasteful furniture and furnishings obviously catering to museum goers. **Sea Street Graphics** (No. 475) specializes in silk-screened designs on T-shirts and clothing (made here, widely distributed); the **Black Parrot** (No. 328) specializes in its colorful fleece-lined reversible garments but carries a mix of clothing, toys, cards, and more; **Caravans** (No. 415) sells clothing we never pass up; **Ravishing Recalls** (No. 389) is a useful trove of secondhand clothing. **Sage Market** (No. 410) is great for reasonably priced wines, artisinal cheese, handmade chocolates, and much more.

Along Rt. 131 to Port Clyde
Check out **St. George Pottery** (4.5 miles south of Rt. 1), George Pearlman's combination studio and contemporary ceramics gallery. **Noble Clay** (529 Port Clyde Rd.) in Tenants Harbor, open year-round, displays Trish and Steve Barnes's white-and-blue-glazed porcelain pottery with whimsical and botanical designs. **Ocean House Gallery** (207-372-6930; www.oceanhousegallery.com), end of Port Clyde Rd., is a seasonal gallery with changing exhibits worth checking.

In South Thomaston
Keag River Pottery (Westbrook St., marked from Rt. 73) offers Toni Oliveri's unusual but functional creations like the glazed vase we bought and love: Its inner ribbons of pottery make it easier to artistically display flowers. **Old Post Office Gallery & Art of the Sea** on Rt. 73 displays nearly 100 museum-quality, full-rigged ships' models; also half models and nautical paintings.

BOOKSTORES **The Reading Corner** (207-596-6651), 408 Main St., Rockland, is a full-service bookstore with an unusual interior.

Rock City Books and Coffee (207-594-4123), 328 Main St., Rockland, carries new and used books, and

ERIC HOPKINS AT ARCHIPELAGO FINE ARTS
Christina Tree

offers a place to drink fine coffee and eat one of the daily sandwich specials while you read.

✐ **The Personal Book Shop** (207-354-8058), 144 Main St., Thomaston. Open year-round 10–6. Marti Reed's shop is more like a book-lined living room than your ordinary bookstore: plenty of places to sit and read but also a large selection of titles; many Maine authors, and a well-stocked children's room.

Dooryard Books (207-594-5080), 438 Main St., Rockland (open Memorial Day–Columbus Day). A good general stock of hardcover and paperback used books.

Breakwater Bookland (207-593-9354; www.booklandcafe.com), 91 Camden St., Rockland, a full-service, waterside bookstore with a café.

Lobster Lane Book Shop (207-594-7520), Spruce Head. Marked from the Off-Island Store. Open May weekends then Thu.–Sun. June–Sept., weekends through Oct., 12:30–5. This stock of 50,000 titles is well known in bookish circles. Specialties include fiction and Maine.

SPECIAL SHOPS **Maine State Prison Showroom** (207-354-9237), Main St. (Rt. 1), Thomaston, at the south end of town. Open daily 9–5. A variety of wooden furniture—coffee tables, stools, lamps, and trays—and small souvenirs, all carved by inmates. The prison has moved to Warren but, happily, the shop is still here. Prices are reasonable, and profits go to the craftsmen.

✱ Special Events

June: **Summer Solstic,** a Main Street Rockland Street Fair.

July: Thomaston **Fourth of July** festivities include a big parade, footraces, live entertainment, a crafts fair, barbecue, and fireworks. The **North Atlantic Blues Festival** (*mid-July*), Harbor Park, Rockland (www.northatlanticbluesfestival.com), is huge. **Maine Windjammer Parade of Sail** (*midmonth*), Rockland Harbor. **Friendship Sloop Days** (*last weekend*) includes a regatta and festivities in Rockland and a parade, BBQ, and children's activities in Friendship.

August: **Maine Lobster Festival** (*first weekend, plus the preceding Wed. and Thurs.*) (www.mainelobsterfestival.com), Harbor Park, Rockland. This is probably the world's biggest lobster feed, prepared in the world's largest lobster boiler. Patrons queue up on the public landing to heap their plates with lobsters, clams, corn, and all the fixings. King Neptune and the Maine Sea Goddess reign over the event, which includes a parade down Main Street, concerts, an art exhibit, contests such as clam shucking and sardine packing, and a race across a string of lobster crates floating in the harbor. **Maine Boats & Harbor Show** (*midmonth*), Harbor Park, Rockland. **Union Fair** and **State of Maine Wild Blueberry Festival** (*third week*) (www.unionfair.org)—a real agricultural fair with tractor- and ox-pulling contests, livestock and food shows, a midway, the crowning of the Blueberry Queen, and, on one day during the week, free mini blueberry pies for all comers.

November–December: **Rockland Festival of Lights** begins on Thanksgiving—parade, Santa's Village, sleigh rides.

MIDCOAST ISLANDS

MONHEGAN; THE FOX ISLANDS: VINALHAVEN AND NORTH HAVEN; MATINICUS

MONHEGAN

Eleven miles at sea and barely a mile square, Monhegan is a microcosm of Maine landscapes, from 160-foot sheer headlands to pine woods, from wild-flower-filled inland meadows to the smooth, low rocks along Lobster Cove. "Beached like a whale" is the way one mariner in 1590 described the island's shape: headlands sloping down to the small off-island of Manana, a blip on Monhegan's silhouette.

Monhegan is known for the quality and quantity of its artists and the grit of its lobstermen, who fish for a period between October through June. The island's first recorded artist arrived in 1858, and by the 1870s a hotel and several boardinghouses were filled with summer guests, many of them artists. In 1903 Robert Henri, a founder of New York's Ashcan School and a well-known art teacher, discovered Monhegan and soon introduced it to his students, among them George Bellows and Rockwell Kent. The island remains a genuine art colony. Jamie Wyeth owns a house built by Rockwell Kent. More than 20 artists open their studios to visitors. Hours are posted on "The Rope Shed" and printed in handouts during summer weeks.

The island continues to draw artists in good part because its beauty not only survives but also remains accessible to all. Prospect Hill, the only attempted development, foundered around 1900. It was Theodore Edison, son of the inventor, who amassed property enough to erase its traces and keep the island's cottages (which still number just 130 or so) bunched along the sheltered harbor, the rest preserved as common space and laced with 17 miles of footpaths.

In 1954 Edison helped organize Monhegan Associates, a nonprofit corporation dedicated to preserving the "natural, wild beauty" of the island. Ironically, this is one of the country's few communities to shun electricity until relatively recently. A number of homes and one inn still use kerosene lamps. Vehicles are limited to a few trucks for those with businesses and golf carts for those with medical needs.

Petroglyphs on Manana Island (just offshore) are said to have been carved by Norsemen, but a plaque beside the schoolhouse states that the island was

Monhegan Island Light, built of granite in 1850 and automated in 1959, caps a hill that's well worth climbing for the view alone. The former keeper's cottage is now the **Monhegan Museum** (207-596-7003; open daily 11:30–3:30 July–Aug., 12:30–2:30 in June and Sept.), $4 suggested donation. A spellbinding display of island art, including prints by George Bellows and Rockwell Kent, and annual special exhibits in the neighboring gallery. There are artifacts, flora, fauna, some geology, lobstering, and island history, including documents dating back to the 16th century. Inquire about viewing James Fitzgerald's work in the Kent-Fitzgerald-Hubert house. Built by Rockwell Kent, it later served as a home and studio for Fitzgerald.

discovered by Captain John Smith in 1614. Native American artifacts on display in the Monhegan Museum may date back 8,000 years. The island's present settlement has been continuous since 1790; it's been a "plantation" since 1839. The year-round population of 70 or so swells in summer to a little more than 600, not counting day-trippers. Visitors come to walk, to paint, to bird, and to reflect. A number of them come alone.

Monhegan has three inns, a B&B, several nightly rentals, and a limited number of weekly rental cottages. Fog and a frequently rough passage insulate it to some degree, but on summer days a high tide of day-trippers from Boothbay Harbor and New Harbor, as well as Port Clyde, washes over this small, fragile island. More worrisome still are skyrocketing real estate prices. Monhegan Island Sustainable Community Association (MISCA) is now dedicated to ensuring affordable housing for year-round residents.

GUIDANCE A booklet guide to the island is available, along with a confirmation of reservations from the Monhegan Boat Line and from Hardy Boat Cruises (see *Getting There*). Also check out **www.monhegan.com**, the site for Monhegan Commons, not your usual chamber of commerce (there isn't one). It's frequently updated and tracks social and political events.

THE ROPE SHED, MONHEGAN ISLAND'S BULLETIN BOARD

Christina Tree

GETTING THERE **Monhegan Boat Line** (207-372-8848; www.monheganboat.com) operates both the sleek *Elizabeth Ann* and the beloved old *Laura B* from Port Clyde; reservations a must. Service is three times daily in-season, less frequent in spring and fall, and only Mon., Wed., and Fri. in winter. It's a 50- or 70-minute trip, depending on which boat you catch. Mid-May through Columbus Day weekend **Hardy Boat Cruises** (1-800-278-3346; www.hardyboat.com) offers a 60-minute run from New Harbor with two daily roundtrtips early June through September. The Ocean House in Port Clyde and the Gosnold Arms in New Harbor are within walking distance of these two services, taking the sting out of making morning boats. The ***Balmy Days II*** (1-800-298-2284; www.balmydaycruises.com) also offers seasonal roundtrips from Boothbay.

Christina Tree

MONHEGAN ISLAND

EQUIPMENT AND RULES Come properly shod for the precipitous paths. Hikers should wear long pants and socks against poison ivy; bring sweaters and windbreakers. Wading or swimming from any of the tempting coves on the back side of the island can be lethal. Kayaking is discouraged. Flashlights, heavy rubber boots, and rain gear are also good ideas. Public phones are few; cell phone reception has improved, thanks to an intrusive tower that now dwarfs the lighthouse, but is still undependable. Camping is prohibited. Do not bring bicycles. Dogs must be leashed at all times. No smoking outside the village, and please don't pick the flowers.

PUBLIC RESTROOMS The two public pay toilets are on a lane behind the Monhegan House.

GETTING AROUND Several trucks meet each boat as it arrives and provide baggage service. Otherwise visitors have no access to motorized transport.

WHEN TO COME The spring migration season brings birds and birders. June can be rainy and foggy but also glorious and always flowery with wild strawberries to be found along hiking paths. July and August are prime time, but September is best for hiking; birds and birders return.

✷ To Do

BIRDING Positioned in the middle of the Atlantic flyway, Monhegan is one of the best birding places on the East Coast. Your local Audubon Society may have a trip going in May or mid- through late September.

COMING ASHORE ON MONHEGAN ISLAND

Christina Tree

HIKING Pick up a current Monhegan Associates Trail Map before setting out on the island's 17-mile network. Day-trippers are advised to take the Burnt Head Trail (No. 4) and loop back to the village via the Whitehead Trail (No. 7), descending by the lighthouse, or vice versa. This way you get a sense of the high bluffs and the unusual rocks in Gull Cove. Beyond this well-trod loop, trails are marked with few guideposts. It's easy to get turned around in Cathedral Woods (justly famed and known for its "fairy houses"), which, along with Pulpit Rock, should be reserved for an unhurried day. The path along the southern outer tip of the island, from Burnt Head to Christmas Cove, is ledgy and unsuitable for children and shaky hikers.

✱ Lodging

All listings are on Monhegan Island 04852

Note: Lodging is limited but remarkably varied.

INNS Island Inn (207-596-0371; www.islandinnmonhegan.com). Open Memorial Day–Columbus Day weekend. This shingled, cupola-topped, gabled, classic 1907 summer hotel with a long, rocker-lined verandah, is steps from the ferry dock and overlooks the boat-filled harbor and Manana Island. In recent years it has been steadily renovated, and public rooms are a winning mix of old-fashioned and chic, with a comfortable living room and book-stocked side porches. The nicely decorated dining room has the harbor view (see *Dining Out*). The 28 rooms and four suites are divided between the main inn and Pierce Cottage behind it. Opt for a room with a view in the inn itself. Just eight rooms still share baths. In high season (late July–Labor Day), $145 per couple (shared bath, meadow view) to $315–340 for suites. Otherwise $115–290, depending on room and week. $4 gratuity added per day and $5 charge for one-night stays. Children under 5 are free if no extra bedding is required. All rates include a full breakfast, served buffet style, usually featuring lobster casserole.

Monhegan House (207-594-7983 or 1-800-599-7983; www.monheganhouse.com), P.O. Box 345. Open Memorial Day–early Oct. Holden and Susan Nelson have revived Monhegan's oldest continuously operating summer hotel, upgrading both infrastructure and decor. Two suites with bath and a deck have been added and more are planned. Built in 1870s in the middle of the village, it offers 31 rooms on four floors. No closets, and most baths and showers (plentiful and immaculate) are in a wing off the middle of the second floor. For couples and families we recommend the third floor; for singles the bargain-priced fourth-floor rooms have the best views (coveted by artists). The downstairs lobby is tastefully decorated, hung with good art, warmed by a gas fireplace, and equipped with books and games. On sunny days guests opt for the porch, watching the comings and goings of everyone on the island. Children are welcome and free under age 3. A full breakfast is included in the rates (singles are $77, doubles $129–140 in high season; $67 and $109 in low); suites are $185. Head for the dining room before 8 AM, because it's open to the public and very popular. Dinner is also good (see *Dining Out*).

The Trailing Yew (207-596-0440). Open mid-May–mid-Oct. This quirky, affordable institution has a loyal following among artists and writers. New England's last genuine 19th-century-style "summer boardinghouse," it's the place for the many solo travelers drawn to Monhegan. The 35 rooms are divided among the main house and adjacent annexes and cottages on the grounds and The Mooring Chain (good only for groups) up the road. Baths are shared but clean and equipped with electricity. Guest rooms are comfortable, lit with kerosene lamps. Dining is at 5:45 at shared tables and the conversation is usually lively (BYOB). Dinner is open to the public but priced to discourage guests. Two rooms in Lower Seagull are geared to families. $90 per person per day includes breakfast and dinner; sliding scale ages 2–11. No credit cards.

Christina Tree
SHINING SAILS GUESTHOUSE WINDOW ART

BED & BREAKFAST "1" **Shining Sails Guesthouse** (207-596-0041; www.shiningsails.com), P.O. Box 346. Open year-round. Lobsterman John Murdock and his wife, Winnie, offer two rooms and five exceptional apartments in their welcoming village home overlooking the water. All five water-view units have a deck, the better to savor the sunset and stars. All rooms are tastefully decorated, featuring original island art. On foggy days a woodstove warms the living room, where an ample continental breakfast is served daily. May through Columbus Day. The Murdocks are helpful hosts and this place is so justly popular, it's advisable to book far in advance for July and August, but there are always some openings. Rooms are $130–185 per night in-season, $820–1060 per week; apartments are $135–225 per night, $865–1400 per week. Also see *Rentals*.

GUEST HOUSES AND DAILY RENTALS Hitchcock House (207-594-8137; e-mail hhouse@midcoast.com), Horn's Hill. Open year-round. Hidden away on Horn's Hill with a delightful garden and a large, sheltered deck, which serves as common space for guests. In the house itself Barbara Hitchcock offers two appealing housekeeping units, both with decks with views down across the meadows to the village and water. There are also two upstairs guest rooms, each with a small fridge and a hot pot, sharing one bath and behind the garden is a cottage with a full kitchen, living room, and bath. July through the Labor Day weekend efficiencies are $120–130 per night, $760–840 per week; rooms are $85 per night, $520 per week, less off-season.

PLEIN AIR PAINTING
Christina Tree

Tribler Cottage (207-594-2445; www.monhegan.biz/tribler.html). Open mid-May–mid-Oct. On the edge of the Meadow, at the base of Lighthouse Hill, this remains in the same family that has been welcoming visitors since the 1920s. Richard Farrell offers four housekeeping apartments and one housekeeping room. All have private bath; one apartment (Hillside) has a sundeck and living room with fireplace, while another (accommodating three) has a gas heater and is available off-season. $80–140 per couple per night based on two-night stay; $525–945 weekly.

Murdock's Fish & Maine (207-596-0041; www.shiningsails.com). Four attractive apartments in the middle of the village, just off Fish Beach, two with harbor views and decks. From $175 per night ($1,120 per week) for a one-bedroom with a full kitchen and gas fireplace to $225 ($1,450 per week) for a two-bedroom with deck and harbor view. Less off-season.

WEEKLY RENTALS Cooking facilities come in handy here: You can buy lobster and good fresh and smoked fish (bring meat and staples) and a limited line of vegetables. **Shining Sails Cottage Rental** (207-596-0041; www.shiningsails.com) manages more than two dozen rental cottages, available by the week. Demand is high, and it's wise to get in your bid in early January for the summer. $900–2,000 per week.

✱ Where to Eat

DINING OUT **The Island Inn** (207-596-0371). Open to the public Memorial Day–Columbus Day for breakfast and dinner. This classic, turn-of-the-century dining room has been has contemporary decor and water views. The breakfast frequently features lobster casserole. Reserve for dinner and request a table overlooking the water. Appetizers usually include lobster stew and a wide choice of entrées. We can vouch for pan-seared scallops on a bed of mixed greens and tangy Maine crabcakes with the house herb and chive aioli. Both came with Israeli couscous and crisp green beans. Entrées $18–36. BYOB.

Monhegan House offers an attractive, many-windowed dining room at the back of the inn, overlooking the village and meadow. Breakfasts feature house-made breads and omelets. The dinner menu changes nightly and always includes a vegetarian option. Starters might include mushroom strudel with Madeira sauce and greens; entrées, fresh haddock with artichokes, olives, wild rice, and a seasonal vegetable, or roasted eggplant Napolean. Leave room for dessert, epecially if it's lemon mousse with blueberry sauce and Chantilly cream. Entrées $14–18. BYOB.

EATING OUT **The Barnacle.** Sited beside the ferry wharf and owned by the Island Inn, there is limited seating on the deck and inside. Sandwiches, soups, and pastries, also espresso and prepared sandwiches. Wine and beer sold.

The Novelty, behind Monhegan House. Pizza, soups and sandwiches, salads and hot wraps. Freshly made hermits and cookies are great hiking fuel as you set off up Horn's Hill. Hand-dipped ice cream and frozen yogurts hit the spot on the way down.

The Fish House Market, Fish Beach. Open daily. The source of all good seafood for anyone with cooking facilities, also of steamed clams and the island's best crab and lobster rolls to eat at picnic tables on Fish Beach.

North End Market (207-594-5546), open year-round 9–7. A general store with good deli sandwiches, wine, and beer.

✱ Selective Shopping

ART GALLERIES **The Lupine Gallery** (207-594-8131; www.lupinegallery.com), 48 Main St. Open early May–Columbus Day, 11–4:30. Bill Boynton and Jackie Bogel offer original works by 100 artists who paint regularly on the island. This is a very special gallery, showcasing the work of many professional artists within walking distance. Sited just uphill from the ferry dock, it's a good place to judge which studios you want to visit. Great cards, prints, and art books, also artists' supplies and framing.

Open studios. More than 20 resident artists welcome visitors to their studios; pick up a map/guide and schedule, check "The Rope Shed," or look for shingles hung outside listing the hours they're open. **Don Stone** is the current dean of Monhegan painters, and his studio on the way to Burnt Head is open by chance or appointment.

SPECIAL SHOPS **Carina**. The spiritual successor to the old Island Spa, the year-round island gathering place to linger in booths over coffee, tea, and fresh-baked goods. It's also a prime source of wines, produce, and daily newspapers.

Winterworks. Open more or less daily Memorial Day–Labor Day, by the ferry dock. A former fish house is now the island co-op, filled with work produced by the island's craftspeople: a surprising variety and quality of knitted goods, jewelry, cards, Christmas decorations, and more.

Black Duck Emporium. Open Memorial Day–Columbus Day. This longtime island gift store has expanded to fill the former general store, offering cappuccino and pastries as well as a selection of imaginative T-shirts, books, kitchenware, pottery, jewelry, and more.

THE FOX ISLANDS: VINALHAVEN AND NORTH HAVEN

The Fox Islands Thoroughfare is a rowable stretch of yacht-filled water that separates Vinalhaven and North Haven, two islands roughly a dozen miles off Rockland. While you can get from one island to the other, no ferry stops at both.

Vinalhaven is heavily wooded and marked by granite quarries that include two public swimming holes. Life eddies around the village of Carver's Harbor, home to Maine's largest lobster fleet. In 1880, when granite was being cut on Vinalhaven to build New York's Customs House, 2,855 people were living here on the island, a number now reduced to less than 1,300—a mix of descendants of 18th-century settlers and the stonecutters who came here from Sweden, Norway, Finland, and Scotland. In recent years the island has also attracted a number of artists, including Robert Indiana. Summer visitors now equal year-round residents, but there is no yacht club or golf course. This is Maine's largest offshore island, its largest year-round island community, and claims the world's largest lobster fleet. It's not an island resort.

North Haven is half as big, with just 350 year-round residents, some 1,500 in summer. Founded well over a century ago by Boston yachtsmen, its summer colony now includes some of the country's wealthiest and most influential families. Over the years some members of these families have married islanders, while others have settled or retired here. The result is a creative mix. Its K–12 school, the smallest in New England, has produced a play (*Islands*) that has been performed on Broadway. The former general store by the ferry dock is now Waterman's Community Center, with a 140-seat state-of-the-art theater, the venue for summer lectures, concerts, and plays.

The village of North Haven offers two gift shops and galleries, two seasonal restaurants, and recently restored Nebo Lodge, with gracious year-round lodging and dining (see *Lodging* and *Dining Out*. Beyond the village a 10-mile loop beckons bicyclists through rolling, open fields, spotted with buttercups and idyllic farmhouses, most of them summer homes. Unusually sheltered Pulpit Harbor is a favorite mooring for windjammers and yachtsmen. There's also a public golf club and a private yacht club, the North Haven Casino, home to the island's distinctive dinghies.

It was British explorer Martin Pring who named the Fox Islands in 1603, ostensibly for the silver foxes he saw there. A dozen miles out in Penobscot Bay, these islands are understandably protective of their considerable beauty, especially in view of their unusual—by Maine island standards—accessibility by Maine State Ferry. Be it said that there is just one inn on North Haven, and lodging is also limited on Vinalhaven.

For the kind of tourist who loves islands, especially less crowded islands with ample places to walk, Vinalhaven is a real find. And contrary to rumor, it's possible to cross the Thoroughfare (see *Getting Around*) to spend the day on North Haven, but you may have to wait a little while for transport. Islands dictate their own terms.

Vinalhaven makes sense as a day-trip destination only if it's a nice day and if you take the early boat. Pick up a map and don't be discouraged by the walk into Carver's Harbor, along the island's least attractive half mile. Don't miss the Historical Society Museum, and walk or bike out to Lane's Island. It's better as a destination for a couple of days or more, and it's a great place to be on the Fourth of July.

GUIDANCE Town offices on **North Haven** (207-867-4433) and **Vinalhaven** (207-863-4471 or 207-863-4393) field most questions. **The Vinalhaven Chamber** site is www.vinalhaven.org. On-island pick up a free copy of *The Wind*, the island's newsletter.

GETTING THERE **The Maine State Ferry Service** (in Rockland: 207-596-2202). The islands are serviced by different ferries, and neither ferry stops at both. From Rockland it's a 75-minute ride; service is frequent. Day-trippers never have a problem walking on; the bike fee is nominal. Each ferry takes a set number of cars, and only a handful of these spaces can be reserved; otherwise, cars are taken in order of their position in line. For the morning boats, it's wise to be in line the night before. During the summer season, getting off the island can be nerve racking. It doesn't make sense to bring a car unless you plan to stay a while.

Note: **Concord Trailways** stops daily at the **Rockland Ferry Terminal**.

Penobscot Island Air (207-596-7500; www.penobscotislandair.com) will fly you in from Portland or Boston as well as Rockland to either Vinalhaven or North Haven. $130 per half hour for up to 5 passengers.

Christina Tree

CARVER'S HARBOR

GETTING AROUND *By boat:* Shuttle service between North Haven and Vinalhaven is possible through **J. O. Brown & Sons Boatyard** (207-867-4621) in North Haven. Try calling from the phone on the boat landing on the Vinalhaven side of the Thoroughfare. On Vinalhaven **Tidewater Motel** rents cars. Also see *Bicycling*.

Note: **Day-trippers** to North Haven will find shopping and food within steps of the ferry dock, but on Vinalhaven it's 0.4 mile from the ferry to Carver's Harbor. It's another mile or so to the quarries and Lanes Island Nature Preserve.

WHEN TO COME Only in July and August can you count on all visitor-geared facilities being open on both these islands. June and September, however, can be as beautiful.

✷ To See

On North Haven

North Haven Village. The village itself is charming, with several shops, galleries, and a choice of places to eat. Pulpit Harbor, the island's second, much smaller community, several miles away, is the site of the general store and the **North Haven Historical Society Museum** (open Tue. in July and Aug., 2–5). A general store, period kitchen and living room, special exhibits.

✷ To Do

BICYCLING If you take care to keep to the roadside, both North Haven and Vinalhaven are suited to bicycling. Bike rentals are available at **Bikesenjava** (see *Bicycling* in "Rockland") near the ferry terminal. A more limited selection is

ON VINALHAVEN

The Vinalhaven Historical Society Museum (207-863-4410; www.vinalhaven historicalsociety.org), top of High St. Open mid-June–mid-Sept., Tues.–Sat. 11–3 and by appointment. Sue Radley is the director of one of Maine's most welcoming and extensive community museums, housed in the former town hall, which has also served as a theater and skating rink. It was built in 1838 in Rockland as a Universalist church, and floated over on a barge in 1878. Displays feature the island's granite industry, with photos of St. John the Divine's massive columns, for instance, quarried here.

The first order for Vinalhaven granite, you learn, was shipped to Boston in 1826 to build a jail, but production really skyrocketed after the Civil War, when granite was the preferred building material for the country's building boom. On an island map, 40 red pins mark the sites of major quarries, but there are also countless "motions," backyard pits.

Museum displays also depict island life and other industries, like fishing (the Lane-Libby Fisheries Co. was once one of Maine's largest fish-processing companies) and lobstering (in the 1880s the Basin, a large saltwater

available at Tidewater Motel on Vinalhaven and Nebo Lodge on North Haven. **Sea Escape Kayak** (see *Sea Kayaking*) offers hiking and biking tours.

On North Haven we recommend the North Shore Rd.

On Vinalhaven we recommend the Granite Island Rd. out along the Basin or following Main St. the other direction out to Geary's Beach (see *Green Space*). The North Haven Rd. is an 8-mile slog up the middle of Vinalhaven, but the rewards are great: Browns Head Light, the Perry Creek Preserve, and views of North Haven.

GOLF **North Haven Golf Club** (207-867-2054), open June–Sept. A waterside course, nine holes.

SEA KAYAKING **Sea Escape Kayak** (207-863-9343; www.seaescapekayak.com), Carver's Harbor, Vinalhaven. Burke Lynch has all the right credentials for guiding novices, from two-hour harbor paddles to two-day camping trips,

SWIMMING ON VINLAHAVEN **Lawson's Quarry**. From the middle of Carver's Harbor, turn (uphill) at the Bank Building and continue up and up High St., past the historical society, and then turn right on the North Haven Rd. for 0.5 mile. For **Booth Quarry** continue east (uphill) on Main St. 1.5 miles past the Union Church. This is a town park and swimming hole.

inlet, was used as a giant holding tank, penning as many as 150,000 lobsters until prices peaked). Knitting horse nets (to keep off flies) in intricate designs was yet another island industry. Check out the nearby Carver Cemetery. A Galamander, a huge wagon such as those used to carry stone from island quarries to schooners, stands in the small park at the top of the hill on the other side of town (junction of Main, Chestnut, Carver, and School Sts. and Atlantic Ave.).

The Victorian-style town of **Carver's Harbor** is picturesque and interesting, its downtown a single street straddling a causeway and narrow land strip between the harbor and Carver's Pond, its estuary. A boomtown dating from the 1880s when *Vinalhaven* was synonymous with *granite,* the village is built almost entirely of wood, the reason why many of the best of its golden-era buildings are missing. The strikingly Victorian Star of Hope Lodge, owned by artist Robert Indiana, is one of two surviving second-empire mansard buildings (there were once four) marking the center of town.

Brown's Head Lighthouse, now automated, commands the entrance to the Thoroughfare from the northern end of Vinalhaven, more than 8 miles from Carver's Harbor.

✷ Green Space

On Vinalhaven

Lane's Island Preserve, on the southern side of Carver's Harbor (cross the Indian Creek Bridge and look for the sign on your left). It includes 45 acres of fields, marsh, moor, and beach. This is a great spot to picnic or to come in the evening. Stroll out along the beach and up into the meadows facing open ocean and filled with wild roses and beach peas.

Armbrust Hill is on the way to Lane's Island, hidden behind the medical center. The first place from which the island's granite was commercially quarried, it remained one of the most active sites on the island for many decades. Notice the many small pits ("motions") as well as four major quarries. The main path winds up the hill for a splendid view.

BOOTH QUARRY

Christina Tree

Grimes Park, just west of the ferry terminal, is a two-acre point of rocky land with two small beaches. Note the rough granite watering trough once used by horses and oxen.

Geary's Beach. Turn right off Main St. a bit farther than the Booth Quarry, just after the Coke Statue of Liberty (you'll see), and bear left for this stony town-owned beach, its trails, and picnic table. The view is off to Isle au Haut, Brimstone, and Matinicus.

The Vinalhaven Land Trust (207-863-2543) maintains several of the preserves mapped on island handouts. This list is just a sampling.

✷ Lodging

On Vinalhaven 04863

Tidewater Motel and Gathering Place (207-863-4618; www.tidewatermotel.com), P.O. Box 546, Carver's Harbor. Open year-round. "I don't want to leave this room," I wrote about number 16, an aerie with a skylight (with shade) above the bed, a window above the raceway, and a deck overlooking a harbor full of lobster boats, all turned into the wind like gulls. Creature comforts include a microwave, coffeemaker, and small fridge, a full bath and small TV. Phil and Elaine Crossman's waterside motel has evolved into a remarkable place to stay in the heart of both the harbor and the village. It spans a tidal stream connecting the harbor with Carver's Pond. The water swooshing under your room once powered a blacksmith shop. Many of the original 11 motel units have decks overhanging the water. Adjacent buildings house eight units—also over the water—including suites and efficiencies, one with a sleeping loft, another with a full kitchen, living room, and dining room, fit for a large family or small conference. Note that the Crossmans also loan out bikes, rent or loan cars, meet the ferry, and help guests get around the island. Elaine Crossman is a noted artist, and Phil's book of essays, *Away Happens*, captures island life and is genuinely funny. $125–240 in high season, $72–140 off-season.

Payne Homestead at the Moses Webster House (207-863-9963 or 1-888-863-9963; www.paynehomestead.com), Atlantic Ave. Open June–Sept. Lee and Donna Payne have young sons of their own and cater to families while offering some romantic rooms in this mansard-roofed, high-Victorian home. We prefer the upstairs rooms over those on the first floor. The five rooms (one with private bath) range $90–145 including breakfast.

Libby House (207-863-4696; www.libbyhouse1869.com), Water St. Open June–Oct.; call for off-season availability (631-369-9172). This rambling home is furnished with Victorian pieces, including heavily carved beds. Two of the three upstairs rooms share a bath. Downstairs common spaces are often filled with music; innkeeper Philip Roberts is a retired music teacher. There's also an enclosed porch with rockers and it's a short walk to Lane's Island Preserve. $80–110 for rooms, $140 for a two-bedroom ground-floor apartment with an eat-in kitchen.

On North Haven 04853

Nebo Lodge (207-867-2007; www.nebolodge.com), 11 Mullins Lane, P.O. Box 358. Open year-round. Built handsomely in 1912 as an inn but privatized in 1956, reopened in 2006 by a dedicated local group of women to serve both as a place for residents to dine together and as an island entrée to visitors. There are nine crisp guest rooms (just four year-round), seven with shared bath. Two third-floor rooms are the brightest and most attractive, both with private bath. The sitting room is delightful, with a rosy rug by island designer Angela Adams. The dining room with its working fireplace is justly busy (see *Dining Out*). Your cell phone may not work here but there's wireless Internet. Bikes are available and the innkeeper will help arrange kayaking or a boat trip. $140–225 in July and August, less in shoulder months and $75–90 in winter.

Our Place Inn and Cottages (207-867-4998; www.ourplaceinn.com), Crab Tree Point Rd. Open year-round. A guest house under many names over the years. Marnelle and Gordon Bubar offers five rooms in the main house 2 miles from North Haven Village, within walking distance of Pulpit Harbor. $75–95 in high season with continental breakfast. There are also three basic efficiency cottages ($125 per night).

COTTAGE RENTALS **Vinalhaven Realty** (207-863-4474; www.vinalhavenrealty.com) specialize in summer rentals. The **Island Group** (207-863-2554) offers both sales and rentals for both islands.

✷ Where to Eat

On Vinalhaven

The Haven Restaurant (207-863-4969), 49 Main St. Open Tue.–Sat. Jun.–Dec. unless Tory Pratt is catering, with a 6 and 8:15 seating harborside, reservations required. On the street side you can eat from a lighter menu, pub style, and do not need a reservation. This island mainstay serves a variety of entrées that change almost nightly, always including fish, meat (with at least one steak), and pasta dishes. Entrées $14–22.

What's Left Lobster Restaurant (207-863-4444; www.whatsleftonvinalhaven.com), 365 North Haven Rd. A ways out of town but call for a pick-up. Open daily year-round, 5:30–9. Richard "Dicky" Hildings claims that he's making the best of what his "X" left him—basically his lobster boat. Nightly specials range from seafood pie to prime rib. Burgers, sandwiches, and local haddock, scallops, or shrimp are on the menu but for nonresidents basically this place is all about lobster. Entrées: $10–$21; market price for lobster. X-wife ale a specialty.

The Harbor Gawker (207-863-9365), Main St., middle of the village. Open mid-Apr.–mid-Nov. Mon.–Sat. 11–8. Lobster rolls, crabmeat rolls, and baskets of just about anything. Homemade soups, chowders, and blueberry pies, along with ice cream and a dairy bar for dessert. Order at the counter and eat at a table with a view of Carver's Pond.

Surfside (207-863-2767), Harbor Wharf, W. Main St. Donna Webster opens at 4 AM for the lobstermen and technically closes at 11 AM. A great harborside breakfast spot with tables on the deck, and specials like a crabmeat or lobster omelet, or a tomato herb cheese omelet with fish cakes.

The Pizza Pit (207-863-4311) Main St., is open daily 4–9 PM, serving more than pizza. Kids love it.

On North Haven

Coal Wharf Restaurant (207-867-4739), hidden away in the J. O. Brown & Sons Boatyard, overlooking the Fox Island Thoroughfare. Open for lunch and dinner in July and Aug., specializing in local seafood and on-island organic produce. Dinner entrées $15–25. Reservations advised.

Nebo Lodge (207-867-2007; www.nebolodge.com), 11 Mullins Ln., North Haven Village. Open seasonally for supper Wed.–Sat. Reserve. The menu changes nightly, depending on what's available locally. On a June night we began with fried green tomatoes with slab bacon and homemade aioli ($9) and dined on homemade "torn" pasta, fresh crabmeat, local pea shoots, and lemon crème fraiche ($18), topped off with rhubarb pie and cardamom-ginger ice cream ($8).

H. J. Blake's. (207-867-4739) Open seasonally 11–11. This snack shop with seating inside and out is at the summer heart of the village. Good burgers, fried foods, and the like.

Waterman's Community Center (www.watermans.org), North Haven Village. Open daily 6:30–4 for coffee, tea, muffins, sodas, and bagels in an airy, comfortable space with couches, tables, board games, and newspapers.

✱ Selective Shopping

In Carver's Harbor on Vinalhaven

The Paper Store (207-863-4826) is the nerve center of the island, the place everyone drops by at least once a day. Carlene Michael is as generous about dispensing directions to visitors as she is news to residents. This is also the place to check for current happenings like plays and concerts, and to get a chart of the island.

New Era Gallery (207-863-9351; www.neweragallery.com), Main St. Open Memorial Day–Dec. Artist Elaine Austin Crossman's recently expanded gallery shows work by some of Maine's most prominent painters, sculptors, photographers, and fiber artists.

Go Fish (207-863-4193), Main St. Open year-round, Tue.–Sat. 10–4:30. A cheerful kids-geared shop with books, games, and candy.

Second Hand Prose, Main St. Open Mon.–Sat. 9–4:30. Run by Friends of the Library and featuring secondhand books. Good selection of Maine and maritime titles.

Island Spirits (207-863-2192). Open Mon.–Sat. 11–6:30 in summer. Some of the "best cheeses you can ever hope for," great wines, beer and olives, and freshly ground coffee.

In North Haven Village

North Haven Gift Shop and Gallery (207-867-4444). Open Memorial Day–mid-Sept. (but closed Sun.), 9:30–5. Since 1954 June Hopkins (mother of Eric) runs this shop with rooms that meander on and on, filled with pottery, books, accessories, jewelry, and much more, including bags by the island's famous young designer, Angela Adams. Gallery exhibits change frequently. Hopkins keeps running accounts for summer families and knows the names of members of as many as six generations of a family when they walk in.

Calderwood Hall and North Island Fiber Shoppe (207-867-2265). Open year-round, daily 9–5, 10–2 Sun. Housed in a weathered building that has served as movie theater and dance hall, featuring paintings by owner Herbert Parsons; also offering an interesting mix of clothing and gifts, many island made, and Mickey Bullock's lustrous yarns, hand spun from her sheep. Wine, beer, and water are also sold.

Eric Hopkins Gallery (207-867-2229; www.erichopkins.com). Open by chance or appointment. Until the opening of Hopkins' Rockland gallery, this was the reason many people come to North Haven. The son of a North Haven fisherman, he is known for bold, distinctive paintings of clouds, deep blue water, and spiky green islands, and most recently, fish.

✷ Special Events

Year-round: **North Haven Arts Enrichment Presentations** include exceptional plays, concerts, and lectures performed in Waterman's Community Center in North Haven Village at the ferry landing. For details, phone 207-867-2100; www.watermans.org.

Summer season: **Concerts**, primarily classical, chamber, and jazz, are staged on both islands, sponsored by **Fox Islands Concerts**.

July–August: **Saturday Farmer's Market** at the ball field, North Haven Village, features crafts as well as produce. **Saturday Flea Market**, 10 AM in the field next to the Galamander, Carver's Harbor, Vinalhaven. **Union Church Baked Bean Supper** (*every other Thursday*), Vinalhaven.

Christina Tree

CALDERWOOD HALL GALLERY, NORTH HAVEN

For details about other regular occurrences on both islands, consult *The Wind*, a weekly newsletter published on Vinalhaven.

MATINICUS

Home to fewer than 60 hardy souls in winter, most of whom make their living lobstering, Matinicus's population grows to about 200 in summer. Maine's outermost island, it lies 22 miles at sea beyond the outer edge of Penobscot Bay. Quiet and unspoiled, it's a haven for birds and birders. Walking trails thread the meadows and shore, and there are two sand beaches—one at each end of the 750-acre island. Matinicus Rock is offshore, a protected nesting site for puffins, a lure for birders in June and July.

GUIDANCE For a brochure and general questions contact the **Matinicus Chamber of Commerce** (207-354-8354), 45 Thatcher St., Thomaston 04861.

GETTING THERE The flying time via **Penobscot Island Air** (207-596-7500) from Owls Head is 15 minutes, but flights may be canceled because of weather—and the fog can hang in there for days. That's when you contact **George Tarkleson** (207-691-9030), June 22–Oct. 20; it's a 70-minute ride. Inquire about puffin-, whale-, and seal-watching trips.

Penobscot Ferry (207-691-6030; www.penferry.com) makes charter runs to Matinicus and Criehaven and carries up to 12 people.

The Maine State Ferry (207-596-2022) takes 2¼ hours to ply between Matinicus and Rockland, four times a month May–Oct., and once a month the rest of the year.

✷ Lodging

Tuckanuck Lodge (207-366-3830; www.tuckanuck.com), Shag Hollow Rd., P.O. Box 217, Matinicus 04851. Open year-round. Well-behaved children and pets welcome. Nantucket native Bill Hoadley offers five rooms (two shared baths), some with a view of Old Cove and the ocean. $70 single, $100 double, including breakfast; half rate for children 12 and under; weekly rates available, less off-season. Guests have kitchen privileges for lunch (bring your own fixings); the lodge offers supper ($18–21 including salad and dessert; BYOB). Baked goods are available on-island, but there's no general store.

Cottage Rentals: See www.matinicusisland.com.

CAMDEN/ROCKPORT AREA

ISLESBORO

Smack on Rt. 1, Camden is the most popular way station between Kennebunkport or Boothbay Harbor and Bar Harbor. Seemingly half its 19th-century captains' homes are now B&Bs. Shops and restaurants line a photogenic harbor filled with private sailing and motor yachts. It's also a poor man's yacht haven—open year-round—with a thriving fishing industry. The ski area would make a good winter vacation destination as well as a summer tour.

Here, in 1935, artist Frank Swift refitted a few former fishing and cargo schooners to carry passengers around the islands in Penobscot Bay. He called the boats windjammers. Half a dozen members of Maine's current windjammer fleet are still based here (the rest are in neighboring ports), and several schooners offer daysails. You can also get out on the water in an excursion boat or a sea kayak.

From the water you can see two aspects of Camden not apparent from land. The first is the size and extent of the Camden Hills. The second is the size and number of the palatial old waterside "cottages" along Beauchamp Point, the rocky promontory separating Camden from Rockport. Here, as in Bar Harbor, summer residents were wise and powerful enough to preserve the local mountains, seeding the creation of the present 6,500-acre Camden Hills State Park, one of Maine's more spectacular places to hike.

Camden's first resort era coincided with those colorful decades during which steam and sail overlapped. As a stop on the Boston–Bangor steamboat line, Camden acquired a couple of big (now vanished) hotels. In 1900, when Bean's boatyard launched the world's first six-masted schooner, onlookers crowded the neighboring ornate steamboat wharf to watch.

In contrast with Boothbay and Bar Harbor, Camden has always been a year-round town and never overdependent on tourism. Camden's early business was, of course, building and sailing ships. By the mid-1800s half a dozen mills lined the series of falls on the Megunticook River, just a block or two from the waterfront. The vast wooden Knox Woolen Company—the "Harrington Mill" portrayed in the movie *Peyton Place*—made the felts used by Maine's paper mills to absorb water from paper stock. It operated until 1988, and now holds a hodgepodge of restaurants and businesses.

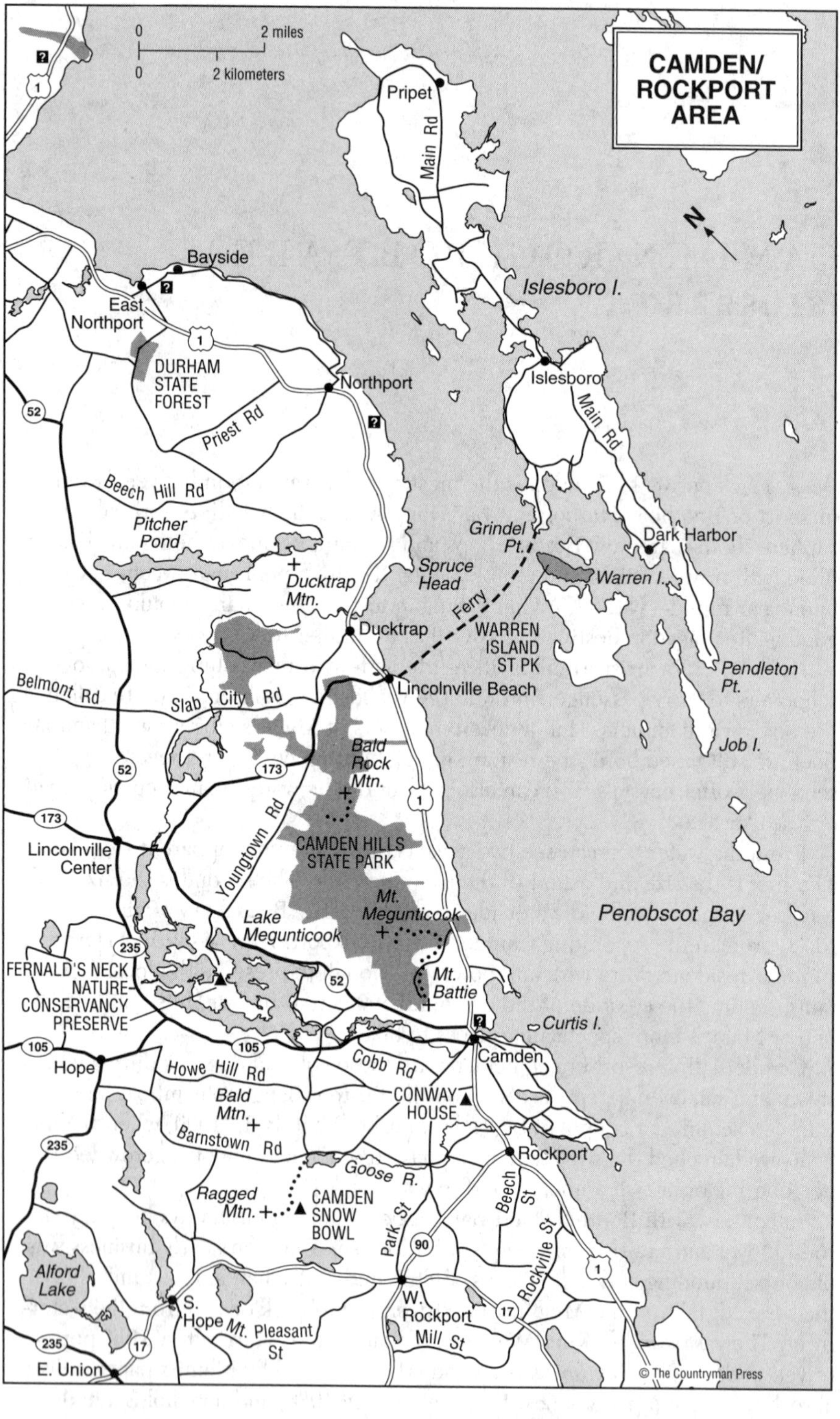

CAMDEN/ ROCKPORT AREA
0 2 miles
0 2 kilometers
N
Pripet
Main Rd
Islesboro I.
Islesboro
Main Rd
Dark Harbor
Grindel Pt.
Warren I.
WARREN ISLAND ST PK
Pendleton Pt.
Job I.
Spruce Head
Ferry
Bayside
East Northport
DURHAM STATE FOREST
Northport
Priest Rd
Beech Hill Rd
Pitcher Pond
Ducktrap Mtn.
Ducktrap
Lincolnville Beach
Belmont Rd
Slab City Rd
Bald Rock Mtn.
Youngtown Rd
CAMDEN HILLS STATE PARK
Lincolnville Center
Mt. Megunticook
Lake Megunticook
Mt. Battie
Penobscot Bay
FERNALD'S NECK NATURE CONSERVANCY PRESERVE
Curtis I.
Camden
Hope
Howe Hill Rd
Cobb Rd
Bald Mtn.
CONWAY HOUSE
Barnstown Rd
Rockport
Goose R.
Ragged Mtn.
CAMDEN SNOW BOWL
Beech St
Park St
Rockville St
Alford Lake
S. Hope
Mt. Pleasant St
W. Rockport
Mill St
E. Union
1
52
173
235
105
17
90
© The Countryman Press

Culturally enriched by its sophisticated populace—workaday residents, retired diplomats, military and intelligence officers, and summer people alike—Camden (along with Rockport) offers a bonanza of music, art, and theatrical productions, all of surprising quality. There are also world-renowned programs in filmmaking, computer science, woodworking, and photography.

Ironically, only a small fraction of the thousands of tourists who stream through Camden every summer take the time to discover the extent of its beauty. The tourist tide eddies around the harborside restaurants, shops, and galleries and continues to flow on up Rt. 1 toward Bar Harbor. Even in August you are likely to find yourself alone atop Mount Battie (accessible by car as well as on foot) or Mount Megunticook (highest point in the Camden Hills), or in the open-sided Vesper Hill Children's Chapel, with its flowers and sea view. Few visitors see, let alone swim in, Megunticook Lake or set foot on the nearby island of Islesboro.

A decade or two ago you could count on your fingers the number of places to stay here, but Camden has since become synonymous with B&Bs. A total of some 1,000 rooms can now be found in hotels, motels, inns, and cottages as well as the B&Bs between Camden and neighboring Lincolnville and Rockport.

GUIDANCE **Camden-Rockport-Lincolnville Chamber of Commerce** (207-236-4404 or 1-800-223-5459; www.visitcamden.com), 2 Public Landing (behind Cappy's), P.O. Box 919, Camden 04843. Open year-round, Mon.–Fri. 9–5 and Sat. 10–5; also open Sun. noon–4, mid-May–mid-Sept. You'll find all sorts of helpful brochures here, plus maps of Camden, Rockport, and Lincolnville, along with knowledgeable people to send you in the right direction. The chamber keeps tabs on vacancies during the high season, as well as on what's open off-season and cottages available to rent (a list is ready for requests each year by Jan.). Be sure to secure the 132-page *The Jewel of the Maine Coast*. Events are listed on the Web site. The Camden-Rockport Historical Society's *A Walking Tour*,

ROCKPORT HARBOR

Kim Grant

which outlines tours of historic districts in Camden and Rockport, is an essential publication that includes a bike and car route.

GETTING THERE *By air:* **Knox County Regional Airport**, at Owls Head, about 10 miles from Camden, offers daily flights to and from Boston. **Bangor International Airport** and **Portland International Jetport** offer connections to all parts of the country.

By bus: **Concord Trailways** (1-800-639-3317) stops on Rt. 1 at the Maritimes Farm, just south of Camden en route from Bangor to Portland and Boston and vice versa.

By limo: **MidCoast Limo** (207-236-2424 or 1-800-937-2424; www.midcoastlimo.com) makes runs from Portland International Jetport by reservation. **Schooner Bay Limo** (207-594-5000; www.alldirections.net) goes to Portland and elsewhere.

By car: Our preferred route, to bypass Rt. 1 traffic, is to take I-295 to Gardiner, then follow signs to Rt. 226. When this road ends, take a right onto Rt. 17, which winds through pretty countryside to Rt. 90, and then intersects with Rt. 1 leading into Camden.

PARKING Parking is a problem in July and August. In-town parking has a stringently enforced two-hour limit (just 15 minutes in a few spots, so be sure to read the signs). There are a few lots outside the center of town (try the Camden Marketplace and a lot on Mechanic St.). There's an advantage here to finding lodging within walking distance of the village. The chamber has a map that highlights all-day parking areas.

WHEN TO COME Camden and Rockport are open year-round with a thriving fishing industry; the ski area makes this area a good winter destination as well as a summer tour. But for sailing and swimming, summer is the time to come, and fall foliage constrasts beautifully with the blue water.

✱ Villages

Rockport's harbor is as picturesque as Camden's, and the small village is set high above it. Its quiet, subdued charm provides a nice respite from the hustle of Rt. 1. Steps (you have to look closely for them) lead down to Marine Park, a departure point in 1816 for 300 casks of lime shipped to Washington, D.C., to help construct the Capitol. In the small park you'll see the restored remains of a triple kiln, a saddleback steam locomotive, and a granite sculpture of André the Seal, the legendary performer who drew crowds every summer in the early and mid-1980s. The village (part of Camden until 1891) includes the restored Rockport Opera House, site of the Bay Chamber Concerts, the noted Center for Maine Contemporary Art, the Maine Photographic Workshops program, and a salting of restaurants and shops.

Lincolnville's landmarks—the Lobster Pound Restaurant, Maine State Ferry to Islesboro, and the Whale's Tooth Pub, formerly a customhouse, with a big fireplace—serve as centerpieces for proliferating shops, restaurants, and B&Bs. The beach offers a nice swimming spot on hot days and good beachcombing when the temperature drops.

✷ To See

LIGHTHOUSE **Curtis Island Light**. A public park, the island is nevertheless accessible only by boat, and the lighthouse is not open to the public. The best views are from sightseeing cruises leaving Camden Harbor, but you can also walk down to where Bayview Street connects with Beacon to find a good look-out.

MUSEUMS ✐ ♿ **Old Conway Homestead and Cramer Museum** (207-236-2257), Conway Rd. (off Rt. 1 at the Camden–Rockport town line). Open July and Aug., Mon.–Thu. 10–4; admission $5 adults, $4 seniors 60-plus, $2 students 6–18, children 5 and under free; 10 percent AAA discount. Open June and Sept. by appointment. Administered by the Camden-Rockport Historical Society, this restored early-18th-century farmhouse features antiques from several periods. The barn holds collections of carriages, sleighs, and early farm tools; don't miss the Victorian privy, blacksmith shop, and 1820 maple sugar house, where sugaring demonstrations are held each spring. **The Cramer Museum** displays local memorabilia and changing exhibits.

Schoolhouse Museum (207-789-5445), Rt. 173, Lincolnville Beach. Open Mon., Wed., and Fri. 1–4 June–Oct., other times by appointment. Admission is free. A small museum detailing the history of Lincolnville, with exhibits that change often and include stereoptics and tintypes, early settlers' tools, and Native American artifacts. The museum also publishes *Ducktrap: Chronicles of a Maine Village*, an excellent book on local history, and *Staying Put in Lincolnville, Maine*, both by local author Diane O'Brien.

SCENIC DRIVE Drive or, better yet, bicycle around **Beauchamp Point**. Begin on Chestnut St. in Camden and follow this peaceful road by the lily pond and on by the herd of **belted Galloway cows** (black on both ends and white in the middle). Take Calderwood Lane through the woods and by the **Vesper Hill Children's Chapel**, built on the site of a former hotel and banked with flowers, a great spot to get married or simply to sit. Continue along Beauchamp Ave. to Rockport Village to lunch or picnic by the harbor, and return via Union St. to Camden.

OTHER SITES **Cellardoor Vineyard** (207-763-4478; www.mainewine.com), 367 Youngtown Rd., Lincolnville. A seven-acre vineyard with 15 varieties of grapes, the winery now makes 13 different wines with, for instance, Vidal Blanc grapes (an American hybrid), Cayuga white grapes, and Niagara grapes (for its Amorosa). The signature red wine is called Trilogy, made with Cabernet Sauvignon, Marechel Foch, and DeChaunac grapes. Open for wine tastings in the 18th-century barn 11–6 daily from mid-May through Oct., when the grapes are harvested.

✱ To Do

BICYCLING **Camden Hills State Park**, Rt. 1, Camden, has a 10-mile (round-trip) ride through the woods on a snowmobile trail. Bikes are not allowed on hiking trails. The **Camden Snow Bowl** also offers a number of rides through woods and swamps, as well as riding on ski trails. It's a hearty ride, but the views from the top are terrific.

Georges River Bikeways. The Georges River Land Trust (207-594-5166) puts out a pamphlet highlighting several good biking routes, with many scenic spots within the Georges River watershed.

Maine Sport Outfitters (207-236-7120 or 1-800-722-0826; www.mainesport.com), Rt. 1, Rockport, rents Raleigh hybrids, as well as bike trailers and car racks for a day or extended periods. Rentals include helmet, lock, water bottles, and cable.

BOAT EXCURSIONS See also *Windjammers*.

Yacht charters are offered spring to autumn along the Maine coast. Most charters run for a week, although sometimes it's possible to charter a boat just for a long weekend, with or without crew. For more information, contact **Johanson Boatworks** (207-596-7060 or 1-877-4JOHANS), which rents everything from J-40 sloops to Ericson 38s. **Bay Island Yacht Charters** (1-800-421-2492; www.sailme.com) has yachts available for bareboat, skippered, or crewed charters out of Rockland as well as other ports the length of Maine's coast. They also run hiking, sightseeing, and kayak tours. **Rockport Charters** (207-691-1066) offers, with advance notice, 20-passenger, three-hour wildlife charters to see puffins, eagles, ospreys, and more. Leaving from both Camden and Rockland, as well as Rockport, Captain Robert Iserbyt also provides transportation for workers out to North Haven.

WINDJAMMERS IN CAMDEN HARBOR
Kim Grant

It would be a shame to be in Camden and not spend some time on the water. **The two-hour sailing excursions** are a wonderful way to get a taste of what the harbor has to offer if your time is limited. Remember to bring a jacket, because the air can get chilly once you're offshore, even on a sunny day. Wander down the wooden boardwalk and check the offerings, which include:

Schooner *Appledore II* (207-236-8353 or 1-800-233-PIER; www.apple dore2.com), an 86-foot schooner (the largest of the daysailing fleet), has sailed around the world and now offers several trips daily, including sunset cruises.

Surprise (207-236-4687; www.camdenmainesailing.com), a traditional, historic, 57-foot schooner, offers entertaining, informative two-hour sails. Capt. Jack and wife Barbara Moore spent seven years cruising between Maine and the Caribbean, educating their four children on board in the process.

Olad (207-236-2323; www.maineschooners.com), a 57-foot schooner, offers two-hour sails and charters.

Schooner Yacht *Heron* (207-236-8605 or 1-800-599-8605; www.woodenboatco .com), runs lobster lunch, mid-afternoon, and evening sails (BYOB, with hors d'oeuvre served) out of Rockport for a maximum of 36 passengers. With typically eight to 20 passengers on the regular sails, this 65-foot schooner, built in 2003 in Camden by its owners, is available for private trips.

Betselma (207-236-4446; www.betselma.com), a motor launch, provides 1-hour coastal and two-hour island trips (owner Les Bex was a longtime windjammer captain) out of the harbor and down the coast. Combine the two for a three-hour journey.

Lively Lady Too (207-236-6672 or 418-839-7933; www3.sympatico.ca/lively .lady), a traditional lobster boat, takes passengers on two-hour ecotours that can include watching lobster traps being hauled and swinging in close to an island for birdwatching. A monitor on the deck shows video of the ocean floor.

Schooner *Lazy Jack II* (207-230-0602; www.schoonerlazyjack.com). Two-hour sails and private charters from Camden Harbor, with Capt. Sean O'Connor.

♿ **Maine State Ferry** from Lincolnville Beach to Islesboro (207-734-6935). At $7.50 round-trip per passenger, $17.75 per vehicle, and $6.25 per bicycle, this is the bargain of the local boating scene. An extra $14 each way secures your reservation. (See *Getting There* under "Islesboro.")

BOWLING **Oakland Park Bowling Lanes** (207-594-7525), 714 Commercial St., Rockport. Susan and Joe Plaskas have updated this old-fashioned bowling alley with new carpeting. Video games, air hockey, and VDR are located in the lower section.

GOLF **Goose River Golf Club** (207-236-8488), Simonton Rd., Rockport. Nine holes, but you can play through twice using different starting tees. Cart rentals; clubhouse. Tee times recommended any time of the week; you can request one 24 hours in advance, but not more than that.

Golfers Crossing Miniature Golf (207-230-0090); water hazards and obstacles complete this mini golf experience on Route 1 in Rockport.

Samoset Resort Golf Course (clubhouse, 207-594-1431), Rockport, has an 18-hole, par-70 course with seven oceanside holes and ocean views from 14 holes. A renovation includes a redesigned 18th hole featuring a stone seawall, a remodeled 185-yard, par-3 5th hole, and renovations to hole 4. The clubhouse has a pro shop, locker rooms, and the **Clubhouse Grille**. Carts are available.

HIKING **Bald Rock Mountain**. This 1,100-foot mountain in Lincolnville once had a ski area at the top. Great views of Penobscot Bay and the Camden Hills. You'll find the trailhead 1.25 miles down a dirt road from the gate on Ski Lodge Rd. (off Youngtown Rd.). The climb is about 0.5 mile long and moderate. Ask about overnight camping at the Camden Hills State Park headquarters on Rt. 1 in Camden.

Georges Highland Path is a 37-mile trail network created and maintained by the Georges River Land Trust (207-594-5166; www.grlt.org). The most recent section travels through the Oyster River Bog, a magnificent semiwilderness area with a 7.2-mile trail that links the Thomaston Town Forest with the Ragged Mountain section. A map put out by the trust details distances and hiking times and shows where the trailheads are.

Bay Island Yacht Charters (see *Boat Excursions*) also offers guided hiking tours.

Coastal Mountain Hiking (207-236-7731), Camden, offers guided hikes and packed lunches.

See also **Camden Hills State Park** in *Green Space.*

SEA KAYAKING **Ducktrap Sea Kayak Tours** (207-236-8608), Lincolnville Beach, offers two-hour and half-day guided tours in Penobscot Bay. No experience is necessary; in fact, most patrons are first-time kayakers. Group and family tours, rentals, and lessons are also available.

Maine Sport Outfitters (207-236-8797 or 1-800-722-0826; www.mainesport.com), on Rt. 1 just south of Rockport, is no mere outfitter—it's a phenomenon. Be sure to stop. They offer courses in kayaking, guided excursions around Camden Harbor and out into Penobscot Bay, and island-based workshops. They also rent kayaks and canoes. Contact them for a catalog of activities (also see *Special Learning Programs*).

SPECIAL LEARNING PROGRAMS **Camden Yacht Club Sailing Program** (207-236-4575; off-season 207-236-7033), Bayview St., Camden, provides sailing classes for children and adults, boat owners and non-boat-owners, during late June, July, and Aug.

Maine Media Workshops (207-236-8581; www.theworkshops.com), Rockport. This nationally respected year-round school for photography, cinematography, television produc-

THE CAMDEN HILLS

Far less recognized than Acadia National Park as a hiking haven, the Camden Hills offer ample challenge and some spectacular views for the average hiker. Mount Battie is accessible by a moderate and sometimes steep 0.5-mile trail just off Rt. 52 and is the only peak also accessible by car. The 1-mile Maiden Cliff Trail (park off Rt. 52, 2.9 miles from Rt. 1) is favored by locals for its views from the top of 800-foot sheer cliffs overlooking Lake Megunticook; it connects with the 2.5-mile Ridge Trail to the summit of Mount Megunticook (1,380 feet).

tion, and related fields offers a choice of 200 programs that vary in length from one week to three months for every skill level. The faculty includes established, recognized professionals from across the country; the students come from around the world. Housing is provided for most of the students, and the school helps arrange accommodations for others. Also a gallery with changing exhibitions, open to the public.

Bay Island Sailing School (1-800-421-2492; www.sailme.com) is headquartered in Camden but based at Journey's End Marina in Rockland. This ASA-certified sailing school offers weeklong, weekend, and private sailing lessons for basic, intermediate, and advanced levels, plus offshore and navigation courses. Enroll online or in person at the school.

The Center for Maine Contemporary Art (207-236-2875; www.artsmaine.org; see *Entertainment* and *Selective Shopping*), 162 Russell Ave., Rockport (formerly Maine Coast Artists). Professional development for artists includes year-round weekend and long-term workshops and lectures for visual artists. Numerous gallery talks and art lectures open to the public.

Maine Sport Outfitters (207-236-8797; www.mainesport.com), Rockport. This Rt. 1 complex is worth a stop whether you're up for adventure sports or not. The place has evolved over the years from a fly-fishing and canvas shop into a multitiered store that's a home base for adventure tours. Inquire about a wide variety of local kayaking tours and multiday kayaking workshops geared to all levels of ability, based at its facilities on Gay Island.

Center for Furniture Craftsmanship (207-594-5611; www.woodschool.com), 25 Mill St., Rockport. June–Oct. Hands-on one- and two-week workshops for novice, intermediate, and advanced woodworkers and cabinetmakers. Twelve-week intensive courses are also offered a couple of times a year. A nine-month comprehensive course runs from Sept. to June.

SWIMMING ✐ Saltwater swimming from Camden's **Laite Memorial Park and Beach**, Upper Bayview St.; at **Lincolnville Beach**, Rt. 1 north of Camden; and in Rockport at **Walker Park**, across the road from Marine Park. Freshwater swimming at **Megunticook Lake**, Lincolnville (**Barret Cove Memorial Park and Beach**; turn left off Rt. 52 northwest of Camden), where you'll also find picnic grounds and a parking area; **Shirttail Beach**, Camden (Rt. 105); and at the **Willis Hodson Park** on the Megunticook River, Camden (Molyneaux Rd.). At the **Penobscot Bay YMCA** (207-236-3375), Union St., visitors can pay a day-use fee that entitles them to swim in the Olympic-sized pool (check hours for family swimming, lap swimming, and other programs), use the weight rooms, and play basketball in the gym.

TENNIS There are two public tennis courts at the **Camden Snow Bowl** on Hosmer Pond Rd. (first come, first served). In addition, **Samoset Resort** (207-594-2511), Rockport, has outdoor courts, as does the **Rockport Recreation Park** (207-236-9648).

WALKING TOUR **The Camden-Rockport Historical Society** (207-236-2257) has prepared a brochure (available at the chamber of commerce and the Cramer Museum) with a 2.5-mile walk past historic buildings. The brochure includes historical details and a sketch map. An expanded bicycle or car tour encompassing two towns is also included.

WINDJAMMERS Windjammer cruises are offered late May–mid-Oct. Fourteen traditional tall ships sail from Camden, Rockland, and Rockport on three- to six-day cruises throughout Penobscot Bay. For brochures and sailing schedules, contact the **Maine Windjammer Association** (1-800-807-WIND; www.sailmainecoast.com).

Angelique (207-785-3020 or 1-800-282-9989; www.sailangelique.com), Camden, is a 95-foot ketch that was built expressly for the windjammer trade in 1980. Patterned after 19th-century English fishing vessels, she offers 15 passenger cabins, a pleasant deck-level salon with piano, belowdecks showers, and rowboats for exploring the coast.

Timberwind (207-236-0801 or 1-800-759-9250; www.schoonertimberwind.com), Rockport. Built in Portland in 1931 as a pilot schooner, this pretty 74-foot vessel was converted to a passenger vessel in 1969. She has an enclosed handheld shower on deck and room for 20 passengers. The only windjammer sailing out of Rockport Harbor, the *Timberwind* welcomes families with children ages 5 and up on most cruises.

Lewis R. French (207-594-2241 or 1-800-469-4635; www.schoonerfrench.com), Camden, was launched on the Damariscotta River in 1871 and is the oldest documented vessel in the windjammer fleet. Before becoming a passenger vessel, the *French* carried cargo such as lumber, firewood, bricks, granite, lime—even Christmas trees—along the coast. She had three major rebuilds, the most recent in 1976 when she was brought into passenger service. Sixty-five feet long, the *French* accommodates 22 passengers in 13 private cabins with freshwater sinks and portholes that open. Hot, freshwater shower on board. Capt. Garth Wells enjoys getting his guests actively involved in the experience of sailing an authentic 19th-century schooner.

Mary Day (1-800-992-2218; www.schoonermaryday.com), Camden, was the first schooner built specifically for carrying passengers. At 90 feet, she's among the swiftest; Capts. Barry King and Jen Martin have extensive sailing experience. Features include a fireplace and parlor organ and hot, freshwater showers on the deck. The *Mary Day* accommodates up to 30 passengers, and meals include a New England boiled dinner, baked goods made in the galley's woodstove, and a lobster bake on six-day cruises.

Grace Bailey, Mercantile, and ***Mistress*** (207-236-2938 or 1-888-692-7245; www.mainewindjammercruises.com), Maine Windjammer Cruises, Camden. For years known as the *Mattie*, *Grace Bailey* took back her original name following a thorough restoration in 1990. Built in 1882 in New York, the 81-foot *Grace Bailey* once carried cargo along the Atlantic coast and to the West Indies. She has belowdecks showers. *Mercantile* was built in Maine in 1916 as a shallow-draft coasting schooner; 78 feet long, she has been in the windjammer trade since its beginning in 1942. There are belowdecks showers. *Mistress*, the smallest of the fleet at 46 feet, carries just six passengers. A topsail schooner built in 1967 along the lines of the old coasting schooners, she is also available for private charter. All three cabins have private head, but there is no shower on board.

✷ Winter Sports

CROSS-COUNTRY SKIING **Camden Hills State Park** (207-236-3109) marks and maintains some trails for cross-country skiing, and there's a ski hut on Mount Battie. (See *Green Space.*)

Tanglewood 4-H Camp (207-789-5868 or 1-877-944-2267), 1 Tanglewood Rd., off Rt. 1 near Lincolnville Beach. Ungroomed, scenic cross-country trails that wend through woodlands and along streams. Maps with a description of trails are found at the kiosk at the head of the trail on the loop of the road.

DOWNHILL SKIING **Camden Snow Bowl** (207-236-3438; www.camdensnowbowl.com), Hosmer Pond Rd., Camden. The only place you can ski overlooking views of the Atlantic Ocean! With a 850-foot vertical drop, 10 trails for beginners through experts, and night skiing, this is a comfortably sized area where everyone seems to know everyone else. Facilities include a base lodge, rental and repair shop, ski school, and cafeteria, plus the Jack Williams Toboggan Chute ($5 per person/per hour) and tube sliding ($5 per person/ per hour). Come the second weekend in February, when the Snow Bowl hosts the hilarious annual U.S. National Toboggan Championship Races at the toboggan chute (right next to the ski area). Outlandishly costumed teams make mad runs down the chute at 40-plus miles an hour, bottoming out on the ice-covered Hosmer Pond.

✷ Green Space

Camden Hills State Park (207-236-3109; off-season, 207-236-0849), 280 Belfast Rd., Rt. 1, Camden. $3 adults, $1 ages 5–11; free under 5 and 65 and older with a Maine state pass. In addition to Mount Battie, this 6,500-acre park includes Mount Megunticook, one of the highest points on the Atlantic seaboard, and a shoreside picnic site. You can drive to the top of Mount Battie on the road that starts at the park entrance, just north of town. At the entrance pick up a *Camden Hills State Park* brochure, which outlines 19 trails with distance and difficulty level. In winter many of the trails convert to cross-country ski runs, given snow. There are 106 campsites available May 15–Oct. 14.

Warren Island State Park, also administered by Camden Hills State Park, is just a stone's throw off the island of Islesboro. The park features picnic tables, trails, and tent sites. Accessibility is the problem: You can arrange to have a private boat carry you over from the mainland, rent your own boat in Camden, or paddle out in a sea kayak. Because of this, the island boasts a peace and quiet often hard to find on the mainland in high season.

Marine Park, off Russell Ave. (just after you cross the bridge), Rockport. A nicely landscaped waterside area with sheltered picnic tables. Restored lime kilns and a locomotive remind visitors of the era when the town's chief industry was processing and exporting lime. During a stroll you're likely to see several painters capturing the picturesque harbor on canvas.

Merryspring Nature Center (207-236-2239; www.merryspring.org), Camden. Open to the public year-round during daylight hours. A 66-acre private preserve with walking trails; herb, lily, demonstration, and rose gardens; raised beds; and an arboretum. The Goose River bisects the preserve, which is accessible via Conway Rd. from Rt. 1 in Camden. Wildlife abounds here, and birders frequent the gardens on the lookout for the kind that flies. If you're lucky you'll see white-tailed deer, ermine, otter, porcupine, raccoon, rabbit, even moose or bobcat. Weekly talks in summer. Free.

Fernald's Neck Preserve (207-729-5181). At the end of Fernald Neck Rd. off Rt. 52, just past the intersection with Youngtown Rd., Lincolnville and Camden. Open during daylight hours; no pets allowed. The preserve's 326 acres cover most of a heavily wooded peninsula that juts into Lake Megunticook. A brochure of walking trails is available at the registration box near the entrance. Trails lead to stunning water views. Trails can be boggy: Wear boots or old shoes.

Amphitheatre and Camden Harbor Park (207-236-3440), Atlantic Ave., Camden. The ampitheatre, designed by Fletcher Steele in 1929, is on the National Register of Historic Places; it's a magical setting for summertime concerts, and a good place to sit, think, or read anytime. Across the street, Harbor Park covers a manicured slope down to the water, with a Megunticook River waterfall in its midst. Picnic on one of the benches overlooking Camden Harbor. The grounds are beautifully maintained after a renovation in 2004.

Curtis Island, in the outer harbor. A small island with a lighthouse that marks the entrance to Camden. It's a public picnic spot and a popular sea kayaking destination.

✷ Lodging

All listings are in Camden 04843 unless otherwise noted

Note: If you choose one of the many B&Bs in historic houses on Elm, Main, or High Sts. (all are Rt. 1), you might want to ask what pains have been taken to muffle the sound of passing traffic.

Camden Accommodations (207-236-6090 or 1-800-344-4830; www.camdenac.com), 43 Elm St., is a vacation rental agency with more than 85 private properties in the Camden area.

Camden Bed & Breakfast Association (innkeeper@camdeninns.com), P.O. Box 553. The brochure lists 13 members with descriptions of each and contact information.

RESORT ♿ **Samoset Resort** (207-594-2511 or 1-800-341-1650; www.samoset.com), 220 Warrenton St., Rockport 04856. The original Samoset lodge burned down in the 1980s. The present resort has just undergone a $5 million renovation; flat screen TVs and fine linens are just part of it. Set on 230 oceanfront acres, the 178 rooms include suites, many with ocean views, balcony or patio; all have private bath and air-conditioning.

Time-share units and the two-bedroom Flume Cottage, perched on a rocky outcropping above the water, are also available (cottage weekly in-season). The Samoset has a world-class 18-hole golf course and golf center, outdoor tennis courts, Nautilus-equipped fitness club, spa and sauna, and indoor and heated, handicapped accessible outdoor pools. Samoset takes wonderful care of families with young children with a children's program during July and August and other school holidays. The dining room, Marcel's (see *Dining Out*), and the adjacent Breakwater Café have a large fireplace and floor-to-ceiling windows overlooking the water. Rooms $269–529, off-season $129–369.

INNS **The Belmont** (207-236-8053 or 1-800-238-8053; www.thebelmontinn.com), 6 Belmont St. Open mid-May–Oct. The peaceful location a few blocks off Rt. 1 combined with Sherry and Bruce Cobb's hospitality make this a favorite inn. An 1890s Edwardian house with a wraparound veranda, the Belmont has six guest rooms, all with private bath and several with a gas fireplace. Full breakfast, afternoon tea, and dessert in the evening. $120–175 per night in-season.

Whitehall Inn (207-236-3391 or 1-800-789-6565; www.whitehall-inn.com), 52 High St. (Rt. 1). Open Memorial Day through the week after Columbus Day. New owners Greg and Sue Marquise preside over the large, low-beamed lobby of this old inn; adjoining parlors are fitted with Oriental rugs and sofas, games, and a guest computer. The Millay Room, with its vintage-1904 Steinway, looks much the way it did on the summer evening in 1912 when a local girl, Edna St. Vincent Millay, read her poem "Renascence" to assembled guests; you can learn about the evening in the words hung on the walls. One of the guests was so impressed that she paid for Millay's Vassar education. Forty guest rooms in the main inn, five more in the Wicker House across Rt. 1, and a three-bedroom suite hold simple, old-fashioned furnishings, but the Italian sheets and duvet covers are ironed daily. Most rooms have private bath, and a heavy old hotel phone the likes of which your children have probably never seen. The bar called Gossip is decorated with *Peyton Place* memorabilia; some of the movie was filmed here. The fresh-cut fruit bowl offered at breakfast is the best I've encountered. A "sneaker" beach (wear shoes because of the rocks) is a short walk away. Rooms $135–170; $85–125 off-season.

The Blue Harbor House (207-236-3196 or 1-800-248-3196; www.blueharborhouse.com), 67 Elm St. Open year-round. This friendly 10-room inn serves dinner to guests (by reservation) as well as breakfast on the spacious sunporch. Breakfast might include Dutch babies (custard-type pancakes with fresh fruit, Maine maple syrup, almonds, and powdered sugar). Fresh Scottish shortbread was baking for the afternoon snack on our visit. Rooms are pleasantly decorated with country antiques and handmade quilts; all have private bath, telephone, air-conditioning, and TV/VCR. The Captain's Quarters has a kitchenette. Doubles $95–205.

Hartstone Inn (207-236-4259 or 1-800-788-4823; www.hartstoneinn.com), 41 Elm St. Open year-round.

Mary Jo and Michael Salmon have created one of the most romantic inns in town. The eight guest rooms and six suites (all with private bath) are tasteful and elaborate, some offering a fireplace and canopy bed. Inn guests and the public alike may stay for dinner, an elegant, multicourse affair served by candlelight on the lovely porch (see *Dining Out*). In high season $125–265 double with full breakfast and afternoon tea and cookies; low season $105–185. Dinner is $45 prix fixe per person. Guests who would like to try professional cooking can sign up for the inn's "Chef for a Day" package and prepare the multicourse dinner. Other food lovers packages involve mushroom hunting and tours of local cheesemakers.

BED & BREAKFASTS **The Camden Maine Stay** (207-236-9636; www.camdenmainestay.com), 22 High St. (Rt. 1). Open year-round. Innkeepers Bob and Juanita Topper keep a high polish on this Greek Revival house, one of the oldest and most famous in Camden's High Street Historic District. Stay in one of four standard rooms and four suites with names like the Common Ground Room, which has a cathedral ceiling and private deck over the garden. The lower-level carriage house room is especially appealing, with well-stocked, built-in bookshelves, a woodstove, and French doors opening onto a private patio with lawn and woods beyond. The two-acre property is embellished with impeccable gardens. You can have breakfast in the formal dining room or on the sunporch overlooking the gardens. Afternoon tea and sweets included in the $125–250 double room rate, in season; $110–185 off.

The Hawthorn (207-236-8842; www.camdenhawthorn.com), 9 High St. (Rt. 1). Open year-round. Owner Maryanne Shanahan has renovated each of the 10 guest rooms at this Victorian inn, a short walk to Camden. The spacious carriage house rooms each have a double Jacuzzi, TV/VCR, fireplace, and private deck. The Queen Anne Tower holds two bedrooms, a Victorian slipper tub, and four shades of violet that make the walls luminous. The innovative breakfast, served alfresco in good weather, may include house hazelnut granola. $129–289 in high season. A landscaped garden spreads out beyond the deck, where breakfast is served in fine weather. Children are welcome in rooms that accommodate more than two people.

Norumbega (207-236-4646 or 1-877-363-4646; www.norumbegainn.com), 63 High St. (Rt. 1). Open year-round. With one of the most imposing facades of any B&B anywhere, this turreted stone "castle" has long been a landmark, just north of Camden. Inside you'll find an ornate staircase with fireplace and love seat on the landing, formal parlor, and dining room with blue-tiled fireplace. Eleven guest rooms and two suites named for European castles come with king or queen bed, private bath, antiques, phone, and TV. Ask for the Library Suite, two rooms with a loft balcony full of books that formed the original castle library. Doubles $160–475, including full breakfast and evening hors d'oeuvres; a 10 percent service charge is added to the bill. Two-night minimum on weekends. The inn welcomes children 7 and up, and offers murder mystery weekends.

The Camden Windward

House (207-236-9656 or 1-877-492-9656; www.windwardhouse.com), 6 High St. (Rt. 1). Open year-round. Kristen and Jesse Bifulco have added a cozy bar upstairs with a second floor deck overlooking Mount Battie; they have been hosting garden weddings and entertaining guests here since 2005. The five guest rooms and three suites all have private bath, air-conditioning, cable TV, and clock-radio with CD player. The Chart Room Suite features a living room with fireplace, TV/DVD, library, sofa, Jacuzzi whirlpool tub, separate bedroom with queen canopy bed, and French doors that open onto a private deck overlooking the garden. Breakfast might include an avocado omelet and in-season fruits and vegetables. $125–280 in high season, $99–199 in low.

A Little Dream (207-236-8742; www.littledream.com), 60 High St. (Rt. 1). Open year-round except Mar. Raised up on a hill over busy Rt. 1, this place feels wonderfully secluded and intimate, while sustaining a high standard of elegance. Seven guest rooms include a carriage house suite called the Isle Watch. Overlooking the harbor and Curtis Island, it has a gas fireplace, king canopy bed, soaking tub, and covered porch complete with porch swing. If you stay here over July 4, you can view three separate fireworks displays right from the inn. $159–295 double includes breakfast, perhaps an apple cheddar omelet or lemon ricotta pancakes. Two-night minimum on holiday weekends. Foreign guests are always welcome: Innkeeper JoAnna Ball speaks Italian, German, and French. Her husband, Bill Fontana, is a sculptor, and many guests are artists.

🐾 ⚭ 🥂 **Inns at Blackberry Common** (207-236-6060 or 1-800-388-6000; www.blackberryinn.com), 82 Elm St. Open year-round. Cyndi and Jim Ostrowski's two buildings hold some of the prettiest interiors in town. Settees covered in silk damask, ornate Oriental rugs, and decorative swords set the style. Stay in the Bette Davis, where the movie star slept after the cast party for *Peyton Place*, with a queen brass bed and antique lighting fixture. The garden rooms are cozy, with fireplace and whirlpool bath. Children are welcome in rooms that can accommodate them. $129–249 in-season, $99–189 off, including a full breakfast served in the dining room or in the courtyard.

♿ **Inn at Ocean's Edge** (207-236-0945; www.innatoceansedge.com), P.O. Box 258, Lincolnville 04849. Look for the entrance off Rt. 1 a couple of miles north of the Camden line. Open year-round. This modern hotel features a main inn with three common areas, a breakfast room, and 18 guest rooms; the Hilltop building with 12 rooms nestled farther from the bay; a restaurant; and a spa. Believe it or not, almost every single room features a water view, and they all have a Jacuzzi, gas fireplace, TV, VCR, stereo, and more. The Spa building holds two luxury suites. Steps lead down to a private shingle beach. The delicious breakfasts include such specials as Grand Marnier French toast. An elegant heated pool, spa with treatment rooms, sauna, and whirlpool are available to guests, and a fine-dining restaurant stands next door (see *Dining Out*). $195–425, depending on room and season, includes breakfast. Children 14 and up welcome.

The Inn at Sunrise Point (207-236-

7716 or 1-800-435-6278; www.sunrisepoint.com), Sunrise Point Rd., P.O. Box 1344, Camden, 04843. Open May–Oct. Set on a four-acre waterfront estate just over the town line in Lincolnville, this small, luxurious B&B was acquired in 2002 by Irishman and raconteur Stephen Tallon and his Australian-raised, American-born wife, Deanna. Four cottages named for Maine painters and writers—among them Winslow Homer and Richard Russo—have an incredible view, fireplace, private deck, and Jacuzzi; the three rooms in the main house feature a fireplace and water views. The Rachel Carson suite and the Wyeth Loft are also on the property, and all offer queen or king bed, phone, and TV/DVD. Common rooms include a glass conservatory, plus a snug, wood-paneled library with fireplace perfect for cooler days. Three rooms, one suite, and the loft are $300–395, cottages $395–595, full breakfast included.

"I" **The Victorian by the Sea** (207-236-3785 or 1-800-382-9817; www.victorianbythesea.com), Lincolnville Beach 04849. Open year-round. Ginny and Greg Ciraldo own this quiet, romantic spot overlooking the water, away from the bustle of Rt. 1. As the name suggests, decor is Victorian. There are seven guest rooms, all with queen bed, private bath, and a fireplace. We especially like the Victorian Suite, with a turret room, fireplace, and lovely water views, in the off-season. The $159–239 summer rate includes full breakfast with, perhaps, crème brûlée French toast, or peach strata, and afternoon sweets. The Ciraldos also own the 13-unit motel at the top of the road and the house between the inn and the bay, and have created a nature path to the top of a 30-foot cliff overlooking Penobscot Bay, where guests have seen porpoises, seals, and bald eagles.

OTHER LODGING **High Tide Inn** (207-236-3724 or 1-800-778-7068; www.hightideinn.com), Rt. 1. Open May–late Oct. Set far enough back from Rt. 1 to preclude traffic noise, this no-frills, easygoing complex appeals to singles and couples (who tend to choose one of the five rooms in the inn) and families (who opt for a cottage, two-bedroom deck house, or motel unit, five with connecting sleeping rooms). Most of the 31 rooms have breathtaking views—especially for the price—and they're all extremely clean. The complex fills seven quiet acres of landscaped grounds that slope to the water, where there's more than 250 feet of private ocean beach. A generous continental breakfast includes just-baked popovers and muffins. Pets allowed in only four of the cottages. The living room and bar have working fireplaces. $85–225. Two-night minimum weekends in July and Aug. and over holidays.

"I" **Lord Camden Inn** (207-236-4325 or 1-800-336-4325; www.lordcamdeninn.com), 24 Main St. Open year-round. This inn is named for the British nobleman who championed the American cause in the House of Lords during the Revolutionary War. Occupying a restored 1893 brick Masonic hall, the Lord Camden sits smack dab in the center of town and takes up several floors above a row of Main St. shops. Six luxury suites line the top floor. The 36 rooms offer cable TV, private bath, telephone, air-conditioning, and elevator. Most rooms have two double beds and private balcony overlooking the town and harbor or the river and hills beyond. In June to Nov., rates include a full breakfast with a make-your-own waffle stand; a continental breakfast is served off-season. Owner Marianne Smith's painted still lifes hang on many walls in the inn. $99–289, depending on the view and season.

Cedarholm Garden Bay Inn (207-236-3886; www.cedarholm.com), Rt. 1, Lincolnville Beach 04849. Guests enjoy the luxuries of these unusual accommodations, and the pleasures of their privacy and setting make a stay extraordinary. Gorgeously landscaped grounds featuring mature trees and gardens lead to the four cottages set off by the sea. Named for birds found on the Maine coast (Osprey, Puffin, Tern, and Loon), these gems set at the edge of Penobscot Bay abound with myriad features: fireplace, Jacuzzi, queen (or king) bed, Thomasville furniture, wet bars with microwave ovens, small fridges, and a fabulous view from a private deck. Two recently renovated upper cottages, closer to Rt. 1, have a private bath, wet bar, and mini-fridge. Continental breakfast includes muffins baked with berries grown here, and fresh fruit. All guests have access to a shared deck right on the beach. Upper units begin at $175 per night. Luxury cottages $300-495 per night.

CAMPING **Megunticook Campground by the Sea** (207-594-2428; www.campgroundbythesea.com), P.O. Box 375, Rockport 04856. Open May 15–mid or early Oct. Wooded, oceanfront campground with 100 sites and 10 rustic camping cabins. Facilities include a store, recreation hall, fishing, heated pool, and oceanfront picnic area and gardens for Saturday-night lobster bakes. $35–45 in-season. **Camden Hills RV Resort** (207-236-2498), 30 Applewood Rd. in Rockport, is a sister park.

✱ Where to Eat

DINING OUT **Francine Bistro** (207-230-0083; www.francinebistro.com), 55 Chestnut St., Camden. Open Tue.–Sat. 5:30–10; reservations recommended. Small, intimate, and a little noisy because everyone is exclaiming about how good the food is. Chef-owner Brian Hill and his partner Lindsey Schechter took this place over after a year of working in it, and he presides in the kitchen like a master. Chewy, dense bread accompanies corn soup or BBQ lamb riblettes to start; grilled swordfish with corn and lobster, or steak frites, are admirable main meals. Entrées $21–29.

The Edge (207-236-4430), P.O. Box Stone Coast Rd., Rt. 1, Lincolnville. Open daily in the summer; call during off-season. You can sit on the ocean-side outdoor patio for a casual menu, or inside by the wood fire in one of the 66 seats at this elegant, high

A CABIN AT CEDARHOLM GARDEN BAY INN
Nancy English

design restaurant next to a luxurious inn (see *Bed & Breakfasts*). Sunday night is pizza night, a great time to savor the chef's inventions. On other nights formal, finely made meals, like dry-aged sirloin with potato leek terrine or seared halibut with sweet corn flan, are served. Appetizers are more fun—maybe miniburgers, or clam fritter with aioli. Entrées $23–35.

Ephemere, a Restaurant and Wine Bar (207-236-4451; www.villagesoup.com/ephermerecafe), 51 Bayview St., Camden. Locals depend on Ephemere for their taste of France year-round, in the irresistible *pommes allumette*, match-stick-thin fried potatoes, for instance. But no one would neglect the masterful crabcake, or the scallop entrées with their perfect risotto. Open for dinner Mon.–Sat. Entrées $18–28.

Natalie's (207-236-7008; www.camdenharborinn.com), at the Camden Harbor Inn, 82 Bayview St., Camden. Open daily for dinner 5:30–9. Smoked trout or seared foie gras with potato dumplings and beets ($17) are mainstay appetizers. Entrées change every month; lamb ($32) "cooked on a nail" goes into the oven spiced with cumin, coriander, paprika, comes with white beans, roasted cauliflower, and tomato, accompanied by cucumber mint salad. Entrées $22–33; $42 for the butter-poached lobster.

✐ ♿ **Marcel's** (207-593-1529), Rockport (at the Samoset Resort). Open daily for breakfast, dinner, and Sunday brunch. Marcel's still offers tableside service, breaking an egg into your Caesar salad for two ($18) or carving grilled châteaubriand for two ($72). The uniformed waiters, well trained and warm, know their stuff. Jackets are suggested but not required for men at dinner; no T-shirts or jeans allowed. $19–37. Reservations suggested. The adjacent **Breakwater Café** offers casual dishes and entertainment.

Hartstone Inn (207-236-4259 or 1-800-788-4823; www.hartstoneinn.com), 41 Elm St., Camden. Open year-round. The menu for the five-course, prix fixe dinner ($45) changes every night—only one is available each night. Menus are listed on the Web site, so you can choose what you prefer. Start with seafood or a beef tenderloin appetizer, then soup or a salad, a cup of sorbet, then rack of lamb or grilled salmon. Desserts might be chocolate cherry soufflé or raspberry praline crème brulée. Make reservations early. Many fine wines, in full and half bottles.

Atlantica (207-236-6011; www.atlanticarestaurant.com), 1 Bay View Landing, Camden. Open for dinner year-round, closed Tue. and Wed.; reservations suggested. Ken and Del Paquin serve creative dishes, lobster tempura or crab and halibut cake to start and roast duck with apricot gatrique and green peppercorns, one example of the good entrées. A wonderful deck on the harbor makes summer evenings here charming. Good cocktails, wine, and beer. Dinner $17–27.

✐ ♿ **Chez Michel** (207-789-5600), Lincolnville Beach (across the road from the beach). Open Apr.–mid-Nov., dinner Tue.–Sun., lunch and dinner on Sun. This pleasant restaurant serves French food that has won a spectrum of loyal customers. The mussels mariniere with garlic, onion, and white wine are a great appetizer, and even better for dinner (with salad, potato, and French bread). New England–style fisherman's chowder, with haddock, Maine shrimp, clams, and scallops, and steak *au poivre* are always good. Raspberry pie in season inspires requests with reservations. Dinner entrées run $17–23.

The Gallery Café (207-230-0061; www.prismglassgallery.com), 297 Commercial St., Rockport. Open Wed.–Sat. 11–3 for lunch and 5–9 for dinner; Sunday brunch 10–3, dinner 4–8. This glassblowing gallery and studio can show off its craft, but even if the artist is absent, the food is so good you might not care. Lobster macaroni and cheese, or swordfish puttanesca, might follow crab artichoke dip. Desserts are often from Sweet Sensations Bakery. Entrées $12–23.

♂ ♿ **Peter Ott's** (207-236-4032), 16 Bayview St., Camden. Open year-round for casual dinner, with a large menu that features sirloin steak and fresh local fish. Entrées are served with the salad bar, unless you choose a lighter entrée. $17–29.

EATING OUT

In Camden

"I" ♿ **McMahon's Knox Grill** (207-236-4431), 43 Mechanic St. Open 11–11 for lunch and dinner, Sunday brunch 11–2. Big pale wooden booths with natural-edge board along the top add rusticity to the exposed brick interior; table also set on a deck that hugs a waterfall. Creamy chowders and cheese-filled onion soup warm you in a chill; wraps, burgers, pizza, pasta steaks, and seafood fill the menu. Live entertainment. Entrées $14–26.

♂ ♿ **Camden Bagel Café** (207-236-2661), 25 Mechanic St. Open Mon.–Sat. 6:30 AM–2 PM, Sun. 7:30–2. Bagels with substance are baked here, some in whole wheat. The plain interior makes a good refuge, and white shutters filter the sun as you enjoy a bagel with cream cheese or with an egg and bacon for breakfast. Soups and chili when things cool down.

♂ ♿ **Cappy's Chowder House** (207-236-2254; www.cappyschowder.com), 1 Main St. Open year-round. Lunch and dinner daily in summer; closing one or two days in winter. Croissant sandwiches, burgers, and full meals for lunch; seafood entrées, special pasta and meat dishes for dinner.

♂ ♿ **Cedar Crest Restaurant** (207-236-7722), 115 Elm St. Open Tues.–Sun. 7 AM–9 PM, fewer days off-season. This is Camden's favorite breakfast spot, and the reasons are clear. The big black coffee carafe stays at your table to empty as you wish, the homemade bread has some real flavor, and the servers are responsive and quick to help you. For dinner and lunch you can find highly praised pizza.

♂ **Quarterdeck Bar and Grill** (207-236-3272), 21 Bayview St. Open daily 12 AM–10 PM (pizza served until 11, and the bar stays open until 1 AM). Menu choices in this harborside setting include brick-oven pizzas, pasta, fresh seafood, and beef. Entrées $8–24.

♂ ♿ **The Waterfront Restaurant** (207-236-3747; www.waterfrontcamden.com), Bayview St. Open for lunch and dinner; you can watch the activity in the harbor. Popular and with a well-trained staff, this place fills up fast and doesn't take reservations, so be prepared to wait. Dinners include lobster entrées and a shore dinner (clam chowder, corn on the cob, steamers, mussels, and a lobster) for $24.95, and steaks.

Village Restaurant (207-236-3232), Main St. Open year-round for lunch and dinner, daily July–Oct.; closed Tue. the rest of the year. Family owned for more than 40 years, this is a longtime favorite with locals, but we found the breaded and fried fish too heavy. Try the broiled and sautéed seafood instead, and the home-baked desserts. Children's menu. The two dining rooms overlook Camden Harbor.

Gilbert's Public House (207-236-4320), Bayview St. Tucked underneath the shops along Bayview (you enter through a side door just off the road), this is a good place for a beer and a sandwich, burgers, chowder, snacks or light meals for the kids, pizza, or a simple supper before the evening's activities. Live music for dancing in the evening on weekends.

Boynton-McKay Food Co. (207-236-2465), 30 Main St. (in the heart of downtown). Open daily year-round for breakfast, lunch, and takeout, closed Nov.–June on Mon. A fun, lighthearted place to have a yummy skillet breakfast, roast turkey wrap, fresh croissants, and *pain au chocolat*. Sit in one of the tall booths in this 1890s-era former apothecary designed by the owner to fit with the decor, and relax.

Fitzpatrick's Café (207-236-2041), Bayview Landing, Bayview St. Open for breakfast and lunch year-round 7–3, dinner nights depend on season. Fitzy's is easy to miss as you walk to the public landing. But it's a find: a wide variety of sandwiches and salads plus daily specials; many Thai dishes are offered on the dinner menu. You order at the counter, and they call you by name when your food is ready, except for the sit-down dinner. Outside patio for summertime dining with views of the Camden Hills.

Camden Deli (207-236-8343; www.camdendeli.com), 37 Main St. Open 7 AM to 10 PM daily. Breakfast, and more than 40 sandwich choices, combining all the regular deli meats and cheeses as well as some less expected choices, like an artichoke and spinach wrap, for lunch. The back dining room overlooks the waterfall in downtown Camden, and another dining room upstairs, with a deck open in summer, also overlooks the water.

In Rockport

Rockport Corner Shop (207-236-8361), Central St. Open 7–2 Mon.–Fri., 7–1 Sat.–Sun. for breakfast only, usually closed in winter for two months. Fresh baked goods daily, sandwiches, soups, and salads for lunch. Breakfast specialties include eggs Benedict and Swedish pancakes. Very reasonable prices.

Sweet Sensations and 3 Dogs Café (207-230-0955; www.mainesweets.com; www.3dogscafe.com), 309 Commercial St. (Rt. 1), Rockport. Open daily 7:30 AM–8 PM in summer; same hours planned in winter. A big, modern building with outdoor seating has replaced Sweet Sensations Bakery's original building; it houses both the bakery and the café, offering wonderful stuff like peanut butter pie and chocolate mousse cake, and meals of soup, salad, and sandwiches. The Vinalhaven is a BLT with applewood smoked bacon on sourdough. Lunch $7–8.

LOBSTER POUND ✐ ♿ **Lobster Pound Restaurant** (207-789-5550), Rt. 1, Lincolnville Beach. Open every day for lunch and dinner from first Sun. in May–mid-Oct. This is a mecca for lobster lovers—some people plan their trips around a meal here. Features lobster, boiled or baked, also clams, other fresh seafood, roast turkey, ham, steaks, and chicken. A family-style restaurant that seats 246 inside and has an outside patio near a sandy beach. Takeout and picnic tables offered across the beach.

TAKEOUT The Market Basket (207-236-4371), Rts. 1 and 90, Rockport. Open Mon.–Fri. 7–6:30, Sat. 8–6:30, Sun. 9–4. This specialty food store offers a wide variety of creative salads, delicious French bread, soups, entrées, sandwich specials for takeout, more than 500 wines from around the world, and more than 75 varieties of cheese.

Scott's Place (207-236-8751), Elm St. (Reny's parking lot), Camden. Open 10:30–4, Mon.–Sat. Since 1974 this tiny building in the parking lot of a small shopping center has served thousands of toasted crabmeat and lobster rolls, chicken sandwiches, burgers, veggie burgers, hot dogs, and chips. Prices are among the best around: $1.79 for a hot dog, under $8.99 for a lobster roll. This is one of several small takeout buildings in the area, but it's the only one open year-round.

✱ Entertainment

Bay Chamber Concerts (207-236-2823; www.baychamberconcerts.org), 58 Bay View St., Suite 1, Camden 04843. This renowned organization has presented outstanding concerts since 1961. In July and August they sponsor Thursday-evening chamber music concerts in the beautifully restored Rockport Opera House with its gilded interior, and Wednesday evening concerts at the beautifully restored Strand in Rockland. Winter-season selections include classical and jazz music concerts and dance performances.

Nancy English

SWEET SENSATIONS BAKERY AND THREE DOG CAFÉ

Camden Civic Theatre (207-236-2281; www.camdencivictheatre.com), Main St., Camden. A variety of theatrical performances are presented in the restored Camden Opera House, a second-floor theater with plum seats and cream-and-gold walls. Tickets are reasonably priced.

✐ ♿ **The Center for Maine Contemporary Art** (207-236-2875; www.cmcanow.org), 162 Russell Ave., Rockport. Open year-round, Tue.–Sat.

SCOTT'S PLACE, A SOURCE OF FIRST-RATE LOBSTER ROLLS.

Nancy English

10–5; also open Sun. 1–5. Call for details about special exhibits. $5 admission for nonmembers; members, children under 18, and Rockport residents free. Promoting contemporary Maine art and artists since 1952 through exhibitions and education. The building, which started out as a late-19th-century livery stable, then became a firehouse, then the town hall, now showcases contemporary Maine art. The gallery sponsors more than 20 shows each season, an art auction, a crafts show, gallery talks, a shop, and an evening lecture series. The shop features a mix of objects for gifts and home use. T-shirts that read FEAR NO ART go for $22.

✷ Selective Shopping

Avena Botanicals (207-594-0694; www.avenabotanicals.com), 219 Mill St., Rockport. Open Mon.–Thu. 9–5, Fri. 9–1. Customers can walk in the botanical garden in growing season, when you can drink in the scents serenaded by the chorus of crickets and honeybees. At the apothecary you can purchase creams, salves, teas, and tincture, during the same hours, year-round. You can also purchase items online. Check the Web site for schedule of free herb walks with Deb Soule, the herbalist founder of this company. "Sacred basil honey" for sale.

ANTIQUES At the chamber of commerce, pick up the leaflet guide to antiques shops scattered among Camden, Rockport, and Lincolnville.

ART GALLERIES **Elan Fine Arts** (207-236-4401; www.elanfinearts.com), 86 Pascal Ave., P.O. Box 300, Rockport. The 1850s former Baptist Church now holds Elan Fine Arts, and reception on the first Friday of the month year-round. It is also the convivial scene of chamber music concerts, when the movable walls slide away and the 21-foot-high tin ceiling regales all with fine acoustics. Come to see Alan Magee's tapestries, hanging in the nave; woven with cotton thread they hold the super-realism of his paintings of Maine stone.

Bay View Gallery (207-236-4534; www.bayviewgallery.com), 33 Bayview St., Camden. One of the largest galleries in the Midcoast area. Original paintings and sculptures by contemporary artists working in Maine. Expert custom framing, too.

A Small Wonder Gallery (207-236-6005; www.smallwondergallery.com), 1 Public Landing (across from the chamber of commerce), Camden. A small gallery with well-chosen, limited-edition graphics, watercolors, hand-painted tiles, porcelain, and original sculpture. Custom framing.

The Northport Landing Gallery (see "Belfast, Searsport") is 10 minutes from Camden.

Prism Glass Gallery (207-230-0061; www.prismglassgallery.com), 297 Commercial St., Rockport. Open Wed.–Sat. 10 AM–9 PM, Sun. 10–8 with exhibits of hand-blown glass. Glassblower and gallery owner Patti Kissinger demonstrates her skills in the barn next door (see *Eating Out* for the café).

ARTISANS **Windsor Chairmakers** (207-789-5188; www.windsorchair.com), Rt. 1, Lincolnville Beach. Filling two floors of an old farmhouse are Windsor chairs and tables, highboys, and four-poster beds, all offered in a selection of finishes. A gallery in a wing of the connected farmhouses shows a line of Shaker-style furniture. Visitors can tour the workshop to see furniture being made.

Maine Artisans (207-789-5376), Rt. 1, Lincolnville Beach. Open daily May–Oct., this charming store sells work by weavers, potters, and sock makers, among others.

The Foundry (207-236-3200; www.remsen.com), 531 Park St., West Rockport (next to the Baptist church). Custom metal castings in bronze and aluminum. Also handblown glass vases, bowls, and goblets, and giant sculptural fishing lures.

Carver Hill Gallery (207-230-0034; www.carverhillgallery.com), 264 Meadow St., Rockport. Furniture makers with a gallery of artwork, rugs, and jewelry, as well as furniture and design by the owners, Phi Home Designs.

BOOKSTORES **ABCD Books** (207-236-3903), 23 Bayview St., Camden. Open June–Aug., Mon.–Sat. 10–9, Sun. 1–5; Sept.–May, 10–5. Sun. by chance in winter. A Camden literary landmark: an unusually extensive and organized collection of rare and used books featuring maritime, art, New England, and history titles.

♿ **Down East** (207-594-9544), Rt. 1, Rockport. The headquarters for Down East Enterprises (publishers of *Down East*, *Fly Rod & Reel*, and *Shooting Sportsman* magazines, as well as a line of New England books) is located in a handsome old mansion that includes a book shop, open 9–5 Mon.–Fri. year-round.

✐ **The Owl and Turtle Bookshop** (207-236-4769 or 1-800-876-4769), 32 Washington St. (one block north of Rt. 1 on Rt. 105), Camden. One of Maine's best bookstores, located in an old mill with old maple floors and dark wood bookcases, with a reading corner by a fireplace. The children's room has a little wishing well with a Plexiglas window on the Megunticook River. One room holds one of the best selections of marine books on the East Coast. Free parking on Mechanic St. and in a lot up the street. Maine history, travel, and art. Great for browsing, and check out their frequent author book signings.

Sherman's Books (207-236-2223 or 1-800-803-5949; www.shermans.com), 8 Bay View St., Camden. Another in the fine chain of Sherman's bookstores on the Maine coast, Camden's branch is filled with a wide variety of books and gifts.

SPECIAL SHOPS

All shops are in Camden and open year-round unless otherwise noted.

Unique 1 (207-236-8717), 2 Bayview St. Woolen items made from Maine wool, designed and hand loomed locally. Also a full yarn shop for knitters and some pottery.

✐ **Once a Tree** (207-236-3995), 46 Bayview St. Wooden crafts, including beautiful clocks, kitchen utensils, desk sets; a large game and toy section.

✐ **The Smiling Cow** (207-236-3351; www.smilingcow.com), 41 Main St. Seasonal. Three generations ago a mother and five children converted this stable into a classic gift shop, one with unusual warmth and scope. We like the Maine-themed items like fragrant, locally made soaps.

✪ **Heavenly Threads** (207-236-3203), 57 Elm St. (Rt. 1). Open

Mon.–Fri. 10–4, Sat. 10–1, closed Mon. off-season. Wealthy summer folks and locals both donate to this extremely clean shop full of surprising finds. We found clothes by Ann Taylor, Calvin Klein, and others for under $5 per garment, as well as books and housewares in excellent shape. Also men's and children's clothing, jewelry, gift items, and coffee-table books. Proceeds benefit Habitat for Humanity, Coastal Hospice, Rockland Soup Kitchen, and others.

Ducktrap Bay Trading Company (1-800-560-9568; www.ducktrapbay.com), 37 Bayview St. Many of these pieces—decoys, wildlife and marine art, scrimshaw, and paintings—have earned awards for their creators.

Danica Candleworks (207-236-3060), 569 West St. (Rt. 90), West Rockport. In a striking building with a Scandinavian-inspired interior, you'll find a candle factory and shop that sells high quality hand-dipped and scented candles and accessories.

✷ Special Events

February: **U.S. National Toboggan Championships**—teams from all over the country compete in two-, three-, and four-person races, often in costume (Camden Snow Bowl).

Mid-July: **Annual Open House and Garden Day**, sponsored by the Camden Garden Club. Very popular tour of homes and gardens in Camden and Rockport held every year for five decades. **Summer HarborArts,** a juried arts and crafts show (*third Saturday and Sunday*), Camden Amphitheatre.

August: **The Center for Maine Contemporary Art's Annual Art Auction**—Maine's largest exhibit and auction of quality contemporary Maine art. **Merryspring's Annual Kitchen Tour**—see uniquely designed kitchens in Camden, Rockport, and Lincolnville, plus demonstrations and tastings from professional growers and chefs.

Late August: **Union Fair** and **Blueberry Festival,** Union Fairgrounds (see "Rockland/Thomaston Area").

Labor Day weekend: **Windjammer Weekend**, Camden Harbor. A celebration of the windjammer industry, featuring a parade of boats, music, nautical history, fireworks, and the Schooner Bum Talent Contest.

September: **Country Roads Artists and Artisans Tour** (207-763-4770; www.artisanstour.com); **Maine Fare** (www.mainefare.org), cooking demonstrations, fine food, wine pairings mostly at the Camden Snow Bowl.

First weekend in October: **Fall HarborArts**, a juried arts and crafts show, Camden Amphitheatre—75 artisans displaying work for sale.

First weekend in December: **Christmas by the Sea**—tree lighting, Santa's arrival, caroling, holiday house tour, refreshments in shops.

ISLESBORO

A 14-mile-long, string-bean-shaped island just 3 miles off Lincolnville Beach (a 20-minute ferry ride), Islesboro is a private kind of place.

There are three distinct communities on the island. The town of Islesboro with the necessary services (town office, post office, health center, and fire department) sits in the center between Dark Harbor and Pripet. Dark Harbor (described by Sidney Sheldon in his best seller *Master of the Game* as the "jealously guarded colony of the super-rich") has long been a summer resort village, where huge "cottages" peek from behind the trees along the road to Pendleton Point. Pripet is a thriving year-round neighborhood of boatbuilders and fishermen.

GETTING THERE The car-carrying **Maine State Ferry** (207-789-5611 or 207-734-6935; $7.50 round-trip per passenger, $17.75 per vehicle, and $6.25 per bicycle, with an extra $14 for a round-trip reservation. Beach lands mid-island at Grindle Point. The crossing is a 3-mile, 20-minute ride, the schedule depending on the season. If you go for a day trip only, pay close attention to when the last ferry leaves the island to avoid being stranded. At the landing you'll find a clean ferry terminal with public restrooms.

GUIDANCE The **Islesboro town office** (207-734-2253), 150 Main Rd., is a great source of information, with friendly service both on the phone and in person. When you board the Maine State Ferry, ask for a map and schedule. The detailed and informative island map shows a full view of the island as well as business locations, a ferry schedule, a brief description of the island, and a historical society events calendar.

WHEN TO COME Only in summer will visitors find a bookstore, two cafés, a gallery, and a few places with rooms to rent.

✷ To See and Do

The old lighthouse on **Grindle Point** (built in 1850, now automated) and keeper's cottage now house the seasonal **Sailors' Memorial Museum** (207-734-2253), open July–Labor Day, 9:30–4:30, closed Wed. and Sun. Look for summer musical and theatrical performances at the **Free Will Baptist Church**. Check out the **Up Island Church**, a fine old structure with beautiful wall stencils and fascinating old headstones in the adjacent graveyard.

The layout of the island makes at least a bicycle necessary to get a real feel for the place. The roads are narrow, winding, and have no shoulder. Bicyclists should use great caution. Even so, after both driving and biking the island, we prefer biking. A drive from one end of the island to the other is a nice way to spend a couple of hours, but on bicycles, it'll take you most of a day. In Dark Harbor you'll see huge "cottages" and impressive architecture. In summer you'll also find a very few shops for browsing, including the **Dark Harbor Shop** (207-734-8878), with souvenirs, gifts, ice cream, and a deli. "We haven't changed in 35 years—it's disgusting," said owner Bill Warren, laughing. Open Memorial Day to

Labor Day. A picnic area and town beach at Pendleton Point have spectacular views. The trip down the other side of the island will take you past the **Islesboro Historical Society** (207-734-6733) in the former town hall, which houses rotating exhibits on the first floor and a permanent collection upstairs.

✷ Lodging

The Islesboro town office (207-734-2253) is a welcoming source of information and can refer you to local real estate agents who handle cottage rentals.

The Village Bed and Breakfast (207-734-9772; www.thevillagebedandbreakfast.com), 119 Derby Rd., Islesboro 04848. Open year-round. Since 2000, Bonnie and Larry St. Peter have hosted guests at this country farmhouse with a wraparound porch. They offer four bedrooms, each with private bath (one room with a king bed, two with queen, and one with two twin bed). $75–125.

Aunt Laura's B&B (207-734-8286; lbebb@aol.com), 812 Main Rd., Islesboro 04848. On the other side of the island, Louanne Bebb offers two guest rooms and a living room for guests in the wing attached to her 1855 Cape.

✷ Where to Eat

The Village Café (207-734-9772; www.thevillagebedandbreakfast.com), 119 Derby Rd. Open daily in-season 5:30–7:30 for dinner by reservation only, off-season Thurs. and Fri. except for inn guests, who can have dinner whenever they stay. "I call it comfort food," Bonnie St. Peter said: meatloaf, baked haddock, and fish chowders are typical of her menus. For dessert there's blueberry pie and profiteroles. Everything is made here. Entrées around $17.

You can often pick up a snack (breakfast specials, burgers, lobster rolls, and such for lunch and dinner) at a takeout stand at the far end of the ferry terminal parking lot. The luncheonette in the **Dark Harbor Shop** is a local gathering place where you can get lunch and ice cream in summer. **Durkee's General Store** (207-734-2201) and **The Island Market** (207-734-6672) both sell sandwiches, pizza, and provisions for picnics.

✷ Selected Shopping

Artisan Books and Bindery (207-734-6852; www.artisanbooksandbindery.com), 509 Pendleton Point Rd., Dark Harbor Village. A nice little bookstore with coffee and muffins, where you can also find custom binding.

BELFAST, SEARSPORT, AND STOCKTON SPRINGS

Belfast's long, Victorian brick Main Street slopes steadily downward, away from Rt. 1, toward the confluence of the tidal Passagassawakeag River and Belfast Bay.

With just 7,100 residents and a small-town feel, Belfast is a city and the seat of Waldo County. Magnificent Greek Revival and Federal homes, proof of early prominence, line High and Church Streets. Lower blocks suggest a checkered commercial history that included a sarsaparilla company, a rum distillery, a city-owned railroad, and, most recently and memorably, poultry slaughtering and shipping.

An artist in one of Belfast's burgeoning galleries observes: "You have to want to come here. People who turn off Rt. 1 and take the downhill plunge are looking for something." What they find is a mix of boutiques and basic shops, trendy cafés, restaurants, and hometown eateries, a supermarket-sized health-food store, a funky old movie house, and live theater, as well as B&Bs that could charge twice as much down the road in Camden. In Belfast the prime employer is now MBNA (credit cards).

High above downtown Belfast, Rt. 1 crosses the Passagassawakeag River into East Belfast, threading a string of shops, restaurants, and a mix of 1940s motor courts and motor inns with water views.

In Searsport Rt. 1 becomes, suddenly and briefly, a mid-19th-century brick-and-granite downtown. Stop at Mosman Park, with its picnic tables and playground right on Penobscot Bay (just down Water Street), for a sense of place. Then visit the Penobscot Marine Museum to learn that more than 3,000 different vessels have been built in and around Penobscot Bay since 1770. Searsport alone launched eight brigs and six schooners in one year (1845), and for many years boasted more sea captains than any other town its size, explaining the dozens of 19th-century mansions lining Rt. 1. What you don't see from the highway is Sears Island and its deepwater harbor, for which a series of projects has been planned in recent decades.

A number of the captains' mansions are now B&Bs, which work not only as way stops but also as hubs from which to explore this part of Waldo County. If you have the time, take the scenic route to this region from Augusta, poking

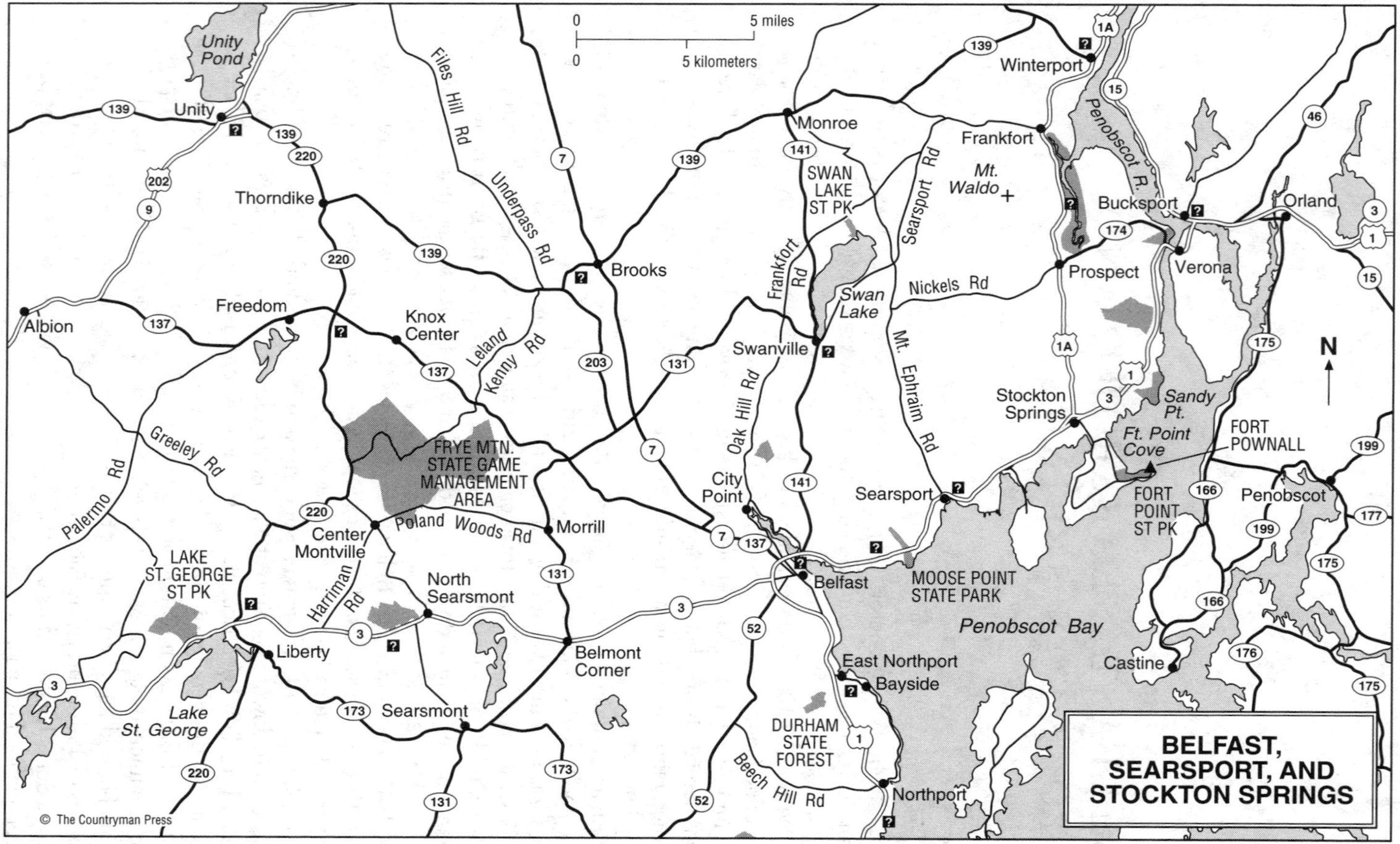

BELFAST, SEARSPORT, AND STOCKTON SPRINGS
0 5 miles
0 5 kilometers
N
Unity Pond
Unity
Thorndike
Freedom
Albion
Knox Center
Brooks
Monroe
Winterport
Frankfort
Mt. Waldo
Bucksport
Orland
Verona
Prospect
Penobscot R.
SWAN LAKE ST PK
Swan Lake
Swanville
Files Hill Rd
Underpass Rd
Leland Rd
Kenny Rd
Searsport Rd
Frankfort Rd
Nickels Rd
Mt. Ephraim Rd
Oak Hill Rd
Stockton Springs
Sandy Pt.
Ft. Point Cove
FORT POWNALL
FORT POINT ST PK
Penobscot
City Point
Searsport
Belfast
MOOSE POINT STATE PARK
Penobscot Bay
Castine
East Northport
Bayside
Northport
DURHAM STATE FOREST
Beech Hill Rd
FRYE MTN. STATE GAME MANAGEMENT AREA
Poland Woods Rd
Morrill
Center Montville
Harriman Rd
North Searsmont
Belmont Corner
Liberty
Searsmont
LAKE ST. GEORGE ST PK
Lake St. George
Greeley Rd
Palermo Rd
© The Countryman Press

through the communities of Unity, Thorndike, and Brooks, detouring to Liberty then down to Belfast. Rt. 1 continues to shadow the shore as it narrows into what seems more like a broad river.

GUIDANCE **The Greater Belfast Area Chamber of Commerce** (207-338-5900; www.belfastmaine.org), P.O. Box 58, Belfast 04915, maintains an information booth on Main St. down near the waterfront; open May–Oct., 10–6.

Waldo County Marketing Association (1-800-870-9934; www.waldocountymaine.com), P.O. Box 139, Searsport 04974. The Web site is exceptional.

GETTING THERE *By air:* For commercial service, see "Rockland/Thomaston," "Bangor," and "Portland."

By car: The most direct route to this region from points south and west is via I-95, exiting in Augusta and taking Rt. 3 to Belfast. A new I-95 exit (113) accesses a new connector to Rt. 3, offering motorists bound for the Midcoast a way around Augusta. If you're coming up Rt. 1, take the first turnoff for downtown Belfast. The approach is down Northport Ave. and Belfast City Park, then down High St.

By bus: **Concord Trailways** (1-800-639-3317) stops in both Searsport and Belfast.

PUBLIC RESTROOMS At the public landing at the bottom of Main Street.

WHEN TO COME The town chugs along through winter, with most inns and restaurants open throughout the year; still, the summer season gives the ocean a friendlier look and fills the farm stands. Come to Belfast anytime to enjoy the downtown, but wait for warm weather to sail, visit the wonderful museum, and eat seafood along the shore.

✷ Villages

Brooks. In the center of this quiet county, surrounded by hills, this town has the most scenic golf course around.

Liberty, straddling Rt. 3, is home to Lake St. George State Park and to the extraordinary **Liberty Tool Company** (207-589-4771; www.jonesportwood.com), Main St. Open June–mid-Oct., daily, fewer days off-season, closed Jan. and Feb. and reopening the first Sat. in Mar. with a big sale on the first Saturday. Antique and used tools, and every other thing that you can imagine—clocks, lanterns, books, postcards. The octagonal Liberty post office, also on Main St., dates from 1867 and houses the Liberty Historical Society (207-589-4393), open weekend afternoons in July and Aug.

DOWNTOWN BELFAST

Kim Grant

Northport. A low-key community with yacht and golf clubs, as well as a mid-19th-century former Methodist campground with hundreds of gingerbread cottages on the bay.

Unity. Home to a rural college, a raceway, and the fairgrounds for the popular late-September Common Ground Fair.

Stockton Springs. Rt. 1 now bypasses this former shipbuilding town. Follow East St. down to Fort Point.

✷ To See

MUSEUMS ✐ **Penobscot Marine Museum** (207-548-2529; www.penobscotmarinemuseum.org), Rt. 1, Searsport. Open May–mid-Oct., Mon.–Sat. 10–5 and Sun. noon–5. $8 adults, children 7–15 are $3. Family rate $18. (The library is open in summer and by appointment in winter.) The 13 buildings include eight on the National Register of Historic Places. The museum shop is at the entrance to the complex, which lies west of Rt. 1. Museum exhibits show off peapods, dories, canoes, and lobster boats, and the artifacts that exemplify the changing faces of Mainers over the centuries, from the first Wabanaki natives to the shipbuilders of the 1800s. Gorgeous nautical paintings convey the ship worship of a time when fortunes were made when the ships came in. The galleries in the **Captain Jeremiah Merithew House** have been refurbished and now hold a collection of paintings by father-and-son marine artists Thomas and James Buttersworth, whose depictions of ships in storm and calm are luminous and exciting. In 1889, 77 deep-sea captains lived in Searsport, 33 of whom piloted full-rigged Cape Horners. The museum displays the scrimshaw—carved whale teeth and bone—that the captains and crew brought home after perfecting their art at sea. Other exhibits focus on the working-class people who made their living here in the granite, lime, ice, fishing, and lobstering industries.

Davistown Museum (207-589-4900; www.davistownmuseum.org), 58 Main St., Liberty. Skip Brack, meticulous owner of Liberty Tool Company, has sorted out the finest antique tools of his collection to create this museum above the power tool annex of his tool store. Contemporary Maine artists exhibit their work in this space, and a permanent collection is also on display, most in the top floors. As the Web site states, the art and artifact combination at Davistown Museum "is unique among Maine's museums and galleries." Early American maritime tools, and Native American artifacts. Scavenger hunts are going on any time; children can make a sculpture out of odds and ends gathered from the tool store. Admission $3.

Belfast Historical Society and Museum (207-338-9229; www.belfastmuseum.org), 10 Market St., Belfast. Open early June–mid-Oct.; in summer Tues.–Sat. 11–4, off-season Fri.–Sat. 11-4; by appointment year-round. Local artifacts, paintings, and changing exhibits. A ship model of the *Charlotte W. White* has been restored for display. A self-guided "Museum-in-the-Streets" walking tour is installed downtown.

Harbor Church, Rt. 1, Searsport. Phone 207-548-6663 or pick up the key across the street and check out the fabulous stained-glass windows in this church, built in 1815. It's now maintained as a meditation space, and holds regular services.

Bryant Museum (207-568-3665), 27 Stovepipe Alley (junction of Rts. 220 and 139), Thorndike. Open year-round, Mon.–Sat. 8–4:30. What began as a stove shop has evolved into a fascinating museum. The front room is crammed with restored woodstoves (for sale). Walk through these to the doll circus, with its array of mechanical, musical dolls from Barbie to Disney characters and everything in between. The back room houses a collection of player pianos, nickelodeons, and vintage automobiles. Worth the drive.

SCENIC DRIVE **Rt. 3**, past Lake St. George and Sheepscot Pond, through the China Lakes region, is the most direct path between Belfast and Augusta, but take time to detour down Rt. 173 to **Liberty** to see the octagonal post office and the **Liberty Tool Company** and **Davistown Museum** (see *To See*). For a leisurely tour of the villages between Belfast and Augusta, head north from East Belfast on Rt. 141 to Monroe. Ask for directions to **Stone Soup Farm** to see their gardens, then check out **Monroe Falls**, just off Rt. 139, and maybe have a picnic. Head out on Rt. 139, through Brooks, and then on toward Thorndike, where you'll want to stop at the **Bryant Museum**. Continue on Rt. 139 to Unity, where you'll pass the new home of the Common Ground Fair. Follow Rt. 139 into Kennebec County to Fairfield to meet up with I-95, or detour yet again onto Rt. 202, which will bring you through the China Lakes region to Augusta.

✷ To Do

BERRY PICKING **Staples Homestead Blueberries** (207-567-3393 or 207-567-3703), 302 Old County Rd., Stockton Springs. Turn at the ball field on Rts. 1/3, then drive 3 miles to the T at County Rd.; turn right. Or ask directions in Stockton Springs Village. Open 8–5 daily while its certified organic berries are in-season (Aug.). Friendly owners Basil and Mary Staples will instruct you in the mysteries of blueberry raking then let you go to it, or you can pick by hand.

BOAT EXCURSIONS **Belfast Bay Cruises** (207-322-5530; www.belfastbaycruises.com), Thompson Wharf, Belfast. June–Oct. daily the M/V *Good Return* cruises Penobscot Bay, offering a choice of itineraries. The 47-passenger wooden boat, built in 1966 in Southwest Harbor, is captained by Maine Maritime graduate Melissa Terry.

BAYSIDE IN NORTHPORT

Christina Tree

GOLF **Country View Golf Course** (207-722-3161) in Brooks is the most scenic in the area: nine holes, par 36, cart and club rentals, lessons, clubhouse.

Northport Golf Club (207-338-2270), Northport. A fully irrigated nine-hole course, pro shop, snack bar, driving range, and rentals.

KAYAKING **Water Walker Sea Kayaks** (207-338-6424; www.touringkayaks.com), Belfast. Ray Wirth, a Registered Maine Guide and ACA-certified open-water instructor, offers tours ranging from several hours in Belfast Harbor or around Sears Island up to full-day trips out among offshore islands and from inn to inn.

SWIMMING **Lake St. George State Park** (207-589-4255), Rt. 3, Liberty. Open May 15–Oct. 15. A great way station for travelers going to or from Down East. A deep, clear lake with a small beach, lifeguard, bathhouse, parking facilities, 31 campsites, and a boat launch. **Swan Lake State Park**, Rt. 141, Swanville (north of town; follow signs), has a beach with picnicking facilities. **Belfast City Park,** Rt. 1, Belfast (south of town), holds a swimming pool, tennis courts, picnicking facilities, and a gravel beach. Sandy Point Beach, off Rt. 1 north of Stockton Springs (it's posted HERSEY RETREAT; turn toward the water directly across from the Rocky Ridge Motel).

✳ Green Space

Also see Lake St. George State Park and Belfast City Park under *Swimming*.

Moose Point State Park, Rt. 1, south of Searsport. Open May 30–Oct. 15. A good spot for picnicking; cookout facilities are in an evergreen grove and an open field overlooking Penobscot Bay. Also check out **Mosman Park** in downtown Searsport with its playground and picnic benches by tidal pools and the public landing.

Fort Pownall and Fort Point State Park, Stockton Springs (marked from Rt. 1; follow the 3.5-mile access road). The 1759 fort built to defend the British claim to Maine (the Penobscot River was the actual boundary between the English and French territories) was burned twice to prevent its being taken; only earthworks remain. The adjacent park, on the tip of a peninsula jutting into Penobscot Bay, is a fine fishing and picnic spot.

Sears Island. After decades of debate about the future of this island (it was slated to be a container port, nuclear power plant site, LNG port, and more), it's open to the public. There are 940 acres and around 5 miles of shorefront to explore, just as the migratory birds do. Good for walking, biking, kayaking, and fishing; visit the sand beaches view the Camden Hills. It's connected to the mainland by a causeway. Off Rt. 1, take Sears Island Rd.

Carleton Pond Waterfowl Production Area, Troy. Part of the National Wildlife Refuge System. One thousand acres are accessible by canoe or kayak. Unstaffed. Contact the Maine Coastal Islands Wildlife Refuge Rockport office (207-236-6970), P.O. Box 495, Rockport, ME 04856, for information.

✷ Lodging

INNS AND BED & BREAKFASTS

In Belfast 04915

Harbor View House (207-338-3811 or 1-877-393-3811; www.harborview house.com), 213 High St. Open year-round. This vintage-1807 Federal mansion turned B&B seems to have it all: Federal-era grace, all the comforts, and a sweeping view of Penobscot Bay from its perch above downtown Belfast on Primrose Hill. All six rooms have a private bath (four with claw-foot tub), working fireplace, and TV/VCR (there's a film library); five have water views. Our favorite is the second-floor Joshua Chamberlain Room ($150) with a queen bed and fire-side rocker. Rates include a full breakfast served in the dining room, or in summer on the deck. Your helpful hosts are Mary Ellen and her sister Trish Jakielski. $105–170, $10 less if single, less off-season.

"1" **The Alden House** (207-338-2151 or 1-877-337-8151; www.thealden house.com), 63 Church St. This gracious 1840 mansion holds Italian marble mantels and sinks and a circular staircase inside its substantial walls. Deborah and Ted Hensley maintain the seven guest rooms, one on the ground floor, and five with private bath. From the charm of the open porch to the substantial Victorian furnishings, their taste is polished and their attention unceasing. In the Hiram Alden Room two antique chairs face a working fireplace. $100–160 includes a full breakfast, served at separate tables.

The Jeweled Turret Inn (207-338-2304 or 1-800-696-2304; www .jeweledturret.com), 40 Pearl St. Open year-round. A handsome 1890s gabled and turreted house that's ornate inside and out. The fireplace in the den is said to be made of stones from every state in the Union at that time. This now-lovely house suffered neglect before Carl and Cathy Heffentrager began transforming it in 1986, reviving its first glory and adding the stone-edged verandas, where guests love to lounge in rockers and a swing. Each of the seven guest rooms has a private bath and is decorated in colors of the gem it's named for. The Opal Room features a marble bath with a whirlpool tub, and the popular Tourmaline Room has a working fireplace. Full breakfast and afternoon sherry with cheese and crackers. Rates $105–159.

ꝏ **The White House** (207-338-1901 or 1-888-290-1901; www.mainebb .com), 1 Church St. The pillared facade of this 1840 Greek Revival mansion with its octagonal cupola is strikingly handsome, set off by its triangular front lawn in the V between

THE PORCH AT THE ALDEN HOUSE

Nancy English

Church and High Streets. The eight guest rooms are elaborately decorated; all have phone, private bath, and a TV/VCR. Weddings are a specialty, and one of the two innkeepers is licensed to officiate. Rates are $115–185 per couple, including a full breakfast.

In Searsport 04974

1794 Watchtide By the Sea (207-548-6575 or 1-800-698-6575; www.watchtide.com), Rt. 1. This bright house faces the sea with a 19-windowed sunporch. The five guest rooms each have a private bath, TV, air-conditioning, and small fridge. Eleanor Roosevelt slept here several times when this was the College Club Inn (opened in 1917), and her namesake, ocean-view room has a two-person Jacuzzi and skylight. $140–190 in high season, lower off-season, includes breakfast. Owners Frank and Patricia Kulla, chefs in former careers, might make a soufflé or serve alpine sweet-ricotta-filled French toast with a sabayon sauce.

Inn Britannia (207-548-2007 or 1-866-466-2748; www.innbritannia.com), 132 W. Main St. (Rt. 1). Formerly the Captain Butman Homestead, this classic 1830s farmhouse has been thoroughly anglicized by Caren Lorelle and Susan Pluff, who have named the seven guest rooms (each with private bath) the Cotswolds, Brighton, Nottingham; we could go on. Windsor features a vaulted ceiling, wet bar, TV, separate sitting room, and well-appointed bath. Breakfast, served in the deep purple dining room lined with teapots, might include Cornish baked eggs—a savory meringue made with eggs from the inn's own chickens—and PG Tips tea. $125–205 in-season, less off-season. Dinners for guests are served by reservation only.

Fairwinds, The Captain Green Pendleton B&B (1-800-949-4403; www.bbmaine.com), Rt. 1. Another fine old captain's home with 80 acres set well back from Rt. 1. The three bedrooms are handsomely furnished, and the spacious common rooms are bright and airy. All guest rooms have a working fireplace; there's a Franklin fireplace in the parlor. A path takes guests around a meadow and woods by a spring-fed trout pond. There's ping-pong in the barn. The Greiners are helpful hosts. $85–125 per night includes a full breakfast.

Wildflower Inn (207-548-2112 or 1-888-546-2112; www.wildflowerinnme.com), 2 Black Rd. S. (corner of Rt. 1). Just off the main road, this attractive 1846 sea captain's home offers a double parlor and four guest rooms, two with king beds and one with a Jacuzzi. A queen room with a day bed and adjoining king room is a good suite for couples traveling together. The gardens fill half an acre with blooms, birdbaths, and water features, which Cathy Keating and Deb Bush keep immaculate. Rooms $85–140, including breakfast; less off-season. A treadmill and other exercise equipment is available for guests.

Carriage House Inn (207-548-2167 or 1-800-578-2167; www.carriagehouseinmaine.com), 120 E. Main St. (Rt. 1). Three rooms with private bath are available in this 1874 Victorian home built by sea captain John McGilvery; it was later impressionist Waldo Peirce's place, and visited by Peirce's friend Ernest Hemingway, whose portrait he painted. Two of the painter's works hang in the room named for him, which also has a view of the sea. A loft space, Peirce's studio paneled with oak and pine, with full kitchen and bath and room for six, rents for $750 a week. There's a resident beagle, gardens, and 200 books on tape. Rates $95–125, less Nov.–mid-May, with full breakfast including muffins, fruit, and sometimes cognac French toast.

COTTAGES ✐ **Bayside Village**, built in the 1800s, has about 50 cottages on Penobscot Bay in Northport available for rent by the week by Bayside Cottage Rentals (207-338-5355; www.baysidecottagerentals.com). Margaret Lacoste's agency is open spring, summer, and fall, renting the cottages out for between $550 and $1,500 a week May–mid-Oct. Originally a Methodist campground, the cottages are ornately trimmed with Victorian gingerbread, some with stone fireplace. The village offers a main common, a swim float and dock on the pebble beach, sailing lessons, and a little yacht club with children's activities in summer.

MOTELS ((1)) 🐾 ✐ **Ocean's Edge Comfort Inn** (207-338-2090 or 1-800-303-5098), 159 Searsport Ave. (Rt. 1), Belfast 04915. Usually we don't include a Comfort Inn in our listings, but the location of this three-story facility is terrific. All 83 units (each with two queen beds) have a balcony overlooking the bay; amenities include a full-service restaurant, guest laundry, indoor pool with sauna and hot tub, and lobby computer. $89–329 in summer includes continental breakfast; less off-season. Try the two-night specials in winter midweek—the pool is heated to 86 degrees.

((1)) 🐾 ✐ **Belfast Harbor Inn** (207-338-2740 or 1-800-545-8576; www.belfastharborinn.com), 91 Searsport Ave. (Rt. 1), Belfast 04915. Set back from Rt. 1 on six acres of lawn that stretch to the rim of the bay, this is an inviting, independently owned two-story motel with 61 units. Price depends on location—from (heated) poolside to ocean view. A generous continental breakfast is included for all rooms. Top rate of $149 in high season, less late Sept.–late June.

✷ Where to Eat

DINING OUT Rhumb Line (207-548-2600; www.therhumblinerestaurant.com), 200 E. Main St. (Rt. 1), Searsport. Open year-round, daily in summer and varying times off-season. Owners Charles and Diana Evans ran a successful restaurant on Martha's Vineyard before coming to Searsport. The menu changes daily but might include oven-poached, horseradish-crusted salmon or grilled rack of lamb with fig-infused mint vinegar ($28). Dessert choices may include French bread pudding or chocolate Grand Marnier mousse cake. Entrées $21–28.

♿ ✐ **The Ocean's Edge Restaurant** (207-338-2090), 159 Searsport Ave., Belfast. Open daily 4–9. Not just an amenity for the Comfort Inn to which it's attached, this spot is a local favorite given the view, the service, and the menu, which ranges from chicken and broccoli alfredo with fettucini to surf and turf. Entrées $9–20. Children's menu.

Darby's Restaurant and Pub (207-338-2339), 155 High St., Belfast. Open daily for lunch and dinner. A storefront café with tin ceilings and local artwork. A reasonably priced dinner might include pecan haddock with mojito sauce, or a black bean enchilada "smothered in cheddar and Ranchero sauce." Soups, salads, and sandwiches are served all day. Entrées $8–22.

EATING OUT **Chase's Daily** (207-338-0555), 96 Main St., Belfast. Breakfast and lunch Tue.–Sat., dinner Fri. from 5:30, Sun. brunch 8-1. This high-ceilinged restaurant features enticing produce from the owners' Chase Farm in Freedom, sold in the back. The freshness of the ingredients and the great cooking combine to make the vegetarian fare wonderful. Pizza with eggplant, tomato, corn, and fontina and Parmesan comes in late summer, along with tomato tarts and lasagne with roasted beets Gorgonzola and mozzarella. Freshly baked bread and treats like sunken chocolate cake for dessert. Meals $7–19.

Anglers (207-548-2405), Rt. 1, Searsport. Open daily 11–8. Buddy Hall's Maine-style diner styles itself "Maine's Family Seafood Restaurant," and the seafood ranges from chowder to fried and broiled fish dinners to lobster every which way. "Land Lovers" get a token chicken Parmesan, barbecued ribs, and prime rib, and the Minnow Menu is for "the smaller appetite" (you don't have to be small). Entrées $7–30.

Bay Wrap (207-338-9757; www.baywrap.com), 20 Beaver St. (off Main), Belfast. Open daily for lunch and dinner, except Sun., closing earlier in winter. An eatery with a next-door coffeeshop called the Hub, where you can eat the wraps. On a foggy day we feasted on warm grilled eggplant with roasted red peppers, ricotta and feta cheeses, mint, field greens, and salsa verde ($7.65 for large).

Bell the Cat (207-338-2084), Reny's Plaza, Rt. 3, Belfast. Open 7:30–7:30, Sun., 9–5. Set inside a spacious upfront corner of Mr. Paperback, this is the local, very casual favorite for designer sandwiches; from breakfast sandwiches to a fat Reuben. Also good for salads, soups, and ice cream. Coffees and teas.

Seng Thai (207-338-0010), 160 Searsport Ave. (Rt. 1), Belfast. Open daily (except Mon.) from 11:30. Not your ordinary Thai. Residents warn you not to try level-five spiciness. An eggplant special with shrimp, chicken, and peppers in black bean sauce was made with fresh ingredients and delicious. Dinner entrées $9–14.

Three Tides (207-338-1707; www.3tides.com), 2 Pinchy Lane, Belfast. Open Tue.–Sat. from 3 PM, Sun. 1–8, later opening in winter. A fun spot with a serpentine concrete bar and an outdoor deck over the river, where you can drink special cocktails and eat pizzettes ($8.50), salads, and quesadillas. The seafood, mussels, steamers, and lobsters are very fresh; the lobsters are from their own lobster pound. The Marshall Wharf Brewing Company has opened on the premises, offering microbrews.

BUY A BEAUTIFUL BOUQUET WHEN YOU LUNCH AT CHASE'S DAILY.

Abbraccci (207-548-2010), 225 W. Main St., Rt. 1, Searsport. A bakery, espresso bar, and lunch spot with pizza, calzone, and quiche.

Also see **Belfast Co-op** under *Selective Shopping.*

ICE CREAM **Scoops** (207-338-3350), 35 Lower Main St., Belfast. This comfortable place to rest and recoup with ice cream. The (homemade) chocolate chip cookie sundae with Round Top Dairy ice cream and hot fudge is $5.50, and a fruit-filled crêpe topped with honey ice cream is $5.75.

LOBSTER POUND **Young's Lobster Pound** (207-338-1160), Mitchell Ave. (posted from Rt. 1 just across the bridge from downtown Belfast), East Belfast. Open in-season 7–9, and year-round (winter closing at 5:30) for live and cooked lobsters, crabs, clams, and mussels, or takeout. A pound with as many as 30,000 lobsters, and seating (indoor and outdoor) to accommodate 500. The view of Belfast across the Passagassawakeag River is beautiful. They pick the lobster meat here fresh everyday.

✷ Entertainment

In Belfast

The Belfast Maskers (207-338-9668; www.belfastmaskerstheatrer.com). A year-round community theater that puts on several shows each season at the Railroad Theater on the waterfront. Schedule available at the theater. They also offer acting workshops and classes for adults and children.

The Playhouse (207-338-5777), 107 Church St. A cozy 36-seat theater offering plays for adults as well as children. Founder Mary Weaver teaches acting, directs, and performs.

The Colonial Theater (207-338-1930; www.colonialtheater.com). The new home of the out-sized carved elephants from a local landmark, Perry's Nut House; three screens with nightly showings in a restored theater in downtown Belfast.

National Theater Workshop of the Handicapped (207-338-6894; www.ntwh.org), 96 Church St., Belfast. Theatrical productions are staged periodically, free and open to the public.

✷ Selective Shopping

ANTIQUES SHOPS Searsport claims to be the Antiques Capital of Maine. **The Searsport Antique Mall**, 149 E. Main St., open more or less daily year-round, is a cooperative of more than 70 dealers, spread over two floors. **The Pumpkin Patch Antiques Center** (207-548-6047), 15 W. Main St., a 20-dealer shop, has been in business 29 years and is widely respected. Cindy Gallant runs **the Hobby Horse Flea Market** (207-548-2981, 379 E. Main St.), which fills a four-acre complex with two retail stores. A flea market surrounds it every day but Tue., and it's open May–Columbus Day. Two other Searsport Flea Markets are held weekends in-season. **Captain Tinkham's Emporium** (207-548-6465; www.jonesport-wood.com), 34 Main St., next to the Penobscot Marine Museum store, is where you can find antique and functional tools, as well as books, records and sheet music, and other finds from the cellars, attics, and workshops of New England.

BOOKSTORES **Left Bank Books**

(207-548-6400; www.leftbankbookshop.com), 21 E. Main St. (Rt. 1), Searsport. There is a cup of tea by the fireplace here, along with 5,000 select titles, from great mysteries to Arctic explorations. This handsome and welcoming bookstore also sells reproduction maps and vintage cards.

Fertile Mind Bookshop (207-338-2498), 105 Main St., Belfast. An outstanding browsing and buying place featuring Maine and regional books and guides, maps, and cards.

Penobscot Books (207-548-6490; www.penobscotbooks.com), 164 W. Main St., Searsport. With art, architecture, and photography books, more than 50,000 titles, this store sells to universities and libraries all over the world.

Victorian House/Book Barn (207-567-3351), 290 Main St., Stockton Springs. Open every day of the year. A landmark collection of 20,000 antiquarian books, and a special find for mystery-book buffs.

GALLERIES, ETC. **Northport Landing Gallery and Espresso Bar** (207-338-2210; www.northportlandinggallery.com), 1330 Atlantic Hwy. (Rt. 1, and 10 minutes from Camden), Northport. Joy Ambrust, the rambunctious owner, runs this handsome two-level gallery—and also serves cappuccinos, chai, tea, and coffee. Outside the gallery are bronze sculptures of a moose, a bear, and deer; a wild mustang and a big-horned sheep are promised for 2008. Watercolors by Tom Hennessey of wildlife and outdoor sportsmen inside, with other artists' work. Open Mon.–Sat. 9–5; closed Jan. and Feb.

A leaflet guide to all current Belfast galleries is available at any one of them. Don't miss **The Art Alliance Gallery**, (207-338-9994), 92 Main St., a cooperative gallery for seven to 10 very different and interesting artists; the **Parent Gallery** (207-338-1553; www.nealparent.com), 92 Main St., displaying fine black-and-white photographs by Neal Parent, and pastels and oils by daughter Joanne; **High Street Studio and Gallery** (207-338-8990; www.highstreetgallery.com), 149 High St., featuring Susan Tobey White's many-peopled landscapes and amazing doll sculptures.

SPECIAL SHOPS

In Northport

Swan's Island Blankets (207-338-9691; www.swansislandblankets.com), 231 Atlantic Hwy. (Rt. 1), Northport. The old looms are in use in the back room, visible through a window from the elegant showroom; and a few of the natural sources of dye stand in jars. But the real draw is the soft, beautiful, expensive blankets made from the owners' sheep, which may be grazing in the field near the store.

In Belfast

Belfast Co-op Store (207-338-2532), 123 High St. Open daily 7:30 AM–8 PM. Everyone needs something in this store and café with its standout deli and lunches. **Coyote Moon** (207-338-5659), 54 Main St., is a nifty, reasonably priced women's clothing and gift store. **All About Games** (207-338-9984), 78 Main St., is a great place to buy traditional board games; **The Game Loft,** 78A Main, over the store, is a youth center where kids can play non-electronic games for free. **Colburn Shoe Store** (207-338-1934), 79 Main St., bills itself as the oldest shoe store in America, open since 1832. **Reny's** (207-338-4588),

Reny's Plaza, Rt. 3 just north of the junction with Rt. 1, is one in Maine's chain of distinctive outlet stores. Always worth a stop (good for everything from TVs to socks).

North along Rt. 1
Perry's Nut House (207-338-1630), Rt. 1 just north of the Belfast Bridge. Reopened and working on being what it used to be. The nut collection is in the Smithsonian. The man-eating clam cannot be located. **Mainely Pottery** (207-338-1108; www.mainelypottery.com), 181 Searsport Ave. (Rt. 1), features the work of owner Jamie Oates and carries varied work by 30 other Maine potters.

In Searsport
Silkweeds (207-548-6501), Rt. 1, Searsport. Specializes in "country gifts": tinware, cotton afghans, wreaths. **Waldo County Co-op**, Rt. 1, Searsport Harbor. Open June–Oct., daily 9–5. A showcase for the local extension service. Dolls, needlework, wooden crafts, quilts, pillows, jams, and ceramics—and lots of them.

✷ Special Events

May–October: **Belfast Farmer's Market** on Tue., Fri., and Sat. at Reny's Plaza, junction of Rts. 1 and 3.

July 4: Parade, fairs, and fireworks in Searsport.

Mid-July: **Belfast Bay Festival**—a week of events, including a giant chicken barbecue, midway, races, and parade.

July–August: Free Thursday-night **street concerts** in downtown Belfast.

August: **Searsport Lobster Boat Races** and related events.

September: **Common Ground Fair** in Unity—organic farm products,

Nancy English

BELFAST CO-OP

demonstrations, children's activities, sheepdog roundup, crafts, entertainment.

October: First Sat., **Church Street Festival** and parade.

Columbus Day weekend: **Fling to Fall celebration**—parade, bonfire, church suppers.

Second weekend in December: **Searsport Victorian Christmas**—open houses at museums, homes, and B&Bs.

ORGANIC PRODUCE AT BELFAST FARMER'S MARKET.

Nancy English

Down East

amazingmaine.com

EAST PENOBSCOT BAY REGION

ACADIA AREA

WASHINGTON COUNTY AND THE QUODDY LOOP

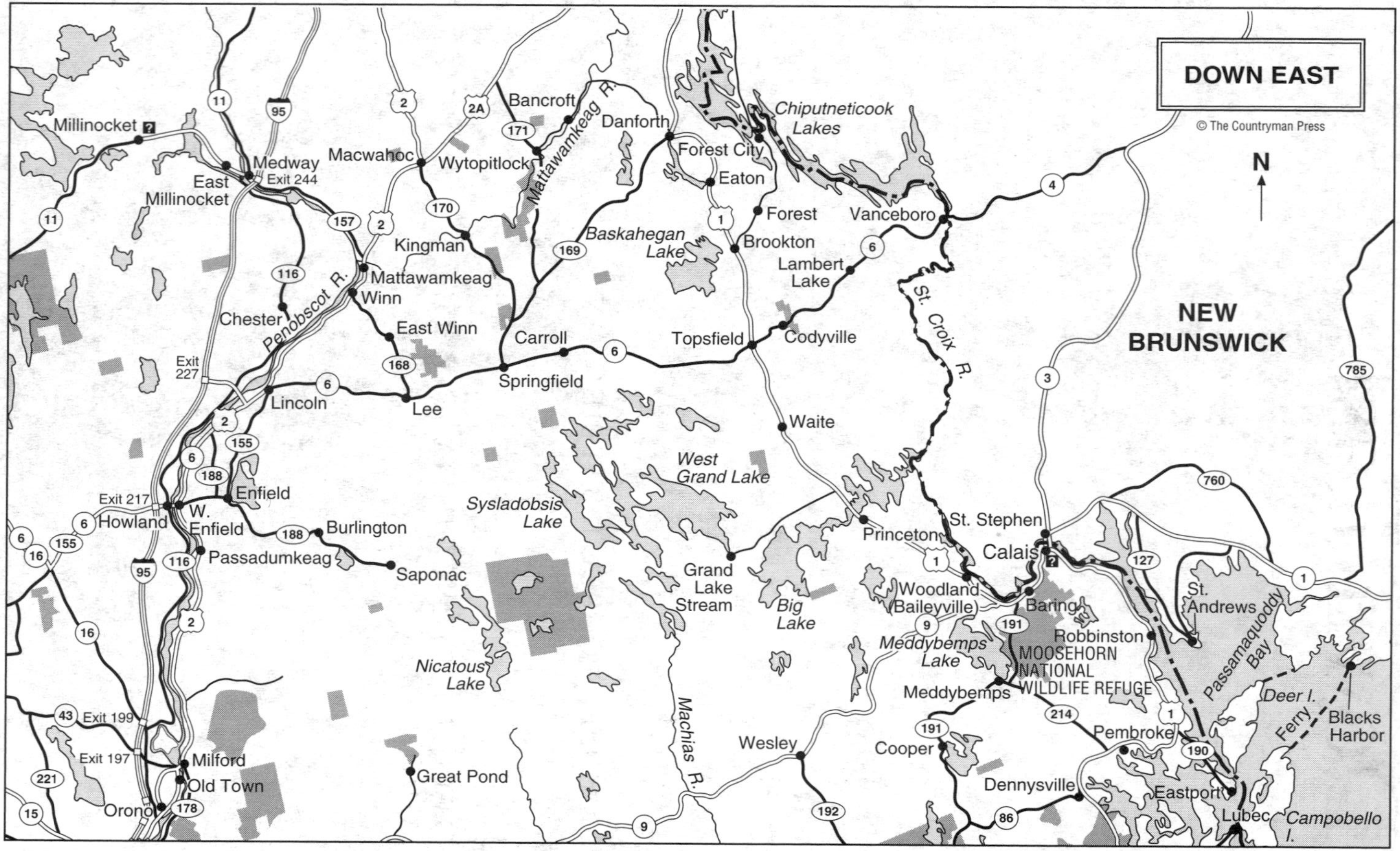
DOWN EAST
© The Countryman Press
N
NEW BRUNSWICK
Millinocket
East Millinocket
Medway
Exit 244
Macwahoc
Wytopitlock
Bancroft
Mattawamkeag R.
Danforth
Forest City
Chiputneticook Lakes
Eaton
Forest
Vanceboro
Brookton
Baskahegan Lake
Kingman
Mattawamkeag
Winn
Chester
Penobscot R.
East Winn
Lambert Lake
Codyville
Topsfield
Carroll
Springfield
Lincoln
Lee
Exit 227
St. Croix R.
Waite
West Grand Lake
Sysladobsis Lake
Exit 217
Howland
W. Enfield
Enfield
Burlington
Passadumkeag
Saponac
Grand Lake Stream
Big Lake
Princeton
St. Stephen
Calais
Woodland (Baileyville)
Baring
Robbinston
MOOSEHORN NATIONAL WILDLIFE REFUGE
Meddybemps Lake
Meddybemps
St. Andrews
Passamaquoddy Bay
Deer I.
Ferry
Blacks Harbor
Nicatous Lake
Machias R.
Wesley
Cooper
Pembroke
Dennysville
Eastport
Lubec
Campobello I.
Exit 199
Exit 197
Milford
Old Town
Orono
Great Pond

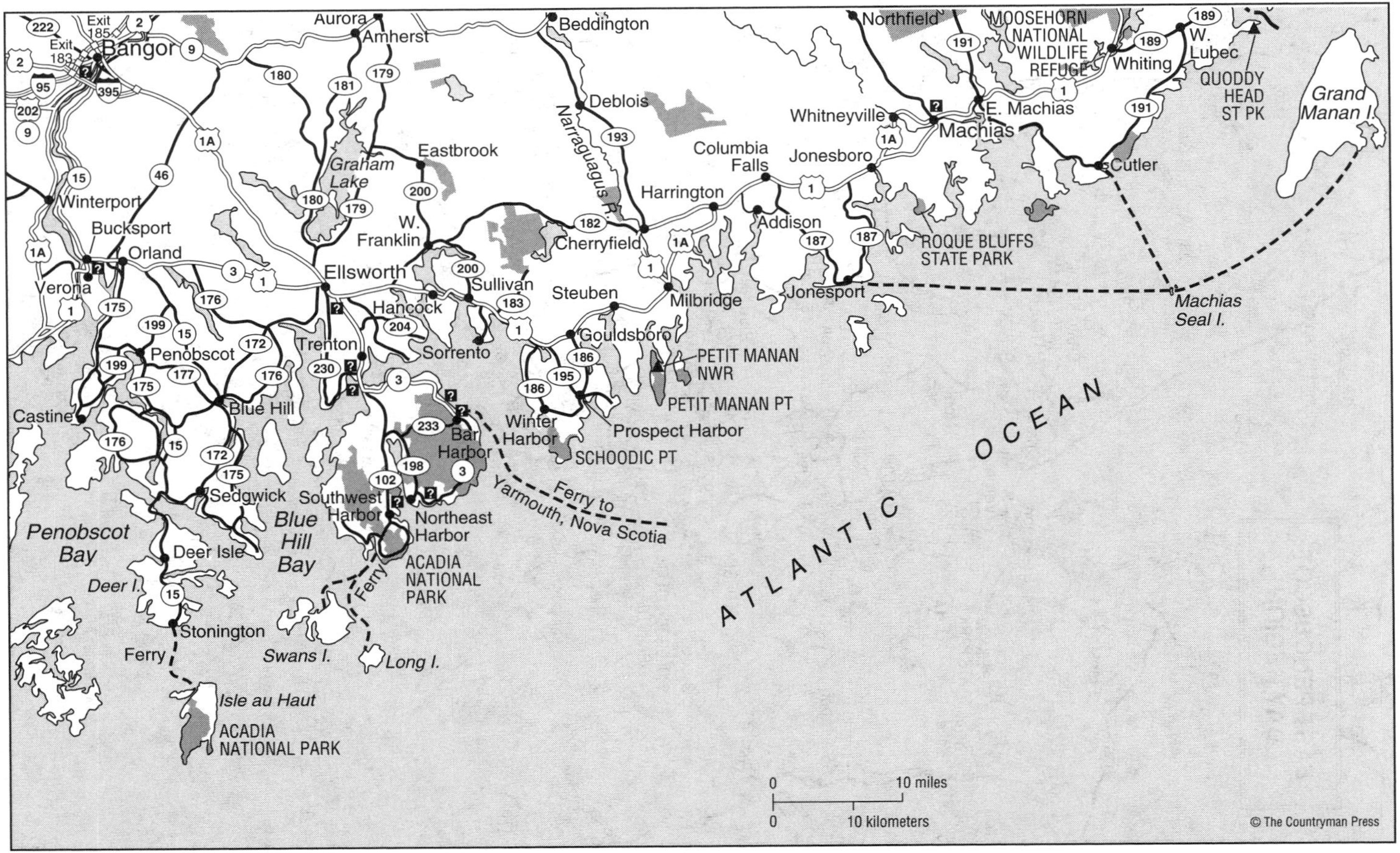

Bangor
Exit 185
Exit 183
Aurora
Amherst
Beddington
Northfield
MOOSEHORN NATIONAL WILDLIFE REFUGE
Whiting
W. Lubec
QUODDY HEAD ST PK
Grand Manan I.
Deblois
Narraguagus R.
Whitneyville
E. Machias
Machias
Eastbrook
Graham Lake
Columbia Falls
Jonesboro
Cutler
Winterport
Bucksport
Orland
Verona
W. Franklin
Harrington
Addison
Cherryfield
ROQUE BLUFFS STATE PARK
Ellsworth
Sullivan
Steuben
Milbridge
Jonesport
Machias Seal I.
Hancock
Penobscot
Trenton
Sorrento
Gouldsboro
PETIT MANAN NWR
PETIT MANAN PT
Castine
Blue Hill
Bar Harbor
Winter Harbor
Prospect Harbor
SCHOODIC PT
Sedgwick
Southwest Harbor
Northeast Harbor
Ferry to Yarmouth, Nova Scotia
ATLANTIC OCEAN
Penobscot Bay
Blue Hill Bay
Deer Isle
Deer I.
ACADIA NATIONAL PARK
Ferry
Stonington
Swans I.
Long I.
Isle au Haut
ACADIA NATIONAL PARK
0 10 miles
0 10 kilometers
© The Countryman Press

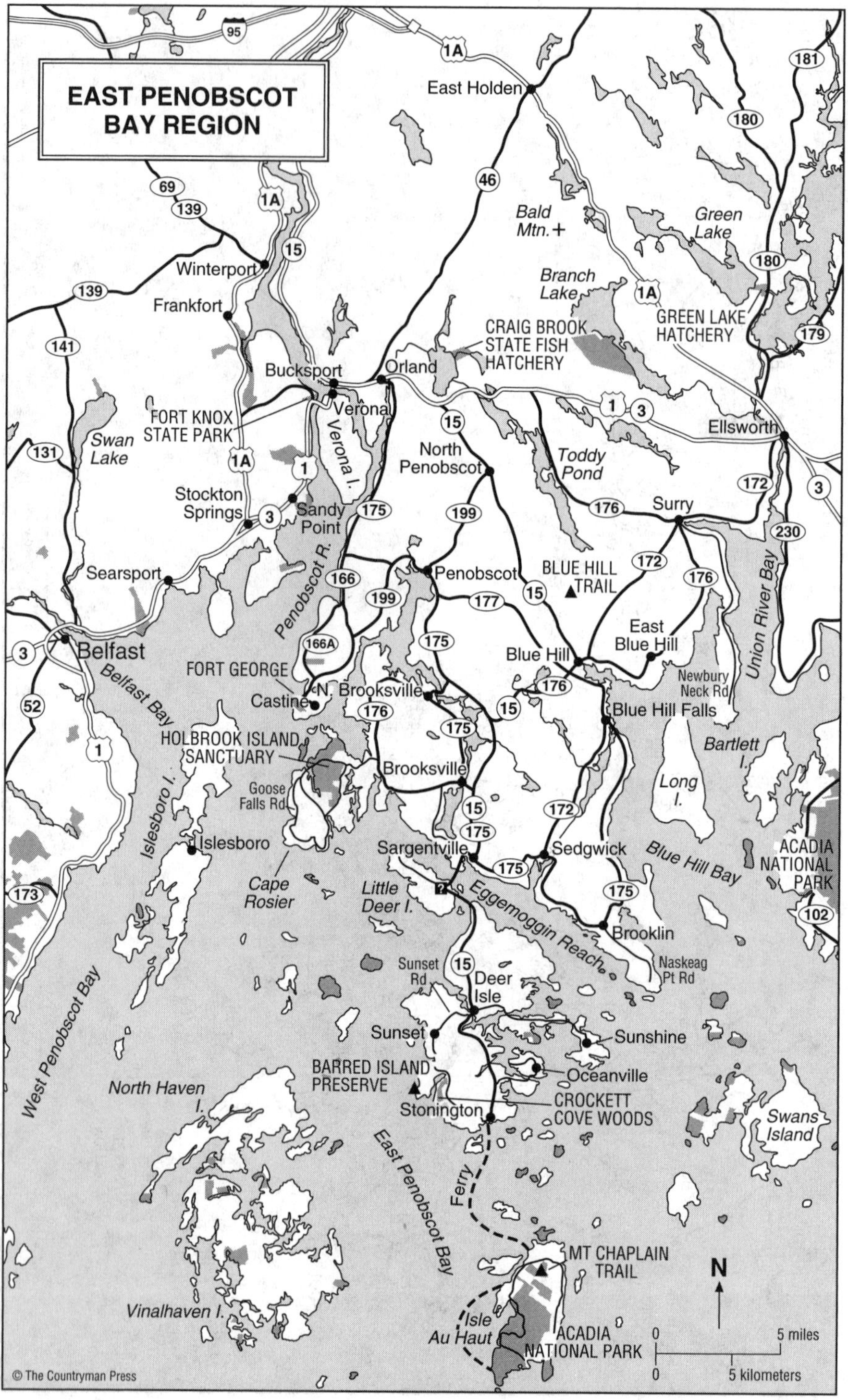
EAST PENOBSCOT BAY REGION
95
1A
East Holden
181
180
46
69
139
1A
Bald Mtn.
Green Lake
Winterport
15
180
Branch Lake
1A
139
Frankfort
CRAIG BROOK STATE FISH HATCHERY
GREEN LAKE HATCHERY
179
141
Orland
Bucksport
Verona
1
3
FORT KNOX STATE PARK
Verona I.
15
Ellsworth
Swan Lake
131
1A
1
North Penobscot
Toddy Pond
172
3
Stockton Springs
Sandy Point
175
199
176
Surry
3
230
Searsport
Penobscot R.
Penobscot
BLUE HILL TRAIL
172
176
166
199
177
15
Belfast
3
166A
175
Blue Hill
East Blue Hill
Union River Bay
Belfast Bay
FORT GEORGE
Castine
N. Brooksville
176
176
15
Newbury Neck Rd
Blue Hill Falls
52
175
HOLBROOK ISLAND SANCTUARY
Bartlett I.
1
Brooksville
Goose Falls Rd
Long I.
Islesboro I.
15
172
175
Islesboro
Sargentville
Sedgwick
ACADIA NATIONAL PARK
175
Blue Hill Bay
Cape Rosier
Little Deer I.
Eggemoggin Reach
175
173
102
Brooklin
Sunset Rd
15
Naskeag Pt Rd
Deer Isle
West Penobscot Bay
Sunset
Sunshine
BARRED ISLAND PRESERVE
Oceanville
North Haven I.
Stonington
CROCKETT COVE WOODS
Swans Island
East Penobscot Bay
Ferry
MT CHAPLAIN TRAIL
N
Vinalhaven I.
Isle Au Haut
ACADIA NATIONAL PARK
0
5 miles
0
5 kilometers
© The Countryman Press

EAST PENOBSCOT BAY REGION

BUCKSPORT/ORLAND AREA; BLUE HILL AREA; DEER ISLE, STONINGTON, AND ISLE AU HAUT; CASTINE

The dramatic new Waldo-Hancock bridge at the Penobscot Narrows links two counties and Midcoast with Downeast Maine. It visually underscores the sense of turning a major coastal corner.

The series of peninsulas and islands defining the eastern rim of Penobscot Bay—an intermingling of land and water along ponds and tidal rivers, as well as bays—is a landscape that's exceptional, even in Maine. Seasonal home to the state's largest concentration of artists and craftspeople, writers and musicians, it's no longer the undiscovered backwater described in earlier editions of this book. On summer days the gallery and shop-lined main streets of Blue Hill, Castine, and Stonington are thronged and reservations are essential at the best restaurants.

Still, the area is webbed with narrow roads threading numerous land fingers, leading to studios of local craftspeople and artists. What you remember afterward is the beauty of clouds over fields of wildflowers, quiet coves, some amazing things that have been woven, painted, or blown, and conversations with the people who made them.

Getting anywhere takes longer than you'll anticipate, and it's best to allow a few days here, perhaps a couple on the Blue Hill and another couple in Castine or Stonington. In recent years the wealth of places to hike has greatly increased, and it's easier than ever to get out on the water, via excursion boat or kayak. Do try to get to Isle au Haut with its hiking trails at Dark Harbor, part of Acadia National Park.

GUIDANCE **The East Penobscot Bay Association** publishes a map/guide covering the entire Blue Hill area, available locally and at **www.penobscotbay.com**. Also pick up the current free copies of the *Browser's Trail* and the *Gallery Guide*.

Also see **www.bluehillpeninsula.org** and **www.deerislemaine.com**.

BUSCKSPORT/ORLAND AREA

Whoosh and the elevator sets you 42 stories above the Penobscot River, atop one of the two obelisk-like pylons anchoring Maine's newest bridge at the confluence of the Penobscot River and Penobscot Bay. Bucksport, beyond the bridge, is a workaday river and paper mill town with a waterfront park, some shopping, restaurants, and a 1916 movie theater/museum showcasing New England films dating back to the turn of the 20th century.

Positioned at the mouth of the Penobscot River, Bucksport was a major shipping port in 1764, the reason it was burned by the British in 1799 and was then occupied by them during the War of 1812. In the 1820s it was the largest town in eastern Maine. Note the former Jed Prouty Tavern in the middle of Main Street, a dining stop for Daniel Webster and a half dozen presidents down through the years. Bucksport overlooks New England's biggest fort, a memorial to its smallest war.

East of Bucksport the town of Orland offers more than meets the eye along Rt. 1. The village itself overlooks the Narramissic River, and in East Orland, Alamoosook Lake is just north of the highway, accessible to the public from the Craig Brook National Fish Hatchery with its innumerable salmon, visitors center, swimming, and hiking trails.

GUIDANCE **Bucksport Bay Area Chamber of Commerce** (207-469-6818; www.bucksportchamber.org). 52 Main St. Open Mon.–Fri. 10–5; brochures available 24 hours.

ALAMO THEATER, BUCKSPORT

Christina Tree

✷ To See and Do

Northeast Historic Film/The Alamo Theatre (207-469-0924; www.oldfilm.org), 85 Main St., Bucksport (entrance on Elm). This 125-seat, vintage-1916 restored theater is open year-round, featuring first-run movies, Dolby digital sound, low prices, and real buttered popcorn. It is also a venue for concerts and live performances. Call for show times. The theater was restored by nonprofit Northeast Historic Film, New England's only "moving-image" archive. Stock footage, technical services, and sales of *Videos of Life in New England* are all available.

Bucksport Historical Society Museum, Main St., Bucksport. Open July–Aug., Wed.–Sat. 1–4, and by appointment: 207-469-3284. Housed in the former Maine Central Railroad

Penobscot Narrows Observatory and Fort Knox State Historic Site, Prospect. (207-469-6553 or 207-469-7719; www.fortknox.maineguide.com), Rt. 174 (off Rt. 1), Prospect. Open daily May–Nov.1, 9 AM–sunset. $5 adults, $3 ages 5–11; $3 adult, $1 child for the fort only.

West of the Waldo-Hancock bridge a traffic light eases access to the Fort Knox grounds, site of the elevator up to the observatory. Access is limited to 49 visitors at any one time, so at the parking-lot gate you receive a ticket stamped with a "go time." In July and August expect a wait. On a sunny Sunday we just had time to picnic at one of the tables overlooking the river, but a larger group might well have had time to explore the fort first. The elevator whisks you to the top (after a few initial hiccups, it's been performing flawlessly). Far below Bucksport is a toy town, and from another window Penobscot Bay sweeps away to the horizon. This is the only bridge with an observatory in the country.

Fort Knox Guided tours are available Memorial Day–Labor Day, then weekends. In the visitors center interpretative panels tell the story: Built in 1844 of granite cut from nearby Mount Waldo, the fort includes barracks, storehouses, a labyrinth of passageways, and picnic facilities. The fort was to be a defense against Canada during the Aroostook War with New Brunswick. The boundary dispute was ignored in Washington, and so in 1839 the new, lumber-rich state took matters into its own hands by arming its northern forts. Daniel Webster represented Maine in the 1842 treaty that formally ended the war, but Maine built this fort two years later, just in case. It was never entirely completed and never saw battle. Troops were, however, stationed here during the Civil War and again during the Spanish-American War. This is a great fort with plenty of tunnels and turrets to explore. It's a venue for reenactments and a wide variety of events, sponsored by Friends of Fort Knox, every weekend, beginning with an Easter egg hunt April and ending with "Fright of the Fort" nights on the two weekends before Halloween. Check the Web site.

PENOBSCOT NARROWS BRIDGE

Christina Tree

Station by the water with some genuinely interesting displays, including one about town founder **Colonel Jonathan Buck**, whose grave (Rt. 1, north of downtown, across from Hannaford's Supermarket), a granite obelisk, is a long-time tourist attraction. The outline of a leg on the stone has spurred many legends, the most popular being that a woman whom Judge Buck sentenced to death for witchcraft is carrying through on a promise to dance on his grave.

Atlantic Salmon Museum (207-469-6701, ext. 215), 306 Hatchery Road, East Orland (marked from Rt. 1). First opened in 1871, this is the country's oldest salmon hatchery. A large visitors center (open year-round, daily 8–3) offers films and interactive displays on Maine rivers, watersheds, and salmon. A small museum exhibits salmon industry memorabilia, open daily noon–3 in summer. The facility also includes a boat launch on Alamoosook Lake, a picnic area and swim beach on Craig Pond, and hiking/skiing trails.

✱ Lodging

Orland House (207-469-1144; www.orlandhousebb.com), Box 306, 10 Narramissic Dr., Orland 04472. This imposing 1820 house stands above the Narramissic River. Alvion and Cynthia (Cindi) Kimball offer four spiffy guest rooms, all with private bath, and kayaks for use on the river. $95–105 in-season (otherwise $10 less) includes a full breakfast. Inquire about weekly rentals for the riverside cottage across the street.

"1" ⚭ **Alamoosook Lakeside Inn** (207-469-6393; www.alamoosooklakesideinn.com), 229 Soper Rd., Orland 04472. Open year-round. This log lodge was built as a corporate retreat by a local paper company. The dining room, jutting out into Alamoosook Lake, is a popular spot for weddings. The six attractive guest rooms all open onto a sunporch. The lake offers good swimming, canoeing, and fishing; also cleared for ice fishing and cross-country skiing in winter. $125 per couple, $105 single with breakfast in summer and fall, less off-season.

Best Western Fort Knox Inn (207-469-3113), Main St., Bucksport 04416. Open year-round. Built as a modern annex to the old Jed Prouty Inn, now offering 40 motel-style rooms with two double beds and great views of Fort Knox across the mouth of the Penobscot River. $79–149 per couple, depending on the season, includes continental breakfast.

✱ Where to Eat

✎ **MacLeods** (207-469-3963), Main St., Bucksport. Open nightly for dinner from 5. Dependable dining in a pubby atmosphere with booths. Entrées ($11–22) range from comfort food like baked meat loaf and barbecued ribs to specials like a baked scallop strudel.

✱ Selective Shopping

h.o.m.e. co-op (207-469-7961; www.homecoop.net), Rt. 1, Orland. Open daily 9–5. A remarkable complex that includes a crafts village (visitors can watch pottery making, weaving, leather work, woodworking); a museum of old handicrafts and farm implements; a large crafts shop featuring handmade coverlets, toys, and clothing; and a market stand with fresh vegetables, herbs, and other garden produce.

"I" **Book Stacks** (207-469-8992 or 1-888-295-0123), 71 Main St., Bucksport. Open Mon.–Sat. 9–8, Sun. 9–5. Not what you would expect to find on this brief Main Street: an inviting full-service bookstore with a cyber café.

✷ Special Events

Note: Check with **Friends of Fort Knox** (www.fortknos.maineguide.com) for colorful events at the fort, staged most weekends from Apr. through Oct.

Late July: **Bay Festival**—Parade, and a variety of events on the river; at the fort and along the Bucksport waterfront.

July–August: **Bucksport Riverfront Market** every Sat. 9–3. Art, crafts, baked goods, and produce.

August: **h.o.m.e's Annual Craft & Farm Fair and Benefit Auction** (207-469-7961; www.homecoop.net). A Saturday blueberry pancake breakfast, poetry readings, music, fish-fry supper, street dance, BBQ, children's games, crafts, and more.

BLUE HILL AREA

In Maine, *Blue Hill* refers to a specific hill, a village, a town, a peninsula—and also to an unusual gathering of artists, musicians, and craftspeople. A shade off the beaten path, one peninsula west of Mount Desert, Blue Hill has its own following—especially among creative people.

Over the entrance of the Bagaduce (sheet music) Lending Library, a mural depicts the area as the center of concentric creative circles. Helen and Scott Nearing, searching for a new place to live "the Good Life" in the 1950s (when a ski area encroached on their seclusion in southern Vermont), swung a dowsing pendulum over a map of coastal Maine. It came to rest on Cape Rosier. For many decades the small town of Brooklin was a familiar byline in the *New Yorker* thanks to E. B. White, who also wrote *Charlotte's Web* and *Stuart Little* here at about the same time millions of children began to read about Blueberry Hill in Robert McCloskey's *Blueberries for Sal* and about Condon's Garage (still a South Brooksville family-owned landmark) in the 1940s classic *One Morning in Maine.*

Energy lines or not, this peninsula is exceptionally beautiful, with views to the east toward Mount Desert as well as back across Penobscot Bay. Pause at the turnout on Caterpillar Hill, the height-of-land on Rt. 15/175 (just north of the Deer Isle Bridge), to appreciate the panorama. Then plunge down the hill to an improbably narrow, soaring suspension bridge.

The 1939 bridge spans Eggemoggin Reach, a 10-mile-long passage dividing the Blue Hill Peninsula from Deer Isle but linking Penobscot and Jericho Bays. A century ago this was a busy thoroughfare, a shortcut from Rockland to points Down East for freight-carrying schooners and passenger steamboats. It remains a popular route for windjammers, yachts, and, increasingly, for sea kayakers. Rt. 175 winds along "the Reach" on its way through Sedgwick to Brooklin.

GUIDANCE **The Blue Hill Peninsula Chamber of Commerce** (207-374-3242; www.bluehillpeninsula.org), 28 Water St. Blue Hill 04614, covers the six peninsula towns, publishing a booklet guide. It maintains a year-round information center, with hours that vary with volunteers.

GETTING THERE *By car:* From points south take I-95 to Rt. 295 to Rt. 3 to Belfast and Rt. 1 to Rt. 15 to Blue Hill. There are many shortcuts through the confusing web of roads on this peninsula; ask directions to your lodging.

By air: The nearest airportis **Bangor International** (www.flybangor.com).

By bus: **Concord Trailways** (www.concordtrailways.com) offers the best service from Boston's Logan International Airport and its South Station: a little more than four hours to Bangor.

WHEN TO COME Blue Hill is very seasonal, but several inns and restaurants remain open year-round.

✷ To See

Johnathan Fisher Memorial (207-374-2459; www.jonathanfisherhouse.org), 0.5 mile south of Blue Hill Village on Rt. 15/176. Open July–mid-Oct., Mon.–Sat. 1–4. A house built in 1814 by Blue Hill's first pastor, a Harvard graduate who augmented his meager salary with a varied line of crafts and by teaching (he founded Blue Hill Academy), farming, and writing. His furniture, paintings, books, journals, and woodcuts are exhibited. Admission.

Holt House, Water St., Blue Hill. Open July–mid-Sept., Tue. and Fri. 1–4, Sat. 11–2. Open year-round on Thu. for research. Donation. The Blue Hill Historical Society collection is housed in this restored 1815 Federal mansion near the harbor and noted for its stenciled walls.

Blue Hill Library (207-374-5515), 5 Parker Point Rd., Blue Hill. Open daily except Sun. A handsome WPA building with periodicals and ample reading space; changing art shows in summer.

Bagaduce Music Lending Library (207-374-5454; www.bagaducemusic.org), Rt. 15, Blue Hill. Open Mon.–Fri. 10–3. This Blue Hill phenomenon features roughly 100,000 sheet music titles (instrumental, keyboard, and vocal), some more than a century old and most special for one reason or another—all available for borrowing. The collection includes 1,400 pieces about Maine, by Maine composers, or published in Maine. Stop by just to see the mural over the entrance.

The Good Life Center (207-326-8211; www.goodlife.org), on the loop road, facing Orrs Cove (opposite side of the road), Harborside, on Cape Rosier. In July, Aug., open daily except. Tue. 1–5; also closed Wed. off-season. Forest Farm, with its stone home built in 1953 by Helen (d. 1995) and Scott Nearing (d. 1983), coauthors of *Living the Good Life* and seven other books based on their simple, purposeful lifestyle, is now maintained by a nonprofit trust. Through a stewardship program a couple maintains the property year-round. The grounds include an intensively cultivated organic garden, a greenhouse, and a yurt. A weekly series of evening talks is offered in summer. Inquire about workshops.

Sedgwick-Brooklin Historical Society & Museum (207-359-8958), Rt. 172, Sedgwick. Open July–Aug., Sun. 2–4. This complex includes the town's original parsonage, a restored schoolhouse, and an 1820s cattle pound. It is part of the Sedgwick Historic District. Note the old cemetery.

Also see *Selective Shopping—Art Galleries*.

Christina Tree

THE GOOD LIFE CENTER

SCENIC DRIVES To come as far as Blue Hill Village and go no farther would be like walking up to a door and not opening it. The beauty of the peninsula lies beyond—via roads that wander west to **Brooksville** by taking Rt. 15 south to Rt. 176/175 north to Rt. 176 (yes, that's right) and across the **Bagaduce River** and south on Rt. 176 (never mind). Turn off at the sign for **Cape Rosier** to see **Holbrook Island Sanctuary** and **Forest Farm**. Return to Rt. 176 and continue into the village of South Brooksville (don't miss **Buck's Harbor**). Rt. 176 rejoins Rt. 175 and then Rt. 15; turn south and follow Rt. 15 south over **Caterpillar Hill**, where a recently expanded pullout permits space to enjoy one of the most spectacular panoramas available from any coastal road, south across Penobscot Bay to the Camden Hills. From this height Rt. 5 plunges downhill. Turn left at the bottom, and drive alongside **Eggemoggin Reach**. The alternate scenic route is Rt. 175 south across Blue Hill Falls and along Blue Hill Bay to **Brooklin** and back along the Reach through Sedgwick. These two routes meet at the **Little Deer Isle Bridge**. Be sure to cross the bridge (see "Deer Isle, Stonington").

✷ To Do

BOATING **Buck's Harbor Marine** (207-326-8839), South Brooksville, rents sail- and motorboats. Inquire about sailing lessons.

Summertime (1-800-562-8290; www.schoonersummertime.com). Capt. Bill Brown offers daysails in early summer and fall; three- and six-day midsummer cruises on his 30-foot pinky schooner depart from Rockland.

Perelandra (207-326-4279). Capt. LeCain Smith offers daysails from Buck's Harbor in his 44-foot steel ketch.

✐ **MERI Summer Eco-Cruises** (207-374-2135). During summer months regularly scheduled eco-cruises and Island Explorer programs are held aboard the 12-passenger, lobster boat–style excursion boat, also special Island Explorer programs for children(see *Learning Programs*).

Also see *Sea Kayaking, Canoeing*.

FISHING **Eggemoggin Guide Service** (207-359-2746; www.eggemogginguide

service.net), Sedgwick. Capt. Pete Douvarjo offers half-day trips for striped bass and full-day float trips on the Penobscot River. Fly-fishing and hand-crafted fishing rods are specialties.

SEA KAYAKING, CANOEING **The Activity Shop** (207-374-3600; www.activityshop.com), 61 Ellsworth Rd. (Rt. 172), north of Blue Hill Village. Old Town canoes, kayak and bicycle rentals. **Rocky Coast Outfitters** (207-374-8866), on Grindleville Rd. off Rt. 15 in Blue Hill, rents and offers free delivery of kayaks, canoes, and bicucles. The **Bagaduce River** north from Walker Pond is a favorite flatwater run for novices, with some popular whitewater at **Blue Hill Falls**, a reversing falls accessible off Rt. 175. Also see *To Do* in the Deer Isle, Stonington, and Castine sections of this chapter.

SPECIAL LEARNING PROGRAMS **WoodenBoat School** (207-359-4651 or 1-800-273-7447; www.woodenboat.com), off Naskeag Point Rd., south of the village of Brooklin. A spinoff from *WoodenBoat* magazine, this seafaring institute of national fame offers summer courses that range from building your own sailboat, canoe, or kayak to navigation and drawing and painting. Accommodations available. The store is a shopping destination in its own right; open weekdays 7:30–6, Sat. 9–5.

Marine Environmental Research Institute (MERI) (207-374-2135; www.meriresearch.org), 55 Main St., Blue Hill. Open year-round except Sun.; weekdays only in the off-season. The focus of this nonprofit is harbor seals. MERI offers a summer schedule of educational, guided cruises plus hands-on ocean science programs, some specially geared to youngsters ages 6–12 and others to older kids. The center is also the scene of lectures, videos, and children's story hours.

Also see **Haystack Mountain School of Crafts** in "Deer Isle, Stonington."

✷ Green Space

Blue Hill. Our friends at the Blue Hill Bookstore tell us that this was not the setting for the children's classic *Blueberries for Sal*, by Robert McCloskey—a longtime summer resident of the area. But we choose to disbelieve them. It looks just like the hill in the book and has its share of in-season blueberries. The big attraction, however, is the view of the Mount Desert mountains from the 934-foot summit. From Rt. 172 take Mountain Rd. to the parking area (on your right). It's a mile to the top via the Hayes Trail through town conservation land, and a little longer if you loop back down to the road via the Osgood Trail through Blue Hill Heritage Trust land.

Blue Hill Heritage Trust (207-374-5118; www.bluehillheritagetrust.org) is steadily increasing the amount of preserved open space throughout the peninsula.

Blue Hill Town Park. Follow Water St. past the hospital to this pleasant waterside park with picnic tables and great rocks for kids.

Caterpillar Hill, Rt. 15, Sedgwick. The spectacular panorama south across

Holbrook Island Sanctuary (207-326-4012), 172 Indian Bar Rd. (off Rt. 176 in West Brooksville on Cape Rosier), is a state wildlife sanctuary of 1,350 acres, including 2.3 miles of shore and 115-acre Holbrook Island. No camping is permitted, but a lovely picnic area adjoins a pebble beach. A network of old roads, paths, and animal trails leads along the shore and through marshes and forest. It's the creation as well as the gift of Anita Harris,who died in 1985 at age 92, the sole resident of Holbrook Island. Her will stipulated that her mansion and all the other buildings on the island be demolished. She was also responsible for destroying all homes within the sanctuary. Wildlife is plentiful and birding is exceptional, especially during spring and fall migrations. Great blue herons nest around the pond and the estuary. Bald eagles and peregrine falcons and an eagle's nest may also be seen. Inquire about guided nature walks on Mon., Wed., and Fri. in July and Aug.

Penobscot Bay to the Camden Hills can now be viewed from an accessible scenic overlook.

✷ Lodging

RESORTS **Hiram Blake Camp** (207-326-4951; www.hiramblake.com), Cape Rosier, Harborside 04642. Open June–Sept. Well off the beaten track, operated by the same family since 1916, this is the kind of place where you come to stay put. All cottages are within 200 feet of the shore, with views of Penobscot Bay. Under the able management of Deborah Venno Ludlow and her husband David, many have been renovated. There are five one-bedroom cottages, six cottages with two bedrooms, and three with three bedrooms; each has a living room with a wood-burning stove; some have a fireplace as well. Each has a kitchen, a shower, and a porch. Guests with housekeeping cottages cook for themselves in the shoulder months, but in July and August everyone eats in the dining room, which doubles as a library because thousands of books are ingeniously filed away by category in the ceiling. There are rowboats at the dock, a playground, and a recreation room with table tennis and board games; also trails. From $600 per week MAP for the one-room Acorn Cottage to $2,400 for a three-bedroom cottage (up to five guests). Additional guests are each $350 per week. Rates drop during "housekeeping months" to $600–850 per week.

INNS AND BED & BREAKFASTS

In Blue Hill 04614

Blue Hill Inn (207-374-2844 or 1-800-826-7415; www.bluehillinn.com), 40 Union St. The inn itself is open mid-May–Oct.; the Cape House is open year-round. A classic 1830s inn on a quiet, elm-lined street in the village. Wisconsin-bred Sarah Pebworth, the new innkeeper, first discovered this area in 1988. She continues to preserve a sense of comfortable elegance in the dozen guest rooms, some with sitting room and/or

Oakland House Seaside Resort (207-359-8521 or 1-800-359-RELAX; www.oaklandhouse.com), 435 Herrick Rd., Brooksville 04617. Most cottages open May–Oct.; Lone Pine and Boathouse cottages are open year-round. The picturesque old mansard-roofed hotel opened by Jim Littlefield's forebears in 1889 now houses only the dining rooms and serves as a centerpiece for this 50-acre property, with a half mile of frontage on Eggemoggin Reach, and with lake as well as saltwater beaches. Scattered through the woods and along the shore are 15 cottages (each different; most with cooking facilities, living room, and fireplace), accommodating one to nine people. There are no TVs (with the exception of Lone Pine), and firewood is free. Families feel particularly welcome. Facilities include a dock, rowboats, badminton, croquet, a recreation hall full of games, and hiking trails. Breakfast and dinner are served in the delightfully old-fashioned dining rooms, one reserved for families, the other adults-only. The current fare is on a par with the best around (see *Dining Out*). Thursday is lobster picnic night. In-season cottages rent by the week: $565–1,375 per adult MAP (children's rates slide) and in shoulder season $475–1,375 per week (housekeeping) per cottage, no meals.

A part of but apart from the larger resort is **Shore Oaks Seaside Inn**, one of the best-kept secrets of the region. Built as a private cottage in 1907, an era when Maine cottage signified something specific—namely, simplicity and a focus on surroundings—it has been sensitively restored by Sally Littlefield, a designer who recognized the quality of its Arts and Crafts–era architecture, detailing, and furnishings, all of which she has amplified. Shaded by huge old oaks and firs, this 10-room "cottage" features a long porch lined with rocking chairs and a gazebo right on the water, commanding sweeping views of Eggemoggin Reach, the Pumpkin Island Lighthouse, and Penobscot Bay beyond. Rooms have deep old tubs. Our favorite is Room 7, a corner room overlooking the water with no less than six windows and a working fireplace, Mission oak furniture, and a sense of space and comfort. We have also stayed on the third floor with shared bath, not a bad option. $74–265 per room B&B.

OAKLAND HOUSE

Christina Tree

working fireplace. The handicapped-accessible Cape House Suite, an adjoining cottage, has a full kitchen and living room with fireplace, good for families. In good weather guests gather for cocktails in the garden. A full breakfast with a choice of entrées, afternoon tea, and hors d'oeuvres are included in $158–285 double (the inn is fully licensed) high season, otherwise $138–175.

Blue Hill Farm (207-374-5126; www.bluehillfarminn.com), 578 Pleasant St., Box 437. Open year-round. Off by itself on Rt. 15 north of Blue Hill Village, a former barn has been reworked as an open-beamed combination breakfast/dining/living room. Upstairs are seven small guest rooms, each with a private bath. The attached farmhouse offers seven more guest rooms with shared baths (including one appealing single) and more common rooms, one with a woodstove. $90–110 double, less single and off-season, includes a generous continental breakfast.

Barncastle Hotel + Restaurant (207-374-2300; www.barncastlehotel.com), 125 South St. A fanciful shingle-style summer mansion, for many years an inn called "Arcady Downeast," has recently been totally renovated by Lori and Isaac Robbins. The guest area is nicely removed from the busy restaurant, but this is on a main drag. The feel is of a boutique hotel rather than an inn. Each of the five rooms has a king bed, flat screen TV, mini-fridge, microwave, coffeemaker, and private bath. $100–150 includes breakfast en suite. (Also see *Dining Out*.)

Capt. Isaac Merrill Inn (207-374-2555; www.captainmerrillinn.com), 5 Union St., Blue Hill. In the middle of Blue Hill Village, this Federal-style home has six guest rooms, four with gas fireplace. Hostess Jane Hemmerly Brown is descended from the captain who built it and enjoys talking with guests during breakfast, included in $95–175.

Elsewhere on the Blue Hill Peninsula

DragonFlye Inn (207-359-5057; www.dragonflyeinn.com), Naskeag Point Rd., P.O. Box 20, Brooklin. Open May–Oct. Joe and Natasha Moore have turned this mansard-roofed Victorian house into a glorious place to stay. Each of the five rooms is thoughtfully decorated (but not overdone), featuring Maine-made furniture and work by local artists. There's also plenty of light, an airy common space, a deck, and a flower garden. Just around the corner from the village, it's within easy walking distance of dinner at the Brooklin Inn and the deli at the general store. $135 in high season includes an organic, continental breakfast. $110–125 in shoulder seasons includes use of bikes. Joe also offers guided sea kayaking tours.

First Light Bed & Breakfast (207-374-5879; www.firstlightbandb.com), 821 E. Blue Hill Rd., Blue Hill 04614. A coveside home with a tower built in the 1970s to resemble a lighthouse. The dining and living rooms have large windows overlooking the picturesque harbor and, on clear days, beyond to Mount Desert Island. Two bedrooms on the second floor share a bath, but the Lighthouse Suite is the real star: a round bedroom with bird's-eye maple dressers built into the curve of the wall and rockers with views, plus a dressing room overlooking the cove (full bath). $135–160 with a full breakfast; two-night stay required.

"1" **The Brooklin Inn** (207-359-2777; www.brooklininn.com), 22 Reach Road, P.O. Box 25, Brooklin 04616. A casual, friendly, year-round inn in the middle of a minute village. Chip (a former tugboat captain) and Gail Angell are clearly the right innkeepers for this landmark that's well known for its restaurant (see *Dining Out*) with an separate, inviting pub. The four pleasant upstairs bedrooms now each have private bath, and another room can be added on to form a suite. $105–125 per couple in summer, $95 in winter includes full breakfast; a $145 winter special adds all you can eat for two. *Note*: Brooklin offers sheltered moorings to yachters.

The Maples (207-359-8309), Rt. 175, P.O. Box 222, Brooklin 04616. Open year-round. Two upstairs rooms share a bath and in summer there are two more very pleasant downstairs rooms, shared bath. We like the hospitable feel of this village guest house with its resident cats, and at age 84 Dorothy Jordan still obviously enjoys her guests. $85 includes morning coffee.

Brass Fox Bed and Breakfast (207-326-0575; www.brassfox.com), 907 Southern Bay Rd. (Rt. 175), Penobscot 04476. Open year-round. This 19th-century farmhouse is filled with antiques. Common space includes two dining rooms (with original tin ceilings), a small library (with phone jack for Internet connection), and parlor. All the second-floor guest rooms (each with bath) share balconies with views off across fields and woods. A full breakfast includes freshly squeezed orange juice, an entrée, and homemade pastries; the Bagaduce Lunch (see *Eating Out*) is handy. Gerry and Dawn Freeman are helpful hosts. $90–115. Pets possible.

COTTAGES AND MORE Peninsula Property Rentals (207-374-2428; www.peninsulapropertyrentals.com), Main St., Blue Hill 04614. A range of area rentals. Also see **Maine Vacation Rentals** (207-374-2444; www.mainevacationrentalsonline.com), 105 Main St., Blue Hill.

The Red Windows (207-326-8235; www.wanamakerraphael.com), 1208 Coastal Rd., Brooksville 03617. Most cottages are weekly rentals, but this lovely second-floor suite, with a panoramic water view, is available nightly, two-night minimum on weekends. It offers a queen-sized beds and two bunks suitable for small children, kitchen facilities. $135 per night.

✱ Where to Eat

DINING OUT Arborvine (207-374-2119; www.arborvine.com), Main St. (Rt. 172), south Blue Hill Village. Open for dinner Tues.–Sun. in-season, Fri.–Sun. off-season. Few Maine restaurants are as widely acclaimed, and reservations may be necessary a couple days in advance. Chef-owner John Hikade was already the area's most respected chef when he and his wife Beth restored the handsome 1820s Hinckley homestead, retaining its original Dutchman's pipe vine above the door. The several open-beamed dining rooms with fireplaces, once the parlors, are simple and elegant. The menu presents local produce in memorable ways, such as Bagaduce River oysters on the half shell with a frozen sake mignotte, or broiled Stonington halibut with grilled polenta, lemon butter crumb crust, an orange-miso sauce and carmelized vidalias. Entrées $25–30. The wine list is extensive and reasonably priced. Also see The Vinery under *Eating Out*.

Wescott Forge (207-374-9909; www.thewescottforge.com), 66 Main St., Blue Hill. Open June–Oct. for lunch and dinner, jazz nights with a raw bar Fri. and Sat. Off-season hours vary. Reservations recommended. Anneliese Riggall has restored the original name of this streamside building to distinguish it from its many lives as Fire Pond. Thoroughly renovated, the upstairs dining room is now a lighter, more casual space with a wine bar. Downstairs is more intimate, with white-clothed tables lining windows by the stream, others by the hearth. Lunch is upstairs. Begin or sup on gazpacho with lobster, flash-fired Spinney Creek oysters with creamed greens, or a selection of locally smoked fish. The menu changes daily to reflect what's locally available but might include seaweed-seared yellowfin tuna and a wakame salad, or a grilled juniper berry pork chop. Entrées $16–25.

The Brooklin Inn (207-359-2777; www.brooklininn.com), 22 Reach Rd. (Rt. 175), Brooklin Village. Reservations advised. Open nightly in summer, closed Mon. and Tues. in winter. This restaurant religiously serves only wild fish and produce that's organic and local. This is a justly popular and hospitable small village inn with a menu that changes nightly. The Bagaduce River oysters might be fried, served with a spicy mustard sauce, and the sesame-crusted blue fin tuna seared rare, served with sweet-and-sour braised cabbage and poached ginger. Entrées from $17 for vegetable bouillabaisse to $35 for sautéed lobster. The wine list and choice of beers are extensive. The downstairs pub, with a menu featuring Guinness beef stew and chicken potpie, is a favorite local gathering spot.

Buck's (207-326-8683), Buck's Harbor Market, middle of the village of South Brooksville, Rt. 176. Open Wed.–Sat. 5:30–8; no reservations. Chef Johnathan Chase has a wide following and this, his latest venture, gets great reviews. The informal dining room behind the village market is all about local ingredients and great, reasonably priced food. Choose from "soups, salads, and small plates" as well as "Buck's specialty sandwiches" (like avocado, artichoke, humus, sprouts, tomato, field greens, and Vermont cheddar on 12-grain bread). Entrées might include baked native haddock with balsamic aioli and a sourdough crumb topping and seared duck breast with cranberry, beer, and maple barbeque sauce. Entrées $16–18.

The Rusticator Restaurant at Oakland House (207-359-8521), off Herrick Rd., Brooksville. Open mid-June–Sept. for dinner 6–8:30 and Sunday brunch 9–11 in July and Aug. On Thursday in July and August a lobster picnic is served, weather permitting, on the beach. Reservations requested. This delightfully old-fashioned dining room is a hidden gem. The five-course menu that changes daily, but always emphasizes seasonal ingredients with organic herbs and edible flowers from the resort's gardens. Outside, guests can order à la carte from a choice of several entrées—perhaps fresh swordfish with citrus butter or seafood fettucini. This isn't a place to skip dessert, maybe a blueberry tart with maple anglaise. Entrées $13–16. In spring and fall dinner is served in the smaller dining room at Shore Oaks Seaside Inn (see *Lodging*).

The Lookout Inn & Restaurant (207-359-2188; www.thelookoutinn.biz), 455 Flye Point Rd., Brooklin. Open for dinner Tues.–Sat. mid-June–mid-Oct., call off-season. Butch Smith has a talent for finding superb chefs, year after year. The setting is one of Maine's oldest family-owned summer hotels, set above gardens and a meadow that slope to the water, a stunning wedding venue. The à la carte menus might include portobello mushrooms, steamed local mussels, and lobster cakes. Entrées always include today's catch, rack of lamb, and duck breast with lemon cranberry glaze. $18–28.

Surry Inn (207-667-5091; www.surryinn.com), Rt. 172, Contention Cove, Surry. Open nightly for dinner except Tue.; just Fri.–Sat. in winter. This pleasant dining room overlooking a cove is well known locally for reasonably priced fine dining, under the same ownership and management for many years. The menu changes often but always includes interesting soups—maybe Hungarian mushroom or lentil vegetable—and a wide entrée selection that might include veal sautéed with sundried tomatoes, blueberry duckling, spicy garlic frogs' legs, and lobster with corn cakes and a scallop mousseline. Entrées $14–23.

Blue Moose Restaurant (207-374-4374), 50 Main St., Blue Hill. Open daily for lunch, dinner, and afternoon tea. "A fusion of foods" is the way chef Mike Menge describes what he serves. At lunch try a Santa Fe salad of grains and local greens with cumin tomato dressing; at dinner, perhaps marinated pork loin with braised red cabbage. All dinner entrées available in small portions. Dinner entrées $9–17 for large portions.

Also see *Dining Out* in Deer Isle, Stonington, and in Castine.

EATING OUT **Barncastle** (207-374-2300), 125 South St., Blue Hill. Open daily 11–9. This former mansion is an unlikely but delightful venue for the area's best pizza. What you need to know is that most of the staff here come from Pie in the Sky, the area's previously best but now-defunct pizza source. The centerpiece of this sleek new restaurant is its wood-fired oven, producing pizza with a choice of more than 30 toppings. The menu also includes sandwiches, subs, and salad featuring local farms. Wine and beer served.

Bagaduce Lunch, Rt. 176, South Penobscot at the reversing falls and the bridge to North Brooksville. A seasonal, hugely popular lunch stand that closes at 3. Fried seafood baskets are the big draw, but we were disappointed on our last visit. Still the ice cream is Gifford's and picnic tables are scattered over a lawn that slopes to the Bagaduce River.

The Vinery (207-374-2441; www.arborvine.com), part of the Arborvine complex on the southern edge of Blue Hill Village. Open Wed.–Sun. for supper, bar open until 10:30. No reservations. Piano bar and local entertainment nightly, a full bar and wine by the glass, light bistro fare such as cod cakes and sweet potato napoleon as well as pastas and pad Thai.

Marlintini's Grill (207-374-2500), The Mines Rd. (Rt. 15/176) south of Blue Hill Village. Local favorite, open for lunch and dinner. There's a sports bar but plenty of space to get away from it. Grilled and fried meat and seafood, salads, hot sandwiches, and nightly specials.

Morning Moon Café (207-359-2373), Rt. 175, Brooklin. Open daily 7 AM–2 PM except Mon.; also for take-out pizza 5–8 PM (days vary with the season). For sale at this writing, but we are assured this will continue to be an oasis in the middle of Brooklin Village, our favorite kind of eatery with deep booths, good salads, pizza and sandwiches, pies, and soups.

The Fish Net (207-374-5240), Blue Hill Village, Rt. 15, across from the turnoff (Rt. 176) to East Blue Hill. Open seasonally 11–8, until 9 on Fri.–Sat. Known for lobster rolls; also a convenient place to feast on lobster and steamers or to buy a cooked lobster to take home, plus the usual fried seafood, burgers, and sandwiches.

Buck's Harbor Market (207-326-8683), Cornfield Hill Rd. (Rt. 176), Brooksville Village. The market has a lunch counter, open year-round for breakfast and lunch. Baking is done here, and the stuffed pockets and breads make great picnic fare.

Blue Hill Food Co-op Café (207-374-2165), Rt. 172 in Green's Hill Place, a small shopping center just north of the village. Open weekdays 8–7, Sat. 8–6, Sun. 10–5. This attractive café is part of a well-stocked market specializing in organic and local produce as well as wines, general health foods, and vitamins. Good organic coffees and teas and a selection of baked goods, soups, sandwiches, and specials. Also a source of premade sandwiches and quiche. *Note*: A great place to eat and sip while washing clothes at the Laundromat across the street.

Blue Hill Hearth, Main St., Blue Hill Village. In 2007 Kathleen McCloskey, locally beloved for her former bakery, Pain de Famille, was producing her artisan breads and pizzas in the back of North Light Books.

Nancy English

BAGADUCE LUNCH

The Pantry Restaurant (207-374-2229), Water St. Open year-round weekdays for breakfast and lunch 7–2. Since 1988 this small eatery has been serving up reasonably priced breakfast and lunch. PB&J is still $2.95, and there are more creative sandwiches. Soups and salads.

El El Frijoles (207-359-2486; www.elelfrijoles.com), Route 15 south of Caterpillar Hill, Sargentville. Open Wed.–Sun. 11–8. We love the takeoff on L.L. Bean. Primarily a take-out, with a few tables inside and out, this is a frankly Californian version of Mexican basics like ceviche, empanadas, and pollo asado, with an emphasis on things fresh and local.

Breakfast at Sunrise Cottages (207-326-9700), 186 Varnumville Rd., Brooksville. Open seasonally, Fri.–Sun. Fred Bull cooked for many years on Woods Hole Oceanographic boats and his breakfasts, served in a small cottage he has built himself (he rents two similar cottages) has become a destination. Fred serves all the basics with home-made fries, muffins, and scones, and there is always a special "Flag," meaning specialties of a particular country. Patrons are asked to guess which one.

Also see *Eating Out* in "Deer Isle, Stonington."

PICNIC FIXINGS Don't waste a nice day by eating inside! For picnic sites, see *Green Space*. **Merrill & Hinckley** on Union St., middle of Blue Hill, is an old-fashioned general store, making good sandwiches fresh each morning and keeping them in a cooler way in back. Also see **Buck's Harbor Market** and the **Blue Hill Food Co-op**, above.

✷ Entertainment

MUSIC ✐ **Kneisel Hall Chamber Music School and Festival** (207-374-2811; www.kneisel.org), Pleasant St. (Rt. 15), Blue Hill. One of the oldest chamber music festivals in the country (dating back to 1924). Faculty present string and ensemble music in a series of Sunday-afternoon and Friday-evening concerts, June–Aug.; inquire about Young Artist Concerts.

WERU (207-469-6600; www.weru.org) is a major nonprofit community radio station based in East Orland (89.9 FM) known for folk and Celtic music, jazz, and reggae.

Bagaduce Chorale (207-667-6084), Blue Hill. A community chorus staging several concerts yearly, ranging from Bach to show tunes.

Flash in the Pans Community Steel Band (www.peninsulapan.org) performs throughout the Blue Hill Peninsula with special performances elsewhere. Check their schedule on the Web site; in summer street dances are generally Monday evenings.

FLASH IN THE PANS COMMUNITY STEEL BAND

amazingmaine.com

✷ Selective Shopping

ANTIQUES Sedgwick Antiques (207-359-8834), Rt. 172, Sedgwick. Tue.–Fri. 10–5, Sat. noon–5. A wide range with emphasis on formal styles. Jill Knowles and Bill Perry buy and sell year-round, but call off-season.

Thomas Hinchcliffe Antiques (207-326-9411), Graytown Rd. (Rt. 176), West Sedgwick. Open 10–5 most days in-season.

ART GALLERIES

In Blue Hill

Leighton Gallery (207-374-5001; www.leightongallery.com), Parker Point Rd. Open June–Columbus Day. One of Maine's oldest and most prominent contemporary art galleries, with exhibits in the three-floor space changing every few weeks. Judith Leighton's own oils alone are worth a stop, as is the amazingly expansive sculpture garden.

Jud Hartman Gallery and Sculpture Studio (207-374-917; www.judhartmangallery.com), Main St. Open mid-June–mid-Sept. daily. Now in newly expanded quarters with a water view, Hartman exhibits his realistic bronze sculptures of northeastern Native Americans.

Randy Eckard (207-374-2510; www.randyeckhardpaintings.com), 4 Pleasant St. Open July–Sept., Tue.–Sat. 11–4. Limited-edition prints of the artist's precise, luminous landscapes.

Liros Gallery (207-374-5370; www.lirosgallery.com), Parker Point Rd., specializes in fine paintings, old prints, and Russian icons; appraisals.

Blue Hill Bay Gallery (207-274-5773; www.bluehillbaygallery.com), 11 Tenney Hill. Open 10–5 Memorial Day–Labor Day; weekends thereafter. Changing exhibits of 19th-century and contemporary art, featuring northern landscapes and the sea.

Elsewhere

The Gallery at Caterpillar Hill (207-359-6577). Positioned right next to the scenic pullout (Rt. 15/17), it offers changing works featuring local landscapes.

Also see *Selective Shopping* in "Deer Isle, Stonington."

ARTISANS **Rowantrees Pottery** (207-374-5535), Union St., Blue Hill. June–Sept., Mon.–Sat., otherwise weekdays. Find your way back behind the friendly white house into the large studio. A Blue Hill tradition since 1934 when, inspired by a conversation with Mahatma Gandhi in India, Adelaide Pearson conceived the idea of using glazes gathered from the town's abandoned copper mines, quarries, and bogs. Watch tableware being hand thrown and browse through the upstairs showroom filled with plates, cups, vases, and jam pots.

Rackliffe Pottery (207-374-2297; www.rackcliffepottery.com), Rt. 172, Blue Hill Village. Open Mon.–Sat. 8–4; also Sun. in July and Aug., noon–4. Since 1968 Phyllis and Phil Rackliffe have produced their distinctive pottery, featuring local clay and their own glazes. Their emphasis is on individual small pieces rather than on sets. Visitors are welcome to watch.

Handworks Gallery (207-374-5613), Main St., Blue Hill. Open Memorial Day–late Dec., Mon.–Sat. 10–5. A middle-of-town space filled with stunning handwoven clothing, jewelry, furniture, rugs, and blown glass.

North Country Textiles (207-374-2715; www.northcountrytextiles.com), Levy House, Main St., Blue Hill. Carole Larson's woven overshot wall hangings, throws, spreads, and place mats are well worth a detour; we have lovely napkins and place mats six years old and going strong in our dining room.

Eggemoggin Textile Studio (207-359-5083; www.chrisleithstudio.com. Rt. 175, Sargentville. Open seasonally Tues.–Sat. Exceptional woven scarves, wraps, hangings, and pillows from hand-dyed silks and wool.

BOOKSTORES **Blue Hill Books** (207-374-5632;www.bluehillbooks.com), 2 Pleasant St. (two doors up from the post office), Blue Hill. A long-established, full-service, two-floor, family-run bookstore with a separate room for children's titles.

North Light Books (207-374-5422), Main St., Blue Hill. Bonnie Myers' full full-service, independent bookstore, also art supplies and cards.

Pushcart Press & Bookstore (207-669-5335), Rt. 172 behind Sedgwick Antiques. Claiming to be the "world's smallest bookstore" this self-serve cottage is crammed with books, and there's space to read on the porch overlooking a meadow. Annually since 1976 PushCart Press has published *The Pushcart Prize*, a collection of short stories, poetry, and essays selected from hundreds of small presses. Current and past editions of the anthology are sold, along with other small-press titles and thousands of books from publisher Bill Henderson's personal library.

SPECIAL SHOPS **Blue Hill Wine Shop** (207-374-2161), Main St., Blue Hill. Open Mon.–Sat. 10–5:30. A long-established shop dedicated to the perfect cup of tea or coffee, a well-chosen wine, and the right blend of tobacco.

Blue Hill Yarn Shop (207-374-5631), Rt. 172 north of Blue Hill Village. Open Mon.–Sat. 10–4. A mecca for knitters in search of a variety of wools and needles. Lessons and original hand knits.

New Cargoes (www.newcargoes.com), 49 Main Street, Blue Hill. Lots of everything, from clothing to housewares to gifts.

The Sow's Ear Winery (207-326-4649), junction of Rt. 176 and Herrick Rd. The winery tasting room is open Tue.–Sat. 10–5. Tom Hoey produces dry, organic wines from locally grown and wild fruits. The sparkling hard cider utilizes apples from his orchard and the sparkling rhubarb begins in his garden. Blueberry and wild berry wine are the other specialties.

Architectural Antiquities (207-326-4942; www.archantiquities.com), Harborside. Call for directions and to let them know what you're looking for. Specialties include brass lighting, hardware and fireplace items, Victorian plumbing fixtures, windows, doors, weather vanes, hand-hewn beams, and more.

PUSHCART PRESS

Christina Tree

✷ Special Events

Memorial Day–mid-October: **Blue Hill Farmer's Market**, Sat., 9–11:30 AM, Blue Hill Fairgrounds, Rt. 15 until mid-Aug., then in the Congregational Church parking lot. Crafts, food, and baked goods as well as seasonal produce and flowers. Guest artists in July and August.

July: **Full Circle Fair** (*third weekend*), Blue Hill Fairgrounds—constant music ranging from traditional folk to hard rock, children's music, contra dancing, sponsored for more than 15 years by WERU.

August: **Academy Antiques Fair** (*first weekend*), George Stevens Academy, Blue Hill, is big. **Downeast Antiques Fairs** (*midmonth*).

Labor Day weekend: **Blue Hill Fair**, at the fairgrounds—harness racing, a midway, livestock competitions; one of the most colorful old-style fairs in New England.

October: **Foliage Food & Wine Festival**.

DEER ISLE, STONINGTON, AND ISLE AU HAUT

The narrow, half-mile-long suspension bridge across Eggemoggin Reach connects the Blue Hill Peninsula with Little Deer Isle, linked in turn by causeways and bridges to Deer Isle and its wandering land fingers. This intermingling of land and water is characterized by the kind of coves and lupine-fringed inlets usually equated with "the real Maine." It's divided between the towns of Deer Isle and Stonington, and there are the villages of Sunset and Oceanville and of Sunshine, home of the nationally respected Haystack Mountain School of Crafts. Galleries display outstanding work by dozens of artists and craftspeople who live, or at least summer, in town.

Stonington, almost 40 miles south of Rt. 1, remains a working fishing harbor, but it, too, now has its share of galleries. Most buildings, scattered on smooth rocks around the harbor, date from the 1880s to the World War I boom years, during which Deer Isle's pink granite was shipped off to face buildings from Rockefeller Center to Boston's Museum of Fine Arts. At the height of the granite boom Stonington's population was 5,000, compared with 1,152 in 2000.

In Stonington life still eddies around Billings Diesel and Marine, and the Commercial Pier, home base for one of Maine's largest fishing/lobstering fleets. But the tourist tide is obviously rising. Galleries and seasonal, visitor-geared shops are multiplying along Main Street; the restored Opera House is the scene of frequent films, live performances, and readings. Hundreds of new houses have been built, and property values have more than doubled in the past three decades.

More than half of Isle au Haut, a mountainous island that's a 45-minute ferry ride from Stonington, is technically part of Acadia National Park. The mail boat makes seasonal stops at Duck Harbor, near the island's southern tip, accessing rugged, coastal hiking trails. The remaining half of the island, which supports less than 80 year-round residents and an old summer colony, is vividly depicted in *The Lobster Chronicles* by Linda Greenlaw.

GUIDANCE **Deer Isle–Stonington Chamber of Commerce** (207-348-6124; www.deerisle.com) maintains an "Information Building" (with facilities) on Rt. 15 at Little Deer Isle, south of the bridge. Open 10–4 mid-June–Labor Day, sporadically after that for a few weeks. Be sure to pick up the chamber's the current map/guide (an outside box is kept stocked), an invaluable tool.

GETTING THERE Follow directions under *Getting There* in "Blue Hill Area"; continue down Rt. 15 to Deer Isle.

GETTING AROUND **Eddie's Island Taxi & Tours** (207-367-5508; www.eddiesislandtaxi.com) offers local and shuttle service to airports, also tours.

✷ To See

Deer Isle Granite Museum (207-367-6331), Main St., Stonington. Open Memorial Day–Labor Day, theoretically Mon.–Sat. 9–5, Sun. 1–4, but call to check. Housed in the former pharmacy, this beautifully conceived and executed small museum features an 8-by-15-foot working model of quarrying operations on Crotch Island and the town of Stonington in 1900. Derricks move, and trains carry granite to waiting ships. Photo blowups and a video also dramatize the story of the quarryman's life during the height of the boom (see the chapter introduction).

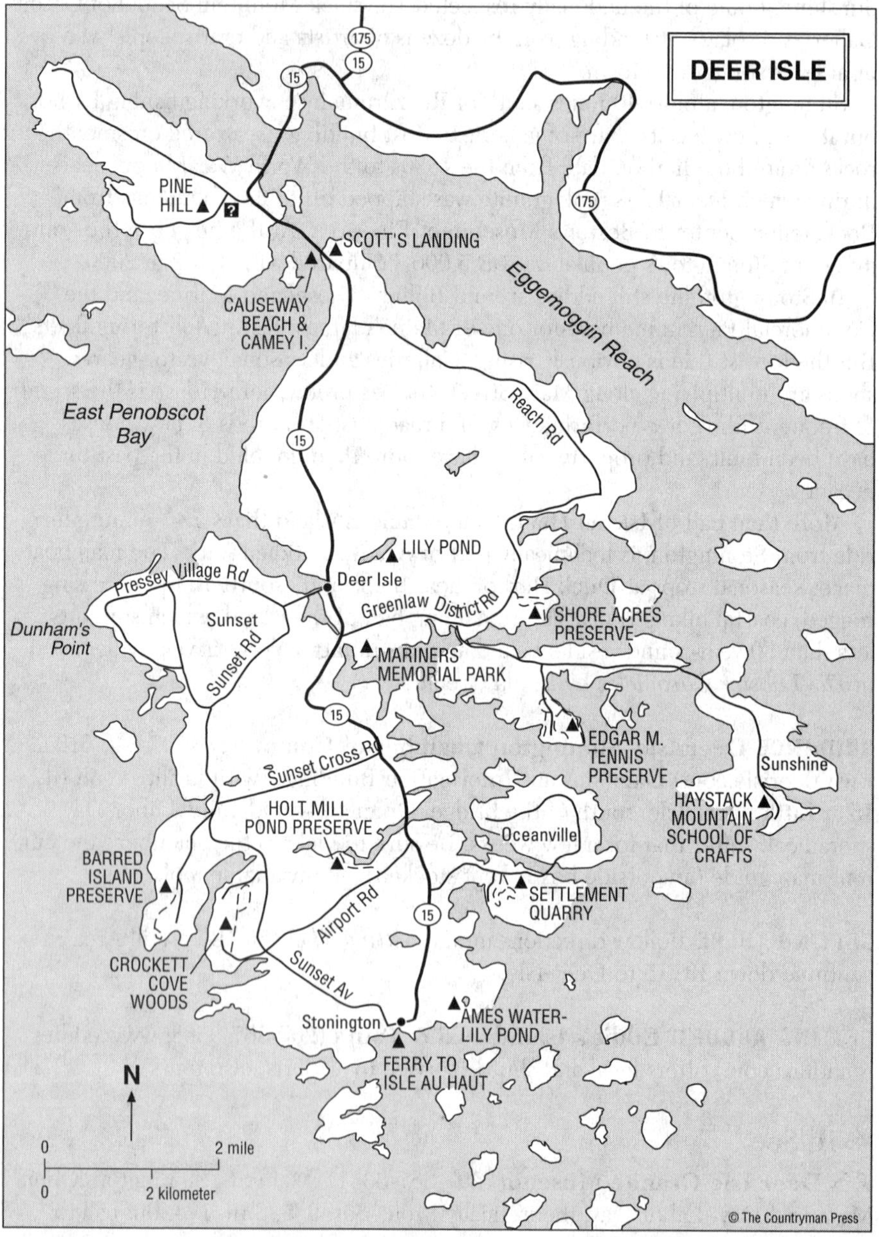

Isle au Haut (pronounced *eye-la-ho*) is 6 miles long and 3 miles wide. More than half the island is part of Acadia National Park (see *Green Space*), but this is a quiet, working island with limited facilities for visitors. Samuel de Champlain named it "High Island" in 1605 and the highest hill (543 feet) is named for him. Most visitors come to hike the 20-mile network of trails around Dark Harbor and along the cliffy southern tip. To really enjoy the island, to swim in Long Pond and to explore without the pressure of needing to catch a boat, you need to spend a couple days. On the other hand, given a beautiful day the 45-minute boat ride is its own reward and a 15-minute walk from the town dock can be a pleasure (see *Lodging* and *Selective Shopping*).

Haystack Mountain School of Crafts (207-348-2306; www.haystack-mtn.org), Deer Isle (south of Deer Isle Village; turn left off Rt. 15 at the Irving station and follow signs 7 miles). This is one of the country's outstanding crafts schools, and the campus itself is a work of art: a series of spare, shingled buildings, studios with a central dining hall and sleeping quarters, all weathered the color of surrounding rocks and fitted between trees, connected by steps and terraced decks, floated above the fragile lichens and wildflowers on land sloping steeply toward Jericho Bay. Given the brevity and intensity of each session (see *Special Learning Programs*), visitors are permitted in the studios only on weekly tours (Wed. at 1 PM) and during the "walk-throughs," in which student and faculty work is displayed (4–6 on the second Thu. of each session, followed by a 7:30 PM auction). The public is also welcome in the Gateway Building auditorium for frequent 8 PM slide lectures, visiting artists' presentations, and occasional concerts. There are also biweekly auctions.

The Salome Sellers House (207-348-2897), Rt. 15A, Sunset. Open late June–late Sept., Wed. and Fri. 1–4. Salome Sellers herself lived to be 108 years old in this snug 1803 red Cape, now the home of the Deer Isle–Stonington Historical Society, displaying ships' models, Native American artifacts, and old photos; interesting and friendly.

Lighthouses. **Pumpkin Island Light**, 3 miles from the chamber booth, at the end of Eggemoggin Road, is now a private home. **Eagle Island Light** can be viewed from Sylvester Cove in Sunset or, better yet, from the Eagle Island mail boat, from which you can also see the **Heron Neck**, **Brown's Head**, and **Goose Rocks Lights**. From Goose Cove Lodge in Sunset you can see and hear the now-automated **Mark Island Light** (its old bronze bell sits on the resort's lawn); the **Saddleback Ledge Light** is also visible on the horizon. (For details about reaching the **Isle au Haut Light**, or about **Old Quarry Ocean Adventures**, which offers a lighthouse cruise, see *Boat Excursions*.

EGGEMOGGIN REACH BRIDGE

Christina Tree

✷ To Do

BICYCLE RENTALS **Old Quarry Ocean Adventures** rents mountain bikes (see *Sea Kayaking and Canoeing*), but we advise using two wheels only on quieter side roads, please, not Rt. 15. **Isle au Haut Ferry Service** rents bikes at the island's town dock. Rentals are $20 both places.

BOAT EXCURSIONS **Isle au Haut Ferry Service** (207-367-5193; www.isleauhaut.com) links Stonington with Acadia/ Duck Harbor twice daily early June–early Sept. This mail boat is the only direct service to this dramatic, trail-webbed part of the island and it's limited to 50 daily passengers. You can reserve space with a credit card. See *Green Space* for more about logistics. $16 (one-way) adults, $8 children, $4 pets (must be leashed). This mail boat also stops at the island's town dock on these runs and several more during summer, daily (except Sunday) but less frequently off-season. It takes kayaks and canoes ($15 one-way) and bicycles ($8 one-way), but not to Duck Harbor. The ferry service also offers seasonal scenic cruises aboard the *Miss Lizzie* (9 AM and 2 PM), with lobster hauling.

Old Quarry Ocean Adventures (207-367-8977; www.oldquarry.com), 130 Settlement Road off the Oceanville Rd. Stonington. Capt. Bill Baker offers seasonal 9 AM runs aboard his 38-foot lobster boat–style *Nigh Duck* to the Isle au Haut town dock (returning 5 PM), carrying bikes and kayaks gratis ($34 round-trip adult, $17 per child); guided kayaking around the island is also available. Stay aboard until noon for an ecotour ($38 adult $22 child). A variety of other cruises are offered throughout the day, as are **sailboat** rentals and lessons. Old Quarry has also become the area's prime source of **kayak** rentals, lessons, and both half- and full-day guided trips, also multiday island camping. The Old Quarry Campground, with its platform tent sites and camp store, caters to kayakers. The waters off Stonington and Merchant's Row—the many islands just offshore—are among the most popular along the coast, but it's imperative for novice kayakers, to explore these waters with a guide. Rental rowboats, canoes, and a house are also available. Inquire about lobster bakes and weddings.

ISLE AU HAUT

Christina Tree

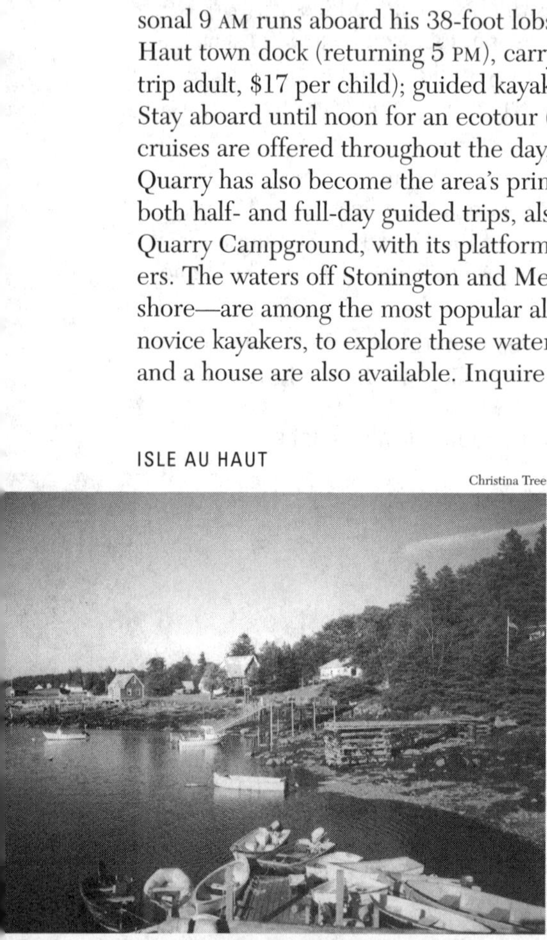

Eagle Island mail boat. Operated by the Sunset Bay Company (207-348-9316), the *Katherine* leaves Sylvester's Cove in Sunset mid-June–mid-Sept., Mon.–Sat., at 9 AM. Half a mile off Sunset, Eagle Island is roughly a mile long with rocky ledges, a sandy beach, and a working lighthouse. Inquire about island rentals. Kayaks are carried.

GOLF AND MINI GOLF **Island Country Club** (207-3 48-2379), 442 Sunset Rd., Deer Isle, welcomes guests mid-May–mid-Oct., 8–7; nine holes; Fairway Café open for lunch except Mon. Lessons, carts, also tennis courts and lessons.

SPECIAL LEARNING PROGRAMS **Haystack Mountain School of Crafts** (207-348-2306; www.haystack-mtn.org), Deer Isle. Two- and three-week sessions, June–Labor Day, attract some of the country's top artisans in clay, metals, wood, fibers, graphics, and glass. From its beginnings Haystack has been equated with cutting-edge design rather than traditional craft, and the architecture underscores the school's philosophy. It's intimate and self-contained, like the summer sessions themselves, each limited to no more than 90 students. Workshop topics are determined by faculty members, and these, like the students, change every two or three weeks. Each group is carefully balanced to include young (minimum age 18) and old, neophytes as well as master craftsmen; repeaters are kept to a third.

The Stonington Painter's Workshop (207-367-2368; off-season, 617-776-3102). Nationally prominent artist and art teacher Jon Imber coordinates and teaches this July series of weeklong landscape workshops.

Seamark Community Arts (207-348-5308), Deer Isle. July and August classes and workshops for residents and visitors of all ages.

SWIMMING **Lily Pond**, off Rt. 15 north of Deer Isle Village. The island's freshwater swimming hole. Ask locally for directions. "Mother's Beach" is a great spot for small children, also for long swims.

Causeway Beach, Rt. 15. South of the information booth (see *Guidance*), a roadside strand that at low tide can fill the bill on a hot day, especially if there are children in the car. Also see **Scott's Landing** in *Green Space*.

Green Space

Island Heritage Trust (207-348-2455; www.islandheritagetrust.org), which maintains an office in Deer Isle Village, publishes detailed maps of the following walking trails, also sponsors walks and talks.

Settlement Quarry, Stonington. A 0.25-mile walk from the parking area follows an old road to the top of this former working quarry for a view off across Webb Cove and west to the Camden Hills. Side trails loop back through woods. It's on Oceanville Rd., 0.9 mile from Rt. 15 (just beyond the turn marked for Settlement Quarry Ocean Adventures); turn at Ron's Mobil.

Scott's Landing A small sign along the causeway points the way to the parking area. Trails web this historic 24-acre point on Eggemoggin Reach, leading to a vintage 1807 dock and a sandy beach. Great views of the bridge and the Reach.

Pine Hill Preserve, Little Deer Isle. The trail from this easy-to-find parking area (0.2 mile down Blastow Cove Rd.) is a short, rugged climb to a bald summit with a sweeping view. It's also of particular interest to geologists, and its vegetation is remarkably varied, some of it rare. Please keep to the path.

Edgar M. Tennis Preserve. Three miles of wooded and shore trails with shore views. Access is off Sunshine Rd., Fire Rd. 523.

amazingmaine.com

STONINGTON HARBOR

Crockett Cove Woods Preserve (a Maine Nature Conservancy property) consists of 100 acres along the water, with a nature trail. Take Rt. 15 to Deer Isle, then Sunset Rd.; 2.5 miles beyond the post office, bear right onto Whitman Rd.; a right turn at the end of the road brings you to the entrance, marked by a small sign and registration box. From Stonington, take Sunset Rd. through the village of Burnt Cove and turn left onto Whitman Rd.

Barred Island Preserve is a two-acre island owned by The Nature Conservancy, just off Stinson Point, accessible at low tide (only) by a wide sandbar; parking is on the road to Goose Cove Lodge. Owned by landscape architect Frederick Law Olmsted around the turn of the century and bequeathed to The Nature Conservancy by his grandniece, this is a very special place, a good walk with small children.

Shore Acre Preserve. A 38-acre preserve with a loop trail to and along the shore with views of Oak Point and Goose Island. Take Sunshine Rd. 1.2 miles, bear left at the fork onto Greenlaw District Rd., and continue 0.9 mile to the parking area.

More public spaces

Ames Pond, east of Stonington village on Indian Point Rd., is full of pink-and-white water lilies in bloom June–early Sept.

Holt Mill Pond Preserve. A walk through unspoiled woodland and marsh. The entrance is on Stonington Cross Rd. (Airport Rd.)—look for a sign several hundred feet beyond the medical center. Park on the shoulder and walk the dirt road to the beginning of the trail, then follow the yellow signs.

Mariner's Memorial Park, Deer Isle. This is a delightful picnic and bird-watching spot with views of Long Cove. Take Fire Rd. 501 off Sunshine Rd., just east of Rt. 15.

Acadia National Park/Isle au Haut (see *To See* and *Boat Excursions*). In summer months the mail boat arrives at Duck Harbor at 11 AM, allowing plenty of time to hike the island's dramatic Western Head and Cliff Trails before returning on the 5:45 PM boat. The logistics are more difficult if you are coming from the town dock. Plan to catch the earliest boat and return on the latest. It's a short walk to the park ranger station (207-335-5551), where you can use the facilities (♿) and pick up a map, but 4 miles to Duck Harbor. You should allow 4 hours to enjoy the dramatic cliff trails at Duck Harbor and around Western Head, Deep Cove, and Barred Harbor. The Duck Harbor trail from the ranger station is through the woods. With a bike you can get there faster on the unpaved road. Bikes are not permitted on the trails, which are largely pineneedle-carpeted and shaded but demanding with cliffy outcroppings. Camping is permitted at Duck Harbor mid-May–mid-Oct. in the five Adirondack-style shelters (each accommodating six people). Reserve on or as soon after April 1 as possible (207-288-8791 or download form at www.nps.gov/acad).

✱ Lodging

INNS AND BED & BREAKFASTS

In Deer Isle 04627

🐾 **Pilgrim's Inn** (207-348-6615 or 1-888-778-7505; www.pilgrimsinn.com). Open mid-May–mid-Oct. Built as a private home in 1793, this gracious, four-story, hip-roofed inn stands in the middle of Deer Isle Village yet both fronts and backs on water. A summer inn since 1899, it features big front parlors and guest rooms of varying sizes, some with gas log fireplaces, all with private bath and water views. There are also three nicely decorated, two-bedroom cottages with kitchens and living rooms. Common space includes formal old parlors and an inviting bar on the garden level. The **Whale's Rib** (see *Dining Out*) is open to the public. Inn rooms $89–$249 depending on the season and the room, including breakfast. $50 charge for pets allowed in cottages.

The Inn at Ferry Landing (207-348-7760; www.ferrylanding.com), Old Ferry Rd., RR 1, Box 163. Overlooking Eggemoggin Reach, Jean and Gerald Wheeler's 1840s seaside farmhouse offers magnificent water views, spacious rooms, patchwork quilts, and a great common room with huge windows and two grand pianos that Gerald plays and uses for summer recitals and spontaneous music sessions. The six guest rooms include a huge master suite with a woodstove and skylights. $120–130 for double rooms, $175 for the suite; less off-season. The Mooring, a two-story, two-bedroom, fully equipped housekeeping cottage, perfect for families, is $1,500 per week. Room rates include a full breakfast; minimum of two nights in high season.

Eggemoggin Inn (207-348-2540), 40 Babson Point Road, Little Deer Isle. Positioned at the eastern entrance to Eggemoggin Reach, this vintage 1906 mansion has been owned by the same family and welcoming guests since 1964. Barbara and Ned Allen don't advertise and are geared "mostly to people who have been here before" but they have worked hard to spruce up the six second- and third-floor rooms, five sharing two baths. Rooms vary in size from small to family-sized. The big attraction here is the spectacular view from most windows and from the wraparound porch. There's a guest fridge and breakfast is $9 (full) or $5 (continental). $85–150 late June to late Sept., $45 for extra cots, less in shoulder weeks. No credit cards.

In Stonington 04681

Pres du Port (207-367-5007; www.presduport.com), W. Main and Highland Ave., P.O. Box 319. Open June–Oct. A find. This cheery, comfortable B&B is an 1849 home built on a rise overlooking Greenhead Cove. Common space includes a light- and flower-filled sunporch overlooking the harbor, filled with as many as many as 400 lobster boats. There are three imaginatively furnished guest rooms, one with a cathedral ceiling and loft, kitchenette, deck access, and private bath. The other two share two baths (each room also has its own sink) and have harbor views, plus there's an outdoor hot tub overlooking the water. There's also a crow's nest, "Charlotte's Folly." Charlotte Casgrain is a warm, knowledgeable hostess who enjoys speaking French. The generous buffet breakfast—perhaps crustless crabmeat and Parmesan quiche—is served on the sunporch. $85–100 per couple, less per single, tax included.

The Inn on the Harbor (207-367-2420 or 1-800-942-2420; www.innontheharbor.com), 45 Main St., P.O. Box 69. Open year-round. Guest rooms come with binoculars, the better to focus on lobster boats and regularly on the schooners in the Maine windjammer fleet, for which each of the14 comfortable rooms (private bath, phone, cable TV), is named. The inn backs on Stonington's bustling Main Street, but most rooms, some with balconies, face the working harbor, one of Maine's most photographed views. Our favorite rooms: The Heritage, with working hearth; the Stephen Taber, a freestanding room retaining its tin walls and ceiling (it used to be a barbershop); and the American Eagle suite with two bedrooms, an open kitchen, dining area, and living room. A flowery ground-floor deck is shared by all. $130–215 summer, $65–130 off-season, includes continental breakfast. In-room spa services are available. Shipps also rents, from this inn, Mountain Glory Farm, a housekeeping duplex in Patten near Katahadin.

DEER ISLE VILLAGE

Christina Tree

On Isle au Haut 04645

The Inn at Isle au Haut (207-335-5141;www.innatisleauhaut.com), P.O. Box 78. Open June–late Sept. This mansard-roofed Victorian-era cottage (four guest rooms share one bath) faces east, with views of the Mount Desert hills. Diana Santospago greets guests at the 4:30 mail boat and serves them a five-course dinner. A full breakfast, a packed lunch, and use of bicycles is included in $275–350. The inn is nicely situated for biking to town, to Long Pond, and to the hiking trails, but Diana cautions that her bikes are fat tired and single speed. You need to be in good shape to enjoy this island, and you need to spend a couple days. No children under age 16.

The Keeper's House (www.keepershouse.com) is currently for sale, but check the Web site.

MOTEL **Boyce's Motel** (207-367-2421 or 1-800-224-2421; www.boycesmotel.com), P.O. Box 94, Stonington 04681. In the heart of Stonington Village, family run, clean, and comfortable, water views from decks. Eleven units have queen or twin beds, and there are several efficiency units—one with two bedrooms, a living room, and kitchen. $65–125 per in high season, $45–90 off-season; $10 per day per pet.

COTTAGES The best selection of rentals on Deer Isle and Isle au Haut is through **Island Vacation Rentals** (207-367-5095; www.islandvacation rentals.biz), 50 Main St., Stonington.

✱ Where to Eat

DINING OUT **Whale's Rib Tavern** in Pilgrim's Inn (207-348-6615; www .pilgrimsinn.com), Main St., Deer Isle Village. Open mid-May–Oct. for dinner, lunch. Reservations advised. Under its most recent change in ownership the Pilgrim Inn's long-popular barn dining room has changed its name and menu. Expect the likes of Maine maple-Moxie ribs, fish-and-chips, and broiled seafood casserole; soups and sandwiches are also available. Daily specials. Dinner entrées $13–24.

Maritime Café (207-367-2600; www .maritimecafe.com), 27 Main St., Stonington. Open daily May–Oct. for lunch and dinner. Reservations advised. This harborside restaurant has an unbeatable view. The menu might include pan-seared halibut served with peach vinaigrette, grilled sirloin and a vegetarian pasta, always lobster served several ways. Entrées $16–23. Beer and wine.

Cockatoo II Portuguese Restaurant at Goose Cove (207-348-2300 or 207-367-0900), formerly the Goose Cove Lodge, marked from Rt. 15, Sunset. Open daily in-season, 11–10. Suzen Carter isn't one to pass up a challenge: Donald Sussman, the new owner of this landmark resort, asked the Azorean-born creator of Cockatoo (see *Eating Out*) to open an upscale version. With a totally renovated kitchen and meat-savvy staff (Suzen's expertise is fish), she opened mid-season in 2007 and the going was a bit bumpy, but we have great faith in Suzen. Dinner entrées: $13–33.

EATING OUT **Lily's Café** (207-397-5936), Rt. 15 at Airport Rd. Open year-round, weekdays for breakfast (7–10) and lunch until 5 with dinners-to-go and occasional dinners in-house. Recently expanded, this series of attractive dining rooms, upstairs and down, is the setting for exceptional food, most of it organic and locally grown or fished. The table we like to lunch on is topped with a sheet of glass over a shell collection. Favorite sandwiches include Lily's nutburger and Ethel's pulled pork. Soups are great too.

🏵 ♿ **Harbor Café**, Stonington. Open year-round, Mon.–Sat. 6 AM–8 PM; in summer, open later on Fri. and Sat., plus Sun. 6–2. Spanking clean and friendly; booths and dependable food. Soups and salads. Seafood rolls, sandwiches and subs, fried and broiled seafood. Friday night it's a good idea to reserve for the all-you-can-eat seafood fries.

🏵 ♿ **The Fisherman's Friend Restaurant** (207-367-2442), 5 Atlantic Ave., Stonington. Open year-round, 11–9 in summer months, until 10 Sat., less off-season. This popular waterfront restaurant (next to the quarryman statue) can seat more than 200 with a second-floor deck. A wide choice of fried and broiled fish, chowders and stews, burgers, and all the usual sandwiches. Children's menu.

🏵 ♿ **The Cockatoo** (207-367-0900), Cottage Lane off Oceanville Rd. (just off Rt. 15; turn at Ron's Mobil). Open Memorial Day–Labor Day, noon–8.

As different from the predictable coastal Maine take-out as a cockatoo is from a seagull. The Carter family's long-established fish shop offers take-out and waterside tables (you can kayak in) at which to enjoy Suzen Carter's seafood creations. These are Portuguese specialties such as kale soup, distinctly Mediterranean fish soup, and mussels, plus "crabmeat snakes" (crabmeat baked in pastry, $15.95). The decor is tropical, lit by tiki-style torches, and includes Peaches and Mango, the family's pet cockatoos. In 2007 prices were up ($30 for paella); this was also a transition year as Suzen opened Cockatoo II (see *Dining Out*) in the former dining room at Goose Cove Lodge across the island. BYOB.

Finest Kind (207-348-7714), marked from Rt. 15 between Stonington and Deer Isle Village. Open Apr.–Nov. for dinner 5–9; nights vary so call. Neat as a pin, a log cabin with counter and booths. The mini-golf course, part of the scene, makes this a favorite with families.

Lodie's (207-248-6346), Rt. 15 (3 miles south of the bridge), Deer Isle. Open 11–7 most of the year. Sandra Eaton's cheerful, spotless diner (named for her dog) is a good bet with a standout fried fish sandwich and deserts.

Harbor Ice Cream (207-348-9949), 11 Main St., Deer Isle Village. Nothing fancy but good burgers, Gifford's ice cream, and daily specials.

COFFEE, TEA AND JAM, ICE CREAM. **Nervous Nellie's Jams and Jellies and Mountainville Café** (207-348-6182; www.nervousnellies.com), 598 Sunshine Rd., Deer Isle. Open May–Oct. 10–5. Sculptor Peter Beerits displays his whimsical life-sized sculptures, sells his jams and jellies (wild blueberry preserves, blackberry-peach conserve, hot tomato chutney), and serves tea, coffee, and scones. Children of all ages love the sculptures, including a big red lobster playing checkers as a 7-foot alligator looks on. From Rt. 15, follow directions for Haystack (see *To See*).

Susie Q's (207-367-2415), 40 School St., Stonington. Open daily 8–4. Susan Scott is at home in this premises from which she and her husband Jack operated the Fisherman's Friend, which her son Tony Bray has since dramatically expanded (see *Eating Out*). Soups and sandwiches at lunch, but this delightful café is really about morning pastries and Susan's great pies.

Sophie's Cup (207-348-5667), 7 Main St., Deer Isle Village. Daily 7:30–4. For those who need their morning cappuccino, this is an unexpected find, especially in a shop that also sells handcrafted jewelry (www.fibulajewelry.com).

Espresso Bay at the Inn on the Harbor (207-367-2420), 45 Main St., Stonington. Open daily in season. Espresso, iced drinks, homemade ice cream, and desserts. In good weather this is a must, an excuse to sit a spell on the inn's flower-filled harborside deck.

✷ Entertainment

Stonington Opera House (207-367-2788; www.operahousearts.org), School St., Stonington. Open year-round. This shingled building with its skinny, four-story "fly tower" dates to 1912, when it replaced a larger, 1880s theater built during the town's boom era. It now stages a full calendar of reasonably priced concerts and original theatrical productions. Movies Fri.–Sun. at 7 PM. Call for schedules of movies and live performances.

✷ Selective Shopping

ART GALLERIES AND ARTISANS

Note: Studio crawling is a popular local pastime. Because local galleries feature work by local artists, it's frequently possible to trace a piece to its creator. Handout studio maps and postcards that picture individual artists' works are also readily available. The following is far from a complete list of galleries.

Deer Isle

Turtle Gallery (207-348-9977; www.turtlegallery.com), Rt. 15, north of Deer Isle Village. Open daily in summer, year-round by appointment. Artist Elena Kubler's gallery showcases exceptional jewelry as well as biweekly changing shows featuring fine art and contemporary crafts. It's housed in the barn in which Haystack faculty work was first displayed, back when adjoining Centennial House was home to Francis ("Fran") Sumner Merritt, the school's founding director, and his wife, Priscilla, a noted weaver.

The Blue Heron (207-348-2267; www.blueherondeerisle.com), Deer Isle Village, beside the libary. In 2008 Sue Wilmot opened this newest incarnation of the island's premier showcase for contemporary work by faculty and students of Haystack Mountain School faculty. There's no offical connection, just a longtime relationship fostered by the gallery's previous owner, Mary Nyberg.

The Lester Gallery (207-348-2676; www.tlesterphotography.com), 4 Main St. Open in-season Mon.–Sat. 10–5; off-season by chance or appointment. Ginger Lester features Terrell Lester's striking local "lightscapes," also photography by other locally-based photographers.

Ronald Hayes Pearson Design Studio and Gallery (207-348-2535), Old Ferry Rd. (off Rt. 15), Deer Isle. Open Mon.–Sat. 10–5, closed Sat. off-season. Creative designs in gold and silver jewelry as well as delicately

TURTLE GALLERY

Kim Grant

STONINGTON, BY JILL HOY

wrought tabletop sculpture in other metals. Farrell Ruppert, the resident artist, is also a sculptor.

Greene-Ziner Gallery (207-348-2601), 73 Reach Rd. (off Rt. 15). Open July–Sept. In a barn surrounded by meadows, iron sculptor Eric Ziner displays his ornate and whimsical creations and potter Melissa Greene, her thrown earthenware pots suggesting Greek amphorae in shape but decorated with designs evoking tribal themes.

Dockside Quilt Gallery (207-348-2531; www.docksidequiltgallery.com), 33 Church St. (Rt. 15), just south of Deer Isle Village. Open weekdays, July–Oct. This is a trove of beautiful quilts made by Nancy Knowlton and Kelly Pratt, whose ancestry goes way back on Deer Isle.

Deer Isle Artists Association (207-348-2330), 6 Dow Rd. Open June–late Sept. A 150-member cooperative gallery with exhibits changing every two weeks.

Stonington

Note: A dozen galleries now fill many of Stonington's old shop fronts and hold receptions on the first Fridays, July through Oct. (www.stonington galleries.com).

♿ **Hoy Gallery** (207-367-2368; www.jillhoy.com), 80 Thurlow Hill. Open daily July–Sept. A big white barn set back from the street, filled with Jill Hoy's bold, bright Maine landscapes.

Watson Gallery (207-367-2900; www.gwatsongallery.com), 68 Main St. Open May–Oct., Mon.–Sat. 10–5, Sun. 1–5. This is a serious gallery, recently expanded, showing prominent contemporary painting and sculpture, featuring local and New England artists.

The Clown (207-367-6348; www.the-clown.com), Main St. Contemporary art, also ceramics, fine wine, and art.

SPECIAL SHOPS

In Deer Isle

Old Deer Isle Parish House Antiques (207-348-9964), Rt. 15. Open daily June–Oct. A combination antiques, quilts, crafts, and whatever shop that's a phenomenon in its own right: handmade quilts, used books, rag rugs, whatever. Browser's heaven.

The Periwinkle, Deer Isle Village. Open June–mid-Oct., a tiny shop with a vintage-1910 cash register, crammed with books and carefully selected gifts.

In Stonington

Dockside Books and Gifts (207-367-2652), 62 W. Main St. Seasonal. Al Webber's waterside bookstore has an exceptional selection of Maine and marine books, also gifts, sweaters by local knitters, and a great harbor view from the balcony.

Stonington Sea Products (888-402-2729; www.stoningtonseafood.com), Rt. 15, north of Stonington village. Open Memorial Day–mid-Sept., Mon.–Fri. 10–4. This is a must-stop for every visitor. The quality of all fish and seafood is as good as it gets, as are the smoked salmon, scallops, and mussels. Also hard-to-find smoked mackerel, and fish pâtés.

The Dry Dock (207-367-5528), Main St. Open daily mid-May–Oct., 9–5. Tempting clothing and craftwork; an outlet for Deer Isle granite products.

"1" **Mr. York's Bookshoppe** (207-669-4431; www.mryorksbookshoppe.com), Open Mon.–Thurs. 10–5; Fri.–Sun. 10–10. Housed in a former schoolhouse, this a bookstore for browsers and bibliophiles of all sorts. The eclectic collection of new and used books runs the gamut from rare and collectible to used paperbacks that owner Stephen York describes as "beachworthy." There's a small café, also poetry readings, author readings, book discussions, and writing workshops.

V&S Variety Stores (207-367-5570), Rt. 15A, Burnt Cove. The many boutiques and galleries have displaced the basic stuff of life—like groceries and everything a five-and-dime once carried. It's all moved out to Burnt Cove, where you'll also find the recycle shop, gas, and plenty of parking. Beside **Burnt Cove Market** (the supermarket, open daily until 9 PM) stands this huge but homespun "variety store," which stocks everything you forgot to bring.

Also see Nervous Nellie's Jams and Jellies under *Where to Eat*. The shop is open year-round, producing 15 flavors of jam, chutney, and marmalade.

Isle au Haut

The Sea Urchin (207-335-2021). A little more than half a mile from the town dock on the town road, toward Moore's Harbor, Martha and Jim Greenlaw offer a fine selection of ship models and mostly Maine-made gifts and souvenirs, some island-made. They feature books by their famous daughter Linda, also sea bags made from recycled sails by Portland-based daughter Elizabeth.

"1" **Black Dinah Chocolatiers** (335-5010; www.blackdinahchoclatiers.com), 100 yards from the Sea Urchin (above). A café with wireless Internet, open July and Aug., serving drinks and pastries as well as delectable chocolates, isn't what you expect to find on a hike. In 2007 Kate and Steve Shaffer began making these amazing chocolates, featuring ingredients from Maine farms, marketing them through mail order. The venture is named for the rock face above their house.

✱ Special Events

Note: The weekly Island Advantages (www.islandadvantages.com) lists and details many more current happenings.

May–October: Friday morning (10–noon) **farmer's market** at the Island Community Center (the former elementary school) in Stonington. This is huge.

May: **Memorial Day parade**.

June: **Lupine Festival**

July: **Independence Day Island-wide festivities:** parade in Deer Isle Village, fireworks at Stonington Fish Pier. **Fisherman's Day**, Stonington. **Deer Isle Jazz Festival** (www.operahousearts.com). **Lobster-boat races** and **Stonington Fisherman's Festival**.

August: **Downeast Race Week** (www.downeastraceweek.com).

December: A weekend of **Christmas celebrations**.

CASTINE

Sited on a fingertip of the Blue Hill Peninsula, Castine is one of Maine's most photogenic coastal villages, the kind writers describe as "perfectly preserved." Even the trees that arch high above Main Street's clapboard homes and shops have managed to escape the blight that felled elms elsewhere, and Castine's post office is the oldest continuous operating post office in the country (since 1833).

Occupying a peninsula at the confluence of the Penobscot and Bagaduce Rivers, the town still looms larger on nautical charts than on road maps. Yacht clubs from Portland to New York visit annually. Castine has always had a sense of its own importance. According to the historical markers that pepper its tranquil streets, it has been claimed by four different countries since its early-17th-century founding as Fort Pentagoet. It was an early trading post for the Pilgrims but fell into the hands of Baron de Saint Castine, a young French nobleman who married a Penobscot Indian princess and reigned as a combination feudal lord and Indian chief over Maine's eastern coast for many decades.

Since no two accounts agree, we won't attempt to describe the outpost's constantly shifting fortunes—even the Dutch owned it briefly. Nobody denies that in 1779 residents (mostly Tories who fled here from Boston and Portland) welcomed the invading British. The Commonwealth of Massachusetts retaliated by mounting a fleet of 18 armed vessels and 24 transports with 1,000 troops and 400 marines aboard. This small navy disgraced itself absurdly when it sailed into town in 1779. The British Fort George was barely in the making, fortified by 750 soldiers with two sloops as backup, but the American privateers refused to attack and hung around in the bay long enough for several British men-of-war to come along and destroy them. The surviving patriots had to walk back to Boston, and many of their officers, Paul Revere included, were court-martialed for their part in the disgrace. The town was occupied by the British again in 1814.

Perhaps it was to spur young men on to avenge this affair that Castine was picked (150 years later) as the home of the Maine Maritime Academy, which occupies the actual site of the British barracks and keeps a training ship anchored at the town dock, incongruously huge beside the graceful, white- clapboard buildings of a very different maritime era.

In the mid–19th century, thanks to shipbuilding, Castine claimed to be the second wealthiest town per capita in the United States. Its genteel qualities were recognized by summer visitors, who later came by steamboat to stay in the eight hotels. Many built their own seasonal mansions.

MAIN STREET, CASTINE

Christina Tree

Castine's current population hovers around 1,300, including the 700 Maine Maritime Academy students. The population roughly doubles in summer. Two of the hotels survive, and a couple of mansions are now inns. The town dock is unusually welcoming, complete with picnic tables, parking, and restrooms. It remains the heart of this walking town, where you can amble uphill past shops or down along Perkins Street to the Wilson Museum. While the remainder of the Blue Hill Peninsula has become notably more touristed in recent years, Castine seems to have become less so, another reason to spend a few days steeping in its beauty.

GUIDANCE **Castine Merchants Association** produces a helpful map/guide, available on request from the town office (207-326-4502) or around town. Also check the town's Web site, www.castine.me.us, as well as www.penobscotbay.com. The obvious place to begin exploring is the **Castine Historical Society** on the common.

GETTING THERE See "Blue Hill Area," but turn off Rt. 1 onto Rt. 175 in Orland and follow signs for Castine.

WHEN TO COME Museums are highly seasonal, but the Maritime Academy contributes to the sense of a college town, a pleasant place to stay through October.

✷ To See

HISTORIC DISTRICT All of downtown Castine is on the National Register of Historic Places. Pick up the pamphlet *A Walking Tour of Castine*—it's free, available at shops—and walk out along Perkins Street and up along Maine to Battle Avenue. Don't miss:

Castine Historical Society (207-326-4118; www.castinehistoricalsociety.org), Abbott School Building, Castine town common. July–Labor Day, Tue.–Sat. 10–4; from 1 on Sun.

The permanent exhibit here is a multimedia presentation about the 1779 Penobscot Expedition (see chapter introduction). Special exhibits and events throughout the summer.

The Wilson Museum (207-326-8545; www.wilsonmuseum.org), 120 Perkins St. Open May 27–Sept. 30, Tue.–Sun. 2–5; free. This fine waterside building was donated by anthropologist J. Howard Wilson, a summer resident who amassed many of the displayed Native American artifacts. There are also changing art exhibits, collections of minerals, old tools, and farm equipment, an 1805 kitchen, and a Victorian parlor. **Hearse House** and a blacksmith shop are open in July and Aug., Wed. and Sun. 2–5. The complex also includes the **John Perkins House**, open July and Aug., Wed. and Sun. 2–5 (admission): a pre–Revolutionary War home, restored and furnished in period style. Guided tours and crafts, frquent special events.

Fort George, Battle Ave. Open May 30–Labor Day, daylight hours. The sorry tale of its capture by the British during the American Revolution (see the chapter introduction) and again during the War of 1812, when redcoats occupied the town for eight months, is told on panels at the fort—an earthworks complex of grassy walls (great to roll down) and a flat interior where you may find Maine Maritime Academy cadets being put through their paces.

State of Maine (207-326-4311), town dock. When in port, the training vessel for Maine Maritime Academy is usually open to visitors daily from the second week in July until mid-Aug.; 30-minute tours on the hour 10–6 are conducted by midshipmen (allow an hour), subject to security checks and alerts. Tours on weekends during the academic year. If this is your prime reason for coming to Castine, call to check if tours are being offered.

✷ To Do

BICYCLING **Mountain Bike Rentals** (207-326-9045), available at Dennett's Wharf.

GOLF AND TENNIS **Castine Golf Club** (207-326-8844), Battle Ave. Offers nine holes and four clay courts.

SEA KAYAKING **Castine Kayak Adventures** (207-326-9045; www.castinekayak.com), Dennets Wharf. Karen Francoeur offers half- and full-day trips plus a number of "unique adventures" such as sunrise and phosphorescent paddles, and "intermediate adventures" to the Bagaduce reversing falls and around Cape Rosier. Also overnight camping and B&B tours and workshops ranging from beginning skills to advanced coastal navigation.

✷ Green Space

Witherle Woods is an extensive wooded area webbed with paths at the western end of town. The ledges below **Dyce's Head Light**, also at the western end of town, are great for clambering. The **Castine Conservation Commission** sponsors nature walks occasionally in July and Aug.; check local bulletin boards.

✷ Lodging

In Castine 04421

🐾 **The Manor Inn** (207-326-4861; www.manor-inn.com), 76 Battle Ave. Open year-round except Christmas–Valentine's Day. This expansive 1890s stone-and-shingle summer mansion is set above its lawns in five acres bordering conservation land. Innkeepers Tom Ehrman and Nancy Watson have renovated throughout, bringing new beds and new life to all 14 rooms, upgrading baths (all are private) and expanding the dining room while preserving private common space for guests. The price of guest rooms varies with size, ranging in high season from $110 for twin-bedded Dices Head to $275 for spacious Pine Tree with its king canopy bed, fireplace, and sitting porch, fit for a governor and his wife (who were checking in as we stopped by). Nancy Watson is a respected Iyengar yoga teacher, and guests are permitted to participate in scheduled classes (we slid into the back row and heartily recommend doing likewise). See *Dining Out* for the restaurant and pub. Rates include a full breakfast and drop to $95–165 in spring and fall, less in winter. Pets are $25 per stay.

🐾 🍴 **Pentagoet Inn** (207-326-8616 or 1-800-845-1701; www.pentagoet.com), Main St., P.O. Box 4. Open May–Oct. A very Victorian summer hotel with a turret, gables, wraparound porch, even awnings. Over the past nine years Jack Burke and Julie Vande-

Graaf have been restoring the 1894 building room by room. Guest rooms are unusually shaped and nicely furnished; one room at **Ten Perkins Street** (a neighboring 200-year-old home that's an annex) has a working fireplace. In all there are 16 guest rooms, each with private bath. Common space includes sitting rooms, the wicker-furnished and flowery veranda and back deck, the fine restaurant (see *Dining Out*), and **Passports Pub**. $95–245 during high season, less in shoulder months, with full breakfast. $25 for pets. Amenities include bicycles and a guest computer.

Castine Inn (207-326-4365; www.castineinn.com), P.O. Box 41, Main St. Open May–Oct. Amy and Tom Gutow put this 1890s summer hotel on the national culinary map, but then stopped serving dinner. (Tom does offer cooking classes.) Guests enter a wide, welcoming hallway and find a pleasant sitting room and a pub, both with frequently lit fireplaces. A mural of Castine by the previous innkeeper covers all four walls of the dining room, and French doors open onto a broad veranda. The 17 rooms are simply furnished, each has private bath. $90–165 for rooms, $230–265 for two-room suites, includes a full breakfast.

Rental cottages are available through **Jean de Raat Realty** (207-326-8448; www.deRaatRealty.com), and **Castine Realty** (207-326-9392).

✱ Where to Eat

All listings are in Castine

DINING OUT **Pentagoet Inn** (207-326-8616), 26 Main St. Open for dinner in-season. Reservations advised. Choose to sit in the airy, candlelit dining room with its well-spaced tables, on the porch, or in Passports Pub. You might begin with a big bowl of Blue Hill mussels, and dine on slow-roasted lamb shank with sage risotto, garlicky Swiss chard, and bitter orange compote. Entrées $18–27. Don't pass up dessert, the pride of innkeeper Julie VandeGraaf, former owner of a well-known Philadelphia pastry shop. Small plates also available, along with a full bar.

The Commodore Room at the Manor Inn (207-326-4861), Battle Ave. Open for dinner Valentine's Day to Christmas, fewer nights of the week off-season. A former enclosed porch has been expanded and transformed into an appealing dining room overlooking the sweeping front lawn and gardens. Co-owner Nancy Watson is the chef. The crabcakes are a family recipe, served as an entrée with mustard and aioli sauces. Other choices on the daily-changing menu might include seared sesame-crusted tuna loin with a lime glaze and aged beef from the local butcher, charbroiled. Entrées $18–27. Full liquor license, and pub food in the **Pine Cone Pub**.

Stella's Restaurant (207-326-9710), 26 Water St. Open Tues.–Sun, 7–10. Reservations advised. There's seating for 40 in this attractive new dining and music space above Bah's Bake House (see *Eating Out*). The menu ranges from light to elaborate fare and the specialty of the house is really live jazz, Thurs.–Sun. Entrées $8.50–18.50.

EATING OUT "1" **Dennett's Wharf** (207-326-904), Sea St. (off the town dock). Open daily May–Columbus Day, 11–9. An open-framed, harbor-side structure said to have been built as a bowling alley after the Civil War, this is the town's informal gathering place. There's a big menu with plenty of salads as well as seafood and BBQ back ribs at lunch, with expanded choices for dinner, a choice of steaks and entrées ranging from vegetable strudel to lobster pie. The home brew is Wharf Rat Ale. Entrées $14–29.

Bah's Bake House (207-326-9510), Water St. Open 7 AM–5 PM daily in-season. A few tables and a great deli counter featuring sandwiches on baguette bread, daily-made soups, salads, and baked goods.

The Breeze (207-326-9034), town dock. Seasonal. When the summer sun shines, this is the best place in town to eat: fried clams, hot dogs, onion rings, and soft ice cream. The public facilities are next door and, with luck, you can dine at the picnic tables on the dock.

T&C Grocery (207-326-4818), 12 Water St. Open 7–9, until 8 Sun. This well-stocked market has a first-rate deli, source of great picnic fixings.

Castine Variety (326-8625), 1 Main St. Open 5 AM–7 PM year-round. The ultimate corner store with an ice cream counter dating back to its 1920 opening. Serving breakfast, light meals, pizza, and ice cream, as well as lobster and crab rolls, newspapers, film, and a lot of other stuff.

Christina Tree

CASTINE VARIETY

✷ Selective Shopping

In Castine

Leila Day Antiques (207-326-8786), 53 Main St. An outstanding selection of early American furniture; also paintings, quilts, and Maine-made Shard Pottery. The shop is in the historic Parson Mason House, and the approach is through a formal garden.

McGrath-Dunham Gallery (207-326-9175; www.mcgrathdunhamgallery.com), 9 Main St. Open May–mid-Oct., 10–5 except Sun. A long-established gallery featuring sculpture and pottery as well as paintings and original prints.

✐ **Compass Rose Bookstore & Café** (207-326-9366 or 1-800-698-9366), 3 Main St. Open Mon.–Sat. 10–6. Sharon Biggie is the new owner of this local institution, featuring children's titles, summer reading, nautical and regional books. Its **Linger Longer Café** servies drinks, snacks, also soups and sandwiches in winter.

Four Flags (207-312-8526), 19 Water St. A long-established gift shop with an eclectic mix of Maine-made and exotic gifts.

Castine Historical Handworks (207-326-4460; www.castinehistoricalhandworks.com), 9 Main St. Jodie White's shop is all about traditional American craftsmanship: pottery, textiles, woodworking, metalwork, and folk art.

Adam Gallery (207-326-8272), 140 Battle Ave. Open weekends in July and Aug., also most days by appointment. Susan Paris Adams's oils are worth a stop.

✷ Special Events

May: **Memorial Day Parade**.

July: **Independence Day parade** and fireworks. **Sea Kayaking Symposium** sponsored by Castine Kayak Adventures.

ACADIA AREA

MOUNT DESERT ISLAND; ACADIA NATIONAL PARK; BAR HARBOR AND ELLSWORTH; THE QUIET SIDE OF MOUNT DESERT; EAST HANCOCK COUNTY

MOUNT DESERT ISLAND

Mount Desert (pronounced dessert) is New England's second largest island, one conveniently linked to the mainland. Two-fifths of its 108 square miles are maintained as Acadia National Park, laced with roads ideally suited for touring by car, more than 50 miles of "carriage roads" specifically for biking and skiing, and 120 miles of hiking trails.

The beauty of "MDI" (as it is locally known) cannot be overstated. Twenty-six mountains rise abruptly from the sea and from the shores of four large lakes. Mount Cadillac, at 1,532 feet, is the highest point on the U.S. Atlantic seaboard; a road winds to its smooth, broad summit for a 360-degree view that's said to yield the first view of dawn (which usually attracts a crowd) in the United States. Sunset, however, attracts a far larger crowd. There are also countless ponds and streams, an unusual variety of flora, and more than 300 species of birds.

Native Americans populated the island for at least 6,000 years before 1604, when Samuel de Champlain sailed by and named it L'Isle de Monts Deserts. In 1613 two French Jesuits attempted to establish a mission on Fernald Point near present Southwest Harbor. They were welcomed by the local Wabanaki chief Asticou but massacred by sailors from an English ship, and for 150 years this part of Maine remained a war zone between French and English. Finally settled in the second half of the 18th century, this remained a peaceful, out-of-the-way island even after a bridge was built in 1836, connecting it to the mainland.

In the 1840s landscape painters Thomas Cole and Frederic Church began summering here, and their images of the rugged shore were widely circulated. Summer visitors began arriving by steamboat, and they were soon joined by travelers taking express trains from Philadelphia and New York to Hancock Point, bringing guests enough to fill more than a dozen huge hotels that mushroomed in Bar Harbor. By the 1880s many of these hotel patrons had already built their own mansion-sized "cottages." These grandiose summer mansions numbered more than 200 by the time the stock market crashed. Many are now inns.

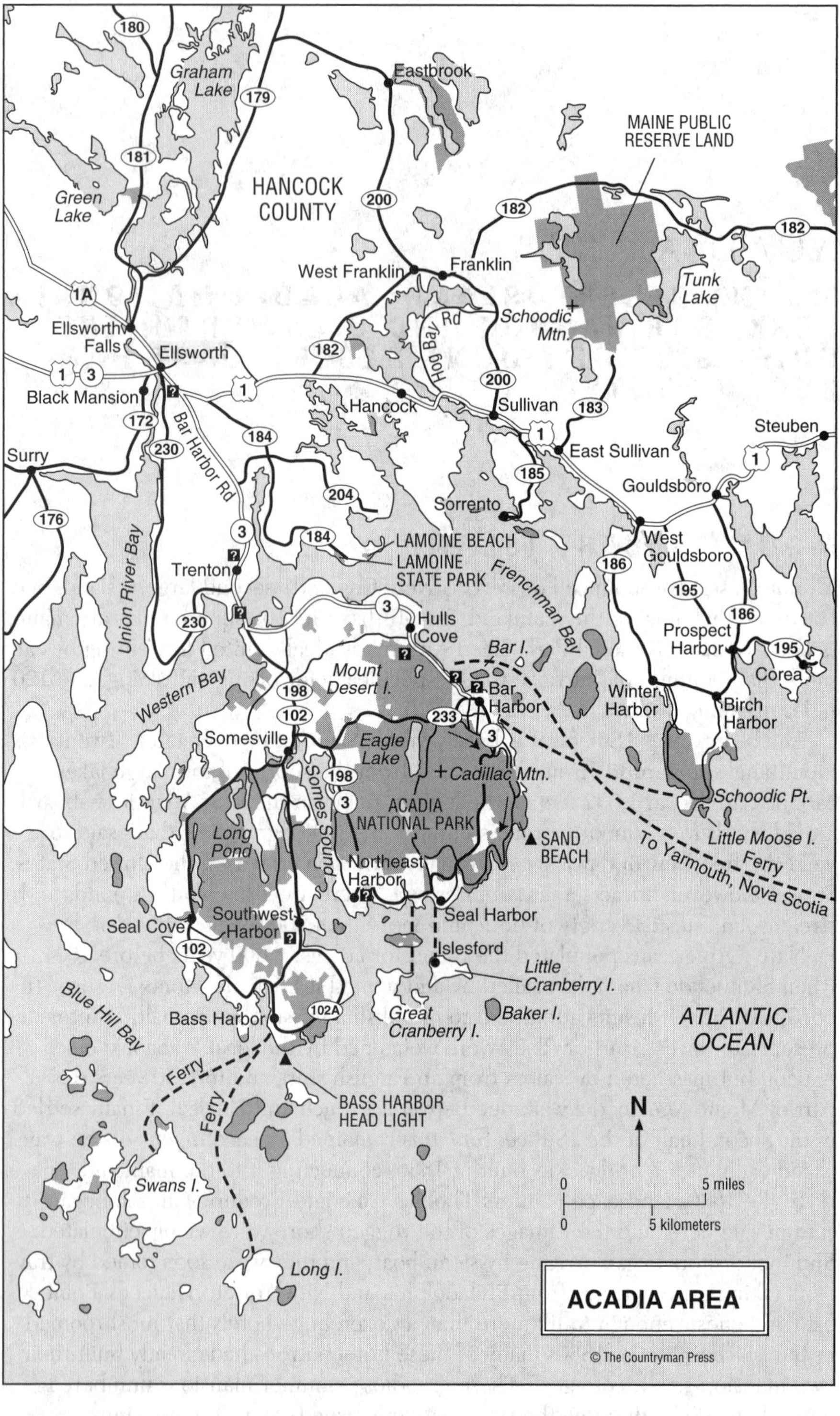

180
Graham Lake
179
Eastbrook
MAINE PUBLIC RESERVE LAND
181
Green Lake
HANCOCK COUNTY
200
182
182
Tunk Lake
West Franklin
Franklin
1A
Hog Bay Rd
Schoodic Mtn.
Ellsworth Falls
Ellsworth
182
1
3
1
Black Mansion
Hancock
200
Sullivan
183
172
Bar Harbor Rd
184
1
East Sullivan
Steuben
Surry
230
1
185
Gouldsboro
204
Sorrento
176
3
184
LAMOINE BEACH
West Gouldsboro
Union River Bay
Trenton
LAMOINE STATE PARK
Frenchman Bay
186
195
230
3
Hulls Cove
186
Prospect Harbor
195
Corea
Bar I.
Western Bay
Mount Desert I.
198
Bar Harbor
Winter Harbor
Birch Harbor
102
233
Somesville
Eagle Lake
3
198
Cadillac Mtn.
Schoodic Pt.
3
ACADIA NATIONAL PARK
Somes Sound
Long Pond
SAND BEACH
Little Moose I.
Northeast Harbor
Ferry
To Yarmouth, Nova Scotia
Seal Harbor
Seal Cove
Southwest Harbor
102
Islesford
Little Cranberry I.
Blue Hill Bay
Bass Harbor
102A
Great Cranberry I.
Baker I.
ATLANTIC OCEAN
Ferry
Ferry
BASS HARBOR HEAD LIGHT
N
0
5 miles
0
5 kilometers
Swans I.
Long I.
ACADIA AREA
© The Countryman Press

Mount Desert Island seems far larger than it is because it's almost bisected by Somes Sound, the only natural fjord on the East Coast, and because its communities vary so in atmosphere. Bar Harbor lost 67 of its 220 summer mansions and five hotels in the devastating fire of 1947, which also destroyed 17,000 acres of woodland, but both the forest and Bar Harbor have recovered, and then some, in recent decades.

Politically the island is divided into four townships: Bar Harbor, Mount Desert, Southwest Harbor, and Tremont. Northeast Harbor (a village in Mount Desert) and Southwest Harbor, the island's other two resort centers, also enjoy easy access to hiking, swimming, and boating within the park. Compared with Bar Harbor, however, they are relatively quiet, even in July and August, and the several accessible offshore islands are quieter still.

Mount Desert's mountains with "their gray coats and rounded backs look like a herd of elephants, marching majestically across the island," travel writer Samuel Adams Drake wrote in 1891, describing the first impression visitors then received of the island. They were, of course, arriving by steamboat instead of traveling down the unimpressive commercial strip that's Rt. 3. Today it's harder to get beyond the clutter and crowds—but not that hard. The memorable march of rounded mountains is still what you see from excursion boats and from Little Cranberry Island, as well as from the eastern shore of Frenchman Bay, the area described in this section as "East Hancock County."

ACADIA NATIONAL PARK

The legacy of Bar Harbor's wealthy "rusticators" is Acadia National Park. A cadre of influential citizens, who included Harvard University's President Charles W. Eliot, began to assemble parcels of land for public use in 1901, thus protecting the forests from the portable sawmill. Boston textile heir George Dorr devoted his fortune and energy to amassing a total of 11,000 acres and persuading the federal government to accept it. In 1919 Acadia became the first national park east of the Mississippi. It is now a more-than-47,000-acre preserve, with 30,300 acres and more than another 10,000 in easements encompassing almost half of Mount Desert Island.

Almost two-thirds of the park's more than 2 million annual visitors get out of their cars and hike the park's trails. Many take the free, white-and-blue Island Explorer buses. They usually begin by viewing the introductory film in the visitors center and then drive the 27-mile Park Loop Road, stopping to see the obvious sites and noting what they want to explore more fully (see below). The park has much more to offer, from simple hikes to rock climbing, horse-drawn carriage rides to swimming, bicycling, canoeing, and kayaking.

OVERLOOKING FRENCHMAN'S BAY

Kim Grant

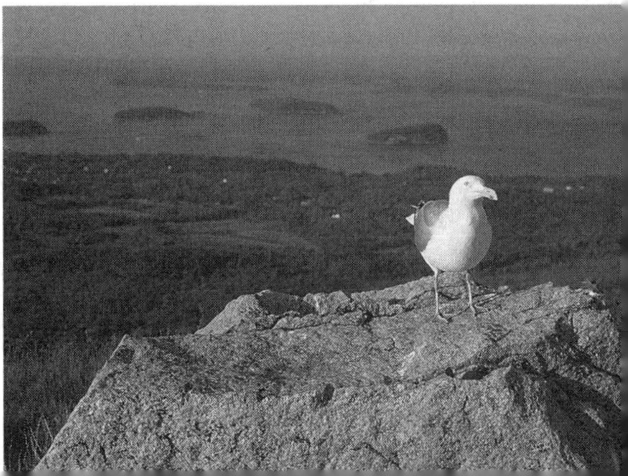

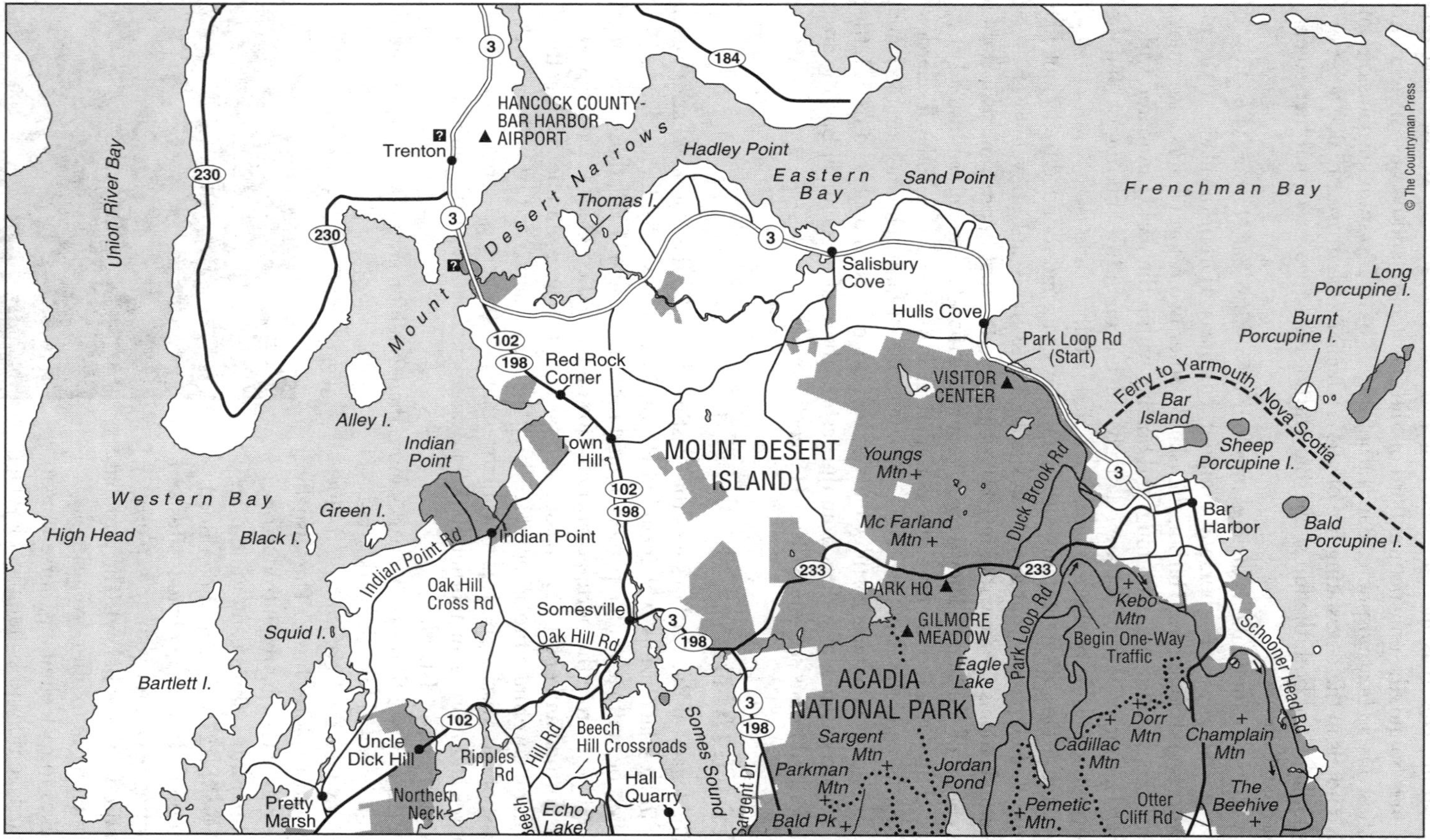

HANCOCK COUNTY-BAR HARBOR AIRPORT
Trenton
Union River Bay
Mount Desert Narrows
Thomas I.
Hadley Point
Eastern Bay
Sand Point
Frenchman Bay
Salisbury Cove
Hulls Cove
Long Porcupine I.
Burnt Porcupine I.
Park Loop Rd (Start)
VISITOR CENTER
Ferry to Yarmouth, Nova Scotia
Bar Island
Sheep Porcupine I.
Bald Porcupine I.
Bar Harbor
Red Rock Corner
Alley I.
Indian Point
Town Hill
MOUNT DESERT ISLAND
Youngs Mtn
Mc Farland Mtn
Duck Brook Rd
Western Bay
Green I.
High Head
Black I.
Indian Point Rd
Oak Hill Cross Rd
Somesville
Oak Hill Rd
PARK HQ
GILMORE MEADOW
Eagle Lake
Park Loop Rd
Kebo Mtn
Begin One-Way Traffic
Schooner Head Rd
Squid I.
Bartlett I.
ACADIA NATIONAL PARK
Sargent Mtn
Parkman Mtn
Bald Pk
Jordan Pond
Cadillac Mtn
Dorr Mtn
Champlain Mtn
Pemetic Mtn
Otter Cliff Rd
The Beehive
Uncle Dick Hill
Ripples Rd
Hill Rd
Beech Hill Crossroads
Somes Sound
Sargent Dr
Hall Quarry
Pretty Marsh
Northern Neck
Beech
Echo Lake
3
184
230
102
198
233
© The Countryman Press

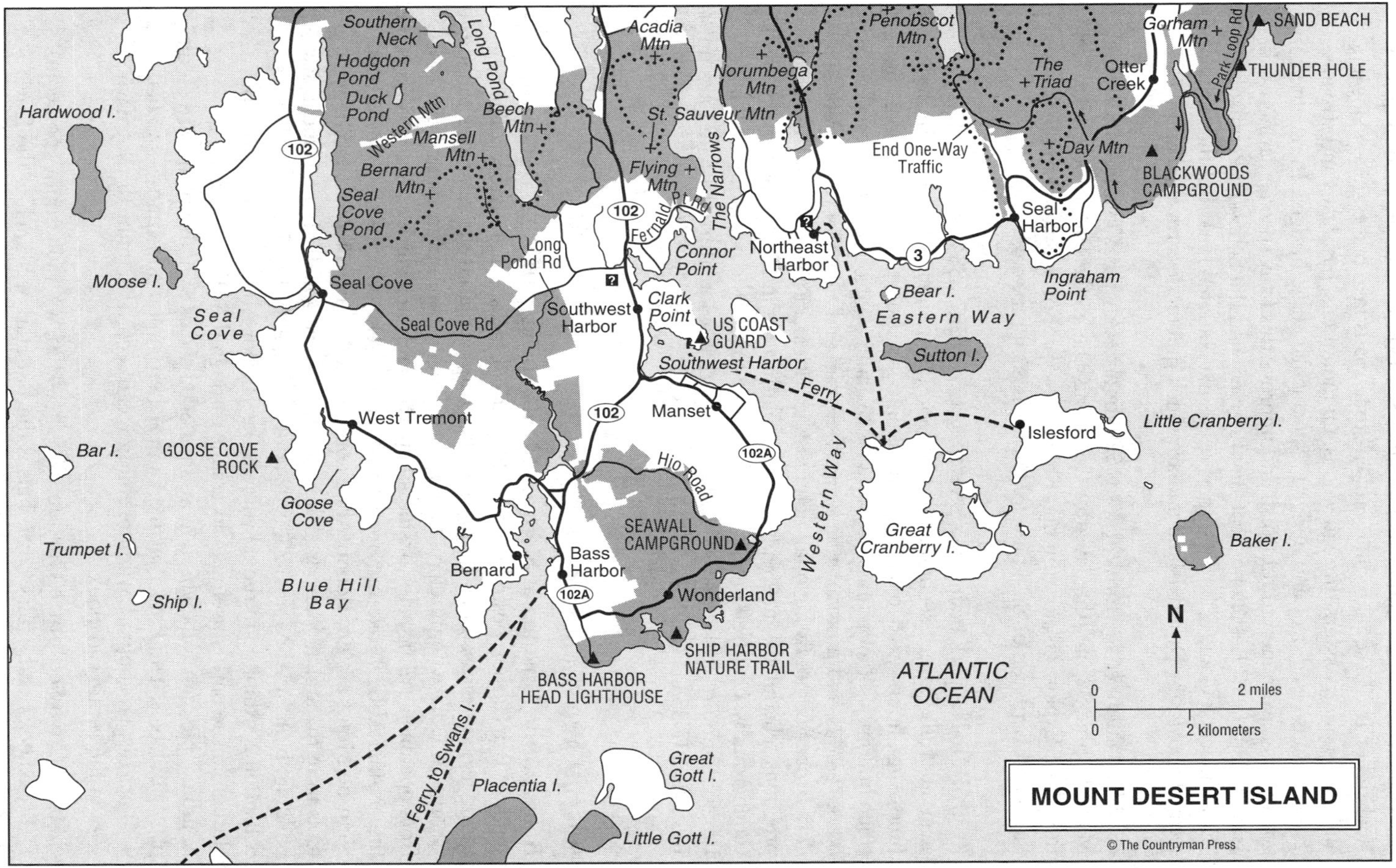
MOUNT DESERT ISLAND
Southern Neck
Long Pond
Hodgdon Pond
Duck Pond
Western Mtn
Mansell Mtn
Bernard Mtn
Seal Cove Pond
Beech Mtn
Acadia Mtn
St. Sauveur Mtn
Flying Mtn
Norumbega Mtn
Penobscot Mtn
The Triad
Day Mtn
Gorham Mtn
Otter Creek
SAND BEACH
THUNDER HOLE
Park Loop Rd
BLACKWOODS CAMPGROUND
End One-Way Traffic
Seal Harbor
Ingraham Point
Northeast Harbor
The Narrows
Fernald Pt Rd
Connor Point
Clark Point
US COAST GUARD
Southwest Harbor
Long Pond Rd
Seal Cove Rd
Seal Cove
Hardwood I.
Moose I.
Bear I.
Eastern Way
Sutton I.
Southwest Harbor Ferry
Western Way
Islesford
Little Cranberry I.
Great Cranberry I.
Baker I.
Manset
Hio Road
SEAWALL CAMPGROUND
West Tremont
GOOSE COVE ROCK
Bar I.
Goose Cove
Trumpet I.
Bernard
Bass Harbor
Wonderland
Blue Hill Bay
Ship I.
SHIP HARBOR NATURE TRAIL
BASS HARBOR HEAD LIGHTHOUSE
ATLANTIC OCEAN
Ferry to Swans I.
Placentia I.
Great Gott I.
Little Gott I.
102
102A
3
N
0
2 miles
0
2 kilometers

Within the park are more than 45 miles of carriage roads donated by John D. Rockefeller Jr. These incredible broken-stone roads take bikers, hikers, joggers, and cross-country skiers through woods, up mountains, past lakes and streams. The paths also lead over and under 17 spectacular stone bridges. In recent years volunteers have rallied to refurbish and improve this truly spectacular network. Isle au Haut (see "East Penobscot Bay Region") and the Schoodic Peninsula (see "East Hancock County") are also part of Acadia National Park, but they are not located on Mount Desert Island and are much quieter, less traveled areas.

FEES The entrance fee for vehicles is $20 for a weekly pass. The fee is $10 from May 1 to June 22, and the day after Columbus Day to the end of October, when the Island Explorer is not running. Free Nov.–Apr. For individuals on foot, on the Island Explorer, or on a bicycle, the fee is $5 for a weekly pass.

GUIDANCE The park maintains its visitors center (207-288-3338; www.nps.gov/acad) at Hulls Cove, a section of Bar Harbor. It's open mid-Apr.–Oct. In mid-June–Aug., hours are 8–6 daily; during shoulder seasons, 8–4:30. The glass-and-stone building, set atop 50 steps, shows a 15-minute introductory film and sells books, guides, and postcards. Pick up a free map and a copy of the current *Acadia's Beaver Log* (a listing of all naturalist activities), and sign up for the various programs scheduled June–Sept. at the amphitheaters in Blackwoods and Seawall Campgrounds. Children of all ages are eligible to join the park's Junior Ranger Program; inquire at the visitors center. The park headquarters at Eagle Lake on Rt. 233 (207-288-3338) is open throughout winter, daily 8–4:30.

* To See

MUSEUM AND GARDENS

Robert Abbe Museum at Sieur de Monts Spring (207-288-3519), 2 miles south of Bar Harbor, posted from Rt. 3 (south of Jackson Laboratory). The spring itself is encased in a Florentine-style canopy placed there by park founder George B. Dorr, who purchased the property to prevent enterprising islanders from opening a springwater business here. It stands in a garden, and beyond is the original **Abbe Museum**, open mid-May–mid-Oct., daily 9–4. On exhibit at Sieur de Monts are Dr. Robert Abbe's original collections of stone and bone tools from the archaic periods. Admission to this octagonal, Mediterranean-style building, built by Abbe in 1928, is $2 adults, $1 ages 6–15. The rest of Abbe's collection is exhibited in the downtown Bar Harbor Abbe Museum (see "Bar Harbor"). The park museum is accessible through the **Wild Gardens of Acadia**, a pleasant walk where more than 300 species of native plants are on display with labels. The **Park Nature Center** here (open mid-June–Sept., daily 9–5) has displays on park wildlife; children can record the animals they have seen in the center's logbook.

Hull's Cove Sculpture Garden (207-288-5126; www.jonesport-wood.com), 17 Breakneck Road, Hull's Cove. This is the Bar Harbor branch of the Davistown Museum in Liberty. Two acres with a path and signage thread through grounds full of work by contemporary Maine artists like Melita Westerlund, who works with polychrome steel, and David McLaughlin, a metal sculptor who put together something that resembles an old car. A picnic area, tree house, and playhouse for children are all open sunrise to sunset (Rocky Mann's studio is next door). You can also park here to walk into Acadia National Park and find a beaver pond.

✷ To Do

BICYCLING The more than 50 miles of broken-stone carriage roads make for good mountain biking. Several outfitters in Bar Harbor (see "Bar Harbor") rent equipment and can help you find good trails.

CAMPING The two campgrounds within the park are Blackwoods, 5 miles south of Bar Harbor, and Seawall, on the quiet side of the island, 4 miles south of Southwest Harbor. Both are in woods and close to the ocean. One vehicle, up to six people, are allowed on each site. Neither campground has utility hook-ups. Facilities include comfort stations, cold running water, a dump station, picnic tables, and fire rings. Showers and a camping store are within 0.5 mile of each. There are also four group campsites at Blackwoods and five at Seawall, for up to 15 people, which must be reserved through the park. Call 207-288-3338 for details.

Blackwoods (207-288-3274), open all year. Reservations required May–Oct. through the National Recreation Reservation Service (1-877-444-6777; www.recreation.gov). Cost of sites is $20 per night during the reservation period; fees vary during the off-season.

Seawall (207-244-3600), near Southwest Harbor, open late May–late Sept. Sites at Seawall are meted out on a first-come, first-served basis. Cost is $20 with a vehicle, $14 if you walk in.

HIKING The park is a mecca for hikers. Several detailed maps are sold at the visitor center, which is also the source of an information sheet that profiles two dozen trails within the park. These range in difficulty from the **Jordan Pond Loop Trail** (a 3.3-mile path around the pond) to the rugged **Precipice Trail** (1.5 miles, very steep, with iron rungs as ladders). There are 17 trails to mountain summits on Mount Desert. **Acadia Mountain** on the island's west side (2 miles round-trip) commands the best view of Somes Sound and the islands. The **Ship Harbor** on Rt. 102A (near Bass Harbor) offers a nature trail that winds along the shore and into the woods; it's also a great birding spot.

HORSE-DRAWN CARRIAGE TOURS ♿ **Carriages in the Park** (207-276-3622), Wildwood Stables, 2 miles south of the Jordan Pond House. One- and two-hour horse-drawn tours in multiple-seat carriages are offered six times a day.

RANGER PROGRAMS A wide variety of programs—from guided nature walks and hikes to birding talks, sea cruises, and evening lectures—are offered

RIDING THROUGH THE PARK

throughout the season. Ask at the visitors center for a current schedule.

ROCK CLIMBING Acadia National Park is the most popular place to climb in Maine; famous climbs include the **Precipice**, **Goat Head**, and **Otter Cliffs**. See "Bar Harbor" for guide services.

SWIMMING Within Acadia there is supervised swimming at **Sand Beach**, 4 miles south of Bar Harbor, and at **Echo Lake**, a warmer, quieter option, 11 miles west (see "The Quiet Side").

WINTER SPORTS More than 50 miles of carriage roads at Acadia National Park are maintained as ski touring and snowshoeing trails. Request the *Winter Activities* leaflet from the park headquarters (write to Superintendent, Acadia National Park, P.O. Box 177, Bar Harbor 04609).

BAR HARBOR AND ELLSWORTH

Bar Harbor is the island's resort town, one of New England's largest clusters of hotels, motels, inns, B&Bs, restaurants, and shops—all within easy reach of the park visitors center and main entrance on the one hand, and an array of water excursions and the ferries to Nova Scotia on the other.

Ellsworth is the shire town and shopping hub of Hancock County, a place with a split personality: the old brick downtown blocks along and around the Union River and its falls, and the strip of malls and outlets along the mile between the junctions of Rts. 1A and 1 and of Rts. 1 and 3. If you're coming down Rt. 1A from Bangor, you miss the old part of town entirely, and it's well worth backtracking. Downtown Ellsworth offers the restored art deco Grand Auditorium, several good restaurants, and rewarding shopping, as well a sense of the lumbering-boom era in which the Colonel Black Mansion, arguably the most elegant in Maine, was built.

The 6 miles of Rt. 3 between Ellsworth and Bar Harbor are lined with a mix of commercial attractions (some of which are vacation savers if you are here with children in fog or rain), 1920s motor courts and 1960s motels, newer motor inns and hotels.

In Bar Harbor itself shops and restaurants line Cottage, Mount Desert, West, and Main Streets, which slope to the Town Pier and to the Shore Path, a mile walk between mansions and the bay. On sunny days most visitors tend to be out in the park or on the water; half an hour before sunset (the time is announced each day in local publications), folks gather on and near the top of Cadillac Mountain for a show that can be truly spectacular. Dinner reservations are advisable because everyone then converges on restaurants at the same time, then walks around; most shops stay open until 9 PM.

PARK LOOP ROAD

The 27-mile Loop Road is the prime tourist route within the park. There is a weekly fee of $20 per car on the road.

The Loop Road officially begins at the visitors center but may be entered at many points along the way. Most of the road is one-way, so be alert to how traffic is flowing. Places of interest along the Loop Road include Sieur de Monts Spring, a stop that could include the Wild Gardens of Acadia, the Abbe Museum, and Park Nature Center as well as the covered spring itself; Sand Beach, which is actually made up of ground shells and sand and is a great beach to walk down and from which to take a dip, if you don't mind 50-degree water (there are changing rooms and lifeguards); Thunder Hole, where the water rushes in and out of a small cave, which you can view from behind a railing; Jordan Pond House, popular for afternoon tea and popovers; and Cadillac Mountain. From Cadillac's smooth summit (accessible by car), you look north across Frenchman's Bay, dotted with the Porcupine Islands, which look like giant stepping-stones, and way beyond Down East. To the west, Jericho and Blue Hill Bays are directly below, and beyond the Blue Hill Peninsula you see Penobscot Bay and the Camden Hills. Many visitors come at sunrise, but sunset can be far more spectacular, a sight not to be missed.

A VIEW FROM PARK LOOP ROAD

Christina Tree

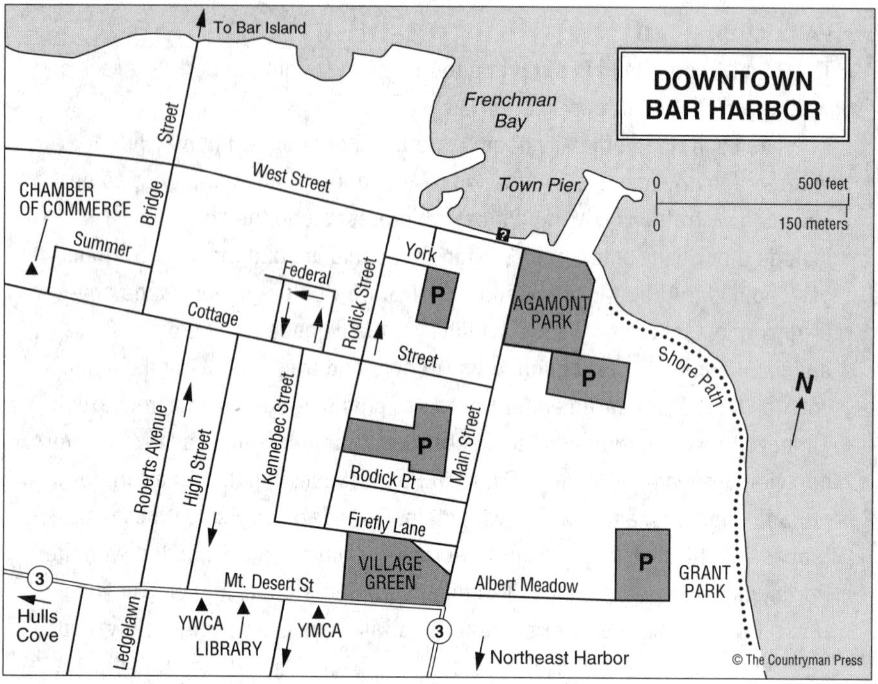

GUIDANCE **Bar Harbor Chamber of Commerce** (year-round 207-288-5103 or 1-888-540-9990; www.barharbormaine.com), 1201 Bar Harbor Rd., Trenton 04605, maintains year-round and a seasonal information booth at the pier in Bar Harbor.

Mount Desert Island Information Center (207-288-3411) is open daily mid-May–mid-Oct. (8:30–6 during high season) on Thompson Island, just after Rt. 3 crosses the bridge. This is the island's most helpful walk-in center, with restrooms and help with lodging reservations on all parts of the island. It keeps track of vacancies at Seawall Campground; park rangers are usually there to sell passes to the park.

Ellsworth Chamber of Commerce (207-667-5584 or 207-667-2617; www.ellsworthchamber.org), 163 High St., Ellsworth 04605, maintains an information center in the Ellsworth Shopping Center on the Rt. 1/3 strip; look for Wendy's. Also see "Acadia National Park."

GETTING THERE *By air:* **Colgan Air** (1-800-428-4322; www.colganair.com) has been absorbed by U.S. Airways but still serves the **Hancock County & Bar Harbor Airport** in Trenton (between Ellsworth and Bar Harbor) from Boston and Rockland. Rental cars are available at the airport. **Bangor International Airport** (207-947-0384; www.flybangor.com), 26 miles north of Ellsworth, offers connections with most American cities.

In 2008 the boat departs both Bar Harbor and Yarmouth, Nova Scotia from May 30 to July 13, and Sept.1 to Oct. 14, 9 AM Mon. and 8 AM Tues. to Thurs. A day trip is feasible Mon. to Wed., but on Thursday the Cat does not make a return trip, heading instead to Portland. Between July 14 and Aug. 31, the Cat leaves Bar Harbor 9 AM Mon. and 8 AM Tues. and Wed., with a day trip possible just Monday and Tuesday.

By private boat: For details about moorings, contact the Bar Harbor harbormaster at 207-288-5571.

By bus: **Concord Trailways** (1-800-639-3317; www.concordtrailways.com) offers unbeatable year-round service from Boston's Logan Airport and South Station (five hours) to Bangor. **Vermont Transit** (1-800-451-3292) runs one bus late May–Labor Day from Bangor at 5:25 PM, with a 6:45 arrival. It returns to Bangor at 9:45 AM.

By car: From Brunswick and points south (including Boston and New York), the shortest route is I-295 to I-95 in Augusta, to Bangor to I-395 to Rt. 1A south to Ellsworth. A slightly slower route that includes some coastal views is I-95 to Augusta, then Rt. 3 east to Belfast (stop for a swim at Lake St. George State Park), and north on Rt. 1 to Ellsworth.

GETTING AROUND Jump on the **Island Explorer** buses operated by Downeast Transportation (207-288-4573; www.exploreacadia.com). The free, propane-powered buses travel eight routes around the island and carry bikes front and back. They will stop on request wherever it's safe. Hikers take note: You can get off at one trailhead and be picked up at another. Bus schedules are timed to coincide with ferry departures to Nova Scotia, Swans Island, and the Cranberry Isles. The bus service starts June 23 every year and ends Columbus Day.

PARKING In high season, parking here is a pain. Note the lots on our Downtown Bar Harbor map. Much of the lodging is downtown (with parking), and the village is compact. Park and walk.

WHEN TO COME Since this is the most crowded summer place on the coast, everyone who lives nearby, from Portland north, prefers a visit in the off-season, preferably early fall. Although the Island Explorer bus's schedule is reduced and the nights are chilly, the scenery is spectacular and the museums are still open. Winter is quiet indeed.

BEAR ISLAND

Nancy English

✷ To See

In Bar Harbor

🖍 ♿ **Abbe Museum** (207-288-3519; www.abbemuseum.org), 26 Mount Desert St. Open mid-May–Oct. daily

10–6, off-season Thu.–Sat. 10–4. $6 per adult, $2 ages 6–15, under 6 free. Native Americans are free, too. The downtown Abbe in the heart of Bar Harbor, facing the village green, is more than eight times the size of its original, seasonal facility. The museum is dedicated to showcasing the cultures of Maine's Wabanaki, the 7,000 members of the Penobscot, Passamaquoddy, Micmac, and Maliseet tribes who live in Maine. The permanent collection of 50,000 objects ranges from 10,000-year-old artifacts to exquisite basketry and crafts from several centuries. The orientation gallery and time line begin with the present and draw visitors back slowly and skillfully through 10,000 years to the core, a circular tower, the "Circle of Four Directions." Exhibits include a fabricated copy of the 1794 treaty between Massachusetts and the Wabanaki that deeded much of Maine to its Native people. Much of the museum space is devoted to changing exhibits.

College of the Atlantic (COA; 207-288-5015 or 207-288-5395; www.coa.edu), Rt. 3. Housed in the original Acadia National Park headquarters, the **George B. Dorr Museum of Natural History** is a good stop (open daily 10–5 in summer, varying days and hours off-season). $3.50 adults, $2.50 seniors, $1.50 teens, $1 children ages 3 and older. Exhibits include the skeleton of a rare true-beaked whale and dioramas of plants and animals of coastal Maine. The **Ethel H. Blum Gallery** (open Tues.–Sat. same hours) holds changing exhibits. Founded in 1969, COA is a liberal-arts college specializing in ecological studies. Its waterside acreage, an amalgam of four large summer estates, is now a handsome campus for 230 students.

Bar Harbor Historical Society (207-288-0000; www.barharborhistorical.org), 33 Ledgelawn Ave. Open June–Oct., Mon.–Sat. 1–4. In winter, open by appointment. Free. Well worth finding. A fascinating collection of early photographs of local hotels, Gilded Era clothing, books by local authors and about Bar Harbor, and the story of the big fire of 1947.

In Ellsworth

Colonel Black Mansion (Woodlawn) (207-667-8671; www.woodlawnmuseum.com), W. Main St. (Rt. 172). Open June–Sept. daily 10–5, with a last tour at 4; May and Oct. Tue.–Sun. 1–4. $7.50 adults, $3 12 and older, children under 12 free. An outstanding Federal mansion built in 1824 by John Black, who moved in with his wife and his three youngest children (five older children had already left home). The bricks were brought by sea from Philadelphia, and it took Boston workmen three years to complete the home. The rooms are furnished just as they were when the Black family used it, and a carriage house holds old carriages and sleighs.

Birdsacre/Stanwood Wildlife Sanctuary (207-667-8460; www.birdscacre.com), Rt. 3. Old homestead and gift shop open May–Oct., daily 10–4; sanctuary open year-round with outdoor shelters that house non-releasable (injured) hawks and owls. A 200-acre nature preserve that is a memorial to Cordelia Stanwood (1865–1958), a pioneer ornithologist, nature photographer, and writer. The 1850 homestead contains a collection of Stanwood's photos.

The Telephone Museum (207-667-9491; www.thetelephonemuseum.org), 166 Winkumpaugh Rd., marked from Rt. 1A north of Ellsworth. Open July–Sept.,

Thu.–Sun. 1–4. $5 adults, $2.50 children. The evolution of telephone service, from 1876 to 1983 (when the museum was founded), is the subject of this quirky museum. Switchboards and phones are hooked up ready for people to place calls—within the museum.

FOR FAMILIES ✐ **Acadia National Park Junior Ranger Programs** (207-288-3338) are the best thing going here for youngsters: First complete the activities in the Junior Ranger booklet, then join a ranger-led program or walk to receive a Junior Ranger patch. Books are for 7 and younger, and 8 and older; the senior ranger book for 18 and older contains much harder activities.

✐ **Family Nature Camp at College of the Atlantic** (see above) offers six one-week programs in which families live in dorms and spend days on field trips led by naturalists in Acadia National Park. Summer Field Studies give children entering first to 12th grades one or two weeks of outdoor exploration.

Rt. 3 attractions

You'll find waterslides, mini golf, and go-carts, as well as:

✐ **Mount Desert Oceanarium** (207-288-5005; www.theoceanarium.com), 1351 State Highway 3, Bar Harbor 04609. Open 9–5 daily, except Sun., late May–mid-Oct. $10–12 adults, $6–7 ages 4–12, depending on what you want to see and do. Tour the lobster hatchery and the Thomas Bay Marsh Walk.

Kisma Preserve (207-667-3244), Rt. 3, Trenton. $25 adults, under 3 free, but check if allowed. Tours are geared toward adults and more mature children. Make your reservation in advance. Thirty-five-acre nonprofit animal preserve with native and non-native animal species. The moose is a draw for tourists who want to see one; but animals from 60 other species are also living here, many retired, injured, or abused.

✐ **The Maine Lumberjack Show** (207-667-0067; www.mainelumberjack.com), Rt. 3, Trenton. Late June–Labor Day, nightly at 7. The show includes ax throwing, log rolling, speed climbing, and more.

✷ To Do

AIRPLANE RIDES **Scenic Flights of Acadia** (207-667-6527; www.mainecoastalflight.com), Rt. 3, Hancock County Airport, Trenton. Sightseeing flights in a Cessna 172 take four different routes over MDI.

Scenic Biplane Helicopter and Glider Rides (207-667-7627; www.acadiaairtours.com), located at the Hancock County Airport. Helicopter, glider, and biplane trips sunrise to sunset, by appointment, depending on weather. The biplane is extremely popular. "No one's done this up here before," said owner Steve Collins. "It's a wonderful way to experience the beauty of the park. It's like riding a Harley at 1,000 feet."

BICYCLING The network of gravel carriage roads constructed by John D. Rockefeller Jr. in 1915 lends itself particularly well to mountain biking. In Bar Harbor, **Bar Harbor Bicycle Shop** (207-288-3886; www.barharborbike.com), 141 Cottage

St., is the oldest bike outfitter in town and still rents only bikes: mountain, tandem, and everything that goes with them. **Acadia Bike & Coastal Kayaking** (207-288-9605; www.acadiafun.com), 48 Cottage St., rents mountain and road bikes with a full bike shop.

BIRDING **Downeast Nature Tours** (207-288-8128; www.downeastnaturetours.com). Michael Good offers guided bird and nature tours daily. Birders can strengthen field identification skills and encounter neotropical migrants in season.

For special programs led by park naturalists, consult *Acadia's Beaver Log*, available at the park visitor center.

BOAT EXCURSIONS **Bar Harbor Ferry Co.** (207-288-2984; www.barharborferry.com) sails from the Bar Harbor Inn Pier, crossing Frenchman Bay to Winter Harbor several times a day; bring a bicycle and bike around Schoodic. **Lulu Lobster Boat Ride** (207-963-2341; www.lululobsterboat.com), Harborside Hotel and Marina, offers sightseeing (*le capitaine parle français*) on Frenchman Bay, with lobstering demonstrations and seal watching. **Dive-in-Theater** (207-288-3483; www.divered.com) operates *The Seal*, an excursion boat from which passengers can watch Diver Ed (through an underwater camera) probe the depths of Frenchman Bay, and then get to touch what he fetches.

BREWERY TOURS **Atlantic Brewing Company** (207-288-BEER; www.atlanticbrewing.com), 15 Knox Rd., in Town Hill (across from the Town Hill Market), has re-created an indoor–outdoor European brewery-pub. Daily tours and tastings at 2, 3, and 4, Memorial Day–Columbus Day. Try **The Knox Road Grille** for its great barbeque next door; Saturday all-you-can-eat cost $15 in 2007.

Bar Harbor Brewing Co. and Sodaworks (207-288-4592; www.barharborbrewing.com), Otter Creek Rd., 1 mile north of Blackwoods Campground, also offers tours, from mid-June through August, 3:30 to 5.

THE *MARGARET TODD* AND AN ERRATIC BOULDER

CANOEING AND SEA KAYAKING Most ponds on Mount Desert offer easy access. **Long Pond**, the largest lake on the island, has three access points. Boats can be launched at **Echo Lake** from **Ike's Point**, just off Rt. 102. **Seal Cove Pond** is less used and accessible from fire roads north of Seal Cove. **Bass Harbor Marsh** is another possibility at high tide. Canoe rental sources offer suggestions and directions. **National Park Canoe Rentals** (207-244-5854) on Long

Pond near Somesville offers tours as well as rentals, including kayaks. In Bar Harbor, **Aquaterra Adventures** (207-288-0007), 1 West St., does guided sea kayak tours and sells gear. **National Park Sea Kayak Tours** (207-288-0342 or 1-800-347-0940; www.acadiakayak.com), 39 Cottage St., gives guided kayak trips on the remote, west side of MDI. **Acadia Bike & Coastal Kayaking** (207-288-9605; www.acadiafun.com), 48 Cottage St., rents kayaks and canoes, and offers kayaking tours, some with camping.

Nancy English

"THE BUBBLES" AT JORDAN POND

GOLF **Kebo Valley Club** (207-288-3000), Rt. 233, Bar Harbor. Open daily May–Oct. Eighteen holes. "Eighth oldest golf grounds in America," since 1888. **Bar Harbor Golf Course** (207-667-7505), Rts. 3 and 204, Trenton. Eighteen holes.

FISHING Several charter boats offer deep-sea fishing. **Downeast Windjammer Cruises** (207-288-4585; www.downeastwindjammer.com) offers a four-hour fishing trip once or twice a day, with bait and tackle provided, leaving from the Bar Harbor Inn pier.

HIKING See "Acadia National Park."

HORSE-DRAWN CARRIAGE TOURS See "Acadia National Park."

ROCK CLIMBING **Acadia Mountain Guides** (207-288-8186; www.acadiamountainguides.com) and **Atlantic Climbing School** (207-288-2521) offer instruction and guiding for beginner through advanced climbers. (Also see "Acadia National Park.")

SAILING The ***Margaret Todd*** (207-288-4585) sails from the Bar Harbor pier late June–early Oct. This 151-foot four-masted schooner, designed and built in 1998 by Capt. Steve Pagels, cruises through Frenchman Bay several times a day in high season, less frequently in slower weeks.

SWIMMING ✐ **Lake Wood** near Hull's Cove is a pleasant freshwater beach, ideal for children. Also see "Acadia National Park."

WHALE-WATCHING The big operator is **Bar Harbor Whale Watch Co.** (207-288-2386; www.barharborwhales.com), 1 West St., Bar Harbor, which also offers seal-watching and lobstering tours. Bring a jacket, sunblock, binoculars, and a camera. Ask how long it takes to get out to the whales and about weather—and sea—conditions on the day you book.

✱ Lodging

Many of Bar Harbor's nearly 2,400 beds, ranging from 1920s motor courts to large chain hotels and motels, are strung along Rt. 3, north of the walk-around town—where a few surviving summer mansions are now B&Bs commanding top dollar. Reservations are not as crucial as they used to be, with a surge in the number of rooms here, but still a good idea. We cannot claim to have inspected every room in town, but we have checked out the most appealing options.

WATER-VIEW BED & BREAKFASTS

In Bar Harbor 04609

Ullikana Bed & Breakfast (207-288-9552; www.ullikana.com), 16 The Field. Open May–Oct. This is our top pick in downtown Bar Harbor, steps from both Main Street and the Shore Path, yet with an away-from-it-all feel. Innkeepers Helene Harton and her husband Roy Kasindorf combine a rare flair for decorating with a genuine warmth that sets guests at ease. They bought Ullikana, a vintage-1885 Tudor-style summer mansion, in 1990 and transformed it with vivid colors and stylish, artful decor. The neighboring Yellow House, another classic Bar Harbor "cottage," flaunts their touch with tiled baths and pretty colors. Breakfast, perhaps a light berry-stuffed soufflé pancake, is served on the terrace overlooking the water or in Ullikana's attractive dining room, where you will feel as if you had returned to the home you always wished for. The 10 guest rooms all have private bath, three have a fireplace. $180–330 in high season, varying with room size and view.

Balance Rock Inn (207-288-2610 or 1-800-753-0494; www.barharborvacations.com), 21 Albert Meadow. The original mansion, built in 1903 for a Scottish railroad tycoon, is augmented by a heated pool. Fourteen rooms, most with ocean view, private balcony, whirlpool bath; some with fireplace. The three suites have a kitchen, living room, and sauna. Rooms and suites, all with breakfast, range from $155–625 depending on season. $30 fee for pets.

The Shore Path Cottage (207-288-0643; www.shorepathcottage.com), 24 Atlantic Ave. Open May–Oct. Roberta Chester has owned this delightful Bar Harbor "cottage" since 1973, and the feel is that of a family home rather than a formal B&B. The dining room, however, has a kind of authentic elegance that can't be imitated, with lovely china and decor. Seven guest rooms (just one without with private bath, a few with claw-foot tub) are named for the youngsters who grew up in them. Roberta is herself a writer, and the house is filled with books and art, along with a classic video library. Both kosher and vegetarian diets are honored, and solo travelers and children are particularly welcome. $120–250.

♿ **The Bass Cottage Inn** (207-288-1234, 1-866-782-9224; www.basscottage.com), 14 The Field, P.O. Box 242. Open May to the beginning of Nov., this 10-room inn was completely redone before reopening in 2004, adding whirlpool tubs, gas fireplaces, and TVs with DVD players (which will be removed if you ask). With a culinary degree to attest to her skill, Teri Anderholm makes lobster quiche or crème brûlée French toast for breakfast served in a bright, elegant sunporch, and fine hors d'oeuvres in the early evening. She and her husband, Jeff Anderholm, run things smoothly in the handsome and comfortable inn, where rates range $195–350 in-season, less before and after.

OTHER DOWNTOWN B&BS

In Bar Harbor 04609

"1" **Manor House Inn** (207-288-3759 or 1-800-437-0088; www.barharbormanorhouse.com), 106 West St. Open mid-April–Oct. No real water views, but a short walk from Bar Island. Nine comfortable rooms with private bath are in the vintage-1887 "Manor" with its rich woodwork. The full acre of landscaped grounds also includes Acadia Cottage with whirlpool, the Chauffeur's Cottage with three guest rooms and two suites, and two garden cottages with gas fireplace. $125–250 (less off-season) includes full breakfast and afternoon tea.

Seacroft Inn (207-288-4669 or 1-800-824-9694; www.seacroftinn.com), 18 Albert Meadow. Open early May to early Nov. Beverly and Dave Brown's gracious, many-gabled old "cottage" is sequestered on a quiet street, steps from the Shore Path. Extended stays are the norm; all seven rooms have a fridge and a microwave, or a kitchen. $99–139 in-season, substantially less off, with housekeeping $10 extra; a two-bedroom apartment can be made of two rooms, sleeping six. Includes a "Breakfast Basket" with fruit, muffin, juice, and yogurt.

"1" 🐾 **Primrose Inn** (207-288-4031 or 1-877-TIME-4-BH; www.primroseinn.com), 73 Mount Desert St. Open mid-May–Oct. This is a spiffy 1878 stick-style "painted lady" Victorian summer cottage. The 15 guest rooms are bright with floral wallpaper and Victorian decor; several have a gas fireplace and private balcony. The nicest rooms in the house have a "bubble massage" Kohler bathtub. Every room has a flat-panel TV with DVD player. Rooms are $145–245, less off-season, and include a great breakfast and afternoon tea. Free soda and water in guest refrigerator.

The Maples Inn (207-288-3443; www.maplesinn.com), 16 Roberts Ave. Open May–Oct. Mark Dresser bought this inn in 2005 and has been decorating with his and his family's antiques; his architectural books are a resource at this pleasant 1903 house on a quiet side street within walking distance of shops and restaurants. The six rooms (all with private bath) are crisply decorated, furnished with a high, antique bed and down comforter. Red Oak, under the eaves, has its own tranquil deck. $125–170 per couple; $90–120 off-season, with a fine breakfast.

Canterbury Cottage (207-288-2112; www.canterburycottage.com), 12 Roberts Ave. Open year-round. Martha Helfrich and Rob Rochon are your hosts at this architecturally interesting Victorian house (its original owner was the B&M stationmaster, and its architect specialized in railroad stations). Rooms each hold a private bath and cable TV. One has a small balcony. $116–130 double in-season includes breakfast served in the pretty dining room.

"1" **Cleftstone Manor** (207-288-8086; www.cleftstone.com), 92 Eden St. Open May–Oct. Located a short drive from downtown, this 1880 mansion once owned by wealthy summer visitors has been an inn for 50 years.

One smallish room called Benjamin Stanwood has a huge bathroom; four have a sofa bed. Joseph Pulitzer summered here, and a few of the original antiques are still in place, like two crystal chandeliers in the dining room. Seventeen rooms with private bath, five with fireplace. In-season rates $130–195, less off-season.

Anne's White Columns Inn (207-288-5357 or 1-800-321-6379; www.anneswhitecolumns.com), 57 Mount Desert St. Open May–Oct. Built in the 1930s as a Christian Science church, hence the columns. The 10 rooms have private bath, air-conditioning, and cable TV. $100–150 July–mid-Oct.; less off-season, including full breakfast and afternoon wine and cheese.

♿ **Mira Monte Inn and Suites** (207-288-4263 or 1-800-553-5109; www.miramonte.com), 69 Mount Desert St. Open May–mid-Oct. Bar Harbor native Marian Burns offers 13 comfortable guest rooms and two suites in her gracious 1864 mansion, many, like Malvern, with a private balcony overlooking the deep, peaceful lawn in back or the gardens on the side. All rooms have private bath, phone, clock-radio, voice-mail, and cable TV; some have a gas fireplace.

BAR HARBOR INN

Nancy English

Rates include a full breakfast and afternoon refreshments. $169–290 for rooms and suites; $95–165 off-season.

HOTELS AND MOTELS

In Bar Harbor 04609

✎ ♿ **Bar Harbor Inn** (207-288-3351 or 1-800-248-3351; www.barharborinn.com), Newport Dr. Open Mar.–Nov. With 153 units, this landmark hotel gets its share of groups, but its downtown waterside location is unbeatable. It's also a genuinely gracious hotel, with a 24-hour front desk, bellhops, a restaurant, and room service. The hotel-sized lobby with its formal check-in desk and seating near the fire is quite grand. Reading Room Restaurant (see *Dining Out*), begun as an elite men's social club in 1887, offers fine dining with water views. The 51 guest rooms in the Main Inn were the first new hotel rooms available in town after the 1947 fire. Of these, 43 were completely rebuilt in 1998; balconies, jetted tubs, and fireplaces were added. The grounds also include a 64-unit Oceanfront Lodge with private balconies on the bay, and the Newport Building—38 equally comfortable rooms without views. All rooms have phone, cable TV, and access to the pool, Jacuzzi, fitness room, and sseven acres of manicured lawns on the water. $199–375 in-season, continental breakfast included.

Harborside Hotel & Marina (207-288-5033 or 1-800-328-5033; www.theharborsidehotel.com), 55 West St. Open May–Oct. Delightful views of the harbor and Porcupine Islands. Luxuriously furnished and accented with marble baths and marble-tiled floors, many rooms and suites are equipped with full kitchens; some have fireplace in the master bedroom and Jacuzzi on the porch. One deluxe ocean-front room ($379 high season) held upscale hotel furniture and a balcony. The on-site marina can dock a 175-foot yacht. **La Bella Vita**, a high-end Italian restaurant, lies off the main lobby. The spa is located in the neighboring Bar Harbor Club with its own restaurant. Tennis courts and a saltwater pool. Standard rooms $275–425, suites $399–1,700 in-season; off-season $99–199, $299–$800.

Wonder View Inn (207-288-3358 or 1-888-439-8439; www.wonderviewinn.com), 50 Eden St., P.O. Box 25. Open May–Oct. Children are welcome in the 75-unit motel built on 14 acres, the site of an estate once owned by Mary Roberts Rinehart, author of popular mystery stories. Near both the ferry terminal and downtown Bar Harbor, the motel overlooks Frenchman Bay and includes a swimming pool and the **Rinehart Dining Pavilion**, which serves breakfast and dinner. $104–219 in summer, less off-season. Most rooms have a balcony with an ocean view.

Bar Harbor Villager Motel (207-288-3211 or 1-888-383-3211; www.barhaborvillager.com), 207 Main St. This reasonably priced motel, owned by the Coston family since 1969, provides immaculately clean and comfortable rooms within an easy walk of everything Bar Harbor offers. With a turquoise, heated pool tucked into a back corner of the parking lot, and a friendly staff, this is the seasonal Bar Harbor stop for Vermont Transit. Summer rates $99–128, $69–98 off-season, children under 10 free.

Sea Breeze Motel (207-288-3565 or 1-800-441-3123; www.seabreeze.us), 323 R.t. 3. Open mid-May–mid-Oct. Watch the sun rise over Frenchman Bay all summer long from the motel's seven-acre hillside location, 4 miles from town. Thirty-six clean, comfortable rooms, most with ocean view, have private bath, mini-fridge, cable TV, air-conditioning, and in-room coffee. Heated swimming pool and hot tub. $114–174, high-season, less off season.

Nancy English

HARBORSIDE HOTEL AND MARINA

In Ellsworth 04605

"T" **Twilite Motel** (207-667-8165 or 1-800-395-5097; www.twilitemotel.com) Rts. 1 and 3. In 2007, Chuck and Ariela Zucker took over this charming motel with flowers spilling out in between the 1950s-style, updated rooms, all with private bath and a little outdoor seating area. Coffee and baked goods are set out in the office in the morning. Coin-operated laundry, and free wireless Internet connection in the lobby. Rates $79–109, less off-season.

COTTAGES **Acadia Cottage Rentals** (207-288-3636; www.acadiarental.com) offers camps, cottages, private homes, and estates for a minimum of one week (Sat.–Sat.).

Emery's Cottages on the Shore (207-288-3432 or 1-888-240-3432; www.emeryscottages.com), Sand Point Rd., Bar Harbor 04609. Open May–late Oct. In the family since 1969, these 22 cottages and an apartment on Frenchman Bay offer electric heat, shower, and cable TV; 14 have a kitchen. Linens, dishes, and cooking utensils provided. Serene, private pebble beach. Telephone available for local calls. No pets. Hikers like to use these cabins as a launching place from which to set out on day trips in Acadia National Park. $550–1,050 per week late June–late Aug.; $450–790 late Aug.–Oct.; less in May and June.

PUBLIC CAMPGROUNDS **Lamoine State Park** (207-667-4778; www.campwithme.com), Rt. 184, Lamoine. Open mid-May–mid-Oct. Minutes from busy Rt. 3 (between Ellsworth and Bar Harbor), this 55-acre waterside park offers a boat launch and 62 campsites (no hookups, but hot showers in a bathhouse), two-night minimum, $20 per night for nonresidents in-season, $15 for residents. Neighboring Lamoine Beach is great for skipping stones. *Note:* There are occasionally vacancies here in July and Aug. when Acadia National Park campsites are full. (For reservations, out-of-state call 207-624-9950, in-state call 1-800-332-1501.)

TWILITE MOTEL

Nancy English

Also see *To Do* in "Acadia National Park." There are more than a dozen commercial campgrounds in this area; check local listings.

✱ Where to Eat

DINING OUT All listings are in Bar Harbor unless otherwise noted.

The Burning Tree (207-288-9331), Rt. 3, Otter Creek. Open June–Columbus Day 5–10; closed Tue., also Mon. after Labor Day. Reservations recommended. Admired for its fresh fish and its own organically grown produce from five gardens. Dine inside or on a lattice-enclosed porch on a wide choice of seafood, chicken, and vegetable entrées, but no red meat. A favorite entrée is yellowfin tuna served rare with ginger tamari and wasabi-lime sauce with sesame spinach ($25). Entrées $18–26.

♿ **Café This Way** (207-288-4483), 14½ Mount Desert St. Open seasonally for breakfast and dinner. Tucked just off the village green, this is a winner. Start dinner with grilled halloumi, a Cypriot cheese, then try, perhaps, pecan-crusted halibut or beef tenderloin with blue cheese. Entrées $14–23. Reservations a good idea. Breakfast is just as good (see *Eating Out*).

Eden (207-288-4422; www.barharborvegetarian.com), 78 West St. Wonderfully made vegetarian meals include a bento box of assorted Asian specialties and luscious lentil stew. The cocktails are organic and guilt-free, and dessert delicious without using any dairy products at all. Entrees $14–19.

Cleonice (207-664-7554; www

.cleonice.com), 112 Main St., Ellsworth. Open year-round for dinner, lunch in summer Mon.–Sat. Chef Rich Hansen is a master of Mediterranean seafood and meat dishes. Bagaduce oysters Rockefeller, weir-caught mackerel, and roasted halibut with mushroom vodka cream were one fall day's specials, but don't skip the tapas. The dark wood bar adds to the illusion of being farther south and east; but the food makes you feel like it's the center of the universe. Entrées $17–24.

✐ **Jordan Pond House** (207-276-3316; www.jordanpond.com), Park Loop Rd., Seal Harbor. Open mid-May–mid-Oct. for lunch and tea 11:30–6 in summer, 5:30 early and late in the season, and for dinner 6–9. Reservations advised. First opened in the 1870s, this landmark was beautifully rebuilt after a 1979 fire, with dining rooms overlooking the pond and mountains. It's best known for popovers and outdoor tea (see *Afternoon Tea*) but is least crowded at dinner (jackets suggested). Prime rib, fresh fish, and baked scallops. Dinner entrées $15–24.

♿ **Havana** (207-288-CUBA), 318 Main St. Open from 5 nightly; reservations suggested. The menu changes weekly, the accent ranges from the Caribbean to Africa and farther east, and people love it. Entrées ($18–27) have included Calle Ocho pork chops with a chipotle glaze, and yellowfin tuna with Thai pesto.

Galyn's (207-288-9706), 17 Main St. Lunch and dinner. Easy to miss among the shops near the bottom of Main St., this is bigger than it looks, with dining rooms upstairs and down, and one of the best bets in town. Try the crabcakes or Frenchman Bay stew. Entrées from $13; $36 for a twin-lobster dinner in 2007.

♿ **Café Bluefish** (207-288-3696; www.cafebluefishbarharbor.com), 122 Cottage St. Dark wood, books, cloth napkins with varying designs, and mismatched china create a pleasant atmosphere. Chef-owner Bobbie Lynn Hutchins, a fourth-generation Bar Harbor native, specializes in chicken, vegetarian, and seafood entrées, plus (Food Network famous) lobster strudel. $18–32.

McKay's Public House (207-288-2002; www.mckayspublichouse.com), 231 Main St. Two floors (with live music upstairs) fill up with dedicated local customers at this year-round place. Farm stand salad, seafood risotto, roasted organic chicken, and a double-cut brined pork chop are possibilities. Entrées $15–18.

Maggie's Restaurant (207-288-9007), 6 Summer St., off Cottage (corner of Bridge). Open June–Oct., Mon.–Sat. 5–9. Maggie O'Neil worked on commercial draggers and sold fish to local restaurants before opening in 1987. Most vegetables and herbs are grown on her farm. Lobster crêpes inspire praise, and a Maine shrimp, cherrystone clam, mussel, and potato stew with chorizo and saffron keeps you warm. Entrées $19–27.

The Reading Room (207-288-3351; www.barharborinn.com), Bar Harbor Inn, Newport Dr. Opened in 1887 as an elite men's club, the horseshoe-shaped formal dining room commands a splendid harbor view; frequent piano music at dinner. Open for all three meals. Dinner entrées range from a Dijon-roasted rack of lamb to lobster pie ($23–37).

✐ **Testa's** (207-288-3327), 53 Main

St. Open 8 AM–10 PM, June–Aug., closing earlier off-season (the family moves to its Palm Beach restaurant Nov.). In Bar Harbor since 1934. Extensive menu, including Italian and seafood specialties. Dinner entrées $16–30. Early-bird and children's menu.

LOBSTER POUNDS Lobster pounds are the best places to eat lobster. The easiest to find are the clutch around the Trenton Bridge on Rt. 3. The **Trenton Bridge Lobster Pound** (207-667-2977), open in-season 8–8, year-round 8–5, has been in George Gascon's family a long time, and the view is great.

♿ **Bar Harbor Lobster Bakes** (207-288-5031), Rt. 3, Hulls Cove, is a twist on the traditional lobster pound. Reservations are a must. Choices are lobster or steak. Watch the lobsters being steamed with your potatoes and corn in the large steel cookers. $32 per person in 2007 includes tip and tax.

Also see **Union River Lobster Pot** under *Eating Out*, as well as *Lobster Pounds* in "The Quiet Side."

EATING OUT

In Bar Harbor

Miguel's Mexican Restaurant (207-288-5117), 51 Rodick St. Open 5–10 nightly. Fajitas, and a crab and avocado salad with Mexican beer hit the spot late one evening. Lively but pleasant; friendly to solo diners.

Lompoc Café (207-288-9392), 36 Rodick St. Open daily 11:30–3 and 5–9:30 for dinner, till 1 for drinks. Billed as the original home of Bar Harbor Real Ale (the Atlantic Brewing Company itself has outgrown its birthplace), this is a congenial oasis with an open knotty-pine dining room, plus porch and terrace tables by a bocce court. Entrée choices include pizzas and salads; live music on weekends.

Rosalie's Pizza (207-288-5666), 46 Cottage St. Locals head for a booth at Rosalie's when they want excellent pizza. Calzones, salads, and baked subs are also served.

Morning Glory Bakery (207-288-3041; www.morningglorybakery.com), 39 Rodick St. Open weekdays 7–7, Sat.–Sun. 8–7. Smoothies, espresso, savory and sweet baked goods, soup, sandwiches. Local meats, produce, and dairy products on the menu; the bacon and fresh eggs are local, Smith Family Farm yogurt, and Sunset Acres Farm goat cheese.

♿ **Poor Boy's Gourmet** (207-288-4148), 300 Main St. Open for dinner from 4:30 nightly. Chef-owner Kathleen Field provides a decent dining experience at reasonable prices. Choices range from vegetarian entrées to a full lobster dinner—including brownie à la mode. Early-bird specials. Wine and beer.

Epi Sub & Pizza (207-288-5853), 8 Cottage St. Open 11–9 June–early Nov., fewer hours off-season, may be closed in winter. Tops for food and value but zero atmosphere. Cafeteria-style salads, freshly baked calzones, pizza, quiche, pasta, and crabmeat rolls.

Café This Way (207-288-4483), 14½ Mount Desert St. Open for breakfast 7–11 Mon.–Sat., 8–1 Sun. The menu ranges from scrambled tofu to steak and includes omelets, eggs Benedict with smoked salmon, and many other appetizing dishes.

Jordan's Restaurant (207-288-3586), 80 Cottage St. Open 4:30 AM–2 PM. Under David Paine's ownership (since 1976), this remains an old-style diner: breakfast all day, specializing in blueberry pancakes and muffins and a wide variety of three-egg omelets. The place to fuel up after watching the sunrise from Cadillac Mountain.

In Ellsworth

Union River Lobster Pot (207-667-5077; www.lobsterpot.com), behind Rooster Brothers at the western edge of Ellsworth. Open daily June–Aug., 11:30–8:30, dinner only until mid-Sept. Brian Langley owns this pleasant riverside restaurant and serves a full menu, including ribs, but the specialty is lobster and seafood cooked four ways. Leave room for pie. Beer and wine, and an eagle overhead.

Calypso (207-667-6554; www.calypsodining.com), 156 Main St. Open 11–9 Mon.–Wed., 11–11 Thur.–Sat., 4–9 Sun. The interior of this diner is the focal point, with big comfortable chairs by the windows. Local produce comes alongside steak, seafood, and vegetarian dishes. Live music on weekends, sushi every Friday.

♿ **Riverside Café** (207-667-7220), 151 Main St. Open 6 AM–3 PM weekdays, 7–3 Sat., 7–2 Sun. for breakfast and lunch in expanded, bright, spacious quarters. Good food and coffees.

In Hulls Cove

Chart Room (207-288-9740), Rt. 3. Open for lunch and dinner. A dependable, family-geared waterside restaurant with seafood specialties; good quiche and Caesar salads.

AFTERNOON TEA **Jordan Pond House** (207-276-3316; www.jordanpond.com), Park Loop Rd., Seal Harbor. Tea on the lawn at the Jordan Pond House (served 11:30–6 mid-July–Aug., till 5:30 early and late in-season) has been de rigueur for island visitors since 1895. The tea comes with freshly baked popovers and homemade ice cream. Reservations suggested.

SNACKS **J. H. Butterfield Co.** (207-288-3386), 152 Main St., Bar Harbor. FANCY FOODS SINCE 1887, the sign says, and John Butterfield preserves the atmosphere of the grocery that once delivered to Bar Harbor's summer mansions. Now featuring Maine specialty foods. Carry sandwiches to a bench on the village green, or to Grant Park overlooking the water. Try the chocolate and lemon cake.

Rooster Brother (207-667-8675; www.roosterbrother.com), Rt. 1, Ellsworth. Just south of the bridge. Gourmet groceries, cheese, fresh-roasted coffee blends, take-out sandwiches.

UNION RIVER LOBSTER POT

Nancy English

✱ Entertainment

MUSIC Bar Harbor Music Festival (207-288-5744, off-season 212-222-1026; www.barharbormusicfestival.org), the Rodick Building, 59 Cottage St., Bar Harbor. Late June–late July. For more than 40 years this annual series has brought up and coming young artists to the island, with opera, jazz, new composers, the Bar Harbor Festival String Orchestra and more. The evening concerts are staged at a variety of sites around town.

Also see *Theater*, below, and *Entertainment* in "The Quiet Side."

FILM Criterion Movie Theater (207-288-3441), Cottage St., Bar Harbor. A vintage-1932, art deco, 891-seat nonprofit performing arts theater, open year-round. Live music and performances as well as first-run and art films nightly. Rainy-day matinées.

Reel Pizza Cinema (207-288-3811), 22 Kennebec Place, Bar Harbor. Pizza and art, foreign, and independent films in a funky setting (beanbag chairs and big sofas). Films at 6 and 8:30 nightly, year-round.

The Grand Auditorium (207-667-9500; www.grandonline.org), Main St., Ellsworth. A classic old theater, restored in 2006. Live performances, musical theater; art and independent films.

Maine Coast Mall Cinemas (207-667-3251), Maine Coast Mall, Rt. 1A, Ellsworth. First-run films.

THEATER See **Acadia Repertory Theatre** in "The Quiet Side" and **Grand Auditorium**, above.

✱ Selective Shopping

ART AND FINE-CRAFTS GALLERIES

Eclipse Gallery (207-288-9048), 12 Mount Desert St., Bar Harbor. Seasonal. A quality gallery specializing in contemporary handblown American glass, ceramics, and fine furniture; also showing metal sculpture.

Island Artisans (207-288-4214; www.islandartisans.com), 99 Main St., Bar Harbor. Open May–Dec. Featuring Maine artists and craftspeople: textiles, pottery, Native American baskets. Glass, silver, and more.

Alone Moose Fine Crafts (207-288-4229), 78 West St., Bar Harbor. A long-established collection of "made in Maine" crafts, specializing in wildlife sculpture in bronze and wood.

Monroe Saltworks (207-667-3349; www.monroesaltworks.com), 150 High St., Ellsworth. This distinctive pottery, which originated in nearby Monroe, now has a wide following around the country.

Rocky Mann Studio Potter and Gallery (207-288-5478), Breakneck Rd., Hulls Cove. Turn off Rt. 3 at the Hulls Cove General Store. In summer open daily 10–5; off-season 11–4, closed Mon. After Christmas by appointment. Rocky Mann's ever-evolving work is worth a trip, with raku and his charming frogs, cranes, and turtles. Paintings and cards by Carol Shutt.

BOOKSTORES Sherman's Bookstore and Stationery (207-288-3161; www.sherman.com), 56 Main St., Bar Harbor. Open 9 AM–10:30 PM in summer, 9–6 daily in winter. A great browsing emporium; really a combination five-and-dime, stationery store, gift shop, and well-stocked bookshop.

Big Chicken Barn Books and

Antiques (207-667-7308; www.bigchickenbarn.com), Rt. 1/3 south of Ellsworth. Open daily year-round; call for hours. Maine's largest used-book store fills the vast innards of a former chicken house. Annegret Cukierski has 120,000 books in stock: hardbacks, paperbacks, magazines, and comics; also used furniture and collectibles.

Also see **Port in a Storm Bookstore** in "The Quiet Side."

✷ Special Events

Throughout the summer: **Band concerts**, Bar Harbor village green (check current listings).

Second Sunday in June: **Working Waterfront Celebration** includes the Blessing of the Fleet.

Mid-June: **Legacy of the Arts**, a week of art and culture with concerts, artists' events, and, at the week's end, **Bar Harbor Chamber of Commerce Art Show**, displaying original work on the Bar Harbor village green (207-288-5103).

July: **Bar Harbor Music Festival** (see *Entertainment*).

July 4 weekend: **Independence Day**—blueberry pancake breakfast, town parade, seafood festival focused on lobster and mussels, and strawberry shortcake. Live music, kids' games, and fireworks from the pier at night. **Native American Festival**—dances and a big sale by the Maine Indian Basketmakers at the College of the Atlantic (207-288-5744).

Late September: **Art in the Park** on the Bar Harbor village green throughout a weekend.

November: **Shopping in your PJs** downtown for extra discounts, with a parade and fashion show at 9 PM, prize for craziest sleepwear.

First weekend of December: **Island Arts Association Holiday Fair** sponsored by YWCA (207-288-5008).

First Friday in December: **Midnight Madness Sale and Village Holidays**, Santa arrives, lights the tree. Discounts from 8 PM to midnight.

THE QUIET SIDE OF MOUNT DESERT

The Quiet Side has come to refer to the longer, thinner arm of land that's divided by Somes Sound from the part of Mount Desert that's home to Bar Harbor, the Acadia National Park visitors center, and Park Loop Road. The name generally also applies to Northeast Harbor.

"Northeast" is a yachting village, with a large marina geared to visiting yacht owners, summer residents, and ferries to the Cranberry Islands. Beyond a brief lineup of boutiques and art galleries, summer mansions trail off along Somes Sound. The village also offers splendid public gardens and a wide choice of ways onto the water. Try to get to Islesford (Little Cranberry Island), and be sure to follow Sargent Drive (rather than Rt. 3/198) along the Sound. The Mount Desert Historical Society in Somesville is well worth a stop. Some of Acadia's best hiking, as well as its best public swimming beach (at Echo Lake) and canoeing (on Long Pond), are found west of Somes Sound.

Southwest Harbor is a boatbuilding center, home of the Hinckley Company, the Rolls-Royce of yacht builders, one of many boatyards in this town that also ranks among Maine's top commercial-fishing harbors. In the neighboring town of Tremont, Bass Harbor is a classic fishing village. It's also the departure point for Swans, a destination in its own right, and several other islands that were once far busier.

Ironically, back in the 1840s Mount Desert's first summer visitors—artists in search of solitude—headed for the Bar Harbor area precisely because it was then far less peopled than the villages on this western side of the island. Much as the Rt. 1 town of Ellsworth is today, Southwest Harbor back then marked the crossroads of Down East Maine, and several island harbors were as busy as any on the mainland today.

GUIDANCE ♿ **Mount Desert Chamber of Commerce** (207-276-5040; www.mountdesertchamber.org), Sea St., Northeast Harbor. A walk-in cottage (with wireless Internet, accessible restrooms, and showers), geared to visitors arriving by water, is open daily June–Sept., 8–5, at the town dock. Pick up a copy of the current *Northeast Harbor Port Directory.*

Southwest Harbor/Tremont Chamber of Commerce (207-244-9264 or 1-800-423-9264; www.acadiachamber.com), 20 Village Green Way, behind the library in the middle of the village. The walk-in info center is open weekdays 9–noon and 1–5; Sat. 9–3, Sun. 10–2.

GETTING THERE *By air and bus:* See *Getting There* in "Bar Harbor."

Note: **Airport & Harbor Car Service** (207-667-5995) meets planes, buses, and boats; serves the entire area.

By boat: Contact the harbormasters in **Northeast Harbor** (207-276-5737) and **Southwest Harbor** (207-244-7913) about transient moorings.

By car: From Ellsworth: Fork right off Rt. 3 as soon as it crosses the Mount Desert narrows; follow Rt. 102/198 to Somesville and Rt. 198 to Northeast Harbor, or Rt. 102 to Southwest Harbor.

THE VIEW FROM LITTLE CRANBERRY ISLAND

amazingmaine.com

GETTING AROUND This is one place in Maine where water transport is still as important as land. **MDI Water Taxi** (207-244-7312) and the ***Delight*** (207-244-5724), an old-style launch, supplement the services out of Northeast and Southwest Harbors listed under *Boat Excursions*, and the **Maine State Ferry Service** (207-244-4353 or 1-800-491-4883) services Swans Island and Frenchboro.

Late June–Columbus Day, the free **Island Explorer Bus Service** (207-

288-4573) stops frequently along the routes from Southwest Harbor to Bernard, up and down both sides of Somes Sound, and into the park and Bar Harbor, connecting with service from Northeast Harbor. Donations welcomed.

amazingmaine.com

ISLESFORD DOCK

✷ To See

In Northeast Harbor

Thuya Garden and **Lodge** (207-276-5130). This is a very special place. Parking is marked on Rt. 3, just east of the junction with Rt. 198. Cross the road and climb the steps with Asticou Terraces, carved in granite beside them. These wind up Asticou Hill, offering a splendid view of Northeast Harbor. Thuya Lodge (open late June into Sept. 10–4:30), a botanic library and a lovely spot to read, is the former home of Joseph Henry Curtis, a landscape architect who began this exquisite system of paths and shelters around 1900 and donated the 140-acre property to the public. It's now maintained by the Mount Desert Land and Garden Preserve to which visitors are asked to donate $3. The two-acre Thuya Garden, behind the lodge, was designed by the Asticou Inn's longtime former innkeeper, Charles Savage, who also designed the 2.3 acre **Asticou Azalea Garden**, (junction of Rt. 3 and Rt. 198), a spectacular show of azaleas and laurels mid-May–mid-June. Stroll down winding paths and over ornamental bridges. Those not wishing to climb the Asticou Terrace steps can take the single road (just past the parking lot) up to the garden and lodge. Also note the 1.4-mile Eliot Mountain Trail behind Thuya Garden, leading up through blueberry bushes to a sweeping view.

Great Harbor Maritime Museum (207-276-5262), 125 Main St. in the Old Firehouse. Open seasonally, Tue.–Sat. 10–5. A collection of model ships, small boats, and historical maritime artifacts from Mount Desert Island, changing exhibits on local boats and boatbuilders.

Petite Plaisance (207-276-3940; petiteplaisance@acadia.net), South Shore Rd. Open mid-June–Aug., 9–4 by appointment. The former home of French author Marguerite Yourcenar has long been a destination for her fans. English translations of her books are available in local bookstores.

ASTICOU AZALEA GARDENS

Kim Grant

In Mount Desert

The tiny white wooden village of Someseville at the head of Somes Sound is a National Historic District; be sure to check out Brookside Cemetery and the Somesville Museum

(207-244-5043; www.mdihistory.org), Rt. 102. Open mid-June into Sept., Tue.–Sat. 1–4 (donation), the Mount Desert Historical Society maintains this lively museum: two tidy buildings, one dating back to 1780, connected by a moon bridge, house many artifacts and photographs of the island's vanished hotels and the shipyards for which this village was once widely known. Inquire about special programs. The MDI Historical Society's headquarters is the vintage 1892 Sound School House Museum, Rt. 3/198 between Somesville and Northeast Harbor, open Memorial Day–Sept., Tue.–Sat. 10–4, housing changing exhibits, a children's program, library, and year-round activities relating to MDI history.

In Southwest Harbor

Wendell Gilley Museum (207-244-7555; www.wendellgilleymuseum.org), Rt. 102. Open May–Dec., 10–4 (10–5 in July and Aug.), daily except Mon.; Fri.–Sun. only in May, Nov., and Dec. $5 adults, $2 ages 5–12. Wendell Gilley was a local plumber who began hand carving birds as a hobby in the 1930s, over more than 50 years carving some 10,000 birds and acquiring a reputation as a master. Friend and patron Steven Rockefeller helped develop this first-rate, handsome museum, housing more than 200 of Gilley's works and changing art exhibits.

The Cranberry Isles (www.cranberryisles.com)

Little Cranberry Island 04646 (www.islesford.com), also known as Islesford, is a 400-acre island 20 minutes offshore. It's exceptionally appealing, both naturally and in the ways visitors can interact with the people who live and summer here. The official "sight-to-see" is the incongruously brick and formal **Islesford Historical Museum** (207-244-9224; open daily mid-June–Sept., 9–12 and 12:30–3:30), built in 1928 with funds raised by Bangor-born, MIT-educated summer resident William Otis Sawtelle to house his fascinating collection of local, historical objects. Acadia National Park maintains the museum (and restrooms), featuring it as part of a ranger-narrated Islesford Historical Cruise. Frankly we prefer to come by mail boat and take our time exploring the island. It's an easy walk up the main road, following signs to Danny and Kate Furnald's **Islesford Artists Gallery** (207-244-3145), specializing in Maine's many excellent island artists. Waterside there's **Winter's Work**, showcasing island-made crafts, and Marian Baker's **Islesford Pottery** (207-244-5686). Next door is **Islesford Dock** restaurant (see *Dining Out*). **Islesford Market** (207-244-7667) is the island's other living room. Pizza and light lunches are available year-round, and island-bred postmistress Joy Sprague sells more stamps per year from her window here than any other post office in Maine, despite the fact that Islesford has just 80 year-round and some 400 summer residents. Requests for Sprague's "Stamps by Mail" come from as far as Fiji, Iceland, and Istanbul—perhaps because with each

In Bass Harbor

Tremont Historical Society (207-244-9753), Shore Rd. near the Swans Island Ferry. Open seasonally Wed. and Sat. 1–4. This 19th-century store is now filled with historic artifacts and photos. Archival records, available by appointment.

In Seal Cove

Seal Cove Auto Museum (207-244-9242; www.sealcoveautomuseum.org), Pretty Marsh Rd. (Rt. 102), between Bass Harbor and Somesville. Open June into Sept., daily 10–5. Squirreled away in a little-trafficked corner of the island across from Cove Pond and Western Mountain, this collection is a real find: more than 100 gleaming antique cars and 30 motorcycles, including the country's largest assemblage of pre-1915 cars—the lifework of a private collector.

ISLANDS **Swans Island** (04685; www.swansisland.org). At the mouth of Blue Hill Bay, 6 miles out of Bass Harbor, with frequent car ferry service (see *Getting Around*), this is a large lobstering and fishing island with a year-round population of 350, a library, a general store (no alcohol), seasonal restaurants, **Quarry Pond** to swim in, and **Fine Sand Beach** to walk. With a bike it's a possible day trip, but be forewarned: The ferry dock is 4 hilly miles from Burnt Coat Harbor, the

order she encloses one of her island photos and a monthly newsletter (her address is USPO, Islesford 04646). Sprague also operates **Joy of Kayaking** (207-244-4309), renting one- and two-person kayaks.

Consider spending the night. Year-round, Franny Jo Bartlett offers three attractive guest rooms sharing a spanking-clean bath ($100) on the second floor of her vintage-1892 **Braided Rugs Inn** (207-244-5943). Rooms are hung with extraordinary turn-of-the-20th-century photos taken by Bartlett's grandfather Fred Morse. Common space includes the big, old-fashioned, sunny kitchen in which Franny Jo serves a full breakfast and dinner (lobster too) on request—and also permits guests to fix their own. Children are welcome, pets possible. At seasonal **Islesford House** (207-244-9309), Evelyn Boxley offers four inviting guest rooms with shared bath; children welcome. $100 includes a full breakfast. To get there see *Boat Excursions*/**Beal & Bunker, Cranberry Cove Boating** and **Great Harbor Tours.**

Great Cranberry is less visitor geared, but the **Seawich Café & Cranberry General Store** (207-244-5336) at the ferry landing offers salads, sandwiches, and daily specials. The evolving **Great Cranberry Historical Society Museum** is 0.7 mile from the dock in the building that also houses the town office, library (with wireless Internet), and school. Open daily mid-June–mid-Sept., it includes an eclectic mix of exhibits. Walk a short way farther to the The **Whale's Rib** (207-244-5153), featuring island-made Lisa Hall Jewelry, also a selection of crafts and art.

picturesque island center with Hockamock Light (built in 1872) at its entrance. Swans works better as an overnight, given its choice of places to stay and the beauty of local hiking trails (check out the new shore path at the light) and of kayaking options.

Swans Island recently gave up two of its three zip codes, but it maintains its historic geographic divisions into Atlantic (where the ferry docks), Minturn (site of the quarry pond and grocery store), and Swans Island Village, which has the Fine Sand Beach and the lighthouse. The island was named for James Swan, its original owner.

Maili Bailey coordinates seasonal property rentals, including cottages, houses, and apartments (**Swans Island Vacations**, 207-526-4350; off-season, 207-474-7370; www.swansislandvacations.com); rentals run $500–1,300 per week. **Harbor Watch Motel** (207-526-4563 or 1-800-532-7928; www.swansisland.com), open year-round at the head of Burnt Coat Harbor, offers four comfortable units, two with a full kitchen ($75–120), and Colleen will pick you up at the ferry. This is also the island's source of kayak and bicycle rentals. Not far from the ferry but off by itself with an ocean view, **Appletree House** (207-526-4438; www.appletreehouse.com) is a classic 1850s house with two upstairs guest rooms; it can be rented in its entirety or by the room ($80–100 with breakfast). Jeannie Joyce offers three rooms, shared bath (**Jeannie's Place**, 207-526-4116), open year-round at Burnt Coat Harbor ($55 double, $45 single). The **Island Bake Shoppe** (207-526-4578), a short walk from the ferry, serving breakfast and lunch, is known for its pastries. **Iverstudio** (207-526-4350) offers weeklong workshops in woodblock printing. **Swans Island Lobster & Marine Museum** (207-526-4423), open mid-June–mid-Sept., displays ships' models, fishing equipment, and photos. The **Swans Island Library** (207-526-4330) has historical displays and sponsors a summer speakers series. The big annual event is the **Sweet Chariot Festival**, usually the first week in August. Folksingers gather from throughout the East, and many members of the **Maine Windjammer Association** sail in to attend.

Frenchboro, 8 miles out of Bass Harbor, is home to 65 year-round residents (up from 38 since 2000), most in Lunts Harbor; two-thirds of the island (nearly 1,000 acres) is preserved by the Maine Coast Heritage Trust as the **Frenchboro Preserve**. A network of hiking trails runs along the shoreline, and the birding is terrific. See *Boat Excursions* for access via the Maine State Ferry and **Island Cruises**. The seasonal **Dockside Deli** (207-334-2902) serves the basics, from veggie wraps to a lobster dinner; the fish chowder is good. The **Frenchboro Historical Society** (207-334-2932), open daily in-season 12:30–5:30, displays old tools, furniture, and local memorabilia, also sells crafted items. *Note:* One day a year (early in August) the island welcomes visitors with a lobster feed, plenty of chicken salad, and pies.

SWAN'S ISLAND

Evie Douglas

SCENIC DRIVES **Sargent Drive**, obviously built for carriages, runs from Northeast Harbor north half a dozen miles right along Somes Sound.

Rt. 102A loop. This isn't the quickest way between Southwest and Bass Harbors, but it's beautiful, following the shore through a section of **Acadia National Park** that includes the **Seawall Campground** (note the oceanside picnic tables) and the **Ship Harbor Nature Trail** down to gorgeous, flat pink rocks. A short ways beyond, be sure to turn onto Lighthouse Road to see **Bass Harbor Light**, a photographer's delight. Continue on into Bass Harbor and Bernard.

✷ To Do

Acadia Ranger Programs. Pick up a copy of *Acadia's Beaver Log* at Seawall Campground (Rt. 102A) if you can't find it in local chambers or shops. The free handout *Acadia Weekly* also lists programs ranging from guided walks and cruises to evening programs. Definitely worth doing.

BICYCLING The network of gravel carriage roads constructed by John D. Rockefeller Jr. in 1915 lends itself particularly well to mountain biking. The fire roads are also good for mountain biking, as is Swans Island. **Southwest Cycle** (207-244-5856 or 1-800-649-5856) in Southwest Harbor rents mountain and touring bicycles, children's bikes, baby seats, car racks, and jog strollers.

BIRDING For special programs led by park naturalists, consult *Acadia's Beaver Log*; also see the **Wendell Gilley Museum** under *To See* in this chapter, *To Do* in "Bar Harbor," and **Island Cruises**, below.

BOAT EXCURSIONS See Cranberry Isles, Swans Island, and Frenchboro under *To See.*

From Bass Harbor

Island Cruises (207-244-5785; www.bassharborcruises.com), Little Island Marine, Bass Harbor. Kim Strauss offers daily (weather-dependent) lunch cruises aboard 40-foot *R. L.Gott* to Frenchboro and around Placentia and Black Islands as well as Great and Little Gott Islands, all depicted in novels by Great Gott native Ruth Moore (1903–89). In *The Weir*, *Speak to the Winds*, and *Spoonhandle*, Moore describes the poignant ebb of life from these islands in the 1930s and 1940s. These are exceptional cruises, given the quality of the historical narration, scenery, and

BASS HARBOR LIGHT

Kim Grant

wildlife: a wide variety of birds, including several bald eagles, and many harbor and gray seals. On Fridays the *R. L.Gott* also serves as the Frenchboro ferry, departing the Maine State Ferry pier at 8 AM and returning at 6 PM, enabling hikers to explore the Frenchboro Preserve.

The car-carrying **Maine State Ferry** (207-244-3254) makes the 40-minute run to Swans Island several times a day, twice weekly to Frenchboro.

From Northeast Harbor: **Beal & Bunker** (207-244-3575) offers year-round mail-boat and ferry service to the Cranberries and Sutton Island. ***Sea Princess Cruises*** (207-276-5352; www.barharborcruises.com) offers seasonal regular cruises with naturalists, including Somes Sound, sunset, and Islesford historical cruises.

From Southwest Harbor: **Cranberry Cove Boating** (207-244-5882) offers frequent service to the Cranberries from both Manset and Southwest. **Great Harbor Tours** (207-244-9160), Clark Point Rd., operates the *Elizabeth T.* mid-May–mid-Oct. to Islesford Dock, two trips per day. **Downeast Friendship Sloop Charters** (207-266-5210; www.sailacadia.com) offers daysails and private charters.

BOAT RENTALS In Southwest Harbor both **Manset Yacht Service** (207-244-4040) and **Mansell Boat Rental Company** (207-244-5625), rent power- and sailboats and offer sail lesson cruises.

CANOEING AND KAYAKING **Long Pond**, the largest lake on any Maine island, has three access points. Boats can be launched at **Echo Lake** on Ike's Point, just off Rt. 102. **Seal Cove Pond** is less used and accessible from fire roads north of Seal Cove. **Bass Harbor Marsh** is another possibility at high tide. Canoe rental sources offer suggestions and directions. **National Park Canoe Rentals** (207-244-5854; www.acadia.net/canoe), on Long Pond near Somesville, offers guided paddles and instruction. Guided half- and full-day paddles are offered by **Maine State Sea Kayak** (207-244-9500; www.mainestatekayak.com), 244 Main St., Southwest Harbor.

GOLF **Causeway Golf Club** (207-244-3780), Fernald Point Rd., Southwest Harbor. Nine-hole waterside course, clubhouse and pull carts, pro shop.

FISHING Deep-sea fishing is offered aboard the party boat ***Masako Queen*** (207-667-1912), departing Beal's Lobster Pier in Southwest Harbor June–Sept.

HIKING The highest mountains on the western side of Somes Sound are Bernard and Mansell, but both summits are wooded. The more popular hikes are up **Acadia Mountain** (3.5 miles round-trip, off Rt. 102) with an east–west summit trail commanding a spectacular view of the sound and islands. Admittedly we have only climbed **Flying Mountain**, a quick hit with a great view, too. The trail begins at the Fernald Cove parking area. Don't miss **Asticou Terraces** (see *To See*) and the **Indian Point Blagden Preserve** (see *Green Space*). **Ship Harbor Nature Trail**, (off Route 102A) winds along the shore and into the woods, with good birding. If a sunny Friday is promised, take advantage of the once-weekly service to Frenchboro (207-244-5785; see *Boat Excursions*) and spend the day hiking in the Frenchboro Preserve.

SAILING **Mansell Boat Rentals** (207-244-5625), Rt. 102A, Manset (near Southwest Harbor), offers sailing lessons; also rents small sailboats. Also check **Hinckley Yacht Charters** (207-244-5008), Southwest Harbor, and **Manset Yacht Service** (207-244-4040) in Manset.

SWIMMING **Echo Lake** offers a beach with a lifeguard, restrooms, and parking (Rt. 102 between Somesville and Southwest Harbor). Another favorite spot is known as "the bluffs" or "the ledges." Park in the Acadia Mountain parking area (about 3 miles south of Somesville on Rt. 102). A short path leads down to the lake.

TENNIS The courts at the Northeast Harbor Marina are open to the public and the Mount Desert Chamber of Commerce (see *Guidance*) offers racquets and balls.

* Green Space

Indian Point Blagden Preserve, a 110-acre Nature Conservancy preserve in the northwestern corner of the island, includes 1,000 feet of shorefront and paths that wander through the woods. It offers a view of Blue Hill Bay and is a tried-and-true seal-watching spot. From Rt. 198 north of Somesville, turn right on Indian Point Rd., bear right at the fork, and look for the entrance; sign in and pick up a map at the caretaker's house.

Seal Cove. An unpublicized waterside park with picnic tables, a beach at low tide, a kayaking put-in. From Rt. 102 turn at the red buoy onto the waterside extension of Seal Cove Rd.

See also **Asticou Terraces**, and Islands in *To See, Hiking*, the Acadia National Park section of this chapter.

* Lodging

INNS AND BED & BREAKFASTS

In Northeast Harbor 04662

Harbourside Inn (207-276-3272; www.harboursideinn.com), P.O Box 178. Open June–Sept. A gracious 1880s shingle-style inn set on four wooded acres, with 11 guest rooms and three suites (two with kitchenette) on three floors, all with phones, private bath; some kitchens. There are also working fireplaces in all the first- and second-floor rooms. This is a very special place, as only an inn with long-term family management can be. Flowers from the garden brighten every guest room. Guests mingle at breakfast over Gerri Sweet's fresh baked blueberry muffins, served on the sunporch. The Asticou Azalea Gardens, extensive woodland walks, shops, and the town landing with its water excursions are all within walking distance. $130–160 for a room; $135–295 for a three-room suite with

TWO GRAND OLD RESORTS

In 1947 many of Bar Harbor's hotels were destroyed by fire, but on the Quiet Side, two Gilded Era resorts survive.

ꝏ **Asticou Inn** (207-276-3344; www.asticou.com), Rt. 3, Northeast Harbor 04662. Mid-May–mid-Oct. The elegant Asticou was built at the head of Northeast Harbor in 1901, replacing an earlier building that burned. Fred Savage, its architect and the son of innkeeper A. C. Savage, also designed many of the shingle-style "cottages" in this area. The hotel continued to prosper under A. C.'s grandson Charles Savage, who also developed the Asticou Azalea Garden (see *To See*). Since the 1960s the hotel has been owned by a consortium of summer residents and business people. It offers fine dining (see *Dining Out*), rooms with water views, public rooms with Oriental rugs and wing chairs by the hearth, and a vast porch overlooking formal gardens. The 48 rooms and suites, all with private bath, are divided among the main house and annexes, which include Cranberry Lodge across the road and the Topsider suites in modern water-view cottages. Lunch is served on the deck overlooking the harbor. Facilities include a cocktail lounge, tennis courts, and a heated swimming pool. In July and Aug., $250–340 EP; from $160 per couple EP off-season.

♿ 🖉 ((↑)) **The Claremont** (207-244-5036 or 1-800-244-5036; www.theclaremonthotel.com), Claremont Rd., Southwest Harbor 04679. Open May–mid-Oct.

kitchen. Inquire about the two-bedroom apartment with a large kitchen, dining area, and working fireplace, available by the week year-round.

🖉 ♿ **The Maison Suisse Inn** (207-276-5223 or 1-800-624-7668; www.maisonsuisse.com), Main St. at Kimball Lane, P.O. Box 1090. Open late May–late Oct. A 19th-century Acadia summer mansion is surrounded by Northeast Harbor's shops and restaurants, but set back behind its garden. All rooms have phone and TV, and three large common rooms are sparely, elegantly furnished, hung with Audubon prints, warmed with fireplaces. High season $175–395, includes breakfast at a café across the street.

Grey Rock Inn (207-276-9360; www.greyrockinn.com), Rt. 3/198. Open mid-May–Oct. An expansive 1910 summer mansion under longtime ownership with seven gracious rooms and a suite, some in-room fireplaces, and property bordering Acadia National Park. $185–375 in high season.

In Southwest Harbor 04679

🖉 ♿ **The Birches** (207-244-5182; www.thebirchesbnb.com), Fernald Point Rd., P.O. Box 178. Open year-round. A very special place. Dick and Rocky Homer's home, built in 1916, commands a water view from its spacious paneled living room and ample grounds, which include a croquet

Gracious but not stuffy, Mount Desert's oldest hotel has the grace and dignity but not the size of a grand hotel. It also has the best views on the island and has benefited from the fact that, since its 1884 opening, there have been just three owners. The McCue family, current owners, have been summering on Mount Desert since 1871. "We didn't expect to make money, just to keep it going and to improve it" is how the late Getrude McCue explained what she and her late husband, Allen, were thinking when they bought the hotel in 1968. All 24 guest rooms have been thoroughly upgraded. All have phone, antiques, and fresh flowers. Wood floors gleam around thick carpets in sitting rooms, the wraparound porch is lined with rockers, and every table in the dining room has a view. Visitors are welcome to lunch at **The Boathouse** (see *Eating Out*), to dine at **Xanthus** (see *Dining Out*), and to attend Thursday-evening lectures (see *Entertainment*). There are large suites in Phillips, Clark, and Cole Cottages, as well as individual cottages, each with living room and fireplace, all with kitchenette. Facilities include tennis on clay courts, two croquet courts, badminton, and water sports; bicycles and rowboats are available. The Croquet Classic in August is the social high point of the season. A room in the hotel is $120–245 B&B; the 12 rooms on the water side are priced slightly higher than those overlooking the tennis courts. Before July 15 and after Labor Day rates drop, and there are childrens' and weekly rates. A 15 percent gratuity is added in the cottages.

court. The three guest rooms (private bath) are furnished in family antiques. $130–140 in high season includes a full breakfast. Inquire about weekly rentals at the five-bedroom Old House.

Cranberry Hill Inn (207-244-5007; www.cranberryhillinn.com), 60 Clark Point Rd. Open mid-May–mid-Oct. This newest addition to Southwest Harbor options is a winner: five rooms, each with private entrance and bath, garden or harbor view, two with Jacuzzi, and all tastefully, cheerfully furnished. We like the feel of the place and the easy hospitality of hosts Patti and Jerry Selig. $110–135 includes a three-course breakfast.

"1" **Lindenwood Inn** (207-244-5335 or 1-800-307-5335; www.lindenwoodinn.com), 118 Clark Point Rd., P.O. Box 1328. This turn-of-the-20th-century sea captain's home set by the harbor among stately linden trees is open all year. Australian-born owner Jim King has a sure decorating touch in the nine rooms (all with private bath), many of which have water views, balcony, and fireplace. The heated pool and hot tub are appreciated after hiking or biking. A full breakfast is served in the paneled dining room, where the fire is lit most mornings. A full bar is also available. $125–295 double in-season, $95–225 in low. The high end is for the penthouse suite, with its own hot tub and a great view; other choices include two housekeeping suites.

"1" **Harbour Cottage Inn and Pier One** (207-244-5738 or 1-888-843-3022; www.harbourcottageinn.com), 9 Dirigo Rd., P.O. Box 258. Don Jalbert and Javier Montesinos have revamped this old landmark to feature creature comforts and romance. The eight standard rooms are equipped with phone, cable TV, and whirlpool bath or steam-sauna shower. The Southwester (sleeping six) and Carriage House (sleeping four), both neighboring cottages, have full kitchens. Five skillfully furnished weekly rental units ($1,260–1,570) with kitchens are clustered by the water, collectively known as Pier One. $117–169 for standard rooms, $145–257 for suites, $135–250 for cottages. Rates include breakfast, snacks, and use of bicycles.

"1" **The Kingsleigh Inn** (207-244-5302; www.kingsleighinn.com), 373 Main St. Open seasonally. The check-in desk is the counter of a large, open kitchen, and the living room has a wood-burning fireplace; wicker chairs fill the wraparound porch. Dana and Greg Moos have added balconies to several rooms to maximize harbor views. We especially like the Chelsea, Abbott, and Hawthorne rooms more than the three-room third-floor suite. $145–195 for rooms, $245–305 for the suite. Breakfast is a production.

♿ **Penury Hall** (207-244-7102; www.penuryhall.com), Main St., P.O. Box 68. Open year-round. An attractive village house with three guest rooms (private bath). This was the first B&B on the island. Toby and Gretchen Strong take their job as hosts seriously. Breakfast includes a choice of eggs Benedict, blueberry pancakes, or a "penurious omelet." $115 May–Oct. also includes modest use of the fridge and laundry facilities, also of the library and music, games (they play backgammon for blood), and sauna.

The Inn at Southwest (207-244-3835; www.innatsouthwest.com), Main St., P.O. Box 593. Open May–Oct. Built in 1884 as a high-Victorian-style annex to a now-vanished hotel. Of the seven guest rooms, all with private bath and named for lighthouses, we particularly like Pemaquid Point, with its chapel-style window and a window seat. There are also a pair of two-room suites. Breakfast might be eggs Florentine. $135–185 per couple in high season; from $105 in shoulder seasons.

In Bass Harbor 04653

Bass Harbor Inn (207-244-5157), P.O. Box 326. Open May–Oct. In an 1870 house with harbor views, within walking distance of village restaurants and the ferry to Swans Island, Barbara and Alan Graff offer seven rooms ranging from doubles with shared baths to a fabulous top-floor studio with kitchenette. One room with half bath has a fireplace, and several have decks. $80–125 in-season, $60–105 off-season, including breakfast.

"1" **Ann's Point Inn & Spa** (207-244-9595, www.annspointinn.com), P.O. Box 398. This secluded, contemporary waterfront home packs some unusual luxuries, like a hot tub, sauna, 32 x 12-foot indoor pool, and two double kayaks, which can be launched from the front lawn. Innkeepers Phil and Lesley DiVirgilio offer four rooms with plenty of space, light, and extras. We like the look of Eagle's Nest, previously an artist's studio. $150–295 depending on room and season, includes a full breakfast.

MOTELS ♿ ✐ **Kimball Terrace Inn** (207-276-3383 or 1-800-454-6225; www.kimballterraceinn.com), 10 Huntington Rd., P.O. Box 1030, Northeast Harbor 04662. Open May–late Oct. A motor inn replacing its predecessor hotel of the same name, this establishment occupies a prime site on the harbor, offering 70 large rooms, 52 with sliding doors opening onto private patios and balconies. Amenities include a full-service restaurant, outdoor pool, and tennis courts. $167–187.

✐ **Harbor View Motel & Cottages** (207-244-5031 or 1-800-538-6463), P.O. Box 701, Southwest Harbor 04679. Open mid-May–mid-Oct. Lorraine and Joe Saunders have owned this 20-unit harborside motel for 40 years. In July and Aug. rooms with decks right on the water are $110–120, while others are $86–90, less in Sept., for solo travelers, and by the week. A third-floor apartment and seven cottages are available in high season by the week ($645–1,075). A continental breakfast is served in the lobby.

Seawall Motel (207-244-3020 or 1-800-248-9250; www.seawallmotel.com), 566 Seawall Rd., Southwest Harbor 04679. Open year-round. Twenty clean, quiet rooms with two queen beds and cable TV, right across the road from the ocean. From $60 in winter to $110 in high season, when rates include continental breakfast.

OTHER LODGING ✐ **Appalachian Mountain Club's Echo Lake Camp** (207-244-3747; www.amcecholakecamp.org), AMC/Echo Lake Camp, Mount Desert 04660. Open late June–Labor Day weekend. Accommodations are platform tents; family-style meals are served in a central hall. There is a rustic library and reading room, and an indoor game room, but more to the point are boats for use on the lake, daily hikes, and evening activities. Reservations should be made on April 1. Rates for the minimum one-week stay (Sat.–Sat.) are inexpensive per person but add up for a family. All meals included.

Dockside Inn (207-244-9144; www.dockside.com), 48 Shore Road, Southwest Harbor 04679. Mid-May–mid-Sept. Six rooms above the Blame It on Rio restaurant (see *Dining Out*) have great water views, two doubles or a king bed, cable, and a fridge; some with kitchenettes. $60–140.

COTTAGES AND EFFICIENCIES Both chambers of commerce listed under *Guidance* keep and publish lists.

✷ Where to Eat

DINING OUT

In the Southwest Harbor area

Red Sky Restaurant (207-244-0476), 14 Clark Point Rd., Southwest Harbor. Open nightly June–Sept. The toast of this restaurant town, a comfortably low-key bistro with food to come back and back for: appetizers like leek and tomato tart with fresh basil and Gruyère cheese, main courses that might include lobster, picked and sautéed with zucchini and baby peas, served over crispy polenta. Ingredients are all as fresh and local as possible; owners Elizabeth and James Lindquist are very much your hosts, and the chef is Adam Bishop. Entrées $19–30.

Xanthus at the Claremont (207-244-5036; www.theclaremonthotel

.com), Clark Point Rd., Southwest Harbor. Open for dinner late June–Columbus Day; lunch at The Boathouse (see *Eating Out*) mid-July–Aug. Also the place for a drink before dinner, with a view that's as spectacular as any on the island from an attractive bar off the dining room. Here most tables have some water view. Both decor and service are traditional, the kind of place it's appropriate (but not required) to dress. In 2007 the chef was Daniel Swimler, and the food was extraordinary. Fresh field greens with thin sliced green apples were dressed with just the right amount of a champagne vinagrette, and the grilled duo of salmon and prawns with fried green tomatoes was perfection; ditto for the pan-crisped duck breast with wild musroom risotto. Plan to come on Thursday and stay for a lecture (see *Entertainment*). Entrées $25–29.

XYZ Restaurant & Gallery (207-244-5221), end of Bennett Lane off Seawall Rd. (Rt. 102A), Manset. Open high season nightly for dinner, varying hours shoulder seasons. Reservations suggested. Janet Strong and Robert Hoyt have acquired an enthusiastic following for their "classical food from the Mexican interior" (*X* is for "Xalapa," *Y* for "Yucatán," and Z for "Zacatecas"). The atmosphere is intimate (just 30 seats) and colorful with Mexican folk art. Entrées change constantly but always include pork and chicken dishes, all $22, including salad. The fresh lime margaritas are legendary. Mexican beer and wine are served.

Café 2 (207-244-4344), 326 Main St., Southwest Harbor. Dinner served Tue.–Sun. 5–9 in-season. Reserve a booth. A vintage car dealership has been transformed into an informal, colorful café with a wide-ranging menu, from pasta to a brace of quail stuffed with lobster. The dinner salads are generous; signature dishes include a seafood pot au feu and sage-rubbed tenderloin of pork. Beer and wine served. Entrées $14–26.

Blame It on Rio (207-244-9144; www.docksidesw.com), 48 Shore Road (by the Manset Town dock). Open seasonally for lunch and dinner except Thursdays. Burgers, salads, and soups (try the pomegranate soup with ground Brazil nuts, chicken stock, cream, and spices) all day. Dinner specialties include a Brazilian feijoada with black beans, linguica, chorizo, kale, and sliced orange. Entrées $16–26.

In Northeast Harbor

Redbird Provisions Restaurant (207-276-3006), 11 Sea St. Open for lunch and dinner June–mid-Oct., Tues.–Sat. in July and August, fewer days in shoulders. A popular newcomer with terrace and inside dining. Begin with roasted butternut squash and apple soup and dine on wild mushroom risotto or seared halibut with braised cabbage, whipped potatoes, and leeks. Entrées $25–34.

Bassa Cocina de Tapeo (207-276-0555; www.bassacocina.com), 3 Old Firehouse Lane. A garden-like setting with the bar set off from the restaurant proper, a wide choice of tapas and drinks, also a menu with a half dozen full entrées such as prociutto tipped fish (of the day) in a pistachio sauce with grilled baby eggplant and couscous. The paella of fresh seafood in a duck sauce gets rave reviews. Entrées $29–33.

Asticou Inn (207-276-3344), Rt. 3. Open for dinner May–mid-Oct., also for lunch and brunch in July and Aug. Grand old hotel atmosphere with water views. Window seats, however, are reserved for longtime guests. Dinner entrées might include lobster ravioli, green tea encrusted salmon, and stuffed Japanese eggplant ($22–35). Reservations required.

Moorings Restaurant & Pier, Shore Rd. beside Hinkley Yachts (207-244-7070). Open seasonally Wed.–Sun. for dinner. This newly resuscitated restaurant has a good reputation and a great view. Entrées $16–28.

ꝏ **Islesford Dock** (207-244-7494), Isleford open mid-June–Labor Day except Mon. for lunch (11–3), Sunday brunch (10–2), and dinner (5-9), another great reason to come to the Cranberry Islands (see box in *To See—Islands*). At lunchtime try to get in before the tour boat. This is also a spectacular place to watch the sun set behind the entire line of Mount Desert's mountains. On weekends, however, it's wise to check on whether the whole place has been reserved for a wedding. Longtime owners Cynthia and Dan Lief grow their herbs and vegetables behind the restaurant and secure most of their seafood and produce within a boat ride of their dock. Try the crabcakes or a whole grilled fish with toasted red pepper, olive vinaigrette, summer vegetables, and mussels. We can vouch for this venue as magical for a wedding reception. Entrées $8–23.

EATING OUT

In Southwest Harbor

Sips (207-244-4550), 4 Clark Point Rd. Open 6:30 AM–10 PM. Almost too good to be true, Sips opens early for fresh brewed coffee, espresso, and full breakfasts, from bagels with homemade spreads to crêpes and Greek omelets. Lunch options include unusual sandwiches and bruschettas as well as salads and seafood. The dinner menu includes crêpes, risotto, vegetarian pastas, and polentas as well as halibut in parchment and black Angus beef. All this plus a pleasant atmosphere and a wine bar. Dinner entrées $10–24.

Little Notch Café (207-244-3357), 340 Main St. Open year-round at 9 for coffee and breads, 8–7 for light meals; closed weekends off-season. The aroma of freshly baked bread is almost impossible to resist. Arthur and Katherine Jacobs specialize in soups and sandwiches like grilled tuna salad with cheddar on wheat; also great pizza. Seating inside and out, take-out.

The Captain's Galley at Beal's Lobster Pier (207-244-3202; www.bealslobsterpier.net), Clark Point Rd. Open daily Memorial Day–Columbus Day, 11–8. The recently expanded dining room on this working pier is all about lobster, crabmeat rolls, chowder, fresh fish specialties, and lobster. This is also a place to buy lobster to ship.

The Boathouse at the Claremont Hotel (207-244-3512), Clark Point Rd. Open July–Aug., serving lunch until 2 PM. This informal dockside facility on the grounds of the island's oldest hotel arguably offers the island's best view, east across the mouth of Somes Sound, with Acadia's mountains rising beyond. Sandwiches, salads, and burgers; also good for drinks at sunset.

Eat-a-Pita (207-244-4344), 326 Main St. Open daily from 8 AM; at dinner this spot turns into Café 2 (see *Dining*

Out). A lively, bright café with soups, salads, and pastas, specialty coffees, and pastries.

Café Drydock (244-5842), 357 Main St. Open daily 11–9:30, Sunday brunch 10–2. Convenient, pleasant, predictable, and dependable. Dinner specialties include shrimp scampi, crabcakes, scallops, and a broiled seafood platter as well as chicken Boursin and steak. Fully licensed. Dinner entrées $15–22, and you can always get a burger.

DuMuro's Top of the Hill Restaurant (207-244-0033), 1 Main St., Rt. 102 north of town. Open seasonally. We have had only good reports about this family-run and -geared place with a very reasonably priced menu ranging from fried chicken and salad plates to mussels marinara.

Westside Grill (207-244-5959), Southwest Food Mart Plaza, Rt. 102 north of the village. Open daily for lunch and dinner. A family find, ideal while using the neighboring Laundromat. Burgers, including "little buckaroos," are a specialty, as are grilled "panini" sandwiches and the salad bar. Grilled fish to Angus steak; senior and children's menu.

In Northeast Harbor

Docksider (207-276-3965), Sea St. Open 11–9. Bigger than it looks, with a no-frills, knotty-pine interior, amazingly efficient, friendly waitresses, passable chowder, and Maine crabcakes; also salads, burgers, clam rolls, and a shore dinner. Wine and beer; lunch all day; early-bird specials 4:30–6.

The Tan Turtle Tavern (207-276-9898), 151 Main St. Open daily year-round for lunch and dinner. The hot spot in this village, a small space (said to be expanding by the 2008 season) with a huge menu and rave reviews. A wide choice of salads, quesadillas, paninis, po-boys, fried baskets, steaks, lobster dishes, and stir fries, plus BBQ, bouillabaisse, and more—at reasonable prices.

The Colonel's Restaurant (207-276-5147), Main St. Open early Apr.–late Oct. Serving breakfast 6:30–11:30, lunch and dinner 11:30–9. A big, informal eatery with some outdoor tables, good for fresh-dough pizzas, burgers, also reasonably priced seafood dinners.

Pine Tree Market (207-276-3335), 121 Main St. Open daily 1–1, Sunday 8–6. Geared to boaters and summer residents, this classic old market prides itself on its meats, wines, and baked goods. Good picnic makings. There's a coin-operated laundry in the cellar.

The Full Belly Deli (207-276-4299), 5 Sea St. A handy source of picnic fixings as you head down to the harbor. Imaginative sandwiches as well as the basics plus baked goods. A few tables.

In Bass Harbor

Thurston's Lobster Pound (207-244-7600), Steamboat Wharf Rd., Bernard. Open Memorial Day–Columbus Day, daily 11–8:30. Weatherproofed, on a working wharf overlooking Bass Harbor and just far enough off the beaten path not to be mobbed. Fresh and tender as lobster can be, plus corn and pie, also seafood stew, sandwiches, and blueberry cheesecake. Wine and beer. All seems well under new ownership (since 2007), except the chowder.

Seafood Ketch (207-244-7463), on Bass Harbor. Open mid-May–mid-Oct., daily 11–9. Longtime ownership by Lisa, Stuart, and Ed Branch has given this place a solid reputation for homemade breads and desserts, and fresh, fresh seafood. On our last visit, however, tables were too tightly packed, service slow, prices substantially up—and table wines over the top. We hope we just hit them on a bad night. Dinner entrées $18-30.

✷ Entertainment

MUSIC **Mount Desert Festival of Chamber Music** (207-276-3988), Neighborhood House, Main St., Northeast Harbor. A series of six concerts presented for more than 37 seasons mid-July–mid-Aug.

See "Bar Harbor" for the Bar Harbor Music Festival.

THEATER **Acadia Repertory Theatre** (207-244-7260), Rt. 102, Somesville. Performances during July and Aug., Tue.–Sun. at 8:15 PM; matinees at 2 on the last Sun. of each run. A regional repertory theater group performs in the Somesville Masonic Hall, usually presenting half a dozen popular plays in the course of the season. Tickets are reasonably priced.

Deck House Restaurant and Cabaret Theatre (207-244-5044; www.deckhouse.com), Great Harbor Marina, Southwest Harbor. June–Sept. A dining/entertainment landmark since 1976. Sitting on and over the water with a stunning view of Great Harbor, this nightly cabaret theater by talented young people has a great reputation. The dining room opens at 6:30, shows begin 7:45. Full bar.

The Claremont Hotel Thursday Evening Lecture Series (207-244-5036), Claremont Rd., Southwest Harbor. July and Aug. An impressive array of authorities speak on a variety of topics (maybe a slide lecture such

Christina Tree

THURSTON'S LOBSTER POUND

as "American Artists at the Seaside"), as well as talks on jazz, mountain climbing, and Mount Desert history. All lectures are at 8:30.

✷ Selective Shopping

In Somesville

Port in a Storm Bookstore (207-244-4114 or 1-800-694-4114; www.portinastormbookstore.com), Rt. 102. Open year-round, Mon.–Sat. 9:30–5:30 and Sun. noon–6. A 19th-century general-store building with water views and two floors of carefully selected books. Specialties include Maine authors and Maine and maritime books, children's and young adult titles. An inviting second-floor space with water views is handy to poetry and books on writing, stationery and cards. Jazz and classical music CDs and cassettes, soft music, reading nooks, coffee. An oasis for book lovers. Frequent readings and book signings. A number of patrons kayak or sail in.

Along Main St. in Northeast Harbor

The quality of the artwork showcased in this small yachting haven is amazing. **The Wingspread Gallery** (207-276-3910) has changing exhibits in the main gallery and a selection by well-established artists. **Redfield Artisans Gallery** (207-276-3609;

www.islandartisans.com) offers a mix of high-end and affordable works. **Moss Gallery** (207-276-4100; www.mossgallery.net), 141 Main Street and **Northeast Fine Art** (207-276-9890) are also worth checking out. **Shaw Contemporary Jewelry** (207-276-5000; www.shawjewelry.com), 100 Main St., open year-round, is an outstanding gallery featuring Sam Shaw's own work. The village anchor stores are the **Kimball Shop** (207-276-3300), an upscale department store geared to summer residents' needs since 1935, as has **Pine Tree Market** (see *Eating Out*). **McGrath's Store** (207-276-5548) Main St., is an old fashioned newspaper/stationery store with some surprises.

In Southwest Harbor
Aylen & Son Fine Jewelry (207-244-7369; www.peteraylen.com), 320 Main St. Open mid-April–Christmas Eve. Peter Aylen fashions gold, silver, pearl, and Maine gemstone jewelry with botanical themes, and Judy Aylen's bead necklaces and work with a variety of stones are also distinctive.

The Sand Castle (207-244-4118), 360 Main St. Open year-round, daily. Creations from and about the ocean and nature by more than 120 Maine artists and craftspeople, 100 more from around the country. Also toys, educational kits, books, videos, music, chimes, and lighthouses.

Carroll Drug Store (207-244-5588), just off Main St. at the north end of the village. A supermarket-sized store with a genuine general-store/five-and-dime feel.

Sawyer's Market (207-244-3315), 344 Main Street. This is a great old grocery store with a good deli counter and good soups on tap.

In Bernard and Seal Cove
E. L. Higgins (207-244-3983; www.antiquewicker.com), Bernard Rd. (the way to Thurston's). Open mid-Apr.–mid-Oct., 10–5 or by appointment. An 1890s schoolhouse filled with Maine's largest stock of antique wicker; also antique furniture and glassware.

Port Side Bookstore (207-244-9114), 30 Steamboat Wharf Rd., is a seasonal branch of Port in a Storm Bookstore in Somesville. It's a short walk from Thurston's (see *Eating Out*).

Seal Cove Pottery and Gallery (207-244-3602), Kelly Town Rd., Seal Cove. Open Apr.–mid-Nov. Ed Davis is a fifth-generation (both sides) MDI native, and this shop with its handsome, functional pottery (glazes are made from scratch) is worth a special trip.

Also see the **Cranberry Isles** sidebar under *To See* for more galleries and studios.

✷ Special Events

July: **Independence Day fireworks** on Somes Sound. **Quietside Festival and Annual Pink Flamingo Canoe Race** at Seal Cove in Tremont (207-244-3713).

Early August: **Sweet Chariot Festival** on Swans Island. **Frenchboro Days** in Frenchboro. **Annual Art Show on the Green**, Southwest Harbor (1-800-423-9264).

September: **Annual MDI Garlic Festival**, Smugglers Den Campground.

Columbus Day weekend: **Octoberfest**—food, crafts, games at Smuggler's Den Campground, Southwest Harbor (1-800-423-9264).

Also see *Entertainment*.

EAST HANCOCK COUNTY

At the junction of Rts. 3 and 1 in Ellsworth, it's Rt. 3 that continues straight ahead and Rt. 1 that angles off, the road less taken. Within a few miles you notice the absence of commercial clutter. Nowhere in Maine does the coast change as abruptly as along this rim of Frenchman Bay.

On the western side is Mount Desert Island with busy Bar Harbor, magnet for everyone from everywhere. The northern and eastern shores are, however, a quiet, curving stretch of coves, tidal bays, and peninsulas, all with views of Acadia's high, rounded mountains. This is an old but quiet resort area with high mountains, hidden lakes, fishing villages, fine inns, and rich cultural life.

In 1889 the Maine Central's Boston & Mount Desert Limited carried passengers in less than eight hours from Boston's North Station to Mount Desert Ferry, the name of the terminal in Hancock. Briefly billed as the fastest train in New England, it connected with ferries to several points on this far side of Frenchman Bay, as well as Bar Harbor. That era's huge old summer hotels are long gone, and only the surviving summer colonies in Sorrento, Grindstone Neck, and Hancock Point evoke the era of steamboats and railroads.

The 27 miles along Frenchman Bay that begin on Rt. 1 at the Hancock/Sullivan bridge and loop around the Schoodic Peninsula to Prospect Harbor are now a National Scenic Byway. Beyond the bridge across the tidal Taunton River, Rt. 1 shadows the bay, offering spectacular views. Be sure to stop at the scenic turnout (the site of a former inn) just before Dunbar's Store.

It's said that on a clear day you can see Katahdin as well as the Acadia peaks from the top of Schoodic Mountain, some 20 miles inland, back up between Sullivan and Franklin and handy to swimming at Donnell Pond. Most travelers who come this far are, however, bound for the Schoodic Point loop around a 2,100-acre headland that's part of Acadia National Park.

"Schoodic" is the name that has come to apply to the entire area along the eastern side of Frenchman Bay. Schoodic Penninsula, however, applies only to the fat finger of land pointing seaward that's now part of the national park—which is really just the tip of what's commonly referred to as the Gouldsboro Peninsula. This larger peninsula is divided between the towns of Winter Harbor and the several villages, including Prospect Harbor and Corea, that comprise the town of Gouldsboro. Sensibly, Louise Dickinson Rich simply titled her 1958 book about this area *The Peninsula*.

At the entrance to the park, Winter Harbor serves the old summer colony on adjacent Grindstone Neck. Until recently it was also home to a U.S. naval base that sent and intercepted coded messages from ships and submarines. Prospect Harbor, at the eastern end of the park, is more of a fishing village, the site of Maine's last sardine-processing plant (Stinson Seafood) and of red-flashing Prospect Harbor Light. Corea, beyond on Sand Cove, is a photogenic fishing village set on pink granite rocks.

Many visitors day-trip to Winter Harbor and Schoodic Point, especially since access has been eased by the seasonal ferry from Bar Harbor. Given the choice of attractive places to stay and to eat, the widely scattered but outstanding art and crafts galleries, the annual arts festival and the hiking, biking, and kayaking possibilities, East Hancock County should loom far larger as a destination in its own right.

GUIDANCE **Schoodic Peninsula Chamber of Commerce** (207-963-7658; www.acadia-schoodic.org), P.O. Box 391, Winter Harbor 04693; request the helpful pamphlet guide.

GETTING THERE *By car:* For a shortcut to Hancock from Bar Harbor, take Rt. 3 north to Rt. 204, posted for Lamoine State Park. Turn left onto Rt. 184, immediately right at the town hall on Pinkham Road, and then left after a mile or so at the sign for Rt. 1 (Mud Creek Rd.).

From points south, see *Getting There* in "Bar Harbor."

By boat: The **Bar Harbor Ferry** (207-288-2984; www.barharborferry.com) offers frequent seasonal service across Frenchman Bay between Bar Harbor and Winter Harbor. There are six round-trips weekdays and five on weekends—but check. Bring a bike.

GETTING AROUND **Island Explorer** (www.exploreacadia.com). In summer months this fabulous, free bus meets the **Bar Harbor Ferry** and makes an hourly circuit from Winter Harbor around Schoodic Point and through Birch and Winter Harbors.

* To See

SCENIC DRIVES **Schoodic Scenic Byway** (see the description in this chapter's introduction). Federal funding has improved signage and turnouts along this breathtakingly beautiful stretch of coast with views back across the bay to Acadia's mountains.

THE VIEW FROM COREA

Christina Tree

Acadia National Park, Schoodic Peninsula. Accessed from Rt. 186 just east of Winter Harbor, this is a one-way, 11.5-mile shore road, 7.2-miles of it within the park. **Frazer Point Picnic Area** (with comfort station) is a good first stop, a place to unload bikes if you want to tour on two wheels. It's said to have been an Indian campsite for thousands of years.

Farther along this stretch note the turnouts with views of the Winter Harbor Light (1856) and across French to Cadillac Mountain.

A little more than 2.5 miles farther along the unmarked, unpaved road up to **Schoodic Head** may or may not be open. Visitors are clearly encouraged to access the long views from this rocky 400-summit via hiking trails (See *Hiking*).

Bear right at the intersection for Schoodic Point (note this portion of the road is two-way). You can pick up a map and hiking advice at the Schoodic Gatehouse (open seasonally, 10–4) at the entrance to the Schoodic Education and Research Center, the site of U.S. Navy base. **Schoodic Point** (plenty of parking) thrusts into the Atlantic and on sunny days tidal pools invite clambering. On stormy days surf and spray can shoot as high as 40 feet, a popular spectacle. That surf can be deadly, so be careful.

Bear right along the drive to the **Blueberry Hill Parking Area** (about a mile beyond Schoodic Point) with its views of Moose and Schoodic Islands and access to most of the area's hiking trails. Continue along the drive 2 more miles to Rt. 186 in the village of Birch Harbor.

✷ To Do

BOAT EXCURSION **Bar Harbor Ferry** (see *Getting There*).

BIKING The 11-and-a-half-mile loop from Winter Harbor around Schoodic Point is a popular bike route. **SeaScape Kayaking** (see *Kayaking*), just off the loop, offers bike rentals.

KAYAKING **Hancock Point Kayak Tours** (207-422-6854; www.hancockpointkayak.com), 58 Point Rd., Hancock. Antonio Blasi offers guided paddling in Frenchman and Taunton bays.

SeaScape Kayaking (207-963-5806; www.seascapekayaking.com), based in Bass Harbor, offers tours and instruction.

GOLF **Grindstone Neck Golf Course** (207-963-7760), Gerrishville. A nine-hole course dating to 1895 as part of this summer colony; open to the public June–Sept.

HIKING **Acadia National Park, Schoodic Penninsula** (*To See*) offers several short hikes, all best accessed from the **Blueberry Hill Parking Area**. The gentle 0.6-mile Alder Trail leads to the steeper 0.6-mile Schoodic Head Trail to the summit of Schoodic Head (440 feet), a vantage point also accessed by the relatively demanding 1.1-mile Anvil Trail. While it's not marked, another popular hike at low tide is out on Little Moose Island. Check the tide and pick up a map at the **Schoodic Gatehouse**.

Schoodic Mountain, off Rt. 183 north of Sullivan, provides one of eastern Maine's most spectacular hikes, with 360-degree views. Maine's Bureau of Parks and Lands (207-287-5936) has improved the parking area and trail system here. Take the first left (it's unpaved) after crossing the railroad tracks on Rt. 183; bear left at the Y and in 0.8 mile bear right to the parking lot. The hike to the top of Schoodic Mountain (1,069 feet) should take around 45 minutes; a marked trail from the summit leads down to sandy **Schoodic Beach** at the southern end of Donnell Pond (good swimming and half a dozen primitive campsites). Return to the parking lot on the old road that's now a footpath (0.5 mile). From the same parking lot, you can also follow a dirt path down to Donnell Pond or hike to the bluffs on **Black Mountain**, a mesmerizingly beautiful hike with summit views north to Tunk Lake and east across Washington County. Another trail descends to Schoodic Beach. This is now part of 14,000 acres known as **Donnell Pond Public Preserved Land**, which also includes Tunk and Spring River Lakes and primitive campsites.

SWIMMING See **Donnell Pond** just above, under *Hiking*. **Tunk Lake** can be accessed from a points off Rt. 183. Ask locally about **Molasses Pond** in Eastbrook.

✱ Lodging

"1" 🐾 ✐ ♿ **Crocker House Country Inn** (207-422-6806 or 1-877-715-6017; www.crockerhouse.com), Hancock Point 04640. Open daily May–Oct., weekends Nov.–New Year's Eve. Billed as "a little out of the way and out of the ordinary," this handsome, shingled inn is midway between the sections of Acadia National Park on Mount Desert and Schoodic Point. Sited at the center of a charming 1880s summer colony, complete with a chapel, tiny post office, an octagonal library, and tennis courts, it's the lone survivor among several once-larger hotels. Since 1980 it's been owned by Richard and Elizabeth Malaby and the welcome is genuine. There are nine antiques-furnished rooms in the inn itself, two in the carriage house, all with private bath and phone, and in addition to the inn's parlor, there's a den with TV (adjoining a room with a hot tub) in the carriage house. The inn is set among flowers and trees but water is a short walk in most directions. $85–165 includes a full breakfast. Moorings are available, and a few touring bikes are kept for guests. The restaurant is a major draw (see *Dining Out*).

🐾 **Le Domaine** (207-422-3395 or 1-800-554-8498; www.ledomaine.com), 1513 Rt. 1, Hancock 04640. Best known for its dining room (see *Dining Out*), this elegant little inn offers three luxurious rooms and suites. Provençal antiques, fabrics, original paintings, and small niceties create real charm and a high comfort level. Bathrooms have a porcelain soaking tub and separate shower as well as a heated towel rack, lighted vanity mirror, and fluffy towels; the suites have a gas fireplace and cathedral ceilings, and all rooms have phone, bed light, and access to the balconies on which you can enjoy the flakiest of croissants with homemade honey and jam and French roast coffee. Pets are accepted for an additional charge. $200 per room, $285 per suite B&B. Add $85 per couple for a complete dinner. Inquire about specials.

The Black Duck (207-963-2689; www.blackduck.com), P.O. Box 39, Corea 04624. Barry Canner and Robert Travers offer their fine old house overlooking one of Maine's most picturesque working harbors. Their four guest rooms and ample common areas are all comfortably, imaginatively furnished with antiques and contemporary art. The sunny dining room is a venue for morning feasts and good conversation. The working harbor is just across the road—unless you happen to be renting one of two housekeeping cottages that sit right on it. You can walk to sand beaches, but the nearby pond is more inviting for swimming. Two dogs will welcome you, so please leave your pets at home. One host can perform weddings. There's a pleasant upstairs room with a harbor view, a first-floor room with deck plus queen and twin beds, a two-bedroom suite, and Harbor Studio (one bed and a kitchenette). $120–145 includes breakfast, Inquire about Harbor Cottage, a weekly rental.

Three Pines B&B (207-460-7595; www.threepinesbandb.com), 274 East Side Road, Hancock 04640. Open year-round. Turn in at this organic farm and follow a private road down through 40 acres of woods and meadow to the edge of Sullivan Harbor. Here Ed and Karen Curtis have built a shingled, timber-frame, passive solar dream house with a separate wing housing two delightful B&B guest rooms, each with a sitting room and water view. Breakfast includes eggs from the farm's chickens, frequently too homegrown vegetables and fruit. Farm animals also include sheep, ducks, and roosters. $85–115 per couple, $15 per extra person.

Acadia View Bed & Breakfast (1-866-963-7457; www.acadiaview.com), 175 US 1, P.O. Box 247, Gouldsboro 04607. Aerospace engineers in a previous life that took them many places, Pat and Jim Close have designed and built this mansion specifically as a B&B. The Great Room, with its wood-burning fireplace, and two of the four guest rooms (private bath) all share splendid views across Frenchman Bay to Acadia. All rooms have private decks with water views. $135–165 includes a full breakfast.

Island View Inn (207-422-3031; www.maineus.com/islandview), 12 Miramar Ave., Sullivan Harbor 04664. Open June–mid-Oct. This is a spacious, gracious, 1880s summer "cottage" with a massive central hearth and airy sitting room set well back from Rt. 1 with splendid views of Frenchman Bay and the mountains on Mount Desert. Evelyn Joost offers four nicely decorated guest rooms, all with private bath and water views. There is a well-equipped guest pantry; a very full breakfast in the dining area overlooking the water is included. $155; $35 per extra person. A canoe and rowboat are available at no charge.

ꝏ ✐ ♿ **Oceanside Meadows Inn** (207-963-5557; www.oceaninn.com), P.O. Box 90, Prospect Harbor 04669. Open May–Oct., off-season by special arrangement. This 200-acre property (a nature preserve) includes an 1860s sea captain's home and neighboring 1820s farmhouse overlooking well-named Sand Cove. Sonja Sundaram and Ben Walter, passionate conservationists who met at an environmental research center in Bermuda, have renovated both houses, with a total of 15 guest rooms, including several suites good for small families. All are within earshot of waves. The farmhouse in particular lends itself to rental as a whole, ideal for family reunions. The meadows and woods are webbed with trails leading to a salt marsh, good for spotting wildlife ranging from moose to eagles. A rehabbed open-timbered barn is the venue for a full schedule of concerts, lectures, and live performances and also works as a conference or wedding reception center. $128–178 for rooms, $178–207 for suites July–Columbus Day weekend, including Sonja's three- to four-course breakfasts. Less in May and June. See *Entertainment* for details about the Oceanside Meadows Institute for the Arts and Sciences.

🐾 ✐ ♿ **Elsa's Inn on the Harbor** (207-963-7571; www.elsasinn.com), 179 Main St., Prospect Harbor 04669. This gabled, mid-1800s house overlooks a working harbor, the last in Maine to retain its sardine cannery. Jeff Alley, a sixth-generation lobsterman, was raised in this house, which is named for his mother. Jeff, his wife Cynthia, daughter Megan Moshier (a veteran of management jobs at hotels from Hawaii to D.C.), and her husband Glenn have together totally renovated the old homestead, creating six bright, spiffy guest rooms with handmade quilts, private baths, and water views, as well as a comfortable living room, veranda, and patio. In all, 16 guests can bed down. $105–155 in high season, from $75 off-season, including a full breakfast that might include crabmeat strata. Lobster bakes ending with blueberry cobbler can be arranged for in-house guests.

🐾 ✐ **Mermaid's Purse Farm** (207-963-7344; www.mermaidspursefarm.com), 50 Lighthouse Point Rd., Prospect Harbor 04669. Open year-round. Penny Altman and Michael Morton are artists, and their rambling 1840s farmhouse is a casual, comfortable haven with six guest rooms fronting on a quarter mile of ocean shore. While in the midst of an unending renovation, the finished rooms are really comfortable and attractive. $125–145 (depending on the season and room), breakfast, with the likes of fresh fruit salad and a mozzarella omelet, included. Two resident sheep dogs welcome canine guests.

🐾 ✐ **Bluff House Inn** (207-963-7805; www.bluffinn.com), 57 Bluff House Road, South Gouldsboro 04607. Open year-round. Mary Moshier is the friendly innkeeper at this modern lodge with a dining room featuring floor-to-ceiling windows and a screened porch overlooking the water and a comfortable sitting area by a stone hearth. The eight guest rooms line the upstairs hall; three have water views. It's set off by itself above the pink granite shore; there's a road down to a beach from which you can launch a kayak onto Frenchman Bay. Inquire about Saturday night lobster dinner and other evening meals. $65–100 varying by the season includes a continental breakfast. A two-bedroom efficiency apartment is $125 per couple.

COTTAGES **Sullivan Harbor Farm** (207-422-3735 or 1-800-422-4014; www.sullivanharborfarm.com), Rt. 1, P.O. Box 96, Sullivan 04664. Three particularly attractive cottages cluster on a nicely sited property with a landscaped pool and a resident host who delights in turning guests on to local hiking, biking, and paddling possibilities. Cupcake, a bright year-round cottage with two working fireplaces, has water views and can sleep six ($1,350 per week; less off-season). Another cottage, Milo, sleeps four adults ($925 per week); Guzzle Cottage ($1,550) is a newly renovated three-bedroom, two-bath 1810 Cape with all conveniences and views across Frenchman Bay. A canoe is available.

Albee's Shoreline Cottages (207-963-2336 or 1-800-963-2336; www.theshorehouse.com), Rt. 186, P.O. Box 70, Prospect Harbor 04669. Open Memorial Day–mid-Oct. The 10 cottages, five directly on the shore, are classic old Maine motor court vintage, but each has been painstakingly rehabbed; all have gas heater, woodstove, or fireplace. Richard Rieth enjoys orienting guests to the best of what's around. $75–114 per night.

Black Duck Properties (207-963-7495; www.blackduck.com) in Corea handles local seasonal rentals.

CAMPGROUND **Ocean Woods Campground** (207-963-7194), P.O. Box 111, Birch Harbor 04613. Open early May–late Oct. Wooded, 70 mostly oceanside campsites, some with hook-ups, some wilderness; hot showers.

✷ Where to Eat

DINING OUT **Le Domaine** (207-422-3395; www.ledomaine.com), Rt. 1, Hancock (9 miles east of Ellsworth). Open for dinner early June–Oct., Tue.–Sun. 6–9, and for Sunday brunch. Reservations recommended. Many summer residents on MDI know the shortcut to Le Domaine (see *Getting There*). Nicole Purlow, the inn's longtime *proprietaire et chef* has retired and the menu has been modified, but her specialties remain. Just 14 tables are nicely spaced in the softly lit dining rooms, decorated in Provençal prints with fresh flowers from the cutting garden and frequently a glowing fire, reflected in gleaming wood and copper. The meal might begin with the legendary *pâté de foie maison* or handmade lobster ravioli. The choice of entrées might include coquilles Saint-Jacques (pan-seared Maine scallops with a roasted tomato beurre blanc), or thin veal escalope lightly breaded, pan seared and served with lemon and capers. The wine list is unusually extensive. The menu is à la carte with appetizers $11.50 and entrées $29–31with "supplements" (gnocchi, potato gratin, or risotto), $7. A prix fixe menu of salad and chicken or salmon with a petite crème brûlée to finish is $35.

Crocker House Country Inn (207-422-6806; www.crockerhouse.com), Hancock Point. Open nightly Apr.–Jan., weekends off-season for dinner, 5:30–9. The main dining room, with its 19th-century leaded-glass windows, is a pleasant setting for reliably fine dining, popular among a wide circle of summer residents. Chef Silas Coffin varies his menu daily to take full advantage of local produce and fish. Staples include Crocker House scallops, sautéed with mushrooms, scallions, garlic, and tomatoes with lemon and wine sauce, and farm-raised semi-boneless roast duckling with Grand Marnier ginger sauce. Entrées $25–31, including fresh bread, salad, starch, and a fresh vegetable. Desserts include homemade ice creams and gelato as well as a sinful Crocker House mousse (layered white and dark chocolate, laced with Myers rum).

Bunkers Wharf (207-963-2244), 260 East Schoodic Dr., Birch Harbor. Open in-season Mon.–Sat. for lunch and dinner; check off-season. Beautifully sited on a small harbor a mile from the park exit, this knotty-pine, many-windowed building offers both patio and fireside tables. Lunch choices include all the seafood staples. The pan-blackened haddock sandwich with greens and roasted red pepper tartar sauce ($8.85) is a real standout. Dinner entrées $11–28. A children's menu is available all day.

Chippers Restaurant (207-422-8238), 193 Main St. (Rt. 1), Hancock. Open year-round for dinner Tue.–Sat. 5–10, Sun. 4–8; Thu.–Sat. off-season. Not much from the road, but inside there's a serious dining atmosphere and menu. All meals begin with a very small bowl of rich haddock chowder. Entrée choices might include roasted salmon or breast of duck ($17.95), Cajun seafood Alfredo ($21.95), and rack of lamb ($24.95).

Fisherman's Inn Restaurant (207-963-5585), 7 Newman St., Winter Harbor. Open Apr.–Oct. for lunch 11:30–2:30; dinner is served year-round 4:30–8:30. Chef-owner Carl Johnson's booth-filled restaurant is pleasant and dependable, with a full menu ranging from pasta to char-grilled filet mignon. Still, seafood is the specialty: lobster several different ways, a Winter Harbor seafood casserole, finnan haddie, haddock stuffed with crabmeat, and crispy cooked salmon fillet with Thai spices. Dinner entrées $17–27 (for the lobster bake).

EATING OUT **Tidal Falls Lobster Restaurant & Take Out** (207-422-6457), 0.7 mile off Rt. 1 (take East Side Rd.), Hancock. Open mid-May–Labor Day, Mon.–Wed. 3–8:30, Thurs.–Sun. 11–8:30. Sited by the reversing falls, home to seals, ospreys, blue herons, and bald eagles, it's now owned by the Frenchman Bay Conservancy. Feast on steamers, lobster, mussels, crabs, and the view. Salads are also served and pork—pulled, ribs, and sausage, all smoked on the premises—is a new specialty. Fish fry every Friday night, 4–8 ($12.95). Another surprise: this is a wireless Internet hotspot. The Captain's Deck, a weatherproofed pavilion, can be reserved. BYOB.

Ruth & Wimpy's Kitchen (207-422-3723), Rt. 1, Hancock. Open year-round. Look for "Wilbur the Lobster." Wimpy Wilbur is a former long-haul truck driver, and this family-run mainstay is decorated with his collection of miniature trucks, license plates, beer bottles, and more. The menu includes burgers and steaks, overstuffed sandwiches, and seafood, including lobster with all the fixings.

Chase's Restaurant (207-963-7171), 193 Main St., Winter Harbor.

Open all year for all three meals. A convenient, local hang-out on Rt. 186 near the entrance to the park. Booths, fried lobsters and clams, good chowder; will pack a picnic.

Mano's Market, (207-422-6500), 1517 Rt. 1, Hancock. Open except Mar., Tue.–Sat. 9–6. Sandwiched between La Domain and Sullivan Harbor Salmon is Adam Bishop's amazing source of sandwiches—with tables on a pleasant deck—as well as dinners to go. Try the chicken salad sandwich with bacon and blue cheese or the hummus melt with fresh veggies, cheese, and avacado. The focaccia is made here and there's a large selection of deli items. For dinner try a naturally raised, local chicken rotisserie or pot pie, or stuffed portobellos. Also a wide selection of wine and cheese.

The Galley (207-422-2059), Rt. 1 on the Sullivan end of the Hancock/Sullivan Bridge. Open year-round for lunch and dinner. In its newest incarnation this handy waystop offers standout crab rolls and -cakes, house-made slaw, rolls, and fries. Deck dining and the promise of a dining room with a water view.

"1" **J. M. Gerrish Market & Café** (207-963-2727), 352 Main St., Winter Harbor. Open July 4–Labor Day, Mon.–Sat. 8–5, Sun. 9–5. No longer the old-fashioned ice cream parlor beloved by generations of the summer community, this is now a coffee bar with ice cream and baked goods; wireless Internet is now its main attraction.

SMOKED SALMON **Sullivan Harbor Salmon** (1-800-422-4014; www.sullivanharborfarm.com), Rt. 1, Hancock Village. Open 9–5 Mon.–Sat.;

Nancy English

RUTH & WIMPY'S

weekdays only off-season. The salmon is carefully chosen, top of the line, and visitors can view the smokehouse through windows in the retail area. Fish are cured in small batches, hand rubbed with a blend of salt and brown sugar, then rinsed in springwater and slowly smoked over a smudge fire of hickory shavings in the traditional Scottish way. No preservatives or additives. Mustards, crackers, breads, and Maine-made items also sold.

Grindstone Neck of Maine (207-963-7347 or 1-800-831-8734; www.grindstoneneck.com), 311 Newman St. (Rt. 186), Winter Harbor. A source of smoked mussels, oysters, scallops, and seafood spreads as well as salmon.

✷ Entertainment

♿ **Schoodic Arts for All** (207-963-2569; www.schoodicarts.org), Hammond Hall, 427 Main St., Winter Harbor. This grassroots nonprofit sponsors music, art, crafts, dance, theater, and film through most of the year. Check the Web site for ongoing events, such as Friday concerts, coffee houses, community theater, and a summer chorus. The **Schoodic Arts Festival**, held the first two weeks in August, is a destination event with dance, theater, visual arts, writing and crafts workshops, and performances staged throughout the area, but otherwise the venue is Hammond Hall, renovated, heated, and handicapped accessible.

Pierre Monteux Memorial Concert Hall (207-422-3931; www.monteuxschool.org), off Rt. 1, Hancock. A series of symphony concerts (Sun. afternoon) and chamber music concerts (Wed. evening) is presented in June and July by faculty and students at the respected Pierre Monteux School for Conductors; inquire about musical events in August.

Oceanside Meadows Institute for the Arts and Sciences (207-963-5557; www.oceaninn.org/omias), Rt. 195, Corea. June–Sept.: a Thursday-evening series of lectures and concerts and other performances—from classical music and light opera to jazz and chamber music—are staged in a renovated, open-beamed barn behind the Oceanside Meadows Inn (see *Lodging*).

✷ Selective Shopping

ART AND FINE CRAFTS GALLERIES

Listed geographically, more or less, heading east along Rt. 1

Gull Rock Pottery (207-422-3990), Eastside Rd. (1.5 miles off Rt. 1), Hancock. Open year-round, Mon.–Sat. 9–5. Tori and Kurt Wray wheel-throw functional blue-and-white stoneware with hand-brushed designs. The studio itself is worth the short detour off Route 1, beyond Tidal Falls (see *Eating Out*). The sculpture garden offers a spectacular view of Frenchman Bay, and seats to enjoy it from. The striking work is by Tori and Kurt's son Russell, who maintains his own **Raven Tree Art Gallery** (207-422-8273; www.raventreegallery.com) nearby at 536 Point Road, Hancock (open Mon.–Sat. 9–5:30) with etchings and sterlng silver as well as sculpture; pottery by Akemi Wray can be found both places.

Barter Family Gallery and Shop (207-422-3190; www.barterfamilygallery.com), 318 Taunton Bay Rd., Sullivan. Open June into Sept., Tues.–Sat. 10–5, or by appointment. Posted from Rt. 1 at Sullivan's common (it's 2.5 miles). "We never get busy here," Priscilla Barter will tell you. Never mind that her husband's paintings hang in museums and fetch big money in the best galleries. This gallery, attached to the small house that Philip Barter built and in which the couple raised seven children, is easily the most colorful in Maine, and still remote enough to keep browsers and buyers to a trickle. Here, added to dozens of distinctive Barter mountains, houses, and harbors, are off-the-wall pieces, wood sculptures, and Barter-made furniture. The gallery also features Matthew Barter's paintings, Priscilla's braided rugs, and Psalm's hand-hooked wall hangings.

Art & Old Things (207-422-3551), 70 Taunton Dr., Sullivan. Open June–Oct., Tues.–Sun. Joe Martell offers an irresistible mishmash of antiques and collectibles plus a first-rate upstairs gallery.

Wildfire Run Quilt Boutique (207-422-3935), 0.7 mile down Taunton Dr. Peg McAloon's quilts, wall hangings, and clothing are well worth a stop.

Lunaform (207-422-0923), marked from Rt. 1 at the Sullivan common. Open year-round, Mon.–Fri. 9–5. Striking handmade, steel-reinforced concrete garden urns (some are huge) as well as pots and planters are made in this former granite quarry.

Also worth a detour

Hog Bay Pottery (207-565-2282; www.hogbay.com), 4 miles north of Rt. 1 on Rt. 200, Franklin. Open year-round. Susanne Grosjean's award-winning rugs and distinctive table- and ovenware by Charles Grosjean.

Spring Woods Gallery (207-442-3007), Rt. 200 (off Rt. 1), Sullivan. Open daily (except Sun.) 10–5. This gallery represents several members of the Breeden family. The adjoining gallery alone is worth a stop.

On the peninsula

Maine Kiln Works (207-963-5819), Rt. 186, West Gouldsboro (0.5 mile off Rt. 1). Over the years Dan and Elizabeth Weaver have come to specialize in distinctive stoneware sinks and towel bars, flameware platters and plates, as well as tableware.

Lee Art Glass Studio (207-963-7280), Rt. 186, 3 miles south of Rt. 1. Open June–Oct., 10–4. It's difficult to describe this fused-glass tableware, which incorporates ground enamels and crocheted doilies or stencils. Wayne Taylor has acquired the secret of creating these distinctive pieces, which he makes and sells in a former post office in South Gouldsboro.

Stave Island Gallery (207-963-2040; www.properclay.com), 636 S. Gouldsboro Rd., (Rt. 186), Gouldsboro. Susan Dickson-Smith hand throws her pottery, from functional tableware to sculptural vases. The gallery also displays her weaving and works of other local craftspeople.

Works of Hand & Winter Harbor Antiques (207-963-7900), Main St., Winter Harbor. Open daily 10–5. This antiques shop and neighboring gallery are set back from the street across from Hammond Hall, and visitors are invited to sit a spell in the flowery garden. The two-floor gallery is well worth a look, presenting the work of more than 50 artists, craftsmen, and a selection of author-signed books.

U.S. Bells and Watering Cove Pottery (207-963-7184; www.usbells.com), 56 East Bay Road (Rt. 186), Prospect Harbor. Open weekdays 9–5, Sat. 9–2, and by appointment. Richard Fisher creates (designs and casts) bells that form musical sculptures, and Liza Fisher creates wood-fired stoneware and porcelain.

SPECIAL SHOPS **Bartlett Maine Estate Winery** (207-546-2408; www.bartlettwinery.com), just off Rt. 1, Gouldsboro. Open for tastings June into October, Tues.–Sat. 10–5 and by appointment. Before Bob and Kathe Bartlett could open Maine's first winery back in 1982, they had to get the law changed. "Prohibition began in Maine," Bob Bartlett will remind you. An architect by training, he designed this low-slung winery sequestered in firs. The wines, which utilize Maine apples, blueberries, raspberries, and honey as well as regional pears and peaches, continue to win top honors in national and international competitions.

Darthia Farm (207-963-7771; www.darthiafarm.com), 51 Darthia Farm Rd. off Rt. 186 (East), Gouldsboro. Open June–Sept. Mon.–Sat. 8–5. A 150-acre organic farm on West Bay with resident sheep, pigs, and turkeys, where much of the farmwork is powered by drafthorses. Cynthia and Bill Thayer's farm stand is justly famed for its vinegars, jams, salsas, and cheeses; Hattie's Shed, a weaving

Christina Tree

HATTIE'S SHED AT DARTHIA FARM

shop also at the farm, features coats, jackets, scarves, shawls, and Cynthia Thayer's well-respected, locally-set novels.

Winter Harbor 5&10 (207-963-7927; www.winterharbor5and10.com), 349 Main St., Winter Harbor. Open daily, year-round. Peter Drinkwater will tell you it isn't easy operating a genuine, old-style five-and-dime these days. While it sells some souvenirs, this is the genuine article with just about everything you come looking for; also the local stop for keys, photo developing, UPS, a copier, fax, and newspapers.

Chapter Two: Corea Rug Hooking Company & Accumulated Books Gallery (207-963-7269), 611 Corea Rd., Prospect Harbor. Open year-round Thurs.–Mon. 11–4. Rosemary's hand-hooked designs and Gary's extraordinary accumulation of books are a winning combination.

✷ Special Events

May: **Annual Trade Day and Benefit Auction**—peninsula-wide yard sales climax with an auction at the Winter Harbor Grammar School.

August: **Sullivan Daze** (*first Saturday*)—an art festival. **Schoodic Arts Festival** (*first two weeks*)—a major event with dozens of nominally priced workshops in a wide variety of arts and many performances at venues scattered throughout the Schoodic Peninsula (www.schoodicarts.org). **Winter Harbor Lobster Festival** (*second Saturday*), Winter Harbor—includes road race, lobster feed, and lobster-boat races.

SCULPTURE AND VIEW AT GULL ROCK POTTERY, HANCOCK

Christina Tree

WASHINGTON COUNTY AND THE QUODDY LOOP

THE ATLANTIC COAST: STEUBEN TO CAMPOBELLO ISLAND (NEW BRUNSWICK)

EASTPORT, COBSCOOK BAY, AND PASSAMAQUODDY BAY

CALAIS AND THE ST. CROIX VALLEY

ST. ANDREWS AND GRAND MANAN (NEW BRUNSWICK)

As Down East as you can get in this country, Washington County is a ruggedly beautiful and lonely land unto itself. Its 700-mile coast harbors some of the most dramatic cliffs and deepest coves—certainly the highest tides—on the eastern U.S. seaboard, but relatively few tourists. Lobster boats and trawlers still outnumber pleasure craft.

Created in 1789 by order of the General Court of Massachusetts, Washington County is as large as the states of Delaware and Rhode Island combined. Yet it's home to less than 34,000 people, widely scattered among fishing villages, logging outposts, Native American reservations, and saltwater farms. Many people (not just some) survive here by raking blueberries in August, making balsam wreaths in winter, and lobstering, clamming, digging sea worms, harvesting sea cucumbers, diving for sea urchins, and "winkling" the remainder of the year. Washington County is the world's largest source of wild blueberries.

A small fraction of Maine's visitors get this far. The only groups you see are scouting for American bald eagles or ospreys in the Moosehorn National Wildlife Refuge; for puffins, auks, and arctic terns on Machias Seal Island; or for whales in the Bay of Fundy. You may also see fishermen angling for landlocked salmon and smallmouth bass in the lakes, and perhaps meet a few people looking to buy some of the most reasonably priced coastal property in Maine.

"For a long time people thought this area would never be developed because it was too far and too foggy," David McDonald, director of Land Protection for the Maine Coast Heritage Trust, has observed. In the late 1980s, however,

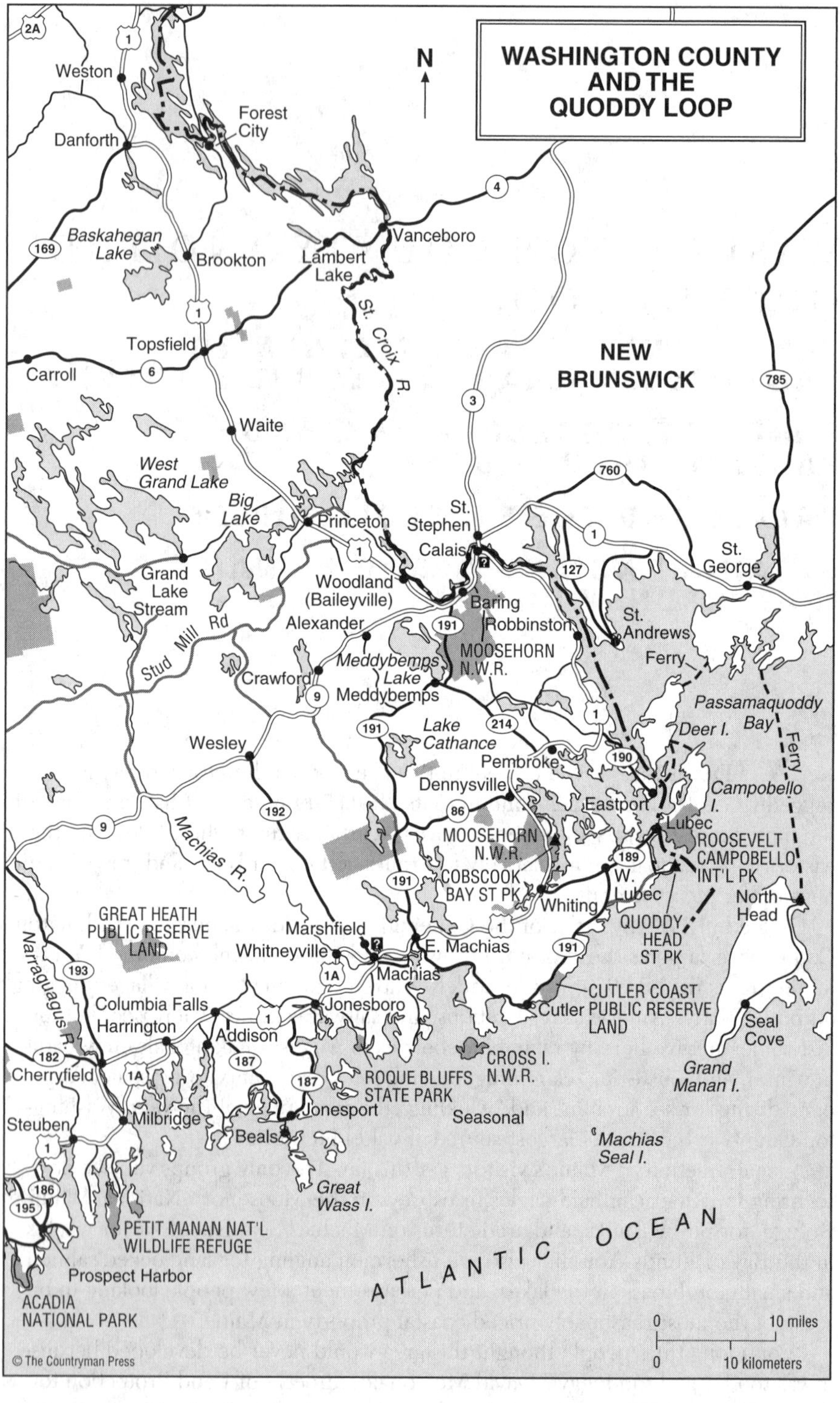
WASHINGTON COUNTY
AND THE
QUODDY LOOP
N
NEW
BRUNSWICK
Weston
Danforth
Forest City
Vanceboro
Baskahegan Lake
Brookton
Lambert Lake
St. Croix R.
Topsfield
Carroll
Waite
West Grand Lake
Big Lake
Princeton
Grand Lake Stream
Stud Mill Rd
Woodland (Baileyville)
Alexander
Crawford
Meddybemps Lake
Meddybemps
St. Stephen
Calais
Baring
Robbinston
MOOSEHORN N.W.R.
St. Andrews
St. George
Ferry
Passamaquoddy Bay
Deer I.
Campobello I.
Lake Cathance
Pembroke
Dennysville
Eastport
Lubec
ROOSEVELT CAMPOBELLO INT'L PK
Wesley
Machias R.
MOOSEHORN N.W.R.
COBSCOOK BAY ST PK
Whiting
W. Lubec
North Head
QUODDY HEAD ST PK
GREAT HEATH PUBLIC RESERVE LAND
Narraguagus R.
Marshfield
Whitneyville
E. Machias
Machias
CUTLER COAST PUBLIC RESERVE LAND
Cutler
Columbia Falls
Harrington
Jonesboro
Addison
Cherryfield
Milbridge
ROQUE BLUFFS STATE PARK
CROSS I. N.W.R.
Seasonal
Seal Cove
Grand Manan I.
Machias Seal I.
Jonesport
Beals
Steuben
Great Wass I.
PETIT MANAN NAT'L WILDLIFE REFUGE
Prospect Harbor
ACADIA NATIONAL PARK
ATLANTIC OCEAN
0 10 miles
0 10 kilometers
© The Countryman Press

developers began acquiring some of the choicest properties, such as Western Head in Cutler and Boot Head to the east.

Cutler fisherman and historian Jasper Cates started a ball rolling, writing letters to the paper, and soon found himself taking Peggy Rockefeller out in his boat to see the "The Bold Coast," this country's easternmost 20 miles, the stretch of dramatically high and wild cliffs between Cutler and West Quoddy Head. In recent decades tens of thousands of acres of shore property, some of the most spectacular in the county, have been acquired by the state and conservation groups; many miles of hiking trails now access remote cliffs and coves. Each public parcel has its own story.

This is former lumbering country. Maine writer Wayne Curtis has noted that it's here that the North Woods meets the shore and "you can set off in search of moose and whales on the same hike." For exploring purposes, Washington County is divided into three distinct regions: (1) the 60-mile stretch of Rt. 1 between Steuben and Lubec (with roughly 10 times as many miles of wandering coastline) and the island of Campobello, N.B., just across the bridge from Lubec; (2) Eastport and Cobscook Bay, the area of the highest tides and an end-of-the-world feel (by water, Lubec and Eastport—respectively the country's easternmost town and city—are less than 3 miles apart, but they're separated by 43 land miles); (3) Calais and the St. Croix Valley, including the lake-splotched backwoods and the fishermen's havens at Grand Lake Stream. In this chapter we also include St. Andrews and Grand Manan, New Brunswick, part of the Quoddy Loop and well worth exploring for anyone who has come this far.

Wherever you explore in Washington County—from the old sardine-canning towns of Eastport and Lubec to the coastal fishing villages of Jonesport and Cutler, and the even smaller villages on the immense inland lakes—you find a Maine you thought had disappeared decades ago. You are surprised by the beauty of old buildings, such as the 18th-century Burnham Tavern in Machias and Ruggles House in Columbia Falls. You learn that the first naval battle of the Revolution was won by Machias men; that some local 18th-century women were buried in rum casks (because they were shipped home that way from the Caribbean); and that pirate Captain Richard Bellamy's loot is believed to be buried somewhere near Machias.

What happened along this particular coastline in prehistoric times has also taken on new interest to scientists studying global warming. Apparently the ice sheet stalled here some 15,300 years ago, evidenced by the region's extensive barrens and number of bogs, eskers, and moraines. A free map/guide to 46 stops on Maine's Ice Age Trail Down East (http://iceagetrail.umaine.edu) is widely available.

Happily, you don't drop off the end of the world beyond Eastport or Campobello Island, even though—since the boundary was drawn across the face of Passamaquoddy Bay—New England maps have included only the Maine shore and Campobello Island in New Brunswick, Canada (linked to Lubec, Maine, by a bridge), and Canadian maps have detailed only New Brunswick. In summer when the ferries are running, the crossing from either Eastport or Campobello to L'Etete, near the resort town of St. Andrews, New Brunswick, is among the most scenic in the East. This circuit, the Quoddy Loop, includes a drive up along the St. Croix River to Calais, and a ferry trip that involves transferring from a small to a larger (free) Canadian ferry on Deer Island in the middle of Passamaquoddy Bay. St. Andrews itself probably offers a greater number and variety of "rooms" and dining than all Washington County combined. We also include the magnificent island of Grand Manan, which lies off Maine's Bold Coast but is part of New Brunswick, accessible from Blacks Harbour not far from St. Andrews.

GUIDANCE **DownEast & Acadia Regional Tourism** (1-888-665-DART; www.downeastacadia.com) is the umbrella tourism organizaton for the area. Also see chambers of commerce listed for specific regions.

The **Maine Tourism Association** maintains a full-service visitors center (207-454-2211) in the **Downeast Heritage Museum**, 39 Union St., Calais. Open July–Oct., daily 8–6, otherwise 9–5:30.

A Quoddy Loop Tour Guide (www.quoddyloop.com) has information and a map of the area from Machias to Calais as well as Campobello Island, Grand Manan, and other communities around Passamaquoddy Bay in Maine and New Brunswick.

Maine's Washington County, Just Off the Beaten Path, a free booklet guide to the county, published annually by Eric Hinson, is available locally or by request from Calais Press Printing Co. (1-800-660-7992).

GETTING THERE *By air:* See "Bar Harbor" and "Bangor Area" for scheduled airline service.

By bus: **Concord Trailways** (1-800-639-331; www.concordtrailways.com) offers the quickest service to Bangor from Augusta, Portland, and Boston while **Vermont Transit** (1-800-451-3292; www.vermonttransit.com) comes via Brunswick, Lewiston, and Waterville. **West's Coastal Connection** (1-800-596-2823; www.westbusservice.com), offers daily, regularly scheduled service year-round between Bangor Airport (stopping at both bus terminals) to Calais, with stops in Machias and Perry, with many flag-down stops (call ahead) in between.

By car: From points south take I-95 to Rt. 295 to I-95 to Bangor. For the westernmost towns take Rt. 1A to Ellsworth, then Rt. 1. For coastal points east of Harrington, you save 9 miles by cutting inland on Rt. 182 from Hancock to Cherryfield but for most easterly points from Bangor, take the Airline Highway (Rt. 9) from which many roads connect to coastal communities. Rt. 9 runs for 100 miles, straight through the blueberry barrens and woods, to Calais.

GETTING AROUND **East Coast Ferries Ltd.** (506-747-2159 or 1-877-747-2159; www.eastcoastferries.nb.ca), based on Deer Island, serves both **Campobello Island** (30 minutes) and **Eastport** (20 minutes). Generally these run every hour from around 9 AM (Atlantic Time, or AT) to around 7 PM (AT), late June–early Sept., but call Stan Lord to check. $15 per car and driver, $3 per passenger (free age 12 and under). The Campobello ferry takes 15 cars, and the Eastport ferry takes eight but gets fewer passengers. "It's not what you usually think of as a ferry," says Velma Lord, about the shape of the two vessels her family operates. *Bay of Fundy* and *Island Hopper* are both tugs with long, hydraulically operated arms linked to barges. Passengers and bikes, cars, and even buses board on ramps lowered to the beach. Once back in deep water the steel arm turns the barge, reversing direction. The Lords go back at least four generations on **Deer Island** (pop. 900), the largest island in Passamaquoddy Bay. It offers lodging and dining but most ferry passengers use it as a stepping stone to the Canadian mainland, accessed from Butler's Point at the opposite end of the island via the free, larger New Brunswick Department of Transportation ferries (506-453-3939). These make the 20-minute run, usually every half hour, from 6 AM–10 PM to **L'Etete**, New Brunswick, handy both to St. Andrews and to Black Harbor (departure point for ferries to Grand Manan). Theoretically the ferry from Campobello to St. Andrews is 100 miles shorter than the drive around the bay, but the two trips may well take the same amount of time. On a beautiful day, however, there's no comparison.

CROSSING THE BORDER Passports are required for reentry to the United States from Canada. For other questions, check: www.DHS.gov or phone U.S. Immigration in Lubec (207-733-4331). Cars are checked more carefully than they were before 9/11. Do *not* bring a radar detector into Canada; they are illegal in the maritime provinces. Also, if you're driving a vehicle other than your own, you must have the owner's written permission, and if you're bringing in a dog or cat for more than a couple of days you must have proof of a rabies vaccination. *Note*: An Immigration official greets arriving ferries in Eastport but there is virtually no line because this is not a commercial crossing.

THE ATLANTIC COAST: STEUBEN TO CAMPOBELLO ISLAND (NEW BRUNSWICK)

GUIDANCE **The Machias Bay Area Chamber of Commerce** (207-255-4402; www.machiaschamber.org). A walk-in information center on Rt. 1 is sequestered between Helen's Restaurant and the Irving station, in the back of the Wall's Appliance building. Open weekdays, 10–3, it's well stocked with brochures and serves the coastal and lake area extending from Jonesboro to Cutler and Whiting.

Cobscook Bay Area Chamber of Commerce (207-733-2201; www.cobscookbay.com) is based at the Puffin Pines Country Gift Store, Rt. 1 in Whiting. Also look for the volunteer-run seasonal information center in the Lubec Historical Society, 135 Main St., a former general store, as you enter town on Rt. 189.

The Campobello Island Tourist Information Center (506-752-7043), just past Canadian customs after crossing the bridge to the island, is open daily May–Columbus Day. New Brunswick tourist information is available from 1-800-561-0123; www.tourismnbcanada.com.

Also see *Guidance* under the Washington County introduction.

✱ To See

Entries are listed geographically, heading east

Steuben, the first town in Washington County, is known as the site of the **Maine Coastal Islands Refuge**. See *Green Space*.

Milbridge (www.millbridge.org). A Rt. 1 town of less than 1,300 residents, with a wandering coastline, is the administrative home Jasper Wyman and Sons, one of one of the oldest wild blueberry processors. The town also supports a Christmas wreath factory and a great little movie theater. **McClellan Park** (207-546-2422), overlooking Narraguagus (pronounced *nair-a-GWAY-gus*) Bay, offers picnic tables, fireplaces, campsites, restrooms, and drinking water. The **Milbridge Historical Museum** (207-546-4471; www.milbridgehistoricalsociety.org), open June–Aug., Sun. 1–4 and by appointment, is a delightful window into this spirited community, with ambitious changing exhibits and displays on past shipyards, canneries, and 19th-century life. **Milbridge Days** in late July has attracted national coverage in recent years; the highlight is a codfish relay.

Cherryfield. A few miles up the Narraguagus River, Cherryfield boasts very early and stately houses (see *Lodging*). The **Cherryfield-Narraguagus Historical Society** (207-546-7979), 88 River Rd., is open July and Aug., Fri. 1–4. Cherryfield (why isn't it called Berryfield?) bills itself Blueberry Capital of Maine; there are two major processing plants in town.

Columbia Falls is an unusually picturesque village with one of Maine's most notable houses at its center: **Ruggles House** (207-483-4637; www.ruggleshouse.org; 0.25 mile off Rt. 1; open June–mid-Oct., Mon.–Sat. for guided tours, 9:30–4:30, Sun. 11–4:30; $5 adults, $2 children 6–12) is a Federal-style mansion built by wealthy lumber dealer Thomas Ruggles in 1818. It is a beauty, with a graceful flying staircase, a fine Palladian window, and superb woodwork. Legend has it that a woodcarver was imprisoned in the house for three years with a penknife, and there is an unmistakably tragic feel to the place. Mr. Ruggles died soon after its completion. The house had fallen into disrepair by the 1920s, and major museums were eyeing its exquisite flying staircase when local pharmacist Mary Chandler, a Ruggles descendant, galvanized local and summer people to save and restore the old place.

Jonesport (pop. roughly 1,400) sits at the tip of a 12-mile-long peninsula facing Moosabec Reach, which is, in turn, spanned by a bridge leading to **Beals Island** (pop. 600). Both communities are all about fishing. Together Jonesport and Beals are home to eastern Maine's largest lobstering fleet, and the bridge is a popular viewing stand for the **July 4 lobster-boat races**. Beals Island, populated largely by Alleys and Beals, is known for the distinctive design of its lobster boats, and it's not hard to find one under construction. Beals is connected, in turn, to **Great Wass Island**, a hiking destination with trails through a 1,579-acre tract maintained by The Nature Conservancy (there's good picnicking on the rocky shore, when you finally reach it). Turn right just before the conservancy parking to visit the **Downeast Institute for Applied Marine Research and Education** (207-497-5769; open to the public year-round, daily 9–4). This recently expanded facility at Black Duck Cove produces millions of seed clams annually for distribution to local clam flats, also thousands of lobsters; old photos depict the history of local clamming.

The village of Jonesport seems small the first time you drive through but grows in dimensions as you slow down. Look closely and you'll find a marina, food, antiques shops, lodging, chandleries, and **puffin trips** to **Machias Seal Island**. Railroad buffs also come to see Buz and Helen Beal's **Maine Central Model Railroad** (call ahead: 207-497-2255), where 380 cars traverse 3,000 feet of tracks that wind through hand-built miniature replicas of local towns and scenery. The Tiffany-style stained-glass windows in the **Congregational church** are a point of local pride. The recently expanded **Peabody Memorial Library** (open Tue., Thu., and Sat., 10–2 and Thu. 6–8) offers wireless Internet, restrooms, exhibits showcasing the work by two dozen local arts, historical exhibits, and computer access to visual and oral histories of over 60,000 residents (present, past, and related). It's also the venue for lectures and concerts. A **Meet the Artists** tour of area studios is usually the first weekend in Aug.

Jonesboro (pop. roughly 600) is represented on Rt. 1 by blueberry barrens, a church, a post office, and (larger than any of these) the White House Restaurant. The beauty of this town, however, is its shoreline, which wanders in and out of points and coves along the tidal Chandler River and Chandler Bay on the way to **Roque Bluffs State Park**, 6 miles south of Rt. 1. A public boat launch with picnic tables is 5 minutes south of Rt. 1; take the Roque Bluffs Rd. but turn right onto Evergreen Point Rd.

Machias (pop. 2,353) is the county seat, an interesting old commercial center with the Machias River running through town and over the Bad Little Falls. **The Burnham Tavern** (207-255-4432; www.burnhamtavern.com), 2 Free St., is open mid-June into Sept., Mon.–Fri. 9–5 and by appointment. A 1770s gambrel-roofed tavern, it's filled with period furnishings and tells the story of British man-of-war *Margaretta*, captured on June 12, 1775, by townspeople sailing the small sloop *Unity*. This was the first naval battle of the American Revolution. Unfortunately, the British retaliated by burning Portland. The **University of Maine at Machias** enrolls some 1,260 students, and its 43-acre campus is just south of downtown. Its art gallery is open weekday afternoons; for special events check: www.umm.maine.edu. There is summer theater and music in Machias, including concerts in the graceful 1836 **Congregational church** (centerpiece of the annual **Wild Blueberry Festival**, the third weekend in August). Also note the picnic tables and suspension bridge at the falls and the many headstones worth pondering in the neighboring cemetery. Early in the 19th century Machias was second only to Bangor among Maine lumber ports. In 1912 the town boasted an opera house, two newspapers, three hotels, and a trot-

JONESPORT

Christina Tree

ting park. Today Main Street (Rt. 1) is pocked with empty storefronts and lots but still offers good places to shop and to eat.

Machiasport (pop. 1,160). Turn down Rt. 92 at Bad Little Falls Park in Machias. This picturesque village includes the **Gates** and **Cooper Houses** (207-255-8461, open July and Aug., Tue.–Fri. 12:30–4:30), Federal-style homes with maritime exhibits and period rooms. **Fort O'Brien** consists of earthen breastworks with cannons and includes the grass-covered remains of the ammunition powder magazine used during the American Revolution and the War of 1812. We recommend that you continue on down this road to the fishing village of Bucks Harbor and on to **Jasper Beach**, so named for the wave-tumbled and polished pebbles of jasper and rhyolite that give it its distinctive color. The road ends with great views and a beach to walk in part of town known as **Starboard**.

Cutler, Little River Light, and **The Bold Coast**. From East Machias, follow Rt. 191 south to this small, photogenic fishing village that's happily shielded from a view of the U.S. Navy communications station's 26 antenna towers (800 to 980 feet tall) that light up red at night and can be seen from much of the county's coast. A portion of this former base is now Beachwood Bay Estates, a housing development with an enterprising general store (see *Selective Shopping*). The vintage 1876 **Little River Lighthouse** (www.lighthousefoundation.org/ALF), set on a 15-acre trail-webbed island at the mouth of the harbor, has been restored through a major volunteer effort and in 2008 opens both for daytime visits and overnight stays in the keeper's house (BYO sleeping bag and food; details at 207-259-3688).

This area was initially about lumbering, not fishing. In 1835 Massachusetts investors built a dam across the upper part of the harbor and a tidal mill to turn spruce into laths and shingles. In the 1850s fires destroyed what was left of the original forest. In 1883 a steamboat wharf was built for the Boston to St. John ferry, and along with it the Hotel Cutler, a truncated version of which survives as Little River Lodge. Cutler (pop. 620) is the departure point for **Bold Coast** coastal excursions and trips to see **puffins** on **Machias Seal Island**, 9.7 miles offshore (see *Birding*). Beyond Cutler, Rt. 191 follows the shoreline through moorlike blueberry and cranberry country, with disappointingly few views from the road but splendid panoramas from the **Bold Coast Trails** (see *Hiking*). In South Trescott bear right onto the Boot Cove road instead of continuing north on Rt. 191 and follow the coast, keeping an eye out for the **Hamilton Cove Preserve**, with a walk to a cobble beach. Continue on to **West Quoddy Light** (see *Lubec*). *Note*: this is at least a day-trip. It's one of the jewels of the entire Maine coast, but requires time to hike and/or get out on the water. Also see *Lodging*.

Lubec (pop. 1,650). The direct route from Machias to **Quoddy Head State Park** (207-733-0911) in South Lubec is via Rt. 1 to the marked Rt. 189 turnoff. The 532-acre park is open mid-May–mid-Oct., sunrise to sunset, with a staffed **visitors center** in the Keepers House (10–4). Displays tell the story of the lighthouse, which dates back to 1858, and of local industries; there's also a gift shop and a gallery with changing art exhibits. Despite its name, the red candy-striped **West Quoddy Head Lighthouse** marks the easternmost tip of the United

States (see Campobello Island for the **East Quoddy Head Lighthouse**). There are benches for those who come to be among the first in the United States to see (fog permitting) the sunrise, a fine view of Grand Manan Island, and a pleasant picnic area. Best of all is the spectacular 2-mile **Coastal Trail** along the cliffs to Carrying Place Cove. Between the cove and the bay, roughly a mile back down the road from the light, is an unusual coastal, raised-plateau bog with dense sphagnum moss and heath.

Christina Tree

WATER STREET, LUBEC

Most visitors just stop to see the lighthouse and then cross the FDR Memorial Bridge to Campobello Island, NB, but there's more to Lubec, from **Water Street,** presently transitioning from sardine cannery row to an interesting lineup of shops, eateries, and galleries, to the many trails (see *Hiking*) that now access some of the most scenic stretches of the town's widely wandering shoreline. The **Lubec Historical Society Museum** (207-733-2274), 135 Main St. (Rte. 189), open seasonally, weekdays 9–3, fills the old Columbian Store and doubles as an information center. It's also base for non-profit Tours of Lubec and Cobscook (1-888-347-9302; www.toursoflubecandcobscook.com), offering local eco- and historic tours, including one of **McCurdy's Smokehouse** on Water St., restored by Lubec Landmarks to evoke the era in which Lubec was home to 20 canneries. Stop by the old town landing with its public boat launch, breakwater, and a view of **Mulholland Point Light** on Campobello Island. The tide rushes in and out through the narrows, and frequently you can see seals playing and fishing in the water. Another light, Lubec Channel Light, better known as **the Sparkplug,** can be viewed from **Stockford Park**, along the water south of the bridge. **SummerKeys** (see *To Do*) offers musical workshops and a series of free Wednesday evening concerts all summer long.

QUODDY LIGHT

Christina Tree

Campobello Island, New Brunswick, is easily accessible from Lubec via the FDR Memorial Bridge. You have to pass through Canadian and U.S. Customs, but there's rarely a wait. Franklin D. Roosevelt's "Beloved Island" (the family summered here for six decades) is 9 miles long with some 3,000 year-round residents living primarily in the fishing villages of Wilson's Beach, Welshpool, and North Road. Granted to Capt.

William Owen in the 1760s, much of the island remained in the family until 1881, when a large part was sold to Boston developers who built three large (long-gone) hotels. Another major real estate development in the 1980s and '90s by the same Arkansas-based company that developed Whitewater (the Clintons were not involved in this one) failed. The International Park aside, Campobello offers whale-watching, golf, some good places to eat and sleep, a (relatively) warm-water beach, and some very good hiking and birding.

✐ **Roosevelt Campobello International Park** (506-752-2922; www.fdr.net), Welshpool, Campobello Island, New Brunswick. Open Memorial Day weekend–mid-Oct., daily 9–5 EDT (10–6 Canadian Atlantic daylight time). This manicured 2,800-acre park with a visitors center and shingled "cottages" is the number one sight to see east of Bar Harbor. The house in which Franklin Delano Roosevelt summered as a boy has disappeared, but the airy 34-room **Roosevelt Cottage**, a wedding gift to Franklin and Eleanor, is sensitively maintained just as the family left it, charged with the spirit of the dynamic man who contracted polio here on August 25, 1921. It's filled with many poignant objects, such as the toy boat FDR carved for his children. During his subsequent stints as governor of New York and then as president of the United States, FDR returned only three times. Neighboring **Hubbard Cottage**, with its oval picture window, gives another slant on this turn-of-the-20th-century resort. There's a visitors center here with an excellent historical exhibit and a 15-minute introductory film. Beyond stretch more than 8 miles of trails to the shore and then inland through woods to lakes and ponds. There are also 15.4 miles of park drives, modified from the network of carriage drives that the wealthy "cottagers" maintained on the island. **East Quoddy Head Lighthouse** is beyond the park, accessible at low tide, a popular whale-watching station but a real adventure to get to (attempt only if you are physically fit).

THE BRIDGE TO CAMPOBELLO ISLAND
Christina Tree

✱ To Do

AIR RIDES **Chickadee Air** (207-255-4193), South Machias. Scenic flights from the Machias Valley in a Cessna 172 (up to three passengers), $25 per person for a 15-minute flight.

BIKING See *Boating and Paddling*.

BOATING AND PADDLING **Roberston Sea Tours Adventures** (207-483-6110; www.robertsonseatours.com) offers a variety of cruises from the Milbridge Marina on the 30-foot lobster boat *Mairi Leigh*, focusing on the 50 miles of coast west to Schoodic.

Downeast Charter Cruises (207-483-4392), South Addison Town Landing. Capt. Paul Ferriero offers coastal tours on his 34-foot lobster boat, the *Honey B.* Six people max, $50 per person; $150 minimum.

Machias River & Bay Boat Tours (207-598-5002), Machias public landing (next to Helen's Restaurant). Capt. Don Green offers seasonal two-and-a-half–three hour tours aboard the 50-foot *Miss T.C.*

Capt. Laura Fish (207-497-3064), Kelley Point Rd., Jonesport. Mid-June–mid-Aug. (weather permitting), the 23-foot *Aaron Thomas*, named for Jonesport's first settler—from whom the captain and first mate are descended—offers three-hour cruises around the islands, lighthouses, and beaches; also a walk around **Mistake Island**, site of 72-foot-high Moosepeak (pronounced *MOOSE-a-peak*) Light. Inquire about deep-sea scuba diving.

Sunrise County Canoe and Kayak (207-255-3375; www.sunrisecanoeandkayak.com), based just off Rt.1 in Machias behind Rae's Restaurant. Rob and Jen Scribner offer kayak rentals and guided tours out in Machias Bay to see the Indian petroglyphs on several private islands. Half-day trips are $48; 24-speed **bicycles** are $15 per day. Shuttles and logistical support for private parties also offered.

For rigorous spring Whitewater Weekends or weeks with wilderness camping, contact Bangor-based Martin Brown at **Sunrise Expedtions International** (www.sunrise-exp.com).

Also see **East Coast Ferries Ltd.** under *Getting Around*; **Bold Coast Charter Co.**, and **Norton of Jonesport** under *Birding*

FISHING Sea-run Atlantic salmon, long the draw for fishermen to the Narraguagus and Machias Rivers, are currently illegal to catch and will be until stocks have been replenished. **Landlocked salmon** are, however, still fair game and can be found in **Schoodic Lake** (8 miles north of Cherryfield), **Bog Lake** in Northfield on Rt. 192 (10 miles north of Machias), **Gardner Lake** in East Machias (look for the new boat ramp and parking area), and **Cathance Lake** on Rt. 191 (some 18 miles north of East Machias with a nice boat landing). Trolling lures, streamer flies, or bait from a boat is the most popular way to catch landlocked salmon.

Brook trout can be caught in May and June in local rivers and streams, but in warm weather they move to deeper water like **Six Mile Lake** in Marshfield (6 miles north of Machias on Rt. 192), Indian Lake along Rt. 1 in Whiting, and **Lily Lake** in Trescott. **Brown trout** are found in **Simpson Pond** in Roque Bluffs (park in Roque Bluffs State Park), as well as in the lakes listed above. **Gregg Burr** (207-255-4210) is an experienced local fishing guide.

CAMPOBELLO ISLAND

Joyce Morell

PUFFIN WATCHING AND OTHER BIRDING This region is said to have every northern forest habitat, from thick stands of boreal softwood to marsh and bog wetlands, clam flats, rocky cliffs, meadows, and blueberry barrens. Thinly populated, it also has two national wildlife refuges and is home or a migratory stop for hundreds of species, many now rare (see www.maine birdingtrail.com/Downeast).The **Annual Down East Spring Birding Festival**, Memorial Day Weekend (www.downeastbirdfest.org), with an associated Elderhostel program, is growing year by year and more than 171 species of birds are usually spotted. By far the area's most famous bird is the puffin, and the place to see it is **Machias Seal Island**, 9.7 miles off Cutler.

Puffins are alcids, sea birds that come to land only to rest. Just about 12 inches tall, these colorful "sea parrots" converge in spring on 15-acre Machias Seal, a rodent-free outcropping of rocks with crevices seemingly designed for birds to lay and nurture eggs. On the June day we visited, Capt. Andy Patterson estimated it was home to 3,000 pairs of nesting puffins, 2,000 pairs of razorbills, 300 arctic terns, and 800 common murres. Visitors are strictly limited to formal groups and herded into blinds, which tend to be surrounded by birds. It's an unforgettable sight—and sound (a chorus of puffins sounds just like a chain saw). The birds are pretty much gone by late August. Although it's just 9 miles off Cutler, Canada maintains and staffs a lighthouse station as well as the wildlife refuge. Reservations are usually required well ahead of time with any of the three outfits with landing permits for the island.

Christina Tree
PUFFINS

Bold Coast Charter Company (207-259-4484; www.boldcoast.com) is based in Cutler. Capt. Andrew Patterson offers daily five-hour puffin-watching trips (weather permitting) May–Aug. Capt. Andy also uses his partially

Saltwater and tidewater fishing is usually for striped bass or mackerel. For information about licenses, guides, and fish, check with the regional headquarters of the **Inland Fisheries and Wildlife Department** in Jonesboro.

GOLF **Great Cove Golf Course** (207-434-7200), 387 Great Cove Rd., Roque Bluffs, offers nine holes, water views, a clubhouse, rental clubs, and carts.

enclosed 40-foot passenger vessel *Barbara Frost* to cruise the Bold Coast, the stretch of high, rocky bluffs east of Cutler. $80 per person for the Machias Island Landing Tour. Tours that circle the island without landing are $80 per adult, $45 per child.

Norton of Jonesport (207-497-5933; www.machiassealisland.com). Capt. Barna B. Norton pioneered bird-watching cruises to Machias Seal, beginning in the late 1940s and furthermore refused to concede the island to Canada. He insisted that it was not formally mentioned in the 1814 Treaty of Ghent that set the international boundaries in this area and was claimed by his grandfather (Tall Barney Beal) in 1865. His son, Capt. John E. Norton, continues to offer birding trips to the island in *Chief*, getting you there in 20 minutes. ($100 per person).

See also **Sea Watch Tours** in "Grand Manan."

For any of these trips come prepared with windbreakers, hats, and mittens for the early morning ride out, usually in fog.

CAPTAIN ANDY ABOARD THE *BARBARA FROST*

Bold Coast Charters

Barren View Golf Course (207-434-7651), Rt. 1, Jonesboro. This new course offers nine holes with views of the blueberry barrens and boasts Maine's largest sand trap. Facilities include a clubhouse plus rental carts and clubs.

Herring Cove Golf Course (506-752-2449), in the Herring Cove Provincial Park (open mid-May–mid-Nov.), has nine holes, a clubhouse restaurant, and rentals.

HIKING Within the past 15 years the number of coastal hiking options has increased dramatically. (See *Green Space*.)

HORSEBACK RIDING **Lucky Star Stables** (207-255-6124), Rim Rd., East Machias. Kellie and Brenda Ramsdell offer ocean-view trail rides as well as lessons.

PICNICKING **McClellan Park**, in Milbridge, 5 miles south of town at Baldwin's Head, overlooks the Atlantic and Narraguagus Bay (from Rt. 1, follow Wyman Road to the park gates). A town park on 10.5 acres donated in 1926 by George McClellan, a one-time mayor of New York City. There's no charge for walking or picnicking.

Roosevelt Campobello International Park's large natural area on Campobello Island, **Quoddy Head State Park** in Lubec, and **Roque Bluffs State Park** also all have picnic areas.

SPECIAL LEARNING PROGRAM (ADULT) **SummerKeys** (207-733-2316; in winter, 973-316-6220; www.summerkeys.com), 6 Bayview St., Lubec. Mid-June–Labor Day. New York piano teacher Bruce Potterton offers weeklong programs for a variety of instruments, but especially piano for beginners to advanced students. Lodging is at local B&Bs.

Elderhostel programs on varied subjects are held on Campobello Island (www.elderhostel.org).

Sunrise Senior College (207-255-2384), an all-volunteer program with widely varied courses, is held at the University of Maine at Machias (www.umm.maine.edu).

LOW TIDE LEAVES LOBSTER BOATS HIGH AND DRY

Christina Tree

SWIMMING ✐ **Roque Bluffs State Park**, Roque Bluffs (6 miles off Rt. 1). The pebble beach on the ocean is frequently windy, but a sheltered sand beach on a freshwater pond is good for children—though the water is cold. Tables, grills, changing areas with vault toilets, and a playground.

Sandy River Beach in Jonesport (off Rt. 187) is a rare white sand beach marked by a small sign, but the water is frigid. On Beals Island the **Backfield Area**, Alley's Bay, offers equally bracing saltwater swimming.

Gardner Lake, Chases Mills Rd., East Machias, offers freshwater swimming, a picnic area, and a boat launch. **Six Mile Lake**, Rt. 192, in Marshfield (north of Machias), is good for a dip.

Campobello Memorial Aquatic Park, Welshpool, Campobello Island. Changing rooms, toilets; this is landlocked saltwater swimming, so it's relatively warm.

WHALE-WATCHING The unusually high tides in the Bay of Fundy seem to foster ideal feeding grounds for right, minke, and humpback whales and for porpoises and dolphins. East Quoddy Head on Campobello and Quoddy Head State Park in Lubec are favored viewing spots. The commercial excursion boats, both based on Campobello Island, are **Captain Riddle's Sea Going Adventures** (1-877-346-2225) and **Island Cruise Whale Watching Tours** (506-752-2213 or 1-888-249-4400).

✷ Green Space

Entries are listed geographically, heading east, and are continued under Green Space in the next two subchapters.

Pigeon Hill and Petit Manan. from Rt. 1 in **Steuben** turn on Pigeon Hill Rd. and after some 5 miles, look for a small graveyard on your left. Stop. The well-trod path up **Pigeon Hill** begins across the road. The climb is fairly steep in places, but it's nonetheless a pleasant 20-minute hike, and the view from the summit reveals the series of island-filled bays that stretch away to the east, as well as mountains inland. Drive another mile down Pigeon Hill Rd. and past the sign announcing that you have entered a 2,166-acre preserve, part of **Maine Coastal Islands Refuge** (www.fws.gov/northeast/mainecoastal), which includes two other parcels and 47 offshore islands. There are two loop trails, and you can drive to the parking lot for the second. This is a varied area with pine stands, cedar swamps, blueberry barrens, marshes, and great birding (more than 250 species have been identified here). Maps are posted at the parking lots. A 0.5-mile shore path hugs the woods and coastline. For details about the entire refuge, contact the main refuge headquarters in Milbridge (207-546-2124).

HIKING THE BOLD COAST

Christina Tree

Great Wass Island. The Maine

chapter of The Nature Conservancy owns this 1,579-acre tract at the southern tip of the Jonesport-Addison peninsula. Trail maps are posted at the parking lot (simply follow the island's main road to its logical end). The interior of the island supports one of Maine's largest stands of jack pine and is a quite beautiful mix of lichen-covered open ledge, wooded path, and coastal peatland. Roughly a third of the 5-mile loop is along the shore. Little Cape Point is a great picnic spot. Wear rubber-soled shoes.

Western Head, off Rt. 191, 11 miles south of East Machias, is maintained by the Maine Coast Heritage Trust, Brunswick (207-276-5156). Take the first right after the Baptist church onto Destiny Bay Rd. and follow it to the sign. The 3- to 4-mile loop trail is through mixed-growth woods and spruce to the shore, with views of the entrance to Cutler Harbor and high ledges with crashing surf, large expanses of open ocean, as well as the high, sheer ledges of Grand Manan to the northeast and Machias Seal Island to the southeast.

Bold Coast Trails. Look for the trailhead marked CUTLER COAST UNIT TRAILS some 4 miles east of Cutler Harbor on Rt. 191. Maine's Bureau of Parks and Lands (207-287-4920) has constructed inner and outer loop trails (one 5 miles, one 10 miles) from the road to the rugged cliffs and along the shore overlooking Grand Manan Channel. The Coastal Trail begins in deep spruce-fir forest, bridges a cedar swamp, and 1.5 miles from the parking lot climbs out of the woods and onto a promontory, continuing to rise and dip along the cliffs to Black Point Cove, a cobble beach. (*Note:* The cliffs are high and sheer, not good for children or shaky adults.) Bring a picnic and allow at least five hours. The trail continues from Black Point Cove to Fairy Head, site of three primitive campsites.

The **Quoddy Regional Land Trust** (207-733-5509; www.qrlt.org), with the help of the Maine Coast Heritage Trust, publishes a thick, ever-expanding booklet titled *Cobscook Trails: A Guide to Walking Opportunities Around Cobscook Bay and the Bold Coast*. It's available locally and from the trust. Descriptions include trails in Lubec to **Morong Cove**, **Mowry Beach** to **Horan Head**, and trails in the **Pike Lands**, in the **Hamilton Cove Preserve** and the **Boot Head Preserve,** and to **Comissary Point** in Trescott.

Quoddy Head State Park, Lubec (follow signs from Rt. 189). The candy-striped lighthouse and visitors center (*To See*) are as far as most people come, but the Coastal Trail, along the cliffs, is one of the most dramatic in Maine,. The views from the trail and from well-placed benches are back to the lighthouse, down the coast, and across to the sheer cliffs of Grand Manan 7 miles offshore. Bring a picnic.

Roosevelt Campobello International Park. At the tourist information center, pick up a trail map. We recommend the trail from Southern Head to the Duck Ponds. Seals frequently sun on the ledges off Lower Duck Pond, and loons are often seen off Liberty Point. Along this dramatic shoreline at the southern end of the island, also look for whales July–Sept.

Herring Cove Provincial Park on Campobello Island offers rewarding hiking trails.

East Quoddy Head Lighthouse, also officially known as Head Harbour Light

Station, is sited at the far northern end of Campobello Island. Very photogenic, a prime whale-watching spot, but accessible only from the parking area at low tide, and a demanding hike.

Lodging

INNS AND BED & BREAKFASTS

Entries are listed geographically, heading east

The Englishman's Bed and Breakfast (207-546-2337; www.englishmansbandb.com), 122 Main St., Cherryfield 04622. This is a beautifully restored four-square 1793 Federal-style mansion (on the National Register) set above the Narragaugus River, with a wide back deck and screened gazebo. Kathy and Peter Winham offer two guest rooms (private bath) in the house itself and a delightful "guest house" unit with a fridge and hot plate. A full breakfast is served by the 18th-century hearth in the dining room. Teas and cream teas are also served, and the Winhams sell and mail order their own high-quality selection. $95 for either room, $155 for both; $115 for the guest house.

Ricker House (207-546-2780), 49 Parker St., Cherryfield 04622. Open May–Nov. A classic Federal house built in 1803 (it's on the National Register) with a double parlor and furnished comfortably with plenty of books, a big kitchen, and an inviting screened-in porch overlooking the river. Two guest rooms with river views, nicely furnished with antiques and old quilts, share a bath. Jean Conway is delighted to help guests explore the area; bicycles and canoe are available to guests. $75 per couple, $65 single ($10 per extra person), includes a full breakfast.

The Guagus River Inn (207-546-9737; www.guagusriverinn.com), 376 Kansas Rd., Milbridge 04658. Billy and Jackie Majors' contemporary house has a hot tub and small indoor lap pool and overlooks the Narraguagus River. Five of the six rooms are rented at any one time (there are five baths), and they are themed: Deer, Fish, Bear, et cetera. All are inviting, but the easy winner is Moose suite, with its big log bed and stained glass above the Jacuzzi. In-season rooms are $70–75; the Moose $150, with a two-night minimum—but that, too, goes down to $120 off-season. A one-bedroom apartment is $450 per week. Set in meadows, the B&B is 1.8 miles up a quiet road from Rt. 1A and the shore.

Pleasant Bay Bed & Breakfast (207-483-4490; www.pleasantbay.com), 386 West Side Rd., P.O. Box 222, Addison 04606. Open year-round. After raising six children and a number of llamas in New Hampshire, Leon and Joan Yeaton returned to Joan's girlhood turf, cleared this land, and built this gracious house with many windows and a deck and porch overlooking the tidal Pleasant River. A living room is well stocked with puzzles and books for foggy days; there's a hammock down by the river for pleasant weather. This is a working llama farm, and guests can meander the wooded trails down to the bay with or without their companionship. The four upstairs guest rooms with views include one family-sized room with private bath and a lovely two-room suite with a living room, kitchenette, and deck overlooking the water. There are moorings for guests arriving by water. $50–85 per couple ($10 per child) and $135 for the suite includes, if you're lucky, Joan's popover/pancake. $15 charge for llama walks.

"1" **Harbor House on Sawyer Cove** (207-497-5417; www.harborhs.com), 27 Sawyer Square, P.O. Box 468, Jonesport 04649. Open year-round. Maureen and Gene Hart have transformed this handsome 1880s house, which at one time included a telegraph office, general store, ship's chandlery, and art gallery, into an attractive B&B and antiques store. Two unusually large, attractive upstairs guest rooms, one with a queen and the other with a king, each have several windows overlooking the marina and harbor as well as a spacious sitting area, cable TV, and private bath. The Harts work hard to make guests not only comfortable, but aware of where they are, sharing their views, bountiful breakfasts (served on the harborside porch), and sense of discovery. $125 in-season, $100 off; weekly rates.

Moose-A-Bec Manor (207-497-2121; www.mooseabecmanor.com), Old House Point, P.O. Box 557, Jonesport 04659. Open year-round for weekly rentals. Charlie and Abby Alley have renovated an 1875 waterside house that's been in Abby's family for generations, turning it into two large waterside apartments, each with two bedrooms plus a sleeper-sofa and full kitchen, including dishwasher, washer-dryer, and cable TV. Views are of Moosabec Reach. $100–125 per night includes linens.

Chandler River Lodge (207-434-2540), 654 Rt. 1, Jonesboro 04648. Open year-round, this comfortable old house welcomed guests in decades past and it's nice to see it restored. Set back in its grounds from Rt. 1, there are four rooms, one with a king-sized bed and spa bath, the others with queens and private bath, although one is down the hall. $100–175 in-season includes a continental breakfast. From $75 off-season. There's no common space, as the first floor is a restaurant (see *Dining Out*).

"1" **Broadway Inn Bed and Breakfast** (207-255-8551; www.broadwayinn.us), 14 Broadway St., Machias 04654. This spacious 1888 home, an inn in the 1920s, has been nicely restored by the Hahn family. Each of the six rooms is named for a Maine author and each is furnished with a writing desk. Edith Wharton has a private bath, but Sarah Orne Jewett, Robert Frost, Robert McCloskey, and Elisabeth Olgive all have shared baths; Henry Wadsworth's shared bath is downstairs. All rooms are nicely decorated in antiques, and there's plenty of comfortable common space as well as an inviting porch. $105–125 includes a full breakfast.

The Blue Butterfly (207-255-0115), 9 Pleasant St., Machias 04654. Liz Flauver's informal, comfortable 1850s downtown house offers two rooms with shared bath. $85–125 per couple includes a full breakfast.

"1" **The Inn at Schoppee Farm** (207-255-4648; www.schoppeefarm.com), RR 1, Box 314, Machias 04654. David and Julie Barker are Machias natives and have spent much of their lives away but returned to buy this landmark farm, set on a 40-acre meadow rise above the Machias River. There are two antiques-furnished rooms, both with whirlpool bath, satellite TV, air-conditioning, a fridge, sitting area, and river view. $85–110, depending on season. A second story "guest house" with two bedrooms, a full kitchen, and living room is $250–900 per week, and also available by the night. No common space downstairs because it's filled with tables (see *Dining Out*), where breakfast is served.

Micmac Farm Guesthouses and Gardner House (207-255-3008; www.micmacfarm.com), 47 Micmac Ln., Machiasport 04655. Open Memorial Day weekend–Oct. This classic Cape, built by Ebenezer Gardner above the Machias River in 1776, is the oldest house in Machias and a real treasure. Home to Anthony Dunn, Bonnie, his wife, and their small daughter, in summer they occupy a separate wing and offer guests the large downstairs bedroom off the living room. Very private—with a deck overlooking the river and a bath with whirlpool tub—it's furnished in family antiques, a desk, and a life's collection of books. Three comfortable, well-designed housekeeping cabins (we had boiled lobsters for five, and feasted on them, in one) each has two double beds and overlooks the river. $80–95 daily for either the guest room or cabin; $495–595 per week. Children are welcomed and pets accepted in the cabins. Ebenezer Gardner was born in Roxbury, Massachusetts, and moved to Nova Scotia in 1763, but because he sided with the Americans in the Revolution he moved back down the coast. He is buried in the family cemetery on the property.

Captain Cates (207-255-8812; www.captaincates.com), 309 Port Rd. (Rt. 92), Machiasport 04655. Open year-round. This 1820s sea captain's house overlooks the tidal river and offers guests six cheerful, antiques-furnished rooms on the second and third floors, sharing three baths. Downstairs there's a lilac-colored front parlor, a library, and a dining room. From $75 for a small single to $95 for rooms with queens, with full breakfast that may well include grits. Rick and Mary Bury offer hospitality with a southern accent and the library now features portraits of Confederate generals and battlefield prints as well as TV, books, and games.

Riverside Inn (1-888-255-4344; www.riversideinn-maine.com), Rt. 1, P.O. Box 373, East Machias 04630. Open year-round. The heart of this vintage 1805 house—actually the first thing guests see—is the kitchen. Innkeepers Ellen McLaughlin and Rocky Rakoczy will probably be there preparing for the evening meal (see *Dining Out*). We recommend one of the two suites (one with a living room, bedroom, and kitchen facilities; the other with two bedrooms) in the Coach House, nearer the river and with decks. There are also two nicely decorated upstairs guest rooms with private bath in the house, which was Victorianized in the 1890s; the clear glass in its fan lights was replaced with red and tin ceilings were added. $95–129 in high season, $85–119 in low, includes a full breakfast.

Little River Lodge (207-259-4437; www.cutlerlodge.com), P.O. Box 251, Cutler 04626. Open Memorial Day–Columbus Day; some rooms open-year round. Built in 1845 to house lumber mill workers, this capacious, beautifully sited (across from

Cutler Harbor) building became a summer hotel in 1870 when passenger steamers began stopping. Innkeepers Larry and Irene Dearborn are happy to steer guests to the nearby hiking trails. The inn is ideally sited for patrons of Capt. Andy Patterson's Bold Coast puffin-watching trips and for hiking the Bold Coast trails. It offers five rooms, two with private bath, all simply, nicely decorated; three have harbor views; two are in the back ell. Downstairs there's plenty of room to relax and read in the living and dining rooms with views of the harbor. $80–135 includes a full breakfast. A brown-bag lunch is $10 and a lobster dinner is available (market price), minimum of six.

West Quoddy Station (1-877-535-7414; www.quoddyvacation.com), The former U.S. Coast Guard station within walking distance of Quoddy Head State Park has been transformed into six attractive units, nicely furnished with antiques, fitted with phones, and TV; upstairs units with sea view. From $110 per day and $700 per week for a one-bedroom to $1,500 per week for a unit with four bedrooms. From $75 off-season.

Whiting Bay Bed & Breakfast (207-733-2463; www.whitingbay.com), Rt. 1, No. 7, Whiting 04651; a few miles from Cobscook Bay State Park and 11 miles from Lubec, set back from Rt. 1 with nicely landscaped grounds bordering tidal water. Richard and Sandra Bradley offer two upstairs rooms (shared bath) in their house. Guests breakfast in the Carriage House, which also contains a ground-floor (handicapped-accessible) unit and one upstairs with a kitchenette and deck. $95–125 includes a full breakfast.

Peacock House (207-733-2403; www.peacockhouse.com), 27 Summer St., Lubec 04652. Open May–Oct. A gracious 1860s house on a quiet side street, home to four generations of the Peacock family, owners of the major local cannery. There are three carefully, comfortably furnished guest rooms and four suites, one handicapped accessible. The most luxurious suite, the Peacock, is especially spacious and has a gas fireplace. Innkeepers Dennis and Sue Baker have the right touch. Rates, which include a full breakfast served at the dining room table (two sittings, 7:30 and 8:30), run $85 for the rooms, $95–105 for three of the suites, and $125 for the Peacock—a good value.

Home Port Inn and Restaurant (207-733-2077 or 1-800-457-2077; www.homeportinn.com), 45 Main St., P.O. Box 50, Lubec 04652. Open May–mid-Oct. Happily, this long-established inn is flourishing under owners Dave and Suzannah Gale. The large, raspberry-colored living room is a great space to read or watch TV, and each of the seven guest rooms (private bath) has been tastefully decorated. We like Room 5, melon colored with a canopy bed. (Also see *Dining Out*.) $90–105 per couple; $10 for a rollaway.

BayViews (207-733-2181; off-season, 718-788-2196), 6 Monument St., Lubec 04652. Open mid-May–Labor Day. An 1894 Victorian with not just bay views but also a porch, hammock, and lawn sloping to Johnson Bay. The house has been lovingly restored by Kathryn Rubeor, filled with period furniture, prints, books, and collectibles, and fitted with two pianos, the better to serve participants in SummerKeys. There are five guest rooms (shared baths): a family suite with a double bed, twins, a child's bed, and private bath; a room with its own piano and bath (twin beds); and three more rooms with double beds, sharing one bath. $60–100 includes a full breakfast.

♿ **Betsy Ross Lodging** (207-733-8942; www.atlantichouse.net), 61 Water St., Lubec 04652. Open most of the year. This shingled building, replicating the Betsy Ross House in Philadelphia, fits into the eclectic lineup on this funky old street. Bill and Dianna Meehan offer four pleasant rooms with private bath. $60–95 includes a credit for breakfast at the Atlantic House Coffee House and Deli across the street (see *Eating Out*). A rental a unit in a former brick bank building, down the street, sleeps five; one bedroom (with fireplace) is in the vault and there's plenty of open space ($800 per week).

Cohill's Inn (207-733-4300; www.cohillsinn.com), 7 Water St., Lubec 04652. Open year-round. Unpromising from the outside, but the nine rooms are fresh-smelling, simply furnished, and have private bath, TV, and a superb view of the narrows and bay. $95–125 includes a continental breakfast. The first floor is an inviting pub and restaurant (see *Eating Out*).

The Owen House (506-752-2977; www.owenhouse.ca), 11 Welshpool St., Welshpool, Campobello, New Brunswick, Canada E5E 1G3. Open late May–mid-Oct. This delightful inn is reason enough to come to Campobello. Built in 1835 by Admiral William Fitzwilliam Owen, son of the British captain to whom the island was granted in 1769, this is probably the most historic house on the island, and it's a beauty, set on a headland

Christina Tree

BAYVIEWS B&B, LUBEC

overlooking Passamaquoddy Bay. Joyce Morrell, a watercolor artist who maintains a gallery here, has furnished the nine guest rooms (seven with private bath) with friendly antiques, handmade quilts, and good art. Room 1 is really a suite with a single bed in the adjoining room; Room 2, the other front room, is our favorite. Guests gather around the formal dining room table for a full breakfast and around one of several fireplaces in the evening. Paths lead through the 10-acre property to the water, and the Deer Island ferry leaves from the neighboring beach. From $102 (U.S.) for the shared-bath third-floor rooms to $195 for the water-view suite; $114–165 for a private room with bath, plus the 14 percent tax.

The Lupine Lodge (1-888-912-8880; www.lupinelodge.com), 610 Rt. 774, Welshpool, Campobello, New Brunswick, Canada E5E 1A5. Open Memorial Day–Columbus Day. The log structures connected by wooden walkways were built in 1915 on a rise overlooking the water for the Frederick Adams family, cousins of the Roosevelts. The big sitting room with its massive fireplace is now a restaurant (see *Eating Out*). Guest rooms, in two separate log buildings, vary from small to spacious with two queen beds, a full bath, and a living room with fireplace ($65–125). A family room has a queen bed and two more twins in a loft. Request an ocean view. The compound has been recently refurbished and is ably managed by a group of women on both sides of the border, the "Lupines." Trails through this former estate lead to Herring Cove. $85–260.

Also, for a weekly rental, see **Columbia Falls Pottery** in *Selective Shopping*.

COTTAGES Check with the **Machias Bay Area** and **Cobscook Bay Chambers of Commerce** (see *Guidance*). Summer rentals in this area still begin at around $600 per week. Also see **Hearts of Maine Waterfront Rental Properties** (207-255-4210; www.boldcoast.com/maine-cottages).

MOTELS 🐾 "1" **Blueberry Patch Motel and Cabins** (207-434-5411), Rt. 1, P.O. Box 36, Jonesboro 04648. This spic-and-span 19-unit motel is next door to The White House restaurant. Each unit has a refrigerator, air-conditioning, a phone, TV, and coffee. There is a pool and sundeck surrounded by berries. The 1930s tourist cabins way in back are surprisingly roomy and comfortable (two double beds), and there are three efficiencies. $48–65 in-season.

🐾 "1" **Machias Motor Inn** (207-255-4861; www.machiasmotorinn.com), Rt. 1 next to Helen's Restaurant, Machias 04654. Bob and Joan Carter maintain a two-story, 35-unit motel; most rooms are standard units, each with two double, extra-long beds, cable TV, and phone. Rooms feature decks overlooking the Machias River. $84 double, more for efficiencies, less off-season. Pets (no cats) are extra.

🐾 **Eastland Motel** (207-733-5501), Rt. 189, Lubec 04652. Open year-round. A good bet if you're taking the kids to Campobello and want a clean, comfortable room with TV; $66–76 double mid-Apr.–mid-Oct., less off-season. Higher prices are for rooms in the newer section.

CAMPGROUNDS **McClellan Park**, marked from Rt. 1, Milbridge. Open Memorial Day–Columbus Day. This waterside town park is free for day use; a nominal fee is charged to stay at one of the 18 campsites (showers available). For details, call the town hall at 207-546-2422.

Henry Point Campground (207-497-9633), Kelly Point Rd., Jonesport 04649. Open May.–Nov. Surrounded on three sides by water. No showers. This is a put-in place for sea kayaks.

Herring Cove Provincial Park (506-752-2396), Campobello Island, New Brunswick. Adjoining the Roosevelt Campobello International Park is this campground offering 87 campsites; there's a beach, golf course, and extensive hiking trails.

Also see **Cobscook Bay State Park** under *Lodging* in "Eastport and Cobscook Bay."

✱ Where to Eat

DINING OUT

Entries are listed geographically, heading east

Chandler River Lodge (207-434-2540), Rt. 1, Jonesboro. Open for dinner Tue.–Sat. 5–8 and for lunch in-season by reservation. Hopefully we just ordered all the wrong things, because we want this pleasant place to succeed. We are familiar with what finnan haddie should taste like and at $30, this wasn't it. The guava mango chicken was so undercooked it was almost inedible and the mango seemed canned ($29); the vegetable manicotti ($28) was a pre-made pasta filled with a skimpy portion of undercooked veggies. Entrées include a salad and rolls. Chef-owner Beth Foss is well known locally as a good cook, having honed he skills at her family-owned Bluebird Ranch Restaurant in Machias.

Artist's Café (207-255-8900), 3 Hill St., Machias. Open late Apr.–Columbus Day, weekdays for lunch and Mon.–Sat. for dinner 5–8. Reservations accepted. Chef-artist Susan Ferro's delightful restaurant is tucked away off Rt. 1 south of the bridge, across from the university. Light, bright rooms are hung with local art, much of it by Ferro. Lunch on sandwiches with artistic names like The Impressionist (natural chicken breast sautéed and sliced on a French baguette with basil pesto mayonnaise). Dinner entrées might include stir-fried vegetables and tofu on brown rice, or rack of veal braised in white wine. Wine and beer. Dinner entrées $24.

Schoppee Farm (207-255-4648), Rt. 1, Machias. Open nightly 5–7:30 in-season, Thurs.–Sat. off-season. Reservations are required and frequently necessary a few nights in advance. David and Julie Baker keep the numbers to 15 most nights, serving a five-course meal in their pine-floored, many-windowed dining room with its view of the Machias River. Much of what's served is grown on this 40-acre farm, or comes from local suppliers. The menu changes constantly but might include pan-seared local scallops in a champagne-vanilla butter sauce or naturally-raised chicken with a locally-made Dijon mustard sauce and a 10-ounce sirloin in port reduction. $36–42 includes appetizer, soup, salad, entrée, and dessert. BYOB.

Riverside Inn (207-255-4134; www.riversideinn-maine.com), Rt. 1, East Machias 04630. Open for dinner year-round; six nights a week in-season, four off-season. Innkeepers Ellen McLaughlin and Rocky Rakoczy have expanded the dining area in their winterized wraparound porch. Still, space is limited, demand is large, and reservations are a must. Rocky is the chef, and the menu ranges from a choice of seafood dishes through dinner salads to steak and Jamaican baby back ribs. House specialties include lobster and scallops in champagne butter sauce and fresh salmon stuffed with shrimp and crabmeat, served with a turmeric-dill sauce. Entrées $22–27, including a salad and herbed bread. Dinner salads are $20. Full liquor license.

Home Port Inn (207-733-2077; www.homeportinn.com), 45 Main St., Lubec. Open July–Labor Day for dinner 5–8. This is the fine-dining option in Lubec. Entrées range from a crab salad in avocado to fresh seafood bouillabaisse to steak *au poivre* ($15–24). A house salad is $4. Wine and beer are served.

EATING OUT

Entries are listed geographically, heading east

✐ **Joshy's Place**, Rt. 1, Milbridge. Good seasonal take-out. Having researched crab rolls up and down the coast, we think Joshy's rates an 8 on a scale of 1–10. Gifford's ice cream.

44 Degrees North (207-546-4440; www.44-deegrees-north.com), 17 Main St., Milbridge. Open daily 11–9 and Fri.–Sat. year-round, otherwise until 8 in winter. This bright, attractive, affordable restaurant is a godsend to the area. Soups and salads, burgers and slow-roasted prime rib, Bourbon Street chicken, grilled swordfish, and beer batter fried shrimp, daily specials, homemade pies, and a full bar (try the blueberry martinis).

The Red Barn (207-546-7721), Main St. (junction of Rts. 1 and 1A), Milbridge. Open daily year-round, 7 AM–8 PM in summer. The main, pine-paneled dining room with its counter and booths is an old reliable with a big menu, but it's looking tired. Fully licensed.

Chicamoose Café, 1 Main St., Milbridge. Open weekdays 9–4:30. An inviting way-stop with wireless Internet, coffees, drinks, sandwiches, pastries, and panini, along with art and some locally crafted items for sale.

Scovils Millside Dining, 1276 Main St., Harrington. Open daily 7–7, until 8 in summer. Jim Scovil's menu is big and reasonably priced, with many breakfast choices and then basics like meatloaf and liver and onions, also pizza and Mexican fare good enough to pass muster with the area's seasonal blueberry pickers. No liquor and no BYOB.

Elmer's Seafood Shack, Rt. 1, Columbia. Open daily except Mon. 11–8. Formerly Perry's Seafood, a spanking clean diner on a rise with a view of the barrens. Good seafood and road food. BYOB at dinner (the package store is next door).

Tall Barney's Restaurant (207-497-2403; www.tallbarneys.com), 52 Main St., Jonesport, across from the Beals Island Bridge. Open daily from 6–2 Sun.–Tue., until 7 Wed.–Sat. This legendary local gathering spot was the subject of an NPR radio story that inspired present owners John and Linda Lapinski to come and buy it. They have expanded the menu to include veggie burgers as well as a wide choice of seafood stews, fried fish, and self-consciously styled "Maine Meals," such as grilled franks and fried onions, along with daily specials. Their **City Girl Market** now offers box breakfasts and lunches (order the day before for early pickup). This place is still particularly welcoming for breakfast on a foggy morning. The long "liar's table" down the middle of the front room is reserved for the local lobstermen, who drift in one by one. Many around here still claim descent from Tall Barney Beal (1835–99), who stood 6 foot 7 inches.

The Pit Stop (207-497-5650), Main St., Jonesport. Open 4 AM–2 PM, later Thur. and Fri. A local gathering spot for the basics.

White House Restaurant (207-434-2782), Rt. 1, Jonesboro. Open 5 AM–8 PM. A classic roadhouse with genuine diner atmosphere and food.

TALL BARNEY'S

Christina Tree

"I" **Whole Life Natural Market & Café** (207-255-8855), 80 Main St., Machias. Open year-round; summer hours Mon.–Sat. 9–6, Sun. 10–2; closed Sundays off-season. A comfortable, window-side corner of the market is furnished with tables. Pick a sandwich or salad from the deli or have one made. Daily soups too. Our spanakopita, warm and flakey, came on a real (not plastic) plate. Wireless Internet too.

Fat Cat Deli & Pizzeria (207-255-6777), 5 Main St., Machias. Open daily 11–9. The decor is all about the blues, and the sandwiches and salads are above average. Try the Broken Record Cheesecake, frozen on a stick and hand-dipped in milk chocolate.

Helen's Restaurant (207-255-8423), 28 East Main St., Machias (north of town on the water). Open 6 AM–8 PM, Fri. and Sat until 8:30. The town's landmark restaurant since 1950, geared to bus groups at lunch. Generous servings and reasonable prices for a wide choice of seafood plus sandwiches, hot dogs, and burgers. Famed for "whipped" pies. Fully licensed. Children's plates.

Blue Bird Ranch (207-255-3351), Lower Main St. (Rt. 1), Machias. Open year-round for all three meals. Family owned with a diner atmosphere and good food. Plenty of fried fish and steak choices, fresh-made chowders and seafood stews, burgers and sandwiches, pies and puddings. Fully licensed.

Rae's Restaurant (207-255-5050), Rt. 1, Machias (north of the dike). Open daily in-season 11–7:30, from 7 on weekends, off-season Thurs.–Sun. Formerly Joyce's, this family restaurant has a limited menu but continues to be known for exceptionally good, homemade food. Wine and beer, served.

Murphy's Village Restaurant (207-733-4440), 126 Main St. (Rt. 189), Lubec. Open daily year-round except Wed., 7AM–8 PM. Peter and Mary Sue Murphy own this local gathering place serving "traditional downeast home-style cooking." It's breakfast all day long, fresh seafood, and homemade pies. Fully licensed.

Uncle Kippy's Seafood Restaurant (207-733-2400), Rt.189, Lubec. Open daily 11–8. Closed Mon. off-season. A local dining landmark known for steak, seafood, and the area's best pizza.

Cohill's Inn (207-733-4300), 7 Water St., Lubec. Open year-round from 11. Blackboard menu featuring fresh, seasonal produce, microbrews, and Guiness chowder. A nice pub atmosphere.

Atlantic House Coffee Shop (207-733-0906), 52 Water St., Lubec. Open seasonally, daily 7–7. A welcome addition to this reawakening street: pastries, pizza, stromboli, calzones, sandwiches, 26 flavors of ice cream, and a back deck on the water.

Phil's Not-So-Famous Ice Cream, Washington St., right before the international bridge. Many flavors of ice cream, sorbet, crêpes, and more are made on the premises.

Lupine Lodge (506-752-2555), Campobello Island, New Brunswick. Open 8 AM–9 PM. This former log "cottage," built by cousins of the Roosevelts, features a great hearth with a chimney built from ship's ballast stones and has some charm. The dinner menu ranges from $11 (Canadian) for vegetarian pasta to $19 for a fried seafood platter. Full liquor license.

Sweet Time Restaurant & Bakery

(506-752-2428), Rt. 174, Welshpool, Campobello Island, New Brunswick. Open 8 AM–9 PM daily in summer, less off-season. Margo Malloch's bakery-turned-restaurant is a find, an island gathering place with "omelets of your choice" or fish cakes topped with fried eggs for breakfast, a wide choice of sandwiches on freshly baked bread for lunch, and superb pies and chowders. Lobster stew and fried fish platters at dinner.

Family Fisheries (506-752-2470), Rt. 774, Wilson's Beach, Campobello Island, New Brunswick. Open from 11:30 through at least 8:30 June–Oct. until 10 CDN (an hour later than Lubec). This is a combination fish market, take-out (there's a screened eating area), and sit-down dining room, a good bet for fish-and-chips, seafood casserole, chowder, lobster, and pizza.

✷ Entertainment

Milbridge Theater (207-546-2038), Main St., Milbridge. Open nightly May–Nov., 7:30 showtime. A refurbished movie house featuring first-runs at affordable prices. Fresh popcorn.

Down River Theatre Co. (207-255-8940) stages plays June–Aug. at University of Maine, Machias. Community theater productions—a mix of safe musicals and original plays. Tickets are very affordable.

Machias Bay Chamber Concerts (207-255-3889), Center Street Congregational Church, Machias. A series of six chamber music concerts, July–early Aug., Tue. at 7:30 PM. Top groups such as the Kneisel Hall Chamber Players and the Vermeer Quartet are featured.

Mary Potterton Memorial Piano Concerts, Sacred Heart Church Parish Hall, Lubec. Wed. evenings (7:30) all summer. Free. Featuring SummerKeys faculty and guest artists. (www.summerkeys.com).

✷ Selective Shopping

Entries are listed geographically, heading east

A&M Chain Saw Sculptures (207-546-3462), Rogers Point Rd., Steuben. Arthur Smith's wooden animals are truly amazing and exhibited in widely respected galleries for many times the price that he will sell them to you for from his roadside house-gallery. Marie Smith is responsible for painting the sculptures.

Columbia Falls Pottery (207-483-4075 or 1-800-235-2512; www.columbiafallspottery.com), 150 Main St., Columbia Falls. Open year-round, June–Oct. daily 10–5, otherwise Thu.–Sat. 10–5. Striking, bright, sophisticated pottery and custom tile designs by April Adams featuring lupines and other wildflowers. Inquire about the upstairs apartment available for short-term rentals.

Wild Blueberry Land (207-483-3583; www.wildbuleberryland.com), Rt. 1, Columbia Falls. The blue geodesic dome suggests a squashed blueberry and houses an assortment of berries—fried, in freshly-made pies, jam, syrup, juice, frozen (will ship), and actual blueberries beyond the usual season.

Jonesport Village has become an antiques center. At **Jonesport Nautical Antiques** (1-800-996-5655; www.nauticalantiques.com), Cogswell and Main Sts., nautical antiques and reproductions are the specialty. **Moospecke Antiques** (207-497-2457) on Sawyer

Square, open seasonally, Tue.–Fri. 10–noon and 1–4, specializes in country furniture, fine arts, and Americana. **Harbor House on Sawyer Cove** (207-497-5417), next door, is worth checking for art, furnishings, and gifts. **Nelson Decoys Gallery and Gifts** (207-497-3488), Cranberry Ln., open May–Dec., sells prizewinning decoys, local art, and Maine-made gifts. At **Downeast Quilting & Interiors** (207-497-2251; www.downeastquilting.com), 178 Main St., Sarah Davis sells quilts, also makes draperies and much more.

Machias Laundromat (207-255-6639). Open in summer daily 8–8, closing in winter at 6. Our favorite Maine Laundromat, spanking clean and sited next to the river (just across the bridge as you come into town) so that you can dump your stuff, poke around, lunch, and come back. For a

MAINE BLACKFLY BREEDER'S ASSOCIATION (www.maineblackfly.org). You may have seen bumper stickers proclaiming SAVE THE BLACKFLY and T-shirts boasting WE BREED 'EM, YOU FEED 'EM. The puzzling message can be traced to Machias's Woodwind Gallery, where owner Holly Garner-Jackson's standard greeting is "May the Swarm be with you." She explains that the nonprofit association traces its conception to the length and boredom level of Washington County winters. Proceeds from sale of all products—which include carved, finger-sized "fly-houses" in a variety of shapes, from trailers to condos—benefit Washington County charities. For $1 the association will send you a "certificate of membership" designed by artist Marilyn Dowling, featuring a blackfly striking an eaglelike pose. Dowling personally renders your name in flowing calligraphy. The source: Woodwind Gallery (207-255-3727), 62 Dublin St. (Rt. 1 south of the bridge), Machias. Open year-round, Tue.–Sun. in July and Aug.; closed Sun. off-season The combination framery and gallery shows some 40 local artists and sculptors. Work includes glass, pottery, photography, paintings, and metal; art supplies, too.

nominal fee they will also wash, dry, and fold for you.

Machias Hardware Co. (207-255-6581), 26 Main St., Machias. An old-fashioned hardware store that's also an unexpected source of reasonably priced herbs and spices in 2-ounce and 1-pound packages. Also local products like those by A. M. Look's Canning (see below).

"1" **Whole Life Natural Market** (207-255-8855), 80 Main St., Machias. Open year-round; summer hours Mon.–Sat. 9–6, Sun. 10–2. Finally, a first-class market featuring organic and local produce and environmentally safe products, beauty aids, and supplements. There's also a resource/lending library and café with wireless Internet (see *Eating Out*).

Tin Ceiling Emporium & Books (207-255-0660), 84 Main St. Open weekdays 9–6, Sat. 9–1. Realtor Sharon Dexter operates this eclectic mix of good things in the storefront adjacent to her office.

Connie's Clay of Fundy (207-255-4574), Rt. 1, East Machias. Open year-round. Connie Harter-Bagley's combination studio-shop is filled with her distinctive glazed earthenware in deep colors. Bowls, pie plates, platters, lamps, and small essentials like garlic jars and ring boxes, also "healing spiritual jewelry."

Maine Sea Salt Company (207-255-3310; www.maineseasalt.com), 11 Church Ln., Marshfield, 2 miles up Rt. 192 from downtown Machias. Salt is produced in shallow pools of seawater insides greenhouses. Tours are offered in summer Tues.–Sat. 10–4, with salt tastings.

Look's Gourmet Food Co. (207-259-3341 or 1-800-962-6258), Rt. 191 south of East Machias. Retail shop open year-round weekdays 8–4. Said to be the first company to successfully can crabmeat and the first to bottle clam juice (the product for which it's most famous) under the Atlantic label, Look's now produces a whole line of specialty products, from lobster spread to Indian pudding, under both the Atlantic and Bar Harbor labels.

A2Z General Store (207-259-3800), Beachwood Bay Estates, Rt. 191, Cutler. Open 6:30 AM–8 PM in summer, otherwise 7–7. This much-needed general store opened in the former naval station complex in 2007. In addition of groceries, pizza, sandwiches, and gas, it carries local products such as Artful Ware (flatware with handles crafted next door from seashells), Look canned seafood products, locally made soaps and salt, and much more.

Bold Coast Smokehouse (1-888-733-0807; www.boldhousesmokehouse.com), 224 County Rd. (Rt. 189), Lubec. Open year-round. Be sure to stop at Vinny Gartmayer's fine smokehouse. Pick up some delectable smoked salmon kabobs, finnan haddie, smoked mussels, or smoked lobster pâté.

Broomstick Creations, (207-733-4999), Rt. 189. Open daily 9–7. A full-service bookstore and giftshop, specializing in crystals and New Age items. Coffee and biscotti available.

Monica's Chocolates (207-733-4500; www.monicaschocolates.com), 56 Pleasant St., Lubec. Open daily, 8–8. Monica Elliott, a native of Peru, pioneered (so to speak) chocolate-making in Lubec, and her store at the foot of the FDR Bridge is a must-stop. Specialties include truffles, crèmes, and bonbons made with her father's special recipe.

Bayside Chocolates (207-733-8880), 37 Water St., Lubec. Super dark chocolate, handmade truffles, chocolate-covered blueberries. This locally owned establishment is also a must-stop.

Northern Tides Art and Gift Gallery (207-733-2500), 24 Water St., Lubec. Debra Ayala's attractive shop features original prints, weaving, wood and stone carving, jewelry, cards, pottery, and more.

Quoddy Mist Sea Salt (207-733-4847; www.quoddymist.com), 72 Water St., Lubec. Occupying the former R. J. Peacock Canning Building, Quoddy Mist revives a tradition of harvesting salt from the Bay of Fundy. Its plant is strategically sited along the Lubec Narrows, fed twice daily by extreme tides. It's possible to arrange a tour and see how the brine from the boiled-down seawater crystallizes on tables, with high trace minerals, low sodium chloride levels, and a fine flavor.

Diane's Glass Gallery (207-733-2458; www.dianesglass.com), 72 Water St. (Peacock Canning Building), open daily June–Sept. Truly exceptional glass jewelry and fused accent plates using recycled glass.

Campobello Island Gift Shop (506-752-2233), Rt. 774, Welshpool, Campobello Island, NB. The specialty of the house is New Brunswick and Celtic folk-music CDs but there's plenty of everything else, from souvenirs (especially lighthouse stuff) to books and local crafts, especially jewelry.

CHRISTMAS WREATHS More than half of Maine's Christmas wreaths are made in Washington County. You can order in fall and take delivery of a freshly made wreath right before Christmas. Prices quoted include delivery. **The Wreath Shoppe** (207-483-4598), Harrington (wreaths decorated with cones, berries, and reindeer moss); and **Flo's Wreaths** (1-800-321-7136; www.floswreaths.net) are a couple among dozens of purveyors.

✷ Special Events

Memorial Day weekend: **Downeast Birding Festival**—guided hikes, cruises, lectures (www.downeastbirdfest.org).

July **Independence Day celebrations** in **Jonesport/Beals Island** (lobster-boat races, easily viewed from the bridge); **Cherryfield** (parade and fireworks); and **Steuben** (firemen's lobster picnic and parade); **Lubec** goes all-out with a grand parade, contests, and fireworks; **Cutler** and **Machias** also celebrate. **Campobello** celebrates Canada Day (July 1) in a big way. Also see the **Eastport** section for the state's biggest celebration. *Last weekend in July:* **Milbridge Days** (207-546-2406) includes a parade, a dance, a lobster dinner, and the famous codfish relay race.

August: **Meet the Artists Tour** in Jonesport (first weekend), **Lights Across the Border** is a day of coordinated activities at all the area's lighthouses. Contact Friends of Little River Light (207-259-3688) in Cutler.

Wild Blueberry Festival and Machias Craft Festival (*third weekend*) in downtown Machias, sponsored by Penobscot Valley Crafts and Center Street Congregational Church—concerts, food, a major crafts fair, and live entertainment.

EASTPORT, COBSCOOK BAY, AND PASSAMAQUODDY BAY

Eastport is just 3 miles north of Lubec by boat but 43 miles by land around Cobscook Bay. *Cobscook* is said to mean "boiling water" in the Passamaquoddy tongue, and tremendous tides—a tidal range of more than 25 feet—seemingly boil in through this passage and slosh up deep inlets divided by ragged land fingers along the north and south shores. One gap between the opposite shores is just 300 yards wide, and the tides funnel through it at 6 to 8 knots, alternately filling and draining the smaller bays beyond. For several hours the incoming tide actually roars through these "Cobscook Reversing Falls."

The force of the tides in Passamaquoddy Bay on Eastport's eastern and northern shores is so powerful that in the 1930s President Roosevelt backed a proposal by hydroelectric engineer Dexter Cooper to harness this power to electrify much of the northeast coast, including Boston. The sardine-canning process in Maine began in Eastport in 1875 and a boom era quickly followed, but today the population of this island "city" has dropped to below 2,000 (from more than 5,000 in 1900). Still, Eastport—which once rivaled New York in shipping—remains a "city" and a working deepwater port, the deepest on the U.S. East Coast. Large freighters regularly dock at the new shipping pier near Estes Head to take on woodland products, a reminder (as is the surviving Federal and Greek Revival architecture) that by the War of 1812 this was already an important enough port for the British to capture and occupy it.

Today there are many gaps in the old waterfront, now riprapped in pink granite to form a seawall. With its flat, haunting light, Eastport has an end-of-the-world feel and suggests an Edward Hopper painting. It's a landscape that draws many artists, and there are galleries along Water Street and they are making a difference. It's also the venue for a series of home repair homicide mysteries by resident Sarah Graves.

Eastport consists entirely of islands, principally Moose Island, which is connected to Rt. 1 by Rt. 190 via a series of causeways (actually, tidal dams built in the 1930s for the failed tidal power project), linking other islands. It's a departure point for the small car ferry and excursion boats that ply Passamaquoddy Bay. Old Sow, a whirlpool between Eastport and Deer Island said to be 230 feet in diameter, is reportedly the largest in the Western Hemisphere. Thanks to the extreme tides and currents, marine life is more varied than in other places. Nutrients that elsewhere settle to the bottom shoot here to the surface and nourish some forms of life that exist nowhere else. The fact that you can see only a short distance down into the water around Eastport is due not to pollution but to this rich nutrient life.

FISHERMAN STATUE

Christina Tree

Rt. 190 runs through the center of Sipayik (pronounced *zeh-BAYH-igh*), the Pleasant Point Indian Reservation, home to some 700 members of the Passamaquoddy Indian tribe. The three-day Indian Ceremonial Days in early August fully celebrate Passamaquoddy culture.

Unfortunately, the 20 miles of Rt. 1 between Whiting (turnoff for Lubec) and Perry (turnoff for Eastport) offer few glimpses of Cobscook Bay. Be sure to take the short detour into Cobscook Bay State Park and into the ghostlike village of Pembroke to find your way to the Reversing Falls Park.

GUIDANCE **Eastport Chamber of Commerce** (207-853-4644; www.eastport.net).

Cobscook Bay Area Chamber of Commerce (207-733-2201; www.cobscookbay.com).

Also check the Web site www.eastportme.info.

For more about the Quoddy Loop around both sides of Passamaquoddy Bay see www.quoddyloop.com.

✷ To See

The Quoddy Dam Museum (207-853-6630), 72 Water St., Eastport, features a 14-by-16-foot concrete model of the Passamaquoddy Tidal Power Project (see the introduction) and is open Memorial Day–Sept., daily except Sun. It triples as a museum, crafts cooperative, and **information center**.

The Tides Institute and Museum of Art (207-853-4047; www.tides.institute.org), 43 Water St., Eastport. Open in summer Tues.–Sun. 1–4; off-season, Wed–Sat. 10–4. Several years ago the city's ornate, vintage-1887 bank building came up for sale and seemed in danger of demolition. It's presently under restoration as a cultural center archiving and exhibiting regional photography, also exhibiting original art and serving as a resource and library. The Web site is worth checking.

Barracks Museum (207-853-6630), 74 Washington St., Eastport. Open July–Aug. Wed.–Sat. 1–4. Originally part of Fort Sullivan and occupied by the

EASTPORT WATERFRONT

Christina Tree

British during the War of 1812, this house has been restored to its 1820s appearance as an officers' quarters and displays old photos and memorabilia about Eastport. Free.

Reversing Falls Park. Turn off Rt. 1 at Rt. 214 into the village of Pembroke; follow the slight jog in the road then Leighton Neck for 3.3 miles, and turn right onto Clarkside Rd. (the sign may or may not be there), then left at the T. This last road turns to dirt before it ends at a parking area for a town park with two short trails to the water. Try to time your visit to coincide with the couple of hours before the height of the incoming tide, which funnels furiously through the gap between Mahar's Point and Falls Island. As the salt water flows along at 6 to 8 or more knots, it strikes a series of rocks, resulting in rapids. At low water this is a great place to hunt for fossils and any time it's well worth finding.

Old Sow. What's billed as the largest whirlpool in the Western Hemisphere, and one of five significant whirlpools in the world, is sited between the tips of Moose and Deer islands. It's said to be produced by 70 billion cubic feet of water rushing into Passamaquoddy Bay, much of which finds its way around the tip of Deer Island and an underwater mountain at this narrow point. The area's smaller whirlpools are called Piglets. See *Boat Excursions* for viewing. The Old Sow is visible from the ferry crossing. We once saw a small cruise ship heel over dramatically when it came too close to the vortex; small craft beware.

✷ To Do

BIRDING is what **Moosehorn National Wildlife Refuge** is about. Vast tidal flats in Eastport are good places to watch migrating plovers, sandpipers, and other shorebirds. American bald eagles are frequently seen around Cobscook Bay; see *Green Space.* For details about the late-May **Down East Spring Birding Festival**, see www.downeastbirdfest.org, and for puffin-watching on Machias Seal Island check out *Birding* in the "Atlantic Coast" and "St. Andrews and Grand Manan" subchapters.

MUSIC AT PEAVEY LIBRARY

Christina Tree

BOAT EXCURSIONS Harris Whale Watching/Eastport Windjammers (207-853-2500 or 207-853-4303; www.eastportwindjammers.com), out of Eastport, is a very special experience. Capt. Butch Harris offers afternoon and sunset cruises on Passamaquoddy Bay aboard the two-masted, 84-foot schooner ***Sylvina W. Beal***, a veteran of many years as a herring and mackerel seiner out of Lubec and Eastport. **Fishing trips** on Passamaquoddy Bay are also offered by the Harris family aboard the 35-passenger ***Quoddy Dam***.

The windjammer ***Halie & Matthew*** (207-853-4500; www.schoonerhaliematthew.com), is a stunning 92-foot, clipper-bowed, gaff-rigged schooner designed, built, and launched in Eastport with a state-of-the-art navigation system in 2005. Approved to carry 100 passengers on day sails, she is outfitted with eight staterooms, each with a double berth, private shower, and electric head. Weekend cruises to Grand Manan are $150–300 per person; four- and five-day cruises from St. Andrews to Bar Harbor are also offered. Rates include meals, including a lobster bake.

Ferry to Deer Island, New Brunswick, with connections to Campobello and the New Brunswick mainland. For details about **East Coast Ferries Ltd.** (506-747-2159; www.eastcoastferries.nb.ca.), see *Getting Around* in "Washington County." Late June–early Sept. the ferry departs every hour from the beach beside Eastport Lobster and Fish House. Be sure to take it at least to Deer Island. We strongly suggest you go the whole way around the Quoddy Loop (see the introduction to "Washington County").

Cobscook Hikes & Paddles (207-726-4776; off-season, 207-454-2130). Registered Maine Guides Stephen and Tess Forek, based in Robbinston, offer guided two- and three-hour kayaking paddles from Whiting to Calais.

MINI GOLF **Downeast Adventure Golf** (207-853-9595), Rt. 1, Perry. An oversized putting course with two acres of terrain including a pond, splash fountains, arched bridges, and a batting cage.

WALKS **Shackford Head State Park** (posted from Rt. 190 near downtown Eastport) is a 90-acre peninsula with several trails including a roughly 0.7-mile path from the parking lot to a 173-foot-high headland overlooking Campobello Island and Lubec in one direction and Cobscook Bay in the other. Another 0.25-mile-long trail leads down the headland and permits access to the shore. Views are of the bay with its floating salmon pens. Look for fossils at low water.

Green Space

The Quoddy Regional Land Trust (207-733-5509) publishes *Cobscook Trails* (see *Hiking* in "The Atlantic Coast").

Moosehorn National Wildlife Refuge, Unit 2, Edmunds (off Rt. 1 between Dennysville and Whiting). Some 7,200 acres bounded by Whiting and Dennys bays and the mouth of the Dennys River. North Trail Rd. is 2.5 miles long and leads to a parking area from which canoes can be launched into Hobart Stream. South Trail Rd. covers 0.9 mile and leads to a parking area for a 10-mile unmaintained trail network. Trails in the Baring section (Unit 1) of the refuge are maintained.

Cobscook Bay State Park (207-726-4412), off Rt. 1 between Dennysville and Whiting, has 888 acres with a 2-mile nature trail with water views and a 0.5-mile Shore Trail. Wildlife and birds are plentiful.

Gleason Point, Perry. Take Shore Rd. next to the Quoddy Wigwam Gift Shop on Rt. 1 and follow signs to the beach and boat landing.

✱ Lodging

INNS AND BED & BREAKFASTS

In Easptort 04631

Weston House (207-853-2907; www.westonhouse-maine.com), 26 Boynton St. Open year-round. An elegant Federal-style house built in 1810 with two large front guest rooms sharing a full bath. One of these has a working fireplace and a tall four-poster, views of the bay and gardens, and antiques, but it was in the other—equally spacious and gracious—room that John James Audubon slept on his way to Labrador in 1833. A small room, tucked into the back of the ell, is perfect for solo travelers. Jett and John Peterson continue to add "rooms"—a bricked terrace here and a rose garden with gazebo, the spot for a wedding. Rates are $70–90 double, including a sumptuous breakfast in the formal dining room: maybe Eastport salmon and eggs Benedict. Jett's four-course dinner or a picnic lunch can be arranged.

Kilby House Inn (207-853-0989 or 1-800-853-4557; www.kilbyhouseinn.com), 122 Water St. A Queen Anne-style house on the quiet end of the waterfront, within walking distance to the Deer Island ferry. The attractive double parlor with a fireplace and grand piano invites you to sit down and read. Innkeeper Gregg Noyes's passions include playing the organ and refinishing antiques. There are five pleasant upstairs guest rooms: the sunny master with its four-poster canopy bed and water view; two more antiques-furnished rooms with private bath. $60–85 includes a very full breakfast on weekends and during summer months when Gregg, who teaches down in Steuben, is on hand to prepare it.

Chadbourne House (1-888-853-2728; www.chadbournehouse.com), 19 Shackford St., P.O. Box 191. Innkeepers Jill and David Wetphal have restored this vintage 1821 Federal-style mansion, furnishing it with antiques. Three of the four guest rooms are suites, one occupying the entire third floor, featuring skylights, a king bed, and a sitting area. The remaining suites have a fireplace and all rooms have private bath. Common areas are spacious and elegantly comfortable; breakfast is served in a formal dining room. Guests are asked to shed their shoes on entering. $110–140 per night, $25 per extra person.

Todd House (207-853-2328), 1 Capen Ave. Open year-round. A restored 1775 Cape, the oldest house in Eastport, with water views. In 1801 men met here to charter a Masonic order, and in 1861 the house became a temporary barracks. The four large double rooms (shared baths) vary in view, and access to baths. Our favorites are the ground-floor Cornerstone Room and the Masonic Room, with a working fireplace. Innkeeper Ruth McInnis welcomes well-behaved children and pets; her own pets include a Maine coon cat and six cockatiels. $60–100.

The Milliken House (1-888-507-9370; www.eastport-inn.com), 29 Washington St. Bill and Mary Williams are the owners of this 1840s house, which retains Victorian charm with a large double parlor, ornate detailing, and some original furniture. There are six guest rooms, all with private bath. $75–85 year-round includes a full breakfast.

MOTEL **The Motel East** (207-853-4747), 23A Water St., Eastport 04631. This two-story motel has 14 units, some handicapped accessible, all with water views, some with balcony. Amenities include direct-dial phones, cable TV, eight kitchenettes. No charge under 18 years. $105–120 per night, less off-season. Guest cottage next door.

OTHER **Tide Mill Farm** (207-733-2110; www.tidemillfarm.com), 40 Tide Mill Rd., Edmunds 04628. This 200-year-old working farm on Whiting Bay and Crane Mill Stream has been in the Bell family since 1765. It is set on 1,600 acres with 6 miles of shorefront. The century-old farmhouse has five bedrooms sharing one and a half baths. $1,200 per week in-season; off-season rates available. Terry and Cathy Bell are maintaining the property as a working organic farm with draft horses, Hereford cattle, chickens, pigs, and organic dairy herd. The ninth generation raises organic produce and animals, with vegetables and eggs available in summer season. Tours of the farm are offered mid-June–early Sept., Wed. 2–4. (www.toursoflubecandcobscook.com).

"1" **The Commons** (207-853-4123; www.thecommonseastport), 51 Water St., P.O. Box 255. Two second-floor units in an 1880s brick commercial building, each offer two bedrooms, bath, kitchen, sitting area, balcony overlooking the harbor, and laundry facilities. $900–950 per week.

House Checkers Maine (207-853-6179; www.housecheckersmaine.com), based in Eastport, offers wide selection of rentals.

CAMPGROUND **Cobscook Bay State Park** (207-726-4412), S. Edmunds Rd. just off Rt. 1, between Dennysville and Whiting. Open mid-May–mid-Oct., 88 acres with 150 campsites, most of them for tents and many with water views. There are even showers (unusual in Maine state campgrounds). The 880-acre park also offers a boat-launch area, picnic benches, and a hiking and cross-country ski trail. Birding is superb.

✱ Where to Eat

In Eastport unless noted

The New Friendly Restaurant (207-853-6610 or 1-800-953-6610), Rt. 1, Perry. Open daily 11–8. Great road food. A homey restaurant with booths and food that's known as the best around: fish stews and chowders, basics like liver and onions, not-so-basics like an elegant crab salad and the most lobster in a lobster sandwich. Desserts include Grape-Nut pudding as well as pies. Beer and wine served.

The Pickled Herring (207-853-2323; www.thepickledherring.com), 32 Water St. Due to open in 2008. Eastport native Gary Craig has totally renovated this prime downtown dining spot (for many years La Sardina Loca). It features a wood-fired grill, local beers and produce. Dinner entrées $8–20.

Eastport Chowder House (207-853-4700), 167 Water St. Open seasonally, daily 11–9. A good location, on what's said to be the site of the country's first fish and sardine cannery. Sandwiches to fish stews and lobster. The downstairs pub on Cannery Wharf is informal, and it's possible to get take-out (and thus park in line) for the ferry that departs from the adjacent beach. The restaurant is barnlike and can be noisy; the outside deck is a blessing. The reasonably priced menu runs from fried haddock and eggplant parmesan to lobster.

Quoddy Bay Lobster Co. (207-853-6640), 7 Sea St. Open seasonally Wed.–Sat. 10–5. Fresh fish and fabulous lobster rolls drizzled with butter, fried clam rolls so thick you have to eat them with a fork, great fish chowder. Outside picnic tables.

Rose Garden (207-853-9598), 9 Dana St. Open year-round with live music Fri. and Sat. at 8 PM. A funky eclectic restaurant on one side, and an antiques shop with a pool table in the back on the other. Linda Salleroli is a locally respected cook, known for her stir-fries, chili, and root beer floats. Inquire about poetry readings.

✐ **The Happy Crab** (207-853-9400), 35 Water St.Open daily 6 AM–9 PM. A cheerful diner with a selection of burgers, seafood baskets, wraps, and sandwiches all made with the specially flavored house mayo.

The Blue Iris Restaurant (207-853-2440), 31 Water St. Open May–mid-Sept. for breakfast and lunch. Theme dinners Sat. evenings. A local gathering spot with a water view from the deck.

WaCo Diner (207-853-4046), Water St. Open year-round, Mon.–Sat. 6 AM–8 PM. Begun as a pushcart in 1924, the WaCo has expanded to include a waterside Schooner Room and a deck dining room overlooking the bay that on a sunny day just could not be more pleasant. The old section features booths and a long shiny counter. You can get a full roast turkey dinner or lazy lobster; also beer and chowder; mixed reviews lately.

Moose Island Country Store (207-853-2622) 109 Water St. Open in summer 6 AM–9 PM, 7–7 off-season. A good bet for early morning coffee and homemade doughnuts, sandwiches, ice cream, and pizza all day.

Rosie's Hot Dog Stand at the breakwater. Open seasonally for decades.

Also see *Selective Shopping* for **The Pantry at Raye's Mustard**.

✷ Entertainment

Eastport Arts Center (207-853-5803; www.eastportartscenter.com), 36 Washington St. The vintage 1837 Washington Street Baptist Church has been restored and fitted with a new heating system as home to six arts organizations, including the Northern Lights Film Society (Sunday evening films at 7 PM on a large screen, great sound).

Stage East (207-853-4747; www.stageeast.org) is a terrific community theater, plus puppetry, changing exhibits by The Eastport Gallery, and a wide variety of concerts. Check the Web site for the current schedule.

SummerKeys via water taxi. See "Atlantic Coast" for details about this summerlong Wed.-evening music series in Lubec. Concerts are at 7:30; the water taxi leaves the Eastport breakwater at 6:30, returning at 9:30. Stop by the *Sylvina Beal* office on Water St. (207-853-2500) for more concert and taxi tickets.

✷ Selective Shopping

Along Rt. 190 and in Eastport

Raye's Mustard Mill and Pantry (207-853-4451 or 1-800-853-1903; www.rayesmustard.com), Rt. 190 (Washington St.). Open daily 9–5 in summer, 10–4 off-season. In business since 1900, this company is the country's last remaining stone-ground-mustard mill. It's the mustard in which Washington County's sardines were once packed, and it's sensational. Sample the many varieties in **The Pantry**, where soup and sandwiches are also served, limited seating. Tours of the mustard mill are offered year-round, daily on the hour (except the lunch hour).

The Commons (207-853-4123; www.thecommonseastport.com), 51 Water St. Open year-round; in summer, Mon.–Sat. 9–6, Sun. 1–5, otherwise Mon.–Sat. 10–6. An outstanding gallery displaying the work of more than 60 Passamaquoddy Bay area artists and artisans: botanical and wildlife paintings, fabric art, carved burl bowls, jewelry, hand-knit sweaters, wooden ware, pottery, and Passamquoddy sweetgrass baskets.

Wood on Water (207-853-9663; www.woodonwater), 75 Water St. Open Apr.–Dec. featuring wood-burning and hand-painting work by Amy Marcotte, also a variety of gifts.

Earth Forms Pottery (207-853-2430; www.djsutherland.com), corner of Water and Dana Sts. Open daily in-season. Nationally known potter Donald Sutherland specializes in large garden and patio pots, also in free-form sculptures and in smaller, functional but striking pieces like our fruit bowl.

The Eastport Gallery (207-853-4166; www.eastportgallery.com), 74 Water St. Open early June–Oct. 1 daily, 10–5. A cooperative gallery representing more than 25 local artists.

Crow Tracks (207-853-2336; www.crowtracks.com), 11 Water St. Open year-round. R. J. LaVallee carves a variety of birds, whales, and fantasy figures, from decoys to Christmas ornaments.

Dancing Dogs Pottery & Art (207-853-6229), 107 Water St. An impressive array of wheel-thrown porcelain and stoneware pottery, also oils, acrylics, and watercolors.

Quoddy Crafts. Sharing space the Quoddy Dam Museum (see *To See*), a local crafts outlet worth checking out.

S. L. Wadsworth & Sons (207-853-4343; www.slwadsworth.com), 42/44 Water St. Billed as the country's oldest ship chandlery and Maine's oldest merchandiser (no one really noticed until the present generation took over), this marine-geared store has recently added "nautical gifts" to hardware. There's no question that it was founded in 1818 by Samuel Wadsworth, son of General Peleg Wadsworth and uncle of poet Henry Wadsworth Longfellow. Buy a rod and fish from the breakwater (you don't need a license).

The Tides Gift Shop (207-853-4805), 123 Water St. Open Mon.–Fri. 9–5, Sat. 10–4. Local books and crafts.

Along Rt. 1, heading north from Whiting

Quoddy Wigwam Gift Shop (207-853-4812), Rt. 1, Perry. Open daily 9–6. This is a prime retail outlet for Passamaquoddy baskets and other crafts, also high-quality Quoddy Trail Moccasins hand-sewn by Kevin and Kirsten Shorey next door (207-853-2488; www.quoddytrail.com). The store is also home to some amazing stuffed wildlife and to Larry the 26-pound lobster.

Maine-ly Smoked Salmon Company (207-853-4794; www.mainelysmokedsalmon.com), 144 South

Meadow Rd., Perry. Hot and cold smoked salmon.

45th Parallel (207-854-9500), "halfway between the Equator and the North Pole," Rt. 1, Perry. Open seasonally. Chicago designers Britani and Philip Pascarekka have filled this space—from floor to 12-foot-high ceilings—with stained glass and antique beds, drawer pulls and lamps, jewelry, bird feeders, and much more.

Katie's on the Cove (207-454-8446; www.katieschocolates.com), Rt. 1, Mill Cove, Robbinston. All handmade and hand-dipped chocolates. Favorites, the luscious truffles aside, include Passamaquoddy Crunch, Maine Potato Candy, and Maine Black Bear Paws, even mustard chocolates using Raye's.

✷ Special Events

Memorial Day weekend: **Downeast Birding Festival**—guided hikes, boat tours, presentations (www.downeastbirdfest.org).

July: **Independence Day** is celebrated for an entire week in **Eastport**, with parades, a military flyover, and fireworks. Eastport's is the first flag in the United States to be raised on July 4 itself (at dawn).

Mid-August: **Annual Indian Ceremonial Days**, Pleasant Point Reservation—a celebration of Passamaquoddy culture climaxing with dances in full regalia.

September: **Paint Eastport Day** (*Saturday after Labor Day*)—artists of all ages are invited to come paint their favorite scene of the island city. At the end of the day artists return to the gallery for a silent auction.

Eastport Salmon (Pirate's) Festival (*Sunday after Labor Day*)—a celebration of Eastport's salmon industry; salmon, trout, and Maine potatoes are grilled dockside, and tours of fish farms in the bay are offered, along with live entertainment, games, an art show, an antiques auction, and a fishing derby.

December: **Festival of Lights**, Eastport. **New Year's Eve** is also big in Eastport, the first American city to welcome in the new year.

CALAIS AND THE ST. CROIX VALLEY

Calais (pronounced *CAL-us*), the largest city in Washington County, is the sixth busiest point of entry into the United States from Canada, just across the St. Croix River from St. Stephen, New Brunswick. The two communities are inextricably linked, celebrating a nine-day International Festival together in August.

The city's present population is less than 3,500, roughly 4,000 less than it was in the 1870s, the decade in which its fleet of sailing vessels numbered 176. The brick downtown was built soon after an 1870 fire had wiped out the previous city center. Happily, the city's wooden residential district seems largely to have escaped the fire and remains the best testament to the city's most prosperous era.

Down by the old waterfront the city shows signs of revival. The brick railroad station has been expanded and transformed into a Downeast Heritage Museum, offering an overview of the region as well as exhibits on the Passamaquoddy

Nation, local history, and the nature of surrounding land and water. It opened in 2004 to celebrate the 400th anniversary of the settling of nearby St. Croix Island, 8 miles downstream in the middle of the river. Rarely mentioned in American schoolbooks, St. Croix looms large in Canadian and French history. It was the first European settlement north of Florida and the beginning of the French presence in North America.

A French expedition was drawn here by the fur trade, and its leader, Pierre Dugua, Sieur de Monts, retained Samuel de Champlain as his mapmaker and chronicler. Probably the first European expedition to push up into Passamaquoddy Bay, they chose this 6.5-acre island for their settlement in June 1604 and set about building a storehouse and dwellings, despite the blackflies. The waters teemed with fish, and the native inhabitants were friendly—but the first snow came in early October, the river froze, and 35 of the 79 settlers died. Finally, on June 15, supply vessels arrived, and Dugua sailed south in search of a better settlement site. He instead returned to Port Royal, Nova Scotia, seeding French culture in Canada.

North of Calais the St. Croix Valley is as heavily forested and known for its fish-filled lakes as any spot in the North Maine Woods. Follow Rt. 1 north from Calais and your nose quickly reveals the area's big employer, the pulp and paper mill in nearby Woodland. Then the woods close in.

This area was first settled by Passamaquoddy Indians, who migrated up from the Bay of Fundy along the inland waterways. The small town of Princeton, flanked by Big Lake and Grand Falls Lake, is home to a number of fishing camps and to the Passamaquoddy community of Odeneg. The center of this Indian township reservation is, however, in Motahkomiqkuk at Peter Dana Point on Big Lake, a village with an Indian cemetery beside the old Catholic mission church of St. Anne's (Mass on Sunday at 11:15).

Grand Lake Stream. To visit Dana Point you have already turned off Rt. 1 on the road to Grand Lake Stream, a plantation that's a famous fishing outpost on West Grand Lake, with access to the vast Grand Lake chain. Grand Lake Stream claims to have been home to the world's biggest tannery, employing more than 500 people for some decades before it burned in the 1870s. The current lures are landlocked salmon, lake trout, smallmouth bass, pickerel, and white perch.

Despite its population of fewer than 200 year-rounders, this spirited and well-connected community has, in recent years, successfully struggled to create a land trust to manage the surrounding woodland. Some outstanding fishing lodges and camps are clustered here, and there are many good and affordable lakeside rental camps, a find for families. Local innkeepers can get you into the historical museum, a trove of Native American artifacts, tannery-era photos, and canoe molding. Inquire about hiking and guided kayaking. The **Grand Lake Stream Folk Festival** in late July draws visitors from far and wide.

GUIDANCE **Maine Tourist Information Center in the Downeast Heritage Museum** (207-454-2211), 39 Union St., Calais. Open year-round; July–Oct. 15, daily 8–6, otherwise 9–5:30. This center, operated by the Maine Tourism Association, is a source of brochures for all of Maine as well as the local area. The staff are friendly and eager to help, and there are public restrooms.

St. Croix Valley Chamber of Commerce (1-888-422-3112; www.visitstcroix valley.com) is helpful. For the **Grand Lake area** also check www.grandlake stream.com.

GETTING THERE *By car:* The direct route to Calais from Bangor and points west of Washington County is Rt. 9, the Airline Highway. From the Machias area, take Rt. 191. The slower but more scenic drive is along coastal Rt. 1.

WHEN TO COME Fly-fishers converge on Grand Lake Stream and the many lakes and ponds of the St. Croix Valley in May and June. The tourist season begins in July, and winter comes early (as Samuel de Champlain discovered). The area's two big events—the Grand Lake Stream Festival in late July and the Calais/St. Stephen International Festival in August—are as colorful as only big celebrations in small places can be.

✱ To See

Downeast Heritage Museum (207-454-7878 or 1-877-454-2500; www.down eastheritage.org), 39 Union St., Calais. Open Memorial–Columbus Day, 10–5. Donations welcomed. The saga of the 1604 settlement of St. Croix Island (see the introduction) is dramatized in French and English. You discover that the settlement's houses and storehouses were half-timbered, with brick chimneys, far more substantial than those the Pilgrims built two decades later at Plymouth. You also learn that the entire group would have perished were it not for help received from the region's Native American residents, the Passamaquoddy.

People of the Dawn, the museum's major exhibit, tells another long-overdue story—that of the Passamaquoddy tribe, whose members have managed, against all odds, to maintain their language, music, and crafts. Displays include replicas of local pictographs, some dating back 6,000 years; one depicts a 17th-century sailing vessel, probably Champlain's, which must have moored in Machias Bay, within view of the Native artist. The Passamaquoddy exhibit isn't large, but it does attempt to be authentic. The mannequins' faces depict actual tribal members. The 18-foot-long oceangoing birch-bark canoe was built by David Moses Brieges exactly as his great-grandfather would have built it, and the centuries-old wampum belt belongs to Donald Soctomah, tribal preservation officer. According to Soctomah, the tribe presently numbers 3,300 widely scattered members, with 800 in Indian Township north of Calais and 250 on the Pleasant Point Reservation near Eastport. Another 500 to 600 live in surrounding Washington County. St. Croix Island itself is flat, unprepossessing, and off-limits to the general public, due to ongoing archaeological excavations. At St. Croix Island's **International Historic Site Overlook**, Rt. 1 in Red Beach (8 miles south of Calais), however, a path leads leads to a bronze replica of the settlement. Along the way you encounter half a dozen haunting, life-sized bronze statues, here elaborately dressed Frenchmen, there a young Passamaquoddy girl.

St. Stephen Chocolate Museum (506-466-7848; www.chocolatemuseum.ca), Rt. 1, St. Stephens, New Brunswick. Open Mar.–Nov. but closed weekends before late June and after Sept. Admission fee. This interesting museum tells the story of the Ganong Bros. Ltd. Company. Displays of old candy boxes, hand-dipping demonstrations, videos, a game to test your packing speed, and free samples. The Ganong Chocolatier sells the tempting goodies.

Dr. Holmes Cottage/Museum (207-454-2604), 245 Main St. The oldest existing house in Calais, built in 1805 by Artemus Ward. Open July until the Friday before Labor Day, Mon.–Fri. 1–4:30. Restored to its 1850 look and maintained by the St. Croix Historical Society. Pick up a *Walking Tour Guide* to the Calais Residential Historic District, which includes several Gothic Revival gingerbread houses on S. Main St.

Whitlock Mills Lighthouse. The northeasternmost lighthouse in the country is best viewed from the Pike Woods Rest Area on Rt. 1, 3 miles south of Calais.

✱ To Do

BIRDING **Moosehorn National Wildlife Refuge** is a prime birding center with some 190 species recorded, as well as resident bald eagles (see *Green Space*).

BOATING **Grand Lake Outfitters** (207-796-5561; stevelaura@aol.com) Steve and Laura Schaefer offer rentals and guided tours of West Grand Lake with an eye out for blue herons, eagles, ospreys, muskrats, and otters as well as moose and deer. Both Steve and Laura are longtime residents, and Steve is a Registered Maine Guide.

Sunrise Expedtions International (www.sunrise-exp.com) offers trips—camping and canoeing—down the St. Croix River.

Cobscook Hikes & Paddles (207-726-4776; off-season, 207-454-2130). Registered Maine Guides Stephen and Tess Forek, based in Robbinston, offer guided two- and three-hour kayaking paddles from Whiting to Calais.

✐ **Up Close Tours** (207-454-2844). Calais-based Capt. Louis Bernardini offers two-hour boat tours downriver to see see ospreys and eagles, haul traps, and circle St. Croix Island.

Also see *Lodging* entries for Princeton and Grand Lake Stream; all fishing camps offer boat rentals. For guides see **www.grandlakestreamguides.com**.

FISHING The St. Croix watershed is famed for its abundance of landlocked salmon, square-tailed trout, and some of the finest smallmouth bass fishing in Maine. Best May–mid-June. When ice is out in spring, trolling starts on West Grand Lake, Big Lake, and Pocumcus Lake. Grand Lake Stream itself, fast-flowing water linking West Grand and Big Lakes, is one of the country's premier fly-fishing spots for landlocked salmon.

DOWNTOWN CALAIS

Christina Tree

Fishing licenses, covering three days to a full season (also necessary for ice fishing), are available, along with lodging and supplies, in the woodland village of **Grand Lake Stream** (www.grandlakestream.com), the focal point of the region and base for the state's largest concentration of fishing guides (www.grandlake streamguides.com). **Princeton**, on the way to Grand Lake Stream, is also worth noting for its waters: Big and Grand Falls Lakes. Both once ran freely into the St. Croix River, but thanks to a series of 19th-century industrial dams, are now known for their shallows and flowage, great for trout as well as moose-watching and canoeing.

Moosehorn National Wildlife Refuge (see *Green Space*). Several lakes and streams within the refuge are open for fishing.

GOLF **St. Croix Country Club** (207-454-8875), River Rd., Calais. A tricky nine-hole course on the banks of the St. Croix River.

SWIMMING **Red Beach on the St. Croix River** is named for the sand on these strands: pulverized deep red granite. There is also swimming in dozens of crystal-clear lakes. **Round Pond** in Charlotte has a free beach and boat launch. North of Calais, follow the Charlotte Rd. 8 miles to the pond.

✷ Green Space

Moosehorn National Wildlife Refuge (207-454-7161; www.moosehorn.fws .gov). This area is the northeast end of a chain of wildlife and migratory bird refuges extending from Florida to Maine and managed by the U.S. Fish and Wildlife Service. The 23,000-acre refuge is divided into two sections some 20 miles apart. The larger, 17,200-acre area is in Baring, 5 miles north of Calais on Rt. 1. Look for eagles, which nest each spring at the intersection of Charlotte Rd. and Rt. 1. The Edmunds division is found by heading south on Rt. 1 from Calais, between Dennysville and Whiting (see "Eastport"). This 7,200-acre area lies on the border of the tidal waters of Cobscook Bay. Volunteer-dependent programs—guided hikes, bike tours, and van tours, which sometimes take you down roads you wouldn't be able to explore on your own—are offered late June–Aug.

ST. CROIX INTERNATIONAL HISTORIC SITE OVERLOOK ON RT. 1, RED BEACH

Christina Tree

WALKS **Calais Waterfront Walkway**. A new 1.5-mile path follows a former railbed along the river, beginning at city landing parking lot. Formally a part of the East Coast Greenway, it's a good venue from which to appreciate the daily 25-foot tidal changes.

Devil's Head. A trail leads to a promontory, said to be the highest point west of Cadillac Mountain; great views. Look for the sign on Rt. 1 south of Heslin's Motel.

✷ Lodging

In Robbinston 04671

Brewer House (207-454-2385; www.thebrewerhousebnb.com), 590 Rt. 1, P.O. Box 88. This columned, 1828 mansion is now owned by Norwegian violinist and director of the Passamaquoddy Bay Symphony Orchestra and concertmaster of the Bangor symphony Trond Saeverud and artist Joan Siem. There are four rooms, all with private bath, three retaining massive carved beds from the previous owner. In the St. Andrews Room the headboard is a former altarpiece and the bath is large, with bay views. Captain John has an antique carved bed and a private bath (shower). Rates June 20–Oct. 15 are $95–155, including a full breakfast; otherwise $85–135. Pets are permitted in the two-bedroom Quoddy Cove Apartment ($95–125), with its own kitchenette and dining area. A gallery showcasing paintings by Joan and others is worth a stop, and chamber music is performed here throughout the summer.

Redclyffe Shore Motor Inn (207-454-3270; www.redclyffeshoremotorinn.com), Rt. 1. Twelve miles south of Calais on Rt. 1, this one-story motel with 16 units is set high above the wide mouth of the St. Croix, many rooms (request one) with river views. The added plus is dinner, a few steps away (see *Dining Out*). $68–78 per couple.

In Calais 04619

Greystone Bed & Breakfast (207-454-2848; www.greystonecalaisme.com), 13 Calais Ave. This 1840s Greek Revival mansion is set back on a quiet street, within walking distance of downtown shops. Alan and Candace Dwelley offer two attractive upstairs guest rooms with private bath, and TV; breakfast at 8 at the dining room table. $70–80 depending on the season.

The International Motel (207-336-7515 or 1-800-336-7515; www.theinternationalmotel.com), 626 Main St. The best lodging views in town are from the 19 Riverview units in this 61-unit motel owned and operated by three generations of the Thomas family. $75 per couple. Dogs accepted but not in Riverview. Meals are next door at the Wickachee.

Calais Motor Inn (1-800-439-5531; www.calaismotorinn.com), 663 Main St. A friendly, locally owned 70-unit motel with the bonuses of a new, indoor Olympic-sized swimming pool (with an aquatic lift), a hot tub and small fitness center, and a licensed restaurant (see *Dining Out*). $79 per couple in-season, $59 off-season.

In Princeton 04668

Lakeside Country Inn and Cabins (207-796-2324 or 1-888-677-2874; www.thelakeside.org), 14 Rolfe St., P.O. Box 36. Open year-round; cabins May–Nov. Built in 1854 with twin chimneys, the inn offers seven guest rooms. There are also five basic housekeeping cabins on Lewy Lake (the outlet to Big Lake). Rooms in the inn are simple, nicely furnished; each has a sink, some share a bath. Hosts Gary and Jennifer seem right for this place, hospitable outdoorspeople who are gardeners and good cooks. Inn rooms are $45 single, $65 double with breakfast; camps are $55–75 per couple with meals additional. Facilties include spa and game rooms. Guide service, boat rentals, and hunting/fishing licenses are available.

In Grand Lake Stream 04637

Leen's Lodge (207-796-2929 or 1-800-995-3367; www.leenslodge.com), P.O. Box 40. This traditional sporting camp faces West Grand Lake. According to guide and owner Charles Driza, this area represents the best woodcock hunting in the United States. July and August are family season, a good time just to fish, kick back, and relax by the lake. Lights are doused by 9 PM, the better to see the amazing sky. The nine cabins (50 beds) are scattered along the wooded shore, ranging in size from one to eight bedrooms, each with a full bath, fireplace or Franklin stove (with gas heat as a backup), and fridge. The dining room overlooks the water. The Tannery, a pine-paneled gathering space with a picture window, is equipped with games, books, and a TV. BYOB. $135 per person per day double occupancy MAP, $155 per person single occupancy, includes breakfast and dinner. Family rates; 15 percent gratuity is added; lunch, boat rentals, and guide service are extra.

Weatherby's (207-796-5558; in winter 207-926-5598; www.weatherbys.com), P.O. Box 69. Open early May–Oct. Jeff McEvoy and Elizabeth Rankin are the owners of this rambling white 1870s lodge set in roses and birches by Grand Lake Stream, the small river that connects West Grand Lake with Big Lake. Each of the 15 cottages is different, but most are log-style with screened porches, a bath, and a Franklin stove or fireplace. Fishing is what this place is about (fly-fishing only—Weatherby's is now an Orvis-sponsored lodge), and it's a great spot for children. $140 per person double occupancy, $162 single; $55 for children under 14 (family rates available) plus 15 percent gratuity. Rates include all three meals, a trail lunch or cookout lunch as well as breakfast and dinner; motorboats are $50 per day, a guide, $200 for two people for fly-fishing on the stream or smallmouth fishing on the lakes. Inquire about scheduled fly-fishing schools for novices and women as well as pros.

Chet's Camps (207-796-5557; www.chetscamps.com). Exceptional lakeside cabins and a central lodge right on Big Lake serve as a base for fly-fishing workshops and canoe expeditions as well as laid-back family vacations. Cabins can accommodate four to 10 people and can be booked on a housekeeping basis ($30–40) with meals available, or $135 per person ($105 per child) including all three meals. Inquire about the Grand Lake Stream Outdoor School. Guided backcountry canoe trips and flat- and whitewater canoeing and kayaking workshops are offered.

The Pines (207-557-7463; off-season, 207-825-4431; www.thepineslodge.com), P.O. Box 158. Open May 15–Oct. 1. Twelve miles and a century in atmosphere away from Grand Lake Stream on Lake Sysladobsis, part of the Grand Lake Stream chain. It's the oldest sporting camp in the area; past guests include Andrew Carnegie and

Calvin Coolidge. There are five cabins, also two housekeeping cottages on small islands. The oldest cabin dates to 1883 and the large, double-porched white-clapboard house from 1884. The upright piano in the living room was ferried over on the *Manhattan*, the launch that served the camp until the 1950s, when the 12 miles of logging roads were built (the last mile or so is a narrow dirt track that peters out into a trail along the edge of the lake). The cabins are heated by woodstoves and have gas lights and a chemical toilet. The main house (which offers flush toilets) and bathhouse are electrified. Cabins are $80 per person per night with three meals, including a packed lunch, $60 for children 3–10. Housekeeping cottages are $550 per week for four or less, $125 per day ($137.50 for more than four people). Steve and Nancy Norris have managed The Pines for the past 17 years.

Indian Rocks Camps (207-796-2822 or 1-800-498-2821; indianrocks@nemaine.com). Open ice-out through October. The Canells offer five century-old log cabins and a central lodge, not quite on the lake but with docking facilities. It's a friendly compound that caters to families and fishermen. $80 per person double occupancy, $82 single, includes all meals; five-day packages. Summer housekeeping cabin rentals are $425 per week. The dining room is open to the public by reservation.

🐾 ✐ **Canal Side Cabins** (207-796-2796 or 1-888-796-2796; www.canalsidecabins.com), P.O. Box 77. Open year-round. These family-run, family-geared cabins sleep between four and eight with a living room and dining area, a furnace or fireplace, full kitchen, and screened porch. Daily rates $35-40 per person, minimum of two; weekly family rates in July and Aug.

✱ Where to Eat

DINING OUT **The Chandler House** (207-454-7922), 9 Chandler St., Calais. Open 4–11 daily except Mon. Chef-owner William Condon specializes in seafood and is widely respected—with reason—in this corner of Maine. On our last visit we began with sautéed mussels served with oyster sauce, fresh peppercorns, and green onions, and scallop chowder. Some two dozen seafood choices might include baked stuffed salmon; prime rib with Yorkshire pudding is a favorite. Entrées $13–26.

Bernardini's (207-454-2237), 257 Main St., Calais. Open year-round (except Sun.) for lunch and dinner. Marilyn and Louis Bernardini's cheerful Italian trattoria glows with stained glass and wooden detailing from the demolished Immaculate Conception Church—and the food is good. Traditional Italian entrées, veal parmigiana, pasta specials, and desserts. Entrées ($13–14) come with salad and pasta or rice.

Redclyffe Shore Dining Room (207-454-3270), Rt. 1, Robbinston. Open May–Oct. 5–9 for dinner. The dining room overlooks the St. Croix River. The vast menu offers pasta, steaks, chicken, and seafood; specialties include baked haddock with lobster sauce. Entrées $15–22. Reserve.

Heslin's (207-454-3762), Rt. 1, Calais (south of the village). Open May into Oct. 5–9. A popular local dining room high above the river, specializing in steak ("the thickest cuts in town!")

and seafood entrées; homemade desserts, fully licensed. Most entrées under $20.

EATING OUT **Wickachee** (207-454-3400), 282 Main St. (Rt. 1), Calais. Open year-round 6 AM–10 PM. Steak and seafood (with a big salad bar) are the dinner specialties. Spacious, clean, and friendly, tiny restrooms.

Calais Motor Inn Restaurant (207-454-7111), 293 Main St. (Rt. 1), Calais. Open for lunch and dinner. A large, comfortable dining room specializing in steak and seafood at dinner.

✷ Selective Shopping

J. B. Siem Gallery (207-454-0333), Rt. 1, Robbinston (12 miles south of Calais). Open Mon.–Sat. 10–5, Sun. noon–5, and by appointment. The gallery features haunting paintings by internationally respected artist Joan Burger Siem, along with guest exhibits.

Downeast Heritage Museum Gift Shop (207-454-7878), 39 Union St., Calais. No museum admission necessary for the shop, which specializes in Passamaquoddy crafts and books and offers a quality selection of gifts.

Calais Bookshop (207-454-1110), 405 Main St., Calais. Carole Heinlen's inviting store stocks new, used, and rare titles. Worth checking.

Chermtos (207-454-3300), 283 Main St., Calais. Open year-round, Mon.–Sat. in-season, otherwise Thu.–Sat. Native American baskets, dream catchers, Maine and children's books, jewelry, notecards, gifts.

The Urban Moose (207-454-8277), 80 Main St., Calais. Souvenirs galore; same owner as 45th Parallel (see *Selective Shopping* in "Eastport"), same fabulously eclectic mix.

Marden's (207-454-1421), 189 Main St. and Rt. 1, Calais. Two representatives of the chain of Maine discount centers, which has been doing business in the state since 1964. Big-time bargains can be found here, from furniture to fabrics, housewares to clothing.

Pine Tree Store (207-796-5027), Water St., Grand Lake Stream. Open daily year-round. Kurt and Kathy Cressey's outpost oasis offers one of the largest selections of fishing flies in Maine; also tackle, clothing, hunting and fishing licenses, groceries, and an astonishing selection of wines "with caps that don't screw" plus great sandwiches to take with you to countless waterside picnic spots.

THE BEACH AT LEEN'S LODGE

Christina Tree

✷ Special Events

Last weekend of July: **Grand Lake Stream Folk Art Festival**—bluegrass and folk music, woodsmen's skills demonstrations featuring canoe building, crafts, dinner cooked by Maine Guides.

August: **International Festival**, Calais and St. Stephen, New Brunswick—a week of events on both sides of the border, including pageants, a parade, entertainment, and more.

ST. ANDREWS AND GRAND MANAN (NEW BRUNSWICK)

Beyond Eastport and Calais, you don't drop off the end of the world. Instead you cross the Canadian border—either via Rt. 1 at Calais or via ferry across Passamaquoddy Bay—into coastal New Brunswick. Suddenly it's an hour later, distance is measured in kilometers, signs are in French as well as English, gas is priced by the liter. Most tourists here are, of course, Canadian.

Historically and geographically, in this area Maine and Canada are intrinsically linked. Both St. Andrews (New Brunswick's liveliest resort town) and the island of Grand Manan (a haven for whale-watchers, birders, and hikers) were settled by loyalists during the Revolution, and Grand Manan, which lies just 9 miles off West Quoddy Light, is geographically closer to Maine than to Canada.

GUIDANCE Complete lodging listings for both St. Andrews and Grand Manan are detailed in the ***New Brunswick Touring Guide***, available by calling 1-800-561-0123 (toll-free in Canada and the United States) or by visiting www.tourismnbcanada.com. A large **Provincial Tourist Information Centre** (506-466-7390), 5 King St., St. Stephen, is housed in a grand old railroad station a few blocks beyond the border crossing, surrounded by banks at which you can exchange American for Canadian dollars (there's also a currency exchange inside the center). The municipal visitors center in **St. Andrews By-the-Sea** (1-800-563-7397; stachamb@nbnet.nb.ca) can mail information that includes ferry schedules.

GETTING THERE In good weather the ride across Passamaquoddy Bay from Eastport or Campobello via Deer Island is a delight, certainly the way to go at least one way to St. Andrews (see "Washington County"). If you're heading directly to Grand Manan, however, it makes more sense to drive to Blacks Harbour and board that island's ferry. From the Calais–St. Stephens border, it's 19 miles to St. Andrews and 35 miles to Blacks Harbour. See "Grand Manan" for details about the ferry.

TIME Note that New Brunswick's Atlantic time is one hour ahead of Maine's eastern time (1 PM ET is thus 2 PM AT). Both Maine and New Brunswick observe Daylight Saving Time.

ST. ANDREWS

Christina Tree

ST. ANDREWS

St. Andrews retains a genteel 19th-century charm. It's a pleasant resort town with shops lining well-named Water Street and plenty of choices for lodging, several restaurants, and a range of activities from historical tours to day adventures.

The big hotel is the Fairmont

Algonquin, a 240-room, many-gabled, neo-Tudor resort dating from 1915. It sits enthroned like a queen mother above this tidy town with loyalist street names like Queen, King, and Princess Royal. St. Andrews was founded in 1783 by British Empire loyalists, American colonists who so strongly opposed breaking away from the mother country that they left the new United States after independence was won. Most came from what is now Castine, many of them unpegging their houses and bringing them along. Impressed by this display of loyalty, the British government made the founding of St. Andrews as painless as possible, granting the settlers a superb site. British army engineers dug wells, built a dock, constructed a fort, and laid out the town on its present grid. Each loyalist family was also given a house lot twice the usual size. The result is an unusually gracious, largely 19th-century town, hauntingly reminiscent of Castine. The focal point remains Market Wharf, where the first settlers stepped ashore—now the cluster point for outfitters offering whale-watching, sailing, and kayaking tours—and Water Street, lined with shops.

GUIDANCE **St. Andrews Chamber of Commerce** (506-529-3555; www.town.standrews.nb.ca), 46 Reed Ave., St. Andrews, New Brunswick, Canada E5B 1A1. The information center is open mid-May–mid-Oct.

For New Brunswick tourist literature, including St. Andrews and Grand Manan, phone 1-800-563-7397 or e-mail stachamb@nbnet.nb.ca.

GETTING THERE *By car:* Rt. 1 via Calais. From the border crossing at Calais, it's just 19 miles (25k) to St. Andrews.

By car ferry: Late June–mid-Sept. only. See *Getting Around* and *Boat Excursions* in "Washington County." The ferry docks in L'Etete, and the road curves up the peninsula through the town of St. George, where you pick up Canadian Rt. 1, following it 13 unremarkable miles to the turnoff (Rt. 127) for St. Andrews.

WHEN TO COME The summer season is late June through September, but December is also big in St. Andrews, with many special events.

✷ To See

♿ **Kingsbrae Horticultural Garden** (506-529-3335; www.kingsbraegarden.com), 220 King St., St. Andrews. Open mid-May–mid-Oct., daily 9–6. Also open Nov.–Jan. with trees decorated for Christmas. $9 adults, $7.50 seniors and students. Even if you aren't a garden buff, this glorious 27 acres of elaborate gardens is a must-see. Walking paths, a delightful café, an art gallery, and a gift shop. Built on the grounds of several long-gone estates, the garden uses mature cedar hedges, flower beds, and old-growth forest in the new design. Specialized areas include display gardens with rare and native plants, a fantasy garden with animals made from moss, demonstration gardens, a woodland trail through the old-growth forest, a therapy garden, bird and butterfly gardens, and much more. For more about the café, see *Eating Out*.

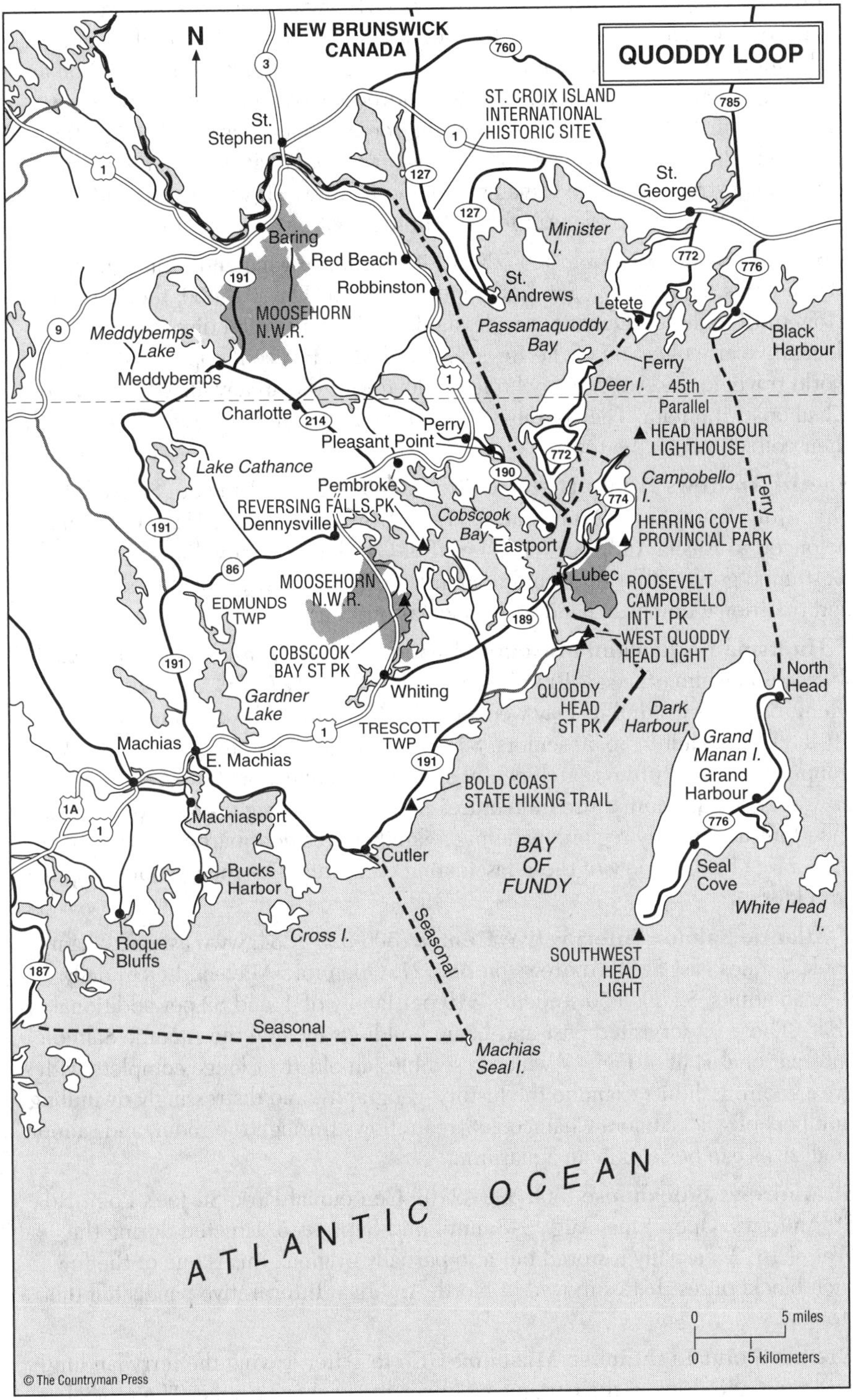
QUODDY LOOP
NEW BRUNSWICK
CANADA
N
St. Stephen
ST. CROIX ISLAND INTERNATIONAL HISTORIC SITE
St. George
Minister I.
Baring
Red Beach
Robbinston
St. Andrews
Letete
Black Harbour
MOOSEHORN N.W.R.
Meddybemps Lake
Passamaquoddy Bay
Ferry
Meddybemps
Deer I.
45th Parallel
Charlotte
Perry
Pleasant Point
HEAD HARBOUR LIGHTHOUSE
Lake Cathance
Campobello I.
Pembroke
REVERSING FALLS PK
Dennysville
Cobscook Bay
HERRING COVE PROVINCIAL PARK
Eastport
Lubec
MOOSEHORN N.W.R.
ROOSEVELT CAMPOBELLO INT'L PK
EDMUNDS TWP
COBSCOOK BAY ST PK
WEST QUODDY HEAD LIGHT
Whiting
North Head
QUODDY HEAD ST PK
Gardner Lake
Dark Harbour
TRESCOTT TWP
Grand Manan I.
Machias
E. Machias
Grand Harbour
BOLD COAST STATE HIKING TRAIL
Machiasport
Cutler
BAY OF FUNDY
Bucks Harbor
Seal Cove
White Head I.
Cross I.
Roque Bluffs
Seasonal
SOUTHWEST HEAD LIGHT
Seasonal
Machias Seal I.
ATLANTIC OCEAN
0 5 miles
0 5 kilometers
© The Countryman Press

Ministers Island Historic Site (506-529-5081; www.ministersisland.org), Chamcook. Open June–mid-Oct. $12 adult, $10 senior and student, free age 6 and under; $40 per family. One of the grandest estates, built around 1890 on an island connected by a "tidal road" to St. Andrews, **Covenhoven** is a 50-room mansion with 17 bedrooms, a vast drawing room, a bathhouse, and a gigantic and ornate livestock barn. The builder was Sir William Van Horne, the driving force in construction of the Canadian Pacific Railway. This is a real island, accessible at low tide; otherwise wait for the shuttle boat or kayak across.

Ross Memorial Museum (506-520-5124), corner of King and Montague Sts., St. Andrews. Open Mon.–Sat. mid-June–Columbus Day 10–4:30, then closed Mon. until mid-Oct. Donations welcomed. An 1824 mansion displaying the fine decorative art collection of the Reverend and Mrs. Henry Phipps Ross of Ohio, world travelers and collectors who fell in love with the area while on a picnic on Chamook Mountain. They purchased the 1824 house and donated it, along with their collections, to the town.

Sheriff Andrews House Historic Site (506-529-5080), King St., St. Andrews. Open June–early Sept., Mon.–Sat. 9:30–4:30, Sun. 1–4:30. An 1820 house that belonged to Elisha Andrews, high sheriff of Charlotte County; fine detailing. Costumed guides offer tours and demonstrate open-hearth cooking techniques and traditional domestic handiwork, such as quilting.

Huntsman Aquarium Museum Marine Science Centre (506-529-1202; www.huntsmanmarine.ca), Brandy Cove Rd. (off Rt. 127), St. Andrews. Open Memorial Day–Columbus Day weekend, 10–6 in July and Aug., otherwise 10–4:30. $7.50 adult, $6.50 seniors, $5 children; ages 3 and under are free. A nonprofit aquaculture research center sponsoring educational programs and cruises. The aquarium museum features hundreds of living plants and animals found in the Quoddy region, including a family of resident harbor seals, providing a rare close-up view of these fascinating creatures. The touch pool is popular with kids.

Atlantic Salmon Interpretive Centre (506-529-1384; www.asf.ca), Chamcook, 5 miles east of St. Andrews on Rt. 127. Open mid-May–mid-Oct., daily 9–5. $5 adults, $2.50–3.50 students, $10 per family of 4, and $2 per additional child. These undervisited post-and-beam buildings include the Atlantic Salmon International Hall of Fame—which resembles an old river lodge complete with great room. Exhibits examine the history, geography, and distressingly dwindling numbers of wild salmon. Chamcook Stream flows through the room, and salmon of all sizes can be seen in an aquarium.

St. Andrews Blockhouse (506-529-4270), Centennial Park, St. Joe's Point Rd., St. Andrews. Open June–Aug., 9–8; until mid-Sept., 9–5. Erected during the War of 1812, partially restored but also partially original, this is one of the few such blockhouses that's survived in North America. Interpretive panels tell the story.

Green's Point Lighthouse Museum, L'Etete. After leaving the ferry landing, turn right and drive to the parking area near the keeper's garage. The official name of the light station is "L'Etete Passage Light."

✱ To Do

GOLF **Algonquin Signature Golf Course** (see *Lodging*). Open May–Oct. The resort's golf course, recently completely redesigned. Thomas McBroom, an award-winning architect, laid out the 18 holes. From oceanfront to forest holes, the natural flow of the course and the scenic views make this an unforgettable golfing experience. Clubhouse, pro shop.

SAILING **Tall Ship Whale Adventures** (506-529-8116), St. Andrews Wharf. June–Oct. Three-hour sails travel Passamaquoddy Bay and up the St. Croix River of the Bay of Fundy, where you can see whales, dolphins, and other wildlife. Passengers are welcome to take the helm or help hoist sails.

SEA KAYAKING AND CANOEING In St. Andrews, **Seascape** (506-529-4866; www.seascapekayatours.com) offers half- and full-day guided tours as well as longer expeditions and lessons. **Eastern Outdoors** (1-800-56-KAYAK; www.easternoutdoors.com), 165 Water St., also offers guided half- and full-day tours; beginners welcome.

SWIMMING **Katy's Cove** (506-529-3433), Acadia Rd., St. Andrews, has (relatively) warm water, a sandy white beach, and a newly renovated clubhouse; nominal fee.

WHALE-WATCHING **Fundy Tide Runners** (506-529-4481; www.fundytiderunners.com). Hurricane boats, and clients wear flashy orange, full-length flotation suits; **Quoddy Link Marine** (506-529-2600; www.quoddylinkmarine.com) offers Whale Search and Island Cruises aboard two larger, slower vessels with enclosed, heated viewing areas as well as outdoor decks; **Island Quest Marine Adventures** (506-529-9885) offers a three-hour tour on a custom-built 38-foot tour boat.

✱ Lodging

All listings are in St. Andrews, New Brunswick, Canada.

RESORT "1" ✐ ♿ **The Fairmont Algonquin Hotel** (506-529-8823; in the U.S., 1-800-441-1414; www.fairmont.com), 184 Adolphus St., E5B 1T7. Fully open mid-Apr.–mid-Nov., but some 50 rooms in the new wing remain open year-round. The last of the truly grand coastal resorts in northeastern America: a 240-room (including 13 suites), Tudor-style hotel with formal common and dining rooms, this hotel was built in 1889 with the castle facade, but only 80 rooms. Ownership began with the St. Andrews Land Company and passed to the Canadian Pacific Railway Company, then to the province of New Brunswick; this is now a Fairmont-

FAIRMONT ALGONQUIN

Christina Tree

managed property. The golf course has undergone extensive renovations in recent years, and there are five dining options, a spa and fitness center, fitness classes year-round, a heated outdoor pool, tennis courts, shuffleboard, and a daily activity program for children in July and August. Bellhops wear kilts. The rack rates are $99–459, $299–$1,169 for suites (Canadian) per couple, but there are many special packages.

INNS "1" **Kingsbrae Arms Relais & Chateaux** (506-529-1897; www.kingsbrae.com), 219 King St., E5B 1Y1. Canada's first five-star inn (as decreed by Canada Select) is this 1897 shingled mansion adjoining Kingsbrae Gardens. The innkeeper is Harry Chancey Jr. with Alan Bell as manager. The softly colored drawing room is elegant with its grand piano and a pool in gardens beyond. A five-course meal is served (see *Dining Out*). Guest rooms are divided between the mansion and newer "wings." Those in the mansion are elegantly formal, while newer units are more spacious and informal, some tailored for families. All have phone and air-conditioning; some have air-pool bathtub and steam shower, fireplace. $690–1,175 (U.S.), including a full breakfast and a four-course dinner. Minimum two-night stay.

THE GARDEN AT KINGSBRAE ARMS

Christina Tree

Rossmount Inn (506-529-3351; www.rossmountinn.com), 4599 Rt. 127, E5B 2Z3. East of town, this boxy three-story hilltop mansion is a period piece—high Victorian with ornate chandeliers, woodwork, and appropriate furnishings. Built at the turn of the 20th century by the same Reverend and Mrs. Ross who endowed the Ross Museum in town, it has been recently revitalized by Chris and Graziella Aerni. A Swiss-born and -trained chef, Chris quickly established the inn as a dining destination (see *Dining Out*). Most rooms are now charmingly furnished with antiques and a choice of double, twin, queen-, and king-sized beds. The extensive property includes a swimming pool and walking trails up Chamcook Mountain, the highest point on this side of Passamaquoddy Bay. $105–135 in high season, otherwise from $76.

BED & BREAKFASTS Check with the chamber of commerce for other reasonably priced B&Bs, many of which seem to change each season.

"1" **Treadwell Inn** (1-888-529-1011; www.treadwellinn.com), 129 Water St., E5B 1A7. Open May–Oct. A real find. Annette and Jerry Mercer offer six spacious rooms, imaginatively furnished in antiques, each with private bath. Two rooms have a balcony overlooking the water (35 feet away). Two third-floor efficiency suites have a sitting area and whirlpool bath with private waterside balcony. Originally built in 1820 by a ship's chandler, eventually the building served as the town's customhouse. $145–250 (Canadian), $95–150 off-season, with breakfast available. Two-night minimum stay in waterfront rooms. Enjoy the street level Snug restaurant and cozy bar with water-view seating (see *Dining Out*).

"1" **Harris Hatch Inn Bed & Breakfast** (506-529-4995; www.harrishatchinn.ca), E5B 1E2. Open year-round, This stately 1840 brick mansion is the long-time home of Jura and Bob Estes. They offer three suites with full bath, two with a fireplace, and one with kitchen facilties. Full breakfast. $100–125 per couple in season, from $75 in winter.

OTHER 🐾 ✐ **St. Andrews Motor Inn** (506-529-4571), 111 Water St., E5B 1A3. A three-story motel with 37 units and a heated indoor swimming pool. All rooms have two queen-sized beds and color TV, some have kitchenette, and all have private balcony overlooking Passamaquoddy Bay. $159–229 (Canadian) plus tax in high season includes coffee. From $80 off-season.

🐾 ✐ **Seaside Beach Resort** (506-529-3846 or 1-800-506-8677; www.seaside.nb.ca), 339 Water St., E5B 2R2. Open early spring through autumn. We like the feel and location of this complex: 24 one- and two-bedroom housekeeping units (towels changed daily) in a mix of old houses and cabins that's been evolving since the 1940s, fronting—with a big shared deck—on Passamaquoddy Bay. Either Beth Campbell or David Sullivan is in the office to meet, greet, and help. High season $90–120, off-season $75–95; $10 per extra person.

CAMPING **Ocean Front Camping** (506-529-3439), Indian Point Rd. Maintained by the Kiwanis Club of St. Andrews, this is a beautifully sited campground with full hook-ups as well as tent sites.

Island View Campground (506-529-3787), Rt. 127, with sites featuring full hook-ups and tent sites, pool, and beach access overlooking historic St. Croix Island.

* Where to Eat

All listings are in St. Andrews.

DINING OUT **Rossmount Inn** (506-529-3351; www.rossmountinn.com), 4599 Rt. 127. East of town, this landmark inn (see *Lodging*) is once more a fabulous place to eat, thanks to Swiss-born and -trained chef-owner Chris Aerni. Reservations a must. The emphasis is on local ingredients—organic when possible—and all pastries are made here. The many-windowed yellow dining room is large and gracious, with crystal chandeliers, stained glass, and contemporary art. There's also a small, ornately comfortable bar. On our most recent visit we began with an heirloom tomato salad with chèvre and black olive tepenade and dined on prosciutto-wrapped pork tenderloin with shitake truffle risotto. Somehow we also managed a lavender-lemon crème brûlée with berry sorbet and citrus gingersnap. Entrées $16–25, more for lobster. Fully licensed.

The Treadwell Snug & Oyster Bar (506-529-8005; www.treadwellinn.com), 129 Water St. Open for lunch and dinner. This attractive waterside restaurant with imaginative decor was serving some of the best food in town in 2007 with Tim Currie, formerly of the Niger Reef Tea House, as chef. You might dine on cedar-planked salmon with a ginger molasses glaze or Dijon-glazed lamb shish kebabs with peppers and red onions. Entrées $19–26.

Kingsbrae Arms (506-529-1897; www.kingsbrae.com), 219 King St. Open for dinner by reservation May–Oct. and during the Christmas season. We celebrated our 35th wedding anniversary here and found ourselves overdressed. Dinner is served in one of the inn's two elegant dining rooms and it was a set menu: the "amuse," locally smoked sturgeon; the "debut," crabcakes from locally caught shellfish; "la suite," roasted leg of caribou with shallot popover; and a choice of "finale," a vanilla maple crème brûlée. $100 per person plus wine.

L'Europa (506-529-3818; www.europainn.com), 48 King St. Open in-season for dinner daily except Mon. Established as a fine restaurant with a German accent in 1983, it continues on both counts under owners master chef Markus Ritter and his wife, Simone, who moved to St. Andrews from Bavaria. Dine on duck a l'orange, or on jagerschnitzel—milk-fed veal scalloppine in a creamy mushroom sauce with vegetables and homemade spaetzle. Entrées $19–28. Fully licensed.

Inn on Frederick (506-529-2603; www.innonfrederick.ca), 58 Frederick St. Open for breakfast, dinner, and a Sunday buffet brunch. Chef-owner James Crouch worked for 25 years at Canadian Pacific hotels, for 10 at the Algonquin before opening his own inn. This is formal dining with entrées like salmon baked in phyllo pastry with cream cheese and scallops, and milk-fed veal quickly sautéed with artichoke hearts, onions, and mushrooms in a light cream sauce. Entrées $23–32.

The Passamaquoddy Dining Room at the Algonquin (506-529-8823), 184 Adolphus St. The dining room is huge, and its most pleasant corner is in the veranda, with windows overlooking formal gardens. The menu is large, featuring local salmon and lobster. Entrées $28–48. Inquire about the hugely popular Sunday buffet.

EATING OUT The Gables (506-529-3440), 143 Water St. Open 11–10. Reasonably priced good food, and a tiered, shaded deck with a water view. Specialties include fresh fish ranging from fried haddock-and-chips to a seafood platter. We recommend the mussels. Fully licensed; wine by the glass and a wide selection of beers.

✎ **Kingsbrae Garden Café** (506-529-3335; www.kingsbraegarden.com), 220 King St. Open May–Oct. Housed in the original manor home on the grounds of this 27-acre formal garden, this delightful café is well worth knowing about before you get there, good for ample but ladylike luncheon salads and sandwiches served on a choice of freshly baked croissant, seven-grain roll, or wrap. Wine and beer. Afternoon tea with scones, finger sandwiches, and a deluxe chocolate brownie is served from 2:30.

Elaine's (506-529-4496), 24 Lower King St. An informal place for a variety of food, salads and burgers to curries, and nori seaweed roll-ups.

Sweet Harvest Market (506-529-6249), 182 Water St. Open for breakfast and lunch, 8–5. Try the salmon mousse with dill, lemon, and mayo.

✷ Selective Shopping

All listings are in St. Andrews.

Cottage Craft Ltd. (1-800-355-9655; www.cottagecraftwoolens.com), 209 Water St. in Town Square. Open year-round, Mon.–Sat. Dating to 1915, Cottage Craft showcases yarns, tweeds, finished jackets, sweaters, and skirts; also distinctive throws handwoven in homes throughout Charlotte County. Upward of 150 knitters produce the sweaters, hats, scarves, and mittens, some wonderfully priced. A wine bar on the water is planned.

Cricket Cove (506-456-3897), 147 Water St. Fine hand knits and designer yarns from around the world.

Serendipin' Art (506-529-3327), 168 Water St. A large selection of handmade New Brunswick crafts, including jewelry, pottery, hand-painted silks, and more.

Christina Tree

DINING AT THE GABLES

✷ Special Events

December: **Winter Festival**—a full range of Christmas activities from a twinkling evening candlelight parade to the "garden of lights" dine-around experience (506-529-3555 or stachamb@nbnet.nb.ca, for a schedule of events and packages).

GRAND MANAN

Little more than 15 miles long and less than 7 miles wide, Grand Manan is Canada's southernmost island, far enough at sea to be very much its own place, a rugged outpost at the mouth of the Bay of Fundy.

Right whales are what draw many visitors. These are the rarest of whales. Just 320 are known to exist worldwide, but many seem to be here in summer months, feeding on krill and other nutrients in the tide-churned waters. Birds are another draw: 240 species frequent the island. Machias Seal Island, the prime viewing place for puffins, is as easily accessible from Grand Manan as from Maine. A 40-mile network of hiking trails is another plus, many miles hugging cliffs that vary from 100 to almost 400 feet.

Fishing boats line the wharves the way they used to in New England. While fish are fewer than they once were here, too, fishing is more profitable than ever. Connors Brothers sardine factory at Seal Cove was the island's largest employer until it closed in the spring of 2005, but salmon farming remains big, along with lobster and clams, periwinkles, and that Grand Manan delicacy: dulse. The hundreds of herring smokehouses for which the island was once known are, however, either gone or standing unused, with one preserved as an unusual museum.

Grand Manan's population has hovered around 2,700 since the late 19th century, clustered in the sheltered harbors and coves along its gentle Bay of Fundy shore, which is protected by many small islands. In contrast, the northern and southern "heads" of the island are soaring cliffs, as is almost the entire western shore. It's a mirror image of Maine's Bold Coast, with only well-named Dark Harbour accessible by car. Trails and boats can make their way to Indian Beach, Money Cove, Bradfords Cove, and Little Dark Harbour.

In many ways Grand Manan remains as out-of-the-way and unspoiled as it was during the 20 summers (1922–42) that Willa Cather spent here, working on some of her most famous novels, including *Death Comes for the Archbishop*. Her cottage on Whale Cove is one among the island's many summer rentals.

GUIDANCE **Grand Manan Tourism Association**, 1141 Rt. 776. The seasonal **Visitor Information Center** (506-662-3442 or 1-888-525-1655; www.grandmanannb.com) is housed at the rear of the museum. Open July–mid-Sept., daily 9–5. The association publishes the inexpensive booklets *Grand Manan Trails* and *Grand Manan Guide*. The Web site is by far the island's best source of information.

GETTING THERE *By car:* From Calais it's 19 miles to St. Andrews and 35 miles to Blacks Harbour.

By ferry: **Coastal Transport** (506-662-3724; www.coastaltransport.ca) operates ferries on the 20-mile, 90-minute sail between Blacks Harbour on the mainland (35 miles from the Calais–St. Stephen border) and North Head on the island. During high season (June 29–Labor Day), ferries run seven times a day, every two hours during summer months beginning at 7:30 AM. Service from the mainland is first come, first served but check to see; this policy is due to change. Things we wish we'd known: (1) The ferry terminal is a couple of miles beyond the village of Blacks Harbour, so you may want to stock up on food and drink before you get in line. (2) Call to check which ferry runs when. At peak times avoid the M/V *Grand Manan*, the smaller seasonal ferry, which takes just around 20 cars or, as on our run, 15 cars (we were car 16) and a few big trucks; the M/S *Grand Manan V* is capable of swallowing many more vehicles. This ferry also has an elevator up from the car level. (3) If you are returning the following day, use the special wall phone in the terminal to reserve your space. Reservations are available a day in advance on trips *from* the island. Food is available on both ferries. Pedestrians and bicyclists have no problem getting on. Parking is ample and free in Blacks Harbour, and whale-watching, sea kayaking tours, and rental bikes are also within walking distance of the ferry terminal on Grand Manan.

✷ To See

✐ ♿ **The Grand Manan Museum** (506-662-3524; www.grandmananmuseum.ca), 1141 Rt. 776, Grand Harbor, across from the school. Open May–Sept., Mon.–Sat. 9–5. $5 adult, $3 senior and student, free age 12 and under. The Allan Moses Bird Collection, an exhibit of more than 300 mounted birds, documents the island's bird life, and the history of the island's smoked herring industry is dramatized in paintings, photographs, and memorabilia. Novelist Willa Cather's typewriter and manuscript table are also here. Inquire about evening slide shows and rainy-day programs.

Dark Harbour. The only road across the width of the island ends abruptly at the harbor (it's a tight turnaround at high tide), the one nick in what is otherwise a wall of cliffs that run the length of the western shore. This is a prime dulse-harvesting spot, but there are no commercial enterprises, just seasonal cottages that are inaccessible except by boat.

Southwest Head. Your first instinct is to drive the length of the island on the one north–south road, grandiosely numbered 776. It ends at Southwest Head Lighthouse, and a path leads along spectacular cliffs.

Hole in the Wall. The view of this much-photographed natural arch near the northern end of the island is most easily accessed via a fairly steep path, from a parking area that lies within Hole-in-the-Wall Park, a former airport that's now a commercial campground. Great viewing spots for whale-watching.

✱ To Do

BIRDING AND NATURE The island is visited annually by 240 species of birds and many, many more individual bird-watchers. Bird species are listed on the island Web site (www.grand manannb.com). Castalia Marsh, accessible via a nature trail in Castalia Provincial Park, is a favorite spot at dawn and dusk. One of the first visitors was John James Audubon, who came in 1831 to check out the unlikely-but-true story that island seagulls nest in trees.

Sea Watch Tours (506-662-8332; www.seawatchtours.com) offers mid-June–early Aug. trips from Seal Cove Grand Manan to Machias Seal Island to see puffins, Arctic terns, and razor-billed auks. Capt. Peter Wilcox is a native of Grand Manan whose ancestors came here from New England during the Revolution. In 1969 his father began offering trips to Machias Seal, which is 10 miles south of the southern tip of in Grand Manan. Be sure to come prepared with windbreaker, wind pants, hat, and mittens for the early morning ride out. For details about Machias Seal Island see *Birding* in the Atlantic Coast subchapter. Whale-watching tours are also offered; no whales, no charge.

MACHIAS SEAL ISLAND

Christina Tree

HIKING Some 45 miles of marked hiking trails cover a variety of terrain along the shore. Pick up a copy of *Heritage Trails and Footpaths* (available in most island stores) and a picnic and you're set.

KAYAKING AND BIKE RENTALS

Adventure High (506-662-3563 or 1-800-732-5492; www.adventurehigh.com), 83 Rt. 776. Guided tours range from a two-hour moonlight trip to six-hour explorations and include Seal

Watch Tours and a Kayak Tour & Dinner on the beach. Mountain and hybrid bikes are also rented. Inquire about the solar-heated rental cottage on a remote cove.

WHALE-WATCHING **Whales-n-Sails Adventures** (506-662-1999 or 1-888-994-4044; www.whales-n-sails.com), North Head, Fisherman's Wharf, offers two daily trips, weather permitting, June–mid-Sept. Sailing and whale-watching are a great combination. The 56-foot, 47-passenger ketch *Elsie Menota* supplements sail with power to reach the deeps in the Bay of Fundy (12 miles northeast of Grand Manan), where Atlantic right whales feed and play, but then it's quiet and pleasant to tack and jibe among these huge creatures. Owner Allan McDonald points out bird and sea life en route.

Sea Watch Tours (see *Birding*) also offers whale-watch cruises, and is the only boat that goes from Grand Manan to Machias Seal Island, the home of the puffins.

✷ Lodging

Note: The choice of lodgings and cottages is large, and most are listed on www.grandmanannb.com. The following represent the best of the inns and B&Bs we checked. All listings are in Grand Manan, New Brunswick, Canada.

✐ "1" **The Inn at Whale Cove Cottages** (506-662-3181; www.holidayjunction.com), 26 Whale Cove Cottage Rd., 35G 2B5. The gray-shingled Main House dates from 1816, overlooking a quiet cove with a large fish weir, backed by rugged Fish Head. It was here in picturesque Orchardside cottage ($900 per week) that Willa Cather first came to write in 1922, eventually building a replica of it a way down the shore (also available for rent, a gem in which we celebrated a birthday). The inn and cottages are owned and operated by Laura Buckley. The Main House parlor has changed little since it began welcoming "rusticators" in 1910. The fireplace is large and usually glowing, and the walls are lined with books. Two-bedroom Cove View, with two decks and a full living room and library, is $800 per week. Coopershop features a huge fireplace and two upstairs bedrooms as well as a living room and kitchen/dining area ($800 per week). There are also the one-bedroom Bungalow ($120 per night) and three delightful rooms in the Main House ($110 single, $120 double per night). Rates include a very full breakfast. Dinner is also served (see *Dining Out*).

❀ **McLaughlin's Wharf Inn** (506-662-8760), 1863 Rt. 776, E5G 3H1. Open July–Aug. Brenda McLaughlin converted the store in Seal Cove that had been in her family for generatons to a combination B&B and restaurant: six upstairs rooms with two shared baths, water views, TV lounge. $79 single to $89 double includes full breakfast. Dinner served. This is a very special spot.

Compass Rose (506-662-8570; off-season, 613-471-1772; www.compassroseinn.com), 65 Rt. 776, North Head, E5G 1A2. Open June–Oct. Within walking distance of the ferry terminal, water excursions, and bike rentals, this is a gem of an inn, overlooking the busy harbor of North Head. Owner Nora Parker has renovated the entire inn. Each of the six guest rooms is furnished in antiques and has a private bathroom and harbor view, but they're also right on the road. The dining room, which is open to the public, is a must-stop for every visitor (see *Dining Out*). $89–129 per couple includes a full breakfast.

The Shorecrest Lodge (506-662-3216; www.shorecrestlodge.com), 100 Rt. 776, E5G 1A1. Open May–Oct. Gunther Bogensperger and Evelyn Paine are steadily renovating this rambling old country inn on the edge of North Head Village. All rooms are nicely, unfussily comfortable and have a variety of bed arrangements and private baths. The food is good. We recommend Room 8. $75–119.

Marathon Inn (506-662-8488; www.angelfire.com/biz2/marathon), North Head, E0G 2M0. Open year-round. This is a big white ark of a place on a hill overlooking the water in North Head. The rooms we saw (there are 24) were clean and cheerful, with tasteful prints and colorful quilts, and there's a pool. We've been warned to avoid the annex. The large, sunny dining room, serving all three meals, is popular with birding groups and Elderhostel. $79–109.

Manan Island Inn B&B (506-662-8624; www.mananinn.com), 22 Rt. 776, E5G 1A1. Open year-round. Conveniently sited in North Head across from the ferry terminal, an 1894 house with nine guest rooms, all with private bath or shower. Guest refrigerator. $79–99 with continental breakfast.

CAMPGROUNDS **The Anchorage** (506-662-7035 or 1-800-561-0123), 136 Anchorage Rd., E5G-2H4. The 100 sites vary from wooded to waterside; 24 accommodate trailers.

Hole-in-the-Wall (506-662-3152 or 1-866-662-4489; www.grandmanancamping.com), 42 Old Airport Rd., E5G 1A9. With 48 sites, there is a wide range in this sprawling property, from RV to wooded—some fairly spectacular.

Forest Edge Camping (506-662-3673; www.forestedgecamping.com). Thirty camper sites, 10 tent sites.

✱ Where to Eat

DINING OUT **The Inn at Whale Cove** (506-662-3181), 25 Whale Cove Cottage Rd., near North Head. Open nightly in-season, 6–8:30. Reservations required. The dining room in the early-19th-century cottage seats just 30 people. It's candlelit and decorated with vintage willowware. Chef-owner Laura Buckley uses local ingredients imaginatively. The set menu changes nightly but always includes three to five courses. Fully licensed. Entrées $20–30.

Compass Rose (506-662-8570), North Head. Open June–Oct. for dinner (except Mon.). The harbor view is unbeatable, and even without it the dining room would strike you as unusually pleasant. Dinner might be seafood lasagna or pan-fried haddock; leave room for double chocolate cheesecake. Entrées $16–25.

McLaughlin's Wharf Inn (506-662-8760), 1863 Rt. 776, Seal Cove. Open July–Aug. for dinner. Begin with fresh mussels steamed in garlic butter or smoked salmon with lemon butter and homemade dill bread, then dine on sea scallops baked in garlic butter, served with vegetables, salad, and a fresh roll or lobster with tarragon cream on farfalle pasta. $11–21.

The Shorecrest Lodge (506-662-3216; www.shorecrestlodge.com), 100 Rt. 776. Open for dinner. Chef-owner Gunther Bogensperger is establishing a reputation for this attractive, old-fashioned hotel dining room. We feasted on scallops and salmon. Entrées $22–28.

EATING OUT ✐ **Gallaways Restaurant** (506-662-8871), Rt. 776, North Head. A sports bar with plenty of room to get away from the bar, the obvious place for a burger and beer, also salads, fried seafood, a kids' menu.

North Head Bakery (506-662-8862), Rt. 776 south of the village. Open 6–6. Seasonal. Using organic flours, no bleach, this is a both a first and last stop for patrons: first stop in the morning for croissants and doughnuts (coffee is served); last stop when leaving the island, taking baguettes and breads home with them.

Keyser's Wharf (506-662-8182), 9 Ferry Wharf Rd. Open daily for breakfast and an all-day menu that includes spring rolls, pan-seared scallops, and pizza. Nice atmosphere.

✷ Selective Shopping

Roland's Sea Vegetables (506-662-3866), 174 Hill Rd. (marked from the Dark Harbour Rd.), is a must-stop. Dulse and other seaweeds are hand harvested at Dark Harbour, then dried and packaged. We wish we had bought more bottles of dulse flakes.

Island Artisans (506-662-3625), North Head. Open seasonally. A mix of quality crafted items and art. Inquire about summer art workshops.

Western Mountains and Lakes Region

SEBAGO AND LONG LAKES REGION

OXFORD HILLS AND LEWISTON/AUBURN

BETHEL AREA

RANGELEY LAKES REGION

SUGARLOAF AND THE CARRABASSETT VALLEY

Christina Tree

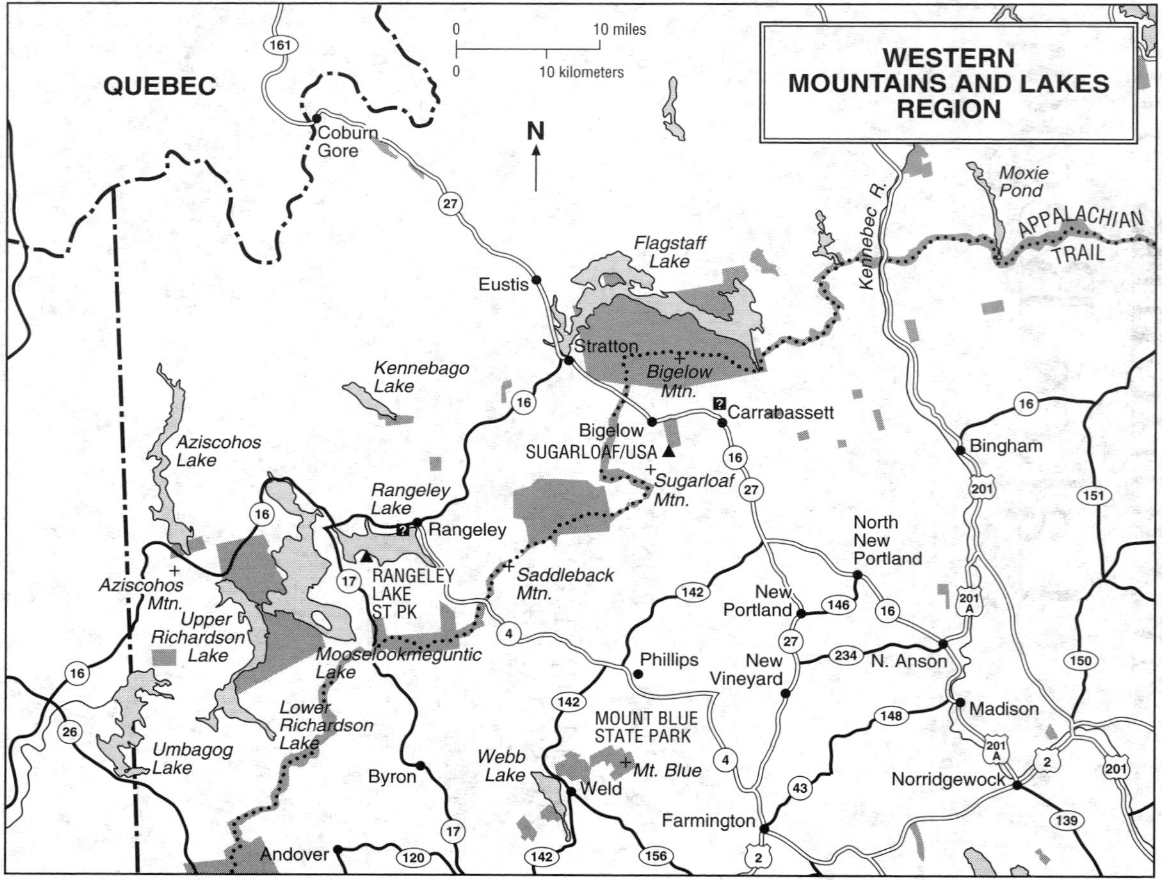
WESTERN
MOUNTAINS AND LAKES
REGION
QUEBEC
0
10 miles
0
10 kilometers
N
Coburn Gore
Eustis
Stratton
Flagstaff Lake
Bigelow Mtn.
Bigelow
Carrabassett
SUGARLOAF/USA
Sugarloaf Mtn.
Kennebago Lake
Aziscohos Lake
Aziscohos Mtn.
Rangeley Lake
Rangeley
RANGELEY LAKE ST PK
Saddleback Mtn.
Upper Richardson Lake
Mooselookmeguntic Lake
Lower Richardson Lake
Umbagog Lake
Byron
Andover
Webb Lake
Weld
MOUNT BLUE STATE PARK
Mt. Blue
Phillips
New Portland
North New Portland
New Vineyard
N. Anson
Farmington
Madison
Norridgewock
Bingham
Kennebec R.
Moxie Pond
APPALACHIAN TRAIL
161
27
16
17
4
142
146
234
148
43
156
120
26
201
201 A
2
139
150
151

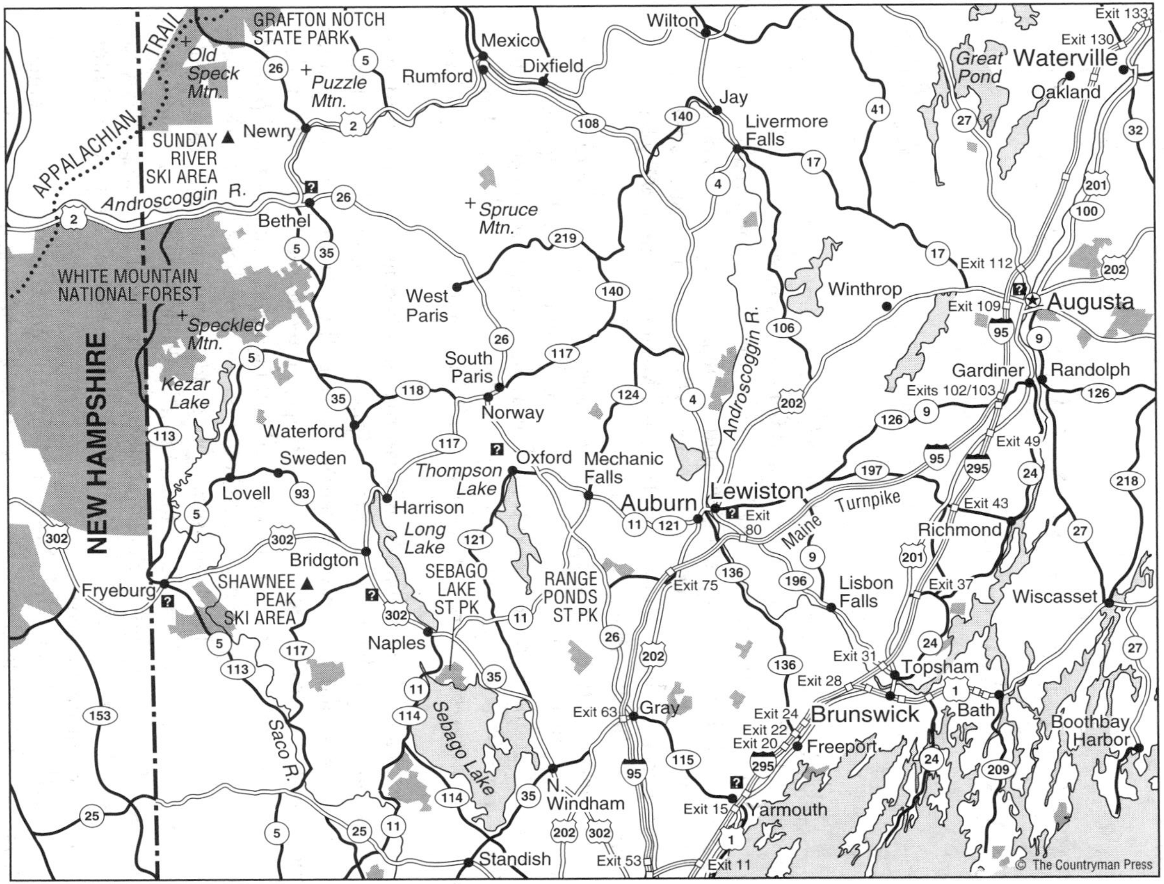
NEW HAMPSHIRE
APPALACHIAN TRAIL
GRAFTON NOTCH STATE PARK
Old Speck Mtn.
Puzzle Mtn.
SUNDAY RIVER SKI AREA
Newry
Rumford
Mexico
Dixfield
Wilton
Jay
Livermore Falls
Androscoggin R.
Bethel
Spruce Mtn.
WHITE MOUNTAIN NATIONAL FOREST
Speckled Mtn.
Kezar Lake
West Paris
South Paris
Norway
Waterford
Sweden
Lovell
Oxford
Thompson Lake
Mechanic Falls
Harrison
Long Lake
Bridgton
Fryeburg
SHAWNEE PEAK SKI AREA
SEBAGO LAKE ST PK
RANGE PONDS ST PK
Naples
Sebago Lake
Saco R.
N. Windham
Standish
Auburn
Lewiston
Exit 80
Maine Turnpike
Exit 75
Gray
Exit 63
Exit 53
Lisbon Falls
Winthrop
Augusta
Exit 112
Exit 109
Gardiner
Randolph
Exits 102/103
Exit 49
Exit 43
Richmond
Exit 37
Wiscasset
Exit 31
Topsham
Exit 28
Brunswick
Bath
Exit 24
Exit 22
Exit 20
Freeport
Exit 15
Yarmouth
Exit 11
Boothbay Harbor
Great Pond
Waterville
Oakland
Exit 130
Exit 133
© The Countryman Press

WESTERN MOUNTAINS AND LAKES REGION

Inland Maine is the most underrated, least explored piece of New England, frequently perceived as an uninterrupted flat carpet of firs.

Larger than Vermont and New Hampshire combined, it is actually composed of several distinct and unique regions and distinguished by a series of almost continuous mountain ranges, more extensive than New Hampshire's White Mountains and higher than Vermont's Green Mountains, but lacking a name (why aren't they the Blue Mountains?).

In contrast with the coast, inland Maine was actually more of a resort area a century ago than it is today. By the 1880s trains connected Philadelphia, New York, and Boston with large resort hotels in Rangeley and Greenville, and steamboats ferried "sports" to "sporting camps" in the far corners of lakes. Many of these historic resorts survive but today require far more time to reach, unless you fly in.

Today inland Maine seems even larger than it is because almost a third of it lies beyond the public highway system, a phenomenon for which we can blame Massachusetts and its insistence that Maine sell off the "unorganized townships" (and divide the profits) before it would be permitted to secede in 1820. In the interim most of this land has been owned and managed by lumber and paper companies. Debate currently rages about the future of these woodlands (somewhere between a third and almost half of inland Maine); many environmental organizations would like to see a Maine North Woods National Park, but locals remain adamantly against such an initiative. The reality of the way public roads run—and don't run—continues to physically divide Maine's mountainous interior into several distinct pieces.

One of these pieces is the Western Mountains and Lakes Region, extending from the rural farmland surrounding the lakes of southwestern Maine, up through the Oxford Hills and into the foothills of the White Mountains and the Mahoosuc Range around Bethel, then on into the wilderness (as high and remote as any to be found in the North Woods) around the Rangeley Lakes and the Sugarloaf area—east of which public roads cease, forcing traffic bound for the Moosehead Lake region to detour south into the farmland of the Lower Kennebec Valley.

The five distinct areas within the Western Mountains and Lakes Region are connected by some of Maine's most scenic roads, with farmhouses, lakes, mountains, and unexpected villages around each bend. Many of these views are not generally appreciated because the area is best known to skiers, accustomed to racing up to Sunday River and Sugarloaf (Maine's most popular ski resorts) by the shortest routes from the interstate. They don't know what they're missing. The roads around Rangeley offer views so spectacular, stretches of two of them (Rts. 4 and 17) are included in a newly designated National Scenic Byway.

In summer and fall we suggest following Rt. 113 through Evans Notch or heading north from Bridgton to Bethel by the series of roads that threads woods and skirts lakes, heading east along Rt. 2, continuing north to Rangeley via Rt. 17 through Coos Canyon and over the spectacular Height o' Land from which you can see all five Rangeley Lakes and the surrounding mountains. From Rangeley it's just another 19 scenic miles on Rt. 16 (better known as Moose Alley) to the Sugarloaf area. You can return to Rt. 2 by continuing along Rt. 16 to Kingfield, then taking Rt. 142 through Phillips and Weld.

SEBAGO AND LONG LAKES REGION

Fifty lakes can be seen from the summit of Pleasant Mountain, 10 within the town of Bridgton itself. These lakes are what draw summer visitors. They swim and fish, fish and swim. They cruise out in powerboats or paddle canoes and kayaks. On rainy days they browse through the area's abundant antiques and crafts stores. In winter visitors ski, downhill at Shawnee Peak (alias Pleasant Mountain) or cross-country almost anywhere.

Before the Civil War visitors could actually come by boat all the way to Bridgton from Boston. From Portland, they would ride 20 miles through 28 locks on the Cumberland & Oxford Canal, then across Sebago Lake, up the Songo River, Brandy Pond, and Long Lake to Bridgton. The first hotel atop Pleasant Mountain opened in 1850, and in 1882 the "2-footer" narrow gauge opened between Hiram and Bridgton, enabling summer visitors to come by train as well.

Today, as in the 1880s, most visitors waste little time getting onto or into water. The Naples Causeway is the base for water sports, and the departure point for cruises on Long Lake and through the only surviving canal lock. Sebago, Maine's second largest lake, is its most popular waterskiing area.

This southwestern corner of the state offers plenty on land, too: hiking, golf, tennis, mineral collecting, and such fascinating historic sights as Willowbrook in Newfield.

Fryeburg, just west of the lakes in the Saco River Valley, is the region's oldest community and the site of the state's largest agricultural fair. It is also headquarters for canoeing the Saco River. Sandy bottomed and clear, the Saco meanders for more than 40 miles through woods and fields, rarely passing a house. Too shallow for powerboats, it is perfect for canoes and kayaks. There is usually just enough current to nudge along the limpest paddler, and the ubiquitous sandbars serve as gentle bumpers. Tenting is permitted most places along the river, and there are public campgrounds. Outfitters rent canoes and provide shuttle service.

In summer most families come for a week to stay in lakeside cottages—of which there seem to be thousands. Motels, inns, and B&Bs still fill on weekends with parents visiting their children at camps—of which there seem to be hundreds. As more travelers discover the beauty and tranquility of the region, the number of these types of lodgings, while nowhere near the glut of such establishments along the coast, is expanding every year.

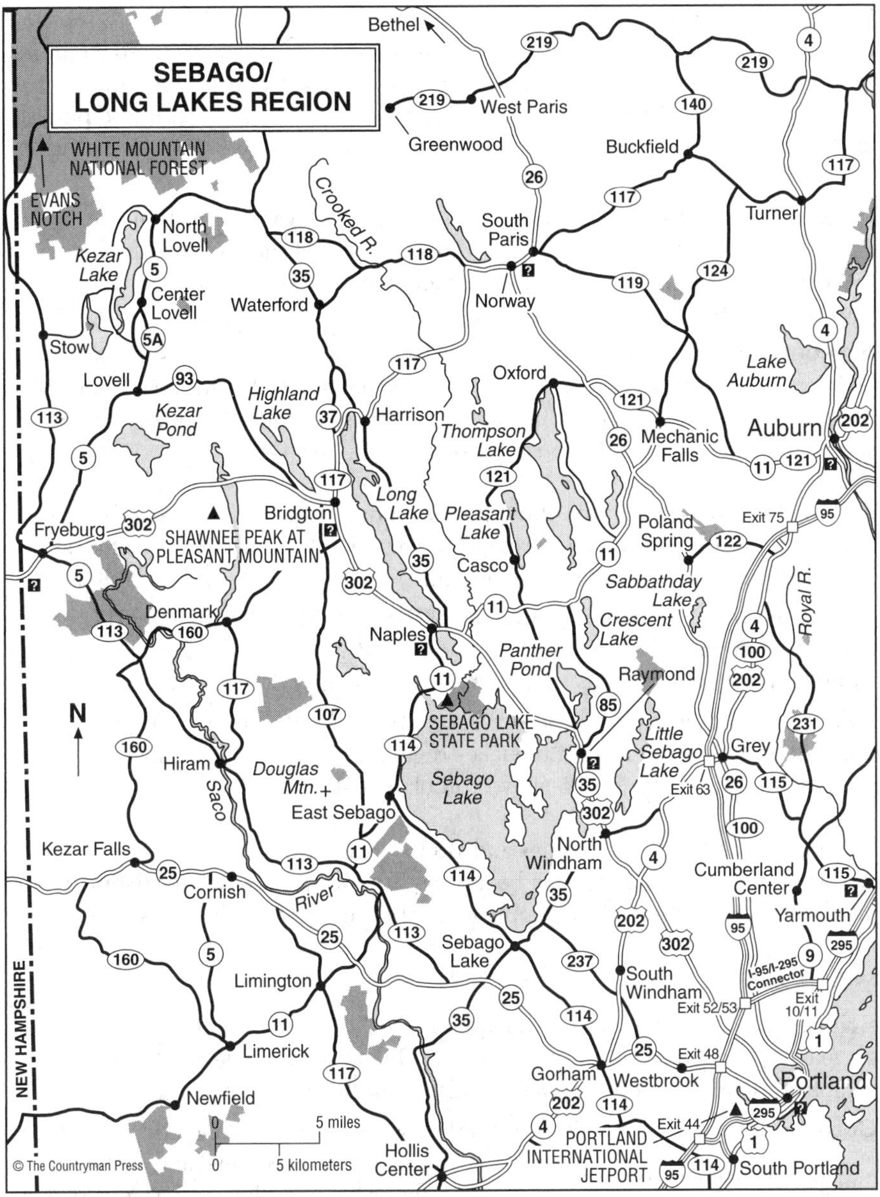

GUIDANCE **Greater Bridgton Lakes Region Chamber of Commerce** (207-647-3472; www.mainelakeschamber.com), 101 Portland Rd. (Rt. 302), Box 236, Bridgton 04009. The chamber maintains a walk-in information center. Request a copy of the *Greater Bridgton–Lakes Region Area Guide*. Year-round information is also available from the **Bridgton town office** (207-647-8786).

Sebago Lakes Region Chamber of Commerce (207-892-8265; www.sebagolakeschamber.com), P.O. Box 1015, Windham 04062, maintains a seasonal information booth at 911 Roosevelt Trail on Rt. 302 and a seasonal information bureau next to the Naples Historical Society Museum on Rt. 302. It also publishes a tourism and information guide that covers the towns of Casco, Gray, Naples, Raymond, Standish, and Windham.

Cornish Association of Businesses (207-625-8083; www.cornish-maine.org), P.O. Box 573, Cornish 04020. Their Web site is one of the most comprehensive in Maine, with maps, information about lodging and dining, shopping and events, and a brief history of the town.

Fryeburg Information Center (207-935-3639; www.mainetourism.com), Rt. 302, Fryeburg 04037. The Maine Tourism Association staffs this new facility with AC and restrooms 500 feet from the New Hampshire line. Pamphlets on the state in general, western Maine in particular.

GETTING THERE *By air:* The **Portland International Jetport**, served by several carriers, is 30- to 60-minute drive from most points in this area. Rental cars are available at the airport. (See "Portland.")

By bus and train: **Concord Trailways** (207-828-1151 or 1-800-639-3317) bus lines and **Amtrak's Downeaster** (1-800-USA-RAIL) serve the Portland area from the clean new rail–bus station on outer Congress St. in Portland.

By car: From New York and Boston, take I-95 to the Westbrook exit (exit 48), then Rt. 302, the high road of the lakes region. For Newfield and south of Sebago area, take Rt. 25 from I-95 at Westbrook (exit 48).

WHEN TO COME With some inns and B&Bs open year-round and good cross-country skiing available, this can be a place for a winter retreat. Ice fishing is another winter pastime some people love. Still, the big time here is summer.

✻ Villages

Bridgton has a plethora of antiques shops, including two country auction houses, making it a good way stop for browsers. Take time for a detour to the pretty campus of Bridgton Academy, a few miles from the center of town.

Cornish. In recent years this pretty little town has been making efforts to attract visitors. The colonial and Victorian homes lining Main and Maple Streets were moved here by teams of about 80 oxen in the 1850s after the arrival of a new stagecoach route. It's halfway between Portland and the Mount Washington Valley in New Hampshire. Pick up a copy of the local pamphlet, which includes a detailed map and business listings, at several area businesses.

BIRCHES NEAR SUGARLOAF

Kim Grant

Fryeburg is an interesting town that sees its share of traffic as travelers pass through en route to North Conway, New Hampshire, and the White Mountains. The traffic clog during the Fryeburg Fair (Maine's largest, most popular agricultural fair) can back up for more than an hour. The village itself is small and unassuming, with a smattering of historic homes (some now inns) and businesses. As noted in the chapter introduction, canoe trips down the Saco originate here.

✷ To See

MUSEUMS **Willowbrook Museum Village** (207-793-2784; www.willowbrookmuseum.org), off Rt. 11, Newfield. Open Memorial Day–Oct., Thurs.–Mon. 10–5. Admission $9 adults, $7.50 seniors, $4 students 6–18. Sandwich shop, ice cream parlor, and stores are free (the shop remains open Fri.–Sun. 11–4 till Dec. 23). Devastated by fire in 1947, the village was almost a ghost town when Donald King began buying buildings in the 1960s. The complex now includes 37 buildings displaying more than 11,000 items: horse-drawn vehicles, tools, toys, a vintage-1894 carousel, and many other artifacts of late-19th-century life. Linger in the ballroom, ring the schoolhouse bell, or picnic in the area provided.

Rufus Porter Museum (207-647-2828; www.rufusportermuseum.org), 67 N. High St. (Rt. 302), Bridgton. Open Memorial Day weekend to mid-Oct., Thu.–Sun. 12–4; weekends only from September. $5 adults, $4 students, 6 and under free. Dedicated to Rufus Porter, a multitalented man, this house contains his 1828 original murals, an icon of folk art. Porter founded the *Scientific American* magazine and invented the Colt revolver; he patented a churn, corn sheller, fire alarm, and cheese press, among many other inventions; and in his spare time painted murals in homes all over New England. A signed set of murals from Westwood, Mass., is now also on permanent display.

HISTORIC BUILDINGS AND MUSEUMS **Daniel Marrett House** (207-642-3032; www.historicnewengland.org), Rt. 25, Standish. Tours on the first and third Saturday of the month beginning at 11, June–Oct. Admission $5. Money from Portland banks was stored in this Georgian mansion for safekeeping during the War of 1812. Built in 1789, it remained in the Marrett family until 1944; architecture and furnishings reflect the changing styles over 150 years. The formal perennial gardens bloom throughout summer and are always open for a visit.

THE MAN SAILING ALONG IN A TOP HAT IS A MOTIF OF PORTER'S MURALS.

???

Parson Smith House, 89 River Rd., South Windham. Open mid-June–Labor Day, Tue., Thu., and Sun. noon–5; admission. A Georgian farmhouse with an exceptional stairway and hall; some original furnishings.

Narramissic (207-647-9954, summer only) Ingalls Rd. (2 miles south of the junction of Rts. 107 and 117), Bridgton. Open June 15–Labor Day,

Fri.–Sat. 1–4. Admission fee. A Federal-period home and a Temperance Barn in a rural setting, this interesting site includes a working blacksmith shop and is the scene of frequent special events; check with the **Bridgton Historical Society Museum** (207-647-3699; www.bridgtonhistory.org), Gibbs Ave., which also maintains a former fire station built in 1902. The collection (open July and Aug., call for hours) includes slide images of the old narrow-gauge railroad.

Naples Historical Society Museum (207-693-4297), village green, Rt. 302, Naples. Open July and Aug., Fri. 10–2. The brick complex includes a rooftop brake coach, a diorama and great memorabilia on the Cumberland & Oxford Canal, photos of and information on the Sebago and Long Lake steamboats and the Songo Locks, and artifacts from vanished hotels, such as the Bay of Naples Hotel.

Hopalong Cassidy in the Fryeburg Public Library (207-935-2731), 98 Main St., Fryeburg. Open year-round, varying days. The library is housed in an 1832 stone schoolhouse and is decorated with many paintings by local artists. It also contains a collection of books, guns, and other memorabilia belonging to Clarence Mulford, creator of Hopalong Cassidy. The **Fryeburg Historical Society** (207-935-4192), 511 Main St., has a library open by appointment.

Harrison Historical Society and Museum (207-583-6225), 121 Haskell Hill Rd., Harrison. Open July and Aug., Wed. 1–4 and by appointment (call 207-583-2213); May–Dec., open the first Wed. of the month at 7 PM. The public is welcome at this small museum full of artifacts, cemetery records, town histories, and news clipping scrapbooks.

OTHER HISTORIC SITES **Songo Locks**, Naples (2.5 miles off Rt. 302). Open May–Oct. Dating to 1830, the last of the 27 hand-operated locks that once allowed people to come by boat from Portland to Harrison still enable you to travel some 40 watery miles. Boat traffic is constant in summer.

✷ To Do

BOAT EXCURSIONS ♿ ***Songo River Queen II*** (207-693-6861), Naples Causeway. Operates daily July–Labor Day; reduced schedule in spring and fall. The *Queen* is a replica of a Mississippi River stern paddle wheeler, with accommodations for 300 passengers, a snack and cocktail bar, and restrooms. Take a two-and-a-half-hour Songo River ride across Brandy Pond and through the only surviving lock from the 1830 canal; the Songo River winds its way to the mouth of Sebago Lake, just 1.5 miles as the crow flies, but 6 miles as the Songo twists and turns. Also, one-hour Long Lake cruises and moonlight charters available.

THE *SONGO RIVER QUEEN II*

BOAT RENTALS Available regionwide. Inquire at local chambers. (Also see *Canoeing and Kayaking*.)

CANOEING AND KAYAKING **Saco River Canoe and Kayak** (207-935-2369; www.sacorivercanoe.com), 1009 Main St. (Rt. 5), Fryeburg (across from the access at Swan's Falls). Fred Westerberg, a Registered Maine Guide, runs Saco River Canoe and Kayak with the help of his wife, Prudy, and daughters, Beth and Chris. They offer shuttle service and canoe and kayak rentals, which come with a map and careful instructions geared to the day's river conditions.

Saco Bound (603-447-2177), Rt. 302, Center Conway, New Hampshire (just over the state line, west of Fryeburg). The largest canoe outfitter around. With its sister company Northern Waters, Saco Bound offers rentals, guided day-trips and whitewater canoeing on the Androscoggin River in summer, a campground at Canal Bridge in Fryeburg, and a shuttle service. Its base is a big glass-faced store stocked with kayaks and canoes, trail food and lip balm. Staff members are young and enthusiastic.

Sportshaus (207-647-3000), 103 Main St., Bridgton, rents canoes and kayaks by the day or week.

Woodland Acres (207-935-2529), Rt. 160, Brownfield. Full-facility camping, canoe rentals, and a shuttle service.

River Run (207-452-2500; www.riverruncanoe.com), P.O. Box 190, Brownfield. Canoe rentals, a shuttle, and parking Memorial Day–Labor Day weekends. They also have camping—see *Lodging*.

FISHING Fishing licenses are available at town offices and online at www.mefish wildlife.com; check marinas for information. Salmon, lake trout, pickerel, and bass abound.

GOLF AND TENNIS **Bridgton Highlands Country Club** (207-647-3491; www .bridgtonhighlands.com), Highland Rd., Bridgton, has an 18-hole course, snack bar, carts, a resident golf pro, and tennis courts. Also 18-hole **Lake Kezar Country Club** (207-925-2462), Rt. 5, Lovell; and 18-hole **Naples Golf and Country Club** (207-693-6424; www.naplesgolfcourse.com), Rt. 114, Naples.

HIKING **Douglas Mountain**, Sebago. A Nature Conservancy preserve with great views of Sebago and the White Mountains. The trail to the top is a 20-minute walk, and there's a 0.75-mile nature trail at the summit; also a stone tower with an observation platform. Take Rt. 107 south from the town of Sebago and turn right on Douglas Mountain Rd.; go to the end of the road to find limited parking.

Pleasant Mountain, Bridgton. Several summits and interconnecting trails, the most popular of which is the Firewarden's Trail to the main summit: a relatively easy 2.5-mile climb from base to peak through rocky woods.

Jockey Cap, Rt. 302, Fryeburg. Watch for the Jockey Cap Country Store and Motel beside a general store. The arch to the right of the motel is the entrance to one of New England's shortest hikes to one of its biggest rewards. A 15-minute climb up the path (steep near the top) accesses a bald, garnet-studded summit with a sweeping view of the White Mountains to the west, lesser peaks and lakes to the east and south, all ingeniously identified on a circular bronze monument designed by Arctic explorer Admiral Peary.

HORSEBACK RIDING **Secret Acres Stables** (207-693-3441; www.secretacresstables.com), 185 Lambs Mill Rd. (1 mile off Rt. 302), Naples, offers trail rides and lessons.

✐ **Carousel Horse Farm** (207-627-4471; www.maine-horse-vacation.com), 69 Leach Hill Rd., Casco. Takes beginning through advanced riders on trail rides with views of lakes and the White Mountains. Ask about summer riding camps for kids, and riding vacations for adults.

MINI GOLF ✐ **Steamboat Landing** (207-693-6782; www.steamboatlandingminigolf.com), Rt. 114, Naples (0.25 mile off the causeway). Open daily Memorial Day weekend–Labor Day, 10–10. A lovely 18-hole course with a Maine theme in a wooded setting. Ice cream parlor with Gifford's ice cream, and game room for pinball and family-oriented video games.

✐ **Seacoast Fun Park** (207-892-5952; www.seacoastfunparks.com), Rt. 302, Windham. Open June–Oct. Elaborate mini golf, driving range, go-carts, bumper boats, arcade, waterslide, and trampoline: a ride that straps you into a bungee cord, hauls you high into the air, then lets you swing.

SAILING **Sportshaus** (207-647-3000 in winter; 207-647-9528 in summer), 103 Main St., Bridgton, rents Sunfish and Rhumbas by the week.

SWIMMING ✐ **Sebago Lake State Park** (Memorial Day–Labor Day, 207-693-6613; otherwise, 207-693-6231), off Rt. 302 (between Naples and South Casco). A great family beach with picnic tables, grills, boat ramp, lifeguards, and bathhouses. Day use only; there is a separate camping area (see *Lodging*). No pets.

The town of Bridgton maintains a tidy little beach on **Long Lake** just off Main St., another on **Woods Pond** (Rt. 117), and another on **Highland Lake**. The town of Fryeburg maintains a beach, with float, on the **Saco River**, and **Casco** maintains a small, inviting beach in its picturesque village.

THE PERRY-DESIGNED MARKER THAT IDENTIFIES THE MOUNTAINS THE TOP OF JOCKEY CAP

Nancy English

✷ Winter Sports

CROSS-COUNTRY SKIING ✐ **Five Fields Farm X-C Ski Center** (207-647-2425; www.fivefieldsfarmx-cski.com), Rt. 107, 6 miles south of Bridgton. Open daily 9 AM–dusk. Pick your own apples in fall. Trails loop around the 70-acre working apple orchard and connect to logging roads. You can snowshoe to the top of Bald Pate Mountain for spectacular views. Full- and half-day rates, rentals, warming hut. A dog-sled race with 70 teams was held here in 2007.

Harris Farm Cross Country Ski Center (207-499-2678; www.harrisfarm.com), 280 Buzzell Rd., Dayton. Open daily 9 AM–dusk when there's snow. This 500-acre dairy and tree farm offers 40 kilometers of groomed trails, from easy to difficult, over hills, by ponds and streams, and through the woods. Rentals available.

DOWNHILL SKIING **Shawnee Peak** (207-647-8444; www.shawneepeak.com), Rt. 302, Bridgton. An isolated 1,900-foot hump, 6 miles west of the center of town. Maine's oldest ski area has a vertical drop of 1,300 feet and offers 40 trails with 98 percent snowmaking capacity, a double, two triples, and a quad lift, plus a surface lift—and the only lit half-pipe in Maine. Open until 9 PM (until 10 Fri. and Sat.), night skiing is big here. Glades and free-style terrain park. Ski and snowboard instruction, rentals, childcare, and base lodge with pub. Rooms in a comfortable self-service guesthouse with private bath start at $79 per room weekdays, including two lift tickets.

Sportshaus (207-647-3000), rental facility on Route 302, also at 103 Main St., Bridgton, rents skis, snowshoes, and snowboards by the day or week.

✷ Green Space

The **Lakes Environmental Association** (LEA; 207-647-8580; www.mainelakes.org), 102 Main St., Bridgton, has been working since 1970 to preserve the clear, unsullied lakes in western Maine from development, invasive species such as milfoil, and overuse. Trails and a boardwalk lead through the **Holt Pond Preserve**, a watershed with a bog, a river, and other wetlands, and a boardwalk over a quaking bog full of sphagnum moss and orchids. The **Stevens Brook Trail** follows the water body from Highland Lake to Long Lake. Tour the LEA's **Harry & Eunice Bradley Lake Center** in Bridgton to see the water-testing lab, buffer gardens, and educational displays.

Kezar Falls, reached from Lovell Rd. off Rt. 35, is a small, pretty waterfall on the Kezar River.

The Sucker Brook Preserve, with a signed, interpretive trail, is part of the Greater Lovell Land Trust, as is **The Kezar Outlet Fen** in Lovell, a 250-acre wetland perfect for eagle-watching and canoeing.

✷ Lodging

RUSTIC RESORTS The Western Lakes area offers unusual old resort complexes, each with cabin accommodations, dining, and relaxing space in a central, distinctively Maine lodge. In contrast to similar complexes found farther north, these are all geared to families or to those who vacation here for reasons other than hunting and fishing.

Migis Lodge (207-655-4524; www.migis.com), off Rt. 302, P.O. Box 40, South Casco 04077. Open early June–Columbus Day weekend. This classic Maine lakeside resort takes excellent care of its guests, tucking them under hand-sewn quilts at night, next to fully tiled baths, with arrival-day fresh flowers. Paintings of Maine landscapes adorn all the cottages. A comforting fire burns constantly in the Main Lodge, fed from fences of stacked firewood that frame the pathways. Deluxe accommodations include six rooms in the two-story Main Lodge and 35 cottages with names like Skylark and Tamarack scattered throughout the pines on 125 acres. All cottages have a fireplace, with daily wood deliveries (and ice for the ice bucket). A private beach, tennis, lawn games, waterskiing, sailboats, canoes, and boat excursions while away the days. Because children 5 and under aren't allowed in the dining during high season, they eat in a family dining room, and are offered supervised dining and playtime 6:30–8:30 PM; older children are welcome to join in. $210–360 per adult per night (cottages) includes three meals. $305 per adult in the lodge rooms. Children's rates available; 15 percent service charge. Spa services—in-room massage, yoga classes—are now offered.

"I" ✐ **Quisisana** (207-925-3500; off-season 914-833-0293; www.quisisanaresort.com), Lake Kezar, Center Lovell 04016. Mid-June–Aug. One-week minimum stay in high season. Guests and staff alike are passionate about this unique lodging, founded in 1917 as a place for music students and music lovers to relax in the pines by one of Maine's clearest lakes. Each evening staff recruited from top music schools perform in the lakeside hall: musical theater, opera, and chamber music concerts might star the tenor who is the long-time business manager, and others with impressive talents. The 75 guest quarters in one- to three-room pine-paneled cottages (some with fireplace) are scattered through the woods or near the soft beach. The lack of phone or TV in the cabins means more time for waterskiing, boating, fishing, croquet, tennis, and swimming. The white-frame central lodge includes a homey sitting room, a bar with tables spread out on a deck, and the kind of dining room you don't mind sitting in three times a day. $175–220 per person double occupancy includes all meals.

BED & BREAKFASTS ✐ **Noble House** (207-647-3733 or 1-888-237-4880; www.noblehousebb.com), 81 Highland Rd., Bridgton 04009. Open year-round. Rick and Julie Whelchel are innkeepers worth seeking out at this former senator's manor. Nine guest rooms (all with private bath) are divided between the original house and the former ell, with luxurious linens and beds in each one. Bridgton Suite's four-poster has sheer curtains, there's also a TV nook and a whirlpool bath. Most rooms in the ell open on a tranquil, private deck overlooking the flowers and lawn. The inn is across the street from a beach. Shawnee Peak stay-and-ski packages take care of winter. $99–225 double includes breakfast and use of the canoe or snowshoes, along with access to the bottomless cookie jar. Lobster quiche, spiced apple pancakes, and organic yogurt and fresh fruit start the days.

✐ **Center Lovell Inn** (207-925-1575 or 1-800-777-2698; www.centerlovellinn.com), Rt. 5, Center Lovell 04016. Closed Nov.–mid-Dec. and Apr.–mid-May. Innkeeper Janice Sage runs this striking old inn with a cupola and busy restaurant (see *Dining Out*). The inn features four guest rooms on the second floor (the two with shared bath can be a suite), nicely furnished with antiques and art. In the 1835 Harmon House there are five cozy rooms, three with private bath. $95–240 with no meals; breakfast and dinner additional.

Oxford House Inn (207-935-3442 or 1-800-261-7206; www.oxfordhouse inn.com), 548 Main St., Fryeburg 04037. Open year-round. John and Phyllis Morris's gracious 1913 house in the middle of Fryeburg enjoys an idyllic view across corn and potato fields and the placid Saco River to the White Mountains in New Hampshire. You won't want to miss dining in John's wonderful restaurant downstairs at sunset (see *Dining Out*), especially at a table by the big windows. Four rooms are large and comfortable, with in-room sinks and small shower and toilet rooms in two, claw-foot tub in one. $95–175 includes a great breakfast overlooking those mountains.

Main Street Bed & Breakfast (207-935-7171; www.mainstbandb .com), Fryeburg 04037. Margaret Cugini has transformed this 1820 farmhouse in the heart of Fryeburg into a stunning and luxurious B&B, with the original woodwork, pumpkin pine floors in the hallway, and oak balustrade. The inn's five guest rooms, three with immaculately tiled, lovely private bath, one with a 6-foot Jacuzzi, are furnished with antiques, updated beds, and lovely linens. Guests also have use of a sitting room with a TV/DVD and shelves with books to choose from. Full breakfast and afternoon tea, cocoa, and pastries included. $79–179.

Admiral Peary House (207-935-3365 or 1-877-423-6779; www.admiral pearyhouse.com), 27 Elm St., Fryeburg 04037. Named for Robert E. Peary, Maine's famed Arctic explorer, this house holds seven casual guest rooms named for Peary's partners, family members, and others; each has a private bath and air-conditioning, three have a gas fireplace, and one a whirlpool. Common space includes two spacious living rooms and an enclosed porch overlooking 6.5 acres of lawn and woods. $129–199 in-season includes a full breakfast; $119–159 off-season.

Sebago Lake Lodge (207-892-2698; www.sebagolakelodge .com), White's Bridge Rd., P.O. Box 110, North Windham 04062. A homey white inn in business since the mid-1980s, set on a narrows between Jordan Bay and the Basin, seemingly surrounded by water. Eight units have kitchenettes, and four standard rooms have kitchen privileges. There are also 12 moderately priced cottages. An inviting beach, picnic tables, and grills; fishing boats, kayaks, canoes, and motorboat rentals. Pets are allowed in cottages. $68 for a room in high season, $160–195 in the main lodge. Cottages by the week only, $800–1,295.

The Inn at Long Lake (207-693-6226 or 1-800-437-0328; www .innatlonglake.com), Lake House Road, P.O. Box 806, Naples 04055. Buddy Marcum has renovated room by room, adding ornamental details like wicker and antique furniture, gas stoves, and fancy fabrics; a honeymoon suite displays an old wedding gown. The four-story clapboard building is just a block from the lake. Sixteen rooms include two suites, most with queen beds. Each has private bath, TV, and air conditioner, and a few offer lake views. $160–200 includes an elaborate breakfast.

Greenwood Manor Inn (207-583-4445; www.greenwoodmanorinn .com), 52 Tolman Rd., Harrison 04040. Open year-round. A former carriage house on 108 hillside acres sloping down to Long Lake, the inn features seven guest rooms and two suites, some with a gas log fireplace, some with whirlpool tub, and all with private bath. The dining and living areas overlook a beautifully landscaped garden. $140–220 in season includes a full breakfast. *Note:* Although this B&B is technically in Harrison, much of its property lies in the town of Bridgton, and it is thus much closer to the Sebago/Long Lakes area than to the Oxford Hills; as a result, we're listing it in both chapters.

Olde Saco Inn (207-925-3737; www.theoldesacoinn.com), Fryeburg. Set in a grove of tall pines, along the quiet meandering Old Saco River, this secluded inn holds seven rooms and one suite, including two rooms that can link to a bunk room for children. A billiard table and trails for snowshoeing and cross-country skiing along with hiking trails on the 65-acre property could fill your days. Kayaks and canoes available for guests, who can also arrange to dine here. Rates $85–189, depending on the season.

MOTELS **Jockey Cap Motel and Country Store** (207-935-2306), 116 Bridgton Rd., Fryeburg 04037. Open year-round. Located at the trailhead for Jockey Cap Mountain, this simple place has been repainted and refurnished by Allyson and Robert Quinn. Four rooms holds two doubles, and three have queens; all have private bath with tub and shower, air-conditioning, cable TV. $49–79 depending on the season. The store sells a good-looking Greek salad for $3.99 (see *Eating Out*); picnic tables under the pines are perfect for a casual lunch.

COTTAGES The **Greater Bridgton Lakes Region Chamber of Commerce** (see *Guidance*) publishes a list of more than two dozen rental cottages, and many in this area are also listed in the *Maine Guide to Inns and Bed & Breakfasts and Camps & Cottages*, free from the Maine Tourism Association (see *Information* in "What's Where").

CAMPGROUNDS See *Canoeing and Kayaking* for information about camping along the Saco River. In addition to those mentioned, the Appalachian Mountain Club maintains a campground at Swan's Falls. The *Maine Camping Guide*, available from the **Maine Campground Owners Association** (207-782-5874), 655 Main St., Lewiston 04240, lists dozens of private campgrounds in the area.

Sebago Lake State Park (207-693-6613; before June 20 and after Labor Day, 207-693-6231), off Rt. 302 (between Naples and South Casco). Open through Oct. 15. Visitors return year after year to these 1,300 thickly wooded acres on the northern shore of the lake, so make your reservations early if you want a good site. The camping area (with 250 campsites, many on the water) comes with its own beach, hot showers, a program of evening presentations such as outdoor

THE JOCKEY CAP, A CLEAN, SPRUCED UP MOTEL

Nancy English

movies, and nature hikes. For information about reservations, call 1-800-332-1501, or 207-624-9950 from outside the state. Go to www.campwithme.com to make reservations online. One hundred sites now have water and electricity.

🐾 ✐ ♿ **Point Sebago Resort** (207-655-3821 or 1-800-655-1232; www.pointsebago.com), 261 Point Sebago Rd., Casco 04015. Open May–Oct. For those who want to camp on a Maine lake cheaply without roughing it, this complex offers a lot. One hundred sites for RV hook-ups on a 775-acre lakeside site, plus hundreds of small, manufactured "Park homes," for rent, some with linens and others empty, requiring you stock the basics. Everyone has access to the beach, marina, pavilion, children's activities, excursion boats, soccer and softball fields, horseshoe pitches, 18-hole championship golf course, 10 tennis courts, video-game arcade, general store, and combination restaurant/nightclub, with DJs, and teen dances.

River Run (207-452-2500), Denmark Rd., P.O. Box 190, Brownfield 04010. Camp on more than 100 acres, with sites in the woods and along the Saco River. Amenities include public phone, group tenting area, swimming beaches, fire rings, picnic tables, and firewood and ice for purchase.

✷ Where to Eat

DINING OUT **Oxford House Inn** (207-935-3442 or 1-800-261-7206), 105 Main St., Fryeburg. Open for dinner every night in summer and fall, Thu.–Sun. in winter and spring. Reservations required. The most romantic spot in western Maine when you sit in the dining room's back porch. Sunset mountain views offer wildlife sightings of an albino woodchuck and passing deer. Chef John Morris served us a fabulous appetizer of scallops baked in the shell with pancetta and crumbs; rare bison sirloin raised in nearby Waterford was meaty and intensely flavored. Grilled duck breast could not have been more tender and luscious. Salad included, and fine wines to accompany all. Entrées $26–31.

Center Lovell Inn (207-925-1575), Rt. 5, Center Lovell. Open for dinner daily in summer; on weekends in winter, but daily again during holiday weeks. Closed Nov.–mid-Dec. and Apr.–mid-May. Call for reservations. Specialties include a wild mushroom crostini appetizer, and entrées like seafood Norfolk—shrimp, scallops, crabmeat, and lobster sautéed with garlic and brandy. Bison from Beech Hill Bison Farm in Waterford is served occasionally, and there is always a fish special. The rack of lamb with port reduction was perfect. $19–29.

Venezia Ristorante (207-647-5333), Bridgton Corners, Rts. 302 and 93, Bridgton. Open for dinner Tue.–Sun. 5–9 in summer, Wed.–Sun. in winter. Dependable, moderately priced Italian dishes.

Olde Mill Tavern (207-583-9077; www.oldemilltavern.com), 56 Main St., Harrison. Open Mon.–Thu. 4–9, Fri.–Sat. noon–10, Sun. 10–8. From

THE OXFORD HOUSE INN

Nancy English

prime rib steak to ribs with bourbon barbeque sauce to smothered pork chops, the meat eater will be well served. Baked fish and seafood casserole too. Entrées $16–24.

Black Horse Tavern (207-647-5300; www.sunnysidevillagemaine.com/blackhorsetavern), Rt. 302, Bridgton. Open daily for lunch and dinner, Sunday brunch from 10 AM. A large filet mignon and honey-glazed ginger salmon are regulars on the changing menu. $11–19.

Tom's Homestead (207-647-5726), Rt. 302, Bridgton. Lunch and dinner are served (closed Mon.) in this 1821 historic home. Fried squash blossoms wowed one diner here, who extolled the lunch.

Chao Thai (207-647-4355), 112 Main St., Bridgton. This is the best Thai food that some customers have ever tasted—and they have been trying it all over. High praise indeed.

EATING OUT **Krista's** (207-625-3600), 2 Main St., Cornish. Open Wed, Thurs. and Sun. 7 AM to 8 PM, Fri. and Sat. until 9. Breakfast is all homemade, with muffins and scones, and special spiced pumpkin waffles likely in fall. Dinner ranges from nachos to roast duck. Entrées $14–25.

Bray's Brew Pub (207-693-6806; www.braysbrewpub.com), Rts. 302 and 35, Naples. Open year-round for lunch and dinner daily. Dinnertime in summer is busy, and there can be a wait. Mike Bray, Michele Windsor, and brewer Rob Prindall brew excellent American ales using grains and malted barley, Oregon yeast, and Washington hops; a beer garden with horseshoe pits and a luxuriant hops vine is a pleasant place on warm nights. The dinner menu runs from grilled salmon to filet mignon; pub menu served till 9:30 PM.

Jockey Cap Country Store and Motel (207-935-2306; www.quinnsjockeycap.com), 116 Bridgton Rd. (Rt. 302), Fryeburg. Open Monday to Saturday 6 AM to 7 PM, Sunday 7 AM to 5 PM. Breakfast sandwiches and pizzas—with bacon, sausage, egg, and cheese—great sandwiches and salads, with picnic tables for al fresco dining by the motel. Just one table and a few seats by the window inside.

Center Lovell Market (207-925-1051), Rt. 5, Center Lovell. This place combines the best of an old-fashioned general store (clothing, groceries, Maine-made items) with a deli and café. Pizza, salads, and more served to go or to eat in the pleasant dining area.

Route 160 Ice Cream and Hot Dog Stand, north of Kezar Falls on Rt. 160. Locals swear by the dogs here, as well as the hamburgers and ice cream. A good place to stop for lunch when traveling between Cornish and Fryeburg.

Beef and Ski (207-647-9555), 243 Portland Rd. (Rt. 302), Bridgton. Serves everything, from hot sandwiches to seafood dinners. Onion rings are hand cut, fish is fresh, turkey and beef are roasted here for sandwiches and dinners. Take-out is the focus, but seating is available. Entrées $6–16. This is a franchise from a North Conway business.

✷ Entertainment

FILM **Windham Hill Mall Cinema** (207-892-7000), Rt. 302, North Windham, shows first-run movies. **Bridgton Drive-In** (207-647-8666), Rt. 302, shows first-run movies in summer.

MUSIC **Sebago–Long Lake Region Chamber Music Festival** (207-583-6747), Deertrees Rd., Deertrees Theatre and Cultural Center, Harrison. A series of five world-class concerts held mid-July–mid-Aug.

The Saco River Festival Association (207-625-7116) holds a chamber music festival in Cornish in July and Aug. Call for a brochure detailing performances.

Stone Mountain Arts Center (1-866-227-6523; www.stonemountainartscenter.com), 695 Dugway Rd., Brownfield. Marty Stuart, Cheryl Wheeler, Asleep at the Wheel, Taj Mahal, and other fine musicians play here, musician Carol Noonan's 200-seat hall in Brownfield. A Friday variety show runs year-round. Brownfield is 20 miles east of Conway, N.H. Noonan wanted to build herself a hall and get herself off the road; now crowds drive to her big red barn where wonderful things keep happening.

THEATER See **Deertrees Theatre and Cultural Center** in "Oxford Hills."

✷ Selective Shopping

ANTIQUES SHOPS Rt. 302 is chockablock full of antiques shops, so stop anyplace that looks interesting. Cornish has also grown into an antiques haven, and we relish the lack of crowds.

The Smith Co. (207-625-6030), 24 Main St., Cornish. Specializes in country-store fixtures and memorabilia—including old Coca-Cola collectibles and advertising signs.

BOOKSTORES **Bridgton Books** (207-647-2122), 140 Main St., Bridgton. More than 20,000 titles, new and used books, books on tape, cards and stationery, music.

EFG Books (207-647-9339; www.efgbooks.com), 186 Main St., Bridgton. New, used, and rare books are sold here—look for everything by the Beat Generation—and a small gallery holds changing exhibits.

SPECIAL SHOPS **The Shops at South Casco** (207-655-5060), Rt. 302, South Casco. A three-building complex. **Cry of the Loon** (207-655-5060) encompasses unique pottery, glassware, and other handmade crafts. **The Nest** (207-655-5034) offers country furniture and other items for your decor, including rugs. In **The Barn** (207-655-5066), you'll find cast-iron toys to wine racks.

The Cool Moose (207-647-3957; www.thecoolmoose.com), 36 Main St., Bridgton. Hand-made belts and leather goods, and other well-made and quirky inventory.

Craftworks (207-647-5436), 79 Main St., Upper Village, Bridgton. Open daily. Fills a former church and two neighboring buildings. Selective women's clothing, pottery, books, linens, handmade pillows, crafted jewelry, Stonewall Kitchen–prepared foods, and wines from all over the world.

Blacksmiths Winery (207-655-3292; www.blacksmithswinery.com), 967

BARGAIN HUNTING IN NAPLES

Kim Grant

Quaker Ridge Rd., South Casco. Open May–Dec. 1, Mon.–Sat. 11–6, Sun. noon–5; Jan.–Apr., Fri.–Mon. 11–5, Sun. noon–5. Visitors can sample the surprisingly good cabernet sauvignon, chardonnay, and blueberry wines, and an ice wine from Ontario grapes. (Other grape juice comes from New York and Washington State.)

✷ Special Events

End of January/beginning of February: **Mushers' Bowl**, a dogsled race at the Fryeburg Fairgrounds with participants from all over the United States. Includes sleigh rides, crafts, dancing, stargazing, ice skating, snowshoeing, ice fishing, and more.

March: **March Maple Syrup Sunday**, with tapping and sugaring-off demonstrations around the area, including Pingree Maple Syrup, High Rd., Cornish; and Highland Farms Sugar Works, Towles Hill, Cornish.

April: **Sheepfest**, Denmark—demonstrations of spinning, carding, combing, knitting, dyeing, sheep shearing, hoof trimming, and more.

July: Independence Day is big in Bridgton and Naples, with fireworks, a parade, and the **4 on the Fourth Road Race**—a 5K walk/run/wheelchair race around Bridgton. Shawnee Peak hosts a **Portland Symphony Orchestra** concert that week on Pleasant Mountain. In **Naples** the fireworks over the lake are spectacular. Harrison and Casco also hold their **Old Home Days** this month, and check out the **Waterford World's Fair**. **Strawberry Festival**, Thompson Park, Cornish.

August: **Windham Old Home Days** (*beginning of the month*)—parade, contests, and public feeds. In Lovell the **Annual Arts and Artisans Fair** (*midmonth*) is held at the new Suncook School—a juried crafts fair. The **Spinners and Weavers Show** at Narramissic has grown in popularity in recent years (see *To See*).

September: **Chili Cook-Off and Road Race**, Waterford. **Cornish Apple Festival**, including crafts booths, food vendors, quilt show, antique auto parade, apple pie contest, and the **Apple Acres Bluegrass Festival**. **Brewers' Festival** at Point Sebago Resort, Casco, offers tastes from microbreweries, with crafts and children's activities; look at www.lakesbrewfest.com for details.

October: **Fryeburg Fair**, Maine's largest agricultural fair, is held for a week in early October, climaxing with the Columbus Day weekend. This is an old-fashioned agricultural happening—one of the most colorful in the country. **Haunted Happenings** with hundreds of pumpkins and refreshments at Mark's Lawn and Garden, Rt. 302, Bridgton; check www.markslawnandgarden.com.

Early November: **Early-Bird Shopping**, featuring discounts at many local retail shops.

Late November–early December: **Christmas in Cornish**—open houses, concerts, Cornish Historical Society Walking Tour, horse-drawn carriage rides, children's story time, poinsettia display, and caroling. **Bridgton's Festival of Lights**—a parade with Santa Claus and tree lighting.

December: **Christmas Open House** and festivals in Harrison.

OXFORD HILLS AND LEWISTON/AUBURN

Over the years many of Maine's small towns have banded together to form distinctive regional identities. One such area, a rolling gem- and lake-studded swatch of Oxford County, is known as the Oxford Hills. Technically made up of eight towns, the region seems to stretch to include many of the stops along Rt. 26, the region's traffic spine, as visitors pass through from Gray (an exit on the Maine Turnpike) to Bethel, an area with both summer attractions and winter ski resorts.

Its commercial center is the community composed of both Norway and South Paris, towns divided by the Little Androscoggin River but joined by Rt. 26. Off Rt. 26 is a quiet part of the Western Lakes and Mountains Region, with startlingly beautiful villages like Waterford and Paris Hill, and genuinely interesting places to see, such as the country's last living Shaker community at Sabbathday Lake.

The Oxford Hills are best known for their mineral diversity. The area's bedrock is a granite composed of pegmatite studded with semiprecious gemstones, including tourmaline and rose quartz. Several local mines invite visitors to explore their "tailings," or rubble, and take what they find.

Otisfield is renowned for a unique summer camp devoted to healing the wounds of war, called Seeds of Peace Camp. It began with Palestinian and Israeli children, and now includes campers from Afghanistan, India, Pakistan, Iraq, and Iran, who spend the summer getting to know children they might have encountered otherwise only as enemies.

Lewiston and Auburn (Maine's "LA"), just east of the Oxford Hills, are the "cities of the Androscoggin" but for most visitors are seen as "the cities on the Turnpike," the exits accessing routes to the Rangeley and Sugarloaf areas. Both are worth a stop. By the 1850s mills on both sides of the river had harnessed the power of the Androscoggin's Great Falls, and the Bates Mill boomed with the Civil War, supplying fabric for most of the Union army's tents.

Today Lewiston is best known as the home of prestigious Bates College (founded in 1855), an attractive campus that's the summer site of the nationally recognized Bates Dance Festival. It's also the home of a growing number of Somali immigrants, who are bringing their own cultural flair to the region. The

Bates Mill is now a visitor-friendly complex housing a museum and restaurants, and both Lewiston and Auburn offer a number of colorful festivals—some, like Festival de Joie, reflecting the rich diversity of the residents.

GUIDANCE **Oxford Hills Chamber of Commerce** (207-743-2281; www.oxfordhillsmaine.com), 4 Western Ave., South Paris 04281, publishes a comprehensive directory to the area.

Androscoggin County Chamber of Commerce (207-783-2249; www.androscoggincounty.com), 415 Lisbon St., P.O. Box 59, Lewiston 04243.

GETTING THERE For the Sabbathday Lake–Poland Spring–Oxford area, take I-95 to Gray (exit 63) and Rt. 26 north. Auburn is exit 75 and Lewiston is exit 80 off the Maine Turnpike.

WHEN TO COME This is lovely country in winter, but dinner choices can be limited to weekends in the countryside. We love the Lilac Festival at the McLaughlin Garden on Memorial Day weekend.

* Villages

Harrison. Once a booming lakeside resort town, Harrison is now a quiet village resting between two lakes. Main Street has a popular restaurant and restored clock tower. In the 1930s many of the country's most popular actors came to perform at the Deertrees Theatre, which is again offering theater, dance, music, and children's shows to the area.

Norway. Making up part of the commercial center of the region, the downtown is quiet and quaint. L. M. Longley's hardware store has items from days gone by, the town is home to Maine's oldest newspaper, and there are interesting art exhibits held by the Western Maine Art Group in the Matolcsy Art Center. The Norway Sidewalk Arts Festival in July features close to 100 artists exhibiting along Main Street.

Paris is a town divided into sections so different they don't feel like the same town at all. Paris Hill has views of the White Mountains and a number of historic houses and buildings, including the Hamlin Memorial Library.

Oxford. Home of the Oxford Plains Speedway, which attracts stock-car-racing fans throughout the season, and the Oxford County Fairgrounds (host to several annual events), Oxford is also the largest manufacturing base in the area, including manufactured homes, information processing, textiles, and wood products.

* To See

The International Sign. At the junction of Rts. 5 and 35 in the village of Lynchville, some 14 miles west of Norway, stands Maine's most photographed roadside marker, pointing variously to Norway, Paris, Denmark, Naples, Sweden, Poland, Mexico, and Peru—all towns within 94 miles of the sign.

FOR FAMILIES ✐ ♿ **Maine Wildlife Park** (207-657-4977), Rt. 26, Gray. Open

Apr. 15–Nov. 11, daily 9:30–4:30 (no one admitted after 4 PM). $6 adults, $4.50 ages 61-plus, $4 ages 4–12, and free for those 3 and under. What started as a pheasant farm has evolved into a wonderful haven for injured animals. The park prepares animals to return to the wild, but while they're here it's a great opportunity to see species you might otherwise never glimpse. The park allows visitors to observe animals as they live in the wild. Nature trails and picnic facilities round out the experience. Animals include moose, lynx, deer, black bears, red foxes, wild turkeys, eagles, and many more.

Beech Hill Bison Ranch (207-583-2515; www.beechhillbison.com), 539 Valley Rd. (Rte. 35), Waterford. Call for hours. Paul and Marcia Hersey are raising a breeding herd of North American bison here, and operate a shop with bison meat and a variety of gifts. There's a chance you can see the buffalo, including Chief Chadwick, who has produced champions.

HISTORIC BUILDINGS **Poland Spring Museum** (207-998-7143; www.polandspring.com), 115 Preservation Way, Poland Spring. Open Memorial Day–Columbus Day, Fri.–Sat. 9–4. The original bottling plant and springhouse for the well-known bottled water, Poland Spring, is its own nonprofit branch set in its business park. The old spa had a renowned visitor list, and photos of some are displayed in the gallery here, like Mae West and Babe Ruth.

State of Maine Building (www.polandspringps.org), Rt. 26, Poland Spring. Open July and Aug., Tues.–Sat. 9–4, fewer hours off-season. Admission. A very Victorian building that was brought back from the 1893 World's Columbian Exposition in Chicago to serve as a library and art gallery for the now vanished Poland Spring Resort (today the water is commercially bottled in an efficient, unromantic plant down the road). Peek into the **All Souls Chapel** next door for a look at its nine stained-glass windows and the 1921 Skinner pipe organ.

Hamlin Memorial Library and Museum (207-743-2980), Hannibal Hamlin Dr. off Rt. 26, Paris Hill, Paris. Open seasonally, call for hours. The old stone Oxford County Jail now houses the public library and museum. Worth a stop for the American primitive art; also local minerals and displays about Hannibal Hamlin (who lived next door), vice president during Abraham Lincoln's first term. The setting is superb: a ridgetop of spectacular early-19th-century houses with views west to the White Mountains.

THE INTERNATIONAL SIGN

Nancy English

MUSEUMS **Sabbathday Lake Shaker Community and Museum** (207-926-4597; www.shaker.lib.me.us), 707 Shaker Rd. (Rt. 26), New Gloucester (8 miles north of Gray). Open Memorial Day–Columbus Day for six two-hour tours daily (except Sun.), 10–4:30; $6.50 adults, $2 ages 6–12. Welcoming the "world's people" has been part of summer at Sabbathday Lake since the community's inception in 1794. Founded by Englishwoman Ann Lee in 1775, Shakers numbered 6,000 Americans in 18 communities by the Civil War. Today, with only three Shaker Sisters and Brothers, this village is the only one in the world that still functions as a religious community. These men and women continue to follow the injunction of Mother Ann Lee to "put your hands to work and your heart to God." Guided tours are offered of some of the white-clapboard buildings; rooms are either furnished or filled with exhibits to illustrate periods or products of Shaker life. The **Shaker Store** sells Shaker-made goods, including oval boxes, knitted and sewn goods, homemade fudge, yarns, souvenirs, antiques, Shaker-style antique furniture, and Shaker herbs. During warm-weather months, services are held at 10 AM on Sunday in the 18th-century meetinghouse on Rt. 26, when Shakers speak in response to the psalms and gospel readings. Each observation is affirmed with a Shaker song—of which there are said to be 10,000. This complex includes an extensive research library housing Shaker books, writings, and records.

♿ **Museum L-A, Museum of Labor and Industry** (207-333-3881; www.museumla.org), 35 Canal St., Box A7, Lewiston. Open Mon.–Sat.10–4. $3 adults, $2 seniors and students. A 50-foot drop in the Androscoggin River powered the mills built along side; in its heyday Lewiston had seven mills turning out elegant bedspreads for Bates Mills. George Washington spreads, matelasse spreads that sandwich fibers inside the weave, were one of their best products. Shoes and bricks were also made in these mills, which prospered until cheaper electricity and labor moved the textile industry to the south in the mid-20th century. One last company still operates in the mills, however, and tours can be arranged with the museum; the Maine Heritage Weavers throws are also for sale in the gift store. Don't miss the jacquard loom, a model for early computers studied by IBM employees for functionality.

Franco-American Heritage Collection, Lewiston-Auburn College/USM (207-753-6545), 51 Westminster St., Lewiston. Open 8:30–5 Mon. and Wed., 8–noon on Thu. The curators of this collection research and promote interest in the French roots of many of the region's inhabitants. Peruse documents, photographs, artifacts, and audiovisual materials.

SABBATHDAY LAKE SHAKER COMMUNITY AND MUSEUM

Kim Grant

Bates College Museum of Art, Olin Arts Center (207-786-6158; www.batescollege.edu), 75 Russell St., Lewiston. Open Tue.–Sat. 10–5. Hosts a variety of performances, exhibitions, and special programs. The museum also houses fine artworks on paper, including the Marsden Hartley Memorial Collection. Lovers of the artist won't want to miss this small but excellent collection of bold, bright canvases by Hartley, a Lewiston native (call ahead to find out what's on display).

Finnish-American Heritage Society of Maine (207-743-5677), 8 Maple St., West Paris. Open in July and Aug., Sun. 2–4, or by appointment. This organization features a museum, library, and gift shop focused on the Finnish settlers in this area. They sponsor a Finnish cultural gathering every third Sun., Sept.–June.

SCENIC DRIVES

Along Rt. 26

Patched with ugly as well as beautiful stretches, the 46 miles between Gray (Maine Turnpike exit 11) and West Paris don't constitute your ordinary "scenic drive," but this is the way most people head for Bethel and the White Mountains. The following sights are described in order of appearance, heading north:

Sabbathday Lake Shaker Community and Museum, New Gloucester (8 miles north of Gray), both sides of the road, is a must-stop (see *Museums*).

State of Maine Building from the 1893 World's Columbian Exposition in Chicago (see *Historic Buildings*). An abrupt right, up through the pillars of the old Poland Spring Resort.

✐ In Oxford two exceptional **farm stands** make ice cream from their own cows' milk. Northbound, don't miss hilltop **Crestholm Farm Stand and Ice Cream** (on your right; 207-539-8832), which has a petting zoo (sheep, goats, pigs, ducks, and more) as well as cheeses, honey, and great ice cream; also a nice view. Southbound, it's **Smedberg's Crystal Spring Farm** (see *Where to Eat—Snacks*).

✐ In South Paris highway hypnosis sets in big time after the light; it's easy to miss **Shaner's Family Dining** (see *Eating Out*).

Across from Ripley Ford, look for the **McLaughlin Garden** (see *Green Space*).

The **Oxford Hills Chamber of Commerce** (207-743-2281), 4 Western Ave., South Paris, is open year-round, and you can pick up the magazine guide to the area here.

Paris Hill is posted just beyond the second light in South Paris. The road climbs steadily up to Paris Hill common, a spacious green surrounded on three sides by early-19th-century mansions, with the fourth commanding a panoramic view of hills and valley and the White Mountains in the distance. Look for **Hamlin Memorial Library and Museum** (see *Historic Buildings*).

Christian Ridge Pottery (see *Special Shops*) is marked from Christian Ridge Rd., a way back to Rt. 26.

✐ **Snow Falls Gorge**, 6 miles south of the center of West Paris on Rt. 26, left as you're heading north. A great picnic and walk-around spot, a rest area with tables and a trail by a waterfall that cascades into a 300-foot gorge carved by the Little Androscoggin.

Trap Corner, an area in West Paris (at the junction Rts. 219 and 26) is rockhounding central (see Perham's in *Rockhounding* below).

Greenwood Shore Rest Area, Rt. 26 just north of Bryant Pond. A good waterside spot for a picnic.

STOCK-CAR RACING **Oxford Plains Speedway** (207-539-8865; www.oxfordplains.com), Rt. 26, Oxford. Weekend stock-car racing, late Apr.–Oct.

✷ To Do

APPLE PICKING **Ricker Hill Orchards** (207-225-5552; www.rickerhill.com), Turner. Maps show you where your favorite varieties can be picked in the big orchard here. Cranberries for sale at the farm stand, along with apple butter. You can also see apple cider making and apple packing in process. In the fall a corn maze can be explored. A petting "ranch" brings you close to goats, pigs, cows, donkeys, and horses.

GOLF **Paris Hill Country Club** (207-743-2371), Paris Hill Rd., Paris, nine holes, founded in 1899, is the epitome of old-shoe; rental carts, snack bar. **Norway Country Club** (207-743-9840), off Rt. 118 on Norway Lake Rd., nine holes, long views. Fourteen holes as well at **Summit Springs Golf Course** (207-998-4515), Summit Spring Rd., Poland.

HIKING **Streaked Mountain**. This is a relatively easy hike with a panoramic view, good for kids. From Rt. 26, take Rt. 117 to the right-hand turnoff for Streaked Mountain Rd. and look for the trailhead on your left. The trail follows a power line up to an old fire tower at just 800 feet. A round-trip hike takes about one-and-a-half-hours. Look for blueberries in-season.

Singlepole Mountain. Also off Rt. 117, nearer South Paris (see the *Maine Atlas and Gazetteer*, published by DeLorme), is a walk up a dirt road (bear left) through the woods to a summit with a view of Mount Washington and the Mahoosuc Mountains.

MOUNTAIN BIKING **Paris Hill Area Park**, near the common. You can bike the ridge roads radiating from here; inquire about routes in Hamlin Memorial Library and Museum.

ROCKHOUNDING **Perham's of West Paris** (207-674-2341 or 1-800-371-GEMS), 194 Bethel Rd., West Paris. Open May–Dec. daily 9–5; Jan.–Apr. open Wed.–Sun. 9–4, closed Mon.–Tues. Looking deceptively small in its yellow-clapboard, green-trim building (right side of Rt. 26, heading north), this business has been selling gemstones since 1919. Aside from displaying an array of locally mined amethyst, tourmaline, and topaz, and selling gem jewelry, Perham's offers maps to five local quarries in which treasure seekers are welcome to try their luck.

Rochester's Eclectic Emporium (207-539-4631), Rt. 26, Oxford. Nicholas Rochester has some of the finest mineral and crystal specimens you can see; he can steer visitors to local mines. Jewelry, beads, loose gems, and a large selection of tourmaline.

SWIMMING **Range Pond State Park** (207-998-4104), Empire Rd., features a beach perfect for spreading out a picnic blanket. Lifeguards, playground, ball field, changing rooms, bathrooms, boat launch, swimming, and fishing, plus 2 miles of easy walking trails. The pond has a 10-horsepower limit—kayakers love it here.

Pennesseewasee Lake in Norway is well off the road, but public and equipped with lifeguards.

✷ Winter Sports

CROSS-COUNTRY SKIING **Carter's X-Country Ski Center** (207-539-4848; www.cartersxcski.com), 420 Main St. (Rt. 26), Oxford. Extensive acreage used to grow summer vegetables is transformed into a ski center in winter. Equipment rentals, lessons, 35 kilometers of groomed trails, and food.

Lost Valley Ski Area (207-784-1561), Lost Valley Rd., Auburn. One continuous trail is more than 5 miles long. Rentals. Tickets $9.

DOWNHILL SKIING **Lost Valley Ski Area** (207-784-1561; www.lostvalleyski.com), Lost Valley Rd., Auburn. With 21 trails and two chairlifts, this small mountain is a favorite for schools and families. Night skiing every night till 9. In 2007–08, weekend adult lift tickets were $35, junior $32.

SNOW TUBING **Mountain View Sports Park** (207-539-2454), Rt. 26, Oxford. A lighted 1,000-foot slope open Fri.–Sun., plus all school vacation days. Tubes, helmets, and a T-bar are the ingredients of this low-tech, low-cost sport. Snowmaking capability means you can enjoy the fun even during a mild winter.

✷ Green Space

The McLaughlin Garden (207-743-8820; www.mclaughlingarden.org), 97 Main St., South Paris. Garden open daily May to October, 8–7. Free admission. In 1936 Bernard McLaughlin, who had no formal horticultural training, began planting his farmstead; now lilacs and established garden beds flourish next to stone walls and a massive barn. After his death in 1995, a nonprofit organization formed to preserve the home, barn, and five-acre floral oasis. In lilac season, with more than 100 varieties, the annual Lilac Festival is a sensual delight. Tours of the garden and lilac

MCLAUGHLIN GARDEN IN SOUTH PARIS HOLDS A HUGE VARIETY OF LILACS.

Nancy English

workshops and sales are offered. The gift shop is open year-round, and the café serving light lunches—including Provençal panini with prosciutto, artichoke hearts, and pesto—is open Memorial Day weekend–Labor Day, Wed.–Sun. 11–3.

Thorncrag Nature Sanctuary in Lewiston is 357-acre bird sanctuary, owned and managed by Stanton Bird Club (207-782-5238; www.stantonbirdclub.org). Six nature trails cross through meadows, forest, wetlands, and vernal pools, all good for bird-watching or walking and jogging. This preserve is accessible through two gates, one at the end of East Avenue, the other on Montello Street. Open dawn to dusk, and free.

✷ Lodging

INNS 🐾 ✐ **The Waterford Inne** (207-583-4037; www.waterfordinne.com), turn off Rt. 37 at Springer's General Store, P.O. 149, Waterford 04088. This striking 1825 farmhouse with its double porch is sequestered up a back road, set on 25 quiet acres of fields and woods. Barbara Vanderzanden opened her inn in July 1978; her unobtrusive style will appeal to those who prefer privacy. Four spacious rooms in an addition and four upstairs, six with private bath, include the Chesapeake Room, with a second-story porch. A full breakfast is included. $100-200 per room; dinner is available (see *Dining Out*) at an additional cost. Pets are accepted; $15 fee.

Kedarburn Inn (207-583-6182 or 1-866-583-6182; www.kedarburn.com), Valley Rd. (Rt. 35), Waterford 04088. Open year-round. London natives Margaret and Derek Gibson offer English hospitality in their seven guest rooms, five with private bath. Margaret's quilts cover beds and the walls. The handsome Balcony Room has a queen bed and loft with two twin beds. The quilt shop on the ground floor is filled with a rainbow of fabric. Quilting weekends and retreats Sept.–June. $75–135 double in-season, including breakfast. Here tea lovers will find "a proper cup of tea, with teapots and proper cups."

Lake House (207-583-4182 or 1-800-223-4182; www.lakehousemaine.com), Rts. 35 and 37, Waterford 04088. Open year-round. This former stagecoach tavern was the first building in Waterford when it was erected in the 1790s; the inn also used to be a sanatorium for ladies and a private residence. The seven spacious guest rooms, all with private bath, include a two-room suite, five queen or king country rooms, and the Grand Ballroom Suite, a 600-square-foot former ballroom with a 10-foot vaulted ceiling and seven windows. Dudley Cottage can be rented daily and weekly. $99–265 includes breakfast.

♿ ⚭ **King's Hill Inn** (207-744-0204 or 1-877-391-5464; www.kingshillinn.com), 56 King Hill Rd., South Paris. Three suites and three rooms, all with private bath. Rooms 4 and 5 offer both a great view of the White Mountains and a gas log fire. Enjoy blueberry pancakes in the morning before a tour of the perennial gardens spreading out on the lawn, a visit with Nessie the Scottish Highlander cow and Katy the miniature horse. Janice and Glenn Davis keeps everything from the grass to the beds in tiptop condition, including an adorable wedding chapel.

$95–150 per night for a double, depending on season.

BED & BREAKFASTS "1" **Bear Mountain Inn** (207-583-4404; www.bearmtninn.com), Rts. 35 and 37, South Waterford 04081. Open year-round. One of our favorite B&Bs in Maine, this 150-year-old farmhouse is set on 52 gorgeous acres next to Bear Pond. Lorraine Blais takes a charming, bubbly, detail-oriented approach. She decorates the 11 rooms, most with private bath, with stuffed bears and everything bear related, and somehow it comes together as snug and welcoming without being cutesy. The Sugar Bear Cottage has a fireplace, kitchenette, claw-foot tub, and terrific views. Private beach with docks and canoes, kayaks, and paddleboats. $120–325 per room includes a full breakfast; one fall morning, peach sour cream pancakes and herbed goat cheese soufflé were served.

Greenwood Manor Inn (207-583-4445; www.greenwoodmanorinn.com), 52 Tolman Rd., Harrison 04040. Open year-round. A former carriage house on 108 hillside acres sloping down to Long Lake, the inn features seven guest rooms and two suites, some with a gas log fireplace, some with whirlpool tub, and all with private bath. The dining and living areas overlook a beautifully landscaped garden. $140–220 in-season includes a full breakfast. *Note:* Although this B&B is technically in Harrison, much of its property lies in the town of Bridgton, and it is thus much closer to the Sebago/Long Lakes area than to the Oxford Hills; as a result, we're listing it in both chapters.

Wolf Cove Inn (207-998-4976; www.wolfcoveinn.com), 5 Jordan Shore Dr., Poland 04274. Open year-round. A romantic, quiet lakeside hideaway. Ten accomodations, each named for a flower or herb, are quaintly decorated. Eight rooms have private bath; three have whirlpool tubs and gas fireplaces. Kayaks and canoes are available for guest. $100-–250 in-season includes a full breakfast.

Nancy English

KING'S HILL INN

OTHER LODGING **Papoose Pond Resort and Campground** (207-583-4470; www.papoosepondresort.com), 700 Norway Rd. (Rt. 118), Waterford 04088 (10 miles west of Norway). Family geared for 40 years, this facility is on 1,000 wooded acres with 0.5 mile of sandy beach on mile-long Papoose Pond. Cabins with or without bath, housekeeping cottages, bunkhouse trailers, tent and RV sites (some with electricity, water, and sewer); rates in high season range from $30 per night for a tent site to $340 for a cottage. Amenities include a recreation hall, store, café, movie tent, canoes, rowboats, paddleboats, kayaks, fishing equipment, and a 1916 merry-go-round.

The Cape (207-539-4404; www.cape-cottages.com), 105 Cape Rd., Otisfield. Ten cottages are set in trees on the edge of Thompson Lake; the Garden House has three bedrooms and a woodstove, while number 7 is off by itself, with a screened porch over the water. $1,000 a week in-season, 15 percent less off-season.

✱ Where to Eat

DINING OUT **Fuel** (207-333-3835; www.fuelmaine.com), 49 Lisbon St., Lewiston. Open for dinner Tues.–Sat. from 4:30. A magnificent renovation of Lyceum Hall now holds Fuel and an art gallery on its first floor. The restaurant feeds appreciative locals bistro-style steak frites and down-home favorites like fried green tomatoes geared up with pungent aioli. Great wine list and elegant bar area. House doughnuts with chocolate sauce or a poached pear for dessert. Entrées mid-$20s.

Fishbones (207-333-3663; www.fishbonesag.com), 70 Lincoln St., Lewiston. Grilled fish in a spacious exciting room full of exposed brick and lively people. Blue crab spring roll, shrimp and scallop flatbread, and grilled salmon with pomegranate glace. Entrées $18–24.

The Waterford Inne (207-583-4037; www.waterfordinne.com), Waterford (turn off Rt. 37 at Springer's General Store). Open by reservation only. Come and enjoy a surprisingly sophisticated meal in this classic country inn. A four-course prix fixe dinner ($37) might include shrimp Pernod over angel-hair pasta, or crab and leek bisque and pork à la Normande with apples and Calvados. BYOB.

Lake House (207-583-4182 or 1-800-223-4182; www.lakehousemaine.com), Rts. 35 and 37, 686 Waterford Rd., Waterford. Choose from entrées like roast duck with a triple berry sauce of blueberries, red raspberries, and blackberries ($25), or filet mignon with bacon gorgonzola sauce ($34). Entrées $21–34.

Maurice Restaurant (207-743-2532; www.mauricerestaurant.com), 109 Main St., South Paris. Open for dinner daily 4–8:30 PM, lunch weekdays 11:30–1:30, Sunday brunch 11–2. Entrées include coquilles Saint-Jacques, scallops and mushrooms in a Mornay sauce, and rack of lamb. Extensive wine list, $15 and up. Reservations recommended. $14–24.

✐ ♿ **The River Restaurant** (207-674-3800; www.riverrestaurant.com), nestled beside Snow Falls, Rt. 26 at West Paris. Open for lunch and dinner daily except Mon. Known for its creative fine dining at a reasonable price. All soups, dressings, and sauces are made in-house, and specialties include fettuccine Alfredo, crabcakes, and prime rib au jus. Entrées $12–20, including soup, salad, and vegetable side dishes.

Sedgley Place (207-946-5990; www.sedgleyplace.com), off Rt. 202, Greene. Reservations required. A Federal-style house with a well-known dining room. Five-course dinners with entrées that change weekly but always include prime rib, fish, poultry, and a fourth selection. Prix fixe $19–26 includes salad and dessert, with greens, meat, and berries from local farms.

EATING OUT **Nezinscot Farm Store** (207-225-3231; www.nezinscotfarm.com), 284 Turner Center Rd., Turner. Open Mon.–Fri. 6–6, Sat. 6–5, closed Sun. Just beyond the store that sells exceptional cheeses, jams, pickles, organic meats, eggs, and vegetables are some tables where a customer can enjoy a perfect organic hamburger on homemade bread. Gloria Varney, her husband, and her large family staff a great kitchen. Eggs, French toast, and omelets for breakfast, grilled organic cheese sandwiches for lunch. The Tea House, serving tea with clotted cream and scones, is open mid-May–Oct. in the garden, amid the strolling chickens.

Olde Mill Tavern (207-583-9077), Main St., Harrison. Open daily for dinner; also for lunch Sun. Popular with local residents and families. Mexican enchiladas, fajitas, chicken Parmesan, chicken Marsala, penne Alfredo with chicken and broccoli, and burgers, among many other things on the varied menu. Entrées $8–22.

DaVinci's Eatery (207-782-2088; www.davinciseatery.com), 35 Canal St., Bates Mill Complex, Lewiston. Open for lunch and dinner. Brick-oven pizza, classic Italian entrées.

Café Bonbon (207-783-8200), 205 Main St., Lewiston. Green Mountain Coffee is in the great iced coffee as well as the hot stuff. The sandwich list turns egg salad into something special. The café also features drum circles and open mic nights.

Cole Farms (207-657-4714; www.colefarms.com), 64 Lewiston Rd. (Rt. 100/202), Gray. Open Mon.–Thu. 5 AM–9 PM, Fri. until 9:30, Sat. 6 AM to 9:30 PM, Sun. 6 AM–9 PM. No credit cards; checks accepted with ID. Maine cooking from family recipes, including fried seafood, hot chicken sandwiches, and daily specials like New England boiled dinner. No liquor. Kids can use a playground.

♿ **Val's Root Beer** (207-784-5592), 925 Sabattus St., Lewiston. Open daily mid-Apr.–mid-Sept. 11–8 except Sun., when they open at noon. A 1950s-style drive-in with carhops and a *Happy Days* theme. Greasy burgers, great onion rings, hot dogs, and the like, and their specialty, homemade root beer. Popular summer hangout among locals. Fried Oreos are a new item (2 for $1.50) and have become a popular dessert.

Chickadee (207-225-3523), Rt. 4, Turner. A longtime local favorite, serving lunch and dinner daily. Specialties include seafood and beef. Entrées $3–20.

Shaner's Family Dining (207-743-6367), 193 Main St., South Paris. Open for breakfast, lunch, and dinner. A large, cheerful family restaurant with booths; specials like fried chicken, liver and onions, and chicken pie; creamy homemade ice cream in a big choice of flavors like Grape-Nut, buttercrunch, and ginger. Entrées $5–8.

SNACKS **Crestholm Farm Stand and Ice Cream** (207-539-2616), Rt. 26, Oxford. Farm stand, cheeses, honey, ice cream, and a petting zoo: sheep, goats, pigs, ducks, and more.

Greenwood Orchards (207-225-3764), 174 Auburn Rd., Turner. Fresh cider in fall, apples, house jams and jellies, and a bakery. Local produce fills this shop through the growing season.

Smedberg's Crystal Spring Farm (207-743-6723), Rt. 26, Oxford, sells its One Cow Ice Cream (there is actually a herd of beef cattle here) in many flavors; also jams, honey, maple syrup, fruits and vegetables, cheese, berries, home-baked pies, and home-grown beef, pork, and lamb.

Springer's General Store (207-583-

2051), 1218 Waterford Rd., Waterford. This little country store makes pizza and soup to eat at one of the picnic tables. Breakfast, lunch, and dinner are served, with prime rib for dinner in fall and 4-ounce lobster rolls in summer. The gas pump is the only one in the area.

✳ Entertainment

Celebration Barn Theater (207-743-8452; www.celebrationbarn.com), 190 Stock Farm Rd. (off Rt. 117 north of South Paris). In 1972 theater and mime master Tony Montanaro founded a performance-arts school in this big old red racing-horse barn high on Christian Ridge. Summer workshops in acrobatics, mime, voice, clowning, and juggling by resident New Vaudeville artists from around the world in summer.

♿ **Deertrees Theatre and Cultural Center** (207-583-6747; www.deertreestheatre.org), Deertrees Rd., Harrison. A 300-seat historic theater, built as an opera house in 1936, saved from being used as an exercise for the local fire department in the 1980s, and restored to its original grandeur complete with perfect acoustics. The nonprofit performing arts center, run by the Deertrees Foundation, is host to the Sebago–Long Lake Music Festival concert series (see below), and the venue for dance, music, and theatrical productions through the summer, as well as children's shows. Assisted audio for the hard of hearing. Also check out fine arts and sculpture in the **Backstage Gallery**, open an hour before showtime.

Sebago–Long Lake Region Chamber Music Festival (207-583-6747), Deertrees Rd., Deertrees Theatre and Cultural Center, Harrison. A series of five world-class concerts held Tue. mid-July–mid-Aug.

The Public Theatre (207-782-3200), 2 Great Falls Plaza, Auburn. Professional Equity theater featuring high-quality productions of Broadway and off-Broadway shows.

L/A Arts (207-782-7228 or 1-800-639-2919; www.laarts.org), 221 Lisbon St., Lewiston. A local arts agency bringing exhibitions, community arts outreach, dance and musical performances, and award-winning educational programs to the area. The new **Gallery 5**, 49 Lisbon Street, will have themed, group exhibits that change every six weeks. In one show, 32 artists exhibited in "Beyond the Palette," including works in digital imagery, photography, and fused glass.

The Maine Music Society (207-782-1403), 215 Lisbon St., Lewiston, is home to both the Maine Chamber Ensemble and the Androscoggin Chorale. A variety of performances throughout the year.

Bates Dance Festival (207-786-6381), Schaeffer Theater, Bates College, Lewiston. Mid-July–mid-Aug. Student, faculty, and professional performances.

✳ Selective Shopping

ANTIQUES **Orphan Annie's Antiques** (207-782-0638), 96 Court St., Auburn. Open Mon.–Sat. 10–5, Sun. noon–5. If you're looking for art deco and art nouveau objects, this is the place. Tiffany, Steuben, Fiestaware, Depression glass, and much more. The vintage fashions are worth a long journey. Three-floor warehouse sale every Mon. 10–1.

Antiques by Zaar (207-777-3800 or 1-866-868-9227), 301 Peacock Hill

Rd., New Gloucester. Open by appointment only. Interesting Asian furniture and home accessories, including 19th-century Chinese pieces.

BOOKSTORES **Books 'n' Things** (207-739-6200; www.bntnorway.com), 430 Main St., Norway. Billing itself as "Western Maine's Complete Bookstore," this is a fully stocked shop with a good children's section. Coffee, muffins, and author events.

Shoestring Books (207-743-9300; www.shoestringbooks.net), 497 Main St., Norway. A used book store in a charming, old building, with thousands of well-organized titles. Specializing in Maine books.

GEM SHOPS See *To Do—Rockhounding*.

SPECIAL SHOPS **United Society of Shakers** (207-926-4597), Rt. 26, New Gloucester. Open Mon.–Fri. 8:30–4:30, Memorial Day–Columbus Day. Sells Shaker herbs, teas, poultry seasoning, mulled cider mix, pumpkin pie spices, and handcrafted items.

Christian Ridge Pottery (207-743-8419; www.applebaker.com), 210 Stock Farm Rd., South Paris (marked from Rt. 26 and from Christian Ridge Rd.). Open Memorial Day weekend–Dec., daily 10–5, except Sun. noon–5. One of Maine's major potters, known for its functional, distinctive stippleware in ovenproof, microwave-safe designs: coffee- and teapots, bowls, and more. Seconds are available.

Creaser Jewelers (207-744-0290 or 1-800-686-7633), 138 Main St., South Paris. Open daily 10–6. Original designs using Maine tourmaline and amethyst. A small room holds specimens of different gems and crystals. You can buy unset stones too.

Kedar Quilts (207-583-6182; www.kedarquilts.com), Rt. 35, P.O. Box 61, Waterford 04088. Margaret Gibson began making quilts as a child in England. Now she makes them for her Kedarburn Inn and for this quaint shop. The inn hosts quilting retreats Sept.–June (see *Lodging*).

OUTLETS **Bates Mill Store** (207-784-7626 or 1-800-552-2837; www.batesmillstore.com), 41 Chestnut St., Lewiston. Bedspreads, towels, and sheets, as well as blankets made by Maine Heritage Weavers are sold only over the phone and Internet. But go to the Museum of Labor and Industry (see Museum L-A in *To See*) to buy them in person.

Marden's Discount (207-786-0313), Northwood Park Shopping Center, Rt. 202, Lewiston. Like Reny's (see "Damariscotta/Newcastle") this is a Maine original, the first store in a Maine chain. The founder died in 2002, but the legend lives on. A mix of clothing, staples, furnishings—whatever happens to have been purchased cheaply, after a hurricane like Katrina, or, memorably, after 9/11, when designer clothes here were going at 90 percent off.

Oxford Mill-End Store (207-539-4451), 281 King St., Oxford. Open Mon.–Fri. 9–4, Sat. 9–1. First quality woolen and quilting fabric store.

New Balance Factory Store (207-539-9022), Rt. 26, Oxford. The running shoes you love at major discounts.

For more shops in this region, also see "Bethel."

✷ Special Events

February: **Norway-Paris Fish and Game Ice Fishing Derby**, on Norway Lake.

May: **Maine State Parade** (*first Saturday*)—the state's biggest parade; theme varies annually. **Lilac Festival** at McLaughlin Garden.

July: **The Oxford 250 NASCAR Race** draws entrants from throughout the world to the Oxford Plains Speedway; Harrison celebrates Old Home Days. **Founders Day** (*midmonth*) on Paris Hill. **Bean Hole Bean Festival** in Oxford draws thousands. **The Moxie Festival** (*second weekend*), downtown Lisbon, features live entertainment, plenty of food, and Moxie (Maine's own soft drink). The **Norway Sidewalk Arts Festival** has more than 100 exhibitors.

July–August: **Sebago–Long Lake Music Festival** at Deertrees Theatre, Harrison.

August: **Deertrees Theatre Festival**, award-winning plays with Equity casts and student acting workshops for all four weeks of the month (207-583-6747; www.deertreestheatre.org). **Gray Old Home Days** (*beginning of the month*)—parade, contests, and public feeds. **Festival de Joie** (*first weekend*), Lewiston—music, dancing, and cultural and crafts displays. **Great Falls Balloon Festival** (*fourth weekend*), Lewiston—music, games, hot-air launches.

September: **Oxford County Agricultural Fair** (*usually second week*), West Paris—all the usual attractions: horse pulls, 4-H shows, fiddling contests, apple pie judging, and a midway.

November: **The Biggest Christmas Parade in Maine**, Thanksgiving Saturday in South Paris and Norway.

December: **Christmas Open House and Festivals** in Paris Hill.

BETHEL AREA

Bethel is a natural farming and trading site on the Androscoggin River. Its town common is the junction for routes west to the White Mountains, north to the Mahoosuc Mountains, east to the Oxford Hills, and south to the lakes.

When the trains from Portland to Montreal began stopping here in 1851, Bethel also became an obvious summer retreat for city people. But unlike many summer resorts of that era, it was nothing fancy. Families stayed the season in the big white farmhouses, of which there are still plenty. They feasted on home-grown and home-cooked food, then walked it off on nearby mountain trails.

Hiking remains a big lure for summer and fall visitors. The White Mountain National Forest comes within a few miles of town, and trails radiate from nearby Evans Notch. Just 12 miles northwest of Bethel, Grafton Notch State Park also offers short hikes to spectacles such as Screw Auger Falls and to a wealth of well-equipped picnic sites. Blueberrying and rockhounding are local pastimes, and the hills are also good pickings for history buffs.

The hills were once far more peopled than they are today—entire villages have vanished. Hastings, for example, now just the name of a national forest campground, was once a thriving community complete with post office, stores, and a wood alcohol mill that shipped its product by rail to Portland, thence to England.

The Bethel Inn, born of the railroad era, is still going strong. Opened in 1913 by millionaire William Bingham II and dedicated to a prominent neurologist (who came to Bethel to recuperate from a breakdown), it originally featured a program of strenuous exercise—one admired by the locals (wealthy clients actually paid the doctor to chop down his trees) as well as by the medical profession. The inn is still known for at least two forms of exercise—golf and cross-country skiing.

Bethel is best known these days as a ski town. Sunday River Ski Resort, 6 miles to the north, claims to offer "the most dependable snow in New England." Powered by its snow guns (powered in turn by snowmaking ponds fed continuously by the Sunday River), the family-geared resort doubled and redoubled its trails, lifts, and lodging regularly between 1980 and 2002. Snowmaking capacity continues to expand. Mount Abram Family Resort, a few miles south of the village, remains an old-fashioned family ski area, with one of the largest snow-tubing parks in Maine.

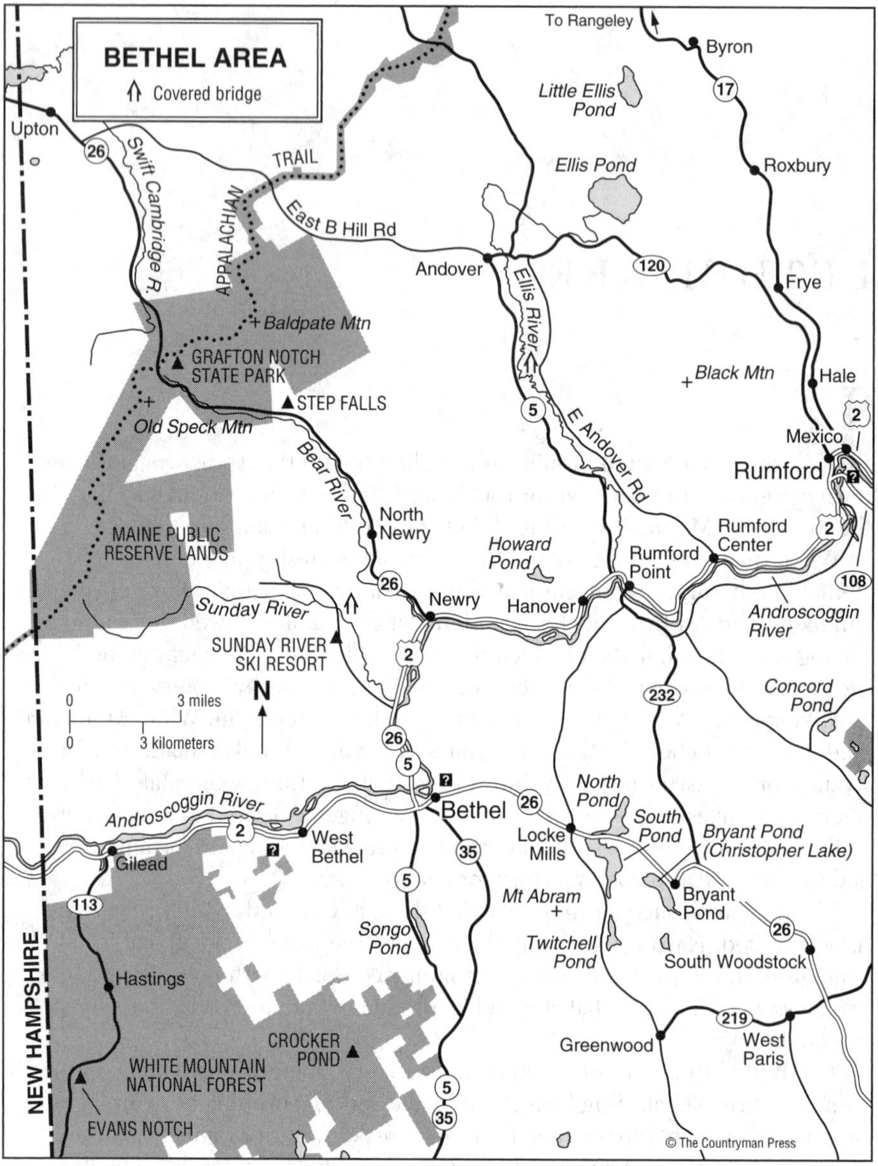

Bethel is also home to Gould Academy, a coed prep school with a handsome campus, and is the summer home of the NTL Institute for Applied Behavioral Science, enrolling participants from all around the world. Hidden away in the Newry woods, an Outward Bound School also contributes to the mix.

For Bethel, tourism has remained the icing rather than the cake. Its lumber mills manufacture pine boards and furniture parts. Three dairy farms ship 7,000 gallons of milk per week. Brooks Bros. is still the name of the hardware store, not a men's clothier.

GUIDANCE **Bethel Area Chamber of Commerce** (207-824-2282 or 1-800-442-5826; www.bethelmaine.com), 8 Station Place, P.O. Box 1247, Bethel 04217, publishes an excellent area guide and maintains a large walk-in information center with restrooms in the depot-style Bethel Station, off Lower Main St. (Rt. 26). Open year-round, weekdays 9–5, varying hours on weekends. See *Lodging* for reservations services.

White Mountain National Forest Service (207-824-2134) maintains an information center, with restrooms, on Rt. 2/5/26 merge, just south of the bridge over the Androscoggin River, next to Crossroads Diner and Rite Aid Pharmacy; open some weekends. It offers detailed information about camping, hiking, and other outdoor activities in the national forest and other nearby natural areas. Pick up a pass for trailhead parking within the White Mountain National Forest.

GETTING THERE *By air:* The **Portland International Jetport**, served by several carriers, is 75 miles from Bethel. All major car rentals are available at the airport (see "Portland"). The **Bethel Airport** (207-824-2669), has a paved 3,818-foot runway, open year-round.

Northeast Charter & Tour (1-888-593-6328) is a 14-passenger van service that runs to the Portland International Jetport; Boston's Logan Airport; Manchester, New Hampshire; and all of New England.

By car: Bethel is a convenient way stop between New Hampshire's White Mountains and the Maine coast (via Rt. 2). From Boston, take the Maine Turnpike to Gray, exit 63; Bethel is 52 miles north on Rt. 26.

GETTING AROUND **Mountain Explorer**. Thanksgiving to Christmas weekends and then daily through the first weekend in April, this free 28-passenger van connects Sunday River with Bethel shops and inns.

WHEN TO COME The ski season, especially Christmas and February vacations, is high season here; given Sunday River's famous snowmaking, snow is fairly dependable through March. April into June is very low season, and summer is quiet but beautiful, with golf, hiking, swimming, llama trekking, horseback riding, mountain and road biking, canoeing, and kayaking all readily available. Fall is even more beautiful, the best season for hiking. Late October through early December is, with reason, low season.

✷ To See

HISTORIC HOMES AND MUSEUMS **Bethel Historical Society's Regional History Center's O'Neil Robinson House** (207-824-2908; www.bethelhistorical.org), 10 Broad St., Bethel. Open year-round, Tue.–Fri. 10–noon and 1–4; also weekends (same hours) in July, Aug., and Dec. No charge for the changing (extensive) exhibits. Built in 1821, the O'Neil Robinson House was remodeled in the Italianate style in 1881 and also houses the museum shop. Next door is the **Dr. Moses Mason House** (open July and Aug., Tue.–Sun. 1–4), an exquisite Federal-style mansion built in 1813, proof of the town's early prosperity. Restored to its original grandeur, it has magnificent Rufus Porter murals in the front hall, fine furnishings in nine period rooms, and well-informed guides to tell you about the items you see throughout the house. Guided tours are $3 adults, $1.50 children. This complex has become a historical exhibit and research center for much of western Maine. Pick up a copy of the historical society's self-guided walking tour of town.

COVERED BRIDGES **Artists' Covered Bridge**, Newry (across the Sunday River, 5 miles northwest of Bethel). A weathered town bridge built in 1872 and painted by numerous 19th-century landscape artists, notably John Enneking. A great spot to sun and swim. Other swimming holes can be found at intervals along the road upstream of the bridge.

Lovejoy Covered Bridge, South Andover, roughly 0.25 mile east of Rt. 5. Built across the Ellis River in 1867, another local swimming hole (it's more than 7 miles north of Rt. 2).

SCENIC DRIVES **Evans Notch**. Follow Rt. 2 west to Gilead and turn south on Rt. 113, following the Wild and then the Cold River south through one of the most spectacular mountain passes in northern New England.

Grafton Notch State Park. A beautiful drive even if you don't hike. Continue on beyond Upton for views of Lake Umbagog; note the loop you can make back from Upton along the old road (East B Hill Road) to Andover (look for the vintage-1867 Lovejoy Covered Bridge across the Ellis River), then south on Rt. 5 to Rt. 2.

Patte Brook Multiple-Use Management Demonstration Area, a 4-mile, self-guided tour with stops at 11 areas along Patte Brook near the national forest's Crocker Pond campground in West Bethel. The tour begins on Forest Road No. 7 (Patte Brook Road), 5 miles south of Bethel on Rt. 5. A glacial bog, former orchards and homesites, and an old dam and pond are among the clearly marked sites.

Rangeley and Weld loops. See the introduction to "Western Mountains and Lakes Region" for a description of these rewarding drives. You can access both by following Rt. 2 north from Bethel along the Androscoggin River, but back-road buffs may prefer cutting up the narrow rural valleys threaded by Rumford Rd. or Rt. 232 from Locke Mills (Greenwood); both join Rt. 2 at Rumford Point.

OTHER SITES **Mount Zircon Bottle**. Walk down Bethel's Broad St. and you'll see this historic bottle-shaped lunch stand, built after the company's second bottling plant opened in 1922.

* To Do

BICYCLING/WALKING The **Bethel Pathway** offers a 1.2-mile round trip along the Androscoggin River beginning in the Davis Park picnic area and playground on the eastern edge of town off Rt. 26.

CAMPING In the **Evans Notch area** of the White Mountain National Forest there are five campgrounds: **Basin** (21 sites), **Cold River** (12 sites), **Crocker Pond** (7 sites), **Hastings** (24 sites), and **Wild River** (11 sites). All accept reservations for May 13–Oct. 11 through the National Recreation Reservation Service: 1-800-280-2267, Mon.–Fri. (Pacific time; from the East Coast, phone weekdays noon–9 PM or Sat. and Sun. 1–6 PM). For information, phone the **Evans Notch Ranger Station** (207-824-2134), West Bethel Rd. (Rt. 2), Bethel.

Also check with the **White Mountain National Forest Service** information center (see *Guidance*) about wilderness campsites, and see *Lodging* for commercial campgrounds.

CANOEING AND KAYAKING Popular local routes include the **Ellis River** in Andover (13 easy miles from the covered bridge in South Andover to Rumford Point); the **Androscoggin River** has become far more accessible in recent years with 10 put-in points mapped and shuttle service offered between Shelburne on the New Hampshire line and the Rumford boat landing; the **Sunday River** (beginning at the covered bridge) also offers great whitewater trips in spring. A chain of water connects **North**, **South**, and **Round Ponds** and offers a day of rewarding paddling, with swimming holes and picnic stops en route. You can learn details about these spots at Round Pond Corner Store, Rt. 26, Greenwood (and find canoe and kayak rentals).

Bethel Outdoor Adventure and Campground (207-824-4224 or 1-800-533-3607), Rt. 2, Bethel, offers shuttle service, canoe and kayak rentals, guided trips, and kayak clinics.

Sun Valley Sports (207-824-7533 or 1-877-851-7533; www.sunvalleysports.com), 129 Sunday River Rd., Bethel, offers guided (and nonguided) kayak and canoe tours and rentals on the Androscoggin River and on local lakes and ponds. They also offer ATV tours and weekly cabin rentals. This is a full-service authorized Orvis dealer, with Orvis-endorsed guides. Wading and drift-boat fly-fishing trips.

Mahoosuc Guide Service (207-824-2073; www.mahoosuc.com), 1513 Bear River Rd., Newry 04261. One- to 10-day canoe trips, including a trip with Cree Indians in Quebec, and western trips too.

FARMS **Sunday River Alpacas** (207-890-3148), 471 Flat Rd., Bethel. Take a farm tour, and feed the fish, chickens, and goats. Alpaca sweaters, capes, mittens, and scarves for sale in the farm store.

FISHING Temporary nonresident licenses are available at the Bethel, Newry, and Woodstock town offices; also at **Dave's Store** in Andover, **Round Pond Corner Store** in Greenwood, **Bethel Outdoor Adventure** in Bethel, and **Sun Valley Sports** (207-824-7533 or 1-877-851-7533; www.sunvalleysports.com), 129 Sunday River Rd., Bethel. Fly-fishing is a growing sport here, especially along the Androscoggin, which is increasingly known for the size of its trout. **Sandy MacGregor** will take you fishing on the Androscoggin: www.mountainranger.com. For guiding and fly-fishing instruction also check with **Aldro French**, based at Middle Dam in Andover (www.rapidriverflyishing.com).

FOR FAMILIES ✐ **The BIG Adventure Center** (207-824-0929), Rt. 2 and North Rd. (adjacent to the Norseman), Bethel. Summer hours, 11–10 daily; winter hours, Mon.–Fri. 5–10 PM, weekends 11–10. Indoor laser tag, indoor rock gym, two-lane waterslide, outdoor 18-hole miniature golf, and four bowling lanes.

GOLF **Bethel Inn Resort** (207-824-2175), Broad St., Bethel. An 18-hole championship-length course and driving range. Mid-May–Oct. the Guaranteed Performance School of Golf (PGA) offers three- and five-day sessions (classes limited to three students per PGA instructor); golf-cart rentals are available.

HIKING **White Mountain National Forest**, although primarily in New Hampshire, includes 41,943 acres in Maine. A number of the trails in the Evans Notch area are spectacular. Trail maps for the Baldface Circle Trail, Basin Trail, Bickford Brook Trail, and Caribou Trail are available from the **Evans Notch Ranger District** (207-824-2134), West Bethel Rd. (Rt. 2), Bethel; open Mon.–Fri. 8–4. Pick up detailed maps from the chamber of commerce.

Grafton Notch State Park, Rt. 26, between Newry and Upton. From Bethel, take Rt. 2 east to Rt. 26 north for 7.8 miles. Turn left at the Bear River Trading Post (Newry Corner) and drive toward New Hampshire for 8.7 miles. **Screw Auger Falls** is 1 mile farther—a spectacular area at the end of the Mahoosuc Range. Other sights include **Mother Walker Falls** and **Moose Cave**, a 0.5-mile nature walk. The big hike is up **Old Speck**, the third highest mountain in the state; round trip is 7.8 miles. Also see *Green Space* below, for the new 35-mile Grafton Loop Trail.

Wight Brook Nature Preserve/Step Falls can be found just before the entrance to Grafton Notch State Park. From Newry Corner, drive 7.9 miles. On your right will be a white farmhouse, followed by a field just before a bridge. There is a road leading to the rear left of the field, where you may park. The well-marked trail is just behind the trees at the back.

In Shelburne there are hiking trails on **Mount Crag**, **Mount Cabot**, and **Ingalls Mountain**, and there are more trails in **Evans Notch**. For details, check the Appalachian Mountain Club's *White Mountain Guide* and John Gibson's *50 Hikes in Coastal and Southern Maine* (Backcountry Guides).

Mount Will Trail. Recently developed by the Bethel Conservation Commission, this 3.25-mile loop is a good family trip; many people choose to climb only to the North Ledges (640 vertical feet in 0.75 mile), yielding a view of the Androscoggin Valley, which only gets better over the next 1.5 miles—climbing over ledges 1,450 feet and then descending the South Cliffs. The trailhead parking lot is opposite the recycling center on Rt. 2, just 1.9 miles east of the Riverside Rest Area (which is just beyond the turnoff for Sunday River).

HORSEBACK RIDING **Sparrowhawk Mountain Ranch** (207-836-2528; www.maineranch.com), 120 Fleming Rd., Bethel. Trail rides, lessons, riding packages with overnight accommodations. **Deepwood Farm** (207-824-2595; www.deepwoodfarm.com), Albany, offers trail rides and summer camps.

LLAMA TREKKING **Telemark Inn** (207-836-2703), 10 miles west of Bethel. Treks offered Apr.–Oct. Primarily for guests of the Telemark Inn, but trips ranging from half day to four days into the surrounding wilderness are available to nonguests as well. Steve Crone offered the first llama treks in New England, and we took one of the first that he offered. The llamas carry your gear, but you walk beside them.

MOUNTAIN BIKING **Bethel Outdoor Adventure** (207-824-4224), Rt. 2, Bethel, offers mountain bike trail maps as well as custom guided tours and rentals.

ROCKHOUNDING This corner of Oxford County is recognized as one of the world's richest sources of some minerals and semiprecious gems. More than a third of the world's mineral varieties can be found here. Gems include amethyst, aquamarine, tourmaline, and topaz. Mining has gone on around here since tourmaline was discovered at Mount Mica in 1821. Jim Mann's **Mt. Mann Jeweler** (207-824-3030), 57 Main St., Bethel, includes a mineral museum. In the cellar kids (of all ages) can explore "Crystal Cave": a dimly lit "mine" in which rockhounds can fill their cardboard buckets (for a nominal fee) and then identify the stones back in the museum. **Perham's of West Paris** (207-674-2341 or 1-800-371-GEMS), open 9–5 daily, offers maps to four local quarries. (Also see "Oxford Hills.") **Songo Pond Mine** (207-824-3898) South Shore Road in Albany Township, is a real mine open to the public with a reservation. Call ahead.

Sunday River Gems (207-824-3414), Sunday River Road, Bethel, is open daily 10–6, and sells local jewelers' one-of-a-kind pieces set with Maine gems, along with other gold and silver jewelry. **Mt. Mica Rarities** (207-875-3060; www.mainetourmalineonline.com), Route 26 (a bright purple building), Greenwood, has a stockpile of tourmaline, amethyst, aquamarine, and smoky quartz, and a collection is on display. Phil McCrillis is the fourth generation of his family to mine Mt. Mica, which was owned by his family until 2003.

The **Annual Gem, Mineral, and Jewelry Show** (second weekend in July) is a mega mineral event with guided field trips to local quarries. (For information contact the Bethel Area Chamber of Commerce, 207-824-2282).

SWIMMING There are numerous lakes and river swimming holes in the area. It's best to ask the chamber of commerce about where access is currently possible. Reliable spots include:

Angevine Park and Swim Pond (207-824-2669). The town of Bethel has created a new swimming spot open to all free of charge. It is located on North Rd., 2.2 miles from Rt. 2 (turn in at Big Adventure Center and the Norseman Inn & Motel). Open daily 10–7, summer only.

Artists' Covered Bridge. Follow SUNDAY RIVER SKI RESORT signs north from Bethel, but bear right at two Y-intersections instead of turning onto either of the ski-area access roads. Look for the covered bridge on your left. Space for parking, bushes for changing.

Wild River in Evans Notch, Gilead, offers some obvious access spots off Rt. 113, as does the **Bear River**, which follows Rt. 26 through Grafton Notch.

✱ Winter Sports

DOGSLEDDING **Mahoosuc Guide Service** (207-824-2073), 1513 Bear River Rd., Newry 04261. Polly Mahoney and Kevin Slater offer combination skiing and mushing trips. You can be as involved with the dogs as you want, for a single or multi-day trips.

Winter Journeys (207-928-2026), based in Lovell. Day, multiday, and custom programs.

Skijoring. Skiing behind dogs is a specialty at the Telemark Inn (see *Lodging*).

CROSS-COUNTRY SKIING **Sunday River Inn and XC Ski Center** (207-824-2410), 23 Skiway Road, Newry. A total of 40 kilometers of double-tracked trails loop through the woods, including a section to Artists' Covered Bridge. Thanks to the high elevation, careful trail prepping, and heavy-duty grooming equipment, snow tends to stick here when it's scarce in much of Maine. The center offers guided night skiing, rentals, instruction, and snacks.

Bethel Inn XC Ski and Snowshoe Center (207-824-2175), Bethel. Redesigned trails meander out over the golf course and through the woods, offering beautiful mountain views, solitude, and challenges for all levels. Skating and classic trails, rental equipment, and lessons available.

Carter's X-Country Ski Center (207-539-4848; www.carterxcski.com), Intervale Rd. (off Rt. 26 south of the village), Bethel. Open daily during winter. Dave Carter, a member of one of Bethel's oldest families and a longtime cross-country pro, maintains some 65 kilometers of wooded trails on 1,000 acres, meandering from 600 up to 1,800 feet in elevation; an easy loop connects two lodges and runs along the Androscoggin River. Reasonably priced equipment rentals and lessons; additional center on Rt. 26 in Oxford.

Telemark Inn (207-836-2703), West Bethel. These 20 kilometers of high-elevation wooded trails and unlimited backcountry skiing terrain frequently represent the best cross-country skiing in the area—but Steve Crone issues a limited number of passes a day, preserving the wilderness feel of his resort for Telemark Inn guests. So call before coming, and inquire about skijoring behind huskies!

SUNDAY RIVER

Mahoosuc Mountain Sports (207-875-3786; www.teleskis.com), Rt. 26, Greenwood, rents and sells telemark skiing equipment.

See also **Mahoosuc Guide Service** in *Dogsledding*, and contact the

Bethel Ranger Station (207-824-2134) for details about cross-country trails in the White Mountain National Forest.

DOWNHILL SKIING **Sunday River Ski Resort** (207-824-3000; resort reservations, 1-800-543-2SKI; www.sundayriver.com), Newry 04217. *Sunday River* has become synonymous with *snow*. Forty-eight miles of trails now lace eight interconnected mountain peaks, including the Jordan Bowl. Challenges include a 3-mile run from a summit and White Heat, considered one of the premier bump runs in the East. The trails are served by 18 lifts: nine quad chairlifts (four high-speed detachable), four triple chairlifts, two doubles, and three surface lifts. The vertical descent is 2,340 feet, and the top elevation is 3,140 feet. Snowmaking covers 92 percent of the skiing and riding terrain. You'll also find one quarter-pipe, one mini pipe, one half-pipe (in-ground competition superpipe), and four terrain parks, including the resort's signature Rocking Chair. Facilities include three base lodges and a Peak Lodge, ski shops, and several restaurants; and a total of 6,000 slope-side beds (see *Lodging*). The Discovery Center ski school offers Guaranteed Learn-to-Ski in One Day and Perfect Turn clinics, Munchkins for ages 4–6, Mogul Meisters for ages 7–12, a Junior Racing Program, and a Maine Handicapped Skiing Program. Two tubing runs and an ice-skating rink are lit at night at the White Cap Base Lodge, which is also the best spot for viewing fireworks on Saturday nights through most of the season. Two-day lift tickets are $130 adults, $114 young adults (13–17), and $86 for juniors and seniors on weekends; less midweek. Many lodging packages available.

Mount Abram Family Resort (207-875-5000; www.mtabram.com), Locke Mills (Greenwood). Open 9–4 Thu.–Sun., Maine school vacation weeks and holidays. This remains a friendly family-owned and -geared ski area: 44 trails and slopes, with well-known learn-to-ski trails, many black-diamond trails, and a "cruiser" trail; 85 percent have snowmaking. The vertical drop is 1,150 feet. Facilities include two double chairlifts and three surface lifts; two base lodges; licensed daycare, cafeteria, retail shop, ski rentals, and tuning center; Loose Boots Lounge; and a PSIA ski school with snowboard and telemark instruction. Three tubing runs at Flying Squirrel Tubing Park, one the longest parks in the state, are open weekends and school vacations. $43 adults, $32 seniors and juniors on weekends and holidays, 5 and under free. Weekday specials include two lift tickets for the price of one Thu. and Fri.

ICE SKATING Skate rentals are available at the public skating rink at Sunday River's White Cap Base Lodge.

SLEIGH RIDES **Bethel Inn Resort** (see *Lodging*) and **Meadowcreek Farm** (207-388-2044; www.meadow-creek-farm.com) offer sleigh rides.

Deepwood Farm (207-824-2595; www.deepwoodfarm.com), Albany. This farm provides the Bethel Inn rides, and offers sleigh rides at their own farm during winter days and evenings, but not Saturday (to give the horse the afternoon off). Their old-fashioned sleigh holds four to five people.

SNOWMOBILING Contact the Bethel Area Chamber of Commerce for information on where to get maps of the trail system. Maine and New Hampshire also maintain 60 miles of trails in the Evans Notch District. **Sun Valley Sports & Guide Services** (207-824-7533 or 1-877-851-7533), 129 Sunday River Rd., Bethel, rents snowmobiles, offers guided snowmobile trips, and rents snowshoes. Also, **Fryeburg Snowmobile Rentals** (1-800-458-1838), 532 Main St., Fryeburg.

✷ Green Space

The Mahoosuc Land Trust (207-824-3806; www.mahoosuc.org), P.O. Box 981, Bethel 04217. Formed in 1988 to preserve land in the Mahoosuc Range and the Androscoggin Valley, the trust owns islands, shoreland, and floodplain land, along with easements on land in the eastern foothills and on the banks of a large pond. Grafton Loop Trail, a new trail about 35 miles long, is a collaborative partnership on land trust land with Maine Appalachian Trail Club (www.matc.org). It can be accessed at the Grafton Loop Trailhead on Route 26, or at the Appalachian Trail parking lot in Grafton Notch State Park.

✷ Lodging

All listings are in Bethel 04217 unless otherwise noted

The **Bethel Area Chamber of Commerce** maintains a lodging reservations service: 207-824-3585 or 1-800-442-5826; www.bethelmaine.com.

Sunday River Ski Resort maintains its own toll-free reservation number, 1-800-543-2SKI, good nationwide and in Canada; the service is geared toward winter and condo information but also serves local inns and B&Bs. Many other condos and rental homes are available in the Bethel area through **Maine Street Realty & Rentals** (207-824-2114 or 1-800-824-6024), **Connecting Rentals** (207-824-4829), and **Four Seasons Realty & Rentals** (207-875-2414). Also see **Lake House** and the **Kedarburn Inn** in "Oxford Hills."

INNS 🍴 🐾 ⛳ ♿ **Bethel Inn Resort** (207-824-2175 or 1-800-654-0125; www.bethelinn.com). This rambling, yellow wooden inn and its annexes frame a corner of the town common (for the history of this special resort, see the chapter introduction). Some Main Inn rooms have a gas fireplace. The formal dining room is truly elegant (see *Dining Out*). The 55 rooms in the inn and guest houses vary widely in size and view (request a larger room in back, overlooking the mountains), but all have air conditioning, phone, cable TV, and private bath, some have a fireplace. Families should opt for one of the 60 one-, two-, and three-bedroom town houses on the golf course and on Mill Hill Rd. There's an indoor–outdoor pool (heated to 92 degrees in winter) that's great year-round; also two saunas, an exercise room, a game room, and a lounge. The 18-hole golf course, with seven holes dating to 1915 and 11 more added by Geoffrey Cornish, is a big draw, with golf-school sessions offered throughout the season. Other facilities also include a Har-Tru tennis court, a boathouse with canoes, and a sandy beach on Songo Pond, as well as an extensive cross-country ski network. From $50 per person in the inn; town houses, $70. Many packages are available, like Golf and Dine for an extra $50 per person. Children age 11 and under stay free in room with parent (plus $20 for the meal plan). Spa services, and a concierge center to "choose your own adventure."

🐾 **Sudbury Inn** (207-824-2174, 1-800-395-7837; www.sudburyinn.com), 151 Main St., P.O. Box 369. A nicely restored village inn built in 1873 to serve train travelers (the depot was just down the street). Innkeeper William White and his wife, Nancy, have made over this inn with good taste. They offer 11 guest rooms and six suites, all different shapes and decors. All have a private bath, TV, and air-conditioning, and two suites have whirlpools. The dining room is popular (see *Dining Out*). Suds Pub (see *Eating Out*) is a year-round evening gathering spot. Pets are accepted only in the Carriage House, an apartment available for rent. Apr.–Nov., $89–300; ski season, $89–450 double; includes breakfast.

🐾 **The Jolly Drayman at the Briar Lea Inn** (207-824-4717 or 1-877-311-1299; www.briarleainn.com), Rt. 2/26. Open year-round. One mile west of town, 5 miles east of Sunday River. Jennifer and Richard Fredricks are innkeepers at this 150-year-old farmhouse, an attractive six-room inn, with private bath, cable TV, phone, and eclectic decor. The English pub is open to the public (see *Dining Out*). The sitting area with a fireplace and polished floors is particularly attractive, as is the neighboring breakfast room. $89–159; pets $10 extra.

🐾 ✐ **L'Auberge** (207-824-2774 or 1-800-760-2774; www.laubergecountryinn.com), 15 L'Auberge Ln. A former barn built in the 1850s for a long-vanished mansion. Innkeepers Sharon and Doron Haendel serve dinner (see *Dining Out*) to the public as well as guests. The property especially lends itself to groups because of its large living room, where you can enjoy a glass of wine by the fire, but it also hums along as a low-key inn. It's around the corner from village shops and restaurants. $89–249 per night for a double with breakfast.

🐾 ♿ **The Victoria Inn and Restaurant** (207-824-8060 or 1-888-774-1235; www.thevictoria-inn.com), 32 Main St. Open year-round. The decor is high Victorian, and under new owners Kamil and Stacey Sahin promises to become ever more polished and elegant, with touches like silk-screened wallpaper. Each of the 14 rooms has a phone along with a TV, and several have extra beds for families. All show an attention to detail and comfort. In-room spa services. A full breakfast is included. $89–279 depending on season. See *Dining Out* for the restaurant.

✐ **Telemark Inn** (207-836-2703; www.telemarkinn.com), RFD 2, Box 800. It is a challenge to describe this unusual retreat, set among birch trees 10 miles from Bethel Village, 2.5 miles off the nearest back road and surrounded by national forest, with a herd of llamas, 60 huskies, four good riding horses, and a tame ox. Steve Crone offers horseback riding (some experience required), as well as hiking, canoeing, and mountain biking; winter brings exceptional cross-country skiing and the opportunity to try "skijoring" (skiing behind huskies) and dogsledding. Meals are served family-style. Six rooms share two baths and accommodate 12 to 17 guests. Two-day packages include room, breakfast, lunch, and guided day activities, $390 adult, $300 child, three-day packages $550 adult, $425 child. Inn rates $125 per room include breakfast.

🐾 ✐ **Philbrook Farm Inn** (603-466-3831; www.philbrookfarminn.com), 881 North Rd., Shelburne, New Hampshire 03581. Open year-round, except Nov.–day after Christmas, and Apr. Twenty miles west of Bethel, just over the New Hampshire line. The long, meandering farmhouse, owned by the same family since 1861, sits above a floodplain of the Androscoggin River with the Mahoosuc Range at its back, with 19 guest rooms furnished with the kind of hand-me-downs that most innkeepers scour the hills for. Second-floor rooms have a private bath; third-floor rooms share. The family-style meals are as old-fashioned as the rest of the place (fish on Friday, ham and beans on Saturday night; BYOB). There are also four housekeeping cottages and two seasonal cabins. $130–150 per couple MAP, plus a 15 percent service charge. B&B rates from $105–130.

BED & BREAKFASTS **A Prodigal Inn & Gallery** (207-824-8884 or 1-800-320-9201; www.prodigalinn.com), 162 Mayville Rd. (Rt. 2). Tom and Marcey White have taken over the old Douglass House, now completely renovated and remodeled, and turned it into a classy bed & breakfast, with a handsome common room with a fireplace, and elegant, deep-hued bedrooms. Audra Suite is a deep purple with a tiled bath, one of four rooms with sitting area and private bath. Tom White's sculptures are scattered in the inn, and for sale; he works in a studio in the barn. $135–155 in winter, $120–140 in summer. Afternoon tea.

"1" ✐ **Chapman Inn** (207-824-2657 or 1-877-359-1498; www.chapmaninn.com), 1 Mill Hill Road. Fred Nolte and Sandra Frye bring years in the hospitality business and energy to this comfortable, rambling white wooden inn on the common. Six units have a private bath, and four share; there's cable TV and air-conditioning in most rooms, and a phone in all. Common space includes, in the barn, a game room with a pool table and two saunas. Handy to cross-country trails at the Bethel Inn, also to village shops and restaurants. $59–99 in summer, $69–129 in winter; $33 per person for the dorm, breakfast included, with fresh fruit, cereals, muffins and pastries, omelet of the day, and other good things.

Austin's Holidae House Bed and Breakfast (207-824-3400, 1-877-224-3400; www.holidae-house.com), P.O. Box 1248, 85 Main St. A gracious Main Street house (the first in Bethel to be electrified), built in the 1890s by a local lumber baron. Laurence and Marcia Austin offer seven rooms furnished in comfortable antiques, with cable TV, phone, and private bath. All have air-conditioning. $100–128 double includes a continental-plus breakfast.

✐ ♿ **Crocker Pond House** (207-836-2027; www.crockerpond.com), 917 North Rd. Off by itself on the Shelburne–Bethel Road (five miles from downtown Bethel), facing south toward Evans Notch, this is a long, shingled, one-room-deep house designed and built by the architect-innkeeper Stuart Crocker. It's a beauty, filled with light and grace, and very quiet. Hiking and snowshoeing or just peace are what it offers, with in-room phones but no TVs. The four guest rooms, one with a loft for children, all have private bath. $95 per couple ($25 per extra person 14 and up) includes a full breakfast, afternoon tea and cookies.

The Gideon Hastings House (207-824-3496; www.gideonhastingshouse.com), 22 Broad St., Bethel. This 1848 Greek Revival house makes an elegant home base for a stay in Bethel. Four bedrooms are bright and gracefully furnished; two have a private bathroom. Play on a professional bocce court in summer. The fine dining restaurant and pub (see *Dining Out*) has an Italian theme. $80–325, with breakfast and afternoon cocktail included.

♂ ♿ **The Norseman Inn and Motel** (207-824-2002; www.norsemaninn.com), Rt. 2, P.O. Box 934. An old farmstead with eight light, pleasant guest rooms, one two-room suite, and 22 motel units in the old barn. Guests can sit by the common room's fireplace made from local stones. The motel units are spacious; amenities include a laundry room and game room, a deck, and walking trails. $45–168 depending on season.

♿ "1" **Bethel Hill Bed & Breakfast** (207-824-2461, www.bethelhill.com), 66 Broad St. Renovated with the needs of a B&B in mind, Scott and Carol Gould host three cushy rooms with whirlpool bath and cable TV, ceiling fans and air-conditioning. $119–169 depending on season, includes complementary pair of bikes; for a fee Scott Gould, a certified staff trainer at Sunday River, can provide ski tuning lessons, Kevlar kayaks, and transportation.

SKI LODGES AND CONDOMINIUMS

♂ **Sunday River Ski Resort** (207-824-3000; resort reservations 1-800-543-2SKI), P.O. Box 450, now offers more than 6,000 "slope-side beds." There are condominium complexes ranging from studios to three-bedroom units. Each complex has access to an indoor pool, Jacuzzi, sauna, laundry, recreation room, and game room; **Cascades** and **Sunrise** offer large common rooms with fireplaces. **Merrill Brook Village Condominiums** have fireplaces, and many have a whirlpool tub. **South Ridge** also offers a fireplace in each unit, which range from studios to three-bedrooms. The 68-room **Snow Cap Inn** has an atrium with fieldstone fireplaces, an exercise room, and an outdoor Jacuzzi; it also offers reasonably priced bunks. The 230-room **Grand Summit Hotel** has both standard and kitchen-equipped units and a health club with a pool, and conference facilities; it offers rooms and studios as well as one- and two-bedroom efficiency units. The 195-room **Jordan Grand Hotel** is off by itself but linked by ski trails as well as road, circled by the mountains of the Jordan Bowl; facilities include a health club, a swimming pool, and restaurants. Hotel prices start at $90. In winter, condo units are based on ski packages, from $60 per night or $299 per person for 5 days. All winter lodging rates include a lift ticket.

♂ ♿ **Sunday River Inn** (207-824-2410 or 1-866-232-4354; www.sundayriverinn.com), 23 Skiway Rd., Newry 04261. Just down the road from the big ski resort but its antithesis: a homey, very personal place. Steve and Peggy Wight have been welcoming guests since 1971, catering to cross-country skiers and to small conferences in other seasons. A game room, sauna, and wood-heated hot tub just outside the back door are also available to guests. The 22 rooms (most with shared bath) range from dorms to private rooms in the inn or adjacent chalet. $40–85 per person B&B includes cross-country ski pass.

CAMPGROUNDS **Littlefield Beaches** (207-875-3290; www.littlefieldbeaches.com), 13 Littlefield Ln., Greenwood 04255.Open mid-May–Sept. Arthur and Lisa Park run a clean, quiet family campground surrounded by three connecting lakes. Full hook-ups, a laundry room, miniature golf, a game room, swimming, kayak rentals. $29–34 daily, seasonal rates available.

Bethel Outdoor Adventure and Campground (207-824-4224 or 1-800-533-3607; www.betheloutdooradventure.com), Rt. 2. Jeff and Pattie Parsons offer RV and tent sites on the Androscoggin River (where you can swim), within walking distance of downtown shops and restaurants. $20–32 daily.

Pleasant River Campground (207-836-2000), 800 West Bethel Rd. (Rt. 2). Wooded sites, restrooms, pool, playground, and many recreational possibilities. In addition to camping, Mike and Michelle Mador offer canoe and kayak rentals, Androscoggin River access, shuttle service, and lobster boils, pig roasts, and barbecues. $20–26 daily.

Also see **Papoose Pond Resort and Campground** in "Oxford Hills." For campgrounds in the White Mountain National Forest, see *To Do—Camping*.

SPECIAL LODGING **The Maine Houses** (1-800-646-8737; www.themainehouses.com), Bryant Pond (reservations: P.O. Box 1138, Yarmouth 04096). Two of the three houses are located on or near Lake Christopher, the third just a short walk away. These unique, self-service guest houses are perfect for small groups or large reunions. The Maine House has eight bedrooms, six and a half baths, a steam room, and a wraparound porch. In the Maine Farmhouse there are seven bedrooms, each with a private bath. The Maine Mountainview House features seven bedrooms, seven full baths, an indoor spa, and a fireplace. All three have fully equipped kitchen, access to the lake, canoes, and outdoor sports equipment, cable TV, DVD/VCR, and all bedding and towels. $20–50 per person per night, but groups of 20 to 94 are the main customers.

Androscoggin Home Rentals (207-824-2461; www.ahr-online.com), 66 Broad St. Scott and Carol Gould rent three cabins and vacation homes: fully outfitted, five-bedroom Village House; secluded River House; and Lake Cottage on remote Concord Pond, without electricity and only cold running water—it's the real thing. $175–450 per night, with weekly and multiday rates.

✻ Where to Eat

All restaurants are in Bethel unless otherwise noted.

DINING OUT **Sudbury Inn** (207-824-2174, 1-800-359-7837; www.sudburyinn.com), Main St., Bethel. Open for dinner 5–9 Tue.–Sun. year-round except Nov. and May, when it's Thu.–Sun. Attractive, traditional dining rooms and a sunporch in a 19th-century village inn. Widely respected chef Peter Bodwell has a fine reputation with a menu that ranges from chicken Sicilian, with mushrooms, tomatoes, artichokes, prosciutto, and spinach ($16), to veal Oscar, with crabmeat and bearnaise sauce. Entrées $16–28.

The Jolly Drayman at the Briar Lea Inn (207-824-4717), Rt. 2/26. The inn's welcoming dining room serves dinner daily. Jennifer Fredricks (who hails from England) and her husband, Richard, have transformed their dining room into an English pub and restaurant. So, here in New England you'll find fish-and-chips and Indian-style curry, as well as other American favorites. A reliably good and reasonably priced place for dinner. Entrées $10–17.

22 Broad Street (207-824-3496; www.gideonhastingshouse.com), 22 Broad St. This new addition to Bethel's dinner places is impressive. The Italian-inspired menu under chef Chris Hascall starts with antipasto like ricotta and scallion stuffed eggplant, *involtini di melanzane,* and escarole and bean soup. A lovely *primi,* first course, might be the ravioli *amatriciana,* with pancetta, onions, and herbs. Among *secondi* there is beloved osso buco, braised veal shank, and braciole alla Siciliana—beef rolls simmered in tomato sauce. Ten tables, plus a martini bar. Entrees $17–22.

The Victoria Restaurant (207-824-8060 or 1-888-774-1235; www.thevictoria-inn.com), 32 Main St. Open year-round. Chef and innkeeper Kamil Sahin pairs pork tenderloin with rhubarb compote, and Gorgonzola butter tops the grilled rib eye. This was one of the rare places that served fresh local strawberries during their brief season, so we'll continue to look for local resources on the menu in Stacey Sahin's elegantly redecorated dining room. Entrées $19–29.

♿ **Bethel Inn Resort** (207-824-2175 or 1-800-654-0125), Bethel Common. Serves breakfast and dinner. An elegant formal dining room with a Steinway, hearth, and large windows overlooking the golf course and hills, plus a year-round veranda. The menu offers a choice of a dozen entrées that might include Maine lobster, beef sirloin, or veal "Jaguar Schnitzel." Entrées $20–27.

S. S. Milton (207-824-2589), 43 Main St. Open for dinner 5–9, lunch in summer. Entrées ($16–23) might include scallops Nantucket with white wine, lemon, and cheddar cheese, topped with Ritz crackers ($18), and Boothbay fettuccine with Maine lobster, scallops, shrimp in a white cream wine sauce ($22). Children's menu.

Sunday River Resort operates several "fine-dining" restaurants: **Legends** (207-824-5858; www.sundayriver.com) at the Grand Summit Resort Hotel, and **Sliders** (207-824-5000) at the Jordan Grand.

Phoenix House & Well (207-824-2222; www.phoenixhouseandwell.com), Skiway Rd., just before South Ridge Base Lodge at Sunday River. With windows on a great view, pick from a list of pasta and sauces, or go for a steak, beef, or tuna. Live music in the Well in winter.

L'Auberge Country Inn and Bistro (207-824-2774), 15 L'Auberge Ln. Open year-round, daily at 5:30 in winter. Reservations suggested. Rack of lamb with raspberry demiglace and haddock provencal are popular items on the menu. Entrées $18–28.

EATING OUT **Café di Cocoa** (207-824-6386; www.cafedicocoa.com), 125 Main St. A market with breakfast and lunch items, and next door a restaurant for dinners on Saturday in winter. Cathy DiCocco's cheerful eatery specializes in vegan and vegetarian dishes using local organic produce. In winter join them for an ethnic dinner party (by reservation only). Full bakery, juice and espresso bars, and wonderful hot chocolate. BYOB ($2-per-party corking fee).

Suds Pub (207-824-6558, 1-800-395-7837), downstairs at the Sudbury Inn, 151 Main St. Open year-round, from 4:30 PM daily. A friendly pub with the largest number of beers on tap west of Portland, and a reasonably priced pub menu with a wide choice of pizzas. Burgers, soups and salads, ribs, and pasta. Kids' menu.

The Funky Red Barn (207-824-3003; www.funkyredbarn.com), 19 Summer St. The Funky Burger is served on a huge Thomas's English muffin—and it looks like the Funky Pizza Muffin is too. Nasty Nachos include black olives and jalapenos to get the digestive turmoil up to speed. This newly reborn popular place used to be the Backstage Lounge.

Crossroads Diner & Deli (207-824-3673), 24 Mayville Rd. (Rt. 2). Breakfast, lunch, and dinner. This is the hangout for the loyal locals.

The Sunday River Brewing Co. (207-824-4ALE), junction of Sunday River Rd. and Rt. 2, North Bethel. Open from 11:30 daily for lunch and dinner. Often has live-entertainment evenings.

Bethel's Best Pizza Grille and Dairy Bar (207-824-3192), just west of Bethel on Rt. 2. Open from 7 AM for a full breakfast. Will deliver, and the pizza is good. Homemade clam "chowdah," chili, burgers, subs, salads, and "lobstah" rolls are also on the extensive menu.

Matterhorn Ski Bar Wood-Fired Pizza and Fresh Pasta (207-824-6271), Sunday River Rd., ski-season only, offers entertainment and steak, seafood, and brick-oven pizza.

Cho Sun (207-824- 7370), 141 Main St., Bethel. Open Wed.–Sun., 5:30–9. Authentic Japanese and Korean cuisine (owner Pok Sun Lee is Korean), sushi, teriyaki steaks, and seafood.

Kowloon Village Chinese Restaurant (207-824-3707), Lower Main St. Simon and his wife are from Kowloon. Eat in or take out.

BBQ Bob's Real Pit Barbeque (207-824-4744), in the parking lot of the Good Food Store, Rt. 2. Cooked over slow heat for hours, this should be the real thing. "You don't need teeth to eat our beef," says the motto.

Milbrook Tavern and Terrace (207-824-2175; www.bethelinn.com) Bethel Common. The big inn has a comfortable barroom and outside terrace, serving pub food and basic dinners.

✷ Entertainment

Casablanca Cinema (207-824-8248), a four-screen cinema in the new Bethel Station development (Cross St.), shows first-run films.

The Mahoosuc Arts Council (207-824-3575) presents the Libbie Goodridge Kneeland Memorial Summer Series, Sunday-afternoon concerts on the Bethel common in memory of a longtime Bethel teacher. Bring a blanket; music begins at 4 PM.

Celebration Barn (207-743-8452; www.celebrationbarn.com), 190 Stock Farm Rd., off Rt. 117 north in South Paris. Programs year-round. In summer this restored barn, set on 10 acres, draws students from around the world for workshops in mime, voice, and clowning, with public performances by students and faculty.

Deertrees Theatre and Cultural Center (207-583-6747; www.deertreestheatre.org), Harrison. From late June–Aug. the stage of this restored summer theater is rarely dark. Call to check.

Also see the **Suds Pub** and **Sunday River Brewing Co.** in *Eating Out*, and *Entertainment* in "Oxford Hills."

✷ Selective Shopping

ANTIQUES **Playhouse Antiques** (207-824-3170), 46 Broad St., Bethel, specializes in antiques from Bethel-area homes. Open June–Oct.

Bennet's Antiques (207-824-2336), 21 Mechanic St. Right in the center of things, this charming store is a great place to pick up an iron frying pan for $8, or fine glass, antique lamps, and furniture.

ARTISANS **Bonnema Potters** (207-824-2821), Lower Main St., Bethel. Open daily 9:30–5:30, except Wed. in winter; call for hours. Distinctive stoneware and porcelain: lamps, garden furniture, dinnerware, produced and sold in Bonnema's big barn. Seconds are available.

GEM SHOPS This area is rich in semiprecious gems and minerals. Jim Mann at **Mt. Mann** (207-824-3030), Main St., Bethel, mines, cuts, and sets his own minerals and gems. **Mt. Mica Rarities** (207-875-3060), Rt. 26 in Locke Mills/Greenwood, is also a source of reasonably priced Maine gemstones. **Sunday River Gems** (207-824-3414), Sunday River Rd., Newry, offers handcrafted pieces with Maine gems, gemstone carvings, and more. Also see *Rockhounding* in "Oxford Hills."

SPECIAL SHOPS **Books-N-Things** (207-824-0275 or 1-800-851-3219), 130 Main St., Bethel. A full-service bookstore in the Pok Sun Emporium.

Brooks Bros. Inc. Hardware Store (207-824-2158), 73 Main St., Bethel. All kinds of old-fashioned hardware, along with up-to-date products and fine service.

Maine Line Products (207-824-2522), Main St., Bethel. Made-in-Maine products and souvenirs, among which the standout is the Maine Woodsman's Weatherstick. We have one tacked to our back porch, and it's consistently one step ahead of the weatherman—pointing up to predict fair weather and down for foul. A second store, an expanded version of this old landmark, is open in Locke Mills/Greenwood: even more pine furniture, toys, wind chimes, buckets, birdhouses.

Groan and McGurn's Tourist Trap

BOOKS-'N-THINGS

Diane Foulds

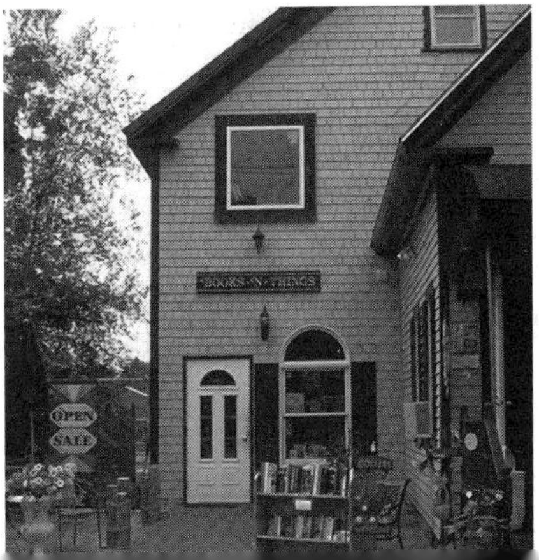

and Craft Outlet (207-836-3645), Rt. 2, West Bethel. Begun as a greenhouse—to which the owners' specially silk-screened T-shirts were added. Now there is so much that an ever-changing catalog is available.

Ruthie's Clothing (207-824-2989), Main St., Bethel. A really wonderful selection of women's clothing.

✷ Special Events

March: **Sunday River Langlauf Races** (*first Saturday*) at the Sunday River Ski Touring Center—for all ages and abilities. **Handicapped Skiing Skiathon** (*third weekend*).

April: **April Fool's Pole, Paddle and Paw Race** (*first Saturday*)—a combination ski-and-canoe event at the end of ski season.

June: **Androscoggin River Canoe/Kayak Race**. **Annual Quilt Show**. **Biannual House Tours**.

July: **Bethel Historical Society Fourth of July Celebration**. **Bethel Annual Art Fair** (*first Saturday*). **Strawberry Festival**, Locke Mills Union Church (date depends on when strawberries are ready; announced in local papers). **Annual Art Fair**. **Annual Bike Rally**—family as well as competitive bicycle loops. The **Annual Gem, Mineral, and Jewelry Show** (*second weekend*) at Telstar High School in Bethel—exhibits, demonstrations, and guided field trips to local quarries. **Mollyockett Day** (*third Saturday*)—festivities include a road race, parade, bicycle obstacle course, fiddler contest, and fireworks, all to honor an 18th-century medicine woman who helped the first settlers.

August: **Annual Maine State Triathlon Classic** (*first Sunday*) Bethel, and the Saturday before, **Kid's Triathlon**. **Andover Old Home Days** (*first weekend*). **Sudbury Canada Days** (*second weekend*), Bethel—children's parade, historical exhibits, old-time crafts demonstrations, bean supper, and variety show.

September: **Bethel Harvest Fest** (*third weekend*).

Columbus Day weekend: **Fall Festival at Sunday River Ski Resort** includes the now world-famous wife-carrying championship—it started here—free chairlift rides, wine tasting, crafts, and much more.

November: **True Hometown Craft and Wares Fair** (*day after Thanksgiving*).

December: A series of Christmas fairs and festivals climaxes with a **Living Nativity** on the Bethel common the Sunday before Christmas. Free horse-drawn wagon rides on Saturdays. **New Year's Bethel**, various venues—music, storytelling, fireworks.

RANGELEY LAKES REGION

Rangeley Lake itself is only 9 miles long, but the "Rangeley Lakes Region" includes 112 lakes and ponds, among them vast sheets of water with names like Mooselookmeguntic, Cupsuptic, and Aziscohos.

The scenery is so magnificent that segments of the two roads leading into Rangeley, Rts. 4 and 17, have been designated National Scenic Byways. In summer be sure to approach the town of Rangeley via Rt. 17 and pull out at the Height o' Land. Below you, four of the six major Rangeley Lakes glisten blue-black, ringed by high mountains. Patterned only by sun and clouds, uninterrupted by any village or even a building, this green-blue sea of fir and hardwoods flows north and west to far horizons.

A spate of 1863 magazine and newspaper stories first publicized this area as "home of the largest brook trout in America," and two local women ensured its fishing fame through ensuing decades. In the 1880s Phillips native Cornelia "Fly Rod" Crosby pioneered the use of the light fly-rod and artificial lure and in 1897 became the first Registered Maine Guide; in 1924 Carrie Stevens, a local milliner, fashioned a streamer fly from gray feathers and caught a 6-pound, 13-ounce brook trout at Upper Dam. Stevens took second prize in *Field & Stream*'s annual competition, and the Gray Ghost remains one of the most popular fishing flies sold.

The Rangeley Lakes Historical Society is papered with photographs and filled with mementos of the 1880s through the 1930s, an era in which trainloads of fishermen and visitors arrived in Rangeley every day throughout the summer, to stay in dozens of wooden summer hotels and numerous sporting camps on islands and outlying lakes.

In the 1940s and 1950s hotels closed and burned, and in the 1980s many sporting camps were sold off as individual "condominiums," but the resort has continued to evolve as a magnificent, low-key destination.

Landlocked salmon now augment trout in both local lakes and streams, and fly-fishing equipment and guides are easy to come by. Moose-watching, kayaking, and canoeing, as well as hiking and golf, are big draws. There are more shops and restaurants, events, and entertainment here than at any time since the 1930s.

Rangeley is a town of 1,500 year-round residents, and "downtown" is a short string of single-story frame buildings along the lake. The village of Oquossoc, 7

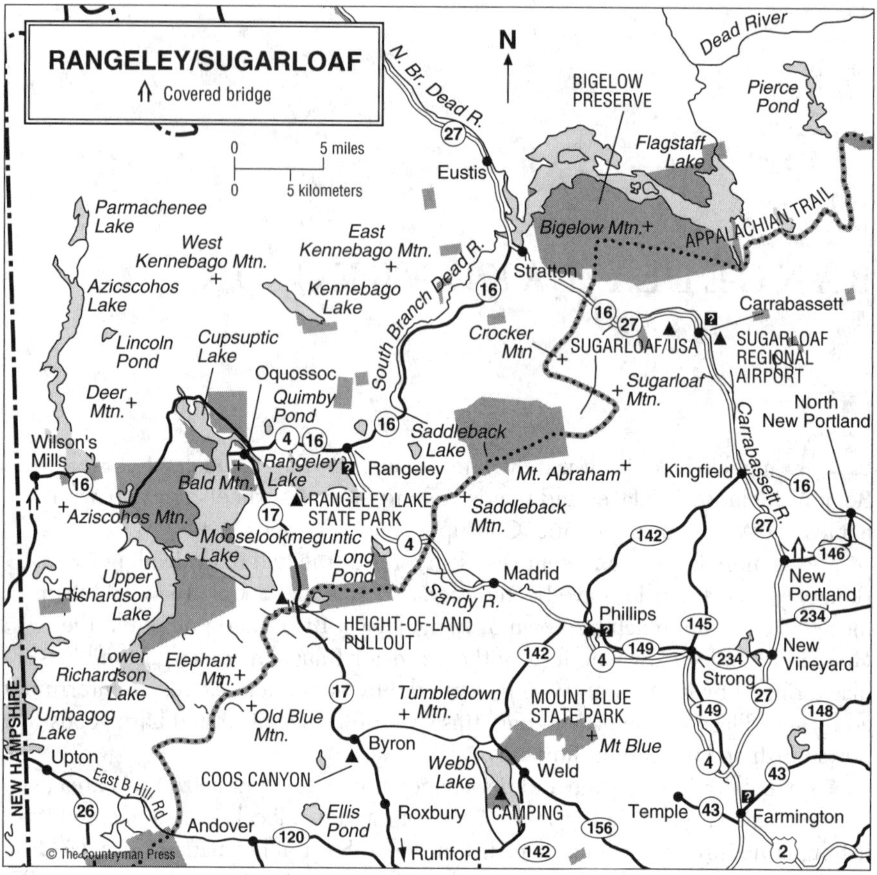

miles west, is just a scattering of shops and restaurants on a peninsula between Rangeley and Mooselookmeguntic Lakes. The summer population zooms to 6,000, but both year-round homes and camps are hidden away by the water, and much of that water is itself sequestered in woodland.

Saddleback, Rangeley's 4,120-foot, 40-trail mountain, is New England's best-kept ski secret, but the word is getting out. Because the area's snow is so dependable, a separate and well-groomed cross-country system has also evolved, and both ski and snowshoeing options in the backcountry abound.

The big news about this western neck of the Maine woods is that it's being preserved. Within the past dozen years hundreds of square miles have been protected through cooperative ventures involving state agencies, timberland owners, and the Rangeley Lakes Heritage Trust.

GUIDANCE Rangeley Lakes Region Chamber of Commerce (207-864-5364 or 1-800-MT-LAKES; www.rangeleymaine.com), P.O. Box 317, Rangeley 04970. Open year-round, Mon.–Sat. 9–5. The chamber maintains a walk-in information center in the village, publishes a handy *Accommodations and Services* guide and an indispensable map, keeps track of vacancies, and makes reservations.

GETTING THERE *By car:* From points south, take the Maine Turnpike to exit 75 (Auburn), then take Rt. 4 to Rangeley. In summer the slightly longer (roughly half an hour) but more scenic route is to turn off Rt. 4 onto Rt. 108 in Livermore, follow it to Rumford, and then take Rt. 17 to Oquossoc. From the Bethel area, take Rt. 17 to Rumford. From New Hampshire's White Mountains, take Rt. 16 east.

WHEN TO COME Rangeley's water is the focus of fishermen and -women in summer and fall, and its hills have good trails. Saddleback Mountain, undergoing an expansion, make this a winter destination as well, as skiers discover the charms of a place still off the radar.

✷ To See

MUSEUMS **Rangeley Lakes Region Historical Society**, 2472 Main St., Rangeley. Open late June–Aug., Mon.–Sat. 10–noon, or when the flag is out. This is a great little museum occupying a former bank building in the middle of town. It features photographs and local memorabilia from Rangeley's grand old hotels, sporting camps, trains, and lake steamers. Note the basement jail cell and the bird's egg collection, coveted by the Smithsonian Museum.

✐ **Wilhelm Reich Museum** (207-864-3443), Dodge Pond Rd., off Rt. 4/16 between Rangeley and Oquossoc. Open July and Aug., Wed.–Sun. 1–5; in Sept. Sun. 1–5. $6 adults, 12 and under free. The 175-acre property, Orgonon, is worth a visit for the view alone. Wilhelm Reich (1897–1957) was a pioneer psychoanalyst with controversial theories about sexual energy. A short documentary video profiles the man and his work. The museum occupies a stone observatory that Reich helped design; it contains biographical exhibits, scientific equipment, paintings, and a library and study that remain as Reich left them. Inquire about special programs. The wooded trails on the property are open daily year round 9–5; leashed pets welcome.

✐ **Rangeley Lakes Region Logging Museum** (207-864-3939 or 207-864-5595), Rt. 16, 1 mile east of Rangeley Village. Open July and Aug. weekends 11–2 or by appointment. Founded by woodsman and sculptor Rodney Richard, the museum features paintings about logging in the 1920s by local artist Alden Grant; also traditional woodcarving and logging equipment. Inquire about Logging Museum Festival Days.

Phillips Historical Society (207-639-3111), Pleasant St., P.O. Box 216, Phillips 04966. Open June–Sept., first and third Sun. 1–3, and the third week in Aug. for Old Home Days; also by appointment. The library and historical society are both in an 1820 house in the middle of the village. Exhibits include a significant Portland Glass collection, as well as pictures of the town's own resort era (it had three hotels) and of the Sandy River Railroad.

Weld Historical Society (207-585-2542), Weld Village. Open July and Aug.,

Wed. and Sat. 1–3, and by appointment. The 1842 house is filled with period furniture, clothing, and photographs. The original Town House (1845) features farming, logging, and ice-cutting tools. Other buildings include Dr. Proctor's 1880s office (containing his equipment), a spruce gum shop that became a library around 1900, and a reconstructed garage/workshop filled with tools, artifacts, and school and post office equipment.

SCENIC DRIVES The roads in this area offer such great scenery that sections of Rts. 4 and 17 are included in a National Scenic Byway.

Phillips/Weld/Byron/Oquossoc/Rangeley loop

Rt. 4 to Phillips and Rt. 142 to Weld. Follow Rt. 4 from Rangeley 12 miles south to **Small's Falls** and on to Phillips, once the center of the Sandy River–Rangeley Lakes "2-footer" line, now a quiet residential area. Plan to come the first or third Sunday of the month, or on foliage weekends, to ride the rails behind the steam train. Stop at the **Phillips Historical Society** and ask directions to **Daggett Rock**, a massive 50-foot-high boulder that glaciers deposited several miles from town (off Rt. 142), having knocked it off Saddleback Mountain (the nearest place that matches it geologically). It's a pleasant mile's walk and has been the local sight-to-see in Phillips for more than a century. From Rt. 4 near Phillips, it's 12 miles on Rt. 142 to **Weld**, a quiet old lake village with several good hiking options, including **Tumbledown Mountain** and **Mount Blue**. You can also swim in **Lake Webb** at **Mount Blue State Park**.

Weld to Byron. From Weld, it's 12 miles to Byron. Drive 2 miles north on Rt. 142 to the STATE BEACH sign; turn left, go 0.5 mile, and turn right on the first gravel road. This is Byron Rd., well packed. Soon you follow the Swift River (stop and pan for gold) down into **Coos Canyon**; the picnic area and waterfalls are at the junction with Rt. 17. This is said to be the first place in America where gold was panned.

Rt. 17 to Oquossoc. From the picnic area, drive north on Rt. 17 for 10 miles to the **Height o' Land** (the pullout is on the other side of the road), from which the view is a spectacular spread of lakes and mountains; the view from the **Rangeley Lake Overlook** (northbound side of the road, a couple of miles farther) offers another panorama.

From Oquossoc, it's a beautiful drive west along the lakes on Rt. 16 to Errol. Roughly 20 miles west of Rangeley, be sure to detour 0.3 mile to see the **Bennett Covered Bridge** (1898–99) spanning the Magalloway River in Wilson's Mills; follow signs to the Aziscohos Valley Camping Area.

Whether you are coming from Bethel or following the above loop, pick up Rt. 17 just beyond the **Mexico Chicken Coop Restaurant** (207-364-2710) on Rt. 2. Despite its exterior, this is a good way stop for Italian food, chicken, a huge salad bar, and fresh pastries.

✱ To Do

BOAT RENTALS Check with the chamber of commerce about the more than a dozen places in town that rent motorboats, canoes, sailboats, and kayaks. **River's**

Edge Sports (207-864-5582), Rt. 4, Oquossoc, rents canoes and kayaks and offers shuttle service. **Oquossoc Cove Marina** (207-864-3463), Rt. 4, Oquossoc, offers the largest choice of motorboats. Be sure to get out on a lake one way or another.

CAMPING Wilderness camping is a part of what this area is about. The chamber of commerce lists more than a dozen sources of information about remote campsites. The **Stephen Phillips Preserve** (207-864-2003), Oquossoc, maintains 70 campsites with fireplaces, picnic tables, and toilet facilities; $16 per site per couple, $8 teenagers or extra person, $5 children. Also see **Rangeley Lake State Park** under *Green Space.* **Aziscohos Valley Camping Area** (207-486-3271) in Wilson's Mills, has 34 sites and offers easy boat access to Magalloway River.

CANOEING AND KAYAKING Rangeley is the departure point for an 8-mile paddle to Oquossoc. On Lake Mooselookmeguntic a 12-mile paddle south to Upper Dam is popular; many people portage around the dam and paddle another 8 miles down Upper Richardson Lake and through the Narrows to South Arm. Kayaks can be rented from **River's Edge Sports** (207-864-5582), Rt. 4 in Oquossoc. They are also available from **Ecopelagicon, A Nature Store** (207-864-2771; www.ecopelagicon.com) in the village of Rangeley, which offers guided tours and kayaking instruction.

A section of the 700-mile **Northern Forest Canoe Trail**, which follows the ancient water route of Native Americans traveling from New York to Fort Kent, comes through Umbagog Lake, the Richardson Lakes, and Mooselookmeguntic and Rangeley Lakes before hitting a long portage to the South Branch of the Dead River. This section takes two to five days to complete. A map, produced by **Native Trails Inc.** (P.O. Box 240, Waldoboro 04572), is available for $5.95 from the Rangeley Lakes Heritage Trust (207-864-7311) and from Ecopelagicon in Rangeley.

FISHING As noted in the chapter introduction, fishing put Rangeley on the map. Both brook trout and landlocked salmon remain plentiful, and while early spring and Sept. remain the big fishing seasons, summer months now also lure many anglers with fishfinders, downriggers, rods, and reels. Rangeley has, however, always been best known as a fly-fishing mecca, and both local sporting stores, **River's Edge Sports** (207-864-5582), Rt. 4 in Oquossoc, and the **Rangeley Region Sport Shop** (207-864-5615), Main St., Rangeley, specialize in fly-tying equipment; they are also sources of advice on where to fish and with whom (a list of local guides is posted). Request a list of members of the **Rangeley Region Guides & Sportsmen's Association**, P.O. Box 244, Rangeley 04970. The group traces its origins to 1896. The current chamber of commerce guide also lists local Registered Maine Guides as well as camps that specialize in boats, equipment, and guides. Guiding service averages $175 per half-day, $300 for a full day. Nonresident fishing licenses, available from sporting stores, are $12 per day, $37 for 7 days, plus $1 agent fee.

FEE-FISHING ✐ **Dunham's Fee Fishing Pond** (207-639-2815; www.dunhamslobsterpot.com), Mount Blue Rd. (off Rt. 4), Avon (between Phillips and Strong). Open year-round, daily in summer 10–7, inquire for hours off-season. A great spot for kids and nonanglers to try their hand at catching rainbow trout. You never miss. Equipment supplied. Dunham's Lobster Pot also sells seafood and a variety of fish.

FITNESS CENTER **Rangeley Region Health Center** (207-864-2900), Dallas Hill Rd., Rangeley. This splendid new community facility offers short-term memberships for anyone wishing to use the equipment or join a variety of exercise classes.

GUIDE SERVICE **Mountain Woman Guide Service** (207-562-4971 or 207-357-4971; www.mountainwomanguideservice.com), Dixfield. Michelle Young is a registered Maine guide who takes individuals and groups on trips into the woods. One tour goes to Forest Lodge, author Louise Dickinson Rich's home on Rapid River where she wrote *We Took to the Woods*; the tour is made with the assistance of Aldro French (see page *What's Where—Books*). $120 per person for a full day. Fly-fishing, hiking on the Appalchian Trail, day hikes tailored to a person's fitness level; also moose tours and gold-panning as an interpretive park ranger at Mount Blue State Park.

GOLD PANNING **Coos Canyon**, on Rt. 17, 23 miles south of Oquossoc, is said to be the first place in America where gold was panned. The Swift River churns through a beautiful natural gorge, and there are picnic tables. Free gold-panning demonstrations are offered, and equipment can be rented or bought at the **Coos Canyon Rock & Gift Store** (207-364-4900).

COOS CANYON

Christina Tree

GOLF **Mingo Springs Golf Course** (207-864-5021), Proctor Rd. (off Rt. 4), Rangeley. A historic (since 1925), par-70, 18-hole course with lake views; instruction, carts, and club rentals.

HIKING **The Rangeley regional map** published by the chamber of commerce outlines more than a dozen well-used hiking paths, including a portion of the Appalachian Trail that passes over **Saddleback Mountain**. The longest hike is up **Spotted Mountain** (4.5 miles to the top), and the most popular is the trail to the summit of **Bald Mountain** (3 miles round-trip); both yield sweeping views of lakes, woods, and more mountains. Other favorites are Bemis Stream Trail up **Elephant Mountain** (six hours round-trip) and the mile walk in to **Angels Falls**—which is roughly 4 miles off Rt. 17; be sure to use a current trail guide.

In Weld the tried-and-true trails are **Mount Blue** (3.25 miles) and **Tumbledown Mountain** (a particularly varied climb with a high elevation).

MOOSE-WATCHING **Rt. 16 north from Rangeley to Stratton** is a good bet for seeing moose at dusk; your chances improve if you drive all the way to dinner at the **Porter House** in Eustis.

RAILROAD EXCURSION ✐ **Sandy River & Rangeley Lakes Railroad** (207-778-3621; www.srrl-rr.org), Phillips. Runs on the first and third Sunday of each month, June–Oct.; runs continuously through Phillips Old Home Days in late Aug. and Fall Foliage Days in late Sept. and mid-Oct., and on other special occasions (check the Web site). $4 adults, free under age 13; $6 if using steam engine. From 1873 until 1935 this narrow-gauge line spawned resort and lumbering communities along its 115-mile length. Begun as seven distinct lines, it was eventually acquired by the Maine Central. Shops and a large roundhouse were built by railroad companies in Phillips. Since 1969 volunteers have been working to rebuild a part of the railroad, producing a replica of the old steam locomotive and the roundhouse, and laying 0.6 mile of track so that you can rattle along in an 1884 car just far enough to get a sense of getting around Franklin County "back when." Two original railroad buildings remain—Sanders Station and a freight shed. A depot houses railroad memorabilia, and rolling stock now includes five boxcars, two coaches, and two cabooses.

SUMMER PROGRAMS **Rangeley Parks and Recreation Department Summer Programs** (207-864-3326), open to everyone vacationing in town, include lessons in fly casting and -tying, golf, canoeing, swimming, tennis, and much more.

SWIMMING **Rangeley Lake State Park** offers a beautiful, secluded grass beach and swimming area and scattered picnic sites. Day-use fee; free under age 12. There is also a town beach with lifeguards, picnic tables, and a playground at **Lakeside Park** in the village of Rangeley. Almost all lodging places offer water access.

Mount Blue State Park also has a nice swimming area.

Coos Canyon, Rt. 17, Byron. It's terrifying to watch kids jump from the cliffs and bridge here, but there are several inviting pools among the smooth rocks and cascades.

✷ Winter Sports

CROSS-COUNTRY SKIING **Rangeley Lakes Trail Center at lower Saddleback Mountain** (207-864-4309). More than 35 kilometers of groomed trails with a skating lane and a track for classic skiing, 4 miles from downtown Rangeley.

Christina Tree

A PEACEFUL TREK THROUGH THE WOODS NEAR RANGELEY

Mount Blue State Park (207-585-2347), off Rt. 156, Weld, offers extensive cross-country skiing trails.

DOWNHILL SKIING ✐ **Saddleback Mountain** (207-864-5671; snow phone, 207-864-3380; www.saddlebackmaine.com), off Dallas Hill Rd., Rangeley. This is a very big downhill ski area with a fiercely loyal following, on the verge of wider popularity under a new owner making a huge investment. Saddleback itself, 4,120 feet high and now webbed with 60 trails serviced by a quad chairlift, two double chairs, and two T-bars, forms the centerpiece in a semicircle of mountains rising above a small lake. Top-to-bottom snowmaking augments more than 200 inches of annual snowfall to keep the slopes open from December into April. Trails and slopes include glade skiing, a 2.5-mile beginner trail, and an above-tree-line snowfield in spring. The vertical drop is 2,000 feet. New in 2006-7, the Black Diamond trail Jane Craig was finished in the summer of 2007. Intermediate runs such as Grey Ghost and Green Weaver are memorable cruising lanes. Experts will find plenty of challenge on Tightline, Wardens Worry, and the Nightmare Glades; and there's a a snowboard park with a 200-foot half-pipe. Facilities include a three-story lodge with cafeteria, lounge, ski school, shop, rentals, nursery, and mountain warming hut. Expansion here was blocked for 26 years by an impasse with the National Park Service over the segment of the Appalachian Trail that passes over Saddleback, but former president Clinton's 11th-hour moves to expand national park holdings cleared the way. The mountain's new owner has more trails under construction and a hotel in the future. $40 adults, $32 ages 13–18 and college students, $30 ages 7–12.

SNOWMOBILING Snowmobiling is huge in this region. The **Rangeley Snowmobile Club** (www.rangeleysnowmobile.com), subsidized by the town, maintains 150 miles of well-marked trails connecting with systems throughout Maine and Canada. Snowmobile rentals are available from **Dockside Sports Center** (207-864-2424) and **River's Edge Sports** (207-864-5582).

SNOWSHOEING Marked trails abound on local conservation land; ask for more information at the Rangeley Lake Region Chamber of Commerce, 207-864-5364.

✷ Green Space

Lakeside Park, in the middle of the village of Rangeley, is a great spot with picnic tables, grills, a playground, portable toilets, and a boat launch.

✐ **Rangeley Lake State Park** (207-864-3858) covers more than 700 acres, including 117 acres on the shore. Open May 15–early Oct. There are 50 scattered picnic sites, a pleasant swimming area, a boat launch, and a children's play area; $3 adults, $1 ages 5–12.

Mount Blue State Park (207-585-2347), off Rt. 156, Weld. Open May 30–Sept. 30. This 6,000-acre park includes Mount Blue itself, towering 3,187 feet above the valley floor, and a beachside tenting area (136 sites) on Lake Webb. The lake is 1.5 miles wide, 7 miles long, and provides good fishing for black bass, white and yellow perch, pickerel, trout, and salmon. There are boat rentals and a nature center complete with fireplace. The view from the Center Hill area looks like the opening of a Paramount picture. Despite its beauty and the outstanding hiking, this is one of the few state camping facilities ($20 for nonresidents) that rarely fills up, except on August weekends. Day-use fee $4 per person, children 5–11 $1.

Small's Falls, Rt. 4, 12 miles south of Rangeley. The Sandy River drops abruptly through a small gorge, which you can climb behind railings. A popular picnic spot. You can follow the trail to **Chandlers Mill Stream Falls**, equally spectacular.

Hunter Cove Wildlife Sanctuary, off Rt. 4/16, 2.5 miles west of Rangeley Village (across from Dodge Pond). A 95-acre Rangeley Lakes Heritage Trust preserve with color-coded trails leading to the cove (boat launch). Bring insect repellent, waterproof footwear, and a picnic (tables are near the parking lot, and benches are scattered throughout).

Rangeley Lakes Heritage Trust (207-864-7311), Rt. 4/16, Oquossoc, open weekdays 9–4:30, Sun. 9–1. Since the trust's founding in 1991, more than 10,000 acres have been preserved, including 20 miles of lake and river frontage, 10 islands, and a 2,443-foot mountain. Request the map/guide and inquire about the guided hikes and nature-study programs offered.

Hatchery Brook Preserve is easily accessible, just 0.5 mile north of town on Rt. 4 (take a left on Manor Brook Rd. and look for the trailhead on your right in another 0.25 mile). We were lucky enough to hike this easy, rewarding loop in blueberry/raspberry season. Yum. There were also bunchberries and nice views of Rangeley Lake. This 50-acre Rangelely Lakes Heritage Trust property was at one time slated for a 50-lot subdivision.

The Stephen Phillips Memorial Preserve Trust (207-864-2003) has preserved many miles of shore on Mooselookmeguntic and maintains a number of campsites (see *To Do—Camping*).

Also see *Lodging—Campgrounds*.

THE SECLUDED BEACH AT RANGELEY LAKE STATE PARK

Nancy English

✷ Lodging

INNS AND LODGES ♿ **Loon Lodge** (207-864-5666; www.loon lodgeme.com), 16 Pickford Rd., P.O.

Box 676, Rangeley 04970. The rusticator of an earlier generation would favor the decor at this charming inn with its log exterior walls and indoor paneling. A large stone fireplace and moose-antler chandeliers add to the away-from-it-all ambiance. But modern amenities and a clean, updated look make all perfect for today's guest, who can settle into Nordic, with its antiques and quilts, for a twilight contemplation of Rangeley Lake. Nine rooms include two suites for families. Two with king bed are on the ground floor, with large picture windows looking at the lake, an exterior entrance, and large bath. The restaurant (see *Dining Out*) is recommended by locals as the best in town. $110–150.

🐾 ♿ **Country Club Inn** (207-864-3831; www.countryclubinnrangeley.com), Rt. 4, P.O. Box 680, Rangeley 04970. Open year-round except Apr. and Nov. This friendly retreat, set on a rise, offers the best views of Rangeley Lake of any lodging in the region. The 20 old-fashioned rooms, all with private bath, have picture windows framing water and mountains. Although set by the Mingo Springs Golf Course, only half its summer patrons even play golf; it was built by millionaire sportsmen as a private club in the late 1920s. Massive stone fireplaces face each other across a living room with knotty-pine walls, plenty of books, and puzzles. Owner-manager Margie Jamison is the second generation of her family to run the inn; her husband, Steve, is chef in the restaurant (see *Dining Out*). In winter you can cross-country ski from the door, and in summer there's an outdoor pool. $125 B&B for two; $185 MAP. Off-season rates available.

LOON LODGE, THE LOCALS' FAVORITE

Nancy English

🐾 ♿ **Bald Mountain Camps** (207-864-3671 or 1-888-392-0072; www.baldmountaincamps.com), Bald Mountain Rd., P.O. Box 332, Oquossoc 04964. Open mid-May–mid-Sept. This is a surviving American Plan (all three meals) fishing resort that dates to 1897, with scalloped oysters, or beef with bourbon BBQ sauce, for dinner. Fireplaces are in 15 cabins that are clean but a little worn; dinner is served in a log-style dining room. Amenities include a safe sand beach; tennis courts; use of canoes, kayaks, and sailboats; and motorboat rentals. Right on Mooselookmeguntic Lake, the camp exudes the kind of hospitality found under long-term ownership of Stephen and Fernlyn Philbrick. Fly-fishing and hiking adventures from here offered as well. $145 adults, meals included, in Aug.; less for children and during May and June; one-week minimum in July and Aug., but occasionally there are a few days open. Some pets accepted. Friday nights feature a lobster cookout.

♿ **Rangeley Inn and Motor Lodge** (207-864-3341 or 1-800-MOMENTS; www.rangeleyinn.com), Rt. 4, Rangeley 04970. Open year-round. This blue-shingled, three-story landmark, on the site of a vanished grand hotel

Nancy English

THE HAMMOCK OFFERS A GREAT VIEW AT BALD MOUNTAIN CAMPS

that stood across the road, overlooking the lake, is owned by Charles and Dominique Gould; the classic old hotel lobby dates from 1907. The 52 guest rooms are divided between the main building, 12 with (somewhat stained) claw-foot tub, some with water views, all comfortably furnished and old-fashioned; unfortunately the TV next door may be audible. Among 15 nicely decorated motel units overlooking Haley Pond, some have kitchenette, whirlpool bath, and woodstove. $84–154 double. Breakfast buffet ($9.50) on weekends, dinner daily in the pub, and special packages available.

BED & BREAKFASTS ✐ ♿ **Kawanhee Inn** (207-585-2000; www.maineinn.net), 12 Anne's Way, Weld 04285. Open Memorial Day–Columbus Day. A traditional Maine lodge set atop a slope overlooking Lake Webb with ten rooms upstairs (six with private bath) and seven cabins (one-, two-, and three-bedroom) down by the lake, each with kitchenette. This is one of the most beautiful old lodges around, and its restaurant opened in 2004. Rooms $85–140 B&B; cabins $165–200 per night, $850–1,150 per week.

✿ ✐ **Lake Webb House** (207-585-2479; www.lakewebbhouse.com), 19 Church St. (Rt. 142), P.O. Box 127, Weld 04285. A pleasant, welcoming 1870 farmhouse with a big porch, near the lake and village. Cheryl England makes the quilts that grace the beds in her three casual guest rooms (four in summer). The rooms share two bathrooms, but one has a private half bath as well. $85–100 double, $65 single, includes a full breakfast. Cheryl also operates the **Morning Glory Bake Shop** (behind the house), good for breads, moose cookies, whoopie pies, and chewy oatmeal cookies. Bakery open daily mid-June till Labor Day, weekends till Columbus Day.

Oquossoc's Own (207-864-5584), P.O. Box 27, Oquossoc 04964. Open daily year-round. Since 1982, Joanne

THE KAWANHEE INN OVERLOOKS LAKE WELD

Nancy English

Nancy English

LAKE WEBB HOUSE IS HOME TO MORNING GLORY BAKESHOP, IN THE BACK.

Koob has been sharing her comfy village home and its four guest rooms, making all the breads to go with a full breakfast, frequently served early enough for men to get out into the woods to work. Coffee is ready at 6 AM. Her friendly, downhome presence makes this a home-away-from-home for many of her repeat guests. Rooms share two baths. $75 double, $45 single, no charge for ages 12 and under.

SPORTING CAMPS Geared to serious fishermen in May, June, and September, and to families in July and August, these are true destination resorts, but don't expect organized activities.

🐾 ✐ **Bosebuck Mountain Camps** (207-670-0013; www.bosebuck.com), Wilson's Mills 03579. Open year-round. Accessible by boat or a 14-mile private gravel road, the camps are sited at the remote end of Aziscohos Lake. We have not visited since ownership changed in 1998. The lodge houses a dining room overlooking the water and a sitting room filled with books. The 12 cabins have a woodstove, electric lights, flush toilet, and shower, powered by a generator that never shuts off. Three full meals are included in the rate, $135 per person per night; inquire about less expensive summer family packages; in mid-Aug., $99 per person per night.

🐾 ✐ **Lakewood Camps** (207-243-2959; www.lakewoodcamps.com), Middle Dam, Lower Richardson Lake, P.O. Box 1275, Rangeley 04970. Open after ice-out through Sept. Owners are Whit and Maureen Carter. Specialty is landlocked salmon and trout; fly-fishing in 5 miles of the Rapid River. Twelve truly remote cabins; meals feature fresh-baked breads, cakes, and pies. Access is by boat only, from Andover. This is very much the same area described in Louise Dickinson Rich's *We Took to the Woods.* $146 per person (two-day minimum), double occupancy, includes three full meals; $60 children under 12, $30 under age 5. $22 pets. Tax and gratuity not included. No credit cards; cash or check only.

COTTAGES AND CONDOS ✐ Rangeley still has an unusual number of traditional family-geared "camps" and second homes available for rental year-round. Check with the chamber of commerce (see www.rangeley.com) for listings and local rental agents.

Clearwater Sporting Camps (207-864-5424; www.clearwatercampsmaine.com), Bald Mountain Rd., Oquossoc 04964. Open from ice-out through Oct. Four cottages, all different, are scattered on private waterfront ledges along Mooselookmeguntic Lake; the fronts of two of the cottages open out almost completely onto the lake. This is a very private, beautiful spot. A year-round log home is also for rent by the week or month. Michael and Tina Warren also offer boat rentals, a boat launch, swimming, and guide service, specializing in fly-fishing. Cabins $140 per day double; $850 per week. Log home $1,300. No pets.

Mooselookmeguntic House (207-864-2962; www.mooselookmeguntic rentals.com), Haines Landing, Oquossoc 04964. Open from ice-out to Columbus Day. The grand old hotel by this name is gone, but the eight log cabins are well maintained and occupy a great site with a beach and marina. Many of the one- and two-bedroom cabins are on the water and have fireplace or woodstove. $600–800 per week.

North Camps (207-864-2247; www.northcamps.com), P.O. Box 341, Oquossoc 04964 (write to E. B. Gibson). Open May–Oct. Twelve cottages on Rangeley Lake among birches on a spacious lawn. Cottages have fireplace or woodstove, modern baths, screened porch, and access to the beach, tennis, sailboats, fishing boats, and canoes. In July and Aug., weekly rentals preferred. $425–775 weekly, $75 to $185 per night for two to eight people.

Hunter Cove on Rangeley Lake (207-864-3383; www.huntercove.com), 334 Mingo Loop, Rangeley 04970. Open year-round. Chris and Ralph Egerhei offer eight nicely equipped one- and two-bedroom lakeside cabins with loft, full kitchen, one with hot tub. $180–210 per night; $950–1,150 per week.

Saddleback, Maine (207-864-5671; www.saddlebackmaine.com), P. O. Box 490, Rangeley 04970. Rock Pond, White Birch, Mountain Brook, and South Branch condominium units are located on the mountain, many with ski in/ ski out access, and with breathtaking views of the Longfellow Mountains and Saddleback Lake. Vacation packages available.

CAMPGROUNDS For reservations in the following state parks, call in-state 1-800-332-1501, out-of-state 207-624-9950.

Rangeley Lake State Park, between Rts. 17 and 4, at the southern rim of Rangeley Lake. Some 50 campsites are well spaced among fir and spruce trees; facilities include a secluded beach and boat launch, picnic sites, and a children's play area. $20 for nonresidents. Some wilderness sites on Mooselookmeguntic Lake are accessible only by boat; inquire at the chamber of commerce.

Mount Blue State Park (207-585-2347), Weld. Campsites here ($20) tend to get filled up later than those in better-known parks.

Coos Canyon Campground (207-364-3880; www.cooscanyoncabins.com), on Rt. 17, 445 Swift River Rd., Byron, 23 miles south of Oquossoc, is only about half an hour from Rangeley, but at these sites you feel as though you're in the middle of the woods. Swimming holes and riverside camping, with kids jumping off the cliffs during the day. Any adults interested? At $14 per night, plus tax, the rates can't be beat. There's a small store and a shower house. Two fully equipped units in a log cabin are $100 per night for two adults and two children under 12. Ten RV sites with hook-ups but no sewer hook-ups (dump station available).

* Where to Eat

DINING OUT Also see *Where to Eat* listings in "Sugarloaf and the Carrabassett Valley." **Porter House**

in Eustis is a popular dining destination for Rangeley visitors.

Loon Lodge (207-864-5666; www.loonlodgeme.com), 16 Pickford Rd., Rangeley. The locals put this at the top of the list, and a visit to the charming dining room proves decor at least, makes for a special meal. Unfortunately the tables were booked on our visit. Sirloin bracciole ($23) with meat from Creekstone Farms stuffed with spinach, garlic, and fontina, or a classic chicken Marsala ($18) are on a summer menu, which begins with appetizers like wild mushroom strudel or grilled scallops in an applejack beurre blanc. Entrées $18–38.

The Gingerbread House (207-864-3602), Rt. 4/16, Oquossoc. Open for breakfast, lunch, and dinner year-round, fewer days in winter, closed Nov. and Apr. An ice cream parlor since the turn of the 20th century, preserved and expanded by the Kfoury family. Lunch might be a barbecued pork sandwich and Black Angus burger—or you can just come for ice cream (Annabel's). At dinnertime the tables are draped in linen, and the menu ranges from grilled filet mignon gratinée with almond gorgonzola ($32) to meatloaf and pot pie. A family-friendly place. Dinner entrées $12–32.

Country Club Inn (207-864-3831), Rangeley. Open for breakfast daily and for dinner Wed.–Sun. in summer and fall; weekends in winter by reservation. The inn sits on a rise above Rangeley Lake, the dining room windows maximize the view, and the food is good. Chef Steve Jamison's menu changes frequently but might include fresh swordfish broiled in wine with lemon-tarragon butter; roast duck with Bing cherry sauce is available every night. Entrées $17–32, including a salad.

Bald Mountain Camps (207-864-3671), Bald Mountain Rd., Oquossoc. Mid-May–beginning of Oct. Dinner by reservation is available to nonguests in this classic sporting camp dining room by the lake; three seatings. The set menu varies with the night; Tuesday might be braised short ribs, Maryland fried chicken, fish cakes, or vegetarian stew. Entrées $1–30. BYOB.

Kawanhee Inn and Restaurant (207-585-2000; www.maineinn.net), 12 Anne's Way, Weld. Start with a calamari fritter or organic beet salad, and dine magnificently on White Marble Farms pork, clams, and chorizo. Seared scallops and free-range chicken, grilled wild sockeye salmon, and venison chops all come to the table with accompaniments out of local summer gardens. Entrées $16–26.

EATING OUT **The Pour in the Rangeley Inn** (207-864-3341), 51 Main St., Rangeley. Every town should have a pub like this, with reasonably priced pub grub such as steakburgers (with bacon and cheese), chicken potpie, and good chowder. Also prime rib and baked haddock. Entrées $17–26.

BMC Diner (207-864-5844), Main St. and Richardson Ave., Rangeley. Open for breakfast all day and lunch; Sun. for breakfast only. The favorite place in town for breakfast; the veggie omelet was full of good spinach and other vegetables. Friendly service.

Red Onion (207-864-5022), Main St., Rangeley. Open daily for lunch and dinner. A friendly Italian American dining place with a sunroom and biergarten; fresh-dough pizzas and daily specials. Entrées $5–16.

Parkside & Main (207-864-3774), 76 Main St., Rangeley. Open 11:30–9 in summer, bar till 10 Fri. and Sat.; in winter open Sun.–Thu. 11:30–8:30, Fri. and Sat. until 9. An attractive dining room with plenty of windows and a deck overlooking the lake. Large menu with burgers, good homemade chowders, seafood, pastas, and daily specials.

The Four Seasons Café (207-864-2020), Rt. 4, Oquossoc. Open 11–9 in summer. A woodstove, tables with checked green cloths, and a big menu with Mexican dishes, salads, good soups, sandwiches, and vegetarian specials all make this a good place to eat, in spite of the bar that "carries on every night." Fresh-dough pizzas are also a specialty. Fish, lobster, clams, and scallops are served as well. Prime rib on Friday night. Entrées $17–29.

Moosely Bagels (207-864-5955), 2588 Main St., Rangeley. Open for breakfast and lunch Mon.–Tues. and Thurs.–Sat. 5:30–2:30, breakfast Sun. 7–11. Closed Wednesday. Great lakeside location and good bagels.

Pine Tree Frosty (207-864-5894), middle of Main St., Rangeley. Try the lobster roll packed full of meat. Gifford's ice cream.

Lakeside Convenience (207-864-5888), Main St., Rangeley. Great fried chicken, usually in at 9 AM and sold out by 2 PM.

✱ Entertainment

Lakeside Youth Theater (207-864-5000), Main St., Rangeley. A renovated landmark that offers first-run films; matinées on rainy days when the flag is hung out. Off-season shows on weekends.

Rangeley Friends of the Performing Arts sponsors a July–Aug. series of performances by top entertainers and musicians at local churches, lodges, and the high school. For the current schedule, check with the chamber of commerce.

✱ Selective Shopping

Alpine Shop (207-864-3741), Main St., Rangeley. Open daily year-round. The town's premier clothing store, with name-brand sportswear and Maine gifts. (Check out its sale store, a walk around the building to the back).

Books, Lines, and Thinkers (207-864-4355), Main St., Rangeley. Open year-round; hours vary depending on season. Wess Connally offers a good selection of art as well as books and music and sponsors a regular book discussion group; the next meeting's selection is featured by the cash register.

The Mad Whittler (207-864-5595), Main St., Rangeley. Rodney Richard sculpts animals and folk characters using a chain saw and jackknife, and his son Rodney Jr. executes his own whimsical creations with similar tools; chances are one or the other will be there working away. Look for the OPEN flag on the shop. Rodney Sr. lives in the neighboring house, so if no one is in the shop, "honk on the horn or bang on the door. Better yet, call ahead."

Ecopelagicon, A Nature Store (207-864-2771), 3 Pond St., Rangeley. In the middle of town but with windows on Haley Pond. Kites, life jackets, camping stuff, and wonderful things for nature lovers, from bird and reptile guides to books on mountain trails and good maps. A line of skin products with fine scents like wild rose and balsam sits in a nook in the front of the store. Also kayak rentals, instruction, and tours (see *Canoeing and Kayaking*).

The Gallery at Stoney Batter Station (207-864-3373), Oquossoc. Open Memorial Day to mid-Oct. daily 10–4; Thurs.–Sun. in winter. Art shares the space with rustic furniture from stick benches and birch log birdhouses. Ceramics, lamps, and much more.

Also see River's Edge Sports and Rangeley Region Sport Shop under *Fishing*.

✷ Special Events

All events are in Rangeley unless otherwise noted

January: **Rangeley Snodeo**—snowmobile rally and cross-country ski races.

February: **Annual Busch East Snowmobile Poker Run for Charity**—with prizes for the best poker hand for participants.

July: **Independence Day** parade and fireworks, silent auction, cookout; **Old-Time Fiddlers Contest**; and **Logging Museum Festival Days**. **Heritage Day Fair** (*final Saturday*) in Weld Village.

Nancy English

THE MAD WHITTLER CARVED THIS SCENE, VISIBLE FROM THE ROADSIDE

August: **Sidewalk Art Show**; **Annual Blueberry Festival**; **Outdoor Sporting Heritage Days**; and **Phillips Old Home Days** (*third week*).

October: **Rangeley Lakes Logging Museum Apple Festival** (*first Saturday*).

December: **Walk to Bethlehem Pageant**, Main St.

SUGARLOAF AND THE CARRABASSETT VALLEY

The second highest mountain in the state, Sugarloaf/USA faces another 4,000-footer across the Carrabassett Valley—a narrow defile that accommodates a 17-mile-long town.

Carrabassett Valley is a most unusual town. In 1972, when it was created from Crockertown and Jerusalem townships, voters numbered 32. The school and post office are still down in Kingfield, south of the valley; the nearest drugstore, chain supermarket, and hospital are still in Farmington, 36 miles away. There are just 399 full-time residents, but there are now more than 5,000 "beds." Instead of "uptown" and "downtown," people say "on-mountain" and "off-mountain."

On-mountain, at the top of Sugarloaf's access road, stands one of New England's largest self-contained ski villages: a dozen shops and more than a dozen restaurants, a seven-story brick hotel, and a church. A chairlift hoists skiers up to the base lodge from lower parking lots and from hundreds of condominiums clustered around the Sugarloaf Inn. More condominiums are scattered farther down the slope, all served by a chairlift. From all places you can also ski down to the Carrabassett Valley Ski Touring Center, Maine's largest cross-country trail network.

More than 800 condominiums are scattered among firs and birches. To fill them in summer, Sugarloaf has built an outstanding 18-hole golf course; maintains one of the country's top-rated golf schools; fosters a lively special-events program; promotes rafting, mountain biking, and hiking; and even seriously attempts to eliminate blackflies.

Spring through fall the focus shifts off-mountain to the backwoods hiking and fishing north of the valley. Just beyond the village of Stratton, Rt. 27 crosses a corner of Flagstaff Lake and continues through Cathedral Pines, an impressive sight and a good place to picnic. The 30,000-acre Bigelow Preserve, which embraces the lake and great swatches of this area, offers swimming, fishing, and camping. Eustis, a small outpost on the lake, caters to sportsmen and serves as a P.O. box for sporting camps squirreled away in the surrounding woodland.

Kingfield, at the southern entrance to the Carrabassett Valley, was founded in 1816. This stately town has long been a woodworking center and produced the first bobbins for America's first knitting mill; for some time it also supplied most of the country's yo-yo blanks. It is, however, best known as the onetime home of the Stanley twins, inventors of the steamer automobile and the dry-plate coating machine for modern photography. The Stanley Museum includes fascinating photos of rural Maine in the 1890s by Chansonetta, sister of the two inventors. Kingfield continues to produce wood products and also offers outstanding lodging and dining.

The Carrabassett River doesn't stop at Kingfield. Follow it south as it wanders west off Rt. 27 at New Portland, then a short way along Rt. 146, to see the striking vintage-1841 Wire Bridge. Continue on Rt. 146 and then west on Rt. 16 if you're heading for The Forks and the North Woods; to reach the coast, take Rt. 27 south through Farmington, a gracious old college town with several good restaurants and an unusual opera museum.

GUIDANCE **Sugarloaf Area Chamber of Commerce Kiosk** (www.sugarloafareachamber.org), on Rt. 27 just south of Sugarloaf/USA, operates a kiosk stocked with brochures on the area as well as statewide information. **Sugarloaf/USA**'s toll-free reservations and information number for the eastern seaboard is 1-800-THE-LOAF; you can also call 207-237-2000, or log onto www.sugarloaf.com. Pick up a copy of *Maine's Western Mountains and Lakes Region*, an area guide available locally.

GETTING THERE *By air:* **Portland International Jetport** (207-779-7301), two-and-a-half hours away, offers connections to all points. **Rental cars** are available at the airport.

By car: From Boston it theoretically takes four hours to reach the Carrabassett Valley. Take the Maine Turnpike to exit 75 (Auburn), then Rt. 4 to Rt. 2, to Rt. 27; or take I-95 to Augusta, then Rt. 27 the rest of the way. (We swear by the latter route, but others swear by the former.)

GETTING AROUND In ski season the **Valley Ski Shuttle Bus** runs from the base lodge to the Carrabassett Valley Ski Touring Center and Rt. 27 lodges.

WHEN TO COME Summer hikes and winter skiing trips work in this area, with its year-round accommodations and restaurants. Sporting camps run from spring ice-out to late fall. Whitewater rafting is at its prime in spring.

✷ To See

MUSEUMS **Stanley Museum** (207-265-2729; www.stanleymuseum.org), 40 School St., Kingfield. Open year-round, Tue.–Sun. 1–4 (closed weekends Nov.–May). $4 adults, $3 seniors, $2 ages 11 and under. Housed in a stately wooden school donated by the Stanley family in 1903, this is a varied collection of inventions by the Stanley twins, F. O. and F. E. (it was their invention of the airbrush in the 1870s that made their fortune). Exhibits range from violins to the steam car for which the Stanleys are best known. Three Stanley Steamers (made between 1905 and 1916) are on exhibit.

Nordica Homestead Museum (207-778-2042), 116 Nordica Ln. on Holley Rd.

(off Rt. 4/27), north of Farmington. Open June–Labor Day, Tue.–Sat. 10–noon and 1–5, Sun. 1–5. Appointment-only till Oct. 15. Adults $2, children $1. This 19th-century farmhouse is the unlikely repository for the costumes, jewelry, personal mementos, and exotic gifts given to the opera star Lillian Norton, who was born here (she later changed her name to Nordica).

Nowetah's American Indian Museum (207-628-4981; www.mainemuseums.org, click on AMERICAN INDIAN), 2 Colegrove Rd., jut off Rt. 27, New Portland. Open daily 10–5; no admission charge. Nowetah Cyr, descendant of St. Francis Abenaki and member of the Paugussett Nation, displays Native American artifacts from the United States, Canada, and South America, with a focus on the Abenaki of Maine. A special room holds more than 400 Native American Maine baskets and bark containers. Almost all the items in the gift shop are made by the Native Americans who run this museum.

Red School House Museum (207-778-6083), Farmington Fairgrounds, Farmington. Open by appointment. A schoolhouse built in 1852 and used as a school until 1958, this building was moved to the fairgrounds in 2006, where it sits near an Agricultural Museum, maple syrup house, and blacksmith forge, popular draws during Farmington Fair in mid-Sept. The schoolhouse has been filled with old school items and artifacts.

Wilton Farm & Home Museum (207-645-2261; www.wiltonmaine.org), Canal St., Wilton. Open by appointment. A Civil War–era building housing displays of items owned by the Bass family, Bass shoes, period costumes, a display on Sylvia Hardy ("The Maine Giantess"), and a large collection of Maine bottles, among other things.

HISTORIC SITES **Kingfield Historical House** (207-265-4032), High St., Kingfield. Open June–Sept. Wed. 9–2, during Kingfield Days in July, and by appointment. Built in 1890, this high-Victorian house museum is operated by the Kingfield Historical Society and full of period furnishings, as well as personal possessions and information about Maine's first governor, William King (where Kingfield got its name). Changing exhibits throughout the house and country store in the barn.

Dead River Historical Society (207-246-2271), Rts. 16 and 27, Stratton. Open weekends in summer 11–3. A memorial to the "lost" towns of Flagstaff and Dead River, flooded in 1950 to create the present 22,000-acre, 24-mile Flagstaff Lake. Artifacts include carpentry and logging tools, china and glass. When the water is low you can still see foundations and cellar holes, including that of a round barn, in the Dead River.

Wire Bridge, on Wire Bridge Rd., off Rt. 146 (not far) off Rt. 27 in New Portland. Nowhere near anywhere, this amazing-looking suspension bridge across the Carrabassett River has two massive shingled stanchions. The bridge is one of Maine's 19th-century engineering feats (it was built in 1841). There's a good swimming hole just downstream and a place to picnic across the bridge; take a right through the ball field and go 0.5 mile on the dirt road. Note the parking area and path to the river.

FOR FAMILIES ✐ **Sugarloaf Outdoor Adventure Camp** (207-237-6909), Riverside Park, Rt. 27, Carrabassett Valley. Runs weekdays mid-July–Aug. Begun as a town program and now operated by Sugarloaf. Open to visitors (reservations required); designed for ages 4–13: archery, swimming, biking, golf, climbing, camping, fly-fishing, and arts and crafts.

✐ **Sugarloaf Dorsets Sheep Farm** (207-582-8539; www.sugarloafdorsets.com), 259 Birmingham Rd., Chelsea (300 feet from the Kingfield town line on Rt. 27 headed north). On the site of a turn-of-the-20th-century sheep farm. Come see lambs being born or just stop to pet the animals.

SCENIC DRIVES **Rt. 142 from Kingfield to Phillips** (11 miles) runs through farmland backed by Mount Abraham. Stop at the **Phillips Historical Society** and **Daggett Rock** and continue to **Mount Blue State Park**; return to Kingfield via New Vineyard and New Portland, stopping to see the **Wire Bridge**. **Rt. 16 though North New Portland and Embden** is the most scenic as well as the most direct route from Kingfield to the Upper Kennebec Valley and Moosehead Lake.

✵ To Do

BOATING See *Fishing* for rental canoes, kayaks, and motorboats.

CANOEING AND KAYAKING The **Carrabassett River** above East New Portland is a good spring paddling spot, with Class II and III whitewater. The north branch of the **Dead River** from the dam in Eustis to the landing after the Stratton bridge is another good paddle, as is the upper branch of the **Kennebago River**.

FISHING Through **Guide Adventures at Sugarloaf/USA**, guests can take spring and summer fly-fishing lessons (207-237-2000). The village of Stratton, north of Sugarloaf/USA, serves as the gateway to serious fishing country. **Northland Cash Supply** (207-246-2376) is a genuine backwoods general store that also carries plenty of fishing gear: "We've got everything, clothing, souvenirs, wine, the Lottery." In Eustis **Tim Pond Wilderness Camps** is a traditional fishing enclave. In Farmington **Aardvark Outfitters** (207-778-3330) offers a wide selection of fly-fishing gear. Inquire about fly-fishing schools at Sugarloaf.

THE WIRE BRIDGE IN NEW PORTLAND

Kim Grant

GOLF **Sugarloaf/USA Golf Club** (207-237-2000), Sugarloaf/USA. This spectacular, 18-hole, par-72 course, designed by Robert Trent Jones Jr, is ranked among the nation's best, as is its golf school. Inquire about weekend and midweek golf programs and packages.

Junior Golf Camp (207-237-2000), Sugarloaf/USA (five midweek days), designed for ages 12–18, is offered several times between mid-June and mid-August.

HIKING There are a number of 4,000-footers in the vicinity, and rewarding trails up **Mount Abraham** and **Bigelow Mountain**. The APPALACHIAN TRAIL signs are easy to spot on Rt. 27 just south of Stratton; popular treks include the two hours to **Cranberry Pond** or four-plus hours (one-way) to **Cranberry Peak**. The chamber of commerce usually stocks copies of the Maine Bureau of Parks and Lands' detailed map to trails in the 35,000-acre **Bigelow Preserve**, encompassing the several above-tree-line trails in the Bigelow Range (the trails are far older than the preserve, which dates to 1976 when a proposal to turn these mountains into "the Aspen of the East" was defeated by a public referendum).

West Mountain Falls on the Sugarloaf Golf Course is an easy hike to a swimming and picnic spot on the South Branch of the Carrabassett River. Begin at the Sugarloaf Clubhouse.

Poplar Stream Falls is a 51-foot cascade with a swimming hole below. Turn off Rt. 27 at the Valley Crossing and follow this road to the abandoned road marked by a snowmobile sign. Follow this road 1.5 miles.

Check in at the Sugarloaf/USA Outdoor Center, then head up **Burnt Mountain Trail**, a 3-mile hike to the 3,600-foot summit. At the top you'll have a 360-degree view of mountains, Sugarloaf's Snowfields, and Carrabassett Valley towns. The trail follows a streambed through soft- and hardwoods.

The Maine Huts and Trails System (207-265-2400; reservations 1-877-634-8824; www.mainehuts.org), 375 N. Main St., Kingfield. This new organization is creating a 180-mile trail for summer hiking and winter snowshoeing and skiing. In the summer of 2007, the first 36 miles were completed from Carrabasset Valley to Dead River; in the spring of 2008 the Poplar Stream Falls hut will open, followed by Flagstaff on Flagstaff Lake. The final route will run from the Mahoosucs to Moosehead, and will hold huts for overnight shelter as well as trails and waterways. The "huts" will be large enough to accommodate 35 to 40 guests, with use under the "leave no trace" system advised. Call the organization for maps and information. (See *Hiking* in Upper Kennebec)

MOOSE-WATCHING **Moose Cruises** (207-237-6830) depart from the Sugarloaf/USA Outdoor Center Wed. and Sat. evenings in early summer: View a video while sipping complimentary champagne, and ride the "Moose Express" van to moose-watching spots.

MOUNTAIN BIKING The **Sugarloaf/USA Outdoor Center** (207-237-2000), Rt. 17, is the hub of a trail system designed for cross-country skiers that also serves bikers well. The more adventurous can, of course, hit any number of abandoned logging roads. Inquire about guided tours. Maps are at the Sugarloafer Shop in the Sugarloaf Village.

A 19.5-mile loop begins at Tufulio's Restaurant (see *Eating Out*). Park there, cross the Carriage Rd. bridge, and turn left onto Houston Brook Rd. This will lead you into the **Bigelow Preserve** on double-track logging roads. When the road forks, heading uphill with a hard right, stay instead to the left on the single-track trail. You'll go past Stratton Brook Pond and the Appalachian Trailhead. When you reach Rt. 27, head south to Bigelow Station. Follow the Narrow Gauge Trail back to Tufulio's. This is a good trip for intermediate-level bikers.

SWIMMING ✐ **Cathedral Pines**, Rt. 27, Stratton. Just north of town, turn right into the campground and follow signs to the public beach, with changing rooms and a playground, on Flagstaff Lake. Free.

✐ **Riverside Park**, Rt. 27, 0.5 mile south of Ayotte's Country Store, is among the Carrabassett River's popular swimming holes. It features a natural waterslide and a very small beach, ideal for small children. Look for a deeper swimming hole off Rt. 27, 0.5 mile south of Riverside Park on the corner of the entrance to Spring Farm.

Also see **Wire Bridge** under *Historic Sites*.

TENNIS **Riverside Park**, Rt. 27, Carrabassett Valley. This municipal park along the Carrabassett River also features volleyball, basketball, a playground, and bathroom facilities.

WHITEWATER RAFTING See the outfitters listed in "Upper Kennebec Valley" and reserve a ride: phone 1-800-RAFT-MEE.

Sugarloaf/USA (1-800-765-RAFT) has entered into a partnership with Northern Outdoors, providing rafting trips and packages.

✷ Winter Sports

CROSS-COUNTRY SKIING **Sugarloaf/USA Outdoor Center** (207-237-6830), Rt. 27, Carrabassett Valley. Open in-season 9 AM–dusk. This is Maine's largest touring network, with 100 kilometers of trail loops, including race loops (with snowmaking) for timed runs. Rentals and instruction are available. The center itself includes the **Bull Moose Cafe**, which serves soups and sandwiches, provides space to relax in front of the fire with a view of Sugarloaf, and rentals.

Titcomb Mountain Ski Touring Center (207-778-9031), Morrison Hill Rd. (off Rt. 2/4), West Farmington. A varied network of 17 kilometers of groomed trails and unlimited ungroomed trails, plus a lodge with snack bar and fireplace and ski rentals. $9 adults, $7 ages 6–12, under 6 free.

DOWNHILL SKIING/SNOWBOARDING ✐ **Sugarloaf/USA** (general information, 207-237-2000; snow report, ext. 6808; on-mountain reservations, 1-800-THE-LOAF; www.sugarloaf.com). Sugarloaf Mountain Corporation was formed in the early 1950s by local skiers, and growth was steady but slow into the 1970s. Then a boom decade produced one of New England's largest self-contained resorts, including a base village complete with a seven-story brick hotel and a forest of condominiums. Sugarloaf has been expanding and improving snowmaking and services ever since. Snowmaking now even covers much of its alpine cap. Trails number 134, and glades add up to 55 miles. The vertical drop is a whopping 2,820 feet. The 14 lifts include two detachable quads, a triple chair, eight double chairs, a T-bar, and a surface lift. Facilities include a Perfect Turn Development Center, a Perfect Kids school, a ski shop, rentals, a base lodge, a cafeteria, a nursery (day and night), a game room, and a total of 12 bars and restaurants. The nursery is first-rate; there are children's programs for 3- to 12-year-olds; also mini mountain tickets for beginners. In 2007–08, one-day lift rates were $69 adults, $59 young adults 13–18, $45 juniors 6–12 and seniors. Also multiday, early- and late-season, and packaged rates. Lifts are free for kids 5 and under.

ICE SKATING **Sugarloaf/USA Outdoor Center** (207-237-6830) maintains an Olympic-sized, lighted rink and rents skates.

SNOWMOBILING Snowmobile trails are outlined on many maps available locally; a favorite destination is **Flagstaff Lodge** (maintained as a warming hut) in the Bigelow Preserve. **Flagstaff Rentals** (207-246-4276) and **T&L Enterprises** (207-246-2922), both in Stratton, rent snowmobiles. Inquire about guided tours.

TUBING **Sugarloaf/USA** offers a Turbo Tubing Park with a surface lift on a special run, to the left as you face the mountain. Tubers fly down the mountain in a huge inner tube, channeled through bumpers of snow and sliding up a ramp to stop. It's fun but can be scary for little ones—and some adults, too.

✷ Lodging

On-mountain

✐ ♿ **Sugarloaf/USA Inn and Condominiums** (207-237-2000 or 1-800-THE-LOAF; www.sugarloaf.com), Carrabassett Valley 04947. More than 250 ski-in, ski-out condominiums are in the rental pool. Built gradually over more than 20 years (they include the first condos in Maine), they represent a range of styles and sites; when making a reservation, you might want to ask about convenience to the base complex, the Sugarloaf/USA Sports and Fitness Club (to which all condo guests have access), or the golf club. The 42-room Sugarloaf Inn offers attractive standard rooms and fourth-floor family spaces with lofts; there's a comfortable living room with fireplace and a solarium restaurant (see The Seasons under *Dining Out*). The front desk is staffed around the clock, and the inn is handy to the health club as well as to the mountain. Packages $69–299 per person in winter, from $109 in golf season.

✐ ♿ **Grand Summit Resort Hotel & Conference Center** (1-800-527-9879), RR 1, Box 2299, Carrabassett Valley 04947. So close to the base complex that it dwarfs the base lodge, this is a massive, seven-story, 120-room brick condominium hotel with a gabled roof and central tower. Rooms feature a small refrigerator and microwave. Request a view of the mountain or you might get stuck overlooking the less attractive back of the hotel. A pair of two-bedroom suites come with a living room and kitchen. The two palatial tower penthouses each hold three bedrooms, three baths, and a hot tub. There's a library and a health club with a large hot tub (opens at 2 PM) and plunge pool, sauna, and steam room. Midwinter $109–159 per night for a one- or two-bedroom, $224–650 for suites; less in summer; multiday discounts.

Off-mountain

INNS AND BED & BREAKFASTS **The Herbert Grand Hotel** (207-265-2000 or 1-888-656-9922; www.herbertgrandhotel.com), 246 Main St., P.O. Box 67, Kingfield 04947. Open year-round. This three-story Beaux Arts–style hotel was billed as a "palace in the wilderness" when it opened in 1918 in the center of Kingfield. The "fumed oak" walls of the lobby gleam. Soak up the warmth from richly upholstered chairs and enjoy music from the grand piano. Look for the sink on the dining room wall, where stagecoach customers used to clean up before dining. The 26 rooms (including four suites) are furnished with antiques and cable TV, and many bathrooms feature a single whirlpool. $79–160 includes tax and a 3 percent gratuity. Pets are welcome, $10 fee.

Three Stanley Avenue (207-265-5541; www.stanleyavenue.com), Kingfield 04947. Designed by a younger brother of the Stanley twins, now an attractive B&B with six Victorian-inspired rooms (three with private bath) next to the ornate restaurant, One Stanley Avenue, also owned by Dan Davis (see *Dining Out*). Breakfast is included in the rates, $65–75.

MOTEL **Spillover Motel** (207-246-6571), P.O. Box 427, Stratton 04982. An attractive, two-story, 20-unit (16 nonsmoking) motel just south of Stratton Village. Spanking clean, with two double beds to a unit, cable TV, and phone. $72–92 per unit includes continental breakfast; $5 pets.

SPORTING CAMPS **Tim Pond Wilderness Camps** (207-243-2947; in winter, 207-897-4056; www.timpond.com), Eustis 04936. Open May–Nov. Located on a pond where there are no other camps, and down a road with gated access, here are 11 log cabins, each with a fieldstone fireplace or woodstove. Fly-fishing only. Deer and moose hunt, mountain bike, hike, moose-watch, swim, or canoe on or around this clear, remote lake surrounded by 4,450 acres of woodland. $155 single per night (plus 15 percent gratuity) includes meals, cabin, boat and motor. Ten percent discount July–Aug. Pets $10. Dinner by reservation July–Oct.

COTTAGES AND CONDOS For a list of rental units ranging from classic old A-frames to classy condos, contact the **Sugarloaf Area Chamber of Commerce** (see *Guidance*).

CAMPGROUNDS **Cathedral Pines Campground** (207-246-3491; www.eustismaine.com), Rt. 27, Eustis 04936. Open mid-May–Sept. Three hundred town-owned acres on Flagstaff Lake, with 100 wooded tent and RV sites set amid towering red pines. Recreation hall, beach, and canoe and paddleboat rentals.

Deer Farm Camps & Campground (207-265-4599 or 207-265-2241; www.deerfarmcamps.com), Tufts Pond Rd., Kingfield 04947.

Open May–mid-Oct. Fifty wooded tent and RV sites near Tufts Pond (good swimming); facilities include a store, playground, and hot showers. $18 tent sites, $22 with water and electric; hook-ups available. $250 per week for cabins.

✷ Where to Eat

DINING OUT ♿ **Porter House** (207-246-7932; www.porterhousemaine.com), Rt. 27, Eustis. Open year-round, closed Mondays. This country farmhouse located 12 miles north of Sugarloaf draws patrons from all over—call for reservations. Roasted half duckling, cedar-plank salmon, or Porter House steak are cooked by chef Brian Anderson, who owns this restaurant with partner Sue Benoit. Entrées $16–29. The Blue Heron Pub has a pub menu, with seafood Alfredo pizza, for instance, and burgers.

♿ **One Stanley Avenue** (207-265-5541), Kingfield. Closed Apr.–Dec., otherwise, open after 5 PM except Mon. Reservations are a must. Guests gather for a drink in the Victorian parlor, then proceed to one of three intimate dining rooms. Entrées include roast duck with rhubarb sauce, and beef and chestnut pie including local produce like fiddlehead ferns. Owner-chef Dan Davis describes his methods as classic, the results as distinctly regional. $21–35 includes fresh bread, salad, vegetables, starch, coffee, and tea, but it's difficult to pass on the wines and desserts.

Hugs (207-237-2392), 3001 Town Line Rd. (Rt. 27). Open mid-July–mid-Dec. Wed.–Sun. for dinner; open every night for dinner in winter. The green metal roof and board-and-batten siding keep this restaurant looking modest—but inside you'll find some great food. Past the shrine to pasta, among festoons of grapevines, you can enjoy wild mushroom ravioli with Gorgonzola, fresh tomato and spinach sauce, accompanied by great pesto bread—or chicken, veal, and seafood. All entrées can be altered, our good waiter told us.

The Double Diamond Restaurant (207-237-2222, ext. 4220), Grand Summit Hotel, Carrabassett Valley. Lounge 7–10, dinner 4–9:30. This is the most ambitious restaurant in the Sugarloaf complex, with some hits and a few misses. The menu ranges from lobster (served nightly from a tank on premises) to prime rib on Thursday. Entrées begin at $13–25.

Bullwinkle's (1-800-THE-LOAF), at the top of Bucksaw chair. On Saturday night (and possibly another night) this place converts from a daytime ski cafeteria into a charming on-mountain full-service restaurant. Reserve early, because it fills up quickly in high season. We were lucky enough to ride up in the Sno-Cat during a lovely snowstorm. Soups like lobster and corn bisque were spectacular, and the venison and lobster filled us up nicely after a day on the slopes. Two sittings per night mean you can have a drink in the **Widowmaker Lounge** at the base of the mountain before or after, watching the powder collect on the runs you'll ski the next morning.

The White Wolf Inn (207-246-2922; www.thewhitewolfinn.com), Stratton. Owner Sandy Isgro runs a restaurant that serves Wolf burgers, turkey potpie, venison, quail, and buffalo. She caters to all kinds of guests, from Appalachian Trail hikers to Europeans who are leaf peeping to snowmobilers and skiers in winter. A pub keeps things informal and serves fine microbrews. Entrées $5–29. Rooms for rent as well.

EATING OUT **The Orange Cat Café** (207-265-2860; www.orangecatcafe.com), The Brick Castle, 329 Main St., Kingfield. Open 7–5 in winter, 7–3 in summer. Run alongside a flower shop, this place is pretty from the door. Good coffee and homemade scones are served under a map of the world; you can also get great lunch dishes, like a jalapeño chicken salad sandwich ($7.50) or bacon and cheese quiche ($3.95); best hot chocolate in the valley.

Longfellows Restaurant (207-265-4394), Main St., Kingfield. Open year-round for lunch from 11 and dinner from 5. An attractive, informal dining place in a 19th-century building decorated with photos of 19th-century Kingfield. A find for budget-conscious families at dinner. Chicken fingers, hot dogs, and PB&J for the kids. Deck overlooking Carrabassett River. Entrées $7–15.

♿ **Tufulio's Restaurant & Bar** (207-235-2010), Rt. 27, Carrabassett (6 miles south of Sugarloaf). Open for dinner 5–9 daily; happy hour begins at 4. A pleasant dining room with large oak booths, specializing in a wide selection of pastas, seafood, steaks, and microbrews. Children's menu and game room.

The Woodsman (207-265-2561), Rt. 27, Kingfield (north end of town). Open Mon.–Sat. for breakfast and lunch; Sun. for breakfast only. Pine paneled, decorated with logging tools and pictures, this is a friendly barn of a place. Good for stacks of pancakes, omelets, homemade soups, and local gossip.

The Rack (207-237-2211; www.rackbbq.com), Sugarloaf Access Rd., Carrabassett. Barbeque, pulled pork, and a "three-legged chicken," are the focus but there are other options, from prime rib to fresh fish and pasta. Roast duck is exceptionally crispy and tender. One of the mountain snowmakers makes the carrot cake. Entrées $10–25 for "a mountain or ribs."

In Farmington

Soup for You! (207-779-0799), 222 Broadway. This small restaurant offers homemade soups, salads, and sandwiches that bear the names of *Seinfeld* characters and other whimsical monikers like Don Quixote and Barking Spider. Smoothies, cappuccino, and espresso, too.

The Granary Brewpub (207-779-0710; www.thegranarybrewpub.com), 147 Pleasant St. Open daily 7 AM–10 PM. Featuring a large menu of soups, sandwiches, and moderately priced entrées like veggie burgers, popcorn shrimp, and French dip, a roast beef sandwich with onion soup.

The Homestead Bakery Restaurant (207-778-6162), 186 Broadway (Rt. 43). Open Tues.–Fri. 11 AM–9 PM, Sat. 8–9, Sun. 8–2, closed Mon. Dinner includes steaks, seafood, and chicken. A good stop en route to Sugarloaf.

Gifford's Famous Ice Cream (207-778-3617), 293 Main St. (Rt. 4/27). Open seasonally from 11 or noon. Nearby Skowhegan is home base for this exceptional ice cream that comes in 40 flavors.

✱ Selective Shopping

Grand Central Station (207-265-2893; www.grandcentralstation.com),

244 Main St., Kingfield. Selling items made by Kingfield Wood Products (www.kingfieldwood.com) and others. Open Mon.–Sat. 10–6, Sun. 11–3. A trove of wooden furniture, housewares, and needlepoint supplies. Also individual shop with handmade socks, cloth bags, and other unusual items, like a mirror made of old skis.

Devaney, Doak & Garret Booksellers (207-778-3454; www.ddgbooks.com), 193 Broadway, Farmington. Open daily. A bookstore worthy of a college town, and one with a good children's section. Comfortable seating invites lingering. Readings from local and Maine authors. You can order online.

Sugarwood Gallery (207-778-9105; www.sugarwoodgallery.com), 248 Broadway, Farmington. A cooperative gallery showing the work of local artists, mostly woodworkers, with stained glass, pottery, and fabric as well.

Mainestone Jewelry (207-778-6560), 179 Broadway, Farmington. Ron and Cindy Gelinas craft much of the jewelry here—made from Maine-mined gems—and carry the work of other local craftspeople. Artists' work is exhibited, too.

Special Events

January: **White White World Winter Carnival**—snow sculpture contest, annual Dummy Jump, and discounts at Sugarloaf/USA.

March: **St. Patrick's Day Leprechaun Loppet**—a 15 kilometers citizens' cross-country race at Sugarloaf/USA Outdoor Center.

April: **Easter Festival at Sugarloaf**—costume parade, Easter egg hunt on the slopes, and sunrise service on the summit. **Reggae Fest weekend**.

June: **Family Fun Days**, Stratton—games and children's events, live entertainment, fireworks, put on by the Flagstaff Area Business Association, 207-246-4221.

Late July: **Kingfield Days Celebration**—four days with parade, art exhibits, potluck supper.

August: **Old Home Days** in Stratton, Eustis, and Flagstaff.

September: **Franklin County Fair**, Farmington.

October: Skiers' Homecoming Weekend, Sugarloaf Mountain.

December: Yellow-Nosed Vole Day, Sugarloaf Mountain. Chester Greenwood Day, Farmington, honors the local inventor of the earmuff with a parade and variety show.

The Kennebec Valley

AUGUSTA AND MID-MAINE, INCLUDING THE BELGRADE LAKES REGION

THE UPPER KENNEBEC VALLEY AND MOOSE RIVER VALLEY, INCLUDING THE FORKS AND JACKMAN

Raft Maine

AUGUSTA AND MID-MAINE INCLUDING THE BELGRADE LAKES REGION

Augusta was selected as the nascent state's capital in 1827 because then as now so many travelers come this way, whether headed up or down the coast, in to or out of Maine's interior. First I-95 and now the Rt. 3 connector make it all too easy, however, to bypass the city.

If time permits, approach Augusta via the Kennebec instead of the highway. Follow Rt. 201, the old river road, at least for the 6 miles from Gardiner up through Hallowell's mid-19th-century Water Street, lined with antiques and specialty shops and restaurants. However you come, don't skip the Maine State Museum, which does an excellent job of showcasing Maine's natural history and traditional industries, as well as tracing human habitation back 12,000 years.

Augusta and neighboring Hallowell both mark the site of Native American villages. In 1625 the Pilgrims came here to trade "seven hundred pounds of good beaver and some other furs" with the Wabanaki for a "shallop's load of corn." They procured a grant for a strip of land 15 miles wide on either side of the Kennebec, built a storehouse, and with the proceeds of their beaver trade were soon able to pay off their London creditors. With the decline of the fur trade and rising hostilities with the Wabanaki, the tract of land was sold to four Boston merchants. It wasn't until 1754, when the British constructed Fort Western (now reconstructed), that serious settlement began.

The statehouse, designed by Charles Bulfinch and built of granite from neighboring Hallowell, was completed in 1832 (it's been expanded and largely rebuilt since). During the mid–19th century, this area boomed: Some 500 boats were built along the river between Winslow and Gardiner, and river traffic between Augusta and Boston thrived.

This Lower Kennebec Valley remains rolling, open farmland with breathtaking views from its ridge roads, spotted with surprisingly large spring-fed lakes. It was the site of numerous, now vanished 19th-century summer hotels and boardinghouses and still is home to numerous summer camps. The Belgrade Lakes Region, just north of Augusta, remains a low-key *On Golden Pond* kind of resort area with old-style family-geared "sporting camps," summer rental cottages, and

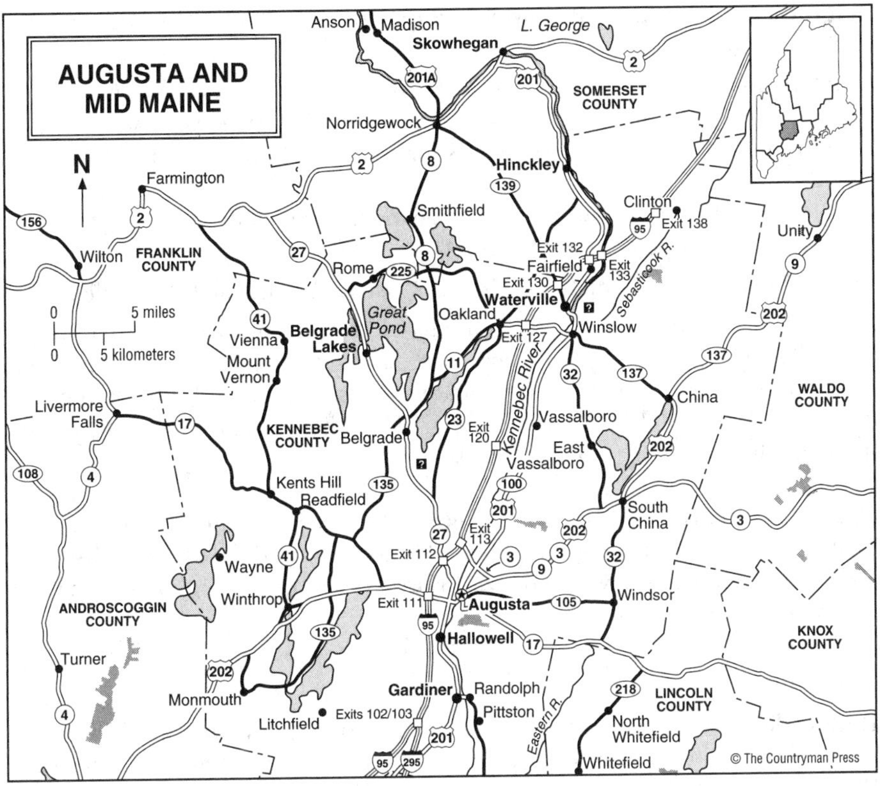

widely scattered B&Bs. East of the city, the China Lakes is another old low-profile summer haven. Golf courses (former farms) are proliferating. The Maine International Film Festival draws cinephiles to Waterville in July and long-established summer theater continues to thrive in Monmouth and Skowhegan.

The latter town, sited at one of the major drops in the Kennebec River, is an obvious road food stop on your way north up the Kennebec Valley. Stroll Skowhegan's reawakening Main Street, and find one of the walking bridges across the gorge or view the Kennebec from the gem of a small museum and research center honoring the late U.S. Senator Margaret Chase Smith, "the Lady from Maine."

Those who would rather shadow the Kennebec north can follow its curve through the gracious old town of Norridgewock and on up Rt. 201A through Anson and Embden (just across a bridge from Solon), where petroglyphs are evidence of a Native American culture that dates back several thousand years.

GUIDANCE **Kennebec Valley Chamber of Commerce** (207-623-4559; www.kennebecvalley.org) runs a Web site worth checking for current updates.

Mid-Maine Chamber of Commerce (207-873-3315; www.midmainechamber.com). Stop by the chamber's pamphlet-stocked office in the former post office building at the corner of Waterville and Main Sts.

Belgrade Lakes Region Business Group, Inc. (207-4952744; www.belgradelakesmaine.com).

Skowhegan Chamber of Commerce (207-474-3621; www.skowheganchamber.org), 23 Commercial St., is open year-round 9–5 weekdays and Sat. 10–2 in summer months. Rt. 201 snakes through downtown, right by this office.

GETTING THERE *By air:* **Augusta State Airport** is served by U.S. Airways Express, which is operated by **Colgan Air** (207-623-7527).

By bus: **Vermont Transit** (1-800-451-3292) serves Augusta and Waterville.

By car: From points south, Rt. 295 is both quicker and cheaper than I-95 (the Maine Turnpike). The two merge just south of Augusta. Note the new connector (Exit 113) bypassing Augusta and facilitating access to Rt. 3 east. For Rt. 3 via downtown Augusta take exit 112; for Belgrade Lakes, exit 127; for Rt. 201 north through Hinkley and Skowhegan, exit 133.

SUGGESTED READING ***A Midwife's Tale***, a Pulitzer Prize winner by Laurel Thatcher Ulrich, vividly describes life in this area from 1785–1812. ***Empire Falls***, a Pulitzer Prize novel by Richard Russo, describes current life in a town resembling Waterville.

✷ Villages

Hallowell (www.hallowell.org). Two miles south of Augusta, this "city" (pop. 2,467), with its line of brick two- and three-story buildings along the Kennebec River, looks much the way it did at the time this, not Augusta, was the region's commercial center. Shipbuilding and granite quarrying were the big industries here, along with ice. Residential streets, stepped into the slope above the shops, are worth driving to see fine houses and churches dating to every decade in the 19th century. The city's revival dates from the 1970s. A road-widening proposal threatened to level most of Water Street, but residents rallied; the anniversary of their protest, the last weekend in July, is now observed as Old Hallowell Day. Walk in Vaughan Woods, part of the city's most historic estate, dating to the 18th century. Water Street, now all a National Historic District, is lined with quality, individually owned shops (no chain stores) and the best restaurants around.

STREET SCENE, HALLOWELL

Christina Tree

Gardiner (pop. 6,198). Sited at the confluence of the Kennebec River and Cobbosseecontee Stream, this old industrial (shoe, textile, and paper)

town has been hovering on the verge of renaissance for more than a decade. The **A1 Diner** is a draw for travelers and locals alike, as are performances at the **Johnson Hall Performing Arts Center** and the increasingly varied shopping along Maine Street.

Waterville. Twenty-five miles north of Augusta on the Kennebec River, Waterville (pop. 15,605) is an old mill town with an interesting ethnic mix, restaurants and shopping worth finding in the downtown beyond the commercial strip, and home to prestigious Colby College with its distinguished art museum. Waterville is the thinly disguised subject of Richard Russo's best-selling novel *Empire Falls*; the television mini-series based on the book was partially filmed in Waterville. Check out the **Waterville-Winslow Two Cent Bridge**, Front St.—one of the only known toll footbridges in the country (although these days it's free). The **Redington Museum and Apothecary** (207-872-9439), 64 Silver St. (open Memorial Day–Labor Day, Tue.–Sat. 10–2) houses the local historical collection: furniture, Civil War and Native American relics, a children's room, period rooms, and a 19th-century apothecary. **Colby College** (207-872-3000; www.colby.edu) is the pride of the city. Founded in 1813, it enrolls some 1,800 students at its 714-acre campus, with brick ivy-covered buildings, a 128-acre arboretum and bird sanctuary (with nature trails and a picnic area), and the 274-seat Strider Theater, offering performances throughout the year. For a self-guided tour, stop by admissions. Also see the **Colby College Museum of Art** under *To See*.

Belgrade Lakes. At the heart of the seven Belgrade Lakes is Belgrade Lakes Village, and at the heart of Belgrade Lakes Village is **Day's Store** (207-495-2205). Open year-round, this general store sells liquor, fishing licenses and gear, boots, and gifts, and is a rainy day mecca. The Belgrade chain consists of East, North, Great, Long, McGrath, and Salmon Ponds and Messalonskee Lake.

Winthrop (pop. 6,475). A proud town with 12 lakes and many summer cottages within its boundaries, Winthrop seems to be thriving despite closure of the woolen mill. There are interesting shops and restaurants here, and downtown is filled with the aroma of roasting Cobbossee Coffee.

Skowhegan (pop. 8,875). In Wabanaki the name is said to mean "watch for fish." This, one of the major falls in the Kennebec River, has been long since harnessed to generate power for both textile and woodworking mills. Skowhegan is also shire town of Somerset County and a major north/south (Rt. 201) and east/west (Rt. 2) crossroads. Stop downtown (there's parking behind the Water St. shops and restaurants) to view the gorge from one of two pedestrian bridges or from Coburn Park on the eastern edge of town. If it's a hot day, Lake George Regional Park (see *Swimming*) is worth the detour. The Kennebec doglegs west here and Rt. 201A follows it up through Norridgewock (see Wabanaki Cultural Landmarks), rejoining Rt. 201 in Solon. Whichever way you go, be sure to stop by the riverside Margaret Chase Smith Library Center. This is really an outstanding small museum (see *To See*). Skowhegan is also home to Gifford's Ice Cream, to the Skowhegan State Fair, and the Skowhegan Lakewood Theater on Lake Wesserunsett, billed as America's Oldest Summer Theater. The prestigious Skowhegan School of Painting and Sculpture (www.skowheganart.org), holds an intensive nine-week summer residency program, squirreled away on a 300-acre campus 4 miles from town, and also opens its evening lectures to the public. The South Solon Meetinghouse (*To See*) showcases work by Skowhegan School artists.

✷ To See

In Augusta

♿ **Maine State Museum** (207-287-2301; www.mainestatemuseum.org), State House Complex, marked from Sewall St., also accessible from State St. (Rt. 201/27). Open Tue.–Fri. 9–5, Sat. 10–4. $2 adults, $1 ages 6–18, $1 seniors. Maine's best-kept secret, this is a superb and fairly large museum, just a few blocks off the interstate but badly posted. It's well worth finding, especially if there are children along.

The *Back to Nature* exhibit features animals such as the lynx and snowshoe rabbit, deer, moose, beaver, and birds in their convincingly detailed habitats (the trout are real) with plenty of sound effects. The *Maine Bounty* exhibits depict the way the state's natural resources have been developed through fishing, agriculture, granite quarrying, ice harvesting, shipbuilding, and lumbering. Exhibits include a gigantic wagon used to haul stone from quarries and the equally huge Lombard Hauler and 1846 narrow-gauge locomotive Lion, used to transport lumber. Archival films such as *From Stump to Ship* (narrated by Tim Sample) bring the era to life. *Made in Maine* depicts more than a dozen 19th-century industrial scenes: textile mills and shops producing shoes, guns, fishing rods, and more, again with sound effects.

Our favorite exhibit, *12,000 Years in Maine,* traces the story of human habitation in the state from the Paleo Indians down through the "ceramic period" (3,000 BC–AD 500) with reproductions of petroglyphs and genuine artifacts. This fascinating exhibit also dramatizes early European explorations and displays 19th-century Penobscot and Passamaquoddy craftsmanship, from highly decorative beaded moccasins and bent-birch boxes to birch-bark canoes.

From I-95 exit 109 follow Eastern Ave. (Rt. 17/202) and turn right at the light across from the armory (posted for the capitol complex). Follow signs for the capitol until you see the museum posted (a right turn onto Sewall St.) and turn into the parking lot. The museum is in the low-slung modern building that also houses the state library and archives. If you miss the first turn, continue around the rotary, take Rt. 27/201 south, then make your first right after passing the capitol. This takes you to the other side of the same parking lot.

FLAG RETIRED AFTER THE BATTLE OF GETTYSBURG, 1863

Maine State Museum, Augusta, Maine

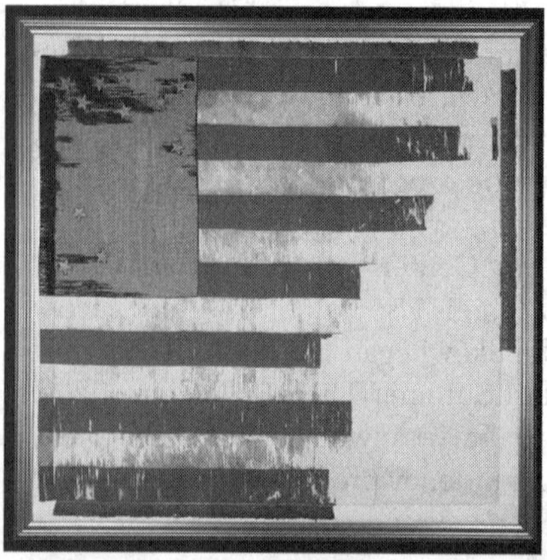

Tours of the State House (by reservation weekdays 9–1) and of the governor's mansion, Blaine House (open

Tue.–Thu. for half-hour guided tours by reservation at 2, 2:30, and 3), are arranged by calling the museum.

Maine State Museum, Augusta, Maine

CABINET MAKER'S SHOP

Old Fort Western (207-626-2385; www.oldfortwestern.org), City Center Plaza, 16 Cony St., Augusta. Open Memorial Day–Labor Day, 1–4; Labor Day–Columbus Day, weekends only, 1–4; Nov.–Jan., first Sun. of every month, 1–3. $6 per adult, $4 ages 6–16. The original 16-room garrison house has been restored to reflect its use as a fort, trading post, and lodge from 1754 to 1810. The blockhouse and stockade are reproductions, but the main house (barracks and store) are original. The fort, a National Historic Landmark, is the oldest surviving wooden fort in New England. Costumed characters answer questions and demonstrate 18th-century domestic activities. Many special events.

In Waterville

Colby College Museum of Art (207-859-5600; www.colby.edu/museum), Colby College, Mayflower Hill Dr. Open Tues.–Sat. 10–4:30, Sun. noon–4:30. Free. Closed Mon. and major holidays. This museum is a sleeper with an outstanding permanent collection of 18th-, 19th-, and 20th-century art. An 11-gallery addition houses some 150 works from the permanent collection; three galleries exhibit 18th-century work, two house 19th-century paintings and sculpture, another is for impressionist paintings, two are for primitive 19th-century work, and two galleries are devoted to 54 works by John Marin, most on Maine subjects, from Mount Katahdin to seascapes. The Paul J. Schupf Wing rotates more than 500 paintings and sculptures by Alex Katz. Significant Maine-based works by Marsden Hartley, George Bellows, and Rockwell Kent are also on display, along with special exhibits; inquire about gallery talks, lectures, and receptions throughout the year.

Fort Halifax, Rt. 201 (1 mile south of the Waterville–Winslow Bridge at the junction of the Kennebec and Sebasticook Rivers). Just a blockhouse remains, but it's original, built in 1754—the oldest in the United States. There's also a park with picnic tables here.

COLBY COLLEGE MUSEUM OF ART

Colby College

Along Route 201 North

L. C. Bates Museum (207-238-4250; www.gwh.org), Rt. 201, Hinckley. A few miles up Rt. 201 from I-95, exit 133. Open Wed.–Sat. 10–4:30, Sun. 1–4:30, but look for the OPEN flag; it's frequently staffed on "closed" days. $2 adults, $1 child. Across the road from the Kennebec River, one in a lineup of brick buildings that are part of the campus of the Good-Will Hinckley School (founded in 1889 for "disadvantaged chidden"), this ponderous Romanesque building houses a large and wonderfully old-fashioned collection, with stuffed wildlife, dioramas by noted American impressionist Charles D. Hubbard, and some significant Wabanaki craftsmanship, with examples ranging from several thousand years old to early-20th-century items. Allow at least an hour. The annual summer art exhibit, usually incorporating work by faculty and/or students at the nearby Skowhegan School of Painting, is a bonus. The 2,540-acre campus includes many miles of walking and biking trails, an arboretum, and a picnic area.

Margaret Chase Smith Library Center (207-474-7133; www.mcslibrary.org), 54 Norridgewock Ave., Skowhegan (turn left at the first traffic light heading north out of town.). Open year-round Mon.–Fri. 10–4. Free. Set in 15 acres above the Kennebec, this expanded version of Senator Smith's home is a major museum to an era as well as to a stateswoman who voted her conscience in the face of overwhelming opposition. She is credited with putting an end to the reign of national paranoia instigated by Senator Joseph R. McCarthy. Well worth a stop for the exhibits. This research and conference center houses over 300,000 documents relating to "the lady from Maine," as Margaret Chase Smith (1897–1995) was known during her years as a congresswoman (1940–49) and U.S. senator (1949–73).

South Solon Meeting House (207-643-2555 or 207-643-2721), South Solon. Turn east off Rt. 201 onto Rt. 43 north to South Solon Meeting House Rd. and the crossroads village with the 1842 Greek Revival meetinghouse at its center. Open daily year-round. The interior is a total work of art, its walls almost entirely frescoed by WPA and Skowhegan School artists.

FOR FAMILIES ✐ **Children's Discovery Museum** (207-622-2209; www.childrensdiscoverymuseum.org), 265 Water St., Augusta. Open Tue.–Thu. 10–4, Fri. and Sat. 10–5, and Sun. 11–4; extended hours during school vacations and summer. $5 per child, $4 per adult. An excellent hands-on museum, with a stage for kids to videotape a performance and then watch themselves on TV; post office, diner, and supermarket play areas; a construction site complete with real equipment; and a weather station and communications center with computers and a ham radio.

MARGARET CHASE SMITH LIBRARY CENTER
Christina Tree

✐ **D.E.W. Animal Kingdom** (207-293-2837), 918 Pond Rd. (Rt. 41), West Mount Vernon. Open May–mid-Sept. daily except Mon., weekends in April and through foliage 10–5. $10 per adult, $8 age 12 and under. Julie

Christina Tree
SOUTH SOLON MEETING HOUSE

and Bob Miner stress that this is a "farm," not a "zoo." But what began as a traditional farm with pigs and cows has evolved into the most exotic menagerie in New England: some 190 animals contained within chain-link pens on 41 wooded acres. What's striking is the way the animals relate to Julie and Bob, who have raised most from birth. Cougars and lions nuzzle them. A female lynx offers her tail to be pulled. The tigers lumber up to be hugged. Eddie the Camel offers slurpy kisses to visitors as well. A wallaby baby peaks from its mother's pouch. Mallard and eider ducks follow you around. It's certainly a magic place. You can feed the several kinds of goats, but this isn't a petting farm—just a place to marvel at animals that are native (deer and black bear) or fairly familiar (ostrich and llamas), and also those you may have only read about—from badgers to black leopards to some so exotic you couldn't have imagined them.

✐ **Norlands Living History Center** (207-897-4366; www.norlands.org), 290 Norlands Rd., Livermore. From Rt. 4 take Rt. 108 east for 1.2 miles, then travel 1.6 miles up Norlands Rd. Open for live-in programs and frequent seasonal events, also by appointment. This 455-acre complex includes a restored Victorian mansion, large barn, farmer's cottage, church, granite library, and a one-room schoolhouse. These buildings and grounds provide the backdrop for rural late-19th-century living history experiences ranging from tours to daylong and overnight programs. Become a scholar in the one-room schoolhouse, hear the story of the Washburn family and their 11 sons and daughters, or take part in the daily chores of the 1870s.

✷ To Do

BALLOONING **Sails Aloft** (207-623-1136; www.sailsaloft.com), Augusta, offers sightseeing flights in central and midcoast Maine.

BICYCLING The **Kennebec River Rail Trail** (www.krrt.org) runs along the river from Augusta (most easily accessed from Capitol Park) to Gardiner (at the Hannaford parking lot and bike).

BOAT EXCURSIONS **Great Pond Marina** (207-495-2213), Belgrade Lakes Village, operates the **Mail Boat on Great Pond** (said to be the inspiration for the book and movie *On Golden Pond*). Also moorings, boat rentals (canoes, sailboards, sailboats, fishing boats), and service.

FISHING **The Belgrade Lakes** are a big lure for anglers. The seven ponds and lakes harbor smallmouth bass, brook, pickerel, and landlocked salmon, among many other species. The sporting camps listed under *Lodging* all offer rental

WABANAKI CULTURAL LANDMARKS

Wabanaki heritage is particularly strong along this stretch of the Kennebec River. Your clue might be the 62-foot-high Skowhegan Indian, billed as "the world's largest sculptured wooden Indian." He stands in the downtown parking lot, visible (and accessible) from Rt. 201. Finding genuine evidence of longtime Indian habitation, however, requires some sleuthing. There are two sites, one commemorating an early-18th-century Indian mission village and the second consisting of genuine Indian petroglyphs. To find the first from Skowhegan, follow Rt. 201A along the Kennebec for just a few miles to Norridgewock. If you are interested only in the petroglyphs, you can remain on Rt. 201 into Solon.

French Jesuit Sebastian Rasle established the mission in Norridgewock, insisting that Native American lands "were given them of God, to them and their children forever." Rasle and his mission were wiped out by the English in 1724. **Norridgewock Oosoola Park** features a totem pole topped by a frog (this is a good picnic spot and boat-launch site). The site of the village itself is marked by a pleasant riverside picnic area in a pine grove.

The **petroglyphs** (pictured in the Maine State Museum) are in Embden on an arrowhead-shaped rock that juts into the Kennebec. From Rt. 201 in Solon, turn at the sign for the Evergreens Campground. Cross the Kennebec and turn south on Rt. 201A. The trail to the river is just down the road; it's not marked, but it's easy to see. If you are coming from the mission village site, continue straight ahead; the road hugs the river all the way to Solon. Also see the **L. C. Bates Museum** in *To See*.

ROCKS FOUND AT AZISCOHOS LAKE, NORTHWESTERN MAINE

Maine State Museum, Augusta, Maine

boats and cater to fishermen, especially in May, June, and Sept. **Day's Store** (207-495-2205) in Belgrade Lakes Village is a source of fishing licenses and devotes an entire floor to fishing gear. Boat rentals are available. **Great Pond Marina** (207-495-2213), Belgrade Lakes Village, rents boats.

GOLF AND TENNIS **Belgrade Lakes Golf Club** (207-495-GOLF), Belgrade, is a new, highly rated 18-hole golf course, designed by renowned English golf architect Clive Clark. Just off Rt. 27 with views of both Great and Long Ponds. Fees vary with season.

Natanis Golf Club (207-622-3561), Webber Pond off Rt. 201, Vassalboro, offers a 36-hole course and tennis courts. **Waterville Country Club** (207-465-9861), Waterville (off I-95), 18 holes, clubhouse with restaurant, carts, and caddies. **Lakewood Golf Course** (474-5955), Rt. 201A, Madison, 18 holes on the west side of Lake Wesserunsett.

KAYAKING AND CANOEING **Belgrade Canoe and Kayak** (207-495-2005 or 1-888-CANOE-11), Rt. 27, Belgrade Lakes, offers rentals, tours, and sales.

Maine Wilderness Tours (207-465-4333; www.mainewildernesstours.com), guided canoe and kayak trips on the Belgrade Lakes and down the Kennebec as well as fishing, moose-watching, and rafting farther afield.

Belgrade Boat Rentals & Storage (207-495-3415), rents small fishing boats, and offers free delivery and pickup.

SPA **The Senator Inn & Spa** (207-622-3138), 284 Western Ave., Augusta. The three-story spa wing contains a fitness center, saltwater lap pool, aerobics and yoga studio, hot tub and steam room, and outdoor pool. A full menu of spa services is offered: hairstyling, manicure and pedicure, coloring, and a long list of skin care, massage, and other treatments for both men and women. All treatments include full use of the facilities.

Apollo Salon/Spa (207-872-2242, www.apollosalonspa.com) 91 Silver St., Waterville. A day spa offering a range of services including facials, body massages, wraps, and use of a Roman-style soaking tub.

SWIMMING ✐ **Peacock Beach State Park**, Richmond (just off Rt. 201, 10 miles south of Augusta). A small, beautiful sand beach on Pleasant Pond; lifeguards and picnic facilities. $3 adults, free under age 12.

Sunset Camps Beach (207-362-2611), on North Pond in Smithfield, and **Willow Beach** (207-968-2421) in China. Although public access is limited at the Belgrade and China Lakes, every cottage cluster and most rental "camps" there are on the water.

Lake George Regional Park (207-474-1292), Rt. 2, 8 miles east of Skowhegan. Open seasonally with two sand beaches on either side of the lake; changing rooms, restrooms, boat launch, and picnicking facilities. $3 adult, $1 child. (Also see *Green Space.*)

Lake St. George State Park (207-589-4255), Rt. 3, Liberty. A pleasant, clean, clear lake with a sandy beach and changing facilities; a perfect break if en route from Augusta to the coast. $4 day-use fee.

✷ Green Space

Capitol Park, across from the State House Complex, is a good place for a picnic. Also located here is the Maine Vietnam Veteran's Memorial, three triangular structures with a cutout section in the shape of soldiers that visitors can walk through.

Pine Tree State Arboretum (207-621-0031), 153 Hospital St., Augusta. (At Cony Circle—the big rotary across the bridge from downtown Augusta—turn south along the river; it's a short way down on the left, across from the Augusta Mental Health Institute.) Open daily dawn to dusk. Visitors center open 8–4 weekdays. There are 224 acres, with trails through woods and fields. More than 600 trees and shrubs (including rhododendrons and lilacs), as well as hostas and a rock garden. Cross-country ski trails, too.

Vaughan Woods, Hallowell. In 1791 Charles Vaughan settled in the town named for his grandfather Benjamin Hallowell; in 1797 his brother Benjamin arrived and built himself a fine house here, transforming the property into an agricultural showplace. A substantial portion of this property remains in the family seven generations later, and 152 acres have been granted as a conservation easement to the Kennebec Land Trust. Vaughan Woods represents the largest acreage open to the public, and it's beautiful: webbed with footpaths through mixed forest and open fields. The best entrance is from Litchfield Rd. at the end of Middle St. Park at the stone wall and look for the path.

Jamies Pond Wildlife Management Area, Meadow Hill Rd., Hallowell. These 800 acres of woodlands, managed by the Maine Department of Inland Fisheries and Wildlife, include 6 miles of trails good for walking and cross-country skiing, and a 107-acre pond. There is a small parking lot and a launch ramp.

Lake George Regional Park (207-474-1292), Rt. 2, 8 miles east of Skowhegan. This 320-acre lakeside park, site of a 19th-century mineral spring resort, then a summer camp, was acquired by the state in 1992 and is maintained by a nonprofit group for year-round use. Ten kilometers of trails for mountain biking and cross-country skiing. Inquire about an evolving museum. Nominal admission charged in summer; see *Swimming*.

Coburn Park, Water St. (Rt. 2 east) on the edge of downtown Skowhegan. This riverside park with a lily pond and formal landscaping hosts a regular concert series in July and August.

✷ Lodging

INNS AND BED & BREAKFASTS ✐ ♿ "1" ⚭ **Maple Hill Farm Bed & Breakfast Inn & Conference Center** (207- 622-2708 or 1-800-622-2708; www.MapleBB.com), 11 Inn Rd. (off the Outlet Rd.), Hallowell 04347. This pleasant old house, not far from the turnpike and downtown Augusta, sits on 130 acres of fields and woods with trails, a spring-fed swimming hole, and a small abandoned quarry adjoining a 800-acre wildlife reservation. Scott Cowger and Vincent Hannan offer eight rooms tastefully furnished, with phone, cable TV, VCR, clock-radio, air-conditioning, and private bath. Some rooms have a whirlpool tub, private deck, and fireplace. As you meander up the driveway, watch for chickens (which provide the morning eggs). Goats, llamas, cows, a pony, and a cat are also in residence. This is, however, more of a grown-up's than family retreat, although children are welcome. The carriage house is perfect for wedding receptions (the inn is fully licensed), and the Gathering Place, seating up to 125 people, hosts functions. In winter trails are maintained for cross-country skiing. A full breakfast, with a choice of dishes, is included. $105–205 per couple in high season; off-season rates.

The Pleasant Street Inn (207-680-2515; www.84pleasantstreet.com), 84 Pleasant St., Waterville 04901, within walking distance of downtown. The three guest rooms, one with a private bath, are bright and cheery with beds covered by colorful quilts. Guests have access to a common area that includes kitchen, dining room, and a living room with TV/DVD. $50–75.

Home-Nest Farm (207-897-4125; www.mainefarmvacation.com/homenest/index.html), 76 Baldwin Hill Rd., Fayette 04349. Open year-round. The main house, built in 1784, offers a panoramic view of the White Mountains. Lilac Cottage (1800) and the Red Schoolhouse (1830) are available for rent as separate units. The property has been in the Sturdevant family for seven generations. $80 for one room, $140 daily, $700 weekly for one- to three-bedroom units with kitchens; all include breakfast. Two-night minimum stay July–Oct.

♿ **A Rise and Shine Bed and Breakfast** (207-933-9876; www.riseandshinebb.com), 19 Moose Run Dr. (Rt. 135), Monmouth 04259. Ten miles west of Augusta, with a distant view of Lake Cobbosseecontee, this rambling house with its even larger stables was for many years a racehorse farm, part of a 2,000-acre spread belonging to the Woolworth family. Locals Tom Crocker and Lorette Comeau have replaced 76 windows, used up some 300 gallons of paint, and installed gas- or pellet-fired hearths in many of the eight guest rooms. Lorette has also painted murals on many walls. Our favorite is the Sunshine Room, the former master bedroom with a king-sized bed, hearth, and steam shower. $125–180, includes a full breakfast. Cottage $300 a night. Horses are welcome, and there's lake access.

Maple Tree Inn B&B (207-377-5787), 34 High St., Winthrop 04364. Open May–Nov. Lloyd and Ann Lindholm have created an attractive suite with its own parlor, kitchen, bedroom, and bath on the second floor of their early-1900s house on a shady dead-end street. $55–85 includes a full breakfast served on a garden-side porch, weather permitting, otherwise in the dining room.

In the Belgrade Lakes region

Wings Hill Inn (207-495-2400 or 1-866-495-2400; www.wingshillinn.com), Rt. 27 and Dry Point Dr., Belgrade Lakes 04918. Open year-round. This 200-year-old white-clapboard farmhouse rambles across a knoll, above its lawns just north of the village of Belgrade Lakes, overlooking

Long Pond. The name recalls a one-time owner, U.S. Air Force general Edmund "Wings" Hill. Current innkeepers Christopher and Tracey Anderson met in culinary school, and the inn is known for fine dining (see *Dining Out*). The six guest rooms, all with private bath (one with a Jacuzzi), have been individually decorated with an eye for romance. $140–180 May–Oct. (less off-season) includes a three-course breakfast and afternoon tea.

The Pressey House Lakeside Bed & Breakfast (207-465-3500 or 1-877-773-7738; www.presseyhouse.com), 32 Belgrade Rd., Oakland 04963. Open year-round. Lorie and Lorne McMillan have divided an 1850s octagonal house on Messalonskee Lake into five guest units, each with its own bedroom, bath, living room with TV, and kitchen. A large common room with a fireplace overlooks the water. Guests can use a canoe, paddleboat, and two kayaks, or swim off the dock. All just 2.5 miles off I-95. Open year-round.$125–215 including breakfast; less off-season.

Yeaton Farm Inn Bed & Breakfast (207-495-7766; www.yeatonfarminn.com), 298 West Rd., Belgrade 04917.

CASTLE ISLAND CAMPS

Christina Tree

This is a classic 1826 Federal-style house on a quiet road. Because it survived in the same family for so long, it retains its original windows and big kitchen hearth as well as detailing. A mother and daughter, both named Connie Parker, are the enthusiastic hosts, offering three bedrooms, each with fireplace, private bath, and air-conditioning. There's also a front parlor with a hearth and upright piano. The Belgrade Lake Golf Course is just up the road. $150 per couple includes a full breakfast and afternoon tea.

Among the Lakes Bed & Breakfast (207-465-4900; www.amongthelakes.com), 58 Smithfield Rd., Belgrade 04917. Open year-round. This is a handsome old house with five bright, comfortable guest rooms, offering a choice of king, queen, or single bed, private or shared bath, and air-conditioning. There's lake access. Polly Beatie and Sandy Famous actually live across the road. Breakfast is included in $120–140 per night.

FAMILY-GEARED SPORTING CAMPS

In the Belgrade Lakes region

Bear Spring Camps (207-397-2341; www.bearspringcamps.com), 60 Jamaica Point Rd., Rome 04957. Open mid-May–Sept. Ron and Peg Churchill run a very special family resort and fishing spot, set on 400 acres of woods and fields and in the family since 1910. Serious anglers come in early May for trout and pike, and in July there's still bass. The 32 cabins are strung along the shore of Great Pond, each with a bathroom, hot and cold water, a shower, heat, an open fireplace, dock, and motorboat. There's a tennis court, a golf driving range, and a variety of lawn games.

The swimming is great (the bottom is sandy). Meals are served in the big white farmhouse set a way back across open lawns from the lake. Weekly rates from $725–800 per couple include all meals; special children's and group rates.

Castle Island Camps (207-495-3312; in winter, 207-293-2266; www.castleislandcamps.com), P.O. Box 251, Belgrade Lakes 04918. Open May–Sept. John and Rhonda Rice are the owners of this great old family compound: a dozen comfortable cottages clustered on a small island (connected by bridges) in 12-mile Long Pond. Geared to fishing (the pond is stocked; rental boats are available). Three daily meals are served in the cozy central lodge, where guests also gather around an open fireplace, and in a recreation room with pool tables, table tennis, and darts. $75 per person double, $511 per week includes all meals; children's rates. No pets.

Alden Camps (207-465-7703; www.aldencamps.com), 3 Alden Camps Cove, Oakland 04963. Founded by A. Fred Alden in 1911 with just one rental unit, it's still in the family with 18 one- to three-bedroom log cabins with screened porch and woodstove or Franklin fireplace, scattered among the pines on the shores of East Pond. Meals are served in a wonderfully rambling old clapboard house with a big dining room, sitting area, and a long porch. Activities include fishing, golf nearby, swimming, waterskiing, boating, tennis, hiking, and several playing fields. Children are welcome, and pets can be accommodated for an extra fee. $79–163 per person per day, and $476–978 per person per week, includes all three meals.

COTTAGES In addition to the full-service, traditional "Maine Camps" listed above, many seasonal rentals are available. Check www.belgrade vacationrentals. com.

MOTEL **Best Western Senator Inn and Spa** (207-622-5804 or 1-877-772-2224; www.senatorinn.com), 284 Western Ave., Augusta 04330. A longtime gathering spot for Maine politicians, this property, with 125 guest rooms and suites, extends far back from the road and offers some amenities rarely found in motor inns—namely one of the area's best restaurants and a full-service spa featuring a glass-walled, Grecian-columned saltwater lap pool, hot tub, and fitness center (see *Dining Out* and *To Do*). Sited right off I-95 and minutes from the Maine State Museum and downtown Augusta, this is a surprisingly quiet, friendly, and relaxing place to stay. There are some genuinely attractive suites with fireplace, writing area, jetted tub, and fridge. You'll also find an inviting little bar. $89–259, depending on room and season. $9 per pet.

* Where to Eat

DINING OUT **Wings Hill Inn** (207-495-2400), Rt. 27, Belgrade Lakes Village. Open for dinner Thu.–Sun. year-round; seatings at 6 and 8. Reservations requested. Chef-owner Christopher Anderson and his wife, Tracey (who makes the desserts), trained at the Culinary Institute of America. Together they orchestrate seasonal five-course prix fixe menus served to a maximum of 16 diners seated in adjoining rooms. An evening's feast might begin with a walnut and feta pâté in a phyllo crust, moving on to curried chicken soup or gazpacho, a salad of greens or a small Caesar, and a choice of four entrées, among them excellent sea bass with chanterelles and leeks, a fantastic eggplant Parmesan, and rack of lamb. To finish, there is frozen Grand Marnier mousse or brown sugar crème brûlée. The menu changes every week. Service is friendly and fast, and tables are set off by themselves. Diners bring their own wine, served by the staff at the table (no corking fee); an 18 percent service fee is added to the $50 prix fixe bill.

Apollo's Bistro (207-872-2242) 91 Silver St., Waterville. Open for dinner Tue.–Sat., 5:30–11. Located on the second floor of a cupola-topped Victorian mansion—the first floor is occupied by a salon and spa under the same management—this restaurant's boast is that it uses locally grown ingredients when ever possible and cooks them slowly and carefully. Proprietor Keli Kenyon says she recently bought a plot of land so she could grow her own herbs. The imaginative menu might include pumpkin bisque with chèvre and walnut oil or crispy frogs legs for appetizers, entrées such as duck leg confit or hand-rolled goat cheese gnocchi; and desserts like pear tart with white chocolate cream and toasted almonds. Entrées $17–26.

Cloud 9 at the Senator Inn & Spa (207-622-5804), 284 Western Ave., Augusta. Open daily 6:30 AM–10 PM. Generally regarded as one of the best places to eat in the Augusta area, this restaurant has an attractive contemporary bistro decor. Maine crabcake, served at both lunch and dinner, is unusually light and tasty, and lobster is served up many ways. Dinner options include country chicken pie in a puff pastry, homemade penne with beef tenderloin, and freshly seared tuna Nicoise. Be warned: Portions are large. Most entrées also include the salad bar. Dinner entrées $16–28, with the shore dinner priced daily. Children's menu. The elaborate Sunday brunch buffet (11–2) is $16, free for children under five.

Slate's (207-622-4104; www.slatesrestaurant.com), 167 Water St., Hallowell. This hugely popular dining landmark was all but destroyed by fire in 2007 but its bakery survived (see *Eating Out*), and the restaurant is scheduled to open again in 2008 for breakfast, lunch, and dinner.

Freedom Café (207-859-8742; www.freedomcafeusa.com), 144 College Ave., Waterville. Open for dinner Wed.–Sat. at four seatings (5, 5:30, 7, and 7:30); reserve. One of central Maine's most unlikely and most popular restaurants. Both James Swinton and wife and executive chef Janice Swinton grew up in the deep south, he in Arkansas and she in Mississippi, and serve what they call "southern comfort food." This means dishes like pork chops with tasso milk gravy, creole fried tilapia with pineapple salsa, and pork ribs in a bourbon seasoned barbeque sauce. Entrées change weekly, sometimes daily, but all have southern roots. Desserts might be white chocolate bread pudding or carrot cake. The dining room has a colorfully eclectic decor. Entrées $19–22, including beverage and dessert. Children 6–10 are $7; under 5 eat free. Beer and wine are served. No credit cards.

The Bread Box Café (207-873-4090), 137 Main St., Waterville. Open for lunch and dinner Tue.–Fri., dinner Sat. Brick walled and dimly lit, good for luncheon sandwiches like hot turkey, Havarti, artichoke, roasted red pepper, and pesto on pumpernickel; grilled eggplant with chèvre, sweet red pepper, and pesto on a roll; or butternut squash ravioli with mascarpone cream. There's also a wide choice of salads. Dinner features salads and entrées such as char-grilled duck breast with apricot ginger glaze, or pan scallops and artichoke hearts tossed with white wine cream and angel-hair pasta. $18–25.

The Last Unicorn (207-873-6378), 8 Silver St., Waterville. Open daily 11–9, until 10 Fri. and Sat.; Sunday brunch until 2:30. Colorful and conveniently sited right off the central parking lot. There are usually 15 different dinner specials; soups, desserts, and most dressings and spreads are made here. The menu ranges from tortellini with mushrooms and cream sauce laced with sherry ($7.95 at lunch, $13.95 at dinner) to grilled beef tenderloin ($21.95).

Village Inn (207-495-3553), Rt. 27, Belgrade Lakes. Open Easter–mid-Oct., daily 5–9 in-season, Thurs.–Sun off-season. This is a rambling old dining landmark with a lake view and lot of atmosphere. The specialty is duckling, roasted for up to 12 hours and served with a choice of sauces, including brandied black cherry, Madagascar with green peppercorn and thai lemon grass. Entrées $16–30.

Heritage House Restaurant (207-474-5100; www.townemotel.com), 260 Madison Ave., Skowhegan. Open for lunch and dinner. Popular restaurant with a strong local following. The large menu always includes six fresh seafood entrées, such as sea scallops tempura with apricot mustard dip, medallions of beef with brandied mushroom sauce, and Cajun chicken breast with wine, lemon, capers, and mushrooms. Most entrees $10–20.

Lakewood Inn Restaurant (207-474-7176; www.lakewoodtheater.org), Rt. 201, Skowhegan. Open Memorial Day–mid-Oct., Tue.–Sat. for dinner plus a Sunday buffet brunch (10:30–2). This vintage-1925 inn served the likes of Humphrey Bogart and Vincent Price. It was on the verge of being razed when it was restored and reopened as an elegant restaurant—in time to celebrate the centennial year of the adjoining summer theater (see *Entertainment*). The à la carte menu ranges from vegetarian fettuccine Alfredo to rack of lamb and prime rib. $12.95 per person for the Sunday brunch buffet.

The Lobster Trap and Steakhouse (207-872-0529), 25 Bay St., Winslow. Open for lunch and dinner. The view of the river and the fresh fish at reasonable prices are what recommend this locally popular place. Fully licensed.

EATING OUT

In Augusta

Riverfront Barbeque & Grill (207-622-8899), 300 Water St. Open daily for lunch and dinner. Patrick Quigg's offshoot of the famous Bath restaurant, and considered by some the best: smoked chicken quesadilla, hickory-smoked ribs, daily-made soups with corn bread, chili, bayou pilaf, and more.

Java Joe's (207-622-1110), 287 Water St. Open weekdays 7 AM–2 PM. A cozy place with baked goods, an interesting lunch menu, and the usual coffee and espresso drinks.

Also see **Cloud 9 at the Senator**

Inn & Spa under *Dining Out*. It makes a reasonably priced bet for breakfast and lunch; also brick-oven pizza.

In Hallowell

Hattie's Chowder House (207-621-4114; www.hattieslobsterstew.com), 103 Water St. Open daily 11–9, Fri. and Sat. until 10. A small space with a big menu. Both chowder and fish are available to take home—and just about everyone around here does. Pick up chowder, a salad, or a sandwich and head for Vaughan Woods or to the bench by the river across the street.

Liberal Cup (207-623-2739), 115 Water St. Open for lunch and dinner, Fri. and Sat. until 10. Mid-Maine's only brewpub, noisy on the bar side, less so in the dining room. Half a dozen good brews (crafted here) on tap. Live music Thu.–Sat. evenings. Most menu items, including sandwiches, are served all day, along with shepherd's pie, fish-and-chips, and drunken pot roast.

Café de Bangkok (207-622-2638), 232 Water St. Just south of the village with river views, this is a highly respected local dining option. The menu includes the usual Tom Yum and miso soups, a soft-shell crispy crab salad with hot chili lime sauce on lettuce, "pad" and fried rice dishes. The chef's specials include crispy fried red snapper with ginger sauce and vegetables, and half a crispy roast duck with peanut sauce and steamed vegetables. Entrées $9–19. Lunch specials include a sushi combo.

THE A1 DINER

Kim Grant

Lucky Garden (207-622-3465), 218 Water St. A popular Chinese restaurant offering Mandarin, Szechuan, and Cantonese dishes. House specialties include General Tso's chicken, crispy shrimp, and Peking duck. Entrees $8–25. The dining room has a river view.

Slate's Bakery (207-622-4104), 169 Water St., is a good source of ready-made take-out sandwiches.

In Gardiner

The A1 Diner (207-582-4804; www.a1diner.com), 3 Bridge St. Open Mon.–Sat. for all three meals, brunch only on Sun. (8–1). A vintage-1946 Worcester diner with plenty of Formica, blue vinyl booths, blue and black tile, and a 14-stool, marble-topped counter. You won't find typical diner fare here, however. The breakfast menu includes banana almond French toast and a wide variety of omelets, as well as eggs and hash; there are always specials, superb soups (this time around we lunched on Tuscan minestrone), and chili. Lunch and dinner specials can include such entrées as adobe grilled pork and Moroccan stew. Beverages range from herbal tea to imported beers and wines. You can often get tapioca pudding, and the route to the restroom is still outside and in through the kitchen door.

A1 To Go Community Market and Café (207-582-5586), 347 Water St. Open Mon.–Fri. 7–6:30; Sat.7–5.

Next door to their famous diner, long-time owners Niel Andersen and Michael Giberson have added its antithesis, a trendy espresso-bar café featuring smoothies, panini, and wraps (try the crab, avocado, and scallions with pickled ginger, nori, and wasabi mayo!); also grilled wraps, soups, and salads. Dinners-to-go are a specialty, just the thing if you're heading for a cottage and don't want to cook when you get there. Wine, beer, and assorted gourmet items are also stocked.

In Waterville/Winslow
Jorgensen's Café (207-872-8711), 103 Main St., Waterville. An inviting café with at least a dozen flavored coffees, as well as tea and espresso choices. The deli serves quiche, soups, salads, and sandwiches. Coffee and tea supplies.

Also see **The Bread Box** and **The Last Unicorn** in *Dining Out*, good lunch options.

In Belgrade Lakes
♿ **The Sunset Grille** (207-495-2439), 4 West Rd., Belgrade Lakes Village. Open year-round, Mon–Thurs.7–9, Fri.–Sat. 7–midnight. Hopping in the summer, casual family fare served waterside. Saturday-evening karaoke.

Lakeside Country Market (207-465-7474), 533 Belgrade Road, Oakland. Lobsters and steamers are available, live or cooked. Also, locally famous for massive sandwiches: small is six inches long; large, a foot. Open daily year-round.

In Skowhegan
Old Mill Pub (207-474-6627), 41-R Water St., Skowhegan. Open daily for lunch and dinner. It's just where you may want to stop en route: a picturesque old mill building set back from the main drag with a seasonal deck overlooking a gorge in the Kennebec, with views downriver as well as of the dam. A friendly bar and scattered tables; sandwiches (a good Reuben), quiche, and specials for lunch; spinach lasagna or stir-fried shrimp for dinner; music on Fri. and Sat.

Empire Grill (207-374-3440), 105 Water St., Skowhegan.Open weekdays 6 AM–8 PM, weekends 6 AM–3 PM. Re-created as a stage set for Empire Falls, this is a classic '50s diner with an eight-stool counter, good coffee and food. Specials on the day we stopped by included kale soup.

Gifford's Ice Cream (207-474-2257; www.giffordsicecream.com), Upper Madison Ave. (Rt. 201 north; look for the big plastic moose), Skowhegan. Proudly served throughout Maine, century-old, family-owned Gifford's is made in Skowhegan, and this is its prime local outlet, a classic ice cream stand, serving 50 flavors, including Lobster Tracks and Maine Birch Bark in cones, cups, parfaits, frappes, sodas, more. Limited picnic tables out back overlook a mini-golf course.

In Winthrop
✐ **Sully's** (207-377-5663), Main St. Open Mon.–Sat. for lunch and dinner, Sun. dinner noon–7. Set back from Main St. with plenty of parking to accommodate its local following. Salads as well as burgers and sandwiches for lunch, seafood dishes, like a seafood medley that includes lobster and salad; liver and onions and an old-fashioned roast turkey dinner ($9.99).

✷ Entertainment

LIVE PERFORMANCES ✐ **Theater at Monmouth** (207-933-2952; www

.theateratmonmouth.org), Main St., Monmouth. Open May–Oct.; Thu.–Sun. in shoulder season, Wed.–Sun. in July, Tue.–Sun. in Aug. Housed in Cumston Hall, a striking turn-of-the-20th-century building designed as a combination theater, library, and town hall. A resident nonprofit company specializes in Shakespeare but also presents contemporary shows throughout the season. Tickets $20–26.

Lakewood Theater (207-474-7176; www.lakewoodtheater.org), off Rt. 201, 6 miles north of Skowhegan on Lake Wesserunsett, billed as America's Oldest Summer Theater, a resident company performs Memorial Day through mid-Sept, Thur.–Sat. at 8, alternate Sundays and Wednesday matinees. The Lakewood Jesters stage morning performances for children.

Waterville Opera House (207-873-7000; www.operahouse.org), 93 Main St., Waterville, presents a number of shows throughout the year, including music performances and theater productions. It's also a prime venue for the ten-day Maine International Film Festival (see *Film*).

Gaslight Theater (207-626-3698; www.gaslighttheater.org), City Hall Auditorium, Hallowell. This community theater stages productions throughout the year.

Johnson Hall Performing Arts Center (207-582-7144; www.johnsonhall.org), 280 Water St., Gardiner. A restored historic space where workshops, dances, and other performances occur frequently.

FILM **Maine International Film Festival** (207-861-8138; www.miff.org) 177 Maine St., Waterville. In existence for more than a decade, this week-long, mid-July festival has evolved into a major event screening scores of films from around the world—although always including some made in Maine—and attracting noted actors, directors, and screenwriters as speakers and lecturers. Tickets to individual screenings are $8, a full festival pass good for admission to all screenings and special events, such as awards ceremonies, is $150.

Railroad Square Cinema (207-873-4021; www.railroadsquarecinema.com), Main St., Waterville. From I-95 exit 130 head toward downtown; turn left between Burger King and the railroad tracks. Art and foreign films, and mid-July home of the Maine International Film Festival.

Skowhegan Drive-in (207-474-9277), Rt. 201 south. A genuine 1950s drive-in with nightly double features "under the stars" in July and August weekends in June.

Strand Cinema (207-474-3451), Court St., Skowhegan. A 1929 jewel, recently, lovingly revamped with nightly films, reasonable prices.

✱ Selective Shopping

ANTIQUES SHOPS A dozen antiques stores cluster in Hallowell, each with a different specialty. **Brass and Friends** (207-626-3287), 154 Water St. (look for the gargoyles atop the building) is a large trove of antique lighting fixtures. **Josiah Smith Antiques** (207-622-4188), 101 Second St., specializes in Asian and British ceramics and early glass. **Johnson-Marsano Antiques** (207-623-6263), 172 Water St., sells Victorian, art deco, and estate jewelry.

Fairfield Antiques Mall (207-453-

4100; www.fairfieldantiquesmall.com). Rt. 201, Hinckley. Open daily 8:30–5, with three floors of antiques under one roof, the largest group shop in central Maine.

Hilltop Antiques (1-800-899-6987), 52 Water St., Skowhegan. Two floors (16 rooms) filled with "fresh picked merchandise."

ART GALLERIES **Kennebec Valley Art Association/Harlow Gallery** (207-622-3813), 160 Water St., Hallowell. A cooperative, good-quality gallery.

BOOKSTORES **Barnes & Noble Booksellers** (207-621-0038), the Marketplace at Augusta, directly across from the Augusta Civic Center. A full-service bookstore with music and computer software sections, as well as a café.

Mr. Paperback (207-873-3935) 13 Elm Plaza, Upper Main St., Waterville. Open Mon.–Sat. 9–9; Sunday 9–5. One of a chain of bookstores in central and northern Maine that despite the name also carries hardback books along with cards, magazines, and gifts.

Apple Valley Books (207-377-3967; www.applevalleybooks.com), 121 Main St., Winthrop. Rita Moran and Eric Robbins run a welcoming full-service bookstore, stocking used as well as new titles.

Re-Books (207-877-2484; www.re-books.com) 25 East Concourse, Waterville. A wide variety of used books, including collectibles.

✐ **Children's Book Cellar** (207-872-4543), 52 Main St., Waterville. Good selection of kids books.

Merrill's Bookshop (207-623-2055), 134 Water St., second floor, Hallowell. This is an antiquarian bookshop among antiquarian bookshops. Some 30,000 titles include many odd and unusual volumes. Particular emphasis on Americana, Maine books, history—including a large Civil War collection—and literature. There is also a room filled with books for a buck.

RiverBooks, 111 Water St., Hallowell. Open 8–6 Mon.–Sat, 12–5 Sun. A quirky little street-level bookstore so narrow and book-packed patrons have to go single file. There is an interesting selection of reasonably priced books, most used but with some new regional titles. Also, books in foreign languages, including Estonian. (Did we mention that this is a quirky bookstore?)

SPECIAL STORES **Brahms Mount Textiles** (207-623-5277; www.brahmsmount.com), 19 Central St., Hallowell. Open weekdays 9–5. Inquire about special sales. The former Bodwell Granite Works holds the antique looms that weave the textiles here, and the showroom displaying exceptional linen and "personal blankets" designed and woven by Claudia Brahms and Noel Mount. Nationally respected through catalog and wholesale distribution, the shop usually has seconds and specials.

Reny's (207-582-4012), 185 Water St., Gardiner, and at 73 Main St. in Madison. Open weekdays 9–5:30, Fri. until 8, Sat. 9–5, Sun. 10–4. Don't pass up this amazing Maine discount department store, good for quality clothing and shoes, for peanut butter, art supplies, and an range of everything in between.

Marden's Discount Store (207-873-6112), 458 Kennedy Memorial Dr.,

Waterville. Maine's salvage and surplus chain with ten stores. The Waterville outlet is well worth checking.

New Balance Outlet Store (207-474-6231; www.newbalance.com), 13 Walnut St., Skowhegan. Rt. 201, south of the bridge. Open Mon.–Sat. 9–6, Sun. 11–5. Housed in a former school, this is a major outlet with a wide selection of athletic gear as well as shoes made in town.

The Green Spot (207-465-7242), Kennedy Memorial Dr., Oakland. Open May–Columbus Day, daily 9–7; closed Tue. A quarter mile or so west of I-95 look for a small yellow store on the left. Locally loved as a source of amazing daily fresh breads, organic produce, fine wines, and terrific deli items, Tanya and Brenda Athanus's small store on the way from Waterville to Oakland is well worth seeking out.

Johnny's Selected Seeds (207-861-3900; www.johnnyseeds.com), 955 Benton Ave., Winslow. Open Mon.–Sat. in-season, selective days off-season. A catalog seed company with more than 2,000 varieties.

The Potter's House (207-582-7985, www.thepottershouse.com), 82 Stevenstown Rd., Litchfield. Mary K. and Jeff Spencer produce outstanding handcrafted and hand-decorated pottery.

Cobbossee Coffee Company, 134 Main St., Winthrop (207-377-2208), Named for a 9-mile-long local lake (said to be the third largest in Maine), this company roasts its coffee in Winthrop and sells it in the retail shop.

✱ Special Events

June–July: During its nine-week sessions the prestigious **Skowhegan School of Painting and Sculpture** (207-474-9345) sponsors a lecture series on weekday evenings that's free and open to the public.

July: The **Whatever Family Festival** (*week preceding the Fourth of July*), Capitol Park—children's performances, soapbox derby, Learn the River Day, entertainment, carnival, and more. **Maine International Film Festival** (*midmonth*) in Waterville. **Old Hallowell Day** (*third weekend*)—parade and fireworks, crafts and games. **Pittston Fair**, Pittston. **Intown Arts Fetival** in Waterville (over 90 artists along Main St.)

August: **Windsor Fair**, Windsor; **Monmouth Fair**, Monmouth; **Skowhegan State Fair**, one of the oldest and biggest fairs in New England—harness racing, a midway, agricultural exhibits, big-name entertainment, tractor and oxen pulls. **China Community Days,** China. Public supper, fishing derby, scavenger hunt.

September: **Oosoola Fun Day**, Norridgewock, includes the state's oldest frog-jumping contest (up to 300 contestants) around a frog-topped totem pole; also canoe races, crafts fair, flower and pet contests, live music, barbecue. **Litchfield Fair**, Litchfield. **Common Ground Country Fair**, Unity, a celebration of rural living sponsored by the Maine Organic Farmers and Gardeners Association (www.mofga.org; also see *What's Where*).

THE UPPER KENNEBEC VALLEY AND MOOSE RIVER VALLEY

INCLUDING THE FORKS AND JACKMAN

By rights this upper stretch of the Kennebec Valley and certainly the Moose River Valley belong in the "Northern Maine" section of this book, but the Kennebec is a classic north–south corridor, linking northern woodland with mid-Maine mills and farms. Solon, with its steepled meetinghouse, still seems a part of the long-settled valley, but Bingham, just 8 miles north, has the feel of the woodland hub that it is.

The 78-mile stretch of Rt. 201 north from Solon to the Canadian border is now officially The Old Canada Road Scenic Byway, with a granite marker and an evolving visitors center at its gateway on Robbins Hill. From this rise the valley rolls away north to the distant, blue peaks of Sugarloaf and the Bigelow Range. Along the way interpretive panels at five more scenic way stops tell the story of this magnificent but haunting valley.

The Kennebec River itself rises in Moosehead Lake and flows south, as did most 19th-century traffic along this route. More than a million French Canadian and Irish families came looking for work in New England logging camps, farms, and factories. This stretch of Rt. 201 is now also a link in the 233-mile Kennebec-Chaudiere International Corridor, stretching from Quebec City to Bath. Whatever its titles, this remains a busy, twisty, two-lane road and traffic flows both ways far too quickly. It's also frequented by both lumber trucks and lumbering moose. Drive carefully!

Once upon a time, the river was the highway. For more than 140 years beginning in 1835, logs were floated down from the woods to the mills. Then in 1976 fishing guide Wayne Hockmeyer discovered the rush of riding the whitewater through dramatic 12-mile-long Kennebec Gorge, deep in the woods, miles northeast of Rt. 201. On that first ride Hockmeyer had to contend with logs hurtling all around him, but as luck would have it, 1976 also marked the year in which environmentalists managed to outlaw log drives on the Kennebec.

Thirteen rafting companies presently vie for space to take advantage of up to 8,000 cubic feet of water per second released every morning from late spring through mid-October from the Harris Hydroelectric Station. In and around **The**

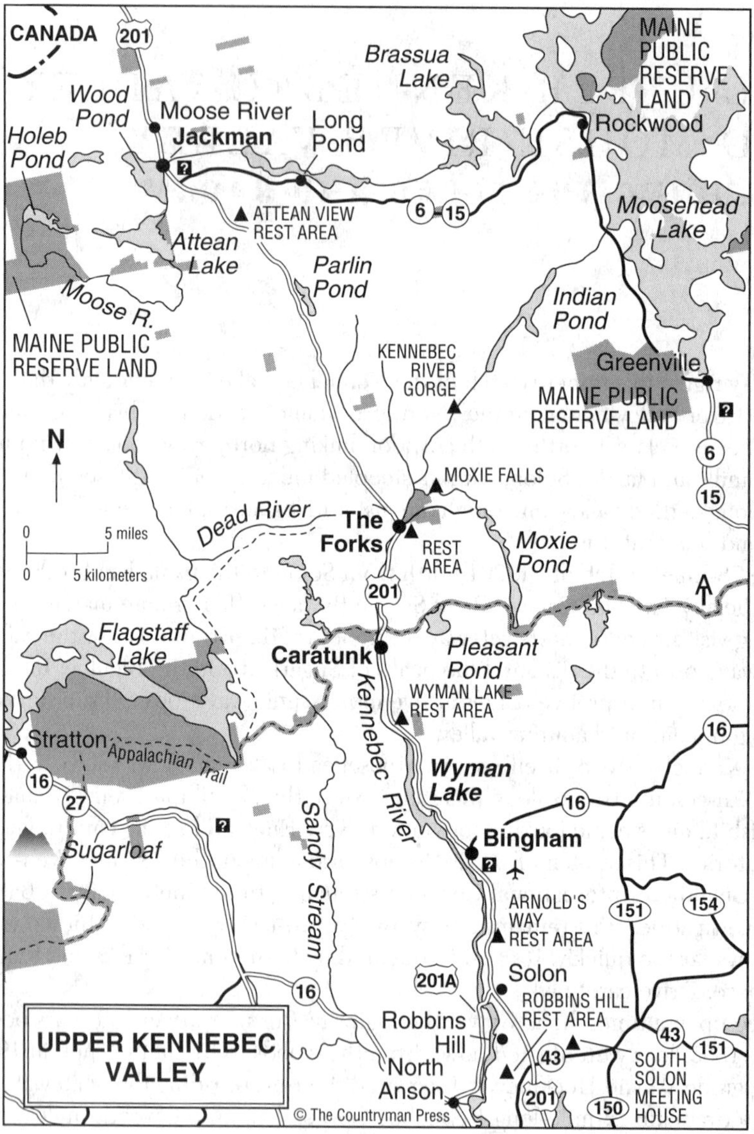
UPPER KENNEBEC VALLEY
CANADA
201
Wood Pond
Moose River
Jackman
Holeb Pond
Long Pond
Brassua Lake
MAINE PUBLIC RESERVE LAND
Rockwood
Moosehead Lake
6
15
ATTEAN VIEW REST AREA
Attean Lake
Parlin Pond
Moose R.
MAINE PUBLIC RESERVE LAND
Indian Pond
Greenville
MAINE PUBLIC RESERVE LAND
KENNEBEC RIVER GORGE
N
MOXIE FALLS
0
5 miles
0
5 kilometers
Dead River
The Forks
REST AREA
Moxie Pond
Flagstaff Lake
Caratunk
Pleasant Pond
WYMAN LAKE REST AREA
Kennebec River
Stratton
Appalachian Trail
16
27
Sandy Stream
Wyman Lake
Bingham
Sugarloaf
ARNOLD'S WAY REST AREA
151
154
201A
Solon
ROBBINS HILL REST AREA
Robbins Hill
43
SOUTH SOLON MEETING HOUSE
North Anson
150
© The Countryman Press

Forks, a community (pop. 60) at the confluence of the Kennebec and Dead Rivers, whitewater rafting has spawned extensive lodging and dining facilities that also cater to snowmobilers, hunters, hikers, and travelers passing through—many of whom spend an extra day or two here once they discover the accessibility of this valley's waterfalls and summits, its remote ponds for fishing and kayaking, and its woods roads for bicycling.

Empty as it seemed when rafting began, this stretch of the Upper Kennebec was a 19th-century resort area. A 100-room, four-story Forks Hotel was built in 1860, and the 120-room Lake Parlin Lodge soon followed. Caratunk, The Forks, and Jackman were all railroad stops and "rusticators" came to fish, hike, and view natural wonders, like 90-foot Moxie Falls. Increasingly whitewater rafting outfitters are styling themselves "adventure companies," offering present-day rusticators a choice of rock climbing, moose safaris, bicycle and kayak rentals, and more.

Bingham (pop. 1,200), 23 miles south of the Forks, is the only sizeable town in Upper Kennebec Valley. It's the obvious stop for road food. Just north of town a 155-foot-high hydro-dam walls back up the river, raising it more than 120 feet and creating wide, shimmering 13-mile long Wyman Lake.

At The Forks, Rt. 201 itself forks off from the Kennebec River, heading northwest through lonely but beautiful woodland. The Parlin Pond pull-out is aptly about moose. Don't fail to stop at the Attean View Rest Area south of Jackman, with its spectacular panorama and panels devoted to 19th-century migration.

Jackman and **Moose River** form a community (divided by a short bridge) on Big Wood Lake. In warm weather you notice that something is missing here and don't realize what it is unless you revisit in winter. It's snow. Winter is actually high-season. Snow softens the severity of this shrunken old border community with its outsized French Canadian Catholic church. Named for the man who built the Canada Road from the border down to The Forks, Jackman boomed after the Canadian Pacific Railroad arrived in 1888, setting the lumbering industry into high gear.

Most of Jackman's mills have disappeared, but this former rail junction is now a major hub of Maine's snowmobiling network and 400 miles of ATV trails. With restaurants and reasonably priced camps, it's also a base for exceptional canoeing and kayaking.

To stay in Maine turn off Rt. 201 onto Rt. 15/6, a lonely 31-mile road that follows the Moose River east to Moosehead Lake. Otherwise it's a roughly three-hour drive from Jackman to Quebec City.

GUIDANCE **Upper Kennebec Valley Chamber of Commerce** (207-672-4100; www.upperkennebecvalley.com) maintains an information center at 356 Main St. (Rt. 201) in Bingham Village, open year-round, weekdays 9–3 and on weekends when volunteers are available. Displays evoke local history. This building also houses offices for the **Old Canada Road National Scenic Byway** (207-672-3971). For more about the Kennebec-Chaudiere International Corridor see www.kennebec-chaudiere.com (1-800-782-6497). Inquire about "Deep Woods and River Roads," the audio tour of Rt. 201 in Maine.

Jackman-Moose River Region Chamber of Commerce (207-668-4171 or 1-888-633-5225; www.jackmanmaine.org) maintains the region's best Web site and a Rt. 201 welcome center near the lakeside town park (rest rooms).

GETTING THERE *By car:* The obvious route from points south and west is I-95 to exit 133, then Rt. 201 north all the way to The Forks. The approach from the Rangeley and Sugarloaf areas, Rt. 16, is also a beautiful drive.

WHEN TO COME Whitewater rafting and fishing commence in April, but we prefer paddling in warmer months. June is buggy. July through mid-October are glorious with fall bringing plenty of color. Hikers should check the "seasons" described under *Hunting*. Snow usually begins in November but has been more plentiful in recent years during late February and March.

✷ To See

Listed south to north along Rt. 201

Note: See the **L. C. Bates Museum**, the **Margaret Chase Smith Library Center**, and the **South Solon Meetinghouse** in the previous chapter's *To See*; all are rewarding stops along Rt. 201 south of Solon.

Old Canada Road rest areas have with interpretative panels (and outhouses). Just north of the junction with Rt. 43 look for **Robbins Hill**, described in the chapter intro. In 2008 it offers picnic shelters, and a visitors center is planned. At **Arnold's Way Rest Area**, on the Bingham town line, panels chronicle the 1775 saga of Colonel Benedict Arnold and his more than 1,000 men traveling this way in a heroic but luckless attempt to capture Quebec. The **Lake Wyman Rest Area** is a pine-shaded and carpeted lakeside spot with picnic tables; panels tell of Indian habitation and the 1932 creation of the lake. **The Forks** pullout is just below the bridge at the actual fork in the river. Panels describe 19th-century lumbering and river runs and logging trucks rumble over the bridge.

Moxie Falls (90 feet high) is said to be the highest falls in New England. From The Forks rest area on Rt. 201, it's 1.8 miles down Lake Moxie Rd. to the parking area. An easy 0.6-mile trail leads to the falls. The pools below are a popular swimming hole.

More Old Canada Road rest areas: Note the pullout at **Parlin Pond**, one of the spots you are most likely to see moose, the subject of its interpretive panels. **Attean View**, the next pullout is a must-see. The view is splendid: Attean Lake and the whole string of ponds linked by the Moose River, with the western mountains as a backdrop. There are picnic tables. Note the trail leading to **Owl's Head** (see *Hiking*).

MOXIE FALLS

Northern Outdoors

Jackman-Moose River Historical Museum, Main St., Jackman. Open Memorial Day–late Sept., Fri. 1–4, more often, volunteers permitting. Housed in a former town hall (with rest rooms), displays convey a sense of this outpost area; note the prisoner-of-war camp once sited on Parlin Pond.

✷ To Do

AIR TOURS **Jackman Air Tours** (207-668-4461), 7 Attean Rd., Jackman. Jim Schoenmann offers scenic air tours of the entire area.

ATVS This is a mecca for people who love to ride their all-terrain vehicles, with 400 miles of trails. Bingham and Jackman are both hubs. Rentals are available from **Northern Rivers** (see *Whitewater Rafting*) in Bingham.

BIKING AND MOUNTAIN BIKING Local terrain varies from old logging roads to tote paths. Rentals are available from many rafting outfitters (see *Whitewater Rafting*). A 7-mile multiuse (ATV/walking/biking) trail now follows the old rail bed along the Kennebec from Solon to Bingham. Check out www.jackmanmaine.org for descriptions (North Country in Bingham rents bikes). The 16.8-mile road from Pleasant Pond to Moxie Falls is also a favorite among bicyclists. Jackman claims to have one of the most extensive mountain bike trail systems in Maine.

BOAT EXCURSIONS Northern Outdoors (see *Whitewater Rafting*) offers a three-hour pontoon boat cruise on Wyman Lake, heading south from their Lakeside Resort Center, passing an active eagle nest on an island, and stopping for swim below 35-foot-high Houston Brook Falls. Must be age 8 or older.

CANOEING AND KAYAKING **The Moose River Bow Trip** is a Maine classic: A series of pristine ponds forms a 34-mile meandering route that winds back to the point of origin, eliminating the need for a shuttle. The fishing is fine, 21 remote campsites are scattered along the way, and the put-in is accessible. One major portage is required. Canoe rentals are available from a variety of local sources. Several rafting companies rent canoes and offer guided trips, but the kayaking specialists here are Registered Maine Guides Andy and Leslie McKendry at **Cry of the Loon Outdoor Adventures** (207-668-7808; www.cryoftheloon.net) east of Jackman, who offer a fully-outfitted and guided Moose River Bow Trip as well as one- to seven-day tours throughout northwestern Maine. They also offer canoe and kayak rentals and shuttle services. In Bingham **Riverside Inn** rents kayaks for a lazy paddle downstream to Solon and shuttle back. Most whitewater outfitters rent kayaks and/or stable "funyaks."

FISHING Fishing is what the sporting camps (see *Lodging*) are all about. The catch is landlocked salmon, trout, and togue. Rental boats and canoes are readily available. Camps also supply guides, and a number of them are listed on the Jackman chamber's Web site.

GOLF **Moose River Golf Course** (207-668-5331), Rt. 201, Moose River (just north of Jackman). Mid-May–mid-Oct.; club rental, putting green, nine holes.

HIKING *Note:* **The Appalachian Trail (AT)** crosses Rt. 201 in Caratunk and climbs Pleasant Pond Mountain (below). It also crosses the Kennebec River here, and Steve Longley runs the **Appalachian Trail Ferry Service** (207-663-4441; www.riversandtrails.com) to get hikers across safely. His **Ferryman's Store** (1603 Rt. 201) is a source of local hiking info.

Maine Huts & Trails (www.mainehuts.org) The first 36-miles of an evolving 180-mile hiking/mountain-biking/skiing trail runs from from Flagstaff Lake (north of Sugarloaf) along the Dead River to The Forks. The first of three staffed, full-service huts opens in 2008. Plans call for the trail to continue east to Mooshead Lake.

Pleasant Pond Mountain in Caratunk. With an open ledge peak at 2,477 feet, the view is 360 degrees. It's a one-and-a-half-hour hike. Turn east off Rt. 201 at the Maine Forest Service Station in Caratunk and head toward Pleasant Pond on the road across from the post office and general store. At the fork (with Pleasant Pond in view), bear left. The pavement ends, the road narrows, and at 5 miles from the post office take Fire Lane 13 on the right. The trail begins on the left just beyond the AT lean-to.

Coburn Mountain is the site of the former Enchanted Mountain ski area. The gravel access road off Rt. 201 begins about 10 miles north of Berry's Store. The Forks snowmobile club maintains a trail to the summit of the mountain, along the old ski area service road. At 3,750 feet, it's the highest groomed snowmobile trail in Maine and can be hiked in summer. The 360-degree view from the open summit and its tower includes Mount Katahdin (68 miles to the northeast) and Sugarloaf Mountain (30 miles southwest).

Owls Head, Jackman. A 0.75-mile hike begins at the Attean View pullout on Rt. 201 (see *To See*) south of Jackman Village. This is one of Maine's most amazing easily accessible panoramas, stretching all the way to the Canadian border and encompassing Big Wood Lake, Slide Down Mountain, and Spencer Valley. The trail begins at the north end of the picnic area.

Moxie Falls is the area's easiest and most famous hike (see *To See*).

HUNTING Deer seasons runs from late Oct. through Nov. Moose hunting usually begins the second week in October (by permit only); bears are hunted Aug.–Nov. and partridge Oct.–Dec.

MOOSE-WATCHING The best time to see a moose is at dawn or dusk. Favorite local moose crossings include Moxie Rd. from The Forks to Moxie Pond; the Central Maine Power Company road from Moxie Pond to Indian Pond; the 25 miles north from The Forks to Jackman on Rt. 201; and the 30 miles from Jackman to Rockwood on Rt. 6/15. Drive these stretches carefully; residents all know someone who has died in a car–moose collision. Moose Safaris are offered May–Oct. by most outfitters.

✱ Winter Sports

SNOWMOBILING Snowmobiling is huge in this region, with The Forks serving as a hub for more than 150 miles of the Interconnecting Trail System (ITS) over

WHITEWATER RAFTING

The 12-mile run down the **Kennebec River** from Harris Dam begins with 4 miles of Class II and IV rapids—notably Magic Falls, though this comes early in the trip—and after that it's all fun. The slightly more challenging run on the **Dead River**, available less often (releases are less frequent) is also offered by most outfitters. The safety records for all outfitters are excellent, or they wouldn't be in this rigorously monitored business.

Basics: Apr.–Oct. rates include a river ride and a chance to view (and buy) slides of the day's adventures. The minimum suggested age is 10 on the Upper Kennebec and 8 on the lower section, compared with 15 on the Dead River.

River trips begin between 7 and 9 and end between 3 and 4. Obviously it makes sense to spend the night before at your outfitter's base camp, hence our attempt to describe what's available.

Variables: The time of the morning put-in, whether you eat along the river or back at camp afterward, the size and nature of the group you will be rafting with, and the comfort level of the lodging. Note that some outfitters are on lakes or ponds, good for kayaking and canoeing. Some outfitters also offer additional activities: overnight camping trips, rock climbing, and more.

Note: Children, seniors, and others who want to experience smaller rapids can join the trip later in the day. Midweek trips are generally more family-geared. Weekends draw a younger, wilder crowd.

Raft Maine (1-800-723-8633; www.raftmaine.com) offers a good Web site and represents a number of outfitters.

Note: Although whitewater rafting began as a big singles sport, it's becoming more and more popular with families, who frequently combine it with a visit to Quebec City. Minimum age requirements vary, but weight is often a consideration (usually no less than 90 pounds). We identify the outfitters who cater to kids or who offer Lower Kennebec trips geared to children as young as .

Northern Outdoors, Inc. (207-663-4466 or 1-800-765-7238; www.northernoutdoors.com). Open year-round. The first and still the biggest outfitter on the Kennebec, now with two distinct bases—**Forks Resort Center** and **Lakeside Resort Center**—with a total of 350 beds year-round plus 100 campsites in summer. The Forks Center is an open-timbered lodge with high ceilings, a huge hearth, comfortable seating, a cheerful dining room, along with a major brewpub, pool, private pond, platform tennis,

RAFTING THE KENNEBEC

Northern Outdoors

volleyball, basketball, sauna, and giant hot tub. Accommodations range from riverside camping to lakeside cabins, from lodge rooms to "logdominiums" (condo-style units with lofts and a kitchen/dining area). The 30-acre Lakeside Resort Center (30 Wyman Lake, 3.5 miles south of the Forks Center) has six guest houses (sleeping up to 10 people) and four luxury rental houses (leather furniture, queen-sized beds, decks). Amenities include an outdoor Jacuzzi, sand volleyball, a dining pavilion, kayak rentals, and pontoon boat cruises. The base lodge has changing rooms, showers, and access to Wyman Lake for boating, fishing, and kayaking. Northern Outdoors also offers float trips, fishing trips, rock climbing, a ropes course, and lake kayak touring. Inquire about "family camps," where children as young as 8 are welcome. In winter the lodge caters to snowmobilers with snowmobile rentals and guided tours. $72–129 for a one-day raft trip. Kids half-price in July and Aug.

✐ **Crab Apple White Water** (207-663-4491 or 1-800-553-7238; www.crabappleinc.com), 3 Lake Moxie Rd., The Forks 04985. A family-owned and -geared outfitter with a base camp that offers eight luxury suites (with wet bar, fridge, Jacuzzi, and deck); also four cottages accommodating four to eight people in bunk-style rooms, six motel units, and a large lodge with a restaurant right in The Forks. "Funyaks" (inflatable kayaks) and half-day float trips are also offered. Rafting/lodging packages are $126–201 per person. Inquire about winter snowmobile rentals and packages.

✐ **Magic Falls Rafting** (207-663-2220 or 1-800-207-7238; www.magicfalls.com), P.O. Box 9, West Forks 04985, has a riverside base camp that includes a pleasant B&B (four rooms), cabin tents, and campsites on the banks of the Dead River in The Forks. **Dead River Lodge**, a new facility at the base camp, has king and queen rooms, each with half-bath, deck, and a living room with big-screen TV. In addition to rafting they offer "funyaks" (inflatable kayaks) and

mountains, rivers, and lakes and through woods with connections to the Rangeley and Moosehead areas, and to Canada (for which trail passes must be purchased). Rentals and guided trips are available from most major rafting companies. Also check with the **Jackman Region Chamber of Commerce** (see *Guidance*) Sled rental prices run around $150 per day single, $175 double, plus insurance.

✱ Lodging

SPORTING CAMPS While these camps were originally geared exclusively to fishermen, they now also welcome families and hikers.

🐾 ✐ **Cobb's Pierce Pond Camps** (in summer, 207-628-2819; in winter, 207-628-3612), North New Portland 04961. Open from ice-out to Oct. 1. Twelve guest cabins accommodate two

rock climbing. Rafting $69–99; rafting/lodging packages $117–154 per person.

Moxie Outdoor Adventures (1-800-866-6943; www.moxierafting.com), HC 63, Box 60, The Forks 04985. This long-established outfitter is based in a set of traditional cabins on Lake Moxie, offering camping, platform tents, and cabin lodging, specializing in two- and three-day canoe trips as well as rafting. Two nights with rafting and four meals is $199 per person in a cabin, substantially less if camping.

Windfall Rafting (207-668-4818 or 1-800-683-2009; www.raftwindfall.com), Rt. 201, P.O. Box 505, Jackman 04945. Based in a classic 1890s schoolhouse in Moose River (just north of downtown Jackman), Windfall has been in business one way or another since 1982. Tim Blake books you into the gamut of what's available; he also offers inflatable-kayak trips on the Kennebec's East Outlet.

Adventure Bound (1-888-606-7238; www.adv-bound.com), The Forks 04985. An offshoot of Northern Outdoors, this is an entirely separate family- and kids-geared outfitter. Facilities include an outdoor pool, indoor climbing wall, and ice cream bar. It has its own base lodge and cabin-tent village.

Professional River Runners (1-800-325-3911; www.proriverrunners.com), P.O. Box 92, West Forks 04985. The specialty is overnight trips, beginning with a run down the East Outlet and campout the night before you run the Kennebec. We were lucky enough to see a spectacular display of the northern lights on our trip, and the campfire food was outstanding. Accommodations are at the **Grand View B&B**, or in one- and two-bedroom condos and a cottage.

North Country Rivers/Maine Whitewater (1-800-348-8871; www.northcountryrivers.com). The former Maine Whitewater base in Bingham is on 60 acres with camping and RV sites, platform tents and basic new log cabins, also a very basic base lodge and a private airport on the riverside grounds. $124–154 per person for rafting/cabin lodging package in-season.

to eight people; each has a screened porch, woodstove, bathroom, and electricity. Home-cooked meals and between-meal snacks are served in the main lodge. This traditional sporting camp dates to 1902, and the Cobb family has been running it for more than 50 years; 90 percent of their guests are repeats. It's the kind of place that doesn't advertise. It has a loyal following among serious anglers; sand beaches nearby. Guiding services available. $105 per person, $192 per couple per day includes three meals; children's rates. Dogs, $15 per day.

Attean Lake Lodge (207-668-3792; www.atteanlodge.com), Jackman 04945. Open Memorial Day weekend–Sept. Sited on Birch Island in Attean Lake, surrounded by mountains, you can get to this resort on their water shuttle. It has been in the Holden family since 1900. The 15 log cabins, luxurious by sports lodge standards, have with full bath, Franklin fireplace, kerosene lamps, and maid service daily. There is a relatively new central lodge (the old one burned) with a dining room overlooking the lake. Fishing boats, kayaks, and canoes are available. $250–300 per couple includes meals; children's rates and weekly rates available; 13 percent service charge added.

OTHER LODGING "1" 🐾 ✐ **Riverside Inn** (207-672-3215), 178 Main St (Rt. 201), P.O. Box 65, Bingham 04920. Maine natives Scott and Vicki Stanchfield have transformed this century-old riverside lodge into an appealing place to stay with eight guest rooms (four shared baths). They've restored the hardwood floors and reopened the wood-burning fireplaces in the twin parlors. Every room has a TV, but there's also of shared space and guests tend to mingle over evening cheese and crackers or later, samosas around the fire pit while Scott strums his guitar. The backyard is fitted with croquet and horseshoes, but Scott urges guests to get out and hike to local beauty spots. He also rents kayaks and offers shuttles from Solon. $60 per room with coffee and muffins. At **Here's the Scoop**, their seasonal snack bar, the Stanchfields serve steamed hot dogs, wraps, and Gifford's ice cream.

Inn by the River (207-663-2181; www.innbytheriver.com), 2777 Rt. 201, The Forks Plantation 04985. Open seasonally. As we go to press this contemporary lodging, built to resemble a 19th century inn, is about to be sold. Well worth checking.

Kennebec Riverside Cabins (1-866-787-7433; www.krcabins.com), Rt. 201, P.O. Box 123, The Forks 04985. Melissa Howes, a Registered Maine Guide when she's not working as an airport controller at Bangor International, has rehabbed five century-old, literally riverside one- and two-bedroom housekeeping cabins across from the Marshall Inn in the middle of The Forks. $140 for up to four people, $35 per extra person (each cabin sleeps 2–8).

🐾 **Sally Mountain Cabins** (207-668-5621 or 1-800-644-5621; www.sallymtcabins.com), 9 Elm St., Jackman 04945. Open year-round. Sited at the end of a quiet street, right on Big Moose Lake, basic but cheerful housekeeping cabins with cable TV, each accommodate two to five people. As many as 10 can stay in larger condo-style units across the street. $30 per person per night, $180 per person per week. Age 4 and under and pets free. Inquire about rental boats, canoes, and ice-fishing shacks.

🐾 ♿ **Cedar Ridge Outfitters** (207-668-4169; www.cedarridgeoutfitters.com), 3 Cedar Ridge Dr., P.O. Box 744, Jackman 04945. Registered Maine Guides Hal and Debbie Blood have been steadily expanding this serious hunting operation. Sited on a quiet road are seven two- and three-bedroom housekeeping cabins with TV, VCR, and phone. Amenities include hot tubs and a heated swimming pool; "adventure packages" include fishing, hunting, guided snowmobiling, and whitewater rafting.

"1" **Bishop's Country Inn Motel** (207-668-3231 or 1-888-991-7669; www.bishopsmotel.com), 461 Main St., Jackman 04945. This two-story motel in the middle of Jackman Village offers clean and spacious rooms and all the bells and whistles it takes for AAA to give it three diamonds.

$90 per couple in winter (high season), $83 per couple in rafting season.

Note: Most lodging described for the outfitters under *Whitewater Rafting* is available to nonrafters.

✷ Where to Eat

Note: In this little-populated area the line between "eating" and "dining" out blurs—and if you're between rafting, hunting, and snowmobiling seasons, it comes down to what's open. Listings are in geographic order along Rt. 201, south to north.

Note: See *Eating Out* in Skowhegan in the previous chapter for suggestions between I-95 and the Canada Road.

In Bingham

Antlers Inn & Restaurant (207-67-3006), 334 Main St. Open daily 11–11 but closed some days off-season, and breakfast served seasonally. The décor is pleasant and the menu ranges from sandwiches to roast duckling filet mignon and lobster. Dinner entrées: $13–20. Fully licensed.

Maplewood Family Restaurant (207-672-3330), 418 Main St. Open Tue.–Sat. 11–9, Sun. from 8 with brunch until 1. Recently expanded to accommodate rafting groups, the large menu specializes in fresh seafood chowder, BBQ, and baby back ribs. There's a Saturday night buffet, full bar, kids' menu, and play area. Sandwiches all day.

Thompson's Restaurant (207-672-3245), Main St. Open daily 5 AM–8 PM. In business since 1929 and still a good bet. Owner Frances Tatkis describes the menu as "home cook'n', period." Regulars come for the pies and doughnuts. Beer and wine served.

Valley View Market (207-672-3322), Rt. 201. Source of pizza and good take-out sandwiches if you're running late or want to eat by the lake.

Also see **Riverside Inn**.

In the Forks

Kennebec River Pub & Brewery, (207-663-4466), Rt. 201 at Northern Outdoors. Open daily year-round for all three meals. This is an inviting brewpub with a half dozen beers ranging from light summer ale to robust stout. There's also a pine-sided, informal dining room hung with archival photos of The Forks in its big-time logging and old resort days. Good for burgers, salads, and baskets, also dinner entrées ranging from stuffed portobello mushrooms to a full rack of Class V Stout BBQ Ribs. Kids'meals all include Gifford's ice cream. Entrées $15–24.

Marshall's Bar and Restaurant (207-663-4455), Rt. 201. Open daily for lunch and dinner. Chris Hewke has revived this century-old hotel, a prime source of pizza, fried baskets, and salads, burgers and steakhouse-style dinner entrées. Live music and "events" on weekends.

Crab Apple (1-800-553-7238), Crab Apple Acres, just off Rt. 201. Open daily for dinner Memorial Day–Labor Day; otherwise check. This outfitter's large base lodge includes both a pub and a more formal restaurant. Dinner options range from vegetable pasta Alfredo to prime rib and Yorkshire pudding ($27.99). Children's menu.

Hawk's Nest (207-663-4430), Rt. 201, West Forks. Open in snowmobiling and rafting seasons. Peter Dostie spent more than a year building this lodge with 100- and 200-year-old logs and elaborate animal carvings. There's a bar, game room, and indoor climbing wall. Sandwiches and burgers all day, also seafood, steaks, and pasta.

Also see **Inn by the River** *Other Lodging*.

In Jackman

Mama Bear's Den (207-668-4222), Rt. 201. Open 4 AM–8 PM, from 6 AM on weekends. We always seem to stop here for lunch. It's totally pleasant with great daily specials and a menu ranging from poutine to surf and turf with Vidalia onions. Fully licensed.

Four Seasons Restaurant (207-668-7778), Jackman. Open 5 AM–9 PM. One big room, booths, good road food, blackboard specials. Fully licensed.

Schmooses (207-668-7799), 513 Main St. Open daily from 11:30. This is a classy North Woods "lounge" with a moose depicted in smoked glass, handsome fieldstone hearths, and a dance floor that comes to life with a DJ Thurs.–Sat. At dinner a 10-ounce steak with king crab is $19.99.

The Bigwood Steakhouse (207-668-5572), 1 Forest St. Open from 4 PM Thur.–Sun. Meal-sized salads, pasta, and Cajun dishes, as well as BBQ ribs, but hand-cut steaks are the specialty, all served in in Kim and Karen Hewke's home ("The kids grew up and moved out. Now they can't come back."). FYI: Son Chris now owns the Marshall's in The Forks. The full menu is available as take-out.

BERRY'S IN THE FORKS

Christina Tree

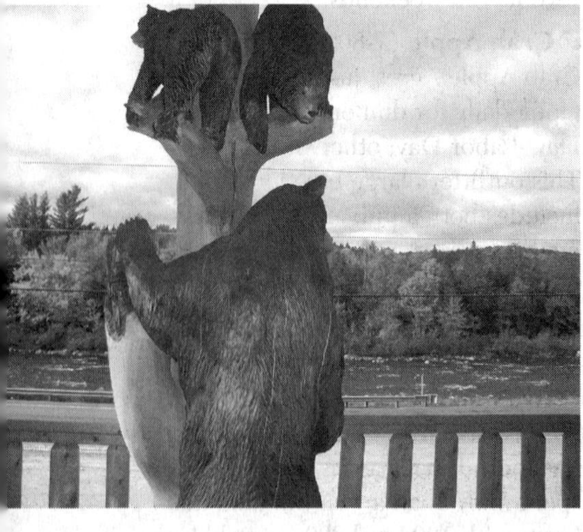

✷ Selective Shopping

General stores in Solon and on up through Jackman are generally the only stores, ergo community centers. Our favorite is **Berry's in The Forks** (open 6 AM–9 PM), a source of fishing/hunting licenses and liquor, lunch, flannel jackets, rubber boots, and groceries, as well as gas. Stuffed birds and other wildlife are scattered throughout the store, most of it shot by Gordon Berry, who has been behind the counter for 40 years. Until the rafting/snowmobiling boom hit, Berry notes, he and his parents could manage the place alone; now it takes a staff of up to 10.

Jackman Trading Post (207-666-2761; www.moosealley.com), 281 Main St. (Rt. 201 south of the village). Open May–Thanksgiving, 8–6. A peerless selection of Far North T-shirts and souvenirs.

✷ Special Events

March: **Northeast Sled Dog Races**, Jackman: a three-day professional race.

Late September: **Fly-In**, Gadabout Gaddis Airport, Bingham (207-672-4100).

November: **Annual Hunter's breakfast and Supper**, Jackman.

Northern Maine

BANGOR AREA

THE NORTH MAINE WOODS

MOOSEHEAD LAKE AREA

KATAHDIN REGION, INCLUDING LOWER PISCATAQUIS AND LINCOLN LAKES

AROOSTOOK COUNTY

Nancy English

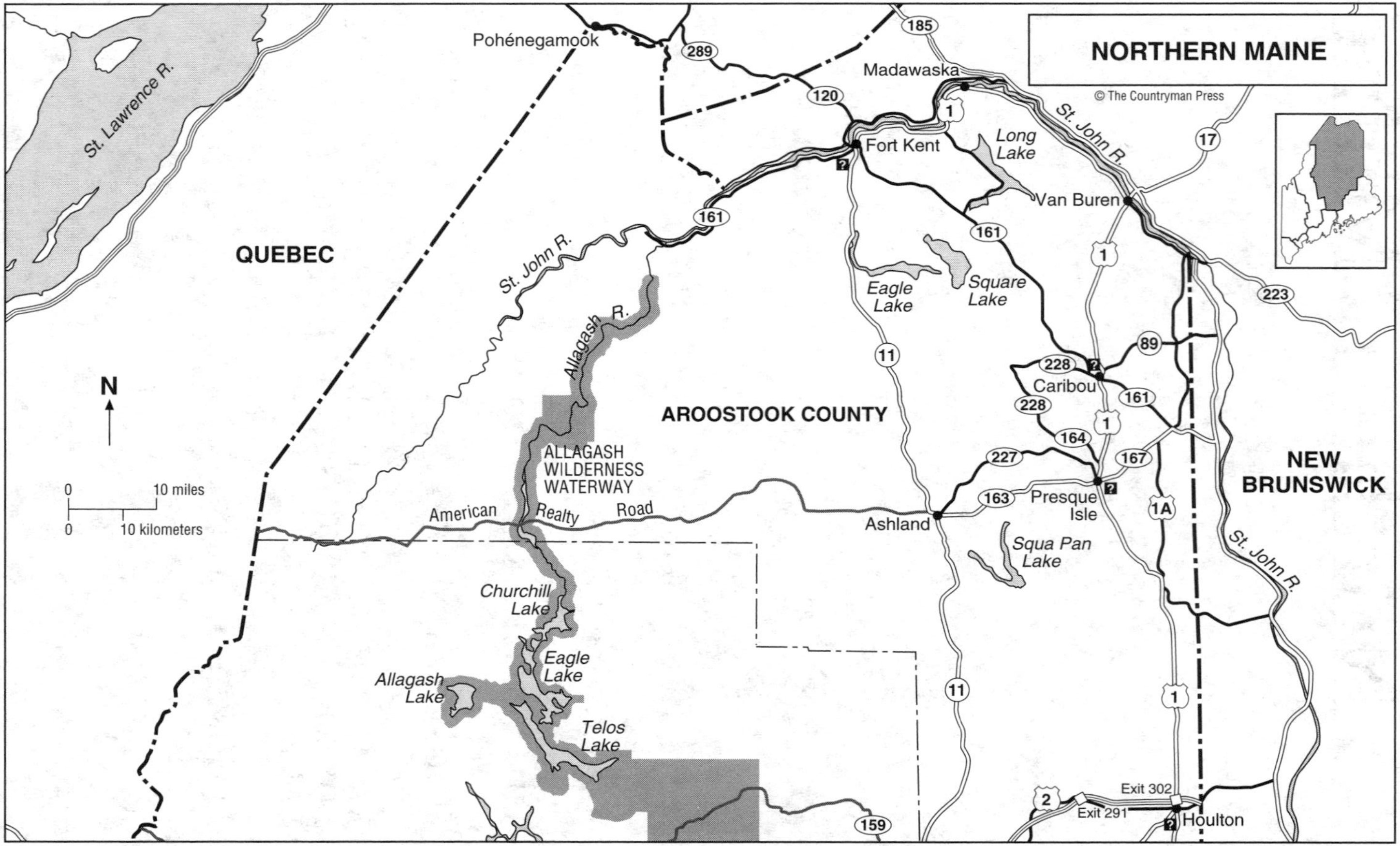
NORTHERN MAINE
© The Countryman Press
QUEBEC
NEW BRUNSWICK
AROOSTOOK COUNTY
St. Lawrence R.
Pohénegamook
Madawaska
Fort Kent
Van Buren
Long Lake
St. John R.
Eagle Lake
Square Lake
Caribou
Presque Isle
Ashland
Squa Pan Lake
Houlton
Exit 302
Exit 291
Allagash R.
ALLAGASH WILDERNESS WATERWAY
American Realty Road
Churchill Lake
Eagle Lake
Allagash Lake
Telos Lake
N
0 10 miles
0 10 kilometers
185
289
120
1
17
161
223
89
228
164
227
167
163
1A
11
2
159

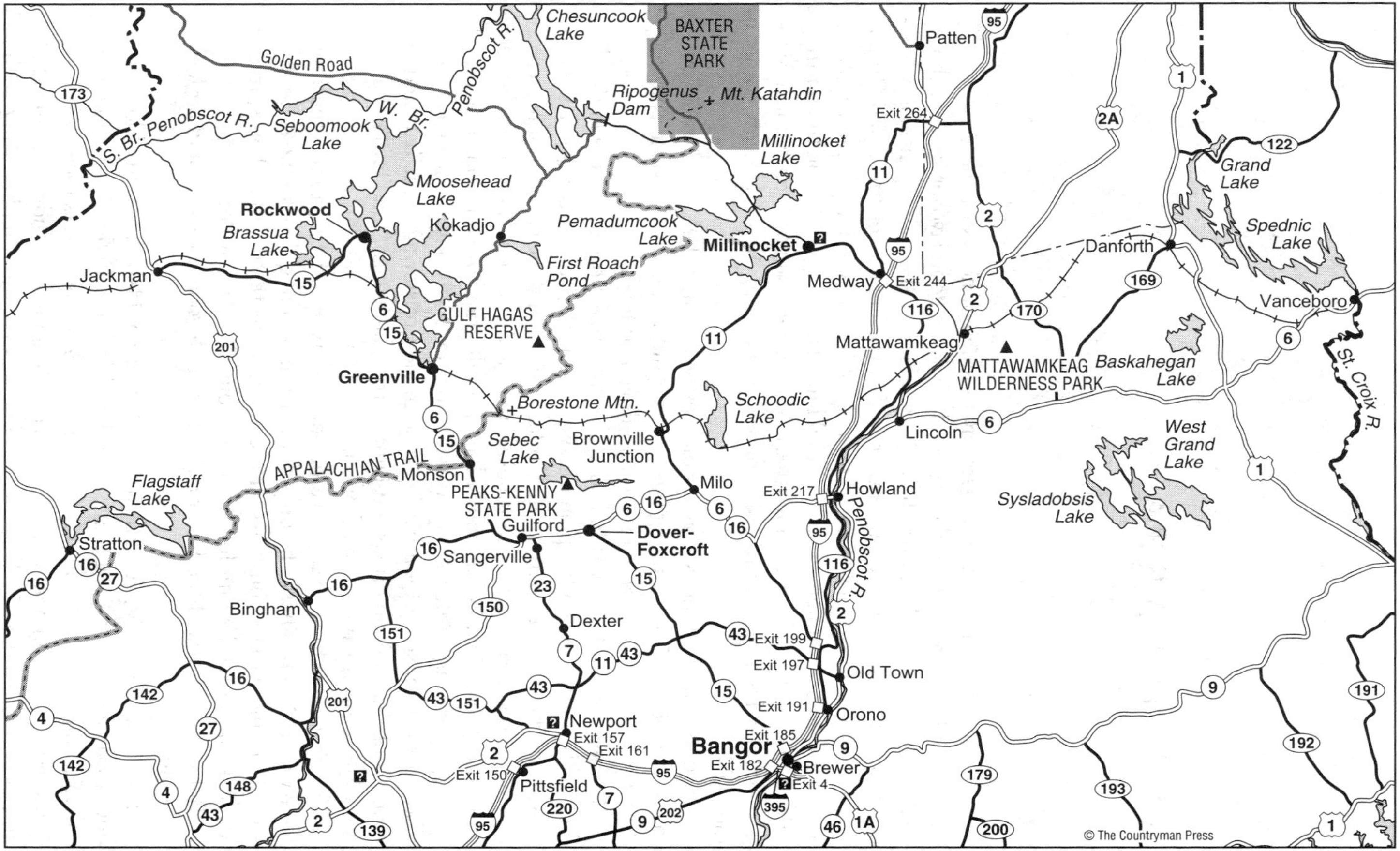
BAXTER STATE PARK
Chesuncook Lake
Golden Road
Penobscot R.
Ripogenus Dam
Mt. Katahdin
Patten
S. Br. Penobscot R.
W. Br.
Seboomook Lake
Moosehead Lake
Millinocket Lake
Exit 264
Rockwood
Kokadjo
Pemadumcook Lake
Brassua Lake
Millinocket
Grand Lake
Spednic Lake
Danforth
Jackman
First Roach Pond
Medway
Exit 244
GULF HAGAS RESERVE
Vanceboro
Mattawamkeag
MATTAWAMKEAG WILDERNESS PARK
Baskahegan Lake
Greenville
St. Croix R.
Borestone Mtn.
Schoodic Lake
Sebec Lake
Brownville Junction
Lincoln
West Grand Lake
APPALACHIAN TRAIL
Monson
Flagstaff Lake
PEAKS-KENNY STATE PARK
Milo
Howland
Exit 217
Sysladobsis Lake
Guilford
Dover-Foxcroft
Stratton
Sangerville
Penobscot R.
Bingham
Dexter
Exit 199
Exit 197
Old Town
Exit 191
Orono
Newport
Exit 157
Exit 161
Exit 185
Bangor
Exit 182
Brewer
Exit 150
Pittsfield
Exit 4
© The Countryman Press

BANGOR AREA

Bangor is both the natural gateway to much of northern and eastern Maine and the largest city in the region. It makes a good layover spot for those venturing into either the Baxter State Park region or the vast expanse of Aroostook County. With Brewer on the other side of the Penobscot River, and Orono, home of the main campus of the University of Maine, the Bangor metropolitan area is a vibrant commercial and cultural hub. The Bangor Mall on the north side of the city is the largest in northern Maine, and Bangor International Airport (referred to locally as BIA) is a departure point for flights to every corner of the globe.

Once the home of the National Folk Festival, Bangor began to host its own folk festival in 2005, celebrating the richness and variety of American culture through music, dance, traditional storytelling, and food.

Residents will tell you wistfully that the city's real glory days were in the mid–19th century, when the pine tree was arboreal gold and Bangor was the most important lumber port in the world. Back then the city was a brawling, boisterous boomtown where fortunes were quickly made and lost in timber deals and land speculation. Local lumber barons built grandiose hilltop mansions, sparing no expense. After a long winter's work in the woods, the loggers who labored for them spent their hard-earned money, roistering in the bars and brothels of the city's notorious red-light district, known as "the Devil's Half Acre," most of which was wiped out in a 1911 fire.

The Bangor of today has recovered some of its notoriety with the enormous Hollywood Slots business, the only slot machine gaming floor in the state. Revenues pouring into this business far exceeded projections, and its hours, from 8 AM to 4 AM, reveal the lure for instate and out-of-state travelers.

But walking tours of the historic districts are a good diversion, and far less expensive.

The West Market Square Historic District is a mid-19th-century block of downtown shops. The Broadway area is lined with the Federal-style homes of early prominent citizens and lumber barons' mansions. Across town, West Broadway holds a number of even more ornate homes, including the turreted and thoroughly spooky-looking Victorian home of author Stephen King, with its one-of-a-kind bat-and-cobweb wrought-iron fence.

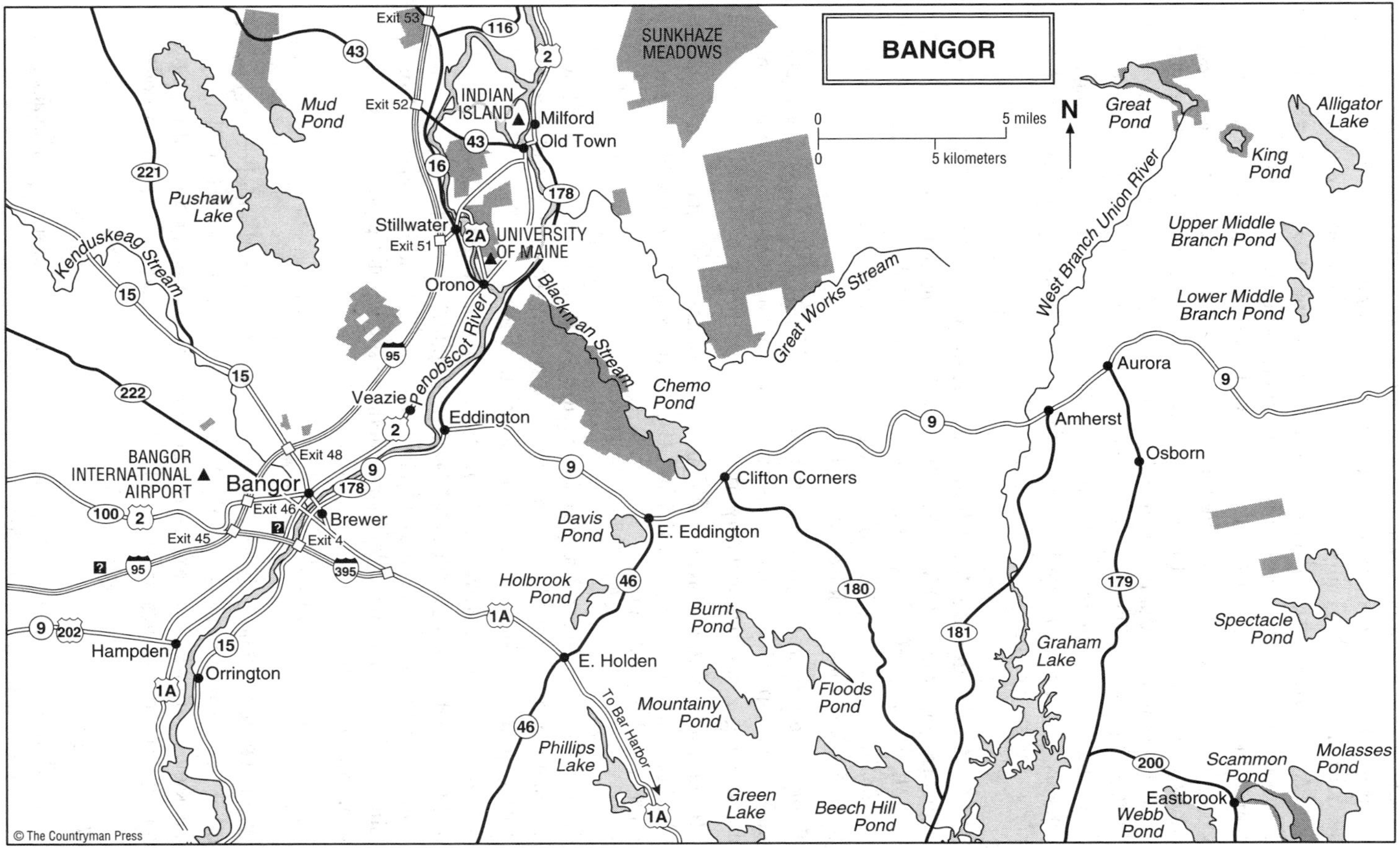
BANGOR
0
5 miles
0
5 kilometers
N
SUNKHAZE MEADOWS
Mud Pond
Pushaw Lake
Kenduskeag Stream
INDIAN ISLAND
Milford
Old Town
Stillwater
UNIVERSITY OF MAINE
Orono
Penobscot River
Blackman Stream
Great Works Stream
Chemo Pond
West Branch Union River
Great Pond
King Pond
Alligator Lake
Upper Middle Branch Pond
Lower Middle Branch Pond
Aurora
Amherst
Osborn
Veazie
Eddington
BANGOR INTERNATIONAL AIRPORT
Bangor
Brewer
Clifton Corners
Davis Pond
E. Eddington
Holbrook Pond
Burnt Pond
Floods Pond
Mountainy Pond
Graham Lake
Spectacle Pond
Hampden
Orrington
E. Holden
To Bar Harbor
Phillips Lake
Green Lake
Beech Hill Pond
Scammon Pond
Molasses Pond
Eastbrook
Webb Pond
Exit 53
Exit 52
Exit 51
Exit 48
Exit 46
Exit 45
Exit 4
© The Countryman Press

The outsized symbol of Bangor's romantic timber boom era is native son Paul Bunyan. The mythical lumberjack superhero was conceived in tall-tale-swapping sessions in the logging camps of northern Maine and the saloons of the Devil's Half Acre. When most of the tall stands of virgin pine in Maine's North Woods had been cut down, ending the boom, lumberjacks began moving west, taking Paul with them—and making him bigger and his feats more incredible with every move. Scattered across the forested northern tier of the United States, all the way to the Pacific Northwest, are villages and small towns named Bangor settled by nostalgic Maine loggers who all had a Paul Bunyan tale to tell.

Paul Bunyan is still very much a presence here: A 31-foot-high fiberglass statue of the great logger, wearing a red-and-black-checked shirt and carrying a huge ax, stands in a city park named for him—and casts a long shadow just across the street from Hollywood Slots.

GUIDANCE **Bangor Region Chamber of Commerce** (207-947-0307; www.bangorregion.com), 519 Main St., P.O. Box 1443, Bangor 04402 (just off I-395 exit 3B, which is off I-95 exit 182A, across from the Holiday Inn), maintains a seasonal visitor information office in Paul Bunyan Park—you can't miss the giant lumberjack statue—on lower Main St. (Rt. 1A).

Bangor Convention and Visitors Bureau (207-947-5205; www.visitbangormaine.com) operates staffed, year-round information centers at 40 Harlow St, and at Bangor International Airport.

Maine Tourism Association maintains two rest areas/information centers on I-95 in Hamden between exits 175 and 180: northbound (207-862-6628) and southbound (207-862-6638).

GETTING THERE *By air:* **Bangor International Airport** (207-942-0384; www.flybangor.com) is served by Delta Air Lines, Northwest Airlink, and U.S. Airways Express. **Rental cars** are available at the airport.

By bus: **Greyhound** (207-942-1700) offers daily service to the downtown terminal. **Concord Trailways** (207-945-5000 or 1-800-639-5150) has express trips, complete with movies and music, daily from Portland and Boston. **Cyr Bus Line** (207-827-2335) provides daily scheduled service all the way to Caribou, with stops in between.

By car: I-95 from Augusta.

WHEN TO COME The Folk Festival draws a lot of folks at the end of August, but other reasons to explore—from the Penobscot Nation Museum in Old Town to Bookseller's Row in downtown—can be enjoyed any time. If you visit in midwinter, you can try to imagine how the lumberjacks managed in the deep woods.

* Villages

Hampden. Adjacent to Bangor, but offering a more rural setting. The academically excellent Hampden Academy is found here.

Orono. A college town, housing the University of Maine, but still a small town where almost everyone knows everyone else. Downtown there are some nice shops and local dining landmarks, and on campus look for a wide variety of cultural activities.

Old Town. Definitely a mill town, but also the home of the famous Old Town Canoe factory. There's a great little museum worth visiting.

Winterport. An old river town, once home of many sea captains and now a quiet little area with a historic district. Walking-tour brochure available from area businesses.

✷ To See and Do

CANOEING AND KAYAKING **Sunrise International** (207-942-9300, 1-888-490-9300; www.sunriseexpeditions.com), 4 Union Plaza, Suite 2, Bangor, is one of the state's best river expedition, guided kayaking and canoeing businesses. Martin Brown started Sunrise County Canoe Expeditions in 1973 in Downeast Maine and moved it to Bangor, where it is now Maine's oldest river guide and outfitter service. A master Maine guide since 1970, Brown has taken his customers out west and far north, to Nunavut, for instance, and Iceland. But the St. Croix, St. John, and Machias River, as well as other eastern and northern Maine waterways, are explored in scheduled trips every summer. Guide author Chris Tree and one of her sons took the St. Croix trip with Brown years ago, and said, "It was fabulous."

MUSEUMS **Cole Land Transportation Museum** (207-990-3600), 405 Perry Rd. (near junction of I-95 and I-395), Bangor. Open May 1–Nov. 11, daily 9–5. $6 adults, $4 seniors, under 19 free. A collection of 200 antique Maine vehicles going back to the 19th century: snowplows, wagons, trucks, sleds, rail equipment, and more. A World War II memorial, Vietnam veterans museum, and Purple Heart memorial are all on-site.

Hose 5 Fire Museum (207-945-3229), 247 State St., Bangor. Open by appointment. A working fire station until 1993, now a museum with firefighting artifacts from the area. Three fully restored fire engines, wooden water mains, and plenty of historical pictures on display. Free, but donations gladly accepted.

University of Maine Museums, Rt. 2A, Orono. **Hudson Museum** (207-581-1901), in the **Maine Center for**

PAUL BUNYAN

Kim Grant

the Arts (open Tue.–Fri. 9–4, Sat. 11–4), is an exceptional anthropological collection including a special section on Maine Native Americans and Maine history. Tour programs are offered by prior arrangement. **University of Maine Museum of Art** (207-561-3350; www.umma.umaine.edu), 40 Harlow St., Bangor, shows a fraction of its 4,500-work collection, which includes an extensive selection of 19th- and 20th-century European and American prints by Goya, Picasso, Homer, and Whistler, as well as modern American paintings by George Inness, John Marin, Andrew Wyeth, and others. Tours are available by prior arrangement, and tours on tape are also available. **Page Farm Home Museum** (207-581-4100; www.umain.edu/page farm), on the University of Maine at Orono campus. Open daily May 15–Sept. 15, 9–4; closed Sun. and Mon. off-season). Free. Historical farm implements and household items from 1865 to 1940.

Old Town Museum (207-827-7256), 353 Main St., Old Town. Open early June–end of Aug., Wed.–Sun. 1–5. A former waterworks building houses a great little museum with exhibits on the Penobscot tribe and on local logging. You'll also find early area photos, an original birch-bark canoe, and well-informed guides.

Old Town Marine Museum, 240 Main St., No. 2, Old Town, displays vintage canoes, boats, and outboard motors. Free.

Maine Forest and Logging Museum (207-581-2871; www.leonardsmills.com), Leonard's Mills, off Rt. 178 in Bradley (take Rt. 9 north from Brewer; turn left onto Rt. 178 and watch for signs). Open during daylight hours. "Living History Days" on two weekends, one in mid-July and another in October, feature people in period attire with horses or oxen. Located on the site of a 1790s logging and milling community, it includes a covered bridge, water-powered sawmill, millpond, saw pit, barn, and trapper's line camp. Other special events include Children's Day and Woodsmen's Day.

HISTORIC HOMES AND SITES **Bangor Museum and History Center** (207-942-1900; www.bangormuseum.org), 115 Main St. (mailing address 25 Broad St.), Bangor. Open Mon.–Fri. 10–5. This temporary location for the history center operates while the new museum is under construction. A curved-front historic building at 25 Broad St. will be the site of this museum in the future; call or visit the Web site for updates. Walking tour maps and tours of Mount Hope Cemetery are available; call for information.

SCULPTURE IN MARKET SQUARE

Kim Grant

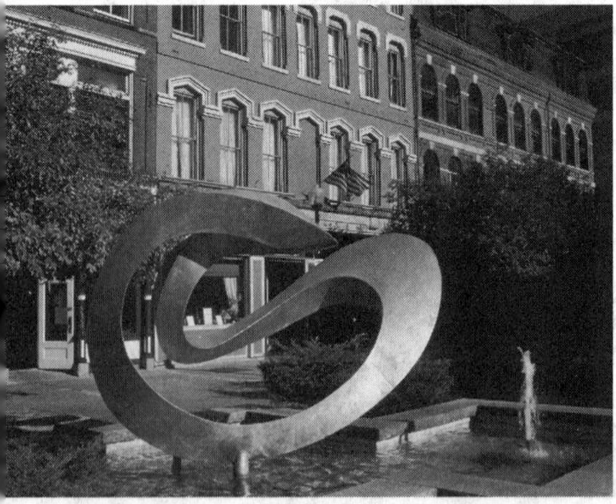

Thomas A. Hill House (207-942-5766); 159 Union St. (at High St.), Bangor. Tours by appointment; $5 adults, children and members free. The downstairs of the Hill House has been restored to its 19th-century grandeur with Victorian furnishings and an elegant double parlor.

INDIAN ISLAND In 1786 the Penobscot tribe deeded most of Maine to Massachusetts in exchange for 140 small islands in the Penobscot River. An 18th-century agreement (discovered in the 1970s) detailed that Indian Island (much of it now valuable) belonged to the tribe and brought the island a new school and a large community center, which attracts crowds to play high-stakes bingo (call 1-800-255-1293; www.penobscotbingo.com, for the schedule). Today the Indian Island Reservation, the Penobscot homeland for more than 5,000 years, and connected by bridge to Old Town, is occupied by about 500 tribal members. At 12 Downstreet St., the **Penobscot Nation Museum** (207-827-4153; www.penobscotnation.org) is open year-round Mon.–Thu. 9–2 and Sat. 10–4. The museum occupies the former Indian agent's office, the fifth building on the right after crossing the bridge. Museum Coordinator James Neptune greets visitors, explaining that the birch table is by the legendary Passamaquoddy craftsman Tomah Joseph (who taught Franklin Roosevelt to paddle a canoe) and that the beaded deerskin dress belonged to Indian Island's Molly Spotted Elk, a dancer, actress, and writer known around the world in the late 1930s. Most items in this authentic and informal collection—which includes a 150-year-old birch-bark canoe and some exquisite beaded works, war bonnets, war clubs, and basketry—have a human story. Several videos about the history of the Penobscot Nation can be shown upon request. The island is accessible from Rt. 2, marked from I-95, exit 197.

Mount Hope Cemetery in Bangor is one of the nation's oldest garden cemeteries, designed by noted Maine architect Charles G. Bryant. Abraham Lincoln's first vice president, Hannibal Hamlin, is buried here.

FOR FAMILIES ✐ **Maine Discovery Museum** (207-262-7200; www.mainediscoverymuseum.org), 74 Main St., Bangor. The largest children's museum in Maine, with three floors of kid-oriented displays and activities. Science and music exhibits on the third floor include a giant body to climb through and the Recollections Room, with lights that follow movement. The second floor displays exhibits about world trade with a cargo ship, warehouses, and an airplane. There is also a gift shop. $6.50 per person, 12 months or older.

GAMBLING **Hollywood Slots at Bangor** (207-561-6100; www.hollywoodslotsatbangor.com), 427 Main St., Bangor. Mon.–Thurs. 9 AM–1 AM, Fri.-Sat. 9 AM–2 AM, Sunday noon–1 AM. This temporary facility has 479 slot machines and a restaurant. You must be 21 to enter and use the slot machines. In the summer of 2008 the new facility is opening 500 Main St., with 1,000 slot machines, a 152-room hotel, 1,500 car parking garage, lounge with live entertainment on weekends, simulcast theater for off-track betting, a buffet, and a snack bar. Hours for the new facility will be Mon.–Sat. 8 AM–4 AM, Sun. noon–4 AM.

GOLF **Bangor Municipal Golf Course** (207-941-0232), Webster Ave., Bangor; 27 holes. **Penobscot Valley Country Club** (207-866-2423), Bangor Rd., Orono; 18 holes. **Hermon Meadow Golf Club** (207-848-3741), 281 Billings Rd., Hermon; eighteen holes.

SWIMMING **Jenkins' Beach**. Popular beach on Green Lake for families with children. Store and snack bar.

Violette's Public Beach and Boat Landing (207-843-6876), Dedham (between Ellsworth and Bangor). $4 admission. Also on Green Lake, a popular spot for college students and young adults. Swim float with slide, boat launch, and picnic tables.

Beth Pancoe Aquatic Center (207-992-4490; www.bangormaine.gov), run by the Bangor Parks and Recreation Department. An outdoor Olympic-sized pool with a waterslide and a couple of fountains, this new facility has a slow slope into the water, easy on the old and young, and was built with a gift from Stephen King, Bangor's best-selling novelist. Open end of June–Aug. $1 children, $2 resident adults; $2 children, $4 adults from away.

DOWNHILL AND CROSS-COUNTRY SKIING **Mt. Hermon Ski Area** (207-848-5192; www.skihermonmountain.com), Newburg Rd., Hermon (3 miles off I-95 from exit 173, Carmel; or off Rt. 2 from Bangor). Popular local downhill skiing area, with a chairlift and a T-bar and 20 runs (the longest is 3,500 feet); rentals available; base lodge, night skiing, snowboarding. A tubing park, with a lift, runs day and night, too. Day passes for adults $20; 12 and under $15.

See also **Sunkhaze Meadows** under *Green Space*.

✷ Green Space

Sunkhaze Meadows National Wildlife Refuge, Milford. Unstaffed. Call the Maine Coastal Islands Wildlife Refuge Rockport office (207-236-6970), P.O. Box 495, Rockport, ME 04856 for information. Just north of Bangor, this 11,500-acre refuge includes nearly 7 miles of Sunkhaze Stream and 12 miles of tributary streams. Recreation activities include canoeing, hiking, and hunting and fishing in accordance with Maine laws. Also excellent bird-watching and cross-country skiing opportunities.

A brochure titled ***Trails in the Bangor Region*** is available at the chamber visitor center and lists close to a dozen trails for biking, walking, picnicking, running, hiking, cross-country skiing, and other outdoor activities.

✷ Lodging

♿ **The Charles Inn** (207-992-2820; www.thecharlesinn.com), 20 Broad St., Bangor 04401. A historic inn on W. Market Square, a vest-pocket park in the heart of downtown Bangor, is a perfect location for getting to know the city. Connie Boivin bought this hotel in 2005; 35 large rooms are pleasant and simple, with solid mahogany or cherry beds. All have private bath, air-conditioning, and TV. A continental, kosher and nonkosher breakfast is served in the café. $69–109 depending on season.

🐾 **Fireside Inn and Suites** (207-942-1234; www.bangorbestinn.com), 570 Main St., Bangor 04401. A 51-room motel that is clean, comfortable, and convenient. Right next door to the new Hollywood Slots, this place is busier than ever. All the basic conveniences, including mini-fridge, microwave ovens, and videos for rent. **Geaghan's**, the on-site restaurant, serves decent food, with Irish specials. $80–120, including continental breakfast. Children under 18 stay free.

Country Inn at the Mall (207-941-0200 or 1-800-244-3961), 936 Stillwater Ave., Bangor 04401. Despite the name, this is essentially a 96-room motel—but brighter and more cozily decorated than most. There's no restaurant, newsstand, or gift shop, but with the Bangor Mall (largest in northern Maine) right next door that's not an inconvenience. $75–111 with continental breakfast.

The Lucerne Inn (207-843-5123 or 1-800-325-5123; www.lucerne inn .com), 2517 Main Rd., Holden 04429. A 19th-century mansion on Rt. 1A, overlooking Phillips Lake in East Holden. Best known as a restaurant (see *Dining Out*), it also has 31 rooms with private bath (whirlpool), working fireplace, heated towel bars, phone, and TV. $99–199 in-season includes continental breakfast. Lower rates off-season.

Note: Bangor also has many hotels and motels, mainly located by the mall and near the airport.

✱ Where to Eat

DINING OUT Thistles Restaurant (207-945-5480; www.thistlesrestaurant .com), 175 Exchange St., Bangor. Open for lunch Tues.–Sat. for lunch 11–2:30 and dinner 4:30–9. A fine dining place that does many things perfectly, the Argentinian dishes in particular. Chef-owner Juan Santiago Rave can put together a tangy chimichurri sauce for steaks and empanadas; the salmon in dill cream sauce wasn't quite as exciting. Entrées $17-25.

The Lucerne Inn (207-843-5123 or 1-800-325-5123; www.lucerneinn .com), 2517 Main Rd., Rt. 1A, East Holden (11 miles out of Bangor, heading toward Ellsworth). Open for dinner daily, as well as a popular Sunday brunch. A grand old mansion with a view of Phillips Lake. Brunch specialties include Belgian waffles and chicken cordon bleu. Entrées start at $16; more than $30 for a steamed lobster and filet mignon.

Captain Nick's (207-942-6444), 1165 Union St., Bangor. Open daily for lunch and dinner. A large, locally popular place with good seafood and steaks.

Governor's (207-947-7704; www .governorsrestaurant.com), 643 Broadway in Bangor; and Stillwater Ave. in Old Town (207-827-4277). Open from early breakfast to late dinner. The Stillwater restaurant is the original in a statewide chain. Popular at all meals, large breakfast menu, hamburgers to steaks; specials like shepherd's pie, fresh strawberry pie, ice cream.

Baldacci's (207-945-5813; www .baldaccis.com), 12 Alden St., Bangor. Family-owned and -operated since 1933, this restaurant is open for lunch and dinner, serving Italian specialties at reasonable prices. The restaurant is run by the nephew of Maine's governor.

EATING OUT Paddy Murphy's Irish Pub (207-945-6800; www.paddy murphyspub.com), 26 Main St.,

Bangor. Some of the best food in town, we heard, with smoky beef chili and a banger sandwich with Guinness barbeque sauce. Corned beef and cabbage pasty, beef and Guinness stew, bangers and mash with pork and apple sausages. Entrées $14–18.

Café Nouveau (207-942-3336), 84 Hammond St., Bangor. An attractive bistro-style restaurant with an interesting international menu. Open Tue.–Fri. 11–2:30 and Tues.–Sat. 5–9. Small portions with high quality are devised to accompany the wines. Full bar with the most wines by the glass in the area.

New Moon Restaurant (207-990-2233; www.newmoondining.com), 49 Park St., Bangor. Spacious and open with interesting art on the walls. Open daily for dinner, with late hours for the bar.

Dysart's (207-942-4878), Coldbrook Rd., Hermon (I-95, exit 180). Open 24 hours. Billed as "the biggest truck stop in Maine," but it isn't just truckers who eat here. Known for great road food and reasonable prices. Homemade bread and seafood are specialties.

Pat's Pizza (207-866-2111), Mill St., Orono. A local landmark, especially popular with high school and university students and families. Now franchised throughout the state, this is the original with booths and a jukebox, back dining room, and downstairs taproom, plus Pat's son Bruce and his family still running the place. Pizza, sandwiches, Italian dinners.

Java Joe's Café (207-990-0500), 98 Central St., Bangor. Breakfast, lunch, and the all-important morning latte. Open Mon.–Sat. 7:30–4, with bagels, eggs, sandwiches, salads and wraps, and Thai specialties.

Sea Dog Brewing Company (207-947-8004; www.seadogbrewing.com), 26 Front St. Open 11:30 AM–1 AM daily. Microbrews and a long menu of seafood, burgers, and steaks. A great deck next to the Penobscot River, and the winter view is good too.

COFFEEHOUSES AND SNACKS

The Store & Ampersand (207-866-4110), 22 Mill St., Orono. A combination health food store, coffee bar, and gift shop. Great for snacks (try the big cookies) and specialty items. Wine and cheese.

Friar's Bakehouse (207-947-3770; www.franciscansofbangor.com), 21 Central St., Bangor. Open Tues.–Fri. 8–2. This bakery run by the Franciscan Brothers of Hungary, a Roman Catholic order from Brewer, makes and sells muffins, chocolate chip cookies, whoopie pies, and lots of bread. A chapel up the stairs is always open for prayer and meditation.

Bagel Central (207-947-1654), 33 Central St., Bangor. Open Mon.–Thurs. 6–6, Fri. 6–5:30, closed Sat., Sun. 6–2. Bagels, bialys, and spinach knish at this Kosher deli. Sarah Faragher of Sarah's Books (see *Bookstores*) said the leek and potato soup is perfect in winter; avocado vegetable sandwich great in summer. There is a line out the door every Sunday.

Entertainment

Maine Center for the Arts (207-581-1805; box office 207-581-1755; www.mainecenterforthearts.org), at the University of Maine in Orono, has become the cultural center for the area. It hosts a wide variety of concerts and events, from classical to country-and-western, children's theater, and dance. Many performances are held in Hutchins Concert Hall, Maine's first concert hall.

Penobscot Theatre Company (207-947-6618), 131 Main St., Bangor. This company has been putting on quality shows for more than 34 years. Performing in the Bangor Opera House, the company performs a variety of plays during the season; *Driving Miss Daisy* was a recent production. In summer the company sponsors the Creative Arts Program for young people.

Maine Masque Theater (207-581-1792), Hauck Auditorium, University of Maine, Orono. Classic and contemporary plays presented Oct.–May by University of Maine theater students.

Bass Park, 100 Dutton St., Bangor. The complex includes **Bangor Auditorium** and **Civic Center** (207-947-5555), **State Fair**, and **Raceway** (207-947-6744) featuring harness racing Thu.–Sun., May–July, and the Hollywood Slots (see *Gambling*). Band concerts in the park by the Paul Bunyan statue on Tuesday in summer.

Bangor Symphony Orchestra (207-942-5555; www.bangorsymphony.com). The symphony began in 1895 and is still going strong, with performances at the Bangor Auditorium and Peakes Auditorium Oct.–May.

✱ Selective Shopping

BOOKSTORES

In Bangor

Bangor has a Bookseller's Row right downtown. The first listings below all cluster together and sell a wonderful range of books, from children's classics to historical works and the latest mysteries. With Java Joe's coffee and the Friar Bakehouse's homemade muffins in the same block, this stretch of downtown is an introvert's paradise.

Sarah's Books (207-992-2080; www.sarahsbooksusedrare.blogspot.com), 32 Central St., second floor. Open year-round Mon.–Fri. 11–5:30, and most Saturdays, same hours. This is our favorite bookstore, beautifully organized, with clean secondhand editions of great books. Emphasis on Maine, history, travel, poetry, and literature. Sarah Faragher's blog details the romance of old books and more.

BookMarcs (207-942-3206; www.bookmarcs.com), 78 Harlow St. A first-rate, full-service downtown bookstore with new, used, and discounted books. Particular specialties are books about Maine and by Maine authors. Java Joe's Café is connected to the store.

W. J. Lippincott Books (207-942-4398), 36 Central St. Open Mon.–Fri. 10–5:30, Sat. 10–5, Sun. 10–3. A large street-level bookstore with some 30,000 used and rare titles, well arranged. Specialties include books on the North Woods, logging, and Indians of the northeastern United States, detective novels, and science fiction.

The Briar Patch (207-941-0255), 27 Central St. A large and exceptional children's book store, with creative toys, puzzles, and games.

Top Shelf Comics (207947-4939; www.tcomics.com), 25 Central St., Bangor. All the newest comics, and more.

Elsewhere

Betts' Bookstore (207-947-7052; www.bettsbooks.com), 584 Hammond St., Bangor. A small bookstore specializing in the works of local author Stephen King, who has used Bangor and surroundings as the setting of several novels. New editions but also used and hard-to-find copies. Also stocks books on aviation and automobiles.

Mr. Paperback (207-942-9191). This

store at the Airport Mall has a good selection of Maine books.

Borders Books and Music (207-990-3300), 116 Bangor Mall Blvd. at Bangor Mall. Part of a nationwide chain, and a good place to both find a book, movie, or CD, and sip an espresso made with Seattle's Best.

CAMPING AND HIKING **The Map Store** (207-827-4511; www.themapstore.biz), 240 Main St., No. 5, Old Town. An independent store stocking a large selection of Maine topographic maps and nautical charts along with U.S. and worldwide maps and aerial photos.

CANOES **Old Town Canoe Visitors' Center and Factory Outlet Store** (207-827-1530), 125 Gilman Falls Ave., Old Town. Varieties of canoes and kayaks sold include fiberglass, wood, Crosslink, and Royalex. Factory-tour video shows how canoes are made. Memorabilia and museum-quality wooden canoes and a birch-bark canoe are on display, not for sale. Many accessories from the parent company Johnson Outdoors, from Eureka Tent, Mecky Kayak, and more.

SPECIAL SHOPS **Winterport Boot Shop** (207-989-6492), 264 State St., Twin City Plaza, Brewer. Largest selection of Red Wing work boots in the Northeast. Proper fit for sizes 4–16, all widths.

Antique Marketplace & Café (207-941-2111; www.antiquemarketplacecafe.com), 65 Main St., Bangor. Booths display antique carpets, china, and more, and the café sells tea, coffee, and pie.

The Grasshopper Shop (207-945-3132; www.grasshoppershop.com), 1 W. Market Square, Bangor. Trendy women's, children's, and infant's clothing, as well as toys, jewelry, gifts, and housewares. Also a branch at Bangor International Airport.

One Lupine Fiber Arts (207-299-6716; www.onelupine.com), 170 Park St., Bangor. Open Mon.–Sat. 9–4. Felting, scrollwork ornaments, and chiffon scarves, in beautiful colors. Also coats, balls, and other felt items.

Wabanaki Arts Center Gallery (207-827-0391; www.maineindianbaskets.org), 240 Main St., Old Town. Open Mon.–Sat. 10–5. Operated by the Maine Indian Basketmakers Alliance, a nonprofit arts service organization, this is a lovely small gallery shop staffed by Native American crafters from the Penobscot, Passamaquoddy, Maliseet, and Micmac tribes, selling beautifully made baskets, carvings, and jewelry. There are also displays of antique baskets and carvings, including some rare and unusual war clubs.

Special Events

April: **Kenduskeag Stream Canoe Race**.

July: **Bangor State Fair**, Bass Park—agricultural fair with harness racing.

August: **WLBZ Sidewalk Art Festival**, downtown Bangor. **American Folk Festival** (*last weekend*), Bangor—a celebration of American culture through song, dance, storytelling, and food. Free.

September: **Paul Bunyan Festival Days**, at Paul Bunyan Park—crafts, food, entertainment.

Mid-December: **Native American basketmaker's market**, Hudson Museum, University of Maine at Orono.

THE NORTH MAINE WOODS

Like "Down East," the "North Maine Woods" may seem a bit of a mirage, always over the next hill. Much of this land lies within the area already described in this book as the "Western Mountains and Lakes Region." However, the one particular tract of forest that tends to be equated with "the Maine Woods" is the section bordered on the north and west by Canada, the one that on highway maps shows no roads. This is the largest stretch of unpeopled woodland in the East, but wilderness it's not.

Private ownership of this sector, technically part of Maine's 10.5 million acres known as the unorganized townships, dates from the 1820s when Maine was securing independence from Massachusetts. The mother state, her coffers at their usual low, stipulated that an even division of all previously undeeded wilderness be part of the separation agreement. The woods were quickly sold by the legislature for 12¢ to 38¢ per acre.

Pine was king, and men had already been working this woodland for decades. They lived together in remote lumber camps such as the one Thoreau visited in 1846 at Chesuncook. They worked in subzero temperatures, harvesting and hauling logs on sleds to frozen rivers. They rode those logs through the roaring spring runoffs, driving them across vast lakes and sometimes hundreds of miles downstream to mills. These were lumberjacks, the stuff of children's stories and adult songs, articles, and books. They were the cowboys of the East, larger than ordinary men.

What's largely forgotten is that by the second half of the 19th century, the North Maine Woods were more accessible and popular with visitors than they are today. By 1853 *Atlantic Monthly* editor James Russell Lowell could chug toward Moosehead on a cinder-spraying train; by 1900 Bostonians could ride comfortably to Greenville in a day, while Manhattanites could bed down in a Pullman and sleep their way to the foot of Moosehead Lake. The Bangor & Aroostook Railroad published annual glossy illustrated guidebooks to Moosehead and its environs, and detailed maps were circulated.

By 1882 the Kineo House, with 500 guest rooms and half a mile of verandas overlooking Moosehead Lake, was said to be the largest hotel in America. In Greenville, Sanders & Sons, the era's L. L. Bean, outfitted city "sports" with the clothing, firearms, and fishing gear with which to meet their guides and board steamers bound for far corners of the lake, frequently continuing on by foot and canoe to dozens of backwoods "sporting camps."

With the advent of World War I, the Depression, and the switch from rails to roads, the North Woods dimmed as a travel destination. In the 1920s the steamboat *Katahdin*, once the pride of the Moosehead fleet, was sold to a logging company as a towboat, and the Maine state legislature refused to protect woodland around Mount Katahdin, the state's highest mountain. Governor Percival Baxter bought the core of current Baxter State Park with his own money. In 1938 the Kineo House burned to the ground.

In ensuing decades the wisdom of Governor Baxter's puchase became increasingly apparent. Mount Katahdin, as the terminus of the 2,144-mile Appalachian Trail from Georgia, attracted recognition and serious hikers from throughout the world. Hunters and fishermen continued to make spring and fall trips to their fathers' haunts, and families to find their way to reasonably priced lake camps. In 1966 a 92-mile ribbon of lakes, ponds, rivers, and streams running northwest from Baxter State Park was designated the Allagash Wilderness Waterway, triggering interest among canoeists—though only a very narrow corridor was actually preserved because the state owns only 400 to 800 feet from the high-water mark. Still, it can control activities up to a mile on each side of the river.

Meanwhile the timber industry was transforming. This woodland was harvested initially for tall timber, but in the late 19th century the value of less desirable softwood increased when the process of making paper from wood fibers was rediscovered. (It seems that the method first used in AD 105 had been forgotten, and New England mills had been using rags to make paper.) By the turn of the 20th century many pulp and paper mills had moved to their softwood source. The city of Millinocket boomed into existence. The population skyrocketed from two families to 2,000 people between 1888 and 1900, and to 5,000 in 1912, around mammoth mills built by Great Northern, which also maintained far-flung farms to support more widely scattered lumber camps.

In 1900 it's said that some 30,000 men worked seasonally in the Maine woods. By 1970, however, just 6,500 loggers were working year-round; by 1988 this number fell to 3,660. On the other hand, the total wood harvest in Maine doubled between 1940 and 1970, and again by the mid-1980s. These numbers mirror technological changes, from axes to chain saws, skidders, and ultimately mammoth machines unselectively cutting thousands of trees per day, creating clear-cuts as large as 8 miles square. Today the Maine Forest Practices Act does not allow clear-cuts larger than 75 acres.

Changes in North Woods ownership in recent years have been cataclysmic. Through most of the 20th century large timber companies assumed much of the management responsibility and taxes as well as the cost of building hundreds of miles of roads (log drives ended in the 1970s) in this area. They also accommodated limited recreation, maintaining campsites and honoring long-term leases for both commercial and private camps. In recent decades, however, mergers and sales have fragmented ownership, and much of this "working forest" has been bought by firms without local ties, and not just by timber companies but by investment businesses as well. During the 1990s, 3,000 seasonal camps were built within the state's unorganized territories (not all of them in this particular area) and far more than half of that 10.5 million acres allocated to private ownership in 1827 has changed hands in the past decade.

The subject of North Woods ownership continues to shift and splinter. On the one hand, the organization RESTORE: The North Woods advocates creation of a North Woods National Park. On the other, park opponents argue that a national park would destroy the traditional economy and lifestyle in the region. Maine's Bureau of Parks and Lands has quietly acquired large tracts, and major nonprofit groups such as The Nature Conservancy, The New England Forestry Foundation, and the Appalachian Mountain Club have secured millions of acres outright and in easements that permit timber management. Grassroots coalition groups like the Northern Forest Alliance work quietly to maintain the balance between economic and recreational needs.

These "recreation needs" have also significantly altered in recent decades, notably with the popularity of snowmobiling and whitewater rafting, thanks to the area's relatively reliable snow cover and even more reliable whitewater releases on the West Branch of the Penobscot River. The resurgence of the moose population has sparked their popularity as something to see rather than shoot. Fly-fishing, kayaking, dogsledding, hiking, and cross-country-skiing all contribute to the rediscovery of the beauty of these magnificent woods, a phenomenon not to be confused with second-home development.

To date the effect of increased visitation has been limited. In the lake-studded area around Millinocket and Mt. Katahdin, increasing numbers of rafting outfitters have established bases and lodging options. On the western shore of Moosehead Lake, the family-owned Birches resort now holds 11,000 acres geared to nonmotorized use, and east of the lake the Applachian Mountain Club (AMC) has acquired 37,000 aces and three historic, full-service sporting camps dedicated to hiking, biking, cross-country skiing, and snowshoeing. The country's oldest nonprofit outdoor recreation and conservation group, the AMC is working to maintain an extensive trail system.

North Maine Woods, a long-established nonprofit cooperative organization of landowners, still maintains hundreds of campsites and operates staffed checkpoints at entry points to industrial logging roads (visitors pay a day-use and camping fee). These roads have themselves altered the look and nature of the North Woods. Many remote sporting camps, for a century accessible only by water, and more recently by air, are now a bumpy ride from the nearest town. However, many of the sporting camps themselves haven't changed since the turn of the 20th century. They are Maine's inland windjammers, holdovers from another era and are a precious endangered Maine species, threatened by competition from the region's new second-home owners as well by land sales and access.

As we go to press Maine's North Woods are at a tipping point. Seattle-based Plum Creek Timber Company, the country's largest landowner, has purchased a half million acres at $200 per acre, zoned for forestry and backcounty recreation. It is presently seeking to rezone 20,500 acres around Moosehead Lake to develop a total of 2,315 resort and residential accommodations. It's said to be the largest single land development proposal in Maine's history, and critics suggest that if this happens, other large land owners may do likewise.

Come soon.

There are four major approaches to the North Woods. The longest, most scenic route is up the Kennebec River, stopping to raft in The Forks, and along the Moose River to the village of Rockwood at the dramatic narrows of Moosehead Lake, then down along the lake to Greenville, New England's largest seaplane base.

From Rockwood or Greenville you can hop a floatplane to a sporting camp or set off up the eastern shore of Moosehead to the woodland outpost of Kokadjo and on up to the Golden Road, a 96-mile private logging road running east from Quebec through uninterrupted forest to Millinocket. As Thoreau did in the 1850s, you can canoe up magnificent Chesuncook Lake, camping or staying in the outpost of Chesuncook Village. With increased interest in rafting down the West Branch of the Penobscot River through Ripogenus Gorge and the Cribworks, this stretch of the Golden Road has become known as the West Branch Region.

The second and third routes, leading respectively to Greenville and Millinocket, both begin at the I-95 exit in Newport and head up through southern Piscataquis County, itself an area of small villages, large lakes, and stretches of woodland that here includes Gulf Hagas, Maine's most magnificent gorge.

For those who come this distance primarily to climb Mount Katahdin and camp in Baxter State Park, or to raft the West Branch of the Penobscot, the quickest route is up I-95 to Medway and in through Millinocket; it's 18 miles to the Togue Pond Gatehouse and Baxter State Park.

While I-95 has replaced the Penobscot River as the highway into the North Maine Woods, it has not displaced Bangor, sited on both the river and I-95 (25 miles east of Newport and 60 miles south of Medway) as the area's commercial hub and gateway. A recent effort seeks to promote the two counties—Penobscot and Piscataquis, which include Moosehead Lake, Baxter State Park, Bangor, and a good portion of the North Maine Woods—as a distinct region named "the Maine Highlands."

Contrary to its potato-fields image, Aroostook County to the north is also largely wooded and includes a major portion of the Allagash Wilderness Waterway. Northern reaches of Baxter State Park and the lakes nearby are best accessed from the park's northern entrance via Patten in "The County." Both Ashland and Portage are also points of entry, and Shin Pond serves as the seaplane base for this northernmost reach of the North Maine Woods.

GUIDANCE **North Maine Woods** (207-435-6213; www.northmainewoods.org) publishes map/guides that show logging roads with current checkpoints, user fees and campsites, and a list of outfitters and camps licensed and insured to operate on the property. The Web site is excellent.

Maine Bureau of Parks and Lands (207-287-3821; www.parksandlands.com) The bureau publishes a map/guide identifying holdings, but what's golden here is the Web site. It details specific areas such as Nahmakanta Public Reserved Land—43,000 acres of backcountry hiking trails and remote campsites.

Maine Sporting Camp Association (www.mainesportingcamps.com) maintains an excellent Web site.

Maine Forest Products Council (www.maineforest.org) offers links to local resources. Also check the **New England Forestry Foundation** (www.newenglandforestry.org), the **Northern Forest Alliance** (www.northernforestalliance.org), and **The Nature Conservancy** (www.nature.org).

SUGGESTED READING *Northeastern Wilds: Journeys of Discovery in the Northern Forest*, photography and text by Stephen Gorman (Appalachian Mountain Club Books, 2002). *The Maine Woods*, by Henry David Thoreau (Penguin Nature Library). *The Maine Atlas and Gazetteer* (DeLorme, 2007), is essential for navigating this region.

MOOSEHEAD LAKE AREA

As Rt. 15 crests Indian Hill, you see for a moment what Henry David Thoreau described so well from this spot in 1858: "A suitably wild looking sheet of water, sprinkled with low islands . . . covered with shaggy spruce and other wild wood." After a sunset by the shore of Moosehead Lake you also see what he meant by: "A lake is the Earth's eye, looking into which the beholder measures the depth of his own nature."

Moosehead is Maine's largest lake—40 miles long, up to 20 miles wide, with some 400 miles of shoreline—and its surface is spotted with more than 50 islands. Greenville at its toe is the sole "organized" town (pop. 1,623 in winter, around 10,000 in summer). Rockwood, with fewer than 300 residents, is halfway up the western shore.

Moosehead's shoreline remains predominantly green, but as we go to press, a massive real estate development is proposed for this shoreline by Seattle-based Plum Creek Timber Company. Some 20,500 acres would be rezoned for development that could include 2,325 residential and resort accommodations. It's the largest such development in Maine's history and local residents are deeply divided on the issue.

Greenville began as a farm town but soon discovered its best crops to be winter lumbering and summer tourists—a group that, since train service and grand hotels have vanished, now consists largely of anglers, canoeists, and whitewater rafters in spring and summer, and hunters in late fall. Thanks to snowmobilers, augmented by skiers, cross-country skiers, and ice fishermen, winter is now almost equally as popular. In late September and early fall when the foliage is most brilliant and mirrored in the lake, leaf-peepers are, however, still surprisingly few.

Unlike 1890s "sports" (the game hunters and trophy fishermen who put Moosehead Lake on the world's resort map), many current outdoors enthusiasts want to watch—not kill—wildlife and to experience "wilderness" completely but quickly; that is, by plunging through whitewater in a rubber raft, pedaling a mountain bike over woods trails, or paddling an hour or two in Thoreau's trail or in search of a moose.

Moosehead has become Maine's moose mecca. Experts debate whether the name of the lake stems from its shape or from the number of moose you can see

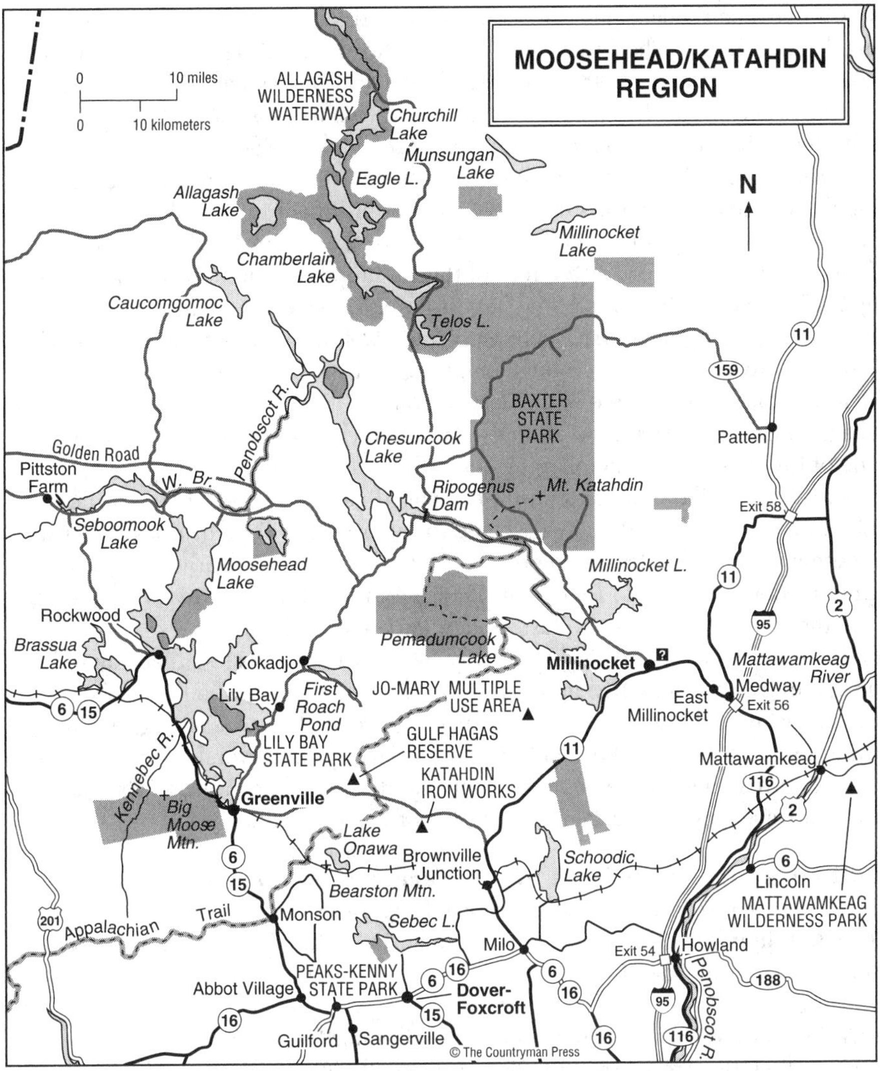

there. During "Moosemainea," a mid-May through mid-June festival that courts Moosemaniacs with a series of special events, moose sightings average 3,500.

Immense and flanked by mountains, the lake possesses unusual beauty and offers families a wide choice of rustic, old-fashioned "camps" at reasonable prices as well as an increasing number of upscale inns and B&Bs. Greenville remains a lumbermen's depot with a salting of souvenir and offbeat shops. It's also still a major seaplane base, with flying services competing to ferry visitors to remote camps and campsites in the working woodland to the north and east.

The community of Rockwood, half an hour's drive north of Greenville on the lake's west shore, is even more of an outpost: a cluster of sporting camps and stores between the lake and the Moose River. Hidden away here on the lake, overlooking Kineo, The Birches is a genuine North Woods resort with traditional lakeside cottages and 11,000 acres stretching back to Brassua Lake.

Rockwood sits at the lake's narrows, across from its most dramatic landmark: the sheer cliff face of Mount Kineo, a place revered by Native Americans. According to local legend, the mountain is the petrified remains of a monster moose sent to earth by the Great Spirit as a punishment for sins. It was also the Native Americans' source of a flintlike stone used for arrowheads. The Mount Kineo House once stood at the foot of this outcropping. First opened as a tavern in 1847, it evolved into one of the largest hotels in America, maintaining its own farm as well as a golf course, yacht club, and stables. It's all but vanished, leaving just a ghostly staff building, a huge elm tree, and a row of shingled Victorian-style summer homes, some available as private rentals. Most of Kineo, an island-like peninsula, is now owned by the state, and the climb to the abrupt summit is one of the most rewarding hikes in Maine.

Most Greenville visitors explore Moosehead's eastern shore at least as far as Lily Bay State Park, and many continue to the outpost village of Kokadjo, prime moose-watching country. It's another 40 miles northeast over private roads to Chesuncook Lake and to Ripogenus Dam, from which logging roads lead north into the Allagash and east to Baxter State Park and Millinocket.

In winter this vast area is dependably snow covered and stays that way well into March, a phenomenon appreciated by snowmobilers—who have become the mainstay of the winter economy, enabling area lodging, including remote camps, to remain open. Formal trail systems, along with several sporting camps, cater to cross-country skiers. Snowshoeing and dogsledding are also popular ways of traversing this backcountry in all its frozen magnificence.

GUIDANCE **Moosehead Lake Region Chamber of Commerce** (207-695-2702 or 1-888-876-2778; www.mooseheadlake.org), is a four-season resource. The walk-in information center up on Indian Hill (Rt. 15 south of town) is open year-round Mon.–Sat. 10–4.

GETTING THERE *By car:* Greenville is 54 miles north of I-95, exit 157, at Newport. Follow Rt. 7 to Dexter, Rt. 23 to Sangerville (Guilford), and Rt. 15 to Greenville. The longer, more scenic route is up Rt. 201 (I-95, exit 133) through The Forks (see "Upper Kennebec Valley" for suggestions about whitewater rafting). From Rt. 201 in Jackman, take Rt. 5/15 east to Rockwood.

GETTING AROUND *By air:* **Currier's Flying Service** (207-695-2778; www.curriersflyingservice.com), Greenville Junction, offers day trips; scenic flights, including Mount Katahdin, Mount Kineo, and others; and service to camps. They will book camps and guides. **Jack's Air Service** (207-695-3020), May–Oct. 1, caters to Allagash canoe trips, fly-ins to housekeeping cottages, and sightseeing flights.

By car: If you plan to venture out on the area's network of private roads, be forewarned that there are periodic gate fees and you need a car with high clearance, preferably four-wheel drive.

WHEN TO COME Greenville's seasons begin with spring fishing, which overlaps with "Moosemainea." June can be uncomfortably buggy (blackflies). The busy season is July 4 through the mid-September annual "fly-in" of floatplanes from all over North America. Fall is beautiful but low-key until deer season begins in mid-November. With snow comes snowmobile season. March has recently been the best month for snowcover.

✱ To See

♿ The **S/S *Katahdin* and Moosehead Marine Museum** (207-695-2716; www.katahdincruises.com), Greenville. This vintage 1914 steamboat sails Tues.–Sun. late June–Columbus Day on a fairly complicated schedule. Three-hour cruises are the most popular ($30 adult, $26 senior, $15 age 6–15), and depart at 12:30 PM. Five-hour cruises are for special events. Private charters available. One of 50 steamboats on the lake at its height as a resort destination, the *Katahdin* was the last to survive, converted to diesel in 1922 and in the 1930s modified to haul booms of logs, something we can remember her doing in 1976, the year of the nation's last log drive. This graceful 115-foot, 225-passenger boat was restored through volunteer effort and relaunched in 1985. The Louis Oakes Map Room displays regional, historical maps, and displays depict the lake's resort history from 1836.

Eveleth-Crafts-Sheridan House (207-695-2909; www.mooseheadhistory.org), 444 Pritham Ave., Greenville. Guided hour-long tours offered June–Sept., Wed.–Fri. 1–4. $4 adults, $2 children under 12. Home of the Moosehead Historical Society, this is a genuinely interesting 19th-century home with displays on the region's history, including postcards and photos picturing early hotels and steamboats, and changing exhibits on the "sunporch." The carriage house has been renovated as a lumberman's museum.

Abbott Museum, Dexter. (www.dexterhistoricalsociety.com). Open mid-June–Sept., daily except Sun. Stop by the information center and gift shop, with a rest room, on Rt. 7 (14 miles north of I-95 exit 157) to get directions to the this unusual local museum housed in an 1854 gristmill that's literally "down" town. It's an added reason to take a break and explore this lively main street, sited several hundred feet lower than the (literal) highway. Best known for Dexter shoes, the town of 4,000 adds another 1,000 or so summer residents along the shores of Lake Wassookeag, which is imore than 400 feet above downtown. The downtown is also noteworthy for its clocktower and several tempting shops, including a big Reny's (see *What's Where*).

MOOSE Don't leave the area without seeing at least one. See *Moose-Watching* under *To Do*.

SCENIC DRIVES

Along the western shore

Follow Rt. 6/15 north through Greenville Junction to Rockwood and take the shuttle to **Mount Kineo**; allow the better part of a day for exploring this dramatic spot. From Rockwood, you can continue north for 20 miles to the North Maine Woods checkpoint (gate fee for out-of-staters). **Pittston Farm**, a short distance beyond, was once the hub of Great Northern's operations for this entire western swath of North Woods. It's now a backwoods lodge that welcomes guests for lunch and dinner. Note that from Rockwood you can also continue on to Quebec City (via Jackman).

Along the eastern shore

Lily Bay State Park (207-695-2700), 8 miles north of Greenville, offers a sandy beach, a grassy picnicking area, and camping. It's a superlatively beautiful spot. $3 day-use fee.

Kokadjo, 18 miles north of Greenville, is a 100-acre parcel of independently owned land on First Roach Pond, in the center of lumber-company-owned forest. Most of the buildings here were once part of a lumbering station and are now camps attached to the Kokadjo Trading Post (serving meals and renting ATVs); Northern Pride Lodge rents canoes and boats. Continuing north, the road turns to dirt and is fairly bumpy for the first few miles. The road surface improves when you pass the (now unstaffed) gate entering paper company land and is fairly smooth (but you must now pull over to let lumber trucks pass); it improves even more in a dozen miles when you hit the Golden Road, where you turn right (east).

Cushing's Landing, at the foot of Chesuncook Lake, is worth a stop. The woodsman's memorial here was created from a post in the doorway of a Bangor tavern; it's decorated with tools of the trade and an iron bean pot. This is also the logical boat launch for visiting Chesuncook Village, one of the few surviving examples of a 19th-century North Maine Woods lumbermen's village, now on the National Register of Historic Places. In summer access is by charter aircraft from Greenville or by boat from Chesuncook Dam. In winter you can come by snowmobile. Writing about the village in 1853, Henry David Thoreau noted, "Here immigration is a tide which may ebb when it has swept away the pines." Today a church, a graveyard (relocated from the shore to a hollow in the woods when Great Northern raised the level of the lake a few years ago), an inn, and a huddle of houses are all that remain of the village.

Ripogenus Dam, just east of Chesuncook Lake, is a spot from which to view the gorge. Rafting trips on the West Ranch of the Penobscot begin a mile downstream, below the power station. This is the most challenging commercial whitewater run in Maine. The river drops more than 70 feet per mile—seething and roiling through Ripogenus Gorge—and continues another 12 miles, with stretches of relatively calm water punctuated by steep drops.

LILY BAY STATE PARK

Christina Tree

The **Telos Road** leads to the Allagash Wilderness Waterway, a 92-mile-long chain of lakes, ponds, rivers, and streams that snakes through the heart of the North Woods. The traditional canoe trip through the Allagash takes 10 days, but two- and three-day trips can be worked out. Brook trout, togue, and lake whitefish are plentiful. For details, see *Canoeing the Allagash* in "What's Where" and *Canoe and Kayak Rentals* and *Trips,* below.

✷ To Do

AIRPLANE RIDES See *Gettting Around.*

ATV TOURING **Kokadjo Trading Post** (207-695-3993) in Kokadjo offers guided tours and sells maps to the surrounding 125-mile trail system.

BIRDING Warblers and many elusive species, including the boreal chicadee, gray jay, black-backed woodpecker, Bicknell's thrush, and white-winged crossbill can be find in local bogs and woodland. Download "Moosehead Lake Birding Guide" from www.mooseheadlake.org; copies are available from the chamber of commerce (see *Guidance*).

Also see the **Borestone Mountain Audubon Sanctuary** under *Hiking.*

The **Appalachian Mountain Club** offers birding programs at its Little Lyford Pond and Medawisla Wilderness camps. See *Remote Sporting Camps.*

BOAT EXCURSIONS See S/S *Katahdin* under *To See.* That's the big one.

The Black Frog (207-695-1100) in Greenville offers a regular evening pontoon-boat cruise in-season on Moosehead Lake.

Kineo Shuttle (207-534-9012). In-season, frequent departures from Rockwood Landing to Kineo for hiking and golf. Both **The Birches Resort** (207-534-7588; www.birches.com) in Rockwood and **Northwoods Outfitters** (207-695-3288; www.maineoutfitter.com) offer excursions on demand.

CANOE AND KAYAKING RENTALS are available in Greenville from **Northwoods Outfitters** (see *Boat Excursions*) and **Indian Hill Trading Post** (207-695-2104) and in Rockwood from **The Birches Resort** (see *Boat Excursions*)

Note: Most sporting camps also rent canoes or kayaks, and flying services will ferry canoes into remote backcountry.

CANOE AND KAYAK GUIDED TRIPS ✐ **Allagash Canoe Trips** (207-237-3077; www.allagashcanoetrips.com), based in Greenville, May–Oct. A family business since 1953, this is the oldest continuously running guided canoe trip service in Maine. It's now operated by third-generation guide Chip Cochrane and offers weeklong expeditions into the Allagash Wilderness Waterway, on the West Branch of the Penobscot, and on the St. John River. Also special teen trips. Sept.–May, Chip (a former member of the U.S. ski team) coaches at Carrabassett Valley Academy at Sugarloaf.

Northwoods Outfitters (see *Boat Excursions*) offers five- to seven-day Allagash and two- to seven-day Penobscot wilderness canoe trips as well as day excursions and overnight camping on Moosehead.

Wilderness Expeditions, at The Birches Resort (see *Sporting Camps*), offers variety of guided kayak trips, including a three-day tour up Moosehead Lake that retraces Thoreau's exact canoe route north from Greenville to Northeast Carry (35 miles).

FISHING Troll for landlocked salmon, togue, and brook trout in Moosehead Lake, and fly-fish in the many rivers and ponds—rental boats and boat launches are so plentiful that they defy listing.

There are two prime sources of fishing information: the state's **Inland Fisheries and Wildlife** office (207-695-3756), Greenville, and the **Maine Guide Fly Shop and Guide Service** (207-695-2266), Main St., Greenville. At the Fly Shop, Dan Legere sells 314 different flies and a wide assortment of gear; he also works with local guides to outfit you with a boat and guide or to set up a river float trip or a fly-in expedition. The resurgence of fly-fishing as a popular sport is reflected in the variety of gear and guides available in this shop. Deep lake trolling is, however, also popular. For a list of local boat rentals as well as a list of local guides, check with the Moosehead Lake Region Chamber of Commerce (see *Guidance*). Also see the listings under *Sporting Camps*, all of which are on water and cater to fishermen.

Ice fishing usually begins in January and ends with March. Icehouse rentals are available locally. Inquire at the chamber.

GOLF **Mount Kineo Golf Course** (207-534-8812). A spectacularly sited nine-hole course at Kineo, accessible by frequent boat service from Rockwood; carts and club rentals.

Squaw Village (207-695-3609), Rt. 15, Greenville, offers nine holes.

HIKING The not-to-be-missed hike in this area is **Mount Kineo**, an islandlike peninsula with trails to the back side of the famous cliff that rises 763 feet above the water and the apron of land once occupied by the Kineo House resort. Most of the peninsula (8,000 acres) is now state owned, and trails along its circumference and up the back of the cliff are maintained. Take the Indian Trail, which heads straight up over ledges that are a distinct green: This is one of the world's largest masses of rhyolite, a flintlike volcanic rock. This trail is shaded by red pines, oaks, and a surprising variety of hardwoods. The view down the lake from the fire tower is spectacular. The Bridle Trail is easier for the descent, and a good option on the way up for small children. A carriage trail also circles Mount Kineo, which is accessible from Rockwood by frequent water shuttle (see *Boat Excursions*). Bring a picnic and lunch at the Kineo House site.

Gulf Hagas, billed as the "Grand Canyon of Maine," is described in the Katahdin Region chapter. It's also accessible from Greenville via Airport Road. When the pavement ends it's another 12.6 miles to the Hedgehog Checkpoint ($9 for out-of-staters), where you can pick up a map. It's another 2 miles to the trailhead parking lot. The gulf is also an easy hike, snowshoe, or ski from **Little Lyford Pond Camps** (see *Remote Sporting Camps*).

OTHER GOOD HIKES INCLUDE ✐ **Borestone Mountain Audubon Sanctuary**, 10 miles out Elliotsville Rd. from Rt. 6/15 at Monson. A good hike for families. The trail begins at the gate (elevation 800 feet) on a 1.3-mile road to the visitors center maintained by Maine Audubon (207-631-4050; www.maineaudubon.org) at Sunrise Pond. A footpath continues another mile up to Borestone's rocky West Peak; a blazed trail continues another 0.5 mile to the East Peak (elevation 2,000 feet) for a 360-degree view.

Check local sources for details about hiking Little and Big Spencer Mountains and Elephant Mountain, and walking into Little Wilson Falls, a majestic 57-foot cascade in a forested setting.

Note: The Moosehead Lake Region Chamber of Commerce publishes a detailed, free hiking guide, available online www.mooseheadlake.org.

HORSEBACK RIDING AND WAGON RIDES See **Northern Maine Riding Adventures** in "Katahdin Region."

Rockies Golden Acres (207-695-3229), Greenville, offers one-and-a-half to two-hour trail rides through the woods to Sawyer Pond; mountain views. Call after 7 PM, or leave a message.

MARINAS **Big Lake Equipment Marina** (207-695-4487) in downtown Greenville offers slips, fuel, and supplies.

Beaver Cove Marina (207-395-3526; www.beavercovemarina.com), 8 miles north of Greenville on the eastern side of the lake, offers slips and a selection of rental boats, parts and service, fuel and clothing.

MOUNTAIN BIKING **Northwoods Outfitters** (207-695-3288), Main St., Greenville, rents bikes and provides trail information. A 17-mile logging road route from **Medawisla** (see *Remote Sporting Camps*) and Little Lyford Pond is suggested by the AMC, which offers a shuttle service back to Medawisla (there's a 2-mile uphill climb the other direction).

MOOSE-WATCHING

"Moosemainea," sponsored by the Moosehead Lake Chamber of Commerce mid-May–mid-June, is the largest, most colorful moose-watching event in New England, maybe anywhere. Still, chances are you can spot the lake's mascot any dawn or dusk at local hangouts like the DOT site on Rt. 15, 4.5 miles south of Indian Hill, Lazy Tom Bog in Kokadjo, or on the road from Rockwood to Pittston Farm. Best, however, to leave the driving to someone else. **Moose cruises** aboard pontoon boats are offered mornings and evenings by **The Birches Resort** (207-534-7305). **Northwoods Outfitters** (207-695-3288) also offers moose-watching excursions by kayak or canoe. Other local outfitters and flying services will also arrange tours; check with the chamber (see *Guidance*).

The Birches Resort (207-534-7305), Rockwood, offers mountain bike rentals for use on its extensive cross-country ski network.

RECREATIONAL FACILITY ✐ **Greenville Athletic Complex** at Greenville High School, Pritham Ave., Greenville. Facilities include an outdoor rink for skateboarding and roller hockey in summer and ice hockey in winter, as well as a 0.25-mile, 8-foot-wide paved in-line skating track; also a sand volleyball court, a 0.25-mile running track, outdoor tennis courts, a basketball court, and a playground.

SWIMMING See **Lily Bay State Park** under *Scenic Drives.*

Red Cross swimming beach, halfway between Greenville Village and the Junction, is a good beach on the lake, with lifeguards.

WHITEWATER RAFTING AND KAYAKING Moosehead Lake is equidistant from Maine's two most popular rafting routes—Kennebec Gorge and Ripogenus Gorge. So see the "Upper Kennebec" and "Katahdin Region" chapters. **Wilderness Expeditions** (207-534-2242), based at The Birches Resort in Rockwood, specializies in half-day whitewater rafting trips on the Kennebec at East Outlet (minimum age is 7).

✷ Winter Sports

CROSS-COUNTRY SKIING Formal touring centers aside, this region's vast network of snowmobile trails and frozen lakes constitutes splendid opportunities for backcountry skiing.

Northwoods Outfitters (207-695-3288), Main St., Greenville, is a full-service retail shop, selling and renting cross-country skis and snowshoes; offering a list of trails.

Birches Ski Touring Center (207-534-7305), Rockwood. The Birches Resort maintains an extensive network of trails, taking advantage of an 11,000-acre forested spread across the neck between Brassua and Moosehead Lakes; you can spend the night in yurts spaced along the trail. You can also ski to Tomhegan, 10 miles up the lake, or out past the ice-fishing shanties to Kineo. Rentals and instruction; snowshoes, too.

The Appalachian Mountain Club (www.outdoors.org) owns Little Lyford Pond and Medawisla camps and maintains and with West Branch Pond Camps (see *Remote Sporting Camps*) offer camp-to-camp cross-country tours with shuttle service and optional dogsledding between. We did this in 2007 and can vouch for the improved access the AMC has brought to one of the most splendid cross-country experiences in New England.

✐ **A Fierce Chase** (207-997-3971), Elliotsville Rd., posted from Rt. 15 (it's 1 mile) in Monson. Open when there's snow, 8 AM–sunset. John and Susan Chase groom 14 kilometers of cross-country ski trails for both classical and skate skiing. Ski and snowshoe sales, rentals, and lessons available. Trail fees $10 adults, $7 students (9–18); ages 8 and under free.

DOGSLEDDING Moose Country Safaris and Dogsled Trips (207-876-4907; www.moosecountrysafaris.com), 191 North Dexter Rd., Sangerville. Ed Mathew offers one- and two-hour trips in the Moosehead Lake region, with heated warming huts along the way. Also see **Maine Dogsledding Adventures** (207-731-8888; www.mainedogsledding.com) in the "Katahdin" chapter. Based at Nahmakanta Lake Camps in Rainbow Township, halfway between Greenville and Millinocket, this is the most extensive dogsledding program in the area. **Song in the Woods** (207-876-4736; www.songinthewoods.com), Abbot. Stephen Medera and his team of huskies offer not only sled rides but also full-day adventures featuring snowshoeing.

DOWNHILL SKIING 🖉 **Big Squaw Mountain Resort** (207-695-1000; www.bigsquawmountain.com), Rt. 15, Greenville. This ski mountain with its 1,750-foot drop, 33 trails, and 52-unit recently renovated lodge is currently closed, as is summer access to the spectacular view. The absentee owner has announced an ambitious expansion. Stay tuned.

SNOWMOBILING Snowmobiling is huge in this area, with 500 well-maintained miles of snowmobile trails. **Moosehead Riders Snowmobile Club** offers a 24-hour trail-condition report (207-695-4561). Its clubhouse is open Sat. and Sun. in winter. The club also sponsors guided tours. Interconnecting Trail System (ITS) Rts. 85, 86, and 87 run directly through the area, and there are many locally groomed trails as well. The 100-mile Moosehead Trail circles the lake. Rt. 66 runs east–west from Mount Kineo to Kokadjo. Snowmobile **rentals** are available from Northwoods Outfitters (207-695-3288) and **Big Lake Equipment** (207-695-4487) in Greenville; from the **Birches Resort** (1-800-825-9453) and **Moosehead Sled** (207-534-2261; www.mooseheadsledrentals.com) in Rockwood; and from **Kokadjo Trading Post** (207-695-3993), among others. Inquire about guided tours.

✷ Lodging

INNS The Blair Hill Inn (207-695-0224; www.blairhill.com), Lily Bay Rd., P.O. Box 1288, Greenville 04441. Overlooking Moosehead Lake from high above, at the top of Blair Hill, this is Maine's most gracious inland inn. The airy 1891 Victorian mansion has been sensitively restored to its original grandeur by Dan and Ruth McLaughlin. The upstairs guest rooms have all been deftly decorated and offer sitting area, a featherbed, fine linens, and CD player. Seven rooms overlook the lake (four have a wood-burning fireplace), and there are two genuine two-room suites, good for families (children must be 10 or older). All baths are private and fitted with hand-cut soaps and terrycloth robes, but there are no Jacuzzis. Our favorites are Room 1, the original master bedroom, with a hearth and a king-sized four-poster, but also Room 6, on the third floor, nestled under the eaves but with the same view. A hot tub on the 90-foot veranda also has magnificent views. From spring through fall the inn is filled with fresh flowers from its garden. $250–450 includes a multicourse breakfast. A

DINING AT BLAIR HILL INN

six-course prix fixe inner is served Fri. and Sat. (see *Dining Out*). Summer Thursday-evening concerts are presented on the lawn.

♿ **The Lodge at Moosehead Lake** (207-695-4400 or 1-800-825-6977; www.lodgeatmooseheadlake.com), 368 Lily Bay Rd., P.O. Box 1167, Greenville 04441. Open year-round. Linda and Dennis Bortis from Missouri are the new owners of his handsome inn with lake views. They offer five guest rooms in the main house, each designed around a theme. Carved four-poster beds depict each theme (moose, bear, loon, totem). All rooms have cable TV, gas fireplace, air-conditioning, and bath with Jacuzzi tub. A carriage house holds three suites, each with double Jacuzzi and private deck. The former owner's quarters are now another large and luxurious suite, comfortably accommodating two couples. Common space includes a living room and an informal downstairs pub with a pool table. A full breakfast is served in the glass-walled dining room, and dinner is served Fri.–Mon. $295–485, $688 for the deluxe suite, includes a full breakfast.

♿ **Greenville Inn** (207-695-2206 or 1-888-695-6000; www.greenvilleinn.com), Norris St., P.O. Box 1194, Greenville 04441. Open all year (B&B Nov.–May). A lumber baron's mansion set atop a hill with a view of Moosehead Lake. Rich wood paneling, embossed walls, working fireplaces, and leaded glass all contribute to the sense of elegance. Terry and Jeffrey Johannemann have added air-conditioning. A master suite with a fireplace in a separate sitting room has a lake view, and there are four more attractive second-floor rooms in the mansion itself, two more spacious suites (one good for a family of six) in the Carrriage House, and six cottages. A separate Tower Suite, painted Valentine red, has been designed for romance with an in-room, two-person Jacuzzi. Rooms $185–220, suites $275–400, cottages $195–225, buffet breakfast included. Less off-season. Also see *Dining Out*.

Lodging note: The above trio of inns represents by far the most elegant inn-style lodging anywhere in inland Maine and are best savored in combination with one of the area's traditional sporting camps. We suggest heading first for the woods, then luxuriating in town.

BED & BREAKFASTS Pleasant Street Inn (207-695-3400; www.pleasantstinn.com), 26 Pleasant St., P.O. Box 1261, Greenville 04441. An 1890s house, built proudly with a square tower and tiger oak woodwork on a quiet side street by the owner of the region's first big outfitter. The six guest rooms vary in size, and each is decorated differently. A fourth-floor Tower Room, available to all, commands a view of the lake. Other common spaces include an upstairs and downstairs sitting room, a well-stocked butler's pantry, and a dining room with a fireplace, the setting for full breakfasts and for dinner by reservation ($35–40). $110–175; suites to $260.

The Evergreen Lodge at Moosehead (207-695-3241 or 1-888-624-3993; www.evergreenlodgemoosehead.com), Rt. 15, P.O. Box 236, Greenville 04441. South of Greenville, this contemporary house is set back in its gardens, surrounded by 30 acres of birches and evergreens. Two sitting rooms have TV and fireplace; the six guest rooms are all brightly, comfortably furnished, all with private bath, two with log fireplace. $115–155 includes a full breakfast.

EASILY ACCESIBLE SPORTING CAMPS **Wilsons on Moosehead Lake** (1-800-817-2549; www.wilsonsonmooseheadlake.com), HC37, Box 200, Greenville Jct. 04442. Open year-round. Scott and Alison Snell and family have rejuvenated this classic complex just south of the East Outlet of the Kennebec River (beloved by firemen and great for family rafting) and right on Moosehead, with 20-mile views across the lake. Its former centerpiece, a tower-topped hotel in which President Grant once spent New Year's Day, is gone, but the area is nicely landscaped. The housekeeping cottages all have screened porches and wood stove or fireplace. Boats, canoes, and kayak rentals, as well as guiding are available. One-bedroom cabins $70–95 per couple, $140–300 for three to five bedroom cottages. Weekly rates available.

✐ 🐾 **Grey Ghost Camps** (207-534-7362; www.GrayGhostCamps.com) P.O. Box 35, Rockwood 02278. A dozen nicely renovated 1950s fishing camps on the Moose River, with access to Moosehead Lake. In the same family for 40 years, now ably managed by Steve and Amy Lane. One and three-bedroom cabins, each with a full kitchen, bath, living room, TV, VCR, and CD. From $80 per night, weekly rates. Kayaks included. Boat rentals, laundry facilities, docking.

MOUNT KINEO FROM ROCKWOOD COTTAGES

Christina Tree

The Birches Resort (207-534-7305 or 1-800-825-WILD; www.birches.com), P.O. Box 41, Rockwood 04478. Open year-round. Over the decades the Willard family has transformed this 1930s sporting camp into a genuine all-season, many-faceted North Woods resort. Its 15 rustic cabins are spaced among birch trees along Moosehead Lake, overlooking Mount Kineo. They range from one to four bedrooms and from traditional hand-hewn log "camps" to a luxurious contemporary cabin with four bedrooms, four baths, and a hot tub. Each has at least a porch and a Franklin stove or fireplace in a sitting room, and all have a kitchen (some don't have an oven), but three meals are offered at the lodge. Inquire about "lakeside homes" and other rentals. The main lodge features a cheerful open-timbered dining room (see *Dining Out*), an inviting lobby, and a living room with a hearth and a corner pub with tree stump stools. Upstairs the four guest rooms have decks overlooking the lake (shared bath); there are also "cabin tents" near the lodge and several yurts scattered along wooded cross-country ski/biking trails. Facilities include an outside hot tub and sauna near the lodge and a fitness center out by the marina. Moose cruises and guided kayak, hiking, backwoods jeep and biking tours are offered, along with fly-fishing, whitewater rafting, and scenic floatplane rides with innkeeper John Willard. Sailboards, sailboats, kayaks, canoes, fishing boats, and mountain bikes are available. In winter this is a major cross-country ski center, but snowmobiles are also rented and there's ice fishing within walking distance of the cabins. $65–115 double in the lodge; $130–200 per night and $750–1,375 per week for one- and two-bedroom "rustic" cabins; $235–295 per night ($1,300–1,625 per week) for the luxury four-bedroom cabin sleeping six. Cabin tents begin at $40 per person per day, and yurts at $35. Inquire about rafting, canoeing, and other packages. Pets are $10 extra.

THE BIRCHES RESORT

Christina Tree

Rockwood Cottages (207-534-7725; www.mooseheadlakelodging.com), P.O. Box 176, Rockwood 04478. Open May–Nov. Ron and Bonnie Searles maintain eight clean, comfortable housekeeping cottages with screened-in porches overlooking the lake and Mount Kineo. Canoe and motorboat **rentals, and hunting and fishing licenses** are available. There's also a sauna and barbecue. From $85 per couple per night, $510 per week.

Beaver Cove Camps (207-695-3717 or 1-800-577-3717; www.beavercovecamps.com), P.O. Box 1233, Greenville 04441. Open year-round. Eight miles north of Greenville on the eastern shore of Moosehead Lake are six fully equipped housekeeping cabins (four waterfront) dating to 1905, each with full kitchen and bath. Owners Dave and Marilyn Goodwin offer launching and docking facilities. $110 per couple per night plus $25 for each additional person; $10 per pet per night. Weekly rates available.

Wilson Pond Camps (207-695-2860; www.wilsonpondcamps.com), P.O. Box 1354, Greenville 04441. Bob and Martine Young are the owners of five modern, waterfront cottages (most with woodstove) and two cottages overlooking Lower Wilson Pond, 3.5 miles from downtown Greenville. A remote cottage called Top Secret Lodge, on Upper Wilson Pond, accepts pets. The housekeeping cottages offer one to three bedrooms, fully equipped kitchen, and screened-in porch. Boats and motors, kayak and canoe rentals are available. From $125 a day for two off-season to $650 a week for three; two-day minimum in July and August.

Maynard's in Maine (207-534-7703; www.maynardsinmaine.com), just off Rt. 6/15 over the bridge in Rockwood 04478. Open May–hunting season. "The only thing we change around here is the linen," says Gail Maynard, who helps run the sportsmen's camp founded by her husband's grandfather in 1919. Overlooking the Moose River, a short walk from Moosehead Lake, Maynard's includes 13 tidy moss-green frame buildings with dark Edwardian furniture, much of it from the grand old Mount Kineo Hotel. The lodge is filled with mounted fish, birds, and other trophies. Two meals a day are served, plus one "packed." Per person $65 with three meals, $40 in a housekeeping cabin (no meals). $20 per pet (for duration of the stay).

REMOTE FULL-SERVICE SPORTING CAMPS (requiring a four-wheel-drive or high-clearance vehicle, and in winter possibly either snowmobile or nonmotorized access; inquire about fly-in access.)

West Branch Pond Camps (207-695-2561; www.westbranchpondcamps.com), P.O. Box 1153, Greenville 04441. A 45-minute drive, 18 miles north of downtown Greenville on the Lily Bay Road, then a 10-mile drive in. Open after ice-out through Oct., and Feb. 1–Mar. 24. Eric Stirling is the fourth generation of his family to run this classic cluster of weathered, waterside log sporting camps and lodge with a view across the lake to the majestic 3,644-feet high bulk of Whitecap Mountain. With the help of his mom, Carol, a legendary cook who herself managed the camps for decades, and his vivacious photographer-wife, Mildred, Eric has opened a new chapter in the long history of these camps. The family now owns the property outright (after almost a century of leasing the land), and easements protect the surrounding woodland from development. Stirling maintains 15 kilometers of trails for nonmotorized recreation. These connect with trails maintained by the Appalachian Mountain Club and in conjunction with them, Stirling offers camp-to-camp cross-country, snowshoeing, and dog-sledding treks (see Little Lyford Pond Camps and Medawisla, below). All cabins have woodstove, electricity, and bath but the plumbing is seasonal: outhouse and wash basin in winter (honestly, it's okay). The furnishings are comfortable, with some rare "rustic" pieces. Motorboats and canoes are available. Food is hearty New England fare with a set menu—prime rib on Thursday and turkey dinner on Sunday—with fresh vegetables and greens from the organic garden June–Sept. and vegetarian fare on request. In summer meals are served in the classic old lodge dining room; in winter guests gather in the big county kitchen. It's no secret that First West Branch Pond is the area's prime moose-viewing spot. $85–95 per person per day includes three meals and use of a canoe; children 5–11 $45–55.

LITTLE LYFORD CAMPS

Christina Tree

Little Lyford Pond Camps (603-466-2727; www.outdoors.org/ lodging/ lyford), P.O. Box 310, Greenville 04441. Open Dec.26–Mar. and early May–Oct. Reservations are required. Little Lyford and 37,000 surrounding acres are now owned by the Boston-based Appalachian Mountain Club, the country's oldest outdoor recreation/conservation group. Sited in a sheltered alpine valley, these camps were built in the 1870s as a logging company station on a "tote road." The seven log cabins (without plumbing or electricity) sleep from one to six. Each has a private outhouse. A bunkhouse sleeps 14. The central lodge houses the dining room and space to relax. A spiffy new bathroom/shower house is open year-round and there's a cedar sauna. Gulf Hagas is a 7-mile round-trip hike or ski, and five other trails start at the camp. In winter you can ski or dogsled to the camps or hitch a snowmobile shuttle, along with your gear. The camps are 2 miles off the Appalachian Trail and 17 miles via a logging road from Greenville. We've come in January and March and enjoyed exceptional skiing both times (March is actually snowier as well as warmer). $65–$99 per person in summer, $75–$120 per person in winter (less for children and AMC members), includes all meals. There's a charge for the snowmobile shuttle and gear shuttle. The KI Jo-Mary gate fee (summer only) is $10. *Note*: Inquire about the **Leon and Lisa Gorman Camps at Chairback Mountain**. Sited on secluded Long Pond, some 5 miles from Little Lyford, this is another classic 19th-century sporting camp now owned by the AMC. It is due to be open on a limited basis beginning in late 2008.

✐ **Medawisla** (603-466-2727; www.outdoors.org/lodging/lodges/medawisla), P.O. Box 310, Greenville 04441. Open Dec. 26–Mar.; early May–Nov. The AMC offers seven fully equipped cabins with woodstove, flush toilet, hot shower, and a propane cookstove, sleeping two to ten people. We love the "reading room," a spot outside overlooking a dam that once held the only road in. Boats and canoes are available. The loons on the soundtrack from the movie *On Golden Pond* were taped here. Rates, all meals included, are $84–99 per person in summer, $102–120 in winter; $47 self-service (summer only); also children's and AMC member rates. This is a cross-country-ski haven with close to 30 miles of trails; dog-sledding trips can be arranged.

🐾 ∞ **Chesuncook Lake House and Cabins** (207-745-5330; www.chesuncooklakehouse.com), Rt. 76, P.O. Box 656, Greenville 04441. Open year-round. At a homey, 1864 farmhouse, David and Luisa Surprenant are carrying on a long-standing tradition of hospitality with four guest rooms (shared bath) and nearby cabins. For an additional charge guests can be shuttled in by boat or snowmobile; they can also hike, fly, ski, or canoe in. With braided rugs, patterned tin walls and ceilings, comfortable furnishings, and woodstoves, not to mention running water, beds with sheets and blankets, and the enticing aromas emanating from the big Vulcan stove in the kitchen, this is a peaceful, magical spot. When we last visited it was winter and our car was parked 14 miles down a snow-covered tote road. $90–120 person per night includes three meals; $30–40 per person in the housekeeping cabins (meals are an option). Small weddings can be arranged, using Chesuncook Village Church.

Historic Pittston Farm (207-280-0000; www.pittstonfarm.com), Rockwood 04478. Overlooking Seboomook Lake, 20 miles north of Rockwood via dirt road, also accessible by sea plane. Great Northern Paper Company built the clapboard lodge and barns here, establishing the farm in the early 1900s as a base for woodland operations. The era of "booming" (floating logs across the lakes) ended in 1971, and the property was used seasonally by the Boy Scouts. Restored as a year-round lodge by the previous owners, it's been further upgraded by Bob and Jen Mills, who offer 15 rooms (shared baths) in the lodge, seven attractive, pine-paneled units with baths in the Carriage House, and seven cabins, each accommodating four to nine people. There are also two mobile home units in the woods, and a campground. All three meals are included (see *Eating Out*). From $94 per person.

CHESUNCOOK LANDING

Christina Tree

MORE REMOTE CAMPS (HOUSEKEEPING) **Spencer Pond Camps** (207-843-5456; www.spencerpondcamps.com), 806 Spencer Pond Rd., East Middlesex Township 04441. Open May–mid-Nov. Bob Croce and Jill Martel maintain the traditions of this long-established cluster of six waterfront housekeeping camps (sleeping two to ten) in an unusually beautiful spot, 14 miles from the closest neighbor. Fly in or drive, 34 miles north of Greenville via a logging road from Lily Bay Rd. Guests are welcome to fresh vegetables from the gardens. Along with gas and kerosene lights and hand-pumped water, each cottage is stocked with cooking utensils and dishes, is furnished with handmade quilts and rocking chairs, and has a private shower room (Sunshower) and outhouse. The camp library is stocked for rainy days, with many reference books for nature study. Canoe, kayak, and mountain bike rentals available. From $70 per couple; family and discount rates available. Dogs accepted in October. Nature-based family adventures are a specialty during summer months.

Tomhegan Wilderness Resort (207-534-7712; www.tomhegan.com), P.O. Box 310, Rockwood 04478. Open year-round. A 10-mile ride up a dirt road from Rockwood Village and then a lengthy, bumpy ride down a private road. The rewards are 1.5 miles of frontage on Moosehead Lake and a string of 1910 hand-hewn two-bedroom housekeeping cottages (one with four bedrooms) set back above lawns, along a wooden boardwalk. Tame deer wander through the grounds. Boats and canoes are available. Cabins range $700–1,295 per week; lodge apartments begin at $155 per night.

LODGING ALONG THE MOOSEHEAD TRAIL IN SOUTHERN PISCATAQUIS COUNTY **Brewster Inn** (207-924-3130; www.brewsterinn.com), 37 Zion's Hill Rd., Dexter 04930. Open year-round. Dexter is a proud old Maine town, and this is its proudest house, built in the 1930s for Governor (later Senator) Ralph Owen Brewster by noted architect John Calvin Stevens. Brits Mark and Judith Stephens offer eight guest rooms and two suites. $59–129 per couple includes breakfast.

The Guilford Bed & Breakfast (207-876-3477; www.guilfordbandb.com), 24 Elm St., P.O. Box 178, Guilford 04443. Harland and Isabel Young offer warm hospitality in their gracious 1905 mansion built by the family of the local woolen mill owner. A great stop on the way to the Moosehead or Katahdin region. Four second-floor rooms (one with two queen beds) are unusually attractive, each with private bath; two delightful third-floor guest rooms, one with a stained-glass window, share a bath (robes provided). $80–115 includes a full breakfast.

RENTALS Private camp rentals are listed with the chamber of commerce and handled by **Century 21 Muzzy Real Estate** (207-695-4741) and **Vacation Rentals, Inc.** (207-534-9703; www.connectmaine.com/vacation).

CAMPGROUNDS **Lily Bay State Park** (207-695-2700). Open May–Oct. 15. Nine miles north of Greenville on the east shore of Moosehead Lake, this 925-acre park contains 91 well-spaced sites, many along the shore. Two are wheelchair accessible;

facilities include a shower house, boat launch, and beach. $19 for nonresidents, $14 for Maine residents.

Seboomook Wilderness Campground (207-280-0555; www.seboomookwildernesscampground.us), HC 85, Box 560, Rockwood. 04478. Open May–Dec. 8. Accessed by dirt road (some 32 miles from Rockwood), in the northwest corner of the lake. Sites for RVs and tents ($18–30); Adirondack shelters ($30) on the water. Photos in the camp store (where there's a lunch counter) document this site's days as a World War II POW camp. $20 per couple for cabins. Canoe, kayak, and boat rentals.

Maine State Forest Service (207-695-3721) maintains free (first-come, first-served) "authorized sites" (no fire permit required) and "permit sites" (permit required) scattered on both public and private land along Moosehead Lake and on several of its islands.

✷ Where to Eat

DINING OUT **Blair Hill Inn** (207-695-0224; www.blairhill.com), Lily Bay Rd., Greenville. Open to the public late June–mid-Oct., Fri. and Sat., also serving inn guests on Sat. evening in winter. Reservations required. A five-course menu with a choice of three entrées, served in the dining room or on the side porch with lake views. In fairness few tables in the dining room itself do not enjoy this view but there are a couple corners and you might request not being stuck in one. Guests tend to come early for a cocktail on the porch. The menu changes daily, depending on the freshest produce available. On a July day appetizers included lobster and corn beignets and pan-fried bean cakes with hot pepper jelly and mango, the soup was ginger carrot with crème fraîche, and the salad was from the inn garden. The fully flavored slow-roasted duck confit and mushroom ragout and the Maine goat-cheese cake with a rhubarb-berry coulis were simply superlative. $55 prix fixe. Blair Hill is the region's outstanding inn; see *Lodging*.

Greenville Inn (207-695-2206 or 1-888-695-6000), Norris St., Greenville. Dinner served in-season late June–mid-Oct., Mon.–Sat., weekends in May and June. Reservations requested. Chef "Bear" Hillard describes his menu as "New American cuisine . . . using fresh, organic, local fare." A summer menu might begin with a smoked seafood salad ($11) and feature a choice of a half dozen entrees ranging from "catch of the day" to venison chops with roasted citrus and port wine with a pistachio-mint and date paté. Entrées: $24–37.

The Lodge at Moosehead Lake (207-695-4400; www.lodgeatmooseheadlake.com), Lily Bay Road, Greenville. Open Fri.–Mon, year-round. The formal dining room in this inn overlooks the lake. A choice of three- and five-course menus ($40 and $55 respectively) are offered. You might begin with grilled Szechuan glazed seafood sausage and dine on grilled rack of lamb or grilled jumbo shrimp and penne. Options in the less formal pub with a similar view range from grilled flatbread pizza to grilled fillet mignon ($10-25).

The Birches Resort (207-534-2242), Rockwood. Open year-round: daily in summer, closed sporadically, please check. This popular resort (see *Lodging*) has one of the area's most attractive dining rooms—log sided with a massive stone hearth, a war canoe turned upside down in the open rafters, and hurricane lamps on the highly polished tables. The dining room's center pole is sculpted by lightning. Add to this a view of the lake. The menu offers grilled or baked options; specialties include baby back ribs, prime rib roast, and Sicilian haddock (baked with Parmesan, black olives, and parsley in red wine and garlic). Entrées $14–18. Reservations suggested. There's also an inviting pub.

Northern Pride Lodge (207-695-2890), Kokadjo. Open year-round. Reservations required. The dining room in this lumber baron's hunting lodge is a heated sunporch overlooking a campground on First Roach Pond. Destination dining combined with moose-watching, a half hour's drive north of downtown Greenfied. Rental canoes and kayaks are offered along with pontoon rides. Dining choices might include roast duckling with crispy skin and tender meat served with a homemade orange sauce, and baked salmon with the house raspberry maple glaze. Entrées $18–21.

Maynard's Dining Room (207-534-7703), off Rt. 6/15, Rockwood. Open Mother's Day–Columbus Day for dinner 6–8. Dine much as your grandparents would have in the traditional old lodge dining room overlooking the Moose River. Choices vary with the night; $16.95 includes entrée, juice or soup, salad, choice of potato or veggie, bread, dessert, and beverage. BYOB. This is known as a first-rate place to dine.

Historic Pittston Farm (207-280-0000; www.pittstonfarm.com), Rockwood 04478. Open year-round 7 AM–7 PM. Destination dining, not because the food is gourmet but because this is a great backwoods destination, a reason to head up the 20-mile road north of Rockwood or to fly in. This classic outpost (see *Lodging*), a wilderness farm on the National Historic Register built in the early 1900s as a major hub of Great Northern's logging operations, offers good home-cooking under current ownership by Jenn and Bob Mills. Buffet all-you-can-eat dinner, 5–7 every night. BYOB.

Rod 'n' Reel Café (207-695-0388), downtown Greenville, across from the lake. Open year-round, 11 AM–closing. Greenville on Sunday night tends to shut down tight by 8 PM, the hour we knocked on the window of this cozy-looking restaurant, which had just closed its kitchen. Karen LeClair, however, is not about to let anyone go hungry, and she fed us, at the bar, one of the best baked haddocks ($11.95) in memory. The daylong menu runs from a hot dog or burger to prime rib (Fri. and Sat. only). Fully licensed. Dinner entrées $10–23. Tadpoles menu and senior discounts.

EATING OUT

In Greenville

The Black Frog (207-695-1100; www.theblackfrog.com), Pritham Ave. Open daily for lunch and dinner. Leigh Turner was a founder of The Road Kill Café in Greenville Junction not that many years ago. Ask and he will recount his brush with Wall Street, a brief period during which Road Kill Cafés proliferated around New England but then went bust. The Black Frog offers waterside dining with a menu featuring the likes of "the chicken that didn't make it across the road," "the moose is loose," and "oops-soups."

✐ **Auntie M's Family Restaurant** (207-695-2238), Lily Bay Rd. Open 5 AM–closing; great breakfast, homemade soups, and specials. We love this place. Everything always tastes good.

Flatlander's Pub (207-695-3373), Pritham Ave. Open daily (except in winter when closed on Wed.) from 11 AM "'til close." Hamburgers, broasted chicken, seafood; homemade desserts.

Stress Free Moose Pub & Café (207-695-3100), 65 Pritham Ave. Lunch–10 PM weekdays, till 11 Fri.–Sat. Dining on the back deck with a lake view in summer, otherwise inside around the bar and with limited seating by the deli; coffeehouse atmosphere upstairs. Regulars swear by the chili.

Beyond Greenville

Kokadjo Trading Post (207-695-3993), Kokadjo. Open 7 AM–9 PM; earlier during hunting season. Fred and Marie Candeloro offer a cozy dining room with a large fieldstone fireplace and a view of First Roach Pond.

Spring Creek Bar-B-Q (207-997-7025), Rt. 15, Monson. Open Thu.–Sun. 10–8. Closed Dec. and Apr. Ribs are the big specialty here, but you might want to reserve (you can call days ahead), because they run out toward the end of the day. Also good for standard road food.

✷ Selective Shopping

Indian Hill Trading Post (207-695-3376), Greenville. Open daily year-round, Fri. until 10 PM. Huge—a combination sports store, supermarket, and general store, stocking everything you might need for a week or two in the woods.

Moosehead Traders (207-695-3806), Moosehead Center Mall, Rt. 15 in downtown Greenville. The most upscale shop in the North Maine Woods: furs, moose antlers and moose antler furnishings (like chandeliers), camp furnishings, antiques, books, and many tempting gifts. The moose is not for sale.

✐ **Breakneck Ridge Farm** (207-997-3922; www.breakneckridgefarm.com), 160 Mountain Rd., Blanchard. Some 200 head of fallow deer and a small herd of buffalo are raised on this farm, which is visitor geared with a shop (tours and shop July and Aug., Wed., Thu., and Sat. noon–4) selling sandwiches, some made from venison and bison. Hayride tours of the farm are offered July and Aug., Wed., Thu., and Sat. at 10; $6 adults, $6 seniors, $5 children, 3 and under free.

Joe Bolf, Woodcarver (207-695-3002; www.joebolf.com), 11 Minden St., across from the firehouse, Greenville. Bolf is the area's outstanding carver of signs (WELCOME TO GREENVILLE is a sample); also chainsaw sculpture, totem poles, figures, and camp furniture.

CHAIN SAW SIGN CARVER

Great Eastern Clothing Company (207-695-0770), a trendy emporium, has replaced the old landmark Indian Store in the Shaw Block.

"1" **Northwoods Outfitters** (207-695-3288), selling sporting gear and wear, now occupies the space vacated by Greenville's other old commercial landmark, Sanders Store. It includes a small cybercafé.

The Corner Shop (207-695-2142), corner of Main and Pritham (across from Great Eastern Clothing), Greenville; gifts, books, magazines.

Moosin' Around Maine (207-695-3939), Pritham Ave., downtown Greenville. Pottery, jewelry, blown glass from Maine and beyond.

See also **Maine Guide Fly Shop** under *Fishing*.

* Special Events

January: **Ice fishing derby**, Greenville

February: **Winter Festival**, Greenville—snowmobile events and poker runs.

Late May–mid-June: **Moosemainea** month, sponsored by the chamber of commerce, takes place throughout the area. It's big; see "What's Where."

July: The **Fourth of July** is big in Greenville, with a crafts fair, food booths, music, parade, fireworks, and street dance.

July–August: **Blair Hill Concert series**, Thurs. on the lawn at Blair Hill Inn (207-695-0224)—jazz, bluegrass, and chamber music concerts. $20 per ticket, with a percentage of all concerts benefiting Greenville High School.

August: **Forest Heritage Days**, Greenville—crafts fair and many forestry-related events.

September: **International Seaplane Fly-In Weekend** (*second weekend*), Greenville.

Columbus Day weekend: **Moose on the Run**, a 5K race.

KATAHDIN REGION

INCLUDING LOWER PISCATAQUIS AND LINCOLN LAKES

Mile-high Mount Katahdin rises massively from a vast green woodland sea, mirrored in nearby lakes and clearly visible from a surprising distance. Maine's highest mountain and the northern terminus of the Appalachian Trail, it's been synonymous with hiking since Henry David Thoreau described his first climb to the top in 1846.

The trails leading to the summit still represent the most popular hikes in the state, but climbers can also choose from several less-trafficked mountains within the surrounding 204,733 acres of Baxter State Park, all with views of Katahdin itself. In all the park offers hiking on 300 trail miles, as well as fishing on remote lakes and ponds.

Hiking is just one of the many ways to accomplish what's described locally as "getting out," which is what this area is all about. Fishing and hunting have long been a way of life, and in recent decades whitewater rafters have been plunging down the West Branch of the Penobscot River through Ripogenous Gorge, the ultimate rafting run in the Northeast.

Early morning and evening moose-watching is another summer ritual. Organized excursions are offered, but there are also some well-known spots where one's likely to see moose at sunset. The winter months are predictably snowy, and there's a big commitment to maintaining snowmobile, cross-country ski, and snowshoeing systems. Dog-sledding and ice-fishing are also draws.

The big town here is Millinocket, a lumbering outpost with some 5,000 souls built by the Great Northern Paper Company around the turn of the 20th century at major drops in the Penobscot River—110 feet in Millinocket itself, and 25 and 50 feet in East Millinocket. In recent years the mills on these sites have changed ownership repeatedly and layoffs have cost some 600 jobs. Currently owned by Brookfield, a Canadian conglomerate, both mills are still operating, producing about what they did decades ago.

Significantly, Millinocket is also the name of the pristine lake east of Mount Katahdin, separated by a narrow causeway from Ambajejus Lake, which becomes Pemadumcook Lake, flowing in turn into North Twin Lake, South Twin

Lake, and Elbow Lake. Even without Katahdin, these lakes would be impressive, and with this magnificent centerpiece they can be downright magical, especially at sunset, when you sit quietly, listening to the haunting call of the loons.

Recreation is visibly becoming the area's future income base. B&Bs are multiplying, a former campground-owner has built a luxurious lakeside log lodge, and an inn has added upscale "suites," supplementing Baxter State Park's cabins and campsites, whitewater base camps and the traditional sporting camps widely scattered through the woods. A 1,450-acre Ktaadn Resort (the spelling is from the Abenaki name) overlooking Millinocket Lake, featuring an organic farm, an 80-room lodge, and a restaurant, is planned.

Southwest of Millinocket, lower Piscataquis County is largely woodland traversed (north–south) by Rt. 11, the old road to Millinocket before the advent of I-95. This is a slice of "the real Maine," with Dover-Foxcroft (pop.: circa 4,300) as its big town. The very real and relatively little-known treasures here are 13-mile-long Sebec Lake, site of Peaks-Kenny State Park, and Gulf Hagas, billed as "Maine's Grand Canyon." Southeast of Millinocket, the Lincoln Lakes region offers some 15 lakes as well as the Penobscot and Mattawamkeag Rivers.

GUIDANCE **Katahdin Area Chamber of Commerce** (207-723-4443; www.katahdinmaine.com), 1029 Central St. (Rt. 11/157), Millinocket 04462. This seasonal information center is open weekdays. An unstaffed information kiosk is sited on Rt. 157 in Medway, just off I-95 exit 244.

The Baxter State Park Headquarters (207-723-5140; www.baxterstatepark authority.com), 64 Balsam Dr., Millinocket 04462, is open Memorial Day–Columbus Day, daily 8–4; otherwise weekdays. Just off Rt. 11/57 on a service road (next to McDonald's), it offers picnic tables, restrooms, and a selection of guides to the park. This is primarily a reservation center (it's 18 miles east of the park itself), but a useful stop if you are coming from I-95 and want to check on conditions (traffic as well as weather) before proceeding. A **Visitor Information Center** located just before Togue Pond Gate (open Memorial Day–Labor Day) offers trip advice, up-to-date weather and trail information, and map/guides.

Southern Piscataquis County Chamber of Commerce (207-564-7533; www.spccc.org), 1033 South St. (Rt. 7). This log information center is open when volunteers are available. The Web site lists many rental camps and other lodging options.

DOGSLEDDING ACROSS RAINBOW LAKE FROM NAHMAKANTA

Christina Tree

GETTING THERE The most direct route is I-95 to exit 244 in Medway (73 miles northeast of Bangor), and 12 miles into Millinocket. From here, it's about 10 miles to Millinocket Lake, and from there another 8 miles to the Togue Pond entrance to Baxter State Park.

From the Moosehead Lake area: Millinocket is 70 miles northeast of

Greenville—but getting there is an adventure. For a detailed description see *Scenic Drives* in the Moosehead Lake Area chapter. The 18 miles to Kokadjo are paved, but the next stretch, "the Greenville Road," is badly marked and maintained. Once you hit the **Golden Road** (turn right), however, the surface improves. This legendary 96-mile logging road, owned by private companies, runs from Millinocket to Quebec. It's mostly paved along the West Branch of the Penobscot; you can cross over onto the paved Baxter State Park Rd. at Ambajejus Lake. Logging trucks, which operate on weekdays, have the right-of-way; slow down and pull to the side to permit them to pass. Your odds of spotting a moose here are high.

GETTING AROUND **Katahdin Air Service Inc.** (207-723-8378; www.katahdinair.com), Millinocket. Available May–Nov. to fly in to remote camps and shuttle in canoes and campers; will drop hikers at points along the Appalachian Trail. **Scotty's Flying Service** (207-528-2626) at Shin Pond also serves wilderness camps, as does **West Branch Aviation** (207-723-4375) in Millinocket.

WHEN TO COME Spring draws fishermen; June brings moose-watching and blackflies; July and August are great for swimming, canoeing, and rafting; September and early October are best for hiking and foliage. Snowfall is dependable February into April, less so in December and January, which bring subzero temperatures. March can be magnificent, the brightest days of the year with intense blue skies above dazzling white lakes and mountains.

✷ To See

KATAHDIN Maine's Mt. Fuji, this is the region's number one, year-round sight-to-see, not just to climb. Check out Baxter State Park in *Green Space* for suggested vantage points within the park. Don't miss a sunset! At dusk locals and visitors alike gather at nearby lakes to watch the big sky as well as big mountain change hues. If you come no nearer than the interstate, don't pass up I-95's **A. J. Allee Scenic Overlook**, some 15 miles beyond the Medway exit. Katahdin is impressive even at that distance.

Patten Lumbermen's Museum (207-528-2650; www.lumbermensmuseum.org), Shin Pond Rd. (Rt. 159), Patten. Open Memorial Day–June, Fri. and Sat. 10–4. July–Columbus Day, Tue.–Sun. 10–4. Nominal admission. The museum, which encompasses more than 4,000 displays housed in nine buildings, was founded in 1962 by bacteriologist

MOOSE-WATCHING

In and around Millinocket

Mainely Photos (207-723-5465; www.mainleyphotos) offers early morning and evening van tours. **New England Outdoor Center** (1-800-766-7238; www.neoc.com) uses boats as well as vans. Both guarantee sightings. Alternatively, ask locally about likely moose-watching spots. There are a number of these within Baxter State Park; staff at the Togue Pond gate dispense maps and direct you.

Lore Rogers and log driver Caleb Scribner. Exhibits range from giant log haulers to "gum books," the lumberman's scrimshaw: intricately carved boxes in which to keep spruce gum, a popular gift for a sweetheart. There are replicas of logging camps from different periods, dioramas, machinery, and photos. This road leads to the Matagamon Gate, the northern, less trafficked corner of Baxter State Park.

The Ambajejus Boom House (www.moreairphotos.com/boomhouse), Ambajejus Lake. Open year-round, $2 donation. Accessible via boat or snowmobile, or even by walking if you don't mind getting your feet wet. River man Chuck Harris has single-handedly restored this old boom house, former quarters for log drivers, as a museum about life during the river drives. Exhibits include tools, paintings, and photographs among the artifacts of the river-driving years. **Katahdin Scenic Cruises** (207-723-2020; www.katahdinsceniccruises.com) offers access on the first and last Sat. of June, July, and Aug.

The Katahdin Iron Works. Open mid-Apr.–Nov. Turn at the small sign on Rt. 11, 5 miles north of Brownville Junction, and go another 6 miles up the gravel road. The spot was a sacred place for Native Americans, who found yellow ocher paint here. From the 1840s until 1890, an ironworks prospered in this remote spot, spawning a village to house its 200 workers and producing 2,000 tons of raw iron annually. Guests of the Silver Lake Hotel (1880s–1913) here came on the same narrow-gauge railroad that carried away the iron. All that remains is a big old blast furnace and an iron kiln. The site may not be worth your effort unless you plan to continue on down the gravel road to hike in **Gulf Hagas** or to camp.

Also see **Abbott Museum, Dexter** in the Moosehead Lake Area chapter.

GULF HAGAS

Timothy Ellis Jr.

✷ To Do

AIR RIDE **Katahdin Air Service, Inc.** (207-723-8378; www.katahdinair.com), based on the Golden Road in Millinocket. Since 1946 Kathadin Air has been serving remote camps and offering fishing on remote ponds. It also offers frequent scenic flights, ranging from a 15-minute flight along the base of Mount Katahdin to a day exploring Henderson Pond and Debsconeag Lake. Inquire about fly-in fishing trips and fly-and-dine packages. **West Branch Aviation LLC** (207-723-4375), based at the Millinocket Municipal Airport (16 Medway Rd.) offers scenic flights and shuttle service using both sea and standard planes. Aircraft rental and hangar space also available.

BOAT CRUISE **Katahdin Scenic Cruises** (207-723-2020; www.katahdinsceniccruises.com). Wildlife cruises on Millinocket Lake daily June–Oct.

CAMPING AND CANOEING EXPEDITIONS This area is often used as a starting point for trips on the Allagash Wilderness Waterway (see "Aroostook County") and St. John River. There is also good canoeing on the East and West (not for beginners) Branches of the Penobscot River as well on the area's many lakes.

Katahdin Outfitters (207-723-5700 or 1-800-862-2663; www.katahdinoutfitters.com), in Millinocket and **Nicatou Outfitters** (207-746-3253; www.mainecampingtrips.com) in Medway offer rentals, planning, transport, and multiday guided and shuttle for trips on the Allagash, St. John, and Penobscot Rivers. **New England Outdoor Center** (207-723-5438 or 1-800-766-7238; www.neoc.com), Rt. 157, Millinocket, offers a canoe and kayak school, guided tours, and rentals. Kayak and canoe rentals are available from most camps (see *Lodging*). **Peaks-Kenny State Park** (see *Green Space*) rents canoes to use on Sebec Lake.

FISHING **Dolby Flowage** is good for bass fishing, and the **West Branch of the Penobscot River** offers good salmon and trout fishing. **New England Outdoor Center** (207-723-5438; see *Whitewater Rafting*) offers guided fishing trips. Licenses are available at the **Millinocket municipal office** on Penobscot Avenue, and at many of the area's stores, including **Lennie's Superette** in Medway, the **Katahdin General Store** in Millinocket, and **North Woods Trading Post** on Millinocket Lake. For a complete list of guide services, contact the **North Maine Woods** office (207-435-6213; www.northmainewoods.org) in Ashland and the **Katahdin Area Chamber of Commerce** (207-723-4443; www.katahdinmaine.com) in Millinocket.

GOLF **JaTo Highlands Golf Course** (207-794-2433), Town Farm Rd., Lincoln; 18 holes with full-service clubhouse, rental carts, and clubs.

Green Valley Golf Course (207-732-3006), Rt. 2, West Enfield. Eight holes. **Hillcrest Golf Course** (207-723-8410), 59 Grove St., Millinocket. Nine holes with full-service clubhouse, rental carts, and clubs.

HIKING See **Baxter State Park** and **Gulf Hagas** under *Green Space*.

HORSEBACK RIDING AND WAGON RIDES ♿ **Northern Maine Riding Adventures** (207-564-3451; www.mainetrailrides.com), Dover-Foxcroft. Judy and Bob Flury-Strehlke, licensed Maine Guides and skilled equestrians, lead rides from their four-season facility into remote backcountry. Half-day and full-day rides, also lessons. Overnight trips offered during foliage season. Special-needs riders are welcome. Judy is a nationally recognized specialist in centered riding.

SWIMMING **Peaks-Kenny State Park** in Dover-Foxcroft is a great family beach, with lawns, playground equipment, and a roped-in swimming area. Hiking trails and camping. $4 per vehicle day-use fee.

Mattawamkeag Wilderness Park (207-736-4881 or 1-888-724-2465), off Rt. 2 in Mattawamkeag (11 miles southeast of I-95's Medway exit), offers a sand beach on the river, also picnic tables, hot showers, a recreation hall, and a playground. Nominal day-use fee.

Medway Recreation Complex in Medway has a family beach, picnic area, volleyball, playground equipment, and a roped-in swimming area on the East Branch of the Penobscot River.

Ambajejus Lake has a public boat landing and also offers a small public beach.

Note: Swimming opportunities abound in Baxter State Park and the many lakes around Millinocket.

WHITEWATER RAFTING The West Branch of the Penobscot represents the ultimate challenge in Maine rafting, best for experienced rafters (to run the whole river you must be at least 15). Rafters are bused from their base camps to the put-in below McKay Station. The 14-mile trip begins with a 2-mile descent through Ripogenus Gorge (Class V rapids), and then drops down through the infamous Cribworks and on to Nesowadnehunk Falls. Trips run late Apr.–mid-Oct., but we suggest midsummer through early foliage season. Rates are lower midweek than on weekends.

New England Outdoor Center (207-723-5438 or 1-800-766-7238; www.neoc.com). Founded by Matt Polstein in 1982, this is by far the oldest outfitter and offers the largest range of lodging options to rafters. **Rice Farm** (off Rt. 157 east of Millinocket) includes popular **River Drivers** (see *Dining Out*), along with a wraparound deck with water views, hot tub, changing room and showers, and complete outfitters shop. A campground offers tent and cabin-tent sites, fire rings, and a shower house. NEOC also operates the **Penobscot Outdoor Center** (www.penobscotoutdoorcenter.com) on Pockwockamus Pond, the closest commercial campground to Baxter State Park. Facilities include **The Katahdin Bar & Grill**, hot tub, game room, sauna, canoes, and kayaks; lodging is at campsites, in cabin tents, and cabins. Nearby **Twin Pine Camps** on Millinocket Lake is a traditional sporting camp set in the woods with a spectacular view of Katahdin (see *Lodging*). Polstien also plans a major resort overlooking Millinocket Lake.

Three Rivers Whitewater (1-800-786-6878; www.threeriverswhitewater.com) maintains a 26-acre Penobscot Outpost facility in Millinocket.

North Country Rivers (1-800-348-8871; www.ncrivers.com) and **Penobscot Adventures** (1-877-356-9386; www.penobscotadventures.com) are based at the **Big Moose Inn, Cabins & Campground** (see *Lodging*).

Christina Tree

CROSS-COUNTRY SKIING

✷ Winter Sports

CROSS-COUNTRY SKIING AND SNOWSHOEING **Millinocket Municipal X-C Ski Area** is the name of the community's free, 40 kilometers-plus network of groomed cross-country ski trails (20 kilometers novice, 10 kilometers intermediate, and 10 kilometers expert terrain). These are divided between two distinct areas, linked by a 5-mile wooded trail. The **Bait Hole Area** is well-marked 2.7 miles south of town on Rt. 11; the **Northern Timber Cruisers Clubhouse** (see *Snowmobiling*) on the Baxter State Park Road is the departure point for the second network. Many skiers also continue on the Baxter State Park Rd. and ski Periphery or Telos Rds. Within Baxter State Park, the road to the **Hidden Springs campground** is maintained for skiers. To check daily conditions during winter months, phone Don Nodine (207-723-4329). Trail maps are available at the area information kiosk on Rt. 244 in Medway, just off I-95. Local skiers take pride in the fact that they can usually ski 100 days of the year.

Note: **Nahmakanta Lake Camps** and **Katahdin Lake Wilderness Camps** cater to cross-country skiers, offering spectacular backcountry trails, and are accessible only by skis. See *Lodging*.

DOGSLED TOURS **Maine Dogsledding Adventures** (207-731-8888; www.mainedogsledding.com), Nahmakanta Lake Camps, Rainbow Township. Don and Angel Hibbs have traveled 40,000 miles by dog team, finishing in the top 10 of the 1995 Yukon Quest—a 1,000-mile race in Alaska—and first in the Labrador 400 (mile) event in Canada. They offer long dogsled runs down wooded trails and across frozen lakes with no need to slow for human traffic. Guests are permitted to drive the teams; inquire about lodging packages ranging from a half day to three days. Winter access is by dogsled or skis; see *Lodging*.

SNOWMOBILING This region offers more than 350 miles of groomed trails, and more than 10 snowmobile clubs in the area to consult. A snowmobile map available at the Katahdin Area Chamber of Commerce shows the Interconnecting Trail System (ITS) trails. The **Northern Timber Cruisers Antique Snowmobile Museum** (207-723-6203), on the Baxter State Park Rd. next to the Northern Timber Cruisers Clubhouse, traces the history of snowmobiling in the region. It's open winter weekends.

Baxter State Park (www.baxterstateauthority.com). Like Acadia National Park, Baxter State Park's acreage was amassed privately and given to the public as a gift. In this case it was the gift of one individual: Percival Baxter (1876–1969). In 1921, at age 44, Baxter became one of the state's youngest governors; he was then reelected for another term. He was unsuccessful, however, in convincing the Maine legislature to protect Katahdin and surrounding lands. Instead, in 1930 he himself paid $25,000 to buy 6,000 acres that included Maine's highest mountain. For the remainder of his life he continued to negotiate with paper companies and other landowners to increase the size of the park. Thanks to his legacy, it continued to grow even after his death and presently encompasses 209,501 acres.

While nominally a state park, it receives no state funds, and the Baxter State Park Authority operates under its own unique and complicated rules, dedicated to ensuring that this preserve "Shall forever be kept and remain in the Natural Wild State." Camping and even day-use admissions to the park are strictly limited. Rental canoes are available at several locations in the park.

There are only two entry points: **Togue Pond Gate**, 18 miles east of Millinocket, by far the most popular, is open 6 AM–9 PM (5 AM during busy summer months and some fall weekends; please call the park to verify), May 15–Oct. 15. **Matagamon Gate**, in the northeast corner of the park, is also open 6 AM–9 PM mid-May–Oct. 15. Vehicles with Maine plates are admitted free, but others pay $12 day-use fee.

The list of rules governing the park is long and detailed. No motorcycles, motorized trail bikes, ATVs, or pets are allowed in. Bicycles can be used on maintained roads only. Snowmobiles are allowed only on the ungroomed main Tote Road in the park. The list goes on; pick up a copy at park headquarters or at the visitors center and read it through before heading in.

The park is open daily, but note the restricted camping periods and the special-use permits required Dec.–Mar. Vehicular access is not guaranteed once snow blocks the roads, usually after Oct. 15, the end of the camping season. Also note that a park prohibition on the collection of any park plants, animals, or artifacts is strictly enforced unless you have applied at least six months in advance and have been approved by the director.

Ever since the 1860s—when Henry David Thoreau's account of his 1846 ascent of "Ktaadn" began to circulate—the demanding trails to Maine's highest summit (5,267 feet) have been among the most popular in the state. Climbing Katahdin itself is considered a rite of passage in Maine and much of the rest of New England. The result is a steady stream of humanity up

PERCIVAL BAXTER AND KATAHDIN

and down the Katahdin trails, while other peaks, such as 3,488-foot Doubletop, offer excellent, less crowded hiking and views of Katahdin to boot.

Day-trippers should be aware that the number of vehicles allowed at specific trailheads is finite; when the parking lots fill, people are turned away. Eighty percent of day-trippers head for lots in the southern end of the park, with access to the most popular trails—but with 42 miles of road, 46 mountain peaks, and 205 miles of trails, there's plenty of room for everyone.

Still, if you are determined to access the parking area for the **Knife's Edge Trail** (the legendary narrow link between Baxter and Pamola Peaks), arrive early, really early. In July and Aug. cars tend to queue at the Togue Pond Gate because the climb to Katahdin's summit and back takes 10 hours. Sleep in if you're heading to one of the less-popular trailheads; later in the day there's rarely a line.

The pamphlet "Day Use Hiking Guide," available at the visitors center (located a short ways before the Togue Pond Gate) locates and describes 32 trails. Park staff, both here and at both gates, suggest appropriate trails, given conditions and the time of day. Arriving midafternoon on a July Sunday we were advised to take the **Hunt Trail** (a popular way to the peak) only as far as **Katahdin Stream Falls**.

Another popular hike is **Sentinel Mountain** from the Kidney Pond Trailhead. The trail traverses moderate wooded terrain until the very end, when it abruptly ascends to a series of excellent vantage points with views in several directions. A flat alternative is the **Daicey Pond Nature Trail,** 1.7 miles around Daicey Pond. **Doubletop Mountain** offers a full day hike with several mileage options: 9.6 miles round-trip hiking up and down from Kidney Pond Trailhead, 6.6 miles round-trip from the Nesowadnehunk Trailhead, and 7.9 miles hiking from Kidney to Nesowadnehunk Trailhead or vice versa. **South Turner Mountain Trail** from Roaring Brook via Sandy Stream Pond (4 miles round-trip) is a good wildlife-watching trail. Many hikers base themselves at Chimney Pond Campground and tackle Katahdin from there on one of several trails. A wide selection of retail maps and trail guidebooks is available at park headquarters. *Katahdin: A Guide to Baxter State Park and Katahdin,* by Stephen Clark, and *50 Hikes in the Maine Mountains,* by Cloe Chunn (Backcountry Guides), detail many of Baxter's trails.

Camping Reservations Camping is permitted May 15–Oct. 15 and Dec.–Apr. 1. Summer reservations for sites throughout the park are on a rolling basis. Space can be reserved four months in advance by mail or in person and still-available sites can also be reserved 14 or fewer days in advance by phone with a credit card. Download the form at wwww.baxterstateparkauthority.com. The 10 campgrounds are widely scattered; there

New England Outdoor Center (207-723-5438 or 1-800-767238; www.neoc.com) has the area's largest rental fleet and clothing at Twin Pines (see *Lodging*). They offer half-day, full-day, and overnight guided snowmobile excursions, overnight and multiday packages, and a complete shop.

Katahdin Power Sports (207-746-9977; www.katahdinpowersports.com) and **Nicatou Outfitters** (207-746-3253; www.nicatououtfitters.com) also rent snowmobiles.

✱ Green Space

Gulf Hagas Reserve is a remote part of the Appalachian Trail corridor, jointly owned and managed by the Appalachian Trail Conference and the National Park Service. It's best accessed (3.1 miles) from the Katahdin Iron Works, marked from Rt. 11 in Brownsville. At the North Maine Woods gate ($9 nonresidents, $6 residents) you can purchase a trail map. The parking area for the trailhead is at Hay Brook. Billed as the Grand Canyon of Maine, this 2.5-mile-long gorge with walls up to 40 feet high was carved by the West Branch of the Pleasant River. At the beginning of the trail you will need to cross the river in ankle- to calf-high water. Bring water shoes for the crossing, or be prepared to take off your shoes

are no hook-ups, and you carry out what you carry in. Two campgrounds, Daicey Pond and Kidney Pond, offer traditional cabins with beds, gas lanterns, firewood, and tables and chairs (summer fees $22 per person per night minimum; $39 minimum for a two-bed cabin, $52 minimum for three-bed cabins, and $65 minimum for a four-bed cabin; ages 1–6 are free, 7–16 are $13 each). Six more campgrounds, accessible by road, offer a mix of bunkhouses, lean-tos, and tent sites (in summer bunkhouses cost $9 per person per night; lean-tos and tenting space are also $9 per person, with a minimum of $18 for both types of sites). Two other popular campgrounds, Chimney Pond and Russell Pond, require hiking in. Several individual backcountry sites are available by reservation for backpackers. Check restrictions before planning your trip. Ideally, allow three to five days at a campground like Trout Brook Farm, in the northern wilderness area of the park, or base yourself at Russell Pond (a 7- or 9-mile hike in from the road, depending on where you begin) and hike to the Grand Falls and Lookout Ledges.

Payment must accompany the reservation request. The mailing address is Baxter State Park, 64 Balsam Dr., Millinocket 04462. Enclose a stamped, self-addressed envelope for confirmation. July through mid-Aug. weekends fill quickly, but tent sites midweek and earlier or later in the season are possible. For a current update on this rolling reservation system, contact the park directly (see *Guidance*) or visit its Web site.

and wade barefoot (be aware that the rocks are very slippery; find a good walking stick to help with balance). The trail threads a 35-acre stand of virgin white pines, some more than 130 feet tall, a landmark in its own right known as The Hermitage and preserved by The Nature Conservancy in Maine. The trail then follows the river, along the Appalachian Trail for a way, but turns off along the rim of the canyon toward dramatic **Screw Auger Falls** and on through The Jaws to **Buttermilk Falls**, **Stair Falls**, and **Billings Falls**. We started early in the day and found ourselves alone for most of the hike. The trail winds through the woods, almost always moving either up or down, with a series of small side paths. Turnouts offer great views of the falls and the gorge. The hike back is flatter, and logs cover mud in some spots. The Gulf Hagas trails are much less traveled than those at Katahdin; many visitors come only as far as the first waterfall for a swim and a picnic. Allow six to eight hours for the hike, and plan to camp at one of the waterside campsites within the **Jo-Mary Lake Campground**. In winter we have also skied into Gulf Hagas from **Little Lyford Pond Camps** (see "Moosehead Lake Area"), a magnificent experience.

Mattawamkeag Wilderness Park (207-736-4881 or 1-888-724-2465), Rt. 2, Mattawamkeag. This town-owned preserve offers 15 miles of hiking trails, campsites, and canoeing and swimming along the Mattawamkeag River 11 miles south of the I-95 Medway exit.

Peaks-Kenny State Park (207-564-2003), Sebec Lake Rd., Dover-Foxcroft. The centerpiece of this park is Sebec Lake (13 miles long, 3 miles wide) with its popular beach, but there are also 9 miles of hiking trails and campsites.

Also see **KI Jo-Mary Multiple Use Forest** under *Campgrounds* and **Borestone Mountain Sanctuary** in "Moosehead Lake Area."

✱ Lodging

Note: For details about motels handy to I-95, check with the **Katahdin Area Chamber of Commerce** (see *Guidance*).

All lodgings in and around Millinocket 04462 unless otherwise noted.

Twin Pine Camps (1-800-766-7238; www.neoc.com), Medway Rd., P.O. Box 669. Sited on Millinocket Lake with a superb view of Katahdin, these 10 housekeeping camps are spaced along the shore under the pines. Owned by New England Outdoor Center, they are just a bit more than 8 miles from the Togue Pond entrance to Baxter State Park. The cabins themselves vary from basic to luxurious (the more primitive old camps are being gradually replaced) and accommodate between six and 14 people. All share a rec lodge with a hot tub, satellite TV, and Ping Pong, and ample outdoor space under the pines, with a swim beach and a glorious view of Mt. Katahdin reflected in the lake. At sunset guests gather around fire circles and along the shore to listen to the loons while the mountain and sky change color. Canoes are available for guests; kayaks and motorboats are rented. With luck, you'll catch Jim Ewing, who manages the camps with his wife Shorey, baking

TWIN PINE CAMPS ON MILLINOCKET LAKE

Kim Grant

beans in his bean hole under a beech tree. In winter Ski-Dos can be rented for use on the adjacent ITS 86. $47.50–77.86 per person, depending on cabin and season.

♿ **5 Lakes Lodge** (207-723-5045; www.5lakeslodge.com), HC 74, Box 544, South Twin Lake 04462. Open year-round. Debbie and Rick LeVasseur, both locally born and raised, have created a luxury lodge on the footprint of a dramatically sited marina on a narrow point of land on South Twin Lake, surrounded by water, with a superb view of Katahdin. Windows maximize lake and mountain views. The five spacious guest rooms are named for the lakes and feature log bed, gas fireplace, cathedral ceiling, and Jacuzzi. Both Debbie and Rick are active outdoor people who been in the local hospitality business since the 1980s and not only know the local waters and woods but how to enjoy them to the max. They enjoy nothing more than tuning guests in and turning them on to the best that this region offers. $175–275, depending on the season, includes a full breakfast. Inquire about a rental cottage.

Big Moose Inn, Cabins & Campground (207-723-8391; www.bigmoosecabins.com), P.O. Box 98. Open June–Oct. and Jan.–mid-Mar. for snowmobiling. This classic 1830s clapboard inn has been run by Laurie Comier's family since 1977, offers a restaurant named for her mother Fredericka (see *Dining Out*) and a pub. There are nine clean and comfortable, antiques-furnished guest rooms with double or twin beds sharing three baths, and five new suites with private bath. There are also 11 cabins, including two large enough for groups, 35 tent-sites, and six lean-tos. Sited between Millinocket and Ambajejus Lakes with access to swimming, this is the nearest full-service facility to Baxter State Park, 8 miles from the Togue Pond entrance and 8 miles from Millinocket. Two rafting companies (see *Whitewater Rafting*) use the premises as a base for trips down the West Branch of the Penobscot. $45–49 per person for inn rooms and $149 per couple for the suites; $42–45 per person for cabins; $10 per person per campsite, $13 for lean-tos. Canoe rentals available. A general store is also part of this complex.

"1" **Keepridge Inn** (1-888-723-68677; www.keepridgeinn.com), 177 Central St. Open May 15–Oct. 15. A fine old home a short walk from Millinocket's downtown eateries, offering eight spacious, nicely decorated guest rooms, each with private bath, one with a Jacuzzi. Common space includes a pleasant breakfast room where coffee, juice, fruit, and yogurt are set out in the morning. $85–95, $120 for the suite with Jacuzzi.

The Young House Bed & Breakfast (207-723-5452; www.theyounghousebandb.com), 193 Central St. Former Floridians Micki and Fred Schumacher have rehabbed a handsome old house across the street from the Keepridge Inn. They offer five cozy rooms, each with queen bed and private bath. $80 per night includes a full breakfast.

Katahdin B&B (207-723-5220), 96 Oxford St. Open year-round. For more than 20 years Marylou and Rodney Corriveau have catered to AT hikers, offering five clean, comfortable rooms with private bath and cable TV. A two-bedroom suite (sleeps five) with private bath and sitting area is great for families. Washer-dryer and kitchen available for guest use; off-street parking. $55–75 includes a full breakfast. Rodney is a Maine Guide.

Baxter Edge Vacation Rentals (www.baxteredge.com) manages and rents a number of area homes and camps.

REMOTE SPORTING CAMPS *Note*: Also see *Remote Sporting Camps* in the preceding and following chapters.

♿ **Bradford Camps** (207-746-7777; www.bradfordcamps.com), P.O. Box 729, Ashland 04732. Open following ice-out through Nov. Sited at the Aroostook River's headwaters, Munsungan Lake, almost 60 miles from the nearest town but easily accessible by commercial floatplane from Bangor, Millinocket, and other points. This is a century-old, classic sporting camp with an unusually tidy lodge set amid well-tended lawns. Eight hand-hewn log, lakeside cabins all have full private bath. Depending on the season, this is all about fly-fishing (landlocked salmon and brook trout) and hunting, but there's also canoeing and kayaking, swimming and fly-out day-trips, including whitewater rafting. $100–137 per person per night includes meals. Guides, boats, and fly-out trips are extra. Family rates in July and Aug. Inquire about two remote outpost cabins ($40 per person). Your hosts are Karen and Igor Sikorsky and yes, Igor is the son of the pioneer aviator best known for developing the helicopter.

🐾 **Frost Pond Camps** (radiophone, 207-695-2821; www.frostpondcamps.com), HC 76, Box 620 Ripongenus Dam, Greenville 04441. Open year-round. Off the Golden Road (35 miles from Millinocket, 45 miles from Greenville) across Ripogenus Dam and 3 miles up along Chesuncook Lake and then down to Frost Pond. Gene Thompson and Maureen Raynes, both Registered Master Maine Guides, are the owners of these seven traditional housekeeping cottages (five on the waterfront) and 10 campsites on the shore of Frost Pond. Cabins have gas lights, refrigerator, and stove and are heated by woodstove in spring, fall, and winter. One has plumbing; each of the others has a clean pit toilet. A great base for exploring the wilderness. $62–164 per person per cabin (one–three people), $55 for each additional person, but $15 for children 15 and under. $24 per night for campsites. Minimum two-night stay. Rental boats, canoes, and kayaks.

Katahdin Lake Wilderness Camps (207-837-1599; www.katahdinlakewildernesscamps.com), P.O. Box 314, Millinocket 04462. Privately owned but on land owned by and accassed through Baxter State Park, these legendery 1880s camps offer the view of Mt. Katahdin depicted by artists from Frederick Church to Marsden Hartley. Spring through fall you can fly-in, or hike the 3.2-mile trail from Roaring Brook Rd. in the park. Dec.–Mar. the camps welcome those hardy souls who ski the 16 miles in from the Abol Bridge Store (gear is transported by snowmobile). Ten log cabins (one to eight people per cabin) and a main lodge (with a library and dining room) are built on a bluff overlooking the lake. All have a woodstove and propane lights; some are fitted out for housekeeping. Facilities include a spring, outhouses, a beach, dock, and canoes. The view of Mt. Katahdin continues to lure artists, and the 717-

acre lake yields native brook trout May–Sept. No access for snowmobilers. The camps are currently owned by Charles FitzGerald and managed by Holly and Bryce Hamilton. $95 per adult, $50 per child per day includes linens and towels, breakfast, dinner, and a trail lunch. The housekeeping rate (BYO sleeping bags, towels, and food) is $25 per adult, $15 per child. Winter rates are slightly higher.

Nahmakanta Lake Camps (207-731-8888; www.nahmakanta.com), P.O. Box 544, Millinocket 04462. Open year-round. Founded in 1872, this is a remote set of eight lakefront cabins (accommodating two to eight people) with picture windows, screened porch, woodstove, gas lights and fridge, and three common shower houses with hot water and flush toilets as well as clean privies to go with each cabin. Guests can choose from housekeeping at $75 per person per day, $95 MAP (breakfast and dinner), or $120 per person with all meals (packed lunch); special children's rates. Boat rentals, guide service, and dogsled tours in winter are the house specialties. Nahmakanta is within walking distance of the Appalachian Trail. In summer access is via road, but in winter you need to ski in—which, may the record reflect, we have done (10 miles).

Nugent's Chamberlain Lake and McNally's Camps (207-944-5991; www.nugent-mcnallycamps.com), HCR 76, Box 632, Greenville 04441. Open year-round. John Richardson and Regina Webster acquired the original 1930s Nugent's Camps from Patty Nugent in 1987, adding a couple of new cabins but retaining the old-fashioned feel. This is sited on the Allagash Wilderness Waterway, 50 miles north of Millinocket between Baxter State Park and Allagash Mountain. It's best reached via floatplane; otherwise, it's a 4-mile boat or snowmobile ride up Chamberlain Lake. The seven housekeeping cabins have the traditional front overhang and outhouses; they sleep two to 16. Boats are available. AP, MAP, or housekeeping plans available. $33–100 per person. John and Regina now also own the even more remote **McNally's Ross Stream Camps**: five classic log structures accommodating two to four people, equipped with flush toilet, sink, and shower in warm-weather months. $100 per person includes all meals; also available in fall.

Shin Pond Village (207-528-2900; www.shinpond.com), 1489 Shin Pond Rd., Mount Chase 04765. Ten miles down Rt. 159 from Patten. Open

NAHMAKANTA CAMPS

Christina Tree

year-round. Craig and Terry Hill run this recreational facility, which offers campsites, housekeeping cottages, and housekeeping "guest suites." The north entrance to Baxter State Park isn't far. Cottages accommodate three to eight people and have full bath, linens, towels, and cookware. Canoe rentals in summer; snowmobile rentals in winter. Cottages are $82 per couple, guest suites $71 and up, more for more people.

CAMPGROUNDS 🐾 ✐ **Katahdin Shadows Campground & Cabins** (207-746-9349 or 1-800-794-5267; www.katahdinshadows.com), Rt. 157, Medway 04460. David and Theresa Violette own this full-service, family-geared four-season campground with a central lodge, swimming pool, dock, weekend hayrides, a big playground, athletic fields, a "community kitchen," tent and hook-up sites, hutniks, and well-designed cabins with kitchen facilities. Pets are welcome. Tent sites $22–28, cabins $25, larger cabins with kitchenettes $56–85. Rates are based on two, $5 per extra person, free under age 18. Weekly rates. Special events.

KI Jo-Mary Multiple Use Forest (207-965-8135). Open May–Oct. A 200,000-plus-acre tract of commercial forest stretching almost from Greenville on the west to the Katahdin Iron Works on the east, and north to Millinocket. There are 150 miles of privately maintained roads (logging trucks have right-of-way) and widely scattered campsites. Seasonal checkpoints charge day-use and camping fees. Good fishing, hunting, and plenty of solitude. The **Jo-Mary Lake Campground** (207-723-8117), open mid-May–Oct. 1, offers 60 campsites, flush toilets, and hot showers, and is handy to Gulf Hagas.

Peaks-Kenny State Park (207-564-2003), Rt. 153, 6 miles from Dover-Foxcroft. Open mid-May–Sept. with 56 campsites on Sebec Lake; $15 per site for Maine residents, $20 for visitors. Reservations are a must; for details see *Camping* in "What's Where."

Mattawamkeag Wilderness Park (207-746-4881; www.mwpark.com), Mattawamkeag (off Rt. 2; half an hour's drive from the I-95 Medway exit). A town-run park with 50 campsites for RVs and tents, 11 Adirondack shelters, bathrooms, hot showers, small store, recreation building, picnic facilities, 15 miles of hiking trails, 60 miles of canoeing on the Mattawamkeag River with patches of whitewater, and bass, salmon, and trout fishing.

Allagash Gateway Campsite and Camps (207-723-9215; www.allagashgateway.com), P.O. Box 396, Millinocket 04462. Open May–Nov.; winter rentals by reservation. Location, location! Off the Golden Road, 28 miles west of Mikllinocket, sited on Ripogeneous Lake, longtime owners Bill and Jan Reeves offer housekeeping cabins, RV and primtive sites, hot showers, a marina, canoe rentals, and shuttle service to the upper West Branch of the Penobscot. Campsites from $12, camps $30.

The Bureau of Parks and Lands (www.parksandlands.com) Northern Region Office in Ashland (207-435-7963) can also supply information and pamphlet guides to campsites in the **Penobscot River Corridor** and other nearby holdings. This is wilderness camping geared to experienced outdoorsmen.

Also see Baxter State Park in *Green Space* and both the Penobscot Outdoor Center (www.penobscotoutdoor center.com) and the Rice Farm Campground (www.neoc.com), described in *Whitewater Rafting*.

✷ Where to Eat

All entries are in Millinocket unless otherwise noted.

DINING OUT ♿ **River Drivers' Restaurant** (207-723-8475), at the New England Outdoor Center's Rice Farm, Old Medway Rd., off Rt. 157. Open for dinner year-round; closed Sun. off-season. Candle light, copper-topped tables, and an elegantly woodsy decor is the setting for a memorable meal. Generally recognized as the best dining experience around. Appetizers range from grilled bourbon-and-garlic marinated beef tenderloin tip skewers to locally vine ripened tomatoes with fresh mozzarella and glazed walnut. A choice of 10 entrées might include pan seared scallops with a corn and mushroom buerre blanc and orzo or double lamb chops with homemade mint pesto. The restaurant is also known for excellent bread and soups and a dessert tray that usually includes its signature flourless chocolate cake. Entrées $18–26. Fully licensed with a separate bar. Children's menu.

♿ **Fredericka's at Big Moose Inn** (207-723-8391), Millinocket Lake, 8 miles west of Millinocket on Baxter State Park Rd. Open for dinner Wed.–Sat., June–early Oct.; also Sun. July–Aug. Hot breakfast is served Sat.–Sun. in-season. Reservations suggested. Accessible by boat, and the most convenient dining to Baxter State Park and to lakeside lodging on the lakes east of Millinocket. We dined here twice on our most recent visit, once on a Saturday night, which was surprisingly uncrowded, and then on Sunday, which was understaffed. We sympathized with the friendly waitresses, who included owner Laurie Cormier (the restaurant is named for her mother), but be prepared to wait. The dining room is pleasant but, on a nice night, the screened-in porch is preferable. We can recommend the spinach and feta spanakopita with spring greens as a starter and the roasted half duck served with shiitake mushroom confit. Fully licensed. Entrées $15–24. The Loose Moose Bar and Grill offers a good pub menu but not much space. Expansion was promised.

EATING OUT **Appalachian Trail Café** (207-723-6720), 210 Penobscot Ave. Open 5 AM–8 PM daily, year-round. Anyone who hasn't stopped by this downtown diner recently is in for a surprise. Still the same good burgers, omelets, superb doughnuts (try the pumpkin), and pies, home cooking and reasonable prices. The difference is in the decor. The walls and back counter are filled with AT photos and memorabilia, and there's a computer for checking e-mail. A couple years ago current owners Paul and Jamie Renaud literally walked into town after completing the 2,175-mile trek from Georgia. They were puzzled by the café's name, given its lack of any obvious link to the trail. They didn't mean to buy it, but it came with the Appalachian Trail Lodge down the street, which they did decide to buy. They kept the cooks, just rehabbed the kitchen and redecorated the café and now they continue to delight old-timers and hikers alike.

Scootic Inn Restaurant (207-723-4566), 70 Penobscot Ave. Open for lunch and dinner Mon.–Sat. from 11, Sun. at 3. George and Bea Simon are third-generation owners. Menu choices include fresh-dough pizza, calzones, pasta entrées, seafood, and smoked baby back ribs. Children's menu.

Orvieto Market & Deli (207-723-8399), 67 Prospect St. Joel and Debra Dicentes's market offers homemade tomato sauce, pastas, stuffed breads, and other makings for dinner at rental camps, also take-out sandwiches and panini.

The Hotel Terrace (207-723-4525), 52 Medway St. Open weekdays 11–9, weekends from 7 AM. Just off Rt. 11/157, informal, seasonal outdoor tables, good food, fully licensed.

Blue Ox Saloon (207-723-6936), 61 Penobscot Ave. The local watering hole with local color, great old local store signs, an open deck in back, and a dozen draft beers.

ROAD FOOD **The Restaurant** (207-943-7432), 66 Park St., Milo. Open for all three meals. Great road food, homemade sandwich bread, wooden booths, blue frilly curtains, dinner specials ranging from liver and onions to salmon steak.

Elaine's Basket Café (207-943-2705), 24 West Main St. Open daily for breakfast and lunch. Open just a few weeks when we stopped by. Pleasant atmosphere, good food, good service, standout pies. The plan was to expand to dinner.

Selective Shopping

In Millinocket

Katahdin General Store (207-723-4123), 160 Bates St. is a source of hunting and fishing licenses, gas, live bait, groceries, cold beer, camping permits, and and the largest selection of camping and sporting gear in the area. Also check out the **Hungry Moose Sandwich Shop & Deli**, good for daily-made sandwiches and soups.

North Light Gallery (207-723-4414; www.artnorthlight.com), 356 Penobscot Ave. Open year-round, Mon.–Sat. 10–6, features the exceptional paintings and drawings by Marsha Donahue, also some of Maine's leading contemporary artists, such as Connie Hayes, Chris Polsen, Abbott Meader, and Elaine Crossman.

Memories of Maine Gallery (207-723-4834; www.memoriesofmaine.com), 80 Penobscot Ave., features art and photography by Jean McLean, also sells jewelry, antiques, and gifts by Maine crafters, also customized laser framing.

Special Events

February: **Winterfest** in Millinocket—snowmobile parade, antique snowmobile display, bonfire, cross-country ski events, and poker run.

July: **Independence Day celebration** in Millinocket features a weekend full of activities and a fireworks display.

August: **Katahdin Area Wooden Canoe Festival** in Medway showcases the wooden canoe with demonstrations, a canoe race, and more.

AROOSTOOK COUNTY

Aroostook is Maine's least populated county but the largest in area, almost as large as all of Massachusetts. Within the state it's usually referred to simply as The County. The name *Aroostook* comes from a Native American word meaning "bright," and that's the best way we can think to describe it. The luminosity of its sky—broader seeming than elsewhere in New England—is The County's most striking characteristic. Bounded by Canada on two sides and the North Maine Woods on the third, Aroostook is so far off traditional tourist routes—it actually gets more visitors in winter than it does in summer—that many New England maps omit it entirely. Maine pundits are fond of noting that Portland is as far from Fort Kent, the northern terminus of Rt. 1, as it is from New York City.

Although admittedly rural, Aroostook has long suffered from the popular misconception that all it has to offer are views of potato fields. In fact, The County is rich in cultural traditions, friendly faces, and has an interesting ethnic heritage that includes a Swedish colony and a string of French-speaking Acadian settlements. Small but fascinating historical museums are scattered from the southern part of The County to its northern tip at the top of the state.

Acadians trace their lineage to French settlers who came to farm and fish in what is now Nova Scotia in the early 1600s and who, in 1755, were forcibly deported by an English governor. This "Grand Dérangement," which dispersed a population of some 10,000 Acadians, brutally divided families (a tale told by Longfellow in "Evangeline"). Many were returned to France, only to make their way back to a warmer New World in Louisiana, and many were resettled in New Brunswick, from which they were once more dislodged after the American Revolution when the British government gave their land to loyalists from the former colonies.

In a meadow overlooking the St. John River behind Madawaska's Tante Blanche Museum (named for an 18th-century local Acadian folk heroine), a large marble cross and an outsized wooden sculpture of a voyageur in his canoe mark the spot on which several hundred of these displaced Acadians landed in 1785. They settled both sides of the St. John River, an area known as Mattawaska ("land of the porcupine"). Not until 1842 did the river—still Rivière St-Jean to Acadians—become the formal boundary dividing Canada and Maine.

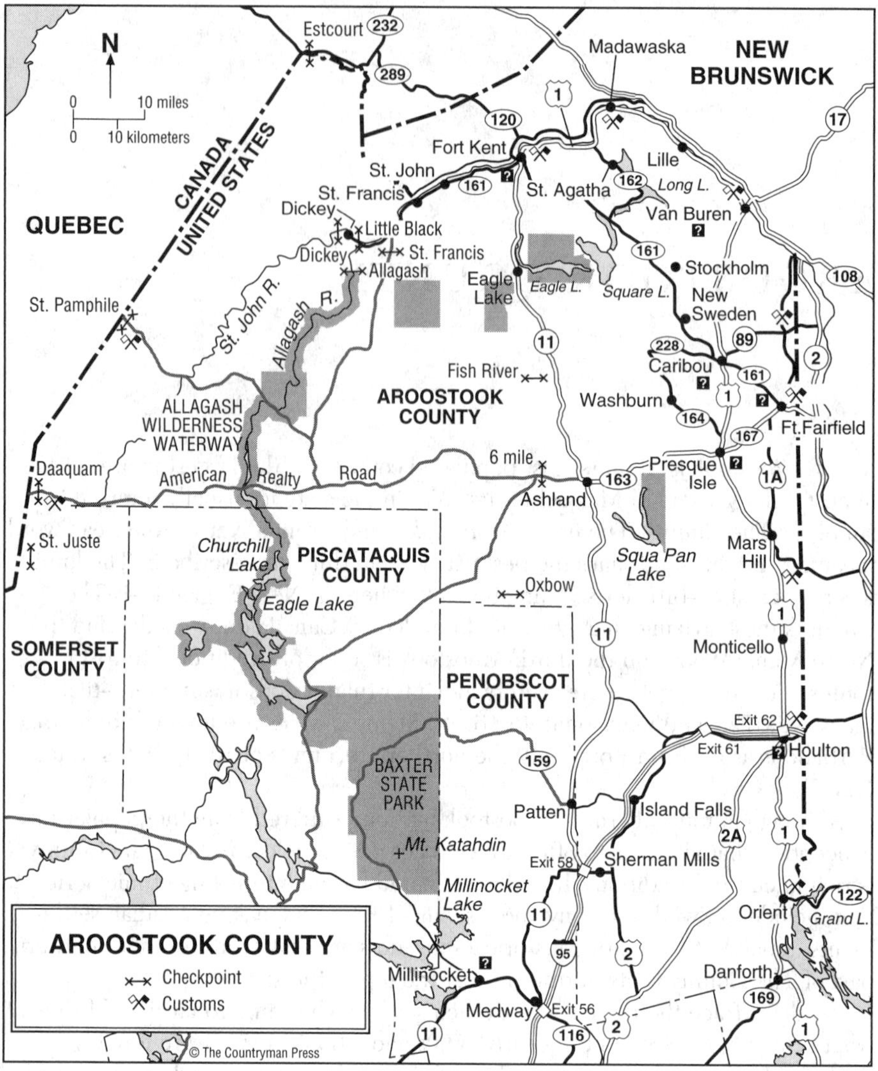

The 1842 Webster-Ashburton Treaty settled the Aroostook War, a footnote in American history recalled in the 1830s wooden blockhouses at Fort Kent and Fort Fairfeld. Until relatively recently this bloodless conflict between the United States and Canada was the area's chief historic claim, but the valley's distinctive Acadian heritage is gaining increasing recognition.

In 1976 Acadian Village, a seasonal living history museum, was created in Van Buren. Now consisting of 16 buildings, many historic and most moved to the Rt. 1 site from around the St. John Valley, it's an interesting place and the scene of many special events. But the Acadian heritage is also visible in the very shape of

St. John Valley towns, where wooden houses are strung out along roads that stretch like arms from the cathedral-sized Catholic churches always at their heart.

Despite intense pressure to assimilate from both civil and ecclesiastical authorities—at one time children could be punished for speaking French anywhere on public school grounds, and parochial schools also discouraged the language—Acadians have stubbornly preserved their traditions and distinctive "Valley French," a blend of old Acadian and Quebec dialects. Today bilingual signage is common in the valley, schools offer French immersion programs, Catholic churches have Masses in both French and English, and there is a bicultural studies program at the Fort Kent campus of the University of Maine, which also has an extensive collection of Acadian historical materials.

Swedes, who settled in and around New Sweden after the Civil War, are a far smaller and more assimilated community than the Acadians but have preserved some colorful Old World traditions. Best known of these is a midsummer festival that attracts Swedish Americans and other visitors from around the country. The Swedes also made an enduring recreational contribution to The County: They are credited with introducing cross-country skiing.

The County cannot be easily categorized topographically. Within the boundaries there are three distinct regions, each with a unique feel and appearance. The Upper St. John Valley, at the top of The County, is a broad ribbon of river land backed by woodland to the west and by a high, open plateau to the east; it has its own distinctly Acadian look, language, and cuisine. Central Aroostook—the rolling farmland around Fort Fairfield, Presque Isle, and Caribou—is generally equated with the entire county. It, too, has its appeal, especially around Washburn and New Sweden, sites of two of New England's more interesting museums. Houlton, the northern terminus of I-95 and the county seat, is in southern Aroostook, a mix of farmland, lonely woods, and lakes.

Four million of Aroostook's 5 million acres are wooded, forestland that includes most of the Allagash Wilderness Waterway and more than 1,000 lakes. Many visitors actually enter The County in canoes, paddling down the Allagash River, which flows north and empties into the St. John River at Allagash, a minuscule hamlet that's become widely known as Mattagash to readers of novels (*The Funeral Makers*, *Once Upon a Time on the Banks*, and *The Weight of Winter*) by native Cathie Pelletier. Local residents will tell you that the names of Pelletier's characters have been changed only as slightly as that of her town, and that the interplay between Catholics and Protestants (descendants of Acadian and Scottish settlers, respectively) chronicled in her books remains very real.

Aroostook County still produces about 1.5 million tons of potatoes a year, but the family farms—once the staple of The County's landscape and social fabric—are fading, replaced by consolidated spreads that grow other crops, notably wheat, broccoli, barley, and sugar beets. The family potato farm is already the stuff of museum exhibits. Our favorites are in the New Sweden Museum, which commemorates not only family farms but also one of the most interesting immigration stories in American history.

Ask locally for directions to the best places to walk, ski, and fish; feast on fiddleheads, ployes (buckwheat crêpes), and poutine (fries with cheese and gravy).

B&Bs are small (often just two or three rooms), with a more personal feel than most downstate.

Winter brings predictable snowfall and is the big draw. Most visitors come in this season to snowmobile (The County has 2,200 miles of maintained snowmobile trails), snowshoe, or dogsled. (Dogsled races are held annually.) The Maine Winter Sports Center, a nonprofit organization that encourages traditional snow sports, recently opened state-of-the-art facilities in Fort Kent and Presque Isle for biathlon and cross-country training, both with free groomed public trail systems.

Winter driving is considered less daunting here than elsewhere in Maine because, thanks to the region's consistently low temperatures, the snow is drier and less icy. Summer temperatures also tend to be cooler, and in early July the potato fields are a spread of pink and white blossoms. Fall colors, which usually peak in the last weeks of September at the end of potato harvest, include reddening barley fields as well as maples.

The conventional loop tour around The County is I-95 to its terminus at Houlton, then Rt. 1 north to Fort Kent and back down Rt. 11. We suggest doing it in reverse—the views from the highway are more scenic going clockwise.

Canada's proximity means that residents of The County are as likely to travel across the border to dine or shop as to venture into other parts of the state. An international bridge over the St. John River links the downtowns of Madawaska and Edmundston, New Brunswick, for instance, making them in effect one mini metropolis. So we also include a few Canadian recommendations within this chapter.

GUIDANCE **Aroostook Tourism** (1-888-216-2463; www.visitarrostook.com), Caribou, can send a regional guide with places to stay and eat; also lists activities and guide services.

Otherwise, The County is divided into three distinct regions. For details about northern Aroostook (the Upper St. John Valley), contact the **Greater Fort Kent Area Chamber of Commerce** (207-834-5354; www.fortkentchamber.com), P.O. Box 430, Fort Kent 04743; and the **Greater Madawaska Area Chamber of Commerce** (207-728-7000; www.townofmadawaska.com), 363 Main St., Madawaska 04756. A walk-in information center at the Fort Kent Blockhouse, staffed by Boy Scouts, is open seasonally. For central Aroostook, contact the **Presque Isle Area Chamber of Commerce** (207-764-6561 or 1-800-764-7420; www.pichamber.org), P.O. Box 672, Presque Isle 04769; and **Caribou Chamber of Commerce** (1-800-722-7648; www.cariboumaine.net), 24 Sweden St., Caribou 04736. For southern Aroostook, see the **Greater Houlton Chamber of Commerce** (207-532-4216; www.greaterhoulton.com), 109-B Main St., Houlton 04730.

SORTING POTATOES DURING HARVEST IN BRIDGEWATER

Nancy English

The big walk-in information center in The County is maintained by the Maine Tourism Association, just off I-95 at the intersection of Rt. 1 in Houlton (207-532-6346).

Note: The North Maine Woods information office on Rt. 1 in Ashland is described under *Guidance* in "The North Maine Woods."

GETTING THERE *By car:* Our preferred route is to take I-95 to Benedicta or Sherman Mills, then Rt. 11 up through Patten, Ashland, and Eagle Lake to Fort Kent, from which you can explore west to Allagash and east along the Upper St. John Valley to St. Agatha and/or Van Buren. Stop at the New Sweden Museum, for a meal in Caribou, and for a final overnight in the Houlton area. An alternate route through The County, especially if you are beginning Down East, is to follow Rt. 1 through rolling hills and past scenic lakes (Grand Lake is breathtaking from the top of one hill), through tiny town centers, to Houlton. From here, continue through Presque Isle and Caribou to Van Buren, then follow Rt. 1 along the St. John River to Fort Kent. Return on Rt. 11 to Sherman Mills, where you can pick up I-95 south.

By plane: Regularly scheduled service to **Presque Isle/Northern Maine Regional Airport** is limited to **U.S. Airways Express** (1-800-428-4322). **Scotty's Flying Service** (207-528-2626), Shin Pond, is a commercial floatplane operation geared to shuttling canoeists, hunters, and anglers to remote lakes and put-in places along the St. John, Allagash, and Aroostook Rivers.

By bus: **Cyr Bus Line** (207-827-2335 or 1-800-244-2335) operates daily between Caribou and Bangor.

WHEN TO COME Snowmobilers and cross-country skiers flock here in the deep of winter to pursue their sports, but the long summer days appeal to many of us. The roads stretch out for miles, inviting the bicycle trips that are a natural for the area, and the lakes and museums along the Acadian region's northern stretch are open and ready for visitors when the weather warms up, when the sporting camps do much of their business. Hunters will want to arrange a visit in fall.

* To See

MUSEUMS A brochure detailing The County's historical museums and attractions is available from most area chambers of commerce. Following are those we found of particular interest (in order of suggested routing). Because most of these museums are entirely run by volunteers, and there are many miles between them, always call before visiting to be sure they are open.

See "Katahdin Region" for details about the **Lumbermen's Museum** in Patten.

Fort Kent Historical Society Museum (207-834-5354), Main and Market Sts., Fort Kent. Open June–Labor Day, Tue.–Fri. 12–4, by appointment off-season. The former Bangor & Aroostook Railroad depot is filled with local memorabilia and exhibits on the economic and social history of the area, focusing on lumbering and agriculture.

Fort Kent Blockhouse Museum, off Rt. 1, Fort Kent. Open Memorial Day–

Labor Day, 9–5, maintained by the town and the local Boy Scout troop. This symbol of the northern terminus of Rt. 1 is a convincingly ancient, if much-restored, two-story 1830s blockhouse with documents and mementos from the Aroostook Bloodless War. Be sure to wander down to the Fish River behind the blockhouse, a pleasant walk to picnic and tenting sites.

Madawaska Historic Center and Acadian Cross Shrine (207-728-3606), Rt. 1, Madawaska. The complex includes the **Tante Blanche Acadia Museum** (local memorabilia) open June–mid-Sept. Wed.–Sun. 11–4, but check for changing hours. If you follow the dirt road behind the museum to the river, you'll see the 18th-century **Albert Homestead**, plus the *Voyageur* statue and stone cross described in the introduction to this chapter.

Acadian Village & Levasseur-Dube Art Museum (207-868-5042; www.connectmaine.com/acadianvillage), Rt. 1, Van Buren. Open mid-June–mid-Sept., daily noon–5. The 17 buildings include a school and store, a barbershop, a train station, old homesteads with period furnishings, a jail, and a reconstructed 18th-century log church. $5 adults, $3 children.

St. Agathe Historical Society Museum (207-543-6911), 534 Main St., St. Agathe. Open late June–early Sept., Tue.–Sun. 1–4. The oldest house in this unusually pleasant village on Long Lake, the Pelletier-Marquis home dates just to 1854; it's filled with a sense of the town's unusually rich ethnic and social history. Enter through **The Preservation Center**, behind the museum, which holds religious, domestic, military artifacts, and an extensive photo collection.

Musée Culturel du Mont-Carmel (207-895-3339), Rt. 1, Lille. Open 12–4 Sun.–Fri. A wooden 1909 church that was never consecrated, this beautiful structure has been painstakingly restored by the Association culturelle et historique du Mont-Carmel. Musicians perform under its now-solid roof. Two gilded archangels blowing trumpets stand at the top of this landmark's two towers. An exhibition space down the street, 122 Main St., a former general store, holds art and history exhibits.

New Sweden Historical Society Museum (207-896-5844), just east of Rt. 161, New Sweden. Open late May–Labor Day, Mon.–Fri. noon–4, weekends 1–4. Entering the community's reconstructed Kapitoleum (meetinghouse), you are faced with the imposing bust of William Widgery Thomas, the Portland man sent by President Lincoln to Sweden in 1863 to halt the sale of iron to the Confederacy. Thomas quickly learned Swedish, married two countesses (the second after her sister, Thomas's first wife, died), and eventually devoted his sizable energies to establishing a colony of Swedish farmers in Maine.

MUSEÉ CULTUREL DU MONT-CARMEL

Nancy English

In 1870 the House of Representatives authorized the project, granting 100 acres of woodland to each Swedish family. A pink granite memorial in a pine grove behind the museum complex commemorates the arrival and hardships of those who settled here between 1870 and 1875. Despite the severe climate and thin soil (Thomas had been struck by the similarities between Sweden and northern Maine), New Sweden prospered, with 1,400 immigrants in 1895 and 689 buildings, including three churches, seven general stores, and two railroad stations. New Sweden's annual festivals draw thousands of local descendants. The museum remains a cultural touchstone for Swedes living throughout the Northeast, and the town continues to attract visitors from Sweden, even an occasional immigrant. Also check out nearby Thomas Park, with a picnic area, the monument and cemetery behind the museum, and the other historic buildings in New Sweden, including the Larsson Ostlund Log Home, Lars Noak Blacksmith and Woodworking Shop, and the one-room Schoolhouse.

The Salmon Brook Historical Society (207-455-4339), Rt. 164, Washburn. Open July 4–Labor Day, Wed. and Sat. afternnoon, tours by appointment. The pleasant 1852 **Benjamin C. Wilder Farmstead** (13 rooms of 1850–1900 period furnishings) and the **Aroostook Agricultural Museum** (potato-harvesting tools and trivia housed in the neighboring barn) offer a sense of life and potato farming in the late 19th century. Washburn's Taterstate Frozen Foods claims to have invented the frozen french fry.

✐ **Nylander Museum** (207-493-4209; www.nylandermuseum.org), 393 Main St., Caribou. Open June–Sept., Tue.–Sat. 12:30–4:30; in winter Mon., Tues., Thurs. 3–7. A small but intriguing museum displaying permanent collections of fossils, minerals and rocks, shells and other marine life, butterflies and moths, birds, and early human artifacts, most collected by Swedish-born Olof Nylander; also a medicinal herb garden in the back with more than 80 specimens.

Caribou Historical Center (207-498-2556), Rt. 1, Caribou. Open June–Aug., Wed.–Sat. 11–5. A log building filled with local memorabilia from the mid–19th century to the 1930s, including antiques, historical papers, photographs, home furnishings, and tools. Also a replica of an 1860s one-room school with a bell in the cupola.

Vera Estey House and the Presque Isle Historical Society (207-762-1151; www.pihistory.org), 16 Third St., Presque Isle. Open by appointment. Many original furnishings, with period additions. The Presque Isle Firehouse is also under restoration, and includes the original area jail. Kim Smith, historical society treasurer, gives guided walking tours of historic Presque Isle while wearing a copy of an 1890s walking dress. Free.

Northern Maine Museum of Science (207-768-9482; www.umpi.maine.edu/info/nmms/museums.html), Folsom Hall, University of Maine at Presque Isle. Open daily. Interesting exhibits, including an herbarium (library of plant species), a coral-reef environment, an extensive display of plant and shell specimens collected by Leroy Norton (a well-known local amateur naturalist), topographic maps, and Aroostook potato varieties, among much more.

The Presque Isle Air Museum (207-764-2542), 650 Airport Dr., Presque Isle.

Open during normal airport hours. The Presque Isle Historical Society has created this museum as a testament to the rich history of air travel in Presque Isle. During World War II, Presque Isle became the departure point for planes and equipment going overseas. An army airfield was created, and more planes left PIAAF bound for Europe than from any other U.S. base. In the early 1960s the missile wing was deactivated and the base was closed.

Aroostook County Historical and Art Museum (207-532-2519), 109 Main St., Houlton. Open Memorial Day–Labor Day, Tue.–Sat. 1–4 and by appointment. Same building as the Houlton Area Chamber of Commerce. A large, well-organized collection of local memorabilia.

Oakfield Railroad Museum (207-757-8575), Station St., Oakfield. Open Memorial Day–Labor Day Sat., Sun., and holidays 1–4. This 1910 Bangor & Aroostook Railroad station is one of three remaining wood-framed railroad stations between Searsport and Fort Kent. Exhibits include photographs from the early days of the railroad, vintage signs and advertising pieces, maps, newspapers, a rail motor car, and a C-66 caboose.

CHURCHES As noted in the introduction to this chapter, tall, elaborate, French Canadian–style Catholic churches form the heart of most Upper St. John Valley villages: **St. Thomas Aquinas** in Madawaska, **St. Louis** in Fort Kent (with distinctive open filigree steeples and a fine carillon), **St. David's** in the village of St. David, and **St. Luce** in Frenchville. When the twin-spired wooden church dominating the village of Lille was decommissioned, it was donated by the bishop of Portland to the **Association culterelle et historique du Mont-Carmel** who converted it into **Musée culturel du Mont-Carmel** (see above), an Acadian cultural center and a setting for concerts and workshops.

OTHER ATTRACTIONS ✐ ♿ **A. E. Howell Wildlife Conservation Center and Spruce Acres Refuge** (207-532-6880; www.spruceacresrefuge.com), 101 Lycette Rd. (off Rt. 1), Amity 04471-5114 (14 miles south of Houlton). Open May–Oct., and weather permitting till Nov. 15, Mon.–Sat. 10–3; $10 adults 15 and older, AARP $2 discount, children 14 and under free. Art Howell Jr, one of the best-known and -respected of more than 90 wild animal rehabilitators in the state, specializes in rehabilitating black bears, moose, deer, wolves, and bald eagles that have been wounded, to return them to the wild if possible. The center has 64 acres of woods with a picnic area and a pond stocked with fish for members; also a camping area. No dogs are allowed. Handicapped accessible. "Moose Man of Baxter Park" Bill Silliker's photographs have been donated to raise funds to benefit wildlife; prints, murals, books are for sale here.

Friends of Aroostook National Wildlife Refuge (207-328-4634; www.friendsofaroostooknwr.org), Limestone. Covering 4,900 acres with six miles of trails for hiking and cross-country skiing, this refuge was created when the Loring Air Force Base in Limestone was decommissioned. Upland sandpipers nest here in summer; boreal birds can be seen. Mink frogs love these wetlands.

The World's Largest Scale Model of the Solar System. Kevin McCartney, a professor at the University of Maine at Presque Isle and director of the Northern Maine Museum of Science, heads the construction by many different schools and organizations of this solar system. The scale model, both in diameter of planets and in distance between planets, is 1:93,000,000. Jupiter, the largest planet, is 5 feet in diameter. Pluto, just an inch in diameter, is located at the Maine Tourism Association's Information Center in Houlton. Dwarf planets more than 90 miles from the "sun" are new additions in Topsfield. An informational brochure details where the planets are along Rt. 1 from Houlton to Presque Isle, and facts about the solar system.

ART **Reed Art Gallery** (207-768-9611), 181 Main St., University of Maine at Presque Isle. Open year-round. About six exhibitions a year are presented here of work from Maine and New Brunswick artists.

SCENIC DRIVES **Flat Mountain**. The single most memorable landscape that we found in all Aroostook is easily accessible if you know where to turn. The high plateau is well named Flat Mountain and is just above but invisible from Rt. 1 east of Fort Kent. Ask locally about the road through the back settlements from Frenchville to St. Agatha, a lake resort with several good restaurants.

Watson Settlement Covered Bridge. Follow Main St. through Houlton's Market Square Historic District (a *Walking Tour Guide* to this area is available from the chamber of commerce) until it turns into Military St. (dating to the Aroostook War). Turn north on Foxcroft Rd.; in 2 miles note your first view of Mars Hill Mountain (the area's only mountain, at 1,660 feet). The mountain's ownership was disputed in the Aroostook War; it is now a ski area. At roughly 3.5 miles, note the road on your left descending to a small iron bridge across the Meduxnekeag River; the covered bridge, built in 1902, is midway down this hill. The road rejoins Rt. 1 10 minutes north of Houlton.

* To Do

BIKING **The Ski Shop** (207-868-2737), 31 Main St., Van Buren, will rent bicycles if used bikes are in stock. Biking on these long slow hills and plains is one of the best ways to tour Aroostook.

Mojo's (207-760-9500; www.melsmojo.com), 719 Main St., Presque Isle. Dynamic owner Melanie Stewart runs clinics, women's programs, and mountain and road group rides. Paddling and river tubing, too. Winter brings group skiing.

Also see **Nordic Heritage Center** in *Winter Sports—Cross-Country Skiing*.

CANOEING **Allagash Wilderness Waterway**. This is considered *the* canoe trip in Maine, and after a three-day expedition we have to agree. The whole trip, 92 miles of lake and river canoeing, takes far longer than three days. We put in at Round Pond and paddled the shorter 32-mile trip to Allagash Village. Though it's possible to shuttle your own vehicles, leaving one at the beginning and one at the end, we recommend using a transportation service, which will bring you, your gear, and your canoes into your put-in spot and retrieve you at take-out. This simplifies the parking issue; also, you won't have to go back into the woods to retrieve your car at the end of the trip, and the transportation companies are experienced in negotiating the bumpy dirt roads that can lead to blown tires and rocks thrown at the windshield. **Norman L'Italien** (207-398-3187), P.O. Box 67, St. Francis 04774, was well informed, helpful, and friendly. After we checked in at the gate (road-use fee of $8 per person for non-Maine-residents per day, $5 for residents; overnight camping fee $5 per person per night for non-Maine-residents, $4 for residents), his driver dropped us off at the bridge just above Round Pond and told us to call when we were off the river. Norman also operates **Pelletier's Campground** (207-398-3187) in St. Francis, a good spot to stay the night before your departure. Keep in mind that the trip to the area from Sherman Mills, where you leave I-95, is at least three hours; head up the night before your trip. Plan to arrive in daylight if you need to set up tents. The **Maine Bureau of Parks and Lands** (207-941-4014) manages the wilderness waterway and is a source of general information as well as a map and a list of outfitters.

Paddling and floating with the current, sunlight twinkling off the water, you'll feel you're truly in a wilderness paradise. Even when the sun hid behind the clouds, the river wasn't the least bit gloomy or less beautiful. We were there on Labor Day weekend, and the weather and bugs cooperated quite nicely—but come prepared for both rain and pests. Blackflies, mosquitoes, and no-see-ums can be brutal, so bring plenty of bug repellent, maybe even protective netting. On our trip, however, bugs were not a problem, and we slept out underneath the stars two of the three nights. Remember that there are no stores around the next corner; if you leave it at home, you do without. Pack light, but bring enough spare clothing so that if some gets wet, you'll still be comfortable. Pack in waterproof backpacks, or seal items in plastic bags to prevent soaking should your canoe tip. Bring extra garbage bags to wrap around sleeping bags and pillows. Don't forget a camera and extra film or disks. **Allagash Falls** is particularly nice, and the portage around the waterfall is an easy 0.5-mile hike. The trail and picnic area are well maintained. This is actually a good place to cook a solid meal, using up your heaviest supplies before carrying your stuff around the falls. The trip after the falls to Allagash is just one more overnight, and if you plan remaining meals accordingly, you can lighten your load around the portage.

Campsites on the waterway are clean and comfortable, with plenty of space for a group to spread out. Sites are available on a first-come, first-served basis, so the earlier in the day you begin paddling, the better choice you have. During our visit the river was far from crowded, even on a holiday weekend. We saw fewer than 15 people outside our group on our three-day journey. The rangers keep track of who is on the river, so there's no need to be nervous that you will be too isolated should something happen. If you're not an experienced canoeist, don't worry: A three-day trip is easily manageable without putting too much strain on infrequently used muscles. Paddling the whole waterway takes seven to 10 days, though it's best to be flexible in case wind or rain delays your trip.

If you aren't comfortable venturing out on your own, several area guides can take you down the river. Following are a few suggestions. Contact **North Maine Woods** (see *Guidance* in "The North Maine Woods") for other options.

Allagash Guide Service (207-398-3418; www.allagashguideservice.com), 928

Allagash Rd., Allagash. Kelley and Sean Lizotte rent paddles and canoes and also offer transport and car pickup. Guided trips here and on the St. John River.

Allagash Canoe Trips (207-237-3077; www.allagashcanoetrips.com). This outfitting company was founded in 1953. Chip Cochrane and other guides lead trips, providing all equipment and meals.

FARM TOUR ✐ **Knot-II-Bragg Farm** (207-455-8386; www.knotiibragg.com), 469 New Dunn Town Rd., Wade 04786. Open by appointment June–Oct., Tue.–Sat. 10–4. $6.50 adults, $5 children. Natalia Bragg, a practicing herbalist and in the sixth generation of women to practice herbal craft in her family, talks about the history and herbal lore of the area. Her company makes Old Log Driver's products, which include natural painkillers; all products are for sale, as is handmade soap and twig furniture. Ask for a copy of the tourist guide to Washburn that she put together, detailing all businesses in the northern Maine community.

FISHING The catch here is so rich and varied that it's recognized throughout the country. Salmon grow to unusual size, and trout are also large and numerous. The 80-mile Fish River chain of rivers and lakes (Eagle, Long, and Square Lakes) is legendary in fishing circles. Fish strike longer in the season than they do farther south, and fall fishing begins earlier. Contact the Maine Department of Inland Fisheries and Wildlife in Ashland (207-435-3231; in-state, 1-800-353-6334).

GOLF The County's topography lends itself to golf, and the sport is so popular that most towns maintain at least a nine-hole course. The most famous course, with 18 holes, is **Aroostook Valley Country Club**, Fort Fairfield (207-476-8083; www.avcc.ca); its tees are split between Canada and Maine. The 18-hole **Va-Jo-Wa Golf Course** (207-463-2128) in Island Falls and the **Presque Isle Country Club** (207-764-0439) are also considered above par. **Houlton Community Golf Club** (207-532-2662) is on offer in the south. **Caribou Country Club** (207-493-3933; www.caribougolf.com), Rt. 161, Caribou, is a nine-hole course designed by Geoffrey Cornish. **Mars Hill Country Club** (207-425-4802; www.golfmhcc.com), 75 Country Club Rd., Mars Hill, has 18 holes.

HIKING See the **Debouille Management Unit** and **Aroostook State Park** under *Green Space*.

Fish River Falls. Ask locally for directions to the trail that leads from the former Fort Kent airport down along the river, an unusually beautiful footway through pines. Note the swimming holes below the falls. **The Dyke in Fort Kent** is also worth finding: a 0.5-mile walk along the Fish River. The trail up **Mount Carmel** (views up and down the river valley) begins on Rt. 1 at the state rest area near the Madawaska–Grand Isle town line.

KAYAKING **Perception of Aroostook** (207-764-5506), Presque Isle. Kayak rentals and river trips. The business offers shuttles for day trips on the Aroostook River; a lunch at Rum Rapids (see lodging below) is featured on one trip.

✷ Winter Sports

CROSS-COUNTRY SKIING The same reliable snow that serves snowmobilers allows residents to take advantage of hundreds of miles of trails maintained exclusively for cross-country skiing by local towns and clubs. Any town office or chamber of commerce will steer you to local trails.

Maine Winter Sports Center (207-328-0991; www.mainewsc.org). The organization, funded by the Libra Foundation, has developed a network of community trails for use by schoolchildren and local residents, and hosted the World Cup Biathlon in 2004, combining rifle marksmanship with cross-county skiing. MWSC has built two nordic events facilities, used for training high school skiers and Olympic hopefuls. **10th Mountain Division Center** (207-834-6203) in Fort Kent includes a biathlon range, links to recreational ski trails, and a handsome lodge. A similar facility, the **Nordic Heritage Center** (207-328-0991) in Presque Isle, focuses on cross-country skiing. Mountain bike races have also been hosted in recent years.

Kate McCartney at the Old Iron Inn in Caribou (207-492-4766) has compiled a brochure of northern Maine's cross-country trails, which lists nine centers dedicated to the sport; her brochure is also available from the chambers.

DOWNHILL SKIING **Big Rock** (207-425-6711, 1-866-529-2695; www.bigrockmaine.com), Mars Hill. A downhill and cross-country facility owned by Maine Winter Sports Center, this place focuses on getting everyone involved, with adult weekday tickets at $23, weekend at $28, seniors and juniors $20, and over 75 and under 5 free.

SNOWMOBILING Snowmobiling is the single biggest reason that visitors come to The County. It's the easiest way to see some of the more remote sporting camps and wilderness areas, since riding over well-maintained trails is often smoother than bumping down logging roads in summer. Trails lead from one end of The County to the other and are far too numerous for us to detail here. Call any Aroostook County chamber of commerce for a *Trail Map to Northern Maine* detailing 2,200 miles of trails maintained by The County's 40-plus snowmobile clubs and including locations of clubhouses, warming huts, and service areas. On the back of the map are ads for several companies that cater to snowmobilers, from rentals and service to lodging and dining.

✷ Green Space

Debouille Management Unit, including Debouille Mountain and several ponds, is a 23,461-acre preserve managed jointly by the state and North Maine Woods (charging gate and camping fees; see *Guidance* in "North Maine Woods"), accessible by gated logging roads from St. Francis and Portage. Campsites are clustered around ponds (good for trout) and near hiking trails leading to the distinctive summit of Debouille Mountain. For details, contact the Bureau of Public Lands in Presque Isle (207-764-2033).

Aroostook State Park (207-768-8341), marked from Rt. 1, 4 miles south of

Presque Isle. Open May 15–Oct. 15. A 600-acre park with swimming and picnicking at Echo Lake; also 30 campsites (June 15–Labor Day only) at 1,213-foot Quaggy Joe Mountain—which offers hiking trails with views from the north peak across a sea of woodland to Mount Katahdin. The monument in the small **Maxie Anderson Memorial Park** next door; a tin replica of the *Double Eagle II* commemorates the 1978 liftoff of the first hot-air balloon to successfully cross the Atlantic.

Aroostook Valley Trail and **Bangor and Aroostook Trail** (207-493-4224). A 75-mile recreational trail system connecting Caribou, Woodland, New Sweden, Washburn, Perham, Stockholm, and Van Buren. Many bogs, marshes, wetlands, and streams lie along these trails, which are owned by the Maine Bureau of Parks and Lands. There are several parking lots and rest areas on the trails as well. Good for biking, walking, cross-country skiing, and snowmobiling.

Also see **Fish River Falls** under *Hiking* and the **Allagash Wilderness Waterway** under *Canoeing*.

✷ Lodging

HOTELS **The Northeastland Hotel** (207-768-5321 or 1-800-244-5321; www.mainerec.com/eastland.html), 436 Main St., Presque Isle 04769. Built in 1934 in the heart of downtown, this 51-room, three-story hotel remains a favorite with business and pleasure travelers. Guest rooms are unusually large, sparely but nicely furnished, and spotless, equipped with a full, mirrored closet, phone, coffeemaker, iron, and blow dryer. The hotel's **Sidewalk Café** serves all three meals and has a liquor license. Double rooms (two queen beds) are $84 year-round, no charge for children; single $78.

🐾 **Caribou Inn and Convention Center** (207-498-3733 or 1-800-235-0466; www.caribouinn.com), junction of Rts. 1 and 164, Caribou 04736. This is a sprawling 73-room motor inn with an indoor pool, hot tub and fitness center, and the full-service **Greenhouse Restaurant**. Rooms are large, suites have kitchenettes, and it fills a need. This is snowmobiler central, the guests mostly male. $94–104; pets are welcome.

🐾 **Presque Isle Inn and Convention Center** (207-764-3321 or 1-800-533-3971; www.presqueisleinn.com), 116 Main St. (Rt. 1), Presque Isle 04769. With 151 guest rooms and suites as well as meeting and banquet space, this is the largest facility of its kind in The County. Amenities include an Italian restaurant, bar and lounge, heated indoor pool, and full fitness center. Like its sister property in Caribou, it's very popular with snowmobilers in winter, when rates are higher. Pets welcome. $96.

🐾 **Northern Door Inn** ("La Porte du Nord") (207-834-3133; www.northerndoorinn.com), 356 W. Main St., Fort Kent 04743. A pleasant and comfortable 43-unit property located directly across from the international bridge to Canada and drawing guests (including many snowmobilers in winter) from both sides of the border. $72 for a double includes continental breakfast. Pet friendly.

BED & BREAKFASTS "1" **Old Iron Inn** (207-492-4766; www.oldironinn.com), 155 High St., Caribou 04736.

Kate and Kevin McCartney offer four rooms (two with private bath, the other two sharing a bath and a half) furnished with attractive antiques and old irons, from tiny little irons for pressing ruffles to big ones; band of trivets to set them on ring the living room wall. The hosts are up to date on everything going on in The County; Kate has a brochure on cross-country ski places, and can recommend fine restaurants. $55–69 includes a good breakfast. A furnished two-bedroom guest cottage is available by the week or month.

The Graham House (207-429-8206; www.thegrahamhouse.com), 5 Church St., Mars Hill 04758. Two bedrooms are connected and share a bath just outside; a second room has its own bath, and an extra room. Both have access to a back second floor deck. $70–150 with a hot breakfast.

Rum Rapids Inn (207-455-8096; www.rumrapidsinn.com), Rt. 164, Crouseville 04738 (not far from Presque Isle). Clifton and Judy Boudman offer candlelight dinners by special arrangement as well as two rooms with private bath and two solar cottages without bathrooms. Guest amenities include a sauna. Multicourse dinners are open to the public by reservation with dishes like tuna steaks with wasabi and green onion mayonnaise. Several courses are $38–48. Room rates start at $99 double, including a full breakfast.

THE OLD IRON INN

Nancy English

SPORTING CAMPS Gardner's Sporting Camps (207-398-3168), P.O. Box 127, Allagash 04774. Open May–Dec. Five tidy camps along a ridge overlooking the confluence of the St. John and Allagash Rivers across the road from Roy and Maude Gardner's welcoming old farmhouse. B&B and hiking, hunting, camping, and fishing guide service also offered. $30 per person per night; $150 per week.

Moose Point Camps (207-435-6156; www.moosepointcamps.com), Portage 04768. Open May 10–early Dec. Ten hewn-log camps on the east shore of Fish Lake (5 miles long and connecting with other lakes linked by the Fish River). The central lodge features a library, a large stone fireplace, and a dining room overlooking the lake where meals are served (BYOB). The camps are 17 miles from Portage, up a paper company road. $395 per person per week or $90 per person per day May–Aug., $495 per week per person Sept.–early Dec. Rates include three meals a day and housekeeping service; children's rates. Boats and canoes available.

Libby Sporting Camps (207-435-8274; www.libbycamps.com), P.O. Box 810, Ashland 04732. Open ice-out through Nov. One of the area's original sporting camps, which has been Libby owned and operated for more than 110 years. The peeled spruce cabins overlook 6-mile-long northern Millinocket Lake and are lighted with propane; handmade quilts cover the beds. In the day guides can take you to 40 lakes and ponds for fishing, orchid hunting, a night at one of 10 outpost cabins, or just exploring. In between, Ellen Libby and daughter-in-law Jessica serve great meals in the lodge, with homemade bread. Matt Libby can tell you where the taxidermied bobcat, lynx, and golden eagle, to name a few in the lodge, arrived from. There is a seaplane based at the camps, available at a fee for day and overnight trips. $155 per person ($180 single) per night includes all meals, boats, motor, kayaks, sailboat, and canoes. Pets welcome, $10 fee. Awarded Orvis Fishing Lodge of the Year 2006–2007.

Red River Sporting Camps (207-435-6207; www.redrivercamps.com), 26 miles from Portage. Open late May–early Oct. Cabins sit next to Island Pond at this remote camp with a reputation for good cooking, run by Mike Brophy. Two small cabins and three larger, with one that holds as many as eight people, are $120 per person American Plan, with housekeeping services, linens, towels, and use of boats, canoes, and more. $60 per person for three housekeeping cabins includes bed linens, woodburning stove, and gas lamps; the private island cabin includes a porch swing.

MOTEL **Long Lake Motor Inn** (207-543-5006), Rt. 162, St. Agatha 04772. Ken and Arlene Lerman pride themselves on the cleanliness and friendliness of this motel overlooking Long Lake. There is a lounge, and continental breakfast is included in $59 for standard room, double occupancy ($49 single); $75 for the suite, which has a whirlpool.

♿ 🐾 ✎ **Brookside Motel** (207-757-8456), 2277 Rt. 2, Smyrna Mills 04780. Just north of exit 291 off I-95, this is a plain place with nine units; the basics are all here, including air-conditioning. You'll also be next door to a wonderful, inexpensive restaurant, the Brookside, that does all the home cooking everybody else used to do (see *Eating Out*). Rates $50 single, $55 double.

✱ Where to Eat

DINING OUT **Canterbury Royale Gourmet Dining Rooms** (207-472-4910), 182 Sam Everett Rd., Fort Fairfield. Reserve one of these two elegant rooms with hand-carved paneling for a special private dinner, with entrées you choose in advance of your visit. Six courses might present chateaubriand or canard a l'orange; Scottish dishes like Chicken Bonnie Prince Charlie. $48 includes all courses.

Horn of Plenty (207-463-2861), 59 Houlton Rd., Island Falls. Written up in Down East Magazine, extraordinary Horn of Plenty features Italian, Portuguese and all-American dishes made by a Johnson & Wales graduate. Entrées $14–19.

Karl's German Cuisine (506-473-6252; www.lakesidelodge.com), Grand Falls, New Brunswick, Canada. Open mid-April–Nov., closed Mon. A reservation is necessary at Karl's, where you will find every kind of schnitzel, homemade spaetzle, and other German specialties. End with Black Forest Torte. Entrées start at $10.

♿ **Long Lake Sporting Club** (207-543-7584 or 1-800-431-7584), Rt. 162, Sinclair. Open daily year-round. Sit down in the lounge with a drink, order, and then go to your table when your meal is ready. Specialties include appetizer platters (wings, mozzarella sticks, ribs, and shrimp), steaks, seafood, jumbo lobsters (3.5-pound hard-shells), and barbecued ribs. Huge portions. Right on Long Lake, with terrific views. Entrées $15–30.

Napoli's (207-492-1102), 6 Center St., Caribou. A friendly Italian restaurant with good spaghetti and sausage, Napoli's is a welcome spot for pizza and generous, fresh salads. The small Greek salad was plenty large, the Chianti on special was tart and fruity, and the marinara sings with flavor. Entrées $7–16.

♿ **Lakeview Restaurant** (207-543-6331), Lakeview Dr., St. Agatha. Open daily for breakfast, lunch, and dinner. Set on a hilltop with a view across the lake and valley. Steak, seafood, and barbecued baby back ribs are the specialties. Most entrées are around $10.

Eureka Hall (207-896-3196), Stockholm. Open for dinner on weekends; reservations recommended. A charming airy room serving with steak, seafood, local organic produce, and homemade breads and desserts. Sunday breakfast in winter features the fabulous homemade Danishes of owner Suzy Anderson, which you can sometimes buy next door at Anderson's store.

EUREKA HALL'S HOMEMADE DANISHES

Nancy English

York's (506-273-2847), Perth Andover, New Brunswick, Canada. Open seasonally (spring–early fall) Tues.–Sun. for lunch and dinner. A large, popular dining room overlooking the St. John River. Home cooking, from steak to lobster and duck. Huge portions are wheeled out in a trolley.

EATING OUT ♿ ✐ **Brookside Restaurant** (207-757-8456), 2277 Rt. 2, Smyrna Mills (at exit 291 off I-95). Old-fashioned the right way, with homemade pies, great meat loaf, and lobster rolls. The fried clams are rated high. And so reasonable. Sunday you can usually find fresh vegetables, turnips, butternut squash, and carrots line up for the fall. Carmel and Carl Watson are the owners.

Cindy's Sub Shop (207-498-6021), 264 Sweden St., Caribou. Open daily 7:30 AM–9 PM, 9–7 on Sun., closed on Sun. between Christmas and Easter. Turkey and bacon sub, great lobster rolls, homemade soups like chicken stew and fish chowder. Homemade pies, "Swirl Delight" squares, and whoopie pies, too.

Doris's Café (207-834-6262), Fort Kent Mills. Open for breakfast and lunch; everything prepared from scratch. What's for breakfast? "Any thing you'd like, Ma'am," the friendly owner said.

Frederick's Southside Restaurant (207-498-3464), 507 Main St., Caribou. Open for lunch and dinner, closed Monday. Good home-style cooking, big portions, reasonable prices. Closed Mon. Entrées $6–14.

Winnie's (207-769-4971), 79 Parsons St., Presque Isle. A small, local favorite for more than 60 years. Burgers, seafood rolls, sandwiches, and a huge variety of ice cream.

The Courtyard Café (207-532-0787; www.thecourtyardcafe.com), 59 Main St., Houlton. Lunch Tues.–Fri. and dinner Wed.-Sat. Sandwiches, daily specials, coffee, and homemade crisps and pies. The "Forget-Me-Not" is a roast beef sandwich made with herb and garlic cream cheese ($6.99).

Elm Tree Diner (207-532-3777), 146 Bangor Rd., Houlton. Reopened after a long hiatus with much praise for all the menus, from 5:30 AM–8 PM daily. The Swiss cheese mushroom burger is recommended by the owner of York's Books (see *Selective Shopping*). Owner Gary Dwyer likes the homemade bread and muffins for breakfast. On weekends the popular roast turkey or pork can come with turnip or squash. Entrées $7–13.

✷ Entertainment

MUSIC **Caribou Performing Arts Center**, (207-493-4278; www.cariboushools.org/PAC), Caribou High School, 308 Sweden St. A full calendar of concerts, dance, ballet, and performances.

✷ Selective Shopping

Bradbury Barrel Co. (207-429-8141 or 1-800-332-6021; www.bradburybarrel.com), 479 Main Rd., Bridgewater. Showroom of white cedar barrels—which used to be the way potatoes traveled around the country—as well as other wood products. Mail-order catalog.

Fish River Tackle (207-834-3951; www.fishrivertackle.com), Fort Kent. Call for directions. Tackle made by Don Baker—one of his big metal flashers secured the $10,000 grand prize in the Lake Champlain Fishing Derby in 1994. He also makes tip-ups for ice fishing.

Bouchard Family Farm (207-834-3237; www.ployes.com), Rt. 161, Fort Kent. Stop by the family kitchen and buy a bag of ploye mix. Ployes are crêpelike pancakes made with buckwheat flour (no eggs, no milk, no sugar, no oil, no cholesterol, no fat—*c'est magnifique*).

Goughan Farms (207-496-1731), Rt. 161, Fort Fairfield. Open weekdays 10–5, Sun. noon–5. Pick-your-own strawberries; also a farm stand and animal barn. Every fall a corn maze covers six acres; $6.50 per person to walk the maze includes an ice cream, made here, and highly recommended. Berries grown here are made into purées to flavor the ice cream. Hayrides on request.

ANTIQUES **Weathervane Antiques** (207-538-9730), 641 Rt. 1, Monticello. Framed heroic prints of Caribou, iron frying pans, antique furniture,

CABBAGES SOLD ON THE HONOR SYSTEM JUST OUTSIDE OF CARIBOU

Nancy English

and tractors at this congenial store in an old barn.

BOOKSTORES **Volumes Book Store** (207-532-7727), 75 Bangor St., Houlton. Volumes boasts the largest selection of used books in The County, some 100,000 of them, and carries new books along with Maine souvenirs and gifts. If you can't find what you're looking for, proprietor Gerry Berthelette can lay his hands on it almost instantly.

York's Books (207-532-3354), 19 Market Square, Houlton. All new book selection.

Mr. Paperback (207-492-2080), 30 Skyway Drive, Caribou. Great selection of books, both hard- and softcover.

Box of Books (207-493-3244), 487 Fort Fairfield Road, Caribou. Colleen Harmon runs a casual used bookstore; buy one, trade one for one, or take a box, fill it up from the unalphebetized but loosely organized piles; the books are likely to be inexpensive.

* Special Events

February: **Mardi Gras** in Fort Kent—the five days before Ash Wednesday bring a parade, ice sculptures, kids' day, Franco-American music, and exhibitions. **International Snowmobile Festival** (*usually first weekend*) in Madawaska—a three-day event that attracts both Canadian and American sledders.

Early March: The **Can Am Sled Dog Race**—Triple Crown 60- and 250-mile races, starting and ending at Fort Kent.

June: **Acadian Festival** in Madawaska—parade, traditional Acadian supper, and talent revue. **"Midsommar"** (*weekend nearest June 21*) is celebrated at Thomas Park in New Sweden and at the New Sweden Historical Society Museum with Swedish music, dancing, and food.

July: **Maine Potato Blossom Festival**, Fort Fairfield—a week of activities including mashed-potato wrestling, Potato Blossom Queen pageant, parade, entertainment, dancing, industry dinner, and fireworks. **Ployes Festival** (*last weekend of the month*), Fort Kent—a celebration of the beloved buckwheat crêpe and other traditional Acadian dishes.

End of July/beginning of August: **Historical Pavilion**, Northern Maine Fair, Presque Isle, in the Forum Building Tues.–Thurs. during fair week. Historical societies put on a show with individual displays, like "freeze-modeling" in antique costumes that won the 2007 "Best Living History Display," by Kim Smith and students from Presque Isle.

August: **Northern Maine Fair**, Presque Isle. **Potato Feast Days** in Houlton—arts and crafts, potato-barrel-rolling contest, potato games, carnival, and more.

First Saturday in December: **Holiday Light Parade**, Presque Isle.

INDEX

B

H

Q

R